YEARS
RING
BRAZIL

D0801627

Brazil Handbook

Alex & Gardênia Robinson

There are few countries as beautiful and vibrant as Brazil with nature so exuberant and people so welcoming. Thousands of miles of pristine and usually deserted beaches line the coast, some pounded by superb surf, others lapped by a gentle sea. They are backed by dunes the size of deserts or forests of swaying coconut palms. Offshore, jewel-like islands offer some of the best diving and snorkelling in the South Atlantic. In the warm shallow waters humpback whales gather to calf and spinner dolphins cavort in the waves. The table-top mountains of the Brazilian interior are covered in medicinal plants and drained by mineral-rich rivers that tumble through gorges and rush over spectacular tiered waterfalls. In the Amazon, virgin forest stretches unbroken for more than 2500 km in every direction and the earth is a tapestry of green broken by a filigree of rivers. There are islands here too – the largest bigger than Denmark, and wilder and more forested than Borneo. The Pantanal, the world's biggest wetland, offers the best wildlife-watching in the western hemisphere.

The tiny cobble and whitewash gold-mining towns of Goiás and Minas Gerais contrast with the busy metropolises of São Paulo, Salvador and Recife, which offer the most exciting and surprising urban culture in Latin America. And then there's Rio – the jewel in the country's urban crown, with its bays and islands, boulder mountains, beaches and beautiful people. But best of all there are the Brazilians, in all their joyful diversity. Portugal, France, Ireland, Holland and Britain all laid claims here and left their cultures to mingle with the indigenous inhabitants; Brazil is home to the greatest numbers of Africans, Arabs and Japanese in the Americas, and bierfests, sushi, bauhaus, rock music and rodeos are as much a part of the culture as bossa nova and football. As yet, the country is undiscovered beyond the clichés, but Brazil is becoming big news, with a World Cup to host in 2014 and the Olympics two years later. So come before Brazil becomes yet another destination on the exotic travel circuit, and have it all to yourself.

This page Sunset on the Pantanal.
Previous page Capoeira, Rio de Janeiro.

Festivals

Carnival

For one raucous week around Shrove Tuesday, the whole country dresses up and stays up all night every night to dance, parade, perform and pose in the world's biggest annual party. There are three principal celebrations, all attended by millions. Salvador's is the largest and wildest, engulfing the entire city centre and beach neighbourhoods in thundering drum-powered processions. Rio's is the most visually spectacular, with jaw-droppingly magnificent parades in the purpose-built sambódromo arena. Pernambuco's is the most traditional, with frenzied *frevo* dancing and mesmerizing *maracatu* drumming reverberating in the colonial streets of Olinda and Recife.

Bumba-Meu-Boi in São Luís

A month of festivities in Brazil's other great African-Brazilian city culminate in this drum-and-sung dance pageant depicting the ritual slaughter of a prize bull, his resurrection by a witch doctor, shaman and Catholic priest, and the rainy season that the magic brings. Bumba-Meu-Boi is also celebrated further north in the Amazon, where it is called Boi Bumba. The biggest party is in Parintins on an island in the middle of the Amazon river – usually at the end of June.

Festas Juninas in Campina Grande and Caruaru

In June partygoers flock to these desert towns in Paraíba and Pernambuco to drink spiced wine, dress up and dance to *forró* – a kind of backlands jig powered by staccato accordion and punchy percussion. Caruaru and Campina Grande are arch rivals – and aficionados of both festivals will assure you that theirs is the best. As the festivals carry on for much of the month (and are at their liveliest on the weekends) it's possible to go to both.

Festa Divino Espírito Santo

The tiny *cerrado* town of Pirenópolis erupts into a week of festivities at Pentecost (50 days after Easter) with colourful processions of cowboys riding on horseback through the cobbled streets, re-enactments of battles fought in Portugal between the Moors and the Christians (complete with jousting and swordplay) and *forró* music reverberating from bars and restaurants from dusk to dawn.

Festa do Bonfim

Bahia's biggest and most colourful festival after Carnival is held in January and sees thousands of Bahians in traditional Yoruba costumes parade from the beachside church of Conceição da Praia to the beautiful colonial church of Bonfim. The festival is nominally Catholic but strongly associated with *candomblé*: Our Lord of Bonfim is also Oxalá, father of the Orixas and creator of humankind.

Bahia, Salvador.

Contents

AMAZON

FORTALEZA

BRASÍLIA,
GOIÁS &
TOCANTINS

RECIFE & THE
NORTHEAST
COAST

PANTANAL

BAHIA

MINAS GERAIS &
ESPÍRITO SANTO

SÃO
PAULO

RIO DE
JANEIRO

IGUAÇU FALLS
& THE SOUTH

Atlantic Ocean

Contents

Essentials

Planning your trip

Where to go

The southeast

The highlight of the southeast is **Rio de Janeiro**. No city on earth has a setting to compare: rainforest-covered mountains rise sheer from a bottle-green ocean and a vast wine-glass bay. And Rio clusters and claws at them; its centre climbing over smaller hills and crowding behind crescent gentle coves; its slums clinging to their smooth granite sides. The beaches and music are wonderful, and carnival – which takes place in a stadium, and not in the streets – is one of the world's great spectacles. Rio's ugly and far less courted big sister, **São Paulo**, lies a few hours' bus ride away. Its interminable labyrinths of concrete are unprepossessing at first, but those who find their way into the maze, preferably with a local guide, discover the best nightlife, restaurants, high-end shopping and popular culture in South America. The land-locked state of **Minas Gerais** is Brazil's literary heartland. Its pastoral landscapes are broken by rocky mountains and dotted with tranquil colonial towns like **Diamantina**, **Ouro Preto** and **Tirandentes**. Minas is infused with a nostalgic lyricism, which inspired Brazil's greatest writer (João Guimarães Rosa), its greatest poet (Carlos Drummond de Andrade), musician, (Milton Nascimento) and footballer (Edson Arantes do Nascimento or Pelé).

Bahia and the northeast

Northeastern Brazil is famous for its beaches and colonial cities. The most popular destination, **Bahia**, offers the best of both with a string of palm-shaded silvery strands lining its coast and islands, and the largest colonial city in the Americas, **Salvador**. Bahia is the home of the martial art dance of capoeira and the African Brazilian candomblé religion – which is related to voodoo. Salvador's street carnival is Brazil's most raucous. The state's arid backlands are broken by dramatic, waterfall-covered mountains in the Chapada Diamantina. **Recife**, capital of Pernambuco, and its twin city **Olinda**, are almost as pretty as Salvador and have an even livelier cultural scene, with some of the most exciting contemporary Brazilian music and the country's largest street carnival. Travelling to the north coast, there are hundreds of beaches to choose from, some highly developed, others less so. You can swim, surf or ride the dunes in buggies in **Jericoacoara** or **Genipabu**, or kitesurf in the neo-colonial settlement of **Cumbuco**. Then there are the vast dune deserts of the **Lençóis Maranhenses** on the windswept Maranhão coast and the last major city before the mouth of the Amazon, **São Luís**, whose centre is covered in colonial tiles, and whose streets reverberate with some of Brazil's best nightlife.

The centre west

The centre west of Brazil is dominated by the expansive grasslands, table-top mountains and scrub forests of the Cerrado and the Pantanal wetlands. The **Cerrado** comprises South America's most acutely threatened biome, almost as rich in unique flora and fauna as the Amazon and, in the wilds of the **Chapada dos Veadeiros** or **Jalapão**, just as magnificent. The rivers, lakes and grasslands of the **Pantanal** are the best place to see wildlife in the Americas; at the end of the dry season, there are few places on earth where birds can be seen in such astonishing numbers. At the eastern end of the centre west is the country's capital, **Brasília**, carved from the *cerrado* in the 1960s and now a World Heritage Site for its repository of striking modernist architecture.

Packing for Brazil

Bag Unobtrusive sturdy bag (either rucksack or bag with wheels) and an inelegant day pack/bag – to attract minimal attention on the streets.

Clothing Brazilians dress casually. It's best to do likewise and blend in. Avoid flashy brands. Thin cotton or a modern wicking artificial fabric are best. Take lightweight trousers, shorts, a long-sleeved shirt, skirts, cotton or wicking socks, underwear, shawl or light water-proof jacket for evenings and a sun hat.

Footwear Light goretex walking shoes (or boots if you intend to trek) are best. Buy from a serious, designated outdoor company like Brasher or Berghaus rather than a flimsy fashion brand. Wear them in before you come. Nothing gives a tourist away more than new shoes.

Sponge bag 2% tincture of iodine; Mercurochrome or similar; athlete's foot powder; tea tree oil; antibiotic ointment; toothbrush; rehydration tablets; Imodium; sun protection (high factor) – this is expensive in Brazil.

Electronics UK, US or European socket adaptor; camera with case to attract minimal attention; torch (flashlight).

Miscellaneous items Ear plugs for surfing, traffic noise and cockerels at dawn; pen knife; strong string (3 m); hooks with a screw-in thread (for mosquito net); gaffer tape; sunglasses (with UV filter); money belt; a sealable waterproof bag large enough for camera and clothes (this is an essential for visits to Iguaçu's Macuco safari.

For rural and beach destinations take a mosquito net impregnated with insect repellent (the bell-shaped models are best) and a water bottle.

What not to pack – to buy there

T-shirts (local brands make you less conspicuous and they are sold everywhere); insect repellent (Johnson's Off! aerosol is best); beachwear (unless you have neuroses about your body – no one cares if their bum looks big in anything in Brazil); flip-flops (Havaianas); pain killers; shampoo and soap; toothpaste; beach shawl (kanga); vitamins; hammock and rope (essential for Amazon boat travel).

Northern Brazil

The north of the country is dominated by the **Amazon**, its forest and its tributaries that spread as wide and thin as the blood vessels in a human body. The first Europeans cut their way into the interior of South America from here in search of an inland sea and an empire rich with gold. And when the river is in full flood its tributaries link through the inundated forest to form what seems like an oceanic labyrinth of lakes. These are served by sea-going cargo boats that call in at river ports along its length. Some ports are little towns while others, like **Belém**, with its cutting-edge alternative music scene, and **Manaus**, with myriad forest lodges, are home to more than a million people. North of Manaus is the overland route through **Boa Vista** to Venezuela. The forest stretches north into Colombia at São Gabriel and Tabatinga, and into Venezuela and the Guianas near Boa Vista, and south to the central tablelands of **Mato Grosso**.

Southern Brazil

With its maté-sipping gaúchos, beer festivals, squeeze-box tango and blonde-haired, blue-eyed supermodels, the three states of southern Brazil feel closer to Uruguay, or even Germany, than they do to the rest of Brazil. Most visitors come for the world's most famous

Brazil's World Heritage Sites

Cultural

Ouro Preto (1980), exquisite Portuguese churches and streets of houses rolling over cobble-covered hills (page 258).

Historic Centre of Olinda (1982), lively culture, raucous carnival and lavish colonial buildings (page 491).

Jesuit Missions (1983), crumbling ruins where indigenous peoples and warrior priests fought a last stand (page 365).

Historic Centre of Salvador de Bahia (1985), colonial splendour and African-Brazilian culture (page 386).

Sanctuary of Bom Jesus do Congonhas (1985), some of the finest baroque carving in the world (page 269).

Brasília (1987), space-age modernist architecture (page 682).

Serra da Capivara (1991), canyons and wild hills preserving perhaps the oldest art in the Americas (page 572).

Historic Centre of São Luís (1997), the best-preserved Portuguese city in the Americas (page 577).

Diamantina (1999), colonial jewel nestled in rugged hills (page 285).

Cidade de Goiás (2001), pretty, timeless and barely visited by tourists (page 697).

São Francisco Square in São Cristóvão (2010), a perfectly preserved Renaissance American village (page 469).

Natural

Iguaçu (1986) – the most spectacular waterfall on Earth, set in a vast forested national park (page 314).

Atlantic Forest South-East Reserves (1999), with the highest endemic biodiversity in South America (page 312).

Discovery Coast Atlantic Forest Reserves (1999), tropical beaches, rainforest and harpy eagle nests (page 434).

Central Amazon Conservation Complex (2000), the largest area of protected tropical forest on Earth (page 631).

Pantanal Conservation Area (2000), the world's largest wetlands and the best place in Brazil for wildlife (page 716).

Chapada dos Veadeiros and Emas (2001), Brazil's most threatened habitat, the stunning Cerrado (page 700).

Fernando de Noronha and Atol das Rocas islands (2001), coral reefs and pearly beaches (page 507).

---

waterfalls, Iguaçu, on the border with Argentina and Paraguay. But there are canyons and good hiking in the **Serra Gaúcha** mountains in Rio Grande do Sul and the **Serra Graciosa** in Paraná, and beautiful beaches around the laid-back city of **Florianópolis** in Santa Catarina and the tranquil sub-tropical island of **Ilha do Mel**. There's also the world's second-largest beer festival in the German-Brazilian enclave of **Blumenau**, every October.

Itineraries

One week

Beach and waterfall Begin in Rio over a weekend and take in the city sights and the nightlife in Lapa. On Monday leave for the beach resort town of Búzios or the pretty colonial port of Paraty, which is surrounded by beautiful beaches, especially near Trindade. Consider taking a trip on the side to the island of Ilha Grande or the rainforests and hiking trails of Itatiaia national park. On Wednesday either take a bus south to Curitiba (via Santos or São Paulo) and take the Serra Verde train to Paranaguá and the Ilha do Mel or return to Rio and fly to the Iguaçu Falls. On Friday fly to São Paulo for a taste of that city's restaurants and nightlife and take a flight home from there.

Carnival hop Fly into Recife on a Friday for Brazil's best, least expensive and most traditional large carnival and mix with the crowds at the Galo da Madruganda opening ceremony hosted by the great Brazilian percussionist Naná Vasconcelos. Spend Sunday and Monday in Recife/Olinda watching the maracatu blocos before flying south to Salvador on Tuesday and spending a few days with the crowds partying in the streets. Fly to Rio for Saturday's champions parade in the Sambódromo; relax on the beach and fly home on Sunday.

Two weeks

Amazon to Recife by beach Head to the vibrant colonial city of Belém at the mouth of the Amazon, being sure to arrive on a weekend to make the most of the fabulous nightlife. Either spend a few days recovering on the beaches of Marajó island or take a bus or flight south to São Luís, one of Brazil's least known colonial highlights with its fascinating architecture and African culture. After a few days' sightseeing in the city and nearby Alcântara, head for the Lençóis Maranhenses – a spectacular sand-dune desert on the wild, windy Atlantic. Continue from the Lençóis to Jericoacoara in Ceará for more beautiful beaches and some of the world's best wind- and kitesurfing. Make a brief stop at Fortaleza for some *forró* dancing and do a hop through one of the smaller beach resorts of Canoa Quebrada and Pipa, in Rio Grande do Norte, before arriving in Olinda and Recife at the weekend. Fly out from Recife.

Salvador to Rio by beach Begin in Salvador, Brazil's first capital, with its impressive historical centre and vibrant African-Brazilian culture. After a few days head to Itacaré, a laid-back surf town to the south, and spend a few days holed up on the beach. Take a long bus journey south to Porto Seguro, where the Portuguese first landed in Brazil and spend a few days here or in the adjacent beach town of Arraial d'Ajuda or, if you feel like a splurge, Trancoso – South America's beach chic capital. Be sure to visit the wildlife reserve at Estação Veracruz Veracel and the Pataxó people. Transfer south to Caravelas for a trip to the Abrolhos islands before taking the long journey south to Rio de Janeiro.

Three weeks

Table-top mountains, rainforests, wetlands and beach Fly into São Paulo and after a day or so in the city take a one-hour flight or a 10- to 14-hour bus ride to Cuiabá and the Pantanal – the best place for wildlife in the Americas. Take a side trip to Cristalino Jungle Lodge in the southern Amazon – one of the finest rainforest lodges in the world – then head to Brasília to see Oscar Niemeyer's modernist fantasy city. From here take a bus north to the wilds of the Chapada dos Veadeiros World Heritage Site to trek, rappel, mountain bike or climb in a landscape of dry forest interspersed with clear-water rivers, canyons and some of the continent's most beautiful waterfalls. Head north to Palmas in Tocantins and visit the forests and waterfalls around that city or take a side-trip into the wild Jalapão table-top mountains. Then fly to Rio or Salvador and the beach.

Colonial cities, waterfalls, wetlands and beach Fly into São Paulo and take a long bus journey to Campo Grande and the southern Pantanal. Stay either in a *fazenda* near Miranda or take a tour with an agency. Fly or bus it to Iguaçu, which at 3 km wide are the world's most impressive waterfalls. Fly from here to Belo Horizonte and a Friday or Saturday of live music, before visiting some of Latin America's prettiest colonial towns – Ouro Preto, Tiradentes or Diamantina – all with stunning baroque buildings set against a backdrop of rugged mountains. From Minas head to the coast, either at Rio or Salvador.

Four weeks

The Amazon heartland to Rio via the beach or via the wild interior The Amazon is not a river – it is 100,000 rivers, brooks and streams, ranging in colour from coffee with milk to cobalt blue to lemon to black. Begin your journey in the Amazon city of Manaus in a nearby jungle lodge or the Mamirauá reserve. Take a passenger boat downstream to lively Belém at the mouth of the river (preferably at the weekend to experience the nightlife). From here follow 'Amazon to Recife by beach' route (see above), then either continue by bus to Salvador and take a flight to Rio, or fly direct to Rio from Recife. It is also possible to take a far wilder and less travelled road to Rio by heading inland from Belém or São Luís and calling in at Palmas (for the vast *cerrado* wilderness near Jalapão); the waterfall-covered mountains of the Chapada dos Veadeiros; the modernist capital of Brasília; Campo Grande (for the Pantanal); and São Paulo.

When to go

The best time for a visit is from April to June, and August to October. Business visitors should avoid mid-December to the end of February, when it is hot and people are on holiday. In these months, hotels, beaches and transport tend to be very crowded. July is a school holiday month. If visiting tourist centres such as Salvador, Rio and the colonial cities in Minas Gerais in the low season, be aware that some tourist sights may be closed.

In Rio de Janeiro conditions during the winter (May to September) are like those of a north European summer, including periods of rain and overcast skies, with temperatures from 14°C to the high 20s. It is more like a Mediterranean autumn in São Paulo and the southern states and it can get very cold in the far south; warm clothing is required as temperatures can change dramatically and it can get cold on high ground anywhere in Brazil, particularly at night. The heaviest rain is from November to March in Rio and São Paulo, and from April to August around Recife (although irregular rainfall causes severe draughts here). The rainy season in the north and Amazônia can begin in December and is heaviest from March to May, but it is getting steadily shorter, possibly as a result of deforestation. Few places get more than 2 m – the coast north of Belém, some of the Amazon Basin, and a small area of the Serra do Mar between Santos and São Paulo, where the downpour has been harnessed to generate electricity. Summer conditions all over the country are tropical, although temperatures rarely reach 40°C.

The average annual temperature increases steadily from south to north, but even on the equator, in the Amazon Basin, the average temperature is not more than 27°C. The highest recorded was 42°C, in the dry northeastern states. From the latitude of Recife south to Rio, the mean temperature is 23-27°C along the coast, and 18-21°C in the highlands. South of Rio, towards the boundary with Uruguay, the mean temperature is 17-19°C. Humidity is relatively high in Brazil, particularly along the coast. The luminosity is also very high, and sunglasses are advisable.

What to do

Birdwatching

Almost a fifth of the world's bird species are Brazilian. The country is home to some 1750 species, of which 218 are endemic – the highest number of any country in the world.

Brazil also has the largest number of globally threatened birds: 120 of 1212 worldwide. This is accounted for partly by the numbers of critically threatened habitats that include the Atlantic coastal rainforest, which recently lost the Alagoas currassow, the *caatinga*, which has lost Spix's macaw, and the *cerrado* which is being cut at an alarming rate to feed the demand for soya.

Compared to Costa Rica or Ecuador, birding in Brazil is in its infancy. But awareness is increasing and there are some excellent birding guides in Brazil. It is no longer necessary to organize a birding trip through an international company (though many choose to do so; see operators below). The best time for birding is Sep-Oct as it is quiet, relatively dry and flights are cheapest.

Contact

For tour operators specializing in birdwatching, see pages 50-53.
Pantanal Bird Club, T065-3624 1930, www.pantanalbirdclub.org, is the best for serious birding in the interior. **Serra dos Tucanos**, www.serradostucanos.com.br, is the best in the Atlantic coastal forest. **Birding Brazil Tours**, www.birdingbraziltours. com, has a good reputation, operates out of Manaus and covers the Amazon and the rest of the country. **Ciro Albano**, www.nebrazil birding.com, and **Edson Endrigo**, www.aves foto.com.br, are excellent guides for the northeast and southeast respectively. **Focus Tours**, www.focustours.com, specializes in birdwatching and responsible travel, while **Ornitholidays**, T01794-519445 (UK), www.ornitholidays.co.uk, is one of the best companies working in Brazil from Europe. 2 comprehensive websites are **www.world twitch.com** and **www.camacdonald.com**.

Caving

There are some wonderful cave systems in Brazil, and Ibama has a programme for the protection of the national speleological heritage. National parks such as Ubajara (see page 551) and Chapada Diamantina (page 285) and the state park of PETAR (page 236) have easy access for the casual visitor, but there are also many options for the keen potholer in the states of São Paulo, Paraná, Minas Gerais and the federal district of Brasília.

Contact

Sociedade Brasileira de Espeleologia, www.sbe.com.br. For cave diving, see Scuba diving, page 23.

Climbing

As Brazil has no mountain ranges of Alpine or Andean proportions, the most popular form of escalada (climbing) is rock-face climbing. In the heart of Rio you can see, or join, climbers scaling the rocks at the base of Pão de Açúcar and on the Sugar Loaf itself. Not too far away, the Serra dos Órgãos provides plenty of challenges, not least the Dedo de Deus (God's Finger, see page 150). In the state of São Paulo a good location for climbing is Pedra do Báu near São Bento do Sapucaí, and Brotas is popular for abseiling (rappel). Pedra Branca and the Serra do Cipó are recommended locations in Minas Gerais. Mato Grosso has the Serra do Roncador and there are other good areas in Paraná and Rio Grande do Sul.

Contact

www.escaladabrasil.com and www.rockclimbing.com/routes/south_ and_central_america/brazil.

Fishing

Brazil is great for sport fishing. Officially, the country's fish stocks are under the control of Ibama (www.ibama.org.br) and a licence is required for fishing in any waters. As states often require permits too it is easiest to organize a trip through an agency. The best areas are the Amazon and Pantanal and the Rio Araguaia. Be aware that many Brazilians do not keep best practice and that rivers are quickly becoming over-fished, especially in the Pantanal, a threat to the world's largest wetland and a unique American biome.

Contact

Amazon Clipper, www.peacocktrips.com, is far and away the best company in the Amazon (page 655). Lodges such as **Barra Mansa**, www.hotelbarramansa.com.br, offer sport fishing in the Pantanal (page 735).

Football nation

Brazilians love football like Indians love cricket and seeing a match live in one of the large cities is an unforgettable experience. The crowd is a sea of waving banners and the noise from the jeers and cheers, drums and whistles is deafening. Football in Brazil is treated with religious reverence. Work is put on hold during an important game. And the country quite literally closes for business during the World Cup.

Brazilians are certain that they are and always will be the best in the world at the sport. German and Italian visitors are afforded token respect; Argentinians, derision; and those from the US, Australia and New Zealand pity. The British should expect mockery. 'Your country invented football' – Brazilians are fond of quipping – 'but we play it'. Brazil may have fared poorly in the last World Cup but they can still justifiably claim to be the best. One popular chant goes 'Tudo o Mundo tenta mais so Brasil e Penta' (every one tries but only Brazil has won [the World Cup] five times – in 1958, 1962, 1970, 1994 and 2002. They've been runners-up twice,

semi-finalists three times and they're the only team to have played in every competition. The best player of all time – as selected by FIFA – is Brazilian: Edson Arantes do Nascimento, aka Pelé, as are the top scorers in history, and the Brazilian national team has been nominated by FIFA as team of the year more than twice as many times as their nearest rivals.

In 2014 the World Cup returns to Brazil – after a 64-year absence. Brazilians will be hoping that they fare better than they did on that occasion. The team had stormed through the competition and were already being hailed as the world champions. When they lost 2-1 to Uruguay, stripped of a title they had already considered theirs, the fans' silence was, in the words of FIFA chairman, Jules Rimet, 'morbid and sometimes too difficult to bear'. The loss became known as the Maracanaço (after the Maracanã stadium in Rio where the match was held) – a word which has since become common parlance in Brazil for any kind of tragedy. To see a game in Rio see page 80.

Hang-gliding and paragliding

There are state associations affiliated with ABVL and there are a number of operators offering tandem flights for those without experience. Rampas (launch sites) are growing in number. Among the best known is Pedra Bonita at Gávea in Rio de Janeiro, but there are others in the state. Popular rampas can also be found in São Paulo, Espírito Santo, Minas Gerais, Paraná, Santa Catarina, Rio Grande do Sul, Ceará, Mato Grosso do Sul and Brasília.

Contact

Associação Brasileira de Vôo Livre (ABVL – Brazilian Hang-gliding Association), R Prefeito Mendes de Moraes s/n, São Conrado, Rio de Janeiro, T021-3322 0266,

www.abvl.com.br, covers both hang-gliding and paragliding. For a full list of launch sites (and much else besides) see the **Guia 4 Ventos Brasil** site, www.guia4ventos.com.br, which also contains information on launch sites in other South American countries.

Horse riding

The Pantanal offers some of the best opportunities for horse riding in Brazil. Almost all the lodges we list offer horse-riding treks into the wetlands – of anything from a few hours to a few days. There are good horse trails in Minas along the routes that used to be taken by the mule trains which transported goods between the coast and the interior. Tours with Tropa Serrana include overnight horse treks and explore many aspects of the Minas Gerais countryside that visitors do not normally see.

Contact
Tropa Serrana, Belo Horizonte, T031-3344 8986, www.tropaserrana.zip.net. Other operators are listed in relevant chapters.

Mountain biking
Brazil is well suited to cycling, both on and off-road. On main roads it is important to obey the general advice of being on the lookout for motor vehicles, as cyclists are very much second-class citizens. Also note that when cycling on the northeastern coast you may encounter strong winds which will hamper your progress. There are endless roads and tracks suitable for mountain biking, and there are many clubs in major cities which organize group rides, activities and competitions. Serra da Canastra in Minas Gerais is a popular area. Tamanduá in São Roque de Minas offer personalized tours and equipment hire.

Contact
Tamanduá, www.tamanduaecoturismo. com.br. Other operators are listed in relevant chapters throughout the book.

Rafting
Whitewater rafting started in Brazil in 1992. **Trópico**, offer trips in São Paulo state (eg on the Juquiá, Jaguarí, Peixe and Paraibuna rivers), in Rio de Janeiro (also on the Paraibuna, at Três Rios in the Serra dos Órgãos), Paraná (Rio Ribeira), Santa Catarina (Rio Itajaí) and Rio Grande do Sul (Três Coroas). There is also good whitewater rafting in the remote Jalapão chapada lands with **Korubo Expeditions**.

Contact
Trópico, www.tropico.tur.br, and **Korubo Expeditions**, www.korubo.com.br, are recommended. Other operators are listed in relevant chapters throughout the book.

Scuba diving
The best diving in Brazil is the Atol das Rocas; only available through private charter through Debopuche; it's very expensive but completely unspoilt, with visibility up to 40 m and with one of the highest levels of biodiversity in the tropical southern Atlantic. Fernando de Noronha has coral gardens, drop-offs and wrecks which include a 50-m Brazilian navy destroyer with full armament. Visibility is up to 50 m, with both current-free and drift diving. Amongst others, divers see at least two species of turtle, spinner dolphins, more than three species of shark, huge snapper and vast shoals of goatfish and jack. The Abrolhos archipelago offers diving of similar quality, with huge brain corals and, in the Brazilian summer, hump-back whale sightings are pretty much guaranteed. Arraial de Cabo is interesting because of the meeting of a southerly cold and northerly

Ten of the best beaches

warm current and has the best marine life in southeast Brazil.

Cave diving can be practised in many of the 200 underwater grottoes such as Bonito, Mato Grosso do Sul, Lapa de São Jorge, 280 km from Brasília, in Chapada Diamantina and Vale do Ribeira located between São Paulo and Paraná.

Contact

Debouche, www.dehouche.com. **American/ Brazilian Dive Club**, www.mergulho.com, with links to other dive sites in Brazil. **Océan**, www.ocean.com.br, is a dive shop and tour operator, based in Rio de Janeiro state (Rio, Angra dos Reis, Ilha Grande, Arraial do Cabo), which has a Diving in Brasil website (Portuguese only).

Surfing

There are good conditions all along the coast. Brazilians love to surf and are well-represented in international competitions, which are frequently held in the country, usually on the beaches near Itacaré in Bahia and on Fernando de Noronha island. Other popular locations include Niterói, Cabo Frio and around, Rio, Ilha Grande, Florianópolis and Ilha de Santa Catarina. See also Footprint's *Surfing the World*.

Contact

Fluir, www.fluir.com.br, the country's biggest surf magazine, has information on surfing (in Portuguese). **Brazil Surf Travel**, www.brazilsurftravel.com (in English).

Wind- and kitesurfing

There's no better place in the Americas for wind- and kitesurfing than Brazil. The northeast coast receives an almost constant wind for pretty much 365 days of the year and, in the last five years, beach towns like Cumbuco (page 548) and Jericoacoara (page 549) in Ceará have turned from small resorts into world wind- and kitesurf capitals. There is good wind- and kitesurfing around Rio too – especially to the east near Cabo Frio (page 138) and in the city itself. Santa Catarina island (page 336) has several popular windsurfing beaches, while the coast along the Linha Verde (page 452) is ideal for windsurfing, owing to constant fresh Atlantic breezes.

Contact

Details on companies offering board rental and tuition are listed in relevant chapters throughout the book. For information on kitesurfing in Cumbuco, visit www.kite-surf-brazil.com.

Getting there

Air

Flights into Brazil generally land in São Paulo, which has direct connections with the rest of **South and Central America**, the **USA**, **Canada**, **Mexico** and **Europe** and **Asia** and indirect connections with **Australasia** via Buenos Aires, Santiago or Los Angeles.

Rio de Janeiro, Brasília, Salvador Belo Horizonte, Fortaleza, Manaus and Recife have connections to the USA and Europe. Many other Brazilian cities have connections to Europe, mostly through Lisbon.

Brazil is connected to Spanish-speaking **Latin America** principally through Rio de Janeiro, São Paulo, Manaus, Porto Alegre and Brasília. It is connected to the **Guianas** through Belém, Fortaleza, Boa Vista and Macapá. Belém also receives flights from the **Caribbean**.

Charter flights, often at very attractive prices, are available from the USA and Europe. For details see www.netflights.com, www.dialaflight.com, www.charterflights.co.uk, www.edreams.co.uk, www.edreams.pt or www.edreams.it.

Prices are cheapest in October, November and after Carnaval and at their highest in the European summer and the Brazilian high seasons (generally 15 December to 15 January, the Thursday before Carnaval to the Saturday after Carnaval, and 15 June to 15 August).

Airport information

For most visitors the point of arrival will be **Cumbica International Airport** at Guarulhos (which it is often used as an alternative name) in São Paulo (see page 178) or **Tom Jobim International Airport** (also known as **Galeão**) on the Ilha do Governador, 16 km from the centre of Rio de Janeiro (see page 60). Details of other entry airports are given in their respective sections. Make sure you arrive two hours before international flights. It is wise to reconfirm your flight as departure times may have changed. ▶ *For airport tax, see page 49.*

International airlines serving Brazil

Aerolíneas, www.aerolineas.com. From Argentina with connections to Europe, Australia, New Zealand and the USA.
Aeroméxico, www.aeromexico.com. From the USA and Mexico via Mexico City to São Paulo.
Aerosur, www.aerosur.com. From Bolivia via Santa Cruz to São Paulo.
Air Canada, www.aircanada.com. From Canada and USA via Toronto to São Paulo.
Air Caraibes, www.aircaraibes.com. From Haiti, Martinique and Paris to Belém.
Air China, www.airchina.com. From China via Beijing to São Paulo.
Air Europa, www.aireuropa.com. From Europe via Madrid to Salvador.
Air France, www.airfrance.com. From Europe via Paris to São Paulo and Rio de Janeiro.

Air Italy, www.airitaly.it. From various Italian airports to Fortaleza.
Alitalia, www.alitalia.com. From Europe via Milan to São Paulo.
American Airlines, www.aa.com. Various non-stop services from key US cities to São Paulo, Rio de Janeiro, Salvador, Recife and Belo Horizonte.
Avianca, www.avianca.com. From Bogotá in Colombia to Rio de Janeiro and São Paulo.
British Airways, www.britishairways.com. From London to São Paulo and Rio Cabo.
Condor, www.condor.com. From Europe via Frankfurt to Recife and Salvador.
Continental, www.continental.com. From the USA via Newark to São Paulo and Rio.
Copa, www.copaair.com. From Panama City and Havana to Manaus and São Paulo.

Delta, www.delta.com. From various US cities via Atlanta to São Paulo and Rio. Emirates, Middle East via Dubai to São Paulo.
El Al, www.elal.co.il. From Tel Aviv to São Paulo.
Emirates, www.emirates.com. From Dubai to São Paulo.
GOL, www.voegol.com.br. From Montevideo, Cordoba and Lima to São Paulo.
Iberia, www.iberia.com. From Madrid to São Paulo and Rio de Janeiro.
JAL, www.jal.co.jp. From Japan via New York and Tokyo to São Paulo.
KLM, www.klm.com. From Europe via Amsterdam to São Paulo.
Korean, www.koreanair.com, Los Angeles and Seoul to São Paulo.
LAN, www.lan.com. From Lima and Santiago to São Paulo and Rio.
Lufthansa, www.lufthansa.com. From Frankfurt, Germany to São Paulo.
META, www.voemeta.com. From Georgetown (Guyana) and Paramaribo (Suriname) to Belém and Boa Vista.
South African, www.flysaa.com. From Johannesburg to São Paulo.
Qatar, www.qatarairways.com. From Doha to São Paulo.

Swiss Air, www.swiss.com. From Zurich to São Paulo.
TAAG, www.taag.aero. From Luanda to São Paulo.
TACA, www.taca.com. From Lima to São Paulo.
TAM, www.tam.com.br. From Asunción, Ciudad del Este, Cordoba, Frankfurt, London, Madrid, Miami, Milan, Montevideo, New York, Paris to São Paulo and Rio.
TAP, www.tap.pt. From Europe via Lisbon and Porto direct or indirect to Aracaju, Belo Horizonte, Brasília, Cuiabá, Curitiba, Fortaleza, Foz de Iguaçu, Goiânia, João Pessoa, Londrina, Natal, Porto Alegre, Porto Seguro, Porto Velho, Recife, Rio Branco, Rio de Janiero, São Luís, São Paulo (Congonhas and Guarulhos), Teresina and Vitória – some on a code-share basis.
Turkish, www.turkishairlines.com, from Istanbul to São Paulo via Dakar (Senegal).
United, www.united.com. From Chicago, Los Angeles, New York, Miami and Washington to São Paulo and Rio.
TACV, www.flytacv.com. From Lisbon and Boston to Fortaleza via Cape Verde.
VistaPluna, www.pluna.aero. From Montevideo to São Paulo and Rio de Janeiro.

Air passes
TAM and **GOL** offer a 21-day **Brazil Airpass**, which is valid on any TAM destination within Brazil. The price varies according to the number of flights taken and the international airline used to arrive in Brazil. They can only be bought outside Brazil. One to four flights start at around US$540, five flights start at US$680, six flights start at US$840, seven flights start at US$990, eight flights start at US$1120, and nine flights start at US$1259. The baggage allowance is the same as that permitted on their international flights. TAM and Gol also operate as part of the **Mercosur Airpass**, which is valid for Brazil, Argentina, Chile, Uruguay and Paraguay using local carriers. It is valid for any passenger with a return ticket to their country of origin, and must be bought with an international flight. The minimum stay is seven days, maximum 45 and at least two countries must be visited. The maximum number of flights is eight. Fares, worked out on a mileage basis, cost between US$295 and US$1195. Children pay a discounted rate, and under-threes pay 10% of the adult rate. Some of the carriers operate a blackout period between 15 December and 15 January.

Baggage allowance
Airlines will only allow a certain weight of luggage without a surcharge; for Brazil this is usually two items of 32 kg but may be as low as 20 kg; with two items of hand luggage weighing up to 10 kg in total. UK airport staff can refuse to load bags weighing more than

30 kg. Baggage allowances are higher in business and first class. Weight limits for internal flights are often lower, usually 20 kg. In all cases it is best to enquire beforehand.

Discount flight agents

Using the web to book flights, hotels and other services directly is becoming increasingly popular. However, cutting out travel agents can end up more costly if you don't know Brazil well, as they can often give you valuable money-saving and itinerary tips as well as quality discount hotel bookings and the benefit of their research.

UK and Ireland
Journey Latin America, 12-13 Heathfield Terrace, Chiswick, London W4 4JE, T020-8747 8315, www.journeylatinamerica.co.uk. Flights and holidays to Latin America.
STA Travel, 86 Old Brompton Rd, London SW7 3LH, T020-74376262, www.statravel.co.uk. Branches throughout the UK. Specialists in low-cost student/youth flights and tours. Good for student IDs and insurance.
Trailfinders, 194 Kensington High St, London, W8 7RG, T020-7938 3939, www.trail finders.com. 18 branches in London and throughout the UK. Also one in Dublin and 5 travel centres in Australia.

USA and Canada
Air Brokers International, 323 Geary St, Suite 411, San Francisco, CA94102, T01-800-883 3273, www.airbrokers.com. Consolidators and specialists on Around the World and Circle Pacific tickets.

Council Travel, www.counciltravel.com. Branches throughout the USA.
Fly Cheap, T1-800-FLY-CHEAP, www.1800 flycheap.com. Consolidator with discount fares from more than 1000 operators.
STA Travel, 5900 Wilshire Blvd, Suite 2110, Los Angeles, CA 90036, T1-800-777 0112, www.sta-travel.com. Also has branches in New York, San Francisco, Boston, Miami, Chicago, Seattle and Washington DC.
TFI, T800-745 8000, www.lowestprice.com. Offers seats unsold elsewhere on bargain-basement clearing basis.
Travel CUTS, 187 College St, Toronto, ON, M5T 1P7, T1-800-667 2887, www.travelcuts.com. Specialist in student discount fares, IDs and other travel services. Branches in other Canadian cities.
Travel Hub, T888-AIR-FARE, www.travelhub.com. Consolidator with discount fares from operators country-wide.
Travelocity, www.travelocity.com. Online consolidator.

Australia, New Zealand and South Africa
Flight Centres, www.flightcentre.com.au, www.flightcentre.co.nz, www.flight centre.co.za. Throughout Australia and NZ.
STA Travel, www.statravel.com.au, www.statravel.co.za and www.statravel.co.nz, Throughout Australia, South Africa and NZ.
Travel.com.au Offices throughout Australia.

River

Boats run from Iquitos in **Peru** to Tabatinga in Brazil. Onward travel is then on a five-day riverboat journey (or when they are available, a flight) to Manaus, the capital of the Amazon. This border can also be crossed by land from Leticia in **Colombia**, which is alongside Tabatinga. Security is tight at these borders and Brazilian immigration occasionally refuse to allow entry to Brazil for more than 30 days.

Brazil is connected to **Venezuela** through Puerto Ayacucho, San Carlos de Rio Negro and Cucui/São Gabriel da Cachoeira. The crossing is difficult. Exit stamps should be secured in Puerto Ayacucho. **Wayumi Airlines** flies to San Carlos. From here it is possible to hitch downstream to Cucui and take a bus to São Gabriel. Entry stamps must be secured in São Gabriel. Boats connect São Gabriel with Manaus (five to seven days).

Road

Bus

Argentina Connected to the south of Brazil at Foz de Iguaçu/ Puerto Iguazú (the Iguaçu falls) in Paraná state, Porto Xavier/San Javier on the Uruguay river and Uruguaiana/Paso de los Libres, both in Rio Grande do Sul state.

Bolivia Connected to Brazil at Puerto Quijarro/Corumbá via road and rail, with onward connections to the rest of Bolivia via Santa Cruz, at Guayara-Mirin, with connections to Porto Velho and at Cobija with fast buses to Rio Branco in Acre.

French Guiana Connected from Cayenne via Oyapock/Oiapoque to Macapá. The road is unpaved in Brazil. It is possible to do a circuit through the Guianas overland from Manaus/Boa Vista to Macapá and onward to Belém, although you will need a visa for Suriname (available in Guyana or Guyane).

Guyana Connected to Brazil at Leticia/Bonfim (by road from Georgetown) and Boa Vista.

Paraguay Reachable via Ciudad del Este/Foz de Iguaçu. Rio de Janeiro and São Paulo can easily be accessed by international buses from Asunción, which has connections with Buenos Aires, Santiago and Montevideo.

Peru Connected to Acre from Puerto Maldonado (reachable by road or plane from Cuzco), with regular fast buses to Rio Branco and onward road connections to the rest of Brazil.

Uruguay Connected to the south of Brazil; as of 2008 all crossings go via Bagé where Brazilian immigration is located. From here there are connections to Aceguá for the Uruguayan town of Melo; Jaguarão for Rio Branco and the Uruguayan border; and Barra do Quaraí/Bella Unión, via the Barra del Cuaraim bridge and Quaraí/Artigas.

Venezuela Connected to Manaus via Santa Elena de Uairen/Boa Vista in Roraima state and a good road.

Car

There are agreements between Brazil and most South American countries (check in the case of Bolivia) whereby a car can be taken into Brazil for a period of 90 days without any special documents. For cars registered in other countries, you need proof of ownership and/or registration in the home country and valid driving licence. A 90-day permit is given by customs or at the **Serviço de Controle Aduaneiro** ① *Ministério da Fazenda, Av Presidente Antônio Carlos, Sala 1129, Rio de Janeiro*, and the procedure is straightforward. Keep *all* the papers you are given when you enter, to produce when you leave.

When crossing the border into Brazil, make sure that there is an official who knows about the temporary import of cars. You must specify which border station you intend to leave by, but application can be made to the customs to change this.

Sea

Travelling as a passenger on a cargo ship to South America is not a cheap way to go, but if you have the time and want a bit of luxury, it makes a great alternative to flying. The passage is often only available for round trips.

Cargo Ship Voyages Ltd, Hemley, Woodbridge, Suffolk IP12 4QF, T01473-736265, www.cargoshipvoyages.co.uk.
Freighter World Cruises, www.freighter world.com. The largest company in the world devoted to cruises on cargo ships.
Strand Voyages, 1 Adam St, London WC2N 6AB, T020-7766 8220, www.strand travel.co.uk. Booking agents for all routes.

Cruise ships
Cruise ships regularly visit Brazil; including Rio and Salvador. The website www.cruisetrans atlantic.com has full details of transatlantic crossings. There are often very good deals off season.

Getting around

Public transport in Brazil is very efficient, but distances are huge. Most visitors will find themselves travelling by buses and planes, except in the Amazon when a boat is often the only way to get around. Train routes are practically non-existent, car hire is expensive and hitchhiking not advisable. Taxis vary widely in quality and price but are easy to come by and safe when taken from a *posto de taxis* (taxi rank).

Air

Because of the size of the country, flying is often the most practical option and internal air services are highly developed. All state capitals and larger cities are linked with each other with services several times a day, and all national airlines offer excellent service. Recent deregulation of the airlines has greatly reduced prices on some routes and low-cost airlines offer fares that can often be as cheap as travelling by bus (when booked through the internet). Paying with an international credit card is not always possible online; but it is usually possible to buy an online ticket through a hotel, agency or willing friend without surcharge. Many of the smaller airlines go in and out of business sporadically. **GOL, Oceanair, TAM, TRIP/Total, Varig**, and **Webjet** operate the most extensive routes. Most of their websites (see below) provide full information, including a booking service, although not all are in English.

Domestic airlines

Abaeté, www.voeabaete.com.br.
Addey Táxi Aéreo, www.addey.com.br.
Aero Star, www.aerostar.com.br.
Air Minas, www.airminas.com.br.
Avianca, www.avianca.com.br.
Azul, www.voeazul.com.br.
GOL, www.voegol.com.br.
Litorânea, www.voelitoranea.com.br.
META, www.voemeta.com.
NHT, www.voenht.com.br.
Pantanal Linhas Aéreas, www.voepantanal.com.br.

Passaredo, www.voepassaredo.com.br.
Puma, www.pumaair.com.br.
Rico, www.voerico.com.br.
Sete, www.voesete.com.br.
TAF, www.voetaf.com.br.
TAM, www.tam.com.br.
TEAM, www.voeteam.com.br.
TRIP and **Total Linhas Aéreas** (operate on a permanent codeshare), www.voetrip.com.br, www.total.com.br.
Varig, www.varig.com.br.
Webjet, www.webjet.com.br.

Rail

There are 30,379 km of railways, which are not combined into a unified system; almost all run goods trains only. Brazil has two gauges and there is little transfer between them. Two more gauges exist for the isolated **Amapá** railway (used to transport manganese from the Serra do Navio) and the tourist-only **São João del Rei** and **Ouro Preto-Mariana** lines. There is also the **Trem do Pantanal** – a tourist-designated train running between Campo Grande and Miranda in the Pantanal.

River

The only area where travel by boat is not merely practical (but often necessary) is the Amazon region. There are also some limited transport services along the São Francisco River and through the Pantanal. ▶▶ *See page 656 for details of river transport in the Amazon.*

Road

The best paved highways are heavily concentrated in the southeast, but roads serving the interior are being improved to all-weather status and many are paved. Most main roads between principal cities are paved. Some are narrow and therefore dangerous; many are in poor condition.

Bus

There are three standards of bus: *Comum*, or *Convencional*, are quite slow, not very comfortable and fill up quickly; *Executivo* are more expensive, comfortable (many have reclining seats), and don't stop en route to pick up passengers so are safer; *Leito* (literally 'bed') run at night between the main centres, offering reclining seats with leg rests, toilets, and sometimes refreshments, at double the normal fare. For journeys over 100 km, most buses have chemical toilets (bring toilet paper). Air conditioning can make buses cold at night, so take a jumper; on some services blankets are supplied.

Buses stop fairly frequently (every two to four hours) at *postos* for snacks. Bus stations for interstate services and other long-distance routes are called *rodoviárias*. They are frequently outside the city centres and offer snack bars, lavatories, left luggage, local bus services and information centres. Buy bus tickets at *rodoviárias* (most now take credit cards), not from travel agents who add on surcharges. Reliable bus information is hard to come by, other than from companies themselves. Buses usually arrive and depart in very good time. Many town buses have turnstiles, which can be inconvenient if you are carrying a large pack. Urban buses normally serve local airports.

Car

Car hire Renting a car in Brazil is expensive: the cheapest rate for unlimited mileage for a small car is about US$65 per day. These costs can be more than halved by reserving a car over the internet through one of the larger international companies such as Europcar (www.europcar.co.uk) or Avis (www.avis.co.uk). Minimum age for renting a car is 21 and it's essential to have a credit card. Companies operate under the terms *aluguel de automóveis* or *auto-locadores*. Check exactly what the company's insurance policy covers.

In many cases it will not cover major accidents or 'natural' damage (eg flooding). Ask if extra cover is available. Sometimes using a credit card automatically includes insurance. Beware of being billed for scratches that were on the vehicle before you hired it.

Documents To drive in Brazil you need an international licence. A national driving licence is acceptable if your home country is a signatory to the Vienna and Geneva conventions.

Fuel Fuel prices vary weekly and between regions. *Gasolina común* is about US$1.65 per litre with *gasolina aditivada* a few cents more. *Alcool* is around US$1. Unleaded fuel is known as *sem chumbo. Comun* (and sometimes in the smaller petrol stations, *aditivada*) is often diluted with acetone as a means of making more profit. This can cause coughs and hiccups and when added in large quantities can damage the engine. Buy from the larger stations to avoid trouble. With alcohol fuel you need about 50% more than regular gasoline as fuel consumption is heavier. Many cars operate a **Flex system** whereby it is possible to put both alcohol and petrol in the same tank.

Insurance Insurance against accident and theft is very expensive. If the car is stolen or written off you will be required to pay very high import duty on its value. The legally required minimum cover for third party insurance is not expensive.

Safety Try to never leave your car unattended except in a locked garage or guarded parking area. Remove all belongings and leave the empty glove compartment open. Also lock the clutch or accelerator to the steering wheel with a heavy, obvious chain or lock. Adult minders or street children will usually protect your car fiercely in exchange for a tip.

Taxi

Rates vary from city to city, but are consistent within each city. At the outset, make sure the meter is cleared and shows 'tariff 1', except (usually) from 2300-0600, Sunday, and in December when '2' is permitted. Check that the meter is working; if not, fix the price in advance. The **radio taxi** service costs about 50% more but cheating is less likely. Taxis outside larger hotels usually cost more. If you are seriously cheated, note the number of the taxi and insist on a signed bill; threatening to take it to the police can work. **Mototaxis** are much more economical, but many are unlicensed and there have been a number of robberies of passengers.

Maps

International Travel Maps (ITM), www.itmb.com, publishes an excellent series of travel maps that feature Brazil, including *South America South*, *North East* and *North West* (1:4M), and *Rio de Janeiro* (1:20,000). Also available is *New World Edition*, Bertelsmann, Neumarkter Strasse 18, 81673 München, Germany, *Mittelamerika*, *Südamerika Nord*, *Südamerika Sud*, *Brasilien* (all 1:4M).

   Stanfords ① *12-14 Long Acre, Covent Garden, London, WC2E 9LP, UK, T020-78361321, www.stanfords.co.uk*, sells a wide variety of guides and maps.

   Editora Abril publishes excellent maps and guides in Portuguese and English. See www.abril.com.br for details.

Sleeping

There is a good range of accommodation options in Brazil. An *albergue* or hostel offers the cheapest option. These have dormitory beds and single and double rooms. Many are part of the **IYHA**, www.iyha.org. **Hostel world**, www.hostelworld.com; **Hostel Bookers**, www.hostelbookers.com; and **Hostel.com**, www.hostel.com, are useful portals. **Hostel Trail Latin America** – T0131-208 0007 (UK), www.hosteltrail.com – managed from their hostel in Popayan, is an online network of hotels and tour companies in South America. A *pensão* is either a cheap guesthouse or a household that rents out some rooms.

A *pousada* is either a bed-and-breakfast, often small and family-run, or a sophisticated and often charming small hotel. A *hotel* is as it is anywhere else in the world, operating according to the international star system, although five-star hotels are not price controlled and hotels in any category are not always of the standard of their star equivalent in the USA, Canada or Europe. Many of the older hotels can be cheaper than hostels. Usually accommodation prices include a breakfast of rolls, ham, cheese, cakes and fruit with coffee and juice; there is no reduction if you don't eat it. Rooms vary too. Normally an *apartamento* is a room with separate living and sleeping areas and sometimes cooking facilities. A *quarto* is a standard room; *com banheiro* is en suite; and *sem banheiro* is with shared bathroom. Finally there are the *motels*. These should not be confused with their US counterpart: motels are used by guests not intending to sleep; there is no stigma attached and they usually offer good value (the rate for a full night is called the '*pernoite*'), however the decor can be a little garish.

It's a good idea to book accommodation in advance in small towns that are popular at weekends with city dwellers (eg near São Paulo and Rio de Janeiro), and it's essential to book at peak times.

Luxury accommodation

Much of the luxury private accommodation sector can be booked through operators. **Angatu**, www.angatu.com, offers the best private homes along the Costa Verde, together with bespoke trips. **Dehouche**, www.dehouche.com, offers upmarket accommodation and trips in Bahia, Rio and Alagoas. **Brazilian Beach House**, www.brazilianbeachhouse.com, has some of the finest houses in Búzios and Trancoso but is not so great at organizing transfers and pick-ups. **Matuete**, www.matuete.com, has a range of luxurious properties and tours throughout Brazil.

Camping

Those with an international camping card pay only half the rate of a non-member at **Camping Clube do Brasil** sites, www.campingclube.com.br. Membership of the club itself is expensive: US$85 for six months. The club has 43 sites in 13 states and 80,000 members. It may be difficult to get into some Camping Clube campsites during high season (January to February). Private campsites charge about US$8-15 per person. For those on a very low budget and in isolated areas where there is no campsite available, it's usually possible to stay at service stations. They have shower facilities, watchmen and food; some have dormitories. There are also various municipal sites. Campsites tend to be some distance from public transport routes and are better suited to people with their own car. Wild camping is generally difficult and dangerous. Never camp at the side of a road; this is very risky.

Sleeping price codes

LL	over US$200	L	US$151-200	AL	US$116-150
A	US$81-115	B	US$51-80	C	US$36-50
D	US$21-35	E	US$10-20	F	under US$10

Prices include taxes and service charge, but not meals. They are based on a double room, except in the E and F ranges, where prices are almost always per person.

Homestays

Staying with a local family is an excellent way to become integrated quickly into a city and companies try to match guests to their hosts. **Cama e Café**, www.camaecafe.com.br, organizes homestays in Rio de Janeiro, Olinda and a number of other cities around Brazil. **Couch surfing**, www.couchsurfing.com, offers a free, backpacker alternative.

Quality hotel associations

The better international hotel associations have members in Brazil. These include: **Small Luxury Hotels of the World**, www.slh.com; the **Leading Hotels of the World**, www.lhw.com; the **Leading Small Hotels of the World**, www.leadingsmallhotels oftheworld.com; **Great Small Hotels**, www.greatsmallhotels.com; and the **French Relais et Chateaux group**, www.relaischateaux.com, which also includes restaurants.

The Brazilian equivalent of these associations is the **Roteiros de Charme**, www.roteiros decharme.com.br, with some 30 locations in the southeast and northeast. Whilst membership of these groups pretty much guarantees quality, it is by no means comprehensive. There are many fine hotels and charming *pousadas* listed in our text that are not included in these associations.

Online travel agencies (OTAs)

Services like **Tripadvisor** and OTAs associated with them – such as **hotels.com, expedia.com** and **venere.com**, are well worth using for both reviews and for booking ahead. Hotels booked through an OTA can be up to 50% cheaper than the rack rate. Similar sites operate for hostels (though discounts are far less considerable). They include the **Hostelling International** site, www.hihostels.com, **hostelbookers.com, hostels.com** and **hostelworld.com**.

Eating and drinking

Food

Brazilians consider their cuisine to be up there with the world's best. Visitors may disagree. Mains are generally heavy, meaty and unspiced. Deserts are often very sweet. That said, the best cooking south of the Rio Grande is in São Paulo and Rio, where a heady mix of international immigrants has resulted in some unusual fusion cooking and exquisite variations on French, Japanese, Portuguese, Arabic and Italian traditional techniques and dishes. The regional cooking in Pará is also a delight – utilizing unusual and unique fruits and vegetables from the Amazon and the sumptuous Amazonian river fish.

Outside the more sophisticated cities it can be a struggle to find interesting food. The Brazilian staple meal generally consists of a cut of fried or barbecued meat, chicken or fish accompanied by rice, black or South American broad beans and an unseasoned salad of lettuce, grated carrot, tomato and beetroot. Condiments are weak chilli sauce, olive oil, salt and pepper and vinegar.

The national dish is a greasy campfire stew called *feijoada*, made by throwing jerked beef, smoked sausage, tongue and salt pork into a pot with lots of fat and beans and stewing it for hours. The resulting stew is sprinkled with fried *farofa* (manioc flour) and served with *couve* (kale) and slices of orange. The meal is washed down with *cachaça* (sugarcane rum). Most restaurants serve the *feijoada completa* for Saturday lunch (up until about 1630). Come with a very empty stomach.

Brazil's other national dish is mixed grilled meat or *churrasco*, served in vast portions off the spit by legions of rushing waiters, and accompanied by a buffet of salads, beans and mashed vegetables. *Churrascos* are served in *churrascarias* or *rodízios*. The meat is generally excellent, especially in the best *churascarias*, and the portions are unlimited, offering good value for camel-stomached carnivores able to eat one meal a day.

In remembrance of Portugal, but bizarrely for a tropical country replete with fish, Brazil is also the world's largest consumer of **cod**, pulled from the cold north Atlantic, salted and served in watery slabs or little balls as *bacalhau* (an appetizer/bar snack) or *petisco*. Other national *petiscos* include *kibe* (a deep-fried or baked mince with onion, mint and flour), *coxinha* (deep-fried chicken or meat in dough), *empadas* (baked puff-pastry patties with prawns, chicken, heart of palm or meat), and *tortas* (little pies with the same ingredients). When served in bakeries, *padarias* or snack bars these are collectively referred to as *salgadinhos* (savouries).

The best cooking in Brazil is not national but regional. **Bahia** offers an African-infused, welcome break from meat, rice and beans further south, with a variety of seafood dishes. Unlike most Brazilians, Bahians have discovered sauces, pepper and chilli. The most famous Bahian dish is *moqueca*, fresh fish cooked slowly with prawns in *dendê* palm oil, coconut milk, garlic, tomatoes, cilantro and chili pepper. A variety served in Espírito Santo, the state south of Bahia, is seasoned with blood-red *urucum* berry and served in a clay pot. Other Bahian dishes include *vatapá* and *Caruaru*, pastes made from prawns, nuts, bread, coconut milk and *dendê* oil, *xinxim de galinha*, a rich, spicy chicken stew, best without *dendê* oil, and *acarajé,* black-eyed peas or beans squashed into a ball, deep-fried in *dendê* oil and served split in half, stuffed with *vatapá* or *Caruaru* and seasoned with chilli.

Minas Gerais and **Goiás** are famous for their buffets of stews served over a wood-fired stove and made from a variety of meats and *cerrado* fruits and vegetables

Eating price codes

🍴🍴🍴 over US$20   🍴🍴 US$8-20   🍴 under US$8

Prices refer to the cost of a two-course meal, not including drinks.

like the *pequi*, which is sucked and never bitten; its flesh covers thousands of tiny, razor sharp spines. Minas specialities include *tutu á mineira* made with bacon, egg, refried beans in a paste, and *feijão tropeiro*, herb-infused beans served with *farofa*. A watery, white soft and almost entirely flavourless cheese, *queijo minas* is often served for dessert with ultra-sweet *guava* paste.

Some of the most interesting cooking comes from the **Amazon**. The river fish here are delicious, especially the firm flesh of the *pacu* and *tambaqui*. The *piracururu* is an endangered species and should only be eaten where it is farmed or fished sustainably, from reserves such as **Mamirauá** (see page 644). The most celebrated regional dish in the Amazon is *tacacá no tucupi*, prawn broth cooked in manioc juice and *jambu* leaf. The soup is infused with an alkaloid from the *jambu* that numbs the mouth and produces an energetic rush to the head.

There are myriad unusual, delicious fruits in the Amazon and Brazil as a whole, many with unique flavours. They include the pungent, sweet *cupuaçu*, which makes delicious cakes, the tart *camu-camu*, a large glass of which holds a gram of vitamin C, and *açaí* – a dark and highly nutritious berry from a varzea (seasonally flooded forest) palm tree, common in the Amazon. *Açaí* berries are often served as a frozen paste, garnished with *xarope* (syrup) and sprinkled with *guaraná* (a ground seed, also from the Amazon, which has stimulant effects similar to caffeine). The *cerrado* gives Brazil fruits such as the delicious *umbu*, *seriguela* and *mangaba*; small pulpy fruits which produce refreshing juices. Brazil also produces some of the world's best mangoes, papayas, bananas and custard apples, all of which come in a variety of flavours and sizes.

Eating cheaply

The cheapest dish is the *prato feito* or *sortido*, an excellent-value set menu usually comprising meat/chicken/fish, beans, rice, chips and salad. The *prato comercial* is similar but rather better and a bit more expensive. Portions are usually large enough for two and come with two plates. If you are on your own, you could ask for an *embalagem* (doggy bag) or a *marmita* (takeaway) and offer it to a person with no food (many Brazilians do). Many restaurants serve *comida por kilo* buffets where you serve yourself and pay for the weight of food on your plate. This is generally good value and is a good option for vegetarians. *Lanchonetes* and *padarias* (diners and bakeries) are good for cheap eats; usually serving *prato feitos*, *salgadinhos*, excellent juices and other snacks.

The main meal is usually taken in the middle of the day; cheap restaurants tend not to be open in the evening.

The national liquor is *cachaça* (also known as *pinga*), which is made from sugar-cane, and ranging from cheap supermarket and service-station fire-water, to boutique distillery and connoisseur labels from the interior of Minas Gerais. Mixed with fruit juice, sugar and crushed ice, *cachaça* becomes the principal element in a *batida*, a refreshing but deceptively powerful drink. Served with pulped lime or other fruit, mountains of sugar and smashed ice it becomes the world's favourite party cocktail, caipirinha. A less potent caipirinha made with vodka is called a *caipiroska* and with sake a *saikirinha* or *caipisake*.

Some genuine Scotch whisky brands are bottled in Brazil. They are far cheaper even than duty free; Teacher's is the best. Locally made and cheap gin, vermouth and campari are pretty much as good as their US and European counterparts.

Wine is becoming increasingly popular, with good-value Portuguese and Argentinean bottles and some reasonable national table wines such as Château d'Argent, Château Duvalier, Almadén, Dreher, Preciosa and more respectable Bernard Taillan, Marjolet from Cabernet grapes, and the Moselle-type white Zahringer. A new *adega* tends to start off well, but the quality gradually deteriorates with time; many vintners have switched to American Concorde grapes, producing a rougher wine. Greville Brut champagne-style sparkling wine is inexpensive and very drinkable.

Brazil is the third most important wine producer in South America. The wine industry is mainly concentrated in the south of the country where the conditions are most suitable, with over 90% of wine produced in Rio Grande do Sul. There are also vineyards in Pernambuco. There are some interesting sparkling wines in the Italian spumante style (the best is Casa Valduga Brut Premium Sparkling Wine), and Brazil produces still wines using many international and imported varieties. None are distinguished – these are drinkable table wines at best. At worst they are plonk of the Blue Nun variety. The best bottle of red is probably the Boscato Reserva Cabernet Sauvignon. But it's expensive (at around US$20 a bottle); you'll get far higher quality and better value buying Portuguese, Argentine or Chilean wines in Brazil.

Brazilian beer is generally lager, served ice-cold. Draught beer is called *chope* or *chopp* (after the German Schoppen, and pronounced 'shoppi'). There are various national brands of bottled beers, which include Brahma, Skol, Cerpa, Antartica and the best Itaipava and Bohemia. There are black beers too, notably Xingu. They tend to be sweet. The best beer is from the German breweries in Rio Grande do Sul and is available only there.

Brazil's myriad fruits are used to make fruit juices or *sucos*, which come in a delicious variety, unrivalled anywhere in the world. *Açai*, *acerola*, *caju* (cashew), *pitanga*, *goiaba* (guava), *genipapo*, *graviola* (*chirimoya*), *maracujá* (passion fruit), *sapoti*, *umbu* and *tamarindo* are a few of the best. *Vitaminas* are thick fruit or vegetable drinks with milk. *Caldo de cana* is a sugar-cane juice, sometimes mixed with ice. *Água de côco* or *côco verde* is coconut water served straight from a chilled, fresh, green coconut. The best known of many local soft drinks is *guaraná*, which is a very popular carbonated fruit drink, completely unrelated to the Amazon nut. The best variety is *guaraná Antarctica*. Coffee is ubiquitous and good tea entirely absent.

Shopping

Arts and crafts

Brazil does not offer the variety and quality of arts and crafts you'll find in the Andes. However, good buys include: beautiful bead jewellery and bags made from Amazon seeds; clay figurines from the northeast, especially from Pernambuco; lace from Ceará; leatherwork, Marajó pottery and fabric hammocks from Amazônia (be sure to buy hooks – *ganchos para rede* – for hanging your hammock at home); carvings in soapstone and in bone; *capim-dourado* gold-grass bags and jewellery from Tocantins; and African-type pottery, basketwork and *candomblé* artefacts from Bahia. Brazilian cigars are excellent for those who like mild flavours.

Jewellery

Gold, diamonds and gemstones are good buys throughout Brazil and there are innovative designs in jewellery. For something special and high quality, buy at reputable dealers such as H Stern, Vartanian or Antonio Bernado. Cheap, fun pieces can be bought from street traders. There are interesting furnishings made with gemstones and marble – some of them rather cheesy – and huge slabs of amethyst, quartz and crystal at a fraction of a new age shop price. More interesting and unusual is the seed and bead jewellery, much of it made with uniquely Brazilian natural products, and based on original indigenous designs. Itacaré in Bahia, Belém and Manaus are good places to buy such items.

Fashion

Brazil has long eclipsed Argentina as the fashion capital of Latin America and São Paulo is its epicentre, hosting the largest fashion show south of New York twice a year at the city's fashion week (www.spfw.com.br). Brazilian cuts, colours and contours are fresh and daring by US and European standards. Quality and variety is very high, from gorgeous bags and bikinis to designer dresses, shoes and denims. In São Paulo the best area for fashion shopping is Jardins (around Rua Oscar Freire) and the **Iguatemi** shopping centre on Avenida Faria Lima, and the city's most exclusive shopping emporium, **Daslu**. In Rio de Janeiro, Ipanema is the place to go for high-end shopping, as well as the **São Conrado Fashion Mall** and **Shopping Leblon**. ▶▶ *See Shopping in Rio de Janeiro, page 122, and São Paulo, page 218.*

Herbal remedies

For those who know how to use them, medicinal herbs, barks and spices can be bought from street markets throughout Brazil. Coconut oil and local skin and haircare products (fantastic conditioners) are better quality and cheaper than in Europe. Natura and O Boticário are excellent local brands, similar in quality to the Body Shop. There are branches in most Shopping Malls in most large Brazilian cities.

Music and instruments

If there is a more musical country on earth than Brazil we are yet to learn of it. Music is as ubiquitous as sunlight in Brazil and browsing through a CD shop anywhere will be sure to result in at least one purchase. See box, page 782, for a list of recommended artists.

Musical instruments are a good buy, particularly Brazilian percussion items. For example: the *berimbau*, a bow with a gourd sound-bell used in *candomblé*; the *cuíca* friction drum, which produces the characteristic squeaks and chirrups heard in samba; assorted hand drums including the *surdo* (the big samba bass drum); and the *caixa, tambor, repinique* and *timbale* (drums that produce the characteristic Brazilian ra-ta-ta-ta-ta). The most Brazilian of hand drums is the tambourine, a misnomer for the *pandeiro* (which comes with bells), as opposed to the *tamborim* (which comes without). There are many unusual stringed instruments too: the *rabeca* (desert fiddle), the *cavaquinho* or *cavaco* (the Portuguese ancestor of ukulele), the *bandolim* (Brazilian mandolin), with its characteristic pear shape, and many excellent nylon-strung guitars.

Festivals and events

Brazil has festivals all year round with most concentrated in Jun and around Carnaval at the beginning of Lent. This list barely skims the surface. See also Festivals, page 10.

January

Procissão de Nosso Senhor dos Navegantes, Salvador, Bahia. A big procession and a key event of the *candomblé* calendar. See www.bahia-online.net/festas.

Festa do Bonfim, see www.bahia-online.net/festas.

São Paulo fashion week, São Paulo and Rio de Janeiro. The most important event on the Latin American fashion calendar attended by models and designers from all over the world. See www.spfw.com.br.

February

Festa de Yemanjá, Rio Vermelho, Salvador, Bahia. Dedicated to the *candomblé orixá* (spirit) of the sea and a great place to hear authentic live Bahian bands. See www.bahia-online.net/festas.

Pré-Caju, a pre-carnival carnival in Aracajú, Sergipe 15 days before Salvador carnival and with a similar vibe, though on a far smaller scale. See www.setur.se.gov.br.

February/March

Carnaval, Brazil's biggest festival takes place throughout the country and most famously in Rio's *sambódromo* stadium. For a wild street party head for Salvador; for something more authentic and traditional, Recife; and for a Brazilian crowd entirely free of foreign

tourists, try one of the cities in Brazil's interior such as Cidade de Goiás, www.vilaboadegoias. com.br/carnaval, or Ouro Preto, www.carnavalouropreto.com.

March

Chocofest, Canela, Serra Gaucha, Rio Grande do Sul. A pre-Easter chocolate-fest with parades, 100,000 visitors and chocolate. See www.canelaturismo.com.br.

April

Festa de Nossa Senhora da Penha, Vila Velha, Vitória, Espírito Santo. A series of spectacular processions celebrating the saint's day of the city's patron. See www.conventodapenha.org.br.

Festa do Açaí, Festa da Castanha and Festa do Cupuaçu, Codajás, Tefé and Presidente Figueiredo, Amazonas. 3 festivals devoted to 3 of the best Amazonian foods: the *açaí* energy berry, *cupuaçu* and the Brazil nut.

Cuiafolia, the biggest festival of the year in Mato Grosso. The capital, Cuiabá, erupts into a mock-Bahian carnival powered by cheesy Bahian *axé* acts. See www.cuiafolia.com.br.

June

Boi Bumba, Parintins, Amazonas. A huge spectacle re-enacting the Boi story, with 2 competing teams, enormous floats and troupes of dancers. On an island in the Amazon. See www.boibumba.com.

Bumba-Meu-Boi, São Luís, Maranhão, see www.saoluisturismo.com.br.

Festas Juninas (Festas do São João), Campina Grande, Paraíba, Caruaru, Pernambuco and throughout Brazil. Brazil's major winter festival when everyone dresses up as a yokel, drinks hot spiced wine and dances *forró*.

July
Anima Mundi, Rio de Janeiro and São Paulo. One of the largest animation festivals in the world; lasts 2 months. See www.animamundi.com.br.
Festa Literária Internacional de Paraty (FLIP), Paraty, Rio de Janeiro. The country's premier literary festival attracting big names such as Salman Rushdie and Alice Walker. See www.flip.org.br.
Fortal Brazil's largest out of season carnival in Fortaleza powered mostly by Bahian music, but with a few more interesting fringe acts. See www.fortal.com.br.

August
Festa da Nossa Senhora D'Ajuda, Arraial d'Ajuda, Bahia. Festivals and processions celebrating the town's patron saint. See www.arraial-dajuda.com.br.
Festival de Gramado, Gramado, Rio Grande do Sul. Latin America's largest film festival. See www.festivaldegramado.net.
Festa do Peão de Boiadeiro, Barretos, São Paulo state. The biggest rodeo in the world, with a legion of Brazil's cheesiest music stars and legions of cowboys riding bulls. See www.festadopeaode americana.com.br.
Festival de Inverno de Garanhuns, Pernambuco. One of the biggest quality music festivals in the northeast, with a big programme of shows by names such as Alceu Valença and Elba Ramalho. Full details of the website, including how to reach the festival and where to stay: www.fig.com.br.

Carnival dates

→ **2011** 5-8 February
→ **2012** 18-21 February
→ **2013** 9-12 February
→ **2014** 1-4 March

October
Brazilian Grand Prix, São Paulo. See www.formula1.com.
Carnoporto, Porto Seguro's huge out-of-season carnival with all the top cheesy Bahian bands and big crowds. See www.axemoifolia.com.br.
Oktoberfest, Blumenau, Santa Catarina. See www.oktoberfest.com.br.
Jogos dos Povos Indígenas, various locations. Indigenous people from throughout the country gather for the Brazilian equivalent of the Highland games, with wrestling, archery, javelin throwing and general celebrations. See www.funai.gov.br/indios/jogos/jogos_indigenas.htm.

November
Círio de Nazaré, Belém and throughout Pará and Amazonas states. One of the largest religious celebrations in Brazil. Huge crowds, long precessions and many live music and cultural events. www.paratur.pa.gov.br.

31 December
Reveillon, New Year's Eve. This is a huge party all over Brazil, and biggest of all on Copacabana beach in Rio. In São Paulo celebrations centre on the city's main Av Paulista, which is lined with sound stages and packed with partygoers.

How big is your footprint?

→ Where possible choose a destination, tour operator or hotel with a proven ethical and environmental commitment – if in doubt, ask.

→ Spend money on locally produced (rather than imported) goods and services, buy directly from the producer or from a 'fair trade' shop, and use common sense when bargaining – the few dollars you save may be a week's salary to others.

→ Use water and electricity carefully – travellers may receive preferential supply while the needs of local communities are overlooked.

→ Learn about local etiquette and culture – consider local norms and behaviour and dress appropriately for local cultures and situations.

→ Protect wildlife and other natural resources – don't buy souvenirs or goods unless they are sustainably produced and are not protected under CITES legislation.

→ Always ask before taking photographs or videos of people.

→ Consider staying in local accommodation rather than foreign-owned hotels – the economic benefits for host communities are greater – and there are more opportunities to learn about local culture.

→ Within cities, local buses and (in São Paulo) metrôs are fast, cheap and have extensive routes. Try one instead of a taxi, and meet some real Brazilians!

→ Long-distance buses may take longer than flying but they have comfortable reclining seats, some offer drinks, and show up-to-date DVDs. They sometimes have better schedules too.

→ Supermarkets will give you a plastic bag for even the smallest purchases. If you don't need one, let them know – plastic waste is a huge problem – particularly in the northeast. When buying certain drinks, look for the returnable glass bottles.

→ Make a voluntary contribution to Climate Care, www.co2.org, to help counteract the pollution caused by tax-free fuel on your flight.

Responsible travel

Sustainable or ecotourism is not just about looking after the physical environment, but also the local community. Whilst it has been slow to catch up with Costa Rica or Ecuador, Brazil now has some first-rate ecotourism projects and the country is a pioneer in urban community tourism in the favelas. Model ecotourism resorts in the forest include **Pousada Uacari** (page 651) and **Cristalino Jungle Lodge** (page 755). **Fazenda San Francisco** in the Pantanal (page 735) runs a pioneering jaguar conservation project; **REGUA** and **Serra dos Tucanos** on the Atlantic coast (page 152) have done a great deal to protect important birding habitats; and resorts such as **Mata N'ativa** in Trancoso (page 446) are taking important first steps in beach holiday areas. In the Amazon, Atlantic coast forest and parts of the *cerrado*, access to certain wilderness areas is restricted to scientists. Having such a low-impact policy over these regions means that their environment is protected from damage or over-use. In much of coastal Brazil, where tourism and property speculation has boomed in the last few years, the impact on local communities is particularly devastating. Some state governments cheerfully exploit the

Brazilian etiquette

In his 1941 travel book, *I Like Brazil*, Jack Harding said of Brazilians that "anyone who does not get along with (them) had better examine himself; the fault is his." And perhaps the best writer on Brazil in English, Joseph Page, observed in his 1995 book *The Brazilians* that "cordiality is a defining characteristic of their behaviour. They radiate an irresistible pleasantness, abundant hospitality, and unfailing politeness, especially to foreigners." It is hard to offend Brazilians or to find Brazilians offensive, but to make sure you avoid misunderstandings, here are a few, perhaps surprising, tips. **Public nudity**, even toplessness on beaches, is an arrestable offence. **Brazilians will talk to anyone, anywhere.** 'Sorry, do I know you?' is the least Brazilian sentiment imaginable and no one ever rustles a newspaper on the metro. **Walks in nature are never conducted in silence.** This has led many Brazilians to be unaware that their country is the richest in terrestrial wildlife on the planet. **Drug use**, even of marijuana, is deeply frowned upon. Attitudes are far more conservative than in Europe. The same is true of public drunkenness. **When driving** it is normal, especially in Rio, to accelerate right up the bumper of the car in the lane in front of you on the highway, hoot repeatedly and flash your headlights. It is considered about as rude as ringing the doorbell in Brazil. **The phrase 'So para Ingles Ver'** ('just for the English to see') is a common expression that means 'to appear to do something by the rule book whilst doing the opposite'. **This is the land of red tape.** You need a social security number to buy a SIM card and fingerprint ID just to go to the dentist. **Never presume a policeman will take a bribe.** And never presume he won't. Let the policeman do the presuming. **Never insult an official.** You could find yourself in serious trouble. **Brazilians are very private** about their negative emotions. Never moan for more than a few seconds, even with justification – you will be branded an *uruca* (harbinger of doom), and won't be invited to the party. **Never confuse a Brazilian footballer** with an Argentinean one. **Brazilians believe that anyone can dance samba.** They can't. **Never dismiss a street seller** with anything less than cordiality; an impolite dismissal will be seen as arrogant and aggressive. Always extend a polite 'não obrigado'. **Brazilian time** Peter Fleming, the author of one of the best travel books about Brazil, once said that "a man in a hurry will be miserable in Brazil." Remember this when you arrive 10 minutes late to meet a friend in a bar and spend the next hour wondering if they've already gone after growing tired of waiting for you. They haven't. They've not yet left home. Unless you specify 'a hora britanica' then you will wait. And wait. And everyone will be mortified if you complain.

colourful local culture while sharing little of the profit. So rather than staying in a big resort and organizing a tour from back home, seek out smaller locally owned hotels and local indigenous guides. Try to visit projects such as the **Pataxó Reserve** in Jaqueira, Porto Seguro, and support the Caiçaras near Paraty.

Essentials A-Z

Accident and emergency

Ambulance T192. **Police** T190. If robbed or attacked, contact the tourist police. If you need to claim on insurance, make sure you get a police report.

Children

Travel with children is easy in Brazil. Brazilians love children and they are generally welcome everywhere. Facilities are often better than those back home.

Some hotels charge a cheaper family rate. Some will not charge for children under 5 and most can provide an extra camp bed for a double room. A few of the more romantic boutique beach resorts do not accept children. If you are planning to stay in such a hotel it is best to enquire ahead.

Most restaurants provide children's seats and menus as well as crayons and paper to keep them happy. Children are never expected to be seen but not heard, and are allowed to run around pretty much everywhere.

Children under 3 generally travel for 10% on internal flights and at 70% until 12 years old. Prices on buses depend on whether the child will occupy a seat or a lap. Laps are free and if there are spare seats after the bus has departed the child can sit there for free.

On tours children under 6 usually go free or it may be possible to bargain a discount rate.

Disabled travellers

As in most Latin American countries, facilities are generally very poor, with notable exceptions such as Sugar Loaf in Rio de Janeiro. Problems are worst for **wheelchair users**, who will find that ramps are rare and that toilets and bathrooms with facilities are few and far between, except for some of the more modern hotels and the larger airports. Public transport is not well geared up for wheelchairs and pavements are often in a poor state of repair or crowded with street vendors requiring passers-by to brave the traffic. Rio and São Paulo metros have lifts and disabled chair lifts at some stations (but not all are operational). Disabled Brazilians obviously have to cope with these problems and mainly rely on the help of others to get on and off public transport and generally move around. Drivers should bring a disabled sticker as most shopping centres and public car parks have disabled spaces.

Disability Travel, www.disabilitytravel.com, is an excellent US site written by travellers in wheelchairs who have been researching disabled travel full-time since 1985. There are many tips and useful contacts (including lists of travel agents on request) and articles, including pieces on disabled travelling through the Amazon. The company also organizes group tours.

Global Access – Disabled Travel Network Site, www.globalaccessnews.com. Provides travel information for 'disabled adventurers' and includes a number of reviews and tips from the public.

Society for Accessible Travel and Hospitality, www.sath.org. Provides some general information, athough there is some specific information on Brazil.

Brazilian organizations include: **Sociedade Amigos do Deficiente Físico**, www.aibr.com.br/sadef, based in Rio and with associate memberships throughout Brazil; and **Centro da Vida Independente**, Rio, www.cvi-rio.org.br. The publisher **O Nome da Rosa**, R Simão Álvares, 484 Pinheiros, T011-3817 5000, www.nome darosa.com.br, publishes a disabled guide to São Paulo entitled *O Guia São Paulo Adaptada*.

There are a number of specialist and general operators offering holidays specifically aimed at those with disabilities. These include: **Responsible Travel**, www.responsibletravel.com; **CanbeDone**, www.canbedone.co.uk; and **Access Travel**, www.access-travel.co.uk, although Brazil was not on their list as of 2008.

Nothing Ventured, edited by Alison Walsh (Harper Collins), has personal accounts of worldwide journeys by disabled travellers, plus advice and listings.

Electricity

Generally 110 V 60 cycles AC, but in some cities and areas 220 V 60 cycles AC is used. European and U.S 2-pin plugs and sockets.

Embassies and consulates

For embassies and consulates of Brazil, see www.embassiesabroad.com.

Gay and lesbian travellers

Brazil is a good country for gay and lesbian travellers as attitudes are fairly liberal, especially in the big cities. Opinions in the interior and rural areas are far more conservative and it is wise to adapt to this. There is a well-developed scene in Rio de Janeiro and São Paulo while Salvador is also a popular destination. Local information can be obtained from the **Rio Gay Guide**, www.riogayguide.com, and in Salvador from the **Centro Cultura**, R do Sodre 45, close to the Museu de Arte Sacra da Bahia, which publishes a guide to the gay scene in the city for US$5.

São Paulo's Pride march (usually in May) is one of the biggest in the world, with more than 2 million people, and there are many supporting cultural and musical events and parties. The Rio de Janeiro Pride march (usually Jun) takes place on Copacabana and is the centrepiece of an annual event that

includes numerous activities, especially around Carnaval (see page 120 for more details). Other festivals include the nationwide **Mix Brasil festival of Sexual diversity**, www.mixbrasil.uol.com.br.

Health → *Hospitals/medical services are listed in the Directory sections of each chapter.*

See your GP or travel clinic at least 6 weeks before departure for general advice on travel risks and vaccinations. Try phoning a specialist travel clinic if your own doctor is unfamiliar with health in the region. Make sure you have sufficient medical travel insurance, get a dental check, know your own blood group and, if you suffer a long-term condition such as diabetes or epilepsy, obtain a **Medic Alert** bracelet (www.medicalalert.co.uk).

Vaccinations and anti-malarials
Confirm that your primary courses and boosters are up to date. It is advisable to vaccinate against polio, tetanus, typhoid, hepatitis A and, for more remote areas, rabies. Yellow fever vaccination is obligatory for most areas. Cholera, diptheria and hepatitis B vaccinations are sometimes advised. Specialist advice should be taken on the best antimalarials to take before you leave.

Health risks
The major risks posed in the region are those caused by insect disease carriers such as mosquitoes and sandflies. The key parasitic and viral diseases are malaria, South American trypanosomiasis (Chagas disease) and dengue fever. Be aware that you are always at risk from these diseases. **Malaria** is a danger throughout the lowland tropics and coastal regions. **Dengue fever** (which is currently rife in Rio de Janeiro state) is particularly hard to protect against as the mosquitoes can bite throughout the day as well as night (unlike those that carry malaria); try to wear clothes that cover arms and legs and also use effective mosquito

repellent. Mosquito nets dipped in permethrin provide a good physical and chemical barrier at night. **Chagas disease** is spread by faeces of the triatomine, or assassin bugs, whereas sandflies spread a disease of the skin called **leishmaniasis**.

Some form of **diarrhoea** or intestinal upset is almost inevitable, the standard advice is always to wash your hands before eating and to be careful with drinking water and ice; if you have any doubts about the water then boil it or filter and treat it. In a restaurant buy bottled water or ask where the water has come from. Food can also pose a problem, be wary of salads if you don't know whether they have been washed or not.

There is a constant threat of **tuberculosis** (TB) and although the BCG vaccine is available, it is still not guaranteed protection. It is best to avoid unpasteurized dairy products and try not to let people cough and splutter all over you.

Another risk, especially to campers and people with small children, is that of the **hanta virus**, which is carried by some forest and riverine rodents. Symptoms are a flu-like illness which can lead to complications. Try as far as possible to avoid rodent-infested areas, especially close contact with rodent droppings.

Websites
www.cdc.gov Centres for Disease Control and Prevention (USA).
www.dh.gov.uk/en/Policyandguidance/Healthadvicefortravellers/index.htm Department of Health advice for travellers.
www.fitfortravel.scot.nhs.uk Fit for Travel (UK), a site from Scotland providing a quick A-Z of vaccine and travel health advice requirements for each country.
www.fco.gov.uk Foreign and Commonwealth Office (FCO), UK.
www.itg.be Prince Leopold Institute for Tropical Medicine.
www.nathnac.org National Travel Health Network and Centre (NaTHNaC).
www.who.int World Health Organisation.

Books
Dawood, R, editor, *Travellers' health*, 3rd ed, Oxford: Oxford University Press, 2002.
Warrell, David, and Sarah Anderson, editors, *Expedition Medicine*, The Royal Geographic Society, ISBN 1 86197 040-4.
Wilson-Howarth, Jane. *Bugs, Bites and Bowels: the essential guide to travel health*, Cadogan 2006.

Internet

Brazil is said to be 7th in the world in terms of internet use. Public internet access is so readily available that it is almost pointless to list the locations. There is internet access on every other street corner in even the smallest towns and cities – look for signs saying 'LAN house' or 'ciber-café'. The facilities usually double-up as computer games rooms for teenagers. There is usually an hourly charge of around US$2, but you can almost always use partial hours at a reduced rate. More and more hotels offer an internet service to their guests – many in-room wireless; usually free but sometimes at exorbitant rates, while some government programmes even offer free use (notably in Manaus and Cuiaba) in public areas. For a regularly updated list of locations around the world, check www.netcafe guide.com.

Language → See also page 812.

Brazilians speak Portuguese, and very few speak anything else. Spanish may help you to be understood a little, but spoken Portuguese will remain undecipherable even to fluent Spanish speakers. To get the best out of Brazil, learn some Portuguese before arriving. Brazilians are the best thing about the country and without Portuguese you will not be able to interact beyond stereotypes and second guesses. Language classes are available in the larger cities. **Cactus** (www.cactuslanguage.com), **Languages abroad** (www.languagesabroad.co.uk) and **Travellers Worldwide** (www.travellersworld

wide.com) are among the companies that can organize language courses in Brazil. **McGraw Hill** and **DK** (*Hugo Portuguese in Three Months*) offer the best teach-yourself books. **Sonia Portuguese** (www.sonia-portuguese.com) is a useful online resource.

Money

Currency

→ *£1 = 2.7; €1 = 2.37; US$1 = R$1.7 (Nov 2010)*.
The unit of currency is the **real**, R$ (plural **reais**). Any amount of foreign currency and 'a reasonable sum' in reais can be taken in, but sums over US$10,000 must be declared. Residents may only take out the equivalent of US$4000. Notes in circulation are: 100, 50, 10, 5 and 1 real; coins: 1 real, 50, 25, 10, 5 and 1 centavo. **Note** The exchange-rate fluctuates – check regularly.

Costs of travelling

Brazil is more expensive than other countries in South America. As a very rough guide, prices are about two-thirds those of Western Europe and a little cheaper than rural USA; though prices vary hugely according to the current exchange rate and strength of the real, whose value has soared since 2008 – with Goldman Sachs and Bloomberg considering the *real* to be the most over-valued major currency in the world in 2009-2010. It is expected to lose value; check on the latest before leaving on currency exchange sites such as www.x-rates.com.

Hostel beds are usually around US$15. Budget hotels with few frills have rooms for as little as US$30, and you should have no difficulty finding a double room costing US$45 wherever you are. Rooms are often pretty much the same price whether 1 or 2 people are staying. Eating is generally inexpensive, especially in *padarias* or *comida por kilo* (pay by weight) restaurants, which offer a wide range of food (salads, meat, pasta, vegetarian). Expect to pay around US$6 to eat your fill in a good-value restaurant.

Although bus travel is cheap by US or European standards, because of the long distances, costs can soon mount up. Internal flights prices have come down dramatically in the last couple of years and some routes work out cheaper than taking a bus – especially if booking through the internet. Prices vary regionally. Ipanema is almost twice as expensive as rural Bahia. A can of beer in a supermarket in the southeast costs US$0.80, a litre of water US$0.60, a single metrô ticket in São Paulo US$1.60, a bus ticket between US$1 and US$1.50 (depending on the city) and a cinema ticket around US$3.60.

ATMs

ATMs, or cash machines, are common in Brazil. As well as being the most convenient way of withdrawing money, they frequently offer the best available rates of exchange. They are usually closed after 2130 in large cities. There are 2 international ATM acceptance systems, **Plus** and **Cirrus**. Many issuers of debit and credit cards are linked to one, or both (eg Visa is Plus, MasterCard is Cirrus). **Bradesco** and **HSBC** are the 2 main banks offering this service. **Red Banco 24 Horas** kiosks advertise that they take a long list of credit cards in their ATMs, including MasterCard and Amex, but international cards cannot always be used; the same is true of **Banco do Brasil**.

Advise your bank before leaving, as cards are usually stopped in Brazil without prior warning. Find out before you leave what international functionality your card has. Check if your bank or credit card company imposes handling charges. Internet banking is useful for monitoring your account or transferring funds. Do not rely on 1 card, in case of loss. If you do lose a card, immediately contact the 24-hr helpline of the issuer in your home country (keep this number in a safe place).

Exchange

Banks in major cities will change cash and traveller's cheques (TCs). If you keep the official exchange slips, you may convert back into foreign currency up to 50% of the amount you exchanged. The parallel market, found in travel agencies, exchange houses and among hotel staff, often offers marginally better rates than the banks but commissions can be very high. Many banks may only change US$300 minimum in cash, US$500 in TCs. Rates for TCs are usually far lower than for cash, they are harder to change and a very heavy commission may be charged. Dollars cash (take US$5 or US$10 bills) are not useful as alternative currency. Brazilians use *reais*.

Credit cards

Credit cards are widely used, although often they are not usable in the most unlikely of places, such as tour operators. Diners Club, MasterCard, Visa and Amex are useful. Cash advances on credit cards will only be paid in *reais* at the tourist rate, incurring at least a 1.5% commission. Banks in small, remote places may still refuse to give a cash advance: try asking for the *gerente* (manager).

Money transfers

Money sent to Brazil is normally paid out in Brazilian currency, so do not have more money sent out than you need for your stay. Funds can ostensibly be received within 48 banking hours, but it can take at least a month to arrive, allowing banks to capitalize on your transfer. The documentation required to receive it varies according to the whim of the bank staff, making the whole procedure often far more trouble than it is worth.

Opening hours

Generally Mon-Fri 0900-1800; closed for lunch some time between 1130 and 1400.
Shops Also open on Sat until 1230 or 1300.
Government offices Mon-Fri 1100-1800.
Banks Mon-Fri 1000-1600 or 1630; closed at weekends.

Post

To send a standard letter or postcard to the USA costs US$1, to Europe US$1.25, to Australia or South Africa US$1. Air mail should take about 7 days to or from Britain or the USA. Franked and registered (insured) letters are normally secure, but check that the amount franked is what you have paid, or the item will not arrive. Aerogrammes are most reliable. To avoid queues and obtain higher denomination stamps go to the stamp desk at the main post office.

The post office sells cardboard boxes for sending packages internally and abroad. Rates and rules for sending literally vary from post office to post office even within the same town and the quickest service is SEDEX. The most widespread courier service is Federal Express, www.fedex.com/br. They are often cheaper than parcel post.

Postes restantes usually only hold letters for 30 days. Identification is required and it's a good idea to write your name on a piece of paper to help the attendant find your letters. Charges are minimal but often involve queuing at another counter to buy stamps, which are attached to your letter and franked before it is given to you.

Safety

Although Brazil's big cities suffer high rates of violent crime, this is mostly confined to the favelas (slums) where poverty and drugs are the main cause. Visitors should not enter favelas except when accompanied by workers for NGOs, tour groups or other people who know the local residents well and are accepted by the community. Otherwise they may be targets of muggings by armed gangs who show short shrift to those who resist them. Mugging can take place anywhere. Travel light after dark with few valuables (avoid wearing jewellery and use a cheap, plastic, digital watch). Ask hotel staff where is and isn't safe; crime is patchy in Brazilian cities.

If the worst does happen and you are threatened, don't panic, and hand over your valuables. Do not resist, and report the crime to the local tourist police later. It is extremely rare for a tourist to be hurt during a robbery in Brazil. Being aware of the dangers, acting confidently and using your common sense will reduce many of the risks.

Photocopy your passport, air ticket and other documents, make a record of traveller's cheque and credit card numbers. Keep them separately from the originals and leave another set of records at home. Keep all documents secure; hide your main cash supply in different places or under your clothes. Extra pockets sewn inside shirts and trousers, money belts (best worn below the waist), neck or leg pouches and elasticated support bandages for keeping money above the elbow or below the knee have been repeatedly recommended.

All border areas should be regarded with some caution because of smuggling activities. Violence over land ownership in parts of the interior have resulted in a 'Wild West' atmosphere in some towns, which should therefore be passed through quickly. Red-light districts should also be given a wide berth as there are reports of drinks being drugged with a substance popularly known as 'good night Cinderella'. This leaves the victim easily amenable to having their possessions stolen, or worse.

Avoiding cons

Never trust anyone telling sob stories or offering 'safe rooms', and when looking for a hotel, always choose the room yourself. Be wary of 'plain-clothes policemen'; insist on seeing identification and on going to the police station by main roads. Do not hand over your identification (or money) until you are at the station. On no account take them directly back to your hotel. Be even more suspicious if they seek confirmation of their status from a passer-by.

Hotel security

Hotel safe deposits are generally, but not always, secure. If you cannot get a receipt for valuables in a hotel safe, you can seal the contents in a plastic bag and sign across the seal. Always keep an inventory of what you have deposited. If you don't trust the hotel, lock everything in your pack and secure it in your room when you go out. If you lose valuables, report to the police and note details of the report for insurance purposes. Be sure to be present whenever your credit card is used.

Police

There are several types of police: **Polícia Federal**, civilian dressed, who handle all federal law duties, including immigration. A subdivision is the **Polícia Federal Rodoviária**, uniformed, who are the traffic police on federal highways. **Polícia Militar** are the uniformed, street police force, under the control of the state governor, handling all state laws. They are not the same as the Armed Forces' internal police. **Polícia Civil**, also state controlled, handle local laws and investigations. They are usually in civilian dress, unless in the traffic division. In cities, the **Prefeitura** controls the **Guarda Municipal**, who handle security. **Tourist police** operate in places with a strong tourist presence. In case of difficulty, visitors should seek out tourist police in the first instance.

Public transport

When you have all your luggage with you at a bus or railway station, be especially careful and carry any shoulder bags in front of you. To be extra safe, take a taxi between the airport/bus station/railway station and hotel, keep your bags with you and pay only when you and your luggage are outside; avoid night buses and arriving at your destination at night.

Sexual assault

If you are the victim of a sexual assault, you are advised firstly to contact a doctor (this can be your home doctor). You will need tests to determine whether you have contracted any STDs; you may also need advice on emergency contraception. You should contact your embassy, where consular staff will be very willing to help.

Women travellers

Most of these tips apply to any single traveller. When you set out, err on the side of caution until your instincts have adjusted to the customs of a new culture. Be prepared for the exceptional curiosity extended to visitors, especially women, and try not to overreact. If, as a single woman, you can befriend a local woman, you will learn much more about the country you are visiting. There is a definite 'gringo trail' you can follow, which can be helpful when looking for safe accommodation, especially if arriving after dark (best avoided). Remember that for a single woman a taxi at night can be as dangerous as walking alone. It is easier for men to take the friendliness of locals at face value; women may be subject to unwanted attention. Do not disclose to strangers where you are staying. By wearing a wedding ring and saying that your 'husband' is close at hand, you may dissuade an aspiring suitor. If politeness fails, do not feel bad about showing offence and departing. A good rule is always to act with confidence, as though you know where you are going, even if you do not. Someone who looks lost is more likely to attract unwanted attention.

Student travellers

If you are in full-time education you will be entitled to an ISIC (International Student Identity Card), which is distributed by student travel offices and travel agencies in more than 77 countries. The ISIC card gives you special prices on all forms of transport and access to a variety of other concessions

and services. If you need to find the location of your nearest ISIC office contact: **ISIC Association**, Box 15857, 1001 NJ Amsterdam, Holland, T+45-3393 9303, www.isic.org. ISIC cards can be obtained in Brazil from **STB** agencies throughout the country, such as Av Brig Faria Lima 1713, São Paulo, T011-870 0555; also try www.carteirado estudante.com.br. Remember to take photographs when having a card issued.

In practice, the ISIC card is rarely recognized or accepted for discounts outside of the south and southeast of Brazil, but is nonetheless useful for obtaining half-price entry to the cinema. Youth hostels will often accept it in lieu of a **IYHA** card or at least give a discount, and some university accommodation (and subsidized canteens) will allow very cheap short-term stays to holders.

Tax

Airport departure tax The amount of tax depends on the class and size of the airport, but the cost is usually incorporated into the ticket.
VAT Rates vary from 7-25% at state and federal level; the average is 17-20%.

Telephone

→ *Country code: +55.*
Ringing: equal tones with long pauses.
Engaged: equal tones, equal pauses.

Making a phone call in Brazil can be confusing. It is necessary to dial a 2-digit telephone company code prior to the area code for all calls. Phone numbers are now printed in this way: 0XX21 (0 for a national call, XX for the code of the phone company chosen (eg 31 for Telemar) followed by, 21 for Rio de Janeiro, for example and the 8-digit number of the subscriber. The same is true for international calls where 00 is followed by the operator code and then the country code and number.

Telephone operators and their codes are: **Embratel**, 21 (nationwide); **Telefônica**, 15 (state of São Paulo); **Telemar**, 31 (Alagoas, Amazonas, Amapá, Bahia, Ceará, Espírito Santo, Maranhão, most of Minas Gerais, Pará, Paraíba, Pernambuco, Piauí, Rio de Janeiro, Rio Grande do Norte, Roraima, Sergipe); **Tele Centro-Sul**, 14 (Acre, Goiás, Mato Grosso, Mato Grosso do Sul, Paraná, Rondônia, Santa Catarina, Tocantins and the cities of Brasília and Pelotas); **CTBC-Telecom**, 12 (some parts of Minas Gerais, Goiás, Mato Grosso do Sul and São Paulo state); **Intelig**, 23.

National calls

Telephone booths or *orelhões* (literally 'big ears' as they are usually ear-shaped, fibreglass shells) are easy to come by in towns and cities. Local phone calls and telegrams are cheap.

Cartões telefónicos (phone cards) are available from newsstands, post offices and some chemists. They cost US$4 for 30 units and up to US$7 for 90 units. Local calls from a private phone are often free. *Cartões telefônicos internacionais* (international phone cards) are increasingly available in tourist areas and are often sold at hostels.

Mobile phones

Cellular phones are widespread and coverage excellent even in remote areas, but prices are extraordinarily high and users still pay to receive calls outside the metropolitan area where their phone is registered. SIM cards are hard to buy as users require a CPF (a Brazilian social security number) to buy one, but phones can be hired. When using a cellular telephone you do not drop the zero from the area code as you have to when dialling from a fixed line.

Time

Brazil has 4 time zones: Brazilian standard time is GMT-3; the Amazon time zone (Pará west of the Rio Xingu, Amazonas, Roraima, Rondônia, Mato Grosso and Mato Grosso do Sul) is GMT-4, the State of Acre is GMT-5; and the Fernando de Noronha archipelago is GMT-2. Clocks move forward 1 hr in summer for approximately 5 months (usually between Oct and Feb or Mar), but times of change vary. This does not apply to Acre.

Tipping

Tipping is not usual, but always appreciated as staff are often paid a pittance. In restaurants, add 10% of the bill if no service charge is included; cloakroom attendants deserve a small tip; porters have fixed charges but often receive tips as well; unofficial car parkers on city streets should be tipped 2 reais.

Tour operators

UK
Austral Tours, 20 Upper Tachbrook St, London SW1V 1SH, T020-7233 5384, www.latinamerica.co.uk. Tours to Rio, the Amazon and the northeast.
Condor Journeys and Adventures, 2 Ferry Bank, Colintraive, Argyll PA22 3AR, T01700-841 318, www.condorjourneys-adventures.com. Tailor-made journeys to standard destinations.
Explore Worldwide, 1 Frederick St, Aldershot, Hants GU11 1LQ, T01252-760 000, www.exploreworldwide.com. Standard small-group trips to the northeast, Amazon and Rio.
Journey Latin America, 12-13 Heathfield Terr, Chiswick, London W4 4JE, T020-8747 8315, www.journeylatinamerica.co.uk. Long-established company with excellent escorted tours to some interesting areas like Goiás and the Chapada Diamantina. They also offer a wide range of good-value flight options.

Last Frontiers, The Mill, Quainton Rd, Waddesdon, Bucks HP18 0LP, T01296-653000, www.lastfrontiers.com. Imaginative tailor-made tours to some interesting out-of-the-way locations including Fernando de Noronha.

Select Latin America, 3.51 Canterbury Court, 1-3 Brixton Rd, Kennington Park Business Centre, London SW9 6DE, T020-7407 1478, www.selectlatinamerica.co.uk. Quality tailor-made holidays and small group tours.

Songlines Music Travel, T020-8505 2582, www.songlines.co.uk/musictravel . Specialist Carnaval packages in Bahia and São Paulo with a break on the beach afterwards. Tour guides offer the chance to meet many of the musicians and to hear the best live music as well as attend the key Carnaval shows.

Steppes Latin America, 51 Castle St, Cirencester, Glos GL7 1QD, T01285-885333, www.steppestravel.co.uk. Tailor-made and group itineraries throughout Brazil and Latin America.

Sunvil Latin America, Sunvil House, Upper Square, Old Isleworth, Middlesex TW7 7BJ, T020-8568 4499, www.sunvil. co.uk. A good range of options throughout Brazil, including some out-of-the-way destinations.

Tell Tale Travel, 25a Kensington Church St, 1st floor, London, T0800-011 2571; www.telltaletravel.co.uk. Imaginative and well-researched bespoke holidays throughout Brazil, with homestays and light adventure trips aiming to integrate locals and visitors and show Brazil from a Brazilian perspective.

Trips Worldwide, 14 Frederick Place, Clifton, Bristol BS8 1AS, T0117-311 4400, www.tripsworldwide.co.uk. Tailor-made trips throughout South America.

Veloso Tours, ground floor, 34 Warple Way, London W3 0RG, T020-8762 0616, www.veloso.com. An imaginative range of tours throughout Brazil and bespoke options on request.

Wildlife and birding specialists
Naturetrek, Cheriton Mill, Cheriton, Alresford, Hants SO24 0NG, T01962-733051; www.nature trek.co.uk. Wildlife tours throughout Brazil with bespoke options and specialist birding tours of the Atlantic coastal rainforests.

Ornitholidays, 29 Straight Mile, Romsey, Hants SO51 9BB, T01794-519445, www.ornit holidays.co.uk. Annual or biannual birding trips throughout Brazil; usually to the Pantanal, Atlantic Coast rainforest and Iguaçu.

Reef and Rainforest Tours Ltd, A7 Dart Marine Park, Steamer Quay, Totnes, Devon, TQ9 5DR, T01803-866965, www.reefandrainforest.co.uk. Specialists in tailor-made and group wildlife tours.

Wildlife World Wide, Long Barn South, Sutton Manor Farm, Bishop's Sutton, Alresford, Hants SO24 0AA, www.wildlife worldwide.com. Wildlife trips to the Amazon (on board the Amazon Clipper), Pantanal, safaris on the Transpantaneira and Iguaçu; with bespoke options available.

Wildwings, 577-579 Fishponds Rd, Fishponds, Bristol BS16 3AF, T0117-965 8333, www.wildwings.co.uk. Jaguar tours around Porto Jofre in the Pantanal with extensions to the Atlantic coastal rainforests and elsewhere.

North America
4starSouth America, T1-800-887 5686, www.4starSouthAmerica.com. Customized or scheduled tours throughout South America. Also has an office in Brazil at Av NS Copacabana 1066/907, Rio de Janeiro, T021-2267 6624.

Brazil For Less, 7201 Wood Hollow Dr, Austin, TX 78731, T1-877-565 8119 (US toll free) or T+44-203-006 2507 (UK), www.brazilforless.com. US-based travel firm with a focus solely on South America, with local offices and operations, and a price guarantee. Good-value tours, run by travellers for travellers. Will meet or beat any published rates on the internet from outside Brazil.

Ela Brasil Tours, 14 Burlington Dr, Norwalk, CT 06851, T203-840 9010, www.elabrasil.com. Excellent bespoke tours throughout Brazil to some very imaginative

destinations. Uses only the best and most responsible local operators.

Ladatco Tours, 3006 Aviation Av 4C, Coconut Grove, Florida 33133, USA, T1800-327 6162, www.ladatco.com. Standard tours to Rio, Iguaçu and Manaus for the Amazon.

Mila Tours, 100 S Greenleaf Av, Gurnee, IL 60031-337, T847-248 2111, T800-387 7378 (USA and Canada), www.milatours.com. Itineraries to Rio, Iguaçu and the northeast.

Wildlife and birding specialists
Birding Brazil, www.birdingbrazil.com. Richard Raby is one of the only US operators taking wildlife and birdwatchers to Bahia.

Field Guides, 9433 Bee Cave Rd, Building 1, Suite 150, Austin, Texas 78733, USA, T1-800-7284953, www.fieldguides.com. Interesting birdwatching tours to all parts of Brazil.

Focus Tours, PO Box 22276, Santa Fe, NM 87502; T(505)216 7780; www.focustours. com. Environmentally responsible travel throughout Brazil with some tour options including parts of Bahia.

Tropical Nature Travel, PO Box 5276, Gainesville, Fl 326270 5276, USA, T352-376 3377, www.tropicalnaturetravel.com. Ecotourism tours to *fazendas* in the northern and southern Pantanal, Cristalino Jungle Lodge, the Amazon (with Amazon Clipper), Iguaçu and the Mata Atlântica.

Brazil
Ambiental, Av Brigadeiro Faria Lima 156, Pinheiros, São Paulo, T011-3818 4600, www.ambiental.tur.br. Trips to every corner of Brazil from Jalapão and Fernando de Noronha to the Pantanal and Iguaçu.

Brazil Always Summer, SEPS EQ 714/914, Bloco E, Sala 409, Edifício Talento, Brasilia-DF, CEP 70390-145, T061-3039 4442, www.brazilalwayssummer.com. Tour operator specializing in holidays to Brazil. Services include hotel booking, Rio Carnaval tickets and excellent car rental rates. English-speaking staff.

Brazil Nature Tours, R Guia Lopes 150, 1st floor, Campo Grande, MS, T067-3042 4659,

www.brazilnaturetours.com. Individual and group tours to the Pantanal and the Amazon.
Cariri Ecotours, R Francisco Gurgel, 9067, Ponta Negra Beach, Natal, T084-9928 0198, www.caririecotours.com.br. If ecotourism means wildlife then Manary are not eco at all, but they do offer unusual, exciting tours to the northeastern *sertão,* including the spectacular Serra da Capivara (to see the rock paintings), Cariri and the fossilized dinosaur prints in Paraíba. Very professional service.
Dehouche, T021-2512 3895, www.dehouche.com. Upmarket, carefully tailored trips throughout Brazil.
Matueté, T011-3071 4515, www.matuete. com. Bespoke luxury options around Brazil including a range of private house rentals.
Tatur Turismo, Av Tancredo Neves 274, Centro Empresarial Iguatemi, Sala 228, Bloco B, Salvador, 41820-020, Bahia, T071-3114 7900, www.tatur.com.br. Very helpful and professional bespoke Bahia-based agency who can organize tours throughout Brazil, especially in Bahia, using many of the smaller hotels.
whl.travel, T031-3889 8596, www.whlbrazil. com. Online network of tour operators for booking accommodation and tours throughout Brazil.

Wildlife and birding specialists
Andy and Nadime Whittaker's Birding Brazil Tours, www.birdingbraziltours.com. Another good company, based in Manaus. The couple worked with the BBC Natural History Unit on David Attenborough's *The Life of Birds* and are ground agents for a number of the major birding tour companies from the US and Europe.
Birding Brazil Tours, www.birdingbrazil tours.com. Bespoke options only.
Ciro Albano, www.nebrazilbirding.com. The best operator for the northeast of Brazil offering the broadest spread of Bahian birding and wildlife sites, including Estação Veracruz, Canudos and the Chapada Diamantina.
Edson Endrigo, www.avesfoto.com.br. Bespoke options only.

Tourist information

The **Ministério do Turismo**, Esplanada dos Ministérios, Bloco U, 2nd and 3rd floors, Brasília, www.turismo.gov.br or www.brazil tour.com, is in charge of tourism in Brazil and has information in many languages. **Embratur**, the Brazilian Institute of Tourism, is at the same address, and is in charge of promoting tourism abroad. For information and phone numbers for your country visit www.braziltour.com. Local tourist information bureaux are not usually helpful for information on cheap hotels – they generally just dish out pamphlets. Expensive hotels provide tourist magazines for their guests. Telephone directories (not Rio) contain good street maps.
   Other good sources of information are:
LATA, www.lata.org. The Latin American Travel Association, with useful country information and listings of all UK operators specializing in Latin America. Also has up-to-date information on public safety, health, weather, travel costs, economics and politics highlighted for each nation. Wide selection of Latin American maps available, as well as individual travel planning assistance.
South American Explorers, formerly the South American Explorers Club, 126 Indina Creek Rd, Ithaca, NY 14850, T607-277 0488, www.samexplo.org. A non-profit educational organization functioning primarily as an information network for South America. Useful for travellers to Brazil and the rest of the continent.

National parks
National parks are run by the Brazilian institute of environmental protection, **Ibama** (**Instituto Brasileiro do Meio Ambiente e dos Recursos Naturais Renováveis**), SCEN Trecho 2, Av L-4 Norte, Edif Sede de Ibama, CEP 70818-900, Brasília, DF, T061-3316 1212, www.ibama.gov.br. For information, contact **Linha Verde**, T0800-618080, linhaverde.sede@ibama.gov.br. National parks are open to visitors, usually with

a permit from Ibama. See also the
Ministério do Meio Ambiente website,
www.mma.gov.br.

Useful websites

www.amcham.com.br American Chamber
of Commerce in São Paulo. A good source of
information on local markets.

www.brazil.org.uk Provides a broad range
of info on Brazilian history and culture from
the UK Brazilian embassy.

www.brazil4you.com Comprehensive
travel and tourism info on everything from
sights to hotels and weather.

www.brazilmax.com Excellent information
on culture and lifestyle, the best available
in English.

www.braziltourism.org The official tourism
website of Brazil, and the best.

www.gringos.com.br An excellent source
of information on all things Brazilian for
visitors and expats.

www.ipanema.com A quirky, informative
site on all things Rio de Janeiro.

www.maria-brazil.org A wonderfully
personal introduction to Brazil, specifically
Rio, featuring Maria's cookbook and little
black book, features and reviews.

www.rainforestweb.org Excellent, accurate
information on rainforest-related issues with
detailed comprehensive information on Brazil
and extensive links.

http://redebma.ning.com/ By far the
best site on Brazilian music with countless
profiles of genres, musicians and bands
and excellent links.

www.socioambiental.org Invaluable for
up-to-the-minute, accurate information on
environmental and indigenous issues.

www.survival-international.org The
world's leading campaign organization for
indigenous peoples with excellent info on
various Brazilian indigenous groups.

www.worldtwitch.com Birding information
and comprehensive listings of rainforest lodges.

Visas and immigration

Visas are not required for stays of up to
90 days by tourists from Andorra, Argentina,
Austria, Bahamas, Barbados, Belgium, Bolivia,
Chile, Colombia, Costa Rica, Denmark,
Ecuador, Finland, France, Germany,
Greece, Iceland, Ireland, Italy, Liechtenstein,
Luxembourg, Malaysia, Monaco, Morocco,
Namibia, the Netherlands, Norway, Paraguay,
Peru, Philippines, Portugal, San Marino,
South Africa, Spain, Suriname, Sweden,
Switzerland, Thailand, Trinidad and Tobago,
United Kingdom, Uruguay, the Vatican and
Venezuela. For them, only the following
documents are required at the port of
disembarkation: a passport valid for at least
6 months (or *cédula de identidad* for nationals
of Argentina, Chile, Paraguay and Uruguay);
and a return or onward ticket, or adequate
proof that you can purchase your return fare,
subject to no remuneration being received
in Brazil and no legally binding or contractual
documents being signed. Venezuelan
passport holders can stay for 60 days
on filling in a form at the border.

Citizens of the USA, Canada, Australia,
New Zealand and other countries not
mentioned above, and anyone wanting to
stay longer than 180 days, *must* get a visa
before arrival, which may, if you ask, be
granted for multiple entry. US citizens must
be fingerprinted on entry to Brazil. Visa fees
vary from country to country, so apply to
the Brazilian consulate in your home
country. The consular fee in the USA is
US$55. Students planning to study in Brazil
or employees of foreign companies can
apply for a 1- or 2-year visa. 2 copies of the
application form, 2 photos, a letter from
the sponsoring company or educational
institution in Brazil, a police form showing
no criminal convictions and a fee of around
US$80 is required.

Extensions

Foreign tourists may stay a maximum of 180 days in any 1 year. 90-day renewals are easily obtainable, but only at least 15 days before the expiry of your 90-day permit, from the Polícia Federal. The procedure varies, but generally you have to: fill out 3 copies of the tax form at the Polícia Federal, take them to a branch of **Banco do Brasil**, pay US$15 and bring 2 copies back. You will then be given the extension form to fill in and be asked for your passport to stamp in the extension. According to regulations (which should be on display) you need to show a return ticket, cash, cheques or a credit card, a personal reference and proof of an address of a person living in the same city as the office (in practice you simply write this in the space on the form). Some offices will only give you an extension within 10 days of the expiry of your permit.

Some points of entry, such as the Colombian border, refuse entry for longer than 30 days, renewals are then for the same period, insist if you want 90 days. For longer stays you must leave the country and return (not the same day) to get a new 90-day permit. If your visa has expired, getting a new visa can be costly (US$35 for a consultation, US$30 for the visa itself) and may take anything up to 45 days, depending on where you apply. If you overstay your visa, or extension, you will be fined US$7 per day, with no upper limit. After paying the fine to Polícia Federal, you will be issued with an exit visa and must leave within 8 days.

Officially, if you leave Brazil within the 90-day permission to stay and then re-enter the country, you should only be allowed to stay until the 90-day permit expires. If, however, you are given another 90-day permit, this may lead to charges of overstaying if you apply for an extension.

Identification

You must always carry identification when in Brazil. Take a photocopy of the personal details in your passport, plus your Brazilian immigration stamp, and leave your passport in the hotel safe deposit. This photocopy, when authorized in a *cartório*, US$1, is a legitimate copy of your documents. Be prepared, however, to present the originals when travelling in sensitive border areas. Always keep an independent record of your passport details. Also register with your consulate to expedite document replacement if yours gets lost or stolen.

Warning Do not lose the entry/exit permit they give you when you enter Brazil. Leaving the country without it, you may have to pay up to US$100 per person. It is suggested that you photocopy this form and have it authenticated at a *cartório*, US$1, in case of loss or theft.

Weights and measures

Metric.

Working in Brazil

Volunteering

The **Task Brasil Trust**, T020-7735 5545, www.taskbrasil.org.uk, is a small UK-based charity set up to help abandoned street children in Brazil. It runs various projects to improve the lives of children and pregnant teenage girls, especially those living on the streets of Rio de Janeiro. You can get involved as a volunteer in Brazil, to help the children with sports, reading and writing, music, art and computer skills. Volunteer at the UK or US offices, or make a donation.

Contents

Footprint features

Rio de Janeiro

At a glance

⊖ **Getting around** Bus, metrô and taxi. Hiring a car is recommended for visiting the more remote areas in Rio state but not for the city.

◉ **Time required** At least 3 days to explore the city; 7-10 days for the city and state.

☼ **Weather** Summer (Dec-Mar) is warm and wet, up to 30°C; winter (Apr-Oct) is dry with blue skies.

✖ **When not to go** Good at any time but wet Dec-Jan. Hotel prices double over New Year and Carnaval.

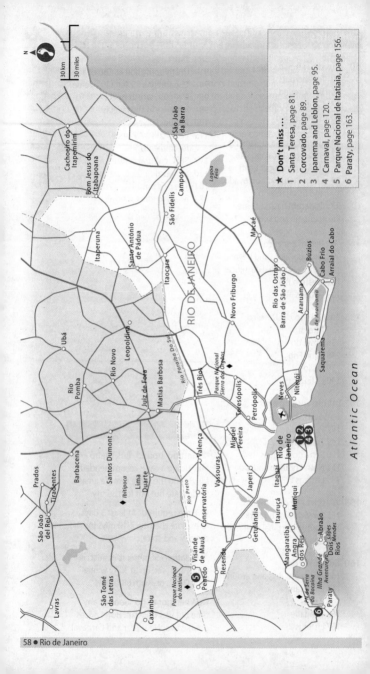

N

30 km
30 miles

★ **Don't miss ...**
1 Santa Teresa, page 81.
2 Corcovado, page 89.
3 Ipanema and Leblon, page 95.
4 Carnaval, page 120.
5 Parque Nacional de Itatiaia, page 156.
6 Paraty, page 163.

São João da Barra

Cachoeiro do Itapemirim

Bom Jesus do Itabapoana

Campos

São Fidélis

Lagoa Feia

Itaperuna

Santo António de Pádua

Macaé

RIO DE JANEIRO

Itaocara

Búzios

Novo Friburgo

Rio das Ostras

Cabo Frio

Barra de São João

Arraial do Cabo

Araruama

L. de Araruama

Ubá

Leopoldina

Rio Novo

Três Rios

Rio Paraíba do Sul

Parque Nacional Sierra dos Orgãos

Saquarema

Rio Pomba

Juiz de Fora

Matias Barbosa

Teresópolis

Petrópolis

Neves

Niterói

Barbacena

Santos Dumont

Miguel Pereira

Rio de Janeiro

Prados

Valença

Japeri

Itaguaí

Tiradentes

Lima Duarte

Ibitipoca

Conservatória

Vassouras

São João del Rei

Rio Preto

Getulândia

Itauruçá

Muriqui

Lavras

São Tomé das Letras

Visconde de Mauá

Resende

Mangaratiba

Angra dos Reis

Abraão

Caxambu

Parque Nacional da Itatiaia

Penedo

Pr. da Serra da Bocaina

Ilha Grande

Cotes

Dois Rios

Aventureiro

Paraty

Atlantic Ocean

Even those who know nothing else of Brazil will have heard of Rio, its Mardi Gras carnival and its spectacular beach and mountain scenery. What many do not realize is that Rio de Janeiro is a state as well as a city, and that this state boasts beaches, forests and mountains just as beautiful as those in its capital. The southern coast, or Costa Verde, is fringed with emerald-green coves and bays that rise steeply to rainforest-covered hills pocked with national parks. Mountains swathed in coffee plantations sit behind Rio itself, with hill retreats once favoured by the imperial family dotted throughout their valleys and remnants of one of the world's most biodiverse forests covering parts of their slopes. To the northeast of the city lies a string of surf beaches and little resorts, the most celebrated of which is Búzios, a fishing village put on the map by Brigitte Bardot in the late 1960s, which has grown to become a chic little retreat for the state's middle classes.

Rio de Janeiro city

→ *Colour map 4, C3. Phone code: 021. Population: 8 million.*

According to Cariocas – the people of Rio de Janeiro – God made the world in six days and then spent the seventh lying on the beach in Ipanema. For in a city as beautiful as this, they say, only the philistine or the ungrateful would do anything else. Indeed, photographs cannot prepare you for Rio. There is far more to the city than Corcovado capped with Christ or the Sugar Loaf; these are overtures to the grand symphony of the scene. Rainforest-covered boulder mountains as high as Snowdon rise sheer from the sea around the vast Guanabara Bay and stretch to the horizon. Their curves and jags are broken by long sweeping beaches of powder-fine sand pounded by the dazzling green ocean, or by perfect half-moon coves lapped by the gentle waters of the bay. The city clusters around them, climbing over hills and crowding behind beaches and lakes. Its neighbourhoods are connected by tunnels bored through the ancient rock or across winding double-decker highways that cling vertiginously to the cliffs above the fierce Atlantic Ocean.

Against this magical backdrop, the famous Carioca day leisurely unwinds. When the sun is up the middle classes head for the beach, wearing nothing but tiny speedos or bikinis. Here they surf, play beach volleyball or football, or soak up the rays between occasional dips into the waves, with the working day just a brief interruption. When the sun is down, still wearing almost nothing, they head for the botecos (street bars) for an ice-cold draught beer or chope. Then they go home, finally put some clothes on and prepare to go out until the early hours of the morning.

From high on the hills, the other Rio watches over the middle classes. Here lie the favelas – slum cities where the poor and predominantly black communities live. These are Rio's engine of blue-collar work, but also its cultural heart; carnival, samba and Brazilian football were born here. Favelas are at the core of the country's cinema resurgence and the soul of the music of Seu Jorge and Afro-reggae. Brazil's joyful spirit can be felt most strongly in the favelas, alongside its greatest misery and its most shocking violence. ▶▶ *For listings, see pages 103-134.*

Ins and outs

Getting there

Air Rio is served by two airports. **Aeroporto Internacional Tom Jobim** ⓘ *Ilha do Governador, 15 km north of the city centre* (formerly known as Galeão and often still called by this name), receives international and domestic flights. There are *câmbios* in the departure hall and on the first floor of international arrivals. The **Banco do Brasil** on the third floor (open 24 hours) has better rates of exchange. There are also ATMs for major Brazilian banks, several of which accept Visa and MasterCard. Duty-free shops are well stocked and open to arrivals as well as departures. There are **Riotur** information booths in the domestic arrivals hall of Terminal 1 (T021-3398 4077, daily 0600-2300), and in the international arrivals hall in Terminal 2 (T021-3398 2245, daily 0600-2400), which provide maps and can book accommodation. **Santos Dumont Airport** ⓘ *in the city centre on Guanabara Bay*, is used for Rio–São Paulo shuttle flights (see Transport, page 128), a handful of other domestic routes, private planes or air taxis. For more information visit www.infraero.gov.br and click on 'aeroportos'.

Taxis can be booked from within the airports or picked up at the stands outside the terminals. Fixed-rate taxis charge around US$30 from Jobim to Copacabana and Ipanema and US$25 to the city centre and Santa Teresa (about half as much from Santos Dumont);

buy a ticket at the counter. Metered taxis cost around US$25 from Jobim to Copacabana, but beware of pirate taxis, which are unlicensed. Fixed-price taxis leave from the first floor of both terminals and have clearly marked booths selling tickets.

There are frequent buses between the two airports, the *rodoviária* (interstate bus station) and the city; the best are the air-conditioned **Real Auto**, T0800-240850, www.realautoonibus.com.br, which leave from outside arrivals on the first floor of terminals 1 and 2 at Tom Jobim (aka Galeão) and run 0500-2400, US$3. There are two routes: *Linha 2018 via Orla da Zona Sul*, runs every 30 minutes, to the Terminal Alvorada bus station in Barra da Tijuca and back again, stopping at the *rodoviária*, Avenida Rio Branco in the centre, Santos Dumont airport, Flamengo, Copacabana, Ipanema, São Conrado and Barra's Avenida das Americas. (This should not be confused with the *Linha 2018 via Linha Vermelha*, which runs a sporadic circular route via Barra and nowhere else of any use to foreign tourists.) *Linha 2145* runs every 25 minutes to Santos Dumont airport and back again, calling at Avenida Rio Branco along the way. Buses can be flagged down anywhere along their route and passengers can request to jump off at any time. There is also a standard Rio bus running along the 2018 line with similar

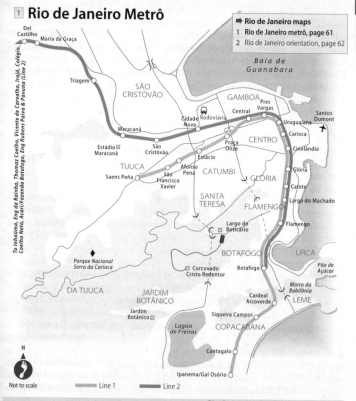

1 **Rio de Janeiro Metrô**

➡ **Rio de Janeiro maps**
1 Rio de Janeiro metrô, page 61
2 Rio de Janeiro orientation, page 62

Line 1
Line 2

Not to scale

② Rio de Janeiro

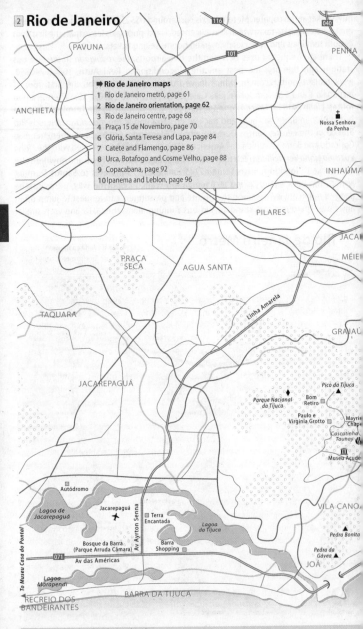

➡ Rio de Janeiro maps
1 Rio de Janeiro métro, page 61
2 Rio de Janeiro orientation, page 62
3 Rio de Janeiro centre, page 68
4 Praça 15 de Novembro, page 70
6 Glória, Santa Teresa and Lapa, page 84
7 Catete and Flamengo, page 86
8 Urca, Botafogo and Cosme Velho, page 88
9 Copacabana, page 92
10 Ipanema and Leblon, page 96

PAVUNA

PENHA

ANCHIETA

Nossa Senhora
da Penha

INHAÚMA

PILARES

JACA

PRAÇA
SECA

AGUA SANTA

MÉIE

TAQUARA

Linha Amarela

GRAJAÚ

JACAREPAGUÁ

Parque Nacional
da Tijuca

Pico da Tijuca ▲

Bom
Retiro

Paulo e
Virginia Grotto

Mayri
Chape

Cascatinha
Taunay

Museu Açude

Autódromo

Lagoa de
Jacarepaguá

Jacarepaguá ✈

Terra
Encantada

Lagoa
da Tijuca

VILA CANO

Pedra Bonita

Bosque da Barra
(Parque Arruda Câmara)

Barra
Shopping

Pedra da
Gávea ▲

To Museu Casa do Pontal

Av das Américas

071

JOÁ

Lagoa
Marapendi

RECREIO DOS
BANDEIRANTES

BARRA DA TIJUCA

Av Ayrton Senna

frequency, US$2. Ordinary city buses also run from the airport to various locations in Rio – from the first floor of both terminals. These are far less secure and are not recommended.
➨ See Transport, page 128.

Bus International and interstate buses arrive at the **Rodoviária Novo Rio** ① *Av Francisco Bicalho 01 at Rodrigues Alves, Santo Cristo, T021-3213 1800, www.novorio.com.br*. There is a **Riotur information centre** ① *T021-2263 4857, daily 0700-1900*, which can help with orientation and accommodation. Left luggage costs US$5. There are *câmbios* (cash only) and ATMs. From the *rodoviária* it is best to take a taxi to your hotel or to the nearest metrô station (Metrô Estácio); taxis can be booked at the booth on the ground floor. The metrô runs south as far as Copacabana (Metrô Cantagalo); for Ipanema and Leblon head to Metrô Siqueira Campos and take a taxi from there, or take bus marked 'Metrô-Gávea'.

The **local bus terminal** is just outside the *rodoviária*: turn right as you leave and run the gauntlet of taxi drivers. The bus station attracts thieves, so exercise caution. The air-conditioned **Real** bus (opposite the exit) goes along the beach to São Conrado and will secure luggage. If you need a taxi collect a ticket from the office inside the entrance as this protects against over-charging; a taxi to Flamengo costs approximately US$12.

Getting around

The city is made up of separate districts connected by urban highways and tunnels heavy with traffic, so it's best to use public transport or taxis to get around. An underground railway, the **Metrô** ① *T0800-2595 1111, www.metrorio.com.br, Mon-Sat 0500-2400, Sun and holidays 0700-2300 and 24 hrs during Carnaval, tickets US$1.60 for a 1-way journey, US$2 for metro and connecting Gávea/Barra bus*, runs from the outer suburbs of the Zona Norte (not of tourist interest), through the city centre (including the Sambódromo and the Maracanã stadium), Glória, Flamengo, Botafogo, Copacabana, the Lagoa to the Arpoador end of Ipanema. The Metrô-Barra buses connect at the penultimate station – General Osório (aka Tom Jobim or Ipanema) – for Leblon, Gávea and Barra. There are plans to extend the service to Rocinha, São Conrado and Barra da Tijuca in time for the 2016 Olympics. Metrô stations often have a number of different access points. **Buses** run to all parts, but should be treated with caution at night, when taxis are a better bet. Buses are usually marked with the destination and any going south of the centre will call at Copacabana and generally Ipanema/Leblon. **Minivans** run from Avenida Rio Branco in the centre as far south as Barra da Tijuca and have the destination written on the window. **Taxis** should always be booked through a hostel or hotel, or caught from a designated taxi *posto*; the name of the *posto* should be written in navy blue on the side of the taxi. Avoid freelance taxis hailed in the street and those without a taxi rank inscription. Santa Teresa is reached by **tram**, which leaves from the Largo da Carioca, near the metrô station and the cathedral, passing over the Lapa viaduct and running along all the main streets in Santa Teresa and eventually reaching either Dois Irmãos or Paula Mattos at the far end of Santa Teresa (see page 81).

Best time to visit

Rio has one of the healthiest climates in the tropics, with trade winds keeping the air fresh. June, July and August are the coolest months, with temperatures ranging from 22°C (18°C in a cold spell) to 32°C on a sunny day at noon. December to March is hot and humid, with temperatures of 32-42°C. October to March is the rainy season; the annual rainfall is about 1120 mm. **Carnaval** is a movable feast, running for five riotous days from the Friday afternoon before Shrove Tuesday to the morning hangover of Ash Wednesday.

Tourist information

Riotur ① *Praça Pio X, 119, 9th floor, Centro, T021-2271 7000, www.rioguiaoficial.com.br,* is the city's government tourist office. There are also booths or offices in **Copacabana** ① *Centro de Atendimento ao Turista, Av Princesa Isabel 183, T021-2541 7522, Mon-Fri 0900- 1800,* and **Copacabana Posto Seis** ① *Av Rainha Elizabeth 36 at NS de Copacabana, T021-2513 0077, Mon-Fri 0900-1800.* The helpful staff speak English, French and German and can provide good city maps and a very useful free brochure. There are further information stands at **Corcovado** ① *R Cosme Velho 513, T021-2258 1329 ext 4, on the upper and lower levels of the elevator,* and at the international airport and Novo Rio bus station. There is also a free telephone information service, *Alô Rio,* in Portuguese and English, T021-2542 8080 or T021-2542 8004.

The state tourism organization is **Turisrio** ① *R da Ajuda 5, 6th floor, Centro, T021-2215 0011, www.turisrio.rj.gov.br, Mon-Fri 0900-1800.* The private sector **Rio Convention and Visitors Bureau** ① *R Visconde de Pirajá 547, suite 610, Ipanema, T021-2259 6165, www.rio conventionbureau.com.br,* also offers information and assistance in English. **Embratur** ① *R Uruguaiana 174, 8th floor, Centro, T021-2509 6017, www.braziltour.com,* provides information on the whole country.

Guidebooks *Trilhas do Rio,* by Pedro da Cunha e Menezes (Editora Salamandra, second edition), US$22.50, describes walking trips around Rio. For a light-hearted approach to living in Rio, see *How to be a Carioca,* by Priscilla Ann Goslin. Danusia Barbara's *Restaurantes do Rio* (Senac Rio) is a widely respected gastronomic guide. Casa da Palavra publishes a series of architectural guides to Rio, *Guia da Arquitetura,* in Portuguese and English. Many hotels provide guests with a useful free tourist booklet, *Guia do Rio,* which is published quarterly and has the most up-to-date listings.

Maps The *Guia Quatro Rodas – Rio* map book is the only completely comprehensive street map and is essential if you are driving. It can be bought at most newsstands.

Newspapers and magazines Advertisements in the classified sections of dailies *O Globo* and *Jornal do Brasil* proffer apartments for rent and other such services. Both have entertainments pages too; *O Globo* has a travel section on Thursday; the *Jornal do Brasil's Programa* on Friday is an essential 'what's-on' magazine. Even better is the Rio supplement to *Veja,* a weekly news magazine. *Caro Amigos,* http://carosamigos.terra.com.br, is Brazil's most influential centre-left magazine.

Websites www.brazilmax.com is by far the best site, with very useful and incisive cultural information, events listings and articles in English on the whole country. www.ipanema.com has practical information about Rio. www.samba-choro.com.br has information about Carioca music, venues and new releases. www.guiadasemana.com.br is an excellent entertainment site, with cinema, theatre and restaurant listings (in Portuguese). There are internet cafés throughout the city and 90% of hotels and hostels offer internet access.

Background

The coast of Rio de Janeiro was first settled about 5000 years ago. When the Europeans arrived, the indigenous inhabitants belonged to the Tupi or Tupi-Guarani, Botocudos, Puri and Maxacali linguistic groups. Tragically, no indigenous people in this region survived the European incursions.

The Portuguese navigator, Gonçalo Coelho, landed at what is now Rio de Janeiro on 1 January 1502. Mistaking the Baía de Guanabara (the name the local people used) to be the mouth of a great river, they called it the 'January River'. But the bay wasn't settled until 1555 when the French, under the Huguenot Admiral Nicholas Durand de Villegagnon, occupied Lage Island. They later transferred to Seregipe Island (now Villegagnon), where they built the fort of Coligny. The fort has been demolished to make way for the Escola Naval (naval college), and the island itself, since the narrow channel was filled up, has become a part of the mainland. Villegagnon set up a colony as the starting point for what he called Antarctic France.

In 1559-1560, Mem de Sá, the third governor of Brazil, mounted an expedition from Salvador to attack the French, who were supported by the indigenous Tamoio. The Portuguese succeeded in capturing the French fort and putting an end to Antarctic France, but did not colonize the area until 1567 when they transferred their settlement to the Morro de São Januário. This is generally considered the date of the founding of the city of São Sebastião do Rio de Janeiro, so called in honour of the Portuguese prince who would soon assume the throne.

Though constantly attacked by local indigenous groups, the new city grew rapidly and when King Sebastião divided Brazil into two provinces, Rio was chosen as capital of the southern captaincies. Salvador became sole capital again in 1576, but Rio again became the southern capital in 1608 and the seat of a bishopric. There was a further French incursion in 1710-1711 as a result of the tension between France and Portugal during the war of Spanish Succession, and because of the flow of gold out of Minas Gerais through Rio. Rio de Janeiro was by now becoming the leading city in Brazil. Not only was it the port out of which gold was shipped, but it was also the focus of the export/import trade of the surrounding agricultural lands. On 27 January 1763, it became the seat of the viceroy. After Independence, in 1834, it was declared capital of the empire and remained so for 125 years.

The shaping of a city

Rio went from a colonial capital to the capital of a large Empire when King João and the entire Portuguese court fled to Brazil in 1808 in fear of Napoleon, abandoning Portugal to a caretaker British Army General. The ideas they brought with them from Europe began to transform Rio. New formal gardens and stately *praças*, graced with faux-European fountains were built to accommodate the court's more refined tastes and lavish mansions and palaces were built to house the royals and their retinue, see pages 786 and 791. Despite his fear of Napoleon, King João invited an artistic mission from France to found academies of fine art and music in Rio in 1816. The architect Grandjean de Montigny, the painter Jean-Baptiste Debret and sculptor Nicolas Antoine Taunay began an artisitic relationship which continued into the 20th century through Le Corbusier and Levi-Strauss and which provided the template for modern Brazil's artistic and academic development. The city also expanded geographically, growing north into São Cristóvão and Tijuca and south through Glória, Catete, Flamengo and Botafogo. It also grew in prosperity, with wealthy coffee barons building *chacaras* – or country houses – in the hills around Tijuca and Santa Teresa, a trend which continued into independence. By the time Brazil had become a republic in 1889, Rio was by far the most important city in the country politically, culturally and economically.

The new Republic was founded on French positivist principles, which were resolutely pragmatic and functionalist – as expressed by the new national motto 'Order and Progress'. The old past were discarded. Sadly it included much of colonial Rio whose beautiful terracotta tiled roofs, old alleys, churches and mansion houses were razed to the ground and replaced by poor versions of US office blocks, lining broad new avenues such as the the 33-m-wide Avenida Central (later renamed Avenida Rio Branco). The disenfranchised poor Brazilian majority, many of whom were recently freed African Brazilian slaves refused work on the plantations, began to cluster on the hills in ungainly shanty towns, or favelas.

In 1960 Brazil entered an era of order and progress when new president Juscelino Kubitschek declared that his country would leap 50 years in just five – equivalent to his term of office. JK shifted the nation's capital several thousand kilometres inland to the new purpose-built Jetson age Brasília, sending the country into bankruptcy and Rio into decline. The commercial centre crumbled, the bright lights of Lapa and Cinelandia flickered and went dim and wealthy Cariocas left for the beaches around Ipanema and São Conrado. Resurrection began in the 1990s, when a new mayor, Luiz Paulo Conde, embarked on a massive programme of regeneration, remodelling the bayside suburbs and attracting residents, artistic endeavours and small businesses to neglected districts. Lapa emerged again as a nightlife centre and Rio began to find its cultural feet again. But years of neglect had left a toll. Contemporary Rio has literally hundreds of favelas and a population chronically divided between the haves, who live in the Cidade Maravilhosa, and the have-nots, who live in the Cidade de Deus or similar slum communities.

Central Rio and Lapa

Hot and sweaty central Rio spreads back from Guanabara Bay in a jumbled grid of streets between Santos Dumont airport and the Jesuit Mosteiro São Bento. It dates from 1567, but much of its architectural heritage has been laid waste by successive waves of government intent on wiping out the past in favour of dubious and grandiose visions of Order and Progress. Nevertheless it remains the centre of Rio's history as well as the city, with some distinguished colonial buildings, Manueline follies and elaborate neoclassical facades huddled together under totalitarian blocks of flats and Le Corbusier-inspired concrete. All watch over a mass of cars and a bustle of people: business suits on lunch, beggars, skateboarders dressed in would-be New York oversized jeans and baseball caps, street performers and opportunists looking to snatch a purse. It can all feel a bit hectic and bewildering. But don't give up. There is plenty to explore here and a wealth of air-conditioned havens in which to escape for respite and a coffee.

The greatest concentration of historic buildings is in the south of the centre, near Santos Dumont airport and around **Praça 15 de Novembro**, from where Rio de Janeiro grew in its earliest days. Here you'll find most of the museums, some of the city's more beautiful little churches and colonial buildings such as the **Paço Imperial** and the **Palácio Tiradentes**. More colonial buildings lie at the centre's northern extremity around Morro de São Bento. These include the finest baroque building in Rio, the **Mosteiro de São Bento**, and the city's most imposing church, **Nossa Senhora da Candelária**.

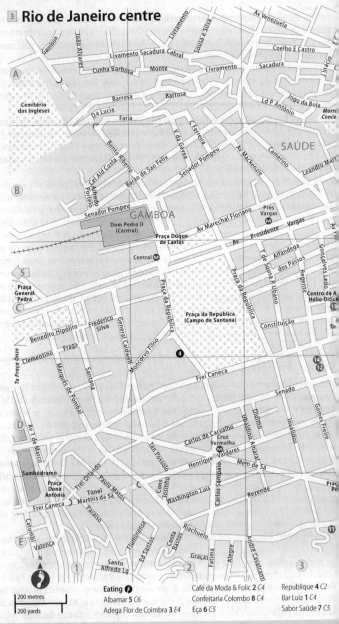

3 Rio de Janeiro centre

Eating ⑦
Albamar **5** C6
Adega Flor de Coimbra **3** E4
Café da Moda & Folic **2** C4
Confeitaria Colombo **8** C4
Eça **6** C5
Republique **4** C2
Bar Luiz **1** C4
Sabor Saúde **7** C5

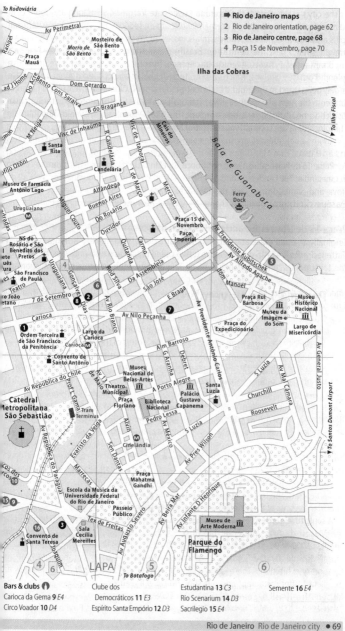

To Rodoviária

Av Perimetral

Rangel

Praça Mauá

Morro de São Bento

Mosteiro de São Bento

Dom Gerardo

Do Acre Bento Cons Saraiva

B do Bragança

Ilha das Cobras

To Ilha Fiscal

Visc de Inhaúma

M. Neiva

Santa Rita

Cais dos Mineiros

Baía de Guanabara

R Candelária

Visc de Itaboraí

Candelária

De Mato

Alfândega

Miguel Couto

Buenos Aires

Do Rosário

Museu de Farmácia Antônio Lago

Uruguaiana

Mercado

Ferry Dock

Ouvidor

Praça 15 de Novembro

Paço Imperial

NS do Rosário e São Benedito dos Pretos

São Francisco de Paula

Gonçalves Dias

Rod Silva

Da Assembleia

Carmo

Av Presidente Kubitschek

Av Alfredo Agache

Av Presidente Antônio Carlos

Teatro João Caetano

7 de Setembro

São José

E Braga

João Manoel

Praça Rui Barbosa

Museu Histórico Nacional

Carioca

Av Rio Branco

Av Nilo Peçanha

Museu da Imagem e do Som

Ordem Terceira de São Francisco da Penitência

Carioca

Largo da Carioca

Alm Barroso

Praça do Expedicionário

Largo de Misericórdia

Convento de Santo Antônio

G Aranha

Debret

Av General Justo

Av República do Chile

Prof L Gama

Av 13 de Maio

Museu Nacional de Belas-Artes

A Porto Alegre

Santa Luzia

S Luzia

Catedral Metropolitana São Sebastião

Teatro Municipal

Praça Floriano

Biblioteca Nacional

Palácio Gustavo Capanema

Churchill

Av Mal Câmara

To Santos Dumont Airport

Tram Terminus

Av República do Paraguai

Evaristo da Veiga

Alvin

Pedro Lessa

Av México

Roosevelt

S Luzia

Sen Dantas

Cinelândia

Av Pres Wilson

cos dos rcos

Martecas

Praça Mahatma Gandhi

Escola da Música da Universidade Federal do Rio de Janeiro

Tex de Freitas

Passeio Público

Av Beira Mar

Av Augusto Severo

Sala Cecília Meireles

Convento de Santa Teresa

São Joaquim

LAPA

Av Infante D Henrique

Museu de Arte Moderna

Parque do Flamengo

To Botafogo

➡ Rio de Janeiro maps
2 Rio de Janeiro orientation, page 62
3 **Rio de Janeiro centre, page 68**
4 Praça 15 de Novembro, page 70

Bars & clubs 🎵
Carioca da Gema 9 *E4*
Circo Voador 10 *D4*

Clube dos Democráticos 11 *E3*
Espírito Santa Empório 12 *D3*

Estudantina 13 *C3*
Rio Scenarium 14 *D3*
Sacrilegio 15 *E4*

Semente 16 *E4*

The city's main artery is the **Avenida Presidente Vargas**, 4.5 km long and more than 90 m wide, which divides these northern and southern sections. It begins at the waterfront, splits around the Candelária church, then crosses the Avenida Rio Branco in a magnificent straight stretch past the **Central do Brasil** railway station. Vargas is dissected by two important arterial streets. **Avenida Rio Branco**, nearest to the sea, was once lined with splendid ornate buildings, which were quite the equal of any in Buenos Aires. These have largely been razed to the ground but a few remain around **Cinelândia**. **Avenida 31 Março**, further to the west beyond the railway station, leads to the **Sambódromo** and the Carnaval district. Some of the better modern architecture is to be found along Avenida República do Chile, including the conical 1960s **Catedral Metropolitana de São Sebastião**.

Ins and outs

For Praça 15 de Novembro, Largo do Carioca, Cinelândia and Lapa take the metrô to Carioca in Cinelândia. For Candelária and São Bento take the metrô to Uruguiana. For the Cidade Nova and Sambódromo take the metrô to Praça Onze. Opening times for churches, museums and public buildings change frequently. All museums close during Carnaval.

Praça 15 de Novembro and the imperial palaces

Originally an open space at the foot of the Morro do Castelo – a hill which has now been flattened – the Praça 15 de Novembro (often called Praça Quinze) has always been one of the focal points in Rio de Janeiro. Today it has one of the greatest concentrations of

4 Praça 15 de Novembro

➡ Rio de Janeiro maps
2 Rio de Janeiro orientation, page 62
3 Rio de Janeiro centre, page 68
4 **Praça 15 de Novembro, page 70**

Eating 🍴
Bar das Artes **1** *C3*
Cais do Oriente **2** *B2*

Bars & clubs 🍸
Mercado 32 **1** *B3*

Shop 🛍
Alequim Música **1** *C3*

historic buildings in the city. Having been through various phases of development, the area underwent major remodelling in the late 1990s. The last vestiges of the original harbour, at the seaward end of the *praça*, were restored. Avenida Alfredo Agache now goes through an underpass, creating an open space between the *praça* and the seafront and giving easy access to the ferry dock for Niterói. The area is well illuminated and clean and the municipality has started to stage shows, music and dancing in the *praça*. At weekends an antiques, crafts, stamp and coin fair (Feirarte II) is held 0900-1900. The rather modest colonial former royal palace, **Paço Imperial** ① *on the southeast corner of Praça 15 de Novembro, T021-2533 4407, www.pacoimperial.com.br, Tue-Sun 1200-1800*, is one of the centre's landmarks. It was built in 1743 as the residence of the governor of the Capitania and was made into the royal palace when the Portuguese court moved to Brazil. After independence it became the imperial palace. It fell into disuse in the mid-20th century to be resurrected as a temporary exhibition space and arts centre. There's often something interesting on display here, and two decent air-conditioned café-restaurants, the **Bistro** and **Atrium**, provide respite from the heat. Just north of the palace is the **Chafariz do Mestre Valentim**, or Chafariz do Pirâmide; a fountain designed by the famous sculptor.

Beside the Paço Imperial, across Rua da Assembléia, is the grand neoclassical **Palácio Tiradentes** ① *T021-2588 1411, Mon-Sat 1000-1700, Sun and holidays 1200-1700, guided visits by appointment only, T021-2588 1251*. It was named in honour of the former dentist (*tiradentes* means teeth puller), Joaquim José da Silva Xavier, who is often seen as the symbolic father of Brazilian independence, and who was held prisoner here and executed nearby. The building itself was constructed between 1922 and 1926 and is now the state legislative assembly. A **statue of Tiradentes** by Francisco de Andrade stands in front.

Largo da Misericórdia and the museums

There is a cluster of interesting little museums south of Praça XV on the way to Santos Dumont airport that can be reached by the Largo da Misericórdia, which runs immediately south of the Palácio Tiradentes. At the end of the *largo* is the **Ladeira da Misericórdia**; the oldest street in Rio and now just a severed stump on the side of the grand Santa Casa da Misericórdia hospital. This hill was once crowned by a magnificent monastery and fort that watched out over the bay. Next door to the hospital, in a series of handsome buildings, is the **Museu Histórico Nacional** ① *Praça Marechal Âncora, T021-2550 9224, www.museuhitoriconacional.com.br, Tue-Fri 1000-1700, Sat and Sun 1400-1800, US$3, free on Sun*. This is one of the city's more distinguished museums, with a collection of magnificent carriages, historical treasures, colonial sculpture and furniture, maps, paintings, arms and armour, silver and porcelain. It also retains a rampart from that first fort that crowned the former Morro do Castelo hill from the 1603 until the 20th century. The building was once the war arsenal of the empire, and was partly constructed in 1762 (this part is called the 'Casa do Trem'). The **Museu da Imagem e do Som (MIS)** ① *at the moment split between 2 centres: R Visconde de Maranguape 15, Largo da Lapa, T021-2332 9508 and Praça Luiz Souza Dantas (aka Praça Rui Barbosa) 01, Praça XV, T021-2332 9068, Mon-Fri 1100-1700, www.mis.rj.gov.br, free, visits by appointment only*, is scheduled to move into a swanky, purpose-built new building in Copacabana in 2012. It currently houses a collection of cinema images, photos of Rio and of Carioca musicians, and recordings of popular music, including early *choro* by artists including Jacob do Bandolim. There are booths for listening to music and a small cinema for watching the 16 mm and 35 mm film archive.

Travessa do Comércio and the Carmelite churches

North of Praça XV, the **Travessa do Comércio** and its continuation to the left, the **Rua do Ouvidor**, are reached via the **Arco do Teles** directly across from the palace. The arch is all that remains of an 18th-century construction, now incorporated into a modern building, and the two streets give an idea of how most of Rio must have looked in the 19th century. Little bars and restaurants line the streets and are very lively after 1800. These include the **Arco Imperial**, where Carmen Miranda lived between 1925 and 1930 (her mother kept a boarding house). There are also some interesting bookshops and one of Brazil's prettiest little baroque churches, **Nossa Senhora da Lapa dos Mercadores** ① *R do Ouvidor 35, T021-2509 2239, Mon-Fri 0800-1400*. This began life as a street oratory erected in a blind alley by market vendors who traditionally petitioned Our Lady of Lapa for help in hard times; it became a church in 1750, was remodelled in 1869-1872 and has now been fully restored.

The busy thoroughfare of Rua 1 de Março cuts across the top of Praça XV and Rua Ouvidor and is littered with Carmelite churches, all of them worth a quick look. The most famous is at the northwestern corner of the *praça*: **Nossa Senhora do Carmo da Antiga Sé** ① *R 1 de Março at R 7 de Setembro 14, T021-2509 2239, Tue-Thu 0900-1700, Sat 1100-1700*, has one of the finest baroque interiors in Rio and occupies the site of the original founding Carmelite chapel, which stood here between 1590 and 1754. The current church dates from 1761. After the arrival of the Portuguese court in 1808 it became the designated Royal Chapel and subsequently the city's first cathedral – between 1900 and 1976. The crypt allegedly holds the remains of Pedro Alvares Cabral, the European discoverer of Brazil; a claim disputed by the town of Santarém in Portugal. Just north of this church and right in front of the end of Rua Ouvidor is the **Igreja da Ordem Terceira do Monte do Carmo** ① *R 1 de Março s/n, Mon-Fri 0800-1400, Sat 0800-1200*. This was built in 1754, consecrated in 1770 and rebuilt in the 19th century. It has strikingly beautiful portals by Mestre Valentim (see Fine art and sculpture, page 786), the son of a Portuguese nobleman and a slave girl. He also created the main altar of fine moulded silver, the throne and its chair and much else. At the rear of the old cathedral and the Igreja da Ordem Terceira do Monte do Carmo, on Rua do Carmo, is the **Oratório de Nossa Senhora do Cabo da Boa Esperança**; one of the few remaining public oratories from the colonial period in Rio.

Candelária and around

Rio's most imposing church lies on an island in a sea of traffic some 500 m north of Praça XV. The mock-Italianate **Igreja de Nossa Senhora da Candelária** ① *Praça Pio X, T021-2233 2324, Mon-Fri 0800-1600, Sat 0800-1200, Sun 0900-1300*, has long been the church of 'society Rio'. Celebrities still gather here in the marble interior for the city's most prestigious weddings. The church is modelled on the Basílica da Estrela in Portugal. The tiles in the dome are from Lisbon, the marble inside is Veronan and the heavy bronze doors were commissioned from France. All were shipped across at vast expense in the late 18th century, during an era when even though such materials were readily available in Brazil at similar quality and far lower prices, snob value demanded that they be imported. The church was built on the site of a chapel founded in 1610 by the Spaniard Antônio Martins Palma who arrived in Rio after surviving a terrible storm at sea. He erected the chapel in homage to Nuestra Señora de Candelária, the patron saint of his home, La Palma island in the Canaries.

There are a number of cultural centres near the church. The **Centro Cultural Correios** ① *R Visconde de Itaboraí 20, T021-2253 1580, www.correios.com.br, Tue-Sun 1200-1900, free* in a smart early 20th-century building with a little private park, is a good stop for an air-conditioned juice or coffee. It has a theatre, a 1000-sq-m concert hall and spaces for temporary exhibitions and cultural events, and a postage stamp fair on Saturdays. Just opposite, with entrances on Avenida Presidente Vargas and Rua 1 de Março 66, is the **Centro Cultural Banco do Brasil (CCBB)** ① *R 1 de Março 66, T021-3808 2020, www.bb. com.br/cultura, Tue-Sun 1000-2100*, in a fine early 19th-century neoclassical building with a beautiful glass domed roof. The centre hosts many of the city's large and distinguished art shows, including some excellent photographic exhibitions. It also has an arts cinema, library, multimedia facilities and lunchtime concerts (around US$5). The restaurant is air-conditioned and the food respectable. At the corner of Rua Visconde de Itaboraí (No 253) and Avenida Presidente Vargas, just opposite Candelária, is the **Casa França-Brasil** ① *R Visconde de Itaboraí 78, T021-2253 5366, www.casafrancabrasil.com.br, Tue-Sun 1000- 2000*, a Franco-Brazilian cultural centre designed by one of the key players in the 19th- century French cultural mission to Rio, Grandjean de Montigny. It holds temporary exhibitions exploring the long relationship between the two countries. The newest of the cultural centres near Candelária is the **Espaço Cultural da Marinha** ① *Av Alfredo Agache, on the waterfront, T021-2104 6025, www.sdm.mar.mil.br/espaco.htm, Tue-Sun 1200-1700, free*. This former naval establishment, built on a jetty over the bay, now contains museums of underwater archaeology and navigation. *Galeota*, the boat used by the Portuguese royal family for sailing around the Baía de Guanabara is kept here and a Second World War submarine and warship, the *Bauru* (not to be confused with the sandwich of the same name), is moored outside. The museum is very popular with Brazilian children and is crowded at weekends.

Just offshore, but connected to the mainland by a causeway to Ilha das Cobras, is the **Ilha Fiscal** ① *Av Alfredo Agache, T021-2233 9165, boats leave Thu-Sun at 1300, 1430 and 1600, closed 1 Jan, Carnaval, Holy Week and Christmas; when the sea is too rough transport is by van*. It was built as a customs house at the emperor's request, but he deemed it too beautiful, and said that it should be used only for official parties. Only one was ever held – a masked ball hosted by the viscount of Ouro Preto in honour of the crew of the Chilean warship, *The Admiral Cochrane*, five days before the republic began. It is now a museum, linked with the Espaço Cultural da Marinha. The island is passed by the ferry to Niterói.

Mosteiro de São Bento

The **Praça Mauá**, which lies north of Avenida Presidente Vargas, marks the end of Centro and the beginning of the port zone. Many of the empty warehouses here are used as workshops by the samba schools for the construction of their beautiful carnival floats. The area would be unremarkable were it not for the **Mosteiro de São Bento** ① *R Gerardo 68, T021-2516 2286, www.osb.org.br, daily 0700-1730, free, guided tours Mon-Sat 0900-1600; modest dress, no shorts; taxi from the city centre US$6*, whose sober Brazilian baroque façade sits on a promontory looking out over the bay. It is widely publicized as a World Heritage Site, which it is not. But of all the city's colonial buildings this is the most worth visiting, both for its magnificent interior and for its significance as the most important Benedictine monument outside Europe. The church began life in 1586 with a group of monks who arrived in Rio from Salvador and it grew to become the most powerful monastery in the city. It preserves a lavish gilt baroque interior but is very poorly lit (the church charges an absurd US$5 to put on all of the electric lights). However, in the gloom it is possible to make out that not an inch remains unadorned. The three doors sculpted by Father Domingos da Conceição, which give access to the nave, and the sculptures of

St Benedict, St Escolastica and Our Lady of Monserrat are particularly remarkable. The last, which is also by Domingos de Conceição, has painted birds' eggs for eyes. The painting is as wonderful as the carving; particularly the panels in the Blessed Sacrament chapel by Inácio Ferreira Pinto and *O Salvador*, the masterpiece of Brazil's first painter, Frei Ricardo do Pilar, which hangs in the sacristy. The enormous candelabra are attributed to Mestre Valentim, Rio's most celebrated church artisan, and are made from solid silver especially imported from Peru and the mines of Potosí in Bolivia at a price higher than Brazil's own gold. The monastery's library (open to men only) preserves a number of priceless religious manuscripts alongside 200,000 other books.

São Bento can be reached either by a narrow road from Rua Dom Gerardo 68, or by a lift whose entrance is at Rua Dom Gerardo 40. Both routes lead to a *praça* with tall trees, but arriving in the lift is more magical as you are whisked from the heat and bustle of the dock area to an oasis of calm, which sets the mood beautifully for a wander around the monastery buildings. If you would rather walk, the monastery is a few minutes from Praça Mauá, turning left off Avenida Rio Branco; Rua Dom Gerardo 68 is behind the massive new RBI building. Every Sunday at 1000 there is a Latin Mass with plainsong. Arrive an hour early to get a seat. On other days, Mass is at 0715 and the monks often sing at vespers.

Largo da Carioca and around

This higgledy-piggledy street of colonial churches, modern buildings and street stalls sits between Rua da Carioca and the Carioca metrô station about 1 km south of Praça XV along Rua da Assembléia. There is a variety of interesting sights here within a very small area. The **Convento de Santo Antônio** ① *T021-2262 0129, Mon, Wed, Thu, Fri 0730-1900, Tue 0630-2000, Sat 0730-1100 and 1530-1700, Sun 0900-1100, free*, the second oldest in Rio, sits on a little hill off the Largo da Carioca. You will often see single women here gathered to pray: there are many more women than men in Brazil and St Anthony is traditionally a provider of husbands. The church interior is baroque around the chancel, main altars and two lateral altars, which are devoted to St Anthony, St Francis and the Immaculate Conception respectively. The beautiful sacristy is decorated with *azulejos* (tiles) and adorned with paintings depicting scenes from St Anthony's life. Many members of the Brazilian imperial family are buried in the mausoleum. Separated from this church only by a fence of iron railings is one of Rio's least-known baroque jewels: the little church of the **Ordem Terceira de São Francisco da Penitência** ① *T021-2262 0197, Mon-Fri 0900-1200 and 1300-1600, free*, which was built between 1622 and 1738. It has a splendid gilt interior by Francisco Xavier de Brito, who is largely credited with introducing baroque to Brazil and who was probably Aleijadinho's teacher in Ouro Preto. There's a also a fine panel depicting the glorification of St Francis by Caetano da Costa Coelho. Behind the church is a tranquil catacomb-filled garden.

A couple of streets north, at the end of Rua do Ouvidor and dominating the square that bears its name, is the twin-towered **Igreja de São Francisco de Paula** ① *Largo São Francisco de Paula, Mon-Fri 0900-1300, free*, with some fine examples of Carioca art including carvings by Mestre Valentim, paintings by Vítor Meireles and murals by Manuel da Cunha. Across the Largo de São Francisco and on the corner of Rua Uruguaiana 77 and Ouvidor is the **Igreja de Nossa Senhora do Rosário e São Benedito dos Pretos** ① *T021-2224 2900, Mon-Fri 0700-1700, Sat 0700-1300, free*. Since the 17th century this church has been at the centre of African Christian culture in Rio. During the 19th century it was the site of an elaborate festival that recreated scenes from the courtly life of the king of Congo. A king and queen were crowned and they danced through the nearby streets followed by long parades of courtiers in fancy dress; a precursor perhaps for Carnaval. It was here that the announcements for the final abolition of slavery were prepared. The church once had a fabulous gilt interior but this was sadly destroyed in a fire in 1967. Next to the church is a small museum devoted to slavery in Brazil, whose collection of instruments of subjugation speaks starkly of life for black people in the last Western country to abolish the slave trade.

The **Real Gabinete Português de Leitura** ① *R Luís Camões 30, T021-2221 3138, www.realgabinete.com.br, Mon-Fri 0900-1800, free*, sits just to the north of Largo São Francisco de Paula on Rua Luís de Camões. This is one of the city's hidden architectural treasures and one of the best pieces of mock-Manueline architecture in Brazil. Manueline architecture is usually described as Portuguese Gothic and takes its name from King Manuel I who ruled Portugal between 1495 and 1521. It is unlike any other European Gothic style, drawing strongly on Islamic and nautical themes – a lavish fusion of Islamic ornamentalism and sculpted seaweeds, anchors, ropes and corals, typified by the Cristo monastery in Tomar and the Mosteiro dos Jerônimos in Lisbon. The modest exterior of the Real Gabinete, which was designed by Portuguese architect Rafael da Silva e Castro in 1880, was inspired by the façade of Jerônimos. It is decorated with statues of Camões, Henry the Navigator, Vasco da Gama and Pedro Álvares Cabral, who claimed Brazil for Portugal. More interesting, however, is the magnificent reading hall built around the oldest central steel structure in Rio. Towering arches decorated with Islamic flourish ascend via coiled wooden ropes to an elaborate painted ceiling with skylights from which a massive iron chandelier is suspended. There are some 120,000 books in the library's collection, many of them very rare. The magnificent belle-époque coffee house, **Confeitaria Colombo**, is a short walk to the east, at Rua Gonçalves Dias 32 (see Eating, page 109).

Praça Tiradentes and the cathedral

One long block behind the Largo da Carioca and São Francisco de Paula is **Praça Tiradentes**, old and shady, with a **statue to Dom Pedro I** carved in 1862 by Luís Rochet. The emperor sits on horseback shouting his famous 1822 declaration of independence, the Grito de Ipiranga: 'Liberty or Death'. The **Teatro João Caetano** sits on the northeastern corner of the *praça* and is named after a famous 19th-century actor. Prince Dom Pedro first showed the green and yellow Brazilian flag in the original building, which was an important venue for meetings discussing Brazilian independence. The current theatre was constructed in 1920 after the original had fallen into disrepair. Two canvases by one of the city's most celebrated artists, Emiliano Di Cavalcanti, hang on the second floor. Just north of the *praça*, in a handsome salmon pink colonial building, is the **Centro de Arte Hélio Oiticica** ① *R Luís de Camões 68, Mon-Fri 1000-1800*, named after another famous Carioca artist and now a smart contemporary art exhibition space with six galleries, a good art bookshop and an air-conditioned café. Important national and international artists exhibit here. Shops in nearby streets specialize in selling goods for *umbanda*, the Afro-Brazilian religion. The **Catedral Metropolitana de São Sebastião** ① *Av República do Chile, T021- 2240 2669, www.catedral.com.br, daily 0700-1900, Mass Mon-Fri 1100, Sun 1000*, lies just south of the Praça Tiradentes and the Largo da Carioca; bordering Cinêlandia to the east and Lapa to the south. It is an oblate concrete cone fronted by a decorative ladder and replete with rich blue stained glass, which looks like a modernist Mayan temple. The design could be mistaken for a Niemeyer, but is in fact by another Brazilian Le Corbusier disciple, Edgar de Oliveira da Fonseca, with heavy modernist statues and panels by Humberto Cozzi. It's best to visit in the late afternoon when the sunlight streams through the immense monotone stained-glass windows. There is a small sacred art museum in the crypt, which has a handful of relics including Dom Pedro II's throne and the fonts used for the baptizing of imperial Brazilian babies. The *bonde* (tram) to Santa Teresa leaves from behind the cathedral, the entrance is on Rua Senador Dantas (see page 81). Soon after leaving the station the tram traverses the Arcos da Lapa offering wonderful views.

One of the city's quirkier museums lies only a short walk from the cathedral. The **Museu de Farmácia Antônio Lago** ① *R dos Andradas 96, 10th floor, T021-2263 0791, www.abf.org.br/museu.html, Mon-Fri 1430-1700 by appointment only via email abf@abf.org.br, US$2*, is a reproduction of a 17th-century Brazilian apothecary's shop, complete with Dr Jekyll cabinets and rows of dubious-looking herbal preparations in glass and porcelain vessels.

Cinelândia and Avenida Rio Branco

The area around Praça Floriano was the liveliest part of the city in the 1920s and 1930s when Hollywood hit Brazil. All of the best cinemas were situated here and their popularity became so great that the *praça* was named after them. Today **Cinelândia** remains lively, especially at the end of the week, owing to its proximity to the city's nightlife capital, Lapa. The 30-m-wide **Avenida Rio Branco**, which bisects Cinelândia, is the financial heart of the city. Lined by an untidy mishmash of modernist and art deco skyscrapers it was built at the turn of 20th the century under the 'tear it down' regime of Mayor Pereira Passos. Rio once had long stately avenues that rivalled the best of Buenos Aires but only clusters have survived. Although it has seen better days, the **Theatro Municipal** ① *Praça Floriano, T021-23329191, www.theatromunicipal.rj.gov.br, Mon-Fri 1300-1700, bilingual guided tours by appointment T021-2299 1667*, remains a splendid piece of French-inspired, lavish neoclassical pomp. The tour is worth it to see front of house and backstage, the decorations and the machine rooms – a luxuriously ornate temple to an early 20th-century Carioca high society. On either side of the ostentatious colonnaded façade are rotundas, surmounted by cupolas. The muses of poetry and music watch over all, alongside an imperial eagle, wings outstretched and poised for flight. The interior is a mock-European fantasy of Carrara-marble columns, crystal chandeliers and gilt ceilings fronted by a vast sweeping, *Gone With the Wind* staircase. The stage is one of the largest in the world. The theatre was designed by Francisco de Oliveira Passos, son of the contemporaneous city mayor, who won an ostensibly open architectural competition together with French architect Albert Guilbert.

Opposite, on the other side of Avenida Rio Branco, is the refurbished **Museu Nacional de Belas-Artes** ① *Av Rio Branco 199, T021-2219 8474, www.mnba.org.br, Tue-Fri 1000-1800, Sat and Sun 1200-1700, US$3, free on Sun*. Fine art in Rio and in Brazil was, as a whole, stimulated by the arrival in 1808 of the Portuguese royal family. In 1816 the Academia de Belas-Artes was founded by another Frenchman, Joaquim Lebreton. This building was constructed 1906-1908 to house the national gallery and contains the best collection of art in the country. This includes depictions of Brazil by European visitors such as Dutchman Frans Post and Frenchman Jean-Baptiste Debret, and the best of 20th-century Brazilian art by important names such as modernist and social realist Cândido Portinari, Emiliano Di Cavalcanti (famous for his iconographic images of black Cariocas at a time when racism was institutionalized in Rio), Tarsila do Amaral (founder of the first major school of Brazilian Art, *antropofagismo*, which strongly influenced *tropicália*) and the brutalist art deco sculptor Victor Brecheret. Another gallery contains further works by foreign artists and the temporary exhibition hall houses many of Rio de Janeiro's most important international exhibitions.

Another of Cinelândia's stately neoclassical buildings is the **Biblioteca Nacional** ① *Av Rio Branco 219/239, T021-3095 3879, www.bn.br, Mon-Fri 0900-2000, Sat 0900-1500, free*, an eclectic Carioca construction, this time with a touch of art nouveau. The library is fronted by a stately engaged portico supported by a Corinthian colonnade. Inside is a series of monumental staircases in Carrara marble. The stained glass in the windows is French. The first national library was brought to Brazil in 1808 by the Prince Regent, Dom João, from a collection in the Ajuda Palace in Lisbon. Today the library houses more than nine million items, including a first edition of the *Lusiad of Camões*, a 15th-century Moguncia Bible and Book of Hours, paintings donated by Pedro II, scores by Mozart and etchings by Dürer.

Nearby, in the former Ministry of Education and Health building, is the **Palácio Gustavo Capanema** ① *R da Imprensa 16, off the Esplanada do Castelo, at the junction of Av Graça Aranha and R Araújo Porto Alegre, just off Av Rio Branco, T021-2220 1490, by appointment only, Mon-Fri 0900-1800*. Dating back to 1937-1945, it was the first piece of modernist architecture in the Americas and was designed by an illustrious team of architects led by Lúcio Costa (under the guidance of Le Corbusier) and included a very young Oscar Niemeyer – working on his first project. Inside are impressive murals by Cândido Portinari, one of Brazil's most famous artists, as well as works by other well-known names. The gardens were laid out by Roberto Burle Marx who was responsible for many landscaping projects throughout Rio (including the Parque do Flamengo) and who worked with Costa and Niemeyer in Brasília.

Lapa → See map, page 84.

Only a decade ago Lapa, which lies just south of the cathedral on the edge of Cinelândia, was a no-go area; tawdry and terrifying, walked only by prostitutes, thugs and drug addicts chasing the dragon in the crumbling porticoes of the early 20th century and art nouveau buildings. The area can still feel a little edgy, especially on weekdays after dark. But it has undergone an unimagined renaissance. This was once the Montmartre of Rio; the painter Di Cavalcanti wrote poetically of wandering its streets at night on his way home to Flamengo, past the little cafés and ballrooms and the rows of handsome town houses. Now the cafés are alive once more, spilling out onto the streets, and the ballrooms and town houses throb with samba and electronica. Opera is once more performed in the concert halls of the Escola de Música, and the area's once notorious thoroughfare, Rua do Lavradio, is now lined with smart little restaurants and clubs, playing host to one of the city's most interesting bric-a-brac and antiques markets on Saturdays. ▸▸ *See Bars and clubs, page 114.*

Although the area is best just for a cautious wander after 2000 at the end of the week, or for the Saturday market, there are a few interesting sights. The most photographed are the **Arcos da Lapa**, built in 1744 as an aqueduct to carry water from Santa Teresa to the Chafariz da Carioca, with its 16 drinking fountains, in the centre of the city. The aqueduct's use was changed at the end of the 19th century, with the introduction of electric trams in Rio. Tracks were laid on top of the arches and the inaugural run was on 1 September 1896. The tram is still in use today and is one of the city's most delightful journeys; it leaves from behind the Catedral de São Sebastião and runs to Santa Teresa, see page 81.

Bars huddle under their southern extremity on Avenida Mem de Sá, one of Rio's most popular nightlife streets. Street performers (and vagrants) often gather in the cobbled square between the *arcos* and the cathedral. There are a number of moderately interesting buildings off this square. The eclectic baroque/neoclassical **Escola da Musica da Universidade Federal do Rio de Janeiro** ① *R do Passeio 98, open officially just for performances*, has one of the city's best concert halls. A stroll away is the bizarre baroque façade of another prestigious classical concert hall, the **Sala Cecília Mereilles** ① *Largo da Lapa 47*. More picturesque are the mosaic-tiled **Ladeira do Santa Teresa** stairs, which wind their way steeply from the square and from the back of Rua Teotônio to Santa Teresa. These are much beloved of music video directors and fashion photographers who use them as a backdrop to carefully produced gritty urban scenes. The steps are tiled in red, gold and green and bordered by little houses, many of which are dishevelled and disreputable but wonderfully picturesque. Be vigilant here.

North of Avenida Mem de Sá is **Rua do Lavradio**. This was one of urban Rio's first residential streets and is lined with handsome 18th- and early 20th-century town houses. These are now filled by samba clubs, cafés, bars and antiques shops. Any day is good for a browse and a wander, and on Saturdays at the end of the month there is a busy antiques market, live street tango, no cars and throngs of people from all sections of Carioca society. Some of the houses here were once grand. Number 84 once belonged to the marquis who gave the street its name. Further along is what was once Brazil's foremost Masonic lodge, the imposing **Palácio Maçônico Grande Oriente do Brasil**, which tellingly has had as its grand masters King Dom Pedro I and one of the country's most important Republican politicians, José Bonifácio Andrada e Silva.

Central do Brasil railway station

Central do Brasil or **Dom Pedro II** railway station, as it is also known, once served much of the country but now serves only Rio. This brutal 1930s art deco temple to progress was one of the city's first modernist buildings and was made famous by the Walter Salles film *Central do Brasil* (Central Station). The film's thronging crowd scenes were set here. For similar shots come with your camera in the morning or evening and watch hundreds of thousands of people bustle in and out of trains leaving for the northern and western parts of Rio.

Gamboa, Cidade Nova and the Sambódromo

In the early 20th century, after the Paraguayan war and the abolition of slavery but before the warehouses were built in **Gamboa**, this northern dockland area was known as 'Little Africa' due to the high number of resident Bahian immigrants. With them, the African-Bahian rhythms of the *candomblé* religion were introduced into the Carioca community and the next generation spawned a host of famous local musicians that included Donga Chico da Baiana and João de Baiana.

The streets and back yards of Gamboa became the birthplace of a new music: samba born of Angolan *semba* rhythms fused with European singing styles and instruments. Donga and João da Baiana used to gather on the Pedra do Sal stairs close to the Praça Mauá to play and hold impromptu music and samba dance parties. Later the dance was incorporated into an alternative Mardi Gras festival as a counterpart to the ballroom dances of the white elite. Street parade clubs were formed by another young Carioca, Hilário Jovino Ferreira. Their structure was copied later by the much larger samba schools that still produce the Carnaval parades today.

In 2008 the city government inaugurated the **Cidade do Samba (Samba City)** ① *R Rivadávia Corréa 60, Gamboa, T021-2213 2503, http://cidadedosambarj.globo.com*

Tue-Sat 1000-1900, both to celebrate samba and to bring the administrative and production houses of the samba schools under one roof. The famous samba schools from the **Liga Independente das Escolas de Samba (LIESA)** now have a permanent carnival production centre of 14 workshops, each of them housed in a two-storey building. Visitors can watch floats and costumes being prepared or watch one of the year-round carnival-themed shows. A visit here is a wonderful experience and a real eye-opener, offering the chance to see how much painstaking work goes into create the floats, costumes and dances of schools such as the **Primeira Estação de Mangueira** (see page 119), for one night's lavish display. Rio's carnival is nailed, glued, stitched and sewn over an entire year. Much of the work is undertaken by **AMEBRAS**, www.amebras.org.br, an association of serious, stern older women who enrol, train and employ dozens of would-be artisans and dressmakers from the favelas. Thus carnival is an industry that revitalizes poor Rio. In the words of Amebras president Célia Regina Domingues "there's no fooling about here – everything we do, from hat-making to foam-sculpting for the floats, is directed towards a profession, post-carnival. People leave our project with real skills." There is a gift shop at the Cidade do Samba where it is possible to buy carnaval costumes and souvenirs many by AMEBRAS, or you can request a visit through their website as part of a visit to the Cidade. The Cidade da Samba has weekly samba shows, tickets for which can be purchased at the booths near the main entrance.

Carnaval happens right next to Gamboa in the **Cidade Nova**. Oscar Niemeyer's 650-m stadium street, the **Sambódromo** ① *R Marquês de Sapucaí s/n, metrô Central or metrô Praça Onze, Cidade Nova, T021-2502 6996, Mon-Fri 0900-1700*, was purpose-built for the annual parades and is well-worth a visit at any time. ▸▸ *See box, page 120.*

Near the Sambodromo, in the Boca do Lixo, an area best reached only by booked taxi. is the **Crescer and Viver circus** ① *R Boca do Lixo, every Thu-Sat from Aug to late Nov, tours are available, see www.crescereviver.org.br; Metrô Praça Onze, but do not walk in this neighbourhood – come by cab*, another of Rio's inspiring community projects. "If it weren't for our circus", says Vinícius Daumas of projeto Crescer and Viver, "I can honestly say that many of these teenagers would be dead. For sure some would be in a trafficking gang." Instead, some 2000 kids from the deprived communities of the Boca do Lixo neighbourhood have gone to circus school and learnt their three Rs whilst also mastering the trapeze and the flic-flac. The current company perform a spectacular show to music composed by Luíz Gonzaga's grandson, Daniel, in a tent in the Boca do Lixo.

Nearby, **Praça Onze** is today the terminus of the city's main thoroughfare, Avenida Presidente Vargas. But it was once a square and an established meeting place for *capoeristas* whose acrobatic martial art to the rhythm of the *berimbau* and hand clap inspired much Carnaval choreography. A replica of the head of a Nigerian prince from the British Museum, erected in honour of **Zumbi dos Palmares**, sits on Avenida Presidente Vargas itself. Zumbi was a Bantu prince who became the most successful black slave emancipator in the history of the Americas, founding a kingdom within Brazil in the 19th century. The **Centro de Memória do Carnaval** ① *Av Rio Branco 4, 2nd floor, T021-3213 5151, www.liesa.com.br, visits by appointment only*, is a research centre and preserves one of the largest repositories of international and Brazilian carnival images, documents and publications in the world.

Cemitério dos Ingleses

Over the Morro da Providência, between the Estação Dom Pedro II and the bay, is the **Cemitério dos Ingleses** ① *R da Gamboa 181*. The cemetery, the oldest in Rio, was granted to the British community by Dom João, Regent of Portugal, in 1810. Catholics who could afford a burial were laid to rest inside their churches (see the numbers on the church floors, marking the graves), but the British in Rio, being non-Catholic, were not allowed to be buried in the religious establishments. There are other interesting cemeteries in Rio, notably **O Cemitério São João Batista** ① *R Real Grandeza, Botafogo, T021-2539 7073*, where many of the city's most famous are buried, including Machado de Assis, Heitor Villa-Lobos, Carmen Miranda, Santos Dumont, Clara Nunes and Tom Jobim. The grand sculptures and mansion-sized mausoleums, many by Brazil's most celebrated sculptors, contrast with the concrete boxes and plastic flowers of the lower middle classes.

Nossa Senhora da Penha

The church of **Nossa Senhora da Penha** ① *Largo da Penha 19, T021-2290 0942, www.santuariodapenhario.com.br, Tue-Sun 1000-1600*, is one of the most important pilgrimage centres in the whole country, especially for black Brazilians. It sits on an enormous rock, into whose side 365 steps have been carved. Pilgrims ascend these on their knees during the festival month of October. The church in its present form dates from the early 20th century, but it was modelled on an early 18th-century chapel and a religious building has been on this site since the original hermitage was built in 1632. There are great views from the summit.

To get there take the metrô to Del Castilho. Leave the station to the left, walk down the passageway and catch microbus (micro-ônibus) No 623 labelled 'Penha-Shopping Nova América 2' to the last stop. Get off at the shopping centre, in front of Rua dos Romeiros, and walk up that street to the Largo da Penha from where there are signposts to the church.

Maracanã stadium

① *Av Prof Eurico Rabelo, T021-2334 1705, www.suderj.rj.gov.br/visitacao_maracana.asp, daily 0900-1700; independent visit Gate 15, guided tour of the stadium from Gate 16 (in Portuguese or English, daily 0930-1700, US$11). Take the metrô to Maracanã station on Linha 2, one stop beyond São Cristóvão. Bus Nos 238 and 239 from the centre, 434 and 464 from Glória, Flamengo and Botafogo, 455 from Copacabana, and 433 and 464 from Ipanema and Leblon all go to the stadium. Trips to football matches can be organized through www.bealocal.com. It is not advisable to drive in this part of Rio. One wrong turn could take you into a dangerous favela.*

Whilst tour guides proclaim Maracanã the largest sports stadium in the world, in fact there are several larger stadiums, including Indianapolis in the USA and Strahov stadium in Prague, Czech Republic. But Maracanã was the largest when it was first built and remains impressive – not least because it is the hallowed temple to the most important religious practice in Brazil – the worship of football. This is where Pelé scored his 1000th goal in 1969. His feet, as well as those of Ronaldo and other Brazilian stars, are immortalized in concrete outside the stadium. The stadium hosted the largest crowd ever to see a football match in 1950 when Brazil lost to Uruguay in front of about 200,000 spectators – an event that shook the national psyche and which is known as the Maracanazo tragedy.

In 2007 the Maracanã was refurbished. The stands were replaced with seats resulting in the decrease of the total capacity to less than 90,000. A further refurbishment is scheduled for the 2014 World Cup, shrinking it even further to less than 80,000 seats. This will take place between September and November 2012, when Maracanã will be closed. The project is controversial, for whilst modest in its aims, it is expected to cost an astounding US$400 million and include the construction of 14,000 new parking spaces, 3000 of which are are going to be allocated inside Quinta da Boa Vista park.

Even if you're not a football fan, matches are worth going to for the spectators' samba bands and the adrenalin-charged atmosphere – especially a local or Rio-São Paulo derby, or an international game. There are four types of ticket: *Cadeira Especial* (special seats), the most expensive; *Arquibancada Branca* (white terraces), which give a good side view of the game; *Arquibancada Verde e Amarela* (green and yellow terraces), with a view from behind the goal; and *Cadeira Comum*. Prices vary according to the game, but it's more expensive to buy tickets from agencies than at the gate or via the internet; it is cheaper to buy tickets from club sites on the day before the match. Average prices are roughly US$46, US$23, US$17 and US$11 respectively. Popular games are more expensive.

Don't take valuables or wear a watch and take special care when entering and leaving the stadium. The rivalry between the local clubs Flamengo and Vasco da Gama is intense, often leading to violence, so it is advisable to avoid their encounters. If you buy a club shirt or favour, don't be tempted to wear it on match day: if you find yourself in the wrong place, you could be in trouble.

Quinta da Boa Vista

ⓘ *Take the metrô to São Cristóvão and follow signs to Quinta da Boa Vista, a 5-min walk. Beware of muggings on weekdays; don't take valuables.*

About 3 km west of Praça da República (beyond the Sambódromo) is the Quinta da Boa Vista, the emperor's private park from 1809 to 1889. The **Museu Nacional** ⓘ *T021-2562 6900, www.museunacional.ufrj.br, Tue-Sun 1000-1600, US$3*, is housed in the former imperial palace. The building is crumbling and the collections dusty and poorly displayed. Only the unfurnished throne room and ambassadorial reception room on the second floor reflect past glories. In the entrance hall is the famous Bendegó meteorite, found in the state of Bahia in 1888; its original weight, before some of it was chipped, was 5360 kg. Besides several collections of foreign pieces (including Peruvian and Mexican archaeology, Graeco-Roman ceramics and Egyptian mummies), the museum contains collections of Brazilian indigenous weapons, costumes, utensils and historical documents. There are also frowsty collections of stuffed birds, beasts, fish and butterflies.

Also in the park is the **Jardim Zoológico** ⓘ *Av Dom Pedro II, T021-3878 4200, Tue-Sun 900-1630, US$4, young children free, students with ID pay half*. The zoo is in the northeastern corner of the park. It has a collection of 2100 animals, most of which are kept in modern, spacious enclosures, and there is an important captive breeding programme for golden-headed and golden lion tamarins, spectacled bears and yellow-throated capuchin monkeys. The aviary is impressive and children can enjoy a ride in a little train through the park.

Santa Teresa

A tram ride from the cathedral to Santa Teresa over the Arcos de Lapa viaduct is an unmissable Rio experience. The old yellow trams clatter up the winding, hilly streets lined with pretty colonial houses and lavish mansions towards the forested slopes of Tijuca National Park, leaving in their wake sweeping views of Guanabara Bay and the Sugar Loaf. Along the way they pass the **Largo do Guimarães** and the **Largo das Neves**, little *praças* of shops and restaurants that feel as if they belong clustered around a village green rather than in a large city. For nowhere in this city of distinct neighbourhoods is more of a world unto itself than Santa Teresa. The neighbourhood has a strong community identity forged by one of the highest concentrations of artists, writers and musicians in the city, who congregate in bars like **O Mineiro** on the Largo dos Guimarães or **Bar Porto das Neves** on the Largo das Neves. At weekends the lively nightlife spills over into clubs like **Espírito Santa** (see page 114) and then into neighbouring Lapa which is only a five-minute taxi ride away. Those who can bear to be away from the beach often find staying in Santa Teresa a far more culturally rewarding experience than the southern suburbs and there are many excellent options.

A sense of separation is reflected not only in the suburb's geography, but also its history. In 1624, Antônio Gomes do Desterro chose the area both for its proximity to Rio and its isolation, and erected a hermitage dedicated to Nossa Senhora do Desterro. The name was changed from Morro do Desterro to Santa Teresa after the construction in 1750 of a convent of that name dedicated to the patroness of the order. The convent exists to this day, but it can only be seen from the outside.

Ins and outs

Getting there and around The best way to visit Santa Teresa is on the traditional open-sided **tram**, the *bondinho*. This can be caught from the terminus next to the Catedra Metropolitana or from Cinelândia: take the metrô to Cinelândia station, go to Rua Senador Dantas then walk along to Rua Profesor Lélio Gama (look for **Banco do Brasil** or the corner); the station is up this street. Take the Paula Mattos line; the fare is US$0.40 one way. Bus Nos 206 and 214 run between Avenida Rio Branco in the centre and Santa Teresa. At night, take a taxi (about US$7 to the centre or Ipanema). In recent years, Santa Teresa has had a reputation for crime, however, the area is much more heavily policed nowadays. Be vigilant with your camera and be particularly wary after dark. Steer clear of any steps that lead down the hill and on Rua Almirante Alexandrino or at the Tijuca end of Largo dos Guimarães.

Sights

Santa Teresa is best explored on foot: wander the streets to admire the colonial building or stop for a beer in a little streetside café and marvel at the view. The better colonia houses, most of which are private residences, include the **Casa de Valentim** (a castle-like house in Vista Alegre), the tiled **Chácara dos Viegas** in Rua Monte Alegre and the **Chal Murtinho**. This was the house in which Dona Laurinda Santos Lobo held her famou artistic, political and intellectual salons at the turn of the 20th century. The house was i ruins until it was partially restored and turned into a cultural centre called **Parque da Ruínas** ⓘ *R Murtinho Nobre 41, daily 1000-1700*. It has superb views of the city, a exhibition space and an open-air stage (live music on Thursday). Next door is the **Chácar do Céu**, or **Museu Castro Maya** ⓘ *R Murtinho Nobre 93, T021-3970 112 www.museuscastromaya.com.br, Wed-Mon 1200-1700, US$1*, housed in the former hom of the Carioca millionaire and art collector, Raymundo Ottoni de Castro Maya. It has a wid range of works by modern painters, including Modigliani and important Brazilian like [Cavalacanti. There are wonderful views out over Guanabara Bay. To get to both th

Chácara and the Parque das Ruínas take the Santa Teresa tram to Curvelo station, walk along Rua Dias de Barros, following the signposts to Parque das Ruínas. There are also superb views from the **Museu Casa de Benjamin Constant** ① *R Monte Alegre 225, T021-2509 1248, Wed-Sun 1300-1700*, the former home of the Carioca military engineer and positivist philosopher who helped to found the Republic.

Glória, Catete and Flamengo

The city centre is separated from Copacabana and the other ocean beaches by a series of long white-sand coves that fringe Guanabara Bay and which are divided by towering rocks. The first of the coves is the **Enseada da Glória**, fronting the suburb of the same name and sitting next to the Santos Dumont airport. Avenida Infante Dom Henrique, a broad avenue lined with an eclectic mix of grand houses and squat office blocks, leads from here to what was once the city's finest beach, **Flamengo**, a long stretch of sand separated from the rest of southern Rio by the Morro da Viúva (widow's peak). The suburb of **Catete** lies just behind Flamengo. These three areas were once the heart of recreational Rio; the posing-spots of choice for the belle-époque middle and upper classes and perhaps the most coveted urban beaches in the world. These days the water is polluted and swimming ill-advised, but the suburbs are pleasant for a stroll.

Ins and outs

Bus No 119 from the centre or No 571 from Copacabana serve the neighbourhoods, as does the metrô. The centrepiece of the three suburbs are the gardens of the Parque do Flamengo, on Avenida Infante Dom Henrique, reached from metrô Glória, Catete, Largo de Machado or Flamengo. Closed to traffic on Sunday. Be careful after dark.

Sights

Before the pollution became too much, Burle Marx, Brazil's 20th-century Capability Brown, designed the **Parque do Flamengo**, a handsome stretch of waterfront to separate Avenida Infante Dom Henrique from the city's most glorious beach, and gave it ample shade with a range of tropical trees and stands of stately royal palms. The gardens stretch from Glória through to the Morro da Viúva at the far end of Flamengo; they were built on reclaimed land and opened in 1965 to mark the 400th anniversary of the city's founding. The lawns and promenade are favourite spots for smooching lovers, especially at sundown. There are children's play areas too and a handful of monuments and museums. These include the impressive postmodern **Monumento aos Mortos da Segunda Guerra Mundial** ① *Av Infante Dom Henrique, Tue-Sun 1000-1700 for the crypt museum; beach clothes and flip flops not permitted*, the national war memorial to Brazil's dead in the Second World War. The gently curved slab is supported by two slender columns, representing two palms uplifted to heaven and guarded by soldiers from the adjacent barracks. In the crypt are the remains of the Brazilian soldiers killed in Italy in 1944-1945. At the far northern end of the Parque do Flamengo is the **Museu de Arte Moderna** ① *Av Infante Dom Henrique 85, T021-2240 4944, www.mamrio.com.br, Tue-Fri 1200-1800, last entry 1730, Sat-Sun 1200-1900, last entry 1830, US$4*, another striking modernist building with the best collection of modern art in Brazil outside São Paulo. Works by many well-known Europeans sit alongside collections of Brazilian modern and contemporary art including drawings by Cândido Portinari and etchings of everyday work scenes by Gregório Gruber.

The beautiful little church on the Glória hill, overlooking the Parque do Flamengo, is **Nossa Senhora da Glória do Outeiro** ① *T021-2225 2869, Tue-Fri 0900-1200 and 1300-1700, Sat and Sun 0900-1200, guided tours by appointment on the 1st Sun of each month.* Built 1735-1791, it was the favourite church of the imperial family and Dom Pedro

⑥ Glória, Santa Teresa & Lapa

➡ **Rio de Janeiro maps**
2 Rio de Janeiro orientation, page 62
6 Glória, Santa Teresa and Lapa, page 84

N

200 metres
200 yards

Sleeping 😴
Casa Áurea 1 *D3*
Glória 2 *D6*
Inglês 4 *D6*
Mama Ruisa 5 *D4*

Novo Mundo 6 *D6*
Rio Hostel 7 *C4*
Santa Teresa 3 *D3*

Eating 🍴
Adega do Pimenta 1 *D4*
Aprazível 9 *D3*
Bar do Arnaudo 5 *D3*
Espírito Santa 3 *D4*

II was baptized here. The building is polygonal, with a single tower. It contains some excellent examples of the best *azulejos* (tiles) in Rio and its main wooden altar was carved by Mestre Valentim. Next door is the small **Museum of Religious Art** ① *T021-2556 6434, same hours as church.*

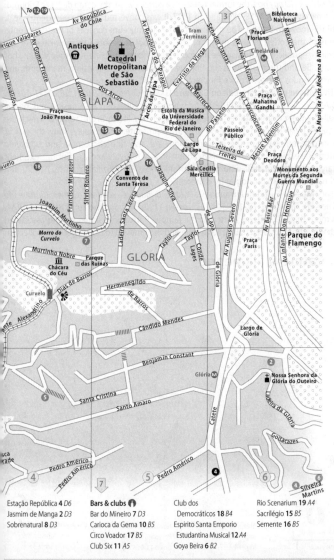

Behind Glória and Flamengo is the rather down-at-heel suburb of Catete, which is dotted with museums. The best of these is the **Museu da República** ① *R do Catete 153, T021-3235 2650, www.museudarepublica.org.br, Tue-Fri 1000-1700, Sat-Sun and holidays 1400-1800, US$4, free Wed and Sun, free for children up to 10 years old and adults above 65, students with ID pay half*, the former palace of a coffee baron, the Barão de Nova Friburgo. The palace was built 1858-1866 and, in 1887, it was converted into the presidential seat, until the move to Brasília. The ground floor of this museum consists of the sumptuous rooms of the coffee baron's mansion. The first floor is devoted to the history of the Brazilian republic. You can also see the room where former president Getúlio Vargas shot himself. Behind the museum is the **Parque do Catete**, which contains many birds and monkeys and is a popular place for practising Tai Chi.

The **Museu do Folclore Edison Carneiro** ① *R do Catete 181, T021-2285 0441, Tue-Fri 1100-1800, Sat and Sun 1500-1800, free*, houses a collection of amusing but poorly labelled small ceramic figures representing everyday life in Brazil, some of which are animated by electric motors. Many artists are represented and displays show the way of life in different parts of the country. There are also fine *candomblé* and *umbanda* costumes, religious objects, displays about Brazil's festivals and a small but excellent library, with helpful staff who can help find books on Brazilian culture, history and anthropology. Flash photography is prohibited.

The **Museu Carmen Miranda** ① *Parque Brigadeiro Eduardo Gomes (Parque do Flamengo), Flamengo, T021-2334 4293, Tue-Fri 1100-1700, Sat and Sun 1300-1700, US$1*, has more than 3000 items related to the famous Portuguese singer forever associated with Rio, who emigrated to Brazil as a child and then moved to Hollywood. The collection

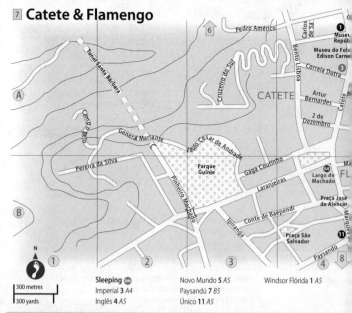

7 Catete & Flamengo

Sleeping 💤
Imperial **3** *A4*
Inglês **4** *A5*
Novo Mundo **5** *A5*
Paysandú **7** *B5*
Único **11** *A5*
Windsor Flórida **1** *A5*

includes some of her famous gowns, fruit-covered hats, jewellery and recordings. There are occasional showings of her films.

Botafogo, Urca and Pão de Açúcar (Sugar Loaf)

Pão de Açúcar, or the **Sugar Loaf**, looms over the perfect wine-glass bay of **Botafogo**, the next of the Guanabara Bay coves after Flamengo. Huddled around the boulder's flanks is the suburb of **Urca**, home to a military barracks and the safest middle-class houses in Rio. Remnant forest, still home to marmosets and rare birds, shrouds the boulder's sides and a cable car straddles the distance between its summit, the **Morro de Urca** hill and the houses below, making one of the continent's most breathtaking views easily accessible. Urca and Botafogo have a few sights of interest and make convenient bases with decent accommodation and restaurant options, particularly in the lower price ranges.

Ins and outs

Botafogo has a metrô station. Buses that run between Copacabana and the centre stop in Botafogo, so take any bus marked 'Centro' from Copacabana or 'Copacabana' from the centre. Bus No 107 (from the centre, Catete or Flamengo) and No 511 from Copacabana (No 512 to return) take you to Urca and the cable-car station for the Sugar Loaf. Alternatively, walk 10 minutes northeast from behind the Rio Sul shopping centre to the cable-car station, which lies on Praça General Tiburcio, next to the Rio de Janeiro federal university. The rides themselves go up in two stages, the first to the summit of Morro da Urca, the smaller rock that sits in front of the Sugar Loaf, and the second from there to the top of the Sugar Loaf itself. Allow at least two hours for your visit.

Parque do Catete

Parque do Flamengo

➡ **Rio de Janeiro maps**
2 Rio de Janeiro orientation, page 62
7 **Catete and Flamengo, page 86**

Pão de Açúcar (Sugar Loaf)

The western hemisphere's most famous monolith rises almost sheer from the dark sea to just under 400 m, towering over Botafogo beach and separating Guanabara Bay from the open Atlantic Ocean. The views from the top, out over Copacabana, Ipanema and the mountains and forests of Corcovado and Tijuca are as unforgettable as the view from New York's Empire State Building or Victoria Peak in Hong Kong. The **cable car** ⓘ *Av Pasteur 520, Praia Vermelha, Urca, T021-2461 2700, www.bondinho. com.br, daily 0800-1950, US$25, free for children under 6, aged 6-12 half price, every 30 mins,* runs to the top where there are extensive paths, plentiful shade and snack bars. Come early for the clearest air, best views and smallest crowds.

Paths up and around the Sugar Loaf
There is more to Sugar Loaf than the views from the top. The surrounding rocks hide

secluded little beaches, remnant forest and small colonial suburbs well worth seeing. The best place to begin is at **Praia Vermelha**, the beach to the south of the rock where there is a simple restaurant, the **Círculo Militar da Praia Vermelha** (no sign) with wonderful views. The walking track, **Pista Cláudio Coutinho** ⓘ *daily 0700-1800*, runs from here along the waterfront around the foot of the rock. You'll see plenty of wildlife at dawn, especially marmosets and colourful tanagers, along with various intrepid climbers scaling the granite. About 350 m from the beginning of the Pista Coutinho is a turning to the left for a path that winds its way up through the forest to the top of **Morro de Urca**, from where the cable car can be taken for US$10. You can save even more money by climbing the **Caminho da Costa**, a path to the summit of the Pão de Açúcar. Only one stretch of 10 m requires climbing gear; wait at the bottom of the path for a group going up. You can then descend to Morro de Urca by cable car for free and walk the rest of the way down. There are 35 rock-climbing routes up the boulder. The best months for climbing are April to August.
➤➤ *For climbing clubs, see Activities and tours, page 126.*

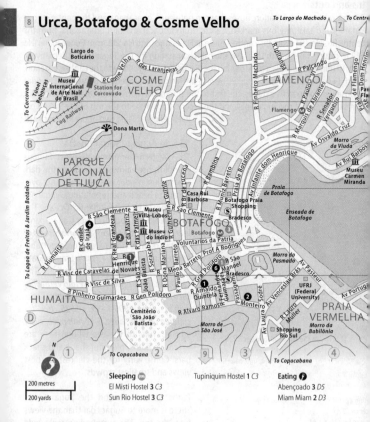

8 Urca, Botafogo & Cosme Velho

Sleeping 🛌
El Misti Hostel **3** C3
Sun Rio Hostel **3** C3

Tupiniquim Hostel **1** C3

Eating 🍴
Abençoado **3** D5
Miam Miam **2** D3

Botafogo

The Funai-run **Museu do Índio** ⓘ *R das Palmeiras 55, T021-3214 8702, www.museudo indio.org.br, Mon-Fri 0900-1730, Sat and Sun 1300-1700, US$2.50, free on Sun, 10-min walk from Botafogo metrô or bus No 571 from Catete*, preserves some 12,000 objects from more than 180 Brazilian indigenous groups, including basketry, ceramics, masks and weapons as well as 500,000 documents and 50,000 photographs. Very few are on display and the museum's few rooms are mostly devoted to information panels and short film shows. The garden includes a Guaraní *maloca* and there is a small, well-displayed handicraft shop and a library of ethnology.

The **Museu Villa-Lobos** ⓘ *R Sorocaba 200, T021-2266 3845, www.museuvillalobos. org.br, Mon-Fri 1000-1700, free, lunchtime concert US$6-17*, is a block east of the Museu do Índio. Such was the fame and respect afforded to Latin America's most celebrated composer that the museum was founded just one year after his death in 1960. Inside the fine 19th-century building is a collection of his personal objects including instruments, scores, books and recordings. The museum has occasional concerts and temporary shows and supports a number of classical music projects throughout Brazil.

➡ Rio de Janeiro maps
2 Rio de Janeiro orientation, page 62
8 Urca, Botafogo and Cosme Velho, page 88

The **Dona Marta viewpoint**, which sits in the forest immediately above Botafogo and is connected by road to Corcovado, offers the best views of the Sugar Loaf in the city. Do not visit after 1730 as robbers from the nearby favelas frequent the roads.

Christ statue at Corcovado and Cosme Velho

Few famous sights in the world live up to the high expectations overexposure has placed on them. The view from **Corcovado mountain** is one of them. Come, if you can, for dusk. Almost 1 km above the city and at the apex of one of the highest pinnacles in Tijuca forest stands **O Redentor** – Christ the Redeemer – lit in brilliant xenon and with arms open to embrace the urban world's most breathtaking view. At his feet to the west are a panoply of bays, fringed with white and backed by twinkling skyscrapers and the neon of myriad street lights. To the east as far as the eye can see lie long stretches of sand washed by green and white surf. And in front and to the south, next to the vast ocean beaches, is the sparkle of Niterói watched over by low grey mountains and connected to Rio by a 10-km-long sinuous bridge that threads its

Praia o Flamengo

Baía de Guanabara

Morro Cara do Cão

Praia da Urca

URCA

Av João Luís Alves

R Cândido Gaffrée

Praia de Fora

ual uaria

Morro de Urca Cable Car

Pão de Açúcar

Gen rcio

Pista Cláudio Coutinho

ha

⑤

⑥

Oui Oui **4** *C1*
aajmahal **6** *C3*
orubá **1** *D3*

Bars & clubs 🍸
Casa de Matriz **1** *C2*
Porão **2** *C2*

way across the 10-km expanse of Guanabara Bay. As the light fades, the tropical forest at Christ's back comes to life in a chorus of cicadas and evening birdsong loud enough to drown even the chatter of 1000 tourists.

At the base of the mountain is the sleepy suburb of **Cosme Velho**, leafy and dotted with grand houses, museums and a little artist's corner called the Largo do Boticario. The two are linked by a 3.8-km railway, opened in 1884 by Emperor Dom Pedro II.

Ins and outs

There are several ways to reach the top of Corcovado. A cog railway and a road connect the city to the mountain from the suburb of Cosme Velho. Both are on the northern side of the Rebouças tunnel, which runs to and from the Lagoa. From the upper terminus of the **cog railway** ① *R Cosme Velho 513, T021-2558 1329, www.corcovado.com.br, daily every 30 mins 0830-1830, 10 min-journey, US$8 one-way, US$15 return*, there is a climb of 220 steps to the top or you can take the newly installed escalator, near which there is a café. Mass is held on Sunday in a small chapel in the statue pedestal. There is a museum at the station with panels showing the history of the statue and the railway.

To get to the cog railway station take a taxi or bus to Cosme Velho and get off at the station. **Buses** are as follows: from the centre or Glória/Flamengo bus No 180; from Copacabana bus Nos 583 or 584; from Botafogo or Ipanema/Leblon bus Nos 583 or 584; from Santa Teresa take the micro-ônibus. **Taxis**, which wait in front of the station, also offer tours of Corcovado and Mirante Dona Marta and cost around US$25.

If going **on foot**, take bus No 206 from Praça Tiradentes (or No 407 from Largo do Machado) to Silvestre, where there is a station at which the train no longer stops. It is a steep 9-km walk from here to the top, along a shady road. Take the narrow street to the right of the station, go through the gate used by people who live beside the tracks and continue to the national park entrance. Walkers are charged entrance fees, even if you walk all the way you still have to pay for the van – it is an illegal charge, but in a country with as high a level of corruption as Brazil they can get a way with it. Allow a minimum of two hours (up to four hours depending on fitness).

By **car**, drive through Túnel Rebouças from the Lagoa and then look out for the Corcovado signs before the beginning of the second tunnel and off to your right. Ignore the clamour of the touts at the beginning of the Corcovado road. They will try to convince you that the road is closed in order to take you on an alternative route and charge a hefty fee. If going by car to Corcovado, avoid going on weekends and public holidays – the slow traffic and long queues are overwhelming. Cars cannot go all the way to the parking outside entrance, which is only for authorized cars and vans, instead you have to park halfway in a designated car park and then either walk or take a van, although you have to pay for the van anyway. Avoid returning after dark; it is not safe.

Almost all the hotels, even the hostels, offer organized **coach trips** to Corcovado, which usually take in Sugar Loaf and Maracanã as well. These offer a fairly brief stop on the mountain and times of day are not always the best for light. **Helicopter tours** are available though these leave from the Sugar Loaf or the Lagoa.

Cosme Velho

The **Museu Internacional de Arte Naïf do Brasil (MIAN)** ① *R Cosme Velho 561, on the same street as the station for Corcovado, T021-2205 8612, www.museunaif.com.br, Tue-Fri 1200-1800, weekends 1200-1900, US$5.70*, is one of the most comprehensive museums of naïf and folk paintings in the world with a permanent collection of 8000 works by naïf

Costly confusion at Corcovado

Corcovado has become so expensive over the last five years that it is now beyond the budget of most holidaying Brazilians. And whilst the views are wonderful, visiting can be a stressful and confusing experience – with long waits and queues, a series of confusing compulsory charges imposed by the management and dozens of touts offering expensive rides.

The cheapest way to get to Corcovado is by bus or tube to Largo do Machado square and then by van (*van* in Portuguese, US$6 per person) or **microbus** (*micrão* in Portuguese, US$9 per person), leaving from Largo do Machado and arriving at the privately owned Hotel das Paineiras car park. Other vans leave from this car park (the last place accessed by car) for the Corcovado entrance some 2 km (25 minutes' walk). The purchase of a **ticket** on these vans is compulsory and is added into the ticket price at the booth in the car park – so even those who choose to walk have to pay for them. The ticket to Corcovado with the van costs US$15. Be prepared for 30-minute queues at the booth. **Touts** in the Largo do Machado, and the Hotel das Paineiras car park offer tickets for as much as US$40. Avoid these. **Taxis** are expensive too – most drivers refuse to go to Corcovado by the meter –

illegally using the ride as a cash cow to charge exorbitant prices. Traffic can be very heavy.

Driving is possible, but there is no signposting and the traffic jams can be almost solid on the way up – especially at weekends and public holidays; with very long waits. Car parking costs US$2 per hour.

Almost as cheap as the van and far less hassle, is the **Corcovado Train** (Trem do Corcovado) to Corcovado. A combined ticket – for train and entrance to the site – costs US$23. Demand is very high and waits can be up to three hours in high season and at weekends or when there are large tour groups visiting.

The confusing bus and van scheme has proved extremely unpopular with local people and has essentially raised prices so high that most Brazilians cannot afford to visit Brazil's most famous sight. There are no concessions for locals and tickets for a family of four, on a standard national wage, would cost some 20% of the family's monthly income. Corcovado is surrounded by favelas whose residents are never able to visit. Cariocas are pressing for the creation of a standard US$1.50 public bus line that goes up to Paineiras parking. There are no formal plans as yet for its implementation.

artists from 130 countries. The museum also hosts several thematic and temporary exhibitions through the year. Parts of its collection are often on loan around the world. There is a coffee shop and a souvenir shop where you can buy paintings, books, postcards and T-shirts. Courses and workshops on painting and related subjects are also available.

The **Largo do Boticário** ① *R Cosme Velho 822*, is a pretty, shady little square close to the terminus for the Corcovado cog railway and surrounded by 19th-century buildings. It offers a glimpse of what the city looked like before all the concrete and highways. That the square exists at all is thanks to concerned residents who not only sought to preserve it but were also instrumental in rebuilding and refurbishing many of the buildings, using rubble from colonial buildings demolished in the city centre. Many of the doors once belonged to churches. The four houses that front the square are painted different colours (white, pale blue, caramel and pink), each with features picked out in decorative tiles, woodwork and stone. Many artists live here and can often be seen painting in the courtyard.

Copacabana and Leme

Copacabana, which is called Leme at its northern end, epitomizes Rio both for better and for worse. Like the city as a whole, it is breathtakingly beautiful from afar and a little ugly close to. At first sight it looks magnificent. The beach is a splendid broad sweeping crescent of fine sand stretching for almost 8 km, washed by a bottle-green Atlantic and watched over by the **Morro do Leme** – another of Rio's beautiful forest-covered hills. Behind it is a wide neon- and argon-lit avenue lined with high-rises, the odd grand hotel and various bars, restaurants and clubs. The tanned and toned flock all around in little bikinis, *sungas* and colourful beach wraps, playing volleyball on the sand and jogging along the wavy black and white dragon's tooth pavements, while others busk, play capoeira and sell their wares. But, like much of Brazil, the devil is in the detail and up close

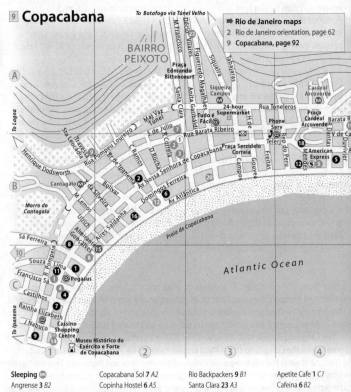

⑨ Copacabana

➡ Rio de Janeiro maps
2 Rio de Janeiro orientation, page 62
9 Copacabana, page 92

Sleeping 🛏
Angrense **3** *B2*
Benidorm Palace **2** *B2*
Copacabana Holiday **4** *A4*
Copacabana Palace
 & Cipriani Restaurant **5** *B4*.
Copacabana Rio **1** *C1*
Copacabana Sol **7** *A2*
Copinha Hostel **6** *A5*
Debret **8** *C1*
Fantastic Rio **13** *B5*
Marriott **20** *B3*
Pestana Rio Atlântica **12** *B2*
Portinari Design **4** *C1*
Rio Backpackers **9** *B1*
Santa Clara **23** *A3*
Sofitel **14** *C1*
Stone of a Beach Hostel **10** *A4*

Eating 🍴
Aipo & Aipim **2** *B2*
Apetite Cafe **1** *C1*
Cafeina **6** *B2*
Cervantes **3** *A5*
Chon Kou **4** *C1*
Churrascaria Palace **5** *B4*
Copa Café **16** *B2*
Eclipse **7** *C1*

Copacabana is a lot less appealing. The sand may be clean enough but those bottle-green waves are far from it. Many of the bars and hotels are tatty and tawdry, some of them frequented by a Pattaya-type crowd of young, thin Cariocas and fat older foreigners looking to buy more than a drink. And at night Copacabana can be dangerous. Soliciting is rife and muggings are not uncommon.

Ins and outs

Buses are plentiful and cost US$1.35; Nos 119, 154, 413, 415, 455 and 474 run between the city centre and Avenida Nossa Senhora de Copacabana. If you are going to the centre from Copacabana, look for 'Castelo', 'Praça XV', 'E Ferro' or 'Praça Mauá' on the sign by the front door. 'Aterro' means the expressway between Botafogo and downtown Rio (not open on Sunday). From the centre to Copacabana is easier as all buses in that direction are clearly marked. The 'Aterro' bus takes 15 minutes. Numerous buses run between Copacabana and Ipanema; the two beaches are connected by Rua Francisco Otaviano or Rua Joaquim Nabuco, immediately west of the Forte de Copacabana. Copacabana has metrô stations a few blocks inland from the beach at Cardeal Arcoverde, Siqueira Campos and Cantagalo. Copacabana metro is linked to Lapa, Centre and Ipanema.

Sights

Copacabana has always been a beach and beyond it there are no sights of any note. The area exploded in population after the construction of the **Túnel Velho** (Old Tunnel) in 1891 and the **New Tunnel** in the early 20th century and has been growing, mostly upward, ever since. Streets are lined with high-rise flats that huddle together even on the seafront, crowding around the stately neoclassical façade of the **Copacabana Palace** hotel, which was the tallest building in the suburb until the 1940s.

Apart from New Year's Eve, when the whole suburb becomes a huge party venue and bands play along the entire length of the beach, Copacabana is a place for little more than landscape and people-watching. It's possible to swim in the sea when the current is heading out from the shore, but otherwise not advisable. The best way to enjoy the area is to wander along the promenade from *posto* (lifeguard

lograma 8 C1
Fiorentina 10 B5
Tratoria 12 B4
ri Mole & Cia 9 C1
mperarte 11 C1
iteurs de France 18 B4

Bars & clubs ()
Bip Bip 15 C2
Clandestino 19 A4

Shop (•)
Modern Sound 1 B2

Copacabana – what's in a name?

Copacabana is most famously a beach in Brazil. However, it is also a beach in New South Wales, a nightclub in New York, a small town in Bolivia and a song by Barry Manilow. All of these, one might think owe their name to Brazil's Copacabana. But it is not so. Copacabana is an Inca word meaning 'beholder of the blue horizon' or 'beholder of the precious stone'. The original Copacabana was a port for the islands of the Sun and the Moon on the shores of Lake Titicaca, endowed with spiritual significance for the Inca people. These islands were the mythical navel of the world and the birthplace of the Inca nation and the sun deities with which they are associated. As far as we know, the Incas never made it to Rio, and certainly were not responsible directly for naming Rio's Copacabana. For this we must thank the Virgin Mary. Sleight of hand from either the church or the Inca people themselves, who often used syncretism to preserve the heart of their spiritual practices led to the Bolivian Copacabana being transformed from an Inca shrine to a Christian one. In 1576, after surviving a storm on the lake, fishermen commissioned Francisco Yupanque, a direct descendant of the Inca nobility to carve a statue in homage to Our Lady whom they credited with having rescued them. The statue, which had strong Inca features was placed inside a purpose built church in the town of Copacabana, which was renamed Nuestra Señora de Copacabana. It quickly became a pilgrimage centre, especially for sailors and copies of the Inca Virgin were often carried on voyages between Spain and the New World. In the 17th century a boat sailing from Spain to South America came into great difficulties during a storm in the Atlantic. The sailors prayed to an image of Nuestra Señora de Copacabana that they had in their possession and, like those Inca fishermen, they were saved. Their captain promised to build a chapel to the Virgin when he reached land, and he did so in Rio de Janeiro. The Chapel, Nossa Senhora de Copacabana and the original image left their by the ship's captain stood at the far end of Copacabana on the Arpoador until 1914 when it was razed to the ground to make way for the Forte de Copacabana.

post) to *posto*, perhaps stopping to enjoy a coconut at one of the numerous beachfront snack bars, and noting the different crowd at each one. Everyone looks at everyone in Rio so don't be afraid to subtly stare.

At the far end of the beach is the **Museu Histórico do Exército e Forte de Copacabana** ⓘ *Av Atlântica at Francisco Otaviano, Posto 6, T021-2521 1032, www.fortedecopacabana. com, Tue-Sun and bank holiday 1000-1800, US$2.30*, a museum charting the history of the army in Brazil through the colonial, imperial and republican periods, with cases of military artefacts and panels in Portuguese on campaigns such as the one fought at Canudos against Antônio Conselheiro. There are good views out over the beaches from the fort and a small restaurant.

Rio's sun worshippers

Ipanema and Copacabana are the most famous beaches in the world and there can surely be no people more devoted to lazing in the sun than Cariocas. But it wasn't always so. In the 19th century Brazilians would only go near sea water if they had been ordered to do so by a doctor. Even then it would only be for a quick dip at the beginning or the end of the day when the sun was weak. A tan was regarded as unhealthy and a sign of being lower class; to actually sit in the sun was a serious breach of social propriety.

All this began to change when the famous French actress Sarah Bernhardt came to Rio in 1886 to star in *Frou Frou* and *The Lady of the Camelias* at the São Pedro theatre. During her time off she caused a scandal, appalling the great

and the good by travelling to then distant Copacabana, throwing on a swimsuit, sunbathing and even swimming in the sea. By the turn of the 20th century others had begun to follow suit, and by 1917 going to the beach had become sufficiently fashionable that the city established strict rules and regulations to govern sun worship. People were permitted to bathe only between 0500-0800 and 1700-1900, had to wear appropriate dress and be quiet and discreet; failure to do so resulted in five years in prison. Official attitudes only began to change in the 1920s with the building of the Copacabana Palace and the arrival of more foreigners who ignored Rio's prudishness and convinced Cariocas to begin to enjoy the beach.

Ipanema and Leblon

Like Copacabana and Leme, Ipanema and Leblon are essentially one long curving beach enclosed by the monolithic Dois Irmãos rocks at the western end and the Arpoador rocks to the east. And, like Copacabana and Leme, they have few sights beyond the sand, the landscape and the beautiful people. Comparisons, however, end there. Ipanema and Leblon are as fashionable and cool as Copacabana is grungy and frenetic. If Copacabana is samba, then Ipanema is bossa nova: wealthy, sealed off from the realities of Rio in a neat little fairy-tale strip of streets and watched over by twinkling lights high up on the flanks of the Morro Dois Irmãos. They look so romantic that it is easy to forget that they come from the world's largest favela.

Closeted and cosseted though it may be, these are the beach suburbs in which to base yourself whilst in Rio. Almost all of the city's best restaurants and bars are here (and in the suburbs of Gávea and Lagoa, which lie behind). The streets are fairly clean and usually walked by nothing more dangerous than a small white poodle; there is plenty of reasonable accommodation, which doesn't rent by the hour at the lower end of the market; and the sea is good for swimming.

Ins and outs

There is a metro station in Ipanema, General Osório, and an overground metro that runs from Ipanema/General Osório to Gávea along Rua Visconde de Pirajá in Ipanema and Avenida Ataulfo de Paiva in Leblon. The destination for buses is clearly marked but, as a rule of thumb, any buses heading east along the seafront go to Copacabana or, if going west, to Barra da Tijuca; those going inland will pass by the Lagoa or Gávea. See metro map, page 61.

Sights

Like Copacabana, Ipanema and Leblon are places for people-watching. A half-day wandering around Ipanema/Leblon followed by a half-day wandering Copacabana/Leme can be most interesting. The crowds are quite different. While Copacabana attracts a real cross-section of Rio society, Ipanema and Leblon are predominantly haunts of the fashionable peacocks, who strut along the beachfront promenade, especially around **Posto Nove**. Beyond the people and the breathtaking landscape, there is little to see here but plenty to do, especially for avid consumers. Shopping is best on and around Garcia D'Avila and at the **Feira Hippy** (see Markets, page 123), where you will find everything from high-quality Brazilian designer swimwear to seed bracelets and T-shirts with pictures of Bob Marley. Those seeking culture but unwilling to leave the beach should head for the **Casa de Cultura Laura Alvim** ① *Av Vieira Souto 176, T021-7104 3603,*

Ipanema & Leblon

Sleeping
Arpoador Inn **12** *C5*
Atlantis Copacabana **13** *C5*
Best Western Sol
  Ipanema **11** *C4*
Caesar Park **1** *B3*
Casa 6 **15** *B4*
Che Lagarto **2** *B3*
Crab Hostel **3** *B4*
Dolphin Inn **5** *B5*

Fasano Rio **14** *C5*
Harmonia **15** *B4*
Ipanema Beach House **18** *B3*
Ipanema Hostel **4** *B5*
Ipanema Inn **6** *B3*
Karisma **15** *B4*
Marina All Suites **8** *B1*
Marina Palace **9** *B2*
Mar Ipanema **7** *B3*
San Marco **10** *B3*

Eating
Alessandro & Frederico **1**
Árabe da Gávea **3** *A1*
Bistrô ZaZá **15** *B4*
Capricciosa **4** *B4*
Carlota **5** *B1*
Casa da Feijoada **17** *B5*
Celeiro **6** *B1*
Empório Saúde **8** *B3*
Fellini **21** *B1*

www.casadelaura.com.br, comprising an arts cinema, art galleries (temporary exhibitions), workshop spaces and a bookshop. If it is pouring with rain you could watch diamonds being cut and set at the **Museus H Stern** ① *R Garcia D'Avila 113, T021-2106 0000*, or **Amsterdam Sauer** ① *R Garcia D'Avila 105, T021-2512 1132*, or hang out in the **Garota de Ipanema**, the bar where the *Girl from Ipanema* was written in the late 1950s (see Bars and clubs, page 116).

Gávea, Lagoa and Jardim Botânico

Just inland from Ipanema and Leblon, nestled under the forested slopes of Corcovado and the Tijuca National Park and spread around the picturesque saltwater lagoon of Lagoa Rodrigo de Freitas, are these three mainly residential suburbs. There are a few sights of

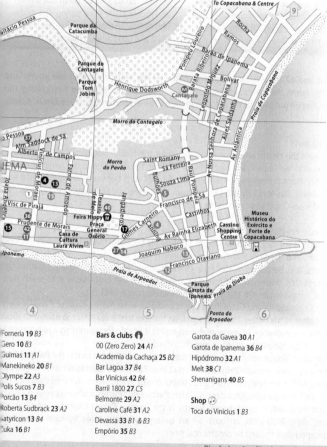

Forneria 19 *B3*
Gero 10 *B3*
Guimas 11 *A1*
Manekineko 20 *B1*
Olympe 22 *A3*
Polis Sucos 7 *B3*
Porção 13 *B4*
Roberta Sudbrack 23 *A2*
Satyricon 13 *B4*
Zuka 16 *B1*

Bars & clubs 🎶
00 (Zero Zero) 24 *A1*
Academia da Cachaça 25 *B2*
Bar Lagoa 37 *B4*
Bar Vinícius 42 *B4*
Barril 1800 27 *C5*
Belmonte 29 *A2*
Caroline Café 31 *A2*
Devassa 33 *B1 & B3*
Empório 35 *B3*

Garota da Gavea 30 *A1*
Garota de Ipanema 36 *B4*
Hipódromo 32 *A1*
Melt 38 *C1*
Shenanigans 40 *B5*

Shop 🛍
Toca do Vinícius 1 *B3*

Violence in the favelas

Brazil's reputation as a violent country comes almost exclusively from the gun fights against the police and the inter-gang wars which take place in the slums of Rio de Janeiro, São Paulo, Belo Horizonte, Salvador and other big cities. Such slums are known as favelas in Portuguese and although visits to are offered on organized tours, many are highly dangerous – closed communities where strangers enter in peril of their life; like the favela so shockingly portrayed in the multi-award-winning film, *Cidade de Deus* (City of God). The film was no exaggeration: Brazil's favela-driven crime statistics speak for themselves. A study undertaken in 2002 by British anthropologist, Luke Dowdney, in conjunction with Brazilian non-governmental organizations working in Rio's slums found that in the 14 years to that date almost 4000 under 18-year-olds were killed by firearms in Rio. Many died in inter-gang wars. Many were shot indiscriminately by the police. This compares with just under 500 children killed in the fighting between Palestinians and Israelis in the same period. The study also estimated that there were between 5000 and 6000 armed children in the city.

interest and all have lively top-end nightlife. **Gávea** tends to attract the young and wealthy, while the 30-somethings dine in the restaurants in **Lagoa** overlooking the lagoon and go out to clubs in **Leblon** or to the exclusive **Jockey Club**. »» *See Bars and clubs, page 113.*

Ins and outs

Buses from the centre are marked 'Gávea', or for the Jardim Botânico, Leblon, Gávea or São Conrado 'via Jóquei'. Bus Nos 571 and 170 from the centre go to the Jardim Botânico or No 172 from Flamengo or Botafogo. Bus No 584 runs between Jardim Botânico and Copacabana. Bus Nos 176 and 178 run from the centre and Flamengo and bus Nos 591 and 592 from Copacabana go to the planetarium.

Lagoa de Freitas

The Lagoa is another of Rio de Janeiro's unfeasibly beautiful natural sights and has long been admired. Darwin and German naturalists Spix and Martius mention it in their accounts. It is best seen in the early evening when thick golden sunlight bathes the rainforest-clad slopes of the **Serra da Carioca**, which rise high above it to reach their spectacular pinnacle with the distant xenon-white statue of Christ.

Like Copacabana and Guanabara Bay, it could be even more beautiful if only it were looked after a little better. The canal that links the lake to the sea is far too narrow to allow for sufficient exchange of water; pollution makes it unsafe for swimming and occasional summer algal blooms have led to mass fish deaths.

The lake is surrounded by a series of parks. Immediately next to it is the **Parque Tom Jobim** and contiguous are **Brigadeiro Faria Lima**, **Parque do Cantagalo** and **Parque das Taboas**. All have extensive leisure areas popular with roller skaters and volleyball players. There are live shows and *forró* dancing in the **Parque dos Patins** and kiosks serve a variety of food from Arabic to Japanese. Nearby is the **Parque Carlos Lacerda** ① *Av Epitacio Pessoa, daily 0800-1900*, an open-air art gallery with sculptures by local artists in a landscaped park shaded by ornamental trees.

Jardim Botânico (botanical gardens)

ⓘ *R Jardim Botânico 1008, T021-3874 1808, www.jbrj.gov.br, daily 0800-1700, US$3.*

These extensive 137-ha gardens protect 9000 rare vascular plants and are home to 140 species of birds, and butterflies including the brilliant blue morphos. There are stately stands of 40-m-high royal palms, large tropical ficus and ceiba trees and pau brasil, from which the country gets its name. Giant Amazonian victoria regia lilies cover many of the ponds and there are views up to Corcovado through the trees. The gardens were founded in 1808 by the king, Dom Joao VI, as a nursery for European plants and new specimens from throughout the world. When the electric tram line arrived in this part of the city, housing and industries soon followed, but the gardens, then as now, remained a haven of peace. There is a herbarium, an aquarium and a library as well as the **Museu Botânico**, housing exhibitions on the conservation of Brazilian flora, and the **Casa dos Pilões**, the first gun-powder factory in Brazil. A new pavilion contains sculptures by Mestre Valentim. Many improvements were carried out before the 1992 Earth Summit, including a new *orquidario*, an enlarged bookshop and a smart café. Birdwatchers can expect to see rarities including the social flycatcher, great and boat-billed kiskadees, cattle tyrants, sayaca, palm and seven-coloured (green-headed) tanagers as well as over 20 different kinds of hummingbird, roadside hawks, laughing falcons and various toucans and parakeets. There are marmosets in the trees.

Less than 1 km from the gardens is the little-visited **Parque Laje** ⓘ *R Jardim Botânico 414, daily 0900-1700, free*, which is more jungle-like than the Jardim Botânico and has a series of small grottoes, an old tower and lakes, as well as the **Escola de Artes Visuais** (visual arts school) housed in a large colonial house in the grounds.

The **Planetario** ⓘ *R Padre Leonel Franco 240, Gávea, www.rio.rj.gov.br/planetario, by appointment, free*, has a sculpture of the Earth and Moon by Mário Agostinelli. On Wednesday evenings at dusk, in clear weather, astronomers give guided observations of the stars. At weekends there are shows for children at 1630, 1800 and 1930. There are occasional *chorinho* concerts on Thursday or Friday.

The **Instituto Moreira Salles** ⓘ *R Marquês de São Vicente 476, Gávea, T021-3284 7400, www.ims.com.br, Tue-Fri 1300-2000, Sat and Sun 1300-1800, free*, is a cultural centre in a modernist mansion with gardens landscaped by Burle Marx. There are exhibition halls for photographic shows and an auditorium for concerts and films.

Rough paths lead to the summit of the flat-topped **Pedra da Gávea** and to magnificent views. Hang-gliders fly to the beach at São Conrado from the **Pedra Bonita** behind the Pedra da Gávea. ▶▶ *See Activities and tours, page 125.*

Barra da Tijuca and beyond

This rapidly developing district, modelled on Miami, is one of the city's principal middle-class residential areas. It focuses on a 20-km sandy beach that is renowned for its surfing, especially at its far westernmost end: **Recreio dos Bandeirantes**. There are countless bars and restaurants, concentrated at both ends, as well as campsites, motels and hotels. Budget accommodation tends to be self-catering.

Ins and outs

Buses from the city centre to Barra are Nos 175 and 176; from Botafogo, Glória or Flamengo take No 179; from Leme Nos 591 or 592; and from Copacabana via Leblon No (45 minutes to one hour). A taxi from the centre costs US$25 (US$35 after 2400) or

A model favela

In the late 1990s, in an attempt to escape favela Pereira da Silva's mixture of boredom and sporadic violence, Cilan Souza de Oliveira, his brother and their schoolboy friends created a model of their home on a patch of wasteland at the edge of the community. 'Soon all the kids began to get involved and we gave the play area a name – Morrinho.' Painted breeze blocks served as model houses, dolls and toy cars gave the model life and soon Morrinho had spread to cover an entire small hillside. 'Then the media started to come and the favela started to get famous for Morrinho instead of violence,' recalls Cilan, 'Even the police changed their attitude. As we turned from children to teenagers they started to treat us differently – 'so you're the kids who built Morrinho?' they'd ask, impressed rather than suspicious. Then people started to call us artists. And we realized we'd made a model of our reality – our world in miniature – from the baile funk parties to the gangs and police raids.' Morrinho is now a tourist attraction and the seat of an international NGO (www.morrinho.com) and favela Pereira da Silva has become one of Rio's least troubled. 'It's great when tourists come,' says Cilan. 'They arrive full of fear and apprehension, and leave thinking that we have a wonderful community. Three foreigners who came as visitors have now moved in to the favela and one had become a baile funk rapper. We call him MC Gringo!'

US$15 from Ipanema. A comfortable bus, **Pegasus**, goes along the coast from the Castelo bus terminal to Barra da Tijuca and continues to Campo Grande or Santa Cruz, or take the free 'Barra Shopping' bus. Bus No 700 from Praça São Conrado goes the full length of the beach to Recreio dos Bandeirantes.

Sights

The **Bosque da Barra/Parque Arruda Câmara** ① *junction of Av das Américas and Av Ayrton Senna, daily 0700-1700*, preserves the vegetation of the sandbanks that existed on this part of the coast before the city took over. The **Autódromo** (motor-racing track) is behind Barra and the Lagoa de Jacarepaguá, in the district of the same name. The Brazilian Grand Prix was held here during the 1980s before returning to Interlagos, São Paulo.

Terra Encantada ① *Av Ayrton Senna 2800, T021-2430 9800, www.terra-encantada. com.br, Thu-Sun 1000-2300*, is a 300,000-sq-m theme park in Barra themed according to the different cultural heritages of Brazil: indigenous, African and European. Among the attractions are roller coasters, river rapids, a cinema and shows. Rides close at 2200 and on the main street restaurants, bars and nightspots open.

A bit further out is the **Museu Casa do Pontal** ① *Estrada do Pontal 3295, Recreio dos Bandeirantes, T021-2490 3278, www.museucasadopontal.com.br, Tue-Sun 0930-1700*. Located in a little wood near Recreio dos Bandeirantes beach, this is one of the finest collections of Brazilian folk art in the country. There are over 5000 works by more than 200 artists from 24 different Brazilian states, accumulated French designer Jacques van de Beuque over a 40-year period. Recommended.

Parque Nacional da Tijuca

① *Daily 0600-2100, see map page 62.*

Corcovado is situated within Tijuca National Park; one of the largest areas of urban rainforest in the world. It is a haven for city-weary Cariocas, as well as for some 200 species of birds, numerous small mammals and primates and hundreds of species of endangered Atlantic coast rainforest plants. The forest has a number of natural springs, many of which have been diverted through bamboo channels to form natural showers – be sure to bring swimming gear. There is plenty of shade and the views from the various vantage points are almost as impressive as those from Corcovado.

The vegetation in the Parque Nacional da Tijuca is not primary; most is natural regrowth and planned reforestation. It is a testament to what humans can do to regenerate lost forest. The first Europeans to arrive in the area cut down trees for use in construction and as firewood. The lower areas were cleared to make way for sugar plantations. When coffee was introduced to Rio de Janeiro in 1760 further swathes were cut down for *fazendas*. But the deforestation destroyed Rio's watershed and in 1861, in one of the world's first conservation projects, the imperial government decided that Tijuca should become a rainforest preserve. The enormous task of reforesting the entire area was given to an army major, Manuel Gomes Archer, who took saplings from other areas of Atlantic forest and replanted Tijuca with native trees and a selection of exotics in fewer than 13 years. The names of the six slaves who did the actual manual work is not known. Reforestation was continued by Tomas de Gama. In 1961 Tijuca was joined to several other patches of remnant forest to form a national park of 3300 ha.

Ins and outs

To get to the park entrance, take bus No 221 from Praça 15 de Novembro, No 233 ('Barra da Tijuca') or No 234 from the *rodoviária* or No 454 from Copacabana to Alto da Boa Vista. There is no public transport within the park and the best way to explore is by trail, tour, bicycle or car. If hiking in the park other than on the main paths, a guide may be useful if you do not want to get lost. Contact the **Sindicato de Guías**, T021-267 4582. ▸▸ *See Hiking, page 126.*

Sights

One of the best walks is to the **Pico da Tijuca** (1022 m). Views from the top are wonderful and the walk offers the chance to see plenty of animals. Allow two to three hours. To get to the trailhead enter the park at **Alto da Boa Vista** and follow the signposts (maps are displayed) to **Bom Retiro**, a good picnic place (1½ hours' walk). At Bom Retiro the road ends and there is another hour's walk up a fair footpath to the summit (take the path from the right of the Bom Retiro drinking fountain, not the more obvious steps from the left). The last part consists of steps carved out of the solid rock. There are several sheer drops at the summit which are masked by bushes – be wary. The route is shady for almost its entire length. The main path to Bom Retiro passes the **Cascatinha Taunay** (a 30-m waterfall) and the **Mayrink Chapel** (1860). Panels painted in the Chapel by **Cândido Portinari** have been replaced by copies and the originals will probably be installed in the Museu de Arte Moderna. Beyond the chapel is the wonderful little restaurant Os Esquilos, which dates from 1945. Allow at least five hours for the walk.

Other viewpoints include the **Paulo e Virginia Grotto**, the **Vista do Almirante**, the **Mesa do Imperador** and the **Vista Chinesa** (420 m), a Chinese-style pavilion with a view of the Lagoa Rodrigo de Freitas, Ipanema and Leblon. **Museu Açude** ① *Estrada do*

Açude 764, Alto da Boa Vista, T021-2492 2119, www.museuscastromaya.com.br, Thu-Sun 1100- 1700, Sun brunch with live music 1230-1700, is in the former home of tycoon Castro Maia with some impressive murals and *azulejos* (tiles).

Western Rio

Almost half of the municipal area of Rio de Janeiro is in what is referred to as the **Zona Oeste** (the West Zone – a region that stretches along the coast beyond Barra da Tijuca in a succession of surf beaches. These include **Prainha** and **Grumari**, both of which are broad sweeps of sand backed by rugged hills and dotted with rustic beach bars. Neither are accessible by public transport, and both are busy at weekends. Further west still are the **Barra de Guaratiba** and **Pedra de Guaratiba** beaches and, finally, those at **Sepetiba**. This stunning coastal road (the start of the Costa Verde highway) is becoming obliterated by executive housing developments, so visit soon.

Sítio Roberto Burle Marx ① *Estrada da Barra de Guaratiba 2019, Barra de Guaratiba, T021-2410 1171, daily 0930-1330, by appointment only*, was, from 1949 to 1994, the home of the great Roberto Burle Marx (1909-1994), world famous as a landscape designer and artist. His projects achieved a rare harmony between nature, architecture and man-made landscapes. He created many schemes in Brazil and abroad; in Rio alone his work includes the Parque do Flamengo, the pavements of the Avenida Atlântica in Copacabana, Praça Júlio de Noronha in Leme, the remodelling of the Largo da Carioca, the gardens of the Museu Nacional de Belas-Artes and of the Biblioteca Nacional and the complex at the Santa Teresa tram station near the Catedral Metropolitana.

Covering 350,000 sq m, the estate contains an estimated 3500 species of plants, mostly Brazilian. It is run now by the **Instituto do Patrimônio Histórico e Artístico Nacional** (**IPHAN**) and one of its main aims is to produce seedlings of the plants in its collection. Also on view are Burle Marx's collection of paintings, ceramics, sculptures and other objets d'art, plus examples of his own designs and paintings. The library houses 2500 volumes on botany, architecture and landscape design.

ⓞ Rio de Janeiro listings

Hotel prices
LL over US$200 **L** US$151-200 **AL** US$116-150
A US$81-115 **B** US$51-80 **C** US$36-50
D US$21-35 **E** US$10-20 **F** under US$10
Restaurant prices
ⵉⵉⵉ over US$20 ⵉⵉ US$8-20 ⵉ under US$8

ⓞ Sleeping

The best places to stay in Rio are **Santa Teresa**, **Leblon**, **Ipanema** and the **Arpoador**, the former for nightlife, culture and easy access to Lapa, the Sambódromo and carnival; the latter 3 (which are contiguous), for the beach. Ipanema is probably the safest area of any in the city. Those looking for hotels with charm and personality will find Rio unremarkable. With a few notable exceptions, those in the higher and mid-range bracket are a mix of anonymous business chain towers and fading leftovers from the 1970s, complete with period decor. Those at the lower end are almost invariably dubious hot-pillow establishments in equally dubious areas. Backpackers, however, are well catered for. Searches on sites such as www.hostels.com or www.hostelworld.com will yield almost 50 options and numbers are increasing every month. There are far too many for us to list them all here, so we have only included our favourites.

All accommodation is considerably pricier over New Year and Carnaval. Reserve well in advance, especially budget accommodation.

Self-catering apartments This is a popular form of accommodation in Rio, available at all price levels. In **Flamengo** furnished apartments for short-term let, accommodating up to 6, cost US$300 per month. In **Copacabana**, **Ipanema** and **Leblon** prices start at about US$25 a day (US$500-600 a month) for a simple studio, up to US$2000 a month for a luxurious residence sleeping 4-6. Heading south past **Barra da Tijuca**, virtually all the accommodation available is self-catering.

Renting a small flat, or sharing a larger one, can be much better value than a hotel room.

Blocks consisting entirely of short-let apartments can attract thieves, so check the (usually excellent) security arrangements; residential buildings are called '*prédio familial*'. Higher floors ('*alto andar*') are quieter.

'Apart-Hotels' are listed in the *Guia 4 Rodas* and *Riotur*'s booklet. Agents and private owners advertise under '*Apartamentos – Temporada*' in publications like *Balcão* (twice weekly), *O Globo* or *Jornal do Brasil* (daily); advertisements are classified by district and size of apartment: '*vagas e quartos*' means shared accommodation; '*conjugado*' (or '*conj*') is a studio with limited cooking facilities; '*3 quartos*' is a 3-bedroom flat. There should always be a written agreement when renting.

Homestays
A range of luxurious private homes throughout Rio and Rio state is offered by www.angatu.com and www.brazilian beachhouse.com.
L-B Cama e Café and Rio Homestay, Rua Laurinda Santos Lobo 124, Santa Teresa, T021-2225 4366, T021-9638 4850 (mob, 24 hrs), www.camaecafe.com and www.riohomestay.com. One of the best accommodation options in Rio with a range of more than 50 homestay deals in Santa Teresa, Cosme Velho and Ipanema from the simple to the luxurious. Included in these are Mestre Valentim's mock neo-Gothic castle and Ronnie Biggs's former home. Homestays are very good value and provide the opportunity to get to know locals and see Rio from the inside. Mixing with your host is at the guest's discretion. Rooms can be treated as impersonally as those in a hotel, or guests can fit in as part of the household. **Cama e Café** work hard to match guests with hosts who share similar interests.

Santa Teresa *p81, map p84*

LL Hotel Santa Teresa, R Almirante Alexandrino 660, www.santa-teresa-hotel.com. This 5-star boutique beloved of package holiday groups is hermetically sealed off from Santa Teresa behind high walls. Within, interior decoration blends panache with prurience. There is a much-vaunted restaurant by chef Damien Montecer, a small poolside spa and a swish bar with views out over Santa Teresa.

LL Mama Ruisa, R Santa Cristina 132, T021-2242 1281, www.mamaruisa.com. French-run boutique hotel with carefully casual public spaces and 4 simply decorated, elegant hard wood and whitewash rooms decorated in a modern French colonial style and named in homage to French artistic icons. Also has a pool and sweeping views.

B-D Casa Áurea, R Áurea 80, T021-2242 5830, www.casaaurea.com.br. Tranquil, friendly, arty hostel and boutique hotel in a colonial house in a Santa Teresa backstreet. All rooms vary in shape, size and colour and they and the public spaces, which include a large garden patio, are decorated with tasteful art and craftwork. 5 languages spoken, attracts an interesting crowd and close to the restaurant areas.

B-E Rio Hostel, R Joaquim Murtinho 361, T021-3852 0827, www.riohostel.com. One of Rio's best small hostels. clinging to the side of a hill, it has spectacular views of the centre and is on the doorstep of the city's best nightlife. Doubles and dorms are simple but well kept and overlook the city or the little pool. Carina, the friendly owner, has an inexplicable love of Jamie Oliver as well as all things British and Australian. Excellent facilities and services such as internet, kitchens, lockers, tours and a shuttle service. There is a new branch in Ipanema.

Glória, Catete and Flamengo
p83, maps p84 and p86

Primarily residential areas between the centre and Copacabana, with good bus and metrô connections. Glória, Catete and Flamengo lie next to a park landscaped

by Burle Marx and a beautiful beach lapped by a filthy sea.

LL Glória, R do Russel 632, Glória, www.hotelgloriario.com.br. A stylish and elegant 1920s hotel, closed for refurbishment at the time of writing but due to re-open in high luxury by the end of 2011. Check the website for details.

L Novo Mundo, Praia Flamengo 20, Catete, T021-2105 7000, www.hotelnovomundo-rio.com.br. Standard 4-star rooms in an art deco building with suites with balcony views of the Sugar Loaf.

L Windsor Flórida, R Ferreira Viana 81, Catete, T021-2195 6800, www.windsor hoteis.com. Business-oriented hotel with a well-equipped business centre, one of the city's largest convention centres, bars (for private hire), a restaurant and modestly decorated no-nonsense modern rooms.

B Imperial, R do Catete 186, Catete, T021-2112 6000, www.imperialhotel.com.br. One of the city's very first grand hotels, built in the late 19th century. Rooms are divided between the old building and the new annexe. The latter has modern US-style motel rooms, which are better equipped but have enclosed views. There is a pool, sauna and gym.

B Inglês, R Silveira Martins 20, Glória, T021-2558 3052, www.hotelingles.com.br. Conveniently located near the metrô Catete and in front of the Museu da República gardens. The better rooms have been refurbished and have a/c and there's a pleasant public balcony overlooking the park.

B Paysandú, Paysandú, R Paissandú 23, Flamengo, T021-2558 7270, www.paysandu hotel.com.br. Old art deco tower next to the Palacio da República and Flamengo gardens, with spartan rooms but helpful staff, good location, tours available. **C** for a single.

B-C Único, R Buarque de Macedo 54, Catete, T021-2205 9932, www.unicohotel.com.br. Pleasant, sunny rooms in a labyrinth of corridors. Check the mattresses; some are spongy. Better-value doubles than many of the hostels.

Camping

If travelling with a trailer, you can park at the **Marina Glória car park**, where there are showers and toilets, a small shop and snack bar. Pay the guards to look after your vehicle. See also www.campingclube.com.br.

Botafogo and Urca *p87, map p88*

B-D El Misti Hostel, Praia de Botafogo 462, casa 9, Botafogo, T021-2226 0991, www.elmistihostel.com. A converted colonial house with 6 dorms, shared bathrooms, kitchen and internet, capoeira classes and tour service. Popular with party-goers.

B-D Sun Rio Hostel, R Praia de Botafogo 462, casa 5, Botafogo, T021-2226 0461, www.sunriohostel.com.br, next door to El Misti. A/c dorms, doubles and en suites, all very well kept and clean. Shared kitchen, internet, bike rental and tours organized. Friendly owner Daniela is very welcoming.

C-D Tupiniquim Hostel, R São Manoel 19, at R da Passagem, Botafogo, T021-2244 1286, www.tupiniquimhostel.com.br. Small-scale hostel in a pretty little town house offering a range of interesting volunteer activities alongside the standard facilities. Friendly staff.

Copacabana *p92, map p92*

Once *the* place to stay in Rio but now increasingly sleazy. Ipanema is a better option. Many hotels charge about 30% more for a sea view, but some town-side upper rooms have good views of the mountains.

LL Copacabana Palace, Av Atlântica 1702, T021-2548 7070, www.copacabanapalace. com.br. Rio's grande dame remains the city's only world-class large hotel, a mantle it has worn since first being made famous by Ginger Rogers and Fred Astaire, who filmed *Flying down to Rio* here. Rooms are quiet, spacious and comfortable, with superb beds, effortless service, and conservative and rather European decor. The hotel restaurant, Cipriani, is of a similar high standard to its celebrated sister restaurants in Venice and New York.

LL Marriott, Av Atlântica 2600, T021-2545 6500, www.marriott.com. Rio's newest top-end business hotel with 245 guest rooms specifically designed for the business traveller, an executive floor, 12 meeting rooms and a whole gamut of other business services.

LL Pestana Rio Atlântica, Av Atlântica 2964, T021-2548 6332, www.pestana.com. The best option in Copacabana after the Palace, with spacious bright rooms and a rooftop pool and terrace with sweeping views. Part of the well-managed Portuguese Pestana group. Very high standards. Highly recommended.

LL Sofitel, Av Atlântica, 4240, T021-2525 1232, www.sofitel.com. One of the best beachfront options in the city, at the safer Arpoadoar end of Copacabana and with easy walking access to Ipanema. The hotel has large, airy modern rooms (the best are on the upper floors, with wonderful views over the beach), a sauna, pool and a French restaurant, Le Pré Catelan, with one of the best kitchens in the city.

L-AL Copacabana Rio, Av N S de Copacabana 1256, T021-2267 9900, www.copacabanariohotel.com.br. Quiet, efficiently run 1970s tower with simple but well-maintained standard 3-star rooms, a little pool and generous breakfasts. Safe area at the Ipanema end of the beach a block from the sand.

L-AL Portinari Design, R Francisco Sá 17, posto 6, T021-3222 8800, www.hotel portinari.com.br. Comfortable mock-boutique suites in a great location at the Arpoador end of Copacabana. Decent breakfast with a view on the top floor, internet and a little spa. Good service.

AL Benidorm Palace, R Barata Ribeiro 547, T021-2548 8880, www.benidorm.com.br. Modern rooms decked out in light wood in a tower fully renovated in 2007. The best and quietest are at the back and have small marble bathrooms. Facilities include a sauna and internet in the lobby.

AL-A Copacabana Sol, R Santa Clara 141, T021-2549 4577, www.copacabanasolhotel.

com.br. Newly refurbished. Tiled, a/c rooms with cable TV, Wi-Fi, safes and en suite bathrooms with marble commodes and showers. Good value.

A Atlantis Copacabana, Av Bulhões de Carvalho 61, T021-2521 1142, www.atlantis hotel.com.br. Fading Arpoador hotel in a quiet, safe street very close to the beach. Small rooftop pool, sauna, and the best hotel rates in the area so close to the beach.

A Debret, Av Atlântica 3564, T021-2522 0132, www.debret.com. Bright, spacious, modern seafront rooms in pastel colours and with separate ante rooms; others are a little dark. Free Wi-Fi.

A Hotel Angrense, Travessa Angrense 25, T021-2548 0509, www.angrensehotel.com.br. Well-kept basic a/c rooms in a little art deco block on a quiet street; 24-hr reception, English-speaking staff, reliable tour agency and good carnival rates.

A Santa Clara, R Décio Vilares 316, Metrô Siqueira Campos, T021-2256 2650, www.hotelsantaclara.com.br. Bright, newly refurbished rooms a few blocks back from the beach. Well maintained, discreet and good value, at the lower end of this price range.

B-E Copinha Hostel, R Felipe de Oliveira 11, T021-2275 8520, www.copinhahostel.com.br. Clean, well-run little lemon-yellow hostel with a range of a/c dorms and doubles in white tile and with en suites. 24-hr reception, kitchen, cable TV and transport services.

B-E Stone of a Beach Hostel, R Barata Ribeiro 111, T021-3209 0348, www.stone ofabeach.com.br. Very popular and well-run hostel with spacious, clean dorms and doubles, a lovely pool and bar on the terrace and one of the best ranges of tours in Rio, including surf classes. Excellent English spoken.

D-E Rio Backpackers, Trav Santa Leocádia 38, on the corner of R Pompeu Loureiro between Barão de Ipanema and R Bolivar, T021-2236 3803, www.riobackpackers.com.br.

Self-catering apartments

Copacabana Holiday, R Barata Ribeiro 90A, T021-2542 1525, www.copacabanaholiday. com.br. Recommended, well-equipped small apartments from US$500 per month, minimum 30-day let.

Fantastic Rio, Av Atlântica 974, apt 501, Leme, T021-3507 7491, http://fantasticrio. vilabol.uol.com.br. All types of furnished accommodation from US$20 per day. Good service, contact Peter Corr.

Ipanema and Leblon *p95, map p96*

LL Best Western Sol Ipanema, Av Vieira Souto 320, Ipanema, T021-2525 2020, www.solipanema.com.br. Part of the US group and world's largest chain, with the usual hotel catalogue rooms. Popular with agencies and business travellers.

LL Caesar Park, Av Vieira Souto 460, Ipanema, T021-2525 2525, www.caesar-park.com. Anonymous chain hotel with mock 19th-century flourishes in a beachfront tower. Some rooms have beach views. Decent service includes beach patrol and child-minding. Pool, sauna, restaurant and business facilities.

LL Fasano Rio, Av Vieira Souto 80, Ipanema, T021-3202 4000, www.fasano.com.br. This Philippe Starck-designed luxury hotel in the tasteful Paulistano hotel chain is by far the best in Ipanema and, aside from **La Suite** in Barra da Tijuca, the best in Rio. The superior **Fasano Al Mare** restaurant serves delicious Italian seafood. There's a spectacular rooftop terrace, pool, fitness centre, sauna and massage, a good bar with live music, and limousine service for airport transfers.

LL Marina Palace and Marina All Suites, Av Delfim Moreira 630 and 696, Ipanema, T021-2294 1794, www.hotelmarina.com.br. 2 towers of 1980s vintage almost next door to each other. The former has smart, modern but standard 4-star rooms, a rooftop pool and occasional discount rates over the internet, the latter is a luxury boutique with designer suites and is favoured by the likes of Giselle Bündchen. By international standards it is shabby, but it has an excellent and fashionable sea view restaurant and bar which is great for breakfast and a light lunch or dinner.

AL-A Arpoador Inn, Francisco Otaviano 177, Ipanema, T021-2523 0060, www.arpoador inn.com.br. One of the best deals on the seafront. Well maintained, with off-season special offers. Recommended.

AL-A Ipanema Inn, Maria Quitéria 27, behind Caesar Park, Ipanema, T021-2523 6092, www.ipanemainn.com.br. A popular package tour and small business hotel less than 100 m from the beach. Good value and location.

AL-A Mar Ipanema, R Visconde de Pirajá 539, Ipanema, T021-3875 9190, www.maripanema.com. Simple, smart, modern rooms a block from the beach. The front rooms can be noisy.

A Dolphin Inn, R Bulhões de Carvalho 480, Casa 6 Ipanema, T021-9672 0025, www.bedandbreakfast.com/brazil-rio-de-janeiro-riodolphininn-page.html. This delightful private house in a safe, quiet, gated street less than 5 mins from the metro and Ipanema and Copacabana beaches, can be rented in whole or part. The American and Carioca surfer owners are warm, welcoming and their home reflects their exuberant personalities, with every room decorated with the arty flotsam and jetsam of a lifetime. Facilities include free internet, cable TV, and a kitchen. A hidden gem, but not for long. Book well ahead.

B San Marco, R Visconde de Pirajá 524, Ipanema, T021-2540 5032, www.sanmarco hotel.net. 2-star with simple rooms and a free caipirinha for every internet booking. Price includes breakfast. 2 blocks from beach. Recommended.

B-E Casa 6, R Barão da Torre 175, casa 6, Ipanema, T021-2247 1384, www.casa6 ipanema.com. This French-owned B&B in townhouses sits on a street filled with hostels, 3 blocks from the beach. It offers good long-stay rates and the small rooms with en suites are decorated in wood and tile and fan-cooled.

B-E Che Lagarto, R Barão de Jaguaripe 208, Ipanema, T021-2247 4582, www.chelagarto. com. Bright red, bustling party hostel with young staff and a terrace with views of Corcovado. Dorms and doubles.

B-E Crab Hostel, R Prudente de Morais 903, Ipanema, T021-2267 7353, www.crabhostel.com.br. Party hostel a block from the beach in a side street behind a set of steel doors. Cable TV, dorms and rooms, all with shared bathrooms.

B-E Harmonia, R Barão da Torre 175, casa 18, Ipanema, T021-2523 4905, www.hostelharmonia.com. 3 blocks from beach, doubles or dorms, kitchen facilities, English, Spanish, German and Swedish spoken, good internet, very popular, welcoming and helpful.

B-E Ipanema Beach House, R Barão da Torre 485, Ipanema, T021-3203 3693, www.ipanemahouse.com. Great little hostel with very friendly staff, pool, internet, outdoor bar, continental breakfast, a range of dorms and doubles and 24-hr check-in.

B-E Ipanema Hostel, R Canning, casa 1, Ipanema, T021-2287 2928, www.riohostel ipanema.com. Sister hostel to the friendly and welcoming **Rio Hostel** in Santa Teresa with a range of small rooms and dorms, a tour operator, internet and a lively crowd.

B-E Karisma, R Barão da Torre 177, Ipanema, T021-2523 1372, www.karismahostel.com. Tranquil little hostel 3 blocks from the beach, small but well-kept dorms and pokey doubles, all up a steep flight of stairs. English spoken, lockers, internet and kitchen.

Gávea *p97, map p62*

LL La Maison, R Sergio Porto 58, T021- 3205 3585, www.lamaisonario.com. Rio's only other decent boutique hotel, also run by the French owners of **La Suite**, sits in a period town house on a quiet backstreet in this residential suburb. The bright spacious rooms are tastefully decorated in primary colours and there are wonderful views of Corcovado from the open-sided breakfast area and the little pool. The beach is a taxi ride away.

Barra da Tijuca and beyond *p99*
Spectacular settings, but isolated and far from centre.

LL La Suite, R Jackson de Figueiredo, 501, Joá, T021-2484 1962, www.lasuiterio.com. Rio's only boutique hotel of distinction with 8 individually themed and exquisitely designed rooms perched like an eyrie over an exclusive beach in Rio's wealthiest small suburb. The rooms, the restaurant and the pool offer magical views. Pelé is a neighbour and the restaurant is run by Ludmila Soeiro, a former chef at one of Rio's best restaurants, **Zuka**.

LL Sheraton, Av Niemeyer 121, Vidigal (a suburb between Leblon and São Conrado), T021-2274 1122, www.sheraton-rio.com. One of the **Sheraton's** poorer hotels – a 1970s slab of concrete in painful need of restyling and refurbishing. Wonderful beach views though and a decent pool area.

C-E Rio Surf n Stay, R Raimundo Veras 1140, Recreio dos Bandeirantes, T021-3418 1133, www.riosurfnstay.com. Hostel and surf camp with double rooms, 6-bed dorms and camping. Free Wi-Fi. Surfing lessons and equipment rental are available.

🍴 Eating

There are many restaurants in Rio but very few good ones. With the arrival of decent food from São Paulo in the 1990s things have been improving, especially in **Leblon**. But it is important not to be taken in by appearances

or hotel concierges. Expect to pay at least US$30 per person in the better restaurants. At the cheaper end of the spectrum, Rio lacks that almost ubiquitous Brazilian institution, the corner bakery. Cariocas generally wolf down their breakfast and snacks on foot at streetside bars so a decent sit-down breakfast that isn't mock-French in appearance (and price) can be hard to find. But there are plenty of stand-up juice booths serving fruit juices made from as many as 25 different fruits from orange to *açai* and carrot to *cupuaçu*, all of which are wonderful. You can eat a filling lunch for an average US$5 per person, less if you choose the *prato feito* (US$1.50-6), or eat in a place that serves food by weight (starting at about US$10 per kg).

Central Rio and Lapa
p67, maps p68 and p84
Restaurants in the business district are generally only open for weekday lunch. Many *lanchonetes* in this area offer good cheap meals. The **Travessa do Comércio** has many extemporaneous street restaurants after 1800, especially on Fri, and is always buzzing with life. **R Miguel Couto** (opposite Santa Rita church) is called the 'Beco das Sardinhas' because on Wed and Fri in particular it is full of people eating sardines and drinking beer.

There are several Arabic restaurants on Av Senhor dos Passos, which are also open Sat and Sun. In addition to those listed there are plenty of cafés, including a few chic new

options on R Lavradio in Lapa, where the lively monthly Sat antiques market is held.

¶¶¶ Adega Flor de Coimbra, R Teotônio Regadas 34, Lapa, T021-2224 4582, www.adegaflordecoimbra.com.br. *Chope* and reliable Portuguese food, including excellent *bacalhau* and sardines in olive oil. This little restaurant bar, founded in 1938, was the home of the Carioca painter Cândido Portinari and was once a haunt of Rio's left-wing intelligentsia who would gather here to discuss political theory over a glass of chilled French wine. Now the eclectic crowd is decidedly capitalist, mostly young after-workers and is particularly lively on Fri.

¶¶¶ Albamar, Praça Marechal Âncora, 186, Centro, T021-2240 8378, www.albamar.com. br. A long-established Rio seafood restaurant as popular with politicians and businessmen as it has been ever since its opening 70 years ago in the old Mercado Municipal. Getulio Vargas, Juscelino Kubitschek, Fernando Henrique Cardoso and almost all the other Brazilian presidents have dined here on dishes such as *bacalhau* with oysters and whiting fillet a la albamar, which have been on the menu for as long as anyone can remember. Great views out across Guanabara Bay.

¶¶¶ Cais do Oriente, R Visconde de Itaboraí 8, Centro, T021-2233 2531, www.caisdooriente. com.br. Wonderful restaurant with a range of different spaces, each with its own atmosphere: from a formal Portuguese-style belle-époque dining room to an informal palm-shaded open-air patio and a terrace with live music. The menu by French chef Alex Giraud is similarly varied with a broad selection of fusions and Mediterranean, Brazilian and oriental dishes.

¶¶¶ Eça, Av Rio Branco 128, T021-2524 2300, www.hstern.com.br/eca. Rio city centre's best business lunch from Frederic de Maeyer – classically trained chef who once cooked in the Michelin-starred L'Escalier du Palais Royale in Brussels.

¶¶¶ Republique, Praça da República 63, 2nd floor, Centro, T021-2532 9000.

A long-established Rio favourite, now newly refurbished by the architect Chico Gouveia (whose decoration is based on the colours of the French flag), serving daring and ambitious South American fusion cooking by distinguished Rio chef Paulo Carvalho.

¶¶¶ Bar Luiz, R da Carioca 39, Centro, T021-2262 6900, www.barluiz.com.br. For 117 years this little bar in one of the few remaining colonial houses in the city centre has been at the heart of Rio life. Almost every Carioca you can name from Di Cavalcanti and Tom Jobim to Ronaldo and Chico Buarque has at one time or another formed part of the lively throng which gathers here on weekday evenings and most particularly on Fri and Sat to drink the famous *chope* and eat tapas. During the day it is a great place for a quiet snack and a respite from the heat and busyness of the city.

¶¶¶ Café da Moda, Loja Folic, R Gonçalves Dias 49, 3rd floor, Centro, T021-2222 0610, www.folic.com.br. An a/c café devoted to the narrow waistline and located within the **Folic** shop. Salads are named after famous models: Gisele Bündchen, Kate Moss, Claudia Schiffer and so on, with more macho options for men, such as Zulu, which comprises buffalo mozzarella, maize, tomato, croutons, lettuce and a garnish of marjoram. Light meals without fashionable names also available.

¶¶-¶ Bar das Artes, Paço Imperial, Praça XV de Novembro 48, Centro, T021-2215 2431, www.pacoimperial.com.br. Neat, clean and peaceful café on the ground floor of the Paço Imperial (formerly the royal palace) in the busy centre of Rio. Salads, sandwiches, light meals and desserts such as strawberry strudel.

¶¶-¶ Confeitaria Colombo, R Gonçalves Dias 32 (near Carioca metrô station), Centro, T021-2505 1500, www.confeitariacolombo.com.br. Afternoons only during the week. The only remaining belle-époque Portuguese coffee house in Rio, serving a range of café food, cakes, pastries and light lunches. The *feijoada colonial* on Sat is accompanied by live *choro*.

¶ Sabor Saúde, R da Quitanda 21, Centro,
T021-2252 6041, www.saborsaude.com.br.
Breakfast and lunch only. Vegetarian and
wholefood including sandwiches (whose
contents you can compile yourself), quiches,
pastries, salads and light dishes such as
grilled salmon with rosti.

Santa Teresa *p81, map p84*
¶¶¶ Aprazível, R Aprazível 62, T021-2508
9174, www.aprazivel.com.br. Decent but
unspectacular Brazilian dishes and seafood
with one of the best restaurant views in the
city: tables are outdoors in a tropical garden
overlooking Guanabara Bay. This is a good
Sun lunch spot when they have occasional
choro and samba.
¶¶ Adega do Pimenta, R Almte Alexandrino
296, T021-2239 9673, www.adegadopimenta.
com.br. Mon-Fri 1200-2200, Sat 1200-2000,
Sun 1200-1800. A very small German
restaurant in the Largo do Guimarães with
excellent sausages, sauerkraut and cold beer.
¶¶¶ Bar do Arnaudo, Largo do Guimarães,
R Almte Alexandrino 316, T021-2252 7246.
A modest-looking restaurant decorated with
handicrafts but serving generous portions of
wonderful northeast-Brazilian cooking. Try
the *carne do sol* (sun-dried beef, or jerky) with
feijão de corda (brown beans and herbs), or
the *queijo coalho* (a country cheese, grilled).
¶¶¶ Espírito Santa, R Almte Alexandrino 264,
T021-2508 7095. Closed Mon; lunch only Tue,
Wed, Sun. Upstairs is a chic boho restaurant
with a view serving sumptuous Amazon
food by Natacha Fink. Downstairs is a funky
weekend basement club. Great cocktails.
¶¶¶ Jasmim Manga, Largo dos Guimarães 143,
T021-2242 2605, www.jasmimmanga.com.
A pretty little cyber café with decent coffee
and a nice view over the square.
¶¶¶ Sobrenatural, R Almte Alexandrino 432,
T021-2224 1003. Simple, elegant seafood
served by sexagenarian career waiters in
bow ties. The huge dining room is always
lively with chatter.

Glória, Catete and Flamengo
p83, map p84 and p86
There are many cheap and mid-range eating
places on **R do Catete**, all fairly similar.
¶¶¶ Alcaparra, Praia do Flamengo 150,
Flamengo, T021- 2558 3937, www.alcaparra.
com.br. Elegant traditional Italian/Portuguese
restaurant overlooking the sea. A long-
established favourite of senior politicians
and business people who often ask for
the *bacalhau*.
¶¶¶ Lamas, R Marquês de Abrantes 18A,
Flamengo, T021-2556 0799, www.cafe
lamas.com.br. This famous café brasserie with
its conservative decor of white tablecloths
and dark wood has been serving steaks,
bacalhau and draught *chopp* to the Rio
intelligentsia since 1874. It is still a wonderful
place to see the city's movers and gives a real
sense of how European the city once was.
¶ Estação República, R do Catete 104, Catete,
T021-2225 2650. A choice of more than 40
dishes, from soups and sushi to salads and
stews, in this pay-by-weight restaurant
housed in the Palácio do Catete.

Botafogo and Urca *p87, map p88*
There are many cheap and mid-range options
in the **Botafogo Praia** shopping centre.
¶¶¶ Abençoado, Morro de Urca s/n
There can be few restaurants anywhere in
the world with a better view than this –
over the bay to Corcovado and the Christ
on one side and the pearly Atlantic beaches
of Copacabana, Ipanema and distant Niterói
on the other. Cooking is described by chef
Natacha Fink as 'rendering Rio de Janeiro
street snacks chic', with a menu of Brazilian
comfort food given a gourmet twist.
Plates include *angu* (corn meal with Santa
Catarina prawns and field mushrooms)
or *escondidinho* (jerk meat with cheese
gratin served on a bed of pureed aipim).
The accompanying caipirinhas and less
alcoholic *batidas* are the best in Rio.
¶¶¶ Miam Miam, General Goes Monteiro 34,
Botafogo, T021-2244 0125, www.miammian
com.br. Closed Mon. The most fashionable c

Rio's alternative fashion set sip caipirinhas here. Frequent visitors include Bebel Gilberto and Adrianna Calcanhotto – both names on the Brazilian music scene. Decoration is retro chic with 1950s and 1960s lounge furniture from the **Hully Gully** antique shop in Copacabana's Siqueira Campos mall and cartoons in homage to cult 1970s Carioca cartoonist, Carlos Zéfiro. Food is light Mediterranean but people come here for the crowd and the cocktails before moving on to Lapa.

¶¶¶ Oui Oui, R Conde de Irajá, 85, T021-2527 3539. Fashionable, arty 30-something Cariocas eat light at Oui Oui, chatting over cocktails before heading to the clubs in Lapa and Sta Teresa – think Bebel Gilberto or Fernanda Abreu. They loiter in the nouvelle art deco lounge bar and sample the *petiscos* – small plates of contemporary Brazilian food served tapas style and ordered in pairs – in the adjacent dining room.

¶ Raajmahal, R General Polidoro 29, Baixo Botafogo, T021-2542 6242, www.raajmahal.com.br. One of the few restaurants in Brazil offering authentic Indian food with a huge menu including a range of vegetarian dishes such as *mater paneer*.

¶ Yorubá, R Arnaldo Quintela 94, Botafogo, T021-2541 9387, www.restauranteyoruba.com.br. Evenings only except weekends, closed Mon, Tue. Rio's favourite Bahian restaurant, and several times voted the best in the city by *Veja* magazine. The menu comprises usual run of Bahian food from *carajé* (beans fried in dendê palm oil) to *atapá* (fish or chicken with coconut milk, shrimps, peanuts, dendê palm oil and chilli) alongside more unusual dishes such as chicken in ginger sauce with cashew nut rice.

opacabana *p92, map p92*

There are stand-up bars selling snacks all around Copacabana and Ipanema. There are plenty of open-air restaurants along **Av Atlântica**, none of which can be recommended for anything but the view.

¶¶¶ Cipriani, Copacabana Palace (see page 105). The best hotel restaurant for formal dining, with a chef from the **Hotel Cipriani** in Venice. Very good seafood and Italian fare.

¶¶¶ Copa Café, Av Atlântica 3056, T021-2235 2947. A French bistro run by São Paulo chef Cássio Machado with light food and fabulous mini burgers with Dijon mustard. Very popular with Carioca celebrities like Caetano Veloso. DJ after dinner in the evenings at weekends.

¶¶¶ La Fiorentina, Av Atlântica 458a, Copacabana, T021-2543 8395, www.lafiorentina.com.br. The best Italian in Copa is famous for its *espaguete com frutos do mar* (seafood spaghetti), served in a light prawn marinade. The bar is a very popular meeting spot for middle class locals and the wine list is reasonable for Rio.

¶¶¶ Siri Mole and Cia, R Francisco Otaviano 90. Excellent Bahian seafood and Italian coffee in elegant a/c surroundings.

¶¶¶-¶¶ Churrascaria Palace, R Rodolfo Dantas 16B, T021-2541 5898, www.churrascaria palace.com.br. Copa's answer to **Porcão** or **Esplanada Grill** with 20 different kinds of barbecued meat served in plush surrounds, under a/c and at your table with buffet salads to accompany.

¶¶ Chon Kou, Av Atlântica 3880, T021-2287 3956, www.chonkou.com.br/site. A traditional Chinese restaurant which also offers an extensive sushi menu. Japanese is far more popular than Chinese in Brazil a/c with piped music; sit upstairs for good views over Copacabana beach. A welcome change from most other options in this area.

¶¶ Kilograma, Av NS Copacabana 1144, T021-3202 9050, www.kilograma.com.br. Open on weekends and holidays. A pay-per-weight meat barbecue with a huge buffet choice and good-value fixed lunch menu.

¶¶-¶ Aipo and Aipim, Av Nossa Senhora de Copacabana 391b and 920 in Copacabana, and R Visconde de Pirajá 145 in Ipanema, T021-2267 8313, www.aipoeaipim.com.br. Plentiful tasty food sold by weight at this popular chain.

Eclipse, Av NS de Copacabana 1309, T021-2287 1788, www.bareclipse.com.br. Spruce, well-run and very popular 24-hr restaurant offering good-value *prato feito* lunches and a generous range of meats, pastas, snacks and sandwiches served in the cool interior or on streetside tables.

Apetite Cafe, R Souza Lima 68, T021-2247 3319. One of Copa's few bakery cafes. Offers a range of breakfasts, respectable coffee, snacks, options for kids and an a/c interior for when it gets too hot.

Cafeina, R Constante Ramos 44, T021-2547 8651, www.cafeina.biz. Very popular breakfast spot with good coffee, tasty pastries and other snacks and ice cold juices.

Cervantes, Barata Ribeiro 07-B at Prado Júnior 335B, T021 2275 6147, www.restaurantecervantes.com.br. Stand-up bar or sit-down a/c restaurant, open all night, queues after 2200. Said to serve the best sandwiches in town. A local institution.

La Tratoria, Rua Fernando Mendes 7A, T021-22553319, www.latrattoriario.com.br, opposite Hotel Excelsior. Good service and Italian food, very reasonable. Recommended.

Temperarte, Av NS de Copacabana 1243, T021-2267 1149, www.temperarte.com.br. Open evenings and holidays. A/c, good-value pay-by-weight food, with mains and a huge range of very sweet desserts.

Traiteurs de France, Av NS de Copacabana 386, T021 2548 6440. Delicious French tarts and pastries, but poor service.

Ipanema and Leblon p95, map p96

Alessandro and Frederico, R Garcia D'Ávila151, Ipanema, T021-2522 5414. Upmarket café with decent café latte and breakfasts.

Bar D'Hotel, Marina All Suites (see Sleeping, page 106). Light but very well-flavoured fish dishes served to people with tiny waists in casual designer cool surrounds. Very good cocktails. The best for breakfast or lunch with a beach view.

Bistrô ZaZá, R Joana Angélica 40, Ipanema, T021-2247 9101, www.zazabistro.com.br.

Hippy chic pseudo-Moroccan/French restaurant that attracts a mix of tourist and bohemian Zona Sul Cariocas. Good fish dishes and cocktails and good fun. Evenings are best for intimate dining when the tables are lit by candles.

Capricciosa, R Vinícius de Moraes 134, Ipanema, T021-2523 3394. The best pizzeria in town and a lynchpin in the TV and fashion scene – the famous and wealthy gather here to gossip and catch up. Queues can be long.

Carlota, R Dias Ferreira 64, Leblon, T021-2540 6821, www.carlota.com.br. The best of many on a street lined with restaurants and bars. Great unpretentious Mediterranean food in an elegant, casual all-white dining room.

Forneria, R Aníbal de Mendonça 112, Ipanema, T021-2540 8045, www.restaurante forneria.com.br. Paulistano restaurateur Rogerio Fasano's latest elegant eating-space in Rio serves supreme burgers in pizza dough and cooked in a wood-fired oven, and other superior bar snacks. Usually full with an elegant after-beach crowd.

Gero, R Aníbal de Mendonça 157, Ipanema, T021-2239 8158, www.fasano. com.br. Tasty Italian fare with excellent fish served to TV *Globo novela* stars and the like in a beautiful minimalist space.

Manekineko, R Dias Ferreira 410, Leblon, T021-2540 7641, www.manekineko.com.br. Rio's best Japanese with a large menu of superb traditional dishes and Japanese, European and South American fusion. The intimate dining area, comprising a corridor of low-lit booths, is always packed.

Porcão, Barão de Torre 218, Ipanema, T021-3202 9158, www.porcao.com.br. One of the city's best *churrascarias* serving all manner of meat in unlimited quantities for a set price.

Satyricon, R Barão da Torre 192, Ipanema T021-2521 0627, www.satyricon.com.br. The best seafood in Rio. Lively crowd in a large dining room which precludes intimacy A favourite with businessmen, politicians and Ronaldo. Avoid Sat when there is a buffet.

Zuka, R Dias Ferreira 233B, Leblon, T021-3205 7154, www.zuka.com.br. One of the most fashionable restaurants in Rio with an exciting and eclectic fusion of everything – French and Japanese, American fast food and Italian – all presented on huge rectangular plates and in a carefully designed modern space.

Casa da Feijoada, Prudente de Morais 10, Ipanema, T021-2247 2776. Serves excellent feijoada all week. Generous portions.

Celeiro, R Dias Ferreira 199, Leblon, T021-22747843, www.celeiroculinaria.com.br. Superior salads and buffet food, which has been consistently voted the best in the city by the magazine, *Veja*.

Big Nectar, R Teixeira de Melo 34, T021-2522 3949. One of the largest range of juices in Rio including uniquely South American and Brazilian fruits such as *seriguela*, *mangaba*, *umbu* and *cupuaçu*.

Fellini, R General Urquiza 104, Leblon, T021-2511 3600, www.fellini.com.br. The best pay-by-weight restaurant in the city with a large range of delicious Brazilian and international dishes, salads and quiches. Plenty of options for vegetarians. Funky website.

New Natural, R Barão da Torre 173, T021-2226 7317. Popular vegetarian and wholefood restaurant with a large range of hot dishes and desserts served per kilo. There's an adjacent natural products shop next door. Service can be poor.

Polis Sucos, R Maria Quitéria 70a, T021-247 2518. A favourite Carioca pre- and post-beach pit-stop offering a huge range of tropical juices and snacks such as *açaí na tigela* (mushed *açaí* berries with *guarana* syrup).

Empório Saúde, R Visconde de Pirajá 414, Ipanema, T021-2247 6361, www.emporio saude.com.br. Closed Sun and evenings. A large variety of vegetarian comfort cooking from quiches to stews in a wholefood shop inside a shopping gallery. Good value.

Gávea, Lagoa and Jardim Botânico
p7, map p62

Gávea is the heartland of trendy 20-something Rio. The neighbourhoods of Jardim Botânico and Lagoa appear at first sight to offer unlimited exciting upmarket dining opportunities. But the restaurants are mostly mutton dressed up as lamb. They look great, cost loads and serve dreadful food. Here are a very few exceptions:

Olympe, R Custódio Serrão 62, Lagoa, T021-2539 4542, www.claudetroisgros.com.br. The Troisgros family were founders of nouvelle cuisine and run a 3 Michelin-star restaurant in Roanne. Claude Troisgros' cooking fuses tropical ingredients with French techniques, exemplified by the roasted quail filled with *farofa* and served with raisins, pearl onions and a sweet and sour *jabuticaba* sauce.

Roberta Sudbrack, R Lineu de Paula Machado 916, Jardim Botânico, T021-3874 0139, www.robertasudbrack.com.br. Roberta was the private chef for President Henrique Cardoso and cooked for all the visiting international dignitaries who dined with him during his term of office. She is celebrated for her European-Brazilian fusion cooking and won *Veja's* coveted chef-of-the-year award in 2006.

Árabe da Gávea, Gávea shopping mall, R Marquês de São Vicente 52, T021-2294 2439. By far the best Arabic restaurant in Rio.

Guimas, R José Roberto Macedo Soares 5, Baixo Gávea, T021-2259 7996. An old favourite for *Globo* actors and low-key celebrities, serving salt Portuguese food in a homely dining room or on the outside veranda on check tablecloths. Very crowded with fashionable under-30s after 2200 on Mon and towards the end of the week.

Mistura Fina, Av Rainha Elisabeth 770, Ipanema, T021-2523 1703. See Bars and clubs, page 116.

Bars and clubs

Rio nightlife is young and vivacious. **Lapa** is a current hotspot at weekends, once down-at-heel and still not entirely safe but undergoing a great renaissance, with a string of clubs along Mem de Sá and R Lavradio and along a little back street known as the **Beco do Rato**. The whole neighbourhood throbs to dance rhythms from samba and *forro* to techno and hip-hop. Similarly busy, even on Sun and Mon, is **Baixa Gávea**, where beautiful 20-somethings gather around Praça Santos Dumont.

Wherever you are in Rio, there's a bar near you. Beer costs around US$2.50 for a large bottle, but up to US$7 in the plusher venues, where you are often given a card that includes 2 drinks and a token entrance fee. A cover of US$3-7 may be charged made for live music, or there might be a minimum consumption charge of around US$3, sometimes both. Snack food is always available. **Copacabana**, **Ipanema** and **Leblon** have many beach *barracas*, several open all night. The seafront bars on Av Atlântica are great for people-watching; but avoid those towards **Leme** as some may offer more than beer.

Clubs on and around Rio's beaches are generally either fake Europe, eg **Melt** and **Bunker** (although decent DJs like Marky play here), or fake US, eg **Nuth** and **00**. Santa Teresa has the most interesting bohemian bars and is a good place to begin a weekend night before heading down the hill to Lapa, Rio's capital of nightlife, with a plethora of samba venues undergoing a steady renaissance. See also Samba schools, page 119.

Central Rio, Lapa and Santa Teresa
p67 and p81, maps p68 and p84

Lapa, Santa Teresa and increasingly the city centre, have Rio's most interesting, bohemian nightlife and shouldn't be missed if you are in Rio over a weekend. Ideally come early on a Sat for the afternoon market and live street tango on **R Lavradio**, eat in Santa Teresa and sample the bars on the **Largo dos Guimarães** and the **Largo das Neves** before returning to Lapa for live samba or funk. Although it is easy to walk between the 2 *bairros*, never walk alone. Always be wary of pickpockets.

Goya Beira, Largo das Neves 13, Santa Teresa, T021-2232 5751. One of several restaurant bars on this pretty little square. This and all the others attract an arty crowd after 2100, especially on the little streetside tables. Decent *petiscos* and a range of aromatic vintage *cachaças*.

Bar do Mineiro, R Paschoal Carlos Magno 99, Santa Teresa, T021-2221 9227, 100 m from Largo dos Guimarães. Rustic *boteco* opening right onto the street and with hundreds of black-and-white photos of Brazilian musicians displayed on the white-tiled walls. Attracts a busy, arty young crowd at weekends, downing Minas *petiscos* and bottled beer.

Carioca da Gema, Av Mem de Sá 79, Centro, near Rio Scenarium, T021-2221 0043, www.barcariocadagema.com.br. One of the longest established samba clubs and daytime cafés in Lapa, with the cream of the live bands and, if you arrive early, sit-down tables. Great little pre-show pizza restaurant upstairs.

Circo Voador. See Music, page 118. One of the best venues in Rio.

Club Six, R das Marrecas 38, Lapa, T021 2510 3230, www.clubsix.com.br. Huge pounding European/NYC dance club with everything from hip-hop to ambient house. A grungy ole dance hall where transvestites gossip on the stairs and bands play Gafieira or dance hall samba. Caetano Veloso's son, Moreno (who invented the new love of dance hall samba in Rio), sometimes plays here with his band **Orquestra Imperial**. If you're a samba lover and 20- or 30-something at heart, this is the place to be. Few tourists, so far …

Clube dos Democráticos, R do Riachuelo 91, T021-2252 4611, www.clubedosdemocraticos.com.br.

Espírito Santa, R Almte Alexandrino 264, Largo do Guimarães, Santa Teresa, T021-2508 7095, www.espiritosanta.com.br. Upstairs restaurant, downstairs lively club where every Sat DJ Zod plays the best in Rio funk and West African dance.

Espírito Santa Empório, R Lavradio 34, www.espiritosanta.com.br. A new lounge bar restaurant next to the Rio Scenarium in

Pedro Luís e A Parede recommends

Pedro Luís and his band play some of the most exciting new samba in Rio, integrating the style with other Brazilian rhythms, modern electronica and indie. They play live in Rio regularly and you can check them out on www.plap.com.br. Here are Pedro's recommendations for what to do in Rio: **Circo Voador**, www.circovoador.com.br and **Fundição Progresso**, T021-2220 5070, www.fundicao.org, are arts and music centres with concert halls, where

some of the city's most exciting new performers and film-makers showcase their talents. The Circo runs a lot of social projects too and is in a beautiful location beneath the Arcos de Lapa. The **Espaço Cultural Municipal Sérgio Porto**, R Humaitá 163, Humaitá, T021-2266 0896, is another arts space with two galleries and a theatre where you can see everything from live music to alternative poetry or performance art – all from some of the freshest and most innovative performers in the city.

Lapa and run by Natacha Fink of the Espírito Santa in Santa Teresa. Come for great comfort food and cocktails, and DJ Zod and DJ Mam's weekend Carioca funk parties.

Estudantina Musical, 3 piso, Praça Tiradentes 79, T021-2232 1149. Closed Mon-Wed. This is one of central Rio's most famous old school gafieira halls. It's at its busiest and liveliest on Thu when hundreds gather to dance samba to some of the best big samba bands in the city. Far less touristy than Lapa.

Mercado 32, R do Mercado 32, Centro, T021-2221 2327, www.mercado32.com.br. Closed weekends. In the heart of the centre in a converted 19th-century building, this little restaurant and bar offers live *MPB* on most nights during the week and live *chorinho* every Thu from 2030.

(closed)Rio Scenarium, R do Lavradio 20, Lapa, T021-3147 9005, www.rioscenarium. com.br. 3-storey samba and dance club in beguilingly spacious colonial house used as a movie prop storage facility by *TV Globo*. Overflowing with Brazilian exuberance and people of all ages dancing furiously, to samba and assorted Euro and Lusitanian club sounds, and the bizarre backdrop of a 19th-century apothecary's shop or mannequins wearing 1920s outfits. Arrive after 2300.

Sacrilégio, Av Mem de Sá 81, Lapa, next door to **Carioca da Gema**, T021-3970 1461,

www.sacrilegio.com.br. Samba, *chorinho*, *pagode* and occasional theatre. Close to many other bars.

Semente, R Joaquim Silva 138, Lapa, T021-2242 5165. Mon-Sat from 2200, US$8 cover, minimum consumption US$7. Popular for samba, *choro* and salsa. Book at weekends. Great atmosphere. Recommended.

The Week, R Sacadura Cabral 154, Zona Portuária, T021-2253 1020, www.theweek. com.br. One of the most popular dance clubs in the city, among Cariocas heaving with a mostly gay crowd and with state-of-the-art dance spaces, DJs and sound systems. Don't expect any Brazilian sounds; it's strictly New York house and Eurotrash here.

Glória, Catete and Flamengo
p83, maps p84 and p86.
Look out for the frequent free live music at the **Marina da Glória** and along Flamengo beach during the summer.

Botafogo and Urca *p87, map p88*
Casa de Matriz, R Henrique de Novaes 107, Botafogo, T021 2226 9691 www.matriz online.com.br. Great grungy club with a bar, Atari room, small cinema and 2 dance floors. Full of Rio students.

The British & Commonwealth Society – Porão, under the Anglican church hall, R Real Grandeza 99, Botafogo, T021 2537 6695,

www.bcsrio.org.br. British ex-pats meet here
on Fri nights.

Copacabana, Ipanema and
Leblon *p92 and p95, maps p92 and p96*
There is frequent live music on the beaches
of Copacabana and Ipanema, and along
the **Av Atlântica** throughout the summer,
especially around New Year.

Academia da Cachaça, R Conde de Bernadotte
26-G, Leblon, T021-2529 2680, with another
branch at Av Armando Lombardi 800, Barra da
Tijuca, www.academiadacachaca.com.br The
best *cachacas* and caipirinhas in the city (try
the delicious *pitanga caipirinha*), and some of
Rio's best *feijoadas* and bar snacks. Good on Fri.

Bar D'Hotel, Marina All Suites, Ipanema
(see page 106). The well-dressed and tanned
drink the excellent house cocktails here
at the cool long bar before dining on
light Mediterranean fare. Beach views.
Good for sunset in smart casual.

Bar do Copa, Hotel Copacabana Palace,
Av Atlântica 1702, T021-2545 8724. This mock
Miami beach cocktail bar next to the pool
at the swish Copacabana Palace hotel is a
favourite high society posing spot and is
much frequented by models and celebrities.
Dress well to get past the velvet rope, and
be prepared to queue.

Barril 1800, Av Vieira Souto 110, Ipanema,
T021-2523 0085, www.barril1800.com.
Pleasant place to watch the sunset with
a cold glass of *chope* beer in hand.
Highly recommended.

Bip Bip, R Almte Gonçalves 50, Copacabana
T021-2267 9696. *Botequim* bar that attracts
a crowd of jamming musicians every Tue.

Clandestino, R Barata Ribeiro 111, T021-
3798 5771, www.clandestinobar.com.br.
A cavernous little cellar bar attracting a lively
young crowd who dance to soul, Rio funk
and occasional live acts. Busiest on Fri.

Devassa, R Rainha Guilhermina 48, Leblon,
and an alternative menu at Ipanema branch,
Av Visconde de Pirajá 539, www.devassa.
com.br/cervejaria.php. A 2-floor pub/bar/

restaurant that is always heaving with the
Ipanema middle-class. Brews its own beer.

Empório, R Maria Quitéria 37, Ipanema,
T021-3813 2526. Street bar that attracts
the hordes. Mon is the busiest night.

Garota de Ipanema, R Vinícius de Moraes 49,
Ipanema. Where the song *Girl from Ipanema*
was written. Now packed with foreigners on
the package Rio circuit listening to bossa.
For the real thing head to **Toca do Vinícius**
on a Sun afternoon (see page 118).

Melt, R Rita Ludolf 47, Leblon, T021-2249
9309, www.melt-rio.com.br. Downstairs
bar and upstairs sweaty club. Occasional
performances by the cream of Rio's new
samba funk scene – usually on a Sun.
Always heaving on Thu.

Mistura Fina, Av Rainha Elisabeth 769,
Ipanema, T021-2523 1703. A venue for the
famous Rio jazz, bossa and MPB club, which
has played host to names from Tom Jobim
to Liza Minelli. Dinner, a cool bar, ocean
views and great music.

Shenanigans, R Visconde de Pirajá 112,
Ipanema, T021-2267 5860,
www.shenanigans.com.br. Obligatory
mock-Irish bar with Guinness and Newcastle
Brown. Not a place to mix with the locals.

Vinícius, R Vinícius de Moraes 39, Ipanema,
http://viniciusbar.com.br. Mirror image of
the **Garota de Ipanema** with slightly better
acts and food.

Gávea, Lagoa and Jardim Botânico *p9*
Bar Lagoa, Av Epitácio Pessoa 1674, Lagoa,
T021-2523 1135, www.barlagoa.com.br.
Attracts an older arty crowd on weekdays.

Belmonte IV, R Jardim Botânico 617,
Jardim Botânico, T021-2239 1649.
Weatlhy middle-class Cariocas come to
this unpretentious little bakery and snack
bar at all hours to have a beer and eat
the delicious *empadas* – little pies stuffed
with crabs, prawns or chicken.

Garota da Gávea, Praça, Santos Dumont 14
Gávea, T021-2274 2347. Closed Mon-Wed.
This corner bar-cum-restaurant is another of

Gávea's informal meeting places. Scores of people gather here for *petiscos* and a cold *chopp* (beer) on weekend and Thu nights.
Hipódromo da Gávea, Praça Santos Dumont 108, Gávea, T021-2274 9720. On weekend and Thu nights this restaurant bar, and its neighbours mentioned above, fill with young middle-class Cariocas who talk and flirt over beer and bar snacks. The crowds from all bars spill out onto Praça Santos Dumont square. Very few tourists make it here.
Caroline Café, R JJ Seabra 10, Jardim Botânico, T021-2540 0705, www.caroline cafe.com. Popular with Rio's young and good-looking middle classes. Kicks off after 2100. Also serves food.
00 (Zero Zero), Av Padre Leonel Franca 240, Gávea, T021 2540 8041, http://www.00site. com.br. Mock-LA bar/restaurant/club with a small outdoor area. Currently the trendiest club in Rio for Brazil's equivalent of 'sloanes' or 'valley girls'. Gay night on Sun.

Barra da Tijuca *p99, map p62*
Nuth, R Armando Lombardi 999, www.nuth.com.br. Barra's slickest club; very mock-Miami and frequented by a mixed crowd of rich-kid surfers, footballers (including Romario) and women with surgically enhanced beauty. The music is a mix of tacky Brazilian and Eurotrash with occasional samba funk live acts. Enormous queues even when the house is empty.

Quiosque do Pepê, Posto 2, Barra da Tijuca beach. One of a string of very popular beach bars frequented by toned, tanned surfers and kitesurfers.

⏺ Entertainment

Rio de Janeiro *p60, maps p62 and p68*
Cinema
There are cinemas serving subtitled Hollywood fare and major Brazilian releases on the top floor of almost all the malls. The normal seat price is around US$10. Discounts on Wed and Thu (students pay half price any day of the week). Alternative and art-house films are shown in the following theatres:
Centro Cultural do Banco do Brasil, R Primeiro de Março 66, Centro, T021-808 2020. One of Rio's better arts centres with the best of the art films and exhibitions from fine art to photography (Metrô Uruguaiana).
Cinemateca do MAM, Infante Dom Henrique 85, Aterro do Flamengo, T021-2210 2188. Cinema classics, art films, roving art exhibitions and a good café with live music. Views of Guanabara Bay from the balconies.
Estaçao Ipanema, R Visconde de Pirajá 605, Ipanema. European art cinema, less-mainstream US and Brazilian releases.

Horse racing
Jockey Club Racecourse, by the Jardim Botânico and Gávea, Praça Santos Dumont

31, T021-3534 9000, www.jcb.com.br, meetings on Mon 1845 Fri 1700 evenings and Sat and Sun 1445, long trousers required, tables can be booked. Take any bus marked 'via Jóquei'. Betting is by tote only.

Live music

Cariocas congregate in Lapa between Thu and Sat for live club music. There are free concerts throughout the summer along the Copacabana and Ipanema beaches, in Botafogo and at the parks: mostly samba, reggae, rock and MPB (Brazilian pop). There is no advance schedule; information is given in the local press. Rio's famous jazz, in all its forms, is performed in lots of enjoyable venues too, see www.samba-choro.com.br for more information.

Canecão, R Venceslau Brás 215, Botafogo, T021-2105 2000, www.canecao.com.br. A big, inexpensive venue for live concerts most nights, and a taste of some purely local entertainment on Mon.

Centro Cultural Carioca, R do Teatro 37, T021-2242 9642, www.centrocultural carioca.com.br, for advance information, 1830-late. This restored old house with wraparound balconies and exposed brick walls is a dance school and music venue that attracts a lovely mix of people. Professional dancers perform with musicians; after a few tunes the audience joins in. Thu is impossibly crowded; Sat is calmer. Bar food available. US$12 cover charge. Highly recommended.

Circo Voador, R dos Arcos, Lapa, T021-2533 0354, www.circovoador.com.br. Lapa's recuperation began with this little concert hall under the arches. Some of the city's best smaller acts still play here – including Seu Jorge who first found fame playing with *Farofa Carioca* at the Circo.

Praia do Vermelha, Urca, www.movimento artistico.org.br/entrada.htm. Bus No 511 from Copacabana. Residents bring musical instruments and chairs onto the beach for an informal night of samba 2130-2400. Free.

Rhapsody, Av Epitácio Pessoa 1104, Lagoa, T021-2247 2104, http://rhapsodypianobar. sites.uol.com.br. Piano-bar restaurant with a mix of Brazilian and Diana Kraal-style crooning.

Toca do Vinícius, R Vinícius de Moraes 129C, Ipanema, www.tocadovinicius.com.br. Rio's leading bossa nova and *choro* record shop has concerts from some of the finest performers every Sun lunchtime.

Theatre

There are about 40 theatres in Rio, presenting a variety of classical and modern performances in Portuguese. Seat prices start at about US$15; some children's theatre is free. For information on particular performances, check on the website www.rioecultura.com.br, in *Veja* at weekends, or ask at the tourist office.

⊕ Festivals and events

Rio de Janeiro *p60, maps p62 and p68*
Carnaval
Tickets → *See also box, page 120.*
Sambódromo, R Marquês de Sapucaí s/n, Cidade Nova. http://carnaval.rioguiaoficial. com.br and www.rioguiaoficial.com.br. The nearest tube is Praça Onze.

The Sambódromo parades start at 1900 and last about 12 hrs. Gates open at 1800. There are *cadeiras* (seats) at ground level, *arquibancadas* (terraces) and *camarotes* (boxes). The best boxes are reserved for tourists and VIPs and are very expensive or by invitation only. Seats are closest to the parade, but you may have to fight your way to the front. Sectors 4, 7 and 11 are the best spots (they house the judging points); 6 and 13 are least favoured (being at the end when dancers might be tired) but have more space. The terraces, while uncomfortable, house the most fervent fans and are tightly packed; this is the best place to soak up the atmosphere but it's too crowded to take pictures. Tickets start at US$100 for *arquibancadas* and are sold at travel agencies as well as the Maracanã Stadium box office (see page 80). Travel agency: **Carnaval Turismo**, Av Nossa Senhora de Copacabana 583, T021-2548 4232, www.carnavalinrio.com.br. Tickets should be bought as far as possible in advance; they are usually sold out before Carnaval weekend but touts outside can often sell you tickets at inflated prices. Samba schools have an allocation of tickets which members sometimes sell, if you are offered one of these check the date. Tickets for the champions' parade on the Sat following Carnaval are much cheaper. Many tour companies offer Rio trips including Carnaval, but tickets are at inflated prices.

Sleeping and security

Be sure to reserve accommodation well in advance. Virtually all hotels raise their prices during Carnaval, although it is usually possible to find a reasonably priced room. Your property should be safe inside the Sambódromo, but the crowds outside can attract pickpockets; as ever, don't brandish your camera, and only take the money you need for fares and refreshments (food and drink are sold in the Sambódromo). It gets hot, so wear shorts and a T-shirt.

Taking part

Most samba schools will accept a number of foreigners and you will be charged from US$175 up to US$435 for your costume depending on which school of samba you choose. This money helps to fund poorer members of the school. You should be in Rio for at least 2 weeks before Carnaval. It is essential to attend fittings and rehearsals on time, to show respect for your section leaders and to enter into the competitive spirit of the event. For those with the energy and the dedication, it will be an unforgettable experience.

Rehearsals

Ensaios are held at the schools' *quadras* from Oct onwards and are well worth seeing. It is

wise to go by taxi, as most schools are based in poorer districts.

Carnaval shows

Tour agents sell tickets for glitzy samba shows, which are nothing like the real thing. When buying a Carnaval DVD, make sure the format is compatible (NTSC for USA or most of Europe; PAL for the UK, region 4).

Samba school addresses and parties

Samba schools hold parties throughout the year, especially at the weekends. These are well worth visiting. See websites for details.
Acadêmicos de Salgueiro, R Silva Teles 104, Andaraí, T021-2238 5564, www.salgueiro.com.br.
Beija Flor de Nilópolis, Pracinha Wallace Paes Leme 1025, Nilópolis, T021-2791 2866, www.beija-flor.com.br.
Imperatriz Leopoldinense, R Prof Lacê 235, Ramos, T021-2560 8037, www.imperatrizleopoldinense.com.br.
Mocidade Independente de Padre Miguel, R Coronel Tamarindo 38, Padre Miguel, T021-3332 5823, www.mocidadeindependente.com.br.
Portela, R Clara Nunes 81, Madureira, T021-2489 6440, www.gresportela.com.br.
Primeira Estação de Mangueira, R Visconde de Niterói 1072, Mangueira, T021-2567 4637, www.mangueira.com.br.
Unidos da Viradouro, Av do Contorno 16, Niterói, T021-2516 1301, www.gresuviradouro.com.br.
Vila Isabel, Boulevard 28 de Setembro, Vila Isabel, T021 2578 0077, www.gresunidosdevilaisabel.com.br.

Transport

Taxis to the Sambódromo are negotiable and will find your gate, the nearest metrô is Praça Onze and this can be an enjoyable ride in the company of costumed samba school members. You can follow the participants to the *concentração*, the assembly and formation on Av Presidente Vargas, and mingle with them while they queue to enter the Sambódromo. Ask if you can take photos.

Carnaval

Carnaval in Rio is as spectacular as its reputation suggests – a riot of colour, flamboyance and artistry unrivalled outside Brazil. On the Friday before Shrove Tuesday, the mayor of Rio hands the keys of the city to *Rei Momo*, the Lord of Misrule, signifying the start of a five-day party. Imagination runs riot, social barriers are broken and the main avenues, full of people and children wearing fancy dress, are colourfully lit. Areas throughout the city such as the Terreirão de Samba in Praça Onze are used for shows, music and dancing. Spectacularly dressed carnival groups throng around the Sambódromo (Oscar Niemeyer's purpose-built stadium, see page 78) strutting, drumming and singing in preparation for their parade. And there are *blocos* (parades) throughout the city, in neighbourhoods such as Santa Teresa and Ipanema. It can be ghostly quiet in the southern beach zones during this time.

Unlike Salvador, which remains a wild street party, Rio's Carnaval is a designated parade, taking place over a number of days and contained within the Sambódromo stadium. Alongside the parade are a number of *bailes* (parties) held within designated clubs, street shows like those held around Praça Onze.

There are numerous samba schools in Rio, which are divided into two leagues before they parade through the Sambódromo. The 14 schools of the *Grupo Especial* parade on Sunday and Monday while the *Grupos de Acesso* A and B parade on Saturday and Friday respectively. There is also a *mirins* parade (younger members of the established schools) on Tuesday. Judging takes place on Wednesday afternoon and the winners of the groups parade again on the following Saturday. Tickets to these winners' parades are always easy to get hold of even when all others are sold out.

Every school comprises 2500-6000 participants divided into *alas* (wings) each with a different costume and parading on or around five to nine *carros alegóricos* (beautifully designed floats). Each school chooses an *enredo* (theme) and composes a samba that is a poetic, rhythmic and catchy expression of the theme. The *enredo* is further developed through the design of the floats and costumes. A *bateria* (percussion wing) maintains a reverberating beat that must keep the entire school, and the audience, dancing throughout the parade. Each procession follows a set order with the first to appear being the *comissão de frente*

see page 78

Useful information

Carnaval week comprises an enormous range of official and unofficial contests and events, which reach a peak on the Tue. **Riotur**'s guide booklet and website gives concise information on these in English. The entertainment sections of newspapers and magazines such as *O Globo*, *Jornal do Brasil*, *Manchete* and *Veja Rio* are worth checking. Felipe Ferreira's guide to the Rio Carnaval, *Liga Independente das Escolas de Samba do Rio de Janeiro*, www.liesa.com.br, has good explanations of the competition, rules, the schools, a map and other practical details.

Other festivals

20 Jan The festival of São Sebastião, patron saint of Rio, is celebrated by an evening procession, leaving Capuchinhos church in Tijuca and arriving at the cathedral of São Sebastião. On the same evening, an *umbanda* festival is celebrated at the *Caboclo* monument in Santa Teresa.
Jun The Festas Juninas are celebrated throughout Brazil. In Rio they start with the **festival of Santo Antônio** on 13 Jun, when the main event is a Mass, followed by celebrations at the Convento do Santo Antônio and the Largo da Carioca. All over

(a choreographed group that presents the school and the theme to the public). Next comes the *abre alas* (a magnificent float usually bearing the name or symbol of the school). The *alas* and other floats follow as well as *porta bandeiras* (flag bearers) and *mestre salas* (couples dressed in 18th-century costumes bearing the school's flag), and *passistas* (groups traditionally of mulata dancers). An *ala of baianas* (elderly women with circular skirts that swirl as they dance) is always included as is the *velha guarda* (distinguished members of the school) who close the parade. Schools are given between 65 and 80 minutes and lose points for failing to keep within this time. Judges award points to each school for components of their procession, such as costume, music and design, and make deductions for lack of energy, enthusiasm or discipline. The winners of the *Grupos de Acesso* are promoted to the next higher group while the losers, including those of the *Grupo Especial*, are relegated to the next lowest group. Competition is intense and the winners gain a monetary prize funded by the entrance fees.

The Carnaval parades are the culmination of months of intense activity by community groups, mostly in the city's poorest districts. Rio´s *bailes* (fancy-dress balls) range from the sophisticated to the wild. The majority of clubs and hotels host at least one. The **Copacabana Palace**'s is elegant and expensive whilst the **Scala** club has licentious parties. It is not necessary to wear fancy dress; just join in, although you will feel more comfortable if you wear a minimum of clothing to the clubs, which are crowded, hot and rowdy. The most famous are the **Red and Black Ball** (Friday) and the **Gay Ball** (Tuesday) which are both televised. Venues then vary.

Bandas and *blocos* can be found in all neighbourhoods and some of the most popular and entertaining are: **Cordão do Bola Preta** (meets at 0900 on Saturday, Rua 13 de Maio 13, Centro); **Simpatia é Quase Amor** (meets at 1600 on Sunday, Praça General Osório, Ipanema) and the transvestite **Banda da Ipanema** (meets at 1600 on Saturday and Tuesday, Praça General Osorio, Ipanema). It is necessary to join a *bloco* in advance to receive their distinctive T-shirts, but anyone can join in with the *bandas*. The expensive hotels offer special Carnaval breakfasts from 0530. **Caesar Park** is highly recommended for a wonderful meal and a top-floor view of the sunrise over the beach.

the state, the **festival of São João** is a major event, marked by huge bonfires on the night of 23-24 Jun. It is traditional to dance the *quadrilha* and drink *quentão*, *cachaça* and sugar, spiced with ginger and cinnamon, served hot. The Festas Juninas close with the **festival of São Pedro** on 29 Jun. Being the patron saint of fishermen, his feast is normally accompanied by processions of boats.
Oct This is the month of the feast of **Nossa Senhora da Penha** (see page 80).
30 Dec Less hectic than Carnaval, but very atmospheric, is the **festival of Yemanjá** when devotees of the *orixá* of the sea dress in white and gather at night on Copacabana, Ipanema and Leblon beaches, singing and dancing around open fires and making offerings. The elected Queen of the Sea is rowed along the seashore. At midnight small boats are launched as offerings to Yemanjá. The religious event is dwarfed, however, by a massive New Year's Eve party, called **Reveillon** at Copacabana. The beach is packed as thousands of revellers enjoy free outdoor concerts by big-name pop stars, topped with a lavish midnight firework display. It is most crowded in front of the Copacabana Palace Hotel. Another good

place to see the fireworks is at the far end of the beach in front of R Princesa Isabel, famous for its fireworks waterfall at about 0010. Many followers of Yemanjá now make offerings on 29 or 30 Dec and at Barra da Tijuca or Recreio dos Bandeirantes to avoid the crowds and noise of Reveillon.

O Shopping

Rio de Janeiro *p60, maps p62 and p68*
Arts and crafts
La Vereda, R Almirante Alexandrino 428, Santa Teresa, T021-2507 0317, www.lavereda.art.br. Colourful arty little boutique filled with crafts, from illuminated favela models to textiles, toys and paintings.
Novo Desenho (ND), Av Infante Dom Henrique 85, Glória (next to MAM), T021-2524 2290, www.novodesenho.com.br. This pocket-sized boutique stocks a range of homeware and furniture from some of Brazil's best small artisan designers. These include established names such as Sergio Rodrigues (whose Mole chair is in MoMa New York's permanent collection) and Mendes-Hirth (who won an award at the 2010 iF Product Design Awards in Germany) alongside up-and-coming designers like Morito Ebine, whose chairs are built entirely of Brazilian wood with hardwood pins instead of screws. Many of the items are small enough to fit in a suitcase.
Santa Sucata, Estudantina Musical Ballroom, 3 piso, Praça Tiradentes 79, Centro. This small workshop above one of central Rio's most famous old school gafieira halls, Estudantina Musical, is home to artists like Maristela Pessoa and Jac Carrara, who work with groups from the favelas to turn rubbish into arts and crafts.

Bookshops
Da Vinci, Av Rio Branco 185, lojas 2, 3 and 9. All types of foreign books, Footprint guides are available.
Folha Seca R do Ouvidor 37, T021-2507 7175. Arty little bookshop tucked away next to

NS de Lapa church and with a good range of Brazilian photography and art books difficult to find elsewhere.
Livraria da Travessa, R Visconde de Pirajá 572, Ipanema, T021-3205 9002. Classy little bookshop with broad selection of novels, magazines and guidebooks in English. Great café upstairs for a coffee while you read.
Saraiva, R do Ouvidor 98, T021-2507 9500. A massive (megastore) bookshop which also includes a music and video shop and a café; other branches in **Shopping Iguatemi** and **Shopping Tijuca**.

Camping equipment
On R 1 de Março, north of Av Pres Vargas, are military shops which sell jungle equipment such as hammocks, mosquito nets and clothing, eg **Casa do Militar**, No 145 and **London**, No 155; you can also buy the Brazilian flag in any size you want here. **Malamada**, R da Carioca 13. Recommended for rucksacks.

Fashion
Fashion is one of the best buys in Brazil, with a wealth of Brazilian designers selling clothes of the same quality as European or US famous names at a fraction of the price. Rio is the best place in the world for buying high-fashion bikinis. The best shops in Ipanema are on Garcia D'Ávila and R Nascimento Silva, which runs off it. This is the home of some of the best Brazilian designers, such as **Andrea Saletto** and **Rosana Bernardes**, together with international big-name stalwarts like **Louis Vuitton** and **Cartier**, and Brazil's classiest jeweller, **Antonio Bernardo**. Most of the international names, together with all the big Brazilian names including **Lenny** (Brazil's best bikinis), **Alberta**, **Salinas**, **Club Chocolate** and so on, are housed in the São Conrado Fashion Mall.

In addition to those listed below, there are some little shops on Aires Saldanha, Copacabana (1 block back from beach), which are good for bikinis and cheaper than in the shopping centres.

Andrea Saletto, R Nascimento Silva 244, Ipanema, T021-2522 5858, and in the fashion mall, loja 211, T021-3225 4235. One of the most sophisticated labels in Rio – elegant and low-profile style, classical cuts and the use of light and tropical fabrics: cotton, linen and silk.

Blue Man, São Conrado Fashion Mall. Tiny, bright bikinis beloved of those with perfect bodies.

Bum Bum, R Visconde de Pirajá 351, Ipanema, T021-2287 9951, www.bumbum. com.br. Together with **Rosa Cha**, one of the most internationally renowned bikini designers, tiny and beautifully cut.

Carlos Tufvesson, R Nascimento Silva 304, Ipanema, T021-2523 9200, www.carlos tufvesson.com. Brazil's latest bright young star who received a standing ovation for his collection at the Barra fashion week in Rio. Sensual evening-wear in high-quality fabric.

Casa Turuna, Av Passos 77, T021-2509 3908, www.casaturuna.com. The places to buy your Carnaval costumes in or out of carnival season, together with samba skirts, masks and general pageantry. Open since 1915.

Lenny, R Visconde de Pirajá, 351, Ipanema, T021-2287 9951, and in the **São Conrado Fashion Mall**. Lenny Niemeyer is widely regarded as Brazil's most sophisticated bikini designer.

Maria Bonita, R Aníbal de Mendonça 135, Ipanema, T021-2540 5354. Impeccably cut, elegantly simple, sophisticated women's wear in high-quality fabrics. One of the oldest labels in Rio de Janeiro.

Osklen, R Maria Quitéria 85, Ipanema, T021-2227 2911, www.osklen.com. Elegant, casual-chic men's wear from a label which has been described as Brazil's answer to Ralph Lauren.

Saara is a multitude of little shops along R Alfândega and R Senhor dos Passos (between the city centre and Campo Santana), where clothing bargains can be found (especially jeans, kanga beach wraps and bikinis); it is known popularly as 'Shopping a Céu Aberto'.

Salinas, R Visconde de Pirajá 547, Ipanema, T021-2274 0644, and fashion mall, T021-2422 0677. Very highly regarded Brazilian bikinis: small, exquisitely made with great attention to detail and using only the best fabrics, in a variety of contemporary styles from hand crochet and beading to reversibles in multiple colour combinations.

Football souvenirs

Loja Fla, Av Nossa Senhora de Copacabana 219C, T021-2295 5057, www.lojafla.com.br. All things related to Brazil's favourite team – Flamengo, from rare and limited edition kit to, balls, boots, DVDs and memorabilia.

Jewellery

Only buy precious and semi-precious stones from reputable dealers. There are several good jewellery shops at the Leme end of Av NS de Copacabana.

Amsterdam Sauer, R Garcia D'Ávila 105. Have 10 shops in Rio and others throughout Brazil, plus St Thomas (US Virgin Islands) and New York; they offer free taxi rides to their main shop.

Antônio Bernado, R Garcia d'Ávila 121, Ipanema, T021-2512 7204, and in the **São Conrado Fashion Mall**. Brazil's foremost jeweller who has been making beautifully understated pieces with contemporary designs for nearly 30 years. Internationally well known but available only in Brazil.

H Stern, R Visconde de Pirajá 490 and R Garcia d'Ávila 113, Ipanema. 10 outlets, plus branches in major hotels throughout the city (as well as elsewhere in Brazil and worldwide).

Markets

The **Northeastern market** takes place at the Centro Luiz Gonzaga de Tradições Nordestinas, Campo de São Cristóvão, www.feiradesaocristovao.org.br, with music and magic, on Fri from 1800, Sat 0800-2200 and Sun 0800-1200 (bus No 472 or 474 from Copacabana or centre). There's a Sat **antiques market** on the waterfront near Praça 15 de Novembro, 1000-1700. Also on Praça 15 de Novembro is **Feirarte II**, Thu and Fri 0800-1800. **Feirarte I** is a Sun open-air handicrafts market (everyone calls it the **Feira Hippy**) at Praça Gen Osório, Ipanema, www.feirahippieipanema.com, Sun 0700-1900, touristy but fun: items from all over Brazil. **Babilônia Feira Hype** is held every other weekend at the Jockey Club 1400-2300. This lively and popular market has lots of stalls selling clothes and crafts, as well as massage and live music and dance performances. A **stamp and coin market** is held on Sun in the Passeio Público. There are **markets** on Wed 0700-1300 on R Domingos Ferreira and on Thu, same hours, on Praça do Lido, both Copacabana. Praça do Lido also has a **Feir arte** on Sat and Sun 0800-1800. There is an **artesania market** nightly by the Othon Hotel, near R Miguel Lemos: one part for paintings, one part for everything else. There's a **Sunday market** on R da Glória, colourful, cheap fruit, vegetables and flowers; and an early morning food market, 0600-1100, R Min Viveiros de Castro, Ipanema. Excellent **food and household goods markets** take place at various places in the city and suburbs (see newspapers for times and places). **Feira do Livro** is a book market that moves around various locations (Largo do Machado, Cinelândia, Nossa Senhora da Paz – Ipanema), selling books at 20% discount.

Music
Arlequim Música, Paço Imperial, Praça XV de Novembro 48, loja 1, T021-2220-8471, www.arlequim.com.br, Mon-Fri 1000-2000 Sat 1000-1800. A good selection of high-quality Brazilian music and film in a shop housed in the Paço Imperial. The **Livraria Imperial** bookshop occupies the same space and sells used books.
Modern Sound, R Barata Ribeiro 502D, Copacabana, T021-2548 5005, www.modern sound.com.br. For one of the best selections of Brazilian music in the city. Live performances most weekday nights from small, classy acts like the Bossa Jazz Trio and Delia Fischer.

Bossa Nova & Companhia, R Duvivier 37a, T021-2295 8096, www.bossanovae companhia.com.br. This long-established music shop underwent a full refurbishment and expansion in 2009, turning its tired wooden floors into chic, wavy dragon's-tooth paving, installing a little music museum in the basement, and re-stocking with the best selection of Bossa Nova, Chorinho and Brazilian jazz in the city. The music shop lies next to the Beco das Garrafas alley, where Tom Jobim and João Gilberto first played together,
Toca do Vinícius, R Vinícius de Moraes 129C, Ipanema, T021 2247 5227, www.tocado vinicius.com.br. Specializes in bossa nova books, CDs and souvenirs, doubles as a performance space.

Shopping centres
Shopping Leblon, Av Afrânio de Melo Franco 290, www.shoppingleblon.com.br. The most fashionable mall in the Zona Sul opened in late 2006. After the São Conrado Fashion Mall, it's the best one-stop shopping mall for Rio's most sought-after labels, which include boutiques from bikini brand Blue Man, Ellus (for jeans), Maria Bonita (for flowing, silk and satin dresses) and Carlos Miele (for dresses in sexy cuts and bold colors). The mall is less than 5 mins' walk from the beach.
Rio Sul, www.riosul.com.br, at the Botafogo end of Túnel Novo, has almost everything the visitor may need. It has been refurbished and is convenient and very safe. Some of the services available are: **Telemar** (phone office) for international calls at A10-A, Mon-Sat 1000-2200; next door is **Belle Tours Câmbio**, A10. There is a post office at G2. A good branch of the bookshop Saravia is at A03. Entertainment includes **Fisico e forma** gym on the 2nd floor; and a cinema, www.gsr.com.br, on the 4th floor. Eating places include fast food restaurants, 2 branches of **Shushi Rio** sushi bar and **Chaika** for milkshakes, ice creams and sandwiches (4th floor, original branch

on Praça NS da Paz, Ipanema). A US$5 bus service runs as far as the Sheraton passing the main hotels, every 2 hrs between 1000 and 1800, then 2130.

Other shopping centres, which have a wide variety of shops and services, include: São Conrado Fashion Mall, Estrada da Gavea 899, T021-2111 4444, www.scfashionmall. com.br; **Shopping Cidade Copacabana**, R Siqueira Campos, www.shoppingcidade copacabana.com.br; **Shopping Botafogo Praia**, Praia de Botafogo 400, T021-3171 9559, www.botafogopraiashopping.com.br; **Norte Shopping** (Todos os Santos); **Plaza Shopping** (Niterói); **Barra** in Barra da Tijuca.

▲ Activities and tours

Rio de Janeiro *p60, maps p62 and p68*
Boat trips
Several companies offer trips to **Ilha de Paquetá**, and day cruises, including lunch, to **Jaguanum Island**, and a sundown cruise around **Guanabara Bay**.
Moreno Urca, Quadrado de Urca, T021-9316 5733, www.morenourca.blogspot.com. Great low-key boat tours of the bay and Atlantic in a fisherman's wooden boat, calling at some of the less-visited sights – like Adam and Eve beach in Jurujuba, the Cagarras islands (for snorkelling) and the Forte São João. From US$45 with breakfast, juices and water and lunch included. Book ahead in high season as it's a litte boat. And bring sun protection.
Pink Fleet, Av Infante Dom Henrique s/n loja 2, Flamengo, T021-2555 4063, www.pink fleet.com.br. Bay and ocean cruises in a very comfortable big iron cruiser, the Spirit of Brazil. Restaurants, bars and plenty of shade on board.
Saveiros Tour, Av Infante Dom Henrique s/n lojas 13 & 14, Mon-Fri 900-1730, Sat-Sun 900-1200, T021-2225 6064, www.saveiros. com.br. Tours in sailing schooners around the bay and down the coast, also 'Baía da Guanabara Histórica' historical tours.

Cycling
Pedalario, Aluguel de Bicicleta (cycle hire), www.mobilicidade.com.br. There are 19 cycle hire stations in Rio (in Leblon, Ipanema, Copacabana and Lagoa). US$6 per day.

Driving tours and personal drivers
Dehouche (see Tour operators, page 127). Luxury tours around Rio city and state in top end a/c saloon cars. Very good English.
Madson Araujo, T021-9395 3537, www.tourguiderio.com. Bespoke personal tours of the Rio city sights and trips into Rio de Janeiro state. Full details on the comprehensive website. Many languages spoken and crisp, efficient service.
Otávio Monteiro, T021-8835 1160 or T021-7841 4799, om2brasil@hotmail.com. Good-value driver and personal tours will go anywhere in Rio or the state. Reliable, good English.
Roz Brazil, T024-9257 0236, www.rozbrazil. com. Some of the best tours around Petrópolis, Teresópolis and the Serra dos Órgãos with British Brazilian Rosa Thompson, who has been living in the area for decades. Pick-ups from Rio.

Football coaching
Pelé da Praia, R Garcia D'Avila, Ipanema, T021-9702 5794, www.peledapraia.com. Football and volleyball coaching from a real Carioca character who has been working on Ipanema beach for many years.

Hang-gliding and paragliding
Delta Flight, T021-3322 5750, T021-9693 8800, www.deltaflight.com.br. Hang-gliding rides above Rio from Pedra Bonita mountain with instructors licensed by the **Brazilian Hang-gliding Association**. 19 years of experience, and equipment is renewed every year. Contact Ricardo Hamond.
Just Fly, T/F021-2268 0565, T021-9985 7540 (mob), www.justfly.com.br. Tandem flights with Paulo Celani (licensed by the **Brazilian Hang-gliding Association**), pickup and

drop-off at hotel included, flights all year, best time of day 1000-1500 (5% discount for Footprint readers on presentation of this book at time of reservation).

Rejane Reis, Exotic Tours, (see Tour operators, page 127), arranges hang-gliding, paragliding, microlight flights, walks and other activities.

Ruy Marra, T021-3322 2286, www.rio superfly.com.br, or find him at the beach. Paragliding from Leblon beach with Brazilian paragliding champion (US$75).

Hiking and climbing

Clube Excursionista Carioca, R Hilário Gouveia 71, room 206, T021-2255 1348, www.carioca.org.br. Recommended for enthusiasts, meets Wed and Fri.

Diogo Monnerat, T021-7712 7489, diogo. monnerat@gmail.com. Hiking and climbing tours in Sugar Loaf and Tijuca's National Park, from beginners to experienced climbers.

Rio Hiking, T021-2552 9204 and T021-9721 0594, www.riohiking.com.br. Hiking tours around Rio city and state, including the Pedra da Gávea, Tijuca Park, Itatiaia and the Serra dos Órgãos and various city tours, including Santa Teresa. Run by friendly and fun Carioca mother and son team who speak excellent English.

Horse riding

See also **Rio Hiking,** above.
Sociedade Hípico Brasileira, Av Borges de Medeiros 2448, Lagoa, T021-2156 0156, www.shb.com.br.

Parachuting

Several people offer tandem jumps; check that they are accredited with the **Associação Brasileira de Vôo Livre,** www.abvl.com.br .

Barra Jumping, Aeroporto de Jacarepaguá, Av Ayrton Senna 2541, T021-3151 3602, www.barrajumping.com.br. Tandem jumping (*vôo duplo*).

Rafting

See **Rio Hiking,** above, for trips on the Paraibuna and Macaé rivers (both around 2 hrs from Rio).

Sailing

Confederação Brasileira de Vela e Motor, Av das AMÉRICAS 500 block 20 room 310, Downtown Barra, T021-3139 9200, www.cbvm.org.br. For information.
Federação de Vela, Praça Mahatma Gandhi 2, 12th floor, T021-2533 0194, www.feverj.org.br. For information.

Sea kayaking

See also **Rio Hiking,** above, for a variety of sea-kayaking tours.

Surfing

For more information on the state of the waves on the beaches in and around Rio de Janeiro, see *Footprint Surfing the World*. See also **Rio Hiking,** above, for surf lessons on Barra, Grumari and Prainha.

Contact **Associação Brasileira de Surf Profissional,** R Serzedelo Correia 15 room 804, Copacababa, T021-2235 3972, www.abrasp.com.br; **Confederação de Bodyboard do Estado do Rio de Janeiro,** R Barata Ribeiro 348/701, Copacabana, T022-2771 1802 ,T021-9219 3038, www.cbrasb.com.br; **Federação de Surf do Estado do Rio de Janeiro,** T021-7884 4226, www.feserj.com.br; **Organização dos Surfistas Profissionais do Rio de Janeiro,** R Visconde de Pirajá 580 shop 213, Ipanema.

Swimming

On all Rio's beaches you should take a towel or mat to protect you against sandflies. In the water stay near groups of other swimmers. There is a strong undertow.

Tour operators

Be A Local, T021-9643 0366, www.bea local.com. The best of the favela tours with walking trips around Rocinha and money going towards community projects; trips to *baile funk* parties at weekends and to football matches.

Cultural Rio, R Santa Clara 110/904, Copacabana, T021-3322 4872 or T021-9911 3829 (mob), www.culturalrio.com.br. Tours escorted personally by Professor Carlos Roquette, English and French spoken, almost 200 options available.

Dehouche, T021-2512 3895, www.dehouche.com. Luxury tailor-made tours throughout Brazil and Rio de Janeiro, including the best private flats, excursions to islands near Angra and the opportunity of driving a Ferrari around the Grand Prix circuit.

Fábio Sombra, T021-9729 5455 (mob), fabiosombra@hotmail.com. Offers private and tailor-made guided tours focusing on the cultural aspects of Rio and Brazil.

Favela Tour, Estr das Canoas 722, bl 2, apt 125, São Conrado, T021-3322 2727, T021-9989 0074 (mob), www.favelatour.com.br. Safe, interesting guided tours of Rio's favelas in English, French, Spanish, Italian, German and Swedish. For the best attention and price call Marcelo Armstrong direct rather than through a hotel desk.

Guanatur Turismo, R Dias da Rocha 16A, Copacabana, T021-2548 3275, www.guanaturturismo.com.br. Sells long-distance bus tickets.

Helisight, R Visconde de Pirajá 580, loja 107, Térreo, Ipanema, T021-2511 2141, www.helisight.com.br. Daily from 0900. Helicopter sightseeing tours. Prices from US$90 per person for 6-7 mins from Morro de Urca or the Lagoa over Sugar Loaf and Corcovado, to US$300 per person for 30 mins over the city.

Metropol, R São José 46, T021-2533 5010, www.metropolturismo.com.br. Cultural, eco, and adventure tours to all parts of Brazil.

Rejane Reis, Exotic Tours, T021-2179 6972, www.exotictours.com.br. Unusual trips throughout Rio such as *candomblé*, rafting or hikes up to the Pedra da Gávea. Cultural and favela tours. Good English spoken.

Rio by Jeep, T021-3322 5750, T021-9693 8800, www.riobyjeep.com. 5-hr tours in open or closed jeeps with local guides showing Rio from 3 perspectives: gorgeous beaches, historical downtown and Tijuca national park. Contact Ricardo Hamond.

Santa Teresa Tour, T021-2507 4417, www.santateresatour.com. Historical tours around the neighbourhood run by **Rio Hiking** (see Hiking, page 126) in a community support project along with people from the local favelas. Daily walks and tram tours from Lapa into Santa Teresa, usually departing from the Largo dos Guimarães or Lapa at 0930 daily. Book ahead.

Volleyball classes

For more general information and other schools see www.voleirio.com.br.

Escola de Vôlei da Leticia, Ipanema beach between R Farme de Amoedo and R Vinicius de Moraes, T021-9841 3833, escoladevolei daleticia@ig.com.br. Classes for adults and

children in Portuguese, Mon-Fri morning and afternoon. Run by Letícia Pessoa who has been working on Ipanema since 1995.
Escola de Vôlei do Renato, Copacabana beach in front of R Hilário de Gouvea, T021-9955 7480. Adult classes Mon-Fri 1900-2100, adult and 8-12 year olds Mon-Fri 0730-0930. Run by Renato França who has been working on the beach for 12 years.

⊖ Transport

Rio de Janeiro *p60, maps p62 and p68*

Air

See Ins and outs, page 60, for airport information. Metered taxis cost around US$30 from Copacabana to Jobim international airport. But the pre-booked (through desks in the airport) taxi – the *taxi especial* is safer. For the airport-based ones you pay a fixed rate before the journey, they are very reliable but also more expensive. Other special taxis run by the meter starting at R$5.70 (US$3.31), adding R$2.46 (US$1.43) per km. There are 2 bus lines with a/c, US$5, to/from the international airport 0530-2300 and 0530-2200 from the final stop in Barra. First bus No 2018, *Via Orla da Zona Sul* (south zone shore) run from the international airport to Av Rio Branco in the centre, Flamengo, Copacabana, Ipanema, Leblon, Gavea, São Conrado, Av das Americas with a final stop at the Terminal Alvorada bus station in Barra da Tijuca and then back on the same route. Second bus No 2018, *Via Linha Amarela* runs from the international airport to the express way Linha Amarela, Av Ayrton Senna, Aeroporto Jacarepagua, Barra Shopping and finally Av das Americas at Barra da Tijuca and then back to the aiport on the same route without a final stop. Contact **Real Auto**, T021-3035 6700, www.realautoonibus.com.br/site, for information. As well as international connections, Rio de Janeiro has flights to all the country's major airports, some via **São Paulo**, **Brasilia** or **Salvador**. The best

deals on flights within Brazil are available through: **GOL**, www.voegol.com.br; **Avianca**, www.avianca.com.br; and **TAM**, www.tam.com.br.
There is a shuttle flight between Santos Dumont airport and **São Paulo** (Congonhas airport, US$250 single, US$450 return). The shuttle operates every 30 mins throughout the day from 0630-2230. Sit on the right-hand side for views to São Paulo, the other side coming back, book flights in advance.

Airline offices
Aerolíneas Argentinas, Av Rio Branco 134 – 7°/701, T021-2103 4201, T0800-707 3313, www.aerolineas.com.ar. **Air France**, Av Pres Antônio Carlos 58, 9th floor, T4003 9955, airport, terminal 1, T021-3398 3686. **American**, Av Pres Wilson 165, 5th floor, Centro, Av das Americas 6700 shop 109/bl2, Barra, T021-4502 5005, airport office terminal 1, T021-3398 4929. **Avianca**, international airport office T021-3398 4648, T4004 4040, T021-2531 0204. **British Airways**, airport terminal 1, T021-3398 3889, T0800-761 0885. **Continental** airport terminal 1, T021-3398 4105, T0800-0702 7500, www.continental.com. **Copa Airlines**, airport terminal 1, T021-3398 3302, T0800-771 2672, www.copaair.com. **Delta Airlines**, airport, T021-3398 3828, www.delta.com. Gol airport terminal 1, T021-3398 3233, www.voegol.com.br. **Iberia**, Av Pres Antônio Carlos 51, 8th and 9th floors, T021-2282 1336, airport terminal 1 T021-3398 3425. **Lan Chile**, airport terminal 1 T021-3398 4390, www.lan.com. **Pantanal**, T0800-702 5888, www.voepantanal.com.br. **Pluna Lineas Aereas Uruguayas**, airport terminal 1, T021-3398 3721, www.pluna.aero. **Taag**, terminal 1, T021-3398 3113, www.taag.com.br. **Taca Peru**, airport terminal 1, T021-3398-5168, T0800-761 8222, www.taca.com. **TAM**, airport terminal 2, T021-3398 2179, www.tam.com.br. **TAP**, Av Rio Branco 311-B, T0300-210 6060, airport terminal 2, T021-3398 3768, www.flytap.com. **United**, airport terminal 2, T021-3398 2461, www.united.com. **US Airways**, airport

terminal 2, T021-3398 2300, www.usairways.
com. **Webjet**, airport terminal 2, T021-3398
2137, www.webjet.com.br.

Bicycle
There are cycle paths all along Rio's beaches
and the number of Carioca cyclists is on the
increase. In total, Rio has about 140 km of
cycle paths and over 6 km run through the
Tijuca National Park. It is the biggest cycle
path in the country and it transports about
300,000 people daily. In the face of ever-more
traffic-choked streets, the local government
has initiated a new scheme to encourage
cyclists called *Pedalario, Aluguel de Bicicleta*
(cycle hire), www.mobilicidade.com.br. There
are 19 cycle hire stations in Leblon, Ipanema,
Copacabana and Lagoa, and 11 more are
being built. The cost of hire is US$6 per day
(you will need a mobile phone and a credit
card in order to hire one) or US$12 per
month. For the monthly scheme it's
necessary to enrol on the website first. In
2009 56 bikes were stolen, so they increased
the security. There is a map with the stations
marked on the website. The website is in
Portuguese. Some hostels also have have
bicycles for rent. Check the cycle path map
on this link: www.ta.org.br/site2/index.htm.
Note that the cycle path is a new space in
Rio that people are learning to respect –
you might find pedestrians, dogs and skaters
on it. Early in the morning it's quieter. Make
sure you lock the bikes well. Be careful on
the roads themselves. Carioca drivers are
generally disrespectful of other road users,
and especially of cyclists.

Bus
Local
There are good services to all parts of the city,
but buses are very crowded and not for the
aged and infirm during rush hours. Buses
have turnstiles which are awkward if you are
carrying luggage. Hang on tight, drivers live
out Grand Prix fantasies. At busy times allow
about 45 mins to get from Copacabana to the
centre by bus. The fare on standard buses is

US$1.40; suburban bus fares are up to US$3
depending on the distance. Bus stops are
often not marked. The route is written on
the side of the bus, but it's hard to see until
the bus has actually pulled up at the stop.
    Private companies, including **Real, Pegaso**
and **Anatur**, operate a/c *frescão* buses, which
can be flagged down practically anywhere.
They run from all points in Rio Sul to the city
centre, *rodoviária* and the airports. Fares are
US$3 (US$5 to the international airport).
    City Rio is an a/c tourist bus service with
security guards, which runs between all the
major parts of the city. Bus stops, marked
by grey poles, are found where there are
concentrations of hotels. Good maps show
what places of interest are close to each bus
stop. Timetables change frequently. Hotels
can provide the latest information on when
the buses run.

Long distance
Rio's interstate bus station, the **Rodoviária
Novo Rio** (see Ins and outs, page 64),
www.novorio.com.br, is just north of the city
centre and can be reached by buses: No 326,
Bancários–Castelo, from the centre and the
airport; No 136: Rodoviária–Copacabana
via Glória, Flamengo, and Botafogo; No127,
Rodoviária–Copacabana (via Tunel do
Pasmado); No 172, Rodoviária–Leblon
(via Joquei and Jardim Botânico); No 128,
Rodoviária–Leblon (via Copacabana and
Ipanema); No 170, Rodoviária–Gávea (via
Glória, Botafogo, Jardim Botânico). The area
around the bus station is not safe after dark
and you should beware of thieves at any
time. Take a taxi to or from the nearest metrô
station (Estácio or Praça Onze) or to your
hotel. **Riotur** has a booth in the bus station
that can help with hotel reservations and
point you to the taxi bookings stand.
    Buses run from Rio to every state capital
and many smaller cities in all parts of the
country from Belém in the far north to
Porto Alegre and the Uruguay border in
the far south. There are departures to major
destinations, such as São Paulo, more than

every hour. It is advisable to book in advance in high season and weekends. Travel agencies throughout the city sell tickets as do many hostels. Otherwise turn up at least 90 mins before your bus leaves to buy a ticket. Timetables, companies and platform information and the most up to date prices are available on www.novorio.com.br; type your destination into the box provided.

Most street travel agents and hostels sell *passagens de onibus* (interstate bus tickets), or will direct you to a company that does so. Agencies include **Dantur Passagens e Turismo**, Av Rio Branco 156, subsolo loja 134, Metro Carioca, T021-2262 3424/3624, www.dantur.com.br; **Guanatur**, R Dias da Rocha 16A, Copacabana, T021-2235 3275, www.guanaturturismo.com.br; **Paxtur Passagens**, R República do Líbano 61 loja L, Center, T021 3852 2277; and an agency at R Visconde de Pirajá 303, loja 114, Ipanema, T021 2523 1000. They charge about US$3 for bookings.

Within Rio state

To **Niteroi**, No 761D Gávea–Charitas (via Jardim Botânico and Botafogo); 751D Galeão–Charitas and 741D Leme–Charitas (via Copacabana, Botafogo, Lapa and Santos Dumont airport), US$3. Frescões Gávea–Charitas, Galeão–Charitas, all run between Rio and Niterói.

To **Búzios**, buses leave every 2 hrs 0600-2000 daily from Rio's *rodoviária* (US$21, 2½ hrs). Go to the **1001** counter, T021-4004 5001 for tickets or buy online at www.autoviacao1001.com.br/en. Buying the ticket in advance is recomended in high season and on major holidays. You can also take any bus from Rio to the town of **Cabo Frio** (these are more frequent), from there take the Viação Salineira bus, it runs every 30 mins, US$2, from where it's 30 mins to Búzios and vice versa.

To **Petrópolis**, buses leave the *rodoviária* every 15 mins throughout the day (US$9.50) and every hour on Sun, buy tickets from **Única & Fácil** counter, www.unica-facil.com.br.

The journey takes 1½ hrs. Sit on the left-hand side for the best views.

To **Angra dos Reis**, buses run at least hourly Mon-Sat from the *rodoviária* with **Costa Verde**, www.costaverdetransportes. com.br, some direct; several go through Copacabana, Ipanema and Barra then take the *via litoral*, sit on the left, US$21, 2½ hrs. You can flag down the bus in Flamengo, Copacabana, Ipanema, Barra da Tijuca, but it may well be full on Sat and bank holidays. To link up with the ferry to Ilha Grande be sure to catch a bus before 1000.

International

There are no direct buses from Rio to **Asunción**. There are direct buses to **Campo Grande**, **Florianopolis**, **Curitiba** and **Foz do Iguaçu**, all of which are reachable from Rio. To **Buenos Aires** (from *rodoviária* buses with **Crucero Del Norte**, T021-2253 2960, ww.crucerodelnorte.com.ar or **Pluma**, www.pluma.com.br), via **Porto Alegre** and **Santa Fe**, 48 hrs, US$146 (book 2 days in advance). Buses also to **Sao Paulo**, **Camburiu**, **Florianopolis** and **Porto Alegre**. To **Santiago de Chile**, (Pluma US$197, or Gen Urquiza), 70 hrs.

Car

Service stations are closed in many places on Sat and Sun. Road signs are notoriously misleading in Rio and you can end up in a favela (take special care if driving along the Estr da Gávea to São Conrado as it is possible to unwittingly enter Rocinha, Rio's biggest slum).

Car hire

There are many agencies on Av Princesa Isabel, Copacabana. A credit card is essential for hiring a car. Recent reports suggest it is cheaper to hire outside Brazil; you may also obtain more comprehensive insurance this way. **Avis**, Antônio Carlos Jobim international airport, T021-3398 5060, Santos Dumont airport, T021-3814 7378, Av Princesa Isabel 150A and B, Copacabana, T021-2543 8481, www.avis.com.br; **Hertz**, international airport, T021-3398 4338, Av Princesa Isabel 500, Copacabana, T021-2275 7440; **Localiza**, international airport, T021-3398 3107 and Santos Dumont airport, T0800-992000, Av Princesa Isabel 150, Copacabana, T021-2275 3340; **Nobre**, Av Princesa Isabel 7, Copacabana, T021-2295 1799; **Telecar**, R Figueiredo Magalhães 701, Copacabana, T021-2548 6778.

Distances and journey times from Rio

Juiz de Fora, 184 km (2¾ hrs); **Belo Horizonte**, 434 km (7 hrs); **São Paulo**, 429 km (6 hrs); **Vitória**, 521 km (8 hrs); **Curitiba**, 852 km (12 hrs); **Brasília**, 1148 km (20 hrs); **Florianópolis**, 1144 km (20 hrs); **Foz do Iguaçu**, 1500 km (21 hrs); **Porto Alegre**, 1553 km (26 hrs); **Salvador**, 1649 km (28 hrs); **Recife**, 2338 km (38 hrs); **Fortaleza**, 2805 km (48 hrs); **São Luís**, 3015 km (50 hrs); **Belém**, 3250 km (52 hrs).

Ferry

Every 10 mins ferries and launches cross Guanabara Bay for **Niterói** from the 'Barcas' terminal at Praça 15 de Novembro, www.barcas-sa.com.br. The journey takes 20-30 mins and costs US$1.70. Catamarans (*aerobarcas*) also leave every 10 mins but take just 12 mins and cost US$1.70 (same price as a *barca* ferry). There are also more expensive catamarans and motor boats that take 9 mins. The slow, cheaper ferry gives the best views. From Niterói, ferries and catamarans return to Rio de Janeiro from the city centre terminal at Praça Araribóia and at Charitas district.

Metrô

See page 64 and map, page 61. www.metrorio.com.br. The current 2 metrô lines are fast, clean, a/c and safe. Most stations are open Mon-Fri 0500-2400, though a few close at different times with a couple closing as early as 1700 (check website or timetable); Sat 0500-2400 with some stations closing at 1400; Sun and bank holiday 0700-2300, with at least 25% of

stations not opening at all. During Carnival most stations are open 24 hrs. The fare is US$1.70 single; multi-tickets and integrated bus/metrô tickets are available. There is also a pre-paid card, *Cartão Pré-Pago* the minimal initial paymet is US$5.85, any minimal additional after that US$3. These can only be bought at the stations. Free metro maps are available at the counter. Note that Rio Metro has a women-only designated wagon Mon-Fri 0600-0900 and 1700-2000, it is the last wagon of each train, and has a pink stripe across the top, but many women still prefer to travel with men and often some distracted men pop into the pink wagon. Substantial changes in bus operations are taking place because of the extended metrô system; buses connecting with the metrô have a blue-and-white symbol in the windscreen. **Line 1 (Orange)** operates between the inner suburb of Tijuca (station Saens Peña), to Ipanema (staion General Osório) via the railway station (Central), Glória, Botafogo, Arcoverde.

Line 2 (Green) runs from the northen outskirt suburb of Pavuna to Botafogo, passing Engenho da Rainha, the Maracanã stadium, Central and then goes along the shore parallel to Line 1.

By 2015 Rio has committed itself to building a new line (**Linha 4**) between the city centre and Barra da Tijuca in the south, in time for the Olympics in 2016. However, it has taken 8 years to complete the last 2 metrô stations in Copacabana and Ipanema so some are sceptical. There are also even grander plans to build Line 3 to Niterói via an underwater tunnel beneath Guanabara Bay, however this is not scheduled for completion before the 2016 Olympics.

Taxi

See also Ins and outs, page 60. The common taxis in Rio are yellow and blue and work by meter. There are 2 price bands, and there is a little flag on the meter that the driver tugs to choose the band. Bandeira 1 runs Mon-Sat 0600-2100, with the meter starting at R$4.30 (US$2.50) and then adding R$1.40 (US$0.81) per km. Bandeira 2 runs, Mon-Sat 21.00-06.00 as well as Sun and bank holiday, it starts at R$5.70 (US$3.32) adding R$2.46 (US$1.43) per km. The websites www.taxisimples.com.br/rio-de-janeiro, www.tarifadetaxi.com/rio-de-janeiro have a Rio map and calculate the approximate taxi price for you. The fare between Copacabana and the centre is around US$30. Tip: print a copy of the map and have it at hand so you can monitor your jouney. Some common taxis drivers sneakily choose the long way round in order to overcharge. Taxis have red number plates with white digits (yellow for private cars, with black digits). Smaller ones (mostly Volkswagen) are marked TAXI on the windscreen or roof. Make sure meters are cleared and on the right price band. It is safest to use taxis from *pontos* – taxi ranks that are abundant throughout the city. *Ponto* taxis have the name of the *ponto* painted on the outside, indicating which *ponto* they belong to. Radio taxis are safer but almost twice as expensive, depending on the co-op they have different colors, eg **Cootramo**, blue, T021-3976 9944, www.cootramo.com.br; **Coopertramo**, white,T021-2209 9292, www.radio-taxi.com.br; **Central Táxi**, yellow and blue, T021-2195 1000, www.centraltaxi.com.br; **Transcoopass**, red, T021-2209 1555, www.transcoopass.com.br; **Coopacarioca**, yellow and blue, T021 2158 1818, www.cooparioca.com.br. If you get a radio/co-op taxi (aka taxi especial) at the airport you will pay in advance, buying the ticket at the airport special taxi booth. In this case the meter will be off but if you get into one outside the airport, the meter should be turned on. It will cost you about US$40 or US$45 to Copacabana, Ipanema. It is better to buy the ticket in advance – you will know for sure how much you are paying.

Train

Buses marked 'E Ferro' go to the train station. There are suburban trains to **Nova Iguaçu**, **Nilópolis**, **Campo Grande** and elsewhere. Supervia is the main company that sells tickets, www.supervia.com.br. None of the destinations are of tourist interest, they can be rough and dangerous, mainly at night. The station Central do Brasil is worth a visit and occasionally hosts cultural events and music concerts, check the program on the Supervia website.

Tram

See also Ins and outs, page 60, and Santa Teresa, page 81. The last remaining tram runs from near the Largo da Carioca (there is a museum open Fri only 0830-1700) across the old aqueduct (Arcos) to Dois Irmãos or Paula Mattos in **Santa Teresa**; a historical and interesting journey, US$0.40.

⊙ Directory

Rio de Janeiro *p60, maps p62 and p68*
Banks
Bradesco, R do Carmo 71 SS, Centro, T021-3970 6555; Banco do Brasil, Av Mal Floriano 114 Centro, T021-2514 8988; Bradesco, Av NS de Copacabana 709 A, Copacabana, T021-32999550; Banco do Brasil, Av NS de Copacabana 1274, Copacabana, T021-32025100; Bradesco, R Visconde de Pirajá 102 B lj A, Ipanema, T021-2522 2611; Banco do Brasil (R Joana Angélica 124, Ipanema, T021-3554 9700; Banco do Brasil, International Airport Antonio Carlos Jobim, T021-3398 4748.

Currency exchange Most large hotels and reputable travel agencies will change currency and TCs. Copacabana (where rates are generally worse than in the centre) is full of *câmbios* and there are also many on Av Rio Branco. **American Express**, Copacabana Palace, Av Atlântica 1702, loja 1, T021-2548 2148, Mon-Fri 0900-1600, Av das Americas 500 bl2 loja 113, Barra da Tijuca and at Antônio Carlos Jobim international airport, T021-3398 4251 (VIP room 1st floor), good rates (T0800-785050 toll-free); **Câmbio Belle Tours**, Rio Sul Shopping, ground floor, loja 101, parte A-1C

Botafogo, www.belletours.com.br, Mon-Fri 1000-1800, Sat 1000-1700, changes cash. In the gallery at Largo do Machado 29 are **Câmbio Nick** at loja 22 and, next door but one, **Casa Franca**.

Dentists

Amílcar Werneck de Carvalho Vianna, Av Visconde de Pirajá 550, Ipanema, T021-2512 7512, English-speaking; **Dr Mauro Svartz**, R Visconde de Pirajá 414, room 509, T021-2521 5196, speaks English and Hebrew, helpful.

Embassies and consulates

Argentina, Praia de Botafogo 228/201, T021-2553 1646, Mon-Fri, 100-1300 and 1330-1530, very helpful over visas; **Australia**, Av Presidente Wilson 231 23rd floor, T021-3824 4624, honconau@terra. com.br; **Austria**, Av Atlântica 3804, Copacabana T021-2102 0020; **Canada**, Av Atlântica 1130, 5th floor, Copacabana, T021-2543 3004; **Denmark**, Av Rio Branco 45 sala 1902, T021-3466 6466; **France**, Av Pres Antônio Carlos 58, T021-3974 6699; **Germany**, R Pres Carlos de Campos 417, T021-2554 0004; **Israel**, Av NS de Copacabana 680, T021-2548 5432; **Netherlands**, Praia de Botafogo 242, 10th floor, T021-2552 9028 (Dutch newspapers here and at KLM office on Av Rio Branco); **Paraguay**, same address, 2nd floor, T021-2553 2294, visas US$5; **Sweden**, **Finland** and **Norway**, Praia do Flamengo 344, 9th floor, T021-2553 5505; **Switzerland**, R Cândido Mendes 157, 11th floor, T021-2221 1867; **UK**, Praia do Flamengo 284, 2nd floor, T021-2555 9600, T021-2553 3223 (consular section direct line), T021-2555 9671, consular section is open Mon-Fri 0900-1230 (consulate 0830-1700), metrô Flamengo, or bus No 170, the consulate issues a useful *Guidance for Tourists* pamphlet; **Uruguay**, Praia de Botafogo 242, 5th floor, T021-2553 6030; **USA**, Av Pres Wilson 147, T021-22927117, Mon-Fri 0800-1100, passports 1330-1500.

Immigration

Federal Police, Av Rodrigues Alves 13th floor Centro T021 2203 4000. To renew a 90-day visa, US$45. Renew at least a week before your visa runs out and allow 4 hrs for the bureaucratic process of queuing and form filling.

Internet

Internet cafés are easy to find throughout the city. There are several places in **Rio Sul** shopping centre, Botafogo; many on Av NS de Copacabana, and others on R Visconde de Pirajá, Ipanema. **Phone Serv**, Av NS de Copacabana 454, loja B, US$3 per hr internet, telephone service. **Tudo é Fácil** has 3 branches in Copacabana: R Xavier da Silveira 19; Av Prado Júnior 78; and R Barata Ribeiro 396, www.tudoefacil.com.br. Well organized, with identification cards so once registered you can bypass the front desk, telephone booths and scanners, US$2 per hr, discounts for extended use.

Language courses

Instituto Brasil-Estados Unidos, Av N Sra de Copacabana 690, www.ibeu.org.br, 5th floor, 8-week course, 3 classes a week, US$150, 5-week intensive course US$260, good English library at same address; **IGI Instituto Globus de Idiomas**, R do Catete 310, sala 303/305, www.institutoglobus.com.br, US$26 per hr for individual lessons, cheaper for groups, helpful staff, recommended.

Laundry

Lavanderia Luar, R Pedro Américo 110, Catete; **Laundromat** at Av NS de Copacabana 1138 shop B; **Lavanderia 5ASec**, Visconde de Pirajá 631A, Ipanema, T021-2294 8142; **Lavelev Flamengo**, R Buarque Macedo 43 B, Catete. In **Rio Sul** there are self-service launderettes such as **Lavelev**, about US$7 for a machine, including detergent and drying, 1 hr. There are also laundrettes at: R Voluntários da Patria 248, Botafogo; and Av Prado Júnior 63B, Copacabana.

Medical services

Hospital Miguel Couto, Mário Ribeiro 117, Gávea, T021-3111 3800, has a free casualty ward. **Hospital Municipal Rocha Maia**, R Gen Severiano 91, Botafogo, T021-2295 2295/2121, near Rio Sul shopping centre, a good public hospital for minor injuries and ailments; free, but there may be queues; **Policlínica**, Av Nilo Peçanha 38, www.pgrj.org.br, for diagnosis and investigation. **Saúde dos Portos**, Praça Mcal Âncora, T021-2240 8628/8678, Mon-Fri 1000-1100, 1500-1800. For vaccinations; vaccination book and ID required.

Post

The **Central Post Office** is on R 1 de Março 64, at the corner of R do Rosário. Also at Av NS de Copacabana 540 and many other locations, www.correios.com.br. All handle international post. There is a post office at Antônio Carlos Jobim international airport; **Federal Express**, R Nair 135, Olaria, is reliable.

Poste Restante at Correios, Av NS de Copacabana 540 and all large post offices (letters held for a month, recommended, US$0.10 per letter).

Students

Student Travel Bureau, Av Nilo Peçanha 50, SL 2417, Centro, T/F021-2544 2627, and R Visconde de Pirajá 550, loja 201, Ipanema, T021-2512 8577, www.stb.com.br, has details of travel, discounts and cultural exchanges for ISIC holders.

Telephone

International telephone booths are blue. International calls can be made at larger **Correios**, eg Av NS de Copacabana 540; larger **Embratel** offices also have telex and fax; at the airports and the Novo Rio *rodoviária*; at R Dias da Cruz 192, Méier-4, 24 hrs, 7 days a week; in Urca, near the Pão de Açúcar cable car; at Praça Tiradentes 41, a few mins' walk from metrô Carioca; at R Visconde de Pirajá 111, Ipanema; and at R do Ouvidor 60, Centro.

Telephone numbers often change in Rio de Janeiro and other Brazilian cities. If in doubt, phone **Auxilio à Lista**, T102, which is the current daily updated directory of telephone numbers. This number can be used all over the country, but if you want to find out a Rio phone number from outside Rio, dial the city code 021, then 121. Note that these services are in Portuguese, so you may need to seek assistance from a hotel receptionist or similar. For further details on Brazil's telephone system, see Essentials, page 49.

Toilets

There are very few public toilets in Rio de Janeiro, but shopping centres, many bars and restaurants (eg McDonald's) offer facilities. Just ask for the *banheiro*.

East of Rio de Janeiro

Rio de Janeiro state is one of Brazil's smallest, but it is packed with great things to see. East of Rio the country gets drier and looks more Mediterranean. The coast, which is lined with fabulous beaches for hundreds of kilometres, is backed by a long series of saltwater lakes and drifting sand dunes. Most visitors ignore Niterói, the city immediately opposite Rio across Guanabara Bay, despite the fact is has ocean beaches as good as or better than Rio's. Instead, they head straight for the surf towns around Cabo Frio or the fashionable little resort of Búzios, which has good beaches and lively summer nightlife. ➤➤ *For listings, see pages 140-146.*

Niterói → *For listings, see pages 140-146. Colour map 4, C3.*

Cariocas are rude about everywhere, but they are especially rude about their neighbour across Guanabara Bay. The only good thing about Niterói, they say, is the view it has of Rio de Janeiro. As a result few visitors make it here. However, its ocean beaches are less polluted and far less crowded than Rio's and the views from them across the bay, especially at sunset, are wonderful. Oscar Niemeyer's Museu de Arte Contemporânea, a flying-saucer-shaped building perched on a promontory in Niterói is one of his very best buildings. There is no reason to stay overnight in Niterói but the city is well worth visiting as a day trip or on the way to Búzios.

Ins and outs

Getting there Ferries and launches to Niterói leave from the 'Barcas' terminal at Praça 15 de Novembro in central Rio, www.barcas-sa.com.br. Boats run every 10 minutes and the journey takes 20-30 minutes, US$1.70. *Aerobarcas* (catamarans) take just three minutes and cost US$1.70. Boats arrive at the Praça Araribóia city centre terminal in Niterói and at Charitas district.

Bus Nos 761D Gávea–Charitas (via Jardim Botânico and Botafogo), 751D Galeão–Charitas, and 741D Leme-Charitas (via Copacabana, Botafogo, Lapa and Santos Dumont airport), US$3, and Frescões Gávea–Charitas, Galeão–Charitas, all run between Rio and Niterói. If you are driving, the bridge across Guanabara Bay is well signposted. There is a toll of US$2.50 per car.

Getting around To get to the ocean beaches from Niterói, take bus Nos 38 or 52 from Praça General Gomes Carneiro or a bus from the street directly ahead of the ferry entrance, at right angles to the coast road. For Jurujuba take bus No 33 from the boat dock; sit on the right-hand side, it's a beautiful ride.

Tourist information Contact **Neltur** ① *Estrada Leopoldo Fróes 773, São Francisco, T021-2710 2727, www.neltur.com.br.*

Sights

Surrounded by long curved walkways, the space-age building of the **Museu de Arte Contemporânea** ① *Mirante da Boa Viagem, T021-2620 2400, www.macniteroi.com.br, Tue-Sun 1100-1800, US$2.90, free Wed,* is rapidly becoming the most famous work by Brazil's celebrated disciple of Le Corbusier, Oscar Niemeyer. It is in a fabulous location, sitting above a long bach with a sweeping view across Guanabara Bay to Rio as a backdrop. The building itself looks like a Gerry Anderson vision of the future; one can almost imagine *Thunderbird 1* taking off through its centre. The main gallery is a white circle of polished concrete perched on a low monopod and sitting in a reflection pool. It is reached by a coiling, serpentine ramp which meets the building on its second storey. The exhibitions comprise seasonal shows and a permanent collection of Brazilian contemporary art of all disciplines. The top level is devoted to temporary displays and the intermediate to the permanent collection. Niemeyer overcomes the problem of the unsuitability of a curved space for the exhibition of art by using an inner hexagonal core enclosed by flat screen walls. More difficult to overcome is that the glimpses of the stunning panorama of Rio through the gaps in the hexagon are far more captivating than most of the art. The building is worth seeing at dusk when it is lit; the sky above the streetlights of Rio is light peacock blue infused with lilac and the distant figure of the Corcovado Christ shines brilliant xenon-white over the dark mass of mountains.

Many buildings associated with the city's period as state capital are grouped around the **Praça da República**. None are open to the public. The city's main thoroughfare, Avenida Ernâni do Amaral Peixoto, runs from the *praça* and is lined with buildings similar to Avenida Presidente Vargas in Rio. At the end of the avenue is the dock for Rio, a statue of the indigenous chief, Araribóia, and **Bay Market Shopping Centre**.

Perched on a rocky promontory at the mouth of Guanabara Bay, the 16th-century **Fortaleza Santa Cruz** ① *Estrada General Eurico Gaspar Dutra, Jurujuba, T021-2711 0462, Tue-Sun 0900-1600, US$2, compulsory guided tour in Portuguese only*, is still used by the Brazilian military and is the most important historical monument in Niterói. As well as the usual range of cannon, dungeons and bulwarks the tour includes a visit to gruesome execution sites and a little chapel dedicated to Saint Barbara. The statue of the saint inside was originally destined for Santa Cruz dos Militares in Rio. However, unlike most Cariocas, the saint obviously prefers Niterói: any attempts to move her image from here have allegedly been accompanied by violent storms.

Beaches

The beaches closest to the city centre are unsuitable for bathing (Gragoatá, Vermelha, Boa Viagem, das Flechas). The next beaches along, also in the city and with polluted water, have more in the way of restaurants, bars and nightlife and some of the best views in the whole country, especially at sunset and sunrise. **Icaraí** is the smartest district, with the best hotels and good nightlife. Together with **São Francisco** and **Charitas**, there are good views out across the bay to Rio. The road continues round the bay, past Preventório and Samanguaiá to **Jurujuba**, a fishing village at the end of the No 33 bus route. About 2 km from Jurujuba along a narrow road are the attractive twin beaches of **Adão** and **Eva** beneath the Fortaleza Santa Cruz with more lovely views of Rio across the bay. These beaches are often used for *candomblé* (Brazilian-African spirit religion) ceremonies.

Piratininga, **Camboinhas**, **Itaipu** and **Itacoatiara**, four fabulous stretches of sand, are the best in the area, about 40 minutes from Niterói through picturesque countryside. Buses leave from the street directly ahead of the ferry entrance, at right angles to the coast road. The undertow at Itacoatiara is dangerous, but the waves are popular with surfers and the beach itself is safe. Itaipu is also used by surfers.

Costa do Sol → *For listings, see pages 140-146.*

To the east of Niterói lies a series of saltwater lagoons, the **Lagos Fluminenses**. Two small lakes lie behind the beaches of Piratininga, Itaipu and Itacoatiara, but they are polluted and ringed by mud. The next lakes, **Maricá** and **Saquarema**, are much larger; although they are still muddy, the waters are relatively unpolluted and wildlife abounds in the scrub and bush around the lagoons. This is a prime example of the *restinga* (coastal swamp and forest) environment. The RJ-106 road runs behind the lakes en route to Cabo Frio and Búzios, but an unmade road goes along the coast between Itacoatiara and Cabo Frio, giving access to the many long, open beaches of Brazil's Costa do Sol. The whole area is perfect for camping.

Maricá → *Colour map 4, C3. Phone code: 022. Population: 60,500.*

The 36-km Itaipu–Açu road, with many wild, lonely stretches, leads to Maricá, a sleepy fishing village with sand streets, on its own lagoon. There is good walking in the **Serra do Silvado**, 14 km away on the road to Itaboraí. Between Maricá and Saquarema are **Ponta Negra** and **Jaconé**, both surfing beaches. Information is available from the **tourist office** ① *Av Ver Francisco Sabino da Costa 945, Centro Maricá, T021-9952 0512, www.marica.rj.gov.br.*

Saquarema → *Colour map 4, C3. Phone code: 022. Population: 44,000.*

Saquarema is a fishing and holiday village, known as the centre for surfing in Brazil. Its cold, open seas provide consistent, crashing waves of up to 3 m. Frequent national and international championships take place here, but beware of strong currents. The lovely white church of **Nossa Senhora de Nazaré** (1675) is on a green promontory jutting into the ocean. Local legend has it that on 8 September 1630, fishermen, saved from a terrible storm, found an image of the Virgem de Nazaré in the rocks. A chapel was founded on the spot and subsequent attempts to relocate the Virgin (as when the chapel was falling into disrepair) resulted in her miraculously returning to the original site. For **tourist information** ① *R Coronel Madureira 77, Centro Saquarema, T022-9972 7251, www.saquarema.rj.gov.br.*

Araruama → *Colour map 4, C3. Phone code: 022. Population: 66,500.*

The **Lagoa Araruama** (220 sq km), is one of the largest lakes in Brazil and is famous for its medicinal mud. The salinity is high, the waters calm and almost the entire lake is surrounded by sandy beaches, making it popular with families looking for unpolluted bathing. The constant breeze makes the lake perfect for windsurfing and sailing. The major industry of the area is salt, and all around are saltpans and wind pumps used to carry the water into the pans. The town itself is at the western end of the lake on the inland shore, 116 km from Rio.

At the eastern end of the lake, also inland, is **São Pedro de Aldeia**, which has a population of 55,500 and, despite intensive development, still retains much of its colonial charm. There is a lovely **Jesuit church** built in 1723, and a **tourist office** ① *Av Brasil 655 Parque Hotel, T022-2665 4145, www.araruama.rj.gov.br.*

Arraial do Cabo → *Colour map 4, C4. Phone code: 022. Population: 21,500.*

This rather ugly little salt-industry town near Cabo Frio is considerably less busy than the resort at Cabo Frio a little to the north, and provides access to equally good beaches and dunes. The lake and the ocean here are divided by the Restinga de Massambaba, a long spit of sand mostly deserted except for the beaches of **Massambaba** and **Seca**, at the western end, and **Grande** in the east at Arraial do Cabo town itself. Arraial has lots of other small beaches on the bays and islands that form the cape, round which the line of the coast turns north, including the long, busy stretch at **Anjos**, **Praia do Forno** and **Prainha**. Excursions can be made by boat around the islets and by jeep or buggy over the sand dunes.

Ins and outs A very steep road connects the beaches of Itaipu and Itacoatiara with RJ-106 (and on to Bacaxá and Araruama) via the village of Itaipu-Açu. Most maps do not show a road beyond Itaipu-Açu; it is certainly too steep for buses. An alternative to the route from Niterói to Araruama through the lagoons is further inland than the RJ-106, via Manilha, Itaboraí and Rio Bonito on the BR-101 and RJ-124; this is a fruit-growing region.

Diving and adventure sports While Arraial is not a dive destination of international quality in its own right, it is one of the best in Brazil and there are a number of sites of varying difficulty with caverns and swim-throughs that are well worth exploring. Cold and warm currents meet here just off the coast and the marine life is more abundant than almost anywhere else on mainland southern Brazil. Expect to see schools of tropical and subtropical reef fish such as batfish and various tangs and butterfly fish, the occasional turtle, colonies of gorgonians and beautiful (though invasive) soft corals probably brought here on oil tankers from the Indo-Pacific. Dolphins are frequent visitors. The best visibility is between November and May. Water temperature is always below 20°C. The little town is also establishing itself as an adventure sports destination with activities including dune boarding, parachuting, kite surfing and kayaking available. ▶▶ *See Activities and tours, page 145.*

Excursions **Praia do Farol**, on Ilha do Cabo Frio, is one of Brazil's best beaches, with sand dunes and crystal-clear water. The **tourist office** ⓘ *T022-2622 1949, www.arraialdocabo-rj.com.br/zarony.html*, is at Praça da Bandeira. ▶▶ *See Activities and tours, page 145.*

Cabo Frio → *For listings, see pages 140-146. Colour map 4, C4. Phone code: 022. Population: 127,000.*

This busy tourist town, 168 km from Rio, is a popular middle-class Brazilian seaside resort, which overflows at the weekend with Cariocas. Although the town itself is very touristy, there are some attractive white-sand beaches, some with dunes and good surf and windsurfing, and accommodation nearby. Bring mosquito repellent.

Cabo Frio vies with Porto Seguro for the title of Brazil's first city. The navigator Amerigo Vespucci landed here in 1503 and returned to Portugal with a boatload of *pau brasil*. Since the wood in these parts was of better quality than that further north, the area subsequently became the target for loggers from France, the Netherlands and England. The Portuguese failed to capitalize on their colony here and it was the French who established the first defended settlement. Eventually the Portuguese took it by force but it was not until the second decade of the 17th century that they planned their own fortification, the **Forte São Mateus** ⓘ *daily 0800-1800*, which was started in 1618 on the foundations of the French fort. It is now a ruin at the mouth of the Canal de Itajuru, with rusting cannons propped up against its whitewashed ramparts. The canal connects Lagoa Araruama with the ocean.

The town beach, **Praia do Forte**, is highly developed and stretches south for about 7.5 km to Arraial do Cabo, its name changing to **Praia das Dunas** (after the dunes) and **Praia do Foguete**. These waters are much more suited to surfing. North of the canal entrance and town is the small under-developed beach of **Praia Brava** (popular with surfers and naturists) and the wine-glass bay of **Praia das Conchas**, which has a few shack restaurants. Next is **Praia do Peró**, 7 km of surf and sand on the open sea with a small town behind it and cheap accommodation. The best dunes are at Peró, Dama Branca (on road to Arraial) and the Pontal dunes at Praia do Forte.

Ins and outs The **airport** ⓘ *Estrada Velha do Arraial do Cabo s/n, T022-2647 9500, www.aero portocabofrio.com.br*, receives flights in high season only, from Rio, Belo Horizonte and Sao Paulo, Ribeirão Preto and Uberlândia. The **tourist office** ⓘ *Av do Contorno s/n, Algodoal, T022-2647 1689, www.cabofrio.tur.br or www.cabofrioturismo.rj.gov.br* , is in the big orange building.

Búzios → For listings, see pages 140-146. Colour map 4, C4. Phone code: 022. Population: 18,000.

Búzios is the principal resort of choice for Carioca and Mineira upper middle classes searching for their idea of St Tropez sophistication. When it was discovered by Brigitte Bardot in 1964 it was little more than a collection of colonial fishermen's huts and a series of pristine beaches hidden beneath steep hills covered in maquis-like vegetation. Now there are strings of hotels behind all of those beaches and the huts have become lost within a designated tourist village of bars, bikini boutiques and restaurants, most of which are strung along the pretty little main street, **Rua das Pedras**. Bardot sits here too – cheesily immortalized in brass, and subsequently in tens of thousands of pictures taken by the troops of cruise line passengers who fill Búzios's streets in high season. St Tropez this is not, but it can be fun for 20-somethings who are single and looking not to stay that way. The beaches are beautiful and there are a few romantic hotels with wonderful views.

Ins and outs

Getting there Buses leave every two hours 0600-2000 daily from Rio's *rodoviária* (US$21, 2½ hrs). Tickets can be bought from the **1001** counter, T022-4004 5001, or buy online at www.autoviacao1001.com.br/en. Buying the ticket in advance is recomended in high season and on major holidays. You can also take any bus from Rio to the town of Cabo Frio (these are more frequent); from Cabo Frio take the Viação Salineira bus, US$2 – it's 30 minutes to Búzios. The Búzios *rodoviária* is a few blocks' walk from the centre. Some *pousadas* are within 10 minutes' walk, eg **La Coloniale** and **Brigitta's**, while for others you'll need to take a local bus (US$1.30) or taxi. The buses from Cabo Frio run the length of the peninsula and pass several *pousadas*. The journey by car along the BR-106 takes about 2½ hours from Rio. Traffic back to Rio can be appalling on Sunday nights and during the peak holiday season.

Tourist information The main **tourist office** ⓘ *Manguinos, Pórtico de Búzios s/n, T022-2633 6200, T0800-249999, 24 hrs*, is at the entrance to town on the western edge of the peninsula. It has helpful staff, some of whom speak English. There's another office at ⓘ *Praça Santos Dumont, T022-2623 2099*, in the centre of Búzios town, which is more limited. For most of the hotels and services on the peninsula check www.buzios online.com.br or www.buzios.rj.gov.br. Maps are available from hotels and tourist offices.

Beaches

During the daytime, the best option is to head for the beaches, of which there are 25. The most visited are **Geribá** (many bars and restaurants; popular with surfers), **Ferradura** (deep-blue sea and calm waters), **Ossos** (the most famous and close to the centre), **Tartaruga** and **João Fernandes**. The better surf beaches, such as **Praia de Manguinhos** and **Praia de Tucuns**, are further from the town centre. To help you to decide which each suits you best, you can join one of the local two- or three-hour schooner trips, which pass many of the beaches, or hire a beach buggy (available from agencies on Rua das Pedras or through most hotels and hostels). These trips cost around US$10-15 and can be arranged through **Escuna Queen Lory** ⓘ *T022-2623 1179, www.queenlory.com.br*.

For Sleeping and Eating price codes and other relevant information, see pages 32-37.

ⓢ Sleeping

Niterói *p135*

AL-A Icaraí Praia, R Belízário Augusto 21, T021-2612 5030, www.icaraipraiahotel.com.br. Plain rooms in a faded 1980s beachfront tower.

AL-A Tower Hotel, Av Almte Ari Parreiras 12, Icaraí, T021-2612 2121, www.towerhotel. com.br. Niterói's smartest hotel (3-star) with ordinary, rather faded rooms, an indoor pool, sauna and reasonable business facilities.

B Pousada Suba e Veja, R Mal Raul Albuquerque 44 (Mirante de Piratininga), Km 18, T021-2619 0823. Wonderful views out over one of the most beautiful beaches on the Costa do Sol. Bar, restaurant, pool and sauna.

Camping

Pousada e Camping Piratininga, Rua dos Tatuís 2, Jardim Imbuí, T021-2618 2566/2562. MT21 9769 4963.

Maricá *p137*

Pousada Luau de Maricá, Cond Condado de Maricá, T021 26377420, www.luaudemarica.com.br.

B Pousada Colonial, Ponta Negra, T/F022-2748 1707. Simple suites and bungalows, with breakfast.

B Solar Tabaúna, Ponta Negra, T022-2648 1626, T021-9923 3101 (mob). Similar to the Colonial but with a pool.

Saquarema *p137*

B Pousada Pedra d'Água Maasai, Trav de Itaúna 17, Praia de Itaúna, T/F022-2651 1092, www.maasai.com.br. Good little beachfront hotel with 18 apartments, pool, sauna and a reasonable seafood restaurant.

C Pousada do Holandês, Av Vilamar 377, Itaúna beach. Many languages spoken by Dutch owner and his Brazilian wife. Good

meals – follow the signs, or take a taxi, from Saquarema. Recommended.

C-D Pousada Canto da Vila, Av Min Salgado 52, T022-2654 1232, www.pousadacanto davila.com.br. 14 little rooms and 2 larger ones. Overlooking the beach. Pokey but well maintained.

D-E Garota de Itaúna, Av Oceânica 165, Itaúna, T022-2651 2321. Very simple rooms next to the beach and a good seafood restaurant.

D-E Ilhas Gregas, R do Prado 671, Itaúna, T022-2651 1008. Youth hostel with a pool, sauna, bar and restaurant.

Camping

Itaúna's, R dos Tatuís 999, access from Av Oceânica, T022-2651 1711.

Araruama *p137*

A Enseada das Garças, R José Costa 1088, Ponta da Areia, about 5 km from São Pedro de Aldeia, T022-2621 1924, www.enseada dasgarcas.com.br. Beautiful little hotel overlooking the sea with access to good walking trails.

A Ver a Vista, R São Sebastião 400, São Pedro de Aldeia, T022-2665 4721, www.veravista hotel.com.br. Small apartment hotel with a sauna, bar and swimming pool.

C Pousada do Peu, RJ-132, Km 12, T022-2661-2066. Basic, popular with families.

E Praia do Sudoeste, R Pedro Américo, Lt 27, T022-2621 2763. Youth hostel with simple rooms, available in high season only.

Camping

Camping da Colina, RJ-106, Km 108, Praia de Teresa, São Pedro de Aldeia, T022-2621 1919. Not much shade.

Arraial do Cabo *p137*

A Pousada Nautillu's, R Marcílio Dias 100, T022-2622 1611, www.pousadanautillus. com.br. Medium-sized *pousada* with a pool, sauna, bar and restaurant. Recommended.

B Pousada dos Atobás, R José Pinto
Macedo 270, Prainha, T022-2622 2461,
www.pousadadosatobas.com.br. Small newly
built hostel with a pool, sauna and bar.
C Orlamar, Av Beiramar 111, Recanto da
Prainha, T/F022-2622 2410, www.pousada
orlamar.com.br. Literally on the beach,
with car access only at low tide. Reasonable
restaurant and bar.

Cabo Frio *p138*

AL-B La Plage, R das Badejos 40, Peró,
T022-2647 1746, www.laplage.com.br/.
Cheaper in low season. Fully equipped
suites; those upstairs have a sea view,
excellent for families. Right on the beach,
services include pool and bar, à la carte
restaurant, hydromassage, sauna, 24-hr
cyber café, garage.
B-C Pousada Água Marinha, R Rui Barbosa
996b, Centro, about 4 blocks from Praia do
Forte, T022-2643 8447, www.pousadaagua
marinhacabofrio.com.br. Cheaper in low
season. Plain white rooms with comfortable
beds, a/c, fan, TV, frigobar, breakfast, pool
and parking. Good choice in the centre.
C-E Pousada São Lucas, R Goiás 266,
Jardim Excelsior, T022-2645 3037,
www.pousadasaolucas.com.br (formerly
a youth hostel). 3 mins from the *rodoviária*.
Price is for double room with TV. Also has
dorms with hot shower, breakfast and
fan (a little cheaper in low season).
E Albergue da Juventude São Lucas,
R Goiás 266, Jardim Excelsior, 3 mins from
the *rodoviária*, T022-2645 3037. IYHA
youth hostel. Price per person.
**E Albergue Internacional da Juventude de
Muxarabi**, R Leonor Santa Rosa 13, Jardim
Flamboyant, T022-2643 0369. Youth hostel.
Price per person.
E Albergue Peró, R Coutrin 13, Peró, T022-
2644 3123. IYHA youth hostel, a stroll from
the Peró beach with bike rental, restaurant,
dorms and doubles.
E Albergue Praia das Palmeiras, Praia das
Palmeiras 1, T022-2643 2866. Youth hostel.

Camping

Camping da Estação, Estr dos Passageiros
370, T022-2643 1786.
Dunas do Peró, Estr do Guriri 1001, T022-
2629 2323, www.pousadadunasdopero.
com.br. Small *pousada* with a campsite on
Praia do Peró.

Búzios *p139*

The best rooms on the peninsula are not on
the beaches but are those with a superb view,
on the Morro do Humaitá hill, 10 mins' walk
from the town centre; hire a beach buggy.
Prior reservations are needed in summer,
during holidays such as Carnaval and New
Year's Eve, and at weekends. For cheaper
options and better availability, try Cabo Frio.
   Several private houses rent rooms,
especially in summer and holidays.
Look for the signs: '*Alugo quartos*'.
LL-L Casas Brancas, Alto do Humaitá 10,
T022-2623 1458, www.casasbrancas.com.br.
Far and away the best hotel in Búzios: a
series of rooms perched on the hill in mock-
Mykonos buildings with separate terraces for
the pool and spa areas. Sweeping views over
the bay. Wonderfully romantic at night when
it is lit by candlelight. If you can't afford to
stay, come for dinner. The **Abracadabra**
next door is owned by Casas Brancas and
is similar though cheaper and less stylish.
LL-L El Cazar, Alto do Humaitá 6, T022-
2623 1620, www.buzioselcazar.com.
Next door to **Casas Brancas** and almost
as luxurious, though a little darker inside.
Beautiful artwork on the walls and Central
Asian kelims on the ipe wood floors.
Tasteful and relaxing.
L-AL Pousada Byblos, Alto do Humaitá 14,
T022-2623 1162, www.byblos.com.br.
Wonderful views out over the bay and bright,
light rooms with tiled floors and balconies.
AL Pousada Pedra da Laguna, R 6, lote 6,
praia da ferradura, T/F022-2623 1965,
www.pedradalaguna.com.br. Spacious
rooms, the best with a view, 150 m from
the beach. Part of the **Roteiros do Charme**
group (see page 34).

A Pousada Hibiscus Beach, R 1 No 22, quadra C, Praia de João Fernandes, T022-2623 6221, www.hibiscusbeach.com. A peaceful spot, run by its British owners, overlooking Praia de João Fernandes, 15 pleasant bungalows, a/c, satellite TV, garden, pool, light meals available, help with car/buggy rentals and local excursions. One of the best beach hotels.

A-B Brigitta's Guest House, Av José Bento Ribeiro Dantas131, T/F022-2623 6157, www.brigittas.com.br. Beautifully decorated little *pousada* where Bardot once stayed, with just 4 rooms on the main street. Its delightful restaurant, bar and tea house overlooking the water are worth a visit.

A-B Casa da Ruth, R dos Gravatás, Geribá, T022-2623 2242, www.buziosturismo.com/casadaruth. Simple mock-Greek rooms in lilac overlooking the beach and pool.

C-E Práia dos Amores, Av José Bento Ribeiro Dantas 92, T022-2623 2422, www.albergue debuzios.com.br. IYHA, not far from the bus station, next to Praia da Tartaruga and just under 1 km from the centre. About the best value in Búzios.

C-E Ville Blanche, R Manoel T de Farias, 222, T022-2623 1201. A hostel and hotel right in the centre in the street parallel to R da Pedras with a/c dorms for up to 10, and light-blue tiled doubles with fridges, en suites and a balcony. Can be noisy.

Camping and chalets
E Country Camping Park, R Maria Joaquina Justiniano 895, (off Praça da Rasa), Praia Rasa, Km 12, T022-2629 1155, www.buzios camping.com.br. Chalets and a well-run shady campsite 1 km from the beach.

🍴 Eating

Niterói *p135*
🍴🍴🍴 **Olimpo**, Estação Hidroviária de Charitas, 2nd floor, Av Quintino Bocaiúva, s/n, Charitas, T021 2711 0554, www.restauranteolimpo. com.br. Brazilian and European cooking in a Niemyer building surrounded by windows overlooking Guanabara bay.
🍴🍴 **Da Carmine**, R Matriz de Barros 305, Icaraí, T021-3602 4988, www.dacarmine.com.br. Decent Italian seafood and pasta and a respectable wine list.
🍴🍴 **La Sagrada Familia**, R Domingues de Sá 325, Icaraí, T021-2610 1683, www.lasagrada familia.com.br/niteroi.htm. The best restaurant in Niterói, varied menu and reasonable wine list and housed in a beautiful colonial building.

Saquarema *p137*
🍴🍴🍴 **Le Bistrô**, Av São Rafael 1134, Itaúna, T022-2651 4594. The best restaurant in the area with good seafood.

Forno a Lenha, R dos Mariscos 511, Itaúna, T022-2651 4088. Mixed menu.

Araruama p137

Don Roberto, Av Getúlio Vargas 272, São Pedro de Aldeia, T022-2621 3913. Wood-fired pizzas.

Becco das Massas, R José Francisco Zeca 57, T022-3637 6398. Italian pasta and salad.

Arraial do Cabo p137

Saint Tropez, Praça Daniel Barreto 2, Praia dos Anjos, T022-2622 1222. Seafood.

Cabo Frio p138

The neat row of restaurants on Av dos Pescadores are worth a browse for good-value seafood and pasta. They have French-style seating on the pavement under awnings.

Picolino, R Mcal F Peixoto 319, Boulevard Canal, T022-2647 6222, www.restaurantepicolino.com.br. In a nice old building, very smart, mixed menu of seafood and a few international dishes.

Gaijin, R José Bonifácio 28, T022- 2643 4922. Reasonable Japanese food, generous portions.

Hippocampus, R Mcal F Peixoto 283, next door but one, T022-2645 5757, www.hippocampuscabofrio.com.br. One of the better seafood restaurants with good robalo (bass) and badejo (whiting).

Chico's, Av Teixeira e Souza 30, upstairs in Centro Comercial Víctor Nunes da Rocha, own centre, T022-2645 7454. Clean, smart, does breakfast, self-service, some more expensive dishes. On the ground floor is the **Coffee Shop**. More a stand than a shop, cheap; but better coffee in **Branca**.

"In" Sônia, Av dos Pescadores 140, loja 04. Good service and tasty fish, many dishes offered for 2 people.

Tonto, Av dos Pescadores, next door to **"In" Sônia**, T022-2645 1886 for delivery. Also serves pizza and has a bar, too.

Branca, Praça Porto Rocha, in the centre of town. Per kilo lunch 1100-1700, also fast food, pizza after 1800, coffee, pastries and cakes, good. A large, popular place.

Chez Michou, Av dos Pescadores. Closed Mon. For crêpes (as in **Rio Sul** shopping centre in Rio de Janeiro). Upstairs are a number of bars and nightclubs, eg **Eleven**, above San Francisco restaurant, and others.

Búzios p139

See also **Casas Brancas**, page 141 (fine views and romantic dining) and **Brigitta's**, page 142 (funky seafood bistro). There are many restaurants on and around Av José Bento Ribeiro Dantas (formerly R das Pedras), now known as Orla Bardot, and one of the charms of Búzios is browsing this street. The cheaper options tend to be off the main drag. There are plenty of beachside barracas (palapas) all over the peninsula serving the usual beans, rice and chips combinations outside of the low season.

There are a few other very cheap places on Praça Santos Dumont, off R das Pedras, and a small supermarket a couple of doors away from **La Prima**.

Acquerello, Av José Bento Ribeiro Dantas 130, Orla Bardot, T022-2623 2817. Smart a/c seafood and Italian restaurant with a reasonable wine list. The best on the street.

Satyricon, Av José Bento Ribeiro Dantas 500, Orla Bardot Praia da Armação (in front of Morro da Humaitá), T022-2623 2691. Búzios's most illustrious restaurant specializing in Italian seafood. Decent wine list.

Moqueca Capixaba, R Manoel de Carvalho 116, Centro, T022-2623 1155. Seafood dishes from Espírito Santo, cooked in coconut, dendê oil and urucum.

Banana Land, R Manoel Turíbio de Farias 50, T022-2623 0855. Cheap and cheerful per kilo buffet.

Chez Michou, Av José Bento Ribeiro Dantas, 90, Orla Bardot, T022-2623 2169, www.chezmichou.com.br. An open-air bar with videos, music and dozens of choices of pancakes accompanied by ice-cold beer. Always busy.

🎵 Bars and clubs

Búzios *p139*

In season, nightlife in Búzios is young, beautiful and buzzing. Out of season it is non-existent. Most of the bars and the handful of clubs are on Orla Bardot. These include **Guapo Loco**, a bizarrely shaped Mexican theme-bar and restaurant with dancing. **Privilege**, Av José Bento Ribeiro Dantas 550, Orla Bardot, Búzios's main club and one of Brazil's best European-style dance clubs with pumping techno, house and hip-hop, and 5 rooms, including a cavernous dance floor, sushi bar and lounge. **Ta-ka-ta ka-ta**, Av José Bento Ribeiro Dantas 256, Orla Bardot is strewn with motorbike parts and has its walls covered completely with graffiti. There are plenty of others including lively options such as **Bar do Zé**, Av José Bento Ribeiro Dantas 382, Orla Bardot T022-2623 4986 and **Alexo**, next door.

❀ Festivals and events

Niterói *p135*

Mar-May Festa do Divino, a festival that traditionally begins on Easter Sun and continues for the next 40 days, in which the *bandeira* (banner) *do Divino* is taken around the local municipalities. The festival ends at Pentecost with sacred and secular celebrations.
24 Jun São João, lots of parades, *forró* dancing and barn-dance costumes.
22 Nov Founding of the town. Parades, concerts and dancing.

Saquarema *p137*

Mar-May Festa do Divino, see Niterói, above.
8 May Founding of the town. Dancing, concerts and plenty of drinking.
29 Jun Festival of São Pedro, at the end of the Festas Juninas.
7 Sep Nossa Senhora de Nazaré, the town's patron saint's day.

Araruama *p137*

16 May Founding of the town.
29 Jun São Pedro, patron saint day of São Pedro de Aldeia.

Arraial do Cabo *p137*

13 May Founding of the town.
May/Jun Corpus Christi.

🛍 Shopping

Búzios *p139*

Many of Brazil's fashionable and beautiful come here for their holidays and Búzios is therefore a good place to pick up the kind of beach clothes and tropical cuts that they would wear. Although seemingly expensive these clothes are a fraction of what you would pay for labels of this quality in Europe, the US or Australia. Shopping is best on R das Pedras. Aside from the boutiques, there is little else of interest beyond the expected range of tourist tack shops. Of the boutiques the best are as follows:
Allegra, R das Pedras. Sexy light dresses, skirts, T-shirts and tops.
Bum Bum Ipanema, Av José Bento Ribeiro Dantas 221, Orla Bardot, T022-2623 4139, www.bumbum.com.br. Bright bikinis in gorgeous cuts.
Farm, Av José Bento Ribeiro Dantas 233, Orla Bardot, T022-2623 7477, www.farmrio. com.br. Cool beachwear and light clothes for 20- and 30-something women by a brand renowned for its soft as silk cotton, bright stamps and elegant but sexy cuts – archetypically Búzios.
Lenny, Av José Bento Ribeiro Dantas 233, Orla Bardot, T022-2623 3745, www.lenny. com.br. The most à la mode bikinis – from the point of view of Brazilians.
Salinas, Av José Bento Ribeiro Dantas, Orla Bardot. Beautifully crafted bikinis and beachwear. Together with **Rosa Chá**, the most la mode – from the point of view of foreigner
Tenda, Av José Bento Ribeiro Dantas, Orla Bardot. A little boutique with the

pick of Brazilian designers including the supermodels' bikini choice – **Rosa Chá**. **Tepo**, R Manoel Turíbio de Farias 202D (parallel to R das Pedras), T022-2623 7140. Upmarket indigenous arts and crafts, jewellery and fashion.

▲ Activities and tours

Niterói *p135*
Rio Cricket Associação Atlética (RCA), R Fagundes Varela 637, T021-2717 5333, www.riocricket.com.br. Bus No 57 from the ferry. **Rio Sailing Club** (late Clube de Niterói), Estr Leopoldo Fróes 418, lote 338, T021-2610 5810, www.ryc.esp.br. Bus No 33 marked 'via Fróes'.

Arraial do Cabo *p137*
Deep Trip, Av Getulio Vargas 93, Praia Grande, Arraial do Cabo, T021-9942 3020 (mob), www.deeptrip.com.br. The only PADI- affiliated dive operator in Arraial, with a range of courses and dive trips. **Gas**, Av Litoranea 80, Praia Grande, T022-9956 1222, www.arraialdocabo-rj.com.br/gas. Various adventure sports including dune boarding, parachuting and kayak surfing. Runs dive trips but is not PADI accredited. **K-Kite School**, R da Alegria 15, M021 9351 7164, www.kkite.hpg.ig.com.br. Windsurfing and kitesurfing, and lessons.

Trips to Ilha do Cabo Frio
Barco Lindo Olhar, T022-2647 4493, ask for Vadinho or Eraldo in the town's main marina. **Zarony tours**, Marina dos Pescadores, 2nd pier on Praia dos Anjos, T02107836 7952 (mob), www.arraialdocabo-rj.com.br/zarony.html.

Búzios *p139*
Malizia, Av José Bento Ribeiro Dantas, Orla Bardot, T022-2623 2022, www.malizia our.com.br. Money exchange, car hire and other services.
Mister Tours, R Germiniano J Luís 3, Centro, 022-2623 2100, www.mistertours.com.br.

◎ Transport

Niterói *p135*
Boat Ferries and launches run between the terminal at Praça Araribóia (for Niteroi city centre) and Charitas beach and the 'Barcas' terminal at Praça 15 de Novembro in **Rio de Janeiro** city centre, every 10 mins (20-30 mins, US$1.70), www.barcas-sa.com.br. There are also catamarans (*aerobarcas*) every 10 mins (12 mins, US$1.70). The slow, cheaper ferry gives the best views.
Bus Buses running between Niterói and **Rio de Janeiro** include No 761D Gávea–Charitas (via Jardim Botânico and Botafogo), 751D Aeroporto Galeão–Charitas 740-D and 741D Leme-Charitas (via Copacabana, Botafogo, Lapa and Santos Dumont airport), US$3. Also available are Frescões Gávea–Charitas, Galeão–Charitas.

Saquarema *p137*
Bus To **Rio de Janeiro** (Mil e Um, 1001), www.autoviacao1001.com.br/en, every 2 hrs 0625-1950, about 2 hrs, US$10.

Arraial do Cabo *p137*
Bus To **Rio de Janeiro**, www.autoviacao1001.com.br/en, US$16.

Cabo Frio *p138*
Air Flights in high season to **Rio de Janeiro**, **Belo Horizonte**, **Sao Paulo**, **Ribeirão Preto**, and **Uberlândia** with GOL, www.voegol.com.br.

Bus
Local Salineira and Montes Brancos run the local services. US$1.35 to places such as **Búzios**, **São Pedro da Aldeia**, **Saquarema**, **Araruama**, **Arraial do Cabo**. The urban bus terminal is near Largo de Santo Antônio, opposite the BR petrol station.
    Long distance The inter-city and interstate *rodoviária* is 2 km from the centre. Buses to **Rio de Janeiro** every 30 mins, 2½ hrs, US$8. To **Búzios**, from the local bus terminal in the town centre, every hr, US$1.

Útil to **Belo Horizonte** US$20. Unifac to **Belo Horizonte**, **Juiz da Fora**, **Petrópolis**. Macaense runs frequent services to **Macaé**. To **São Paulo**, at 2100, US$22.60.

For the route from Cabo Frio to **Vitória** either take Macaense bus to **Macaé** (5¼ hrs), or take **1001** to **Campos** (3½ hrs, US$5.60), and change. **1001** stops in Campos first at the **Shopping Estrada** *rodoviária*, which is the one where the bus connection is made, but it's outside town (US$3 taxi to the centre, or local bus US$0.35). The **1001** then goes on to the local *rodoviária*, closer to the centre, but there are no long-distance services from that terminal. Shopping Estrada *rodoviária* has a tourist office, but no cheap hotels nearby. **Aguia Branca** buses to **Vitória** at 0900 and 1900, US$8.10, 3 hrs 40 mins.

Búzios *p139*
Beach buggies A popular way to get around the cobbled streets of Búzios. Buggy rental available through most *pousadas* and travel agencies on the Rua das Pedras or throught **Malízia**, T022-2623 2022, www.maliziatour.com.br or **Stylus**, T022-2623 2780.

Bus The Búzios *rodoviária* is a few blocks' walk from the centre. **1001**, T021- 4004 5001, www.autoviacao1001.com.br/en, to **Rio de Janeiro** US$18, 3½ hrs (be at the bus terminal 20 mins before departure), 7 departures daily. Buses running between the *rodoviária* Novo Rio in **Rio de Janeiro** and **Cabo Frio** stop at Búzios and are more frequent. Cabo Frio is a 30-min journey from Búzios. Buying the ticket in advance is only recommended on high season and major holidays.

Car
By car via the BR-106 takes about 2½ hrs to **Rio de Janeiro** and can take far longer on Sun nights and on Brazilian public holidays.

ℹ Directory

Niterói *p135*
Banks Banco 24 Horas, Niterói Shopping, R da Conceição 188; Bradesco, R Gavião Peixoto 108. **Internet** O Lido Cyber C@fé, Av Rui Barbosa 29, loja 124, São Francisco. **Laundry** Lavlev, R Pres Backer 138. **Medical services** Universitário Antônio Pedro, Av Marques do Paraná, T021-2620 2828.

Saquarema *p137*
Banks Bradesco, Rod Amaral Peixoto 83.

Araruama *p137*
Banks Bradesco, Av São Pedro 120, São Pedro de Aldeia.

Arraial do Cabo *p137*
Banks Bradesco, R Sen Macedo Soares 44, Ponta Negra. Unibanco, R Dom Pedro, will not change cheques and has no ATM.

Cabo Frio *p138*
Banks Banco do Brasil, Praça Porto Rocha 44, the only bank with exchange, *câmbio* 1100-1430; Bradesco, Av Assunção 904, has Visa ATM; HSBC, Av Assunção 793, has ATM for AmEx, Visa/Plus, MasterCard/Cirrus. **Internet** Aç@i, Av João Pessoa, near R Casemiro de Abreu, US$0.75 per 30 mins, older machines, not always open; Cyber Mar, Nunes da Rocha, Av Teixeira e Souza 30, new, a/c, minimum US$1.50 for 30 mins, US$2.20 per hr, daily 0800-2000; Cyber Tel, Praça Porto Rocha 56, T022-2649 7575, in gallery next to Banco do Brasil. Only 3 machines, but good and fast, US$2 per hr.

Búzios *p139*
Banks There are banks and money exchanges on Orla Bardot; Banco do Brasil, R Manuel de Carvalho 70, Centro, T022-2623 2302. **Internet** There are cyber cafés along Av J B Ribeiro Dantas, Orla Bardot, US$6, 30 mins-1 hr.

Inland resorts and coffee towns

The mountain resorts of Petrópolis, Teresópolis and Nova Friburgo are set high in the scenic Serra do Mar behind Rio. All three are lovely mountain retreats with accommodation in charming fazendas (coffee estates). The imperial city of Petrópolis retains many of its original buildings and boasts what is perhaps Brazil's finest museum. This is a beautiful area and is becoming increasingly popular for walking, as well as horse riding and other activities. The resorts were originally established because the cool mountain air offered a respite from the heat of Rio and from yellow fever and other diseases that festered in the unhealthy port in the 19th century. They also provided the routes that brought first gold, then coffee from the interior to the coast. ➤➤ For listings, see pages 151-154.

Petrópolis → For listings, see pages 151-154. Colour map 4, C3. Phone code: 024. Population: 290,000.

Emperor Pedro I, who tired of the sticky summer heat in Rio, longed for a summer palace in the cool of the Atlantic coast mountains but abdicated before he could realize his dream. When the new emperor, Pedro II, took the throne, he soon approved plans presented by the German architect Julius Friedrich Köler for a palace and a new city, to be settled by immigrants. The result was Petrópolis. The city was founded in 1843 and in little over a decade had become a bustling Germanic town and an important imperial summer retreat. The emperor and his family would spend as much as six months of each year here and, as he had his court in tow, Köler was able to construct numerous grand houses and administrative buildings. Many of these still stand – bizarre Rhineland anomalies in a neotropical landscape.

Ins and outs

There are buses from the *rodoviária* in Rio every 15 minutes throughout the day and every hour on Sundays. The journey takes about 1½ hours, US$8. Sit on the left-hand side for best views and bring travel sickness pills if you are prone to nausea on winding roads. Return tickets are not available, so buy tickets for the return journey on arrival in Petrópolis. The main **tourist office** ① *Praça da Liberdade, Mon-Sat 0900-1800, Sun 0900-1700*, is at the far southwestern end of Avenida Koeler. It has a list of tourist sights and hotels, a good, free, colour map of the city, and a useful pamphlet in various languages. Some staff are multilingual; all are helpful.

Sights

Three rivers dominate the layout of Petrópolis: the **Piabanha**, **Quitandinha** and the **Palatino**. In the historic centre, where most of the sites of tourist interest are to be found, the rivers have been channelled to run down the middle of the main avenues. Their banks are planted with flowering trees and the overall aspect is unusual in Brazil; you quickly get a sense that this was a city built with a specific purpose and at a specific time in Brazil's history.

Petrópolis's main attraction is its imperial palace. The **Museu Imperial** ① *R da Imperatriz 220, T024-2237 8000, Tue-Sun 1100-1730, last entry 1700, US$4, under 6s free, expect long queues on Sun during Easter and high season*, is Brazil's most visited museum and is so well kept you might think the imperial family had left the day before, rather than in 1889. It's modest for an emperor, neoclassical in style and fully furnished, and is worth a visit if just to see the Crown jewels of both Pedro I and Pedro II. The palace gardens in front are filled with little fountains, statues and shady benches. Descendants of the original family live in a house behind the palace. Horse-drawn carriages wait to be hired outside the gate; not all the horses are in good shape.

Opposite the Museu Imperial is the handsome **Palácio Amarelo** ① *Praça Visconde de Maúa 89, T024-2291 9200, Tue-Sun 0900-1800, US$1*, built in 1850 as the palace of another Brazilian baron and now the Câmara Municipal (town hall). The twin shady *praças* **dos Expedicionários** and **Dom Pedro II** (which has a pigeon-covered statue of the emperor) lie opposite each other at the junction of Rua do Imperador and Rua da Imperatriz, 100 m south of the Museu Imperial (left as you leave the museum). A small **market** is held here on Sundays and there are a handful of cafés and restaurants.

At the northern end of Rua da Imperatriz (turn right out of the museum and follow the river as it curves left along Avenida Tiradentes) is the Gothic revival **Catedral de São Pedro de Alcântara** ① *R São Pedro de Alcântara 60, T024-2242 4300, Tue-Sun 0800-1200 and 1400-1800, free*, where Emperor Pedro II, his wife Princesa Teresa, Princesa Isabel and Count D'Eu are entombed in mock-European regal marble. This lies at the end of the city's most impressive avenue, **Avenida Koeler**, which is lined with mansions built by the imperial and republican aristocracy. Among them are the neoclassical **Palácio Rio Negro** ① *Av Koeler 255, T024-2246 9380, Mon 1200-1700, Wed-Sun 0930-1700, US$1.50, under 6s free, multilingual guides*, built in 1889 by the Barão do Rio Negro as the summer retreat of Brazilian presidents, and the **Casa da Princesa Isabel** ① *Av Koeler 42, outside visits only*, the former residence of Dom Pedro II's daughter and her husband the Count D'Eu.

Avenida Koeler ends at the **Praça da Liberdade** (formerly known as Praça Rui Barbosa) where there are cafés, goat-drawn carts for children and very photogenic views of the cathedral. A further 100 m west of the *praça* (away from Avenida Koeler) is the

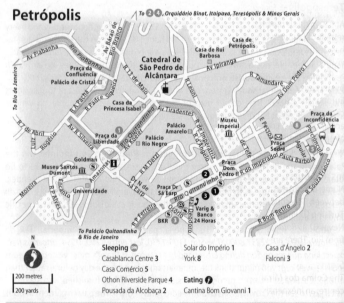

Petrópolis

To ② ④, Orquidário Binot, Itaipava, Teresópolis & Minas Gerais

Sleeping	Solar do Império 1	Casa d'Ángelo 2
Casablanca Centre 3	York 8	Falconi 3
Casa Comércio 5		
Othon Riverside Parque 4	Eating	
Pousada da Alcobaça 2	Cantina Bom Giovanni 1	

200 metres
200 yards

Museu Santos Dumont ① *R do Encanto 22, T024-2247 3158, Tue-Sun 0930-1700, US$1.50, free for under 6s.* The summer home of Alberto Santos Dumont, who Brazilians claim was the first man to fly an aeroplane, was designed in 1918 as a mock-Alpine chalet. Santos Dumont called it 'the enchanted one', and it is a delightful example of an inventor's house. Steps to the roof lead to an observation point and are carefully designed to allow visitors only to ascend right foot first. His desk doubled up to become his bed. The alcohol-heated shower is said to be the first in Brazil.

The city has a handful of other interesting buildings. The **Casa de Rui Barbosa** ① *Av Ipiranga 405, private residence,* was the home of the Bahian media mogul and writer who was instrumental in abolishing slavery in Brazil. The **Casa de Petrópolis** ① *Av Ipiranga 716, outside visits only,* is a magnificent Gothic folly set in formal French gardens and was built in 1884 by José Tavares Guerra, the grandson of the founder of industrialization in Brazil, the Barão de Maúa. Taking centre stage in the Praça da Confluência is the **Palácio de Cristal**, which was commissioned and built in France following London's great exhibition, when such palaces were all the rage in Europe. It opened to great aplomb, fell into disrepair in the 20th century and is now the home of weekend concerts and shows.

Some 10 km from the centre, on the way to the BR-040 to Rio, is the **Palácio Quitandinha** ① *Av Joaquim Rolla 2, T024-2237 1012, Tue-Sun 0900-1700, US$2.50,* a vast mock-Bavarian edifice that was built in 1944 to be the largest casino in South America. The lake in front of the building is in the shape of Brazil. Further out of town still is the **Orquidário Binot** ① *R Fernandes Vieira 390, T024-2248 5665, Mon-Fri 0800-1100 and 1300-1600, Sat 0700-1100.* This nursery has one of the best collections of Brazilian orchids in the state and is well worth visiting even if you don't intend to buy.

Teresópolis → *For listings, see pages 151-154. Colour map 4, C3. Phone code: 021. Population: 140,000.*

At 910 m this is the highest city in the state of Rio de Janeiro. It was the favourite summer retreat of Empress Teresa Cristina and is named after her. Development in recent years has destroyed some of the city's character, but most visitors use the town as a base for visiting the Serra dos Órgãos, which lie nearby.

Because of its altitude and the relatively cool temperatures, the area was not exploited by the early colonists since they could not grow the tropical crops that were in demand in Europe. The existence of *fazendas* in the region was first documented in the early 19th century, the best known being that of George March, an Englishman. In order to accommodate a constant stream of visitors, March added lodgings to his farm; not long after other landowners followed suit. Before taking the name of the empress, the parish was called Santo Antônio de Paquequer.

Ins and outs
Numerous buses run between Teresópolis and Rio's *rodoviária* daily. Eight buses a day run between Teresópolis and Petrópolis. Information is available from the **Secretaria de Turismo** ① *Praça Olímpica, T021-2742 3352, ext 2082,* and **Terminal Turístico Tancredo Neves** ① *Av Rotariana, T021-2642 2094, www.teresopolis.rj.gov.br,* at the entrance to town from Rio. There are very good views of the serra from here.

Sights
The **Colina dos Mirantes** is a 30-minute steep climb from Rua Jaguaribe (2 km from the centre; an inexpensive taxi ride), and offers sweeping views of the city and surroundings.

Around the town are various attractions, such as the Sloper and Iaci lakes, the Imbui and Amores waterfalls and the **Fonte Judith**, which has mineral-rich water, and is accessed from Avenida Oliveira Botelho, 4 km southwest. Just off the road to Petrópolis is the **Orquidário Aranda** ⓘ *5 km from the centre, Alameda Francisco Smolka, T021-2742 0628.*

The road to Nova Friburgo (see page 151) is known as the **Vale das Hortaliças** because it passes through a zone where vegetables and flowers are cultivated. There is an interesting rock formation called **A Mulher de Pedra**, 12 km out of Teresópolis on this road.

Serra dos Órgãos → For listings, see pages 151-154.

These mountains near Teresópolis, named after their strange rock formations, which are said to look like organ pipes, preserve some of the most diverse stretches of Atlantic coast forest in the state of Rio de Janeiro. The wildlife, plant and birdwatching here are excellent, as are the walking and rock climbing. The best way to see the park is on foot. A number of trails cut through the forest and head up into the alpine slopes, including the ascent of the **Dedo de Deus** (God's Finger); a precipitous peak that requires some climbing skills. Other trails lead to the highest point in the park, the **Pedra do Sino** (Bell Rock), 2263 m, a three- to four-hour climb up a 14-km path. The west face of this mountain is one of the hardest climbing pitches in Brazil. Other popular walks include the **Pedra do Açu trail** and paths to a variety of anatomically named peaks and outcrops: O Escalavrado (The Scarred One), O Dedo de Nossa Senhora (Our Lady's Finger), A Cabeça de Peixe (Fish Head), A Agulha do Diabo (The Devil's Needle) and A Verruga do Frade (The Friar's Wart).

Ins and outs

If you have a car, a good way to see the park is to do the Rio–Teresópolis–Petrópolis– Rio road circuit, stopping off for walks in the forest. This can be done in a day. The park has two ranger stations, both accessible from the BR-116: the **Sede** (headquarters, T/F021-2642 1070) is closer to Teresópolis (from town take Avenida Rotariana), while the **Sub-Sede** is just outside the park proper, off the BR-116. By the Sede entrance is the Mirante do Soberbo, with views to the Baía de Guanabara. Both the Sede station and the Mirante can be reached on the bus marked 'Mirante do Soberbo', which leaves every half an hour from the Teresópolis *rodoviária* and city centre.

Anyone can enter the park and hike the trails from the Teresópolis gate, but if you intend to climb the Pedra do Sino, you must sign a register (those under 18 must be accompanied by an adult and have permission from the park authorities). Entrance to the park is US$2, with an extra charge for the path to the top of the Pedra do Sino. For information, contact the Rio de Janeiro branch of **Ibama**, T021-2231 1772.

Flora and fauna

The park belongs to the threatened *Mata Atlântica* coastal rainforest, designated by **Conservation International** as a global biodiversity hot spot and the preserve of what are probably the richest habitats in South America outside the Amazonian cloudforests. There are 20- to 30-m-high trees, such as paineiras (floss-silk tree), ipês and cedros, rising above palms, bamboos and other smaller trees. Flowers include begonias, bromeliads, orchids and quaresmeiras (glorybushes). The park is home to numerous rare and endemic birds including cotingas, the rarest of which is the grey-winged cotinga, guans, tanagers, berryeaters and trogons. Mammals include titi and capuchin monkeys, all of the neotropical rainforest cats including jaguar and oceleot, tapir and white collared peccary. Reptiles include the sapo-pulga (flea-toad), which at 10 mm long vies with the Cuban pygmy frog as the smallest amphibian in the world.

Nova Friburgo and around → For listings, see pages 151-154. Colour map 4, C3.
Phone code: 024. Population: 175,000.

This town, standing at 846 m in a beautiful valley with excellent walking and riding, is a popular resort during the summer months. It was founded by Swiss settlers from Fribourg, the first families arriving in 1820. Apart from tourism, Nova Friburgo has an important textile industry, specializing in lingerie, and also produces cheeses, preserves, sweets and liqueurs. Information is available from the **Centro de Turismo** ① Praça Demerval Barbosa Moreira, T024-2523 8000, ext 236.

A cable car, US$5, from Praça dos Suspiros goes 650 m up the **Morro da Cruz**, for a magnificent view of the rugged country. Most of the interesting sites are in the surrounding countryside, so a car may be necessary to see everything. About 10 km northeast are the **Furnas do Catete**, an area of forest, caves, waterfalls and rock formations, one of which is called the **Pedra do Cão Sentado** (The Seated Dog); there is a small entry fee. Other natural attractions are the **Pico da Caledônia** (2310 m) 15 km southwest, and the **Véu de Noiva waterfall**, 9 km north.

The district of **Lumiar**, 34 km southeast, has beautiful scenery, waterfalls, natural swimming pools and good canoeing in the Rio Macaé and Rio Bonito. These two rivers meet at a point called **Poço do Alemão**, or Poço Verde, 4.5 km south of Lumiar.

◉ Inland resorts and coffee towns listings

For Sleeping and Eating price codes and other relevant information, see pages 32-37.

◉ Sleeping

Petrópolis *p147, map p148*
Good budget accommodation is hard to find, but bargaining is possible Mon-Fri.
LL Locanda della Mimosa, Alameda das Mimosas, Vale Florido, T024-2233 5405, www.locanda.com.br. A 6-room *pousada* in a terracotta Palladian villa in the mountains near town, overlooking a little pool. The owner is one of the finest chefs in Brazil, see page 153.
LL Solar do Império, Av Koeler 376, T024-2103 3000, www.solardoimperio.com.br. A luxury boutique hotel with period furniture in a converted mansion opposite the Palácio Rio Negro. Excellent spa and restaurant.
L Pousada da Alcobaça, R Agostinho Goulão 298, Correas, T024-2221 1240, www.pousadadaalcobaca.com.br. In the

Roteiros de Charme group (see page 34). Delightful, family-run large country house set in flower-filled gardens leading down to a river, with pool and sauna. Worth stopping by for tea on the terrace, or for dinner at the restaurant. Recommended.
A Othon Riverside Parque, R Hermogéneo Silva 522, Retiro, 5 mins from the centre, T024-2246 9850, www.hoteis-riverside. com.br. Mock-colonial hotel with a nice outdoor pool set in attractive gardens with views of the surrounding countryside. The helpful owner can arrange tours.
B Casablanca Centre, R General Osório 28, T024-2242 2612, www.casablancahotel. com.br. Old 1960s block, reasonable rooms and restaurant. Somewhat faded.
B York, R do Imperador 78, near the *rodoviária*, T024-2243 2662, www.hotel york.com.br. Convenient package-tour hotel with faded 1980s rooms, decent breakfast.

C Casa Comércio, R Dr Porciúncula 56, opposite the *rodoviária*, T024-2242 3500. One of the cheapest options. Clean but simple with shared baths or en suites. Linked to a tour agency, www.rioserra. com.br/trekking, which offers trips in the surrounding mountains.

Camping
Associação Brasileira de Camping and YMCA, Araras district. Space can be reserved through Rio YMCA, T024-2231 9860.

Teresópolis *p149*
Many cheap hotels on R Delfim Moreira.
L Fazenda Rosa dos Ventos, Km 22 on the road to Nova Friburgo, T021-2644 9900, www.hotelrosadosventos.com.br. Part of the Roteiros do Charme chain. One of the best hotels in inland Rio with a range of chalets in 1 million sq m of private forest and with wonderful views. Excellent restaurant.
C Várzea Palace, R Sebastião Teixeira 41, T021-2742 0878. Simple hotel with very friendly staff. Highly recommended.
D-E Recanto do Lord Hostel, R Luiza Pereira Soares 109, Centro-Artistas, T021-2742 5586, www.teresopolishostel.com.br. Family-oriented hostel with rooms and dorms, kitchen, cable TV and barbecue area. Breakfast included. Tours, treks and climbing in the mountains can be organized. Book in advance for Jan and Feb. Camping is permitted beside the hostel.

Camping
Quinta de Barra, R Antônio Maria 100, Km 3 the road to Petrópolis, T021-2643 1050.

Serra dos Órgãos *p150*
Ibama has some hostels, US$5 full board, or US$3 first night, US$2 thereafter, a bit rough.
L Reserva Ecológica de Guapi Assu (REGUA), Cachoeiras de Macacu-RJ, T021-2745 3998, www.regua.co.uk. A British-run conservation NGO and ecotourism project focused on a large main house with several rooms, set in primary rainforest. Expert guided walks into the reserve, in one of the richest areas in the state for birds, mammals and orchids.
L Serra dos Tucanos, Caixa Postal 98125, Cachoeiras de Macacu, T021-2649 1557, www.serradostucanos.com.br. One of the best wildlife and birdwatching lodges in Brazil with excellent guiding, equipment and accommodation in a comfortable lodge set in the Atlantic coastal rainforest.

Camping
Two sites in the Sub-Sede part, one close to the museum, the other not far from the natural swimming pool at Poço da Ponte Velha; one site in the Sede part. The Sede has a restaurant and the Sub-Sede a *lanchonete*.

Nova Friburgo *p151*
AL Bucsky, 5 km on the road to Niterói, T021-2522 5052. Meals, tours and guided walks.
AL Pousada do Riacho, Estr Nova Friburgo Km 8, Cardinot, T021-2522 2823, www.pousadadoriacho.com. Charming upmarket Roteiros do Charme hotel with extensive gardens and surrounded by gentle mountains.
A Fazenda São João, 11 km from Garlipp (same ownership) up a side road, T021-2542 1304. Riding, swimming, sauna, tennis, hummingbirds and orchids. The owner will meet guests in Nova Friburgo or even in Rio.
A Garlipp, Muri, 8 km south, Km 70 from Rio, T/F021-2542 1173. German-run chalets.
B Fabris, Av Alberto Browne 148, T021-2522 2852. Central, with plain en suite rooms with TVs hot showers. Large breakfast buffet.
C-D Maringá, R Monsenhor Miranda 110, T021-2522 2309. Standard but with a very good breakfast. Recommended.

Camping
Camping Clube do Brasil has sites on the Niterói Rd, at Caledônia (7 km out, T021-2522 0169) and Muri (10 km out, T021-2542 2275).
Fazenda Sanandu, 20 km out on the same road. Private campsite.

🍴 Eating

Petrópolis *p147, map p148*

Bakeries and cheap eateries by the *rodoviária*.

¶¶¶ Locanda della Mimosa, Alameda das Mimosas, Vale Florido, T024-2233 5405, www.locanda.com.br. One of the best in Brazil, with fusion cooking with a focus on game. Danio Braga was 4 times *Quatro Rodas* chef of the year. The 3000-bottle wine cellar includes heavyweights like 1990 Château Haut-Brion.

¶ Cantina Bom Giovanni, R do Imperador 729, T024-2242 5588. A 1st-floor simple, canteen-style Italian restaurant. Justifiably popular for self-service lunch and dinner.

¶ Casa d'Ángelo, R do Imperador 700, by Praça Dom Pedro II. A traditional, long-established teahouse, self-service food. Also a bar at night.

¶ Falconi, R do Imperador 757, T024-2242 1252. Traditional restaurant with rustic elegance that has been serving Italian food since 1914. Pasta and pizza for US$3. Recommended.

Teresópolis *p149*

There is a good café in the **ABC** supermarket.
¶¶¶ Dona Irene, R Tte Luís Meireles 1800, T021-2742 2901, www.donairene.com.br. Very popular upmarket Russian restaurant. Reservations necessary.

¶¶ Bar Gota d'Água, Praça Baltasar da Silveira 16. A little bar, simple fish dishes and *feijoada*.

¶¶ Taberna Alpina, Duque de Caxias 131. Excellent German cuisine.

Nova Friburgo *p151*

Many restaurants offer European cuisine, reflecting the people who settled in the area. Also Brazilian food, pizzas and *confeitarias*.
¶¶¶ Chez Gigi, Av Euterpe Friburguense 21, T024-2523 0107. Excellent Brazilian-French fusion cooking with dishes such as duck's breast in *jabuticaba*, pear and damson sauce.

¶¶ Auberge Suisse, R 10 de Outubro, T024-2541 1270. Fondue, *roschti* and other Swiss options alongside very good steak.

🎉 Festivals and events

Petrópolis *p147, map p148*
16 Mar Foundation day.
Jun Bohemia Beer Festival. Brazil's earliest beer dates from 1853 and was originally brewed in the city. Although production has been moved to Rio, the festival is still celebrated here.
29 Jun São Pedro de Alcântara, the patron saint of Petrópolis.

Teresópolis *p149*
May Festa das Colônias.
13 Jun Santo Antônio, the town's patron saint.
29 Jun São Pedro, celebrated with fireworks.
7 Jul Foundation day.
15 Oct Santa Terezinha.

Nova Friburgo *p151*
May Maifest festival, celebrated all month.
16 May Founding of Nova Friburgo.
24 Jun São João Batista, patron saint's day.

🛍 Shopping

Petrópolis *p147, map p148*
R Teresa, southeast of the centre, is where the textile industry exhibits its wares. In common with Itaipava, it draws buyers from all over the country and is a good place to find high-quality knitwear and bargain clothes. Closed Mon morning and Sun.

🔺 Activities and tours

Petrópolis *p147, map p148*
Rio Serra, T024-2235 7607, www.rioserra. com.br/trekking. Horse riding, trekking, whitewater rafting and a range of trips into the scenic mountain area, multilingual guides.
Roz Brazil, T024-9257 0236, www.rozbrazil. com. Some of the best drive and light walk tours around Petrópolis, Teresópolis and the Serra dos Órgãos with British Brazilian Rosa

Thompson, who has been living in the area for decades. Pick ups from Rio.

Serra dos Órgãos *p150*
Tours are available through the tourist office or the IYHA Recanto do Lord in Teresópolis. See also Roz Brazil, above.
Lazer Tours, T024-2742 7616. Tours of the park are offered by Francisco (find him at the grocery shop on R Sloper 1). Recommended.

⊖ Transport

Petrópolis *p147, map p148*
Bus Buses run to **Rio de Janeiro** every 30 mins throughout the day (US$10), Sun every hr, 1½ hrs. Sit on the right-hand side for best views, www.unica-facil.com.br. Ordinary buses arrive in Rio at the *rodoviária*; a/c buses run hourly and arrive at Av Nilo Peçanha, US$4. Book your return journey as soon as you arrive in Petrópolis. Bus to **Niterói**, US$11; to **Cabo Frio**, US$26. To **Teresópolis**, 8 a day, US$3. To **São Paulo** daily at 2330.

Teresópolis *p149*
Bus The *rodoviária* is at R 1 de Maio 100. Buses to **Rio de Janeiro** Novo Rio *rodoviária* every 30 mins. Book your return journey as soon as you arrive in Teresópolis. Fare

US$3.60. From Teresópolis to **Petrópolis**, 8 a day, US$3.

Nova Friburgo *p151*
Bus Bus station, Ponte da Suadade, T024-2522 0400. To **Rio**, every hr, 2 hrs, US$4.

❻ Directory

Petrópolis *p147, map p148*
Banks Banco do Brasil, R Paulo Barbosa 81; Banco 24 Horas ATM is by the Varig office at R Mcal Deodoro 98. Travel agents with *câmbios*; BKR, R Gen Osório 12; Goldman, R Barão de Amazonas 46 (between Praça da Liberdade and the university); Vert Tur, R 16 de Março 244. **Internet** Compuland, R do Imperador opposite Praça Dr Sá Earo, US$1.50 per hr. **Post office** R do Imperador 350 in the Palácio dos Correios. **Telephone** R Mcal Deodoro, just above Praça Dr Nelson de Sá Earp, no fax.

Teresópolis *p149*
Banks Cash/TCs at Teretur, Trav Portugal 46. **Internet** Cott@ge Cybercafe, R Alfredo Rebello Filho 996, 2nd floor, US$3 per hr.

Nova Friburgo *p151*
Banks Bradesco, Praça Demerval Barbosa Moreira.

West of Rio de Janeiro

Towns to the west of Rio are mostly spread along the ugly Rio–São Paulo motorway known as the Via Dutra. None are appealing. But the mountains that watch over them preserve important tracts of Atlantic coast rainforest, particularly around Itatiaia. This is one of the best places close to Rio for seeing wild animals and virgin rainforest and is the country's oldest protected area. The little mock-Alpine resort of Visconde de Mauá sits in the same mountain chain a little further towards São Paulo, although the forest here is less well preserved. ➠ For listings, see pages 158-159.

Serra da Mantiqueira → *For listings, see pages 158-159.*

This lush mountain range separates Rio de Janeiro and from Minas Gerais state and is one of few remaining areas with extensive *Mata Atlântica* (Atlantic coastal rainforest) in southeastern Brazil. It is dotted with pretty little towns and national and state parks.

Penedo → *Colour map 4, C3. Phone code: 024. Population: 8000. Altitude: 600 m.*

The small town of Penedo, 175 km from Rio, attracted Finnish settlers in the 1930s who brought the first saunas to Brazil. There is a Finnish museum, a cultural centre and Finnish dancing on Saturdays. This popular weekend resort also provides horse riding and swimming in the Portinho River. There are five buses a day from Resende. There is a **tourist office** ① *Av Casa das Pedras, T024-3351 1876*, and plenty of mid-range and cheap hotels in town.

Visconde de Mauá → *Colour map 4, C3. Phone code: 024. Altitude: 1200 m.*

About 33 km beyond Penedo (part of the road is unpaved) is the charming small village of Visconde de Mauá in the **Serra da Mantiqueira**. In the early 20th century Swiss and German immigrants settled in the town, which is popular with tourists today. The surrounding scenery is lovely, with green valleys, clear rivers, wild flowers and opportunities for good walks and outdoor activities. Many places offer acupuncture, shiatsu massage and macrobiotic food and there is a hippy feel to the crafts on sale. Horses can be hired in Visconde de Mauá from Berto (almost opposite Vendinha da Serra), or Pedro (Lote 10) and many places in Maringá arrange riding. The **Rio Preto** is good for canoeing and there is an annual national event (dates change; check in advance). The **tourist office** ① *T024-3387 1283*, is closed out of season.

Three other small hill towns are nearby: **Mirantão**, at 1700 m, with semi-tropical vegetation; **Maringá**, just across the state border in Minas Gerais and a delightful two-hour walk; and **Maromba**. On the way to Maromba is the **Mirante do Posto da Montanha**, a lookout with a view of the Rio Preto, which runs through the region and is the border between Rio de Janeiro and Minas Gerais states. Also in Minas Gerais, 6 km upriver from Maringá but on a different road, are the **Santa Clara falls** (turn off before Maromba). Between Visconde de Mauá and Maringá is a natural pool in the river (turn left before crossing the bridge). After Maromba follow the signs to **Cachoeira e Escorrega**, a small waterfall and waterslide with a cold natural swimming pool, a 2-km walk. A turning off this road leads to another waterfall, the **Cachoeira Véu da Noiva**.

Although served by buses from both São Paulo and Rio, *pousadas* are spread out and the area is best visited with a car. For **tourist information**, the website www.guia maua.com.br lists many of the hotels and restaurants and gives a good overview of the area (in Portuguese but with pictures).

Parque Nacional de Itatiaia → *For listings, see pages 158-159. Colour map 4, C3.*

Deep valleys shrouded in pristine rainforest hiding rocky clear-water rivers and icy waterfalls. Little winding trails through a whole swathe of different ecosystems, watched over by some of world's rarest birds and mammals. Hotels and guesthouses to suit all budgets from which to explore them. And all within easy reach of Rio or São Paulo.

Itatiaia is a must for those who wish to see Brazilian forest and animals and have a restricted itinerary or limited time. This 30,000-ha mountainous park is Brazil's oldest. It was founded in 1937 to protect Atlantic coast rainforest in the Serra de Mantiqueira mountains, and important species still find a haven here, including jaguars and pumas, brown capuchin and black-faced titi monkeys. This is good hiking country with walks through subtropical and temperate forests, grasslands and *paramo* to a few peaks just under 3000 m. The best trails head for Pedra de Taruga, Pedra de Maçã and the Poranga and Véu de Noiva waterfalls. The Pico das Agulhas Negras and Serra das Prateleiras (up to 2540 m) offer good rock climbing. There is a **Museu de História Natural** ① *Tue-Sun 1000-1600*, near the park headquarters with a depressing display of stuffed animals from the 1940s.

Ins and outs

Getting there and around Itatiaia lies just off the main São Paulo–Rio highway, the Dutra. A bus marked '504 Circular' runs from Itatiaia town run four times a day (variable hours) to the park, calling at the hotels in town. The bus can also be caught at Resende, at the crossroads before Itatiaia. Tickets are sold at a booth in the large bar in the middle of Itatiaia main street.

The alternative option involves adding another 10- to 15-km on to your journey depending on where you are staying in town. There is one bus that goes to the park used mostly by the park employees. The bus leaves at 0700 from the road that leads to the park's gate. It takes about 30 minutes and costs about R$3; stay in the bus until the last stop. Check out the return time in advance. There are also guides that provide their own transport. A local guide for this trek costs R$30 per person.

The best way to see the park is to hire a car or with a tour operator. There is only one way into the park from Itatiaia town and one main road within it – which forks off to the various hotels, all of which are signposted. **Ralph Salgueiro**, T024-3351 1823/024-9952 5962, www.ecoralph.com, takes general tours. **Edson Endrigo**, www.avesfoto.com.br, is one of Brazil's foremost birding guides and offers wildlife tours in Itatiaia and throughout Brazil. English spoken.

Tourist information Entry per day is US$10 per car. Basic accommodation in cabins and dormitories is available in the village strung along the road leading to the park. There are some delightful options inside the park but they are more expensive. Avoid weekends and Brazilian holidays if wildlife watching is a priority. Information and maps can be obtained at the **Administração do Parque Nacional de Itatiaia (park office)** ① *Estrada Parque Km 8.5*, www.ibama.gov.br/parna_itatiaia. Information can also be obtained from **Ibama** ① *T024-33521461 for the local headquarters, or T021-3224 6463 for the Rio de Janeiro state department*. The **Administração do Parque Nacional de Itatiaia** operates a refuge in the park, which acts as a starting point for climbs and treks. Information on trekking can be obtained from **Clube Excursionista Brasileiro** ① *Av Almirante Barroso 2, 8th floor, Rio de Janeiro, T021-2252 9844* www.ceb.org.br.

Flora and fauna

The park is particularly good for birds. It has a list of more than 350 species with scores of spectacular tanagers, hummingbirds (including the ultra-rare Brazilian ruby, with emerald wings and a dazzling red chest), cotingas (included the black and gold cotinga, which as far as we are aware has never been photographed) and manakins. Guans squawk and flap right next to the park roads.

The vegetation is stratified by altitude so that the plateau at 800-1100 m is covered by forest, ferns and flowering plants (such as orchids, bromeliads, begonias), giving way on the higher escarpments to pines and bushes. Higher still, over 1900 m, the distinctive rocky landscape has low bushes and grasses, isolated trees and unique plants adapted to high winds and strong sun. There is also a great variety of lichens.

Sights and hikes

The park also offers excellent trail walking. There are peaks with magnificent views out over the Atlantic coastal forest and the Rio de Janeiro coastline and a series of beautiful waterfalls; many of which are easily accessible from the park road. The trails, most of which begin just behind the Hotel Simon or around the visitors' centre, cut through the forest, bushland and up into the alpine paramo, dotted with giant granite boulders. The views from here are breathtaking. Walking the trails can be one of the best ways of seeing a good cross section of the habitats and their flora and fauna. Be sure to take plenty of water, repellent and a fleece for the higher areas. Temperatures can get well below 0°C in the winter. Information on the trails is available from the visitors' centre, which holds maps and gives directions to all the trail heads (though English is poor). The adjacent museum has a depressing display of stuffed animals from the 1940s; all of whom exist in fully animated form in the park itself.

Maçico das Prateleiras peak, one of the highest in the park (2548 m) is a full day's walk for experienced hikers. When there is no mist the views are magnificent. To reach there, take the trail from Abrigo Rebouças mountain lodge, reached from the BR354 road that heads north out of Engenheiro Passos – the next town beyond Itatiaia on BR116 (The Dutra). From here it is around one hour 30 minutes. **Pico das Agulhas Negras** is the highest point in the park (2787 m) and is reached via the same route as Maçico das Prateleiras, but with a turn to the east at the Abrigo Rebouças (instead of west). The upper reaches are only accessible with a rope and moderate climbing experience. This is another full day's walk. **Tres Picos** is a six-hour walk, leaving from a trail signposted off to the right, about 3 km beyond the visitors' centre. It is one of the best for a glimpse of the park's various habitats. The first half of the trail is fairly gentle, but after about an hour the path gets progressively steep. An hour or so beyond the steep trail is the **Rio Bonito** – a great place for a break, where there is a beautiful waterfall for swimming and refreshment. There are wonderful views from the top, which is another 45 minutes further on. The **Piscina do Maromba** is a natural pool formed by the Rio Campo Belo and situated at 1100m. It's one of the most refreshing places to swim in the park – although most Brazilians find it far too cold. Trails leave for here from behind Hotel Simon.

There are a number of **waterfalls** in the park; most of which have pools where you can swim. The most accessible is **Cachoeira Poranga** – left off the park road about 3.5 km beyond the visitors' centre. **Itaporani** and **Véu da Noiva** are reached by a path just beyond the Poranga trail; which leaves from next to the road bridge and divides after about 1 km left for Véu da Noiva, right for Itaporani.

Engenheiro Passos → *Phone code: 024. Population: 3500.*
Further along the Dutra highway (186 km from Rio) is the small town of Engenheiro Passos, from which a road (BR-354) leads to São Lourenço and Caxambu in Minas Gerais (see page 398). By turning off this road at the Registro Pass (1670 m) on the Rio-Minas border, you can reach the **Pico das Agulhas Negras**. The mountain can be climbed from this side from the **Abrigo Rebouças** refuge at 2350 m, which is manned all year round; US$2.50 per night, take your own food.

◉ West of Rio de Janeiro listings

For Sleeping and Eating price codes and other relevant information, see pages 32-37.

◉ Sleeping

Visconde de Mauá *p155*
There are many *fazendas*, *pousadas* and chalets in the vicinity, but very little budget accommodation.
LL Fronteira, Estr Visconde de Mauá-Campo Lindo, Km 4, T024-3387 1219, www.hotelfronteira.com.br. A **Roteiros de Charme** hotel (see page 34). Huge cabins with tiny private gardens set in a forested garden with wonderful views. Sauna, pool and a good restaurant and bar.
C-D Encanto, on the road to Maringa, Km 7, T024-3387 1155, www.pousadadoencanto maua.com.br/. 7 chalets in woodland and a sauna. Popular with 20- and 30-somethings.
C-D Fazenda Boa Vista, Vale das Flores, on the road to Maringa, Km 15, T024-9983 2751, www.fazendaboavista.com.br. Great views, a pool and a range of organized activities. The simple chalets sit in a private rainforest reserve. Minimum 2-day stay.
C-D Sitio Portal da Travessia, on the road to Maringa, Km 7, T024-3387 1154, www.portaldatravessia.com.br. 6 chalets next to a mountain stream and with a spring-water natural pool. The range of activities include hikes and horse riding.

Camping
Barragen's, Maringá, T024-3387 1354. One of several campsites in the area.

Parque Nacional de Itatiaia *p156*
A Hotel Donati, T024-3352 1110, www.hoteldonati.com.br. One of the most delightful hotels in the country – mock-Swiss chalets and rooms, set in tropical gardens visited by animals every night and early morning. A series of trails leads off from the main building and the hotel can organize professional birding guides. Decent restaurant and 2 pools. Highly recommended.
B-C Hotel Cabanas de Itatiaia, T024-3352 1252, www.hotelcabanasdeitatiaia.com.br. Magical views from these comfortable but rather ridiculous Swiss chalets on the hillside. Pool and good restaurant too.
B-C Hotel do Ypê, T024-3352 7453. Inside the park with sauna and heated pool.
C-D Pousada Aldeia dos Passaros, T024-3352 1152. 10 chalets with fireplaces and balconies in secondary forest overlooking a stream in the lower reaches of the park. Great breakfasts, good off-season rates and a riverside sauna.
C-D Pousada Country, Estrada do Parque Nacional 848, T024-3352 1433. A bit cheaper but outside the park on the paved access road. There are a couple of other smaller hotels and a restaurant close by.
E Ipê Amarelo, R João Maurício Macedo Costa 352, Campo Alegre, T/F024-3352 1232. IYHA youth hostel.

Engenheiro Passos *p158*
Around Engenheiro Passos there are
many *fazenda* hotels.
LL Hotel Fazenda 3 Pinheiros,
Caxambu, Km 23, T024-2108 1000,
www.3pinheiros.com.br. Large resort
charging all inclusive rates with 3 meals
provided. Special rates for trekkers that
only sleep over are negotiable.
L Fazenda Villa Forte, 1 km from town,
T/F024-3357 1122, www.villa-forte.com.br.
With meals, bar, sauna, massage, gym and
other sports facilities.
AL Itamonte MG, Pousada Fragária,
T035-3366 1443. Cosy chalets, good
food, sauna. Sleeping place of choice
for many trekkers.
A Fazenda Palmital, Km 11, BR-354 towards
Caxambu, T/F024-9226 6423, www.hotel
fazendapalmital.com.br. Chalets on the edge
of the national park, arranged around a lake
in a garden and with a waterfall nearby.
Facilities include a pool, sauna, horse riding
and a play area for kids.

🍴 Eating

Visconde de Mauá *p155*
Everywhere in town shuts at about 2200.
† Gosto com Gosto, R Wenceslau Brás,
Mineiro. Self-service Minas Gerais dishes
that are heavy on meat and flavour.
Bar do Jorge. Café.

Parque Nacional de Itatiaia *p156*
The hotels in the park all have restaurants.
Hotel Donati and **Cabanas de Itatiaia**,
the latter with a view, have the best
(see Sleeping, above).
†† Via Park, 1441 Estr Parque, Itatiaia town,
km before the park entrance, T024-9268 7934.
Delicious trout with Brazilian accompaniments,
in super-generous portions.

🎵 Bars and clubs

Visconde de Mauá *p155*
Adega Bar, open till 2400, live music
and dancing (Sat only).
Forró da Marieta for *forró* dancing.

🥾 Activities and tours

Parque Nacional de Itatiaia *p156*
Wildlife guides
Ralph Salgueiro, T024-3351 1823,
www.ecoralph.com; and Edson Endrigo,
T024-3742 8374, www.avesfoto.com.br, offer
birdwatching trips in Itatiaia and throughout
Brazil, English spoken.

Engenheiro Passos *p158*
Local guide
Levy, T024-3352 6097, T024-8812 0006 (mob),
www.levyecologico.com.br. Experienced guide
that takes trekking groups to the high region
of Itatiaia Park. Portuguese only.
Miguel, T024-3360 5224, T024-78342128
(mob). Local guide know the region really
well. Portuguese only.

🚌 Transport

Visconde de Mauá *p155*
Bus From Visconde de Mauá to **Resende**,
2 hrs, at 0830 and 0900, returning from
Resende at 1500 and 1630, US$5. Direct bus
to/from **Rio de Janeiro**, Cidade de Aço,
2 daily, 3½ hrs, US$7.

Parque Nacional de Itatiaia *p156*
Bus Bus '504 Circular' to/from **Itatiaia town**
4 times daily, picks up from **Hotel Simon**
in the park and stops at **Resende** (at the
crossroads before Itatiaia) and hotels in town.
  Itatiaia town has bus connections with
São Paulo and **Rio de Janeiro** and it's
possible to buy through tickets from
the middle of the main street.

Costa Verde

The Rio de Janeiro–Santos section of the BR-101 is one of the world's most beautiful highways, hugging the forested and hilly Costa Verde southwest of Rio. The Serra do Mar mountains plunge down to the sea in a series of spurs that disappear into the Atlantic to reappear as a cluster of islands offshore. The most beautiful of these is Ilha Grande: an 80,000-ha mountain ridge covered in rainforest and fringed with wonderful beaches. Beyond Ilha Grande, further down the coast towards São Paulo, is one of Brazil's prettiest colonial towns, Paraty, which sits surrounded by long white beaches in front of a glorious bay of islands. Seen from the harbour in the morning light, this is one of Brazil's most photographed sights. ▸▸ *For listings, see pages 167-174.*

Ins and outs

The BR-101 is paved all the way to Santos (see page 226), which has good links with São Paulo. Buses from Rio run to Angra dos Reis, Paraty, Ubatuba, Caraguatatuba and São Sebastião, where it may be necessary to change for Santos or São Paulo. Hotels and *pousadas* have sprung up all along the road, as have expensive housing developments, though these have not spoiled the views. The drive from Rio to Paraty should take four hours, but it would be better to break the journey and enjoy some of the attractions. The coast road has lots of twists and turns so, if prone to motion sickness, get a seat at the front of the bus to make the most of the views.

Mangaratiba → *Phone code: 021. Population: 25,000.*

About 22 km down the coast, this fishing village is halfway between Rio and Angra dos Reis. It stands on a little bay within the Baia de Sepetiba and in the 18th century was a port for the export first of gold, later coffee, and for the import of slaves. During the coffee era, it was the terminus for the Estrada São João Marcos highway from the Rio Paraíba do Sul. Mangaratiba's beaches are muddy, but the surroundings are pleasant and better beaches can be found outside town. These include **Ibicuí** (2 km) and **Brava** (between Ibicuí and Saí) to the east, at the head of the bay **Saco**, **Guiti** and **Cação**, and further west **São Brás**. There are numerous hotels in town. Boats run to Ilha Grande several times a day. Times vary according to the season but the last usually departs around 1400. ▸▸ *See Ins and outs, page 162.*

Angra dos Reis and around → *For listings, see pages 167-174. Colour map 4, C3.*
Phone code: 024. Population: 120,000.

The vast bay of Angra dos Reis is studded with more lush islands than there are days in the year. Some are the private playgrounds of Carioca playboys. Others are media islands owned by magazines devoted to the cult of the Brazilian celebrity, and permanently twinkling with camera flashes. A few are thronged with bikinis and board shorts in high season and pulsate to *forró* and samba beats. And many are as wild and unspoilt as they were when the Portuguese arrived 500 years ago. Yachts and speedboats flit across the bay, ferrying their bronzed and smiling cargo between the islands and beaches. In between, they dock at floating bars and restaurants for an icy caipirinha or catch of the day, and at night to dance or be lulled by the gentle sound of bossa nova.

Angra town itself is scruffy and down at heel – little more than a jumping-off point to the private islands and to Ilha Grande – but it's an increasingly popular destination for

The caiçaras

Brazilians of mixed Indian, African and Portuguese race living on the coast and leading traditional lives fishing and hunting are known as *caiçaras*. Until the 1970s almost all the beaches and islands between Rio de Janeiro and Santos were home to caiçara communities. But then the Rio to Santos main highway was constructed and floods of visitors began to pour in. With them came developments – for luxury private houses, hotels and condominiums like Laranjeiras – which is home to members of Brazil's wealthy and allegedly highly corrupt elite. *Caiçara* communities were bought off for pittance or forced from their land with threats of violence or even death. And an entire way of life and knowledge of the Atlantic coast forest, strongly rooted in indigenous traditions is in danger of being entirely lost. All the favelas in Angra dos Reis bear the name of a different beach on Ilha Grande or the beaches and islands around the bay. Nowadays there are *caiçara* communities only on a few isolated stretches between Rio and Santos – like the Ponta da Joatinga peninsula south of Paraty and Aventureiros beach in Ilha Grande. Many think that carefully managed, sensitive ecotourism will help protect them and spread the story of their plight, which is little known even within Brazil.

international travellers. This is a result of the migration of the wealthy out of Rio and their acquisition of beaches and property from the local fishermen, whose families now live in the favelas that encrust the surrounding hills (see box, above).

Angra was once a pretty colonial town like Paraty further along the coast, and several buildings remain from its heyday. Of particular note are the church and convent of **Nossa Senhora do Carmo**, built in 1593 on Praça General Osório, the **Igreja Matriz de Nossa Senhora da Conceição** (1626) in the centre of town and the church and convent of **São Bernardino de Sena** (1758-1763) on the Morro do Santo Antônio. On the Largo da Lapa is the church of **Nossa Senhora da Lapa da Boa Morte** (1752) and a **Museum of Sacred Art** ⓘ *Thu-Sun 1000-1200, 1400-1800.*

On the Península de Angra, west of the town, is the **Praia do Bonfim**, a popular beach; offshore is the island of the same name, on which the **hermitage of Senhor do Bonfim** (1780) is located. Some 15 km east are the ruins of the **Jacuecanga seminary** (1797).

Angra is connected to Rio and Paraty by regular buses, to Ilha Grande by ferry and fishing boat, and to Ilha do Gipóia by fishing boat. The **tourist office** ⓘ *Av Julio Maria, 024-3365 2041, www.angra-dos-reis.com, www.angra.rj.gov.br,* is just behind the Cais de Santa Luiza quay. The websites have more information than the office.

Ilha Grande → *For listings, see pages 167-174. Colour map 4, C3. Phone code: 021.*

Ilha Grande is a mountain ridge covered in tropical forest protruding from the emerald sea and fringed by some of the world's most beautiful beaches. There are no cars and no roads, just trails through the forest, so the island is still relatively undeveloped. With luck it will remain so, as much of Ilha Grande forms part of a state park and biological reserve, and cannot even be visited.

That the island has so much forest is largely a fluke of history. The island was a notorious pirate lair in the 16th and 17th centuries and then a landing port for slaves.

By the 20th century it was the site of an infamous prison for the country's most notorious criminals, including the writer Graciliano Ramos (see Literature, page 784), whose *Memórias do Cárcere* relate his experiences. The prison closed in 1994 and is now overgrown. Since then Ilha Grande has been a well-kept Brazilian secret, and is gradually becoming part of the international backpacker circuit.

Ins and outs

Fishing boats and ferries (**Barcas SA**, T021-2533 7524), leave from Angra dos Reis and Mangaratiba taking two hours or so to reach Vila do Abraão, the island's only real village. From Angra they only leave in the morning and early afternoon and must be chartered (US$60-100 per boat; it is usually possible to get a group together in high season). The weather is best from March to June and the island is over-run during the Christmas, New Year and Carnaval periods. There is a helpful **tourist office** on the jetty at Abraão. Further information and pictures can be found at www.ilhagrande.com. Be wary of undercover police searching for backpackers smoking cannabis on Ilha Grande's beaches.

Beaches and walks

The beach at **Abraão** may look beautiful to new arrivals but those further afield are far more spectacular. The two most famous are: **Lopes Mendes**, a long stretch of sand on the eastern (ocean side) backed by flatlands and patchy forest; and **Aventureiro**, fringed by coconut palms and tropical forest, its powder-fine sand pocked with boulders and washed by a transparent aquamarine sea. Lopes Mendes is two hours' walk from Abraão. Aventureiro is over six hours, but it can be reached by boat. A few fishermen's huts and *barracas* provide food and accommodation here but there is no camping. Good beaches closer to Abraão include the half-moon bay at **Abraãoozinho** (15 minutes' walk) and **Grande das Palmas**, which has a delightful tiny whitewashed chapel (one hour 20 minutes' walk). Both lie east of the town past **Hotel Sagu**. There are boat trips to **Lagoa Azul**, with crystal-clear water and reasonable snorkelling, **Freguesia de Santana** and **Saco do Céu**.

There are a couple of good treks over the mountains to **Dois Rios**, where the old jail was situated. There is still a settlement of former prison guards here who have nowhere to

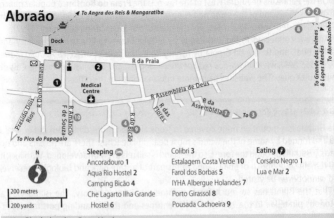

Abraão ◄ *To Angra dos Reis & Mangaratiba*

To Grande das Palmas & Lopes Mendes
To Abraãoozinho

Dock

R da Praia

Medical Centre

R Assembléia de Deus

R da Assembléia   *To ③*

R das Flores

R do Bicão

Presidio Dois Rios
R Dona Romana
R Amâncio F de Souza

To Pico do Papagaio

N
200 metres
200 yards

Sleeping
Ancoradouro 1
Aqua Rio Hostel 2
Camping Bicão 4
Che Lagarto Ilha Grande Hostel 6

Colibri 3
Estalagem Costa Verde 10
Farol dos Borbas 5
IYHA Albergue Holandes 7
Porto Girassol 8
Pousada Cachoeira 9

Eating
Corsário Negro 1
Lua e Mar 2

go. The walk is about 13 km each way, takes about three hours and [...]
scenery and superb views. Another three-hour hike is to **Pico do Pa[...]**
through forest; it's a steep climb for which a guide is essential, however, th[...]
top is breathtaking. **Pico da Pedra d'Água** (1031 m) can also be climbed.

Paraty → *For listings, see pages 167-174. Colour map 4, C2. Phone code: 024. Population: 30,000.*

Paraty is one of Brazil's prettiest colonial towns and one of Rio de Janeiro state's most
popular tourist destinations. It is at its most captivating at dawn, when all but the dogs
and chickens are sleeping. As the sun peeps over the horizon the little rectilinear streets
are infused with a rich golden light, which warms the whitewash and brilliant blue-and-
yellow window frames of the colonial town houses and the façades of the Manueline
churches. Brightly coloured fishing boats bob up and down in the water in the foreground
and behind the town the deep green of the rainforest-covered mountains of the Serra da
Bocaina sit shrouded in their self-generated wispy cloud. The town was founded in the
17th century as a gold port and most of its historic buildings date from this period.

At the weekend Paraty buzzes with tourists who browse in the little boutiques and art
galleries or buy souvenirs from the indigenous Guarani who proffer their wares on the
cobbles. At night they fill the numerous little bars and restaurants, many of which, like the
pousadas, are owned by the bevy of expat Europeans who have found their haven in
Paraty and who are determined to preserve its charm. During the week, especially off
season, the town is quiet and intimate, its atmosphere as yet unspoilt by the increasing
numbers of independent travellers.

The town's environs are as beautiful as Paraty itself. Just a few kilometres away lie the
forests of the **Ponta do Juatinga Peninsula**, fringed by wonderful beaches, washed by
little waterfalls and still home to communities of Caiçara fishermen who live much as they
have done for centuries. Islands pepper the bay, some of them home to ultra-rare animals
such as the tiny golden lion tamarin monkey, which is found nowhere else. The best way
to visit these destinations is on a boat trip with one of the town's fishermen from the quay.

Ins and outs

The *rodoviária* is at the corner of Rua Jango Padua and Rua da Floresta. There are direct
bus connections with Rio and São Paulo several times daily, and with a number of
destinations along the coast. Taxis charge a set rate of US$4 from the bus station to the
historic centre, which is pedestrianized and easily negotiable on foot. Staff at the **Centro
de Informações Turísticas** ① *Av Roberto Silveira, near the entrance to the historic centre,
024-3371 1266*, are friendly and helpful and some speak English. There is a good town
map in the *Welcome to Paraty* brochure, www.eco-paraty.com. More information is
available at www.paraty.com.br. The wettest months are January, February, June and
July. In spring, the streets in the colonial centre may flood, but the houses remain above
the waterline. ▶▶ *See Transport, page 174.*

Sights

In keeping with all Brazilian colonial towns, Paraty's churches were built according to
social status and race. There are four churches in the town, one for the 'freed coloured
men', one for the blacks and two for the whites. **Santa Rita** (1722), built by the 'freed
coloured men' in elegant Brazilian baroque, faces the bay and the port. It is probably the
most famous picture postcard image of Paraty and houses a small **Museum of Sacred Art**

Sun 0900-1200, 1300-1800, US$1. **Nossa Senhora do Rosário e São Benedito** *do Comércio, Tue 0900-1200*, (1725, rebuilt 1757) built by black slaves, is small and simple; the slaves were unable to raise the funds to construct an elaborate building. **Nossa Senhora dos Remédios** ① *Mon, Wed, Fri, Sat 0900-1200, Sun 0900-1500*, is the town's parish church, the biggest in Paraty. It was started in 1787 but construction continued until 1873. The church was never completely finished as it was built on unstable ground; the architects decided not to add weight to the structure by putting up the towers. The façade is leaning to the left, which is clear from the three doors (only the one on the right has a step). Built with donations from the whites, it is rumoured that Dona Geralda Maria da Silva contributed gold from a pirate's hoard found buried on the beach. **Capela de Nossa Senhora das Dores** ① *Thu 0900-1200* (1800), is a chapel facing the sea. It was used mainly by wealthy 19th-century whites.

There is a great deal of distinguished Portuguese colonial architecture in delightful settings. **Rua do Comércio** is the main street in the historic centre. It was here that the prominent traders lived, the two-storey houses having the commercial establishments on the ground floor and the residences above. Today the houses are occupied by restaurants, *pousadas* and tourist shops.

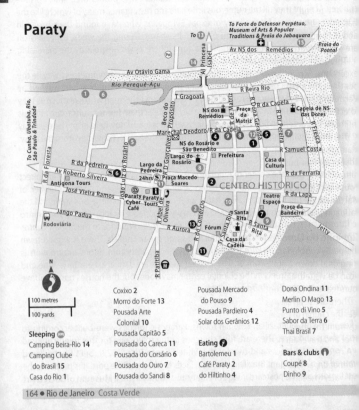

Paraty

Sleeping
Camping Beira-Rio 14
Camping Clube
  do Brasil 1
Casa do Rio 1
Coxixo 2
Morro do Forte 13
Pousada Arte
  Colonial 10
Pousada Capitão 5
Pousada do Careca 11
Pousada do Corsário 6
Pousada do Ouro 7
Pousada do Sandi 8
Pousada Mercado
  do Pouso 9
Pousada Pardieiro 4
Solar dos Gerânios 12

Eating
Bartolemeu 1
Café Paraty 2
do Hiltinho 4
Dona Ondina 11
Merlin O Mago 13
Punto di Vino 5
Sabor da Terra 6
Thai Brasil 7

Bars & clubs
Coupé 8
Dinho 9

The **Casa da Cadeia**, close to Santa Rita Church, is the former jail, complete with iron grilles in the windows and doors. It is now a public library and art gallery.

On the northern headland is a small fort, **Forte do Defensor Perpétuo**, built in 1822, whose cannon and thick ruined walls can be seen. From the fort there are good views of the sea and the roofs of the town. It's about 15 minutes' walk from the centre. To get there, cross the Rio Perequê Açu by the bridge at the end of the Rua do Comércio; climb the small hill, which has some attractive *pousadas* and a cemetery, and follow the signs. Also here is the **Museum of Arts and Popular Traditions** ① *Wed-Sun*, in a colonial-style building. It contains carved wooden canoes, musical instruments, fishing gear and other items from local communities. On the headland is the gunpowder store and enormous hemispherical iron pans that were used for extracting whale oil, which was used for lamps and to mix with sand and cement for building.

Boat trips and beaches

The most popular trip, and highly recommended, is a five-hour **schooner tour** around the bay for swimming (US$15, lunch is an optional extra). Smaller boats are available for US$10 an hour or US$20 for three hours. Many beautiful beaches are visited.

Praia do Pontal is the town beach, five minutes' walk from the historic centre: cross the bridge and turn right along the river. The water and sand are not very clean but the handful of *barracas* under the trees are a nice place to hang out. **Praia do Jabaquara** is about 20 minutes away on foot: cross the bridge and continue straight up the hill. There are a few *barracas* here and the sand is cleaner, but the water tends to be muddy.

There are other beaches further from town, many of which make worthwhile excursions. Scruffy **Boa Vista** is just south of town and beyond this (reachable only by boat) are, in order, the long, broad and clean stretches of **Praia da Conçeicao**, **Praia Vermelha** and **Praia da Lula**, all of which have simple restaurants and are backed by forest and washed by gentle waves. The **Saco da Velha**, further south still, is small and intimate, protected by an island and surrounded by rainforested slopes.

The small town of **Paraty Mirím**, is 17 km away and has a vast sweeping beach with a Manueline church built on the sand and some ruined colonial buildings. It is reached by boat or by four buses a day (three on Sunday) and has simple restaurants and places to camp. Fishing boats leave from here for other islands and beaches including the **Praia do Pouso da Cajaíba**, which has lodgings of the same name, and the spectacular sweep at **Martim do Sá**. The **Saco do Mamanguá** is a long sleeve of water that separates the Ponta da Juatinga and Paraty Mirím, which has good snorkelling.

Caminho do Ouro (Gold Trail) → www.caminhodoouro.com.br.

This partly cobbled trail through the mountains was built by slaves in the 18th century to bring gold down from Ouro Preto before transporting it to Portugal. Recently restored, it can be visited, along with the ruins of a toll house, on foot or horseback as a day trip. Tours leave at 1000 from the **Teatro Espaço** ① *R Dona Geralda 327, T024-3371 1575*.

There are several *cachoeiras* (waterfalls) in the area, such as the **Cachoeira da Penha**, near the church of the same name. It is 10 km from town on the road to Cunha; take a local bus from the *rodoviária*, US$1, there are good mountain views on the way. The tourist office and travel agencies have details on the waterfalls and hikes.

A recommended excursion is to **Fazenda Murycana** ① *T024-3371 3930 for tours and information*, an old sugar estate and 17th-century *cachaça* distillery with original house and waterwheel. You can taste and buy the different types of *cachaça*; some are aged in oak barrels for 12 years. Try the *cachaça com cravo e canela* (with clove and cinnamon). There is an excellent restaurant and horse riding is available but English is not spoken by the employees. Mosquitoes can be a problem at the *fazenda*, take repellent and don't wear shorts. To get there, take a 'Penha/Ponte Branca' bus from the *rodoviária*, four a day; alight where it crosses a small white bridge and then walk 10 minutes along a signed, unpaved road. There is a good chance of hitching a lift back to Paraty.

Trindade → *For listings, see pages 167-174. Colour map 4, C2.*

Ramshackle little Trindade (pronounced *Tringdajee*) may not be as beautiful in its own right as Paraty but its setting, sandwiched between rainforested slopes and emerald sea, is equally spectacular. And, unlike Paraty, it has a long, broad beach. The town has long been a favourite hang-out for young middle-class surf hippies from São Paulo and Rio, who come here in droves during the holiday period. It is now also finding its place on the international backpacker circuit and it's easy to see why. The beach is spectacular, the *pousadas* and restaurants cheap and cheerful, and there are a number of campsites. Sadly there is no sewage treatment and when the town is full, foul black water flows onto the sand. There are plenty of unprepossessing restaurants along the town's main drag, **Avenida Principal**. All serve the usual 'beans and rice and chips' combinations. Avoid coming here during Christmas, New Year, Carnaval and Easter.

Ins and outs Trindade is 30 km south of Paraty. It is reached by a steep, winding 7-km road branching off the Rio–Santos road (BR-101). Buses that run between Paraty and Ubatuba all pass the turning to Trindade and will drop you or pick you up here. Ask for 'Patrimonio' or 'Estrada para Trindade'. In high season there are vans from here to Trindade (US$2). In low season you'll have to hitch or walk; cars pass regularly. Be wary of carrying any drugs – the police at the turn-off post are very vigilant and searches are frequent. Tourist information is available at the booth at the entrance to town (no English spoken) or through the Paraty website, www.paraty.com.br and tourist office. Trindade has no banks.

Around Trindade

Beyond Trindade and the upmarket condominium at **Laranjeiras** there is a series of beaches. **Sono** is a long, sweeping stretch of sand backed by *barracas*, some of which have accommodation to rent. Sanitation is a problem, however. **Ponta Negra** is a little *caiçara* village, beautifully situated in a cove between rocky headlands. It has its own beach, simple but elegant homestay accommodation, fishing-boat trips and organized treks into the surrounding forest, which is rich in birdlife and full of waterfalls. It is possible to climb to the highest peak on the peninsula for views out over the Paraty area. The community is traditional and conservative; visits should be arranged in advance through village leaders. ▶▶ *See Sleeping, page 170.*

Ins and outs Sono and Ponta Negra are reached from the Sono trailhead, which lies at the end of the bus route to Trindade/Laranjeiras. The path is easy to find and follow. Allow 1½ hours for Sono and three hours for Ponta Negra. There are several buses a day to Trindade and the trailhead from Paraty. ▶▶ *See Transport, page 174.*

Costa Verde listings

For Sleeping and Eating price codes and other relevant information, see pages 32-37.

Sleeping

Angra dos Reis and around *p160*
Only stay in Angra town if you miss your bus or boat. There are a few cheap hotels near the port and main *praça*.
L do Frade, on the road to Ubatuba, Km 123 BR-101, 33 km from Angra, T024-3369 2244. Luxury hotel on the Praia do Frade with bar, restaurants, sauna and sports facilities.
AL Pestana, Estr do Contorno 3700, Km 13, T024-3367 2754, www.pestanahotels.com.br. A range of bungalows on a forested hillside overlooking an emerald-green sea. Very pretty, peaceful and secluded with a decent open-sided restaurant and bar overlooking the water and excellent service.
B-C Caribe, R de Conceição 255, T024-3365 0033, www.angra2reis.com.br/caribe. Central and well kept with rather cheesy 1970s rooms in a tower near the centre. A good option for those who miss the Ilha Grande boat and need to stay overnight.

Ilha Grande *p161, map p162*
Accommodation on the island is in *pousadas* at Vila do Abraão or camping elsewhere. It is possible to hire a fisherman's cottage on Aventureiro Beach, which can be reached on the *Maria Isabel* or *Mestre Ernani* boats (T021-3361 9895 or T021-9269 5877) that leave from the quay in front of the BR petrol station in Angra dos Reis. Alternatively boats can be chartered direct from Angra dos Reis (2-3 hrs). There is a handful of upmarket options in isolated locations reachable only by boat.

Abraão
Reservations are only necessary in peak season or on holiday weekends.
A Ancoradouro, R da Praia 121, T024-3361 5053, www.pousadancoradouro.com.br.

Clean, simple rooms with en suite in a beach-front building, 10 mins' walk east of the jetty.
B-C Farol dos Borbas, Praia do Abraão, T024-3361 5866, www.ilhagrandetour.com.br. 1 min from the jetty. Simple, well-maintained, fan-cooled rooms with tiled floors and breakfast tables and chairs. The best have balconies. The worst have no windows. Boat trips organized.
C Porto Girassol, R do Praia 65, T024-3261 5277, www.portogirassol.com.br. Simple rooms in a mock-colonial beach house, 5 mins' east of the jetty.
C-E Aqua Rio Hostel, Town Beach, Abraão, T024-3361 5405, www.aquariohostel.com. Party hostel on a peninsula overlooking the beach. Dorms, scruffy rooms, a large, relaxing bar area, seawater pool and great ocean views.
C-E Che Lagarto Ilha Grande Hostel, Town Beach, Abraão; book through the website www.chelagarto.com. Large beachside party hostel with well-kept dorms, doubles, bar and tours including trail walking and kayaking.
C-E IYHA Albergue Holdandes, R Assembleia de Deus, T024-3361 5034, www.holandeshostel.com.br. Book ahead. Dorms, doubles and 4 little chalets in the forest on the edge of town. Breakfast included, laundry and advice on boats and tours. Good atmosphere.
C-E Pousada Cachoeira, 12-min walk from centre, T024-3361 5083, www.cachoeira.com. Price per person. Great little *pousada* full of character, with small rooms in chalets in a forest garden. Run by a German-Brazilian couple; English spoken. Good breakfast.
D Colibri, R da Assembléia 70, T024-3361 5033, www.colibriresort.com. Smart little Swedish-owned resort with rooms decorated with a personal touch and an outdoor breakfast area. Tours around the island offered.
D Estalagem Costa Verde, R Amâncio Felicio de Souza 239a, ½ a block behind the church, T024-3104 7490, www.estalagemcosta verde.com.br. Bright hostel with light,

well-maintained rooms decorated with a little thought. Great value.

Camping Camping Bicao, R Rua do Bicão s/n, T024-3361 5061. Hot showers, lockers, electricity a campsite with lots of shade. There are plenty of other campsites – see www.ilhagrande.com for details in English.

Paraty *p163, map p164*
There are many options in Paraty and 2 beautiful places in the hills nearby. Also browse www.paraty.com.br/frame.htm.
LL Angatu, T011-3872 0945, www.angatu. com. The very best private houses in the region, including Prince João de Orleans e Braganza's waterfront home and luxury villas on the surrounding islands. Each comes with a yacht and, if you choose, guides and tours around the bay and to Ilha Grande.
L Bromelias Pousada and Spa, Rodovia Rio–Santos, Km 562, Graúna, T/F024-3371 2791, www.pousadabromelias.com.br. An Asian-inspired spa *pousada* with its own aromatherapy products and a range of massage treatments. Accommodation is in tastefully decorated chalets perched on a hillside forest garden overlooking the sea and islands. Pool, sauna and restaurant.
L Pousada do Ouro, R Dr Pereira (or da Praia) 145, T/F024-3371 1311, www.pousada ouro.com.br. Near Paraty's eastern waterfront and built as a private home with a fortune made on the gold route. Plain rooms in an annexe and suites in the main building.

The tropical garden houses an open-air poolside pavilion. Pictures of previous guests such as Mick Jagger, Tom Cruise and Linda Evangelista adorn the lobby.
L Pousada do Sandi, Largo do Rosário 1, T024-3371 2100, www.pousadadosandi. com.br. The most comfortable in town set in an 18th-century building with a grand lobby, comfortable mock-colonial rooms and a very good adjoining restaurant and pool area. Superior breakfast, parking and excellent tours organized through www.angatu.com.
L Pousada Pardieiro, R do Comércio 74, T024-3371 1370, www.pousadapardieiro.com.br. Tucked away in a quiet corner, with a calm, sophisticated atmosphere. Attractive colonial building with lovely gardens, delightful rooms facing internal patios and a little swimming pool. Always full at weekends. No children under 15.
AL Hotel Coxixo, R do Comércio 362, T024-3371 1460, www.hotelcoxixo.com.br. A converted colonial building in the heart of the 17th-century town, which has been turned into a temple to its Brazilian movie-star owner, Maria Della Costa. Black-and-white pictures of her from the 1950s adorn every corner. Rooms are decked out in Catholic kitsch. The best rooms in the hotel and in Paraty are the plush colonial suites.
A-B Le Gite d'Indaitiba, Rodovia Rio–Santos (BR-101) Km 562, Graúna, T024-3371 7174, www.legitedindaiatiba.com.br. French-owned *pousada* with one of the best restaurants in southeastern Brazil. Carefully

designed stylish chalets set in gardens on a hillside overlooking a mountain stream. Sweeping views of the sea and bay of islands and a 2-m-wide spring water swimming pool.

A-B Morro do Forte, R Orlando Carpinelli, T/F024-3371 1211, www.pousadamorrodoforte.com.br. Lovely garden, good breakfast, pool, German owner Peter Kallert offers trips on his yacht. Out of the centre. Recommended.

B Pousada Capitão, R Luiz do Rosário 18, T024-3371 1815, www.paraty.com.br/capitao. Converted colonial building, close to the historic centre, swimming pool, English and Japanese spoken.

B Pousada do Corsário, Beco do Lapeiro 26, T024-3371 1866, www.pousadacorsario.com.br. With a pool and its own gardens, next to the river and 2 blocks from the centre. Simple, stylish rooms, most with hammocks outside. With a branch in Búzios (see website).

B Pousada Mercado do Pouso, Largo de Santa Rita 43, T/F024-3371 1114, http://mercadodepouso.com.b. Historic building close to waterfront decked out in lush wood, good sea views. Family atmosphere, no pool.

B-C Pousada Arte Colonial, R da Matriz 292, T024-3371 7231, www.pousadaartecolonial.com.br. One of the best deals in Paraty. A beautiful colonial building in the centre decorated with style and a personal touch by its French owner, with artefacts and antiques from all over the world. Friendly, helpful and with breakfast. Highly recommended.

B-E Geko Hostel, R Orlando Carpinelli, 3 Praia do Pontal, T024-3371 2507, www.gekohostel.com. Doubles and dorms (**E** pp), breakfast included, free pickup from bus station, Wi-Fi, tours arranged.

B-F Misti Chill Hostel and Pousada, R Orlando Carpinelli, 3-Praia do Pontal, T024-3371 2545, www.mistichill.com. Beachfront accommodation from dorms to private rooms with a/c.

C-D Solar dos Gerânios, Praça da Matriz, T/F024-3371 1550, www.paraty.com.br/geranio. Beautiful colonial family house on main square in traditional rustic style that is a welcome antidote to the more polished *pousadas*. Rooms have lovely wooden lattice balconies – ask for the corner one which has 2. Very reasonably priced, English spoken. Warmly recommended.

D-E HI Paraty Hostel Casa do Rio, R Antônio Vidal 120, T024-3371 2223, www.paratyhostel.com. Youth hostel in a little house with riverside courtyard and hammocks. There's a kitchen and price includes breakfast. Trips by jeep or on horseback to waterfalls, mountains and beaches. Dorms a little crowded.

D-E Pousada do Careca, Praça Macedo Soares, T024-3371 1291, www.paraty.com/pousadadocareca. Simple rooms. Those without street windows are musty.

Camping
Camping Beira-Rio, just across the bridge, before the road to the fort.

Camping Clube do Brasil, Av Orlando
Carpinelli, Praia do Pontal, T024-3371 1877.
Small, good, very crowded in Jan and Feb,
US$8 per person.
Praia Jabaquara, T024-3371 2180.

Trindade *p166*
Expect no frills in Trindade.
D Chalé e Pousada Magia do Mar, T024-
3371 5130. Thatched hut with space for 4.
Views out over beach.
D Pousada Marimbá, R Principal, T024-
3371 5147. Simple colourful rooms and
a breakfast area.
**D-F Ponta da Trindade Pousada and
Camping**, T024-3371 5113. Simple fan-
cooled rooms and a sand-floored campsite
with cold showers and no electricity.

Around Trindade *p166*
C-D Ponta Negra homestays, Ponta Negra,
contact **Teteco**, T024-3371 2673, teteco@
paratyweb.com.br, or Cauê, francocvc@
hotmail.com.

🍴 Eating

Ilha Grande *p161, map p162*
Aside from **Sito do Lobo** (guests only, see
Sleeping, above), food on the island is fairly
basic: fish, chicken or meat with beans, rice
and chips. There are plenty of restaurants
serving these exciting combinations in
Abraão. We list the very few better options.
♦♦♦ Lua e Mar, Abraão, on the waterfront,
T024-3361 5113. A few more adventurous
fish-based options than the other restaurants.
♦♦ Corsário Negro, R da Vila, T024-3361
5321. The best in Abraão with good seafood,
vegetarian food and excellent caipirinhas.
The owner is a mine of information about
the island and is fascinating to chat to.

Paraty *p163, map p164*
The best restaurants in Paraty are in the
historic part of town and are almost as
good as you will find in Rio or São Paulo.

Watch out for surreptitious cover charges
for live music, which are often very discreetly
displayed. The less expensive restaurants,
those offering *comida a quilo* (pay by weight)
and the fast-food outlets are outside the
historic centre, mainly on Av Roberto Silveira.
  Paraty's regional specialities include *peixe
à Parati* (local fish cooked with herbs and
green bananas), served with *pirão* (a mixture
of manioc flour and the sauce that the fish
was cooked in). Also popular is the *filé de
peixe ao molho de camarão* (fried fish fillet
with a shrimp and tomato sauce). There is
plenty of choice in Paraty so have a browse.
Also see **Le Gite d'Indaitiba**, page 168.
♦♦♦ Bartolomeu, R Samuel Costa 179,
T024-3371 5032. Argentinian steaks, fish
(including good ceviche) and great cocktails
from ex-*Elite* fashion model-turned-gourmet
cook, Deborah Cortes.
♦♦♦ do Hiltinho, R Mcal Deodoro 233,
historical centre, T024-3371 1432.
Decent seafood, including local dishes.
♦♦♦ Merlin O Mago, (next to **Hotel Coxixo**),
R do Comercio 376, historic centre, T024-
3371 2157, www.paraty.com.br/merlin.htm.
Franco-Brazilian cooking in an intimate
dining room/bar, by a German cordon
bleu chef and illustrious photojournalist.
Decent wine list. Highly recommended.
♦♦♦ Punto Di Vino, R Mcal Deodoro 129,
historical centre, T024-3371 1348. The best
for seafood in town; owned and run by
a Neapolitan who catches his own 'catch
of the day'. Great wood-fired pizza, live
music and an excellent selection of wine.
♦♦♦ Thai Brasil, R Dona Geralda 345,
historic centre, T024-3371 0127, www.thai
brasil.com.br. Beautiful restaurant decorated
with handicrafts and furnished with hand-
painted chairs and tables. The cooking
comprises well-executed Thai standards
without spices (Brazilians yelp in pain
at the sight of a chilli).
♦♦♦ Café Paraty, R da Lapa and Comércio,
historic centre. Open 0900-2400. Sandwiches,
appetizers, light meals, also bar with live music
nightly (cover charge). A local landmark.

¶¶ **Catimbau**, Baía de Paraty, T024-3371 1847.
A restaurant and bar sitting between 2 giant
boulders on a tiny island in the bay. It is run
by ex-Hollywood line producer and local
fisherman Caca and his Dutch wife Mimi
and serves simple but very fresh seafood
accompanied by ice-cold beer or caipirinhas.
Can be visited by request on any bay tour.
¶¶ **Dona Ondina**, R do Comércio 2, by the
river, historic centre. Closed on Mon, Mar
and Nov. Family restaurant with well-
prepared simple food. Good value.
¶ **Vila Verde**, Estr Paraty–Cunha, Km 7, T024-
3371 7808, www.vilaverdeparaty.com.br.
It's worth a stop off here on the way to or
from the waterfalls, the Caminho Douro or
Cunha. The restaurant serves light Italian
and its open sides overlook a tropical garden
that attracts numerous morpho butterflies,
humming birds and tanagers.
Kontiki, Ilha Duas Irmãs, T024-999
9599, www.paraty.com.br/kontiki.htm.
Daily 1000-1500 and Fri and Sat for dinner.
A tiny island, 5 mins from the pier where
a small speed boat runs a (free) shuttle
service. Wonderful island setting; ordinary
food. Reservations recommended.
Sabor da Terra, Av Roberto Silveira, next to
Banco do Brasil. Closes 2200. Reliable, if not
bargain-priced self-service food.

Bars and clubs

Paraty p163, map p164
The best way to sample Paraty's nightlife
is to wander its handful of streets.
Bar Coupé, Praça da Matriz. A popular
hang-out with outside seating. Good
bar snacks and breakfast.
Bar Dinho, Praça da Matriz at R da Matriz.
Good bar with live music at weekends,
sometimes mid-week.
Amoya, R Comendador José Luiz. Video
bar and café, live music at weekends.

● Entertainment

Paraty p163, map p163
Dance
As well as the Dança dos Velhos, another
common dance in these parts is the *ciranda*,
in which everyone, young and old, dances
in a circle to songs accompanied by guitars.

Theatre
Teatro Espaço, R Dona Geralda 327, T024-
3371 1575, ecparati@ax.apc.org. Wed, Sat
2100, US$12. This world-famous puppet
show should not be missed. The puppets
tell stories (in mime), which are funny, sad,
even shocking, with incredible realism. The
short pieces (lasting 1 hr) are works of pure
imagination and emotion and a moving
commentary on the human condition.

❀ Festivals and events

Angra dos Reis and around p160
New Year Festa do Mar, boat processions.
5 Jan Folia dos Reis, the Three Kings,
culmination of a religious festival that
begins at Christmas.
6 Jan Founding of Angra dos Reis.
May Festa do Divino and, on the 2nd Sun,
the Senhor do Bonfim maritime procession.
Jun As elsewhere in the state, the **Festas
Juninas** are celebrated.
8 Dec Festival of Nossa Senhora
da Conceição.

Paraty p163, map p164
Feb/Mar Carnaval, hundreds of people
cover their bodies in black mud and run
through the streets yelling like prehistoric
creatures (anyone can join in).
Mar/Apr Semana Santa (Easter Week)
with religious processions and folk songs.
Jun FLIP (Easter Week).
Mid-Jul Semana de Santa Rita, traditional
foods, shows, exhibitions and dances.

Aug Festival da Pinga, the *cachaça* fair at which local distilleries display their products and there are plenty of opportunities to over-indulge.
Sep (around the 8th) **Semana da Nossa Senhora dos Remédios**, processions and religious events.
Sep/Oct Spring Festival of Music, concerts in front of Santa Rita Church.
31 Dec New Year's Eve, a huge party with open-air concerts and fireworks (reserve accommodation in advance).

O Shopping

Paraty *p163, map p164*
Shopping here is by and large a disappointment. There are many shops but most sell the kind of tack you'd find in any tourist town in the world; key rings, fridge magnets, cheesy T-shirts and so on. The best items are fine art (which tends to be overpriced), and artisan ware: fish trays, small wooden canoes and boats. The Guarani people sell their arts and crafts on the R da Matriz. Paraty *cachaça* is some of the best in the state, although it can't compare with bottles from Minas.

▲▲ Activities and tours

Angra dos Reis and around *p160*
See **Angatu**, under Paraty, below.

Ilha Grande *p161, map p162*
Boat trips
These are easy to organize on the quay in Abraão on Ilha Grande.

Scuba diving
Ilha Grande Dive, R da Praia s/n, Vila do Abraão, T021-3361 5512, igdive@bol.com.br (next to the *farmacia* on the seafront). Offers trips around the entire bay.

Paraty *p163, map p164*
Angatu, T011-3872 0945, www.angatu.com. The best private tours and diving around the bay in luxurious yachts and motor cruisers, with private entries to the exclusive island parties. Also offers private villa rental in and around Paraty (see Sleeping, page 168). Book well ahead. Highly recommended.
Antígona, Praça da Bandeira 2, Centro Histórico, T/F024-3371 1165, www.anti gona.com.br. Daily schooner tours, 5 hrs, bar and lunch on board. Recommended.
Paraty Tours, Av Roberto Silveira 11, T/F024-3371 1327, www.paratytours.com.br. Good range of trips. English and Spanish spoken.
Rei Cigano, contact through **Bartolomeu** restaurant (see Eating, page 170), or ring Tuca T024-7835 3190, thiparaty@ hotmail.com. Day excursions and overnights or even expeditions along the Brazilian coast in a beautiful 60-ft sailing schooner with cabins.
Soberana da Costa, R Dona Geraldo 43, in **Pousada Mercado do Pouso**, T/F024-3371 1114, see Sleeping, page 169. Schooner trips. Recommended.

⊖ Transport

Angra dos Reis and around *p160*
Bus Costa Verde buses run at least hourly to the *rodoviária* in **Rio de Janeiro**, some are direct, others take the *via litoral* and go through Barra, Ipanema and Copacabana, US$10, 2½ hrs. Sit on the right for the best views. Busy at weekends. There are also regular buses to and from **São Paulo**, **Paraty**, **Ubatuba** and the São Paulo coast.

Ferry Ferries run to **Ilha Grande**, see the timetable on page 173. Fishing boats will also take passengers for around US$5 per person before 1300 or when full. Boat charter costs around US$60-100.

Boats to Ilha Grande

	Monday-Thursday	Friday	Weekends and holidays
Mangaratiba–Abraão	0800	0800, 2200	0800
Abraão–Mangaratiba	1730	1730	1730
Angra–Abraão	1530	1530	1330
Abraão–Angra	1000	1000	1000

Ferries (T0800-704 4113) cost US$3.50 Monday-Friday (one way) and US$8 (one way) and US15 (return) on weekends.

Faster catmarans between Angra and Abraão leave from the Santa Luiza pier (not the ferry pier) and take 45 minutes.

Angra–Abraão	0800, 1100, 1600	0800, 1100, 1600	0800, 1100,1600
Abraão–Angra	0930, 1230, 1700	0930, 1230, 1700	0930, 1230, 1700

Catamarans (T024-3365 6426) cost US$15 (one way) on weekdays. Buy at least an hour in advance to ensure this price, and a place.

Saveiro Resta 1, Samurai and Rei Tomás sailing boats boats also run between Angra and Abraão as follows:

Angra-Abraão	0800, 1700	0800, 1700	0730, 1100, 1530, 1700
Abraão-Angra	1000, 1700	1000, 1700	0930, 1000, 1300, 1700

Saveiro Resta 1 (T024-3365 6426), Samurai & Rei Tomás (T024-3361 5920) cost US$7-9 (one way). There are also occasional sailings (usually Mon-Fri at 0730 in high season) with Saveiro Água Viva – ask at the docks.

Saveiro Acalanto II sailing boats run between Mangaratiba and Abraão.

Mangaratiba-Abraão	1400	1400	1400
Abraão-Mangaratiba	0800	0800	0800

Saveiro Acalanto II (T024-3361 5920) boats cost US$6 (one way).

There are also sailing boats (Saveiros Andréa) running between the town of Conceição de Jacareí and Abraão. Conceição de Jacareí. Conceição has a few buses daily to Rio and Angra.

Conceição de Jacareí –Abraão	0900, 1130, 1500, 1815	0900, 1130, 1500, 1845, 2100	0900, 1130, 1500, 1815
Abraão–Conceição de Jacareí	0800, 1000, 1300, 1700	0800, 1000, 1300, 1700	0800, 1000, 1300, 1700

Saveiros Andrea (T021-9744 0732) boats cost US$6 (one way).

For the most up-to-date timetables see www.ilhagrande.org.

Ilha Grande *p161, map p162*
Bicycles Can be hired and tours arranged; ask at *pousadas*.

Ferry Ferries run between Ilha Grande and Angra dos Reis. See Angra dos Reis and the timetable, above.

Paraty *p163, map p164*
Bus On public holidays and in high season, the frequency of bus services usually increases. **Costa Verde** runs 9 buses a day to **Rio de Janeiro** (241 km, 3¾ hrs, US$8.10). To **Angra dos Reis** (98 km, 1½ hrs, every 1 hr 40 mins, US$4); 3 a day to **Ubatuba** (75 km, just over 1 hr, **São José** company, US$4), **Taubaté** (170 km) and **Guaratinguetá** (210 km); 2 a day to **São Paulo**, 1100 and 2335 (304 km via **São José dos Campos**, 5½ hrs, US$8.50 (**Reunidas** book up quickly and are very busy at weekends), and **São Sebastião**.

Taxi Set rate of US$4 for trips within the historic centre.

Trindade and around *p166*
Paraty–Ubatuba buses all pass the turning to Trindade and will pick you up from here. In high season there are vans from Trindade to the turning (US$2). In low season you'll have to hitch or walk. Frequent cars pass and hitching here is normal. There are 4 or 5 direct buses a day which also call in on **Laranjeiras** for the trailhead to **Sono** and **Ponta Negra**.

❶ Directory

Angra dos Reis and around *p160*
Banks There are several banks in town, with ATMs and money-changing facilities. These include **Banco 24 Horas**, R do Comércio 250, and **Bradesco**, R do Comércio 196.

Ilha Grande *p161, map p162*
Banks Only open at weekends.

Paraty *p163, map p164*
Banks Banco do Brasil, Av Roberto Silveira, just outside the historic centre, ATM. Exchange 1100-1430, ask for the manager.
Internet Connections are plentiful, but are slow and expensive. **Paraty Cyber Café**, Av Roberto Silveira 17. Friendly, 0900-2300, coffee and snacks served. US$3 for 30 mins.
Laundry **Paraty Wash**, Shopping Martins, loja 15, opposite the bus station. **Medical services** Hospital Municipal São Pedro de Alcântara (Santa Casa), Av Dom Pedro de Alcântara, T024-3371 1623. **Post office** R da Cadeia and Beco do Propósito, Mon-Sat 0800-1700, Sun 0800-1200.
Telephone International calls can be made from Praça Macedo Soares, opposite the tourist office. Local and long-distance calls can be made from public phones; buy phone cards from newspaper stands in the centre.

Contents

Footprint features

São Paulo

At a glance

⊝ **Getting around** Metrô, city bus and long-distance bus. Taxi is the only option for some journeys. Car hire recommended for the coast.

◉ **Time required** 2-3 days for the city; preferably over a weekend for nightlife. 5-7 days to visit the city and parts of state.

☀ **Weather** Warm and wet summer (Oct-Mar) on the coast; drier inland with blue skies. Cool winter (Apr-Sep) with blue skies. Temperatures can drop to below 10°C during a cold front.

✕ **When not to go** Jan-Feb is very wet.

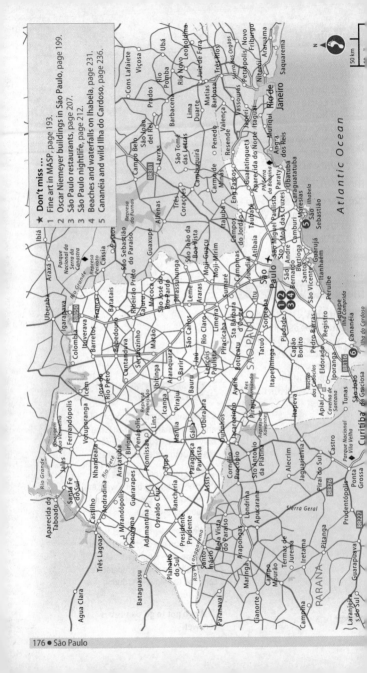

★ **Don't miss …**

1 Fine art in MASP, page 193.
2 Oscar Niemeyer buildings in São Paulo, page 199.
3 São Paulo restaurants, page 207.
3 São Paulo nightlife, page 212.
4 Beaches and waterfalls on Ilhabela, page 231.
5 Canáneia and wild Ilha do Cardoso, page 236.

N

50 km

Atlantic Ocean

PARANÁ

São Paulo is as famous for its ugliness as Rio is for its beauty. But while Rio looks marvellous from a distance and less than perfect close to, São Paulo is the opposite. Restaurants, shops, hotels and nightlife here are infinitely better than in Rio. And, while wandering and browsing in plush neighbourhoods such as Jardins, it is even possible to forget that few cities in the world have quite so much relentless concrete punctuated with quite so few green spaces; or have rivers quite so disgracefully polluted as the Tietê. Marlene Dietrich perhaps summed it up when she said – "Rio is a beauty – but São Paulo; ah … São Paulo is a city."

Indeed, São Paulo is more than a city. It is also a state a little larger than the UK; and while most of its interior is dull agricultural hinterland, its coast is magnificent; just as beautiful as Rio de Janeiro's but far less visited by international tourists. The northern beaches are long and glorious and pounded by some of South America's finest surf. Brazil's largest island, which is every bit as pristine and romantic as Ilha Grande, lies a short boat ride off shore. The beaches further south are less beautiful but far wilder; behind them, stretching into the neighbouring state of Paraná, are the largest expanses of primary forest on Brazil's Atlantic coast.

São Paulo city

→ *Colour map 5, A5. Phone code: 011. Population: 18-20 million. Altitude: 850 m.*
São Paulo is vast and can feel intimidating on first arrival. But this is a city of separate neighbourhoods, only a few of which are interesting for visitors, and once you have your base it is easy to navigate. São Paulo is the intellectual capital of Brazil. Those who don't flinch at the city's size and leave, who are instead prepared to spend time (and money) here, and who get to know Paulistanos, are seldom disappointed and often end up preferring the city to Rio. Nowhere in Brazil is better for concerts, clubs, theatre, ballet, classical music, all-round nightlife, restaurants and beautifully designed hotels. You will not be seen as a gringo in São Paulo, and the city is safer than Rio if you avoid the centre after dark and the outlying favelas (which are impossible to stumble across). ➤➤ *For listings, see pages 203-225.*

Ins and outs

Getting there

Air São Paulo is the cheapest and the principal entry point to Brazil and is one of the key entry points to South America. All international flights (except a handful to Bolivia) and many of the cheapest internal flights arrive at **Guarulhos airport** ① *Guarulhos, 25 km northeast of the city, T011-2445 2945, www.infraero.gov.br*, officially known as **Cumbica**. There are plenty of banks and money changers in the arrivals hall, open daily 0800-2200, and cafés, restaurants and gift shops on the second floor and arrivals lobby. There is a post office on the third floor of Asa A. Tourist information, including city and regional city maps and copies of the entertainment section from the Folha de São Paulo newspaper with current listings, is available from **Secretaria de Esportes e Turismo (SET)** ① *ground floor of both terminals, Mon-Fri 0730-2200, Sat, Sun and holidays 0900-2100.*

Airport taxis charge US$65 to the centre and operate on a ticket system: go to the second booth on leaving the terminal and book a co-op taxi at the Taxi Comum counter, these are the best value. **Guarucoop** ① *T011-6440 7070, 24 hrs, www.guarucoop.com.br*, is a leading, safe radio taxi company operating from the airport. The following **Emtu buses** ① *www.emtu.sp.gov.br/aeroporto*, run every 30-45 minutes (depending on the bus line), from Guarulhos between 0545 and 2215, to the following locations: **Nos 257** and **299** - Guarulhos to Metrô Tatuape (for the red line and connections to the centre), US$2; **No 258** for Congonhas airport via Avenida 23 de Maio and Avenida Rubem Berta, US$15; **No 259** for the Praça da República via Luz and Avenida Tiradentes, US$15; **No 316** for the principal hotels around Paulista and Jardins via Avenida Paulista, Rua Haddock Lobo and Rua Augusta, US$15; **No 437** for Itaím and Avenida Brigadeiro Faria Lima in the new business district, via Avenida Nove de Julho and Avenida Presidente Juscelino Kubitschek; and **No 472** for the Barra Funda Rodoviária and metrô station via the Rodoviária Tietê. A full timetable for each line with precise leaving times is listed on the website. **Airport Bus Service Pássaro Marron** ① *T0800-285 3047, www.airportbusservice.com.br*, also run buses between the airport, the city centre, *rodoviária*, Congonhas airport, Avenida Paulista and Jardins hotels, Avenida Faria Lima, metrô Tatuape, *rodoviária* Tietê and the Praça da República. Buses leave every 10 minutes from 0500-0200 costing US$12.50, children under five free. All are air conditioned and a free paper and bottle of water is provided for the journey. They also run a service directly from the airport to Ubatuba and São Sebastião (for Ilhabela). Full details of this and other services are listed on their website. Th

Arriving late at night

São Paulo's international airport, Cumbica in Guarulhos, has 24-hour facilities (for food, banking and of course taxis) in case you arrive late at night or in the early hours of the morning. It is a long drive from the airport to the city and the a/c bus to Praça da República does not operate between 0200 and 0500 and the service to Avenida Paulista does not run from 2315 to 0645. A taxi to the centre of the city will cost around US$65.

Congonhas airport, which is connected to most of Brazil's major cities, is in the city centre. Although there are no 24-hour services there are hotels across the road from the terminal (via the footbridge) and most areas in and around the centre are a maximum of US$30 taxi ride away.

company have waiting rooms in terminals 1 and 2 at Guarulhos – look for their distinctive red and blue logo or ask at the tour information desk if you can't find the lounge.

Flights with the Brazilian franchise of the US budget airline, Azul ① *www.voeazul.com.br*, have begun to run from **Viracopos airport** in the city of **Campinas** just under 100 km from São Paulo, which the company cheekily calls São Paulo Campinas airport. Fares are very competitive and the company runs a bus connection between Campinas and São Paulo which connects with the flights. Azul buses leave from Terminal Barra Funda and Shopping Eldorado (Estação CPTM Hebraica Rebouças) around every 30 minutes – details on website.

The domestic airport, **Congonhas** ① *Av Washington Luiz, 7 km south of the centre, 5 km from Jardins, T011-5090 9000*, is used for the Rio–São Paulo shuttle (about 400 flights a week, US$150 single, US$300 return) and some other domestic services including Salvador, Belo Horizonte and Vitória. A taxi to the city centre or Jardins costs about US$30.

Bus There are four main bus terminals (*rodoviárias*) in São Paulo. Most buses arrive at the **Rodoviária do Tietê** ① *the largest bus terminal in Latin America situated 5 km north of the centre, T011-2223 7152, www.passagem-em-domicilio.com.br (with details of bus times and prices in Portuguese)*. Left luggage costs US$6 per day per item. You can sleep in the bus station after 2200 when the guards have gone; showers US$6. There is a metrô with connections throughout the city, US$1.20, and buses to the centre (less safe), US$0.80. Taxis to Jardins cost US$25, US$30 at weekends. Buses from the São Paulo state coast and Paraná arrive at **Barra Funda** ① *T011-3666 4682, www.passagem-em-domicilio.com.br*, while buses from Minas Gerais arrive at **Bresser** ① *T011-6692 5191*. Buses from Santos and the coast arrive at **Jabaquara** ① *T011-5581 0856*. All are connected to the centre by metrô. ➤ *See Transport, page 222.*

Train Railways are being privatized and many long-distance passenger services have been withdrawn. São Paulo has four stations but the only one useful for tourists is **Estação da Luz** ① *Metrô Luz, T0800-550121*, which receives trains from the northwest and southeast of São Paulo state and connects with the tourist train from Paranapiacaba to Rio Grande da Serra. See CPTM and Metrô, pages 223 and 224.

Getting around

Bus Buses in São Paulo are operated by **SP Trans** ① *www.sptrans.com.br*, who have an excellent bus route planner on their website. The system is fairly self-explanatory even for non-Portuguese speakers – with boxes allowing you to select a point of departure (*de*) and destination (*para*). It also enables you to plan using a combination of bus, metrô and urban light railway (*trem*). Google maps mark São Paulo bus stops and numbers. Right clicking on the number shows the bus route and time and there is a search facility for

São Paulo Metrô & CPTM urban rail

Due for completion 2011-2014

planning routes. There is a flat fee of US$1.20 for any bus ride – payable to a conductor sitting behind a turnstile in the bus. The conductors are helpful in indicating where to hop on and off. Buses are marked with street names indicating their routes, but these routes can be confusing for visitors and services slow due to frequent traffic jams. However,

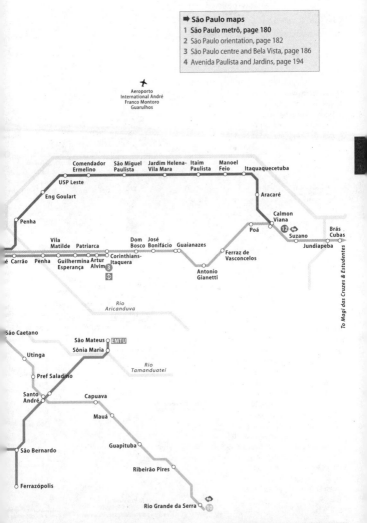

➡ São Paulo maps
1 São Paulo metrô, page 180
2 São Paulo orientation, page 182
3 São Paulo centre and Bela Vista, page 186
4 Avenida Paulista and Jardins, page 194

2 São Paulo orientation

➡ **São Paulo maps**
1 São Paulo metrô, page 180
2 São Paulo orientation, page 182
3 São Paulo centre and Bela Vista, page 186
4 Avenida Paulista and Jardins, page 194

Sleeping
Blue Tree Towers 1
Casa Club 7
Grand Hyatt São
  Paulo 2
Hilton 5
Praça de Árvore
  IYHA 3
Sampa 8
Unique Garden
  Spa 4
Vergueiro Hostel 6

Eating
Café de Pinacoteca 1
Carlotta 17
Eñe 2
Genial 9

Prêt 5

Bars & clubs
A Marcenaria 7
Bambu 8
Bar do Alemão 18
Berlin 19
CB Bar 20
D Edge 21
Di Quinta 3
Grazie o Diao 10
O de Borogodó 12
Pacha 4
Posto 6 13
Sub Astor 14
The Week 22

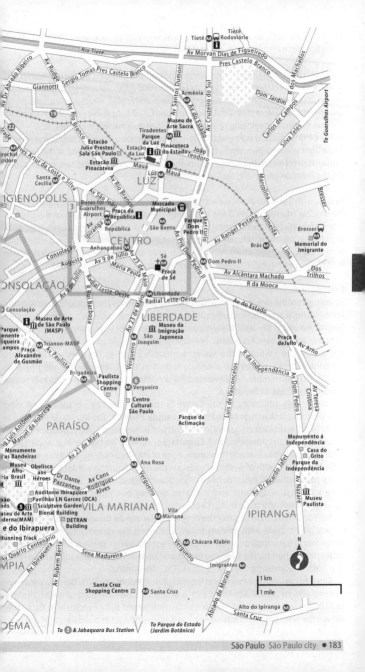

buses are safe, clean and only crowded at peak hours (0700-0900 and 1700-1830). Maps of the bus and metrô system are available at depots, eg Anhangabaú.

Metrô and the CPTM Urban light railway The best and cheapest way to get around São Paulo is on the excellent **metrô system** ① *daily 0500-2400, www.metro.sp.gov.br, with a clear journey planner and information in Portuguese and English*, which is clean, safe, cheap and efficient. It is integrated with the overground CPTM light railway. São Paulo's was the first metrô in Brazil, beginning operations in 1975. It now has five main lines.

The **CPTM** (Companhia Paulista de Trens Metropolitanos) ① *www.cptm.sp.gov.br*, is an urban light railway which serves to extend the metrô along the margins of the Tietê and Pinheiros rivers and to the outer city suburbs. There are six lines, which are colour-coded like the metrô. ▸▸ *For details, see Transport, page 223.*

Taxi Taxis in São Paulo are white with a green light on the roof. They display their tariffs in the window (starting at US$5) and have meters. Ordinary taxis are hailed on the street or more safely at taxi stations (*postos*), which are never more than five minute's walk away anywhere in the city. Hotels, restaurants and some venues will call a taxi on request – either from a *posto* or a taxi driver himself. Radio taxis are more expensive but less hassle. ▸▸ *See Transport, page 224, for recommended companies.*

Orientation

At the heart of the city, the **Centro Histórico** is a place to visit but not to stay. Most of the historical buildings and former beauty are long gone, but its pedestrianized streets are fascinating and gritty, with lively markets and a cluster of interesting sights lost in the concrete and cobbles. For a birds' eye view of the city, head to the lookout platform at the top of the **Edifício Italia** tower, preferably at dusk. The commercial district, containing banks, offices and shops, is known as the **Triângulo**, bounded by Ruas Direita, 15 de Novembro, São Bento and Praça Antônio Prado, but it is rapidly spreading towards the Praça da República.

Immediately southwest of the Centro Histórico is the city's grandest and most photo- graphed skyscraper-lined street, **Avenida Paulista**. The Museo de Arte de São Paulo (MASP), the best art gallery in the southern hemisphere, is here. North of Avenida Paulista is the neighbourhood of **Consolação**, centred on tawdry Rua Augusta but undergoing a Renaissance at the cutting edge of the city's underground live music and nightlife scene. South of Avenida Paulista is the neighbourhood of **Jardins**. This is the city's most affluent inner neighbourhood with elegant little streets hiding Latin America's best restaurants and designer clothing boutiques. There are plenty of luxurious hotels and some budget options.

Next to Jardins, 5 km south of the centre, the **Parque do Ibirapuera** is the inner city's largest green space, with running tracks, a lake and live concerts. Like Brasília, it is a repository of historically important Oscar Niemeyer buildings, many of which are home to interesting museums. The adjoining neighbourhoods of **Vila Mariana** and **Paraíso** have a few hotel options and great live music at SESC Vila Mariana.

Situated between Ibirapuera and the river, **Itaim**, **Moema** and **Vila Olímpia** are among the nightlife centres of São Paulo with a wealth of streetside bars, ultra-chic designer restaurants and European-style dance clubs. Hotels tend to be expensive as these areas border the new business centre on Avenida Brigadeiro Faria Lima and Avenida Luís Carlos

Berrini, in the suburb of **Brooklin. Pinheiros and Vila Madalena** are less chic, but equally lively at night and with the funkiest shops.

Tourist information

There are tourist information booths with English-speaking staff in international and domestic arrivals (ground floor) at **Cumbica airport** (Guarulhos). There are also tourist information booths in the **bus station** and in the following locations throughout the city: **Praça da Luz** ① *in front of the Pinacoteca cafe, daily 0900-1800*; **Avenida São João** ① *Av São João 473, Mon-Fri 0900-1800*; **Avenida Paulista** ① *Parque Trianon, T011-3251 0970, Sun-Fri 0900-1800*; and **Avenida Brig Faria Lima** ① *opposite the Iguatemi shopping centre, T011- 3211 1277, Mon-Fri 0900-1800*. An excellent map is available free at these offices.

 Editora Abril publishes maps and the excellent *Guia de São Paulo – Sampa* guide (in Portuguese only). For cheap travel, *Viajar Bem e Barato*, is available at news-stands and bookshops throughout the city.

Websites The best website in English is www.brazilmax.com. www.guiasp.com.br has comprehensive entertainment listings in Portuguese, but is readily understandable. Also see http://vejasaopaulo.abril.com.br for entertainment, restaurants and general information in Portuguese.

Background

The history of São Paulo state and São Paulo city were much the same from the arrival of the Europeans until the coffee boom transformed the region's economic and political landscape. According to John Hemming (*Red Gold*, see Books page 807), there were approximately 196,000 indigenous inhabitants living in what is now São Paulo state at the time of conquest. Today their numbers have been vastly diminished and of the few who survived, some live in villages within São Paulo itself and can be seen selling handicrafts in the centre.

 The first official settlement in the state was at São Vicente on the coast, near today's port of Santos. It was founded in 1532 by Martim Afonso de Sousa, who had been sent by King João III to drive the French from Brazilian waters, explore the coast and lay claim to all the lands apportioned to Portugal under the Treaty of Tordesillas.

 In 1554, two Jesuit priests from São Vicente founded São Paulo as a *colégio* (a combined mission and school) on the site of the present Pátio de Colégio in the Centro Histórico. The Jesuits chose to settle inland because they wanted to distance themselves from the civil authority, which was based in Bahia and along the coast. Moreover, the plateau provided better access to the indigenous population who they hoped to convert to Catholicism. Pioneers seeking to found farms followed in the Jesuits' wake and as the need for workers on these farms grew, expeditions were sent into the interior of the country to capture and enslave the indigenous people. These marauders were known as *bandeirantes* after the flag wielder who ostensibly walked at their head to claim territory. Most of their number were the culturally disenfranchised offspring of the indigenous Brazilians and the Portuguese – spurned by both communities. São Paulo rose to become the centre of *bandeirante* activity in the 17th century and the *bandeirantes'* ignominious expeditions were responsible for the opening up of the country's interior and supplying the indigenous slave trade. A statue by one of Brazil's foremost modernist sculptors, Victor Brecheret, sits on the edge of Ibirapuera in homage to the *bandeirantes*. Yet whilst

São Paulo was their headquarters, the *bandeirantes'* success in discovering gold led to the economic demise of the city in the 18th century. The inhabitants rushed to the gold fields in the *sertão*, leaving São Paulo to fall to ruin and fall under the influence of Rio de Janeiro. The relative backwardness of the region lasted until the late 19th century when the coffee trade spread west from Rio de Janeiro. Landowners became immensely rich. São Paulo changed from a small town into a financial and residential centre. Exports and imports flowed through Santos and the industrial powerhouse of the country was born. As the city boomed, industries and agriculture fanned outwards to the far reaches of the state.

Between 1885 and the end of the century the boom in coffee and the arrival of large numbers of Europeans transformed the state beyond recognition. By the end of the 1930s

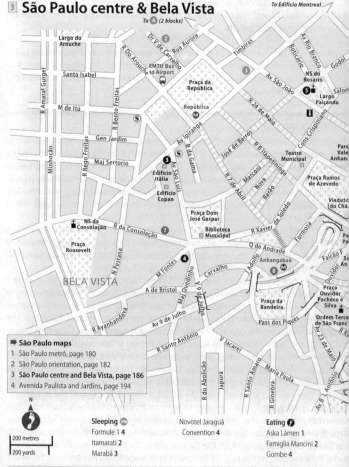

3 São Paulo centre & Bela Vista

➡ **São Paulo maps**
1 São Paulo metrô, page 180
2 São Paulo orientation, page 182
3 **São Paulo centre and Bela Vista, page 186**
4 Avenida Paulista and Jardins, page 194

N

200 metres
200 yards

Sleeping 🛌
Formule 1 **4**
Itamarati **2**
Marabá **3**
Novotel Jaraguá
Convention **4**

Eating 🍴
Aska Lámen **1**
Famiglia Mancini **2**
Gombe **4**

more than a million Italians, 500,000 Portuguese, nearly 400,000 Spaniards and 200,000 Japanese had arrived in São Paulo state. São Paulo now has the world's largest Japanese community outside Japan. Their main contribution to the economy has been in horticulture, raising poultry and cotton farming, especially around cities such as Marília. Nowadays, increasing numbers of Japanese-Brazilians work in the professions and the music industry. Significant numbers of Syrian-Lebanese arrived too, adding an extra dimension to the cultural diversity of the city. Many of the city's wealthiest dynasties are of Middle Eastern descent. São Paulo also has a large and successful Jewish community.

Much of the immigrant labour that flooded in during the early years of the 20th century was destined for the coffee *fazendas* and farms. Others went to work in the industries that were opening up in the city. By 1941 there were 14,000 factories and today the city covers more than 1500 sq km – three times the size of Paris – and greater São Paulo has a population of around 20 million.

Centro Histórico

São Paulo's city centre was once one of the most attractive in South America. English visitors in the 19th century described it as being spacious, green and dominated by terracotta-tiled buildings. There were even macaws and sloths in the trees. Today they are long gone and the centre is dominated by towering (and rather ugly) buildings, broken by a handful of interesting churches and cultural centres, and criss-crossed by narrow pedestrian streets. These are lined with stalls selling everything from shoes to electronics, second-hand goods and bric-a-brac, throughout the week. The best way to explore the area is by metrô and on foot, but don't stay after dark as the area is unsalubrious.

Praça da Sé and around → *Metrô Sé.*

The best place to begin a tour is at the **Praça da Sé**, an expansive square shaded by tropical trees and dominated by the hulking Catholic **Catedral Metropolitana** ① *Praça da Sé, T011-3107 6832, Mon-Sat 0800-1800, Sun 0830-1800, free, Metrô Sé.* This is the heart of the old city and has been the site of Brazil's largest public protests. Crowds gathered here in the late 1980s to demand the end to military rule. And, in

To Estação da Luz (500m)

Av Tiradentes
Santa Ifigênia
R F de Abreu
R 25 de Março
Abdo Schahin
25 de Março Shopping Area
R B Duprat
R Cantareira
Mercado Municipal

São Bento
Largo de São Bento
M São Bento
B Jafet
Porto Geral
Via Diário Popular

Edifício Banespa
Edifício Martinelli
Praça Antônio Prado
R Boa Vista
Centro Cultural Banco do Brasil
R 15 de Novembro
Sutaco
Banco do Brasil
R General Carneiro
Parque Dom Pedro II

Quitanda
R Álvares
R Direita
Pátio do Colégio & Museu de Anchieta
R 25 de Março
R B Rodrigues

Anchieta
Peixoto
é Bonifácio
Br de P
V Bras
Av Rangel

Constant
Conjunto Cultural da Caixa
Praça da Sé
Santa
Teresa
M Sé
Praça Clovis Bevilaqua
Ordem Terceira do Carmo

Catedral Metropolitana
Praça Dr João Mendes
S Martins

To Liberdade
To ❶❹❻ (500-700m)
R Tabatinguera

Ponto Chic 5
Sushi Yassu 6
Terraço Italia 3

Clubs ⬤
Clube Royal 7
Cambridge 8

1992, they demanded the impeachment and resignation of the new Republic's second elected president, Fernando Collor – the first in a seemingly never-ending series of corrupt leaders who in 1990 had frozen the country's savings accounts and personally pocketed millions. The *praça* is always busy with hawkers, beggars, shoeshiners and business men rushing between meetings. Evangelists with megaphones proselytize on the steps of the cathedral – a symbol of the war between Christians for the souls of the poor that dominates contemporary urban Brazil. The *praça* is a great spot for street photography though be discreet with your camera and check that you aren't followed after taking your shots. Like São Paulo itself, the cathedral is more remarkable for its size than its beauty and is an unconvincing mish-mash of neo-Gothic and Renaissance. A narrow nave is squeezed uncomfortably between two monstrous 97-m-high spires beneath a bulbous copper cupola. It was designed in 1912 by the inappropriately named engineer Maximiliano Hell, inaugurated in the 1950s and fitted with its full complement of 14 towers only in 2002. The interior is bare but for a few stained glass windows designed in Germany and capitals decorated with Brazilian floral motifs. In the basement there is a vast, pseudo-Gothic crypt.

There are a few other sights of interest around the *praça*. Next door to the cathedral itself and housed in a 1930s art deco building is the **Conjunto Cultural da Caixa** ① *Praça da Sé 111, T011-3321 4400, www.caixacultural.com.br, Tue-Sun 0900-2100, US\$2, Metrô Sé,* a gallery that hosts excellent small international art and photography exhibitions by day, and, in the evenings, a boutique theatre. It also has a small banking museum with colonial furniture, on one of its upper floors. Two minutes' walk immediately to the west of the cathedral, squeezed between ugly modern buildings at the end of Rua Senador Feijó, is the **Igreja da Ordem Terceira de São Francisco** ① *Largo de São Francisco 133, T011-3106 0081, closed at time of publication, Metrô Sé.* This is one of the city's oldest churches, preserving a modest baroque interior (parts of which date to the 17th century) painted in celestial blue. It is quiet and meditative inside. The exterior is largely an 18th-century excrescence. The church is often referred to as 'O Convento de São Francisco' after a beautiful baroque convent that stood here until the 1930s. This was demolished along with vast swathes of the old colonial centre and sadly the Igreja da Ordem Terceira is in danger of undergoing the same fate – it was condemned in 2008 and remains closed pending donations for a restoration project. There are now only two churches in the centre of one of Brazil's oldest cities which retain any baroque remnants – the Igreja de Santo Antônio (see page 190) and the **Igreja da Ordem Terceira do Carmo** ① *R Rangel Pestana 230, Tue-Sun 0900-2100, free, Metrô Sé.* This church sits just off the far northeastern corner of the Praça da Sé, dates from 1632 and preserves its original gilt baroque altarpiece together with some other stucco work, religious paintings and artefacts. It is a peaceful little place in all the heat, hustle and bustle, and has with few visitors.

Pátio do Colégio and around → *Metrô Sé.*

The site of the founding of São Paulo can be reached by walking north from the bottom of the Praça da Sé (farthest from the cathedral) along Rua Santa Teresa and to the Praça Pátio do Colégio. Here lies the **Pátio do Colégio and Museu de Anchieta** ① *Praça Pátio do Colégio, T011-3105 6899, www.pateodocollegio.com.br, museum: Tue-Fri 0840-1630, US\$3, free on the last Sun of the month, Metrô Sé.* Jesuit priests, led by 18-year-old Padre José de Anchieta arrived here in 1554, when the area was a tiny clearing on a hill in the midst of a vast forest. They made camp and instructed their domicile indigenous Guarani to construct a simple wattle and daub hut. They inaugurated the building with a celebration of Mass on 25 January 1554, the feast of the conversion of São Paulo. Their simple hut took the saint's name, the 'Colégio de São Paulo de Piratinga'. The hut became a school for converted indigenous Brazilians seduced from the forests around. The school became a church and the church gave its name – São Paulo – to a settlement for *bandeirante* slaving raids into the Brazilian interior. In 1760, the Jesuits were expelled from the city they founded, for opposing the *bandeirantes* and their indigenous slave trade. But the Pátio do Colégio (as the complex of buildings came to be known) remained, becoming the palace of the fledgling province's Portuguese colonial captains general, and then of its Brazilian imperial governors. The church's tower fell down in 1886, and shortly after the whole building, but for one piece of wattle and daub wall, was demolished. The Jesuits didn't return to São Paulo until 1954 but they had long memories and immediately set about building an exact replica of their original church and college, which is what stands today. Most of the buildings are occupied by the **Museu Padre Anchieta**. This preserves, amongst other items, a modernist and not altogether sympathetic painting of the priest, by Italian Albino Menghini, bits of his corpse (which is now that of a saint after Anchieta was canonized by Pope John Paul II), a 17th-century font used to baptize the indigenous Brazilians and a collection of Guaraní art and artefacts from the colonial era. The Pátio has a great little al fresco café with a view, serving good snacks and light meals.

The exhibition spaces, cultural centres and concert halls of the **Centro Cultural Banco do Brasil** ① *R Álvares Penteado 112, T011-3113 3651, www.bb.com.br, Mon-Fri 0900-1800, free except for exhibitions, Metrô Sé or São Bento*, can be reached by turning immediately west from the front of the Pátio do Colégio along Rua do Tesouro and then right for a block along Rua Álvares Penteado. These are housed in an attractive art deco building with a pretty glass ceiling. Many of the galleries are contained within the banks original vaults, some of which retain their massive iron doors. The cultural centre has a diverse programme of art and photography shows, cultural events and, in the evenings, theatre, music and cinema. It is always worth a visit in passing.

Mosteiro do São Bento and around → *Metrô São Bento.*

The most beautiful of all the churches in São Paulo is the Benedictine Basilica de Nossa Senhora de Assunção, known as the **Mosteiro São Bento** ① *Largo São Bento, T011-3228 3633, www.mosteiro.org.br, Mon-Fri 0600-1800, Sat and Sun 0600-1200 and 1600-1800, Latin Mass with Gregorian chant Sun 1000; Latin vespers Mon-Fri 1725, Sat 1700, free, Metrô São Bento*. Benedictines arrived on this site in 1598, shortly after the Jesuits and, like them, proceeded to proselytize the indigenous people. Despite their long history in the city the monastery is a modern church dating from 1914. It was designed by Munich-based architect Richard Bernl in homage to the English Norman style. Its façade is strikingly similar to Southwell cathedral in Nottinghamshire, though with added Rhineland roofs and baroque revival flourishes. But few visit São Bento for the exterior. The church preserves a striking Beuronese interior painted by Dom Adelbert Gresnicht, a Dutch Benedictine monk. The style is named after techniques developed by Benedictines in the monastery of Beuron in southwest Germany in the late 19th and early 20th centuries. It finds much inspiration in Byzantine art and is characterized by compressed perspective and iconic, almost exaggerated colours. São Bento is one of the finest Beuronese churches in the world. The stained glass (and much of the statuary) is also by Dom Adelbert. Most of the windows show scenes from the life of St Benedict with the most beautiful, at the far end of the nave, showing Our Lady ascending to heaven guided by the

Holy Spirit in the form of a dove. The church has Brazil's finest organ which is given its own festival in November and December every year. And with this being a Benedictine monastery, there is of course a temple to commerce: the shop sells delicious sweets home-made by the monks in their bakery.

Immediately in front of the monastery, at the corner of Avenida São João and Rua Libero Badaró, is the **Edifício Martinelli (Martinelli Building)** ① *Av São João 35, not open to the public, Metrô São Bento*. This was the city's first skyscraper and, when it was built, looked out over a sea of terracotta roofs and handsome tree-lined avenues. The building is reminiscent of New York's upper east side but is by no means as distinguished: while colonial São Paulo was unique and beautiful, the buildings that replaced it looked tawdry and crowded next to the New York it longed to imitate.

Around the corner is another architectural pastiche, the **Edifício Altino Arantes** (aka **Edifício Banespa/Santander Cultural**) ① *R João Bricola 24 (Metrô São Bento), T011-3249 7466, Mon-Fri 1000-1500, free, passport ID is required, visits limited to 10 mins (dusk visits are limited to those with prior appointments), daypacks must be left in reception, no tripods or bags can be taken to the viewing deck*, looking a bit like a wan Empire State Building, small enough to collapse under the weight of King Kong. The view of the city from the observatory is awe-inspiring. On its fringes are the vast favelas and new distant neighbourhoods with infant skyscraper flats and hundreds of helicopters whirling busily overhead like giant buzzing flies.

Less than 50 m from the Edifício Altino Arantes is the oldest church in São Paulo's city centre, the **Igreja de Santo Antônio** ① *Praça do Patriarca s/n, Mon-Fri 0900-1600, free Metrô São Bento*, with parts dating from 1592. It was fully restored in 2005 and together with the Igreja do Carmo is the only church in the city centre with a baroque interior - although much of what you see today is from reforms in 1899. It's a tranquil spot in the middle of one of the world's busiest city centres.

The streets between São Bento and Luz are some of the busiest shopping districts in the city. The partially covered **Rua 25 de Março** ① *daily 0700-1800, Metrô São Bento shopping complex*, runs north to Rua Paula Sousa and Luz Metrô station. Two blocks to the east of 25 de Marco along Rua Comendador Afonso Kherlakian is the beautiful art deco **Mercado Municipal** ① *R da Cantareira 306, Centro, T011-3326 3401, www.mercad municipal.com.br, Mon-Sat 0600-1800, Sun 0600-1600, free, Metrô São Bento or Luz (see page 220)*. The area offers some of the best people-watching and shopping adventures in the city. It's an easy walk from the market or Rua 25 de Março to Luz, though caution should be observed at all times. The streets to the west, between the centre and Júli Prestes station, should be avoided. This is a notorious area for crack dealing.

Praça da República → *Metrô República.*
There are a few interesting sites here. Most notable is the **Edifício and Terraço Itália** ① *Av Ipiranga 344, T011-2189 2990 and T011-2189 2929, www.edificioitalia.com.br, restauran www.terracoitalia.com.br, US$8, Metrô República*, a rather unremarkable restaurant in the city's tallest building with a truly remarkable view from the observation deck. Arrive ha an hour before sunset for the best balance of natural and artificial light, and bring a tripo The skyscraper immediately in front of the *terraço* is Oscar Niemeyer's **Edifício Copa** ① *Av Ipiranga 200, not open to the public though some visitors are allowed to go to th terraço at the discretion of security, Metrô República*, built in 1951 in a spate of design by th architect, which also included the nearby **Edifício Montreal** ① *Av Ipiranga at Cásp Líbero,* and the **Edifício Califórnia** ① *R Barão de Itapetininga*. Edifício Copan was th

setting for a series of memorable short stories, dissecting daily life and class in São Paulo written by the Paulistano writer Regina Rheda, and published in English as *First World, Third Class and Other Tales of the Global Mix* in 2005.

From the corner of Praça da República, a 10-minute walk southeast along Rua 24 de Maio brings you back into the main part of the city centre and Metrô Anhangabaú, via the **Teatro Municipal Opera House** ① *Praça Ramos de Azevedo s/n, T011-3397 0300, www.prefeitura.sp.gov.br/cidade/secretarias/cultura/teatromunicipal/, box office Mon-Fri 1000-1900, Sat 1000-1700, tickets from US$5, Metrô Anhangabaú, República or São Bento,* based on the 1874 Beaux-Arts, Palais Garnier, but stunted in comparison, in dull stone and with huge baroque flourishes on the roof which make it look rather ridiculous. Maria Callas, Nureyev and Fonteyn and Duke Ellington have all graced the concert hall and the venue continues to host a slice of the better classical music, theatre and ballet performances in the city. Next to the theatre is the **Viaduto do Chá**, a steel bridge riding over the attractive but scruffy Vale de Anhangabaú park and the traffic-heavy Avenida 23 de Maio and 9 de Julho urban highways.

North of the centre

Luz → *Metrô Luz or Metrô Tiradentes, CPTM Luz or Júlio Prestes.*

Some of São Paulo's finest museums are to be found a few kilometres north of the city centre in the neighbourhood of Luz. The area is dominated by two striking 19th- and early 20th-century railway stations, both in use today: the **Estação da Luz** ① *Praça da Luz 1, T0800-550121 for information on suburban trains,* and **Estação Júlio Prestes** ① *Praça Júlio Prestes 51, www.estacoesferroviarias.com.br/j/jprestes.htm*. The former marked the realization of a dream for O Ireneu Evangelista de Sousa, the Visconde de Mauá, who was Brazil's first industrial magnate. A visit to London in the 1840s convinced de Sousa that Brazil's future lay in rapid industrialization – a path he followed with the founding of an ironworks employing some 300 workers from England and Scotland. It made him a millionaire and in 1854 he opened his first railway, designed and run by the British. It linked Jundiaí, in the heart of the São Paulo coffee region, with Santos on the coast via what was then the relatively small city of São Paulo. The line is still extant; though passenger trains only run on the Jundiaí to São Paulo section (see page 224). The grandness of the Estação de Luz station, which was completed in 1900, attests to the fact that the city quickly grew wealthy by exploiting its position at the railway junction. By the time the Estação Júlio Prestes was built, Britannia no longer ruled the railways. This next station was modelled on Grand Central and Penn in New York. In 1999 the enormous 1000-sq-m grand hall was converted into the magnificent, cathedral-like **Sala São Paulo concert hall** ① *Praça Júlio Prestes 51, T011-3337 9573, www.salasaopaulo.art.br, guided visits Mon-Fri 1300-1630, Sat 1330, Sun 1400 (when there is an evening performance) or 1230 when there is an afternoon performance), US$2.50, free on weekends, foreigners should book ahead through the website as English-speaking guides must be arranged, box office 011-3223 3966, Mon-Fri 1000-1800, Sat 1000-1630, concerts from US$10, Metrô Luz, CPTM Luz or Júlio Prestes,* Brazil's most prestigious classical music venue (see page 217).

The city's finest collection of Brazilian art lies 100 m from the Estação da Luz in the **Pinacoteca do Estado** ① *Praça da Luz 2, T011-3324 0933, www.pinacoteca.org.br, Tue-Sun 1000-1800 (last entry at 1730), Sat 1000-1730, US$3, free on Sat, Metrô Luz, CPTM Luz, excellent museum shop and café*. Here you will find works by Brazilian artists from the colonial and imperial eras, together with paintings by the founders of Brazilian modernism, such as Lasar Segall, Tarsila do Amaral, Candido Portinari and Alfredo Volpi. The gallery also contains sculpture by Rodin, Victor Brecheret and contemporary works by artists such as the Nipo-Brazilian painter Tomie Ohtake. The excellent photography gallery in the basement displays some of the world's greatest black-and-white photographers, many of whom are from Brazil. The museum overlooks the **Parque da Luz**, a lovely shady green space dotted with modernist sculpture and shaded by large tropical figs and palms. Take care in this area after dark.

The Pinacoteca's sister gallery, the **Estação Pinacoteca and Memorial da Resistência museum** ① *Largo General Osório 66, T011-3337 0185, daily 1000-1730, US$2, free for the Memorial da Resistência and for the galleries on Sat, very good café restaurant, Metrô Luz, CPTM Luz and Júlio Prestes*, is just over 500 m west of the Pinacoteca along Rua Mauá, next to the Estação Júlio Prestes and Sala São Paulo. It houses 200 of the country's finest modernist paintings from the archive of fthe Fundação José e Paulina Nemirovsky, including further key pieces by Tarsila do Amaral, Emiliano Di Cavalcanti, Portinari Anita Malfatti, Victor Brecheret and Lasar Segall. International art includes Chagall, Picasso and Braque. The building was once the headquarters of the Departamento Estadual de Ordem Politica e Social do Estado de São Paulo (DEOPS/SP) – the counter insurgency wing of the Policia Militar police force. Thousands of Paulistanos were tortured and killed here between 1940 and 1983, during the Vargas years and the military dictatorship. The Memorial da Resistência de São Paulo museum on the ground floor tells their story in grisly detail – through panels, documents and photographs – and shows how the CIA supported the oppression.

Luz's other excellent museum is the **Museu de Arte Sacra** ① *Av Tiradentes 676, 400 m north of the Pinacoteca, T011-3227 7687, www.museuartesacra.org.br, Mon-Fr 1000-1700, Sat and Sun 1000-1900, US$2, Metrô Tiradentes, CPTM Luz*. This superb little museum is often overlooked by visitors, yet it is one of the finest of its kind in the Americas and lies almost immediately opposite the Pinacoteca. The collection i housed in a large wing of one of the city's most distinguished colonial buildings, the early 19th-century Mosteiro da Luz. Parts of the monastery are still home to Conceptionist sisters and the entire complex is imbued with a restful sense of serenity. Even those who are not interested in church art will find the galleries a delightfull peaceful haven from the frenetic chaos of São Paulo. The collection, however, i priceless and of international importance. Rooms house various objects and artefacts from lavish monstrances and ecclesiastical jewellery to church altarpieces. Of particula note is the statuary, with pieces by many of the most important Brazilian baroqu masters. Amongst objects by Aleijadinho, Mestre Valentim and Frei Agostinho d Piedade is a wonderful Mary Magdalene by Francisco Xavier de Brito, displaying a effortless unity of motion and melancholy contemplation. There are sculptures b (anonymous) Brazilian indigenous artists, a majestic African-Brazilian São Bento (wit blue eyes) and an extraordinarily detailed 18th-century Neapolitan nativity cr comprising almost 2000 pieces, which is the most important of its kind outside Naples.

Barra Funda and Higienópolis → *Metrô Palmeiras-Barra Funda, CPTM Barra Funda.*

The monumentalist group of modernist concrete buildings making up the **Memorial d América Latina** ① *Av Mário de Andrade 664, next to Metrô Barra Funda, T011-3823 460 www.memorial.org.br, Tue-Fri 0900-2100, Sat 0900-1800, Sun 1000-1800, free*, we designed by **Oscar Niemeyer** and built in March 1989. They comprise a monument 85000-sq-m-complex of curvi-linear galleries, conference spaces, walkways, bridges a squares, broken by an ugly, urban highway and dotted with imposing sculptures. The largest of these is in the shape of an outstretched hand. The complex was built with the grand aim of integrating Latin American nations, culturally and politically, but it is sorely underused. Occasional shows (details on the website) include the annual Latin American art exhibition in the Pavilhão de Criatividade.

A few kilometres west of Barra Funda – and a quick hop along the CPTM's Linha Rubi, in the emerging nightlife district of **Água Branca**, is **SESC Pompeia** ① *R Clélia 93, T011-3871 7700, www.sescsp.org.br, CPTM Água Branca, 10 minswalk southeast or US\$3 in a taxi*, an arts complex housed in a striking post-industrial building designed by Lina Bo Bardi (see page 213), which together with SESC Vila Mariana (see page 198) showcases some of the best medium-sized musical acts in the city – names like João Bosco, CéU and Otto. It is a vibrant place, with a theatre, exhibitions, workshops, restaurant and café, as well as a gym and areas for sunbathing and watching television.

The upper middle-class neighbourhood of **Higienópolis** lies between Barra Funda and Consolação. It is a favourite haunt of artists and musicians; particularly the **Bretagne building** ① *Av Higienópolis 938, T011-3667 2516*, one of a handful of delightful mid-20th-century blocks of flats whose curved lines, brilliant mosaics and polished stone looks like a film set for an arty 1960s picture. Higienópolis also boasts one of the city's plushest shopping malls, the **Patio Higienópolis** ① *Av Higienópolis 618, T011-3823 2300, www.patiohigienopolis.com.br*.

West of the centre

Avenida Paulista → *Metrô Vergueiro or Paraíso for the southeastern end of Paulista.*

Southwest of the Centro Histórico, Avenida Paulista, is lined by skyscrapers and is thick with six lanes of cars. It is one of São Paulo's classic postcard shots and locals like to compare it to Fifth Avenue in New York. In truth, it's more commercial and lined with functional buildings, most of which are unremarkable individually and awe-inspiring as a whole.

The avenue was founded in 1891 by the Uruguayan engineer Joaquim Eugênio de Lima, who wanted to build a Paulistano Champs-Élysées. After he built a mansion on Avenida Paulista, many coffee barons followed suit and by the early 20th century, Paulista had become the city's most fashionable promenade. The mansions and the rows of stately trees that sat in front of them were almost all demolished in the 1940s and 1950s to make way for ugly office buildings, and in the 1980s these were in turn demolished as banks and multinationals established their headquarters here.

The highlight of Avenida Paulista is the **Museu de Arte de São Paulo (MASP)** ① *Av Paulista 1578, T011-3251 5644, www.masp.art.br, Tue-Wed and Fri-Sun 1100-1800, Thu 1100-1900, US\$5, Metrô Trianon-MASP*. This is the most important gallery in the southern hemisphere, preserving some of Europe's greatest paintings. If it were in the US or Europe it would be as busy as the Prado or the Guggenheim, but here, aside from the occasional noisy group of schoolchildren, the gallery is invariably deserted. Even at weekends, visitors can stop and stare at a Rembrandt or a Velazquez at their leisure. The museum has a far larger collection than it is able to display and only a tiny fraction reaches the walls of the modest-sized international gallery. France gets star-billing, with 11 Renoirs, 70 Degas, and a stream of works by Monet, Manet, Cezanne, Toulouse-Lautrec and Gauguin. Renaissance Italy is represented by a Raphael Resurrection, an impeccable Bellini and a series of exquisite late 15th-century icons. The remaining walls are adorned with paintings by Bosch, Goya, Van Dyck, Turner, Constable and many others, cherry-picked from post-War Europe. A gallery downstairs, the Galeria Clemente de Faria, houses temporary exhibitions, mostly by contemporary Brazilian artists and photographers, and the museum has a decent and good-value restaurant serving buffet lunches (see page 209) and a small gift shop. On Sunday, an antiques fair is held in the open space beneath the museum.

Opposite MASP is the **Parque Tenente Siqueira Campos** ① *R Peixoto Gomide 949 and Av Paulista, daily 0700-1830*, also known as Parque Trianon, covering two blocks on either side of Alameda Santos. It is a welcome, luxuriant, green area located in what is now the busiest part of the city. The vegetation includes native plants typical of the *Mata Atlântica*. Next to the park is the smaller Praça Alexandre de Gusmão.

Consolação and the Pacaembu Museu do Futebol → *Metrô Consolação.*

Consolação, which lies between the northeastern end of Avenida Paulista and the Edifício Italia and Praça República in the city centre, is emerging as the edgiest and most exciting nocturnal neighbourhood in São Paulo. Until a few years it was home to little more than

④ Avenida Paulista & Jardins

➡ São Paulo maps
1 São Paulo metrô, page 180
2 São Paulo orientation, page 182
3 São Paulo centre and Bela Vista, page 186
4 Avenida Paulista and Jardins, page 194

rats, sleazy strip bars, street-walkers and curb-crawlers, but now it harbours a thriving alternative weekend scene. Its untidy streets are lined with grafitti-scrawled shop fronts, the deep velvet-red of open bar doors, go-go clubs with heavy-set bouncers outside and makeshift street bars. On Fridays and Saturdays from 2200 a jostle of hundreds of young Paulistanos down bottles of cooler-fresh Bohemia beer at rickety metal tables, and lines of sharply dressed and well-toned 20- and 30-somethings queue to enter a gamut of fashionable bars, clubs and pounding gay venues, including one of Brazil's most exciting underground venues: **Studio SP** (see Bars and clubs, page 214).

Just north of Consolação, on the other side of the Sacramento Cemetery and rushing Avenida Doutour Arnaldo, is the beautiful art deco **Estádio Pacaembu** which hosts domestic games and big international rock concerts. It sits in a square named after Charles Miller, the Englishman who brought football to Brazil. Inside is the **Museu do Futebol** ① *Metrô Clinicas, Estádio do Pacaembu, Praça Charles Miller, T011-3663 3848, www.museudofutebol.org.br, Tue-Sun 1000-1700, US$3, free on Thu, children under 7 go free, restaurants next to the museum in the stadium, Metrô Sumaré (20-min walk),* which cost US\$15 million and which was inaugurated by Pelé in September 2008. The World Cup, which Brazil have won more often than any other team, is the principal focus. One gallery is devoted to the tournament, profiling the games and what was happening in the world at the time, and telling both stories through video footage, photographs, memorabilia and newspaper cuttings. Music from the likes of Ary Barroso and Jorge Ben forms the soundtrack, along with recordings of cheering fans. A second gallery showcases Brazil's greatest stars, including Garrincha, Falcão, Zico, Bebeto, Didi, Romário, Ronaldo, Gilmar, Gérson, Sócrates, Rivelino, Ronaldo (who is known as Ronaldinho or Ronaldinho Fenomeno in Brazil) and, of course, Pelé. The shirt he wore during the 1970 World Cup final – a game frequently cited as the greatest ever played when Brazil beat Italy 4-1 to take the title for the third time – receives pride of place. A third gallery is more interactive, offering visitors the chance to dribble and shoot at goals and test their knowledge on football facts and figures.

Jardins → *Metrô Consolação.or Oscar Freire (Linha Amarela from 2012).*

Immediately west of Avenida Paulista, an easy 10-minute walk from Consolação Metrô along Rua Haddock Lobo, is the plush neighbourhood of Jardins. This is by far the most pleasant area to stay in São Paulo; it has the best restaurants, shops and cafés and is a tranquil spot for a strong coffee and people-watching, or an urban boutique browse. Jardins is in reality a series of neighbourhoods – each with its own name – the stretches closest to Paulista are known as **Cerqueira César** (to the northwest) and **Jardim Paulista** (to the southeast). These two areas have the bulk of the boutique shops, swanky hotels and chic restaurants. The most self-consciously chic of all is the cross section between Rua Oscar Freire, Rua Bela Cintra and Rua Haddock Lobo, where even the poodles wear collars with designer labels and everyone, from the shop owner to the doorman, addresses people as *'Querida'* (Darling).

Immediately west of Jardim Paulista and Cerqueira César, and separated from those neighbourhoods by a stately city highway preserving a handful of coffee Baron mansions (Avenida Brasil), are three more Jardins. **Jardim Paulistano** is dominated by Avenida Gabriel Monteiro da Silva, which is lined by very expensive, internationally reknowned home decor and furniture stores. Between Jardim Paulistano and Ibirapuera Park are **Jardim America** and **Jardim Europa**, both made up of leafy streets lined with vast mansion houses, almost completely hidden behind towering walls topped with razor wire and formidable electric fencing. Their idyllic seclusion is spoilt only by the stench of raw favela sewage from the nearby River Pinheiros.

The **Museu Brasileiro da Escultura** (**MUBE**) ① *Av Europa 218, T011-2594 2601 www.mube.art.br, Tue-Sun 1000-1900, free,* showcases contemporary Brazilian sculpture through visiting exhibitions. Most are rather lacklustre and the museum merits a visit more for the building itself, which is by Brazil's Prtizker prize-winning architect Paulo Mendes da Rocha. Like many Brazilian architects Espírito Santo-born Rocha is celebrated for his inventive, minimalist use of concrete. The museum is made up of a series of massive, grey, bunker-like concrete blocks which contrast starkly with the surrounding gardens (by Burle Marx), but which integrate them with the underground exhibition spaces. To get there from Metrô Consolação, take bus 702P-42, marked 'Butantã', from the corner of Rua Augusta and Avenida Paulista.

The **Museu da Casa Brasileira** ① *Av Brigadeiro Faria Lima 2705, T011-3032 3727, Tue-Sun 1000-1800, US$2,* preserves a collection of antique (mostly baroque) Brazilian and Portuguese and contemporary international furniture in one of the few remaining coffee baron mansions. The museum also hosts the annual Prêmio Design MCB design award, which has become one of the most celebrated in Brazil. Temporary exhibition space showcase the winners and the museum has a pleasant garden (with live music on Sundays) and a good café-restaurant. From CPTM Cidade Jardim it's 10 minutes' walk; from Pinheiros head east along Rua Professor Artur Ramos to Avenida Brigadeiro Faria Lima.

Vila Madalena and Pinheiros → *Metrô Madalena.*

If Jardins is São Paulo's upper East Side or Bond Street, Vila Madalena and neighbouring Pinheiros are its East Village or Notting Hill – still fashionable, but younger, less ostentatiously moneyed and with more of a skip in their step. Streets are crammed with bars, restaurants and an array of the city's freshest designer labels, clambering over the steep hills and buzzing with young and arty middle-class Paulistanos. Younger boutique brands have set up shop in Vila Madalena (see Shopping, page 218). Galleries such as **Choque Cultural** ① *R João Moura 197, T011-3061 4051, Mon-Fri 1000-1700, Sat 1100-1700, www.choquecultural.co.uk,* sell work by the newest wave of the city's increasingly famous street artists (as well as prints available online through their UK website).

There's music on every corner in both neighbourhoods – from spit-and-sawdust samba bars to mock-Bahian *forró* clubs and well-established live music venues. The area attracts the artistically rich and famous: Seu Jorge lives and drinks in Vila Madalena, as does leading avant garde musician, Max de Castro. The only sight of any consequence is the **Instituto Tomie Ohtake** ① *R dos Coropés 88, T011-3814 0705, www.instituto tomieohtake.org.br, Tue-Fri 1000-1800, US$3*, a monolithic, rather ungainly red and purple tower by Unique Hotel architect Ruy Ohtake. It has galleries inside devoted to the work of his Japanese-Brazilian artist mother, Tomie, and a series of other exhibition halls with work by up-and-coming artists. To get there, go to Metrô Vila Madalena, then take bus 701-10 southwest along Rua Purpurina and Rua Fradique Coutinho, getting off at the stop at Fradique Coutinho 1331. Leave the stop and turn right onto Rua Wisard. After 200 m continue onto Rua dos Miranhas. After 400 m continue onto Rua dos Tamanás and after 150 m turn right into Rua dos Coropés.

South of the centre

Liberdade → *Metrô Liberdade.*

Liberdade was the first centre for the Japanese community in São Paulo; a city with more ethnic Japanese than any other outside Japan. It lies directly south of the Praça da Sé and can easily be reached on foot in under 10 minutes. There are all manner of Asian shops selling everything from woks to *manga* and the streets are illuminated by lights designed to resemble Japanese lanterns. A market selling Asian produce and food is held every Sunday in the Praça da Liberdade and there are many excellent Japanese restaurants.

The **Museu da Imigração Japonesa** ① *R São Joaquim 381, 3rd floor, T011-3209 5465, www.nihonsite.com/muse, Tue-Sun 1330-1730, US$3, Metrô Liberdade*, in the Japanese-Brazilian cultural centre, is a modern, well-kept little museum with exhibitions telling the story of the Japanese migration to Brazil, a replica of the first ship that brought the Japanese to Brazil, reconstructions of early Japanese Brazilian houses, artefacts.

Bela Vista

Bela Vista lies immediately west of Liberdade and east of Consolação between the city centre and Avenida Paulista. In the late 19th and early 20th century the neighbourhood was a centre of Italian immigration. It is a higgledy-piggledy mass of small streets lined with residential houses. There are few sights of interest but the area is a pleasant place for a wander – especially at weekends. On Sunday there is an antiques market, the **Feira das Antiguidades** ① *Praça Dom Orione, Bixiga, Sun 1000-1500*, sometimes with live *chorinho*. There are Italianate houses nearby on Rua dos Ingleses, and a number of little cafés and bars. During carnival the **Vai Vai samba school** ① *R São Vicente 276, T011-3266 2581, www.vaivai.com.br, US$6 for the carnival party*, opens its doors to as many as 4000 visitors who come to dance samba and process through the nearby streets. They often throw a smaller *feijoada* party at weekends. **Rua Avanhandava**, which runs off Rua Martins Fontes in the north of Bela Vista, was closed to traffic in 2007, and has since become one of the prettiest streets in the neighbourhood, lined with some traditional Italian restaurants.

Paraíso and Vila Mariana

Southwest of Liberdade and beginning where Avenida Paulista becomes Rua Vergueiro, are the neighbourhoods of Paraíso and Vila Mariana. Paraíso is dominated by the hulking dome of the the **Catedral Ortodoxa** ⓘ *R Vergueiro 1515, Paraiso, T011-5579 3835, www.catedralortodoxa.com.br, Mon-Fri 0900-1300 and 1500-1800, Sat 1000-1300, Mass at 1015 on Sun, Metrô Paraíso*. The church is modelled on the Hagia Sofia in Istanbul and is one of the largest Antiochian Orthodox churches in the world. Most of the worshippers are Brazilians of Syrian and Lebanese descent. The church of Antioch is one of the five original churches and was founded in Antioch, Turkey by the apostles Peter and Paul. It's seat is in Damascus, Syria and the current patriarch is His Beatitude Patriarch Ignatius IV (Hazim) of Antioch and all the East. Vila Mariana is principally a residential neighbourhood abutting Ibirapuera park. The **SESC Vila Mariana** ⓘ *R Pelotas 141, Vila Mariana, T011-5080 3000, www.sescsp.org.br, daily 1000-2000*, is a cultural centre with a swimming pool, internet, a gym and a concert hall which hosts some of the best small acts in São Paulo. From Metrô Ana Rosa, it's 10 minutes' walk south of Ana Rosa, east along Avenida Cnso Rodrigues Alves, right onto Rua Humberto I (after 500 m) and left onto Pelotas (after 200 m).

Parque do Ibirapuera
ⓘ *Entrance on Av Pedro Álvares Cabral, daily 0500-2400, T011-5573 4180, www.parquedo ibirapuera.com, free, unsafe after dark, www.parquedoibirapuera.com. Metrô Ana Rosa is a 15-min walk east of the park: turn right out of the station and walk due west along Av Conselheiro Rodrigo Alves, continue onto Av Dante Pazzanese which comes to the Av 23 de Maio urban freeway, the park sits in front of you on the other side of the road and can be reached via a footbridge 200 m to the right in front of the Detran building; alternatively bus 5164-21 (marked Cidade Leonor, direção Parque do Ibirapuera) leaves every 30 mins from Metrô Santa Cruz for Ibirapuera; any bus to DETRAN (the Driver and Vehicle licensing building, labelled in huge letters) stops opposite Ibirapuera. Lines include 175T-10, 477U-10 and 675N-10.*

The park was designed by architect Oscar Niemeyer and landscape artist Roberto Burle Marx for the city's fourth centenary in 1954. It is the largest of the very few green spaces in central São Paulo and its shady woodlands, lawns and lakes offer a breath of fresher air in a city that has only 4.6 sq m of vegetation per inhabitant. The park is also home to a number of museums and monuments and some striking Oscar Niemeyer buildings that were designed in the 1950s but which have only been constructed in the last five years. These include the Pavilhão Lucas Nogueira Garcez, most commonly referred to as the **Oca** ⓘ *Portão 3, open for exhibitions*, a brilliant white, polished concrete dome, built in homage to an indigenous Brazilian roundhouse. It stages major international and exhibitions (see the Ibirapuera website, above, for what's on). Next to it is the **Auditório Ibirapuera** ⓘ *Portão 3, www.auditorioibirapuera.com.br*, a concert hall shaped like a giant wedge. The **Fundação Bienal** ⓘ *Portão 3, http://bienalsaopaulo.globo.com, open for exhibitions*, (Bienal buildings) are also by Niemeyer and house the city's flagship fashion and art events: the twice yearly **São Paulo fashion week** and the **Art Biennial**, the most important events of their kind in the southern hemisphere.

A **sculpture garden** separates the Bienal from the Oca; this garden is watched over by the **Museu de Arte Moderna (MAM)** ⓘ *Portão 3, T011-5085 1300, www.mam.org.br, Tue-Sun 1000-1800 (ticket office closes at 1730), US$2.50*. This small museum, with a giant mural outside by Os Gêmeos, showcases the best Brazilian contemporary art in temporary exhibitions. There is always something worth seeing and the gallery has an excellent buffet restaurant and gift shop. MAM is linked by a covered walkway to the **Museu Afro-Brasil** ⓘ *Portão 10, T011-4004 5006, www.museuafro brasil.com.br, Tue-Sun 1000-1800, US$4*, which lies inside Niemeyer's spectacular, stilted **Pavilhão Manoel d**

Oscar Nieymeyer in São Paulo

São Paulo is home to many impressive buildings by South America's most important modernist architect, Oscar Nieymeyer. Many have only opened to the public in the last few years.

→ **Auditório Ibirapuera** (Parque Ibirapuera), a stunning door-wedge shape with a sinuous portal entrance.

→ **Bienal buildings** (Parque Ibirapuera), home of Fashion Week and the Art Bienal; the serpentine walkways are fabulous.

→ **Edifício Copan** (Centro/Consolação), a tower built as a swirling wave.

→ **Ibirapuera museums and walkways** (Parque Ibirapuera), minimalist blocks with vast interior spaces linked by classic Niemeyer curving walkways.

→ **Memorial da América Latina** (Barra Funda), a gargantuan concrete wave between towering rectilinear monoliths.

→ **The Oca** (Parque Ibirapuera), a bright white concrete half-dome, in homage to indigenous communal houses.

→ **Sambódromo do Anhembi** (Anhembi), the stadium venue for São Paulo carnival built right after Rio's.

Nobrega building and devotes more than 12,000 sq m to a celebration of black Brazilian culture with regular films, music, dance, and theatrical events and an archive of over 5000 photographs, paintings, ritual objects and artefacts which include the bisected hull of a slaving ship showing the conditions under which Africans were brought to Brazil.

A few hundred metres to the west of here, on the shores of the artificial lake, the **Planetário e Museu de Astronomia Professor Aristóteles Orsini** (Planetarium) ⓘ *Portão 10, T011-5575 5206, www.prefeitura.sp.gov.br/astronomia, Sat and Sun 1200-1800, US$5*, was restored in 2006 with a new projection ceiling and state-of-the-art Star Master projection equipment by Carl Zeiss, and is now one of the most impressive in Latin America. Shows are in Portuguese.

Less than 100 m to the south, is the **Pavilhão Japonês** ⓘ *Portão 10, T011-5081 7296, Wed, Sat, Sun and holidays 1300-1700, free except for exhibitions*. The building is a reproduction of the Palácio Katsura, in Tokyo, built in Japan in strict adherence to Japanese aesthetic principles and re-assembled next to the park's largest lake (which has illuminated fountain displays on weekday evenings). The pavilion on the lower floor has an exhibition space devoted to Japanese-Brazilian and Japanese culture and a traditional Japanese tearoom upstairs.

The park also has a **running track** (with pit stops for exercise with pull-up bars, weight machines and chunky wooden dumbells), football pitches and hosts regular open-air concerts on Sundays. Those seeking something quieter on a Sunday can borrow a book from the portable library and read it in the shade of the **Bosque da Leitura** or 'reading wood'. Bicycles can be hired in the park (US$3 per hour) and there are dozens of small snack vendors and café-restaurants.

Ibirapuera also has a few monuments of note. **O Monumento as Bandeiras**, which sits on the northern edge of the park, is a brutalist tribute to the marauding and bloodthirsty slave traders, or *bandeirantes*, who opened up the interior of Brazil. It was created by Brazil's foremost 20th-century sculptor, Victor Brecheret. The **Obelisco aos Héroes de 32**, on the eastern edge of the park, is a monumental Cleopatra's needle built in honour of the Paulistano rebels who died in 1932 when the dictator Getúlio Vargas crushed resistance to his Estado Novo regime. Above the rushing Sena Madureira urban highway – where it thunders into the tunnel which passes beneath the park – is **Velocidade, Alma e Emoção**

(Speed, Soul and Emotion), a bronze tribute to one of São Paulo's favourite sons, the Formula One driver **Ayrton Senna**, by local artist Melinda Garcia.

A bridge leads across the 16-lane Avenida 23 de Maio urban highway in the southeast corner of the park near Portao 4 to the former DETRAN building, which is a giant oblong on stilts by Oscar Niemeyer. Until 2007 it was home to the state transit authority. In late 2011 it is ostensibly due to reopen as the new home of the **Museu de Arte Contemporanea de São Paulo** (**MAC**).

Itaim Bibi, Vila Olímpia and Moema
→ *Metrô Faria Lima (from 2012), CPTM Vila Olímpia and Cidade Jardim.*

Business mixes with pleasure in these plush neighbourhoods south of Jardins and near Ibirapuera park. By day they are filled with office workers; by night, especially at weekends, hundreds of street bars and clubs are busy with partying Paulistano professionals. There are also many glamorous shops, including the city's notorious temple to excess, **Daslu**, see page 221, a shop so exclusive that it sits behind its own security gate, shirks changing rooms in favour of women- and men-only shopping galleries, and which boasts a roof covered in helipads for its preferred clientele. It is possible to spend a fortune and an entire day in Daslu, which is dotted with exclusive cafés and restaurants and even has its own private party area on the upper floor.

Further afield

Brooklin and the New Business District → *Metrô Brooklin.*
Brooklin's Avenida Engenheiro Luís Carlos Berrini has taken over from Avenida Paulista as the business centre of the new São Paulo. Many of the larger companies, banks and international corporations now have their South American headquarters here, making this a likely centre of operations for those visiting the city for a work trip.

Parque do Estado
This large park housing the botanical and zoological gardens is 15 km south of the centre at **Água Funda**. The **Jardim Botânico** ① *Av Miguel Estefano s/n, Agua Funda, T011-5073 6300, www.ibot.sp.gov.br, Tue-Sun 0900-1700, US$1.50, Metrô São Judas and then bus 4742 marked Jardim Climax, or taxi from Metrô Jabaquara (US$8),* has a vast garden esplanade surrounded by magnificent stone porches, with lakes and trees and places for picnics, and a very fine orchid farm worth seeing during the flowering season (November to December). More than 19,000 different kinds of orchids are cultivated. There are orchid exhibitions in April and November. The astronomical **observatory** nearby is open to the public on Thursday afternoons. Howler monkeys, guans and toco toucans can be seen here towards the end of the day. To get there take the metrô to São Judas on the Jabaquara line, then take a bus.

The **Jardim Zoológico** ① *Av Miguel Estefano 4241, Água Funda, T011-5073 0811, www.zoologico.com.br, Tue-Sun 0900-1700, US$7, children 7-12 US$3, children under 7 free, Metrô Jabaquara (shuttle from the metrô station to the zoo, US$2, tickets to the zoo can be bought at the metrô ticket office in Jabaquara),* is the biggest zoo in the country and claims that it is the fourth biggest in the world, with 3200 animals, including the big international mammals and many rare and endangered Brazilian species. These include jaguar, puma (in small enclosures), Spix's macaw (which is extinct in the wild), Lear's macaw (which is critically endangered), Harpy eagle, bush dog and maned wolf.

Butantã and the Cidade Universitária

Instituto Butantã/Butantã Institute and Venomous animal and Museum ① *Av Dr Vital Brasil 1500, T011-3726 7222, Tue-Sun 0845-1615, www.butantan.gov.br, US$5, children half price under 12, under 7 free, Metrô Butantan (from 2012)*, on the university campus is one of the most popular tourist attractions in São Paulo. The Butantã Institute was founded at the start of the 20th century when Sao Paulo's governors looked to Brazilian scientists after an outbreak of bubonic plague in the port city of Santos. Over the decades, with Sao Paulo a booming centre of coffee production, researchers sought vaccines against snake bites to protect coffee harvesters working in the fields. The snakes are in pits and a large walk-through vivarium which also houses venomous spiders and scorpions. There is also a well-displayed, modern microbiology museum at the institute. The animals are milked for their venom six times a day and the antidotes have greatly reduced deaths from snakebite in Brazil. The centre also deals with spider and scorpion venom, has a small hospital and is a biomedical research institute responsible for producing about 90% of vaccines used in Brazil, including recent vaccines against H1N1 flu. Recent years have seen the institute invest in the hunt for natural vaccines in the Amazon rainforest. Visitors are not likely to see the venom being milked, but there is a museum of poisonous animals, which is well organized and educational, with explanations in Portuguese and English. The institute suffered a serious fire in May 2010, with the loss of the 85,000-strong preserved snake collection and 450,000 spider and scorpion specimens. It was the largest such collection in the world. The vivarium and public museum areas of the institute were not affected.

In the Prédio Novo da Reitoria, the **Museu de Arte Contemporânea (MAC)** ① *T011-3091 3039, www.mac.usp.br, Mon-Fri 1000-1800, Sun 1000-1600, free, Metrô Butantã (from 2012)*, has an important and beautifully presented collection of Brazilian and European modern art, with pieces by Braque, Picasso, Modigliani, Matisse and Tarsila do Amaral. Also in the university is the **Museu de Arqueologia e Etnologia (MAE)** ① *R Reitoria 1466, T011-3812 4001*, with an ill-kept collection of Amazonian and ancient Mediterranean material.

On the west bank of the Rio Pinheiros, just southeast of the campus, is the palatial **Jockey Club de São Paulo** ① *Av Lineu de Paula Machado 1263, T011-3811 7799*, a racecourse in the Cidade Jardim area. Race meetings are held on Monday and Thursday at 1930 and on weekends at 1430. The racecourse is easily accessible by bus from Praça da República.

Ipiranga and the Parque da Independência

① *To get to the park, take the Metrô to Alto do Ipiranga station, walk 30 m east to Av Dr Gentil de Moura and catch bus 478P-10 Sacoma-Pompeia to Av Nazaré (4 stops), get off and walk north for 200 m to the Parque da Independencia. It is also possible to catch the CPTM to Ipiranga station and walk east across the Viaduto Pacheco Chaves bridge and along R dos Patriotas (for 1 km). Bus No 478P (Ipiranga–Pompéia for return) runs from Metrô Ana Rosa and bus No 4612 from the Praça da República.*

The **Parque da Independência** ① *Av Nazare s/n, Metrô Alto de Ipiranga*, is a large, formal park on the site where Brazilian independence was declared, and littered with monuments to independence and Brazil's early Imperial past. It is watched over by a faux-French chateau, recalling Versailles, which houses one of the city's largest museums. Dominating the northern end of the park is the **Monumento à Independência**, depicting the first Brazilian Emperor, Dom Pedro, brandishing a furled flag and uttering his famous 'grito de Ipiranga' (Ipiranga cry) – 'Independence or Death!', which declared Brazil's separation from Portugal (see Background, page 768). Beneath the monument is the **imperial chapel** ⓘ *Tue-Sun 1300-1700*, containing Dom Pedro and Empress Leopoldina's tomb. The monument was built to commemorate the centenary of Independence in 1922. The **Casa do Grito** ⓘ *Tue-Sun 0930-1700*, is a replica of the tiny house where Dom Pedro I spent the night before uttering his grito. At that time, Ipiranga was outside the city's boundaries, in a wooded area on the main trade route between Santos and São Paulo. Bricks were made here from a local red clay called Ipiranga – in the Tupi language. This clay has given its name to the surrounding neighbourhood.

The **Museu Paulista** ⓘ *T011-2065 8000, www.mp.usp.br, Tue-Sun 0900-1645, US$2*, is housed in a huge palace at the top of the park. The original building, later altered, was the first monument to Independence. The museum contains old maps, traditional furniture, collections of old coins, religious art and rare documents, and has a department of indigenous ethnology. Behind the museum is the **Horto Botânico/Ipiranga Botanical Garden** ⓘ *Tue-Sun 0900-1700*, and the **Jardim Francês**, designed as a garden for plant study, now a recreational area. There is a light and sound show on Brazilian history in the park on Wednesday, Friday and Saturday at 2030.

Mooca and the Zona Leste

São Paulo's Zona Leste is predominantly a blue collar residential region that becomes progressively poorer the farther from the centre you go, eventually tailing off into vast sprawling favelas, like the Favela do Sapo, on the city's outskirts. Most of the city's domestic workers live here (or in similar marginalized communities such as Paraisópolis in the north), near Ipiranga or Jardim Angela (in Capão Redondo in the city's far south). One of the few well to do neighbourhoods, **Mooca**, is home to the impressive **Memoria do Imigrante** ⓘ *R Visconde de Parnaíba 1316, Mooca, T011-2692 1866, www.memoria doimigrante.org.br, Tue-Sun 1000-1700, US$3, Metrô Bresser, from where an original 1912 tram runs to and from the museum during opening hours*, dedicated to the hundreds of thousands of Europeans who flooded into the country from the late 19th century to harvest coffee and work the plantations. Most came on government-funded programmes similar to the one pound pacakage which populated Australia with British emigrants in the 20th century. As many as 10,000 Germans, Italians, Ukrainians, Spanish and Portuguese came to Brazil every day from the arrival of the first boat in 1870 until the last at beginning of Second World War. They were housed and fed for free for eight days before being left to the mercy of often ruthless landowners who had only recently abandoned slavery. Treatment was often so bad that adverts were run in Europe advising people not to leave for Brazil. This museum tells little of that story, or of the African-Brazilians who were denied work in favour of Europeans, in what amounted to kind of employment apartheid, but there are fascinating exhibits on life in the early 20th century Brazil and the lifestyle of the first immigrants.

The suburbs

Parque Burle Marx

ⓘ *Av Dona Helena Pereira de Moraes 200, Morumbi, daily 0700-1900, CPTM Estação Gran Julieta or Metrô Santo Amara, and taxi (US$10, no buses and unsafe to walk)*, was designed by the famous landscape designer Burle Marx. It is the only place in the city where you can walk along trails in the *Mata Atlântica* (Atlantic rainforest), but it is unsafe after dark as lies very close to Paraisópolis, the second largest favela in São Paulo (after Heliópolis).

Santo Amaro Dam

The **Brazilian Grand Prix** is staged at the **Autódromo de Interlagos** ① *Av Senador Teotônio Vilela 261, Interlagos, T011-5666 8822, www.autodromointerlagos.com,* overlooking a vast artificial lake set in remnant forest in the far southeast of the city. There are races all year round – with details of prices and what's on on the website. For information on the Brazilian Grand Prix see box, page 217. São Paulo merges with the beautiful misty mountains and cloud forests of the Serra do Mar beyond Interlagos, its concrete gradually giving way to fresh air and trees. At **Parelheiros** there is access to the the **Mata Atlântica** Atlantic coastal rain, cloud and elfin forests in and around the **Parque Estadual Serra do Mar**, a state park and protected area offering wonderful day hiking and excellent birdwatching. Maned wolf and ocelot still live in the area and brown capuchin monkeys are a common sight.

Paranapiacaba

① *Suburban trains leave from the Estação da Luz every 15 mins for Rio Grande da Serra (Line 10 – the turquoise line), US1.50, 55 mins. From Rio Grande da Serra station, bus No 424 runs to Paranapiacaba hourly during the week, every 30 mins at weekends. The journey is around 1 hr. A tourist train is schelduled to run hourly from Estação da Luz on Sun from 2011 – see www.cptm.sp.gov.br/e_operacao/exprtur/parana.asp for the latest details.*

This tiny 19th-century town, nestled in the cloudforest of the Serra do Mar about 50 km southeast of São Paulo, was built by English railway workers who constructed the São Paulo–Santos railway. Almost all of the houses are made of wood and many look like they belong in suburban Surrey. There is a small railway museum and a handful of little pousadas and restaurants. It is easily visited in a day trip from São Paulo.

The Serra da Cantareira

Whilst the Serra do Mar mountains bring greenery to São Paulo's southern edges, the Serra da Cantareira provides fresh air and forest to its north. Unlike the Serra do Mar, the Serra da Cantareira is cut by small roads, and at weekends Paulistanos traditionally love to slip on their Timberlands, climb into the car and drive through the hills in search of nothing wilder than a steakhouse. But there are trails, and if you're prepared to walk you can get lost in some semi-wilderness. It's best to go with a guide – through local company **Tropico**, www.tropico.tur.br, who offer guided hikes to rushing rainforest waterfalls with grassy plunge pools, and to boulder mountains with sweeping views of the skyscraper city over a canopy of trees.

São Paulo listings

For Sleeping and Eating price codes and other relevant information, see pages 32-37.

Sleeping

São Paulo has the best hotels in Latin America and by far the best city hotels in Brazil. There are designer hotels that Ian Shrager would be proud of, including business towers that combine all the requisite facilities with an almost personal touch. However, rooms are expensive and while there are some reasonable budget options they are not in the best locations. Sampa (as São Paulo is affectionately known) is a place where you have to spend money to enjoy yourself. The best places to stay are **Jardins** (the most affluent area) and on and around **Av Paulista** (close to one of the business centres). Backpackers should consider **Vila Madalena** – a lively nightlife centre with a recently opened hostel. Business travellers will find good hotels on **Faria Lima** and **Av Luís Carlos Berrini** (in the new centre in the south of the city). Some of the better hostels are in seemingly random locations and there are cheap options in the seedy centre, which is an undesirable place to be at night.

Centro Histórico *p187, map p186*
Metrô República and Anhangabaú

The city centre is very busy during the day but decidedly sketchy after dark. Consider taking a cab from your hotel door and be extra careful if you resolve to walk around. Be sure to book rooms on upper floors of hotels, preferably not facing the street for a quiet night in the city centre.

AL Novotel Jaraguá Convention, R Martins Fontes 71, T011-2802 7000, www.novotel. com. This freshly refurbished chain hotel with Wi-Fi in all rooms is the only business hotel of quality in the old centre. It sits in a convenient location right off Av 9 de Julho (with fast taxi access to the airports and business districts) and R Augusta (for Av Paulista), 5 mins' walk from Metrô Anhangabaú. The hotel has a convention centre and a large exhibition and lounge space in the marble lobby, bright, no-nonsense rooms in white and blonde wood with sturdy wooden workplaces a fresh bathrooms, a gym and disabled access to some rooms.

AL-A Marabá, Av Ipiranga 757, T011-2137 9500, www.maraba.com.br. By far the best small hotel in the city centre, this newly refurbished building has colourful, well-appointed modern rooms with concessions to boutique hotel design. The hotel has a small but cosy bar, a restaurant and a pocket-sized gym. Metrô República is a few mins' walk.

C-D Itamarati, Av Dr Vieira de Carvalho 150, T011-3474 4133, www.hotelitamarati.com.br. This long-standing cheapie is popular with budget travellers and represents the best value for money of any hotel in the city centre. The rooms are simple white cubes with little more than a bed, Brazilian TV, retro (or just antique) fridges, a small desk and a

wardrobe, and the whole building has seen better days, but the location is excellent – just over 100 m from the EMTU airport bus stop and Metrô República.

D Formule 1, Av São João 1140, Centre, just off Praça da República, T011-6878 6400, www.accor.com.br. With pre-payment and short shrift service, you'll feel like you're part of a process rather than a guest at this tall chain hotel tower. However, the modern, functional and anonymous little a/c boxes they sell as rooms are spick and span and come with en suites, TVs, work places and space for up to 3 people. 5 mins' walk from Metrô República.

Avenida Paulista and Jardins
p193 and p195, maps p182 and p194
Metrô Brigadeiro, Trianon MASP, Consolação and Oscar Freire (under construction)

These plush neighbourhoods are among the safest in the city and offer easy walking acces: to São Paulo's finest restaurants, cafés, and shops. Those close to Av Paulista are a stroll from one of a string of metrô stations. A new metrô is under construction at R Oscar Freire (due 2012-2013) in the heart of Jardins.

LL Emiliano, R Oscar Freire 384, T011-3069 4369, www.emiliano.com.br. Together with the **Fasano** and **Unique**, these are best suite: in the city: bright, light and beautifully designed with attention to every detail. No pool but a relaxing small spa. Excellent Italian restaurant, location and service.

LL Fasano, R Vittorio Fasano 88, T011-3896 4077, www.fasano.com.br. One of the world's great hotels. There's a fabulous pool, a spa and the best formal haute-cuisine restaurant in Brazil. The lobby bar is a wonderful place to arrange a meeting. Excellent position in Jardins.

LL L'Hotel, Av Campinas 266, T011-2183 0500, www.lhotel.com.br. Part of the Leadir Hotels of the World group, with a series of suites decorated with mock-European paintings and patterned wallpaper, in emulation of the classic hotel look of New York's Upper East Side. The St Regis this is r but it's comfortable, intimate, offers good, discreet service and a respectable French restaurant and it's a convenient base for Paulista.

LL Renaissance, Alameda Santos 2233 (at Haddock Lobo), T011-3069 2233, www.marriott.com. This tall tower designed by Ruy Ohtake is the best business hotel for business around Av Paulista, with spacious and well-appointed rooms (the best with wonderful city views), a good spa, gym, pool and 2 squash courts. There are excellent business and conference facilities including a full business centre, secretarial services and airline booking and Wi-Fi comes in all areas.

L Unique, Av Brigadeiro Luís Antônio 4700, Jardim Paulista, T011-3055 4700, www.hotel unique.com. The most ostentatiously designed hotel in the country: an enormous half moon on concrete uprights with curving floors, circular windows and beautiful use of space and light. The bar on the top floor is São Paulo's answer to the LA Sky Bar and filled with the beautiful and famous.

L Tivoli Mofarrej, R Alameda Santos 1437, Jardins, T011-3146 5900, www.tivolihotels. com. A selection of plush, modern carpeted suites and smaller rooms, the best of which are on the upper storeys and have superb city views. The hotel has the best spa in the city – run by the Banyan Tree group, pool, business facilities, free Wi-Fi and well-equipped gym. Service is patchy, however, and beware of making phone calls from the rooms – they are very expensive.

L-AL George V, R Jose Maria Lisboa 1000, T011-3088 9822, www.george-v.com.br. This tower block in the heart of Jardins offers some of the largest rooms in central São Paulo – albeit with dull Argos-like furnishings. Apartments cover 60-180 sq m, with living rooms, fully equipped kitchens (with dishwashers and washing machines), huge bathrooms, closets and comprehensive business services. Shared facilities include sauna, indoor pool and modern gym. Special deals available on the website.

A Golden Tulip Park Plaza, Alameda Lorena 360, T011-2627 6000, www.goldentulippark plaza.com. Modern tower with apartments of 30 sq m, spa, worn-out gym and internet. Rooms are in desperate need of a re-vamp. The location is excellent – safe and with easy walking access to Jardins restaurants and Paulista. Good views from the upper storeys.

A Transamérica Ópera, Alameda Lorena 1748, T011-3062 2666, www.transamerica flats.com.br. Conservatively decorated but elegant and well-maintained modern flats of 42 sq m in a tower between the heart of Jardins and Av Paulista. At the bottom end of this price range. Gym, free Wi-Fi, parking and room service.

B Landmark Residence, Alameda Jaú 1607, T011-3082 8600, www.landmarkresidence. com.br. Spacious apartments with tired catalogue furnishings (saggy sofas, uninspiring wall prints), broadband in all rooms, a gym, gardens and a modest business centre. The location, however, is excellent – with easy walking to the chic shops, cafés and restaurants.

B-C Ibis São Paulo Paulista, Av Paulista 2355, T011-3523 3000, www.accorhotels. com.br. Great value. Modern, business-standard rooms with a/c in a tower right on Av Paulista. Cheaper at weekends. Online reservations.

C Paulista Garden, Alameda Lorena 21, T/F011-3885 8498, www.paulistagardenhotel. com.br. Small, simple wooden rooms with a/c, cable TV and fridges but no workspaces. 10 mins' walk uphill to Paulista (for Brigadeiro Metrô), 15 to Ibirapuera park and 20 to the heart of Jardins. There are plenty of restaurants nearby and the area is safe. Tiny gym and rooftop patio with a view.

C Pousada Dona Zilah, Alameda Franca 1621, Jardim Paulista, T011-3062 1444, www.zilah. com. Little *pousada* in a renovated colonial house with plain but well-maintained rooms and common areas decorated with thought and a personal touch. Excellent location, bike rental and generous breakfast included. Triple rooms available (**D**).

C Estan Plaza, Alameda Jau 497, Jardins, T011-3016 0000, www.estanplaza.com.br. Well-kept, simple and pocket-sized rooms in a well-situated tower block close to both the restaurants of Jardins and to Av Paulista. Rooms are at a similar price to hostel doubles making this excellent value.

Vila Madalena and Pinheiros *p196, map p182*

Metrô Vila Madalena and Pinheiros (under construction)

These is a great neighbourhoods to stay in – with a wealth of little shops, café-restaurants, bars and nightclubs. The metrô station is 10 mins' walk from most of the action but there are fast subway trains from here to the city centre and connections to Paulista and the *rodoviária*. There are only 2 accommodation options for now. But more will surely come.

C-D Casa Club, R Mourato Coelho 973, T011 3798 0051, www.casaclub.com.br. There are only 4 rooms in this tiny hostel and whilst they're all dorms they can be booked as private rooms – hence the price discrepancy. One is for women only. The hostel began life as a bar and the after-hours party atmosphere remains to this day, so its not an option for those craving peace or privacy. Free Wi-Fi and a restaurant.

B-D Sampa Hostel, R Girassol 519, T011-3031 6779, www.hostelsampa.com.br. This small hostel is in the heart of Vila Madalena, close to shops, cafés and bars. The 2 private rooms fill up quickly so book ahead, the rest of the accommodation is in dorms. All are fan cooled. Prices include breakfast. Wi-Fi is available throughout the hostel at a flat one-off US$3.50 fee.

South of the Centre *p197, map p182*

Metrô Anhangabaú, Liberdade, Paraíso and Vergueiro

B-C Formule 1, R Vergueiro 1571, T011-5085 5699, www.accorhotels.com.br. Another great-value business-style hotel, with a/c apartments big enough for 3 (making this an **E** option for those in a

group). Right next to Paraíso Metrô in a safe area.

B-D Vergueiro Hostel, R Vergueiro 434, Liberdade, T011-2649 1323, www.hostel vergueiro.com. This 2009 opening has simple eggshell blue or burnt ochre rooms with parquet wood or square-tile floors, some of which have balconies. Studio apartments come with either double beds or 3 singles and shared rooms have 6 beds in wooden bunks. Rooms have private bathrooms, there is free Wi-Fi and breakfast is included.

C-E Pousada dos Franceses, R dos Franceses 100, Bela Vista, T011-3288 1592, www.pousadadosfranceses.com.br. Price per person. A plain little *pousada* with an attractive garden, a BBQ area, laundry facilities, dorms, doubles and singles. 10 mins' walk from Brigadeiro Metrô. Free internet, TV room and breakfast included.

B-E Praça da Árvore IYHA, R Pageú 266, Saúde, T011-5071 5148, www.spalbergue. com.br.This pleasant little hostel with friendly helpful (and English-speaking staff) lies 2 mins from the Praça do Arvore Metrô – some 20 mins' ride from the city centre. It is situated in a large residential house in a quiet back street. Facilities include a kitchen, laundry and internet service.

C-E 3 Dogs Hostel, R Cel Artur Godoi 51, Vila Mariana, T011-2359 8222, www.3dogs hostel.com.br. Double rooms and dorms, breakfast and bed linen included, with garden and free Wi-Fi.

Itaim Bibi, Vila Olímpia and Moema *p200, map p182*

Metrô Faria Lima (from 2012), CPTM Vila Olímpia and Cidade Jardim

AL-L Blue Tree Towers, Av Brigadeiro Faria Lima 3989, Vila Olímpia, T011-3896 7544, www.bluetree.com.br. Modern business ho with discreetly designed rooms and excelle service. Ideally positioned for Faria Lima's business district and the restaurants and nigh life of Vila Olímpia and Itaim. Pool, massage gym, sauna and well-equipped business cent

Brooklin and the New Business District *p200, map p182*

This is São Paulo's new business capital. Most hotels are to be found on Av Brigadeiro Faria Lima and Av Luís Carlos Berrini.

L-L Grand Hyatt São Paulo, Av das Nações Unidas 13301, T011-2838 1234, www.saopaulo.hyatt.com. A superb business hotel close to Av Luís Carlos Berrini, which successfully fuses corporate efficiency and exquisite services with designer cool. Spa, pool, state-of-the-art business centre and marvellous views from the upper-floor suites.

L-L Hilton São Paulo, Av das Nações Unidas 12901, T011-2845 0000, www.hilton.com. This tall tower in the heart of the new business district overlooks the new Octavio Frias de Oliveira twin suspension bridge and boasts a vast marble lobby with Wi-Fi access (none in rooms), business and conference facilities and a 24-hr spa. Rooms come with marble bathrooms, an office workstation with broadband and sweeping city views from the upper floors. Suites have separate living rooms, kitchenettes and a second bathroom with Jacuzzin and a TV.

The suburbs *p202*

Unique Garden Spa, Estrada 3500, Serra da Cantareira, T011-4486 8724, www.unique garden.com.br. The über-cool style of hotel Unique (see page 205) transposed into a natural setting of the Serra da Cantareira subtropical forest, 40 mins north of São Paulo. The buildings are equally impressive, with

Ruy Ohtake's iron-grey post-industrial half-moon replaced with a series of Frank Lloyd Wright-inspired post-modernist bungalows. The spa treatments are wonderful. Shuttles can be organized through hotel **Unique**.

🍴 Eating

Those on a budget can eat to their stomach's content in per kilo places or, if looking for cheaper still, in *padarias* (bakeries). There is one of these on almost every corner. They all serve sandwiches such as *Misto Quentes*, *Beirutes* and *Americanos* – delicious Brazilian burgers made from decent meat and served with ham, egg, cheese or salad. They always have good coffee, juices, cakes and *almoços* (set lunches) for a very economical price. Most have a designated seating area, either at the *padaria* bar or in an adjacent room; you aren't expected to eat on your feet as you are in Rio. Restaurants in São Paulo are safe on the stomach. Juices are made with mineral or filtered water.

Centro Histórico *p187, map p186*
Metrô Luz, República, São Bento, Anhangabaú, Sé

You are never far from a café or restaurant in the city centre and Luz. The Pinacoteca galleries, the Centro Culutral Banco do Brasil and the Pátio de Colégio all have decent cafés, and there are dozens in the streets around the Mosteiro São Bento and the

Teatro Municipal. Most tend to be open during lunchtime only and there are many per kilo options and *padarias*.

Terraço Italia, Av Ipiranga 344, T011-3257 6566. An overpriced Italian restaurant, with stodgy pasta, lukewarm risottos and a huge menu of very mediocre pan-European food and the best views in the city of any dining room in São Paulo. Come for a coffee only, although there's a minimum charge of US$12.

Luz *p191, map p182*

Café da Pinacoteca, Pinacoteca Museum, Praça da Luz 2, Luz, T011-3326 0350. This Portuguese-style café with marble floors and mahogany balconies overlooks the Parque da Luz on the basement floor of the Pinacoteca gallery. It serves great coffee, sandwiches, snacks and cakes. There is also a café of similar quality in the Estação Pinacoteca gallery.

Ponto Chic, Largo do Paiçandu 27, T011-3222 6528; www.pontochic.com.br. Paulistanos rave about this rather unpre-possessing little corner café in the heart of the city. A slice of Brazilian culinary history, the *Bauru* sandwich was born here in 1922. A bronze bust of Casemiro Pinto Neto, who apparently first conceived the ground-breaking idea of combining cheese, salad and roast beef in a French bread roll, adorns the back wall. The sandwich itself has a page of the menu devoted to its history, but arrives with little ceremony on a plain white plate, overflowing with gooey cheese and thick with fine-cut beef.

Barra Funda and Higienópolis *p192, map p182*

AK Delicatessan, R Mato Grosso 450, Higienópolis, T011-3231 4497. After moving back to her native São Paulo from New York, former film-producer Andrea Kaufmann resolved to open a New York style deli and an upstairs restaurant decorated with strips of retro wall paper and dedicated to Jewish home cooking. Dishes include Eastern European veal goulash with spätzle, pearl

onions and sour cream and, in the deli, warm bagels and pastrami. The restaurant has won numerous awards, including the Folha de São Paulo restaurant-of-the-year award.

Anita, R Mato Grosso 154, T011-2628 3584 www.restauranteanita.com.br. Simple but elegantly prepared comfort food in this little restaurant next to the AK Delicatessan. Lunchtime is especially popular when fashionable 20-something girls pull up here to lunch on filet mignon or linguini with mushrooms and cracked pepper, after spending the morning browsing in nearby Jardins.

Carlota, R Sergipe 753, Higienópolis, T011 3661 8570, www.carlota.com.br. Chef Carla Pernambuco was a pioneer of fine dining in Brazil when she first opened her restaurant in the mid-1990s. Her recipe of unpretentious, homey surrounds, warm service and Brazilian and Mediterranean fusion cooking has been copied by numerous others in São Paulo. Dishes include fillet of grouper with plantain banana purée and fresh asparagus.

Avenida Paulista and Consolação *p193, map p194*

Metrô Consolação, Trianon-MASP, Brigadeiro.
Restaurants in this area lie along the course of Av Paulista or in the up-and-coming nightlife are of Consolação to its north. Jardins lies within easy access to the south.

Spot, Av Ministro Rocha Azevedo 72, T011-3284 6131, www.restaurantespot. com.br. This chic São Paulo take on an American diner has been a favourite before-and-after club spot for fashionable Paulistanos for more than a decade. The wealthy, beautiful and well-dressed gather here to eat easy-on-the-waistline plates like grilled steak poivre, salmon with balsamic vinegar and seared tuna with soy and lime sauce.

Sujinho, R da Consolação 2068 and 206 Consolação, T011-3231 1299, www.sujinh com.br. Burgers, pastas, salads, grilled fish, spit-roast chicken and sizzling meat all ser in large portions. Home delivery available.

ᵀᵀ-ᵀ America, Av Paulista 2295, Consolação, T011-3067 4424, www.americaburger. com.br. This immensely popular a/c tribute to the New York diner and the North American burger is a great choice for families. Food comes quickly in Texan portions and with crisp waiter service. There are veggie options alongside the huge hunks of beef, a salad bar and a generous choice of sticky puddings and sugar-saturated shakes.

ᵀᵀ Restaurante do MASP, Av Paulista 1578, T011-3253 2829 (see page 193). This bright, hospital clean buffet restaurant in the basement of the museum serves good-value comfort food such as lasagne and stroganoff, accompanied by salad from the buffet bar.

ᵀᵀ-ᵀ Fran's Café, Av Paulista 358, and all over the city. Open 24 hrs. Coffee chain serving aromatic, strong, richly flavoured coffee at a civilized temperature and in European-sized china cups, together with a menu of light eats.

Jardins p195, map p194
Metrô Oscar Freire (from 2013), Consolação or Trianon-MASP 10 mins' walk

Most of the city's fine dining restaurants lie in this upmarket grid of streets to the south of Av Paulista.

ᵀᵀᵀ Charlô Bistro, R Barão de Capanema 440 (next to D.O.M), T011-3087 4444, with another branch at the high-society set **Jockey Club**, Av Lineu de Paula Machado 1263, Cidade Jardim, T011-3034 3682. One of the premier VIP and old family haunts in the city. Decked out in tribute to a Paris brasserie and a menu of simple but elegant Mediterranean and fusion dishes such as Mediterranean squid with black rice and duck risotto with almonds and a curry sauce.

ᵀᵀ Dalva e Dito, R Padre Joao Manoel 1115, T011-3064 6183, www.dalvaedito.com.br. Brazil's most internationally vaunted chef, Alex Atala, opened his new dining room in 2009 to serve Brazilian home cooking with a gourmet twist. Dishes include roast pork with pureed potato and catfish with aromatic apim-santo grass from the plains of the

Brazilian interior. A long open kitchen cuts through the middle of the bright, soaring dining room. The food is better value than it is in D.O.M and the atmosphere more familial.

ᵀᵀᵀ D.O.M, R Barão de Capanema 549, T011-3088 0761. This has been Jardins' evening restaurant of the moment for almost a decade. The kitchen is run by chef Alex Attala, who has won the coveted *Veja* award several times. Contemporary food fuses Brazilian ingredients with French and Italian styles and is served in a large, open, modernist dining room to the sharply dressed.

ᵀᵀᵀ Dui, Alameda Franca 1590, T011-2649 7952, www.duirestaurante.com.br. Sumptuous, light Brazilian-Asian-Mediterranean fusion. Great cocktails in the downstairs bar.

ᵀᵀᵀ Eñe, R Dr Mario Ferraz 213, T011-3816 4333, www.enerestaurante.com.br. Brazil's foremost modern Spanish restaurant is helmed by Sergio and Javier Torres Martínez who have worked with Alain Ducasse and Josep Lladonosa of the Escola Arnadí. The *degustação* is a smorgasbord of Spanish and Brazilian-inspired tapas with choices such as breaded mussels and cream of white carrot with tapioca pearls. They come accompanied with the best choice of Spanish wines in Brazil.

ᵀᵀᵀ Fasano, Fasano Hotel (see Sleeping), R Fasano, T011-3062 4000, www.fasano. com.br. The flagship restaurant of the Fasano group has long been regarded as the best restaurant for gourmets in São Paulo. The menu offers a huge choice of modern Italian and French cooking, modelled on the best of Milan from chef Salvatore Loi and served in a magnificent room where diners have their own low-lit booths and are served by flocks of black-tie waiters. The wine list is exemplary and the dress formal dress.

ᵀᵀᵀ Figueira Rubaiyat, R Haddock Lobo 1738, T011-3063 1399, www.rubaiyat.com.br. The most interesting of the **Rubaiyat** restaurant group, with steaks prepared by Brazilian chef, Francisco Gameleira. Very lively for lunch on a Sun and remarkable principally for the space:

open walled, light and airy and shaded by a huge tropical fig tree.

♔♔♔ Gero, R Haddock Lobo 1629, T011-3064 0005, www.fasano.com.br. Fasano's version of a French bistro serves pasta and light Italian food in carefully designed, casually chic surrounds. The evening clientele includes some of the best-known and most expensively reconstructed faces in São Paulo high society – making this a prime spot for people-watching, but be prepared for a long wait at the bar alongside people who are there to be seen. No reservations.

♔♔♔ La Tambouille, Av 9 de Julho 5925, Jardim Europa, T011-3079 6277, www.tambouille.com.br. The favourite fusion restaurant of the city's old-money society. Chef Giancarlo Bolla, a native of San Remo in northern Italy, learnt his trade on the Italian Riviera and prepares dishes like fillet of sole with passion fruit sauce served with banana and shrimp farofa and filet mignon wrapped in parma ham and cooked in red wine and served with brie ravioli. Excellent wine list. The restaurant offers a good-value three course gourmet lunch Tue-Fri.

♔♔♔ Massimo, Alameda Santos 1826, Cerqueira César, T011-3284 0311. One of São Paulo's longest-established Italian restaurants serving simple northern Italian dishes and a wide selection of very fresh, grilled seafish to the city's politicians and business executives. The wine list stretches to 100 bottles and credit cards are not accepted, despite the elevated price.

♔♔♔-♔♔ Marakuthai, Alameda Itu 1618, T011-3061 1015, www.marakuthai.com.br. A Paulistano take on Indian and Southeast Asian food. Dishes are Brazilian experiments with Asian ingredients.

♔♔ A Mineira, Alameda Joaquim Eugenio de Lima 697, T011-3283 2349. This self-service restaurant offers Minas food by the kilo from a buffet which sizzles in earthenware pots over a woodfire stove. There's plenty of choice and a small draft of *Cachaça* and desserts are included in the price.

♔♔ Baalbek, Alameda Lorena 1330, T011-3088 4820. Lebanese cooking, with great falafel, Arabic salads and sweet desserts. Closed in the evenings.

♔♔ Kayomix, R da Consolação 3215, T011-3082 2769. Brazilian-Oriental fusions with dishes such as salmon taratare with shimeji and shitake.

♔♔ Sattva, Alameda Itu 1564, T011-3083 6237, www.sattvanatural.com.br. Light vegetarian curries, stir fries, salads, pizzas and pastas all made with organic ingredients. There is a great-value dish of the day lunchtime menu on weekdays and live music most nights.

♔♔ Santo Grão, R Oscar Freire 413, T011-3082 9969, www.santograo.com.br. This smart café with tables spilling out onto the street is a favourite coffee and cakes or light lunch stop for wealthy society shoppers. The coffee is superb, freshly roasted and comes in a number of varieties.

♔ Cheiro Verde, R Peixoto Gomide 1078, Jardins, T011-3262 2640 (lunch only), www.cheiroverderestaurante.com.br. Hearty vegetarian food, such as vegetable crumble in gorgonzola sauce and wholewheat pasta with buffalo mozzarella and sundried tomato.

Vila Madalena and Pinheiros *p196, map p182*

The streets of Vila Madalena are lined with restaurants and cafés – many on **Aspicuelta** and **Girassol**. Most of the bars and clubs serve food too, and some – such as **Grazie o Dio!** – have designated restaurants. Pinheiros has some of the best fine dining restaurants in the city.

♔♔♔ Jun Sakamoto, R Lisboa 55, Pinheiros, T011-3088 6019. Japanese cuisine with a French twist. Superb fresh ingredients, some of it flown in especially from Asia and the USA. The dishes of choice are the degustation menu and the duck breast teppaniyaki.

♔♔♔ Mani, R Joaquim Antunes 210, Pinheiros, T011-3085 4148. Superior light Mediterranean menu, which utilizes Brazilian ingredients and perfectly complements the waistlines of the celebrity crowd. Daniel Redondo and partner

Helena Rizzo have worked in Michelin-starred restaurants in Europe.

♥-♥ Deli Paris, R Harmonia 484, Vila Madalena, T011-3816 5911, www.deliparis.com.br. This Paulistano homage to a French café serves light and flavourful sweet and savoury crepes, sickly sweet petit gateaux au chocolat, cheese-heavy quiches, salads and crunchy sandwiches to a busy lunchtime and evening crowd.

♥-♥ Genial, R Girassol 374, T011-3812 7442. This bar, with a black and white mosaic floor and black-tie waiters, is decorated with LP covers by famous traditional musicians such as João do Vale and Luiz Gonzaga. The *chope* is creamy and best accompanied by a *petisco* bar snack – like *caldinho de feijão* (bean broth) or *bolinhos de bacalhau* (codfish balls), both of which are among the best in Vila Madalena. There's a hearty and very popular *feijoada* on Sat and Sun lunch.

South of the Centre *p197, map p182*
Liberdade is dotted with Japanese restaurants and has a lively market on Sun with plenty of food stalls. Bela Vista is replete with Italian restaurants, most of them rather poor – with todgy pasta and gooey risotto. Ibirauera Park has lots of mobile snack bars selling ice cream, sugar cane juice, hot dogs and snacks, and there is a good-value buffet restaurant lose to the Museu Afro Brasileiro.

♥-♥ Famiglia Mancini, R Anhandava, T011-255 6599, www.famigliamancini.com.br. This pretty little pedestrianized street 10 mins' walk from the Terraço Italia is lined with Italian restaurants and delicatessans, almost all of them in the locally owned Famiglia Mancini group. Here, the big dining room with formal waiters and an enormous menu of meats, pastas, risottos, fish and (inevitably for São Paulo) pizzas, is the family's flagship restaurant. Walls are lined with the faces of famous Brazilians who have dined here. The restaurant is very busy with families on weekends and reservations are necessary.

♥ Aska Lámen, R Galvão Buemno 466, Liberdade, T011-3277 9682. One of

Liberadade's more traditional Japanese restaurants with a bar overlooking an open kitchen where chefs serve piping ramen noodle dishes to lunchtime diners who are 90% *issei* (Japonese immigrants and their descendants).

♥ Prêt, Museu de Arte Moderna (MAM), Parque Ibirapuera, T011-5574 1250, www.mam.org.br. Closed evenings. This lunchtime buffet serves the best food in the park – ultra-fresh pre-prepared soups, salads, chicken, fish, meat and vegetarian dishes. It sits in a semi-circular dining room at the front of MAM, bathed in light from 3-m-high glass windows and looking out over the sculpture garden and Niemeyer's Oca. The Bienal building (for Fashion Week and the Art shows) is less than 200 m away.

♥ Gombe, R Tomás Gonzaga 22, T011-3209 8499. Renowned for ultra-fresh seared tuna and steaming hot udon and ramen dishes.

♥ Sushi Yassu, R Tomas Gonzaga 98, T011-3288 2966, www.sushiyassu.com.br. The best of Liberdade's traditional Japanese restaurants with a large menu of sushi/sashimi combinations, teishoku (complete set meals with cooked and raw dishes) and very sweet Brazilianized desserts.

Itaím, Vila Olímpia and Moema
p200, map p182
These areas, south of the centre, have dozens of ultra-trendy restaurants with beautiful people posing in beautiful surroundings. We include only a handful of the best.

♥♥♥ 348 Parrilla Porteña, R Comendador Miguel Calfat, 348, Vila Olímpia, T011-3849 0348, www.restaurante348.com.br. An Argentinian restaurant with the best steak in the country from the choicest cuts available only on export from Buenos Aires. The *ojo del bife* cuts like brie and collapses in the mouth like wafered chocolate. The accompanying wines are equally superb, especially the 2002 Cheval dos Andes. Great, unpretentious atmosphere.

♥♥♥ JAM Warehouse, R Lopes Neto 308, Itaim, T011-3473 3273, www.jamwarehouse.com.br.

Japanese restaurant serving Japanese food with a Brazilian twist – with grilled and seared tuna and salmon, sushi stuffed with foie gras and cream cheese and sweet sushi dishes for dessert. There's more style than substance to the cooking, but the atmosphere is congenial, with live music every night and there's always a smart 'A' list crowd eager to be ogled.

♥♥♥ Kinoshita, R Jacques Félix 405, Vila Nova Conceição, T011-3849 6940, www.restaurantekinoshita.com.br. Tsuyoshi Murakami offers the best menu of traditional cooked or Kappo cuisine in Brazil, dotted with creative fusion dishes in a Nobu vein. His cooking utilizes only the freshest ingredients and includes a sumptuous degustation menu with delights such as tuna marinated in soya, ginger and garlic, served with ponzo sauce and garnished with Kaiware (sprouted daikon radish seeds). Murakami trained in the ultra-traditional 100-year-old **Ozushi** restaurant in Shambashi Tokyo, **Shubu Shubu** in New York and **Kyokata** in Barcelona.

♥♥♥ Kosushi, R Viradouro 139, Itaim Bibi and in Shopping Cidade Jardim, T011-3167 7272, www.kosushi.com.br. The first of São Paulo's chic Japanese restaurants, which began life in Liberdade and is now housed in a beautifully designed Asian modernist space. The rich and famous come here to be seen eating chef George Yuji Koshoji's huge sushi and sashimi combinations.

♥♥♥ Parigi, R Amauri 275, Itaim, T011-3167 1575, www.fasano.com.br. One of the premier places to be seen; celebrity couples come here for intimate, public-view Franco-Italian dining. The menu also has classical French dishes such as *coq au vin*. Attractive dining room, beautifully lit, and decked out in lush dark wood.

♠ Bars, clubs and live music

→ *See Music and dance central colour section.*
São Paulo has more nocturnal panache than Rio. There is great live music on most nights of the week. Large concert venues, such as

the **Pacaembu Stadium**, host the likes of U2 or Ivete Sangalo. Medium-sized venues, such as **Credicard Hall**, are played by acts like Caetano Veloso, Gilberto Gil and Chico Buarque. Smaller venues include SESCs (cultural centres with excellent concert halls), and are found in Vila Mariana and Pompéia. They host smaller, classy artists such as Otto, Naná Vasconcelos, João Bosco and Seu Jorge. It is also worth checking out the established smaller live venues in and around Vila Madalena and Itaim, such as **Bourbon St**, **A Marcenaria** and **Grazie a Dio** for samba-funk acts such as Tutti Baê and Funk como le Gusta, designated samba bars like **Ó do Borogodó** (also in Vila Madalena) and venues on the burgeoning alternative music scene, such as the **CB Bar** and **Studio SP** in Barra Funda and Consolação, respectively.

DJs like Marky and the sadly deceased Suba made the São Paulo club scene world famous, but gone are the days when Marky was resident DJ at the Lov.E Club and the city danced to homegrown sounds in clubs like Prime. São Paulo's sound systems and clubs are slicker and swankier than they have ever been, but the music is painfully derivative of New York and Europe.

The city has a bar at every turn – from spit-and-sawdust corner bars serving cold lager beer to an unpretentious blue-collar cord, to smarter mock-Portuguese *boteco* bars where penguin-suited waiters whirl around the tables brandishishing frothy glasses of draught lager or *chope* (pronounced 'chopee') and self-consciously chic cocktail bars where Paulistano high society flashes its jewels and flexes its pecs. Almost all serve food and many have live music. Beer and snacks are also available at the bar in any *padaria* (bakery).

Barra Funda *p192, map p182*
This dark and edgy neighbourhood northwest of Luz is gradually emerging as a new nightlife venue to rival Consolação. It's more Bohemian than the latter, with a sweep of bars and venues playing host to a

bewildering variety of acts which have little to nothing in common beyond existing beyond the mainstream. It's not safe to walk around here after dark. Take the metrô and a cab.

Aldeia Turiassú, R Turiassú 928, T011-3865 3055, www.aldeiaturiassu.com.br, http://bandagloria.com.br. On Fri this vast concert hall plays host to one of the best live samba gafieira acts in Brazil, Banda Glória, who play smoking dance-hall samba to a seething crowd of middle-class Paulistanos. 2 of the band's singers – Rubi and Andreia Dias – have become big names on São Paulo's alternative scene, signing up for record deals with cult record label Scubidy productions.

Bar do Alemão, Av Antártica 554, Água Branca, T011-3879 0070, http://bardo alemao.zip.net. This cosy little brick-walled bar and restaurant, on an ugly main road in a semi-residential quarter of Barra Funda, is famous for its live samba. There are samba shows most nights with an especially lively crowd at the weekends. Clara Nunes used to play here and famous samba musicians often appear still – including Paulo Cesar Pinheiro and Eduardo Gudin.

Berlin, R Cônego Vicente Miguel Marino 85, T011-3392 4594, www.clubeberlin.com.br. This cool, low-lit, long bar attracts an intelligent, arty crowd of 20- and 30-somethings, who gather from Tue-Sat to hear live contemporary Brazilian jazz with a psychedelic twist on Tue, Brazilian alternative and indie on Thu and pan-Latin American dance fusion on Fri.

CB, R Brigadeiro Galvão 871, T011-3666 8971, www.cbbar.com.br. This low-lit alternative rock and vanguarda venue is one of the best places in the city to hear interesting new acts. The line-up is eclectic, with local and out-of-state bands opening from Tue-Sat and alternating with Paulistano DJs.

D-Edge, Alameda Olga 170, T011-3667 8334, www.d-edge.com.br. This is one of the few São Paulo clubs to play Brazilian as well as international sounds. However, those searching for the shock of the new will still be disappointed by the homages to Ibiza and New York which dominate on most nights.

Pacha, R Mergenthaler 829, Vila Leopoldina, T011-2189 3700, www.pachasp.com.br. Those looking to come to São Paulo and experience Ibiza nightlife will love this gaudy temple to Ibiza, with decks manned by the world's top DJs and dance floors packed with the city's wealthiest and most expensively clad. But with the US$1000 entrance fee to the VIP area, it would be cheaper for Europeans at least to opt for the real thing in Ibiza. Those without a Dubai prince's urge to be seen to spend can enter the dance area, reserved for the hoy poloy, for a 20th of the price.

SESC Pompeia, R Clélia, 93. Pompéia, T011-3871 7700, ww.sescsp.org.br. There's always a great show at this arts and cultural centre in the neighbouring bairro to Barra Funda. Some of Brazil's best small acts play at weekends.

The Week, R Guaicurus 324, Barra Funda, T011-3872 9966, www.theweek.com.br. One of the city's biggest gay- and lesbian-dominated dance clubs, whose party to attend is Babylon (in the VIP room on Sat nights). It's packed with pill-popping gym bodies gyrating to progressive trance. There are a further 6000 sq m of dance floor and there's even a pool for when it all gets too hot.

Avenida Paulista and Consolação
p193, map p194

Until a few years ago the dark streets of Consolação were home to little more than rats, sleazy strip bars, street-walkers and curb-crawlers, but now it harbours a thriving alternative weekend scene. Shortly after R Augusta crosses Av Paulista from Jardins, it leaves the smart and swanky for a mish-mash of untidy streets, grafitti-scrawled shop fronts broken by the deep velvet-red of open bar doors. Go-go clubs with heavy-set bouncers loitering outside sit alongside makeshift street bars where a jostle of hundreds of young Paulistanos down bottles of Bohemia beer at rickety metal tables or brush aside their emo fringes as they queue to enter a gamut of fashionable bars, clubs and pounding gay venues.

Clube Royal, R Consolação 222, T011-3129 9804, www.royalclub.com.br. One of the most fashionable funk and rare groove clubs on the young and need-to-be-seen São Paulo circuit is decorated like a New York dive bar in Brazilian tropical colours. Celebrities who choose to dance here include Gisele Bundchen and the hottest night are Desire and Shine on Fri and Sat respectively. Don't expect to hear any Brazilian music.

Hotel Cambridge, Av 9 de Julho 210, Centro, www.noitesdocentro.com.br/index.php? destino=cambridge. In the 1950s, the Cambridge was been a bastion of the city's bossa nova scene. Nowadays its frayed post-war deco provides the backdrop for alternative bands and DJs who gather here throughout the week but particularly on Fri and Sat to hear an assortment of bands.

Outs Club, R Augusta 486, T011-6867 6050, www.clubeouts.com. One of the bastions of the alternative, rock and hard rock scene with a mix of DJs playing everything from UK indie to heavy Brazilian metal bands.

Sonique, R Bela Cintra 461, Consolação, T011-2628 8707, www.soniquebar.com.br. The crowd in the neon-lit, high-ceilinged cavern of a room which comprises this club may look alternative but they are merely climbing on the grunge bandwagon. Whilst it's a great spot for people-watching, the club sounds are mainstream but anyone coming from Europe or the USA. The venue is intended as a warm-up for the larger clubs around town, with an airport-like messageboard announcing what is happening where.

Studio SP, R Augusta 591, T011-3129 7040, www.studiosp.org. A show hall on the neighbourhood's main thoroughfare. Turning up for the support act (usually before 2200) means getting in for free to see the main show. Bands like Trash pour Quatro, www.trashpour4.com, offer bossa nova

re-workings of kitsch classics like *Material Girl*, in the spirit of Berk and the Virtual Band. Singers such as Andreia Dias, www.andreia dias.com.br, offer smoky, seductive electronica mixed with lilting Brazilian rhythms. They intersperse with harder mangue beat acts like Mombojo from Pernambuco, www.mombojo.com.br.

Volt, R Haddock Lobo 40, Consolação, T011-2936 4041, www.barvolt.com.br. Just across Av Paulista from Consolação, a hip creative industry crowd sip fruit *batidas* to Brazilian drum and bass and Chicago house in this 400-sq-m space. It's lit with luminescent pink and green strip lights and decorated with a mirror wall, vertical fern garden and Eames wooden chairs and is a favourite pre- and post-club stop.

Vegas Club, R Augusta 765, T011-3231 3705, www.vegasclub.com.br. International and local DJs spin a predictable menu of techno, psi-trance and house to a mixed gay and straight crowd dancing on 2 sweaty floors from Tue-Sat.

Jardins p195, map p194

Bar Balcão, R Doutor Melo Alves 150, T011-3063 6091. After-work meeting place, very popular with young professionals and media types who gather on either side of the long low wooden bar, which winds its way around the room like a giant snake.

Barretto, in the **Fasano Hotel** (see Sleeping). A rather conservative atmosphere with heavy dark wood, mirrors and cool live bossa jazz. The crowd is mostly the Cuban cigar type with a sprinkling of the tanned and toned, in figure-enhancing designer labels.

Emiliano Bar, Emiliano Hotel (see Sleeping). Similar crowd to **Skye** but despite its popularity, it can feel like a sterile corridor rather than an intimate space. DJs play on Fri nights.

Dry Bar, R Padre João Manuel 700, T011-3729 6653, www.drybar.com.br. This low-lit, dark bar, with walls decorated with black pooltable balls, is a favourite with Jardins' rich, young and single, who throng here in the late evening to drink from a menu of more than a dozen dry martinis. The bar also serves excellent, expensive bar snacks.

Finnegan's Pub, R Cristiano Viana 358, Pinheiros, T011-3062 3232, www.finnegan. com.br. One of São Paulo's Irish bars. This one is actually run and owned by an Irishman and is very popular with expats.

Casa de Francisca, R José Maria Lisboa 190 at Brigadeiro Luís Antônio, T011-3493 5717, www.casadefrancisca.blogspot.com, This intimate, live music restaurant bar plays host to the refined end of the musical spectrum with acts such as virtuoso guitarist and composer Chico Saraiva, multi-instrumentalist Arthur de Faria or pianist Paulo Braga. The tables to book are those on the upper deck.

Skye, the rooftop bar at **Unique Hotel** (see Sleeping). Another fashionable spot with a definite door policy. The views of glistening skyscrapers pocked by patches of green and red tile are wonderful.

Mokai, R Augusta 2805, T011-3081 3103, www.mokai.com.br. This cool, concrete rectangle with headphones on the walls playing the latest club sounds from the world over, and dance floor lit by twinkling 550-sq-ft LED ceilings, is owned by Amir Slama (creator of Brazil's most internationally successful label, Rosa Chá) and his millionaire playboy friend Rico Mansur. There is a strict door policy. Dress down but well, book ahead through a concierge or someone pretending to be so, and enjoy the people-watching.

Vila Madalena and Pinheiros
p196, map p182

Vila Madalena and adjacent Pinheiros lie just northeast of Jardins. A taxi from Jardins is about US$7; there is also a metrô station, but this closes by the time the bars get going. These suburbs are the favourite haunts of São Paulo 20-somethings, more hippy chic than Itaim, less stuffy than Jardins. This is the best part of town for live Brazilian music and uniquely Brazilian close dances such as *forró*, as opposed to international club sounds.

It can feel grungy and informal but is buzzing. The liveliest streets are **Aspicuelta** and **Girassol**.

A Marcenaria, R Fradique Coutinho 1378, T011-3032 9006, www.amarcenaria.com.br. This is the Vila Madalena bar of choice for the young, single lovers of Brazilian rock who gather here from 2130; the dance floor fills up at around 2300.

Bambu, R Purpurina 272, Vila Madalena, T011-3031 2331, www.bambubrasi bar.com.br. A kind of backland desert jig called *forró* has everyone up and dancing in this slice of mock-Bahia, with live northeastern accordion and *zabumba* drum bands in the front room and a hippy middle-class student crowd downing industrial strength caipirinhas out back.

DiQuinta, R Baumann 1435, T011-5506 0100, www.diquinta.com.br. Mainstream medium-sized acts play here and at other venues in Vila Madalena such as **Grazie o Dio**. This club is one of the few to be busy on a Thu night.

Grazie a Dio, R Girassol 67, T011-3031 6568, www.grazieadio.com.br. The best bar in Vila Madalena to hear live music – there's a different band every night with samba on Sun. Great for dancing. Always packed.

Ó do Borogodó, R Horácio Lane 21, Vila Madalena, T011-3814 4087. It can be hard to track down this intimate club opposite the cemetery. It's in an unmarked house next to a hairdressers on the edge of Vila Madalena. The tiny dance hall is always packed with people between Wed and Sat. On Wed there's classic *samba canção* from retired cleaner Dona Inah who sings material from the likes of Cartola and Ataulfo Alves; and on other nights there's a varied programme of *choro*, *forró* and MPB from some of the best samba players in São Paulo.

Posto 6, R Aspicuelta 644, Vila Madalena, T011-3812 7831. An imitation Rio de Janeiro *boteco* with attractive crowds and backdrop of bossa nova and MPB. Busy from 2100.

Sub Astor, R Delfina 163, Vila Madalena, T011-3815 1364, www.subastor.com.br. This velvety mood-lit lounge bar looks like a film set from a David Lynch movie and is filled with mols, vamps and playboys from the upper echelons of São Paulo society. The cocktails are superb – especially the fruity caipirinhas, and there is no better place in the neighbourhood to see the Vanity Fair.

Itaím, Vila Olímpia and Moema
p200, map p182

This area, just south of Ibirapuera and north of the new centre, is about US$10 by taxi from Jardins and US$15 from the centre, but well worth the expense of getting here. It is packed with street-corner bars, which are great for a browse. The bars here, although informal, have a style of their own, with lively and varied crowds and decent service. The busiest streets for a bar wander are **R Atilio Inocenti** near the junction of Av Juscelino Kubitschek and Av Brigadeiro Faria Lima, **Av Hélio Pellegrino** and **R Araguari**, which runs behind it.

3X4, R Bandeira Paulista 676, Itaím, T011-2122 4051, www.3p4.com.br, This achingly chic place to be seen in owned by fashion impresario Amir Slama has furniture by Philippe Starck and photography by Brazilian Vogue snapper André Schiliró. It's nominally a restaurant, offering light Asian-Mediterranean cooking, but really a club. The dressed-up fashiony crowd who are to waistline conscious to eat anything delightful to the palate and comer here to dance after midnight.

Bourbon Street, R dos Chanés 127, Moema, T011-5095 6100, www.bournbonstreet. com.br. Great little club with acts like funkster Tutti Bae and international acts like BB King.

Columbia, R Estados Unidos 1570. Lively. **Hell's Club** downstairs. Opens 0400, techno, wild.

Disco, R Professor Atílio Inocennti 160, Itaím, T011-3078 0404, www.clubdisco.com.br. One of the city's plushest high-society discos and a favourite with leading socialites and models, especially during fashion week. The decor is by Isay Weinfeld who designed the Fasano, and the music standard Eurotrash and US club sounds.

Na Mata Café, R da Mata 70, Itaím, T011-3079 0300, www.namata.com.br. Popular flirting and pick-up spot for 20- and 30-something rich kids who gyrate in the dark dance room to a variety of Brazilian and European dance tunes and select live bands.

◉ Entertainment

São Paulo *p178, maps p182, p186 and p194*
For listings of concerts, theatre, museums, galleries and cinemas visit www.guiasp. com.br, or look in the *Guia da Folha* section of *Folha de São Paulo*, and the *Veja São Paulo* section of the weekly news magazine *Veja*.

Art galleries
Casa da Fazenda, Morumbi, exhibits in 19th-century house. **Espaço Cultural Ena Beçak**, R Oscar Freire 440. **Galeria São Paulo**, R Estados Unidos 1456.

Cinema
Entrance is usually half price on Wed; normal seat price is US$5 in the centre, US$5-6 in R Augusta, Av Paulista and Jardins. Most shopping centres have multiplexes showing the latest blockbuster releases. These are usually in their original language with Portuguese subtitles (*legendas*). Where they are not, they are marked 'DUB' (*dublado*).
  There are arts cinemas at the SESCs (notably at the **Cine Sesco**, R Augusta 2075, Jardins, T011-3087 0500, www.cinesescsp. org.br, and at **Pompeia** and **Vila Mariana**, www.sescsp.org.br); at the **Centro Cultural Banco do Brasil** (page 189).
  Other arts cinemas are at **Belas Artes** (R da Consolação 2423, T011-3258 4092, www.confrariadecinema.com.br); **Espaço Unibanco** (R Augusta 1470/1475, www.unibancocinemas.com.br); **Museu da Imagem e do Som** (Av Europa 258, T011-2117 4777, www.mis-sp.org.br); **Itaú Cultural**, www.itaucultural.org.br; and **Centro Cultural São Paulo**, www.centro cultural.sp.gov.br (see below).

The Brazilian Grand Prix

Motor racing has had a long and distinguished history in Brazil and the first race day at Interlagos took place on 12 May 1940. The first Brazilian Grand Prix was held here in 1972 and Emerson Fittipaldi drove to victory in front of a home crowd in 1973 and 1974. The following year another Brazilian, José Carlos Pace (after whom the track is officially named Autódromo José Carlos Pace), was first to cross the chequered flags.

During the 1980s the Grand Prix race was held at the Jacarepaguá racetrack in Rio where the outspoken Nelson Piquet won twice in 1983 and 1986 with some of the fastest lap times seen on this track.

The race returned to the improved Interlagos track during the 1990s, and the legendary Aryton Senna won here in 1991 and 1993. After his tragic death in 1994, as a result of mechanical failure, Brazilian viewing figures for motor racing fell drastically but picked up with the success of Rubens Barrichello and Felipe Massa in the new millennium.

The Brazilian Grand Prix is usually the last race of the season, held in October or November. The race consists of 72 laps with a total distance of 309.024 km. Approximately 55,000 people attend, in addition to millions watching around the world. The training session takes place on Friday morning; the time trial on Saturday morning and the race itself on Sunday afternoon with warm-ups and the drivers' parade in the morning.

Tickets can be bought from the racetrack during the whole week or by contacting ABN Amro Bank on T011-5507 2500 from abroad and T0800-170200 inside Brazil. Minimum ticket price is US$100 rising to US$350 depending on the viewing sector. Sectors A and G are uncovered and the cheapest, whilst sector D is covered, provides a better view and is more expensive. Tickets for the training sessions are cheaper and can be bought from 0700 on the day from the box office at the circuit. VIP hospitality is readily available but at a high price.

There is no parking for private vehicles at the racetrack, but park-and-ride facilities (US$5) are available on Saturday from Shopping SP Market, Avenida das Nações Unidas 22540, and on Sunday from Hipermercado, Avenida das Nações Unidas 4403 and Shopping Interlagos, Avenida Interlagos 2255. There are also buses (Saturday-Sunday) from Praça da República, between Rua do Arouche and Rua Marquês de Itu (No 295), from Praça Com Lineu Gomes at Congonhas airport and from Rua dos Jequitibás in front of the Jabaquara bus station (No 189). All buses have coloured stickers to indicate which drop-off point they serve. Further information about the Grand Prix in English can be obtained from www.gpbrasil.com, www.gpbrasil.com.br or www.formula1.com. Matueté (see page 222) can organize packages to the Grand Prix, with all transport, accommodation and pick-up from the airport.

Classical music, ballet and theatre

Centro Cultural São Paulo, R Vergueiro 1000, T011-3397 4002, www.centrocultural.sp. gov.br. A 50,000-sq-m arts centre with concert halls, where there are regular classical music and ballet recitals – with an orchestral performance most Sun afternoons and a concerto most lunchtimes (in the Sala Adoniran Barbosa), a library with work desks, theatres and exhibition spaces.

Sala São Paulo, see page 191. This magnificent neo-gothic hall with near perfect acoustics is the city's premier classical music venue and is home to Brazil's best orchestra, the Orquestra Sinfônica do Estado de São Paulo (www.osesp.art.br), which is under the helm of French conductor, Yan Pascal Tortelier, former Chief conductor at the BBC Philarmonic and Principal Guest Conductor at the Pittsburgh Symphony Orchestra. The OSESP has been cited as one of 3 up-and-coming ensembles in the ranks of the world's greatest orchestras by the English magazine *Gramophone*. They have a busy schedule of performances with details available on their website and concerts usually every Thu, Fri and Sat.

Teatro Municipal Opera House, see page 191, is used by visiting theatrical and operatic groups, as well as the City Ballet Company and the Municipal Symphony Orchestra, who give regular performances.

There are several other 1st-class theatres: **Aliança Francesa**, R Gen Jardim 182, Vila Buarque, T011-3259 0086; **Itália**, Av Ipiranga 344, T011-3257 9092; **Paiol**, R Amaral Gurgel 164, Santa Cecília, T011-3221 2462; free concerts at **Teatro Popular do Sesi**, Av Paulista 1313, T011-3284 9787, Mon-Sat 1200, under MASP.

⊛ Festivals and events

São Paulo *p178, maps p182, p186 and p194*
Throughout the year there are countless anniversaries, religious feasts, fairs and exhibitions. To see what's on, check the local press or the monthly tourist magazines. Fashion week is in the **Bienal Centre** (Bienal do Ibirapuera) in Ibirapuera Park, Parque do Ibirapuera, T011-5576 7600.
25 Jan Foundation of the city.
Feb Carnaval. *Escolas de samba* parade in the Anhembi Sambódromo. During Carnaval most museums and attractions are closed.
Jun Festas Juninas and the Festa de São Vito, the patron saint of the Italian immigrants.
Sep Festa da Primavera.
Oct Formula One Grand Prix at Interlagos.
Dec Christmas and New Year festivities.

⊙ Shopping

São Paulo *p178, maps p182, p186 and p194*
São Paulo isn't a good place to shop for souvenirs, but it remains Latin America's fashion and accessory capital and, with the possible exception of Melbourne and Sydney (whose industries are far smaller), it is the best location in the southern hemisphere for quality fashion and jewellery.

Books and music
Livrarias Saraiva and **Laselva** are found in various shopping malls and at airports, they sell books in English. **FNAC**, Av Paulista 901 (at Metrô Paraíso) and Praça Omaguás 34, Pinheiros (Metrô Pinheiros), www.fnac.com.br. With a huge choice of DVDs, CDs, books in Portuguese (and English), magazines and newspapers.

Fashion boutiques
São Paulo is one of the newest hot spots on the global fashion circuit and is by far the most influential and diverse fashion city in South America. The designers based here have collections as chic as any in Europe or North America, but at a fraction of the price. Best buys include smart casual day wear, bikinis, shoes, jeans and leather jackets. Havaiana flip flops, made famous by Gisele Bundchen and Fernanda Tavares, are around 10% of the price of Europe. The best areas for fashion shopping are **Jardins** (around R Oscar Freire) and the **Iguatemi shopping centre** (Av Faria Lima). The city's most exclusive shopping emporium is **Daslu**, see page 221.
Adriana Degreas, R Dr Melo Alves 734, Jardins, T011-3064 4300, www.adriana degreas.com.br. Adriana opened her flagship store in Jardins with a zesty collection premiered at Claro Rio Summer fashion show. She now sells at Barneys and Bloomingdales in New York and in Selfridges in London.
Adriana Barra, Alameda Franca 1243, T011-2925 2300, www.adrianabarra.com.br. Showroom in a converted residential house whose façade is entirely covered with vines,

bromeliads and ferns. Adriana was already well known for her long dresses and bell-sleeved tunics, made of silk and jersey and printed with designs which take classic belle époque French floral and abstract motifs and reinterpret them in 1970s tropicalia-laced colors and patterns. She now sells homeware – from sofas and scatter cushions to bedspreads, amphorae and notebooks.

Alexandre Herchcovitz, R Haddock Lobo 1151, T011-3063 2889. The most famous Brazilian designer, using brightly coloured materials to create avant garde designs strongly influenced by European trends.

Carina Duek, R Oscar Freire 736, T011-2359 5972, www.carinaduek.com.br. Another rising young star opened this boutique in Oct 2009, designed by Fasano architect Isay Weinfeld. Her simple, figure-hugging light summer dresses and miniskirts – are favourites with 20-something Paulistana socialites.

Fause Haten, Alameda Lorena 1731, Jardins, T011-3081 8685. One of Brazil's most internationally renowned designers who works in plastic, lace, leather, mohair and denim with laminate appliqués, selling through, amongst others, **Giorgio Beverly Hills**.

Forum, R Oscar Freire 916, Jardins T011-3085 6269, www.forum.com.br. A huge white space attended by beautiful shop assistants helping impossibly thin 20-something Brazilians squeeze into tight, but beautifully cut, jeans and other fashion items.

Hotel Lycra, R Oscar Freire 1055, Jardins, T011-3897 4401, www.hotellycra.com. A favourite shopping spot for the Jardins teenybopper set who park their expensive open-top 18th birthday presents outside and pop in to browse the collection from a rotating selection of young, new Brazilian designers.

Iodice, R Oscar Freire 940, T011-3085 9310, and **Shopping Iguatemi**, T011-3813 2622, www.iodice.com.br. Sophisticated and innovative knitwear designs sold abroad in boutiques like **Barney's NYC**.

Lenny, **Shopping Iguatemi**, T011-3032 2663, and R Escobar Ortiz 480, Vila Nova Conceicao, T011-3846 6594, www.lenny.com.br. Rio de Janeiro's premier swimwear designer and Brazil's current favourite.

Mario Queiroz, R Alameda Franca 1166, T011-3062 3982, www.marioqueiroz.com.br. Casual and elegant clothes with a strong gay element, for 20-something men.

Ricardo Almeida, Daslu and **Shopping Iguatemi**, T011-3812 6947. One of the few Brazilian designers who styles for men. His clothes are a range of dark suits and slick leather jackets aimed at would-be bit-part actors from *The Matrix*.

Ronaldo Fraga, R Aspicuelta 259, Vila Madalena, T011-3816 2181, www.ronaldo fraga.com. Fraga's adventurous collection combines discipline with daring, retaining a unified style across the sexes yet always surprising and delighting with its off-the-wall creativity.

Rosa Chá, Shopping Higienópolis, Av Higienópolis 418, Metrô Marechal Deodoro, T011-3823 2630, www.rosacha.com.br. One of the world's most sought-after fashion labels for designer swimwear. Beautifully cut bikinis in top-quality materials. Shops in Brazil have cuts exclusive to the country and unavailable in the New York outlet and in London department stores.

UMA, R Girassol 273, T011-3813 5559, www.uma.com.br. Raquel Davidowicz offers rails of sleek contemporary cuts set against low-lit, cool white walls with a Japanese-inspired monochrome minimalism mixed with colourful Brazilian vibrancy.

Victor Hugo, R Oscar Freire 816, T011-3082 1303, www.victorhugo.com.br. Brazil's most fashionable handbag designer.

Walter Rodrigues, R Natingui 690/696, Vila Madalena, T011-3031 8562. Haute couture for women, renowned for evening gowns that are fluid, sensual and very much inspired by the belle époque.

Zoomp, R Oscar Freire 995, T011-3064 1556, **Shopping Iguatemi**, T011-3032 5372, www.zoomp.com.br. Zoomp have been famous for their figure-hugging jeans for nearly 3 decades and have grown to become a nationwide and now international brand.

Bargain fashion If the upper crust shop and sip coffee in Jardins, the rest of the city buys its wares in the contiguous area of **Bom Retiro**. At first sight the neighbourhood is relentlessly urban: ugly concrete with rows of makeshift houses converted into hundreds of shops selling a bewildering array of clothing. Much of it is trash, and during the week wholesale stores may specify a minimum number of items per buyer. But a few hours browsing will yield clothing bargains to rival those in Bangkok. Many of the outfitters manufacture for the best mid-range labels in São Paulo, including those in **Shopping Ibirapuera** (see below). The best shopping is on and around **R José Paulino** – a street with more than 350 shops. The best day to come is Sat from 0800, when most items are sold individually.

Shopping **25 de Março**, R 25 de Março, www.25demarco.com.br, Metrô São Bento, in the city centre offers a similarly large range of costume jewellery, toys and small decorative items (best on Sat 0800-1430) and the neighbourhood of **Brás** stocks cheaper but lower quality items. For more information see www.omelhordobomretiro.com.br.

Handicrafts
São Paulo has no handicrafts tradition but some items from the rest of Brazil can be bought at **Parque Tte Siqueira Campos/Trianon** on Sun 0900-1700.
Casa dos Amazonas, Av Jurupis 460.
Galeria Arte Brasileira, Av Lorena 2163, T011-3062 9452, www.galeriaartebrasileira. com.br. Stock folk art from the northeast, including the famous clay figurines from Caruaru, Ceará lace, Amazonian hammocks, carved wooden items from all over the country and indigenous Brazilian bead and whicker art.
Sutaco, R Boa Vista 170, Edifício Cidade I, 3rd floor, Centro, T011-3241 7333, www.sutaco. com.br. Handicrafts shop selling and promoting items from the state of São Paulo.

Jewellery
Brazil is one of the world's foremost gemstone producing countries and the largest producer of emeralds. Jewellery is a good buy; though prices are high compared to the rest of Latin America, the stones, setting and craftsmanship of high-end jewellery is on a par with Europe.
H Stern, www.hstern.com.br, with shops all over the city, including R Augusta 2340, R Oscar Freire 652, at Iguatemi, Ibirapuera, Morumbi, Paulista and other shopping centres, at large hotels and at the international airport. Brazil's biggest jewellers, represented in 18 countries. In Brazil they have designs based on Brazilian themes – including Amazonian bead art and Orixa mythology.
Vartanian, NK, R Haddock Lobo 1592, Jardins, T011-3062 2349, www.jackvartanian.com. Jack Vartanian creates fashion jewellery with huge Brazilian emeralds and diamonds set in simple gold and platinum – much beloved of Hollywood red-carpet walkers including Zoe Saldana, Cameron Diaz and Demi Moore. His low-lit Jardins shop showcases jewellery only available only in Brazil.
Antonio Bernardo, R Bela Cintra 2063, Jardins, T011-3083 5622, www.antonio bernardo.com.br. Bernardo is as understated as Vartanian is bling, and offers elegant, contemporary gold and platinum designs and exquisite stones. The designer has branches all over the city and in locations throughout Brazil – full details on website.

Markets
Ceasa flower market, Av Doutor Gastão Vidigal 1946, Jaguaré. Tue and Fri 0700-1200. Should not be missed.
MASP antiques market, takes place below the museum. Sun 1000-1700. Some 50 stalls selling everything from vintage gramophones to ceramics, ornaments and old vinyl.
Mercado Municipal, R da Cantareira 306, Centro, T011-3326 3401, www.mercado

municipal.com.br, Metrô São Bento. This newly rennovated art deco market was built at the height of the coffee boom and is illuminated by beautiful stained-glass panels by Conrado Sorgenicht Filho showing workers tilling the soil. It's worth coming here just to browse aisles bursting with produce – *açaí* from the Amazon, hunks of *bacalhau* from the North Sea, mozzarella from Minas, sides of beef from the Pantanal and 1000 other foodstuffs. The upper gallery has half a dozen restaurants offering dishes of the day and a vantage point over the frenetic buying and selling below.

Oriental Fair, Praça de Liberdade. Sun 1000-1900. Good for Japanese snacks, plants and some handicrafts, very picturesque, with remedies on sale, tightrope walking, gypsy fortune tellers, etc.

Praça Benedito Calixto, Pinheiros, the best bric-a-brac market in São Paulo takes place here, www.pracabeneditocalixto.com.br. Sat 0900-1900. Live *choro* and samba 1430-1830, Metrô Pinheiros. Stalls in the square and in the surrounding streets sell arts, crafts, CDs, T-shirts and second-hand goods. There is live *choro* and *samba* music and good food and there are many stylish arts and crafts and fashion shops, restaurants and cafés around the square.

Av Lorena, which is one of the upmarket shopping streets off R Augusta in Jardins, has an open-air market on Sun selling fruits and juices. There is a flea market on Sun in Praça Don Orione (main square of the Bixiga district).

Shopping malls and department stores For more information on shopping malls, see www.shoppingsdesaopaulo.com.br. **Daslu**, Av Chedid Jafat 131, T011-3841 3000, www.daslu.com.br. This temple to snobbery is worth visiting if only for anthropological reasons. It is the fashion store of choice for South America's high society and it's not uncommon for customers to fly in from

Argentina or Mato Grosso on private planes and spend up to US$50,000 in a single shopping spree. Collections include that of **Daslu** itself, alongside up-and-coming Brazilian names like **Juliana Jabour**, **Cris Barros**, www.crisbarros.com.br, and **Raia de Goeye**, www.raiadegoeye.com.br, and big-name international designers. These sit alongside boutiques selling everything from high-class wines to beautiful coffee-table books. **Shopping Cidade Jardim**, Av Magalhães de Castro 12000, T011-3552 1000, www.cidade jardimshopping.com.br, CPTM Hebraica-Rebouças (and then 5-10 mins by taxi). The city's newest upmarket mall is a vast, neoclassical edifice with a lush tropical garden in its interior and towering skyscraper apartment blocks above. It is filled with Brazilian names like **Carlos Miele** and **Osklen**, whose casual beach and adventure clothes look like Ralph Lauren gone tropical and are aimed at a similar yacht-and-boardwalk crowd. International names include **Hermes** and there is a branch of **Daslu**, which, unlike their store across the river, has changing rooms. There's a spa at the mall, too, as well as a branch of the informal Italian bistro **Nono Ruggero** and an outpost of the popular upmarket Brazilian-Japanese chain **Kosushi**. The shopping mall has a cinema.
Shopping D, Av Cruzeiro do Sul 1100, Canindé, T011-3311 9333. Some 320 shops with many clothes in the middle to low price ranges. On the edge of the city near the river And immediately opposite the Terminal Tietê *rodoviária*. With a cinema.
Shopping Ibirapuera, Av Ibirapuera 3103, www.ibirapuera.com.br, Metrô Ana Rosa and bus 695V (Terminal Capelinha). A broad selection of mid-range Brazilian labels and general shops including toy and book shops.
Shopping Iguatemi, Av Brigadeiro Faria Lima 2232, www.iguatemisaopaulo.com.br. Another top-end shopping mall just south of Jardins with a healthy representation of most of Brazil's foremost labels.

▲ Activities and tours

São Paulo *p178, maps p182, p186 and p194*
Football
The most popular local teams are Corinthians, Palmeiras and São Paulo who generally play in the Morumbi and Pacaembu stadiums.

Tour operators
São Paulo has several large agencies offering tours around the country.
Ambiental Viagens e Expedições, www.ambiental.tur.br. Good for trips to less well known places throughout the country like Jalapão. English and Spanish spoken, helpful.
Matueté, R Tapinás 22, Itaim, T011-3071 4515, www.matuete.com. Luxury breaks throughout Brazil and city tours, including personal shopping. Ask for Camilla. English spoken.
Trip on Jeep, R Arizona 623, Brooklin, T011-5543 5281, www.triponjeep.com. Wonderful day or weekend trips away from the heat and the dust of São Paulo city to the lush, green bird and wildlife filled forests nearby, to the caves in PETAR and destinations throughout the state of São Paulo. The company run tours in comfortable Land Rovers and these are conducted by English-speaking zoologists and botanists. The Parelheiros trip includes organic lunch at the Centro Paulus – a delightful haven in secondary forest. Highly recommended.
Tropico Turismo, T011-4025 9281, www.tropico.tur.br. Adventure day trips around São Paulo including rappelling, zip-lines and canopy walking, whitewater rafting and hikes. English spoken. Well organized.

☉ Transport

São Paulo *p178, maps p182, p186 and p194*
Air
See also Ins and outs, page 178.
Guarulhos international airport (Cumbica) operates services to all parts of the world and much of Brazil. The cheapest internal flights are with TAM, www.tam.com.br, GOL, www.voegol.com.br, Azul, www.voeazul.com.br (who fly from Campinas, page 179), and Avianca, www.avianca.com.br. To get to the airport, Emtu buses run every 30 mins from Praça da República 343 (northwest side, corner of R Arouche), 0530-2300, and from Rodoviária Tietê, US$6.50, 30-45 mins. Buses also run from Bresser bus station and there are buses from Jabaquara bus terminal, without luggage space, usually crowded. Taxi fares from the city to the airport are US$60-80. Rush-hour traffic can easily turn this 30-min journey into an hour or even longer. Be sure to arrive with plenty of time for checking in as long queues form for immigration and customs: passenger numbers have doubled at Cumbica over the past decade and the airport is becoming increasingly crowded.

Congonhas domestic airport is used for flights within Brazil, including the shuttle flight with **Rio de Janeiro** (Santos Dumont airport, US$100-150 single, depending on availability). The shuttle services operate every 30 mins throughout the day from 0630-2230. Sit on the left-hand side for views to Rio de Janeiro, the other side coming back, book flights in advance. To get to Congonhas airport, take an **Emtu** bus the centre or a taxi, US$20.

Bus
There are 4 bus terminals: Tietê, Barra Funda, Bresser and Jabaquara. All are connected to the metrô system. To search for bus routes and times, see www.passagem-em-domicilio.com.br/terminal-tiete.asp. The site gives times and routes and redirects to the

O Bilhete Único

This electronic ticket is similar to a London Oyster card – integrating bus, metro and light railway in a single, rechargeable plastic swipe card. US$2 serves for one metro or CPTM journey and three bus journeys within the space of three hours. Swipe cards can be bought at metro stations. The initial minimum charge is US$10.

bus company website for the service, through which it is possible to buy tickets. **Rodoviária Tietê** This is the main bus station and has a convenient metrô station. Unfortunately the only way to the platforms is by stairs which makes it very difficult for people with heavy luggage and almost impossible for those in a wheelchair. Tietê handles buses to the interior of São Paulo state, to all state capitals and international destinations. To **Rio**, 6 hrs, every 30 mins, US$12.50 (*leito* US$35), special section for this route in the *rodoviária*, request the coastal route via Santos (*via litoral*) unless you wish to go the direct route. To **Florianópolis**, 11 hrs, US$120 (*leito* US$150). To **Porto Alegre**, 18 hrs, US$160 (*leito* US$190). To **Curitiba**, 5 hrs, US$80. To **Salvador**, 30 hrs, US$130 (*leito* US$170). To **Recife**, 40 hrs, US$160-180. To **Campo Grande**, 14 hrs, US$80. To **Cuiabá**, 24 hrs, US$110. To **Porto Velho**, 60 hrs (or more), US$160. To **Brasília**, 16 hrs, US$100 (*leito* US$120). To **Foz do Iguaçu**, 16 hrs, US$90. To **São Sebastião**, 4 hrs, US$30 ask for 'via Bertioga' if you want to go by the coast road, a beautiful journey but few buses take this route as it is longer). **International connections** Buses to Uruguay include: **Montevideo**, via Porto Alegre, cold a/c at night, plenty of meal stops, bus stops for border formalities, passengers disembark only to collect passport and tourist card on the Uruguayan side. Buses to Paraguay include: **Asunción** (1044 km), 18 hrs with Pluma, US$180 (*leito* US$200), Brújula (US$170) or RYSA (US$200), all stop at **Ciudad del Este** US$100, US$130 and US$150 respectively, (*uma leito* US$180). Cometa del Amambay runs to **Pedro Juan Caballero** and

Concepción. To **Buenos Aires** (Argentina), Pluma, 36 hrs, US$240. To **Santiago** (Chile), (Pluma or Chilebus, 56 hrs, US$240 (Chilebus, poor meals, but otherwise good, beware of overbooking).

Barra Funda (Metrô Barra Funda), to cities in southern **São Paulo state** and many destinations in Paraná, including **Foz do Iguaçu** (check for special prices on buses to **Ciudad del Este**, which can be cheaper than buses to Foz). Buses run to **Cananéia** daily at 0900 and 1430, 4 hrs. Alternatively go via **Registro** (buses hourly), from where there are 7 buses daily to Cananéia and regular connections to **Curitiba**.

Bresser (Metrô Bresser), for Cometa (T011-6967 7255) or Transul (T011-6693 8061) serving destinations in Minas Gerais. **Belo Horizonte**, 10 hrs, US$80, 11 a day (*leito* US$100), 9 a day with Gontijo. Translavras and Util also operate out of this station. Prices are given under destinations. See www.passagem-em-domicilio.com.br for more information including bus times and the latest prices.

Jabaquara (at the southern end of the metrô line), is used by buses to **Santos**, US$5, every 15 mins, taking about 50 mins, last bus at 0100. Also serves destinations on the southern coast of São Paulo state.

Car hire
The major names all serve São Paulo and have offices at the airports.

CPTM (urban light railway)
→ *See map, p180*
Ticket prices on the CPTM are the same as the metrô (see below and box, above).

Linha 7 Rubi (ruby) runs from Jundiaí, a satellite commuter town, to the Estação da Luz via Barra Funda and the Palmeiras football stadium.

Linha 8 Diamante (diamond) runs from Amador Bueno to the Estação Júlio Prestes railway station in Luz, near the Pinacoteca and next to the Estação da Luz.

Linha 9 Esmeralda (emerald) runs between the suburb of Osasco and the suburb of Grajaú in the far south. This is the most useful line for tourists as it runs along the Pinheiros river, stopping at the Cidade Universitária (for Butantã), Hebraica-Rebouças (for shopping Eldorado and the Azul bus to Campinas airport, see page 179), Cidade Jardim (for Shopping Cidade Jardim and Daslu malls, see page 221), Vila Olímpia (close to one of the nightlife centres) and Berrini (in the new business district). The line connects with the metrô at the new Pinheiros metrô station on the Linha Amarela.

Linha 10 Turquesa (turquoise) runs from Rio Grande da Serra in the Serra do Mar mountains (from where there are onward trains to Paranapiacaba, see page 203) to the Estação da Luz.

Linha 11 Coral (coral) runs from the Estudantes suburb to the Estação da Luz.

Linha 12 Safira (sapphire) runs from Calmon Viana suburb to Brás.

Metrô → *See map, p180*
Directions are indicated by the name of the terminus station. Network maps are displayed only in the upper concourses of the metrô stations; there are none on the platforms. Many of the maps on the internet are confusing as they incorporate the CPTM overground train routes, also with colour codes. Journeys can get extremely crowded at peak times (0700-1000, 1630-1900). Services are also plagued by unannounced and unexplained stops and cancellations. Fares are at a flat rate of US$1.50, or R$20 for a book of 10 tickets. A combined bus and metrô ticket costs R$2.20; useful for getting to Congonhas airport; see also box, page 223.

Linha 1 Azul (blue), runs from Tucuruvi in the north to the Rodoviária Jabaraquara in the south and passing through Luz, the centre and Liberdade.

Linha 2 Verde (green) runs from Vila Madalena to Vila Prudente, via Av Paulista and the MASP art gallery.

Linha 3 Vermelha (red) runs from the Palmeiras football stadium in Barra Funda to the Corinthians football stadium in Itaquera, via the city centre.

Linha 4 Amarela (yellow) running between between Morumbi football stadium (which will be used for the World Cup) and Luz, via USP University at Butantã, Oscar Freire in Jardins and Av Paulista; due to open in 2011.

Linha 5 Lilás (lilac) running in São Paulo's far southwest, between Capão Redondo favela and Adolfo Pinheiro, with an extension to Chacara Klabin on the 2 Verde line with stations opening between 2011 and 2014.

Taxi
Taxis display cards of actual tariffs in the window (starting price US$4). There are ordinary taxis, which are hailed on the street, or at taxi stations such as Praça da República, radio taxis and deluxe taxis. For Radio Taxis, which are more expensive but involve fewer hassles, **Central Radio Táxi**, T011-6914 6630; **São Paulo Rádio Táxi**, T011-5583 2000; **Fácil**, T011-6258 5947; **Aero Táxi**, T011-6461 4090; or look in the phone book; calls are not accepted from public phones.

Trains
From **Estação da Luz** and **Estação Júlio Prestes** (Metrô Luz).

ⓘ Directory

São Paulo *p178, maps p182, p186 and p19*
Banks Banking hours are generally 1000-1600, although times differ for foreign exchange. For ATMS, the best bank to use is Bradesco, www.bradesco.com.br or HSBC, www.hsbc.com.br, which have branches on

every other street corner and ATMs in the airport and all the major shopping malls. Be wary when using ATMs and never use street machines after dark. Most ATMs do not function between 2200 and 0600. **Banco do Brasil** will change cash and TCs and will advance cash against Visa. All transactions are done in the foreign exchange department of any main branch (eg Av São João 32, Centro), but queues are long and commission very high. **Embassies and consulates** Argentina, Av Paulista 2313, T011-3897 9522 (0900-1300), argentina.visahq.com, very easy to get a visa here. **Australia**, 9th floor, Unit 92 Edifício Trianon Corporate, Alamenda Santos 700, Jardins, T011-2112 6200, www.brazil.embassy.gov.au. **Bolivia**, Av Paulista 1439, T011-3289 0443, www.cgb.org.br. **Canada**, Av das Nações Unidas 12901, 16 andar, T011-5509 4343, www.canadainternational.gc.ca. **France**, Av Paulista 1842, 14th floor, T011-3371 5400, saopaulo.ambafrance-br.org. **Germany**, Av Brigadeiro Faria Lima 2092, T011-3097 6644, www.brasil.diplo.de. **Ireland**, Honorary Consul, Al Joaquim Eugenio de Lima 447, T011 3147 7788, www.dfa.ie. **Israel**, Av Brig Faria Lima 1713, T011-3031 6594. **New Zealand**, Av Campinas 579, T011-3148 0489. **Paraguay**, R Bandeira Paulista 600, 5th floor, T011-3167 6397, www.paraguay.com.br. **Peru**, R Guadelupe 28, T011-3063 1152, www.consuladopersp.com.br. **South Africa**, Av Paulista 1754, T011-3253 8806. **UK**, R Ferreira de Araujo 74, 2 Andar Pinheiros, T011-3094 2700, ukinbrazil.fco.gov.uk **Uruguay**, R Estados Unidos 1284, T011-2879 900, www.emburuguai.org.br). **US**, R Henri Dunant 500, Chácara Santo Antônio, T011-186 7000, www.embaixada-americana.g.br **Venezuela**, R General Fonseca Teles,

564, T011-3887 2535. **Immigration** Federal Police, R. Hugo D'Antola 95, Lapa de Baixo, T011-3538 5000, www.dpf.gov.br. For visa extensions. Allow all day and expect little English (1000-1600). **Internet** Too ubiquitous to list – look for any LAN house sign. **Language courses** The official Universidade de São Paulo (USP) is situated in the Cidade Universitária (buses from main bus station), beyond Pinheiros. They have courses available to foreigners, including a popular Portuguese course. Registry is through the Comissão de Cooperação Internacional, R do Anfiteatro 181, Bloco das Colméias 05508, Cidade Universitária, São Paulo. Other universities include the Pontifical Catholic University (PUC), and the Mackenzie University. Both these are more central than the USP, Mackenzie in Higienopolis, just west of the centre, and PUC in Perdizes. Take a taxi to either. Both have noticeboards where you can leave a request for Portuguese teachers or language exchange, which is easy to arrange for free. Any of the *gringo* pubs are good places to organize similar exchanges. **Laundry** Chuá Self Service, R Augusta 728, limited self-service, not cheap. **Di-Lelles**, R Atenas 409, pricey. **Medical services** Hospital das Clínicas, Av Dr Enéias de Carvalho Aguiar 255, Jardins, T011-3069 6000. **Hospital Samaritano**, R Cons Brotero 1468, Higenópolis, T011-3824 0022. Recommended. Both have *pronto-socorro* (emergency services). Contact your consulate for names of doctors and dentists who speak your language. **Emergency and ambulance**: T192. **Fire**: T193. **Post office** Correio Central, Correios – yellow and blue signs – eg Praça do Correio, corner of Av São João and Prestes Máia, T011-3831 5222.

The coast of São Paulo

São Paulo's coast is packed at the weekend (when the city dwellers leaves for the beach) and deserted during the week. There are many beautiful beaches to choose from: some backed by rainforest-covered mountains and all washed by a bottle-green warm Atlantic. The best are along the northernmost part of the state coast, the Litoral Norte, around Ubatuba, and along the Litoral Sul near Cananéia. There are beautiful islands too including Brazil's largest, Ilhabela, and her wildest, Ilha do Cardoso. The dividing point between the Litoral Norte and Litoral Sul is the historic city of Santos; made most famous by Pelé (there's a museum devoted to him), and dotted with a few interesting buildings and museums in a spruced-up, attractive colonial city centre. ▶▶ For listings, see pages 237-244.

Santos and São Vicente → For listings, see pages 237-244. Colour map 5, A6. Phone code: 013.
Population: 418,000.

The Portuguese knew how to choose a location for a new settlement. **Santos** stands on an island in a bay surrounded by towering mountains and extensive areas of lowland mangrove forest – a setting equally as beautiful as that of Salvador or Rio. When it was dominated by colonial houses, churches and clean white-sand beaches Santos itself must have been one of Brazil's most enchanting cities. But in the 20th century an evil reputation for yellow fever and industrial pollution from nearby Cubatão left the city to decay and lost much of its architecture along with its charm. Contemporary Santos, however, is getting its act together. The old colonial centre has been tidied up and Scottish trams ferry tourists past the city's sights. These include a series of colonial churches and the Bolsa do Café – a superb little museum whose café-restaurant serves the most delicious espresso in Brazil. Santos is also Pelé's home and the city he played for almost all his career. Santos FC has a museum devoted to the club and to Pelé and it is easy to attend a game.

On the mainland, **São Vicente** is, to all intents and purposes, a suburb of Santos having been absorbed into the conurbation. It was the first town founded in Brazil, in 1532, but nowadays it is scruffy and with very few sights of interest but for the rather dilapidated colonial church, the Matriz São Vicente Mártir (1542, rebuilt in 1757) in the Praça do Mercado. The Litoral Sul (see page 234) begins after São Vicente.

Ins and outs
Getting there Santos is served by regular buses from São Paulo as well as towns along the Litoral Norte and Litoral Sul, such as Curitibia, Rio de Janeiro and Florianópolis. Buses arrive at the **rodoviária** ⓘ *Praça dos Andradas 45, T013-3219 2194*, close to the colonial centre. Those from São Paulo also stop at Ponta da Praia and José Menino, which are nearer to the main hotel district in Gonzaga. A taxi to Gonzaga from the bus station costs about US$7; all taxis have meters.

Getting around The best way to get around the centre of Santos is by the newly restored Victorian trams, which leave on guided tours (Tue-Sun 1100-1700) from in front of the Prefeitura Municipal on Praça Visconde de Maúa. The tram passes most of the interesting sights, including the *azulejo*-covered houses on Rua do Comércio, the Bolsa do Café and some of the oldest churches. Local buses run from the colonial centre and *rodoviária* to the seafront – look for Gonzaga or Praia on their destination plaque. Bus fares within Santos are US$0.60; to São Vicente US$0.90.

Orientation The centre of the city is on the north side of the island. Due south, on the Baía de Santos, is **Gonzaga**, São Paulo's favourite beach resort where much of the city's entertainment takes place. Between these two areas, the eastern end of the island curves round within the Santos Channel. At the eastern tip, a ferry crosses the estuary to give access to the busy beaches of Guarujá and Praia Grande. The city has impressive modern buildings, wide, tree-lined avenues, and wealthy suburbs.

Santos

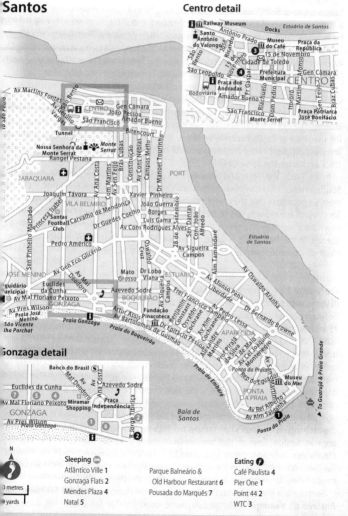

Centro detail

Gonzaga detail

Sleeping		Eating
Atlântico Ville **1**	Parque Balneário &	Café Paulista **4**
Gonzaga Flats **2**	Old Harbour Restaurant **6**	Pier One **1**
Mendes Plaza **4**	Pousada do Marquês **7**	Point 44 **2**
Natal **5**		WTC **3**

Tourist information There are **SETUR** offices at the *rodoviária*, at Praía do Gonzaga on the seafront (in a disused tram – very helpful, lots of leaflets), and next to the British railway station – Estação do Valongo, Largo Marquês de Monte Alegre s/n, T013-3201 8000 www.santos.sp.gov.br, Monday-Friday 1000-1600, Saturday 1000-1400. Although poverty is apparent, the city is generally safe. However, it is wise to exercise caution at night and near the port.

Background

Santos is one of Brazil's oldest cities and has long been its most important port. The coast around the city is broken by sambaqui shell mounds that show the area has been inhabited by humans since at least 5000 BC (see page 762). When the Portuguese arrived, the Tupinikin people dominated the region. However, the first settlements at neighbouring São Vicente (1532) were constantly under attack by the Tamoio who were allies of the French. The French were defeated at Rio in 1560 and the Tamoio massacred soon after.

By the 1580s Santos was a burgeoning port with some 400 houses. The first export was sugar, grown as cane at the foot of the mountains and on the plateau. By the late 19th century this had been replaced by coffee, which rapidly became Brazil's main source of income. The city was connected to São Paulo and the coffee region by the British under the guidance of Barão Visconde de Mauá, and the city grew wealthy. The seafront was lined with opulent coffee mansions and the centre was home to Brazil's most important stock exchange, the Bolsa do Café.

In the 1980s, the hinterland between the sea and mountains became the site of one of South America's most unpleasant industrial zones. The petrochemical plants of Cubatão were so notorious that they were referred to in the press as the 'The Valley of Death'. Santos and around was said to be the most contaminated corner of the planet, with so much toxic waste undermining the hills that the whole lot threatened to slip down into the sea. In the late 1980s, a spate of mutant births in Cubatão eventually prompted a clean-up operation, which is said to have been largely successful.

Sights

The heart of the colonial centre is **Praça Mauá**. The surrounding streets are very lively in the daytime, with plenty of cheap shops and restaurants. The most interesting buildings are to be found here and all can be visited by tram. The most impressive is the **Museu do Café** ① 15 de Novembro 95, T013-3219 5585, www.museudocafe.com.br, Tue-Sat 0900-1700, Su 1000-1700, US$2, housed in the old Bolsa Oficial de Café. Its plain exterior hides a grand marble-floored art deco stock exchange and museum, with a café serving some of the best coffee and cakes in South America. The building was once open only to wealthy (and exclusively male) coffee barons who haggled beneath a magnificent stained-glass skylight depicting a bare-breasted Brazil – the *Mãe Douro* – crowned with a star in a tropical landscape populated with tropical animals and perplexed indigenous Brazilians. The skylight and the beautiful neo-Renaissance painting of Santos that decorates the walls of the exchange is by Brazil's most respected 19th-century artist, Benedito Calixto, who was born in Santos. One of the few remaining coffee baron mansions, the **Fundação Pinacoteca** ① Av Bartolomeu de Gusmão 15, T013-3288 2260, www.pinacoteca.unisanta. Tue-Sun 1400-1900, free, on the seafront, is now a gallery housing some of his paintings, most of them landscapes, which give some idea of the city's original beauty.

Santos has a few interesting and ancient colonial churches. Only the **Santuário San Antônio do Valongo** ① Marquez de Monte Alegre s/n, Tue-Sun 0800-1700, guided to *most days after 1000, in Portuguese only*, is regularly open to the public. Its twee mock-baroque interior is from the 1930s, but the far more impressive original 17th-century altarpiece sits in the Franciscan chapel to the left of the main entrance. The statue of Christ is particularly fine. Next door to the church is the British-built terminus of the now defunct Santos–São Paulo railway, which serves as a small museum. The tourist office sits above it.

On Avenida Ana Costa there is an interesting monument to commemorate the brothers Andradas, who took a leading part in the movement for Independence. There are other monuments on Praça Rui Barbosa to Bartolomeu de Gusmão, who has a claim to the world's first historically recorded airborne ascent in 1709; in the Praça da República to Brás Cubas, who founded the city in 1534; and in the Praça José Bonifácio to the soldiers of Santos who died in the Revolution of 1932.

Brazil's iconic football hero, Pelé, played for Santos for almost all his professional life, signing when he was in his teens. **Santos Football Club** ① *R Princesa Isabel 77, Vila Belmiro, T013-3257 4000, http://santos.globo.com, Mon 1300-1900, Tue-Sun 0900-1900, US$3, for tours of the grounds call T013-3225 7989,* has an excellent museum, the Memorial das Conquistas, which showcases not only Pelé (with his kit, boots and other assorted personal items on display), but the history of the club. Its collection of gold and silver includes several international championship trophies. Pelé still lives in the city and can sometimes be seen at matches. It is possible to see Santos play; details available on their website.

Monte Serrat, just south of the city centre, has at its summit a semaphore station and look-out post which reports the arrival of all ships in Santos harbour. There is also an old church, **Nossa Senhora da Monte Serrat**, where the patron, Our Lady of Montserrat, is said to have performed many miracles.

The top can be reached on foot or by **funicular**, which leaves every 30 minutes (US$6). Seven shrines have been built on the way up and annual pilgrimages are made by the local people. There are fine views.

In the western district of José Menino is the **Orquidário Municipal** ① *Praça Washington, orchid garden Tue-Sun 0900-1700, bird enclosure 0800-1100, 1400-1700, US$0.50.* The flowers bloom from October to February and there is an orchid show in November. Visitors can wander among giant subtropical and tropical trees, amazing orchids and, when the aviary is open, meet macaws, toucans and parrots. The open-air cage contains hummingbirds of 10 different species and the park is a sanctuary for other birds.

Beaches

Santos has 8 km of beaches stretching round the Baía de Santos to those of São Vicente at the western end. From east to west they are **Ponta da Praia**, below the sea wall and on the estuary, no good for bathing, but fine for watching the movements of the ships. Next are **Aparecida, Embaré, Boqueirão, Gonzaga** and **José Menino** (the original seaside resort for the merchants of Santos). São Vicente's beaches of **Itararé** and **Ilha Porchat** are on the island, while **Gonzaguinha** is on the mainland. The last beach is **Itaquitanduva**, which is in a military area but may be visited with authorization. In all cases, check the cleanliness of the water before venturing in (a red flag means it is too polluted for bathing).

Excursions from Santos

The small island of **Ilha Porchat** is reached by a bridge at the far end of Santos/São Vicente bay. It has beautiful views over rocky precipices, of the high seas on one side and of the city and bay on the other. At the summit is **Terraço Chopp** ① *Av Ary Barroso 274*, a restaurant with live music most evenings and great views. On summer evenings the queues can be up to four hours, but in winter, even if it may be a little chilly at night, you won't have to wait.

Litoral Norte → *For listings, see pages 237-244.*

The resorts immediately north of Santos – Guarujá, Praia Grande and Bertioga – are built-up and none too clean. It becomes more beautiful at Camburi, the southernmost beach of São Sebastião province, named after the historical town that sits in front of Ilhabela, an island fringed with glorious beaches. Further north, Ubatuba, borders the state of Rio de Janeiro and has dozens of beautiful stretches of golden sand backed by forest-covered mountains.

Camburi, Camburizinho and Maresias → *Phone code: 012.*

Beyond Boracéia are a number of beaches, including Barra do Una, Praia da Baleia and **Camburi**. The latter is the first beach in São Sebastião province and is surrounded by the *Mata Atlântica* forest. It has a long stretch of sand with some surf, many *pousadas* and two of the best restaurants in São Paulo state. The best place for swimming is at **Camburizinho** (though you should avoid swimming in the river which is not clean). You can walk on the Estrada do Piavu into the *Mata Atlântica* to see vegetation and wildlife, bathing in the streams is permitted, but use of shampoo and other chemicals is forbidden. About 5 km from Camburi is **Praia Brava**, 45 minutes' walk through the forest. The surf here is very heavy, hence the name. Camping is possible.

The road continues from Camburi, past beaches such as **Boiçucanga** (family orientated with many *pousadas*) to **Maresias**, which is beloved of well-to-do Paulistas who come here mostly to surf. It has some chic *pousadas* and restaurants and tends to be younger and less family orientated than Camburi.

São Sebastião → *Colour map 5, A6. Phone code: 012. Population: 59,000.*

From Maresias it is 21 km to São Sebastião, which was once as attractive as Paraty and still retains a pretty colonial centre. Ferries leave from here for the 15-minute crossing to **Ilhabela** (see page 231), the largest offshore island in Brazil, which is shrouded in forest on its ocean side and fringed with some of São Paulo's best beaches.

The city was founded at the time when Brazil's rainforest stretched all the way from the coast to the Pantanal, and all the land north to Rio de Janeiro was ruled by the indigenous Tamoio and their French allies. The settlement was initially created as an outpost of the indigenous slave trade and a port from which to dispatch armies to fight the French and claim Rio for the Portuguese crown. After this was achieved and the Tamoio had been massacred, São Sebastião grew to become one of Brazil's first sugar-exporting ports and the hinterland was covered in vast fields of cane tilled by the enslaved indigenous Brazilians. When the number of local slaves became depleted by the lash and disease, the city became one of the first ports of the African slave trade.

Ins and outs São Sebastião is served by regular buses from Ubatuba and Santos and is also connected to São Paulo. Ferries (for cars as well as passengers), US$2, from Ilhabela run 24 hours a day (see page 243) and take 15 minutes. The **tourist office** ⓘ *R Sebastião Silvestre Neves 214, T012-3892 5323, www.saosebastiao.sp.gov.br, daily 1000-1700,* lies on the waterfront one block towards the sea from Praça Major João Fernandes. Staff are very

Great Burnt Island

Off the shore of Brazil, almost due south of the heart of São Paulo, is Allha de Queimada Grande – Great Burnt Island – untouched by human developers and feared by locals. And for good reason – zoologists estimate that there are between one and five snakes per square metre on the island; a figure which might be tolerable were they harmless garter snakes. However, Queimada Grande's snakes are a unique species of pit viper, the golden lancehead. The lancehead genus of snakes is responsible for 90% of Brazilian snakebite-related fatalities. Golden lanceheads on Queimada Grande grow to well over half a metre long, and they possess a powerful fast-acting poison that melts the flesh around their bites. This place is so dangerous that a permit is required to visit.

elpful and can provide maps and information on ferries to Ilhabela and beaches in the entire São Sebatstião province. The city is far cheaper for accommodation than Ilhabela.

ights São Sebastião's remaining colonial streets are in the few blocks between the horeline and the Praça Major João Fernandes, which is dominated by the **Igreja Matriz** ① *daily 0900-1800*. Although this retains remnants of its original 17th-century design, this predominantly a 19th-century reconstruction devoid of much of its original church art. owever, the newly refurbished **Museu de Arte Sacra** ① *1 block south of the praça, Sebastião Neves 90, T012-3892 4286, daily 1300-1700, free*, in the 17th-century chapel of ão Gonçalo, preserves a number of 16th-century statues found in cavities in the wall of the greja Matriz during its restoration in 2003.

The city has a few sleepy streets of Portuguese houses, fanning out from the square, nd a handful of civic buildings worth a quick look before the ferry leaves for Ilhabela. The ost impressive is the **Casa Esperança** ① *Av Altino Arantes 154, not open to the public though they often let visitors in on request*, on the waterfront. It was built from stone and attle and daub glued together with whale oil, and then whitewashed with lime from ousands of crushed shells collected on the beaches of Ilhabela. The interior has some eeling 17th-century ceiling paintings.

habela (Ilha de São Sebastião)
Colour map 5, A6. Phone code: 012. Population: 21,000 (100,000 high season).

abela is Brazil's largest oceanic island and one of its prettiest. It is wild enough to be home ocelots, and the lush forests on its ocean side (80% of which are protected by a state park) p with waterfalls and are fringed with glorious beaches. Its centre is crowned with craggy aks, often obscured by mist: **Morro de São Sebastião** (1379 m), **Morro do Papagaio** 309 m), **Ramalho** (1285 m) and **Pico Baepi** (1025 m). Rainfall on the island is heavy, about 00 mm a year, and there are many small biting flies known locally as *borrachudos*.

The island is considered the 'Capital da Vela' (capital of sailing) because its 150 km of astline offers all types of conditions. The sheltered waters of the strait are where many ors learn their skills and the bays around the coast provide safe anchorages. There are, wever, numerous tales of shipwrecks because of the unpredictable winds, sudden mists d strange forces playing havoc with compasses, but these provide plenty of adventure divers. There are over 30 wrecks that can be dived, the most notable being the *Príncipe Asturias*, a transatlantic liner that went down off the Ponta de Pirabura in 1916.

Ins and outs There are good transport connections with the mainland. **Litorânea** buses from São Paulo connect with a service right through to Ilhabela town. Ferries run day and night and leave regularly from the São Sebastião waterfront, taking about 20 minutes; free for pedestrians, cars US$1 weekdays, US$10 at weekends. It is very difficult to find space for a car on the ferry during summer weekends. A bus meets the ferry and runs to Ilhabela town and along the west coast. Try to visit during the week when the island feels deserted, and avoid high season (December to February) at all costs. Hotels and *pousadas* are expensive; many people choose to stay in São Sebastião instead. For information contact the **Secretaria de Turismo** ① *Praça Ver, José Leite dos Passos 14, Barra Velha, T012-3895 7220, www.ilhabela.sp.gov.br.* ▸▸ *See Transport, page 243.*

Sights Most of the island's residents live on the sheltered shore facing the mainland, along which are a number of upmarket *pousadas*. Swimming is not recommended on this side of the island within 4 km of São Sebastião because of pollution. Watch out for oil, sandflies and jellyfish on the sand and in the water.

About 20 minutes north of the ferry terminal is the main population centre **Vila Ilhabela**. The village has some pretty colonial buildings and the parish church, **Nossa Senhora da Ajuda e Bom Sucesso**, dates from the 17th century and has been restored. There are restaurants, cafés and shops. Four kilometres north of Ilhabela, **Pedras do Sino** (Bell Rocks) are curious seashore boulders which, when struck with a piece of iron or stone, emit a loud bell-like note. There is a beach here and a campsite nearby.

From Vila Ilhabela, the road hugs the coast, sometimes high above the sea, towards the south of the island. An old *fazenda*, **Engenho d'Água**, a few kilometres from town in grand 18th-century mansion (not open to the public), gives its name to one of the busier beaches. About 10 km further, you can visit the old **Feiticeira** plantation. It has underground dungeons, and can be reached by bus, taxi, or horse and buggy. A trail leads down from the plantation to the beautiful beach of the same name.

On the south coast is the fishing village of **Bonete**, which has 500 m of beach and can be reached either by boat (1½ hours), or by driving to Borrifos at the end of the road, then walking along a a rainforest-covered trail for three hours – a beautiful walk.

Much of the Atlantic side of the island is protected by the **Parque Estadual de Ilhabela**. There is a dirt road across to the east of the island, but it requires a 4WD. A few kilometres along this road is a turning to the terraced waterfall of **Cachoeira da Toca** (US$4). Set in dense jungle close to the foot of the Baepi peak, the cool freshwater pool are good for bathing and attract lots of butterflies. The locals claim that there are more than 300 waterfalls on the island, but only a few of them can be reached on foot; those that can are worth the effort. There is a 50-km return trek from Vila Ilhabela over the hump of the island down towards the Atlantic. The route follows part of the old slave trail and requires a local guide as it negotiates dense tropical forest. It takes at least two days.

Some of the island's best beaches are on the Atlantic side of the island and can only reached by boat. **Praia dos Castelhanos** is recommended. At the cove of **Saco do Sombrio** English, Dutch and French pirates sheltered in the 16th and 17th centuries. Needless to say, this has led to legends of hidden treasure, but the most potent story about the place is that of the Englishman, Thomas Cavendish. In 1592 he sacked Santos and set it on fire. He then sailed to Saco do Sombrio where his crew mutinied, hanging Cavendish, sank their boats and settled on the island.

This is one of the most beautiful stretches of the São Paulo coast and has been recognized as such by the local tourist industry for many years. In all, there are 72 beaches of varying sizes, some in coves, some on islands. Surfing is the main pastime, of which it is said to be capital, but there is a whole range of watersports on offer, including sailing to and around the offshore islands. The **Tropic of Capricorn** runs through the beach of Itaguá, just south of the town.

The commercial centre of Ubatuba is at the northern end of the bay by the estuary, by which the fishing boats enter and leave. A bridge crosses the estuary, giving access to the coast north of town. A small jetty with a lighthouse at the end protects the river mouth and this is a pleasant place to watch the boats come and go. The seafront, stretching south from the jetty, is built up along its length, but there are hardly any high-rise blocks. In the commercial centre are shops, banks, services, lots of restaurants (most serving pizza and fish), but few hotels. These are mainly found on the beaches north and south and can be reached from the Costamar bus terminal.

Ins and outs

The road from São Sebastião is paved, so a journey from São Paulo along the coast is possible. Ubatuba is 70 km from Paraty (see page 163). There are regular buses from São Paulo, São José dos Campos, Paraibuna, Caraguatatuba, Paraty and Rio de Janeiro. The beaches are spread out over a wide area, so if you are staying in Ubatuba town and don't have a car, you will need to take one of the frequent buses. Taxis in town can be very expensive. ▶▶ *See Transport, page 244.*

The **tourist office** ① *R Guarani 465, T012-3833 9007, www.ubatuba.sp.gov.br,* is on the seafront. The area gets very crowded at carnival time as Cariocas come to escape the crowds in Rio. There is a small airport from which stunt fliers take off to wheel and dive over the bay. In summer 10-minute panoramic flights and helicopter rides over Ubatuba are offered from US$45.

Background

This part of the coast was hotly contested between the local indigenous population and the Portuguese. The Jesuits José Anchieta and Manuel Nóbrega came to the village of Iperoig, as it was called in 1563, to put a stop to the fighting; the former was even taken hostage by the locals during the negotiations. A cross on the Praia do Cruzeiro (or Iperoig) in the centre commemorates what the town proudly claims to have been the first peace treaty on the American continent. The colonists eventually prevailed and the town of Vila Nova da Exaltação da Santa Cruz do Salvador de Ubatuba became an important port until Santos overtook it in the late 18th century. In the 20th century its development as a holiday resort was rapid, especially after 1948 when it became an Estância Balneária. The shortened name of Ubatuba derives from the Tupi-Guarani, meaning 'place of ubas', a type of tree used for making bows and canoes. Cariocas disparagingly refer to it as Uba 'chuva' – as it can rain heavily here at any time.

Sights

Ubatuba has a few historic buildings, such as the **Igreja da Matriz** on Praça da Matriz, dating back to the 18th century. It has only one tower, the old 19th-century prison, which now houses the small historical museum. Other interesting buildings include:

Cadeia Velha on Praça Nóbrega; the 18th-century **Câmara Municipal** on Avenida Iperoig; and the **Sobrado do Porto**, the 19th-century customs house at Praça Anchieta 38, which contains **Fundart** (the Art and Culture Foundation). Mostly, though, it is a modern, functional town. In the surrounding countryside there are *fazendas* which are often incorporated into the *trilhas ecológicas* (nature trails) along the coast.

The **Projeto Tamar** ① *R Antonio Athanasio da Silva 273, Itaguá, T012-3432 6202, www.ubatuba.com.br/tamar*, is a branch of the national project which studies and preserves marine turtles. The **Aquário de Ubatuba** ① *R Guarani 859, T012-3432 1382, www.aquariodeubatuba.com.br, Fri-Wed 1000-2200*, has well-displayed Amazon and Pantanal species including caimans and piranhas.

Beaches
The only place where swimming is definitely not recommended is near the town's outflow between Praia do Cruzeiro and Praia Itaguá. The sand and water close to the jetty don't look too inviting either. The most popular beaches are **Praia Tenório**, **Praia Grande** and **Praia Toninhas** (4.5 km, 6 km and 8 km south respectively). Condominiums, apartments, hotels and *pousadas* line these beaches on both sides of the coast road. Of the municipality's 72 beaches, those to the south are the more developed although the further you go from town in either direction, the less built up they are. Boogie boards can be hired at many of the beaches, or you can buy your own in town for around US$5.

Saco da Ribeira, 13 km south, is a natural harbour that has been made into a yacht marina. Schooners leave from here for excursions to **Ilha Anchieta** (or dos Porcos), a popular four-hour trip. On the island are beaches, trails and a prison, which was in commission from 1908 to 1952. The **Costamar** bus from Ubatuba to Saco da Ribeira runs every half an hour (US$0.85) and will drop you at the turning by the **Restaurante Pizzeria Malibu**. It's a short walk to the docks and boatyards where an unsealed road leads to the right, through the boatyards, to a track along the shore. It ends at the **Praia da Ribeira** from where you can follow the track round a headland to the beaches of **Flamengo**, **Flamenguinho** and **Sete Fontes**. It's a pleasant stroll (about one hour to Flamengo), but there is no shade and you need to take water. Note the sign before Flamengo on one of the private properties: "*Propriedade particular. Cuidado c/o elefante!*".

Litoral Sul → *For listings, see pages 237-244.*

Unlike the Linha Verde, the Litoral Sul between Santos and Cananéia has not been continuously developed. From São Vicente to Itanhaém, the whole coast is completely built up with holiday developments, but beyond Itanhaém the road does not hug the shore and a large area has been left untouched. Some 80% of the region is now under some form of environmental protection. An organization called **SOS Mata Atlântica** ① *R Manoel da Nóbrega 456, São Paulo, www.sosmatatlantica.org.br*, aims to help preserve what is left of the coastal vegetation but is part owned by a large paper company.

Itanhaém → *Phone code: 013. Population: 72,000.*
Itanhaém lies 61 km south of Santos. Its pretty colonial church, **Sant'Ana** (1761) on Praça Narciso de Andrade, and the **Convento da Nossa Senhora da Conceição** (1699-1713, originally founded 1554), on the small hill of Morro de Itaguaçu, are reminders of the Portuguese dedication to converting the indigenous Brazilians to Catholicism. Also in the town is the **Casa de Câmara e Cadeia**, but the historic buildings are quite lost amid the

modern development. The beaches here are attractive, but like those at Mongaguá and Praia Grande, several stretches are prone to pollution. Excursions can be made by boat up the **Rio Itanhaém**. Frequent buses run from Santos, an hour away. There are several good seafood restaurants along the beach, hotels and camping.

Peruíbe → Colour map 5, A5. Phone code: 013. Population: 52,000.

Some 31 km further down the coast, there are more beaches at Peruíbe, but some fall within the jurisdiction of the Estação Ecológica Juréia-Itatins (see below). While the beach culture has been well developed here with surfing, windsurfing, fishing and so on, a number of 'alternative' options have recently flourished. The climate is said to be unusually healthy owing to a high concentration of ozone, which helps to filter out harmful ultraviolet rays from the sun. UFO watchers and other esoterics claim that it is a very mystical place. Local rivers have water and black mud proven to contain medicinal properties. And the neighbouring ecological station is a major draw now that ecotourism has become big business in São Paulo state. Peruíbe's history dates back to 1530 when the village of Abarebebê was founded; about 9 km northeast of here, the ruins can be visited, with its church built of stone and shells. There is a **Feira do Artesanato** ① Av São João, Sat and Sun 1400-0100 (1400-2300 in winter).

Buses connect the town with Santos, for São Paulo. For information, contact the **Secretaria de Turismo** ① R Nilo Soares Ferreira 50, T013-3455 2070. You may have to ask permission in the **Departamento da Cultura** ① Centro de Convenções, Av Sã João 545, T013-3455 2232, to visit Abarebebê and other sites. Also at this address is the **Secretaria Estadual do Meio Ambiente** ① T013-3457 9243, for information on the **Estação Ecológico Juréia-Itatins**.

Estação Ecológico Juréia-Itatins

① Special permission is required to enter Juréia and the surrounding protected areas. They can only be visited on an organized tour with Waldhaus Ecopousada (see page 240) or Trip on Jeep (see page 222). Contact the company with at least 5 days' notice. Trip costs vary depending on duration and number of people.

Peruíbe marks the northernmost point of the Estação Ecológico Juréia-Itatins, 820 sq km of protected Mata Atlântica. The four main ecosystems are restinga, mangrove forest, Mata Atlântica and the vegetation at about 900 m on the Juréia mountains. Its wildlife includes many endangered species including rare flowers and other plants. There are deer, jaguar, monkeys, dolphins, alligators and birds, including the yellow-headed woodpecker and toucans. Human occupation of the area has included sambaqui, builders, fazendeiros and present-day fishing communities who preserve an isolated way of life.

The ecological station was founded in 1986. Tourism is very carefully monitored and only certain areas are open to the public. Hikers can walk the 4-km **Trilha do Arpoador** and the 5-km **Trilha do Imperador**, but both need prior reservation and numbers are limited; similarly for the **Despraiado mountain bike trail**. Trips can be made, with authorization, up the **Rio Guaraú** (8 km from Peruíbe) and the **Rio Una do Prelado** (25 km from Peruíbe). Other places of interest are **Vila do Prelado**, which was a stop on the Imperial São Vicente-Iguape post route (electric light was only installed in 1995), and the **Casa da Farinha**, where manioc flour is made, 28 km from Iguape.

Iguape and Ilha Comprida → Colour map 5, A5. Phone code: 013. Population: 28,000.

At the southern end of the ecological station is the town of Iguape, founded in 1538. In the early days of its existence, ownership of the town was disputed between Spain and

Portugal because it was close to the line drawn by the Pope marking their respective territories in the 'New World'. Typical of Portuguese architecture, the small **Museu Histórico e Arqueológico** ① *R das Neves 45, Tue-Sun 0900-1730*, is housed in the 17th-century Casa da Oficina Real de Fundição. There is also a **Museu de Arte Sacra** ① *Praça Rotary, Sat and Sun 0900-1200, 1330-1700*, in the former Igreja do Rosário. The main church, the **Basílica de Bom Jesus**, is a mid-19th-century construction. Information is available from **Prefeitura Municipal** ① *R 15 de Novembro 272, T013-3841 1626*.

The main attractions for tourists are yachting, fishing and half a dozen beaches. Excursions include the ruined *fazenda* of **Itaguá**. Handicrafts include items made from wood and clay, basketware and musical instruments.

Opposite Iguape is the northern end of the **Ilha Comprida** with 86 km of beaches, some of which are disappointing. This **Área de Proteção Ambiental** is not much higher than sea level and is divided from the mainland by the Canal do Mar Pequeno. The northern end is the busiest and on the island there are hotels, a supermarket and some good restaurants; the fresh fish is excellent.

Caverns of the Vale do Ribeira and PETAR (Caverna do Santana) → *Colour map 5, A5.*

This cave system, 40 km from Eldorado, west of the BR-116, forms one of the largest concentrations of caverns in the world. Among the best known is the 8-km Gruta da Tapagem or **Caverna do Diabo** (Devil's Cave) ① *Mon-Fri 0800-1100, 1200-1700, Sat, Sun and holidays 0800-1700, US$2.* It is as huge as a cathedral with well-lit formations in the 600 m that are open to the public.

Some 43 km north of the Caverna do Diabo is the **Parque Estadual Turístico do Alto Ribeira (PETAR)** ① *www.petaronline.com.br*, which includes three groups of caves. The Núcleo Santana, contains the Cavernas de Santana (5.6 km of subterranean passages and three levels of galleries), Morro Preto and Água Suja, plus a 3.6-km ecological trail to the waterfalls in the Rio Bethary, and the Núcleo Ouro Grosso. This section of the park is 4 km from the town of Iporanga. Iporanga is the most convenient town for visiting all the caves it is 64 km west of Eldorado Paulista, 42 km east of Apiaí, on the SP-165, 257 km southwest of São Paulo. The third group, Núcleo Caboclos, near the town of Apiaí.

Ins and outs The nearest towns to the caves are Iporanga and Apiaí; buses run to both from the Rodoviária Barra Funda in São Paulo or you can take a bus to Registro and change there. If coming to Iporanga from Curitiba, change buses at Jacupiranga on the BR-116 for Eldorado Paulista. Most people who visit the caves use their own transport and there is little transport infrastructure for those who come without a car. However the **Pousada Quiririm** (see Sleeping, page 240), 3 km from PETAR, rents boats and can organize trips into the caves with advance notice. All trips in PETAR must be made with an accredited local guide. Tours to the region can also be organized with Trip on Jeep (see page 222).

Cananéia → *Colour map 5, A5. Phone code: 013.*

The 18th-century façades of the little port town of **Cananéia** stand, gradually decaying, at the heart of the wildest region in southeastern Brazil. Extensive mangrove wetland, lowland forests and porpoise-filled estuaries surround the town on all sides. Rising up behind them are the rugged, rainforest-covered mountains of the Serra do Mar, which stretch all the way into neighbouring Paraná. The white sands of **Ilha do Cordoso** are accessible by boat, and the long broad beaches of **Boqueirão Sul**, southern Ilha Comprida, are just five minutes by ferry across the little brackish river that fronts the town

Although this is one of the country's oldest cities (it was one of Martim Afonso de Souza's landfalls), Cananéia lacks the twee charm and tourist facilities of its cousins, Morretes to the south and Paraty to the north. The 17th-century **Igreja de São João Batista** has plants growing out of its belltower and the façades of its colonial buildings are crumbling in the humidity. The only time of year that sees many visitors is Carnaval and New Year. This is a town with an *Under the Volcano* atmosphere; it feels like the end of the line. *Pousadas* open their doors at whim. Restaurants are limited to fish, beans and rice served on plastic tables by friendly waiters. However, for those seeking out-of-the-way places, herein lies its appeal.

Ins and outs Cananéia can be easily visited on the way from São Paulo or Santos to Curitiba. At least two buses a day run to those destinations from the little *rodoviária*, a block west of the central Praça Martim Afonso de Souza.

Car and passenger ferries leave every 30 minutes from in front of the *praça* for the beach at Boqueirão Sul in southern Ilha Comprida. It takes about an hour to walk from the ferry dock to the beach. A few simple *pousadas* line the way. It is also possible to take boats all the way to Ilha do Mel in Paraná (see page 312).

Ilha do Cardoso

The densely wooded Ilha do Cardoso is a Reserva Florestal e Biológica. **Marujá**, the only village on the island, is tiny and has no electricity. There are some very rustic *pousadas* and restaurants and camping is allowed at designated places, but the island is otherwise uninhabited. There are lots of idyllic beaches, where spectacled caiman can be spotted lazing on the virtually untouched white sand. The best place for surfing is **Moretinho**.

Ins and outs There are three daily ferry services from Cananéia, the journey takes four hours (the ticket office as it Rua Princesa Isabel, T013-3841 1122). Boats run tours from the rocks for around US$7 per person in high season and at weekends. Launches can be hired for about US$70 for a full day at other times. Speedboats to Ilha Cardoso must be chartered in Cananéia (US$60-80 for up to five people). *Escunas* (larger boats) generally leave daily in the morning for the fishing community of Marujá and more regularly at weekends and during the high season (US$12 each way). Alternatively, drive 70 km along an unpaved road, impassable when wet, to **Ariri**, from where the island is 10 minutes by boat. Trips can also be organized with **Trip on Jeep** in São Paulo (see page 222).

The coast of São Paulo listings

For Sleeping and Eating price codes and other relevant information, see pages 32-37.

Sleeping

Santos *p226, map p227*

Discounts up to 50% during low season. There are many cheap hotels near the Orquidário municipal a few blocks from the beach.

L-L Mendes Plaza, Av Floriano Peixoto 42, block from the beach in the main shopping area, T013-3208 6400, www.mendeshoteis.

com.br. A large, newly refurbished, 1970s business-orientated hotel with 2 restaurants and a rooftop pool.

LL-L Parque Balneário Hotel, Av Ana Costa 555, Gonzaga, T013-3289 5700, www.parque balneario.com.br. The city's 5-star hotel, with full business facilities and a rooftop pool overlooking the beach. Close to the shops and restaurants. Recently renovated.

A Atlântico Ville, Av Pres Wilson 1, T013-3289 4500, www.atlantico-hotel.com.br. A/c rooms in a newly renovated, well-kept

1930s hotel on the seafront. All rooms have TV; the best are in the upper floors with sea views. There's a decent business centre, sauna, bar and restaurant.

B Gonzaga Flats, R Jorge Tibiriçá 41, Gonzaga, T013-3289 5800, www.gonzaga flat.tur.br. Apartments in a 1990s block, all with kitchenettes and small sitting rooms with sofa beds. Space for up to 4 people.

C-D Hotel Natal, Av Mal Floriano Peixoto 104, Gonzaga T013-3284 2732, www.hotel natal.com.br. Fan-cooled or a/c apartments with or without bathrooms. Cable TV.

C-D Pousada do Marquês, Av Floriano Peixoto 202, Gonzaga, T013-3237 1951, www.pousadadomarques.hpg.ig.com.br. Very simple en suite rooms with fan and cable TV.

Camburi, Camburizinho and Maresias *p230*

A-B Camburyzinho, Estr Camburi 200, Km 41, Camburizinho, T012-3865 2625, www.pousada camburizinho.com.br. 30 smart rooms in mock-colonial annexes gathered around a pool, with a bar and beach service.

B Piccolo Albergo, R Nova Iguaçu 1979, Maresias, T012-3465 6227. 5 smart chalets in a forest setting near a waterfall. With sauna and a natural swimming pool.

B Pousada das Praias, R Piauí 70, Camburizinho, T012-3865 1474, www.pousadadaspraias.com.br. A lovely little beachside *pousada* in tropical gardens, with annexes of thatched-roof wooden rooms with large glass windows and terraces overlooking a pool and sauna. The *pousada* contributes part of its profits to the local community.

São Sebastião *p230*

The city itself is not particularly desirable so only stay here if you have to, otherwise it's best to head for Ilhabela. There are a few cheap places near the main *praça* and *rodoviária*.

C-E Roma, Praça João Fernandes 174, T012-3892 1016, www.hotelroma.tur.br. Simple but well-maintained rooms around

a fig-tree filled courtyard. The simplest are a little scruffy. Includes breakfast.

Camping

Camping do Barraqueçaba Bar de Mar de Lucas, near the beach about 6 km south of São Sebastião. Hot showers, English spoken, cabins available. Recommended.

Ilhabela *p231*

There are a number of moderate and cheap hotels on the road to the left of the ferry.

LL-L Maison Joly, R Antonio Lisboa Alves 278, Morro do Cantagalo, T012-3896 1201, www.maisonjoly.com.br. Exquisite little *pousada* perfect for couples. Each cabin is tastefully decorated in its own style and has a wonderful view out over the bay. Great restaurant and pool. Private, intimate and quiet. No children allowed.

L-AL Barulho d'Agua, R Manoel Pombo 250, Curral, Km 14, T012-3894 2021, www.barulho dagua.com.br. Intimate little cabins with thatched roofs and rustic, chunky wood furniture set in rainforest next to a clear river. Very romantic and with a good restaurant.

A Ilhabela, Av Pedro Paulo de Morais 151, Saco da Capela. T012-3896 1083, www.hotel ilhabela.com.br. One of the larger *pousadas*, orientated to families and with a well-equipped but small gym, pool, restaurant and bar and good breakfast. Recommended

A Porto Pousada Saco da Capela, R Itapema 167, T012-3896 8020, www.sacodacapela.com.br. 18 carefully decorated cabins set in a rocky forest garden on a steep hill. Good pool and breakfast.

B Pousada dos Hibiscos, Av Pedro Paulo de Morais 714, T012-3896 1375, www.pousada doshibiscos.com.br. Little group of cabins set around a pool with a sauna, gym and bar. Nice atmosphere. Recommended.

B Vila das Pedra, R Antenor Custodio da Sil 46, Cocaia, T012-3896 2433, www.viladas pedras.com.br. 11 chalets in a forest garden. Tastefully decorated and a very nice pool.

C Canto Bravo, Praia do Bonete, T012-9766 0478, www.pousadacantobravo.com.br.

Set on a secluded beach 1½ hrs' walk (or 20-min boat ride) from Ponta de Sepituba. Modest and elegantly decorated cabins and excellent simple breakfast and lunch included in the price).

C-D Tamara, R Jacob Eduardo Toedtli 163, Itaquanduba, T012-3896 2543, www.pousada-tamara.com.br. 17 *cabañas* with a/c around a small pool.

C-E Ilhabela, R Benedito Serafim Sampaio 371, Pereque, T012-3896 2725, www.bonnsventos hostel.com.br. A well-kept and well-run mock-colonial hostel with terracotta tiled roofs and solid wooden and whicker furniture in smart, airy public areas. Dorms are stark and simple – with little more than beds and lockers. Suites are more spacious and brighter, with metal tables outside and en suite bathrooms. The hostel has a pool, a large garden and sits a short walk from the beach.

Camping

In addition to **Pedra do Sino**, T012-3896 5266, www.campingpedradosino.com.br, there are campsites at **Pereque**, T011-7202 3840, www.ilhabela.com/camping, near the ferry dock, and at **Praia Grande**, T012-3894 1506, www.cantogrande.com.br, a further 1 km south.

Ubatuba *p233*

Very cheap accommodation is hard to come by and at all holiday times no hotel charges less than US$30.

São Charbel, Praça Nóbrega 280, T012-3832 5007, www.saocharbel.com.br. Plain white a/c rooms with floor tiles, double beds with fitted bedside tables and Brazilian TV. The hotel sits on the busy main square. The advertised rooftop 'pool' is, in reality, a tiny plunge pool.

São Nicolau, R Conceição 213, T012-3832 5007, www.hotelsaonicolau.com.br. Very simple a/c rooms sitting over a colourful restaurant, a 3-min walk from the bus station. The *pousada* is convenient for the town beach restaurants and services. Friendly and well looked after, with a good breakfast.

C Xaréu, R Jordão Homem da Costa 413, T012- 3832 1525, www.hotelxareu batuba.com.br. 3-min walk from the bus station, convenient for the town beach restaurants and services. Pretty rooms with wrought-iron balconies in a pleasant garden area. Good value, excellent breakfast.

Beach hotels

L Recanto das Toninhas, Praia das Toninhas, T012-3842 1410, www.toninhas.com.br. Part of the **Roteiros de Charme** group (see page 34). Elegant *cabañas* and suites of rooms in a large thatched-rofed building. The best with have sea views and are set around a very pretty pool with a full range of services and activities, including a sauna, restaurant, bar, tennis court and excursions.

AL Refúgio do Corsário, Baia Fortaleza, 25 km south of Ubatuba, T012-3443 9148, www.corsario.com.br. A clean, quiet hotel on the waterfront with a large pool set on a palm-shaded lawn overlooking the ocean. Prices are for full board and the hotel offers a range of activities including sailing and swimming. Very relaxing.

AL Saveiros, R Laranjeira 227, Praia do Lázaro, 14 km from town, T012-3842 0172, www.hotel saveiros.com.br. Pretty little *pousada* with a pool and a decent restaurant. English spoken.

A Solar das Águas Cantantes, Estr Saco da Ribeira 253, Praia do Lázaro, Km 14, T012-3842 0178, www.solardasaguascantantes. com.br. A mock-Portuguese colonial house replete with *azulejos* and set in a shady tropical garden. The restaurant is one of the best on the São Paulo coast and serves excellent seafood and Bahian dishes.

B-C Rosa Penteado, Av Beira-Mar 183, Praia de Picinguaba, T012-3836 9119, www.pousadarosapicinguaba.com.br. 4 pretty beachside *cabañas* decorated with paintings and objects made by the owner. The price includes a very good breakfast and dinner.

D-F Tribo Hostel, R Amoreira 71, Praia do Lázaro, 14 km from Ubatuba,

T012-3432 0585, www.ubatubahostel.com.
Great value hostel on one of the prettiest
beaches in Ubatuba. Simple tiled dorms and
doubles, all fan-cooled and with shared
bathrooms. The hostel has a pool and a
simple restaurant and attracts a busy party
crowd at weekends, but is quiet from Sun to
Thu night. Details on how to get to the hostel
from Ubatuba town on the website.

Camping

Be careful camping around Ubatuba,
especially on weekends. Robbery and
assault are increasingly common.
Camping Clube do Brasil, Lagoinha, 25 km
from town, T012-3443 1536, www.camping
clube.com.br; also at Praia Perequê-Açu,
2 km north, T012-3432 1682. There are
about 8 other sites in the vicinity.

Peruíbe p235

A Piero Al Mare, R Indianópolis 20, Praia Orla
dos Coqueiros, T013-458 2603. Modest, plain
rooms with breakfast and a restaurant.
**B-C Waldhaus Ecopousada Casa da
Floresta**, R Gaviota 1201, Praia do Guaraú,
T013-3522 4122, www.jureiaecoadventure.
com.br. A big, brightly coloured mock-
German chalet in glorious surrounds – set in
a sloth and hummingbird-filled tropical
garden on a cape with sweeping views over
the beach to the forests of Juréia. Rooms
are plain but comfortable – decked out in
polished wood and with doubles and sofa
beds and the *pousada* offer trips into Juréia
by foot, jeep or canoe. Money from the hotel
goes towards community projects.
C-D Vila Real, Av Anchieta 6625, T013-
3458 2797. Basic but well looked after
and with good staff.

Iguape and Ilha Comprida p235

The northern part of Ilha Comprida is reached
from Iguape. The southern part of Ilha
Comprida is closer to Cananéia. There are
hotels in the southern end too, reachable from
Cananeia. All those listed here are in Iguape.

B Silvi, R Ana Cândida Sandoval Trigo 515,
Iguape, T013-3841 1421, silvihotel.com.br.
Very simple rooms in a low-rise concrete
complex in the town. Staff are friendly and
see very few foreigners.
C-D Solar Colonial Pousada, Praça da
Basilica 30, Iguape, T013-3841 1591. A range
of rooms in a converted 19th-century house.

Camping

There is a campsite at Praia da Barra da
Ribeira, 20 km north, and wild camping is
possible at Praia de Juréia, the gateway
to the ecological station.

Caverns of the Vale do Ribeiro p236

B-C Pousada Quiririm, Rodovia Antonio
Honório da Silva, Km 156, 6 Bairro da Serra,
Iporanga, www.pousadadoquiririm.com.br.
Pretty litte *pousada* with chalets set in a
sub-tropical garden overlooking the forest.
Organizes trips to the caves. Full board.
Book ahead, especially at weekends.
C Pousada das Cavernas, Iporanga,
T015-3556 1168 or T011-3543 3082,
www.pousadadascavernas.com.br.
Pleasant, simple with breakfast.
D Pousada Rancho da Serra, Iporanga,
T015-3556 1168 or T011-3588 2011,
www.ranchodaserra.com.br. Friendly staff
who can organize trips into PETAR. Rooms
are very simple.

Cananéia p236

There are a few cheap hotels in Cananéia
town and other more expensive options
across the water (2 mins on ferry and about
30-min walk) on the southern end of Ilha
Comprida (see page 235). R Tristã Lobo
lies a few blocks inland from the *praça*
and runs parallel to the shoreline.
B-C Pousada do Pedrinho, R Tristão Lobo
49, Cananéia historical centre, T013-3851
1368. Simple, a/c motel-like rooms with tiled
floors and TVs and a small restaurant. No sig
outside the hotel. R Tristão Lobo lies 2 block
inland from the main *praça*.

D-E Villa (São João Baptysta) de Cananéa, R Tristã Lobo 289, T013-3851 3367, www.pousadavilladecananea.com.br. A small, charming family *pousada* in a converted 18th-century house. Simple but welcoming with chunky faux-antique furniture, friendly staff and a big breakfast. The hotel can organize fishing trips and excursions.

Ilha do Cardoso *p237*

C-D Pousada do Sossego, Praia do Marujá, Ilha do Cardoso, T013-3852 1141, www.cananet.com.br/sossego. Simple rooms in shacks right on a pristine, lonely stretch of beach. The *pousada* can organize trail walks, boat trips and fishing.

C-D Pousada Ilha do Cardoso, Praia do Marujá, Ilha do Cardoso, T013-3852 1613. A little concrete house near the beach and on the edge of the fishing village, with terraces and breakfast included.

Eating

Santos *p226, map p227*

Old Harbour, Av Ana Costa 555, in the Parque Balneário Hotel, T013-3289 5700. Traditional Brazilian fare with daily lunch buffets and a hearty *feijoada* on Sat lunch.

Pier One, Av Almirante Saldanha da Gama, Ponta da Praia. Good evening option in a restaurant perched over the water next to the Ponte Edgard Perdigao bridge. Very good *peca santista* – a local fish speciality served with banana, manioc flour and bacon – and live music at weekends.

WTC, R 15 de Novembro 111/113, Centro Histórico, T013-3219 7175. A business man's club housed in a handsome 19th-century building. Popular with local bigwigs. One of the best restaurants in the city with Mediterranean-influenced menu.

Point 44, R Jorge Tibiriçá 44. Great lunchtime buffet with enormous choice of *churrascaria*, in a large bustling dining room. Bar snack menu, live music Tue-Sat evening and dancing on Tue, Thu and Sat.

Café Paulista, Praça Rui Barbosa 8 at R do Comércio, Centro Histórico, T013-3219 5550. A Santos institution. Founded in 1911 by Italians, this place has been serving great Portuguese dishes such as *bacalhau*, and bar snacks (such as *empada camarão*), and coffee.

Camburi, Camburizinho and Maresias *p230*

There are numerous cheap and mid-range restaurants with bars and nightclubs along the São Sebastião coast and some excellent restaurants around Camburizinho.

Acqua, R Estr. Do Camburi 2000, Camburizinho, T012-3865 1866. Superb food with a view – out over Camburi and Praia de Baleia beach. Come for a sunset cocktail and then dine by candlelight.

Manacá, R do Manacá, Camburizinho, T012-3865 1566. Closed Mon and Wed. One of the best restaurants on the São Paulo coast and one of the best in the state, using French cooking techniques with Brazilian, Asian and seafood ingredients. Specialities include sole in orange and ginger sauce, puréed potato and wasabi. Very romantic setting, in a tropical rainforest garden reached by a candlelit boardwalk. Come for dinner. Worth a special trip.

São Sebastião *p230*

São Sebastião bar and restaurant, Praça Major João Fernades 278, diagonally opposite the Igreja Matriz, T012-3892 4100. Generous *pratos feitos*, fish and chicken and great juices. Very good value.

Ilhabela *p231*

There are cheap places in the town, including a decent *padaria* (bakery) and snack bars.

Pizzabela, Hotel Ilha Deck, Av Alm Tamandaré 805, Itaguassu, T012-3896 1489. Paulistanos consider their pizza the best in the world. This is one of the few restaurants outside the city serving pizza, São Paulo-style. Expect lots of cheese. Nice surrounds.

Viana, Av Leonardo Reale 1560, Praia do Viana, T012-3896 1089. The best and most

The biggest rodeo in the world

The world's biggest annual rodeo, the Festa do Peão Boiadeiro, is held during the third week in August in Barretos, some 115 km northwest of Ribeirão Preto. The town is completely taken over as up to a million fans come to watch the horsemanship, enjoy the concerts, eat, drink and shop in what has become the epitome of Brazilian cowboy culture. There are over 1000 rodeos a year in Brazil, but this is the ultimate. The stadium, which has a capacity for 35,000 people, was designed by Oscar Niemeyer and the wind funnels through the middle, cool the competitors and the spectators. Since the 1950s, when Barretos' rodeo began, the event grew slowly until the mid-1980s when it really took off.

Tours from the UK are run by **Last Frontiers**, www.lastfrontiers.co.uk.

expensive restaurant on the island, with excellent seafood and light Italian dishes. Good wine list. Book ahead.

Ubatuba *p233*
There is a string of mid-range restaurants along the seafront on Av Iperoig, as far as the roundabout by the airport.
¶¶¶ Giorgio, Av Leovigildo Dias Vieira 248, Itaguá. Sophisticated Italian restaurant and bar.
¶¶¶ Solar das Águas Cantantes, (see Sleeping). Very good seafood and Bahian restaurant in elegant surrounds.
¶¶ Pizzeria São Paulo, Praça da Paz de Iperoig 26. Undeniably chic gourmet pizzeria in beautifully restored building. Owned by a young lawyer who brings the authentic Italian ingredients for the gorgeous pizzas from São Paulo every weekend.
¶¶ Senzala, Av Iperoig. Established 30 years ago, this Italian has a lovely atmosphere. Don't miss the seafood spaghetti. Recommended.
¶ Armazém da Praia, R Cel Ernesto de Oliveira 149, opposite the post office. Open for lunch only. Pretty, family-run self-service.
¶ Sérgio, R Prof Thomaz Galhardo 404. Open for dinner, weekends only. Serving ice-cream, pizza and, at weekends, *feijoada*.

✪ Festivals and events

Santos *p226, map p227*
Throughout the summer there are many cultural, educational and sporting events.
26 Jan Foundation of Santos.
Mar/Apr Good Fri.
Jun Corpus Christi; Festejos Juninos.
8 Sep Nossa Senhora de Monte Serrat.

São Sebastião *p230*
20 Jan Festival of the Patron Saint, featuring *congadas*, a song and dance derived from slaves from the Congo.

Ilhabela *p231*
There are sailing weeks and fishing contests throughout the year; dates change annually.
Feb Carnaval.
May Ilhabela is rich in folklore and legends. Its version of *congada* is famous, particularly at the Festival of São Benedito.
28 Jun São Pedro, with a maritime procession
1st week of Jul Santa Verônica in Bonete.
Sep The town's anniversary.

Ubatuba *p233*
Feb Carnaval.
End Jun São Pedro.
Jul Festa do Divino Espírito Santo.
Sep Ubatuba is known for its handicrafts (carved wood, basketware) and it holds an annual Festa da Cultura Popular.
28 Oct Ubatuba's anniversary.

Peruíbe *p235*
18 Feb Founding of Peruíbe.
Jun Festival do Inverno.
Oct Mês das Missões.

Iguape and Ilha Comprida *p235*
Throughout the year there are various
sporting and cultural events.
Jan/Feb Summer festival in Iguape.
Feb Carnaval on Ilha Comprida.
Mar/Apr Semana Santa.
Jun Corpus Christi.
Aug The month of the pilgrimage
of Senhor Bom Jesus de Iguape.
3 Dec Iguape's anniversary.

▲ Activities and tours

Caverns of the Vale do Ribeiro *p236*
Tour operators
Agência de Monitores Parque Aventuras,
Bairro da Serra, Iporanga, T015-3556 1485,
www.parqueaventuras.com.br. Trips to the
caves, waterfalls and forests around PETAR
and light adventure activities including
rapelling. Come during the week. At
weekends big groups from São Paulo
make things noisy and boyish.
Trip on Jeep, see page 222. Run trips to
wildlife destinations along the São Paulo
coast, including Jureia and PETAR.

⊕ Transport

Santos *p226, map p227*
Bus To **São Vicente**, US$0.90. For most
suburbs buses leave from Praça Mauá,
in the centre of the city. Heading south,
several daily buses connect Santos to
Peruíbe, **Iguape** and **Cananeia** for
Ilha Comprida and **Ilha do Cardoso**.
   There are buses to **São Paulo** (50 mins,
US$5) approximately every 15 mins,
from the *rodoviária* near the city centre,
José Menino or Ponta da Praia (opposite the
ferry to Guarujá). Note that the 2 highways

between São Paulo and Santos are
sometimes very crowded, especially at
rush hours and weekends. To **Guarulhos/
Cumbica airport**, Expresso Brasileiro at
0600, 1330, 1830, return 0550, 0930, 1240,
1810, US$20, allow plenty of time as the bus
goes through Guarulhos, 3 hrs. **TransLitoral**
from Santos to **Congonhas airport** then to
Guarulhos/Cumbica, 4 daily, US$12, 2 hrs.
To **Rio de Janeiro**, Normandy, several
daily, 7½ hrs, US$40. To Rio along the coast
road is via **São Sebastião** (US$10, change
buses if necessary), **Caraguatatuba**
and **Ubatuba**.

Taxi All taxis have meters. The fare from
Gonzaga to the bus station is about US$15.
Cooper Rádio táxi, T013-3232 7177.

São Sebastião *p230*
Bus 2 buses a day to **Rio de Janeiro** with
Normandy, 0830 and 2300 (plus 1630 on Fri
and Sun), can be heavily booked in advance,
US$30 (US$10 from Paraty) 6½ hrs; 12 a day
to **Santos**, via Guarujá, 4 hrs, US$11; 11 buses
a day also to **São Paulo**, US$15, which run
inland via **São José dos Campos**, unless you
ask for the service via **Bertioga**, only 2 a day.
Other buses run along the coast via **Maresias**,
Camburi or north through **Ubatuba**. Last
bus leaves at 2200.

Ferry Free ferry to **Ilhabela** for foot
passengers, see below.

Ilhabela *p231*
Bus A bus runs along the coastal strip facing
the mainland. **Litorânea** runs buses from
Ilhabela town through to **São Paulo** (office
at R Dr Carvalho 136) but it is easiest to reach
the island by taking a bus from São Paulo
to São Sebastião across the water and then
the ferry across to Ilhabela.

Ferry The 15- to 20-min ferry to **São
Sebastião** runs non-stop day and night.
Free for foot passengers; cars cost US$1
weekdays, US$10 at weekends.

Ubatuba *p233*

Bus There are 3 bus terminals.
Rodoviária Costamar, R Hans Staden and R Conceição, serves all local destinations.

The *rodoviária* at R Prof Thomaz Galhardo 513, for São José buses to **Paraty**, US$2.25, some **Normandy** services to **Rio de Janeiro**, US$9 and some Itapemirim buses.

Rodoviária Litorânea is the main bus station. To get there, go up Conceição for 8 blocks from Praça 13 de Maio, turn right on R Rio Grande do Sul, then left into R Dra Maria V Jean. Buses go to **São Paulo**, 3½ hrs, frequent, US$8, **São José dos Campos**, US$6, **Paraibuna**, US$5, **Caraguatatuba**, US$2.

Iguape and Ilha Comprida *p235*

Bus Buses run from Iguape to **São Paulo**, **Santos** or **Curitiba**, changing at Registro.

Ferry A continuous ferry service runs from Iguape to Ilha Comprida (free but small charge for cars); buses run until 1900 from the ferry stop to the beaches. From Iguape it is possible to take a boat trip down the coast to **Cananéia** and **Ariri**. Tickets and information from Dpto Hidroviário do Estado, R Major Moutinho 198, Iguape, T013-3841 1122. It is a beautiful trip, passing between the island and the mainland.

Caverns of the Vale do Ribeiro *p236*

Bus Buses from Apiaí run to the Barra Funda *rodoviária* in **São Paulo**, US$22. If heading to **Curitiba**, take the bus from Iporanga to Jacupiranga on the BR-116 and change.

Cananéia and Ilha do Cardoso
p236 and p237

Bus Buses run twice daily from Cananéia to **São Paulo** (Barra Funda). Alternatively go via **Registro** (from where there are buses hourly to Barra Funda).

❶ Directory

Santos *p226, map p227*
Banks Open 1000-1730. ATMs in Santos are very unreliable and often out of order. Visa ATMs at Banco do Brasil, R 15 de Novembro 195, Centro and Av Ana Costa, Gonzaga. Many others. **Embassies and consulates** France, R General Câmara 12, sala 51, T013-3219 5161. Germany, R Frei Gaspar 22, 10th floor, T013-3219 5092. UK, R Tuiuti 58, 2nd floor, T013-3219 6622. **Immigration** Polícia Federal, Praça da República. **Internet** F hop, Shopping Parque Balneário. US$3 per hr. **Laundry** Av Mcal Floriano Peixoto 120, Gonzaga, self-service, wash and dry US$5. **Medical services** Ana Costa, R Pedro Américo 42, Campo Grande, T013-3222 9000; Santa Casa de Misericórdia, Av Dr Cláudio Luiz da Costa 50, Jabaquara, T013-3234 7575. **Post office** R Cidade de Toledo 41, Centro and at R Tolentino Filgueiras 70, Gonzaga. **Telephone** R Galeão Carvalhal 45, Gonzaga.

Ilhabela *p231*
Banks Bradesco, Praça Col Julião M Negrão 29 in Vila Ilhabela.

Ubatuba *p233*
Banks There is a Banco 24 Horas next to the tourist office and an HSBC ATM at 85 R Conceição. The Banco do Brasil in Praça Nóbrega does not have ATMs. **Internet** Chat and Bar, upper floor of Ubatuba Shopping. US$3 per hr, Mon-Sat 1100-2000. **Post office** R Dona Maria Alves between Hans Staden and R Col Dominicano. **Telephone** On Galhardo, close to Sérgio restaurant.

Contents

Footprint features

Minas Gerais & Espírito Santo

At a glance

⊖ **Getting around** Buses and internal flights for Diamantina and the north.

◎ **Time required** 5-7 days for the southern colonial towns, Belo Horizonte and Diamantina.

☼ **Weather** Summer (Apr-Oct) is hot and dry; winter (Oct-Mar) is hot and wet. Cold fronts can cause temperature drops at any time.

✖ **When not to go** Dec-Jan are the wettest months.

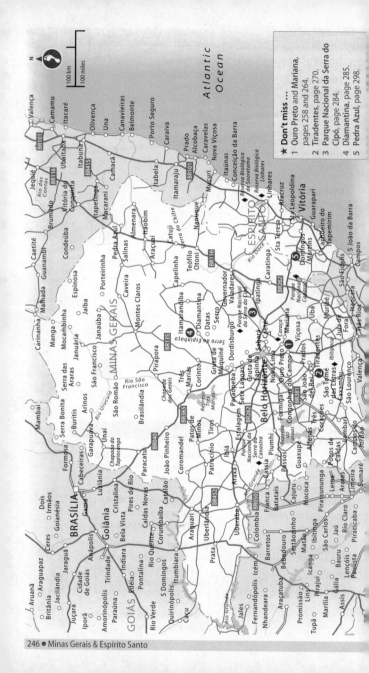

★ Don't miss ...
1 Ouro Preto and Mariana, pages 258 and 264.
2 Tiradentes, page 270.
3 Parque Nacional da Serra do Cipó, page 284.
4 Diamantina, page 285.
5 Pedra Azul, page 298.

Atlantic Ocean

100 km
100 miles

N

The inland state of Minas Gerais ('General Mines'), was once described as having a heart of gold and a breast of iron. The state was founded solely to provide precious metals for the imperial coffers. As the gold-mining camps grew and prospered they became towns of little cobbled streets crowned with opulent Manueline churches. Many of the towns are well preserved and these, and the rugged forested hills around them, are the principal reasons to visit.

The state is a little larger than France and almost as mountainous. In the south the land rises to over 2700 m on the border of Itatiaia national park in Rio, and in the east, to 2890 m at the Pico da Bandeira in the Caparaó national park. Both these areas of highland are part of the chain of forest-clad mountains that forms the escarpment, which cuts Minas Gerais off from the coastal lowlands of the states of Rio de Janeiro and Espírito Santo. The north of Minas is a dry and desolate region known as the sertão, protected by the large national park, Grande Sertão Veredas, which contains significant areas of cerrado forest and the groves of buriti palms (veredas), which give the park its name. Some of the country's rarest and most intriguing animals, such as the maned wolf and giant anteater, live here. The foremost of the colonial towns are Tiradentes, Ouro Preto and Diamantina. Many of these have churches decorated with carvings by the country's most celebrated sculptor, Aleijadinho. The state capital, Belo Horizonte, has few attractions but good transport links.

Espírito Santo, immediately to the east of Minas, is less visited. But although its coastline is not as pretty as that of Bahia to its north, it is far less developed. Beaches here can be almost deserted but for the visiting turtles. The state's interior is rugged, swathed in coffee and eucalyptus and dotted with giant granite rocks even larger than those to the south in Rio de Janeiro. The most famous and striking is Pedra Azul, which is on the main highway between Espírito Santo and Minas.

Belo Horizonte

→ *Colour map 4, B3. Phone code: 031. Population: 5 million.*

The capital of Minas Gerais, Belo Horizonte, is the third largest city in Brazil. Although moderately attractive it offers little in the way of sights, beyond a handful of museums and parks. Most travellers come here to change bus on the way to Ouro Preto or Tiradentes, or to find work as an English language teacher. The bustling modern skyscraper-filled centre sits in a bowl circled by dramatic mountains, which regularly trap pollution as the city strains under ever-increasing tides of rural migration. The city is pocked with hills that rise and fall in waves of red-tiled houses, tall apartment blocks and jacaranda- and ipe-lined streets. These are clogged with cars, particularly during the rush hour, a situation that has led the municipal government to introduce an efficient integrated public transport system linking the bus and metrô networks, in imitation of Curitiba in Paraná.
➤➤ *For listings, see pages 252-256.*

Ins and outs

Getting there
International and many national flights land at **Tancredo Neves International Airport**, more commonly referred to as **Confins** ① *39 km north of Belo Horizonte, T031-3689 2700, www.infraero.gov.br*. A taxi to the centre costs US$50. Buses from Confins, either *executivo* (from the exit, US$15), or the comfortable normal bus (**Unir**, from the far end of the car park, hourly, US$5), go to the *rodoviária*. The domestic airport is at **Pampulha** ① *9 km north of the centre, T031-3490 2000*. Blue bus No 1202 to the city centre leaves across the street from the airport (25 minutes, US$1.50), passing the *rodoviária* and the cheaper hotel district. Interstate buses arrive at the *rodoviária* next to Praça Rio Branco at the northwest end of Avenida Afonso Pena. The bus station is clean and well organized with toilets, a post office, telephones, left-luggage lockers (US$2, open 0700-2200) and shops. ➤➤ *See Transport, page 256.*

Getting around
The city has a good public transport system. **Red** buses run on express routes and charge US$1.50; **yellow** buses have circular routes around the Contorno, US$1; **blue** buses run on diagonal routes charging US$1.50. Some buses link up with the regional overground metrô. At present, the metrô is limited to one line and covers a limited portion of the north and west of the city and few areas of interest to tourists. However, there are plans to extend the service to Pampulha airport and the centre, US$0.90.

Orientation
Belo Horizonte centres on the large Parque Municipal in the heart of downtown Belo Horizonte and on the broad main avenue of Afonso Pena. This is constantly full of pedestrians and traffic, except on Sunday morning when cars are banned and part of it becomes a huge open-air market. Daytime activity is concentrated on and around the main commercial district on Avenida Afonso Pena, which is the best area for lunch. At night, activity shifts to Savassi, southwest of the centre, which has a wealth of restaurants, bars and clubs.

Best time to visit
Central Minas enjoys an excellent climate (16-30°C) except for the rainy season (December to March); the average temperature in Belo Horizonte is 21°C.

Tourist information

The municipal office, **Belotur** ⓘ *R Pernambuco 284, Funcionários, T031-3220 1310, www.turismo.mg.gov.br, www.belotur.com.br; also on Parque Municipal, at the airports and rodoviária*, has lots of useful information and maps. The free monthly *Guía Turística* lists events and opening times. The tourism authority for Minas Gerais, **Turminas** ⓘ *Praça Rio Branco 56, T031-3272 8573, www.turminas.mg.gov.br/intminas.html*, is very helpful, as is its booklet *Gerais Common Ways*. **Instituto Chico Mendes de Conservação da Biodiversidade (ICMBio)** ⓘ *Av do Contorno 8121, Cidade Jardim, T031-3337 2624*, has information on national parks. The website www.belohorizonteturismo.com.br is also useful.

1 Belo Horizonte orientation & Pampulha

➡ Belo Horizonte maps
1 Belo Horizonte orientation and Pampulha, page 249
2 Belo Horizonte centre, page 250

Sleeping 🛏
Ouro Minas Palace **3**

2 km
2 miles

As in any large city, watch out for sneak thieves in the centre and at the bus station. The Parque Municipal is not safe after dark, so it is best not to enter alone.

Sights

Although dotted with green spaces like the **Parque Municipal** ① *Tue-Sun 0600-1800*, and a few handsome buildings such as the arts complex at the **Palácio das Artes** ① *Afonso Pena 156*, central Belo Horizonte has few sights of interest beyond a handful of small

Belo Horizonte centre

➡ Belo Horizonte maps
1 Belo Horizonte orientation and Pampulha, page 249
2 Belo Horizonte centre, page 250

Sleeping 🛏
Best Western Sol Belo Horizonte 12
Continental 1
Dayrell Minas 3
Esplanada 2
HI Chalé Mineiro 4
Le Flamboyant Flats 6
Liberty Palace 5
Mercure 11
O Sorriso do Lagarto Hostel 7
Othon Palace 8
São Salvador 9
Villa Emma Flats 10

Eating 🍴
A Cafeteria 1
Café da Travessa 2
Café Tina 3
Dona Derna 4
Kauhana 5
La Traviata 6
Sushi Beer 7
Taste Vin 8
Vecchio Sogno 9

museums. The **Museu Mineiro** ① *Av João Pinheiro 342, T031-3269 1168, Tue-Fri 1000-1700, Sat and Sun 1000-1600*, houses religious and other art in the old senate building, close to the centre. There is a section dedicated specifically to religious art, with six pictures attributed to Mestre Athayde (see pages 259, 262 and 263), exhibitions of modern art, photographs and works by *naïf* painters. Also of interest are the woodcarvings by Geraldo Teles de Oliveira (GTO). The **Museu Histórico Abílio Barreto** ① *Av Prudente de Morais 202, Cidade Jardim, T031-3277 8861, Tue, Wed, Fri, Sun 1000-1700, Thu 1000-1200,* is in an old *fazenda* which has existed since 1883, when Belo Horizonte was a village called Arraial do Curral d'el Rey. The *fazenda* now houses antique furniture and historical exhibits. To get there, take bus No 2902 from Avenida Afonso Pena.

Pampulha

The city's most interesting attraction by far is the suburb of Pampulha: a complex of Oscar Niemeyer buildings set around a lake in formal gardens landscaped by Roberto Burle Marx. The project was commissioned by Juscelino Kubitschek in the 1940s, when he was governor of Minas Gerais and a decade before he became president. Some see it as a proto-Brasília, for this was the first time that Niemeyer had designed a series of buildings that work together in geometric harmony. It was in Pampulha that he first experimented with the plasticity of concrete; the highlight of the complex is the **Igreja São Francisco de Assis** ① *Av Otacílio Negrão de Lima, Km 12, T031-3441 9325, daily 0800-1800*. This was one of Niemeyer's first departures from the orthodox rectilinear forms of modernism and one of the first buildings in the world to mould concrete, with its series of parabolic waves running together to form arches. Light pierces the interior through a series of louvres and the curves are offset by a simple free-standing bell tower. The outside walls are covered in *azulejo* tiles by Candido Portinari, Brazil's most respected modernist artist. These were painted in a different style from his previous social realism, as exemplified by pictures such as *O Mestiço*. The building provoked a great deal of outrage because of its modernist design. One mayor proposed its demolition and replacement by a copy of the church of Saint Francis in Ouro Preto.

There are a number of other interesting Niemeyer buildings on the other side of the lake from the church. With its snaking canopy leading up to the main dance hall, the **Casa do Baile** ① *Av Octacílio Negrão de Lima 751, Tue-Sun 0900-1900, free*, is another example of his fascination with the curved line. There are wonderful views out over the lake. People would dance here and then take a boat to the glass and marble **Museu de Arte de Pampulha** (MAP) ① *Av Octacílio Negrão de Lima 16585, T031-3443 4533, www.comarte virtual.com.br, Tue-Sun 0900-1900, free*, which was then a casino set up by Kubitschek. Today it houses a fine collection of Mineira modern art and more than 900 works by national artists.

Just 700 m south of the lake are the twin stadia of **Mineirão** and **Mineirinho**, clear precursors to the Centro de Convenções Ulysses Guimarães in Brasília, which was designed by Niemeyer's office though not the architect himself. Mineirão is the second largest stadium in Brazil after the Maracanã in Rio, seating 92,000 people.

Around Belo Horizonte → *For listings, see pages 252-256.*

Parque Natural de Caraça

This remarkable reserve sits in the heart of the Serra do Espinhaço mountains about 120 km east of Belo Horizonte and is perhaps the best place in South America for seeing maned wolf. The park ranges in altitude from 720 m to 2070 m. The lower areas are rich in Atlantic forest while the higher areas support *cerrado*, grassland and other mountain habitats. There are lakes, waterfalls and rivers. Since the early 1980s, the monks have been leaving food for maned wolves on the seminary steps, and at least four can usually be seen in the every evening. Other endangered mammals in the park include southern masked titi monkeys, which can often be spotted in family groups, tufted-eared marmosets and brown capuchin monkeys. Birdlife includes various toucans, guans and hummingbirds (such as the Brazilian ruby and the white-throated hummingbird), various tanagers, cotingas, antbirds, woodpeckers and the long-trained and scissor-tailed nightjars. Some of the bird species are endemic, others are rare and endangered.

The trails for viewing the different landscapes and the wildlife are marked at the beginning and are quite easy to follow, although a guide (available through the seminary) is recommended.

The **seminary buildings** and the church are beautifully set in a shallow valley 1220 m above sea level and surrounded on three sides by rugged mountains that rise to 2070 m at the Pico do Sol. The name Caraça means 'big face', so called because of a hill that is said to resemble the face of a giant who is looking at the sky. This can be best appreciated by climbing up to the cross just above the church. The church itself has a painting of the Last Supper attributed to Mestre Athayde (see pages 259, 262 and 263) with a trompe l'oeil effect. The eyes of Judas Iscariot (the figure holding the purse) seem to follow you as you move. Part of the seminary has been converted into a hotel, which is the only place to stay in the park (see Sleeping, page 253). It is also possible to stay in **Santa Bárbara**, 25 km away on the road to Mariana, which has a few cheap hotels, and hitchhike to Caraça.

Ins and outs   The park is open 0700-2100; if staying overnight you cannot leave after 2100. Entry to the park costs US$5 per vehicle. Santa Bárbara is served by 11 buses a day from Belo Horizonte (fewer on weekends). There is also a bus service to Mariana, a beautiful route, via Catas Altas, which has an interesting church and a *pousada* belonging to the municipality of Santa Bárbara. To get to the park, turn off the BR-262 (towards Vitória) at Km 73 and go via Barão de Cocais to Caraça (120 km). There is no public transport to the seminary. Buses go as far as Barão de Cocais, from where a taxi is US$12. Book the taxi to return for you, or hitch (which may not be easy). The park entrance is 10 km before the seminary. The alternative is to hire a guide from Belo Horizonte, which costs about US$75 including transport and meals. For more information see the seminary website: www.santuariodocaraca.com.br.

◉ Belo Horizonte listings

For Sleeping and Eating price codes and other relevant information, see pages 32-37.

▣ Sleeping

Belo Horizonte *p248, maps p249 and p250*
There are cheap options near the *rodoviária* and on R Curitiba, but many of these hotels are hot-pillow establishments; you'll have a more comfortable stay in one of the youth hostels. You can spend the night in the *rodoviária* if you have an onward ticket (police check at 2400).

L Dayrell Minas, R Espírito Santo 901, T031-3248 1000, www.dayrell.com.br. One of the best and most central business hotels, with a very large convention centre and full business facilities, fax and email modems in the rooms. Rooftop pool. Not much English spoken.
L Le Flamboyant Flats, R Rio Grande do Norte 1007, Savassi, T031-3261 7370, www.clan.com.br. Well-maintained 1980s flats with a pool. Separate sitting rooms with TVs, and kitchens with cookers. Some have 2 bedrooms.
L Liberty Palace Hotel, R Paraíba 1465, Savassi, T031-2121 0900, www.libertypalace.

com.br. A designated business hotel right in the heart of the Savassi restaurant district, with a plush Phantom of the Opera marble lobby and pleasant but unremarkable business rooms with spacious marble bathrooms, 24-hr room service, IDSL in all rooms and a well-appointed business centre.

L Ouro Minas Palace, Av Cristiano Machado 4001, T031-3429 4001 (toll free T0800-314000), www.ourominas.com.br. The most luxurious hotel in the city with palatial suites, including several for women only. Excellent service, a pool, sauna, gym with personal trainers and good business facilities. Not central but within easy reach of the centre and airports.

AL Othon Palace, Av Afonso Pena 1050, T031-2126 0000, www.hoteis-othon.com.br. A 1980s chain hotel with a rooftop pool, good service and an excellent location in the centre opposite the Parque Municipal. Rooms on lower floors can be noisy.

A Best Western Sol Belo Horizonte, R da Bahia 1040, T031-3311 1300, www.hotel solbh.com.br. Well-renovated 1990s business hotel in the centre with a pool, sauna and respectable service. Recently taken over by the Best Western group.

A Villa Emma flats, R Arturo Toscanini 41, Savassi, T031-3282 3388, www.clan.com.br. Spacious flats in need of a lick of paint, with 2 bedrooms, separate living areas and a kitchen. Internet access in some rooms.

B Mercure, Av Do Contorno 7315 (Santo Antonio), T031-3298 4100, www.mercure. com. The newest of the city's business hotels with a good pool, sauna, gym and rooms decked out in standard business attire.

C Esplanada, Av Santos Dumont 304, T031-273 5311, www.hotelesplanadabh.com.br. plusher than usual cheapie with bright en suite rooms with soap and towels provided and generous breakfasts. Triples available for little more than doubles; prices re negotiable. 700 m from the *rodoviária*.

C Continental, Av Paraná 241, T031-3201 944, www.hotelminascontinental.com.br. entral, quiet, with small interior rooms newly renovated, modern fittings. Recommended.

D São Salvador, R Espírito Santo 227, T031-3222 7731. Small well-kept rooms, the best of which are the triples with en suites. Reasonable breakfast and a public telephone. One of many similar cheapies in the area.

D-E O Sorriso do Lagarto hostel, R Padre Severino 285, Savassi, T031-3283 9325, www.osorrisodolagarto.com.br. Simple little hostel in a converted town house with kitchen, internet and fax service, breakfast, lockers, washing machines and a living area with DVD player. With a branch in Ouro Preto.

E-F HI Chalé Mineiro, R Santa Luzia 288, Santa Efigênia, T031-3467 1576, www.chale mineirohostel.com.br. Attractive and well maintained, with dorms and doubles, a small pool and shared kitchen, TV lounge and telephones. Towels and bed linen are extra. To get here take bus No 980 from the *rodoviária*.

Parque Natural de Caraça *p251*
AL-B Santuário do Caraça, reservations: Caixa Postal 12, Santa Bárbara, T031-3837 2698, www.santuariodocaraca.com.br. This on-site hotel has reasonable rooms, the restaurant serves good food, lunch 1200-1330. No camping is permitted.

🍴 Eating

Belo Horizonte *p248, maps p249 and p250*
Mineiros love their food and drink and Belo Horizonte has a lively café dining and bar scene. **Savassi** overflows with bohemian streetside cafés, bars and restaurants and is the best place in the city for a food browse. There is a lively, cheap street food market on **R Tomé de Souza**, between Pernambuco and Alagoas in Savassi every night around 1900-2300: think Bangkok with Minas food and buzzing bars. **Pampulha**, on the outskirts, has the best of the fine-dining restaurants, which are well worth the taxi ride. There are plenty of cheap per kilo restaurants and *padarias* near the budget hotels in the centre. Seriously cheap *comida mineira* is served in the restaurants around the *rodoviária*, *prato feito* US$1.50.

Aurora, R Expedicionário Mário Alves de Oliveira 421, São Luís, T031-3498 7567. Closed Mon and Tue. One of the best restaurants in the city, in a garden setting next to the Lago da Pampulha. Imaginative menu with dishes fusing Mineira and Italian techniques and making use of unusual Brazilian fruits. Respectable wine list.

Taste Vin, R Curitiba 2105, Lourdes, T031-3292 5423. Decent, if a little salty mock-French food. Celebrated for its soufflés and provençale seafood. The respectable wine list includes some Brazilian options. Recipient of the *Veja* best restaurant award 2007/2008.

Vecchio Sogno, R Martim de Carvalho 75 and R Dias Adorno, Santo Agostinho, under the Assembléia Legislativo, T031-3292 5251. Lunch only on Sun. The best Italian in the city with an inventive menu fusing Italian and French cuisine with Brazilian ingredients. Excellent fish. Good wine list.

Xapuri, R Mandacaru 260, Pampulha, T031-3496 6198, www.restaurantexapuri.com.br. Closed on Mon. *Comida mineira*, great atmosphere, live music, very good food, expensive and a bit out of the way but recommended.

Dona Derna, R Tomé de Souza, Savassi, T031-3223 6954. A range of restaurants in one. Upstairs is Italian fine dining with excellent dishes and a respectable wine list. Downstairs on weekdays is traditional Italian home cooking and by night a chic pizzeria called **Memmo**.

La Traviata, Av Cristovão Colombo 282, Savassi, T031-3261 6392. An atmospheric little Italian with a terrace overlooking the dragon's tooth pavements of Cristovão Colombo. The menu is strong on meat and fish with reasonable pasta and pizzas. Modest wine list, good-value house bottles.

Kauhana, R Tomé de Souza, Savassi, T031-3284 8714. Tasty wood-fired pizzas. Pleasant open-air dining area.

Sushi Beer, R Tomé de Souza, Savassi, T031-3221 1116. A large open-air dining area overlooked by a long bar and with a lively crowd and good atmosphere. Food ranges from superior per kilo Minas and Japanese food to meats and pizzas. Respectable range of beers and whiskies.

A Cafeteria, Av Cristovão Colombo 152, Savassi, T031-3223 9901. Salads, great sandwiches in pitta bread and a range of mock-Italian standards served to a lively young crowd and accompanied by live music most nights. One of several café-bars on the corner of Colombo and Albuquerque.

Café da Travessa, Av Getúlio Vargas 1405 at Praça Savassi, T031-3223 8092. Great little café-bookshop. Dishes range from rosti to Brazilian tapas, pasta and wraps. Pizza upstairs. Good coffee and a tasteful choice of books and Brazilian CDs. Breakfast till late.

Café Tina, Av Cristovão Colombo 336, Savassi, T031-3261 5068. Closed Mon. Bohemian café in a 19th-century town house serving soups, risottos and delicious puddings to an arty young crowd.

🎵 Bars and clubs

Belo Horizonte *p248, maps p249 and p250*
Bars
There are plenty of bars around Tomé de Souza in Savassi, where a young and arty crowd spills out onto the street, and the beer and caipirinhas are cheap and plentiful. Always lively are **Bar do James**, Vargas at Tomé de Souza and **Koyote**, R Tomé de Souza 1012.

Clubs
Clube da Esquina acts play at the city's theatres. Look out for information on www.guiadasemana.com.br and follow the link for Belo Horizonte.
A Obra, R Rio Grande do Norte 1168, Savassi, T031-3215 8077, www.aobra.com.br. The leading alternative music venue in the city. Great for the best new Minas acts.

🎬 Entertainment

Belo Horizonte *p248, maps p249 and p25*
Cinema
Belo Horizonte is a good place to watch high-quality Brazilian and foreign films. There are

many art cinemas and cineclubs in the centre such as the **Espaço Unibanco**, R Guajajaras 37.

Theatre
Belo Horizonte has at least a dozen theatres, including **Teatro Alterosa**, Av Assis Chateaubriand 499, Floresta, T031-3237 6610; **Teatro da Cidade**, R da Bahia 1341, T031-3273 1050; and **Teatro Marília**, Av Alfredo Balena 586, Centro, T031-3222 4445. The city prides itself on its theatre and dance companies (look out for the *Grupo Galpão*); don't expect to find many shows in any language other than Portuguese. See the local press for details.

⊕ Festivals and events

Belo Horizonte *p248, maps p249 and p250*
Maundy Thu Corpus Christi.
15 Aug Assunção (Assumption).
8 Dec Conceição (Immaculate Conception).

○ Shopping

Belo Horizonte *p248, maps p249 and p250*
Bookshops
Acaiaca, R Tamóios 72. Good for dictionaries.
Daniel Vaitsman, R Espírito Santo 466, 17th floor, T031-3222 9071. English-language books.
Livraria Alfarrábio, R Tamóios 320, T031-271 3603. Used foreign-language books.
Livraria Van Damme, R das Guajajaras 505, 031-3226 6492. Brazilian and Portuguese.

Gems and jewellery
Manoel Bernardes, Av Contorno 5417, Savassi, T031-3225 4200. Attractive jewellery. Very reasonable prices.

Markets
Mercado Central, Av Augusto de Lima 744. Large and clean, open every day until 1800 selling arts, crafts and bric-a-brac. There is Sun handicraft fair on **Av Afonso Pena**.

Hippies still sell their wares on **R Rio de Janeiro**, 600 block, each evening. A **flower market** is held at Av Bernardo Monteiro, near Av Brasil, every Fri 1200-2000. Also here on Sat is a **food and drinks market**.

Music
Cogumelo, Av Augusto de Lima 399, T031-3274 9915.

▲ Activities and tours

Belo Horizonte *p248, maps p249 and p250*
Ecotourism and adventure sports
Associação Mineira dos Organizadores do Turismo Ecológico (Amo-Te), R Monte Verde 125, Lípio de Melo, T031-3477 5430, oversees ecotourism in the state of Minas Gerais. This includes trekking, riding, cycling, rafting, jeep tours, canyoning, national parks and *fazendas*. For companies that arrange special-interest tours, speak to *Amo-Te* first.
Tropa Serrana, T031-3344 8986, T031-9983 2356 (mob), http://tropa.serrana.zip.net Horse-riding trips around Belo Horizonte and especially in the Serra do Cipó. There are various packages detailed on their website.

Tour operators
Ametur, R Alvarengo Peixoto 295, loja 102, Lourdes, T/F031-3292 4157, www.ametur.tur.br/. Information on *fazendas* that welcome visitors and overnight guests.
Master Turismo (American Express representative), R da Bahia 2140, T031-3330 3655, www.masterturismo.com.br, at Sala VIP, Aeroporto de Confins and Av Afonso Pena 1967, T031-3330 3603. Very helpful.
Ouro Preto Turismo, Av Afonso Pena 4273, grupo 109, Serra, T031-3223 7484, www.ouropretoturismo.com.br. A long established tour agency running excursions to the historical cities in Minas and offering booking services. With an office in Ouro Preto.

⊖ Transport

Belo Horizonte *p248, maps p249 and p250*
Air
Confins A taxi to Trancredo Neves International Airport from the centre costs US$40. Buses run every 30 mins 0415-2300 from the *rodoviária*: *convencional linha 5250* (US$3), *executivo* (US$11) www.conexaoaero porto.com.br, taking 40-60 mins.

Belo Horizonte has connections with **São Paulo** and **Rio de Janeiro** and several Brazilian cities with Azul, www.voeazul. com.br. **webjet**, www.webjet.com.br. **GOL**, www.voe gol.com.br, **Avianca**, www.avianca. com, **Pantanal**, www.voepantanal.com.br, and **TAM**, www.tam.com.br. There are international flights to **Paris** (TAM), **Lisbon** (TAP), **Buenos Aires** (TAM), **Miami** (American Airlines) and **Panama City** (COPA), with connections throughout the Americas. **Pampulha** Almost all the *convencional* bus services (see above) also stop at the domestic airport (25 mins, US$1.50) double check before you board. From Pampulha there are increasingly few flights, but shuttle services remain to several cities including **Rio de Janeiro**, **Salvador** and **São Paulo**. Airlines serving the airport are limited to Passaredo, www.voepassaredo.com.br, TRIP, www.www.voetrip.com.br.

Bus
For information on the bus station and local buses, see Ins and outs, page 248. For bus routes, companies, prices and times see www.rodoviariabelohorizonte.com.br.

To **Rio** with Cometa, T031-3201 5611 and Util, T031-3201 7744 (6½ hrs, US$50 and *leito* US$70). To **Vitória** with São Geraldo, T031-3271 1911 (US$40 and *leito* US$50). To **Brasília** with Itapemirim, T031-3291 9991, and Penha, T031-3271 1027 (10 hrs, 6 a day including 2 *leitos*, only 1 leaves in daylight at 0800, US$50, *leito* US$65). To **São Paulo** with Cometa and Gontijo, T031-3201 6130 (10 hrs, US$40). To **Foz do Iguaçu** (22 hrs, US$70). To **Salvador** with Gontijo

(24 hrs, at 1900 daily, US$60), and São Geraldo (at 1800). São Geraldo also goes to **Porto Seguro** (17 hrs, direct, via Nanuque and Eunápolis, US$60). To **Recife** with Gontijo (2000, US$100); to **Fortaleza** (US$110); to **Natal** (US$110. To **Belém** with Itapemirim, US$120). To **Campo Grande** with Gontijo (at 1930) and Motta (3 a day), T031-3464 0480, US$50, a good route to Bolivia, avoiding São Paulo. For buses within Minas Gerais, see under each destination.

Car hire
All the major companies have offices at Confins airport and in the city.

Around Belo Horizonte *p251*
Bus Buses (Útil) to the **Gruta de Lapinha** leave daily at 1015 and 1130, returning 1600, also Mon at 1830 (1¼ hrs, US$3.25 one way). **Belo Horizonte–Lagoa Santa** every 30 mins (US$2). Bus **Lagoa Santa–Lapinha** every 30 mins. The local bus stop for Lagoa Santa is 2 km downhill from the Lapinha caves. To **Gruta de Maquiné**, several buses daily with Irmãos Teixeira (2¼ hrs, US$8).

ⓘ Directory

Belo Horizonte *p248, maps p249 and p250*
Banks Banco do Brasil, R Rio de Janeiro 750, Av Amazonas 303. Visa ATM at Bradesco, R da Bahia 947. **Citibank**, R Espírito Santo 871. Changing TCs is difficult, but hotels will change them for guests at a poor rate. **Immigration** Polícia Federal, R Nascimento Gurgel 30, T031-291 0005. For visa extensions. To get there take bus No 7902 from the corner of R Curitiba and Av Amazonas and get off at the Hospital Madre Teresa. **Internet** Internet Café Club, R Fernandes Tourinho 385, Plaza Savassi, US$5 per hr. There are others throughout the city. **Medical services** Mater Dei, R Gonçalves Dias 2700, T031-3339 9000. Recommended. **Post office** Av Afonso Pena 1270. Poste restante is behind the main office at R de Goiás 77. The branch on R da Bahia is less slow.

Colonial cities near Belo Horizonte

Streets of whitewashed 18th-century houses with deep-blue or yellow window frames line steep and winding streets leading to lavishly decorated churches with Manueline façades and rich gilt interiors. Behind lies a backdrop of grey granite hills and green forests, still filled with tiny marmoset monkeys and flocks of canary-winged parakeets. The colonial gold-mining towns of southern Minas are the highlights of any visit to the state: islands of history and remnant forest in an otherwise dull agricultural landscape. Most lie south of Belo Horizonte and many people choose to visit them on the way to or from Rio. However, they make a far more charming and restful base than Belo Horizonte and we would recommend spending your time here, with just a quick stop in the capital on the way north or south. ▸▸ *For listings, see pages 277-283.*

Ins and outs

The cities fall into three groups: south of Belo Horizonte (Ouro Preto, Mariana, Congonhas do Campo, São João del Rei and Tiradentes); east (Sabará and Caeté); and north (Diamantina and Serro). All of the southern towns are on the main Rio highway (Ouro Preto being the closest to the state capital and São João del Rei the furthest from it). The towns to the east are on the main highway to Espírito Santo. Those to the north are a longer journey from Belo Horizonte, off the inland route to Bahia.

The most famous of the towns, **Ouro Preto**, can be visited in a day trip from Belo Horizonte. However, one day is not enough and the town is a much more interesting and pleasant place to stay than the capital. **Mariana** is easy to see in a day trip from Ouro Preto – either by bus or the recently inaugurated Maria Fumaça steam train. The spectacular Aleijadinho church in **Congonhas do Campo**, further south, requires only a few hours to visit and is reachable by a new highway. There is no need to stay overnight. **Tiradentes**, further south still, is the prettiest, best preserved and most visited of all the cities but feels somewhat touristy and twee. Nearby, **São João del Rei** is more decrepit but very much a real city. They are linked at weekends by a 30-minute steam train ride and daily by frequent buses. **Sabará** and **Caeté**, to the east of the capital, can be visited as an easy day trip from Belo Horizonte or on the way to Espírito Santo. **Diamantina** and **Serro** are far to the north, on one of the routes to Bahia from Belo Horizonte, and are easiest to see en route to Bahia. Diamantina is perhaps the best preserved and least touristy of all the colonial towns.

Background

Like the Spanish, the Portuguese looked to their colonies for easy money. Outside the Jesuit reduction cities, there were never plans to invest in empire, only to exploit the land and the local people as ruthlessly as possible. At first it was wood that attracted the Portuguese, and then indigenous slaves for the cane plantations that stretched along the northern coast. But it was the ultimate in rich pickings that led to colonial Brazil becoming more than a coastline empire. In 1693, whilst out on a marauding expedition, a Paulista *bandeirante* found *ouro preto* – gold made black by a coat of iron oxide – in a stream south of modern Belo Horizonte. When news reached home, an influx of adventurers trekked their way from São Paulo through the forests to set up makeshift camps along the gold streams. These camps developed into wealthy towns such as Ouro Preto and Mariana. Later, with the discovery of diamonds and other gemstones, a captaincy was established and named, prosaically, 'General Mines'.

The wealth of Minas was reflected in its streets and in the baroque churches, whose interiors were covered in gold plate and decorated with sculptures by the best artisans in

Brazil. And with the wealth came growing self-importance. The Inconfidência Mineira (see box, page 266), the most important rebellion in colonial Brazil, began in Ouro Preto in the late 18th century under a group of intellectuals educated in Portugal who were in contact with Thomas Jefferson and English industrialists. The Inconfidência never got beyond discussion but it was decided that the only non-aristocratic member of the group, José Joaquim da Silva, would be in charge of taking the governor's palace, occupied by the hated Visconde de Barbacena, who was responsible for levying the imperial taxes. Da Silva was derisively known as Tiradentes (the tooth puller) by his compatriots. Today he is the only Inconfidênte rebel that most Brazilians can name and he is celebrated as a folk hero – one of the common people who dared to challenge the powerful elite, and who was cruelly martyred as a result.

After Brazil changed from an empire into a republic, Minas Gerais vied for power with the coffee barons of São Paulo and, in the 20th century, produced two Brazilian presidents. Juscelino Kubitschek, an establishment figure chosen by the electorate as the best alternative to the military, opened up Brazil to foreign investment in the 1960s, and founded Brasília. Tancredo Neves also opposed the Brazilian military, was elected to power in 1985. A few days before his inauguration, he died in mysterious circumstances. His last words were reportedly "I did not deserve this". He was replaced by José Sarney, a leading figure in the Brazilian landowning oligarchy.

Ouro Preto → *For listings, see pages 277-283. Colour map 4, C3. Phone code: 031. Population: 67,000. Altitude: 1000 m.*

Ouro Preto, named after the black iron oxide-coated gold that was discovered here by the adventurer Antônio Dias, was one of the first of the Minas gold towns to be founded. As a former state capital, it became the wealthiest and most important town in the region. Although it now has a hinterland of ugly blocks of flats and crumbling favelas, it preserve some of the most significant colonial architecture in Brazil and remains, at heart, an 18th-century city of steep church-crowned hills, cobbled streets, *azulejos*, plazas and fountains. In homage to its historical importance Ouro Preto becomes the capital of Minas Gerais once again every year for one day only, on 24 June. The modern city bustles with young Brazilians studying and partying at the various local universities and has a thriving café and nightlife scene. Sadly the historic centre, once closed to traffic, is now thick with buses and cars, which is taking its toll on some of the beautiful buildings.

Ins and outs

Getting there Ouro Preto's **rodoviária** ① *R Padre Rolim 661, T031-3559 3225*, is 1 km north of Praça Tiradentes. A 'circular' bus runs from the *rodoviária* to Praça Tiradentes, US$0.4. Taxis charge exorbitant rates. There are frequent bus connections with Belo Horizonte and daily buses to Rio and São Paulo as well as other cities throughout Minas, including Congonhas; some buses pass through Conselheiro Lafaiete. ▶▶ *See Transport, page 282.*

Tourist information The **tourist office** ① *Praça Tiradentes 41, T031-3559 3269, www.ou preto.org.br, 0800-1800*, has details of accommodation in *casas de família, repúblicas* and other places. It also has leaflets showing the opening times of sights, which change frequently and can organize a local guide from the **Associação de Guias de Turismo** (AGTOP) ① *R Padre Rolim s/n, T031-3551 2655, Mon-Fri 0800-1800, Sat and Sun 0800-1700, little English spoke* which has its own office opposite the bus station. Cássio Antunes is a recommended guide

Milton Nascimento – the voice of Minas

Milton Nascimento is the most influential Brazilian singer and composer not to have come out of Bahia or Rio. He has produced some of Brazil's most haunting music, been nominated for a Grammy and had songs covered by almost as many artists as Paul McCartney.

Milton grew up in rural Minas in a town like many others – lost in a landscape of lush green hills and cattle pasture and where life focussed on the *praça* and local church. He was raised by his stepmother who'd once sung in a choir conducted by Villa-Lobos, and who exposed him to religious music from an early age.

Catholicism came to underlie both his musical style and lyrical themes, which were expressed most memorably on a string of ground breaking 1970s albums. The music on these is unique, with rich choral harmonies, jazz interludes and sweetly melancholic melodies interplaying with Afro-Brazilian rhythms and sound effects. Lyrics poetically exalt the day to day life of the oppressed. And Milton's golden voice soars over the top.

You'll hear Milton's songs throughout Ouro Preto. If you are tempted to buy one of his records, opt for *Clube de Esquina*, his 1972 classic.

Praça Tiradentes and around

The city has a number of churches and chapels as well as some excellent examples of *chafariz* (public fountains), *passos* (oratories) and stone bridges. The best place to start exploring the city is the central **Praça Tiradentes**, where you'll see a **statue of Tiradentes**, the leader of the Inconfidêntes (see box, page 266). Another Inconfidênte, the poet Tomás Antônio Gonzaga, lived at Rua Cláudio Manoel 61 near the São Francisco de Assis church, and was exiled to Africa. Most Brazilians know his poem based on his forbidden love affair with the girl he called *Marília de Dirceu*. Visitors are shown the bridge and decorative fountain where the lovers held their trysts. The house where she lived, on the Largo Marília de Dirceu, is now a school.

On the north side of Praça Tiradentes is a famous **Escola de Minas (School of Mining)**. It was founded in 1876, is housed in the fortress-like Palácio dos Governadores (1741-1748) and includes the **Museu de Mineralogia e das Pedras** ① *No 20, Mon, Wed-Fri 1200-1645, Sat and Sun 0900-1300, US$1.50*, which has displays of rocks, minerals, semi-precious and precious stones from all over the world. Just north of the *praça*, towards the rodoviária, is the church of **Nossa Senhora das Mercês e Misericórdia** (1773-1793).

On the south side of the *praça*, next to Carmo church, is the **Museu da Inconfidência** ① *No 139, T031-3551 1121, Mon-Fri 0800-1800, US$1.50*, a fine historical and art museum in the former Casa de Câmara e Cadeia, containing drawings by Aleijadinho and the Sala Manoel da Costa Athayde.

West of Praça Tiradentes

The church of **Nossa Senhora do Carmo** ① *R Brigadeiro Mosqueira, Tue-Sun 1300-1700, entry shared with Nossa Senhora do Pilar*, built 1766-1772, was planned by Manoel Francisco Lisboa, and both his son and Mestre Athayde worked on the project. It was a favourite church of the aristocracy. The best of the city's museums is housed in an annexe of the church, the modern and well-appointed **Museu do Oratório** ① *T031-3551 5369, daily 0930-1200, 1330-1730*. Inside is a selection of exquisitely crafted 18th- and 19th-century prayer icons and oratories, many of them with strong indigenous design and some disguised as bullet cases. On the opposite side of the road, the **Teatro Municipal** ① *R Brigadeiro Musqueiro, daily 1230-1800*, is the oldest functioning theatre in Latin America, built in 1769.

A block north of the theatre, **Casa Guignard** ① *R Conde de Bobadela 110, T031-3551 5155, Tue-Fri 1200-1800, Sat, Sun and holidays 0900-1500, free*, displays the paintings of Alberto da Veiga Guignard. Further west, just before the river, the **Casa das Contas** ① *R São José 12, T031-355 1444, Tue-Sat 1230-1730, Sun and holidays 0900-1500, US$0.50*, built 1782-1784, houses a museum of money and finance on its upper storeys. Far more interesting is the damp, dark basement where slaves were formerly housed. In colonial Preto a slave's life was literally worth less than a chicken: swapping an African Brazilian for poultry was considered a good deal.

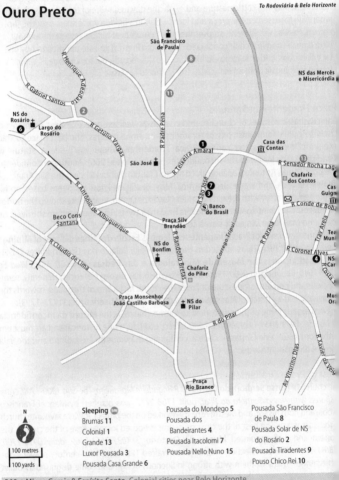

Ouro Preto

To Rodoviária & Belo Horizonte

Sleeping 🛏
Brumas **11**
Colonial **1**
Grande **13**
Luxor Pousada **3**
Pousada Casa Grande **6**
Pousada do Mondego **5**
Pousada dos
 Bandeirantes **4**
Pousada Itacolomi **7**
Pousada Nello Nuno **15**
Pousada São Francisco
 de Paula **8**
Pousada Solar de NS
 do Rosário **2**
Pousada Tiradentes **9**
Pouso Chico Rei **10**

Following Rua Teixeira Amaral across the river, the church of **São José** was begun in 1752, but not completed until 1811; some of the carving is by Aleijadinho. Up on the hill, **São Francisco de Paula** ⓘ *0900-1700*, was started in 1804, making it the last colonial church in Ouro Preto. Further west, on the Largo do Rosário, the church of **Nossa Senhora do Rosário** dates from 1785, when the present church replaced a chapel on the site. It has a curved façade, which is rare in Brazilian baroque. The interior is more simple than the exterior, but there are interesting side altars.

One of the city's grandest churches, **Nossa Senhora do Pilar** ⓘ *just north of R do Pilar, Tue-Sun 0900-1100 and 1200-1700,* was attended by the Portuguese upper classes. The ceiling painting by João de Carvalhães features a trompe l'oeil effect – as you walk to the

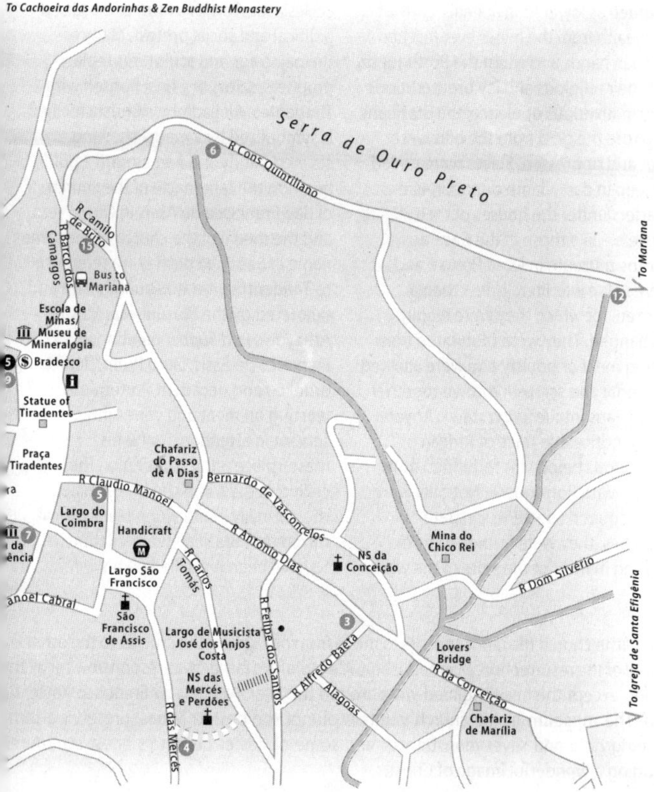

To Cachoeira das Andorinhas & Zen Buddhist Monastery

Serra de Ouro Preto

R Cons Quintiliano

R Camilo de Brito

R Barão dos Camargos

Bus to Mariana

Escola de Minas/ Museu de Mineralogia

Bradesco

Statue of Tiradentes

Praça Tiradentes

Chafariz do Passo de A Dias

Bernardo de Vasconcelos

R Cláudio Manoel

Largo do Coimbra

Handicraft

R Antônio Dias

Mina do Chico Rei

NS da Conceição

R Dom Silvério

Largo São Francisco

R Carlos Tomás

São Francisco de Assis

Largo de Musicista José dos Anjos Costa

R Felipe dos Santos

R Alfredo Baeta

Alagoas

Lovers' Bridge

R da Conceição

To Igreja de Santa Efigênia

NS das Mercés e Perdões

R das Mercés

Chafariz de Marília

anoél Cabral

To Mariana

Racism under the Portuguese

To Brazilians under the shackles of Portuguese colonial rule, Tiradentes was far more than a failed revolutionary. He was a hero who had risen from the oppressed classes to dare to stand up against the tyrannical Portuguese rule and was revered as a saint and martyr after his death. Under the Portuguese the black, indigenous and mixed race majority were regarded as lower than animals. Little of the wealth from the mines ever reached Brazilian hands and whilst the Portuguese and their religious and lay brotherhoods lived in luxurious opulence, the Brazilians who tore the gold from the hills were poor and oppressed. Slaves were forced to sleep in dark, damp dungeon-like quarters under the houses of their masters – like those in the **Casa dos Contos** museum in Ouro Preto – and there value was literally less than a chicken, for which they were readily exchanged. They were prohibited from eating meat or poultry and were allowed only offal and scraps – thrown together with beans into *feijoada* stews. Anyone with a noticeable trace of African or indigenous blood was forbidden from mixing with Portuguese. Not only were they required to attend separate churches; they were forbidden from passing in front of the spire of the white

church as it would cause offence to God. The mulatto artists and their sympathizers, like Aleijadinho and Mestre Athayde (whose wife was a black Brazilian), also experienced prejudice and were known as 'artistas de sangue sujo' or artists with dirty blood; relegated to the level of craftsmen rather than true fine artists. They in turn used their ecclesiastical art as a form of disguised political and social protest. Many of the paintings and sculptures replace prophets, saints or Christ himself with Tiradentes. Aleijadinho's Christ crucified is symbolized by a medal showing severed hands and feet around a gold heart on the tabernacle of the church of **São Francisco de Assis** in Ouro Preto and the medal of the church of the same name in São João del Rey – a reference to Tiradentes who was hung drawn and quartered by the Portuguese. Mestre Athayde's *Last Supper* painting in São Francisco de Assis, Ouro Preto, depicts drunken and decadent Portuguese feasting on meat and wine with a servant in attendance, and his masterpiece – the painting on the ceiling of the same church – replaces the normally white virgin Mary with a mixed race Brazilian woman, thought to have been modelled on his wife.

front of the church the lamb appears to move from one side of the crucifix to the other – symbol of the resurrection. Manoel Lisboa, Aleijadinho's father, was responsible for all the carving except the heavily gilded work around the altar, which is by Francisco Xavier de Brito. The **museum** in the church vaults is one of the best in Minas, preserving some stunning gold and silver monstrances and some of Xavier de Brito's finest sculptures including a wonderful image of Christ.

East of Praça Tiradentes

A block southeast of Praça Tiradentes, on the Largo São Francisco is the grand **São Francisco de Assis** ① *Largo de Coimbra, Tue-Sun 0830-1150, 1330-1640, US$2; the ticke also permits entry to NS da Conceição, keep your ticket for admission to the museun* considered to be one of the masterpieces of Brazilian baroque. Built 1766-1790

Aleijadinho worked on the general design and the sculpture of the façade, the pulpits and many other features. The harmonious lines of the exterior and the beauty of the interior are exceptional; the church feels like a model of Catholic reverence and propriety. It is far from it. Aleijadinho was a mulatto – as were Mestre Athayde's wife and children – and as such they were prohibited from entering white churches like São Francisco, from eating any meat other than offal, ears and trotters and they had no rights in civil society. Mulatto sculptors were not even considered to be artists; they were referred to as artisans or *artistas de sangue sujo* (artists of dirty blood). The church is full of subtle criticisms of the Portuguese encoded in the art by Athayde and Aleijadinho. The model for the Virgin (depicted in the highest heaven, surrounded by cherubs and musicians and saints Augustine, Hieronymous, Gregory and Ambrosius), is said to have been Mestre Athayde's mulatto wife. She has her breasts showing, open legs and her face shows African traces; all of which can only be noticed with careful attention and all of which would have been anathema to the Portuguese. The *Last Supper* painting in the sanctuary replaces the apostles with Portuguese feeding on meat and being attended to by Brazilian servants. And Aleijadinho's *Sacred Heart of Jesus* near the altar has its hands and feet cut into quarters in a reference to the fate that befell Tiradentes at the hands of the Portuguese. A **museum** at the back of the church has a small selection of paintings of serious-looking saints and a fountain by Aleijadinho depicting Blind Faith holding up a banner saying "such is the path to heaven". In the largo outside São Francisco is a handicraft market. South of here, the church of **Nossa Senhora das Mercês e Perdões** ① *R das Mercês, Tue-Sun 1000-1400* (1740-1772), was rebuilt in the 19th century. Some sculpture by Aleijadinho can be seen in the main chapel.

Further east, **Nossa Senhora da Conceição** ① *Tue-Sat 0830-1130, 1330-1700, Sun 1200- 1700*, was built in 1722 and is the parish church of Antônio Dias (one of the original settlements that became Vila Rica de Albuquerque). It is heavily gilded and contains Aleijadinho's tomb. It has a **museum** devoted to him but with very few of his pieces. Be sure to see the exquisite miniature crucifixion on the basement floor. Across the river, the **Mina do Chico Rei** ① *R Dom Silvério, 0800-1700, US$1.50*, is not as impressive as some other mines in the area, but is fun to crawl about in and has a restaurant attached. The Chico Rei was supposedly an African king called Francisco, who was enslaved but bought his freedom working in the mine.

On the eastern edge of town, **Santa Efigênia** ① *Ladeira Santa Efigênia and Padre Faria, Tue-Sun 0800-1200*, built 1720-1785, has wonderful panoramic views of the city. This was a church used by black Brazilians only and the gilt that lines the interior is said to have been made from gold dust washed out of slaves' hair. Manuel Francisco Lisboa (Aleijadinho's father) oversaw the construction and much of the carving is by Francisco Xavier de Brito (Aleijadinho's mentor).

Around Ouro Preto

The town is dominated by a huge cross, easily reached from the road to Mariana, which affords lovely views of the sunset; but don't go alone as it's in a poor district.

The **Cachoeira das Andorinhas**, a waterfall north of town, is reached by taking a bus to Morro de Santana and then walking 25 minutes. To walk all the way takes 1½ hours. Near the waterfall it is possible to visit the **Zen Buddhist monastery** ① *apply in advance to Mosteiro Zen Pico de Rajos, Morro de São Sebastião, Caixa Postal 101, 35400-000, Ouro Preto, T31-3961 2484*. Excursions of 2½ hours are arranged at 0830 and 1430 visiting many cultural and ecological sites of interest.

Parque Estadual de Itacolomi and the Estação Ecológica do Tripuí are protected areas close to the city. The former (a three-hour walk from the centre, cars prohibited) includes the peak of Itacolomi, which the first gold prospectors used as a landmark, the source of the Rio Doce as well as endangered wildlife and splendid views. Tripuí is in the valley where the first gold was found; it protects a rare flatworm, *Peripatus acacioi*. It can also be reached on foot, or the bus to Belo Horizonte will drop you near the entrance.

Minas da Passagem

① T031-3557 5000, www.minasdapassagem.com.br, Mon and Tue 0900-1700, Wed-Sun 0900-1730, visits should be booked in advance.

The world's largest gold mine open to the public lies mid-way between Ouro Preto and Mariana. Its gloomy passages and clunking machinery date from 1719. A 20-minute guided tour visits the old mine workings and underground lake (take bathing suit). There is a waterfall too, the Cachoeira Serrinha, where swimming is possible; walk 100 m towards Mariana then ask for directions. There is also the opportunity to pan for gold on the tour. Note that some signs say 'Mina de Ouro', omitting 'da Passagem'.

The nearest town to the mine is Passagem de Mariana. The bus stops at the edge of town by the Pousada Solar dos Dois Sinos, which has a church behind it. Tours can be organized from hotels or agencies in town.

Mariana → *For listings, see pages 277-283. Colour map 4, C3. Phone code: 031. Population: 47,000. Altitude: 697 m.*

Mariana is the oldest of the colonial mining towns in Minas Gerais, founded by *bandeirantes* a few years before Ouro Preto, on 16 July 1696. At first, when it was little more than a collection of huts, it was called Arraial de Nossa Senhora do Carmo. But by 1711 it had become the town of Vila de Nossa Senhora do Carmo, and by the mid-18th century it had grown to be the most important administrative centre in the newly created Capitania de São Paulo e Minas do Ouro. Its name was changed to Mariana in honour of the wife of Dom João V, Dona Maria Ana of Austria. It retains many fine colonial buildings, most of them constructed in the second half of the 18th century. The artist Mestre Athayde was born here, as was the Inconfidênte Cláudio Manuel da Costa. The town was declared a national monument in 1945.

Unlike its more famous neighbour, Ouro Preto, in whose shadow the town tends to sit, Mariana has remained a working mining centre. For many years the Companhia do Vale do Rio Doce (CVRD), the state mining company, had major operations here and provided a great deal of assistance for the restoration of the colonial heritage. Since CVRD's concentration on its new investments at Carajás, and its subsequent privatization, there have been doubts about its commitment to mining in Mariana and to the town itself.

Ins and outs

Getting there Buses from Ouro Preto and Belo Horizonte stop at the *rodoviária*, out of town on the main road, then at the Posto Mariana, before heading back to the centre at Praça Tancredo Neves. Many buses seem to go only to the *posto* (petrol station) above the town, but it's a long walk from the centre. A bus from the *rodoviária* to the centre via the *posto* and Minas da Passagem costs US$1. Maria Fumaça steam trains run between Ouro Preto and Mariana. ▶▶ *See Transport, page 283.*

Tourist information The **tourist office** ① *Praça Tancredo Neves, T031-3557 9044, www.mariana.mg.gov.br,* can organize guides and has a map and free monthly booklet, *Mariana Agenda Cultural,* full of information. **Mariana Turismo** ① *R Direita 31,* is also helpful.

Sights

The historic centre of the town slopes gently uphill from the river and the **Praça Tancredo Neves**, where buses from Ouro Preto stop. The first street parallel with the Praça Tancredo

Mariana

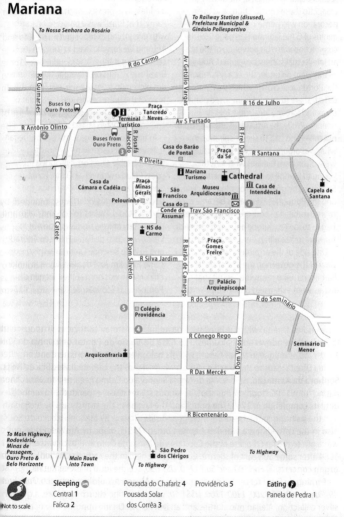

To Nossa Senhora do Rosário

To Railway Station (disused), Prefeitura Municipal & Ginásio Poliesportivo

R do Carmo

RA Guimarães

Av Getúlio Vargas

R 16 de Julho

Buses to Ouro Preto

Praça Tancredo Neves

Terminal Turístico

R Antônio Olinto

Av S Furtado

R Frei Durão

R Santana

Buses from Ouro Preto

R Josafá Macedo

Casa do Barão de Pontal

Praça da Sé

R Direita

Mariana Turismo

Cathedral

Casa da Cámara e Cadéia

Praça Minas Gerais

São Francisco

Museu Arquidiocesano

Casa de Intendência

Capela de Santana

Pelourinho

Casa do Conde de Assumar

Trav São Francisco

NS do Carmo

R Catete

R Dom Silvério

R Silva Jardim

R Barão de Camargo

Praça Gomes Freire

Palácio Arquiepiscopal

R do Seminário

R do Seminário

Colégio Providência

R Cônego Rego

R Dom Vicoso

Seminário Menor

Arquiconfraria

R Das Mercês

R Bicentenário

To Main Highway, Rodoviária, Minas de Passagem, Ouro Preto & Belo Horizonte

Main Route into Town

São Pedro dos Clérigos

To Highway

To Highway

Not to scale

Sleeping 🛏
Central 1
Faísca 2

Pousada do Chafariz 4
Pousada Solar
dos Corrêa 3

Providência 5

Eating 🍴
Panela de Pedra 1

Tiradentes and the Inconfidência Mineira

In the last quarter of the 18th century, Vila Rica de Nossa Senhora do Pilar do Ouro Preto was a dynamic place. Gold had brought great wealth to the city and this was translated into fine religious and secular buildings. Much of the artistry that went into these constructions and their decoration was home-grown, such as the genius of O Aleijadinho (see page 269). In conjunction with this flowering of the arts an intellectual society developed. And yet all this went on under the heavy hand of the Portuguese crown, which demanded its fifth share (the *quinto*), imposed punitive taxes and forbade local industries to operate. While the artists and artisans could not travel and had to seek inspiration in what was around them, the intellectuals were often from families who sent their young to Europe to further their education. So, when the gold yields began to decline and the Portuguese demands became even more exorbitant, some members of society began to look to Europe and North America for ways to free Minas Gerais from the crown.

One side of the argument was the view of the governor, the Visconde de Barbacena, who refused to admit that the mines were exhausted and that poverty was beginning to affect the community. As far as he was concerned, there was no gold because it was being smuggled out of the captaincy and there was no economic problem, just a large unpaid debt to the Portuguese crown. On the other side was the ideà, as expressed by the French poet Parny, that Brazil was a paradise on earth, with everything except liberty. The Jesuit Antônio Vieira, who lived in the previous century, put it thus: "the cloud swells in Brazil and it rains on Portugal; the water is not picked up from the sea, but from the tears of the unfortunate and the sweat of the poor, and I do not know how their faith and constancy has lasted so long."

In the late 1780s a group of people began to have secret discussions on how to resolve the intolerable situation. It included the poets Cláudio Manuel da Costa, Tomás Gonzaga and Ignacio de Alvarenga, the doctors Domingos Vidal Barbosa and José Alvares Maciel, Padres Toledo and Rolim and the military officers Domingos de Abreu Vieira, Francisco de Paula Freire de Andrade and José de Resende Costa. Into this group came Joaquim José da Silva Xavier, a junior officer, who was born at the Fazenda de Pombal near São João del Rei in about 1748.

Neves is Rua Direita, which is lined with beautiful, two-storey 18th-century houses with tall colonial windows and balconies. The **Casa do Barão de Pontal** ⓘ *R Direita 54, Tue 1400-1700*, is unique in Minas Gerais, with its balconies carved from soapstone.

Rua Direita leads to the **Praça da Sé**, on which stands the cathedral, **Basílica de Nossa Senhora da Assunção**. Before Vila de Nossa Senhora do Carmo became a town, a chapel dating from 1703 stood on this spot. In various stages it was expanded and remodelled until its completion in 1760. The portal and the lavabo in the sacristy are by Aleijadinho and the painting in the beautiful interior and side altars is by Manoel Rabello de Sousa. Also in the cathedral is a wooden German organ (1701), made by Arp Schnitger, which was a gift to the first diocese of the Capitania de Minas do Ouro in 1747. It was restored in 1984 after some 50 years of silence. Concerts are held in the cathedral including regular **organ concerts** ⓘ *Fri 1100 and Sun 1200, US$7.50*, see the local press for details.

Turning up Rua Frei Durão, on the right is the **Museu Arquidiocesano** ⓘ *R Frei Durão 49, Tue-Sun 0900-1200, 1300-1700, US$1.50*, which has fine church furniture, a gold and silver collection, Aleijadinho statues and an ivory cross. On the opposite side of the street

He was also a dentist and became known by the nickname Tiradentes – tooth-puller. Already dissatisfied with the way the army had treated him, by failing to promote him among other things, in 1788 he was suspended from active duty because of illness. The subsequent loss of pay roused him further. In trying to get reinstated he met Freire de Andrade and Alvares Maciel and later conversations prompted him to tell them of his idea of an uprising against the Portuguese. The Inconfidência grew out of these types of meeting, some planning action, others the future political and economic organization of a new, independent state.

The conspirators worked to gain support for their cause, but one soldier they approached, Coronel Joaquim Silverio dos Reis, used the information he had been given to betray the cause. The governor received reports from other sources and began to build up a picture of what was going on. Tiradentes was the first to be arrested, at the beginning of May 1789, in Rio de Janeiro. It seems that the plotters at this time still had no clear idea of what their ultimate aim was, nor of the importance of their attitudes. They never got the chance

anyway because all were arrested soon after Tiradentes. They were imprisoned and kept incommunicado for two years while the case against them was prepared. Tiradentes was singled out as the most important member of the group and, under questioning, he did not disabuse his captors, taking full responsibility for everything. A defence for the Inconfidêntes was prepared, but it almost totally ignored Tiradentes, as if he were being made a scapegoat. It made no difference, though, because the defence lost; 11 Inconfidêntes were sentenced to death in November 1791. Soon afterwards the authorities in Brazil read out a surprising letter from the queen, Dona Maria I, commuting the death sentence for 10 of the conspirators to exile in Portugal or Africa. The 11th, Tiradentes, was not spared. On 21 April 1792 he was hanged and his body was quartered and his head cut off, the parts to de displayed as a warning against any similar attempts to undermine the crown. Even though Tiradentes would never have been freed, one of the astonishing things about the queen's letter was that it was dated 18 months before it was brought to light.

the **Casa da Intendência/Casa de Cultura** ⓘ *R Frei Durão 84, 0800-1130, 1330-1700,* which holds exhibitions and has a museum of music. The ceilings in the exhibition rooms are very fine; in other rooms there are *esteiro* (flattened bamboo) ceilings.

The large **Praça Gomes Freire** was where horses would be tied up (there is an old drinking trough on one side) and where festivals were held. Now it has pleasant gardens. On the south side is the **Palácio Arquiepiscopal**, while on the north side is the **Casa do Conde de Assumar**, home of the governor of the capitania from 1717 to 1720; it later became the bishop's palace.

Praça Minas Gerais has one of the finest groups of colonial buildings in Brazil. In the middle is the **Pelourinho**, the stone monument to justice at which slaves used to be beaten. The fine **São Francisco church** ⓘ *daily 0800-1700,* built 1762-1794, has pulpits, a fine sacristy and an altar designed by Aleijadinho, and paintings by Mestre Athayde, who is buried in tomb No 94. The statue of São Roque is most important as he is the patron saint of the city (his day is 16 August). Among Athayde's paintings are the panels showing the life of St Francis, on the ceiling of the right-hand chapel. The church is one of the most simple in Mariana but, in terms of art, one of the richest. There is a small exhibition of the restoration work funded by CVRD.

At right angles to São Francisco is **Nossa Senhora do Carmo** ① *daily 1400-1700*, built 1784, with steatite carvings, Athayde paintings, and chinoiserie panelling. Some consider its exterior to be the most beautiful in Mariana. Unfortunately this church was damaged by fire in 1999. Across Rua Dom Silvério is the **Casa da Cámara e Cadéia** (1768), once the Prefeitura Municipal. It is a superb example of civic colonial construction.

On Rua Dom Silvério the **Colégio Providência** at No 61 was the first college for boarding students in Minas Gerais. Also on this street is the **Igreja da Arquiconfraria** and, near the top of the hill, the **Chafariz de São Pedro**. On Largo de São Pedro is the church of **São Pedro dos Clérigos**, founded by Manuel da Cruz, first bishop of the town (1764), one of the few elliptical churches in Minas Gerais. It is unadorned, although there is a painting by Athayde, *A Entrega do Menino Jesus a Santo António*. The cedar altar was made by José Pedro Aroca. Look for the cockerel, carved in memory of the biblical verses about St Peter betraying Christ before the cock has crowed three times. Ask to see the view from the bell tower.

The **Capela de Santo António**, wonderfully simple and the oldest in town, is some distance from the centre on Rua Rosário Velho. Overlooking the city from the north, with a good viewpoint, is the church of **Nossa Senhora do Rosário** ① *R do Rosário*, dating back to 1752, with work by Athayde and showing Moorish influence.

Outside the centre to the west, but within easy walking distance, is the **Seminário Menor**, now the Instituto de Ciencias Históricas e Sociais of the federal university.

South of the river, Avenida Getúlio Vargas leads to the new **Prefeitura Municipal**. It passes the **Ginásio Poliesportivo** and, across the avenue, the **railway station**. This is a romantic building with a clock tower, but it is rapidly falling into disrepair.

Around Mariana

The small village of **Antônio Pereira**, 24 km north of Mariana, is where imperial topaz i mined. Tours can be made of an interesting cave with stalactites. Local children will show you around for a small fee. ▶▶ *See Transport, page 283.*

Congonhas do Campo → *For listings, see pages 277-283. Colour map 4, C3. Phone code: 031* *Population: 42,000. Altitude: 866 m.*

In the 18th century, Congonhas was a mining town. Today, in addition to the busines brought by the tourists and pilgrims who come to the sanctuary, it is known for it handicrafts. There is little need to stay in Congonhas as the town's main sigh Aleijadinho's beautiful church and chapel-lined stairway, can be seen in a few hour between bus changes. Leave your bags at the information desk in the bus station.

Ins and outs

Getting there The *rodoviária* is 1.5 km outside town; a bus to the centre costs US$0.40. town, the bus stops in Praça JK from where you can walk up Praça Dr Mário Rodrigu Pereira, cross the little bridge, then go up Rua Bom Jesus and Rua Aleijadinho to the Pra da Basílica. A bus marked 'Basílica' runs every 30 minutes from the *rodoviária* to Bo Jesus, 5 km, US$0.45. A taxi from the *rodoviária* will cost US$5 one-way, US$10 retu including the wait while you visit the sanctuary.

O Aleijadinho

Brazil's greatest sculptor, Antônio Francisco Lisboa (1738-1814), son of a Portuguese architect and a black slave woman, was known as O Aleijadinho (the little cripple). A debilitating disease – probably leprosy – left him so badly maimed that he was forced to work on his knees and later on his back with his chisels strapped to his useless hands. Like Mestre Athayde and many other Mineira baroque artists his art was political. He was strongly sympathetic with the Inconfidêntes movement and was probably a friend of Tiradentes. Many of his sculptures contain subtle references to Tiradentes's martyrdom and veiled criticisms of the Portuguese. His most remarkable works are the haunting, vivid statues of the prophets in Congonhas (which are so lifelike that they almost seem to move), and the church decoration in Ouro Preto.

Tourist information Fumcult ① *in the Romarias, T031-3731 1300 ext 114*, acts as the tourist office and is very helpful. On the hill are a tourist kiosk, souvenir shops, the **Colonial Hotel** and **Cova do Daniel** restaurant. There are public toilets on the Alameda das Palmeiras.

O Santuário de Bom Jesus de Matosinhos

① *Tue-Sun 0700-1900. No direct bus from Congonhas do Campo or Rio to the sanctuary; change at the town of Conselheiro Lafaiete, from where there is a frequent service, US$1.*

The great pilgrimage church and its Via Sacra dominate the town. The idea of building a sanctuary belonged to a prospector, Feliciano Mendes, who promised to erect a cross and chapel in thanks to Bom Jesus after he had been cured of a serious illness. The inspiration for his devotion came from two sources in Portugal, the cult of Bom Jesus at Braga (near where Mendes was born) and the church of Bom Jesus de Matosinhos, near Porto. Work began in 1757, funded by Mendes' own money and alms he raised. The church was finished in 1771, six years after Mendes' death, and the fame that the sanctuary had acquired led to its development by the most famous architects, artists and sculptors of the time as a Sacro Monte. This involved the construction of six linked chapels, or *pasos* (1802-1818), which lead up to a terrace and courtyard before the church.

There is a wide view of the country from the church terrace, below which are six small chapels set in an attractive sloping area with grass, cobblestones and palms. Each chapel shows scenes with life-size Passion figures carved by Aleijadinho and his pupils in cedar wood. In order of ascent they are: the chapel of the Last Supper; the chapel of the Mount of Olives; the chapel of the betrayal of Christ; the chapel of the flagellation and the crowning with thorns; the chapel of Jesus carrying the Cross; and the chapel of Christ being nailed to the Cross.

On the terrace stand the 12 prophets sculpted by Aleijadinho 1800-1805; these are thought of as his masterpieces. Carved in soapstone with a dramatic sense of movement, they constitute one of the finest works of art of their period in the world. Note how Aleijadinho adapted the biblical characters to his own cultural references. The prophets are sculpted wearing leather boots, as all important men in his time would have done. Daniel, who entered the lion's den, is represented with the artist's own conception of a lion, never having seen one himself: a large, maned cat with a face rather like a Brazilian monkey. Similarly, the whale that accompanies Jonah is an idiosyncratic interpretation. Each statue has a prophetic text carved with it. The statues "combine in a kind of sacred ballet whose movements only seem uncoordinated; once these sculptures cease to be considered as isolated units, they take

nce as part of a huge composition brought to life by an inspired genius."
n Baroque, edited by Henri Stierlin) The beauty of the whole is enhanced by
of church, Via Sacra and landscape over which the prophets preside.

urch, there are paintings by Athayde and the heads of four sainted popes
rome, Ambrose and Augustine) sculpted by Aleijadinho for the reliquaries on
the high altar. Other artists involved were João Nepomuceno Correia e Castro, who painted
the scenes of the life and passion of Christ in the nave and around the high altar, João
Antunes de Carvalho, who carved the high altar, and Jerônimo Félix and Manuel Coelho
who carved the crossing altars of Santo António and São Francisco de Paula. Despite the
ornate carving, the overall effect of the paintwork is almost muted and naturalistic, with
much use of blues, greys and pinks. Lamps are suspended on chains from the mouths of black
dragons. To the left of the church, through the third door in the building alongside the church
is the Room of Miracles, which contains photographs and thanks for miracles performed.

Up on the hill, the Alameda das Palmeiras sweeps from the **Hotel Colonial** round to the
Romarias, a large, almost oval area surrounded by buildings. This was the lodging where
the pilgrims stayed. It now contains the **Espaço Cultural** and tourist office, as well as
workshops, the museums of mineralogy and religious art, and the **Memória da Cidade**.

Of the other churches in Congonhas do Campo, the oldest is **Nossa Senhora do Rosário**,
Praça do Rosário, built by slaves at the end of the 17th century. The **Igreja Matriz de Nossa
Senhora da Conceição**, in Praça 7 de Setembro, dates from 1749; the portal is attributed to
Aleijadinho, while parts of the interior are by Manuel Francisco Lisboa. There are also two
18th-century chapels, **Nossa Senhora da Ajuda**, in the district of Alto Maranhão, and the
church at **Lobo Leite**, 10 km away.

Tiradentes → *For listings, see pages 277-283. Colour map 4, C3. Phone code: 032. Population: 600*

Aside from Ouro Preto, Tiradentes is the most visited of the Minas colonial towns. Its
winding, hilly streets lined with carefully restored baroque Portuguese churches and near
whitewashed cottages huddle around the Santo Antonio river, beneath the rugged hills of
the Serra de São José. Inside are art galleries, restaurants, souvenir shops and *pousadas*, all
busy with tourists even during the week. Horse-drawn carriages clatter along the cobble
and at weekends a steam train towing Pullmans full of delighted children puffs its way
slowly below the mountains to the pretty colonial town of **São João del Rei** (see page 273).

Ins and outs

Tiradentes and São João del Rei lie within less than 30 minutes of each other and buses
leave every 30 to 40 minutes. Tiradentes is the more twee; São João is uglier but more of a
real town. Tiradentes has a far greater choice of accommodation. São João has better bus
connections with Rio, São Paulo, Belo Horizonte, Mariana and Ouro Preto. The **touri**
office ① *R Resende Costa 71*, is in the *prefeitura*.

Sights

A suggested walking tour is as follows. From the main *praça*, **Largo das Forras**, take R
Resende Costa up to the Largo do Sol, a lovely open space where you'll find the simpl
church of **São João Evangelista** ① *Wed-Mon 0900-1700*. Built by the *Irmandade d*
Homens Pardos (mulattos), it has paintings of the four Evangelists and a cornice painted
an elaborate pattern in pink, blue and beige. Beside the church is the **Museu Padre Toled**
the house of this leader of the Inconfidência Mineira, which is now a museum protecti

some handsome colonial furniture and a painted roof depicting the Five Senses. The **Casa de Cultura** in the row of 18th-century houses on Rua Padre Toledo, which leads from Largo do Sol to the Igreja Matriz de Santo Antônio, is protected by the same organization.

The **Igreja Matriz de Santo Antônio** ① *daily 0900-1700, US$1, no photography*, first built in 1710 and enlarged in 1736, contains some of the finest gilded woodcarvings in the country. The main church is predominantly white and gold. Lamps hang from the beaks of golden eagles. The symbols on the panels painted on the ceiling of the nave are a mixture of Old Testament and medieval Christian symbolism (for instance the phoenix, and the pelican). A carved wooden balustrade separates the seating in the nave from richly carved side chapels and altars. The principal altar is also ornately decorated, as are the walls and ceiling around it. The church has a small but fine organ brought from Porto in the 1790s. The upper part of the reconstructed façade is said to follow a design by Aleijadinho. In front of the church, on the balustrade which overlooks the main street and the town, are also a cross and a sundial by him.

From Santo Antônio, it is well worth taking a detour up to the **Santuário da Santíssima Trindade**. The chapel itself is 18th century while the Room of Miracles associated with the annual Trinity Sunday pilgrimage is modern.

Heading back down past Santo Antônio along Rua da Câmara, you come to the **Casa da Câmara e Antigo Fórum**. Here the road divides, the left-hand street, Jogo de Bola, leads to the Largo do Ó (which rejoins the main street), while Rua da Câmara goes to the crossroads with Rua Direita. At this junction is the **Sobrado Ramalho**, said to be the oldest building in Tiradentes. It is believed to be where the gold was melted down, and contains many soapstone carvings. It has been beautifully restored as a cultural centre.

Before taking Rua Direita back to Largo das Forras, carry straight on towards the river and cross the bridge to the magnificent **Chafariz de São José** (public fountain), installed in 1749. The water is brought by a stone aqueduct from springs in the forest at the foot of Serra São José. It is still used for drinking, washing and watering animals.

Rua Direita has some interesting old buildings. The charming **Nossa Senhora do Rosário** ① *Praça Padre Lourival, Wed-Mon 1200-1600, US$0.50*, has fine statuary and ornate gilded altars. On its painted ceiling colonnades rise to heaven; two monks stand on a hill and the Virgin and Child are in the sky. Other ceiling panels depicting the life of Christ are in poor shape. The church contains statues of black saints, including São Benedito, patron saint of cooks; in one of the statues he is holding a squash. The church dates from 1727, but building by the 'Irmandade dos Pretos Cativos' (black slave brotherhood) began as early as 1708.

Opposite Praça Padre Lourival, is the **Antiga Cadeia** (18th-19th century) which now contains the **Museu de Arta Sacra**. Rua Direita meets the Largo das Forras at the **Prefeitura Municipal**, a two-storey building with an extra room under the roof. It now houses the tourist, post and phone offices.

If you have any energy left, there are other churches and chapels in the town, including the **Igreja de Bom Jesus da Pobreza**, on the Largo das Forras. Across the river, the 18th-century **Nossa Senhora das Mercês** ① *Largo das Mercês, Sun 0900-1700*, has an interesting painted ceiling and a notable statue of the Virgin. On the grassy Morro de São Francisco is the small chapel of **São Francisco de Paula** (mid-18th century).

Excursions from Tiradentes

The **steam trains** ① *Fri-Sun and holidays, 1000 and 1415 from São João del Rei, returning from Tiradentes at 1300 and 1700, US$8*, which run on the 76-cm gauge track between São

João del Rei and Tiradentes (13 km) have been in continuous operation since 1881 – a testament to the durability of the rolling stock and locomotives made by the Baldwin Company of Philadelphia. The maximum speed is 20 kph. To get to the railway station from the centre of the village you have to cross the river and head out of town on the Rua dos Inconfidêntes. Follow this road until it becomes the Rua Antônio Teixeira Carvalho, which carries on to the bridge over the Rio das Mortes. On the opposite bank is a small park and the station. For the railway museum at the railway station in São João del Rei, see page 275.

A recommended walk from Tiradentes is to the protected forest on the **Serra de São José**. The easiest access is from behind the Chafariz, where a black door in the wall is opened at 0730 (Wednesday to Sunday). In just five minutes you are in the forest following the watercourse, where monkeys and birds can be seen. Alternatively, you can walk up into the **Serra** from behind the Mercês Church; ask for directions. It is recommended that you take a guide if you wish to walk along the top of the Serra.

There is a good one- or two-hour walk from Tiradentes to the **Balneário de Águas Santas**, which involves crossing the Serra. At the *balneário* is a swimming pool, a lake and a *churrascaria*, **Senzala**. A map can be obtained from the **Solar da Ponte**, or ask locally for directions (taxi US$15). On the way you pass **Parque Frei Mariano Vellozo**, which contains the Cachoeira do Mangue falls. It is busy at weekends and can be reached by car on the old road to São João.

Tiradentes

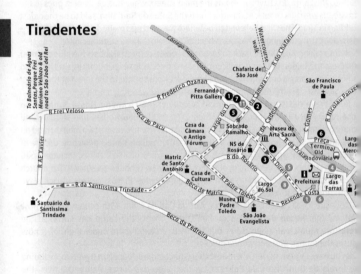

N

| 200 metres |
| 200 yards |

Sleeping
Ponto do Morro **1**
Porão Colonial **2**
Pousada do Alferes **3**
Pousada do Arco Iris **11**

Pousada do Largo **4**
Pousada do Laurito **5**
Pousada Mãe d'Água **6**
Pousada Maria Bonita **7**
Pousada Três Portas **8**

Pouso das Gerais **10**
Solar da Ponte **9**

Eating
Aluarte **1**

São João del Rei lies at the foot of the Serra do Lenheiro, astride what once must have been a winding little stream. This has now sadly been transformed into a concrete gutter with grass verges. Eighteenth-century bridges cross the stream leading to streets lined with colonial buildings and plazas with crumbling churches, the most interesting and best preserved of which is the church of **São Francisco**. The town feels far less of a tourist museum piece than nearby Tiradentes. There is a lively music scene, with two renowned orchestras and an annual arts festival in July, and the bars are filled with locals rather than tourists waiting for their coach. There is a good view of the town and surroundings from **Alto da Boa Vista**, where there is a **Senhor dos Montes** (Statue of Christ).

São João del Rei is famous as the home of Tiradentes and of Tancredo Neves. The former was born in the **Fazenda de Pombal**, about 15 km downstream from Tiradentes on the Rio das Mortes. After his execution, the *fazenda* was confiscated. It is now an experimental station owned by **Instituto Chico Mendes de Conservação da Biodiversidade (ICMBio)**. Tancredo Neves, to whom there is a memorial in the town, was the man who would have become the first civilian president of Brazil after the military dictatorships of the mid-20th century, had he not mysteriously died before taking office.

los Inconfidentes ⑩
Sílvio
Ooncelos
R. de Moraes ② ③
Antônio Carvalho ⑦
Henrique Diniz
Rio Das Mortes
Praça
da Estação
To Train Station & São João del Rei

alagem **2**
aria Luisa Casa de Chá **7**
artier Latin **6**
into de Ouro **4**
eatro da Vila **3**

Virados do Largo **5**

Walking tour - - ▶ - -

Ins and outs

The *rodoviária*, 2 km west of the centre, has a telephone office, toilets, luggage store, *lanchonetes* and a tourist office. São João is a good base for visiting Tiradentes (or vice versa); less than 30 minutes away by bus or an hour away at weekends via one of Brazil's most memorable steam train rides.

Many streets seem to have more than one name, which can be a little confusing, but as the town centre is not large, it is hard to get lost. One such street crosses the Ponte da Cadeia from Rua Passos; it has three names: Rua da Intendência, Manoel Anselmo and Artur Bernardes. The **Secretaria de Turismo** ① *in the house of Bárbara Heliodora, T032-3372 7338, open 0900-1700*, provides a free map.

Sights

The Córrego do Lenheiro, a stream with steep grassy banks, runs through the centre of town. Across it are two fine, stone bridges, **A Ponte da Cadeia** (1798) and **A Ponte do Rosário** (1800), as well as several other modern bridges. Both sides of the river have colonial monuments, which are interspersed with modern buildings.

On the north side are many streets with pleasant houses, but in various states of repair. **Rua Santo Antônio** has many single-storey eclectic houses from the imperial period, which have been restored and painted. **Rua Santo Elias** has several buildings all in the same style. Behind the church of Nossa Senhora do Pilar (see below), the **Largo da Câmara** leads up to **Mercês church**, which has quite a good view. Throughout the city you will see locked portals with colonial porticos. These are *passinhos*, shrines that are opened in Holy Week. They can be seen on **Largo da Cruz** and **Largo do Rosário**.

São Francisco de Assis ① *Praça Frei Orlando, Tue-Sun 0830-1700, US$1*, built 1774, is one of the most beautiful churches in Brazil. Although often attributed to Aleijadinho, it was designed and decorated by two almost completely undocumented artists, Francisco de Lima Cerqueira and Aniceto de Souza Lopes (who also sculpted the Pelourinho in the Largo da Câmara). The magnificent but modest whitewash and stone façade sits between two cylindrical bell towers and is decorated with an ornately carved door frame and a

São João del Rei

Sleeping
Aparecida 1
Beco do Bispo 6
Brasil 2
Lenheiro Palace 4
Ponte Real 5
Pousada Casarão 3
Pousada São Benedito 7
Sinha Batista 8

Eating
611 4
Chafariz 3
Churrascaria Ramón 1
Quinto do Ouro 2

superb medal of St Francis receiving illumination. The *praça* in front is shaped like a lyre and, in the late afternoon, the royal palms cast shadows that interconnect to form the lyre's strings. The six carved altars inside have been restored, revealing fine carving in sucupira wood. Their artistry is wonderful and the three pairs of altars mirror each other, each pair in a different style (note the use of pillars and the different paintings that accompany each altar). The overall shape of the nave is elliptical, the gold altar has spiralling columns and an adoring St Francis kneels atop.

The cathedral, **Basílica de Nossa Senhora do Pilar** ① *R Getúlio Vargas (formerly R Direita), daily 1000-1600*, was built in 1721, but has a 19th-century façade which replaced the 18th-century original. It has rich altars and a brightly painted ceiling (Madonna and Child in the middle, saints and bishops lining the sides). Note the androgynous gold heads and torsos within the eight columns set into the walls either side of the main altar. There is a profusion of cherubs and plants in the carving. This abundance and angelic innocence contrasts with the suffering of the Passion and the betrayal of the Last Supper (two pictures of which are before the altar), all common themes in Brazilian baroque. In the sacristy are portraits of the Evangelists.

The **Memorial Tancredo Neves** ① *R Padre José Maria Xavier 7, Wed-Fri 1300-1800, weekends and holidays 0900-1700, US$1*, is a homage to the man and his life. A short video on São João del Rei is shown. It also holds exhibitions and has a bookshop.

The **Museu Ferroviário (Railway Museum)** ① *Av Hermílio Alves 366, T032-371 8004, US$0.50*, is well worth exploring. The museum traces the history of railways in general and in Brazil in brief. There is an informative display of the role of Irineu Evangelista de Souza, Barão de Mauá, who was a pioneer of both industry and the railways following his visit to England in 1840. The locomotive that ran on the first railway from Rio de Janeiro to the foot of the Serra do Mar was called 'A Baronesa' after his wife. The railway to São João, the Estrada de Ferro Oeste de Minas, was not a success, but it was instrumental in the development of the region. In the museum is an 1880 Baldwin 4-4-0 locomotive from Philadelphia (No 5055) and a 1912-1913 VIP carriage, both still used on the steam journey to Tiradentes. Outside, at the end of the platforms are carriages and a small Orenstein and Koppel (Berlin) engine. You can walk along the tracks to the round house, where there are several working engines in superb condition, an engine shed and a steam-operated machine shop, still working. It is here that the engines get up steam before going to couple with the coaches for the run to Tiradentes. On days when the trains are running, you can get a good, close-up view of operations even if not taking the trip. Highly recommended. For the steam train to Tiradentes, see page 271.

Sabará → *For listings, see pages 277-283. Colour map 4, B3. Phone code: 031. Population: 116,000.*

Some 23 km east of Belo Horizonte is the colonial gold-mining (and steel-making) town of Sabará. The town is strung along the narrow steep valleys of the Rio das Velhas and Rio Sabará. Since the late 17th century, the Rio das Velhas was known as a gold-bearing river and a community soon grew up there. By 1702 it was the most populous in Minas Gerais. In 1711, the name Villa Real de Nossa Senhora da Conceição de Sabará was given to the parish and in 1838 it became the city of Sabará.

Ins and outs

There are regular buses from Belo Horizonte, US$0.75, 30 minutes. If travelling by car, there is a road, mostly unpaved, that runs to Sabará from Ravena on the BR-381 Belo

Horizonte–Vitória highway, which crosses the hills and is a pleasant drive. Tourist information is available from the **Secretaria de Turismo** ① *R Pedro II 200, T031-3671 1522. Passeio a Sabará*, by Lúcia Machado de Almeida, with splendid illustrations by Guignard, is an excellent guide to the town.

Sights

There are a number of old churches, fountains, rambling cobbled streets and simple houses with carved doors of great interest. From the bus terminus, walk up Rua Clemente Faria to Praça Santa Rita, where there's a large *chafariz* (fountain). The square adjoins Rua Dom Pedro II, which is lined with beautiful 18th-century buildings. They include the **Solar do Padre Correa** ① *R Dom Pedro II 200* (1773), now the Prefeitura, a mansion with a rococo chapel and *salão nobre* (main reception room); the **Casa Azul** ① *R Dom Pedro II 215*, (1773), now the INSS building, with a chapel and a fine portal; and the **Teatro Municipal**, former opera house, built in 1770 and the second oldest in Brazil. It has a superb interior, with three balconies, a carved wooden rail before the orchestra pit, wooden floors and *esteiro* (flattened, woven bamboo) ceilings.

At the top of Rua Dom Pedro II is the Praça Melo Viana, in the middle of which is **Nossa Senhora do Rosário dos Pretos** ① *Tue-Sun 0800-1100, 1300-1700*, left unfinished at the time of the slaves' emancipation. Behind the façade of the building are the chancel, sacristy (both 1780) and the first chapel (1713). There is a museum of religious art in the church. To the right of the church is the **Chafariz do Rosário**. Also on the *praça* are the ornate Fórum Ministro Orozimbo Nonato and two schools. From Praça Melo Viana, take Rua São Pedro to the church of **São Francisco** (1781); beyond the church is the **Chafariz Kaquende**.

In Rua da Intendência is the museum of 18th-century gold mining, the **Museu do Ouro** ① *Tue-Sun 1200-1730, US$1*. It contains exhibits of gold extraction, as well as religious items and colonial furniture. The building itself is a fine example of colonial architecture. Sources disagree as to its date of construction, but the general view is that it was before 1730. Originally the foundry, it became the Casa da Intendência in 1735. For most of the 19th century it was abandoned and became the gold museum in 1945.

Another fine example of civil colonial architecture is the **Casa Borba Gato** ① *R Borba Gato 71*, so called because tradition has it that it belonged to the famous *bandeirante*, Manoel de Borba Gato, one of the first to settle on the Rio das Velhas, but exiled from the region after the murder of the king's representative, Rodrigo de Castel Blanco in 1682. The building currently belongs to the Museu do Ouro.

On Rua do Carmo is the church of **Nossa Senhora do Carmo** ① *US$1, leaflet provided* (1763-1774), with doorway, pulpits and choir loft by Aleijadinho and paintings by Athayde From the ceilings, painted blue and grey and gold, religious figures look down surrounding the Virgin and Child and the Chariot of Fire. In the chancel, the Ten Commandments in blue work have a distinctly Moorish air, what with the tents and the night-time scenes.

Similar in style externally is the **Capela de Nossa Senhora do Pilar**, which is beside the municipal cemetery and in front of a large building with blue gates and doors.

Nossa Senhora da Conceição ① *Praça Getúlio Vargas, free* (1720), has a lot of visible woodwork and a beautiful floor. The carvings have a great deal of gilding, there are painted panels, and paintings by 23 Chinese artists brought from Macau. The clearest Chinese work is on the two red doors to the right and left of the chancel.

Nossa Senhora do Ó, built in 1717 and showing unmistakable Chinese influence (paintings in need of restoration), is 2 km from the centre of the town at the Largo Nossa Senhora do Ó. To get there, take the local bus marked 'Esplanada' or 'Boca Grande'.

If you walk up the **Morro da Cruz** hill from the **Hotel do Ouro** to a small chapel, the **Capela da Cruz**, or Senhor Bom Jesus, you can get a wonderful view of the whole region. Look for beautiful quartz crystals while you are up there.

Excursions from Sabará

Some 25 km from Sabará and 60 km from Belo Horizonte is **Caeté**. The town, originally called Vila Nova da Rainha, has several historical buildings and churches. On the Praça João Pinheiro are the **Prefeitura** and **Pelourinho** (both 1722), the **Igreja Matriz Nossa Senhora do Com Sucesso** ① *daily 1300-1800* (1756, rebuilt 1790) and the **Chafariz da Matriz**. Also on the *praça* is the **tourist information office** ① *Casa da Cultura, T031-3651 1855*. Other churches are **Nossa Senhora do Rosário** (1750-1768), with a ceiling attributed to Mestre Athayde, and **São Francisco de Assis**. The **Museu Regional** ① *R Israel Pinheiro 176, Tue-Sun 1200-1700*, in the house of the Barão de Catas Altas, or Casa Setecentista, contains 18th- and 19th-century religious art and furniture. The house itself is a fine example of 18th-century civic architecture, with two floors and an interior patio. From Caeté you can go to the **Serra da Piedade** mountains.

⊙ Colonial cities near Belo Horizonte listings

For Sleeping and Eating price codes and other relevant information, see pages 32-37.

⊖ Sleeping

Ouro Preto *p258, map p260*
Many hotels will negotiate lower prices off season. Ask at the tourist office for reasonably priced accommodation in *casas de família*. Avoid touts who greet you off buses and charge higher prices than those advertised in hotels; it is difficult to get hotel rooms at weekends and holiday periods. Rooms can be booked through www.ouropretotour.com or www.ouropreto.com.

AL Grande Hotel, R das Flores 164, Centro T031-3551 1488, www.grandehotelouro preto.com.br. One of a handful of gorgeous Niemeyer hotels dotted throughout Minas, newly restored and with views over the city.

A Pousada do Mondego, Largo de Coimbra 38, T031-3551 2040, www.mondego.com.br. Beautifully kept colonial house in a fine location by São Francisco Church, room rates vary according to view, small restaurant, Scotch bar, popular with groups. Recommended (a **Roteiros de Charme** hotel, see page 34), the hotel runs a *jardineira* bus

tour of the city, 2 hrs, minimum 10 passengers, US$18 for non-guests.

A Pousada Solar de NS do Rosário, Av Getúlio Vargas 270, T031-3551 5200, www.hotelsolardorosario.com.br. Fully restored historic building with a highly recommended restaurant, bar, sauna, pool; all facilities in rooms.

B Luxor Pousada, R Dr Alfredo Baeta 16, Praça Antônio Dias, T031-3551 2244, www.luxorhoteis.com.br. Converted colonial mansion, no twin beds, comfortable and clean but spartan, good views, restaurant good but service slow.

C Pousada Casa Grande, R Conselheiro Quintiliano 96, T/F031-3551 4314, www.hotelpousadacasagrande.com.br. A large colonial town house with 21 smart, but simply appointed rooms with polished wooden floors, en suites and some with views out over the city.

D Colonial, Trav Padre Camilo Veloso 26, close to Praça Tiradentes, T031-3551 3133, www.hotelcolonial.com.br. A little colonial house with 14 rooms. All are well maintained. Some are distinctly smaller than others so it is worth looking at a few. Decor is modest, with furniture sitting on a polished wooden floor.

D Pousada Itacolomi, R Antônio Pereira 167, T031-3551 2891, www.pousadaita colomi.com.br. Small but well kept with good rates for the 3-room apartments. Recommended. Next door to the Museu da Inconfidência.

D Pousada Nello Nuno, R Camilo de Brito 59, T031-3551 3375, www.pousadanello nuno.com.br. The cheaper rooms have no bath. The friendly owner, Annamélia, speaks some French. Highly recommended.

D Pousada Tiradentes, Praça Tiradentes 70, T031-3551 2619, www.pousadatiradentesop. com.br. The rooms are spartan but well kept and moderately comfortable. Each has a TV, fridge. Conveniently located.

D Pouso Chico Rei, R Brig Musqueira 90, T031-3551 1274, www.pousodochicorei. com.br. A fascinating old house with Portuguese colonial furnishings, very small and utterly delightful, book in advance (room No 6 has been described as a 'dream').

D Solar das Lajes, R Conselheiro Quintiliano 604, T/F031-3551 1116, www.hotelsolardas lajes.com.br. A little way from the centre but with an excellent view and a pool. Well run.

E Pousada dos Bandeirantes, R das Mercês 167, T031-3551 1996, www.hotelpousada bandeirantes.com.br. Behind the São Francisco de Assis Church and offering beautiful views.

E Pousada São Francisco de Paula, R Pe José Marcos Pena 202, next to the São Francisco de Paula church, T031-3551 3456, www.pousadasaofranciscodepaula.com.br. One of the best views of any in the city; from the rooms or from a hammock in the garden. Services and facilities include the free use of a kitchen, multilingual staff, excursions. The hostel has 8 rustic rooms including a dormitory, which come with or without a simple breakfast, private or communal bathrooms. Full breakfasts and snacks are available, 100 m from the *rodoviária*. Recommended.

F Brumas, R Pe José Marcos Pena 68, T031-3551 2944, www.brumashostel.com.br. 150 m downhill from *rodoviária*, just below São Francisco de Paula church. Dormitory, kitchen and laundry and superb views. Don't walk down from the bus station after dark.

Student hostels
During holidays and weekends students may be able to stay at the self-governing hostels, known as *repúblicas* (described as very welcoming, 'best if you like heavy metal music' and 'are prepared to enter into the spirit of the place'). The *prefeitura* has a list of over 50 *repúblicas* with phone numbers, available at the **Secretaria de Turismo**. Many are closed between Christmas and Carnaval.

Camping
Camping Clube do Brasil, Rodovia dos Inconfidêntes, Km 91, 2 km north, T031-3551 1799. Quite expensive but very nice.

Mariana *p264, map p265*
Most of these hotels are housed in colonial buildings. Further details can be found on www.mariana.mg.gov.br.

C Faísca, R Antônio Olinto 48, T031-3557 1206. Up the street from the tourist office. Suites and rooms, breakfast included.

C Pousada Solar dos Corrêa, R Josefá Macedo 70 and R Direita, T/F031-3557 2080. A restored 18th-century townhouse with spacious a/c rooms.

D Pousada do Chafariz, R Cônego Rego 149, T031-3557 1492, www.pousadado chafariz.hpg.com.br. A converted colonial building with parking, breakfast and a family atmosphere. Recommended.

D Providência, R Dom Silvério 233, T031-3557 1444. Has use of the neighbouring school's pool when classes finish at noon.

D-E Central, R Frei Durão 8, T/F031-3557 1630. A charming but run-down colonial building on the Praça Gomes Freire. Recommended but avoid the downstairs rooms.

Congonhas do Campo *p268*
C Colonial, Praça da Basílica 76, opposite Bom Jesus, T031-3731 1834, www.hotel colonialcongonhas.com.br. This converted

colonial townhouse is in a superb location right next to the sanctuário at the top top of the hill. Rooms are spacious but can be noisy. Breakfast extra, cheaper without bath. Fascinating restaurant, **Cova do Daniel**, downstairs is full of colonial handicrafts and good local food.

D Freitas, R Marechal Floriano 69, T031-3731 1543. Basic, with breakfast, cheaper without bath.

Tiradentes *p270, map p272*

Prices drop in the more expensive hotels Sun-Thu. www.tiradentesturismo.com.br has details and pictures of many of the *pousadas*.

AL Solar da Ponte, Praça das Mercês, T032-3355 1255, www.solardaponte.com.br. The atmosphere of a country house, run by John and Anna Maria Parsons, the price includes breakfast and afternoon tea, only 12 rooms, fresh flowers, bar, sauna, lovely gardens, swimming pool, light meals for residents only. Highly recommended (it is in the Roteiros de Charme group, see page 34).

B Pousada Mãe D'Água, Largo das Forras 50, T032-3355 1206. One of the larger *pousadas*, with an outdoor pool set in a small garden, sauna, pool room and a/c rooms. Price includes breakfast.

B Pousada Três Portas, R Direita 280A, T032-3355 1444. Charming central hotel in a restored town house with 8 rooms and a suite. Facilities include a heated indoor pool, sauna and room service. Great for couples.

B-C Pouso das Gerais, R dos Inconfidêntes 109, T032-3355 1234, www.pousodasgerais. hpg.com.br. Spotless, fresh fan-cooled rooms with parquet flooring, desk, TV and marble basins in the bathrooms. Central, quiet, pool and breakfast included. Recommended.

C Ponto do Morro, Largo das Forras 2, T032-3355 1342. A central motel, just off the main square. Avoid the darker, lower rooms.

C Porão Colonial, R dos Inconfidêntes 447, T032-3355 1251. Pleasant, though a little out of town. With a pool, sauna and parking.

C Pousada Maria Bonita, R Antônio Teixeira Carvalho 134, T/F032-3355 1227,

www.tiradentesgerais.com.br/mariabonita. A motel with a pool and a garden full of gnomes leading down to the river. About 10 mins out of town, near the station. At the weekend the price includes breakfast, lunch and an evening snack.

C-D Pousada do Arco Iris, R Frederico Ozanan 340, T032-3355 1167, www.arcoiristiradentesmg.com.br. The best of a string of family-run *pousadas* in houses on this stretch of road just out of town. Rooms are small but scrupulously clean with parquet floors and little more than a bed. They look over a swimming pool. Very popular and only 5 rooms, so book ahead. Price includes breakfast.

D Pousada do Alferes, R dos Inconfidêntes 479, T032-3355 1303. Simple but central on the main shopping street close to the square.

D Pousada do Largo, Largo das Forras 48, T/F032-3355 1219. With a pool, sauna and rooms with Brazilian TV.

D Pousada do Laurito, R Direita 187, T032-3355 1268. Central, cheap and good value. Very popular with international backpackers.

São João del Rei *p273, map p274*

B Lenheiro Palace, Av Pres Tancredo Neves 257, T/F032-3371 8155. Modern hotel with good facilities, parking, cheaper in low season, teahouse, breakfast.

C Ponte Real, Av Eduardo Magalhães 254, T/F032-3371 7000. Modern, comfortable, sizeable rooms, good restaurant.

C-D Beco do Bispo, Beco do Bispo 93, 2 mins west of the São Francisco church, T032-3371 8844, www.becodobispo.com.br. The best in town. Well-kept, bright a/c rooms, hot showers, cable TV, a pool, convenient location and a very helpful English-speaking staff. Organizes tours. Highly recommended.

D Aparecida, Praça Dr Antônio Viegas 13, T032-3371 2540. Unillustrious but centrally located by the bus and taxi stop, with a restaurant and *lanchonete*.

D Pousada Casarão, Ribeiro Bastos 94, opposite São Francisco church, T032-3371 7447. Housed in a delightful converted mansion. The decent-sized rooms have firm beds. Also a games room with a pool table.

E Brasil, Av Pres Tancredo Neves 395, T032-3371 2804. In an old house full of character, on the opposite side of the river from the railway station, cheap. Recommended but basic, no breakfast.

E Pousada São Benedito, R Mcal Deodoro 254, T032-3371 7381. Price per person. Basic, with shared rooms and bathrooms.

E Sinha Batista, R Manock Anselmo 22, T032-3371 5550. The best of the cheaper options. With largish rooms in a colonial building conveniently located by the central canal.

Sabará *p275*

B Del Rio, R São Francisco 345, T031-3671 3040. Standard 3-star rooms. Reasonable service.

C Solar das Sepúlvedas, R da Intendência 371, behind the Museu do Ouro, T031-3671 2708. Grandiose, popular with Brazilian families and with a pool.

E Hotel do Ouro, R Santa Cruz 237, Morro da Cruz, T031-3671 5622. Rooms with en suite bathrooms, hot water, breakfast and a marvellous view, great value.

⊙ Eating

Ouro Preto *p258, map p260*
Try the local firewater, *licor de jaboticaba*, made from a sweet Brazilian tropical fruit.

ŦŦŦ Le Coq D'Or, R Getúlio Vargas 270 (next to the Rosário church), T031-3551 5200. Brazilian-French fusion cooking in a smart dining room with live music. One of the city's best.

ŦŦ Adega, R Teixeira Amaral 24, T031-3551 4171. Open 1130-1530. Vegetarian smorgasbord, US$5, all you can eat. Highly recommended.

ŦŦ Beijinho Doce, R Direita 134A, Café Gerais, 124 R Direita. Decent *bacalhau* and steak, delicious pastries, lousy coffee. Try the truffles.

ŦŦ Café e Compania, R São José 187, T031-3551 0711. Closes 2300. Very popular, *comida por kilo* at lunchtime, good salads and juices.

ŦŦŦ Deguste, R Coronel Alves 15, T031-3551 6363. Large portions, good value.

ŦŦŦ Pasteleria Lampião, Praça Tiradentes. Good views at the back (better at lunchtime than in the evening).

ŦŦŦ Taverna do Chafariz, R São José 167, T031-35512828. Good local food. Recommended.

Ŧ Forno de Barro, Praça Tiradentes 54. Decent Mineira buffet with varied plates and sweet puddings. Generous portions.

Ŧ Vide Gula, R Sen Rocha Lagoa 79a. Food by weight, friendly atmosphere. Recommended.

Mariana *p264, map p265*
ŦŦŦ Engenho Nôvo, Praça da Sé 26. Bar at night, English spoken. Recommended.

ŦŦŦ Mangiare della Mamma, D Viçoso 27. Italian. Recommended.

ŦŦŦ Tambaú, R João Pinheiro 26. Regional food.

Ŧ Panela de Pedra, in the Terminal Turístico. Serves food by weight at lunchtime.

Congonhas do Campo *p268*
Ŧ Estalagem Romaria, 2 mins from **Hotel Colonial** in the Romarias. Good restaurant and pizzeria, reasonable prices.

Tiradentes *p270, map p272*
There are many restaurants, snack bars and *lanchonetes*. your fancy.

ŦŦŦ Estalagem, R Min Gabriel Passos 280, T032-33551144. Excellent and generous traditional Mineira meat dishes.

ŦŦŦ Quartier Latin, R São Francisco de Paula 46, Praça da Rodoviária, T032-3355 1552. French-trained cordon bleu chef with a menu of French-inspired, Italian and seafood. Salads are made from their own organic vegetables. Respectable wine list. Good but expensive.

ŦŦŦ Quinto de Ouro, R Direita 159. Mineira and international dishes. Recommended.

ŦŦŦ Theatro da Vila, R Padre Toledo 157, T032-3355 1275. A gourmet restaurant with Italian, French and Brazilian fusion cooking and an excellent wine list. Good views out over the little garden and performances in summer in the restaurant's garden theatre.

ŸŸŸViradas do Largo, Largo do Ó, T032-3355 1111. The best Mineira restaurant in town together with **Estalagem**.
ŸŸAluarte, Largo do Ó 1, T032-3355 1608. Bar with live music in the evening, nice atmosphere, US$4 cover charge, garden, sells handicrafts. Recommended.
ŸMaria Luisa Casa de Chá, Largo do Ó 1, diagonally opposite **Aluarte**, T032-3355 1502. Tea, cakes and sandwiches in an arty Bohemian atmosphere. Great for breakfast.

São João del Rei *p273, map p274*
ŸŸŸChurrascaria Ramón, Praça Severiano de Resende 52. One of the better *churrascarias*, generous portions, plenty of side dishes.
ŸŸŸQuinto do Ouro, Praça Severiano de Resende 04, T032-3371 7577. Tasty and well-prepared regional food at reasonable prices. Said to be the best Mineira cooking in town.
ŸŸChafariz, R Quintino Bocaiuva 100, T032-3371 8955. The best per kilo restaurant with a huge choice and plenty of vegetarian options.
ŸRestaurant 611, R Getúlio Vargas 145. Cheap but excellent Mineira cooking. Eat all you like for US$2. Plenty of choice. A local favourite.

Sabará *p275*
ŸCê Que Sabe, R Mestre Caetano 56. Mineira and other Brazilian fare. Recommended.

⊕ Entertainment

São João del Rei *p273, map p274*
Music
São João del Rei has 2 famous orchestras which play baroque music. In colonial days, the music master not only had to provide the music for Mass, but also had to compose new pieces for every festival. All the music has been kept and the Ribeiro Bastos and Lira Sanjoanense orchestras preserve the tradition. Both have their headquarters, rehearsing rooms and archives on R Santo Antônio (Nos 54 and 45 respectively). The Orquestra Ribeiro Bastos plays at Mass every Sun in São Francisco de Assis at 0915 and

Fri 1900 at the Matriz do Pilar, as well as at many religious ceremonies throughout the year (eg Holy Week). The **Orquestra Lira Sanjoanense**, which is said to be the oldest in the Americas (founded in 1776), plays at Mass in Nossa Senhora do Pilar at 1900 every Thu and on Sun in Nossa Senhora do Rosário at 0830 and Nossa Senhora das Mercês at 1000, as well as on other occasions. It is best to check at their offices for full details. There are similar orchestras in Prados and Tiradentes, but the latter is not as well supported as those in São João.

⊕ Festivals and events

Ouro Preto *p258, map p260*
Many shops close during Holy Week and on winter weekends.
Feb Carnaval attracts many people.
Mar/Apr Ouro Preto is famous for its Holy Week processions, which actually begin on the Thu before Palm Sun and continue (but not every day) until Easter Sun. The most famous is that commemorating Christ's removal from the Cross, late on Good Fri.
Jun Corpus Christi and Festas Juninas.
Jul The city holds the Festival do Inverno da Universidade Federal de Minas Gerais (UFMG), the 'Winter Festival', about 3 weeks of arts, courses, concerts and exhibitions.
8 Jul Anniversary of the city.
15 Aug Nossa Senhora do Pilar, patron saint of Ouro Preto.
12-18 Nov Semana de Aleijadinho, a week-long arts festival.

Mariana *p264, map p265*
Feb Carnaval
Mar/Apr Traditional Holy Week celebrations.
29 Jun São Pedro.
Jul Mariana shares some events of Festival do Inverno da UFMG with Ouro Preto.

São João del Rei *p273, map p274*
Feb Carnaval is lively and popular here and going through a bit of a renaissance.
Apr Semana Santa.

15-21 Apr Semana da Inconfidência.
May/Jun Festival do Inverno, with many cultural events.
Jul FUNREI, the university (on R Padre José Maria Xavier), holds Inverno Cultural.
Aug First 2 weeks, Nossa Senhora da Boa Morte, with *novena barroca* (baroque music).
12 Oct Nossa Senhora do Pilar, patron saint of the city.
8 Dec Founding of the city.

Sabará *p275*
25 Dec-6 Jan Folia de Reis.
Jun Festas Juninas and Festival da Cachaça.
Oct 2nd Sun. Festival of Nossa Senhora do Rosário, the patron saint.

○ Shopping

Ouro Preto *p258, map p260*
Buy soapstone carvings at roadside stalls rather than in the cities; they are much cheaper. Many artisans sell carvings, jewellery and semi-precious stones in the Largo de Coimbra in front of São Francisco de Assis Church. Also worth buying is traditional cookware in stone, copper or enamelled metal.

Gems and jewellery
Gems are not much cheaper from freelance sellers in Praça Tiradentes than from the shops. If buying gems on the street, ask for the seller's credentials.
Gemas de Minas, Conde de Bobadela 63. One of the city's better jewellers.
Videmaju, R Conselheiro Santana 175. Vincente Júlio de Paula, a professor at the School of Mines, sells stones at very good prices.

Tiradentes *p270, map p272*
Art galleries
Oscar Araripe, R da Câmara. Paintings of Tiradentes and other local scenes in bright colours, popular and commercial.

São João del Rei *p273, map p274*
The pewter factory, Av Leite de Castro 1150, T032-3371 8000, 10 mins' walk from the *rodoviária*, 0900-1800. Run by Englishman John Somers and his son Gregory, is worth a visit for both its exhibitions and its shop. The nearby town of Resende Costa (30 km north) is known for its textile handicrafts.

▲▲ Activities and tours

Ouro Preto *p258, map p260*
Yoga centre, down an alley between Nos 31 and 47 (Cine Teatro Vila Rica), Praça Alves de Brito, T031-3551 3337. Offers shiatsu and Kerala massage.

Tiradentes *p270, map p272*
For horse-riding treks, contact John Parsons at the Solar da Ponte, see page 279.

● Transport

Ouro Preto *p258, map p260*
Bus There are 11 buses a day to/from **Belo Horizonte**, 2 hrs, Pássaro Verde, US$10. Day trips are possible; book your return journey to Belo Horizonte early if returning in the evening; buses get crowded. To **Mariana**, buses run from the Escola de Minas near Praça Tiradentes every 30 mins, US$2, all passing **Minas da Passagem** (buses also leave from Ouro Preto *rodoviária*).

There is a bus to **Rio**, Útil at 0705, 1715 and 2000 (US$50, 12 hrs; from Belo Horizonte or Juiz de Fora, 8 hrs); to **Brasília** at 1830 (12 hrs); to **Vitória** at 2100 (8 hrs). There are also Útil buses to **Conselheiro Lafaiete**, 3-4 a day via Itabirito and direct services to **Congonhas do Campo** via the new Caminho de Ouro highway. Other Útil services to **Rio**, **Barbacena**, **Conselheiro Lafaiete** and **Congonhas** go via Belo Horizonte. Direct buses to **São Paulo**, 3 a day with **Cristo Rei** (10 hrs, US$45). Gontijo go to **Salvador** via **Belo Horizonte**.

Train Maria Fumaça, Praça Cesário Alvim s/n, T031 3551 7705, leaves Fri-Sun at 1100 and 1600, returning from **Mariana** at 0900 and 1200, US$15 return. This 19th-century steam train runs the 18 km through the hills to Mariana. For the best views, sit on the right side and in the back carriages. The train waits just 1 hr in Mariana before returning to Ouro Preto. To avoid a rushed visit consider staying overnight or taking a bus back.

Mariana *p264, map p265*
Bus Buses to **Ouro Preto** can be caught by the bridge at the end of R do Catete, every 30 mins, US$0.60, all passing **Minas da Passagem**. There is a bus to **Belo Horizonte** (via Ouro Preto), US$10, 2¼ hrs. Buses for **Santa Bárbara** (near Caraça) leave from the *rodoviária*.

Around Mariana *p268*
Bus There are 3 buses a day from Mariana to **Antônio Pereira**, Mon-Fri, 0800, 1200, 1445, plus 1100, 1750 and 2100 on Sat.

Congonhas do Campo *p268*
Bus A bus marked 'Basílica' runs every 30 mins from the *rodoviária* to **Bom Jesus**, 5 km, US$1. A taxi from the *rodoviária* will cost US$5 one way, US$10 return including the wait while you visit the sanctuary.

Buses run to **Belo Horizonte**, 1½ hrs, US$4, 8 times a day. To **São João del Rei**, 2½ hrs, US$5, tickets are not sold until the bus comes in. To **Ouro Preto** or **Rio**, buses go via Belo Horizonte, Murtinho or Conselheiro Lafaiete. There is a frequent bus service to **Conselheiro Lafaiete**, US$2.

Tiradentes *p270, map p272*
Bus Last bus back to **São João del Rei** is 1815, 2230 on Sun.

Taxi Around town there are pony-drawn taxis; ponies can be hired for US$5 per hr. A taxi to **São João del Rei** costs US$15.

Train See page 271 for the train between Tiradentes and **São João del Rei**.

São João del Rei *p273, map p274*
Bus Buses to **Rio**, 5 daily with **Paraibuna** (3 on Sat and Sun), 5 hrs, US$40. **Cristo Rei** to **São Paulo**, 8 hrs, 5 a day (also to Santos), and **Translavras**, 4 a day (also to Campinas), US$14. **Belo Horizonte**, 3½ hrs, US$20. To **Juiz de Fora**, US$15, at least 8 a day with Transur. Frequent service to **Tiradentes** with Meier, 8 a day, 7 on Sat, Sun and holidays, US$3; on the return journey to São João, the bus stops outside the railway station before proceeding to the *rodoviária*.

Sabará *p275*
Bus To/from **Belo Horizonte** with Viação Cisne, US$0.75, 30 mins, from separate part of Belo Horizonte *rodoviária*.

⊙ Directory

Ouro Preto *p258, map p260*
Banks Banco 24 Horas, Praça Alves de Brito, next to Correios with a Visa ATM; Banco do Brasil, R São José 189, good rates, also for TCs; Bradesco, corner of Sen Rocha Lagoa and Padre Rolim, opposite the Escola de Minas with a Visa ATM. **Internet** There are many around town, eg **Point**, R Xavier da Veiga 501A, language school and cultural centre. **Post office** Praça Alves de Brito.

Tiradentes *p270, map p272*
Post office and telephone Combined office on Largo das Forras in the Prefeitura Municipal, R Resende Costa 71. It closes at 1200 for lunch.

São João del Rei *p273, map p274*
Banks Bradesco, Av Hermílio Alves 200, next to the Theatro Municipal, has an exchange, 1000-1600 and a Visa cashpoint.

Northern and western Minas Gerais

The population thins out in Northern Minas and as it stretches into the sertão backlands and the state of Bahia, the landscape gets ever more arid. Water mostly comes from the river São Francisco, a blue streak cutting through the beiges and browns of the semi-desert. Few tourists, however, get further than the colonial mining town of Diamantina, recently declared a World Heritage Site and every bit as pretty as its more famous contemporaries to the south. There are extensive tracts of beautiful cerrado forest towards the border with Goiás, parts of it protected by the Serra do Cipó and Grande Sertão Veredas national parks. Western Minas is less visited still, yet there are some beautiful stretches of forest in the Serra da Canastra, which can be visited on the way to or from Mato Grosso or Goiás.➤➤ *For listings, see pages 289-291.*

Parque Nacional da Serra do Cipó → *For listings, see pages 289-291.*

ⓘ *Information from Instituto Chico Mendes de Conservação da Biodiversidade (ICMBio) in Belo Horizonte, T031-3291 6588, www.icmbio.gov.br.*

The Serra do Cipó, 100 km northeast of Belo Horizonte, protects 33,400 sq km of important *cerrado* and gallery forest, which provide a home for ultra-rare bird species such as *cipo canastero* and grey-backed tachuri. Endangered mammals are also found here, including one of the more wimpy carnivores, the maned wolf, looking like a giant fox with overly long legs, which hunts small grassland rodents with its feet. There are also masked titi and brown capuchin monkeys and a number of endemic carnivorous plants. The walks that cut through the park pass through some of the most beautiful rugged grassland country in the state, leading to waterfalls and strands of tropical forest.

Ins and outs

At least eight buses daily run from Belo Horizonte along the MG-010 to Serra do Cipó town. There are *pousadas* all along the MG-010 and the bus will stop at them on request. The road through the park has been newly paved and runs through Conceição do Mato Dentro (36 km) and Serro (99 km) and on to Diamantina. *Pousadas* can organize guides for the park. There is excellent walking and many trails. For tourist information see the websites: www.guiaserradocipo.com.br, www.serradocipoturismo.com.br and www.serradocipo.com, all of which have details of tour operator and accommodation.

The route to Diamantina → *For listings, see pages 289-291. Colour map 4, B3.*

Conceição do Mato Dentro and the Tabuleiro waterfall → *Phone code: 038.*

A newly paved road climbs into the hills from Serra do Cipo town to **Conceição do Mato Dentro**, a sleepy 17th-century town nestled in the rugged folds of the **Serra do Espinhaço**. These mountains run from Central Minas all the way up to the Chapada Diamantina in Bahia and beyond. The surrounding countryside has well-preserved *cerrado* forest and bushland and is gushing with waterfalls. The most spectacular of all is Brazil's third tallest waterfall, the **Cachoeira do Tabuleiro**, Conceição, a sliver of water that plunges some 273 m from a *cerrado*-covered escarpment into a crystal-clear pool. The waterfall lies in the **Parque Natural Municpal Ribeirão do Campo** (Parque do Tabuleiro), which preserves the falls and around 3000 ha of *cerrado*. There are some 1700 species of vascular plants here, including 150 very rare orchids, alongside similar bird species to the Serra do Cipó.

Serro

This unspoiled colonial town sits on the banks of the Rio Jequitinhonha in the heart of lush hilly dairy farm country dotted with *cerrado* forest and waterfalls. The town preserves many pretty, crumbling churches and leafy squares and the locals make some of the best Minas Gerais cheese, *queijo mineiro*, in Brazil. This watery, milky putty is adored by all Brazilians (though foreigners often wonder what all the fuss is about) and is traditionally eaten with guava jam. Serro makes a good stop-off on the route south or north. It receives very few visitors and you will feel like a curiosity. There are a few buildings worth visiting. The prettiest church is **Santa Rita**, on a hill in the centre of town, reached by a long line of steps. On the main Praça João Pinheiro, by the bottom of the steps, is the arcaded **Nossa Senhora do Carmo**, with original paintings on the ceiling and in the choir. The town has two large mansions: **Barão de Diamantina** ① *Praça Presidente Vargas*, is in ruins, but **Barão do Serro** ① *R da Fundição, Tue-Sat 1200-1700, Sun 0900-1200*, across the river, is beautifully restored and used as the town hall and Casa de Cultura. There are old mine entrances in the hillside behind the courtyard. The **Museu Regional Casa dos Ottoni** ① *Praça Cristiano Ottoni 72*, is an 18th-century house now containing furniture and everyday objects from the region. The Ottoni brothers, who were born here, were prominent naval officers turned politicians in the 19th century. The even sleepier and prettier villages of **São Gonçalo do Rio das Pedras** and **Milho Verde** are a short bus ride away in the surrounding hills and are well worth a visit.

Ins and outs

Conceição do Mato Dentro and Serro are served by at least eight buses daily from Belo Horizonte, via the Serra do Cipó, on a newly paved road. Both towns also have bus connections with Diamantina several times daily. There are plenty of accommodation options. For information on Conceição and the Tabuleiro waterfall contact the **Secretária do Turismo** ① *Conceição do Mato Dentro, T031-3868 2423/2431, www.conceicaodomato dentro.com.br*. Their office lies in the centre and the town is tiny. The park itself should be visited with a guide, available through the Secretária or hotels in the town. Expect to pay around US$30 for a half-day round-trip with a guide and an additional US$5 to enter the park. Take walking shoes, swimming gear and water. For information on Serro, São Gonçalo and Milho Verde, contact the **Secretária de Turismo** ① *Chácara do Barão do Serro, T038-3541 1368 ext 234, www.serro.mg.gov.br*.

Diamantina → For listings, see pages 289-291. Colour map 4, B3. Phone code: 038. Population: 48,000. Altitude: 1120 m.

Diamantina, a UNESCO World Heritage Site and northern Minas's prettiest colonial town, sits nestled in rugged hills 300 km north of Belo Horizonte. The town's churches are less spectacular than those in Ouro Preto or São João del Rey, but the city has a wonderful architectural unity and is better preserved and less touristy.

The *cerrado* forests that swathe the countryside around the town are home to some of the rarest birds and mammals on the continent. The recently opened São Gonçalo do Rio Preto state park, 45 km from Diamantina, is the best base from which to explore them. Regular flights from Belo Horizonte to Diamantina have made visiting far easier than it used to be; it is now possible to continue overland from the town to Bahia.

Ins and outs

Getting there The **airport** ① *a few kilometres from town, T038-3531 9176*, receives three flights a week from Belo Horizonte or Pampulha with **Trip**, www.voetrip.com.br. A taxi to the centre costs US$7. The **rodoviária** ① *3 km east of the centre, T038-3531 9176*, has regular bus connections with Belo Horizonte and the Serra do Cipó. Diamantina is connected to Brasília through Curvelo, and Araçuaí and Itaubim from Porto Seguro in Bahia. Taxis are expensive. Excursions in the area can be organized through **Real Receptivo**. There are numerous car hire companies, including **Localiza**. ▸▸ *See Activities and tours, and Transport, page 291.*

Tourist information The **tourist office** ① *Casa de Cultura, Praça Antônio Eulálio 53, 3rd floor, T038-3531 1636, www.diamantina.mg.gov.br*, is friendly and helpful and provides pamphlets and a reliable map, as well as information about church opening times, buses and local guides. The websites www.diamantina-travel.com.br and www.diamantina.com.br, are very useful alternatives (the former in English, the latter in Portuguese), and lists hotels and tour operators.

Background

Like Minas's other colonial towns, Diamantina owes its existence and colonial finery to mining wealth, in this case diamonds, which were first discovered here in 1728. The settlement became known as Arraial do Tijuco and grew rapidly into a city. As the city's wealth increased, so did the feelings of resentment at the Portuguese tyranny. The majority black and mixed-race population were treated as subhuman. They were considered of such low birth that they were banned from walking in front of façades of the white churches as it would be an affront to God. They remained largely in poverty, leading many of the citizens to sympathize with the Inconfidêntes (see page 266). One local priest, José da Silva de Oliveira Rolim (Padre Rolim), joined the movement.

Sights

Diamantina is easily manageable on foot; the city centre is compact and there are plenty of little street-side cafés and bars. The best place to start exploring is the **Praça Guerra** (Praça do Sé) which is dominated by the towering 1930s cathedral. The most interesting church, **Nossa Senhora do Carmo** ① *R do Carmo, Tue-Sat 0800-1200, 1400-1800, Sun 0800-1200*, is a short walk west along Rua Carmo Quitanda. It is most remarkable for its beautiful interior paintings, carried out by José Soares de Araujo, a former bodyguard from Braga in Portugal. Many of the city's churches are painted by him, but this is by far his finest work. The Carmelite are said to have been founded before the time of Christ by the prophet Elijah, who is depicted on the magnificent ceiling, ascending to heaven in a chariot of fire, and brandishing a sword on one of the side altars. Another ceiling painting shows the patron saint and founder of the Third Order of Mount Carmel, the 12th-century English saint, St Simon Stock, receiving scapular from the Virgin. The placing of the church tower at the back of the building was ostensibly to please Chica Silva, the black slave of Padre Rolim. In an era when black Brazilians were valued less than chickens she achieved liberty, married the wealthy diamond merchant João Fernandes de Oliveira and became the most influential woman in the city, living in luxury with him and their 14 children in a house overlooking the Praça Lobo de Mesquita. The house is now a museum, the **Casa de Chica da Silva** ① *Praça Lobo Mesquita 266, free*.

Just south of Nossa Senhora do Carmo is the church of **Nossa Senhora do Rosário dos Pretos** ① *Largo Dom Joaquim, Tue-Sat 0800-1200 and 1400-1800, Sun 0800-1200*, designated for the black underclass who were not permitted to attend mass at Nossa Senhora do Carmo. Its simple interior has a magical meditative silence. Outside is a original 18th-century public fountain, the Chafariz do Rosário where water pours from the mouths of distinctly African faces.

Diamantina has a number of other interesting small museums worth exploring. The **Museu do Diamante** ① *R Direita 14, Tue-Sat 1200-1730, Sun 0900-1200, US$1*, in the house of Padre Rolim houses an important collection of the materials used in the diamond industry, together with some beautiful 18th- and 19th-century oratories and icons and the iron collars that were once fitted to the slaves that worked the mines.

The **Biblioteca Antônio Torres** ① *R Quitanda 48, Mon-Fri 1400-1700*, is a smart 18th-century townhouse, which is also known as the **Casa Muxarabie** after the enclosed Moorish balcony on one of the windows.

Behind the 18th-century building that now houses the **Prefeitura Municipal** (originally the diamond administration building) at Praça Conselheiro Matta 11, is the

Diamantina

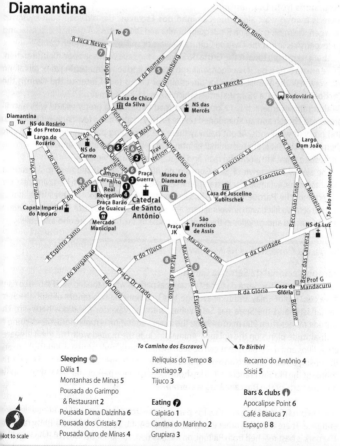

Mercado Municipal or **dos Tropeiros** (muleteers) ① *Praça Barão de Guaicuí*. It was built in 1835 as a residence and trading house before being expanded and has wooden arches. The **Casa da Glória** ① *R da Glória 297*, is the city's most photographed building. Two houses on either side of the street are connected by a covered corridor-bridge. This was once part of a convent school and the girls would laugh and flirt through the small windows. It is now part of a university.

President Juscelino Kubitschek, the founder of Brasília, was from Diamantina and his house is now a **museum** ① *on the outskirts of town, R São Francisco 241, Tue-Sun 1000-1200 and 1400-1800, US$2*. Try and be in the city for the regular **Vesperata** festivals when groups of musicians serenade passers-by from the city's numerous balconies, especially around the Praça Guerra; a tradition that began in the 17th century.
▶ *See Festivals and events, page 290.*

Excursions from Diamantina

There is a good walk along the **Caminho dos Escravos**, the old road built by slaves between the mining area on Rio Jequitinhonha and Diamantina. A guide is essential and not expensive; ask at the Casa de Cultura. Beware of snakes and thunderstorms.

About 9 km from town is the **Gruta de Salitre**, a big cave with a strange rock formation. There are no buses, but it is a good walk and you can find some interesting minerals along the way. Ask the tourist office for directions, or take a taxi. Closer to the town is the **Cachoeira da Toca**, a 15-m waterfall, which is good for swimming.

Along the riverbank it is 12 km on a dirt road to **Biribiri**, a pretty village with a well-preserved church and an abandoned textile factory. It also has a few bars and is popular and noisy at weekends. About halfway there are swimming pools in the river; opposite them, on a cliff face, are red animal paintings of unknown age and origin. There is some interesting plant life along the river and beautiful mountain views.

The sleepy little town of **São Gonçalo do Rio Preto**, which sits next to a beautiful mountain river, is famous for its traditional festivals. It lies some 60 km from Diamantina or the edge of the **Parque Estadual de São Gonçalo do Rio Preto** – an area of stunning pristine *cerrado* filled with flowering trees and particularly rich in birdlife. There are *pousadas* in São Gonçalo and *cabañas* in the park (reachable by taxi). Guides are also available.

Serra da Canastra → *For listings, see pages 289-291.*

Parque Nacional da Serra da Canastra

South of Araxá is the Serra da Canastra national park, in which the Rio São Francisco rises. It is a cool region (May and June average 18°C), comprising two ranges of hills, the Serra da Canastra and the Serra das Sete Voltas, with the Vale dos Cândidos between. The altitude ranges from 900 m to 1496 m; the lower vegetation is mostly grassland, rising to high-altitude plants on the uplands. Animals include the maned wolf, the great anteater, armadillos and deer. Birds that can be seen include rheas, owls, seriema, king vulture and the diving duck. There are also other birds of prey, partridges and tinamous. Besides the source of the Rio São Francisco (6.5 km from the São Roque park entrance), visitors can see the two parts of the **Dasca d'Anta waterfall**.

Ins and outs Gates close at 1800. The park has a **visitor centre**, at the São Roque de Minas entrance. There are three other entrances: Casca d'Anta, São João Batista and Sacramento. The park is best reached from Piumhi, on the MG-050, 267 km southwest of Belo Horizonte.

(this road heads for Ribeirão Preto in São Paulo). From Piumhi you go to São Roque de Minas (60 km). Information is available from **Instituto Chico Mendes de Conservação da Biodiversidade (ICMBio)** ① *Av do Contorno 8121, Cidade Jardim, Belo Horizonte, T031-3291 6588 ext 119/122; or from Caixa Postal 01, São Roque de Minas, T031-3433 1195.*

◉ Northern and western Minas Gerais listings

For Sleeping and Eating price codes and other relevant information, see pages 32-37.

◉ Sleeping

Parque Nacional da Serra do Cipó *p284*
LL Toucan Cipó, booked exclusively through www.dehouche.com as part of a tour. A British-owned luxury *fazenda* in pristine *cerrado* forest cut by clear-water streams. Very rich in bird and mammal life.
AL-A Cipó Veraneio, Rodovia MG-10, Km 95, Jaboticatubas, www.cipoveraneiohotel. com.br. Comfortable a/c rooms with cable TV, fridges and en suites in terraces of stone cabins next to the road that cuts through the park. The hotel has a pool, sauna, very good tour operator and a *cachaça* distillery just up the road, which produces some of Minas's finest.

Camping
Camping Véu da Noiva, Km 101, Santana do Riacho, T031-3201 1166, www.acmmg. org/veudanoiva.html. Pretty little campsite in a forest grove near one of Brazil's most impressive waterfalls. Swiss-style chalets (from **D** per person).

Conceição do Mato Dentro and the Tableiro waterfall *p284*
B-C Pousada da Gameleira, R Eloi Chaves 78, Tabuleiro, T031-3868 2337, www.pousadadagameleira.com.br. A rustic farmhouse set in the countryside near the park, with blocky a/c rooms set along corridors. The hotel organizes and runs land rover and walking tours.
-D Pousadinha Adentro, R Dr Basílio Santiago 55, T031-3868 1294, T031-9714 434 (mob). 3 little spruce suites, with shared balconies in a pretty little house

in the town centre. Generous breakfast and a friendly family owner.
D Hotel Cuiabá, Av Bias Fortes, 17, centro, T031-3868 1413. A very simple town house right in the centre of Conceição, with 6 bare double rooms some with en suites.
E-F Bromelia, R Principal 72, Tabuleiro, T031-9683 9284, ask for Zaide. Very simple concrete house near to the park with boxy tiled rooms a little larger than a bed. Friendly owner and breakfast included. More expensive in high season.

Serro *p285*
B Pousada Vila do Príncipe, R Antônio Honório Pires 38, T/F038-3541 1485. Very clean, in an old mansion containing its own museum. The artist Mestre Valentim is said to have been born in the slave quarters.
C-D Pousada Mariana, Praça Floriano Peixoto 44, T031-3541 1569. A small town hotel with basic a/c and fan-cooled rooms run by a local family. There are other cheap hotels nearby.

Diamantina *p285, map p287*
Rooms are usually half price for those travelling alone. Unless otherwise stated, all are within 10 mins' walk of the centre.
A Tijuco, R Macau do Melo 211, T038-3531 1022, www.hoteltijuco.com.br. A wonderful Niemeyer design that looks like a building from Thunderbird island. The large rooms have been refurbished whilst staying true to the original 1960s kitsch. The best rooms are at the front with balconies and glorious views.
A Pousada do Garimpo, Av da Saudade 265, T/F038-3532 1040, www.pousadadogarimpo. com.br. Plain well-kept rooms in a smart hotel on the outskirts of town, a taxi ride from the centre. There's a pool, sauna and a restaurant

serving some of the city's best Minas cooking from celebrated chef, Vandeka.

A Relíquias do Tempo, R Macau de Baixo 104, T038-3531 1627, www.pousada reliquiasdo tempo.com.br. Cosy wood-floored rooms with en suites in a pretty 19th-century house just off Praça JK. Public areas are decorated like a colonial family home. Breakfasts are generous.

B-C Montanhas de Minas, R da Romana 264, T038-3531 3240, www.grupo montanhasdeminas.com.br. Spacious rooms with stone floors and en suites, some with balconies. Decent breakfasts.

C-D Hotel Santiago, Largo Dom João 133, T038-3531 3407, http://santiagohotel.com.br. Plain, small but spruce rooms with en suites. Reasonable breakfast.

C-D Pousada dos Cristais, R Joga da Bola 53, T038-3531 3923, www.pousadadoscristais. com.br. A range of simple, large rooms in white, with wooden floors. Situated on the edge of town with views out across the mountains.

C-D Pousada Ouro de Minas, R do Amparo 90A, T038-3531 3240, www.grupomontanhas deminas.com.br. Simple well-kept rooms with stone floor rooms with tiny bathrooms in a converted colonial house.

Camping

Wild camping is possible near the waterfall just outside town.

🍴 Eating

Diamantina *p285, map p287*

🍴🍴🍴 **Cantina do Marinho**, R Direita 113, T038-3531 1686. This formal restaurant decorated with bottles of wine and attended by black-tie waiters is celebrated for its *salmão provençale* and *bacalhau*.

🍴🍴🍴 **Grupiara**, R Campos Carvalho 12, T038-3531 3887. Decent regional cooking, a convivial atmosphere and good-value per-kilo options at lunch.

🍴🍴 **Caipirão**, R Campos Carvalho 15, T038-3531 1526. Minas cooking with a lunchtime buffet cooked over a traditional wood-fired clay oven and evening à la carte.

🍴🍴 **Recanto do Antônio**, Beco da Tecla 39, T038-3531 1147. Minas food and decent steak served in a chic rustic dining room in a colonial house.

🍴 **Sisisi**, Beco da Mota 89, T038-3531 3071. Pasta, Minas cooking and a very good-value *prato feito* at lunchtime.

🍸 Bars and clubs

Diamantina *p285, map p287*

Apocalipse Point, Praça Barão de Guaicuí 78, T038-3531 9296. *Sertaneja* music, *axe* and live music upstairs. Lively at weekends with a 20- and 30-something crowd.

Café a Baiuca, R da Quitanda. Coffee bar by day with old men reading the paper, and by night a funky little bar with music DVDs and a crowd spilling out onto the street.

Espaço B, R Beco da Tecla. A bookshop-café serving crêpes and draught beer to an arty crowd until the small hours.

✹ Festivals and events

Diamantina *p285, map p287*

During the famous **Vesperatas**, musicians and singers serenade from balconies along the colonial streets and drum troupes and bands parade along them. Twice a month on a Sat.

Feb Carnaval is said to be very good here.

May-Jun Corpus Christi.

13 Jun Santo Antônio.

Jul 50 days after Pentecost, O Divino Espírit Santo, is a major 5-day feast.

12 Sep O Dia das Serestas, the 'Day of the Serenades', for which the town is famous; this is the birthday of President Juscelino Kubitschek, who was born here.

Oct First half of the month, Festa do Rosári

▲ Activities and tours

Diamantina p285, map p287

There are a few tour operators in the city, but they come and go like the wind and none are firmly established. The tourist office can help organize trips to São Gonçalo do Rio Preto and the surrounding area. **Diamantina Travel**, R Direita 120 sl 06, Centro, T038-3531 6733, www.diamantina-travel.com.br. Trips in and around Diamantina, including Biribiri, cerrado waterfall day tour and the city itself. Come during the week to avoid the crowds. Unusual places visited on the day trips include the Cachoeira da Água Santa (Holy Water Waterfall), which falls into a dark pool in the heart of beautiful cerrado forest. The waterfall is said to have healing properties.

⊕ Transport

Diamantina p285, map p287

Air There are 3 weekly flights to **Belo Horizonte** (Pampulha airport) with Trip, www.voetrip.com.br.

Bus There are 6 buses a day to **Belo Horizonte** (5 hrs) US$30, via Curvelo (for connections to Brasília, 10 hrs), with Pássaro Verde. There are daily buses to **Montes Claros**, with daily connections here for **Brasília** and **Parque Nacional Grande Sertão Veredas**. For the **Serra do Cipó** take the bus to Serro (2 daily) and change for Santa Ana do Riacho and the Serra do Cipó. There is one bus per day to **São Gonçalo do Rio Preto**.

If en route to Bahia, there are 2 daily buses to **Araçuaí** (4 hrs) from here *combis* and buses run to **Itaobim** (US$8, 2 hrs) from where there are connections to **Vitória da Conquista** (US$11, 4 hrs) and on to **Porto Seguro** and other destinations in Bahia. (If you get stuck in Araçuaí there is a Pousada Tropical opposite the *rodoviária*, T038-3731 1765, with bath, clean, cheap and friendly.) The BR-116 passes interesting rock formations at Pedra Azul (see page 298) before crossing the border with Bahia.

❶ Directory

Diamantina p285, map p287

Banks There is a Banco do Brasil and a Bradesco, in the centre.

Eastern and southern Minas Gerais

The border area between Minas and Espírito Santo is the most rugged part of the state. Marked by the ridges of the Serra do Caparaó mountains, it is home to some of the country's highest peaks and covered with eucalyptus plantations and remnant Mata Atlântica forest. It remains an important centre for semi-precious stone processing and crystal carving. The two principal towns, Governador Valadares and Teófilo Otôni, are on the BR-116 inland Rio–Salvador road, and both have good connections with Belo Horizonte. ▸▸ *For listings, see pages 294-295.*

Caratinga Biological Station

* US$15 per person per day, payable only in reais. Trips can be arranged through Focus Tours, www.focustours.com, see page 52.

The privately owned Caratinga Biological Station, set in 880 ha of mountainous, inland Atlantic forest, is protected by a conscientious family and **Conservation International**. The reserve is home to four rare primates: half of the world's northern muriquis (*Brachyteles hypoxanthus*), a sub-species of woolly spider monkeys, which are the largest primates in the Americas and one of the most critically endangered; the brown (or black-capped) capuchin; the brown howler monkey and the buffy-headed marmoset (a sub-species of tufted eared marmoset). Also at the station are brown-throated three-toed sloths and one of the largest inventories of birds outside the Andean regions of the Amazon – 217 species at last count. The primates and many of the birds are easily seen.

Parque Estadual do Rio Doce

① *T031-3822 3006, or phone the Instituto Estadual de Florestas T031-3330 7013. Access is by the BR-262 or 381, from which you have to turn off onto dirt roads to get to the park.*

The Parque Estadual do Rio Eoce is 248 km east of Belo Horizonte in the municipalities of Dionísio, Timóteo and Marliéria. Between 230 m and 515 m above sea level and covering almost 36,000 ha, this is one of the largest tracts of *Mata Atlântica* in southeast Brazil. As well as forest there are a number of lakes, on which boat trips are possible, besides swimming and fishing. The park is home to a great many birds and animals. There is an information centre, a campsite 6 km into the park and trails that have been marked out for hiking.

Parque Nacional Caparaó → *For listings, see pages 294-295.*

This is one of the most popular parks in Minas, with good walking through strands of Atlantic rainforest, *paramo* and to the summits of three of Brazil's highest peaks, **Pico da Bandeira** (2890 m), **Pico do Cruzeiro** (2861 m) and the **Pico do Cristal** (2798 m). Wildlife is not as plentiful as it is in Caratinga as the park has lost much of its forest and its floral biodiversity. However, there are still a number of Atlantic coast primates here, such as the brown capuchins, together with a recovering bird population.

From the park entrance (small entry fee) it is 6 km on a poorly maintained road to the car park at the base of the waterfall. From the hotel, jeeps (US$20 per jeep) run to the car park at 1970 m (2½ hours' walk), then it's a three- to four-hour walk to the summit of the Pico da Bandeira, marked by yellow arrows. There are plenty of camping possibilities all the way up, the highest being at **Terreirão** (2370 m). It is best to visit during the dry season (April to October), although it can be quite crowded in July and during Carnaval.

Ins and outs

The park is 49 km by paved road from Manhuaçu on the Belo Horizonte–Vitória road (BR-262). If you have your own transport, drive from the BR-262, go through Manhumirim Presidente Soares and Caparaó village, then 1 km further to the **Hotel Caparaó Parque**. There are bus services from Belo Horizonte (twice a day), Ouro Preto or Vitória, to Manhumirim, 15 km south of Manhuaçu. From Manhumirim, take a bus direct to Caparaó or to Presidente Soares (7 km), then hitch 11 km to Caparaó.▶▶ *See Transport, page 295.*

To contact the park write to Caixa Postal 17, Alto Jequitibá, or telephone T255, via the operator on 101-PS 1, Alto do Caparaó. **Instituto Chico Mendes de Conservação da Biodiversidade (ICMBio)**① *T031-291 6588 ext 119/122, www.icmbio. com.br,* also has information.

São Tomé das Letras → *For listings, see pages 294-295. Colour map 4, C2. Phone code: 035.*
Population: 6750.

São Tomé das Letras, 35 km from Três Corações, is a beautiful hilltop town which is very popular at weekends. The streets were once lined with houses made of local stone, giving the town a distinctive architectural identity, but its popularity as a tourist destination has seen many of these replaced or overshadowed by ugly concrete buildings and São Tomé is sadly beginning to lose its charm.

Rock paintings found in caves nearby have been dated to about 2000 BC. Inscriptions in the caves have lent the town a mystical reputation, attracting new-age travellers. Many believe it is a good vantage point for seeing UFOs (some claim that the inscriptions are extraterrestrial in origin), and that there are places with special energies. The **Carimbado cave** is rich in myths and legends, such as that its passages lead to an underground civilization and that its powers form an energy source linked to Machu Picchu in Peru.

The Shangri-lá rapid, which is a beautiful spot, is also called the **Vale do Maytréia**. The shops reflect this atmosphere and the hotels are classified by UFOs instead of stars. Whatever you think of it, São Tomé is certainly an unusual place.

Ins and outs

There are three daily buses (two on Sunday) from Três Corações, 1½ hours (the first 30 minutes is on a paved road); take the one that leaves Três Corações at dawn to see the mist in the valleys. If driving to the town, take care at the unsigned road junctions. After the pavement ends, at the next main junction, turn right.

At 1291 m it is one of the five highest places in Brazil. The average maximum temperature is 26°C and the minimum is 14°C. The rainy season is October to March. There is a **tourist office** ① *R José Cristiano Alves 4*, for information.

Background

A quarry town since the beginning of the 20th century, there is evidence of the industry everywhere you look. Settlement in colonial times dates from the mid- to late-18th century when the *bandeirantes* from São Paulo moved into this area, displacing the indigenous inhabitants. Even before the 20th-century 'alternative' arrivals, the hill acquired the following legend: at the end of the 18th century, an escaped slave hid in a cave for a long time. A finely dressed man appeared, asking him why he was living there. On hearing the slave's story, the man gave him a message on a piece of paper which, on presentation to his master, would earn the slave forgiveness. The slave duly did as the man said and the master, impressed by the writing and the paper, went to the cave to seek the mysterious man for himself. He found no one, but instead a statue of São Thomé (St Thomas). The master therefore built a chapel at the site, which was replaced by the Igreja Matriz in 1784, now standing beside the cave. The inscriptions, in red, can just about be seen in the cave; they are the 'Letras' of the town's name.

Sights

The town is almost at the top of the hill. Behind it are rocky outcrops on which are the **Pyramid House**, the **Cruzeiro** (cross) at 1430 m, with good 360-degree views, the **Pedra da Bruxa** and paths for walking or, in some parts, scrambling.

The bus stops at the main *praça*, where there is the frescoed 18th-century **Igreja Matriz** beside the fenced cave. A second church, the 18th-century **Igreja das Pedras** (Nossa Senhora do Rosário) is on a *praça* to the left as you enter town (Rua Ernestina Maria de Jesus Peixoto). It is constructed in the same style as many of the charming old-style buildings, with slabs of the local stone laid on top of each other without mortar.

Tours from São Tomé das Letras

In the surrounding hills are many caves: **Sobradinho**, 12 km; **Carimbado**, 5 km; **Gruta do Feijão**, a short walk from town; **Gruta da Bruxa**, 6 km. Seven waterfalls are also close by, including: **Cachoeira de Eubiose**, 4 km; **Véu de Noiva**, 12 km; **Paraíso**, near Véu de Noiva; **Vale das Borboletas da Lua**, 8 km; and **do Flávio**, 6 km. There are also rapids such as **Shangri-lá**, 17 km, and **Vale dos Gnomos**, near the Vale das Borboletas. Some of these places make a good hike from the town, but you can also visit several in a day on an organized tour. ▸▸ *See Activities and tours, below.*

◉ Eastern and southern Minas Gerais listings

For Sleeping and Eating price codes and other relevant information, see pages 32-37.

🛏 Sleeping

Parque Nacional Caparaó *p292*
B-C Caparaó Parque, 2 km from the park entrance, 15 mins' walk from the town of Caparaó, T032-3747 2559, www.caparao parquehotel.com.br. In a spectacular location right next to a series of rainforest-swathed mountain ridges and with hiking and other adventure activities organized.

São Tomé das Letras *p292*
There are lots of *pousadas* and rooms to let all over town. Streets are hard to follow because their names can change from one block to the next; numbering is also chaotic.
C-E Rancho Paraíso, 8 km on the road to Sobradinho, T035-3237 1342. Basic lodging, campsite, restaurant, garden and trekking.
D Pousada Arco-Iris, R João Batista Neves 19, T/F035-3237 1212. Rooms and chalets, sauna, swimming pool.
E Fundação Harmonia, on the road to Sobradinho (4 km), Bairro do Canta Galo, T035-3237 1280. Cheap and cheerful, price per person. The community emphasizes principles of healthy lifestyle, for mind and body, 'new age', workshops, massage, excursions, veggie food (their shop's on the main *praça*).
E Hospedaria dos Sonhos I, R Gabriel Luiz Alves. Price per person. Clean, with bath, no TV, restaurant, shop, groups accommodated.
E Mahã Mantra, R Plínio Pedro Martins 48, T035-3989 5563. IYHA hostel.

E Pousada Baraunas, R João Cristiano Alves 19, T035-3346 1330. Basic youth hostel with dorms and double. Price per person.
E Pousada Novo Horizonte, R João Cristiano Alves 10. Price per person. Simple rooms, friendly staff, information on local attractions.
E Sonhos II (do Gê), Trav Nhá Chica 8, T035-3237 1235. Price per person. Very nice, restaurant, swimming pool, sauna, television in rooms. Recommended.

🍴 Eating

São Tomé das Letras *p292*
▯▯▯ O Alquimista, R Capt Pedro Martins 7. Closed Mar-Jun and Aug-Nov. The best in town, with a decent menu of Minas dishes.
▯▯ das Magas, R Camilo Rosa. A varied menu of Minas and pasta dishes. Good lasagne.
▯ Padarias Bom Dia, opposite the bus stop on the main *praça*. Pleasant bakery with a range of cheap lunches and sandwiches.
▯ Veranda Pôr-do-Sol, R Plínio Pedro Martins, *comida caseira*. Pizza. Brazilian home-cooking including a range of Minas dishes and pizzas.
▯ Ximama, Martins at the corner of G L Alve Simple pizza restaurant with generous lashings of cheese on the toppings.

▲ Activities and tours

São Tomé das Letras *p292*
Tours to the caves, waterfalls and rapids surrounding the town can be arranged. To t

waterfalls Flávio, Eubiose, Paraíso and Véu de Noiva, US$50; Shangri-lá, US$70; Vale das Borboletas, Gruta do Carimbado and Ladeira do Amendoim (a slope on which cars appear to run uphill when in neutral, like the one in Belo Horizonte), US$50, T035-3237 1283 or enquire at the **Néctar** shop on R José Cristiano Alves.

The tourist office has a list of accredited guides for both ecotourism and adventure tourism: **Departamento de Turismo, Cultura E Proteção ao Patrimônio,** R José Cristiano Alves 04, T035-3237 1461, www.visitesaothome.com.br.

● Transport

Parque Nacional Caparaó *p292*
Bus There are direct services to **Manhumirim**, 15 km south of Manhuaçu,

US$1, from where there are connections to **Belo Horizonte** (twice a day with Pássaro Verde), **Ouro Preto** or **Vitória**. Or hitch the 11 km to **Presidente Soares** and take a bus to Manhumirim from there (several daily, 7 km).

São Tomé das Letras *p292*
Bus To **Três Corações**, 3 daily buses (2 on Sun), US$7, 1½ hrs.

● Directory

São Tomé das Letras *p292*
Bank There is a Bradesco in the main *praça*.
Post office In the group of buildings at the top right of the *praça*, facing the Gruta São Tomé.

Espírito Santo

Sandwiched between Rio de Janeiro, Minas Gerais and Bahia, the coastal state of Espírito Santo is relatively unknown, except by Mineiros heading for the coast for their holidays. It has many beaches, but they are overshadowed by those of its northern and southern neighbours. There are a number of nature reserves and turtle-breeding grounds in Espírito Santo, and European immigration has given the towns a distinctive atmosphere. The state capital, Vitória, is also the main industrial and commercial centre. People here are known as Capixabas, after a former tribe.

The state has a hot, damp seaboard with a more-or-less straight, low coastline and long beaches open to the Atlantic. The south is mountainous and dotted with vast granite boulders even larger than Sugar Loaf in Rio. The most spectacular is Pedra Azul. The slopes are covered with pine plantations and remnants of Mata Atlântica rainforest. The coast is covered with restinga scrub and grassland. The north of the state is flat and dominated by vast eucalyptus plantations which run down to the long coastal sand dunes. ➤➤ *For listings, see pages 300-302.*

Background

Espírito Santo was one of the original captaincies created by the Portuguese in the 16th century, but their colony was very precarious in its early days. During the struggle for supremacy, the son of Mem de Sá (the governor in Bahia) was killed, but, as elsewhere, the invaders eventually prevailed, though not as successfully as in many of the other captaincies, as the Portuguese were only able to gain a foothold on the coastal plains. When the focus of attention moved to the mines in Minas Gerais in the 18th centuries, the state became strategically important. Initially it was not on the gold exporting route, but after iron mining began a trail from Belo Horizonte to Vitória was created. This remains one of the major economic corridors in the country.

Vitória → *For listings, see pages 300-302. Colour map 4, C5. Phone code: 027. Population: 266,000.*

The town of Vitória is beautifully set on an island, its entrance second only to Rio's. The beaches are just as attractive, but smaller, and the climate is less humid. Five bridges connect the island with the mainland. Vitória dates from 1551 and takes its name from a battle won by the Portuguese over the local indigenous people. There are a few colonial remnants, but it is largely a modern city and port. The upper, older part of town, reached by steep streets and steps, is much less hectic than the lower harbour area which suffers dreadful traffic problems. A rail connection westwards to Minas Gerais provides transport for export of iron ore, coffee and timber. Port installations at Vitória and nearby Ponta do Tubarão have led to some beach and air pollution.

Ins and outs

Aeroporto Das Goiabeiras ① *10 km north of the city centre, Av Fernando Ferrari s/n, T027-3235 6300*, has connections with Belo Horizonte, Brasília, Rio de Janeiro, Salvador and São Paulo amongst others. From the airport, a taxi to the centre costs US$25, or take bus No 212. The *rodoviária* is 15 minutes' walk west of the centre.

Vitória

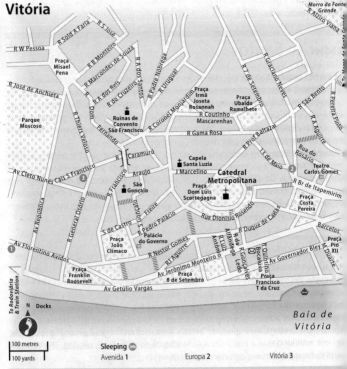

Sleeping
Avenida **1**
Europa **2**
Vitória **3**

Information is available from **Setur** ⓘ *R Marília de Resende Scarton Coutinho 194, Enseada do Suá, T027-3636 8026, and at the rodoviária*, with friendly staff and a free map; or **Instituto Jones dos Santos Neves** ⓘ *Av Marechal Campos 310, Edif Vitória Center, T027-3322 2033 ext 2215, www.setur.es.gov.br.*

Sights

On Avenida República is the huge **Parque Moscoso**, an oasis of quiet, with a lake, playground and tiny zoo. Other parks are the **Morro da Fonte Grande**, with good views from the 312-m summit, and the **Parque dos Namorados**, 6 km from the centre at Praia do Canto. Two islands reached by bridge from Praia do Canto are **Ilha do Frade** and **Ilha do Boi**.

Colonial buildings still to be seen in the city are the **Capela de Santa Luzia**, Rua José Marcelino in the upper city (1551), now an art gallery; the church of **São Gonçalo**, Rua Francisco Araújo (1766) and the ruins of the **Convento São Francisco** (1591), also in the upper city. In the **Palácio do Governo**, or **Anchieta**, on Praça João Climaco (upper city), is the tomb of Padre Anchieta, the 16th-century Jesuit missionary and one of the founders of São Paulo. The **Catedral Metropolitana** was built in 1918 and stands in Praça Dom Luís Scortegagna. The **Teatro Carlos Gomes**, on Praça Costa Pereira, often presents plays as well as holding jazz and folk festivals.

Vila Velha, reached by a bridge across the bay, has an excellent beach, but is built up and noisy: take a bus from Vitória marked Vilha Velha. Visit the ruined, fortified monastery of **Nossa Senhora da Penha**, on a hill above Vila Velha; the views are superb. The Dutch attacked it in 1625 and 1640. There is also a pleasant ferry service to Vila Velha.

Beaches

Urban beaches such as **Camburi** can be affected by pollution (some parts of it are closed to bathers), but it is quite pleasant, with fair surf. South of the city is Vila Velha (see above), but for bigger waves go to **Barra do Jucu**, which is 10 km further south.

There is a hummingbird sanctuary at the **Museu Mello Leitão** ⓘ *Av José Ruschi 4, T027-259 1182, Tue-Fri 0800-1200, 1300-1700*, a library including the works of the hummingbird and orchid scientist, Augusto Ruschi. Hummingbird feeders are hung outside the library. Also in the municipality is the **Dr Augusto Ruschi Biological Reserve** (formerly the Nova Lombardia National Biological Reserve), a forest rich in endemic bird species, including several endangered hummingbirds, Salvadori's antwren, cinnamon-vented Piha, russet-winged spadebill, Oustalet's tyrannulet, rufous-brown solitaire and hooded berryeater. Before visiting, permission to visit must be obtained from **Instituto Chico Mendes de Conservação da Biodiversidade (ICMBio)** ⓘ *Av Marechal Mascarenhas de Moraes 2487, Caixa Postal 762, Vitória ES, CEP 29000, www.icmbio.gov.br.*

Coastal mountains → *For listings, see pages 300-302.*

Mountains separate Vitória from Minas. These were once covered in lush Atlantic coastal rainforest, which now survives only in isolated patches and has been replaced by pine and coffee plantations. The road to Minas is nonetheless picturesque, climbing steeply off the coastal plain and winding its way around the hills and through steep valleys. Many of the towns here were settled by Germans and Swiss and their alpine heritage lives on in a curiously kitsch way: the temperature never drops below freezing, but the tourist chalets are built with long sloping roofs that look like they could fend off a ton of snow. Some customs brought over in the 1840s by the first German and Swiss settlers, are loosely preserved in the villages of **Santa Leopoldina** and **Domingos Martins**, both around 45 km from Vitória, less than an hour by bus (two companies run to the former, approximately every three hours). Domingos Martins (also known as Campinho) has a Casa de Cultura with some items of German settlement. Santa Leopoldina has an interesting **museum** ① *Tue-Sun 0900-1100, 1300-1800*, covering the settlers' first years in the area. **Santa Teresa**, which lies beyond them, is a favourite weekend retreat for people from Vitória. It is linked to Santa Leopoldina by a dirt road.

Whilst these towns are moderately interesting, the only real reason to break the journey between Vitória and Minas is to see **Pedra Azul**, www.pedraazul.com.br, a giant granite mountain that juts out of the nearby hills and changes colour from slate blue to deep orange as the day passes. Although surrounded by pine plantations it preserves a little indigenous forest around its flanks, and the state park in which it sits is good for a day's light walking.

South of Vitória → *For listings, see pages 300-302.*

Cachoeiro do Itapemirim is a busy city straddling both banks of the fast-flowing Rio Itapemirim. **Cachoeira Alta**, with a natural swimming pool, is 38 km away on the road to Castelo. The countryside south of Vitória is flat and uninteresting, broken only by fields of sugar cane and the occasional granite mountain looming over the plain. The beaches that dot the coast are less beautiful than those in the north of the state and considerably less beautiful than those in neighbouring Rio. The most popular are those at **Guarapari**, some 50 km south of Vitória on the coast road. The town gets very crowded at holiday times especially mid-December to the end of February when Mineiros flood down from Belo Horizonte. The sand here is mildly radioactive but if the Casa de Cultura in town is to be believed, the radiation is good for the health. Plenty of Capixabas and Cariocas seem to agree, as they come here to cure everything from rheumatism to backache. There are many hotels and plenty of cheap seafood restaurants in town and by the beach.

A little further south is the far quieter village of **Ubu** and, 8 km beyond, **Anchieta** which has a small estuarine river much beloved of water birds. Boatmen from the Colônia da Pesca charge about US$20 for a short trip along the river. Close by is **Iriri**, a small village in a beautiful setting with two beaches, Santa Helena and Inhaúma. There are a few hotels. Five kilometres beyond is **Piúma**, a calm, little-visited place, renowned for its craftwork in shells, a skill that has been passed down through generations of craftsmen and women. The name derives from the indigenous word *pium*, meaning mosquito. The resort town of **Marataízes** is the last before the border with Rio de Janeiro state.

North of Vitória → *For listings, see pages 300-302.*

Linhares and Sooretama reserves → *Colour map 4, B5.*
The town of **Linhares**, 143 km north of Vitória on the Rio Doce, has good hotels and restaurants but is otherwise dull. However, it is a convenient starting place for visiting the turtle beaches. Besides the one at the mouth of the Rio Doce, there is another **Tamar** site at **Ipiranga**, which is 40 km east of Linhares by an unmade road.

Linhares is close to two other nature reserves. The **Linhares Reserve** ① *permission from the director must be obtained to visit, T027-3374 0016*, owned by **CVRD** (the former state-owned mining company, now privatized), is possibly the largest remaining lowland tract of Atlantic forest. There is very good birdwatching in the reserve and specialities include red-billed curassow, minute hermit, rufous-sided crake, blue-throated (ochre-cheeked) parakeet, black-billed scythebill and black-headed berryeater.

The **Sooretama Biological Reserve** ⓘ *45 km north of Linhares, 65 km south of Conceição da Barra, on the BR-101*, protects tropical Atlantic rainforest and fauna. It contains several bird species not found in the Linhares Reserve, and much of the wildlife is rare and endangered. Both Sooretama and Linhares have orchids apparently not found anywhere else. Sooretama has been protected since 1969. With year-round tropical humidity, vegetation here is dense with ancient trees reaching over 40 m in height. Two rivers, the Barra Seca and the Cupido, cross the reserve and, together with Lagoa Macuco, provide marshlands, which attract migratory birds as well as numerous resident flocks. The reserve is strictly monitored by **Instituto Chico Mendes de Conservação da Biodiversidade (ICMBio)**. It is not open to the public, but drivers and cyclists can cut across it by road.

São Mateus, 88 km north of Linhares, is another unillustrious but inoffensive inland town, which is another base for **Tamar** ⓘ *T027-3761 1267, www.tamar.com*. It is 13 km from good beaches at **Guriri**.

Conceição da Barra → *Colour map 4, B5. Phone code: 027. Population: 25,500.*

The most attractive beaches in Espírito Santo are around Conceição da Barra, 261 km north of Vitória. It is an organized town that welcomes visitors. Many people come in summer and for **Carnaval**, otherwise it is quiet. Viewed from its small port, the sunsets are always spectacular. **Corpus Christi** (early June) is celebrated with an evening procession for which the road is decorated with coloured wood chips. The town has an office for **Tamar** ⓘ *Caixa Postal 53, Conceição da Barra, T027-3762 1124, www.tamar.com*.

Itaúnas

Itaúnas, 27 km north of Conceição, is an interesting excursion (it has some *pousadas* and a small campsite). The small town has been swamped by sand, and has been moved to the opposite riverbank. There is now a fantastic landscape of 30-m-high dunes, coastal swamp land (with numerous capybara) and deserted beaches. From time to time, winds shift the sand dunes enough to reveal the buried church tower. The theory is that the sudden encroachment of the sands in the 1970s was caused by massive deforestation of the surrounding area. The coast here, too, is a protected turtle breeding ground; for information contact **Tamar** in Conceição da Barra (see above).

The beach of **Meleiras**, 3 km south, is accessible only on foot or by boat and is one of a number of pleasant trips. It is 12 km long and offers fabulous diving and fishing. **Guaxindiba**, 3 km north, is partially developed, with hotels and restaurants, but the natural vegetation is still intact. It is possible to drive all the way along dirt roads into Bahia if you have a 4WD.

Buses run to Itaúnas three to four times a day from Conceição da Barra. The town is very popular in high season with middle-class Mineiros and Paulistanos who regard it as less spoilt than Trancoso and the other once laid-back resort towns of southern Bahia. For information on *pousadas* and excursions, visit www.guiaitaunas.com.br.

◉ Espírito Santo listings

For Sleeping and Eating price codes and other relevant information, see pages 32-37.

● Sleeping

Vitória *p296, map p296*
There are a string of adequate but scruffy hotels opposite the *rodoviária* and plenty of others in the beach areas: **Camburi** to the north, **Vila Velha** to the south, both about 15 mins from city centre. Accommodation is very easy to find here except in high season.
AL Senac Ilha do Boi, R Bráulio Macedo 417, Ilha do Boi, T027-3345 0111, www.hotelilhado boi.com.br. The most luxurious in town with its own marina, bay views, restaurant and pool.
A Best Western Porto do Sol, Av Dante Michelini 3957, Praia de Camburi, 7 km from the centre, T027-3337 2244. A beachside hotel built in the 1980s, with a restaurant, pool, sauna and bar.
B Pousada da Praia, Av Saturnino de Brito 1500, Praia do Canto, T/F027-3225 0233. Ordinary little hotel near the beach. Pool.
C Avenida, Av Florentino Avidos 347, T027-3223 4317. Adequate but undistinguished rooms with a/c and a decent breakfast. Recommended.
C Vitória, Cais de São Francisco 85, near Parque Moscoso, T027-3223 0222. Basic hotel with a reasonable restaurant. Recommended but look at a variety of rooms before committing yourself.
D Europa, 7 de Setembro, T027-3323 0108, at the corner of Praça Costa Pereira. Hotel and restaurant, noisy but cheap. Offers advice on nearby veggie restaurants.
D-E Cidade Alta, R Dionísio Rosendo 213, T027-3222 1855. Cheap little fan-cooled boxes opposite the cathedral in heart of the city centre. The area can be a little sketchy at night.
E Príncipe Hostel, Av Dario Lourenço de Souza 120, Ilha do Príncipe, T027-3322 2799, hotelp@terra.com.br. The IYHA youth hostel, housed in a big blocky former budget hotel near the *rodoviária*.

Coastal mountains *p297*
C Pousada Peterle, Estr Pedra Azul, Domingos Martins, T027-3248 1171, www.pousada peterle.com.br. Spacious mock-Swiss chalets set in a little garden with views of the rock. No restaurant but generous breakfast.

South of Vitória *p298*
There are plenty of hotels and *pousadas*. The most popular beach is **Castelhanos** and its extension **Guanabara**, which separates Anchieta from Ubu. Gunanbara is quieter. Both have calm waters.
AL Flamboyant, Km 38, Rod do Sol, Guarapari, T/F027-3229 0066, www.hotel flamboyant.com.br. *Fazenda* hotel with fishing and horse riding. Good internet rates for weekends and longer stays in low season.
A Thanharu Praia, R Jovina Serafim dos Anjos, Praia de Castelhanos, between Anchieta and Ubu, T/F028-3536 1246, www.thanharu.com.br. A big Costa del Sol-style concrete block of a beachside hotel with a pool and sauna. Popular with families and on one of the livelier beaches.
A-B Porto do Sol, Av Beira Mar 1, Praia do Morro, Guarapari, T027-3161 7100, www.hotelportodosol.com.brl. Mediterranean-style village on a rocky point overlooking a calm beach, pool, sauna.
A-B Praia Costa Azul, Iriri, T028-3534 1599. A standard, uninspiring beach hotel with rooms gathered around a pool. Lodging in private houses is also possible. A regular bus runs from Guarapari.
B Pontal de Ubu, R Gen Oziel 1, Praia de Ubu, T028-3536 5065, www.hotelpontalde ubu.com.br. Popular family hotel with a pool saunas, bike rental and organized activities.
B-C Monte Aghá Pousada Haras, R das Castanheiras, Piúma, T028-3520 1363. *Fazenda* hotel with horse riding.
B-C Pousada da Meméia, R Manuel Alves Abrantes, Iriri, T028-3534 1534, www.pousad damemeia.com.br. A range of rooms in a medium-sized *pousada* with a bar and sauna

C Costa Sul, R Getúlio Vargas 101, Guarapari, T027-3261 2942. Basic, friendly, clean and good breakfast. Much beloved of Brazilians and mosquitoes.

C-D Alto da Praia, Av Estr Dos Cancelas 111, Alto da Praia, Marataízes, T028-3532 3630, www.altodapraia.com.br. Small *pousada* with a/c rooms and a pool.

C-D Coqueiros Praia, Av D Helvécio 1020, Praia dos Namorados, Iriri, T028-3534 1592, www.coqueirospraiahotel.com.br. Small but well-kept and intimate beachside *pousada* with a/c rooms and a play area for kids.

C-D Dona Judith, Av Lacerda de Aguiar 353, Marataízes, T028-3532 1436. Basic but friendly.

E Guarapari Hostel, Av F, quadra 40, Guarapari, T027-3261 5210. Simple hostel at Guarapari popular with students.

Camping

Marataízes, Praia do Siri, 9 km south of Marataízes, T027-3325 2202. Municipal site.

Praia de Itapessu, R Antônio Guimarães s/n, quadra 40, Guarapari, T027-3261 0475. Turn left out of the *rodoviária*, then right and right again, past **Pousada Lisboa**, 2 blocks, across a dual carriageway (Av Jones de Santos Neves), 1 block to the campground, US$10 with good breakfast. Recommended.

Linhares and Sooretama reserves *p298*

B-D Reserva Natural da Vale do Rio Doce, BR-101, Km 120, T027-3371 9797, www.cvrd.com.br/linhares. Beautiful location within the reserve. Great for birds and wildlife. With a bar, sauna and simple but pleasant rooms.

B-D Virgínia, Av Gov Santos Neves 919, Linhares, T/F027-3264 1699. Modern building with a range of rooms at different prices. Good if you get stuck in town.

Conceição da Barra *p299*

There are plenty of beach hotels to choose from here and you will have no problem finding one after a short browse, as long as it is not high season.

C Pousada Gandia, Av Atlântica 1054, Praia de Guaxindiba), T/F027-3762 1248.

Small *pousada* with simple rooms, a pool, baby sitting services and helpful staff.

C Praia da Barra, Av Atlântica 350, T/F027-3762 1100, www.hotelpraiadabarra.com.br. Simple and friendly 50-room *pousada* with a/c or fan, a pool and sauna.

D Caravelas, Av Dr Mário Vello Silvares 83, a block from the beach, T027-3762 1188. Basic with shared bathrooms and a light breakfast. Recommended.

E Pousada Pirámide, next to the *rodoviária*, T027-3762 1970. The owner, Lisete Soares, speaks English, good value, 100 m from beach. Recommended.

Camping

Camping Clube do Brasil, Rod Adolfo Serra, Km 16, T027-3762 1346. Site with full facilities.

Itaúnas *p299*

There are numerous attractive little *pousadas* on and around the town's grassy main square.

C Pousada Bem Te Vi, R Adolpho Pereira Duarte 41, T027-3762 5012, www.pousada bemtevi.com. One of the few *pousadas* in town with a pool, with a range of modern rooms organized around a courtyard; all with a/c or fans, TVs, fridges and breakfast.

C Pousada Cambucá, just off Praça Principal, T027-3762 5004, www.portonet.com.br/cambuca. Wooden-floored rooms, some with balconies and a decent seafood restaurant.

C-D Casa da Praia, R Dercílio Fonseca, T027-3762 5028, www.casadapraiaitaunas.com.br. Simple *pousada* close to the beach.

🍴 Eating

Vitória *p296, map p296*
Moqueca capixaba, a seafood dish served in an earthenware pot, is the local speciality. It is a variant of the *moqueca*, which is typical of Bahia.

₤₤₤ **Lareira Portuguesa**, Av Saturnino de Brito 260, Praia do Canto, T027-3345 0329. Portuguese, expensive.

₤₤ **Mar e Terra**, opposite the *rodoviária*. Good food, live music at night.

¶¶ Pirão, R Joaquim Lírio 753, Praia
do Canto. Regional food.
¶ Lavacar, Praia Camburi. One of many
similar on this beach, serves food and
has live music.

South of Vitória *p298*
¶ Peixada do Garcia, Av Magno Ribeiro
Muqui, Guarapari. Respectable seafood.
¶ Peixada do Menelau Garcia, Av Mário
Neves, Guarapari. More respectable seafood.

Conceição da Barra *p299*
There are plenty of simple seafood restaurants
town and some basic *palapas* on the beach.
¶ Tia Teresa, R Dr Mário Vello Silvares 135.
Brazilian food, self-service, good value.

⊖ Transport

Vitória *p296, map p296*
Air Bus 212 runs between the airport city
centre waterfront and the *rodoviária*. Flights
to **Belo Horizonte** (Confins airport), **Brasília**,
Curitiba, **Rio de Janeiro**, **São Paulo**, **Natal**,
Fortaleza and **Salvador** amongst others.
   Airline offices TAM, Av Fernando
Ferrari 3055, Goiaberas, T027-3327 0868.

Bus To **Rio**, 8 hrs, US$35 (*leito* 45). To **Belo
Horizonte**, US$25 (*leito* 35). To **Salvador**,
18 hrs, US$45; to **Porto Seguro** direct 11 hrs
with lots of stops, US$25 (also *leito* service);
alternatively, take a fast bus to Eunápolis,
then change for Porto Seguro and other
destinations on the Bahia coast. For
Caravelas the **Abrolhos islands** in
Bahia, change at Teixeira de Freitas.

Car hire Several including a Localiza
at the airport.

South of Vitória *p298*
Bus There are regular buses to **Gurarpari**
from Vitória and onward from here to the
other resorts down the coast. The **Alvorada**
bus company has a separate *rodoviária* from
Itapemirim/Penha, **Sudeste**, São Gerardo and
others. They are close together, 15 mins' walk
from the city centre or US$10 by taxi. **Penha**
tickets are sold at **R-Tur Turismo**, in the centre
at R Manoel Severo Simões and R Joaquim da
Silva Lima, where air tickets, free brochures,
maps, and hotel addresses can also be
obtained. To **Vitória**, 1 hr with **Sudeste**, US$8.
To **Rio** with **Itapemirim**, 2 a day, US$35.

Linhares and Sooretama reserves *p298*
Bus Frequent buses from Vitória. Most
Bahia-bound buses stop at Linhares.

Itaúnas *p299*
Bus Bus from the *padaria* in Conceição
da Barra at 0700, returns 1700.

⊕ Directory

Vitória *p296, map p296*
Banks Bradesco, Banco do Brasil and
other major banks throughout the city.

South of Vitória *p298*
Banks Banco 24 Horas, Praça do Coronado
Praia da Areia, Guarapari; **Banco do Brasil**,
R Joaquim da Silva Lima 550, Guarapari;
Bradesco, R Henrique Coutinho 901,
Guarapari; **Banco do Brasil**, Av Lacerda
de Aguiar 356, Marataízes.

Contents

Border crossings

Iguaçu Falls & the south

At a glance

⊖ **Getting around** Buses and internal flights. Car hire a possibility.

◉ **Time required** 2 days for Iguaçu, 5 days for Iguaçu and Ilha do Mel or Florianópolis. 7-10 days for 3-4 destinations.

☼ **Weather** Varies across this large region. Summer (Oct-Mar) tends to be warm and dry; winter (Apr-Sep) is cool and wet. Nov is best for Iguaçu, when the falls are fullest. It can freeze in the mountains Jun-Jul.

✖ **When not to go** In Jun-Aug the sea is cold.

PARAGUAY

Eldorado
Mundo Novo
Guaíra
Represa
de Itaipu
Ciudad
del Este
Foz do
Iguaçu
Parque Nacional
Foz do Iguaçu
Iguaçu
Falls
Rio Iguaçu

ARGENTINA

Salto do
Yucumã
Santo
Tomé
Santo
Ângelo
São Borja
São Miguel
das Missões
Itaqui
Uruguaiana
Barra do
Quaraí
Quaraí
Bella
Unión
Rosário
do Sul
Rivera
Santana do
Livramento

URUGUAY

Rio Branco

Santa Vitória
do Palmar
Chuí

Ubitajara
Paranavaí
Cianorte
Maringá
Longina
Londrina
Apucarana
Campo
Mourão
Campina
Toledo
PARANÁ
Pitanga
Cascavel
Prudentópolis
Guarapuava
Represa de
Salto Santiago
Pato
Branco
Represa de
Foz do
Areia
São Miguel
d'Oeste
Treze Tílias
Iraí
Barragem
Passo
Fundo
Erexim
Porto Xavier
RIO GRANDE DO SUL
Cruz Alta
Passo Fundo
Soledade
Bento
Gonçalves
Candelária
Garibaldi
Santa
Maria
Manuel
Viana
Alegrete
São Gabriel
Caçapava
do Sul
Encruzilha
da do Sul
Bagé
Aceguá
Pelotas
Rio Grande
Cassino
Jaguarão
Lagoa
Mirim
Curral Alto
Estação Ecológica
do Taim
Laguna
Mangabeira

Sto Antonio
da Platina
Alecrim
Jaguariaíva
Curitiba
Paranaguá
Matinhos
Joinville
São Francisco
do Sul
SANTA CATARINA
Joaçaba
Curitibanos
Blumenau
Florianópolis
Lages
São
Joaquim
Vacaria
Canela
Gramado
São Leopoldo
Osório
Porto Alegre
Aguas
Brancas
Capivari
Tapes
Lagoa dos
Patos
Tavares
Canguçu
Dunas
São José do Norte
Rio Branco

Lençóis
Paulista
Ourinhos
Pitaju
Avaré
Itapeva
Apiaí
Capã
Boni
Parque
Nacional
Vila Velha
Parque
Nacional
Superaguí
Ilha
Mel
Itapo
Penha
Itajaí
Camboriú
Porto Belo
Ilha
San
Catar
Praia
da
Rosa
Imbituba
Laguna
Içara
Araranguá
Arroio do Silva
Torres
Arroio do Sul
Tramandaí
Cidreira
Quintão
Bacopari

Atlantic
Ocean

Parque Nacional
Lagoa do Peixe
Mostardas
Bojuru

BR376
BR227
BR285
BR116
BR290
BR293

N

100 km

100 miles

★ Don't miss ...
1 Serra da Graciosa, page 309.
2 Ilha do Mel and the Parque Nacional
   de Superagüi, pages 312 and 314.
3 Iguaçu Falls, page 314.
4 Florianópolis, page 336.
5 São Miguel das Missões, page 365.
6 Parque Nacional Aparados da Serra, page 366.

Southern Brazil is famous first and foremost for one sight: Iguaçu. These are the world's mightiest and grandest waterfalls, surrounded on all sides by lush subtropical forest, stretching for almost 3 km, and falling in a thunderous two-tier curtain from a height almost twice that of Niagara. But although Iguaçu is undoubtedly the highlight, it would be a shame to rush in and out of southern Brazil without seeing anything else. There are many other spectacularly beautiful natural sights: toy trains winding their way through jagged, verdant mountains to some of the largest stretches of lowland coastal forest in South America; bays studded with islands, each of which is home to different and often unique fauna; the crumbling ruins of Jesuit monasteries; and, of course, miles of glorious beaches.

The feel of the south is very different to the rest of Brazil; towns are more European and made up of settlers from the Ukraine, Germany and Italy. In Joinville and Blumenau an archaic Bavarian dialect is still widely spoken and there is an annual *bierfest*. Buses run on time, streets are relatively clean and people don't talk much. Things change again in the border country with Argentina and Uruguay, which retains an insular and macho *gaúcho* culture that seems to have more in common with the Argentine pampas than Brazil.

Paraná

Paraná is most famous for the Iguaçu Falls, the largest and most magnificent waterfalls in the Americas. No guidebook can do justice to the spectacle and they are a must on any itinerary to Brazil. Besides Iguaçu, Paraná has a great deal to offer those in search of pristine nature: the largest area of coastal rainforest in Brazil swathes the mountains of the northern coast, while little beach-fringed islands, such as Ilha do Mel, sit a short way offshore. Both are easily reached from the neat and tidy capital, Curitiba, on one of the continent's most impressive railway journeys. The interior of the state is dotted with villages and towns founded by the European settlers that flocked here at the end of the 19th century.

The area of what is now Paraná was neglected by the Portuguese until the beginning of the 17th century when gold was discovered. The region fell under the control of São Paulo, but there was no great success in the extraction of gold, partly because of a lack of indigenous labour (they had all been sent elsewhere or had died of disease). As soon as the precious metal was discovered in Minas Gerais, the mines shut down in Paraná. Instead, the colonists turned to agriculture and cattle-raising and, in the 18th and 19th centuries, the state was dominated by fazendeiros and drovers. Until 1853, the area was controlled from São Paulo. When the new province was created, cattle and maté-growing were the most important activities, but with the coming of the railways at the end of the 19th century, timber became equally significant.

When it became apparent in the second half of the 19th century that the province of Paraná would not develop without a major increase in the population, an official immigration policy was launched. The Italians were the first, but later settlers came from all over Europe and, since the start of the 20th century, from Japan, Syria and the Lebanon. ▸▸ *For listings, see pages 324-335.*

Curitiba → *For listings, see pages 324-335.* *Colour map 5, A4. Phone code: 041. Population: 1.6 million. Altitude: 908 m.*

Paraná's capital is a Brazilian Milton Keynes – celebrated by locals for its civic planning and quality suburban life. It's hardly a tourist draw. Most visitors who end up here do so to change bus or plane en route to or from Iguaçu or the beaches of Ilha do Mel. However those who have a few hours to spare should consider a visit to the **Oscar Niemeyer museum**, a stunning modernist building that looks like a giant eye. This can happily be seen in a few hours between transport connections. Curitiba also marks the start of one of South America's most spectacular railway journeys: to Morretes and the Baía de Paranaguá via the Serra da Graciosa mountains.

Ins and outs

Getting there **Afonso Pena airport** ① *18 km south of the city centre, T041-3381 1515* receives international flights from Paraguay and Argentina and has direct connections with São Paulo, Rio de Janeiro, Porto Alegre and other state capitals. There are car rental booths, banks with international ATMs and cafés along with buses (US$1) and taxis (US$28) to the centre. International and interstate buses arrive at the combined bus and railway station, the **Rodoferroviária** ① *Av Alfonso Camargo, www.rodoviariaonline. com.br*, where there are restaurants, banks, shops, phones, a post office, pharmacy, tourist office and other public services. The website has timetables and prices. Trains run along the Serra Verde between Curitiba and Paranaguá (see box, page 334).

Getting around Within the city there is an integrated transport system with several types of bus route; pick up a map in one of the tourist booths for details. The 'Transport–City Circular–Linha Turismo' circles the major transport terminals and points of interest in the city centre and costs US$16 for five stops. ▶▶ *See Transport, page 332.*

Tourist information The main office is in the **Instituto Municipal de Turismo/Curitiba Turismo** ① *R da Glória 362, 1st floor, T041-3250 7728, Mon-Fri 0800-1200 and 1400-1800*. There is also an office at the **rodoferroviária** ① *Av Presidente Afonso Camargo 330, T041-3320 3121, daily 0800-1800*.

Sights

The city has extensive open spaces and some attractive modern architecture. There is a good panoramic view from the glass observation deck of the telecommunications tower, **Torre Mercês**, built by Telepar and so is also known as the **Telepar Tower** ① *R Jacarezinho, corner of R Professor Lycio Veloso 191, T041-3322 8080, Tue-Fri 1230-2030, Sat and Sun 1030-2030, US$1.70*. The 110-m tower stands at an elevation of 95 m above sea level. There is a map of the city on the floor so that you can locate key sites.

The commercial centre is the busy Rua 15 de Novembro, part of which is a pedestrian area called **Rua das Flores**. Since urban planning first began in 1720, the Rua das Flores has been a focus for street life and street entertainment and is now perennially decorated with flowers and trees, and lined with benches, cafés, restaurants, cinemas and shops. At its southern end, the **Boca Maldita** is particularly lively and a popular meeting place.

On Praça Tiradentes is the **cathedral** ① *R Barão do Serro Azul 31, T041-3324 5136*, built in neo-Gothic style and inaugurated in 1893 (restored in 1993). Behind the cathedral, near Largo da Ordem, is a pedestrian area with a flower clock and old buildings. It is very atmospheric in the evening when it is illuminated by old gas lamps. City centre bar and nightlife is concentrated here. There is an art market on Sunday morning in **Praça Garibáldi**, beside the attractive Rosário church.

Museums worth visiting include the **Museu Paranaense** ① *R Kellers 289, Alto São Francisco T041-3304 3300, www.museuparanaense.pr.gov.br, Tue-Fri 0900-1700, Sat and Sun 1100-1500*, which has temporary shows and concerts in the garden on Sunday, alongside a collection of ethnological and historical material, and the **Museu de Arte Contemporânea** ① *R Desembargador Westphalen 16, Praça Zacarias, T041-3222 5172, www.mac.pr.gov.br, Tue-Fri 1000-1900, Sat and Sun 1000-1600*, which showcases Brazilian contemporary works, with an emphasis on artists from Paraná.

Nearby is the **SESC Paraná** ① *Paço da Liberdade, Praça Generoso Marques, Centro T041-3234-4200, www.sescpr.com.br/eventos/pacodaliberdade*, one of the cultural centres in the excellent SESC network (see box, page 117). It occupies the old Museu Paraense building – a beautiful neoclassical edifice dating from 1916 – and hosts events and exhibitions as well as concerts from leading small Brazilian artists. The air-conditioned café-restaurant is a good spot for lunch or tea.

Unlike most Brazilian cities, Curitiba has plenty of green spaces. The most popular is the **Passeio Público** ① *closed Mon*, in the heart of the city, with three lakes, each with an island, and a playground. About 4 km east of the *rodoferroviário*, the **Jardim Botânico Fanchette Rischbieter**. This has a fine glass house, again with domes, curves and lots of steel, inspired by the Crystal Palace in London. The gardens are in French style and there is also a **Museu Botânico** ① *R Ostoja Roguski (Primeira Perimetral dos Bairros), T041-3362 1800,* *www.cultura-arte.com/curitiba/museu-botanico.htm*. It can be reached by the orange Expreso buses from Praça Rui Barbosa.

Near the shores of Lagoa Bacacheri, on the northern edge of the city, is one of Brazil's many hidden quirks: an **Egyptian temple** ① *R Nicarágua 2453*. The temple is devoted to the Rosicrucian cult: a 19th-century offshoot of Theosophical occultism that has taken hold in Brazil alongside many other arcane religions. This is surely the only country on Earth where Rosicrucians advertise themselves with car bumper stickers. Visits can also be arranged to the Brazilian centre of the Rosicrucians; take the Santa Cândida bus to Estação Boa Vista, then walk.

Museu Oscar Niemeyer (MON)
① *3 km north of the centre, R Marechal Hermes 999, T041-3350 4400, www.museuoscar niemeyer.org.br, Tue-Sun 1000-1800, US$2.25, buses from the rodoviária.*

Curitiba

Not to scale

	Del Rey 5	Lumini 18	**Eating** ⑦
	Deville Express 4	Mercure Curitiba Centro 3	Baviera 11
	Deville Rayon 6	Nova Lisboa 15	Casa Lilas 16
Sleeping	HI Curitiba Eco-hostel 7	Paraty 19	Durski 6
Bourbon & Tower 1	HI Hostel Roma 2	Slaviero Braz 8	Green Life 9
Centro Europeu Tourist 12	Kings 13	Slaviero Palace 10	Makado 1

The Museu Oscar Niemeyer was designed by, and is devoted to, the famous Brazilian modernist architect who designed Brasília and was a disciple of Le Corbusier, together with other Parananese artists. The stunning principal building is shaped like a giant eye and the whole museum serves as a gallery for diverse shows, which in the past have ranged from Picasso drawings to modern Japanese art. An underground passage, also lined with a range of (always high quality) exhibits and photographs links the eye to a sculpture garden.

Curitiba to Paranaguá → For listings, see pages 324-335.

Serra da Graciosa and Parque Nacional Marumbi

When the first European ships arrived at Paraná in the mid-16th century, they would have been daunted by the prospect of conquering the lands of southern Brazil. From the sea, the thickly forested and steep crags of the **Serra da Graciosa** must have seemed an insurmountable wall fortifying the continent from the coast. But in a cruel twist of fate, it was native trails cutting through the mountains that led to inland Paraná being colonized. After the paths were discovered, the Portuguese forced African slaves to pave them with river stones. Miners and traders were soon dragging mules laden with gold, silver, textiles and *herva maté* up and down the mountains. As trade grew, the port at Paranaguá became the most important south of Santos and little towns of whitewashed churches and smart Portuguese buildings like Morretes and Antonina grew up along the trails. In 1885 the routes were busy enough to merit the construction of a railway, which wound its way around the slopes, across rushing rivers and through the forest to the sea.

Ins and outs

Two roads and a railway run from Curitiba to Paranaguá. The railway journey on the **Trem da Serra do Mar** (aka Serra Verde Express), is the most spectacular in Brazil, cutting through numerous tunnels, crossing dizzy viaducts (especially imported from Belgium), offering sudden views of deep gorges and high peaks and waterfalls before arriving at at the little mountain town of Morretes and on Sundays, the sea at Paranaguá (the port for the Ilha do Mel). Near Banhado station (Km 66) is the waterfall of **Véu da Noiva**, and from the Marumbi station at Km 59 you can reach the Marumbi mountain range.

uintana 5
accy 3
almão 7

The Farm 13
Schwarzwald 15
Tuba's 12

ars & clubs
re Fox 4

For timetables, see box, page 334, and the Serra Verde website (www.serraverdeexpress.com.br), as schedules frequently change). If you plan to do a round-trip to Ilha do Mel from Curitiba, but want to ride on the train to see the views, the best value is to take the bus from Curitiba to Paranaguá and the train back.

The principal trail, the **Estrada da Graciosa** – between Curitiba and Paranaguá – is now a spectacular cobbled road that runs for 15 km through the mountains and the Marumbi national park. There are fire grills, shelters and camping at the various rest stops. You can also hike the original mule trail, which follows the road and passes the rest stops; trails leave from just outside Morretes railway station and are well signposted. Take food, water and plenty of insect repellent.

The **Serra da Graciosa Marumbi national park** has recently opened up to guided trekking, rock climbing and light ecotourism. Companies like **Calango Expedições**, www.calangoexpedicoes.com.br, and the Florianópolis-based travel company, **Brazil Ecojourneys**, www.brazilecojourneys.com, offer tours. There is good climbing and hiking in the park. ›› *See Activities and tours, page 331.*

Morretes, Antonina and around → *Colour map 5, A5.*

Morretes was founded in 1721 and is one of the prettiest colonial towns in southern Brazil. A parade of whitewashed Portuguese colonial buildings with painted window frames straddle the pebbly river, and church spires stick up from a sea of red-tiled roofs against the backdrop of the deep-green forest-swathed hills.

The **Estrada da Graciosa** road passes through Morretes, and there are numerous daily buses from Curitiba and Paranaguá. The train terminates here, apart from weekends when it stops for a lunch break. There are a handful of *pousadas* and numerous restaurants serve the local speciality, *barreado* (meat stew cooked in a clay pot), which was originally served a day in advance of **Carnaval** in order to allow women to escape from their domestic cooking chores and enjoy the party. The **tourist office** ① *T041-3462 1024 or see www.morretes.pr.gov.br,* is by the river.

Around Curitiba

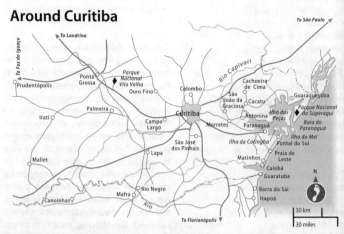

The town itself is tiny and easily negotiated on foot. A series of walks lead from the town into the **Serra da Graciosa** mountains. The most popular trails run to the **Salto dos Macacos** and **Salto da Fortuna waterfalls**, which take between three and four hours there and back from town. Walks can be organized through **Calango Expedições**.
» *See Activities and tours, page 331.*

Antonina, just 14 km from Morretes, is almost as picturesque and sits on the Bahia do Paranaguá. It was once an important port town but is now sleepy and little visited, except during the lively **Carnaval**. It can be reached by local bus from Morretes.

Paranaguá and around → *For listings, see pages 324-335. Colour map 5, A5. Phone code: 041. Population: 128,000.*

After the endless lorry parks and the messy dual carriageway leading into the town, the centre of Paranaguá, 268 km south of Santos, comes as a pleasant surprise, especially around the waterfront. Colonial buildings decay quietly in the heat and humidity, some are just façades encrusted with bromeliads; and fishermen get quietly drunk in little *botiquines*.

There's not much to do in the town but stroll along the cobbles and while away the time in the interesting city museum, **Museu de Arqueologia e Etnologia** ⓘ *R 15 Novembro 575, T041-3423 2511, www.proec.ufpr.br, Tue-Fri 0900-1200, 1330-1800, Sat-Sun 1200-1800, US$1,* housed in a formidable 18th-century **Jesuit convent**. It showcases aspects of the city's interesting past. Other attractions include a 17th-century fountain, the church of **São Benedito**, and the shrine of **Nossa Senhora do Rocio**, 2 km from town. The town is more remarkable for what lies on its doorstep: the **Ilha do Mel** and **Baía do Paranaguá**, see page 312.

Ins and outs
Tourist information is available from **FUMTUR** ⓘ *R Padre Albino 45, Campo Grande, T041-3420 2940.*

Background
Before it became Paranaguá, the region was an important centre of indigenous life. Colossal shell middens, called *sambaquis* (see the Museu Arqueológico do Sambaqui in Joinville, page 346) have been found on the surrounding estuaries, protecting regally adorned corpses. The mounds can be as high as a two-storey building and date from between 7000 and 2000 years ago. They were built by the ancestors of the *tupinguin* and *carijo* people who were here when the first Europeans arrived. The bay's outer islands were initially claimed and occupied by the Spanish (who thought they had reached the coast near Potosí in Bolivia, thousands of miles inland, when they first saw the Serra da Graciosa). But in the late 16th century a *bandeira* expedition under Heiliodoro Eobano found gold in Paranaguá. When the Portuguese realized the importance of the area, they beat the Spanish off the land and fortified the southern end of Ilha do Mel, establishing a port at Paranaguá.

Excursions from Paranaguá
Matinhos, 40 km south, is a medium-sized Mediterranean-style resort, invaded by surfers in October for the Paraná surf competition. About 8 km further south is **Caiobá**, at the mouth of a bay, the other side of which is **Guaratuba**, which is less built up than Caiobá. The ferry between the two towns is frequent and is a beautiful crossing (free for

pedestrians, US$3.80 for cars). Each of these towns has a few hotels but most close in winter; there is camping at Matinhos and Guaratuba.

On the road to Ponta Grossa is a recently created state park, the **Parque Estadual da Vila Velha** ① *T042-3228 1138, Wed-Mon 0800-1730, closed Tue, tickets costs US$14 for foreigners, purchase tickets at the entrance, last bus back is at 1715 and costs US$11*, 97 km from Curitiba and 10 km from Ponta Grossa. The sandstone rocks have been weathered into fantastic shapes, although many have been defaced by thoughtless tourists. Nearby are the **Lagoa Dourada**, surrounded by forests, and the **Furnas**: three waterholes, the deepest of which has a lift shaft which descend 54 m almost to the level of the lake. The lift was inactive as this book went to press as it was damaging the sandstone. The park office is 300 m from the highway and the park a further 1.5 km. Allow all day if visiting all three sites (unless you hitch, or can time the buses well, it's a lot of walking).

Baía de Paranaguá → *For listings, see pages 324-335.*

The Baía de Paranaguá is one of Latin America's biodiversity hotspots and the best place on the Brazilian coast to see rare rainforest flora and fauna. Mangrove and lowland subtropical forests, islands, rivers and rivulets combine to form the largest stretch of Atlantic coast rainforest in the country. The area protects critically endangered species like the black-faced lion tamarin, which was only discovered in 1990, and the red-tailed Amazon parrot (which despite its name is only found here), alongside a full gamut of South American spectaculars including jaguars. Most of the bay is protected by a series of national and state parks (see Parque Nacional de Superagüi, page 314), but it is possible to visit on an organized tour from Paranaguá (or with more difficulty from **Guraquecaba** on the northern side of the bay). The **BARCOPAR boatman's cooperative** ① *Associação dos Proprietários de Barcos de Turismo e Transporte do Estado do Paraná, R General Carneiro 32, Paranaguá, T041-3425 6173, www.barcopar.com.br*, offers a range of excellent trips in large and small vessels ranging from two hours to two days and from US$15 per person to US$100.

Ilha do Mel → *Colour map 5, A5.*

Ilha do Mel is a weekend escape and holiday island popular with Paraná and Paulista surfers, 20-something hippies and day-tripping families. There are no roads, no vehicles and limited electricity. Outside of Carnaval and New Year it is a laid-back little place. Bars pump out Bob Marley and *maranhão* reggae; spaced-out surfers lounge around in hammocks; and bare-footed couples dance *forró* on the wooden floors of simple beachside shacks. Much of the island is forested, its coastline is fringed with broad beaches and, in the south, broken by rocky headlands. Its location in the mouth of the Bahía de Paranaguá made it strategically important to the Portuguese in the 18th century. The lighthouse, **Farol das Conchas**, was built in 1872 to guide shipping into the bay. The cave of **Gruta das Encantadas** is surrounded with myths and legends about mermaids, enchanting all who came near.

The island divides into two sections connected by a spit of sand at the **Nova Brasília** jetty, the principal port of arrival. The rugged eastern half, where most of the facilities are to be found, is fringed with curving beaches and capped with a lighthouse. The flat, scrub forest-covered and balloon-shaped western half is predominantly an ecological protection area and visits are not allowed. Its northern side is watched over by the **Fortaleza Nossa Senhora dos Prazeres**, a fort built in 1767 on the orders of King José I of Portugal, to defend what was one of the principal ports in the country. In 1850, a British warship captured three illegal slave-trading ships, giving rise to a battle known as **Combate Cormorant**. The view from the 20th-century gun emplacements on the hill above the fort is the best on the island.

The best surf beaches are **Praia Grande** and **Praia de Fora**, both about 20 minutes' walk from the Nova Brasília jetty. **Fortaleza** and **Ponta do Bicho** on the north shore are more tranquil and are safe for swimming; they are about 45 minutes' walk from the jetty or five minutes by boat. **Farol** and **Encantadas** are the liveliest and have the most accommodation, restaurants and nightlife. However, Encantadas has become somewhat polluted, with the cesspits overflowing into open sewers in the wet.

Walking on Ilha do Mel A series of well-signposted trails lead throughout Ilha do Mel and its coast. The most walked are as follows: the **lighthouse trail from Farol beach** (20 minutes), which is paved but steep; the views are wonderful. The **Nova Brasília to Encantadas trail** (three hours) offers a series of beautiful views, paths through the forest and stretches of semi-deserted beach. However, once you reach the end of the trail, you will either have to return the same way or take a boat taxi around the rocks back to Nova

Ilha do Mel

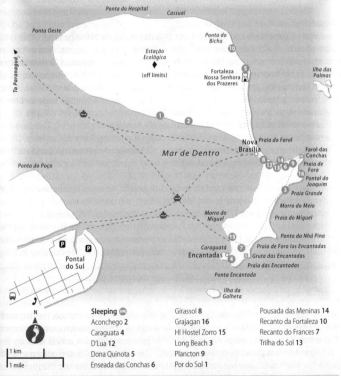

Sleeping	Girassol 8	Pousada das Meninas 14
Aconchego 2	Grajagan 16	Recanto da Fortaleza 10
Caraguata 4	HI Hostel Zorro 15	Recanto do Frances 7
D'Lua 12	Long Beach 3	Trilha do Sol 13
Dona Quinota 5	Plancton 9	
Enseada das Conchas 6	Por do Sol 1	

Brasília. This involves clambering over rocks at the end of Praia Grande; take appropriate footwear. The **Nova Brasília to Fortaleza trail** takes 1½ hours. It is also possible to spend a full day walking around the entire island along the beaches (apart from the stretch between Encantadas and Nova Brasília, which requires a boat taxi). Bear in mind that you won't be able to walk on the protected western side of the island.

Ins and outs There are two main routes. From Paranaguá, large ferries leave from Rua General Carneiro (Rua da Praia) in front of the tourist information kiosk and run to Encantadas and Nova Brasília (twice daily, 0800 and 1500, one hour 45 minutes, US$15 return). Alternatively, there are regular buses from Paranaguá to Pontal do Sul, from where a small boat runs to the island, daily 0800-1730, US$13 return (hourly at weekends, less frequently during the week). There are souvenir and handicraft stalls at the ferry point. The last bus back to Paranaguá leaves at 2200. There aren't any ATM or money exchange booths on the island (although some *pousadas* might change dollars at an exorbitant rate), so bring cash with you. Some restaurants take cards but not all of them.

There are tourist booths at Encantadas beach and Nova Brasília (T041-3426 9091, Tuesday to Sunday 0800-1800). See also www.ilhadomelonline.com.br and www.ilha domel.com. There are no shops on the island so stock up before you go. Many of the hotels have internet access and there are a few internet cafés.▸▸ *See Transport, page 334.*

Parque Nacional de Superagüi

The island of **Superagüi** and its neighbour, **Ilha das Peças**, lie at the heart of the largest single stretch of Atlantic Coast rainforest in the country and are the focus for the Guaraqueçaba Environmental Protection Area, which is part of the **Nature Conservancy's Parks in Peril Programme**, www.parksinperil.org. They also form a national park and UNESCO World Heritage Site. Many endangered endemic plants and animals live in the park, including hundreds of orchids, Atlantic rainforest-specific animals such as brown howler monkeys and large colonies of red-tailed Amazons (a parrot on the 'red list' of critically endangered species and which can be seen nowhere else but here). There are also rare neotropical animals here like jaguarundi, puma and jaguar. There are several Guarani villages in the area; other inhabitants are mostly of European descent, making a living from fishing. There is superb swimming from deserted beaches, but watch out for stinging jellyfish.

Ins and outs Access to the park and accommodation can be arranged through the village on Superagüi beach, just north of Ilha do Mel. Boats run from Paranaguá on Monday, Wednesday and Friday at 1400 and return on Monday, Wednesday and Friday at 0700, US$11 one way. The boat takes about two hours. Private boats from Praia da Fortaleza on Ilha do Mel run if the weather is good, there are plenty of tour operators on the island. It is possible to use the route through Superagüi as an alternative route from Paraná into São Paulo state.

Iguaçu Falls → *For listings, see pages 324-335. Colour map 5, A2. Phone code 045, www.fozdoiguaçu.pr.gov.br.*

Foz do Iguaçu, or Las Cataratas del Iguazú as they are known in Spanish, are the most overwhelming and spectacular waterfalls in the world. Situated on the Rio Iguaçu (meaning 'big water' in Guarani), which forms the border between Argentina and Brazil, they are made up of no less than 275 separate waterfalls. The Paraguayan city of Ciudad del Este is just a few kilometres away but Paraguay does not own territory at the falls themselves.

The most spectacular part is the **Garganta do Diabo** (Devil's Throat), the mouth of a 28-km-long gorge that stretches downstream to the Alto Río Paraná. It is best visited from the Argentine side (see Ins and outs, below, and page 319).

Viewed from below, the water tumbles and roars over the craggy brown cliffs, framed by verdant rainforest encrusted with bromeliads, orchids, begonias and dripping ferns. A seemingly perpetual rainbow hovers over the scene and toco toucans, flocks of parakeets, caciques and great dusky swifts dodge in and out of the vapour whilst a vast number of butterflies dance over the forest walkways and lookouts.

Ins and outs

The town nearest the falls is also, confusingly, called Iguaçu – or to give it its full name – Foz de Iguaçu. Around 80% of the falls lie in Argentina, which offers the most spectacular views and the best infrastructure. Tickets costs about US$22 on both sides (discount for Mercosur members). The Argentine side only accept Argentine pesos (ATMs at the entrance); dollars and euro can be used as reais on the Brazilian side. There are national parks protecting extensive rainforest on both sides. Transport between the two parks is via the Ponte Tancredo Neves, as there is no crossing at the falls themselves.

The **Brazilian park** offers a superb panoramic view of the whole falls and is best visited in the morning (four hours is enough for the highlights) when the light is better for photography. The **Argentine park** (which requires at least half a day) includes a railway trip in the entrance fee as well as offering closer views of the individual falls. To fully appreciate the forest, with its wildlife and butterflies, you need to spend a full day and get well away from the visitor areas. Both parks can, if necessary, be visited in a day, starting at about 0700. However, in the heat, the brisk pace needed for a rapid tour is exhausting. Sunset is best from the Brazilian side.

The busiest times are holiday periods and on Sunday, when helicopter tours are particularly popular. Both parks have visitor centres, though the information provided by the Argentine centre is far superior to that in the Brazilian centre. Tourist facilities on both sides are constantly being improved.

There are many advantages to staying in Foz do Iguaçu town and commuting to the Argentine side; it has, for example a much bigger choice of hotels and restaurants. Whichever side you decide to stay on, most establishments will accept reais, pesos or dollars. Cross-border transport usually accepts guaraníes as well.

A useful guidebook is *Iguazú, The Laws of the Jungle* by Santiago G de la Vega, Contacto Silvestre Ediciones (1999), available from the visitor centre.

Getting to the falls from Brazil Buses leave Foz do Iguaçu town from the **Rodoviária Terminal Urbana** ① *Av Juscelino Kubitschek, 1 block from the infantry barracks.* The grey or red **Transbalan** service runs to the falls every half an hour 0530-2330, past the airport and **Hotel Tropical das Cataratas** (40 minutes, US$1.25 one way, payable in reais only). Return buses run 0800-1900. The bus terminates at the visitor centre, where you must pay the entrance fee and transfer to the free park shuttle bus, which leaves every five minutes 0830-1900. If driving, cars must be left in the visitor centre car park. Taxis from Foz do Iguaçu charge US$20 one way. You can negotiate in advance the return trip, including waiting and pay separately for each journey. Many hotels organize tours to the falls, which have been recommended in preference to taxi rides. Be wary of transfer offers from Iguaçu's travel agencies – they are often even more expensive than taking your own taxi.

Getting to the falls from Argentina **Transportes El Práctico** buses run every half hour from the Puerto Iguazú bus terminal, stopping at the park entrance to buy entry tickets. Fares US$1 return to the visitor centre. The first bus leaves at 0700, and the last return is at 1900, journey time 30 minutes. Buses are erratic, especially when wet, even though the times are clearly indicated. There are fixed rates for taxis, US$15 one-way, up to five people. A tour from the bus terminal, taking in both sides of the falls, costs US$21.

Clothing In the rainy season when water levels are high, waterproof coats or swimming costumes are advisable for some of the lower catwalks and for boat trips. Cameras should be carried in a plastic bag. Wear shoes with good soles, as the rocks can be very slippery in places.

Background

The Caiagangue people originally inhabited the region, but the first European visitor to the falls was the Spaniard Alvaro Núñez Cabeza de Vaca in 1541. He nearly fell off one of the waterfalls on his search for a connection between the Brazilian coast and the Río de la Plata, and named them the Saltos de Santa María (Santa Maria waterfalls). Though the falls were well known to the Jesuit missionaries, they were largely forgotten until the

① Iguaçu Falls orientation

Sleeping 🛏	IYHA Paudimar	Bars & clubs 🎵
Hostel Natura **1**	Campestre **1**	Oba! Oba! **1**
	Suiça **2**	

area was explored by a Brazilian expedition sent out by the Paraguayan president, Solano López, in 1863.

Parque Nacional Foz do Iguaçu (Brazil)

The Brazilian national park was founded in 1939 and designated a World Heritage Site by UNESCO in 1986. The park covers 185,262 ha on the Brazilian side and 67,000 ha on the Argentinian side, extending along the north bank of the Rio Iguaçu, then sweeping northwards to Santa Tereza do Oeste on the BR-277. The subtropical rainforest benefits from the added humidity in the proximity of the falls, creating an environment rich in flora and fauna. Given the massive popularity of the falls, the national parks on either side of the frontier are surprisingly little visited.

Fauna The parks on both sides of the falls are replete with wildlife and are a haven for birders. The most common mammals seen are coatis, which look like long-nosed racoons and squeakily demand food from visitors; do not be tempted as these small animals can be aggressive. There are other mammals here too, including jaguar, puma, ocelot and margay, which can occasionally be seen along the park roads just before and after dawn. They are wary of humans, although in 2003 a jaguar broke into the Parque das Aves (see page 320) and ate the zoo's prize caiman. Most frequently encountered are little and red brocket deer, white-eared opossum, *paca* (which look like large dappled guinea pigs) and a subspecies of the brown capuchin monkey. Other mammals include white-lipped peccary, bush dog and southern river otter. The endangered tegu lizard is common. Over 100 species of butterflies have been identified, among them the electric blue morpho, the poisonous red and black heliconius and species of papilionidae and pieridae.

The birdlife is especially rewarding. Five members of the toucan family can be seen: toco and red-breasted toucans, chestnut-eared araçari, saffron and spot-billed toucanets. From the bamboo stands you may see spotted bamboo wren, grey-bellied spinetail, several antshrikes and short-tailed ant-thrush. In the forest you might see rufous-thighed kite, black-and-white hawk-eagle, black-fronted piping-guan, blue ground dove, dark-billed cuckoo, black-capped screech-owl, surucua trogon, rufous-winged antwren, black-crowned tityra, red-ruffed fruitcrow, white-winged swallow, plush-crested jay, cream-bellied gnatcatcher, black-goggled and magpie

Iguaçu Falls maps
Iguaçu Falls orientation, page 316
Iguaçu Falls, page 318
Foz do Iguaçu, page 321

Parque das Aves

Rio Iguaçu Superior

Argentine Visitor Centre

Circuito Inferior

Brazilian Visitor Centre

Circuito Superior

Isla San Martin

Garganta do Diabo

To Porto Canoas

Floriano Falls

Iguaçu Falls

Parque Nacional Iguazú

To Bernardo de Yrigoyen

To Airport

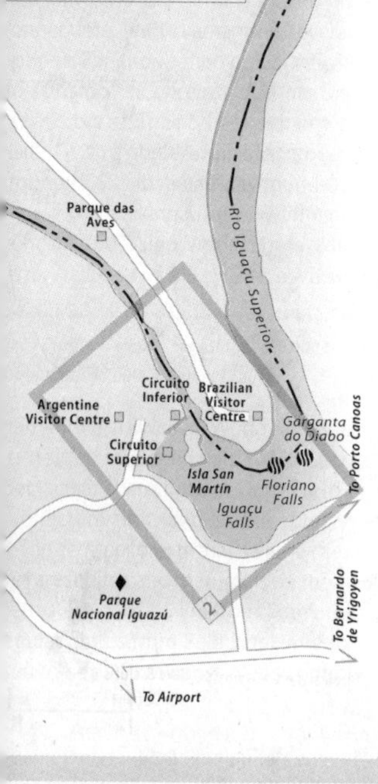

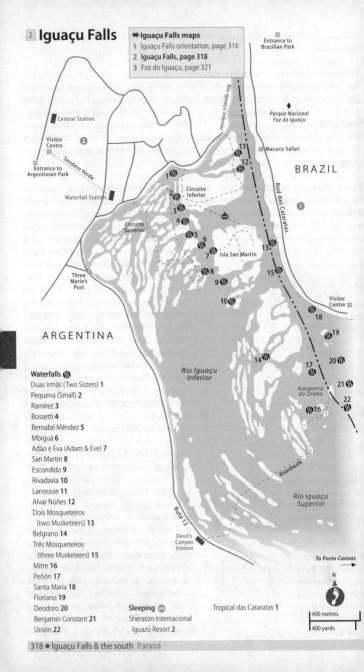

2 Iguaçu Falls

→ **Iguaçu Falls maps**
1 Iguaçu Falls orientation, page 316
2 **Iguaçu Falls, page 318**
3 Foz do Iguaçu, page 321

Entrance to
Brazilian Park

Central Station

Visitor
Centre

Entrance to
Argentinian Park

Sendero Verde

Waterfall Station

Circuito
Superior

Three
Marie's
Port

Rio Iguaçu Inferior

Parque Nacional
Foz do Iguaçu

Macuco Safari

BRAZIL

Rod das Cataratas

Circuito
Inferior

Isla San Martín

Visitor
Centre

ARGENTINA

Rio Iguaçu
Inferior

Garganta
do Diabo

Boardwalk

Rio Iguaçu
Superior

Ruta 12

Devil's
Canyon
Station

To Porto Canoas

N

400 metres

400 yards

Waterfalls
Duas Irmãs (Two Sisters) **1**
Pequena (Small) **2**
Ramírez **3**
Bossetti **4**
Bernabé Méndez **5**
Mbiguá **6**
Adão e Eva (Adam & Eve) **7**
San Martín **8**
Escondido **9**
Rivadavia **10**
Lanousse **11**
Alvar Núñes **12**
Dois Mosqueteiros
  (two Musketeers) **13**
Belgrano **14**
Três Mosqueteiros
  (three Musketeers) **15**
Mitre **16**
Peñón **17**
Santa Maria **18**
Floriano **19**
Deodoro **20**
Benjamin Constant **21**
Unión **22**

Sleeping
Sheraton Internacional
Iguazú Resort **2**

Tropical das Cataratas **1**

318 ● Iguaçu Falls & the south Paraná

tanagers, green-chinned euphonia, black-throated and utlra-marine grosbeaks, yellow-billed cardinal, red-crested finch. (Bird and mammal information supplied by Douglas Trent, **Focus Tours** – see Essentials, page 52.)

The falls All cars and public buses stop at the visitor centre, where there are souvenir shops, a **Banco do Brasil** ATM and *câmbio* (1300-1700), a small café and car park. If possible, visit on a weekday when the walks are less crowded. The centre is open daily in winter 0900-1700 and in summer 0900-1800. There is a R$12 (US$6.80) car-parking fee, payable only in Brazilian currency. This includes a transfer to the free park shuttle bus.

The first stop on the shuttle bus is the overpriced **Macuco Safari** ⓘ US$90 (bookable *through most agencies, which may charge a premium for transfers*). The safari takes one hour 45 minutes, leaving every 15 minutes, and visits the forest near the falls on an electric jeep and with a short trail walk climbing down to to a beach on the Garganta do Diabo. From here there are great views of the falls from below and the option to take a boat to the falls themselves; trips dunk visitors under one of the smaller cascades. Be sure to bring a fully waterproof, sealable plastic or rubber bag. Despite what guides say to the contrary, you and all your belongings will get completely soaked on this boat trip, which is the only part of the safari that can't be done solo. Visitors to Iguaçu will see as much wildlife and forest walking their own trails and boardwalks as they will with Macuco.

Iguazu Explorer ⓘ Sheraton Hotel, www.iguazujungle.com, offer a 'Great Jungle Adventure' for US$45 – a shorter trip modelled than Macuco's, but inferior. It involves bombing through the jungle in a noisy truck followed by a short walk and a boat trip up the Garganto do Diabo to the falls. A better deal is the 12-minute solo boat trip up the Garganta for US$20, without the truck and trail walk.

The second stop is the **Cataratas Trail** (starting from the hotel of the same name, non-residents can eat at the hotel, midday and evening buffets). This 1.5-km paved walk runs part of the way down the cliff near the rim of the falls, giving a stupendous view of the whole Argentine side of the falls. It ends up almost under the powerful **Floriano Falls**; from here there is a lift to the top of the Floriano Falls; a path adjacent to the lift leads to Porto Canoa. A catwalk at the foot of the Floriano Falls gives a good view of the **Garganta do Diabo**.

The **Porto Canoas** complex, with its snack bar, toilets, souvenir shops and terraces with views of the falls, was completed in 2000 after some controversy. Its restaurant serves a US$22.50 buffet, which is good for a memorable meal.

Parque Nacional Iguazú (Argentina) → International phone code + 54.

Created in 1934, the park extends over an area of 67,620 ha, most of which is covered by the same subtropical rainforest as on the Brazilian side. It is crossed by Route 101, a dirt road that runs southeast to Bernardo de Yrigoyen on the Brazilian frontier. Buses operate along this route in dry weather, offering a view of the park.

Fauna You would have to be very lucky to see jaguars, tapirs, brown capuchin monkeys, collared anteaters and coatimundi. As in Brazil, very little of the fauna in the park can be seen around the falls; even on the nature trails described below you need to go in the early morning and have luck on your side. Of the 400 species of birds, you are most likely to spot the black-crowned night heron, plumed kite, white-eyed parakeet, blue-winged parrolet, great dusky swift, scale-throated hermit, suruca trogon, Amazon kingfisher, co toucan, tropical kingbird, boat-billed flycatcher, red-rumped cacique, and the colourful purple-throated euphonia.

The falls The park is open daily 0800-1800 in summer and 0800-1700 in winter. Entry costs US$22, cash payment in Argentine pesos only. There are two cash machines by entrance. Guests at **Hotel Sheraton** should pay and get tickets stamped at the hotel to avoid paying again. The visitor centre includes a museum of local fauna and an auditorium for slide shows (available on request, minimum of eight people). It also sells a good guide book on Argentine birds. Food and drinks are available in the park but are expensive, so it is best to take your own. There is a **Telecom** kiosk at the bus stop.

A free train service leaves every 30 minutes from the visitor centre, departing for the start of two sets of walkways, both taking about an hour. The 'Circuito Inferior' or **Lower Trail**, leads down very steep steps to the lower falls and the start of the boat trip to Isla San Martin (see below). The easy 'Circuito Superior', **Upper Trail**, follows the top of the falls, giving panoramic views. The **Sendero Verde** path, taking about 20 minutes from near the visitor centre, leads to the start of the Upper and Lower trails. A second train route takes visitors to the start of an easy walkway that leads just over 1 km to the **Garganta del Diablo** (Devil's Throat). A visit here is particularly recommended in the evening when the light is best and the swifts are returning to roost on the cliffs, some behind the water.

Below the falls, a free ferry leaves regularly, subject to demand, and connects the Lower Trail with **Isla San Martín**. A steep path on the island leads to the top of the hill, where there are trails to some of the less-visited falls and rocky pools (take bathing gear in summer).

Activities and tours A number of activities are offered, both from the visitor centre and through agencies in Puerto Iguazú (Argentina), see page 332. On clear nights the moon casts a blue halo over the falls. During the full moon, there are sometimes night-time walking tours between the **Hotel Sheraton** and the falls (or from the **Hotel Tropical das Cataratas** on the Brazilian side, see page 327). For serious birdwatching and nature walks with an English-speaking guide, contact the **Pantanal Bird Club**, page 758.

Foz do Iguaçu and around → For listings, see pages 324-335. Colour map 5, A2.
Phone code: 045. Population: 260,000.

The proximity of the falls have made Foz the third most visited town in Brazil. It has no attractions of its own but is only 28 km from the falls and although there are some upmarket hotel options, the town has a greater range of cheap accommodation and restaurants.

From the town it is possible to visit a number of beaches on the shores of **Lake Itaipu** (see Itaipu Dam, page 323); the closest are at **Bairro de Três Lagoas** (Km 723 on BR-277) and in the municipality of **Santa Terezinha do Itaipu** (US$1.70), 34 km from Foz. The leisure parks have grassy areas with kiosks, barbecue sites and offer fishing as well as bathing. It is also possible to take boat trips on the lake.

The bird park, **Parque das Aves** ① *Rodovia das Cataratas Km 16, www.parquedas aves.com.br, US$12,* is well worth visiting. It contains rare South American (and foreign) birds including various currasows, guans, parrots, macaws and toucans. These are housed in large aviaries through which you can walk, with the birds flying and hopping around you. There is also a butterfly house. The bird park is within walking distance of the Hotel San Martín. The HI Paudimar Falls Hostel (see Sleeping, page 329) offers a discount for its guests. The national park bus stops here, 100 m before the entrance to the falls.

Ins and outs

Getting there Foz do Iguaçu's **Aeroporto Internacional de Cataratas** ① *Rodovia BR-469, Km 16.5, T045-3521 4200*, is 12 km from the town centre and receives flights from Belém, Brasília, Curitiba, Macapá, Manaus, Rio de Janeiro and São Paulo. The airport has a **Banco do Brasil**, a **Bradesco** and a *câmbio*, car rental offices, a tourist office and an official taxi stand. Taxis cost US$22 to the town centre and vice versa. **Transbalan** (Aeroporto/Parque Nacional) buses run to town, US$1.20, but don't permit large amounts of luggage (backpacks okay); they run every 20 minutes 0545-2400. The buses go to the Terminal de Transporte Urbano in the centre. There are two terminals in Iguacu so sometimes you

3 Foz do Iguaçu

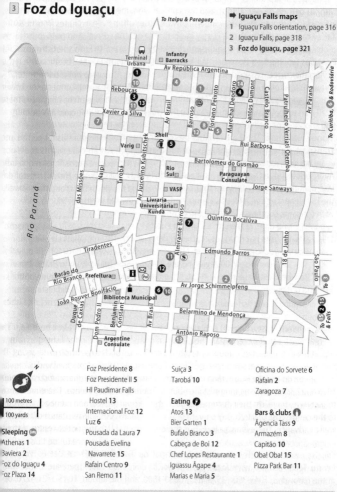

➡ **Iguaçu Falls maps**
1 Iguaçu Falls orientation, page 316
2 Iguaçu Falls, page 318
3 Foz do Iguaçu, page 321

100 metres
100 yards

Sleeping 🛏
Athenas **1**
Baviera **2**
Foz do Iguaçu **4**
Foz Plaza **14**

Foz Presidente **8**
Foz Presidente II **5**
HI Paudimar Falls
  Hostel **13**
Internacional Foz **12**
Luz **6**
Pousada da Laura **7**
Pousada Evelina
  Navarrete **15**
Rafain Centro **9**
San Remo **11**

Suíça **3**
Tarobá **10**

Eating 🍴
Atos **13**
Bier Garten **1**
Bufalo Branco **3**
Cabeça de Boi **12**
Chef Lopes Restaurante **1**
Iguassu Ágape **4**
Marias e Maria **5**

Oficina do Sorvete **6**
Rafain **2**
Zaragoza **7**

Bars & clubs 🍸
Agencia Tass **9**
Armazém **8**
Capitão **10**
Oba! Oba! **15**
Pizza Park Bar **11**

Border essentials: Brazil–Argentina

Foz do Iguaçu (Brazil)–Puerto Iguazú (Argentina)

It takes about two hours to get from Brazilian falls to the Argentine falls, very tiring when the weather is hot. From October to February Brazil is one hour ahead of Argentina.
Immigration A Brazilan exit stamp is required for all foreigners leaving the country even if only for one day. Take your passport and your entry card and make sure you get your exit stamp when you cross the bridge. The Brazilian–Argentinian border at Foz do Iguacu has the reputation of being lax, with people easily crossing, often without getting proper stamps, and then proceeding onwards to other destinations in Brazil (or Argentina). Taxis, vans and private buses often even avoid the border stop if they can get a way with it. It is very important to get the correct stamps to avoid problems on exiting Brazil or with spot checks by federal police within the country. Penalties for improper documentation in Brazil (and Argentina) are stringent and having the correct passport stamp is the responsibility of the individual traveller. Even if you are returning on the same day it's safer to get your exit stamps on the way out of Brazil and an entry stamp into Argentina, an exit stamp in Argentina on return and, finally, an entry stamp and entry card on the way back to Brazil again. When entering you should expect to receive an entry stamp and an entry card; make sure you do.
Money exchange There are facilities beside the Argentine immigration.
Transport Buses marked 'Puerto Iguazú' run every 30 minutes Monday-Saturday and every hour on Sunday and bank holidays, from the Terminal de Transporte Urbano (TTU), Av Juscelino Kubitscheck in the center of Foz do Iguaçu. Make sure you get an international company, they are the ones that cross the bridge. Keep the ticket in case the bus driver can't wait for you at immigration, but note the ticket will be only valid with the same company. There are three companies covering this route. The waiting can take a long time. At the bus terminal in Puerto Iguazu, take the bus to the Argentine falls. Taxis run from Foz do Iguaçu to the border, waiting at immigration, US$10.
Note Be sure you know when the last bus departs from Puerto Iguazú for Foz (usually 1930); last bus from Foz 1900. If visiting the Brazilian side for a day, get off the bus at Hotel Bourbon, cross the road and catch the bus to the falls, rather than going into Foz and out again.

---

have to change buses, but you only pay once so the system acts a bit like a metro – it's a integrated transport system. Many hotels run minibus services for a small charge. From th airport buses run to cities throughout southeastern Brazil and to Asunción in Paraguay. Th rest of Argentina can easily be reached from Puerto Iguazu just across the border.

The **Foz do Iguaçu Rodoviária** ① *Av Costa e Silva, 4 km from centre on road to Curitib T045-3522 3633*, receives long-distance buses. There is a tourist office, **Cetreme** desk f tourists who have lost their documents, *guarda municipal* (police) and luggage store. Bus to the centre cost US$1.20. Buy onward tickets on arrival if possible as seats get booked well in advance. There is also a local bus station, **Terminal Urbana**, in the centre of town

Tourist information The **Secretaria Municipal de Turismo** ① *Praça Getulio Vargas Centro, T0800-451516, www.fozdoiguacu.pr.gov.br, daily 0700-2300*. There are tourist boot at the *rodoviária, T045-3901 3575, daily 0630-1800*, and the airport, *T045-3521 4276, op*

Border essentials: Brazil–Paraguay

Foz do Iguaçu (Brazil)–Ciudad del Este (Paraguay)
The Ponte de Amizade/Puente de Amistad (Friendship Bridge) over the Río Paraná, 6 km north of Foz, leads straight into the heart of Ciudad del Este. It's also possible to cross by ferry. Note that Paraguay is one hour behind Brazil.

Immigration Paraguayan and Brazilian immigration formalities (open until 1700) are dealt with at opposite ends of the bridge. A large new customs complex has been built at the Brazilian end of the bridge. The area is intensively patrolled for contraband and stolen cars; ensure that all documentation is in order.

Transport Buses marked 'Cidade-Ponte' leave from the Terminal Urbana in Foz do Iguaçu, to the Ponte de Amizade, US$2. There is an hourly passenger ferry service from Porto de Lanchas and Porto Guaíra to Salto del Guayra on the Paraguayan side, US$1.50, and an hourly car ferry from Porto Guaíra (US$4 for car with two people). The car ferry runs until 1830 (Brazilian time).

Guaíra (Brazil)–Saltos del Guairá (Paraguay)
Another crossing to Paraguay is at Guaíra, at the northern end of the Itaipu lake. It is five hours north of Iguaçu by road and can be reached by bus from Campo Grande and São Paulo. Ferries cross to Saltos del Guairá on the Paraguayan side.

...or all arriving flights, with a free map and bus information, and Terminal de Transporte Urbano, T045-3523 7901, daily 0700-1800.

Itaipu Dam → *Colour map 5, A2.*
ⓘ *Visitor centre, T045-3520 6999, www.itaipu.gov.br, tours are free but in groups only; tours daily Mon-Sat, the first at 0800, the last at 1500; 'technical' visits can also be arranged. Buses marked 'Usina Itaipu' run from Foz do Iguaçu's Terminal Urbana, US1.50.*

The Itaipu Dam, on the Río Paraná, is the site of the largest single power hydroelectric power station in the world built jointly by Brazil and Paraguay. Construction of this massive scheme began in 1975 and it came into operation in 1984. The main dam is 8 km long, creating a lake that covers 1400 sq km. The height of the main dam is equivalent to a 65-storey building, the amount of concrete used in its construction is 15 times more than that used for the Channel Tunnel between England and France. The Paraguayan side may be visited from Ciudad del Este. Both governments are proud to trumpet the accolade, one of the seven wonders of the modern world' (the only one in South America), which was given to it by the American Society of Civil Engineering in *Popular Mechanics* in 1995. Whatever your views on the need for huge hydroelectric projects, it is worth visiting Itaipu to gain a greater understanding of the scale and impact of such constructions.

The **Ecomuseu de Itaipu** ⓘ *Av Tancredo Neves, Km 11, T045-520 5813, Tue-Sun 1830-1730, closed on Mon,* and **Tatí Yupí Sanctuary Centre** ⓘ *panoramic tour with guide US$11, 9 times daily 0800-1600, other special tours available,* are geared to inform about the preservation of the local culture and environment, or that part of it which isn't underwater. A massive reforestation project is underway, and over 14 million seedlings have already been planted. Six biological refuges have been created on the lakeshore.

If it's sunny go in the morning as the sun is behind the dam in the afternoon and you will get poor photographs. The visitor centre has a short video presentation (ask for the English version) with stunning photography and amazing technical information. The spillways are capable of discharging the equivalent of 40 times the average flow of the Iguaçu Falls. If you are lucky, the spillways will be open. After the film and a brief visit to the souvenir shop where an English guidebook is available, a coach will take you to the dam itself. As it crosses the top, you get a stomach-churning view of the spillways and really begin to appreciate the scale of the project.

To get to Itaipu, the 'executive' bus and agency tours are an unnecessary expense. Take bus lines **Conjunto C Norte** or **Conjunto C Sul** from Foz do Iguaçu TTU Terminal de transporte Urbano, tickets US\$1.20.

> *The dam's 18 turbines have an installed capacity of 12,600,000 kw and produce about 75 billion kwh a year, providing 80% of Paraguay's electricity and 25% of Brazil's.*

◉ Paraná listings

For Sleeping and Eating price codes and other relevant information, see pages 32-37.

⌂ Sleeping

Curitiba *p306, map p308*
General information can be found on the websites: www.ondehospedar.com.br/pr/curitiba.php and www.cmoraes.com.br/webhotelshtml/curitiba.shtml. There are good hotels southeast of the centre in the vicinity of the *rodoferroviária*, but the cheaper ones are seedy and close to the wholesale market, which operates noisily throughout the night.

LL Bourbon & Tower, R Cândido Lopes 102, T041-3322 4600, www.bourbon.com.br. One of the better modern hotels in the centre with a mock old-fashioned charm engendered by wood panelling and fake period furniture. Rooms have jacuzzis. Business facilities.

AL-A Deville Rayon, R Visconde de Nacar 1424, T041-2108 1100 or 0800 703 1866, www.deville.com.br. Central, refurbished in 2008, a good option for business travellers. All the expected services including pool, saunas, well-equipped gym and travel agency. Good online promotions.

A Mercure Curitiba Centro, R Emiliano Perneta 747, T041-3234 1212, www.mercure.com.br. Standard business hotel in the centre

with large rooms – most with separate living area, a pool and business centre.

A-B Del Rey, R Ermelino de Leão 18, T/F041-2106 0099, www.hoteldelrey.com.br. Central, upmarket yet relaxed, refurbished, large rooms and suites, a good restaurant and gym. Good-value online rates.

A-B Deville Express, R Amintas de Barros 73, T041-3322 8558, www.deville.com.br. In the city centre with a bar, small modest restaurant. All rooms a/c with fridge.

A-B Slaviero Palace, R Sen Alencar Guimarães 50, T041-3017 1000, www.hotelslaviero.com.br. The best of the 2nd-grade business hotels in the centre. Anonymously decorated but with a business centre and airport transfer.

B Slaviero Braz, Av Luís Xavier 67, T041-332 2829, www.hotelslaviero.com.br. Refurbishe hotel in a 1940s building preserved as '*Patrimonio Histórico*'. Large rooms, handsome public areas and business facilitie

C Centro Europeu Tourist, Praça Gen Osóri 61, T041-3021 9900. On one of the city's mo attractive squares, in the centre with a range of plain but smart rooms which are quietest at the top of the hotel.

C-D Kings, Av Silva Jardim 264, T041-3022 8444, www.kingshotel.com.br. Modern, secure and well-maintained apartment hotel available only for monthly rental.

C-D Lumini, R Gen Carneiro 1094, T041-3264 5244, www.hotellumini.com.br. Good a/c apartment hotel in a quiet street.

C-D Paraty, R Riachuelo 30, T041-3223 1355, www.hotelparati.com.br. Well-maintained flats with kitchenettes in an anonymous 1980s block next to the Federal University of Paraná, near the centre. Breakfast included.

D-E Nova Lisboa, Av 7 de Septembro 1948, T041-3264 1944, www.hotelnovalisboa.com.br A very simple small hotel near the *rodoviária*, housed in an ugly concrete building above a shop. Price includes breakfast, cheaper without.

D-F HI Curitiba Eco-hostel, R Luiz Tramontin 1693, Campo Comprido, T041-3274 7979, www.curitibaecohostel.com.br. A relatively new hostel with all services. Situated in the Tramontina borough and set in attractive gardens with their own sports facilities. The lowest rates are per person.

D-F HI Hostel Roma, R Barão do Rio Branco 305, T041-3224 2117 or T041-3322 2838, www.hostelroma.com.br. Smart hostel with 110 beds in single-sex dorms. All have private bathrooms. TV room, fax, internet and a member's kitchen. Breakfast included. The lowest rates are per person.

Camping

Camping Clube do Brasil, BR-116, Km 84, 16 km in the direction of São Paulo, T041-3358 6634.

Morretes, Antonina and around p310

For information see www.morretes.com.br.

L-AL Santuário Nhundiaquara, www.nhundiaquara.com.br. A range of chalets set around a tinkling stream in 100 ha of private rainforest under the Pico do Marumbi. They range from super-luxurious rock-Alpine *malocas* with plunging roofs to simpler rooms in annexes. Kids are welcome and there's a lovely, if chilly, spring-water swimming pool.

Pousada Graciosa, Estrada da Graciosa Km 8 (Porto da Cima village), T041-3462 807, www.pousadagraciosa.com. Simple but comfortable wooden chalets set in rainforest

some 10 km north of Morretes. Very peaceful and green but no children under 12.

A-B Hakuna Matata, Reta Porto de Cima s/n Km 2.5, T041-3462 2388, www.pousada hakunamatata.com.br. Stylish *pousada* set in beautiful grounds 15 km from Antonina with luxury apartments and chalets equipped with a/c, frigobar and TV. Also has pool and great restaurant. Perfect for nature lovers reluctant to abandon creature comforts.

C Pousada Cidreira, R Romulo Pereira 61, T041-3462 1604, www.morretes.com.br/ pousadacidreira. Centrally located with characterless but clean rooms, most with balconies and all with TV and en suites. Some rooms have space for 3. Breakfast included.

C-D Atlante, Praça Coronel Macedo 266, 14 km from Morretes in Antonina. Large, frowsty rooms in a converted colonial mansion house in the town centre, all fan-cooled or a/c and with terraces. Good breakfasts.

C-D Hotel Nhundiaquara, R General Carneiro 13, Morretes, T041-3462 1228, www.nundia quara.com.br. A smart whitewashed building beautifully set on the river whose exterior appearance and excellent restaurant belie the hotel's small, plain but recently painted rooms. With breakfast.

Paranaguá p311

For information see www.paranagua.pr.gov.br.

AL Hotel Camboa, R João Estevão (Ponta do Caju), T041-3423 2121, www.hotelcamboa. com.br. Family resort with tennis courts, large pool, saunas, trampolines, restaurant and a/c rooms. Out of town near the port. Book ahead.

AL-A São Rafael, R Julia Costa 185, T041-3423 2123, www.sanrafaelhotel.com.br. Business hotel with plain tiled rooms, a business centre, restaurants, pool and jacuzzis in the en suites.

D Hotel Ponderosa, R Pricilenco Corea 68 at 15 Novembro, a block east and north of the boat dock, T041-3423 2464. Tiled rooms with en suites, some rooms have a sea view.

D Pousada Itibere, R Princesa Isabel 24, 3 blocks east of the boat dock, T041-3423 2485. Very smart spartan rooms with polished wood floors, some with sea views. Friendly service from the Portuguese owner.

Camping
Arco Iris, Praia de Leste, on the beach, 29 km south of Paranaguá, T041-3458 2001.

Excursions from Paranaguá *p311*
There are 4 campsites and a few other cheap *pousadas* in Matinhos.
B Praia e Sol, R União 35, Matinhos, T041-3453 3133. Recommended *pousada*.

Ilha do Mel *p312, map p313*
For information see www.ilhadomel online.com or www.pousadasilhadomel. com.br. All rooms are fan-cooled unless otherwise stated.

You can rent a fisherman's house on Encantadas – ask for **Valentim's Bar**, or for Luchiano. Behind the bar is **Cabanas Dona Maria**, shared showers, cold water; food available if you ask in advance. Many *pousadas* and houses with rooms to rent (shared kitchen and living room). Shop around, prices from about US$10 double, low season, mid-week.
L Grajagan, Praia Grande, T041-3426 8043, www.grajagan.com.br. The smartest *pousada* on the island, Granjagan is right on Praia Grande, making it an excellent surf resort. Lovely suites, the most luxurious ones – complete with plasma screen TVs – have sea views.
AL Enseada das Conchas, Farol, T/F041-3426 8040, www.pousadaenseada.com.br. With 4 individual theme decorated rooms with associated colours: Amanhecer (morning) in light gold, Mata Atlântica (Atlantic rainforest) in green, Azul do Mar (sea blue) and Luz do Sol (sunlight) in burnished orange. Set in a lush garden overlooking the sea. Lots of rescued cats. Great breakfast.
A Long Beach, Praia Grande, T041-3426 8116, www.lbeach.cjb.net. The best on this beach with comfortable chalets for up to 6 with en suites. Very popular with surfers. At the upper end of the price category. Book in advance.

A Caraguata, Encantadas, T041-3426 9097 or T041-9998 7770, www.caraguata-ilhadomel.com.br. A/c en suites in wood with fridge and Monet prints on walls. Very close to the jetty.
A Pousada das Meninas, Praia do Farol, T041-3426 8023, www.pousadadas meninas.com.br. Lovely *pousada* filled with fun Brazilian artefacts the friendly owners have collected throughout the years. Cosy and comfortable wooden chalets and good breakfasts. There are DVD players and TVs for rainy days.
B Aconchego, Nova Brasília, T041-3426 8030, www.cwb.matrix.com.br/daconchego/. 10 scrupulously clean rooms in a house behind an expansive beachside deck strewn with hammocks. Public TV and breakfast areas. Charming. Includes breakfast.
B Dona Quinota, Fortaleza, T041-3423 6176. 3 km from Nova Brasília, right on the beach. Little blue-and-cream cottages with polished wood floors and en suites. Price includes breakfast and supper. **Dona Clara** next door is very similar in yellow instead of blue.
B Plancton, Farol at Fora, T/F041-3426 8061, www.pousadaplancton.com.br. A range of wooden buildings in a hummingbird filled garden. Rooms for 5 split over 2 levels. Wood and slate-tiled en suites. Clean, fresh. Italian food available in high season.
B Por do Sol, Nova Brasília, T041-3426 8009, www.pousadapordosol.com.br. Simple but elegant en suite rooms in grey tile and wood around a garden shaded by sombrero trees. A large deck with hammock-strewn *cabañas* sits next to the beach. Includes breakfast.
B-C D'Lua, Farol, T041-3426 8031, www.pousadalua.com.br. Basic and surfer-hippy with a very friendly new-age owner, Jo and legions of cats.
B-C Girassol, T041-3426 8006, www.ilha domelgirassol.com.br. Wooden rooms with en suites in a little bougainvillea and fruit tre garden. Very close to jetty. Includes breakfas
B-C Recanto da Fortaleza, Ponta do Bicho, T041-3275 4455, www.ilhadomelpousada. com.br. The best of the 2 next to the fort.

Basic cabins with en suites and tiled floors. Free pick-up by boat from Nova Brasília (ring ahead), bike rental. Price includes breakfast and dinner.

B-C Recanto do Frances, Encantadas, T041-3426 9105, www.recantodofrances.com.br. 5 mins from Prainha or Encantadas. French-owned and full of character, with each chalet built in a different style to represent a different French city. Good crêpe restaurant. With a sister *pousada* nearby

B-C Trilha do Sol, Farol, T041-3426 8025. Simple wooden rooms with en suites.

D-E HI Hostel Zorro, Encantadas, T041-3426 9052, www.hostelzorro.com.br. A party hostel overlooking the beach. Small but clean wooden rooms and dorms, and all the usual facilities.

Camping

There are mini campsites with facilities at Encantadas, **Farol** and **Brasília**. Camping is possible on the more deserted beaches (good for surfing). If camping, watch out for the tide, watch possessions and beware of the *bicho de pé*, which burrows into feet (remove with a needle and alcohol) and the *borrachudos* (discourage with **Autan** repellent).

Parque Nacional de Superagüi *p314*

D-E Pousada Sobre as Ondas das Cataratas, www.superagui.net/br. Chalets and rooms with private or shared bathrooms.

Iguaçu Falls *p314, maps p316 and p318*
Brazil

The best hotels with the most modern facilities and the easiest access to Iguaçu are all near the falls. There is little here for budget travellers. Sleeping in your car inside the park is prohibited. You can camp at the **HI Paudimar**, but it's pretty cold and damp in winter.

L Tropical das Cataratas, directly over-looking the falls, 28 km from Foz, T045-521 7000, www.hoteldascataratas.com.br. This grand hotel in the Orient Express group has been has been refurbished in the new millenium and is the only establishment within

the park on the Brazilian side. It is housed in a mock-belle époque building with generous rooms, grand public areas and a poolside garden. The hotel is right next to the falls, offering by far the easiest access and the best chance to beat the crowds. The restaurant overlooking the falls has excellent Brazilian-Mediterranean cooking and there is an additional grill restaurant next to the pool. The only other restaurant options are a pricey cab ride away in Foz de Iguaçu town. Non-resident evening diners will be in the park after it closes and must take a taxi back to town.

C-F Hostel Natura, Rodovia das Cataratas Km 12.5, Remanso Grande, T045-3529 6949, www.hostelnatura.com (near the Paudimar). Rustic hostel with a small pool set in fields pocked with large ponds and on the road to the park. Public areas include a pool table, TV lounge and a small kitchen. Rooms are fan-cooled and the hostel can arrange visits to the falls. Their website has detailed instructions for how to reach them including bus times and a map.

C-F HI Paudimar Campestre, Rodovia das Cataratas Km 12.5, Remanso Grande, near airport, T045-3529 6061, www.paudimar. com.br. Youth hostel with spotless single-sex dorms, pool, communal kitchen, football pitch, camping. The gardens are visited by birds and small mammals. From the airport or town take the Parque Nacional bus (0525-0040) and alight at the Remanso Grande bus stop, by **Hotel San Juan**, then take the free shuttle bus (0700-1900) to the hostel, or walk the 1200 m from the main road. Breakfast included. Tours arranged. There's a **Paudimar** desk at the *rodoviária*. Only HI members in high season when the hostel gets very busy. Low prices are per person.

Argentina
Camping is possible at **Camping Puerto Canoas**, 600 m from Puerto Canoas, with tables, but no other facilities, the nearest drinking water is at the park entrance.

AL Sheraton Internacional Iguazú Resort, Parque Nacional Iguazú, www.starwood.com.

A 1970s wedge of concrete built on the opposite side of the falls from the **Hotel das Cataratas**. Views are spectacular, especially out over the pool from the room balconies on the upper storey. But the falls are a 20-min walk from the hotel. Well maintained, well run. Babysitting service available.

Foz do Iguaçu *p320, map p321*
Many hotels offer excursions to the falls. In a bid to get their commission, touts may tell you the hotel of your choice no longer exists, or offer you room rates below what is actually charged. In high season (eg Christmas-New Year) you will not find a room under US$15, but in low season there are many good deals.
LL-L Internacional Foz, R Alm Barroso 2006, T045-3521 4100, www.internacionalfoz. com.br. The only 5-star hotel in the region with excellent business and conference facilities. Spacious but very standard upmarket hotel rooms and services.
AL-A Rafain Centro, Mcal Deodoro 984, T/F045-3521 3500, www.rafaincentro.com.br. The smart and upmarket communal areas and attractive pool area belie the rather well-worn rooms.
A Suiça, Av Felipe Wandscheer 3580, T045-3525 3232, www.hotelsuica.com.br. Old 1970s hotel with rather dark tile-floor rooms and a pool. Helpful Swiss manager. The extensive facilities include a fitness centre, gym, play area for kids and several pools.
B Baviera, Av Jorge Schimmelpfeng 697, T045-3523 5995, www.hotelbavieraiguassu. com.br. A mock-Bavarian folly with a chalet-style exterior. On the main road, central for bars and restaurants. The rooms look as if they haven't been renovated since the 1980s.
B Foz do Iguaçu, Av Brasil 97, T045-3521 4455, www.hotelfozdoiguacu.com.br. Another vast and gloomy 1970s hotel with faded rooms. With large breakfasts included in the price.
B Foz Plaza, R Marechal Deodoro 1819, T/F045-3521 5500, www.fozplaza.com.br

Serene and well-refurbished 1980s hotel with a restaurant and a bar, swimming pool, souvenir shop, sauna and a games room.
B Foz Presidente, R Xavier da Silva 1000, T/F045-3572 4450, www.fozpresidente hoteis.com.br. Restaurant, pool, with breakfast, convenient for buses. Brighter and more modern than most of Foz's offerings.
B Foz Presidente II, R Mcal Floriano Peixoto 1851, T/F045-3572 4450, www.fozpresidente hoteis.com.br. Smaller and a little more expensive than its sister hotel (with whom it shares leisure areas), but also with pool, bar and restaurant.
B-C Luz, Av Costa e Silva Km 5, near *rodoviária*, T045-3522 3535, www.luzhotel. com.br. Well-kept but bog standard small 1980s hotel with a buffet restaurant. Rooms have a/c and Brazilian TV.
B-C Pousada Evelina Navarrete, R Irlan Kalichewski 171, Vila Yolanda, T/F045-3574 3817, www.pousada evelina.com.br. Lots of tourist information, internet, well-maintained dorms, doubles and singles (some with a/c) and good breakfast. English, French, Italian, Polish and Spanish spoken. Helpful staff with lots of useful tourist information and organized walks. The *pousada* is near Av Cataratas on the way to the falls; take a bus to Parque Nacional from the bus station and ask to be let off after 3.5 km, near the **Chemin** supermarket. R Irlan Kalichewski is down the hill, 3 blocks towards the city on the left.
C-D Tarobá, R Tarobá 1048, T045-2102 7700, www.hoteltaroba.com.br. Good value. Clean with modern, smart rooms, a tiny indoor pool and helpful staff. There is a travel agency in hotel. Near Terminal Urbana.
D Pousada da Laura, R Naipi 671, T045-3572 3374. Secure and run by the enthusiastic Laura who speaks some Spanish, English, Italian and French. The hostel has a kitchen, laundry facilities and en suites and is a good place to meet other travellers. Good breakfast
D San Remo, R Xavier da Silva 563 at Tarobá T045-3523 1619, roberto_171@hotmail.com Scrupulously clean though small rooms with TVs and writing desks. All-you-can-eat

breakfast. English, Spanish and Hebrew spoken. In-house travel agency.

D-E HI Paudimar Falls Hostel, R Antônio Raposo 820, T045-3028 5503, www.paudimar falls.com.br. Despite its name, the companion hostel to the **Paudimar** near the falls, is in the centre of town. It has similar facilities, with doubles, cramped dorms, pool and the usual hostel services.

E Athenas, R Almte Barroso 2215 on corner of Rebouças, T045-3574 2563. Very shabby, but cheapest place in town for those on a tight budget, some rooms with shared baths, fan, TVs in rooms, breakfast extra, beers sold.

Camping

E Pousada Internacional, R Manencio Martins 21, Vila Yolanda, T045-3529 8183, www.campinginternacional.com.br. US$15 per person (half this price for camping), pool, clean basic cabins. Park vehicle or put tent away from trees in winter in case of heavy rainstorms. The food here is poor and the refectory closes at 2300.

Eating

Curitiba *p306, map p308*

Hot sweet wine is sold on the streets in winter to help keep out the cold. There are a couple of *lanchonetes* in the market which close to the *rodoferroviária*. Also good meals in the bus station.

† Armazém Romanus, R Visc do Rio Branco 41, T041-3462 1500. Family-run restaurant with the best menu and wine list in the region. Dishes made from home-grown ingredients include excellent *barreado* and flambéed desserts.

† Casa Lilás, Claudino dos Santos 90, T041-3324 9755, www.casalilas.com.br. Pretty purple building in the heart of Curitiba's old town. Inside, the cosy café serves up delicious home-made cakes and snacks. There's also a lovely patio and a shop selling regional handicrafts.

††† Durski, R Jaime Reis, 254 (centre), T041-3225 7893. Good Eastern European food, including a locally celebrated and lavish banquet of pâtés, borcht, *platzki*, filled pasties and a variety of meat dishes.

††† Guega, R Vol da Pátria 539 (centre), T041-3224 8244. Closed on Sun. The city's most celebrated restaurant serving a mix of French, Italian cooking to a smart crowd. Reasonable wine list.

††† Quintana, Av do Batel 1440, T041-3078 6044. www.quintanacafe.com.br. Café and restaurant serving organic buffet in posh Batel neighbourhood. Wooden decor, lovely arty vibe. Bookshelves filled with books you can borrow for free.

† Baviera, Alameda Augusto Stellfeld, Av Dr Murici (centre), T041-3232 1995. Open 1830-0100. A Curitiba institution, established over 30 years and serving pizza in an intimate beer cellar setting. Delivery service.

† Green Life, R Carlos de Carvalho 271 (centre), T041-3223 8490. Open for lunch only. Vegetarian buffet restaurant.

† Mikado, R São Francisco 126, T041-3323 6709. Centrally located lunchtime buffet place. Great value, serving mostly vegetarian food. US$5 set price all you can eat.

† Saccy, R São Francisco 350, at Mateus Leme. Pizza, tapas and a popular bar with live music, see Bars and clubs, page 331.

† Salmão, R Emiliano Perneta 924, T041-3225 2244. Open until 0100. Restaurant in historic house, delicious fish and pizza, often special promotions, live music every night. Short taxi ride from centre.

Morretes *p310*

† Madalozo, R Alm Frederico de Oliveira 16, overlooking the river, T041-3462 1410. Good *barreado* and generous salads.

† Terra Nossa, R XV Novembro 109, T041-3462 2174. *Barreado*, pasta pizzas and fish. Middle of the road but generous portions and a small wine list. From R$25 for a 2-person *prato da casa*.

Paranaguá *p311*
The choice here is poor.
♥♥ **Danúbio Azul**, R XV Novembro 95, T041-3423 3255, www.restaurantedanubioazul.com.br. The best in town with a range of fish and chicken dishes, pastas and pizzas; all in enormous quantities. 1 block back from the sea at the east end of town.
♥♥ **Divina Gula**, R Baronesa do Cerro Azul, 1357. T041-3425 5006. Open until 1400 only. Seafood buffet and *feijoada* at weekends. 3 blocks east of the Ilha do Mel dock.

Ilha do Mel *p312, map p313*
Many *pousadas* also serve food, some only in season (Christmas to Carnaval). Many have live music or dancing (especially in high season). Things kick off after 2200.
♥♥ **Fim da trilha**, Prainha (Fora de Encantadas), T041-3232 1314. Spanish seafood restaurant. One of the best on the island.
♥ **Bee House**, Farol, T041-3426 8029. Snacks, crêpes, good cakes and puddings.
♥ **Mar e Sol**, Farol, T041-3426 8021. Huge portions of fish and chicken, all with chips and rice. Also a small selection of more adventurous dishes like bass in shrimp sauce.
♥ **Recanto do Frances**, Encantadas. French crêpes and Moroccan couscous.
♥ **Toca do Abutre**, Farol. Live music and the usual huge portions of fish or chicken with rice, beans and chips.
♥ **Zorro**, Encantadas. One of several cheap fish, beans and rice restaurants on the seafront, shaded by palapas. *Forró* dancing at night.

Iguaçu Falls *p314, maps p316 and p318*
Brazil
♥♥♥ **Tropical das Cataratas**, the nearest dining to the falls themselves (see Sleeping).

Foz do Iguaçu *p320, map p321*
♥♥♥ **Bufalo Branco**, R Rebouças 530, T045-3523 9744, superb all-you-can-eat *churrasco*, includes *filet mignon*, salad bar and dessert. Sophisticated surroundings and attentive service.

♥♥♥ **Cabeça de Boi**, Av Brasil 1325, T045-3523 2100. *Churrascaria* with live music and a buffet, coffee and pastries also.
♥♥♥ **Chef Lopes Restaurante**, Av Rep, Argentina 632 (esquina R Tarobá), T045-3025 3334, www.cheflopes.com.br. Smart per kilo place serving good quality beef and excellent salads. Popular with well-heeled Brazilian tourists.
♥♥♥ **Zaragoza**, R Quintino Bocaiúva 882, T045-3574 3084. Large and upmarket, for Spanish dishes and seafood. Respectable wine list.
♥♥ **Atos**, Av Juscelino Kubitschek 865, T045-3572 2785. Lunch only. Per kilo buffet with various meats, salads, sushi and puddings.
♥♥ **Bier Garten**, Av Jorge Schimmelpfang 550. Bustling pizzeria, churrascaria and *choperia*.
♥♥ **Rafain**, Av das Cataratas, Km 6.5, T045-3523 1177. Closed Sun. Set price for excellent buffet with folkloric music and dancing (2100-2300); touristy but very entertaining. Out of town, take a taxi or arrange with travel agency.
♥ **Iguassu Âgape**, R Marechal Deodoro 1819, T045-3521 5544. Good value per kilo place next to Hotel Foz Plaza. *Feijoada* on Sat.
♥ **Marias e Maria**, Av Brasil 505. Good *confeitaria*.
♥ **Oficina do Sorvete**, Av Jorge Schimmelpfeng 244. Daily 1100-0100. Excellent ice creams, a popular local hang-out.

🅞 Bars and clubs

Curitiba *p306, map p308*
A cluster of bars at the square of Largo da Ordem have tables and chairs on the pavement, music which tends to be rock, and bar food: **Fire Fox**, Av Jaime Reis 46, flanked by **Tuba's** and **The Farm**. Av do Batel (or Batel district) has good bars and restaurants catering to the well-to-do/middle-class.
Schwarzwald (aka **Bar do Alemão**), R Claudino dos Santos 63, T041-3223 2585, www.bardoalemaocuritiba.com.br. This German-themed bar serves an impressive range of quality brews and hearty, Teutonic grub. Kitsch but very popular.

Saccy, R São Franscisco, 350, corner with
Mateus Leme, 12. Pizza, tapas and lively
bar with live music.

Foz do Iguaçu *p320, maps p316 and p321*
Most bars double as restaurants and are
concentrated on Av Jorge Schimmelpfeng
for 2 blocks from Av Brasil to R Mal Floriano
Peixoto. Wed-Sun are best nights; the
crowd tends to be young.
Agência Tass, Av Jorge Schimmelpfeng 350,
T045-3523 5373, www.agenciatass.com.
Chic club with swish interior playing dance
and house tunes.
Armazém, R Edmundo de Barros 446,
intimate and sophisticated, attracts
discerning locals, good atmosphere,
mellow live music, US$1 cover.
Capitão Bar, Av Jorge Schimmelpfeng 288
and Almte Barroso, T045-3572 1512. Large,
loud and popular, nightclub attached.
Oba! Oba!, Av das Cataratas 3700, T045-
3574 2255 (Antigo Castelinho). Live samba
show Mon-Sat 2315-0015. Very popular,
US$9 for show and includes 1 drink.
Pizza Park Bar, R Almirante Barroso 993,
specializes in vodka and whisky brands.
Wi-Fi zone.
Rafain, Av das Cataratas Km 6.5. With floor
show and food, see page 330.

Entertainment

Foz do Iguaçu *p320, map p321*
Casinos
Organized tours to casinos (illegal in Brazil)
over the border in Paraguay and Argentina
take 3 hrs.
Casino Iguazú, Ruta 12 Km, 1640, Puerto
Iguazú (Argentina), T3757-498000. Weekdays
1500-0500, 24 hrs weekends. Restaurant on site.

Cinema
Boulevard, Av das Cataratas 1118, T045-
3523 4245. Large complex open from 1700
and all day Sun. Also bowling, games
rooms and bingo.

O Shopping

Foz do Iguaçu *p320, map p321*
Av Brasil is the main shopping street.
Bookshop Kunda Livraria Universitária,
R Almte Barroso 1473, T045-3523 4606.
Guides and maps of the area, books on the
local wildlife, novels, etc in several languages,
including French and English.

Souvenirs and handicrafts Tres
Fronteiras, Rodovia das Cataratas, Km 11.
Large shop on road to falls, frequent stop
on tours. Chocolates, and huge selection of
crafts and jewellery, some of it overpriced.

▲ Activities and tours

Serra da Graciosa and Morretes
p309 and p310
Tour operators
Calango Expedições, Praça Rocha Pombo
s/n, Estação Ferroviária, Morretes, T/F041-
3462 2600, www.calangoexpedicoes.com.br.
Brazil Ecojourneys, Estrada Rozália Paulina
Ferreira 1132, Armação, Florianópolis, T048-
3389 5619, www.brazilecojourneys.com.

Parque Nacional Iguazú (Argentina)
p319
Tour operators
Most of the mid range and smart hotels
have in-house tour agency. Packages and
prices vary little.
Explorador, Perito Moreno 217 (and the
Sheraton hotel, see page 327), T03757-
421632, www.rainforestevt.com.ar.
A range of rainforest safaris and the
standard excursions to the falls.
Iguazu Explorer, visitor centre, Argentine
side of the falls, T+54-0375 742 1696,
www.iguazujungle.com. The Argentinean
counterpart to Macuco, with combinations
of trail walks, boat rides and 4x4 truck safaris.
The latter are noisier than the Brazilian
operator, **Macuco Safari**, as they use petrol
rather than electric engines, but with **Iguazu**

Explorer it's possible to do just the boat trip and tours are a little cheaper: boat trip US$25; jeep, trail and boat excursion US$50.
STTC Turismo, Av das Morenitas 2250, Jardim das Flores, T045-3529 6464. Standard packages to the Brazilian and Argentine side of the falls.

The following excursions are easily organized through the Puerto Iguazú visitor centre: **Aventura Náutica** is a journey by launch along the lower Río Iguazú, US$25. **Safari Náutico**, a 4-km journey by boat above the falls, US$15. **Gran Aventura**, an 8-km ride through the jungle, with commentary on the flora and fauna in English and Spanish, followed by a boat trip on the rapids to the Devil's Throat, US$50. This trip is longer and better value than the Macuco Safari on the Brazilian side. The full day combines Safari Náutico with Aventura Náutica, US$45 (5 hrs), or US$60 with Gran Aventura (7 hrs).

Birding Iguazu Birdwatching, Perito Moreno 217, T+54 3757 421 922, www.iguazubirdwatching.com.ar. The forests and national park around Iguaçu have a broad range of Atlantic coastal rainforest species, especially off the beaten tracks or at the beginning and end of the day. Argentine birder, Daniel Somay, speaks good English and knows his birds, where to find them and can organize equipment given an little notice.

Foz do Iguaçu (Brazilian Side) p320, map p321
Helicopter tours
Helicopter tours over the falls leave from the Hotel das Cataratas, US$60 per person, 10 mins. Booked through any travel agency or direct with **Helisul**, T045-3529 7474, www.helisul.com. Apart from disturbing visitors, the helicopters are also reported to present a threat to some bird species which are laying thinner-shelled eggs. As a result, the altitude of the flights has been increased, making the flight less attractive. 10-min flights from US$100.

Tour operators
Beware of touts at the bus terminal who often overcharge for tours (they have been known to charge double the bus station price) and be sure that the park entrance fees of around US$25 and all the transfer fees are included in the price. There are many travel agents on Av Brasil and in almost all the hotels and hostels. Most do not accept credit cards.
Acquatur, R Almirante Barroso 733, T045-3523 9554, www.acquaturturismo.com.br. Offer full range of tours in executive cars with bilingual guides and airport transfers.
Macuco Safari, Rodovia das Cataratas, Km 25 Parque Nacional do Iguaçu T045-3529 7976 www.macucosafari.com.br. A much tourist-tramped 2-hr walk, with an electric car ride and boat trip (the whole package must be taken), from US100. The trails cut through subtropical forest next to Iguaçu to get up close to the base of the falls themselves. The tour is only worth taking for the boat trip (there is better walking for free on the Argentine side of the falls). Be sure to bring your own, completely waterproof, sealable bag strong enough to withstand total immersion. You will get completely soaked on this excursion and the bags provided by the company are inadequate.

⊖ Transport

Curitiba p306, map p308
Air
Two types of bus run from the *rodoferroviári* to the airport, making several stops along th way: **Aeroporto Executivo**, daily 0500-2330, 20 mins, US$5; regular city bus, 40 mins, US$1.50. There are daily flights to **Rio de Janeiro** and **São Paulo**, and connections to **Fortaleza**, **Foz do Iguaçu**, **Florianópolis** (and cities in the interior of Paraná), the **Pantanal**, **Amazon**, **Mato Grosso**, as well as to **Argentina**, **Chile** and **Uruguay**.
Airline offices Gol, T0300-3789 2121 www.voegol.com.br. NHT, www.voenht. com.br. Avianca, T0300-3789 8160,

www.Avianca.com.br. **Passaredo**, www.voe passaredo.com.br. **Pluna**, www.flypluna. com. TAM, R Ermelino Leão 511, T041-3219 1200, www.tam.com.br, also at airport, T041-3236 1812. **Trip**, at airport, T041-3381 1710. **Webjet**, T0300-3210 1234, www.webjet.com.br.

Bus
See also Ins and outs, page 307.
For detailed timetables of buses from Curitiba see www.rodoviariaonline.com.br.
  Local There are several route types on the integrated transport system; pick up a map for full details. There are 25 transfer terminals along the exclusive busways and trunk routes, allowing integration between all the different routes. **Express** are red, often articulated, and connect the transfer terminals to the city centre, pre-paid access, they use the 'tubo' bus stops. **Feeder** are orange conventional buses that connect the terminals to the surrounding neighbourhoods. **Interdistrict** green conventional or articulated buses run on circular routes, connecting transfer terminals and city districts without passing through the centre. **Direct** or **speedy** silver grey buses use the 'tubo' stations (3 km apart on average), to link the main districts and connect the surrounding municipalities with Curitiba. **Conventional** yellow buses operate on the normal road network between the surrounding municipalities, the Integration terminals and the city centre. **City circular** white minibuses, **Linha Turismo**, circle the major transport terminals and points of interest in the traditional city centre area. US$3.50 (multi-ticket booklets available), every 30 mins from 0900-1700, except on Mon. First leaves from R das Flores, narrow street in front of McDonald's. 3 stops allowed.
  Long distance Frequent buses to **São Paulo** (6 hrs, US$40) and **Rio de Janeiro** (2 hrs, US$60). To **Foz do Iguaçu**, 10 a day, 10 hrs, US$50; **Porto Alegre**, 10 hrs, US$50; **Florianópolis**, every 2 hrs, 4½ hrs, US$35; **Blumenau**, 4 hrs, US$25, 7 daily with

Penha/ Catarinense; good service to most towns in Brazil. **Pluma** bus to **Buenos Aires** and to **Asunción**. TTL runs to **Montevideo**, 26 hrs, 0340 departure (*semi-cama*).

Car hire Avis, at the airport, T041-3381 1370. Localiza, at the airport and Av Cândido de Abreu 336, T041-3888 8788.

Train Passenger trains to **Paranaguá**, see below.

Curitiba to Paranaguá *p309*
Train For current train times see box, page 334. There are 2 trains running on the line from Curitiba to **Morretes** and **Paranaguá** on the Serra Verde Trem da Serra do Mar line through the mountains.
  The **Litorina de Luxo** is a modern a/c railcar with on-board service and bilingual staff, which stops at the viewpoint at the Santuário da Nossa Senhora do cadeado and Morretes. It does not go as far as Paranaguá. Hand luggage only. Tickets can be bought 2 days in advance and cost US$110 one-way to Morretes (3 hrs) and a further US$100 for the return leg to Curitiba. The ticket includes a drink, biscuits and a tiny cake. The windows don't open and are scratched, so not ideal for photos.
  The **Trem Classe Convencional**, runs daily to Morretes, with a stop at Marumbi on the mountain, and continues to Paranaguá on Sun only, buy tickets 2 days in advance, *turístico*, US$40 (US$25 for return leg), *executivo* US$55 (US$37 for return leg), an *econômico* fare (US$23/US$18 for return leg) is available from the ticket office only, best about 2 weeks in advance. 4 hrs to Paranaguá.
  Schedules change frequently; delays are to be expected. Check times in advance with Serra Verde Express (Trem da Serra do Mar), T041-3888 3488, www.serraverde express.com.br. Tickets sold at the *rodoferroviária*, Portão 8, 0700-1830 (till 1200 on Sun). Sit on the left-hand side on the way from Curitiba. On cloudy days

Trem da Serra do Mar timetable

For a description of the journey, see Curitiba to Paranaguá, page 309.

Curitiba–Paranaguá From Curitiba the train leaves daily at 0815, stopping at Marumby at 1035, Morretes at 1115. It continues to Paranaguá only on Sundays, arriving at 1215. A litorina service runs at weekends, leaving Curitiba at 0915.

Paranaguá–Curitiba Monday to Friday from Morretes at 1500 (1600 on Sundays), stopping at Marumby at 1540 and Curitiba at 1800. At weekends the train runs from Paranaguá at 1400, stopping at Morretes at 1600, Marumby at 1640 and reaching Curitiba at 1900.

Schedules change frequently and at short notice. For the latest consult www.serraverdeexpress.com.br and select Trem da Serra do Mar.

---

there's little to see on the higher parts. The train is usually crowded on Sat and Sun. Many travellers recommend returning by bus (1½ hrs, buy ticket immediately on arrival, US$6.50), if you do not want to stay 4½ hrs. A tour bus meets the train and offers a tour of the town and return to Curitiba. Serra Verde Express also gives information about trips by car on the Estrada de Graciosa and sells various packages to the coast.

Morretes p310

Bus The Paranaguá–Antonina bus stops at Morretes, 12 daily: to **Paranaguá**, US$3, 17 daily to **Antonina** US$3. 12 daily to **Curitiba** US$10.

Paranaguá p311

Bus All operated by Graciosa, www.viagraciosa.com.br. To **Curitiba**, US$10, many 1½ hrs (only the 1500 to Curitiba takes the old Graciosa road); 8 buses a day to **Guaratuba** (US$3, 2 hrs), **Caiobá** and **Matinhos**. The buses to Guaratuba go on the ferry, as do direct buses to Joinville, 0600, 1600.

Ferry to Ilha do Mel Ferries from R Gen Carneiro (R da Praia) in front of the tourist information kiosk run to **Ilha do Mel** at 0930 and 1500 (1 hr 40 mins, US$4). Alternatively, go to the small harbour in Paranaguá and ask for a boat to Ilha do Mel, US$15 one-way (no

shade). Make sure the ferry goes to your chosen destination (Nova Brasília or Encantadas are the most developed areas). In high season (mid-Dec-New Year and Carnival), there are alternative times that change every season – but generally around 5 sailings a day/price is around US$8 one-way.

Car hire Interlocadora, T041-3423 4425.

Excursions from Paranagúa p311
Parque Estadual da Vila Velha

Bus Take a bus from Curitiba to the national park (leaving 0745, 1415 and 1715, US$10), not to the town 20 km away. Ask the bus driver where you should get off. Princesa dos Campos bus from Curitiba at 0730 and 0930, 1½ hrs, US$5.65 (return bus passes park entrance at 1600); it may be advisable to go to **Ponta Grossa** and return to Curitiba from there.

Last bus to Ponta Grossa from Vila Velha at 1900. Also ones at 0935 and 1600. US$$2.50, 4.5 km to turn-off to Furnas (another 15-min walk) and Lagoa Dourada (it's not worth walking from Vila Velha to Furnas because it's mostly uphill along the main road).

Ilha do Mel p312, map p313

Ferry See Ins and outs, page 314. Boats run from Encantadas and Nova Brasília to

aranaguá and **Pontal do Paraná** (Pontal
o Sul). The last bus from Pontal do Paraná
o Paranaguá leaves at 2200.

oz do Iguaçu *p320, map p321*
ir Daily flights to Rio, **São Paulo**, **Curitiba**
nd other Brazilian cities with Gol, Tam, and
rip. Airport is 12 km from centre.

us For transport to the falls and crossing into
rgentina, see page 315 and box, page 322.
  To get to the long-distance bus station
few kilometres outside of town, take
ny bus that says 'rodoviária'. To **Curitiba**,
luma, Sulamericana, 9-10 hrs, 3 daily,
aved road, US$15; to **Guaíra** via Cascavel
nly, 5 hrs, US$10; to **Florianópolis**,
atarinense and Reunidas, US$28, 14 hrs;
eunidas to **Porto Alegre**, US$30; to **São**
aulo, 16 hrs, Pluma US$30, *executivo* 6 a
ay, plus 1 *leito*; to **Rio** 22 hrs, several daily,
S$38. To **Asunción**, Pluma, RYSA (direct
1430), US$11.
  To **Buenos Aires** (Argentina), there is
bus direct from Foz (Pluma daily 1200,
S$46). It is cheaper to go to **Posadas**
a Paraguay. To **Asunción** (Paraguay),
uma (0700), RYSA (direct at 1430, 1830),
om *rodoviária*, US$16.50 (cheaper if
ought in Ciudad del Este).

ar hire Avis, airport, T045-3523 1510.
caliza at airport, T045-3529 6300, and
v Juscelino Kubitschek 2878, T045-3522
08. **Unidas**, Av Santos Dumont, 1515,
ar airport, T/F045-3339 0880.

axi Only good value for short distances
en you are carrying all your luggage.

Directory

Morretes *p310*
Banks Banco do Brasil, does not officially
change money, but friendly staff will
sometimes do so. It has an ATM.

Paranaguá *p311*
Banks Banco do Brasil, Largo C Alcindino
27. Bradesco, R Faria Sobrinho 188. Câmbio,
R Faria Sobrinho. For cash.

Foz do Iguaçu *p320, map p321*
Banks There are plenty of banks and travel
agents on Av Brasil. Santander, Al Barroso
1062, has ATM. Bradesco, Av Brasil 1202, Visa
ATMs. Banco 24 Horas at Oklahoma petrol
station, Visa ATMs. HSBC, Av Brasil 1151, ATM.
Embassies and consulates Argentina,
Trav Eduardo Bianchi 26, T045-3574 2969
(Mon-Fri 1000-1430). France, R Federico
Engels 48, Villa Yolanda T045-3574 3693.
Paraguay, Bartolomeu de Gusmão 480,
T045-3523 2898. **Internet** Throughout
the town, eg at Boulevard, Av das Cataratas
1118, T045-3523 4245. Provenet, Jorge
Sanways 773, T/F045-3523 2122, US$1 per hr;
also phone, fax and photocopying. Ask for
fastest machine, Mon-Sat 0900-2300 and Sun
afternoon. Pla4lan, Av Jorge Schimmelpfeng
636. R$3 per hr. **Laundry** Guia Mar, R
Tarobá 827, only US$2.50 per kg, open Sat.
Medical services There is a free 24-hr
clinic on Av Paraná, 1525, opposite Lions
Club, T045-3573 1134. Few buses so take taxi
or walk (about 25 mins). **Post office** Praça
Getúlio Vargas 72. **Telephone** Telepar on
Edmundo de Barros.

Santa Catarina

The state of Santa Catarina is famous above all for its beaches, especially those around the cities of Florianópolis and Laguna. These are among the most beautiful in southern Brazil, and have the best surf in the country. The state is also famous for its beautiful people who, defying the national stereotype, are often tall, blonde and blue-eyed. For this was an area that saw much northern-European immigration in the 19th and 20th centuries. The Portuguese from the Azores settled along the coast, the Germans moved along the Itajaí Valley, the Italians headed for the south and into Rio Grande do Sul, while in the north there are Ukrainians, Japanese, Africans, Hispanics and Indians. Immigrant communities still give a unique personality to a number of the state's towns and districts, as each group maintains its traditions and festivals, its architecture, food and language or accent. German and Ukrainian are spoken as much as Portuguese, and every year one million people visit the Oktoberfest in Blumenau. The vast majority of people today can trace their family to these ethnic origins.

As well as each region having its own distinctive culture, Santa Catarina also has its own climate and scenery. The highlands, just in from the coast, are among the coldest in Brazil and are covered in remnant aracauria pine forest, a tree related to the Chilean monkey puzzle. Except for the summer months of January and February, Santa Catarina's beaches are pleasant and uncrowded. The best months to visit are March, April and May before the water gets too cold for swimming. ►► *For listings, see pages 349-357.*

Florianópolis and around → *For listings, see pages 349-357. Colour map 5, B5. Phone code: 048. Population: 345,000.*

Halfway along the coast of Santa Catarina is the state capital Florianópolis, founded in 1726 as the gateway to Ilha de Santa Catarina. The natural beauty of the island, beaches and bays make it a magnet for holidaymakers in summer. The southern beaches are good for swimming, the eastern ones for surfing (but be careful of the undertow) and many visitors choose to stay here rather than in the city centre. 'Floripa' is accepted as shortened version of Florianópolis, with the people known as 'Floripans', although they like to call themselves 'Ilhéus', or islanders.

Ins and outs

Getting there International and domestic flights arrive at **Hercílio Luz airport** ① *Av Diomício Freitas, 12 km south of town, T048-3331 4000*. There are car hire booths, shops, cafés and a small tourist information office in the airport. Aeroporto/Corredor Sudoeste buses run between the airport terminal and the **local rodoviária** ① *city centre, R Antônio Luz 260, Forte de Santa Bárbara, T048-3324 1415*, every 20 minutes until midnight. A taxi to the city costs around US$25.

The main bus station **Rita Maria rodoviária** ① *15 mins' walk from the centre, Av Paulo Fontes 1101, T048-3224 2777*, is served by buses from all major cities in the south and southeast, with frequent connections to Curitiba, Porto Alegre, São Paulo, Rio and Santos. There are also buses between the city and Joinville, Blumenau, Gramado, Foz do Iguaçu and connections to Uruguay and Argentina. ▸▸ *See Transport, page 355.*

Getting around The city is fairly small and compact, quite hilly, but easy and safe to walk around. Standard buses, and more expensive yellow microbuses, run to nearly every important point on the island. There are buses to the eastern and southern beaches (beaches and sights like Joaquina, Lagoa, Lagoa do Peri and Pantano do Sul) from the local *rodoviária* on Rua Antônio Luz 260. Buses to the north of the island leave from another local *rodoviária* on Rua Francisco Tolentino, immediately in front of the long-distance *rodoviária*. There are also *combis* to the beaches leaving from Praça 15 de Novembro in the city centre.

Tourist information The main tourist office is **SETUR** ① *R Tenente Silveira 60, Centro, T048-3952 7000, www.visitefloripa.com.br, Mon-Fri 1300-1900*. There are also information booths in the **rodoviária** ① *T048-3228 1095* and at the **airport** ① *Mon-Fri 0700-1800, Sat and Sun 0800-1800*. All have maps and some pamphlet information in English. Useful websites include www.guiafloripa.com.br.

Sights

Florianópolis is a pleasant, clean, safe and well-organized city linked to the mainland by a picturesque little suspension bridge. It has few sights but is a good base for exploring the Ilha de Santa Catarina, which has many fine beaches. The 19th-century port area, the **Alfândega** ① *R Conselheiro Mafra, T048-3224 0189, Mon-Fri 0900-1800, Sat 0900-1200, closed Sun*, and **Mercado Público** ① *R Conselheiro Mafra T048-3224 0189, Mon-Fri 0700-1900, Sat 0700-1500, fish stalls on Sun*, have been restored and now house cafés, shops and little arts and crafts stalls. The **Catedral Metropolitana** ① *Praça 15 de Novembro*, was built in 1773 on the site of the first chapel erected by the founder of the city, Francisco Dias Velho. Inside is a life-size sculpture in wood of the flight into Egypt, originally from the Austrian Tyrol.

There are a few museums to while away a rainy day. The **Forte Sant'Ana** (1763) houses **Museu de Armas Major Lara Ribas** ① *beneath the Ponte Hercílio Luz, R Osvaldo Rodrigues Cabral 525, T048-3229 6263, Mon 1400-1800, Tue-Sun 0830-1200, 1400-1800, free*, with a collection of guns and other items, mostly post Second World War. The **Museu Histórico de Santa Catarina** ① *Praça 15 de Novembro, T048-3028 8091, www.mhsc.sc.gov.br, Tue-Fri 1000-1800, Sat, Sun and holidays 1000-1600, US$1.50*, in the 18th-century Palácio Cruz e Souza, has a lavish interior with highly decorated ceilings and contains furniture, documents and objects belonging to governors of the state. The **Museu de Antropólogia** ① *T048-3331 8821, Mon-Fri 0900-1200, 1300-1700*, at the Universidade Federal de Santa Catarina Campus, has a dusty collection of stone and other archaeological remains from the indigenous cultures of the coast. It is also possible to visit the former home of Imperial Brazil's foremost propaganda painter, **A Casa Victor Meirelles** ⓘ *R Victor Meirelles 59, T048-3222 0692, Tue-Fri 1300-1800, US$1 (donation).* The

Florianópolis

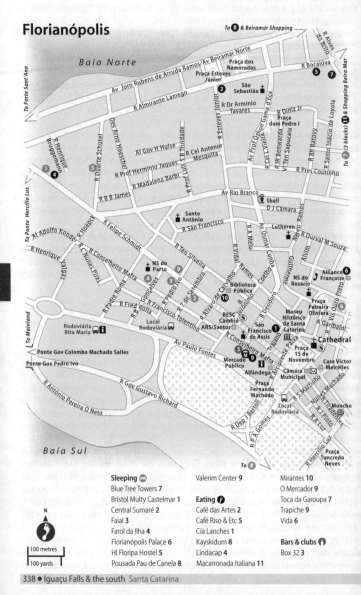

Sleeping 🛏️
Blue Tree Towers **7**
Bristol Multy Castelmar **1**
Central Sumaré **2**
Faial **3**
Farol da Ilha **4**
Florianópolis Palace **6**
HI Floripa Hostel **5**
Pousada Pau de Canela **8**

Valerim Center **9**

Eating 🍴
Café das Artes **2**
Café Riso & Etc **5**
Cía Lanches **1**
Kayskidum **8**
Lindacap **4**
Macarronada Italiana **11**

Mirantes **10**
O Mercador **9**
Toca da Garoupa **7**
Trapiche **2**
Vida **6**

Bars & clubs 🍸
Box 32 **3**

Catarinense painter was responsible for various apotheoses of colonization, such as *Primeira Missa no Brasil* (the First Mass in Brazil) and the war against the Dutch in Pernambuco, *A Batalha de Guararapes*.

There is a lookout point at **Morro da Cruz** (take the **Empresa Trindadense** bus, US$1, which waits for 15 minutes then returns; or walk back).

Ilha de Santa Catarina → *For listings, see pages 349-357.*

Santa Catarina island is often referred to as Florianópolis or Grande Florianópolis. It is fringed with some 42 beautiful beaches; all are easily accessible and many offer accommodation. In general, the north is more heavily visited and has the bulk of the resorts and busiest beaches, whilst the south and east are somewhat quieter. The most popular surf beaches are at **Praia Mole**, and **Joaquina** in the north and **Barra da Lagoa** to the east. **Campeche** and the southern beaches offer more peace and quiet, and the **Lagoa de Conceição** just east of Florianópolis city has windsurfing and lively nightlife. Surfing is prohibited 30 April-30 July because it is the breeding season of the *tainha* (flathead mullet), a popular table fish.

Ins and outs

Almost all the beaches on the Ilha de Santa Catarina are easily reached by standard public buses (US$1.50), air-conditioned *executivo* buses, or *colectivos* (minivans), which run regularly. Buses to the eastern, southern and northern areas (including Joaquina, Lagoa, Lagoa do Peri and Pantano do Sul) leave from the local Terminal Urbano Centro (TICEN) *rodoviária* on Avenida Paulo Fontes s/n. There is a more comfortable *executivo* bus – the yellow bus – which is air conditioned, costs US$3 and goes around the island. This leaves from the side of Terminal Rita Maria. **Note** There is an integrated system: one bus takes you from centre to a local terminal and there you change bus to get to the *bairros*: (for Campeche you take the bus at Rio Tavares). Schedules and further information are available from the tourist office (see page 337) and there is a full timetable on http://portal.pmf.sc.gov.br/servicos/index.php?pagina=onibus.

The temperature in the north of the island can differ from the south by several degrees.

Northern and central Ilha de Santa Catarina

Santo Antônio de Lisboa Heading north from Florianópolis on the SC 401 highway, **Santo Antônio de Lisboa** is the first town of any size that you come to, after about 10 km. The main beach here is **Sambaqui**, a calm bay named after a huge shell midden once discovered here, and now used more for oyster cultivation than for swimming. The town has a few sights of interest though and is one of the oldest settlements on the island, founded by fishermen from the Azores in the 18th and 19th centuries. There's a little art gallery, the **Casa Açoriana** ⓘ *R Cônego Serpa 30, Santo Antônio de Lisboa, T048-3235 1262, Mon-Thu 1000-2000, Fri-Sat 1000-2200, Sun 1000-2100*, which displays works from some 50 local artists, together with objects remembering the Azores. There are some pleasant cafés and restaurants on the waterfront and a handful of places to stay.

To get to Santo Antônio, take **Trindadense** bus No 331, or any bus going north, to the turn-off to the village on the way to Sambaqui beach (fare US$1.50).

Jurerê and Canasvieiras Beyond Santo Antônio, the island becomes increasingly commercial; around **Ponta Grossa**, **Jurerê**, **Canasvieiras** and, in the far north, **Ponta das**

Canas. Together these resort towns make a mini-conurbation of hotels and services, clustered behind some of the islands' prettiest, if most heavily developed, beaches: Praia do Forte, Praia Jurerê, Praia Canasvieras and Praia Ponta das Canas. **Praia do Forte** is overlooked by the **Forte São José da Ponta Grossa** ⓘ *US$2*, a beautifully restored colonial

Ilha de Santa Catarina

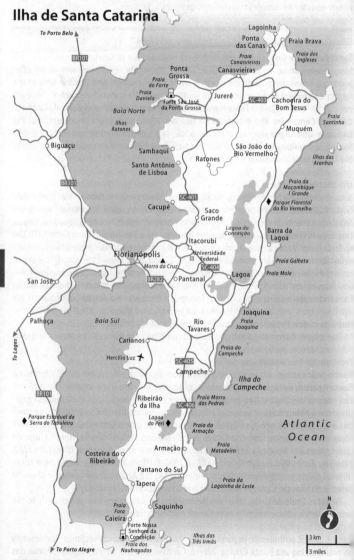

fort with a small museum about its history. The latter three all offer good windsurfing and buzzing in-season beach and bar life. There are plenty of hotel options here.

Praia Brava and the northeast A half-hour walk of the far end of Ponta das Canas beach brings you to the first ocean beach, **Praia Brava**, which is backed by condominiums, sometimes polluted but good for surfing. Just south of here, is **Praia dos Ingleses** (bus No 602), which gets its name from an English ship that sank in 1700. The area is urban, popular with families and with many lively bars in high season. Dunes separate this beach from **Praia Santinho**, where Carijó inscriptions can be seen on the cliffs. Both Ingleses and Santinho have decent surfing. A 2-km trail continues south from Santinho to **Praia do Moçambique**, a glorious 8-km stretch of golden sand backed by an environmental protection area, the **Parque Florestal do Rio Vermelho**, which has some of the best surfing on the island.

Lagoa da Conceição The far end of Praia do Moçambique, near the cape, is known as Praia da Lagoa after **Lagoa da Conceição**, which lies less than a kilometre inland to the east, separating the Atlantic coast from Florianópolis city. This is a good place to stay with frenetic bar and nightlife in season. The lake and coastline are forested, pocked with dunes and offer great windsurfing and fishing. The town of Lagoa da Conceição has a pretty 18th-century church, **Nossa Senhora da Conceição** (1730). It also has a market on Wednesday and Saturday. Hang-gliding and paragliding can be organized from here or through the efficient English-speaking **Brazil Ecojourneys** ① *Estrada Rozália Paulina Ferreira 1132, T048-3389 5619, www.brazilecojourneys.com*. From the Centro da Lagoa on the bridge there are regular boat trips to **Costa da Lagoa**, which run around the lake stopping at various points (Monday to Friday until 2130, weekends and holidays until 1830; check when you buy your ticket, every 30 minutes, US$3 return). The service is used mostly by the local people who live around the lake and have no other form of public transport. The ride is spectacular and there is a charming restaurant to greet you at the end of a thirsty journey. A recommended meal is the *tainha* (local mullet) with salad, chips and an abundance of rice.

Barra da Lagoa, Praia Mole and around Immediately east of the lake and south of Praia Moçambique, **Barra da Lagoa** is a pleasant fishing village and beach, lively in the summer season, with plenty of good restaurants and a popular youth hostel. You can walk across the wooden suspension bridge to a restaurant overlooking the bay, a spectacular setting for a meal. It is reached by **Transol** bus No 403 (aka Lagoa da Conceiçao bus, every 15 minutes from Terminal Urbano, 55 minutes, US$1.50). The same bus goes to the beaches immediately to the south at **Mole**, which is a soft-sand beach, good for walking and with championship surfing. In season, it has some of the liveliest beach and nightlife with a 20-something crowd. **Joaquina**, immediately to the south of Mole and served by the same bus, has some of the best surfing on the island; championships are held here in January. There is sandboarding on the towering powdery dunes that separate the beach from the Lagoa da Conceição.

Southern Ilha de Santa Catarina
Campeche **Praia do Campeche**, 30 minutes by bus (**Pantano do Sul** or **Costa de Dentro**) from Florianópolis is one of the most popular places to stay in the island. It has long been a hippy and new age hang-out, perhaps initially in homage to the French writer Antoine de Saint-Exupéry, author of *Le Petit Prince*, who visited here several times in the 1920s when he was working as a pilot of Ligne Latécoère. The tiny town's main street is named after

his book. There are several beaches around Campeche. **Praia da Armação** is the busiest, with many bars and restaurants overlooking a powdery surf beach. From here there are trips offshore to the **Ilha do Campeche** (US$20), an island with a fine white-sand beach broken by boulders, scrubby subtropical forest and good diving. It is protected by the **Instituto de Patrimônio Histórico Nacional (IPHAN)** because of the myriad petroglyphs, paintings and inscriptions that pepper the islands' rocks.

Armação, Lagoa do Peri and the far south The beaches immediately to the south of Campeche are called **Morro das Pedras** and **Armação**. Both have good surfing, especially the north end of Armação, which is considered one of the most challenging surf spots on the island. Armação village was an important whaling centre in the 19th and early 20th centuries. A few hundred metres inland from Armação beach is the **Lagoa do Peri**, a protected area and the largest stretch of freshwater on the Santa Catarina coast.

Around 4 km after Armacao town, look for a bar by the roadside called **Lanchonete e Bar Surf** (if travelling by bus, it's the last stop on the bus before the road curves around to the right). Just before the bar there is a road to the left. Walk up a red clay path and after about 200 m you should see a path (unsignposted) on the left, leading up into the hills. A steady walk of up to two hours will lead you over two *montes* (hills) with a fabulous view over **Praia da Lagoinha de Leste**. This beach rarely gets crowded, even in the summer months. Camping is permitted and if you don't fancy the walk, you can pay one of the fishermen to take you from the Azorean fishing village of **Pantano do Sul**, immediately to the south. This is an unspoilt, relaxed spot with a long, curved beach and lovely views across to the Três Irmãs islands. There are several *pousadas*, bars and restaurants, though not much nightlife. For **Praia dos Naufragados**, at the southern tip of the island, take a bus to Caieira da Barra do Sul and walk for an hour through fine forests. From the lighthouse and fishing village, it's possible to visit the small island of **Forte Nossa Senhora da Conceição**, just offshore You can take a boat trip with **Scuna Sul** (see Activities and tours, page 355) from Florianópolis.

Ribeirão da Ilha and the southwest
A trail (or boat ride, US$6) leads from the village of dos Naufragados to **Caieiras do Sul**, which is connected to Florianópolis city on the SC401 road. The beach here is lapped rather than pounded by waves as it is the first southern beach round from the cape. Heading north on the SC401 is the village of **Tapera do Sul**, surrounded by mangroves. The road leads on to the pretty Azorean fishing village of **Ribeirão da Ilha**. This is the best-preserved of all Florianópolis's 18th-century settlements, with streets of colourful low houses topped with terracotta tile and fronted by rather unprepossessing concrete cobbles. The village is one of the most popular places in southern Brazil to eat oysters either with the local producer, **Ostravagante**, or one of the many oyster restaurants in town and many buses for the 27-km return ride to Florianópolis city.

North of Florianópolis (mainland) → For listings, see pages 349-357. Colour map 5, B5.

Porto Belo and around → *Phone code: 047. www.portobelo.com.br.*
The coast north of Florianópolis is dotted with resorts. They include **Porto Belo**, a fishing village on the north side of a peninsula settled in 1750 by Azores islanders, with a calm beach and a number of hotels and restaurants. Around the peninsula are wilder beaches reached by rough roads: **Bombas**, **Bombinhas** (both with the same sort of accommodation

as Porto Belo), **Quatro Ilhas** (quieter, good surfing, 15 minutes' walk from Bombinhas), **Mariscal** and, on the southern side, **Zimbros** (or Cantinho). Many of the stunning beaches around Bombinhas are unspoilt and accessible only on foot or by boat. The clear waters around the peninsula offer good snorkelling and reasonable diving. The floating restaurants in the rocky bay of **Caixa d'Aço** are a popular spot.

Southwest of Porto Belo, reached by turning off the BR-101 at Tijucas and going west for 30 km, is **Nova Trento**, a small town in a valley first colonized by Italians and still showing heavy Italian influence. The local cuisine includes cheese, salami and wine such as you might find in Italy; there are several Italian restaurants and wine producers where you can buy *vinho artesanal*. There is a good view of the Tijucas valley and as far as the sea (on a clear day) from the **Morro da Cruz**, at 525 m. West of Porto Belo is **Praia de Perequê**, with a handful of hotels on the long beautiful beach.

Itapema, 60 km from Florianópolis, is another former fishing village on a wide sweep of sandy beach now dominated by tourism. In high season the town accommodates around 300,000 visitors. The **Plaza Itapema Resort e Spa**, T047-3261 7000, is all inclusive and the best such establishment on this part of the coast. Around the headland there are several smaller and quieter beaches, **Praia Grossa** being one of the best, with good surf.

Blumenau → *For listings, see pages 349-357. Colour map 5, B4. Phone code: 047. Population: 262,000.*

Blumenau is in a prosperous district settled mostly by Germans. A clean, orderly city with some almost caricatured Germanic architecture, the *enxaimel* design (exposed beams and brickwork) typifies some of the more famous buildings such as the **mayor's residence**, the **Moelmann Building**, built to resemble a medieval German castle, and the **Museum of the Colonial Family** ① *Av Duque de Caxias 78, Tue-Fri 0900-1700, Sat, Sun 1000-1600, US$1.50*, the German immigrant museum, dating back to 1868.

The first Germans to arrive were the philosopher Herman Bruno Otto Blumenau and 16 other German explorers, who sailed up the river in 1850. Work began on building schools, houses and the first plantations; the city soon became a notable textile centre. Today, software, service and electronics industries are replacing textiles as the town's economic mainstay. There is a helpful **tourist office** ① *R 15 de Novembro, on the corner of R Nereu Ramos*.

Sights of interest include the **German Evangelical Church**, and the house of **Fritz Müller**, now a museum – the **Museu da Ecólogia Dr Fritz Müller** ① *0800-1200 and 1330-1730, free*, and are worth a visit. Müller, a collaborator of Darwin, bought the Blumenau estate in 1897 and founded the town. The **Museu da Cerveja** ① *Praça Hercílio Luz, 160, T047-3326 6791*, examines the history of the region's breweries and the origins of **Oktoberfest**.

Excursions from Blumenau

The **Parque Ecológico Spitzkopf** ① *R Bruno Schreiber 3777, Progresso, T047-3336 5422, US$4*, makes a pleasant day-trip for hiking. It has very pleasant walks through the forest, including a 5.5-km trail passing waterfalls and natural pools up to the Spitzkopf Peak at 936 m, from where you get a wonderful view of the region. If you are not into hiking up hills, there are paths around the lower slopes which will take you half a day. To get there, take the 'Garcia' bus from Avenida 7 de Setembro via Rua São Paulo to Terminal Garcia, then change to 'Progresso' until the end of the paved road, US$1.50 each bus. Then walk 5 km to the park entrance, There's a small zoo and cabins to rent (German spoken).

Blumenau's Oktoberfest

Blumenau's Bierfest is the largest Germanic festival in the Americas. The festival started in 1984 after the city suffered a dreadful flood and sought both to reclaim its civic pride and celebrate its unique culture. Whilst the whole city participates, the party officially takes place in the Parque Vila Germânica, usually in the first half of October. During the day the narrow streets are packed around the Moelmann Shopping Centre, which is where many locals like to begin their festivities before the Oktoberfest Pavilion opens, with drinking and dancing in the local bars. At 1900 the doors to the main pavilions open. There are four in total, all decorated in a Brazilian rendition of traditional Germany. The pavilions host

different events – from drinking competitions to 'sausage Olympics', all accompanied by non-stop traditional German music. The cultural pavilion holds traditional dress and cake-making competitions, as well as organized public singing, which grows steadily worse as the evening rolls on. There is also a funfair and folk dancing shows. Food around the stalls is German and half a litre of *chopp* will cost you around US$2.50. Brazilian popular bands are slowly being introduced, much to the disapproval of the older inhabitants. Visitors report it is worth attending on weekday evenings as weekends are too crowded. The festival is repeated in miniature (and not every day) during the summer.

From the riverside road opposite the *prefeitura* in Blumenau, you can take a bus past rice fields and wooden houses set in beautiful gardens to **Pomerode**, 33 km north of Blumenau. There's an interesting **zoo** ① *R Hermann Weege 160, US$5.50*, founded in 1932 and the oldest in the state, which houses over 600 animals of different species. Next door, **Schornstein** is a restaurant with its own microbrewery, serving excellent German food. Nearby is the **Museu Pomerano** ① *Rodovia SC 418, Km 3, T047-3387 0477*, which tells the story of the colonial family.

There is a **tourist office** ① *R 15 de Novembro, T047-3387 2627*, daily 0800-1800, and the **Associação dos Artistas e Artesãos de Pomerode** ① *next door to the prefeitura municipal*, with a souvenir and bric-a-brac shop. The north German dialect of Plattdeutsch is still spoken here and there are several folkloric groups keeping alive the music and dance of their ancestors: Alpino Germânico, Pomerano, Edelweiss and Belgard. Shooting and hunting is also traditional in the area and there are 16 **Clubes de Caça e Tiro** which are active at all festivities. The men compete for the title of '*Rei do Tiro Municipal*' in July and the women compete for the '*Rainha do Tiro Municipal*' in November.

A half-day excursion to **Gaspar** (15 km) allows you to visit the cathedral, **Igreja Matriz São Pedro Apóstolo**, set high above the river. To get here take a **Verde Vale** bus from the stop outside the huge Shopping Newmarket supermarket on Rua 7 de Setembro in the centre of Blumenau (for tickets, see Transport, page 356). There are four water parks in Gaspar with water slides and other amusements. Two of the best are; **Parque Aquático Cascanéia** ① *R José Patrocínio dos Santos, T047-3397 8500*, with chalets, parking restaurants; and on the same street, **Cascata Berlim** ① *T047-9991 4898/0779*, with camping facilities, a natural pool and a restaurant.

Further west along the Rio Itajaí–Açu, around Ibirama, the river is good for whitewater rafting. You can take a break between rapids to bathe in the waterfalls.

Blumenau to Iguaçu

An alternative to taking a direct bus from Florianópolis or Blumenau to Iguaçu, is to travel through rich and interesting farming country in Santa Catarina and Rio Grande do Sul, stopping at the following places. **Joaçaba** is a town of German immigrants, in the centre of the Vale do Contestado; for information call T047-3522 3000. **Erexim** has a strong *gaúcho* influence. **Iraí**, a town with thermal springs, is situated in an Italian immigrant area and is good for semi-precious stones. From any of these places you can go to Pato Branco and Cascavel and then to Foz do Iguaçu.

Two hours from Joaçaba is **Treze Tílias**, a village where 19th-century Tyrolean dialect is still spoken and the immigrant culture is perfectly preserved. It was settled in 1933 by a group led by Andreas Thaler, who had been the Austrian minister of agriculture. Dairy farming is the main economic activity and children are taught German and Portuguese in school. The style of architecture has been lifted straight from the Alps and the city prides itself on being in the mountains, with all the associated romanticizing of European mountain life found in such resorts throughout Brazil. It may get a bit chilly but it never snows. The major festivity of the year is the four-day **Tirolerfest** in October, celebrating the customs of the Tirol, with food, sculpture and art. There's **tourist office** ① *Praça Andreas Thaler 25*, and buses run to and from Joaçaba and Blumenau.

Joinville → *For listings, see pages 349-357. Colour map 5, B5. Phone code: 047. Population: 430,000.* *www.joinville.sc.gov.br.*

The state's largest city lies 2 km from the main coastal highway (BR-101), within a two-hour drive of Curitiba and Florianópolis. Joinville is known as the 'city of the princes' for its historical connections with royalty. It is also nicknamed the 'city of flowers', and even 'Manchester Catarinense'. The large German population gives it a distinctly European feel, and the city is well-ordered, attractively maintained and easy to navigate on foot.

Ins and outs

Ins and outs **Lauro Carneiro de Loyola airport** ① *13 km from the city centre*, receives flights from São Paulo; a taxi from the airport to the centre costs US$25. Joinville is connected by bus to the larger cities in the south and southeast of Brazil. The **rodoviária** ① *2.5 km outside the town, south exit, T047-3433 2991*, has regular bus services to the centre.

Tourist information You can find information on the city on www.portaljoinville.com.br. There is a **tourist office** ① *R 15 de Novembro 4315, T047-3453 2663, www.turjoinville. com.br.* There are also tourist boards at the airport and *rodoviária*, and information is also available from **Promotur** ① *Centreventos, Av José Vieira 315, sala 20, T047-3453 2633, www.promotur.com.br.*

Sights

The **Museu Nacional da Imigração e Colonização** ① *R Rio Branco 229, Tue-Fri 0900-1700, Sat and Sun 1100-1700, www.museunacional.com.br*, in the impressive **Palácio dos Príncipes**, has a collection of objects and tools from the original German settlement and other items of historical interest. **Arquivo Histórico de Joinville** ① *Av Hermann August Lepper 650, T047-3433 0177, Mon-Fri 0830-1745*, houses a collection of documents dating from the town's foundation.

The **Museu Arqueológico do Sambaqui** ① *R Dona Francisca 600, T047-3433 0144, Tue-Sun 0900-1200, 1400-1800*, has a collection dating back to AD 5000, with an exhibition devoted to the life of the indigenous people who built the sambaqui shell mounds along the south coast of Brazil. There are also two archaeological reserves: **Sambaqui do Rio Comprido**, carbon dated to AD 2855, and **Sambaqui Morro do Ouro**.

The Alameda Brustlein, better known as the **Rua das Palmeiras**, is an impressive avenue of palm trees, leading to the Palácio dos Príncipes. The trees were planted in 1873

Joinville

Sleeping	Joinville Palace 3	Eating
Blue Tree Towers 7	Mattes 5	China 2
Das Palmeiras 4	Tannenhof 9	Sopp 4
Germânia 1		Trento Queijos
HI Joinville Hostel 6		e Vinhos 5

by Frederico Brustlein with seeds brought in 1867 by Louis Niemeyer. The **railway station** ① *R Leite Ribeiro, T047-3422 2550*, dates from 1906 and is a fine example of the German style of architecture; the **Mercado Municipal** ① *Praça Hercílio Luz*, is in the *enxaimel* style. At the other end of the spectrum, the **cathedral**, on Avenida Juscelino Kubitscheck at Rua do Príncipe, is futuristic with spectacular windows recounting the story of man. The **Cemitério dos Imigrantes** ① *R 15 de Novembro 978, Mon-Fri 0800-1700*, is interesting; the attached **Casa da Memória do Imigrante** ① *Mon-Fri 0830-1200 and 1400-1700*, has information on the town's history, with audiovisual and documentary displays.

The **Parque Zoobotânico** ① *R Pastor Guilherme Rau 462, T047-3431 5016, Tue-Sun 0900-1800, 15 mins' walk in the direction of Mirante*, is a good zoo and park, with many local species of birds and animals and a children's park. From here it is 25 minutes' walk to the **Mirante** for a beautiful view of the town and the bay. The tower on the top is at an altitude of 250 m and you can walk up a spiral staircase on the outside for a panoramic view. An **orchid farm** ① *R Helmuth Fallgatter 2547, 0800-1200, 1330-1800*, is open to the public for sales or just to look around.

At **Expoville** ① *4 km from the centre on BR-101 (continuation of 15 de Novembro), daily 0800-2200*, is an exhibition of Joinville's industry, although it is used for many other exhibitions and festivals as well. The multi-functional **Centreventos Cau Hansen** has been built to house sporting activities, shows, festivals, conferences and other events. It is home to the only **Bolshoi Ballet School** outside of Moscow. The tiled mural around the entrance, by Juarez Machado, depicts a circus. There are some hundreds of industries in the manufacturing park, many of which are substantial exporters.

Excursions from Joinville

You can take a boat trip on the **Príncipe de Joinville III** ① *from Lagoa Saguaçu, Bairro Espinheiros, 9 km from the centre, T047-3455 0824, www.barcoprincipe.com.br, departs 1030, returns 1500, US$45 per person including lunch*, past 14 islands to São Francisco do Sul. Stops include the **Museu Nacional do Mar**, the port, lunch at a fish restaurant, Ilha da Rita and Ilha das Flores.

The festival of **São João** in June can be seen best in Santa Catarina at **Campo Alegre**, the first town on the road inland to Mafra. There are bonfires, a lot of (German) folk dancing, and large quantities of local specialities, *quentão* (spiced red wine) and *pinhões* (giant 3-cm-long pine nuts). It is a beautiful cl imb on the road from the BR-101 to Campo Alegre.

At the mouth of the Baia de Babitonga, **São Francisco do Sul** is the port for the town of **Joinville**, 45 km inland at the head of the Rio Cachoeira. It is the country's third oldest city (Binot Paulmier de Gonneville landed here in 1504), after Porto Seguro in Bahia and São Vicente in Rio de Janeiro. The colonial centre has over 150 historical sites and has been protected since 1987. There are good beaches nearby.

South of Florianópolis → *For listings, see pages 349-357.*

The **Parque Estadual da Serra do Tabuleiro**, just south of the BR-282, is the largest protected area in Santa Catarina, covering 87,405 ha, or nearly 1% of the state. Apart from its varied and luxuriant flora, which is home to many birds and animals, it is also important to Florianópolis for its water supply. There is a small **reserve** ① *park office, near Paulo Lopes, Km 252, BR-101, daily 0800-1700*, where animals and birds previously in captivity are rehabilitated before returning to the wild.

Continuing south, two beaches worth a stop are **Pinheira** and **Guarda do Embaú**, which you get to by crossing a river in a canoe. The surfing is excellent here; Guarda in particular is a favourite spot of surfers from Rio and São Paulo (except during the fishing season 15 May-15 July). **Garopaba**, 89 km south of Florianópolis, is a village of 11,000, which swells to 100,000 during the holidays. Its indigenous Carijó name 'Y-Gara-Paba' means 'much water, many fish and many hills'. There is a simple colonial church and a sandy coast.

Silveira, 3 km east, is considered one of Brazil's finest surfing spots. Swimming can be risky, though, because of the surf and sudden drops in the ocean floor. There is good fishing for *tainha*, lobster, anchovy and other varieties. **Praia do Rosa**, 18 km south, is a 3.5-km beach with good swimming, fishing, diving and pleasant coastal walks. It is also one of Brazil's prime whale-watching sites, with southern right whales coming to the bay to calve between June and November. The headquarters of the **Baleia Franca** project is **Pousada Vila Sol e Mar** ① *Estrada Geral da Praia do Rosa, Ibirapuera, T048-3355 6111, www.vidasolemar.com.br, whale-watching trips cost US$50 per person Mon-Fri, US$85 Sat and Sun*, which has cabins for rent and a youth hostel (see Sleeping, page 351). Dolphin-watching and birdwatching trips are available year round.

Laguna → *Colour map 5, B4. Phone code: 048. Population: 48,000.*

The small fishing port of Laguna in southern Santa Catarina (124 km south of Florianópolis), founded in 1676, was a focal point of defence against Spanish invasions and still retains vestiges of its turbulent past. These days Laguna serves mainly as a holiday resort, perched between the ocean and a chain of three lakes. In 1839, Laguna was the capital of the Juliana Republic, a short-lived separatist movement led by Italian idealist Guiseppe Garibáldi. At that time he met a devoted lover, Ana Maria de Jesus Ribeiro, who followed him into battle, was taken prisoner, escaped and rejoined Garibáldi at Vacaria. Their first son, Menotti, was born in Rio Grande do Sul, but the family moved to Montevideo in 1841, where they lived in poverty. They later moved to Argentina and then to Italy, where they fought for the unification of the peninsula. Ana Maria (or Anita) died near Ravenna in 1849 while they were fleeing to Switzerland from the Austrian army. She became a heroine in both Brazil and Italy and there are monuments to her in Rome, Ravenna, Porto Alegre, Belo Horizonte, Florianópolis, Juiz da Fora, Tubarão and Laguna. At Laguna is the **Anita Garibáldi Museum**, containing documents, furniture and her personal effects.

Laguna's well-preserved historic centre boasts many attractive colonial buildings but lacks good accommodation. Resort-style hotels, popular with families, can be found at **Mar Grosso**, Laguna's beach. This heavily developed stretch of sand is 2 km from the centre, but you'll find nicer beaches and dunes 16 km away (accessible by ferry and road) at **Cavo de Santa Marta**.

Also from Laguna, it's possible to take a bus to **Farol**; a beautiful ride that involves crossing the mouth of the Lagoa Santo Antônio by ferry (10 minutes) – look out for fishermen aided by *botos* (dolphins). Here is a fishing village with good surf, deserted beaches and a lighthouse, the **Farol de Santa Marta**. This is the largest lighthouse in South America with the third largest view in the world. It was built by the French in 1890 of stone, sand and whale oil. Guided tours are available (taxi, US$10, not including ferry toll). There are countless inexpensive *pousadas* in the village, as well as several campsites.

West of Florianópolis → *For listings, see pages 349-357.*

From Florianópolis, the BR-282 heads west to Lages. About 12 km along are the hot springs at **Caldas da Imperatriz** (41°C) and **Águas Mornas** (39°C). The latter are open to the public Monday to Friday morning only. Both have good spa hotels (see page 352).

Lages and around → *Colour map 5, B4. Phone code: 049. Population: 160,000.*

The area around Lages is particularly good for 'rural tourism', with lots of opportunities for hiking, horse riding, river bathing and working on a farm. The weather can get really cold in winter and even the waterfalls have been known to freeze. Many of the local *fazendas* are open for visitors and offer accommodation. This is *gaúcho* country and you will get *gaúcho* hospitality, culture and food.

◉ Santa Catarina listings

For Sleeping and Eating price codes and other relevant information, see pages 32-37.

◉ Sleeping

Florianópolis *p336, map p338*
The following hotels are in Florianápolis city. Many visitors to Florianópolis prefer to stay on the beaches, see Ilha de Santa Catarina, below.
L Blue Tree Towers, R Bocaiúva 2304, next to Shopping Beiramar, T048-3251 5555, www.bluetree.com.br. Very smart, well-equipped, modern business hotel. Good restaurant, pool, gym and sauna.
B Bristol Multy Castelmar, R Felipe Schmidt 260, T048-3952 3200, www.bristolhoteis. com.br. Standard 1980s business hotel with restaurant, gym, pool and sauna. There are great views from the upper-floor rooms.
B Faial, R Felipe Schmidt 603, T048-3203 2766, www.hotelfaial.com.br. Comfortable and traditional with simple rooms and a good restaurant. Wi-Fi and lobby bar.
B Florianópolis Palace, R Artista Bittencourt 14, T048-2106 9633, www.floph.com.br. Once the best hotel in town, now a 1970s throwback but with a decent pool, sauna and large a/c rooms.
B Valerim Center, R Felipe Schmidt 554, T048-3225 1100. Functional 2-star with large rooms, hot water and hard beds.
B-C Pousada Pau de Canela, Rio Taveres 606, T048-3338 3584, www.pousadapaudecanela.

com.br. Well-located *pousada* with 10 personalized rooms, restaurant, bar and swimming pool. Cheaper without breakfast.
C Farol da Ilha, R Bento Gonçalves 163, T048-3203 2760, www.hotelfaroldailha.com.br. Well-kept 1990s hotel with 35 a/c rooms, owned by the hotel **Faial**. Convenient for the bus station.
C-D Central Sumaré, R Felipe Schmidt 423, T048-3222 5359. Clean and friendly, good value but some rooms are significantly better than others so look at several. Breakfast included. More expensive with bath.
E HI Floripa Hostel, R Duarte Schutel 227, T048-3225 3781, www.floripahostel.com.br. Price per person. HI hostel, breakfast included, cooking facilities, clean, some traffic noise, very friendly, will store luggage. Prices rise Dec-Feb; more expensive for non-members.

Ilha de Santa Catarina *p339, map p340*
LL Porto Ingleses, R das Gaivotas 610, Praia dos Ingleses, T048-3269 1414, www.porto ingleses.com.br. Small resort with rooms in a 4-storey concrete block overlooking a pool and with a play area for kids, restaurant and beach service. All accommodation has a/c and is spacious. The price includes both breakfast and dinner.
LL Quinta das Videiras, R Afonso Luis Borba, 113. T048-3232 3005, www.quintadas videiras.com.br. Charming colonial style boutique hotel in Lagoa. The loft room has

its own private terrace with mini pool and wonderful views of the Lagoa.

L Pousada Natur Campeche, Servidão Familia Nunes, 59. T048-3237 4011. www.naturacampeche.com.br. Lovely *pousada* with pool and an eco-friendly vibe, steps away from Riozinho beach. All suites are tastefully themed on a country or city and deluxe suites have jacuzzis.

A-B Lexus Beira Mar, R Antônio Prudente de Morais, 814, T048-3266 0909, www.hotel lexus.com.br. 1- and 2-bed studio flats on the beach, with breakfast. Friendly.

A-B Sitio dos Tucanos, Estr Geral da Costa de Dentro 2776, near Pântano do Sul, T048-3237 5084. English, French, Spanish spoken, spacious bungalows in garden setting. Excellent organic food. Take bus to Pântano do Sul, walk 6 km or telephone and arrange to be picked up by German owner.

B-C Pousada 32, on the beach, Barra da Lagoa, T/048-3232 4232, www.pousada32. com.br. Comfortable apartments with kitchen, sleeping 4-7.

C Bangalôs da Mole, Rodovia Jornalista Manoel de Menezes 1005, Praia do Mole, T048-3232 0723, www.bangalosdamole. com.br. Modern tile-roof cabins tucked away from the beach on a little headland; some with kitchenettes and decks with a view.

C Samuka Hotel, Av das Rendeiras c/ Trav Pedro Manoel Fernández 96, Lagoa. T048-3232 5024, www.samukahotel.com.br. Simple, clean and modern apartments for up to 5 people with a/c, frigobar and TVs.

C-D Lagoa Hostel, R José Enrique Veras 469, Lagoa. T048-3234 4466, www.lagoahostel. com.br. Well-located hostel off a side-street of the main going out strip in Lagoa. Attractive garden and terrace. Popular games room with darts board and snooker table.

D Barratur, R Felipa Benta Ramos 18, Barra da Lagoa, T048-3232 3000. Brightly painted beach chalets, the largest of which sleep up to 6, good value.

D Pousada Dona Zilma, R Geral da Praia da Joaquina 279, Lagoa da Conceição,

T048-3232 5161. Quiet, safe and simple with helpful staff.

D-E The Backpackers Sharehouse, Estr Geral, Barra da Lagoa (across hanging bridge, opposite **Pousada Floripaz**), T048-3232 7606. This large, busy hostel is in a prime location and offers free surfboard rental as well as cable TV.

D-E HI Hostel Canasvieiras, R Dr João de Oliveira 517, esq Av das Nações, Canasvieiras, T048-3266 2036, www.floripahostel.com.br. Open 15 Dec-15 Mar. HI hostel, 2 blocks from sea with well-kept dorms and doubles.

E-F Albergue do Pirata, Pântano do Sul, www.alberguedopirata.com.br. Doubles and dorms with breakfast in natural surroundings with lots of trails.

Camping
Camping Clube do Brasil, São João do Rio Vermelho, north of Lagoa da Conceição, 21 km out of town; also has sites at Barra da Lagoa, Lagoa da Conceição, Praia da Armação, Praia dos Ingleses and Praia Canasvieiras.

Wild camping is allowed at **Ponta de Sambaqui** and the beaches of **Brava**, **Aranhas**, **Galheta**, **Mole**, **Campeche**, **Campanhas** and **Naufragados**.

'Camping Gaz' cartridges from **Riachuelo Supermercado**, on R Alvim and R São Jorge.
Camping Fortaleza da Barra, Estrada Geral da Barra da Lagoa 3317, T048-3232 4235. Basic facilities but clean site. Helpful owner, will hold valuables.

Porto Belo and around *p342*
Lots of campsites around the peninsula.
LL Ponta dos Ganchos, 30 mins' drive north of Florianópolis, just south of Porto Belo, Governador Celso Ramos, T048-3262 5000, www.pontadosganchos.com.br. One of the most luxurious resorts in Brazil; isolated on its own steep peninsula with bungalows tucked away on the higher slopes. The best are almost 100 sq m with sweeping (private) views out over the Atlantic. Good restaurant and excellent service. Pick-up service from

Florianópolis airport. The very high price includes all meals (3 per day) and non-alcoholic drinks.

B Hotel Pousada Zimbros, Estrada Geral Zimbros s/n, T047-3393 4087. Cheaper off-season, on beach, sumptuous breakfast, restaurant.

B Porto Belo, R José Amâncio 246, Porto Belo T047-3369 4483. HI. Lots of apartments, most sleep 4-6, good value for a group.

C-D Blumenauense Praia Hotel, Av Sen Atílio Fontana, Praia do Perequê, T047-3369 8208. Simple rooms with en suites and breakfast. On the beach.

Blumenau p343

B-C Glória, R 7 de Setembro 954, T047-3326 1988, hotelgloria@hotelgloria.com.br. Modern resort hotel with a pool and gym. Comfortable though anonymous rooms.

D-E Hermann, Floriano Peixoto 213, T047-3322 4370, www.hotelhermann.com.br. This modest brick home with exposed beams is one of the oldest houses in Blumenau and one of the few that looks authentically European rather than ersatz. Rooms with or without bath, good breakfast, German spoken.

Excursions from Blumenau p343

A-AL Fazzenda Park Hotel, Estrada Geral do Gasparinho 2499, Gaspar, T047-3397 9000, www.fazzenda.com.br. Swimming pool, fishing, walking and riding.

C Pousada Max, R 15 de Novembro 257, Pomerode, T047-3387 3070. A good option.

C Schroeder, R 15 de Novembro 514, Pomerode, T047-3387 0933. A good option.

D Pousada Ecológica Spitzkopf, R Bruno Schreiber 3777, T047-3336 5422. Beautiful, clean and extremely quiet, with pool, eating and a bar, but no restaurant.

Joinville p345, map p346

Tannenhof, R Visc de Taunay 340, T/F047-433 8011, www.tannenhoff.com.br. 4-star, pool, gym, traffic noise, excellent breakfast, restaurant on 14th floor.

A Hotel Germânia, R Ministro Calogeras 612. T047-3433 9886. www.hotelgermania. com.br. Modern building with pretty garden. Pool, reading room, fitness centre.

A Blue Tree Towers, Av Juscelino Kubitschek, 30, T047-3461 8000, www.bluetree.com.br. Smart business hotel with very good service and facilities. Spick and span modern rooms. Sauna, gym and an excellent restaurant and bar.

B-C Joinville Palace, R do Príncipe 142, T047-3433 6111, www.joinvillepalace hotel.com.br. Simple a/c rooms with heating and TV. Visa accepted.

C Das Palmeiras, R 7 de Setembro 40, T047-3433 1288, www.daspalmeiras.com.br. Smart though anonymous 3-star with a pool, bar and restaurant.

D-E HI Joinville Hostel, R Dona Francisca 1376. T047-3424 0844, www.joinvillehostel. com.br. Friendly hostel located about 1 mile from city centre. Garden with hammocks and vegetable patch, bicycles for rent and convenience store. Discounts for HI members.

D-E Mattes, 15 de Novembro 801, T047-3433 9886. Simple but with good service and facilities and a big breakfast. More expensive rooms have cable.

E Flor do Brasil, opposite bus station. Basic but clean rooms with ceiling fan, TV and private bath.

South of Florianópolis p347

LL Quinta do Bucanero, Estr Gerald a Rosa, Praia da Rosa, T048-3355 6056, www.bucanero.com.br. Closed Jun-Jul. Tastefully decorated luxury resort with private access to the beach. Set in lush vegetation in a protected area with a range of activities, from horse riding to boat trips, available. No children.

LL-L Morada do Bouganvilles, Estr Geral do Morro, Praia da Rosa, T048-3355 6179. Luxurious chalets in a bougainvillea-filled garden with a small pool and a bar.

L Pousada Vila Sol e Mar, Estrada Geral da Praia do Rosa, Ibirapuera, T048-3355 6111. The *pousada* has cabins for rent, with kitchen,

TV, restaurant, sushi bar, tennis, surf school. Dolphin-watching and birdwatching trips are available year round. minimum stay 7 nights in high season: US$1150.

L-AL Pousada da Lagoa, R Rosalina de Aguiar Lentz 325, Garopaba, T/F048-3254 3201, www.pousadadalagoa.com.br. Comfortable countryside *pousada* with an outdoor pool, reasonable restaurant and bar and a series of trails running into the environs.

E Praia do Ferrugem, Estr Gerals do Capão, Garopaba, T048-3254 0035. HI youth hostel. Price per person.

Camping

4 km south of Florianópolis, there is a camping site with bar at **Praia do Sonho**. Beautiful, deserted beach with an island fort nearby.

Laguna *p348*

B Flipper, Av Senador Gallottti 680, Mar Grosso, T048-3647 0558, www.flipper hotel.com.br Resort hotel with large rooms, pool, and friendly staff. Good for families.

D Beiramar, 100 m from **Recanto**, opposite Angeloni Supermarket, T048-3644 0260. Clean, TV, rooms with view over lagoon.

D-E Recanto, Av Colombo 17, close to bus terminal. With breakfast. Modern but basic. Cheaper without private bath. The hotel owns snack bar next door.

West of Florianópolis *p349*

L Águas Mornas Palace Hotel, R Coronel Antônio Lehmkuhl 2487, Águas Mornas, T048-3245 7015, www.aguasmornaspalace hotel.com.br, at the springs. Well-maintained luxury spa with a range of treatments. All meals included in the price.

AL Caldas da Imperatriz, SC 432, Rodovia Princesa Leopoldina Km 4, Caldas da Imperatriz, Santo Amaro da Imperatriz, T048-3245 7088, www.hotelcaldas.com.br. A grand, old-fashioned European spa built in 1850 under the auspices of Empress Teresa Cristina, originally with public baths. All meals are included in the price.

Lages and around *p349*

A Grande, R João de Castro 23, T/F049-3251 7000, www.hotellages.com.br. Standard 3-star town hotel.

D Rodeio, T049-3223 2011. One of 3 similar hotels near the *rodoviária* with rooms with or without bath and a good breakfast.

Fazendas near Lages

All on working farms. Prices include all meals.

LL Fazenda do Barreiro, Rod SC 438, Km 43, T049-3222 3031. Games room, library, horses, pool, fishing, boats, TV. All meals included in the price.

LL Fazenda Rancho do Boqueirão, BR-282, Km 4, Saída São José do Cerrito, T049-3221 9900, www.fazendaboqueirao.com.br. Heating, TV, library, games room, pool, horses, bicycles, good walking, fishing.

L Fazenda Aza Verde, Antiga BR-2, Soroptimista 13, T049-3222 0277. Horses, fishing, boats, games room, heating, pool. All meals included in price.

L Fazenda Dourado Turismo Rural, Estr Lages–Morrinhos Km 14, T049-3222 2066/ T049-9982 2094. Simple but comfortable a/c chalets surrounding a grassy lawn and in the edge of Araucária pine forest. With restaurant, pool and live music at weekends. All meals included.

L Fazenda Refúgio do Lago, Rod SC 438, Km 10, Pedras Brancas, T049-3223 1416, www.pousadarefugiodolago.com.br. Pool, games room, library, horses, shooting, fishing, boats, river beach.

🍴 Eating

Florianópolis *p336, map p338*

Take a walk along R Bocaiúva, east of R Almte Lamego, to find the whole street filled with Italian restaurantsand BBQ places.

♗♗♗ Café Riso & Etc, R Bocaiúva 2090, T048-3223 8753, www.caferisoetc.com.br. Smart café and restaurant serving gourmet food and wonderful cakes. Popular with business executives on lunch meetings.

Toca da Garoupa R Alves de Brito 178, just off R Bocaiúva. The city's best seafood restaurant housed in a rustic-chic wood slat house.

Lindacap, R Felipe Schmidt 1162, T048-3222 4002, www.lindacap.com.br. Closed Mon; Sun lunch only. Fish, chicken and meat *pratos* as well as seafood, smart, good buffet.

Macarronada Italiana, Av Beiramar Norte 2458. Good, comfortable, upmarket Italian, with a decent pizzeria next door. In front of the Blue Tree Towers hotel.

O Mercador, Box 33/4 Mercado Público. Excellent self-service specializing in fish and seafood, tables outside on cobbled street.

Trapiche, Box 31, Mercado Público. Self-service fish and seafood, tables on pavement.

Vida, R Visc de Ouro Preto 298, next to Alliance Française. Decent vegetarian set meals and pay by weight.

Café das Artes, at north end of R Esteves Junior 734. Nice café, excellent cakes.

Cía Lanches, Ten Silveira e R Trajano, downstairs, and, in Edif Dias Velho, Av R Felipe Schmidt 303. A wide selection of juices and snacks.

Kayskidum, Av Beiramar Norte 2566. Lanchonete and crêperie, very popular.

Mirantes, R Alvaro de Carvalho 246, Centro, with other branches on R Branco and a churrascaria on R 7 de Setembro. Buffet self-service, good value food with set menu for less than US$5 per kilo.

Ilha de Santa Catarina *p339, map p340*

Ostradamus, Rodovia Baldicero Filomeno, 640, Ribeirão, T048-3337 5711, www.ostra damus.com.br. Smart oyster restaurant by the seafront. Waiters in kitsch attire serve up oysters in every imaginable way – from martini and tabasco oysters, to rosemary oysters. Great wine list.

Bar do Vadinho, Praia do Pantano do Sul, on (last bar on the left), T048-3237 7305. Wonderfully simple place looking out to sea. There's no menu, instead you pay a set price for various regional fish dishes – a selection of whatever fish has been caught that day. The fried swordfish is excellent.

Niguri Sushi Bar, Av Afonso Delambert Neto, 413, Lagoa da Conceição, T048-3232 5761, www.nigirifloripa.com.br. Smart, all-you-can-eat sushi place near Lagoa's integrated bus terminal, serving up all the traditional Japanese delicacies.

Pizzaria Mão na Massa, R Henrique Veras do Nascimento, 255, Lagoa. Cosy pizzeria in Lagoa, with outside space. Excellent pizzas.

Ponta das Caranhas, Estr Geral da Barra da Lagoa 2377. Good seafood and chicken dishes in a romantic waterside setting with outdoor seating.

Oliveira, R Henrique Veras, Lagoa da Conceiçao. Closed Tue. Excellent traditional seafood in pleasant surrounds.

DNA Natural, R Manoel Severino de Oliveira, 360, Lagoa, T048-3207 3441. Popular, healthy snack bar serving imaginative juices, as well as sandwiches and salads. Try the bowl of *açai* with granola.

Joinville *p345, map p346*

The Müeller Shopping has a good food hall.

Chimarrão, R Visconde de Taunay 343, T047-3027 7632. Good churrascaria serving many types of meat, rodizio-style.

China, R Abdon Batista 131, opposite the cathedral, T047-3422 3323. Eat in or home-delivery service for oriental food.

Sopp, R Mcal Deodoro 640, on corner with R Jaraguá, T047-3422 3637. Eclectic menu incorporating German, Brazilian and Japanese dishes. Good chopp.

Trento Queijos e Vinhos, R 15 de Novembro 2973, T047-3453 1796. Traditional Italian with reasonable pastas and pizza.

Biergarten, R Visconde de Taunay 1183, T047-3423 3790. Good-quality German meals, snacks and beers at this combination restaurant and bar.

🍷 Bars and clubs

Florianópolis *p336, map p338*
To find out about events and theme nights check the Beiramar Shopping Centre for

notices in shop windows, ask in surf shops or take a trip to the University of Santa Catarina in Trindade and check out the noticeboards. The newspaper *Diário Catarinense* gives details of bigger events, eg Oktoberfest.

The Mercado Público in the centre, which is alive with fish sellers and stalls, has a different atmosphere at the end of the day when hard-working locals turn up to unwind. However, this area is not particularly safe at night and most bars and restaurants are closed by 2200. The stall, Box 32, is good for seafood and has a bar specializing in *cachaça*, including its own brand. Empórium, Bocaiúva 79, is a shop by day and popular bar at night.

You may need a car to get to other clubs and bars or the hot spots at the beaches. Café Matisse, Av Irineu Bornhausen 5000, inside the Centro Integrade de Cultura, www.cafematissefloripa.com.br. A colourful little café decorated with impressionist prints and art by local artists and which plays hosts to live bands and DJs.
El Divino, Av Beiramar Norte, T048-3225 1266, www.eldivinobrasil.com.br. Wed-Sun from 2000, US$5. Bars, restaurant, dancing, sophisticated.
Ilhéu, Av Prof Gama d'Eça e R Jaime Câmara, US$5. Bar open until early hours, tables spill outside, very popular with locals, fills up quickly, venue for live music rather than a disco (tiny dancefloor).

Ilha de Santa Catarina *p339, map p340*
Throughout the summer, the beaches open their bars day and night; during the rest of the year the beginning of the week is very quiet. The beach huts of Praia Mole invite people to party all night (bring a blanket), while Barraco da Mole in particular heaves with beautiful party people (T048-3232 5585). There are clubs too. Megaclub Pacha, Rodovia Maurício Sirotsky Sobrinho, T048-3282 2054, www.pachafloripa.com.br, and chi-chi Praia Café, Av dos Merlins; T048-3282 1325; www.praiacafedelamusique.com.br, attract a

Gucci-attired crowd who party until the early hours. And Confraria Chopp da Ilha, in Lagoa, gets packed at weekends and is also good for watching football matches (open from 1900). The Black Swan pub in Lagoa is also worth a visit for homesick Brits in need of a pint of ale. They put on excellent live music performances and also host a pub quiz night once a week.

Any bars are worth visiting in the Lagoon area, although Barra da Lagoa becomes quiet after nightfall, even in high season. Around the Lagoa the Brazilian phrase *'qualquer lugar é lugar'* (any place is the place to be) perfectly captures the laid-back beach mood. Other clubs and bars generally require a car: Latitude 27, near Praia Mole, good for live music.

⦿ Entertainment

Florianópolis *p336, map p338*
Cinema The cinema at Shopping Centre Beiramar has international films with subtitles.
Music Free live music every Sat morning at the marketplace near the bus terminal.

⦿ Festivals and events

Florianópolis *p336, map p338*
Easter Farra de Boi (Festival of the Bull). It is only in the south that the bull is actually killed on Easter Sun. Despite being controversial, the festival arouses fierce local pride and there is much celebration. The Portuguese brought the tradition of the bull, which has great significance in Brazilian celebrations.
Dec-Jan The island dances to the sound of the Boi-de-Mamão, a dance that incorporate the puppets of Bernunça, Maricota (the Goddess of Love, a puppet with long arms to embrace everyone) and Tião, the monkey.

Blumenau *p343*
Oct Oktoberfest, see box, page 344.

Joinville *p345, map p346*
Jul Joinville hosts one of the largest dance festivals in the world, the Joinville Dance Festival; around 4000 dancers stay for 12 days and put on shows and displays, ranging from jazz and folklore to classical ballet, seen by some 30,000 spectators in a variety of locations.
Oct Fenachopp, beer festival.
Nov Annual flower festival, mostly orchids, disappointing, US$1.50 entry.

O Shopping

Florianópolis *p336, map p338*
Shopping Centre Beiramar is the largest mall with the usual range of fashion (with plenty of surf wear), music and assorted shops. There are many smaller shopping malls dotted around the resorts. Bargain hunters are better off bartering in the family-run businesses at the **Mercado Público**. Here, Casa da Alfândega, has a good selection of crafts and souvenirs.

▲ Activities and tours

Florianópolis *p336, map p338*
Brazil Ecojourneys, Estrada Rozália Paulina Ferreira 1132, Armação, T048-3389 5619, T048-9111 6366 (mob), www.brazilecojourneys.com. One of the most efficient operators in southern Brazil. Trips around Santa Catarina, with hiking in the Serra and Paraná and Rio Grande do Sul and numerous activities around Florianópolis from trail walking to para- and hang-gilding, surfing and sandboarding.
Scuna Sul, T048-3222 1806, www.scunasul. com.br. Very popular scheduled or bespoke boat trips around the Ilha de Santa Catarina from US$15.

Excursions from Blumenau *p343*
Activities include parapenting, a jeep club (www.jeepclubedeblumenau.com.br), horse riding, and swimming pools with water slides. Ask at the tourist office for details.

⊖ Transport

Florianópolis *p336, map p338*
Air
To get to the airport take a Ribeiroense bus 'Corredor Sudoeste' from Terminal Urbano. Flights to **São Paulo** (Congonhas), **Rio de Janeiro**, **Porto Alegre** and **Curitiba**.
   Airline offices Aerolíneas Argentinas, R Tte Silveira 200, 8th floor, T048-3224 7835. GOL, T0300-3789 2121, www.voegol.com. br. **Nordeste/Rio Sul**, Jerônimo Coelho 185, sala 601, T048-3224 7008, airport T048-3236 1779. **Avianca**, T0300-3789 8160, www.Avianca.com.br. **TAM**, at airport, T048-3236 1812, www.tam.com.br. **Varig**, Av R Branco 796, T048-3224 7266.

Bus
Local There are 3 bus stations for routes on the island, or close by on the mainland: **Terminal de Ônibus Interurbano** between Av Paulo Fontes and R Francisco Tolentino, west of the Mercado Público; **Terminal Urbano** between Av Paulo Fontes and R Antônio Luz, east of Praça Fernando Machado; and a terminal at **R Silva Jardim** and R José da Costa.
   Yellow microbuses (**Transporte Ejecutivo**), starting from the south end of Praça 15 de Novembro, charge US$2.50 depending on the destination. Normal bus fares cost from US$1.40.
   Long distance International buses and those to other Brazilian cities leave from the *rodoviária* Rita Maria on the island, at the east end of the Ponte Colombo Machado Salles.
   Regular daily buses to **Porto Alegre** (US$16, 7 hrs), **São Paulo**, 9 hrs (US$23.75, *leito* US$36.25), **Rio de Janeiro**, 20 hrs (US$31 *convencional*, US$42 executive, US$55 *leito*); to **Foz do Iguaçu** (US$22, continuing to **Asunción** US$30). To **São Joaquim** at 1145, 1945 with Reunidos, 1815 with Nevatur, 5-6 hrs, US$9.30; to **Laguna** US$5.25. No direct bus to Corumbá, change at Campo Grande.

To **Montevideo** (Uruguay), US$52, daily, by TTL. **Buenos Aires** (Argentina), US$55, Pluma, buses very full in summer, book 1 week in advance.

Car hire
Auto Locadora Coelho, Felipe Schmidt 81, vehicles in good condition. Interlocadora, T048-3236 0179, at the airport, rates from US$40 a day before supplements. Localiza at the airport, T048-3236 1244, and at Av Paulo Fontes 730, T048-3225 5558.

Porto Belo and around *p342*
Bus To **Florianópolis**, several daily with Rainha, US$5, fewer at weekends, more frequent buses to **Tijucas**, **Itapema** and **Itajaí**, all on the BR-101 with connections. Catarinense runs several buses daily to **Blumenau**, US$5.50. Local buses run from Porto Belo to the beaches on the peninsula.

Blumenau *p343*
Bus Coletivos Volkmann (T047-3395 1400), run to **Pomerode**, roughly every 40 mins, check schedule at the tourist office, *rodoviária* or www.turismovolkmann.com.br. Also several buses daily with Catarinense and Reunidos, 40 mins, US$2.50. Regular buses with Catarinense to **Curitiba**, US$13-18, **Florianópolis**, US$15, and **Joinville** US$9. Timetables and fares at www.catarinense.net twice daily from Blumenau to **Porto Alegre** with Penha/Itapemirim, 10 hrs, US$50/45.

Excursions from Blumenau *p343*
There are buses from Pomerode to **Jaraguá do Sul**, **Joinville**, **São Bento do Sul**, **Florianópolis**, **São Paulo**, **Curitiba** and other local places with União, Reunidas, and Catarinense.

Joinville *p345, map p346*
Air The airport is 13 km from the city; a taxi from the centre costs US$10. GOL and TAM fly to **São Paulo**.

Airline offices TAM, T047-3433 2033. Varig/Rio Sul, R Alexandre Dohler 277, T047-3433 2800.

Bus Regular buses run to the *rodoviária* is 2.5 km outside the town, south exit. To **Blumenau**, US$3, 2¼ hrs. To **Porto Alegre**, 1½ hrs US$15, with Santo Anjo da Guarda; same company goes to **Florianópolis**, 5 daily (2 hrs, US$25); to **Tubarão**, every hr with Alvorada (US$3, 30 mins). To **Farol** with Lagunatur or Auto Viação São José, 8 buses a day Mon-Fri, 3 on Sat, 2 on Sun (US$5.50), a beautiful ride.

Car hire Interlocadora, R do Príncipe 839, T047-3422 7888. Localiza, R Blumenau 1728, T047-3433 9393, or at the airport T047-3467 1020. Olímpia, R 9 de Março 734, T047- 3433 1755.

Excursions from Joinville *p347*
São Francisco do Sul
Bus The bus terminal is 1.5 km from the centre. Bus to the centre (Terminal Municipal), 'Rodoviária' runs Mon-Fri only, or 'Dom Pedro II' every 40 mins at weekends. There is 1 direct bus daily to **Curitiba** with Penha (www.penha.locaweb.com.br) and 2 daily with Catarinense (www.catarinense.net), US$10, 3 hrs.

Laguna *p348*
Bus To **Porto Alegre**, US$21½ hrs, with Santo Anjo Da Guarda; same company goes to **Florianópolis**, 2 hrs, US$12, 5 daily; to **Tubarão**, every hr with Alvorada, 50 mins. To **Farol** with Lagunatur or Auto Viação São José (8 buses a day Mon-Fri, 3 on Sat, 2 on Sun, US$2.50, a beautiful ride).

Lages and around *p349*
Bus The bus station is 30 mins' walk southeast of the centre. To **Florianópolis**, 6-8 buses daily on the direct road (BR-282), 5 hrs, US$22; twice daily to **Caxias do Sul**, 4 hrs, US$15.

Florianópolis *p336, map p338*
Banks Açoriana Turismo, Jaime Câmara 106, T048-3251 3939, takes Amex. Money changers on R Felipe Schmidt outside BESC. **Banco do Brasil**, Praça 15 de Novembro, exchange upstairs, 1000-1500, huge commission on cash or TCs. Lots of ATMs downstairs. **Banco Estado de Santa Catarina** (BESC), *câmbio*, R Felip, Schmidt e Jerônimo Coelho, 1000-1600, no commission on TCs. ATM for MasterCard/Cirrus at **Banco Itaú**, Shopping Centre Beiramar (not in the centre, bus Expresso). **HSBC**, ATM, R Felipe Schmidt 376, corner with R Álvaro de Carvalho. **Lovetur**, Av Osmar Cunha 15, Ed Ceisa and **Centauro Turismo**, same address.
Embassies and consulates Chile, R Av Rio Branco 387, 4th floor, Edif Mapil, T048-3224 2394. **France**, Alliance Française, T048-3223 2469 (Fri 0900-1200). **Spain**, R Almte Alvim 24, Casa 9, T048- 3222 1821.

Uruguay, Av Rio Branco 387, 5th floor, T048-3222 3718 (0800-1200, 1400-1800). **Internet** Moncho, Tiradentes 181. **Language schools** Step 1 Idiomas, R Joe Collaço 99, Córrego Grande, T048-3233 6605, www.step1.com.br. Portuguese classes for foreigners with short and longer-term courses. **Laundry** Lav e Lev, R Felipe Schmidt 706, opposite Valerim Plaza. **Post office** Praça 15 de Novembro 5. **Telephone** Praça Pereira Oliveira 20.

Joinville *p345, map p346*
Banks There are Bradesco and Banco do Brasil banks in the city. **Internet** Biernet Bar, R Visconde de Taunay 456, and numerous others. **Medical services** 24-hr pharmacies: Drogaria Catarinense, FR Blumenau 138, T047-3433 1518, or Filial São João, Av Getúlio Vargas 1343, T047-3455 2910. **Farmacia** Catarinense, R 15 de Novembro 503, T047-3422 2318.

Rio Grande do Sul

Brazil's southernmost state regards itself as different from the rest of the country and once fought a war for independence. Its people identify themselves as much with Uruguay and Argentina and, like their counterparts on the pampas, refer to themselves as gaúchos.

The scenery is different too. An escarpment, in places over 1000 m high, runs down the coastal area as far as Porto Alegre providing escape from the summer swelter. The state capital is the most industrialized and cosmopolitan city in the south and tops the country's 'urban quality of life' rankings. All along the coast, the green hills of Rio Grande do Sul are fringed by sandbars and lagoons, forming one of the world's longest beaches. On the border with Santa Catarina in the north is the remarkable Aparados da Serra national park, where there is often snow.

In southern Rio Grande do Sul, the grasslands stretch as far as Uruguay to the south and more than 800 km west to Argentina, and are scattered with the remains of Jesuit missions. This is the distinctive land of the gaúcho (cowboy) and the herders are regularly seen in traditional garb. In restaurants, steaks the size of Texas are the order of the day; look out for local specialities such as 'comida campeira', 'te colonial' and 'quentão'.

The state is famous for its music. Perhaps the country's greatest ever female singer – Elis Regina – was a gaucha, as are current big names such as Adriana Calcanhotto, Arthur de Faria and cheesy popster Xuxa. There's live music in Porto Alegre most nights and a series of contemporary and traditional music festivals all over the state. ▶ For listings, see pages 369-378.

Background

The first people to settle in the area were pioneer farmers, and the traditional dress of the *gaúcho* (pronounced ga-oo-shoo in Brazil) can still be seen: the flat black hat, *bombachas* (baggy trousers) and poncho. The indispensable drink of the southern cattlemen is *ximarão* (*mate* without sugar, also spelt *chimarrão*). The *gaúcho* culture has developed a sense of distance from the African-influenced society further north. Many people will tell you they have more in common with Uruguayans or Argentines than Brazilians – apart from when it comes to football. Today, there are many millions of cattle, sheep and pigs, and the state produces some 75% of all Brazilian wine.

Porto Alegre → For listings, see pages 369-378. Colour map 5, B3. Phone code: 051.
Population: 1,361,000.

Whilst it has no obvious sights to draw visitors, Porto Alegre is one of Brazil's more pleasant cities: situated at the confluence of five rivers and freshened by over a million trees. Culturally rich, ethnically diverse and progressive, it is the capital of the southern frontier and the hub of trade with Argentina and Uruguay. It is a good base for exploring the rest of Rio Grande do Sul's natural beauty and historical sites.

Porto Alegre is the seat of the annual **World Social Forum** (www.forumsocia mundial.org.br) – the counter to Davos, which attracts hundreds of thousands of NGC delgates and supporters of alternative political agendas.

Ins and outs

Getting there International and domestic flights arrive at **Salgado Filho airpor** ① *R Severo Dullius 90010, 8 km from the city, T051-3358 2000*, which is one of Brazil's best - with restaurants and cafés, a tourist booth, a post office, a pharmacy, a shopping centre and a cinema; making it one of the few in the world where waiting for flight can actually be pleasureable experience. There are regular buses to the bus station and a metrô service to the city centre. International and interstate buses arrive at the **rodoviária** ① *Larg Vespasiano Júlio Veppo, Av Mauá with Garibáldi, T051-3286 8230, www.rodoviaria poa.com.br*, an easy walk from the city centre. There are good facilities, including a pos office and long-distance telephone service until 2100. ▸▸ *See Transport, page 376.*

Getting around *Lotação* (first-class minibuses), painted in a distinctive orange, blue an white pattern, stop on request. They are safer and more pleasant than normal buses an cost about US$1.50. The **Trensurb metrô** ① *T051-2129 8477, www.trensurb.com.br, sing journey US$1.50*, runs from the southern terminal at the Mercado Público (station beside the market), as far north as Sapucaia do Sul. The second station serves the *rodoviária*, an the fifth station serves the airport (10 minutes). A good way to get your bearings in the cit is to take the **Linha Turisma** ① *buses leave from the Secretaria do Turismo building, Trav Carmo 84, Cidade Baixa, T051-3289 6744, www2.portoalegre.rs.gov.br/turismo, US$5, daily 0900 (around the Centro Histórico), 1030 (around the Zona Sul only), 1330 (around the Zon Sul only) and 1530 (around the Centro Histórico), reservations sometimes necessary in hig season, tickets should be bought 30 mins before departure at other times*, a popular open-te tourist bus around the city with commentary in Portuguese, Spanish and English.

Best time to visit Standing on a series of hills and valleys on the banks of Lake Guaíba, Porto Alegre has a temperate climate for most of the year, although temperatures often exceed 40°C at the height of summer and drop below 10°C in winter.

Tourist information The **Secretaria do Turismo (SETUR)** ① *Trav do Carmo 84, Cidade Baixa, T051-3288 5400, www.portoalegre.rs.gov.br/turismo*, is very helpful, with English speakers, maps and excellent general information and tips about the city. Also helpful are the **Central de Informações Turísticas** ① *R Vasco da Gama 253, Bom Fim, T051-3311 5289, daily 0900-2100*, and Setur ① *Borges de Medeiros 1501, 10th floor, T051-3228 5400, also at the airport and rodoviária*, which provides free city maps. There are free guided walks on Sunday at 1500 or 1600 from Praça da Alfândega or on Saturday from Praça da Matriz, T0800-517686. Contact the tourist office, or ask in the Mercado Público. The state tourism website is www.turismo.rs.gov.br.

Sights

The older residential part of the town is on a promontory, dominated previously by the **Palácio Piratini** (governor's palace) and the imposing 1920s metropolitan **cathedral** on the **Praça Marechal Deodoro** (Praça da Matriz). Also on, or near, this square are the neoclassical **Theatro São Pedro** (1858), the **Solar dos Câmara** (1818), now a historical and cultural centre) and the **Biblioteca Pública**, but all are dwarfed by the skyscraper of the **Assembléia Legislativa**. Down Rua General Câmara from Praça Marechal Deodoro is the **Praça da Alfândega**, with the old customs house, the **Museu de Arte de Rio Grande do Sul**, the old post office and the Banco Meridional. A short walk east from here, up Rua 7 de Setembro, is the busy **Praça 15 de Novembro**, where the neoclassical **Mercado Público** sells everything from religious artefacts to spice and meat. You'll find plenty of food cafés, here, and the pavement bars outside are busy at lunch-times and during 'happy hour'. Opposite the market is the bar/restaurant **Chalé da Praça XV**, a Bavarian-style building dating back to 1874. This is a very popular meeing spot and its outdoor seats are perfectly placed for people watching.

Do not miss the pedestrianized part of **Rua dos Andradas** (Rua da Praia). It is the city's principal outdoor meeting place, the main shopping area, and by around 1600 it is jammed full of people. Heading west along Rua dos Andradas, you pass the pink **Casa de Cultura Mário Quintana** in the converted **Hotel Majestic** (see Entertainment, page 375). A little further along is a wide stairway leading up to the two high white towers of the church of **Nossa Senhora das Dores**, the only National Heritage graded church in the city. Many tall buildings in this part of the city rise above the fine, sometimes dilapidated, old houses and the streets are famous for their steep gradients. On the banks of Lake Guaíba, the **Usina do Gasômetro** is Porto Alegre's answer to London's Tate Modern. Built 1926-1928 as a thermoelectric station, it was abandoned in 1974 before being converted to showcase art, dance and film in 1992. Its 117-m chimney has become a symbol for the city. There is a café at the bottom of the chimney, and the sunset from the centre's balcony is stunning. In the **Cidade Baixa** quarter are the colonial **Travessa dos Venezianos** (between Ruas Lopo Gonçalves and Joaquim Nabuco) and the **house of Lopo Gonçalves** ① *R João Alfredo 582*, which houses the **Museu de Porto Alegre Joaquim José Felizardo** ① *Tue-Sun 0900-1200 and 1330-1800, free*, with exhibits about the city's history.

The **Museu Júlio de Castilhos** ① *Duque de Caxias 1231, Tue-Sun 0900-1700*, has a permanent collection on the history of Rio Grande do Sul state, as well as temporary exhibits. The **Museu de Arte do Rio Grande do Sul** ① *Praça Senador Florêncio (Praça da*

Alfândega), Tue 1000-2100, Wed-Sun 1000-1700, free, is interesting. It specializes in art from Rio Grande do Sul, but also houses temporary exhibitions. **Museu de Comunicação Social** ① *R dos Andradas 959, T051-322 44252, Mon-Fri 1200-1900*, in the former *A Federação* newspaper building, deals with the development of the press in Brazil since the 1920s.

Parks

Porto Alegre is well endowed with open spaces. Many of the trees are of the flowering varieties, such as jacarandas and flamboyants. There are seven parks and 700 squares in the city, of which the most traditional is **Parque Farroupilha** (Parque Redenção), a fine park near the city centre. It has a triangular area of 33 ha between Avenida Osvaldo Aranha, Avenida José Bonifácio and Avenida João Pessoa, and contains a lake, mini-zoo, amusement park, bicycle hire, the Araújo Viana auditorium and a monument to the

Porto Alegre

Sleeping
América **14**
Blue Tree Millennium Flat **1**
Comfort **5**
Conceição Center **2**
Continental **3**
Eko Residence **10**
Embaixador **4**
Everest **12**
Lancaster **6**
Palácio **7**
Plaza São Rafael **8**
Ritter **9**
Uruguay **11**

Eating
Al Dente **1**
Café do Cofre **9**
Chopp Stübel **5**
Galpão Crioulo **2**
Koh Pee Pee **6**
Nova Vida **8**

Bars & clubs
Apolinário **9**
Bar de Beto **10**
Boteca Dona Neusa **7**
Mufuletta **11**
Opinião **12**
Ossip **13**
Santissimo **14**
Zelig **15**

N

200 metres
200 yards

Second World War. On Sundays there is a *feira* of antiques and handicrafts at the José Bonifácio end, where locals walk, talk and drink *chimarrão*, the traditional *gaúcho* drink. **Parque Moinhos de Vento** is popular for jogging and has a replica of a windmill in the middle of the park; there used to be several working mills here, which gave the *bairro* its name. The riverside drive, Avenida Edvaldo Pereira Paiva, around Parque Maurício Sirotsky Sobrinho, is closed to traffic on Sunday for cycling, skating, jogging and strolling. **Marinho do Brasil** is another large park between the centre and the *zona sul*, where there are lots of sporting activities. The **botanic gardens** ① *R Salvador França 1427, zona leste, US$1.50, Tue-Sun 0800-1700, take bus No 40 from Praça 15 de Novembro to Bairro Jardim Botânico*, are a short bus ride from the city centre and well worth a visit. The interesting **Museu de Ciências Naturais** is also housed in the garden's grounds.

The 5-km-wide **Lake Guaíba** lends itself to every form of boating and there are several sailing clubs. Two boats run trips around the islands in the estuary: **Cisne Branco** ① *T051-3224 5222, www.barcocisnebranco.com.br, several sailings daily, from 1 hr, US$8*, from Cais do Porto, near Museu de Arte de Rio Grande do Sul; and **Noiva do Caí** ① *T051-3211 7662, several on Sun, some mid-week, 1 hr, US$1.90, check winter schedules*, from the Usina do Gasômetro. Jet-skiers jump the wake of the tour boats. **Ipanema beach**, on the southern banks of the river, has spectacular sunsets. You can see a good view of the city, with glorious sunsets, from the **Morro de Santa Teresa** (take bus No 95 from the top end of Rua Salgado Filho, marked 'Morro de Santa Teresa TV' or just 'TV').

Around 30 km north of Porto Alegre on the BR-116 is the very good **Parque Zoológico** ① *BR-116, Parada 41, Tue-Sun 0830-1700, US$2.50*, set in 780 ha and home to more than 2000 animals, birds and reptiles.

Excursions from Porto Alegre

A paved road runs south from the town of Tramandaí (mostly prohibited to trucks) along the coast to **Quintão**, giving access to many beaches. One such beach is **Cidreira**, 26 km south of Tramandaí; it is not very crowded and has **Hotel Farol** on the main street. A bus from Porte Alegre costs US$3.40. A track continues to charming **Mostardas** and along the peninsula on the seaward side of the Lagoa dos Patos to São José do Norte, opposite Rio Grande (see

Excursions from Rio Grande, page 364). There is accommodation in **Palmares do Sul** (across the peninsula from Quintão) and Mostardas. The latter also has a Banco do Brasil and good pizzeria (Rua Luís Araújo 941, closed Monday). About 30 km south of Mostardas is **Tavares**, with a barely passable hotel (**F**) in the *praça*.

Mostardas makes a good base for visiting the **Lagoa do Peixe National Park** ⓘ *information at Praça Luís Martins 30, Mostardas, T051-3673 1464*, one of South America's top spots for migrating birds. Flamingos and albatrosses are among the visitors. There is free access to the park, but there is no infrastructure. From Mostardas you can hop off the bus (daily at 1045) that passes through the northern end of the park on its way to the beach, where there are basic hotels and restaurants. The main lake, which has the highest bird concentration, is about 20 km from both Mostardas and Tavares.

Serra Gaúcha → *For listings, see pages 369-378.*

Some of the Serra Gaúcha's most stunningly beautiful scenery is around the towns of Gramado and Canela, 130 km north of Porto Alegre. There is a distinctly Swiss/Bavarian flavour to many of the buildings in both towns. In spring and summer the flowers are a delight, and in winter there are frequent snow showers. December is the busiest month for tourism, with Brazilian and Argentinian families flocking here in droves to see the genuinely impressive Christmas displays.

This is excellent walking and climbing country among hills, woods, lakes and waterfalls. The Rio Paranhana at Três Coroas, 25 km south of Gramado, is well known for canoeing, especially for slalom. Local crafts include knitted woollens, leather, wickerwork and chocolate.

Gramado → *Colour map 5, B4. Phone code: 054. Population: 28,600.*

At 850 m above sea level, Gramado provides a summer escape from the 40°C heat of the plains. The town lies on the edge of a plateau with fantastic views. It is clean and full of Alpine-style buildings making it feel like a Swiss Disneyworld. Famous for its chocolate, Gramado survives almost entirely through tourism. Its main street, Avenida Borges de Medeiros, is full of kitsch artisan shops and fashion boutiques. In the summer, thousands of *hortênsias* (hydrangeas) bloom. Among its parks are **Parque Knorr** and **Lago Negro** and **Minimundo** ⓘ *T054-3286 1334, Tue-Sun 1300-1700*, a collection of miniature models such as European castles. About 1.5 km along Avenida das Hortênsias heading toward Canela is the **Prawer chocolate factory** ⓘ *Av das Hortênsias 4100, T054-3286 1580, www.prawer.com.br, Mon-Fri 0830-1130 and 1330-1700*, which offers free tours of the truffle-making process and free tastings. Opposite is the **Hollywood Dream Car Automobile Museum** ⓘ *Av das Hortênsias 4151, T054-3286 4515, 0900-1900, US$8*, which has an excellent collection of American gas-guzzlers dating back to a 1929 Ford Model and Harley-Davidson motorbikes from 1926. For a good walk or bike ride into the valley, take the dirt road Turismo Rural 28, 'Um Mergulho no Vale' (A Dive into the Valley), which starts at Avenida das Hortênsias immediately before the (the Brazilian Environment Ministry) chocolate factory. There are two **tourist information offices** ⓘ *Av da Hortênsias (Pórtico), T054-3286 1418*, and ⓘ *Praça Maj Nicoletti/Av Borges de Medeiro 1674, T054-3286 1475, www.gramadosite.com.br.*

Canela and around → *Colour map 5, B4. Phone code: 054. Population: 33,600.*

A few kilometres along the plateau rim, Canela has been spared the plastic makeover of its neighbour and offers more affordable sleeping and eating options. The painted wooden buildings provide a certain downtown charm. Canela is surrounded by good parks and is developing as a centre of adventure tourism, with rafting, abseiling and trekking on offer. There's a **tourist office** ① *Laga da Fama 227, T054-3282 2200, www.canelaturismo.com.br.*

Just outside Canela is the **Mundo à Vapor** ① *RS 235, Rodovia Canela–Gramado T054-3282 1115, daily 0915-1700, US$5*, an interesting museum dedicated to steam power. The main attraction is the dramatic reconstruction of the famous 1895 rail disaster in Montparnasse, Paris. Kids and adults clamour to have their picture taken alongside a giant steam train that appears to have burst through the front of the building.

Canela is surrounded by beautiful parks, including **Parque Caracol** ① *T054-3278 3035, 0830-1800, US$4.50*. Here, you'll find the Rio Caracol, a spectacular 130-m-high waterfall, which emerges from thick forest and tumbles like dry ice from an overhanging elliptical escarpment. Just outside the park is **Parque do Teleférico** ① *www.canelatelerifico.com.br*, where you can take a 20-minute ski lift ride over the trees, canyons and falls (US$10). The falls are east-facing, so photography is best before noon. A 927-step metal staircase leads to the plunge pool. If cycling, there is an 18-km circular route continuing on to **Parque Ferradura** (along a 4-km spur), where there is a good view into the canyon of the Rio Cai. From the Ferradura junction, turn right to continue to the national forest **Floresta Nacional** ① *T054-3282 2608, 0800-1700, free*, run by **Instituto Chico Mendes de Conservação da Biodiversidade (ICMBio)**, with woodland walks. From here, the dirt road continues round to Canela. Another good hike or bike option is the 4-km dirt track southeast of Canela past **Parque das Sequóias to Morro Pelado**. At over 600 m, there are spectacular views from the rim edge.

Army maps (1:50,000) are available from military posts in Caxias do Sul and Porto Alegre. The urban department in Canela's prefeitura municipal, Rua Dona Carlinda, and the environmental lodge in Parque Estadual do Caracol have copies available for viewing only.

South of Porto Alegre → *For listings, see pages 369-378. Colour map 5, C3.*

Pelotas → *Phone code: 053. Population: 323,200.*

Pelotas, Rio Grande do Sul's second largest city, was founded in the early 19th century and grew rich on the *charque* (dried beef) trade. It has a very strong and vibrant African-Brazilian identity and hosts lively festivals. The city lies 271 km south of Porto Alegre, on the banks of the muddy Rio São Gonçalo, which connects the Lagoa dos Patos with the Lagoa Mirim. The city's heyday was 1860-1890 and most of the sun-baked colonial churches and pastel coloured townhouses date from this period. Together with a sleepy overall atmosphere, they give Pelotas the feel of being stuck in a time warp: a low-key little city with much typically Brazilian charm. The city centre is pedestrianized, filled with an array of shops and broken up by dozens of pleasant parks and green spaces. It's a pleasant place to wander around and is small enough to be easy to navigate without a map. There is a 19th-century cathedral, **São Francisco de Paula**, and, as testament to British settlers of the time, an Anglican church, **Igreja Episcopal do Redentor**, a couple of blocks from the main square on Rua XV de Novembro. Pelotas is famous for its cakes and sweets; try some of the preserved fruits from the many small confectioners.

Ins and outs The **airport** ① *8 km from the town centre*, receives flights from Porto Alegre. The *rodoviária* is out of town, with a bus every 15 minutes to the centre. There's no official tourist information centre but **Terrasul** ① *R Gen Neto 627, T053-3227 9973, www.terra sulpelotas.com.br*, has local maps and can organize good-value city and regional tours.

Excursions from Pelotas

Within a radius of 60 km (about an hour's drive), there are numerous excursions to the farms of settlers of German descent in the hilly countryside (for example Cerrito Alegre and Quilombo), where you can find simple and clean accommodation, with cheap, good and plentiful food.

West of town, the **Lagoa dos Patos** is very shallow; at low tide it is possible to walk 1 km out from the shore. During heavy rain, saltwater entering the lake brings with it large numbers of crabs, which are a local delicacy. Fishermen are generally happy to take tourists out on sightseeing or fishing trips for a small fee (it's best to go in a group). **Praia do Laranjal** is full of local beach houses and there are several friendly bars. **Barro Douro** is very green with a campsite but no beach. It's the site of a big local festival for *Iemanjá* on 1-2 February; well worth visiting. From Pelotas, take a **Ze3** bus (or taxi US$30).

South of Pelotas, on the BR-471, is the **Reserva Ecológica do Taim** ① *information from Instituto Chico Mendes de Conservação da Biodiversidade (ICMBio) in Porto Alegre T051-3225 2144, www.icmbio.gov.br*, Taim Water Reserve, on the Lagoa Mirim. The road cuts the reserve in two and capybaras, killed by passing traffic, are sadly a common sight along the route. Black-necked swans, southern screamers, roseate spoonbills, southern lapwings, half a dozen heron species, small mammals and spectacled caiman are easy to spot here, nesting in the open grasslands and restinga scrub or wading in the Lagoa. There are no facilities. About 5 km from Taim there is the **ecological station**, where there's a small museum of regional animals; there is some accommodation for scientists or other interested visitors, however, most visitors stay in Rio Grande, 80 km away, or in Pelotas.

Rio Grande → *Colour map 5, C3. Phone code: 053. Population: 186,500.*

At the entrance to the Lagoa dos Patos, 274 km south of Porto Alegre, is Rio Grande, founded in 1737. The city lies on a low, sandy peninsula, 16 km from the Atlantic Ocean. Today it is the distribution centre for the southern part of Rio Grande do Sul, with significant cattle and meat industries.

During the latter half of the 19th century, Rio Grande was an important centre. It has lost much of its importance but is still notable for the charm of its old buildings. The **Catedral de São Pedro** dates from 1755-1775. The **Museu Oceanográfico** ① *2 km from the centre on Av Perimetral, T053-3231 3496, daily 0900-1100, 1400-1700*, has an interesting collection of 125,000 molluscs. To get there take bus No 59 or walk along the waterfront. At Praça Tamandaré is a small zoo. There is a **tourist office** at the junction Rua Duque de Caxias and Rua Gen Becaler.

Excursions from Rio Grande

Cassino is a popular seaside town with hotels and shops, 24 km from Rio Grande via a good road. There are several beaches within easy reach of Cassino, but they have no facilities. A wrecked ship remains on the shore where it was thrown by a storm in 1975. Travelling south the beaches are, in order: **Querência** (5 km), **Stela Maris** (9 km), **Netuno** (10 km), all with surf.

The *barra* (breakwater), 5 km south of Cassino, through which all vessels entering and leaving Rio Grande must pass, is a tourist attraction. Barra–Rio Grande buses, from the east side of Praça Ferreira, pass the *superporto* where there is very good fishing. The coastline here is low and straight, lacking the bays found to the north of Porto Alegre. One attraction is railway flat-cars powered by sail (agree the price in advance); the railway was built for the construction of the breakwater.

Across the inlet from Rio Grande, the little-visited settlement of **São José do Norte** makes a pleasant trip. Founded in 1725 and still mostly intact, the village depends on agriculture and crab fishing. There are only three hotels and a good campsite, **Caturritas**, T053-3238 1476, in pine forests 5 km from the town. There are also several long beaches. Ferries (departing every half-hour, 30 minutes) link São José with Rio Grande; there are also three car ferries daily, T053-3232 1500. Information is available from the **tourist office** ① *R General Osório 127.*

Bagé and the border with Uruguay
There are *pousadas* and cheap guest houses in Bagé. See www.bage.rs.gov.br for more information on the town. Getting to and from Bagé is a struggle, although this will surely change with the closing of the Brazilian side of the border at Chuí. Currently the only bus connections are via Pelotas, Cassino and Santana do Livramento.▸▸ *See Transport, page 377.*

Santo Ângelo and the Jesuit Missions → *Colour map 5, B2. Phone code: 055.*
Rio Grande's only UNESCO-listed World Heritage Site are the Jesuit colleges and churches, sitting near the sleepy village of **São Miguel das Missões**, some 50 km from the western Rio Grande do Sul regional centre of Santo Ângelo. The buildings were constructed in the 18th century to protect the indigenous Guarani people from the *bandeirante* slave trade, and to convert them to Christianity.

Fierce battles were fought over the missions between the Jesuit priests and the *bandeirantes*, who scoured the entire Brazilian backland for human cattle required to work the sugar and coffee plantations to the north. Slaves had a life expectancy of only a few years. The Jesuits, under **Father Antônio Vieira**, campaigned fiercely against the *bandeirantes*, whose practices were officially banned by both the Pope and the Portuguese crown. But Europe was a month away by sea and policing was non-existent. The Brazilian colonial Portuguese, determined not to lose the source of their new-found wealth, campaigned so fervently against the fathers that they succeeded in expelling the priests from the Americas, and subsequently in having the Jesuit order disbanded. The missions were ransacked, the Guarani women raped, the children murdered and the men enslaved. The story is told in Roland Joffe's landmark 1986 film, *The Mission*. A walk around the ruins is haunting. They sit in a a grassy paddock just outside São Miguel. At night they are beautfully illuminated and sit under a dome of stars. There is a small museum, the **Museu da Missões** ① *0900-1800, entrance to the ruins US$3.*

Ins and outs
Whilst the ruins are in São Miguel (which has a few basic *pousadas*), Santo Ângelo, some 50 km away, has a better infrastructure and is connected to São Miguel by hourly buses (US$2, 45 minutes). Santo Angelo is served by regular buses from Porto Alegre and is a pleasant town with a quiet atmosphere and friendly residents. It has a missionary museum in the main square with a **cathedral** whose fresco shows missionaries proselytizing the indigenous population. It is difficult to find a good place to eat in the evening; although there is a reasonable pizzeria next to the *rodoviária* or you could try a

snack bar for hamburgers. *Gaúcho* festivals are often held on Sunday afternoons, in a field near the mission (follow the music). For more information on São Miguel das Missões, see www.saomiguel-rs.com.br.

It is possible to continue into Argentina directly from Santo Ángelo town to visit other UNESCO-protected ruins at San Ignacio Mini and Posadas. Direct buses leave Santo Angelo for those towns with a stop at the border for passport stamps and customs. Be sure to get the correct stamps.

Porto Xavier and the Argentine missions
You can continue into Argentina to see the mission ruins at San Ignacio Miní and Posadas by getting a bus from Santo Ângelo (0600, 0900, 1300,1545, 1930) to the quiet border town of **Porto Xavier** (four hours, US$10), on the Rio Uruguay. Buses also run to Porto Xavier from Porto Alegre (one daily), and Santa Maria.

Salto do Yucumâ
Between November and April, the Rio Uruguay overflows along its east bank for over 1800 m, creating the world's longest waterfall. The 12-m-high Salto do Yucumâ is in the 17,000-ha **Parque do Turvo**. Its isolation (530 km northwest of Porto Alegre on the Argentine border) means few tourists visit. Accordingly it is a wildlife haven with over 220 bird species and 34 mammal species (12 threatened). The nearest town, **Derrumbadas**, 4 km from the park and has an **information point** ① *T054-3551 1558, ext 228*. Lemon extract production is an important local industry.

Northern Rio Grande do Sul: the Serra Geral → *For listings, see pages 369-378.*

This spectacular mountain range some 170 km south of Florianópolis rises steeply from the southern Santa Catarina coast near Praia Grande, ascending from sea level to almost 2000 m in just over 20 km. It is cut by dozens of majestic canyons formed when the African and American plates pulled apart ripping great gashes in the hills. Each of these canyons has its own microclimate, ranging from verdant and mossy to dry and cool. The canyons and the rugged, semi-wild country that surrounds them offers some of the best hiking in southern Brazil. The *serra* is protected by two contiguous national parks: Parque Nacional Aparados da Serra and Parque Nacional de Serra Geral.

In the wet season, the canyons are lush with an abundance of ferns, lichens and mosses and in the misty mornings it's common to hear the eerie roar of red howler monkeys. Birds and butterflies are abundant, including spectaculars such as the red-breasted toucan, endemics like the vinaceous Amazon (a chunky green parrot with a bloody beak) and rarities like the red-legged seriema, which looks a little like a wispy secretary bird in scarlet tights. Mammals include howler and brown capuchin monkeys, ocelot, grey foxes, agouti, paca and armadillos.

Parque Nacional Aparados da Serra
① *T054-3251 1277, open year-round Wed-Sun 0900-1700, US$6.00 plus US$2.50 for a car.*
This park is famous for its much-photographed **Itaimbezinho canyon**, some 8 km long and 720 m deep and fringed with subtropical forest. Two waterfalls cascade 350 m into a stone plunge pool in the base that spills over into the silver sliver of the Rio do Boi, which

Border essentials: Brazil–Uruguay

As of 2008 the border at Chuí was closed and all crossings into Uruguay now go via Bagé where Brazilian immigration is located. Before crossing into Uruguay, you must visit Brazilian Polícia Federal in Bagé to get an exit stamp; if not, the Uruguayan authorities will send you back.

Public transport to these crossings is from Bagé. Bagé is not connected to Porto Alegre by regular bus; it may be better to book crossings through a tour operator in Porto Alegre (see page 375) as they will know the current situation regarding how to get the exit stamp and link this with transport. **Brazil Ecojourneys** in Florianópolis also provides reliable information, see page 355.

Barro do Quaraí (Brazil)–Bella Unión (Uruguay)
This is the most westerly crossing in Rio Grande do Sul, and is via the Barra del Cuaraim bridge, near the confluence of the Uruguai and Quaraí rivers. Bella Unión has three hotels and a campsite in the Parque Fructuoso Rivera; the Brazilian consulate is at Calle Lirio Moraes 62, T055-3739 2054. There are onward buses to Salto and Montevideo.

Quaraí (Brazil)–Artigas (Uruguay)
The crossing from Quaraí to Artigas is in a cattle-raising and agricultural area. The Brazilian consulate is at Calle Lecueder 432, T055-8642 2504. Artigas has hotels, a hostel and campsites. Buses run from the border to Salto and Montevideo.

Santana do Livramento (Brazil)–Rivera (Uruguay)
Santana do Livramento is the main town in this area. Its twin Uruguayan city is Rivera. All one need do is cross the main street to Rivera, but by public transport this is not a straightforward border. The town has hotels and a youth hostel and Banco do Brasil (Avenida Sarandí). The *rodoviária* is at General Salgado Filho and General Vasco Alves. To Porto Alegre, two daily, seven hours, US$20; three daily to Urugaiana (four hours, US$10), services also to São Paulo and other destinations.

Aceguá (Brazil)–Melo (Uruguay)
60 km south of Bagés, 59 km north of the Uruguayan town of Melo.

Jaguarão (Brazil)–Río Branco (Uruguay)
The most easterly border crossing is from Jaguarão to Río Branco via the 1.5-km Mauá bridge across the Rio Jaguarão. The police post for passport checks is 3 km before the bridge; customs is at the bridge.

winds its narrow way along the canyon bottom. A steep rocky path leads to river from the canyon rim, but it's a tough, hair-raising walk that shouldn't be undertaken lightly – or without a guide. It's also possible to do a three-day trek along the banks of the Rio Boi itself, or a series of hikes along the upper rim of the canyon and ultimately to the beach at Praia Grande, around 20 km away.

Border essentials: Brazil–Argentina

Porto Xavier (Brazil)–San Javier (Argentina)
From Santo Angelo it is a four-hour bus ride to the border town of Porto Xavier and an easy crossing (short ferry ride across the Río Uruguay) into Argentina. For exit and entry stamps, visit the federal police at the ferry stations on either side. The five-minute crossing (US$3.75) takes passengers to San Javier, from where there are regular buses, via Posadas, to Iguazú. From the Argentine ferry station it is a short bus or taxi ride to the town centre, with cashpoints, shops, and the *rodoviária*.

Uruguaiana (Brazil)–Paso de los Libres (Argentina)
It is also possible to cross the border through Uruguaiana, a cattle centre 772 km from Porto Alegre, and its twin Argentine town of Paso de los Libres in the extreme west. A 1400-m bridge over the Rio Uruguay links the two cities.

Brazilian immigration and customs are at the end of the bridge, five blocks from the main *praça*. Buses connect the bus stations and centres of each city every 30 minutes. If you have to disembark for visa formalities, the next bus will pick you up without extra charge. Buses run from Uruguaiana via Barra do Quaraí/Bella Unión (US$4.50) to Salto and Paysandú in Uruguay. Exchange and information is available in the same building. Exchange rates are better in the town than at the border. There are a number of cheap and mid-range hotels in town. A taxi or bus across the bridge is about US$3.50.

Parque Nacional da Serra Geral
ⓘ *T054-3251 1320, open year-round daily 0800-1800, free.*
This park has a similar landscape to Aparados da Serra but even deeper gorges. The most impressive are Malacara and Fortaleza; the latter an astounding 1170 m deep. There are spectacular views to the coast from the top of both and wild, remote hiking.

Ins and outs If you plan to hike in the *serra* it is best to go on an organized trip with **Brazil Ecojourneys**, http://brazilecojourneys.com. However, it is possible to visit independently. The most convenient base is **Cambará do Sul**, www.cambaradosul.tur.br. The Aparadas da Serra park entrance is 18 km from Cambara and there are numerous *pousadas*, some of which organize trips into the mountains. The best time to visit is June to August when skies are clear but it can be very cold; temperatures on the high peaks fall well below zero and it can even snow. Rain is heaviest in April, May and September.

Cambará do Sul can be reached from Praia Grande, Caxias, São Francisco de Paula, São José dos Ausentes and Porto Alegre (the latter bus is very slow). Buses run from the *rodoviária* in Cambará do Sul, T054-3251 1567, with **Consórcio São Marcos/União**, to Criciúma stopping at the entrance to the park (four hours, US$15), and leaving Monday to Saturday at 0945 and an additional bus on Monday, Wednesday and Saturday at 1145. There is no bus on Sunday.

*For Sleeping and Eating price codes and other
relevant information, see pages 32-37.*

◎ Sleeping

Porto Alegre *p358, map p360*

Hotels in the area around R Garibáldi and
Voluntários da Patria between Av Farrapos
and *rodoviária* are overpriced and many
rooms are rented by the hour.

L Plaza São Rafael, Av Alberto Bins 514,
T051-3220 7000, www.plazahoteis.com.br.
Recently refurbished 1970s luxury hotel
with excellent service and business facilities
including laptop computer rental and 2 free
internet lines in each room. Gym and sauna.
The best for the city centre.

L Sheraton, R Olavo Barreto Viana 18,
Moinhos do Vento, T051-2121 6000,
www.sheraton-poa.com.br. The most
comfortable stay in the city, with plush
no-nonsense, business-orientated rooms
overlooking the leafy streets of the best
restaurant neighbourhood in the city, Moinhos
do Vento, some 2-3 km from the centre.

AL Blue Tree Millennium Flat, Av Borges
de Medeiros 3120, Praia de Belas, T051-
3026 2200, www.bluetree.com.br. Smart
mini-apartments with microwave, study
and breakfast bar. The rooftop pool, gym
and bar have stunning sunset views.

AL Continental, Largo Vespasiano Júlio
Veppo 77, T051-3027 1900, www.hoteis
continental.com.br A tall tower close to the
rodoviária with newly refurbished rooms,
decked out in soft colours and with views
over the city from the upper floors. Facilities
include a pool and gym and there are
attractive discounts through the website.

AL-B Eko Residence, R Des André da Rocha
1, T051-3225 8644, www.residencehotel.
com.br. This great little hotel is situated
within walking distance of both the city
centre and the Cidade Baixa. Rooms are
simple, but modern, comfortable and very
well appointed. All come with free Wi-Fi,

decent pine workstations and colourful little
en suites with shower cublices. The hotel
prides itself on its sustainability. A wind
turbine and solar panels on the roof power the
hot water, heat the roof-top pool and provide
much of the electricity. Water and rubbish are
recycled and the façade is covered with a
vertical garden. Excellent online promotional
rates can drop the price to **B**.

AL-B Embaixador, R Jerônimo Coelho 354,
T051-3215 6600, www.embaixador.com.br.
One of the city's older grand dame hotels,
refurbished in 2009 and with a marble
chandelier-hung lobby, a wood-pannelled
cigar and piano bar and large mock New
York luxury hotel suites (with plaid carpets
and heavy counterpanes and curtains)
and rather tired-looking tile-floor doubles.
Facilities include a rather stuffy restaurant,
pool, gym (with modern equipment),
business centre, conference facilities
and Wi-Fi. Online discounts.

A Everest, R Duque de Caxias 1357, T051-
3215 9500, www.everest.com.br. A tower hotel
conveniently located close to the nightlife area
in the Cidade Baixa, with suites of modern,
cleanly decorated, quiet and spacious rooms
all with Wi-Fi and decent work desks, and a
little coffee shop in reception.

B Comfort, R Loureiro da Silva 1660, Cidade
Baixa. T051-2117 9000, www.atlanticahotels.
com.br. Standard 3-star hotel with gym, Wi-Fi,
breakfast and suites of hotel rooms with
budget corporate-design and MDF fittings.
Handy for Cidade Baixa nightlife.

B Ritter, Lg Vespasiano Júlio Veppo 55,
opposite the *rodoviária*, T051-3228 4044,
www.ritterhoteis.com.br. A tired, old grand
dame near the *rodoviária*, with wood-
pannelled floors, grandmother carpets and
room decor and a *churrascaria*, café and tiny
bar on site. Facilities include a pool, sauna
(both newly refurbished) and paid internet.
Attractive online and OTA rates.

C Conceição Center, Av Sen Salgado Filho 201,
T051-3227 6088, www.conceicaocenter com.br.

Simple but respectable town hotel with murky public spaces in the interior. There's a need for a change of carpets, but the plain but clean a/c rooms with fridges are quieter than most in the centre – especially on the upper floors at the back. Internet in the lobby.

B-C Lancaster, Trav Acelino de Carvalho 67, T051-3224 4737, www.hotel-lancaster-poa. com.br. Rooms in an attractive 1920s art deco building in the centre, whose over-inflated price is justifiable only because of the location. A pokey granite lobby leads to tiny plain rooms with rather tired carpets and minimal decor. Children under 10 stay for free and rates are cheapest at the weekend – ask for a discount.

C-D Palácio, Av Vigário José Inácio 644, T051-3225 3467. Centrally located, with hot water, family rooms and a safe. Frayed and tired but good value if you are in a group – the quadruples with a shared bath push the hotel into the lower **D** category.

E América, Av Farrapos 119, T/F051-3226 0062, www.hotelamerica.com.br. The pokey public areas in this hotel lead to surprisingly large singles, doubles and triples with spartan tiled floors, eggshell blue walls and spongey beds. The hotel is sorely in need of a fresh lick of paint and a change of furnishings but is the best value in the centre and has particularly good rates for single travellers.

E Uruguay, Dr Flores 371. It's hard to imagine fan-cooled rooms simpler than those at the Uruguay. Carpets are old and worn, tiling chipped, but whilst unkempt, the hotel is clean, friendly and in a good location.

Camping

Praia do Guarujá, 16 km out on Av Guaíba.

Excursions from Porto Alegre *p361*

B Beira-Mar, Av Emancipação 521, Tramandaí beach, T051-3661 1234, www.hotelbeiramarrs. com.br. Pleasant but simple hotel with a thermal pool and sports facilities.

D São Jorge, F Amaral 19, Tramandaí beach, T051-3661 1154, www.hotelsaojorgelitoral. com.br. A 2-storey motel (in the US sense of

the word) with simple but well-kept rooms with parquet floors and en suite bathrooms, a small restaurant serving a generous breakfast and a bar and pool room. 2 blocks from the lagoon.

Gramado *p362*

LL-A Ritta Höppner, R Pedro Candiago 305, T051-3286 1334, www.rittahoppner.com.br. Luxurious, well-appointed and spacious bungalows. The most expensive have private mini-pools. Friendly, good breakfasts. Afternoon tea included in price. German owners also run Mini Mundo theme park and guests have free entrance.

AL Serra Azul, R Garibáldi 152, T054-3295 7200, www.serraazul.com.br. Sauna, massage, tennis and 2 pools, one of which is thermal.

A Chalets do Vale, R Arthur Reinheimer 161 (off Av das Hortênsias at about 4700), T054-3286 4151, www.chaletsdovale.com.br. 3 high-quality chalets in lovely wood setting, 2 double beds, kitchen, TV. Good deal for groups of 4 or families.

A Estalagem St Hubertus, R da Carriere 974, Lago Negro, T/F051-3286 1273, www.sthubertus.com. A big lakeside house set in gardens. Rooms are spacious and luxuriously appointed. All are decorated in an individual style, and most have pretty lake views. Part of the **Roteiros de Charme** group, see page 34.

A-B Pousada Bella Terra, Av Borges de Medeiros 2870, T054-3286 3333, www.pousadabellaterra.com.br. A very comfortable mock-European hotel with comfy sofas in the lobby and bright rooms flooded with light from big windows, and decorated in warm soft colours. Good central location, friendly and helpful.

B Pequeno Bosque, R Piratini 486, located i wood close to Véu da Noiva waterfall, T051-3286 1527, www.hotelpequenobosque. com.br Brick cabins set in a hydrangea-filled garden set in a small wood on the outskirts of Gramando. The simple exteriors lead to surprisingly comfortable rooms with heavy linens, comfy sofas and flatscreen TVs and trails lead into the forest – for a range of short but delightful walks.

B-C Pousada Zermatt, R da Fé 187, Bavária, T/F051-3286 2426, www.pousadazermatt. com.br. One of Gramado's simpler mock-European *pousadas*. The simplest rooms in cream paint and dark wood, are decked out with solid beds and little coffee tables covered in faded linen. Lusher suites have thick, exposed beams and warmer colours. iServices include internet and a lounge area with a TV and DVD player. Lower price range for the quadruple and triple rooms.

D Dinda, R Augusto Zatti 160, T055-3286 1588. Basic but one of the cheapest in town.

E Gramado Hostel, Av das Hortênsias 3880, T054-3295 1020, www.gramadohostel. com.br. Good HI hostel with dorm beds, doubles and family rooms. 24-hr internet, parking, breakfast. Nice grounds.

Camping
Camping Gramado, R Venerável 877-B, Av Central, T054-3286 2615.

Canela and around *p363*
AL Laje de Pedra, R das Flores 272, T051-3012 7240, www.lajedepedra.com.br. Big, busy mountain resort hotel with 3 restaurants, pool, thermal pool, sauna, tennis and plenty of options for kids.

A Vila Suzana Parque, R Col Theobaldo Fleck 15, T054-3282 2020, www.hotelvila suzana.com.br. Whitewash and terracotta tile-roofed chalets in a sub-tropical garden with aheated pool, and welcoming owners.

C Canela, R Ernesto Dorneles 333, T054-3282 8410, www.pousadacanela.com.br. Breakfast, English-speaking staff.

Pousada das Sequóias, R Godofredo Raymundo 1747, T054-3282 1373, www.sequoias.com.br. Pretty forest cabins in national park, 2 km from city centre.

Pousada Schermer, Trav Romeu 30, 054-3282 1746. Basic backpacker accommodation but very friendly, well kept.

HI Hostel Viajante, R Ernesto Urbani 132, behind *rodoviária*, T054-3282 2017,

www.pousadadoviajante.com.br. Youth hostel offering dorms and doubles with kitchen facilities.

Camping
Camping Clube do Brasil, 1 km from waterfall in Parque do Caracol, 1 km off main road (signposted), take bus for Parque Estadual do Caracol, 8 km from Canela. Excellent honey and chocolate for sale.

Sesi, R Francisco Bertolucci 504, camping and smart cabins in lovely parkland setting, 2.5 km outside Canela, T/F054-3282 1311. Restaurant, clean, barbeque facilities. Helpful staff.

Pelotas *p363*
A-B Manta, R Gen Neto 1131, T053-225 2411, www.hoteismanta.com.br. Blocky 1970s hotel with a pool, restaurant and bar. The best in town though somewhat frayed.

D Aleppo Hotel, R Gen Osório 708, T/F053-3225 3950, www.aleppohotel.com.br. Bright, clean and big rooms and breakfast.

Rio Grande *p364*
B Atlântico Rio Grande, R Duque de Caxias 55, T/F053-3231 3833, www.hoteis atlantico.com.br/riogrande. Standard town hotel with a/c rooms. Good value.

B Europa, R Gen Neto 165, main square, T053-3232 8133. Conveniently located in the centre of town with a range of a/c rooms.

D Paris, R Mcal Floriano Peixoto 112. An old colonial building. Charming.

Bagé and the border with Uruguay *p365*
B-C Pousada do Sobrado T053-3242 2713 www.pousadadosobrado.com.br. Rooms in a gorgeous converted colonial ranch house (and ugly modern brick annexe), decorated with heavy antique furniture. In the countryside outside town.

C-D Obinotel, Av 7 de Setembro 901, T053-3242 8211, www.redeversare.com.br. An old 1960s 2-star in the centre of town with a restaurant and large, rather frayed rooms.

Santo Ângelo and the Jesuit Missions p365

São Miguel das Missões

C Hotel Barrichello, Av Borges do Canto 1567, T055-3381 1272. Nice, clean and quiet. It also has a restaurant, **Churrasco**, for lunch.

C Wilson Park, R São Miguel 664, T055-3381 2000, www.wilsonparkhotel.com.br. A sprawling ranch house hotel set on a grassy lawn, with a big pool, tennis courts, football pitches and big hacienda rooms with vast beds and faux-antique furnishings.

C-E Pousada das Missões, next to the ruins, T055-3381 1030, www.albergues.com.br/sao miguel/. Very good youth hostel. Private rooms with a/c and TV, lovely grounds with pool, friendly.

Santo Ângelo

C Turis Hotel, R Antônio Manoel 726, Centro T055-3313 5255. Good-value rooms with a/c and fridge. Good breakfast. Internet access, good, cheap pizzeria on the terrace on the main square. The hotel is about 5 mins' walk from the ferry at the end of the main street.

D-E Hotel Nova Esperança, Trav Centenario 463, T055-3312 1173, behind the bus station. Simple, reasonably well maintained but with no breakfast.

Porto Xavier and the Argentine missions p366

D Rotta, Av Mal Fl Peixoto 757, near the *praça*. Plain rooms with or without a/c, and/or TV, bath, very good breakfast.

Salto do Yucumã p366

There are several cheap hotels in the area.

C-D Hotel Imperial, Av Jn Castilhos 544, Três Passos, 28 km from the park, T055-3522 2135. Standard small town hotel, breakfast included.

In Tenente, 16 km from the park are:
F Hotel Avenida, beside the petrol station, T055-3551 1859; and **F Hotel Iucuma**, R Tapulas 271, T055-3551 1120.

Serra Geral p366

L Parador Casa da Montanha, Estr Parque Nacional, T054-3504 5302, reservations T054-9973 9320, www.paradorcasada montanha.com.br. 7 cabins up a precarious dirt road and perched in the edge of a canyon. A have stunning, dizzying views. Very beautiful. Full board included in the price and optional excursions into the park on horseback or foot. Minimum stay 2 days.

L Rio do Rastro, Rodovia SC – 438 Km 130, Bom Jardim da Serra, T048-9931 6100, www.riodorastro.com.br. Luxury, all inclusive complex set in beautiful grounds, owned by friendly character Ivan. Cottages include fireplace and jacuzzis. Activities include horse-riding, canoeing and trekking. Gourmet meals in restaurant and Sat night entertainment.

AL Refugio Rio Canoas, Rodovia SC 439 – Serra do Corvo Branco Km 27, Urubici, www.riocanoas.com.br This lovely refuge tucked away in the mountains consists of pretty, comfortable rooms near the main house. Sit by the fireplace and read while dinner is being cooked (there is not another restaurant, shop or bar for miles so meals are eaten at the house). The owners are keen trekkers and will take you on all day walks to see spectacular scenery. Cheaper accommodation down the road (hostel): R$25 per person. (Reservations must be made via website – no telephone)

C Pousada Itaimbeleza, Rodoviária, Cambará do Sul, T054-3251 1365, www.itaimbezinho. tur.br. A range of rooms in 2 properties: one in the town near the *rodoviária* (with plain motel like rooms with or without a/c and/or bathroom) and the other rustic log cabins with room for up to 4 in the countryside and on the edge of the park. Children under 7 stay free, there's a pool and breakfast and advice on tours.

⊙ Eating

Porto Alegre *p358, map p360*
Gaúcho cooking features large quantities of
meat, while German cuisine is also a strong
influence. *Campeiro* (regional farm food), now
a dying art, uses plenty of rice, vegetables,
and interesting sauces. Vegetarians might try
some of the *campeiro* soups and casseroles
and growing number of alternative or natural
restaurants, otherwise stick to Italian
restaurants or *churrascaria* salad bars.

Apart from the many good restaurants,
much of the tastiest food can be found in
street stalls and cheap *lancherias*; the central
market along the *praça* is lined with them.
††† Chez Philippe, Av Independência 1005 at
Fernandes Vieira, T051-3312 5333. One of the
finest French-Brazilian fusion restaurants in
southern Brazil, with a small but beautifully
prepared menu of dishes like lobster with
pupunha fruit and herb oil and peppered
steak with Dijon sauce. Housed in a pretty
19th-century building and with dining areas
outside on a garden patio or indoors in a
mood-lit, informal dining room.
††† Galpão Crioulo, Av Loureiro da Silva
(Parque da Harmonia also known as Maurício
Sirotsky Sobrinho, Cidade Baixa), T051-
3226 8194. Open 1130-1600, 1900-0100.
Good *churrascaria* with a show and dancing.
††† Koh Pee Pee, R Schiller 83, T051 3333
5150. Mon-Sat 1930-2400. Sophisticated
restaurant serving excellent Thai cuisine.
Seafood dishes are especially good.
† Al Dente, R Mata Bacelar 210, T051-
3343 1841. Mon-Sat 1900-2400. Wonderful
home-made pastas of every variety, and a
staggering array of sauces to choose from.
Romantic atmosphere.
† Chopp Stübel, R Quintino Bocaiúva 940,
Moinhos de Vento, T051-3332 8895. Mon-Sat
1800-0030. One of the best in the city for
reasonably priced German food.
† Le Bon Gourmet, Av Alberto Bins 514
(in Plaza São Rafael hotel). Mon-Sat 1900-
2300. Steaks, pasta and fine fish dishes. The
24-hr **514 Bar** is at the back of hotel lobby.

††-† Nova Vida, R Demétrio Ribeiro 1182,
Cidade Baixa, T051-3226 8876. A little lunchtime
vegetarian buffet restaurant serving a good
range of mains and puddings and selling natural
products in an adjacent wholefood grocery.
† Café do Cofre, R Siqueira.

Gramado *p362*
There's no lack of choice with plenty
of decent, if pricey, restaurants along
Av Borges de Medeiros.
††† Bella du Valais, Av das Hortensias 1432
T054-3286 1744, expensive but very good
Swiss cuisine, including wonderful fondues.
††† Churrascaria Patrão Velho, Av das
Hortênsias 4759, T054-3286 0823.
Very good meat and side dishes.
† Restaurante Hakone, R Garibaldi 271,
T654-3286 1403. One of very few moderately
priced places to eat in Gramado. Good fixed-
price lunchtime buffet and evening *rodizio*
of pizza, pasta, salad and soup.

Canela and around *p363*
††† Empório Canela, Felisberto Soares 258,
T054-3031 1000. Pleasant bistro with a
good range of soups, pastas and traditional
campeiro dishes. Decent wine list and *petiscos*.
† Café Canela, Praça Joã Correa 7, T054-3282
4422. Good meat and cheese dishes.
† Parati Lanches, Praça Joã Correa 97.
Daily 0800-2400. Traditional watering
hole with pool tables.

Pelotas *p363*
††† El Paisano, R Mcal Deodoro 1093, T053-
3227 1507. Closed Mon, opening hours vary
seasonally. Legendary Uruguayan steak.
††† Lobão, Av Bento Gonçalves 3460, T053-
3225 6197. Standard barbecue *churrascaria*,
plenty of side dishes.
† Mama Pizza, R Gen Osório 720. Good
affordable pizza run by **Hotel Manta**.

Rio Grande *p364*
††† Blue Café, R Luís Loréa 314. Open 0830-
1930 (Fri until 2300 Fri). Expresso machine
and good cake. Jazz/blues music on Fri.

ｉ Barrillada Don Lauro, R Luís Loréa 369, T053-3233 2037. Uruguayan steak in pleasant restaurant.

ｉ Rio's, R Val Porto 393, T053-3231 1180. Vast but good *churrascaria*.

◑ Bars and clubs

Porto Alegre *p358, map p360*
The busiest areas are the Cidade Baixa, with a thriving alternative scene recalling Buenos Aires (though on a tinier scale), and Moinhos de Vento, the city's richest suburb (a US$10 taxi ride from downtown), which is more upmarket, with classy bars, cafés and bistros. Most of the activity in the latter is centered around the streets Padre Chaves and Fernando Gomes. Most Porto Alegre bars also serve food.

On weekend nights, thousands head for the Cidade Baixa and spill out of the bars and clubs along R da República and José do Patrimonio.

Apolinário, R Jose do Patrocinio 527, Cidade Baixa, T051 3013 0158, www.apolinariobar. com.br. A little *boteco* with a handful of outdoor tables and an intimate little indoor bar serving some of the best beer in the Cidade Baixa.

Bar do Beto, Av Venâncio Aires 876, Cidade Baixa, T051-3332 0063. Open 1700-0300. Serves food too.

Bar do Goethe, R 24 de Outubro 112, Moinhos de Vento, T051-3222 2043, www.bardogoethe.com.br. Excellent range of artisan beers (said to be the best in the city), and good German snacks.

Bar do Nito, Av Cel Lucas de Oliveira 105, Moinhos de Vento, T051-3333 4600. Popular music bar.

Boteco Dona Neusa, R Gen Lima e Silva 800, Cidade Baixa, T051-3013 8700. This faux Rio de Janeiro samba bar-restaurant with bright murals, an expansive open-plan dining area, and a big menu of hearty *petisco* bar snacks, ice cold draught *chopp* beer is busy on any night. There is occasional live music at weekends.

Cult, R Comendador Caminha 348, Moinhos de Vento, T051-3346 2257, www.cultpub. com.br. A lively little alternative bar and small live music venue with an eclectic crowd, a range of different areas and good live music. Open 2000-late, also serves decent food.

Dr Jekyll, Trav do Carmo 76, Cidade Baixa, T051-3221 5751, www.drjekyllbar.com.br. Nightclub open from 2200, closed Sun, Tue. Live bands Mon-Thu, Fri and Sat playing everything from 1970s retro to the latest Rio Grande do Sul rock.

Opinião, R José do Patrocínio 834, Cidade Baixa T051-3211 5668, www.opiniao.com.br Tue-Sat 2200 until the last customer leaves. Long-standing favourite with fashionable 20-somethings, with rock DJs and regular live music. Great cocktails and good *petiscos*.

Ossip, Av República 677 (corner with João Afredo). Pleasant wine bar with a lively crowd on weekends and occasional live music.

Muffuletta, R da República 657, Cidade Baixa, T051-3224 1524, www.muffuletta.com.br. A faux-Buenos Aires corner café bar with heavy wooden tables, arty-kitsch decor, live music and famous 'muffuletta' toasted sandwiches. Always lively.

Santissimo, R Sacramento Leite 888 at Lima e Silva, Cidade Baixa, T051-3024 1939, www.santissimobar.com.br. An attractive brick-walled bar and restaurant with exposed beams in the ceiling, big glass windows and a more conservative, wealthy crowd most evenings. Good bar snacks and light meals.

Sargent Pepper's, Dona Laura 329, Moinhos de Vento, T051-3331 3258, www.peppers.com.br. Closed Mon. A very popular bar with live music from a range of well-established local acts Thu-Sat. Good beer, bar snacks and light meals and a congenial mock-English pub atmosphere

Tortaria, R Fernando Gomes 114, Moinhas de Vento, T051-3395 5599, www.tortaria.com.br Serving well-kept *chopp* alongside delicious cakes, this popular spot is open until 0100 and makes a good starting point for a night's bar hopping.

Zelig, R Sarmento Leite 1086, Cidade Baixa, T051-3286 5612, www.zelig.com.br. Open from 2000 until the last customer leaves. Off-beat restaurant, bar and exhibition space. Good, diverse menu and DJs covering a broad musical spectrum. Very busy Sun.

Entertainment

Porto Alegre p358, map p360
Arts and theatre
Casa de Cultura Mário Quintana, R dos Andradas 736, T051-3221 7147. Tue-Fri 0900-2100, Sat-Sun 1200-2100. A centre for the arts, exhibitions and theatre.
Theatro São Pedro, Praça Mcal Deodoro, T051-3227 5100. Tue-Fri 1200-18.30, Sat and Sun 1600-1800. Theatre with regular free concerts, art gallery, café.
Usina do Gasômetro, Av Pres João Goulart 551, T051-3212 5979. Tue-Sun 0900-2200. Art gallery with displays by young artists.

Cinema
Cine Guion, Shopping Nova Olaria, R Gen Lima e Silvva 776, T051-3221 3122, www.guion.com.br. Great little arts cinema showing English-language films with subtitles and housed in a small, arty shopping centre with plenty of cafés and restaurants.

Festivals and events

Porto Alegre p358, map p360
2 Feb The main event is the festival of Nossa Senhora dos Navegantes (*Iemanjá*), whose image is taken by boat from the central quay in the port to the industrial district of Navegantes.
Sep Semana Farroupilha celebrates *gaúcho* traditions with parades in traditional style, its main day being 20 Sep. The **Carnaval** parade takes place in Av A do Carvalho, renamed Av Carlos Alberto Barcelos (or Roxo) for these 3 days only, after a famous carnival designer.
Oct-Nov Each year a month-long **Feira do Livro** (book festival) is held in Praça da

Alfândega. See www.feiradolivro-poa.com.br for details.

Gramado p362
Aug Festival of Latin American cinema.

Shopping

Porto Alegre p358, map p360
Markets
There is a **street market** (leather goods, basketware) near the central post office. Sun morning handicraft and bric-a-brac market (plus sideshows), Av José Bonifácio (next to Parque Farroupilha).

Music
Boca do Disco, R Marechal Floriano Peixoto 474, T051-3408 1294. The best place in the city to buy rare vinyl, second-hand CDs and gaúcho rock and alternative music.

Shopping centre
The **Praia de Belas** shopping centre, is among the largest in Latin America. US$5 taxi ride from town.

Activities and tours

Porto Alegre p358, map p360
Swimming Forbidden from the beaches near or in the city because of pollution – except for **Praia do Lami**, in the south of the city, which has been cleaned up. Beaches in Belém Novo and Ipanema are OK too.

Tour operators
Caminhos Rurais, www.caminho esrurais.com.br, is a cooperative with an extensive online directory of wine tasting, horse riding and hiking tour operators.
See also the 'Turismo' section in *Zero Hora* classifieds (Tue) for four company adverts.
Porto Brasil, R Hilario Ribeiro 202, Moinhos de Vento, Porto Alegre, T051-3025 2626,

www.portobrasil.com.br. Sells air and bus fares and can help with general travel queries.
Rota Cultural, Av Do Forte 1281, Porto Alegre, T051-3348 1649, www.rota cultural.com.br. Agency running eco trips into rural Rio Grande do Sul. Also organizes boat and air tours.

Canela and around p363
Atitude, Av Osvaldo Aranha 391, T054-3282 6305, www.atitude.tur.br. Rafting, waterfall abseiling, and trips to Aparados da Serra National Park.
Black Bear Adventure, R Ernesto Riegel 713, Gramado, T054-9939 7191, www.black bearadventure.com.br. Rafting, waterfall abseiling, climbing and trekking tours.

Santo Ângelo and the Jesuit Missions p365
Caminho das Missões, R Marquês do Herval 1061, T055-3331 29632, www.caminhodas missoes.com.br. 3- to 13-day 'pilgrimages' (80-180 km) between the various ruins. Also organizes bike tours and trips to Foz do Iguaçu. Open to all beliefs.

⊖ Transport

Porto Alegre p358, map p360
Air
See also Ins and outs, page 358. Regular buses run from the bus station to the airport; or take the metrô. There are international flights to Uruguay and Argentina as well as internal connections with **Curitiba**, **São Paulo**, **Rio de Janeiro** and **Florianópolis**.

Bus
There are 2 sections to the *rodoviária*; the ticket offices for interstate and international destinations are together in 1 block, beside the municipal tourist office (very helpful). The intermunicipal (state) ticket offices are in another block; for travel information within the state, ask at the very helpful booth on the station concourse.

To **Rio**, US$80, 24 hrs (Itapemirim www.pluma com.br); **São Paulo** (Itapemirim, www.itapemerim.com.br), *leito* US$67 (18 hrs), standard US$56; **Brasília** (Real Expresso www.real expresso.com.br), US$110, 34 hrs; **Uruguaiana** (Pluma), US$17.50, 8 hrs; Florianópolis, US$30-60, 7 hrs with **Santo Anjo** (take an *executivo* rather than a *convencional*, which is a much slower service); **Curitiba** (Itapemirim), standard US$40 coastal and *serra* routes, 12 hrs; **Rio Grande**, US$25 every 2 hrs from 0600, 4 hrs. **Foz do Iguaçu**, *leito* US$70, standard US$35 (Unesul, www.unesul.com.br). To **Cascavel** in Paraná for connections to Campo Grande, Cuiabá and Porto Velho, 4 daily, US$45, 12 hrs (Unesul). To **Jaguarão** on the Uruguayan border at 2400, US$22, 6 hrs. To **Florianópolis** *leito* US$49, standard US$24.

International buses Take your passport and tourist card when purchasing international bus tickets. To **Montevideo** (Uruguay), with **TTL**, www.ttl.com.br, *executivo* daily 2030 US$80; *leito* Fri only at 2100, US$80.

To **Asunción** (Paraguay) with Unesul at 1900, Tue, Fri, 18 hrs via Foz do Iguaçu, US$40.

To **Santiago** (Chile), with Pluma 0705, Tue and Fri, US$135.

There are bus services to **Buenos Aires** (Argentina) with Pluma, US$68, 19 hrs (depending how long the border takes), daily at 1805, the route is via Uruguaiana, Paso de los Libres, Entre Ríos and Zárate. For **Misiones** (Argentina), take the 2100 bus (not Sat) to Porto Xavier on the Río Uruguay 11 hrs, US$36-45, get your exit stamp at police station, then take a boat across to San Javier, US$3.50, and go to Argentine immigration at the port, then take a bus heading to Posadas.

Excursions from Porto Alegre p361
Bus To Tramandaí, 5 a day, US$3.50. To Osório–Mostardas/Tavares, daily at 1600, US$4.40. To **Torres**, 9 a day, US$6; **Tramandaí** daily at 1300 and 1700, **Osório**

daily at 0630, 1100, 1300 and 1830. There are 3 buses a week from Mostardas and Tavares to **São José do Norte** (130 km) via **Bojuru** (leaving Mostardas 0630 and **Tavares** 0700 Sun, Wed, Fri, 5 hrs, US$4.50). If travelling northwards from **São José do Norte**, the bus leaves 0800 on Tue, Thu and Sat. There is also a daily bus from both **Tavares** and São José do Norte to **Bojuru**, where there is a basic hotel. The road south of Tavares is called the **Estrada do Inferno**. Car drivers should carry a shovel and rope. 4WD only after rains.

Taxi For local transport from Mostardas, try José Carlos Martins Cassola, T051-3673 1186, or Itamar Velho Sessin, T051-3673 1431.

Gramado *p362*
Bus Buses to **Canela**, 10 mins, run every 20 mins. Several daily buses to **Porto Alegre** US$10-14.

Canela and around *p363*
Bus To **Parque Estadual do Caracol**, from outside Parati Lanches, Praça Joã Correa, 0800, 1200, 1730 (returning at 1220, 1800), US$1.30. Several daily to **Caxias do Sul**, 2 hrs, US$2. Every 2 hrs to **São Francisco de Paula**, US$2.60. (Take the 0800 for the connection to Cambará for **Parque Nacional de Aparados da Serra**.) To **Florianópolis**, it is quickest to go via Porto Alegre (US$11).

Bike hire From Pousada das Sequóias or Pousada Casa Rosa, R Gov Flores da Cunha 150, T054-3282 2400.

Pelotas *p363*
Air The airport is 8 km from the centre. Mon-Fri flight to **Porto Alegre** (1530, US$60) with NHT, www.voenht.com.br.
Bus Frequent daily buses to **Porto Alegre**, 244 km (US$18, 3-4 hrs, paved road).
Rio Grande (US$4.50, 1 hr). TTL bus services (Montevideo–Porto Alegre) depart daily at 2400, US$70. To **Buenos Aires** via

Uruguaiana (0710, 2030, US$40). From Bagé, where there is a police post, the Uruguayan company **Núñez** runs buses 3 times a week to **Melo**, via Aceguá. Good direct road northwest to **Iguaçu** via **São Sepé**, **Santa Maria** and **São Miguel** mission ruins. **Santa Maria** (5 daily, US$8.80, 4 hrs) and **Santa Ângelo** (daily at 0805, US$16, 8 hrs).

Taxi Radio Taxi Princesa, T053-3225 8466.

Rio Grande *p364*
Boat There's a boat trip across mouth of Lagoa dos Patos, to the pleasant village of **São José do Norte**, every hr from Porto Velho.

Bus To **Pelotas**, every 30 mins (1 hr, 56 km, US$1.75); to **Santa Vitória**, 220 km; to **Porto Alegre**, 5 a day, US$10, 4 hrs; to **Itajaí**, 14 hrs, US$15. All buses to these destinations go through Pelotas. Bus tickets to **Punta del Este** or **Montevideo** (daily 2330) at *rodoviária* or Benfica Turismo, Av Silva Paes 373, T054-3232 1807.

Bagé and the border with Uruguay *p365*
The only current bus connections to and from Bagé are as follows: through **Pelotas** and **Cassino** (on the route Bage–Terminal Cee–Pinheiro Machado–Pelotas–Cassino) on Sun and Mon leaving Cassino at 0700 and 2000 respectively, 5 hrs); through Cassino and Pelotas (on the route Santanado Livramento–Ipamaroti–Dom Pedrito–Ferraria–Bagé–Vila Operaria–Pinheiro Machado–Pelotas–Cassino), leaving on Sun at 1800 from Cassino, 4-5 hrs; and through **Torres** and **Tramandai** (on the Livramento–Dom Pedrito–Bagé–Tramandai–Capao Da Canoa–Arroio Do Sal–Torres route), leaving Torres at 1930 on Sun, 5 hrs.
    To Uruguay To Montevideo (COT, Cynsa, both on Av Brasil between Olivera and Artigas, or **Rutas del Sol**, on L Oliveria), US$13, 5 hrs.

Santo Ângelo and the Jesuit Missions *p365*

Bus To **Porto Alegre**, 5 *convencional* daily, 6 hrs, US$32. To **São Miguel**, 0715, 1100, 1530, 1700 (Sat 1000, 1330, Sun 0930, 1830), 1 hr, US$2. To **Foz do Iguaçu**, via Cascavel, 1930, 13 hrs, US$21.

Salto do Yucumã *p366*

Bus There are 4 buses daily from **Três Passos** to Santo Ângelo. 2 daily **Tenente Portela**–Santo Ângelo.

⊙ Directory

Porto Alegre *p358, map p360*

Banks Banco do Brasil, Uruguai 185, 9th floor (1000-1500), good rates for TCs. Bradesco, Praça Sen Florência. Visa machine. Citibank, R7 de Setembro 722, T051-3220 8619, exchange on Av Borges de Medeiros, good rate, cash only. **Cultural centres** Sociedade Brasileira da Cultura Inglesa, Praça Mauricio Cardoso 49, Moinhos de Vento. Instituto Goethe, 24 de Outbro 122 (Mon-Fri 0930-1230, 1430-2100), occasional concerts, bar recommended for German *Apfelkuchen*. See also Casa de Cultura Mário Quintana and Usina do Gasômetro, see page 375. **Embassies and consulates** Argentina, R Coronel Bordini 1033, Moinhos de Vento, T/F051-3321 1360 (0900-1600). Germany, R Prof Annes Dias 112, 11th floor, T051-3224 9255 (0830-1130). Italy, Praça Marechal Deodoro 134, T051-3228 2055 (0900-1200). UK, R Itapeva 110, Sala 505, Edif Montreal, Bairro Passo D'Areia, T/F051-3341 0720 (0900-1200, 1430-1800). USA, R Riachuelo 1257, 2nd floor, T051-3226 3344 (1400-1700). Uruguay, Av Cristóvão Colombo 2999, Higienópolis, T051-3325 6200 (0900-1500). **Internet** Ciber Café, Câncio Gomes e C Colombo 778, T051-3346 3098 (0900-2300). Dot.Com Cyber Café, R da Praia Shopping, S17, R dos Andradas 1001, T051-3286 4244, www.com-cybercafe.co.br.

US$3 per hr. Livraria Saraiva Megastore, Shopping Praia de Belas, T051-3231 6868, www.livraria saraiva.com.br (Mon-Sat 1000-2200). PC2 Publicidad Café, Duque de Caxias 1464, T051-3227 6853, pc2.com@terra.com.br. US$2 per hr. Portonet, R Maracheal Floriano 185, T051-3227 4696 (0900-2100), US$2.50 per hr. **Language courses** Portuguese and Spanish, Matilde Dias, R Pedro Chaves Barcelos 37, Apdo 104, T051-3331 8235, malilde@estadao.com.br. US$9 per hr. **Laundry** Several along Av Andre da Rocha including Lavandería Lav-Dem, No 225. US$1.50 per kg wash and dry. **Post office** R Siqueria Campos 1100, Centro (Mon-Fri 0800-1700, Sat 0800-1200). UPS, T051-3343 4972 (Alvaro). **Telephone** R Siqueira de Campos 1245 and upstairs at the *rodoviária*.

Gramado *p362*

Banks Banco do Brasil, R Garibáldi corner Madre Verónica. **Internet** Cyber, Av Borges de Medeiros 2016, T054-3286 9559 (1300-2300), US$2.80 per hr.

Canela and around *p363*

Banks Banco do Brasil, Av Julio de Castilhos 465. **Internet** Posto Telefónico, Av Júlio de Castilhos 349, Sala 5, T054-3282 3305 (0800-2100, Sat 0900-2000, Sun 1000-1200, 1400-1800).

Pelotas *p363*

Banks Banco do Brasil, corner R Gen Osório and R Lobo da Costa. Also at R Anchieta 2122. Will change TCs. It is difficult to change money at weekends.

Santo Ângelo and the Jesuit Missions *p365*

Banks Banco do Brasil charges a commission of US$15 for TCs. Good rates for cash at the garage with red doors opposite Hotel Maerkli on Av Brasil.

Contents

Footprint features

Bahia

At a glance

⊙ **Getting around** Buses and internal flights. Car hire a possibility for the coast.

◎ **Time required** 2-3 days for Salvador; 5 days for Salvador and beaches; 7-10 days for Salvador, the Chapada Diamantina and beaches.

☼ **Weather** Varies greatly over such a large region. Hot summer (Oct-Mar), warm winter (Apr-Sep). Hot and dry in the *sertão* all year round except Dec-Feb.

✖ **When not to go** Apr-May and Nov-Dec are wettest on the coast. Dec-Feb are wet in the *chapada*.

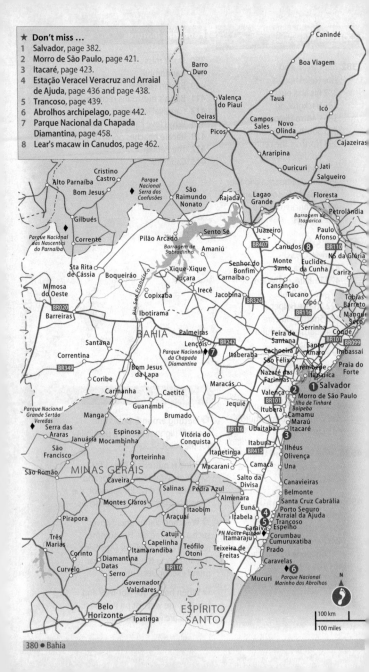

White-sand beaches backed by coconut palms, steep winding streets lined with pastel-coloured houses, ornate baroque churches, Afro-Brazilian ceremonies, gymnastic martial art ballet, the rhythm of the *berimbau*, the aroma of spices … Bahia conjures up as many exotic images, sounds and smells as Rio de Janeiro and has as an equally strong claim to be the heart of Brazil. The state capital, Salvador, was the country's first city for far longer than any other, and is considered by many to be the country's cultural centre.

Brazil's most famous novelist, Jorge Amado, was a Bahian, as were many of its greatest musicians; it was Bahia that gave the world samba, capoeira, Carnaval and *candomblé*. The state has some of the best cuisine in the country, along with many of its best beaches. Bahia's beautiful coast stretches far to the north and south of Salvador and is dotted with resorts along its length: laid-back little places like Itacaré, Morro de São Paulo and Trancoso, and larger more hedonistic party-towns like Porto Seguro and Arraial de Ajuda. Inland, in the wild semi-desert of the *sertão*, is one of Brazil's premier hiking destinations, the Chapada Diamantina, whose towering escarpments are cut by clear-water rivers and dotted with plunging waterfalls.

Salvador and the Recôncavo

→ *Colour map 4, A6. Phone code: 071. Population: 3.2 million.*

Salvador is the capital not just of Bahia but of African Brazil. The country's African heritage is at its strongest here – in the ubiquitous Orixá spirit gods and goddesses, the carnival rhythms of the drum troupe orchestras of Ilê Aiyê and Olodum, the rich spicy cooking, the rituals of candomblé (Brazil's equivalent of santeria) and in the martial art ballet of capoeira. You will see the latter being played on Salvador's beaches and in the squares and cobbled streets of the city's historical centre, the Pelourinho. The Pelourinho is also home to one of the most impressive collections of colonial architecture in South America. There are myriad baroque churches here. Some, like the Convento do São Francisco, have interiors covered with tons of gold plate. Others, like Nossa Senhora do Rosário, are decorated with statues of black saints and art that celebrates African Brazilian culture. The city is famous for its frenetic carnival which, unlike Rio's, takes place in the streets to the pounding rhythms of axé music. The crowds are overwhelming and move like a human wave.

The Baía de Todos os Santos is Brazil's largest bay and is dotted with islands; many of them are privately owned by the northeast's wealthy, others serve as weekend resorts for people from Salvador. The best known is Itaparica, a long, thin island lined with palms, with a pretty colonial capital and some reasonable beaches. Many buses run from here, and taking the ferry across from Salvador and then road transport from Itaparica is the quickest way to get to southern Bahia. Behind the bay is the Recôncavo, a fertile hinterland – where agriculture in Brazil was born, and where hundreds of thousands of indigenous Brazilians and enslaved Africans sweated and died to harvest sugar cane, cocoa and coffee. It is dotted with sleepy colonial towns, the most famous of which are Cachoeira and its twin across the Paraguaçu river, São Felix. ►► *For listings, see pages 402-419.*

Ins and outs

Getting there

Air Domestic and international flights arrive at the new **Luís Eduardo Magalhães airport** ① *32 km east of the centre, Praça Gago Coutinho, São Cristóvão, T071-3204 1010, www.infraero.com.br,* previously known as Dois de Julho. ATM machines are tucked away round the corner on the ground floor to the right as you arrive. The tourist information booth (open 24 hours, English spoken), has a list of hotels and a useful map. An air-conditioned *executivo* bus service runs from the airport to the historic centre (every 30 minutes, Monday to Friday 0500-2200, weekends 0600-2200, US$4). This service stops at all the hotels along the coast road en route – a long way round if you are going to the centre. *Ônibus coletivo* (city buses), US$1.20, are more direct but more crowded. Fixed-rate taxis go both to Barra and the centre; tickets can be bought from the desk next to the tourist information booth) for around US$35. Ordinary taxis leave from outside the airport, US$30.

Bus Interstate buses arrive at the **rodoviária** ① *5 km east of the centre, near Iguatemi Shopping Centre.* There are regular bus services to the centre, Campo Grande, Barra and Rio Vermelho (marked Praça da Sé/Centro). An executive bus leaves from outside the shopping centre (reached from the bus station by a walkway; be careful at night) and runs to Praça da Sé or the lower city (Comércio) via the coast road. Taxi to the centre, US$20. ►► *See Transport, page 416.*

Ferries and catamarans The main ferry dock, principally for car ferries although also for catamarans and passenger boats, is the **Marítimo de São Joaquim** ① *Av Oscar Pontes 1051, T071-3254 1020, www.twbmar.com.br.* It is known colloquially as 'ferry-boat' (pronounced 'fairhee bort'). The terminal has a bank, cafés and some small shops. Ten car ferries per day arrive here from the little town of Bom Despacho on Itaparica as well as catamarans from Morro de São Paulo (two hours).

Salvador's other boat terminal is smaller and serves only passengers. It lies opposite the Mercado Modelo, five minutes' walk from the historic centre, and is known as the **Terminal Marítimo de Mercado Modelo** or Terminal Marítimo Turístico. Ferries and catamarans run between here and the Baía de Todos os Santos, including the village of Mar Grande on Itaparica (every 30 minutes) and there are catamarans from Morro de São Paulo (five a day in high season; three in low season; the last leaves at 1400).

1 Salvador orientation

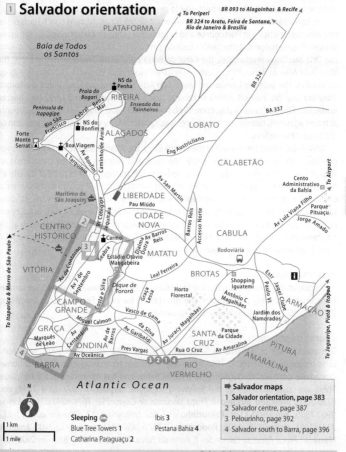

➡ **Salvador maps**
1 Salvador orientation, page 383
2 Salvador centre, page 387
3 Pelourinho, page 392
4 Salvador south to Barra, page 396

Sleeping 😴
Blue Tree Towers 1
Catharina Paraguaçu 2
Ibis 3
Pestana Bahia 4

Getting around

The city is built on a broad peninsula and is at the mouth of the Baía de Todos os Santos. On the opposite side of the bay's entrance is the Ilha de Itaparica (see page 398). The commercial district of the city and its port are on the sheltered, western side of the peninsula; residential districts and beaches are on the open, Atlantic side. Barra lies at the point of the peninsula.

The centre of the city is divided into two levels, the **Cidade Alta** (Upper City) where the historic centre and Pelourinho lies, and the **Cidade Baixa** (Lower City), which is the commercial and docks district. The two levels are connected by a series of steep hills called *ladeiras*. The easiest way to go from one level to the other is by the *Lacerda* lift, which connects Praça Municipal (Tomé de Sousa) in the Upper City with Praça Cairu and the famous Mercado Modelo market. There is also the *Plano Inclinado Gonçalves*, a funicular railway that leaves from behind the cathedral going down to Comércio, the commercial district. The airport bus (see above) runs between the historic centre, Barra and the beaches and offers the best way to get around.

The **Salvador Bus** ① *T071-8845 9878, www.salvadorbus.com.br*, runs coach tours of the city with commentary in Portuguese and English. Buses are air-conditioned on the lower deck and open-topped above (with a covering for when it rains) and call at Rio Vermelho, the Orla Marítima (esplanade), the Farol da Barra lighthouse and beach, the Forts, the Museu de Arte da Bahia, Praça Castro Alves, the Pelourinho, Elevador Lacerda, The Igreja do Bonfim, the Solar de Unhão and Museu de Arte Moderna, and the Dique do Tororó. They are hop-on, hop-off with a wristband ticket (US$15 adults and US$7 for children under six). Five buses run a day, currently between 0830 and 1900. Tickets can be bought at travel agencies, hotels, commercial centres, Iguatemi Shopping (Salvador) and also on the buses themselves.

Most visitors limit themselves to the centre, Barra, the Atlantic suburbs and the Itapagipe peninsula, which is north of the centre. The roads and avenues between these areas are straightforward to follow and are well served by public transport. Other parts of the city are not as easy to get around, but are of less interest to most visitors. If you go to these areas, a taxi may be advisable until you are familiar with Salvador. The website www.transalvador. salvador.ba.gov.br/transporte has details of bus routes in Salvador with a search facility and prices. Buses are fast and frequent. The main bus stop in the Centro Histórico is at the southern end of Praça Municipal (Tomé de Sousa). Buses from the city centre to Bonfim leave from Avenida da França near the Mercado Modelo. ▸▸ *See Transport, page 416.*

Best time to visit

It can rain at any time of year, but the main rainy season is between May and September. The climate is usually pleasant and the sun is never far away. Temperatures range from 25°C to 32°C, never falling below 19°C in winter.

Tourist information

The main office of **Bahiatursa** ① *Av Simon Bolivar, 650, T071-3117 3000, www.bahiatursa.ba.gov.br, Mon-Fri 0830-1800*, has lists of hotels and accommodation in private homes can advise on travel throughout the state of Bahia, and has noticeboards for messages. There are also branches at the following locations: **airport** ① *T071-3204 1244, daily 0730-2300*; **Mercado Modelo** ① *Praça Visconde de Cayru 250, T071-3241 0242, Mon-Sat 0900-1800, Sun 0900-1330*; **Pelourinho** ① *R das Laranjeiras 12, Pelourinho, T071-332 2133/2463, daily 0830- 2100*; **Rodoviária** ① *T071-3450 3871, daily 0730-2100*; **Instituto Mauá** ① *Praça Azevedo Fernandes 1, Porto da Barra, T071-3264 4671, Mon-Fri 0900-1800*,

Sat 1000-1500, **Shopping Barra** ① *Av Centenário, 2992, Chame-Chame, T071-3264 4566, Mon-Fri 0900-1900, Sat 0900- 1400*, **Shopping Iguatemi** ① *Av Tancredo Neves 148, Pituba, T071-3480 5511, Mon-Fri 0900- 2130, Sat 0900-1330*. The website www.bahia-online.net lists cultural events and news.

Safety

There is a lot of paranoia about safety in Salvador but as long as visitors follow common sense and a few rules they should be fine. The civil police are helpful and resources have been put into policing Barra, the Pelourinho and the old part of the city. All are well lit at night, however, police are little in evidence after 2300. The Pelourinho area is generally safe, although there's plenty of begging/touting and pick-pocketing and even occasional muggings do occur. Avoid going to the toilet on the Praça do Reggae and other large communal washrooms on show nights as we have had reports of intimidation by groups of thieves; choose a restaurant loo instead. Be vigilant and wary at all times after dark and avoid carrying credit cards or wads of cash. Buses and the area around the Lacerda lift are unsafe at night. Never venture into the favelas unless on a tour or with a trustworthy local friend. Foreign women often receive unwelcome amounts of attention, especially during Carnaval when levels of physical contact in crowds can be very unpleasant.

Background

On 1 November 1501, All Saints' Day, the navigator Amérigo Vespucci discovered the bay and named it after the day of his arrival – Baía de Todos os Santos. The bay was one of the finest anchorages on the coast, and became a favourite port of call for French, Spanish and Portuguese ships. However, when the Portuguese crown sent Martim Afonso to set up a permanent colony in Brazil, he favoured São Vicente in São Paulo.

It was not until nearly 50 years later that the bay's strategic importance was recognized. When the first governor general, Tomé de Sousa, arrived on 23 March 1549 to build a fortified city to protect Portugal's interest from constant threats of Dutch and French invasion, the bay was chosen as the place from which the new colony of Brazil was to be governed. Salvador was formally founded on 1 November 1549 and, despite a short-lived Dutch invasion in 1624, remained the capital of Brazil until 1763.

The city grew wealthy through the export of sugar and the import of African slaves to work on the plantations. By the 18th century, it was the most important city in the Portuguese empire after Lisbon and ideally situated on the main trade routes of the 'New World'. Its fortunes were further boosted by the discovery of diamonds in the interior. However, as the sugar industry declined, the local economy could not rival the gold and coffee booms of the southeast and this led to the loss of capital status and the rise of Rio de Janeiro as Brazil's principal city. Nevertheless, the city continued to play an influential part in the political and cultural life of the country.

African presence

For three centuries, Salvador was the site of a thriving slave trade, with much of the workforce for the sugar cane and tobacco plantations coming from the west coast of Africa. Even today, Salvador is described as the most African city in the Western hemisphere, and the University of Bahia boasts the only choir in the Americas to sing in the Yoruba language. The influence permeates the city: food sold on the street is the same as in Senegal and Nigeria, the music is fused with pulsating African polyrhythms, men and women nonchalantly carry enormous loads on their heads, fishermen paddle dug-out canoes in the bay, and the pace of life is more relaxed than in other parts of the country.

Modern Salvador

Salvador today is a fascinating mixture of old and modern, rich and poor, African and European, religious and profane. The city has 15 forts, 166 Catholic churches and 1000 *candomblé* temples. It remains a major port, exporting tropical fruit, cocoa, sisal, soya beans and petrochemical products. However, its most important industry is tourism, and it is the second largest tourist attraction in the country, after Rio.

Local government has done much to improve the fortunes of this once run-down, poor and dirty city. Major investments are being made in its infrastructure and public health areas. A new comprehensive sewage system has been installed throughout the city, with a view to improving living conditions and dealing with pollution.

The once-forgotten Lower City, Ribeira and the Itapagipe Peninsula districts have received major facelifts. Bahia has become more industrialized, with major investments being made by multinational firms in the automotive and petrochemical industries, principally in the Camaçari complex, 40 km from the city. The Bahian economy is currently the fastest growing in the country.

Centro Histórico

Most of the interesting sights in Salvador are concentrated in the Centro Histórico in the **Cidade Alta** (Upper City). This is where the Portuguese founded the first capital of Brazil in November 1549. The entire 2-km stretch between the Praça Municipal in the South and the Carmelite churches (Carmo) in the north is a World Heritage Site.

This is the vibrant and colourful heart of Salvador. The colonial houses are painted in pastel colours, and many have been converted into restaurants, small hotels or bars, whose tables spill out onto the patios behind the houses; they host live music several times a week. The entire area proliferates with handicraft shops, artist ateliers and African-Brazilian cultural centres.

Note Most of the churches and museums in the Centro Histórico prohibit the taking of pictures; even without a flash.

Praça Municipal (Tomé de Souza) and the Praça da Sé

These adjacent squares (connected by the Rua da Misericordia), link with neighbouring Terreiro de Jesus (Praça 15 de Novembro) to form an almost entirely pedestrianized zone. A decade ago this area was tawdry, but it has been tidied up in recent years. There's arts and crafts, music and souvenir shopping at the many street-side stores and stalls and plenty of places for snacks and refreshments.

The **Praça Municipal** is the oldest part of Salvador – where the first governor **Thome de Souza** built the first administrative buildings and churches (after unceremoniously clearing an indigenous Tupinambá village from the site). A statue of the soldier stands on a plinth gazing wistfully out to sea at the southern end of the *praça*. From here the city grew in a bewildering panoply of architectural styles, many of which can be seen around the square. Dominating the view are the neoclassical columns of the former council chamber (1660), now the **Paço Municipal** ① *Praça Municipal s/n, T071-3176 4200, Tue-Sa 0930-1700, free*, and the imposing **Palácio Rio Branco** ① *Praça Municipal s/n, T071-317 4200, Tue-Sat 0930-1700, free*. Like many of Brazil's opulent buildings, this was built i

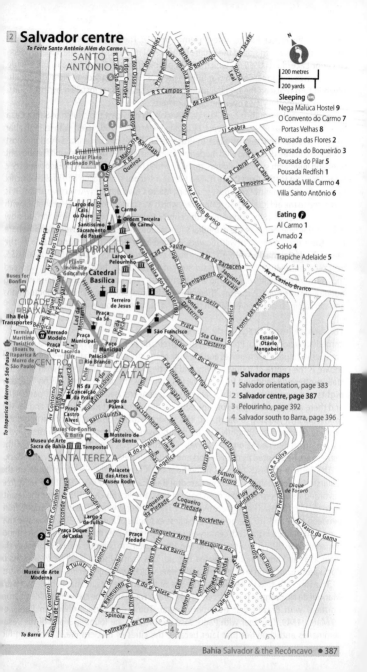

Salvador centre

To Forte Santo Antônio Além do Carmo

SANTO ANTÔNIO

➡ Salvador maps
1 Salvador orientation, page 383
2 **Salvador centre, page 387**
3 Pelourinho, page 392
4 Salvador south to Barra, page 396

Sleeping
Nega Maluca Hostel 9
O Convento do Carmo 7
Portas Velhas 8
Pousada das Flores 2
Pousada do Boqueirão 3
Pousada do Pilar 5
Pousada Redfish 1
Pousada Villa Carmo 4
Villa Santo Antônio 6

Eating
Al Carmo 1
Amado 2
SoHo 4
Trapiche Adelaide 5

Funicular Plano Inclinado Pilar

Largo do Cais do Ouro
Carmo
Santíssimo Sacramento do Passo
Ordem Terceira do Carmo

PELOURINHO

Plano Inclinado Gonçalves
Largo de Pelourinho
Catedral Basílica

Buses for Bonfim

CIDADE BAIXA

Ilha Bela Transportes

Terreiro de Jesus

Terminal Marítimo Turístico (Boats to Itaparica & Morro de São Paulo)

Mercado Modelo
Praça Cairu
Praça da Sé
Paço Municipal
São Francisco

Elevador Lacerda Lift
Palácio Rio Branco

CENTRO
CIDADE ALTA

NS da Conceição da Praia

Praça Castro Alves

Buses for Bonfim & Barra

Museu de Arte Sacra de Bahia Tempostal

Mosteiro de São Bento

SANTA TEREZA

Palacete das Artes & Museu Rodin

Largo 2 de Julho
Praça Piedade

Praça Duque de Caxias

Coqueiro da Piedade
Coqueiro da Piedade

Museu de Arte Moderna

To Barra

Estádio Otávio Mangabeira

Dique de Tororó

homage to the French for the state-governor, in 1918. The palace now houses municipal offices. On the western side of the square is the star of many postcards: the huge, art deco **Elevador Lacerda** ① *US$0.05*, which whisks people from the Cidade Alta to the Cidade Baixa, 70 m below, in seconds. It was built in the late 1920s to replace an old hydraulic lift, which in turn replaced the original rope and pulley system first installed by the Jesuits. There are wonderful views over the bay from here.

Heading north from the *praça*, Rua da Misericórdia runs past the church of **Santa Casa Misericórdia** ① *T071-3322 7666, open by arrangement 0800-1700* (1695), with its high altar and beautiful painted *azulejos* (tiles), to **Praça da Sé**. This is one of central Salvador's most attractive squares, decorated with modernist fountains, shaded by mimosa and flamboyant trees and lined with stately buildings, many of which house smart shops or European-style cafés. Look out for the **Cruz Caída** (Fallen Cross), a sculpture of a fallen and broken crucifix by one of Latin America's foremost sculptors, **Mário Cravo Junior** (www.cravo.art.br). It is dedicated to the old Igreja da Sé (cathedral), which was pulled down in 1930, together with an entire street of 18th- and early 19th-century townhouses, to make way for the now defunct tramline. Some of the cathedral's foundations have been uncovered and lie bare near the Cruz, covered in wild flowers. Immediately opposite the Cruz Caída is the **Memorial da Baiana do Acarajé** ① *Praça da Sé s/n, Mon-Fri 0900-1200 and 1400-1800;US$5*, a museum and cultural centre telling the story of the *Baianas* – the Bahian women who lead the Lavagem do Bonfim parade and who participate in carnaval throughout Brazil wearing traditional large swirling dresses. There are panels, ritual objects and historic photographs and the café next door serves Bahian snacks and has a small souvenir shop.

Terreiro de Jesus (Praça 15 de Novembro)

Immediately northeast of Praça da Sé, the Terreiro de Jesus is a large *praça* surrounded by handsome colonial townhouses and the bulk of the city's fabuous baroque churches. The square is the centre of tourist activity and bustles with bars, cafés and myriad souvenir stalls proffering everything from *acarajé* to *berimbaus*. It's particularly lively on **Tuesday nights** and weekends when there are shows or concerts (see Bars and clubs, page 410), and there are regular displays of **capoeira** – generally presented without joy and for the tourist dollar; if you stop to watch, you'll be expected to pay. Beware, too, of the persistent *Baianos* offering *fitas* (brightly coloured ribbons given as a good luck present), who swoop down like hawks on new arrivals. The streets that run off the south side of the Terreiro are frequented by drug dealers and beggars – best avoided, especially after dark.

The Terreiro de Jesus takes its name from the 'Church of the Society of Jesus' (ie the Jesuits) that dominates it. It is now **Catedral Basílica** ① *daily 0900-1200, 1400-1800, free* devolving its ownership to the main body of the Catholic church in 1759, after the Jesuits were expelled from all Portuguese territories. The cathedral, whose construction dates from between 1657 and 1672, is one of the earliest examples of baroque in Brazil – a style that came to dominate in the 18th century and reached its full glory in Minas Gerais. The interior is magnificent: the vast vaulted ceiling and 12 side altars, in baroque and rococo, frame the main altar and are completely leafed in gold. This lavish display is offset by a series of Portuguese *azulejos* on in blue, white and yellow, which swirl together in a tapestry pattern

The church is said to be built on the site of the original Jesuit chapel built by **Padre Manuel da Nóbrega** in the 16th century. Nóbrega was part of the crew on that came from Portugal with Brazil's first governor-general, Tomé de Sousa, arriving in Bahia on 29 March 1549. Together with Padre José de Anchieta, he founded many of the Jesuit seminaries and churches that later became the cities of modern Brazil, including Rio

Candomblé

Candomblé is a spiritual tradition that developed from religions brought over by Yoruba slaves from West Africa. It is focused on relationships with primordial spirits or *orixás* who are linked with natural phenomena and the calendar. The *orixas* are invoked in *terreiros* (temples). These can be elaborate, decorated halls, or simply someone's front room with tiny altars. Ceremonies are divided into two distinct parts. The first is when the *orixás* are invoked through different rhythms, songs and dances. Once the dancers have been possessed by the *orixá*, they are led off in a trance-like state to be changed into sacred, often very elaborate costumes, and come back to the ceremonial area in a triumphant procession in which each one dances separately for their deity. Overseeing the proceedings are *mães* or *pães de santo*, priestesses or priests.

Candomblé ceremonies may be seen by tourists, usually on Sundays and religious holidays – although many are just for show and not the real thing. The ceremonies can be very repetitive and usually last several hours, although you are not under pressure to remain for the duration. Appropriate and modest attire should be worn; visitors should not wear shorts, sleeveless vests or T-shirts. White clothing is preferred, black should not be worn especially if it is combined with red. Men and women are separated during the ceremonies, women always on the left, men on the right. No photography or sound recording is allowed. Most temples are closed during Lent, although each one has its own calendar. **Bahiatursa** (see page 384) has information about forthcoming ceremonies, but accurate information on authentic festivals is not always easy to come by.

Recife and São Paulo. **Antônio Vieira**, one of the greatest orators in Portuguese history and a campaigner for the protection of the indigenous Brazilians in the Amazon, preached some of his most famous sermons in the church. He died a sad and disgraced old man of nearly 90 in July 1697, condemned by the Dominican-run Inquisition and prohibited from either preaching or writing after being slanderously accused by his enemies of conniving in the murder of a colonial official. The cathedral also preserves the remains of **Mem de Sá**, the great and brutal Portuguese conquistador and third governor-general of Brazil, who perhaps more than anyone was responsible for the establishment of the Brazilian territories. He ruthlessly crushed the Tupinambá along the Bahian coast and, in liberating Rió from the French, he quelled an insurrection that threatened to overthrow the fledgling Brazilian colony. Note the interesting sculptures, particularly those on the altar of Saint Ursula in a huge chest carved from a trunk of Mata Atlântica *jacarandá*, encrusted with ivory, bone and turtle shell.

Across the square is the church of **São Pedro dos Clérigos** ① *Praca 15 de Novembro, T071-3321 9183, Mon-Fri 0900-1200 and 1400-1800, free*, which is beautifully renovated. Alongside is the church of the early 19th-century **Ordem Terceira de São Domingos** ① *Praca 15 de Novembro, T071-3242 4185 Mon-Fri 0900-1200, 1400-1700, free*, which has a beautiful 18th-century, painted wooden ceiling attributed to **José Joaquim da Rocha**, the father of the Bahian School – perhaps the first Brazilian school of art to adopt the contemporaneous European trompe l'oeil style – which used perspective to create the illusion of three-dimensions.

There are two interesting museums on the square, both housed in the former Jesuit College (and subsequent Bahian School of Medicine building). The **Museu Afro-Brasileiro**

(MAfro) ① *Mon-Fri 0900-1800, Sat and Sun 1000-1700, US$3 for a joint ticket with MAE*, charts the history of Africans in Bahia. Between 1440-1640, Portugal monopolized the export of slaves from Africa and they were the last European country to abolish it. Over the course of 450 years, they were responsible for transporting more than 4.5 million Africans – some 40% of the total. There are countless exhibits, from both Brazil and the African continent itself, including fascinating ritual objects, musical instruments and textiles. Panels compare West African and Bahian *orixás* (deities) and in a gallery all to themselves are some beautiful wooden carved effigies by the artist Carybé (Hector Julio Páride Bernabó) who lived most of his life in Bahia. Carybé became famous with the *antropofagismo* movement, illustrating Mario de Andrade's *Macunaíma*, and won the prize as the best draughtsman in Brazil in 1955. He was later celebrated for his depictions of *candomblé* rituals and *orixás*. In the basement of the same building, the **Museu de Arqueologia e Etnologia (MAE)** ① *Mon-Fri 0900-18700, Sat and Sun 1000-1700, US$3 for a joint ticket with MAfro*, houses indigenous Brazilian artefacts collected from all over Brazil over the centuries by the Jesuits, alongside archaeological discoveries from Bahia, such as stone tools, clay urns and rock art.

The Largo Cruzeiro de São Francisco and the Franciscan churches

Facing Terreiro de Jesus is the **Largo Cruzeiro de São Francisco**, crowded with souvenir stalls and dominated by a large wooden cross and the church and the modest façade of the convent of **São Francisco** ① *Largo do Cruzeiro de São Francisco, T071-3322 6430; Mon-Sat 0800-1700, Sun 0800-1600, US$2*. The convent is the jewel in Salvador's baroque crown and one of the finest baroque churches in Latin America. The entrance leads to a sanctuary with another spectacular trompe l'oeil painting by **José Joaquim da Rocha** (1777) and to a set of cloisters decorated with minutely detailed and hand-painted *azulejos*; many are by the celebrated Portuguese artist **Bartolomeu Antunes de Jesus**. Each tile is based on illustrations to epigrams by Horace by the 17th-century Flemish humanist and teacher of Peter Paul Rubens, Otto Venius. 'Quem e Rico? Quem nada ambiciona', proclaims one – 'Who is rich? He who is ambitious for nothing'. The picture shows a man crowned from behind by a bare-breasted woman (representing glory) whilst simultaneously pushing away golden crowns – representing the trappings of aristocracy and establishment. It's hard not to regard this as irony when entering the church itself. It took 64 years to cover the interior with plated gold and iconic art; almost all of it paid for by that same establishment who had grown wealthy on the sugar trade. The irony is compounded by more *azulejos* around the altar showing scenes from St Francis' life – which was remarkable for the saint's Siddhartha-like rejection of his aristocratic birth right, in favour of mendicancy.

Irony aside, only a resolute inverted snob could fail to be transfixed by the artistry inside church. The main body of the church is the most opulent in Brazil – a vast, ornate exuberance of woodcarving in *jacarandá* depicting a riot of angels, animals, floral designs and saints, covered with some 800 kg of solid gold. It's easy to see that the work is by Africans and native Brazilians. Look out for the mask-like faces on the top right- and left-hand corners of the sacristy – an allusion to contemporary African art; and the cherubs below the pulpit and encrusted into the walls, whose genitals were hacked off by Portuguese far more prudish than those who carved their church. There are wonderful individual pieces too, including a beautiful sculpture of St Peter of Alcântara (venerated for his mystical visions attained in a state of painful ecstasy), agonisingly captured by the one of the fathers of Bahian baroque sculpture, **Manoel Inácio da Costa**. He was born in Camamu and known as 'Seis Dedos' (six fingers) to his contemporaries. And he chipped the figure from a single hunk of rainforest wood. Other unspecified statues are known to be by Bento dos Reis, born to African slaves and celebrated for the emotion he imparts to his figures.They may include a serene statue of the patron saint of African-Brazilians – the hermit Saint Benedict, born to Ethiopian slaves in Messina in Sicily in 1524 (beatified by Pope Benedict XIV in 1743), and invited to join the Franciscans order after suffering a racist jibe. He carries the Christ child in his arms. The names of the painters of the dozens of magnificent ceiling panels remain unknown.

Next door is the church of the **Ordem Terceira de São Francisco** ① *Ladeira da Ordem Terceira de São Francisco 3, T071-3321 6968, Mon-Sat 0800-1700, Sun 0800-1600, US$2* (1703), with an intricate sandstone façade in the Spanish Churrigueresque style – an elaborate rococo form characterised by exuberant carving. It is one of only two such churches in the country and its carvings were completely covered over with plaster until the early 20th century, probably in protest against associations with Spain. There's a huge and intricately decorated altar piece inside, a chapterhouse covered in striking images of the Order's most celebrated saints and a series of *azulejos* many depicting scenes of Lisbon before the devastating earthquake in 1755.

The Pelourinho

The streets north of the Terreiro de Jesus, which run over a series of steep hills to the neighbourhood of Santo Antônio, are referred to as the Pelourinho. The area takes its name from the whipping post where the African slaves were auctioned off or punished by their Brazilian-Portuguese masters. Its steep cobbled streets are lined with brightly painted townhouses leading to little pracas and always thronging with people. The bulk of the restaurants, small hotels and shops in the Centro Histórico are to be found here, and the streets are great for a browse.

The Pelourinho's main thoroughfares run north off the Terreiro de Jesus. **Rua Alfredo Brito** (aka Portas do Carmo) and **Rua João de Deus** and the side streets that run off them are lined with three- or four-storey townhouses occupied by shops, restaurants and boutique hotels. Both descend in steep cobbles to the **Largo de Pelourinho**, a large sunny square watched over by one of Salvador's most important African-Brazilian monuments, the church of **Nossa Senhora do Rosário dos Pretos** ① *Praça Jose Alencar s/n, Largo do Pelourinho, T071-3241 5781, Mon-Fri 0830-1800, Sat-Sun 0830-1500 and with African-Brazilian mass every Tue at 1800, free*, built by former slaves over a period of 100 years, with what little financial resources they had. In colonial times, black Bahians were not even allowed to walk in front of the churches reserved for the white elite, let alone go inside them, and had to worship in their own building.The side altars honour black saints such as São Benedito (see Convento do São Francisco, above) and the painted ceiling and panels are by Jose Joaquim da Rocha (see above). The overall effect is of simple tranquillity, in contrast to the busy opulence of the cathedral and the São Francisco church. The church remains a locus for black Bahian culture and has strong connections with *candomblé*. On Tuesdays, following a show by Olodum on the Pelourinho, there is an African-Brazilian mass with singing accompanied by percussion from repiques, tambors and tamborins. Be sure to visit the haunting **slave cemetery** at the back of the building.

At the corner of Alfredo Brito and Largo do Pelourinho is a small museum dedicated to the work of Bahia's most famous author Jorge Amado, **Fundação Casa de Jorge Amado** ① *Largo do Pelourinho s/n, T071-3321 0070, www.jorgeamado.org.br, Mon-Fri 0900-1800, at 1000-1600, free*. Amado was born and brought up around Ilhéus but spent much of his life in this house. The people of this part of Salvador provided the inspiration for the

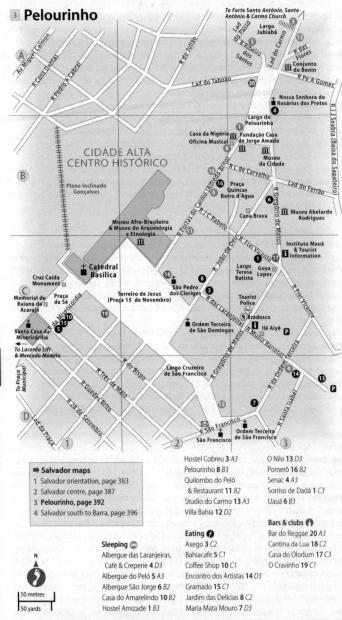

3 Pelourinho

To Forte Santo Antônio, Santo Antônio & Carmo Church

Largo Jubiabá

Largo do Passo

R Ribeiro dos Santos

Lad do Carmo

R das Flores

Conjunto do Benin

R Pe A Gomes

Av Miguel Calmon

R Cons Dantas

R Pedro A Cabral

R do Jitão

Lad do Taboão

Nossa Senhora do Rosários dos Pretos

R J J Seabra (Baixa do Sapateiro)

CIDADE ALTA CENTRO HISTÓRICO

Plano Inclinado Gonçalves

Largo de Pelourinho

Casa da Nigéria
Oficina Musical

Fundação Casa de Jorge Amado

Museu da Cidade

R de Carvalho

Lad do Ferrão

Praça Quincas Berro d'Agua

R Gregório de Matos

Museu Abelardo Rodrigues

Cana Brava

R J C Rabelo

Museu Afro-Brasileiro & Museu do Arqueologia e Etnologia

R João de Deus

R Frei Vicente

Instituto Mauá & Tourist Information

Catedral Basílica

Largo Teresa Batista

Goya Lopes

R Frei Vicente

Cruz Caída Monument

São Pedro dos Clerigos

R das Laranjeiras

Tourist Police

Memorial de Baiana do Acarajé

Praça da Sé

Terreiro de Jesus (Praça 15 de Novembro)

Bradesco

Ilê Aiyê

R Muniz Barreto

Santa Casa da Misericórdia

Ordem Terceira de São Domingos

R Gregório de Matos

To Lacerda Lift & Mercado Modelo

R do Bispo

Largo Cruzeiro de São Francisco

R da Ordem Terceira

R Tres de Maio

R Santa Isabel

To Praça Municipal

R Guedes de Brito

R São Francisco

R 28 de Setembro

São Francisco

Ordem Terceira de São Francisco

Lad da Praça

Salvador maps
1 Salvador orientation, page 383
2 Salvador centre, page 387
3 **Pelourinho, page 392**
4 Salvador south to Barra, page 396

N

50 metres
50 yards

Sleeping
Albergue das Laranjeiras, Café & Creperie 4 *D3*
Albergue do Pelô 5 *A3*
Albergue São Jorge 6 *B2*
Casa do Amarelindo 10 *B2*
Hostel Amizade 1 *B3*

Hostel Cobreu 3 *A3*
Pelourinho 8 *B3*
Quilombo do Pelô
   & Restaurant 11 *B2*
Studio do Carmo 13 *A3*
Villa Bahia 12 *D2*

Eating
Axego 3 *C2*
Bahiacafe 5 *C1*
Coffee Shop 10 *C1*
Encontro dos Artistas 14 *D3*
Gramado 15 *C1*
Jardim das Delícias 8 *C2*
Maria Mata Mouro 7 *D3*

O Nilo 13 *D3*
Pomerô 16 *B2*
Senac 4 *A3*
Sorriso de Dadá 1 *C3*
Uauá 6 *B3*

Bars & clubs
Bar do Reggae 20 *A3*
Cantina da Lua 18 *C2*
Casa do Olodum 17 *C3*
O Cravinho 19 *C1*

arger-than-life characters that populate some of his most famous novels including *Dona Flor e seus dois Maridos* (*Dona Flor and Her Two Husbands*, 1966). Information is in Portuguese only, but the walls of the museum café are covered with colourful copies of his book jackets in scores of languages, and all of his work is on sale.

Next door is the **Museu da Cidade** ① *Praça Jose de Alencar 3, Largo do Pelourinho, T071-3321 1967, Tue-Fri 0900-1830, Sat 1300-1700, Sun 0900-1300, free*, in two adjacent 18th-century houses and with exhibitions of arts and crafts, old photographs of the city, many fascinating objects from *candomblé* rituals and effigies of the *orixás*. A further room is devoted to the life and ouvre of the 19th century abolitionist Antônio Frederico de Castro Alves (1847-1871), and from the higher floors there is a good but seldom photographed view of the Pelourinho.

Just around the corner from the Largo do Pelourinho is the **Museu Abelardo Rodrigues** ① *Solar do Ferrão, R Gregório de Matos 45, T071-3320 9383, Tue-Sat 1300-1800, US$2*, preserves one of the most important and impressive collections of religious art outside the São Paulo's Museu de Arte Sacra (see page 192). It is housed in one of the Pelourinho's best-preserved and most stately 18th-century townhouses – once a Jesuit college – and showcases some impressive statuary, engravings, paintings and lavish monstrances from Brazil, all over Latin America and the Far East. All were collected by the Pernambucan who gave the museum its name. There is also a smaller and less illustrious sacred Art Musuem, the **Museu de Arte Sacra da Bahia**, see page 395.

Below Nossa Senhora do Rosario dos Pretos is the **Conjunto do Benin** ① *R Padre Agostinho Gomes 17, Pelourinho, T071-3241 5679, casadobenin@yahoo.com.br, Mon-Fri 1300-1800*, which has displays of African-Brazilian crafts, photos and a video on Benin and Angola. It hosts exhibitions, dance shows and other artistic events. The **Casa da Nigéria** ① *R Alfredo de Brito 26, Pelourinho, T071-3328 3782*, offers a similar programme orientated more to Yoruba culture and has showcases of African and African Brazilian arts and crafts, photographs and an important library. Yoruba language classes are available here and both cultural centres are important nexuses of African-Brazilian culture and society in Bahia. The **Quilombo do Pelô** hotel (see page 403), also serves as a cultural centre for Jamaican culture. There are occasional shows in the restaurant – where Jamaican food is served – and the hotel receives many Jamaican celebrity guests. There's also Jamaican-Brazilian fusion music played in the **Bar do Reggae** (see page 410).

Morro do Carmo and Santo Antônio

The Ladeira do Carmo climbs up the steep **Morro do Carmo** hill running north from the Largo do Pelourinho, past the **Igreja do Santissimo Sacramento do Passo** and the steps that lead up to it (which were the setting for the city scenes in Anselmo Duarte's award-winning socio-political tragedy, *O Pagador de Promessas*, 'keeper of the promises'), to the **Largo do Carmo**. This little *praça*, at the junction of the Ladeira do Carmo and Rua Ribeiro dos Santos, is watched over by a series of Carmelite buildings. The most impressive is the **Igreja da Ordem Terceira do Carmo** ① *Morro do Carmo s/n, Mon-Sat 0900-1130, 1400-1730, Sun 1000-1200, US$1*, once a piece of striking baroque dating from 1709 but completely gutted in a fire 67 years later and restored in the 19th century. It is in poor state of repair but houses one of the sacred art treasures of the city, a sculpture of Christ made in 1730 by **Francisco Xavier 'O Cabra' Chagas** ('the Goat'), a slave who had no formal training but who is celebrated by many locals as the Bahian Aleijadinho, who carved *O Cabra*. Two thousand tiny rubies embedded in a mixture of whale oil, ox blood and banana resin give Christ's blood a ghostly, almost transparent appearance and the statue itself is so lifelike it appears almost to move. There is a small museum with a collection of ornate icons and period furniture. The adjacent **Igreja do Carmo** ① *Morro do Carmo s/n, Mon-Sat 0800-1200, 1400-1800, Sun 0800-1200, US$1*, a magnificent painted ceiling by the freed slave, José Teófilo de Jesus, while the **Convento do Carmo**, which served as a barracks for Dutch troops during the 1624 invasion, has been tastefully converted into Salvador's most luxurious hotel (see Sleeping, page 402).

Rua do Carmo continues to climb north from the Morro do Carmo into the neighbourhood of Santo Antonio, where dozens of the pretty colonial houses have been converted into tasteful boutique hotels and *pousadas*, the best of which have gorgeous bay views. The street eventually reaches the Barão do Triunfo (Largo de Santo Antônio), after a little over a kilometre. This handsome square (with barely a tourist in sight), is watched over by the hulking **Forte de Santo Antônio além do Carmo fortress** ① *Barão do Triunfo s/n Santo Antônio, T071-3117 1488, http://fortesantoantonio.blogspot.com, Mon-Sat 0900-1200 and 1400-1700, US$4*, and another impressive church, the **Igreja de Santo Antônio Além do Carmo** ① *Largo Barão do Triunfo s/n, Santo Antônio, T071-3242 6463, Mon-Sat 0900-1200 and 1400-1730, free*. The fort dates from the last decade of the 17th century and is known locally as the Forte da Capoeira as it is home to half a dozen capoeira schools. It was restored at the turn of the 20th century and there are beautiful views over the bay from its walls.

Cidade Baixa and Mercado Modelo

Salvador's Cidade Baixa (lower city), which sits at the base of the cliff that runs from Santo Antônio in the north to Praça Municipal and Lacerda lift in the south, was once as delightful and buzzing with life as the Pelourinho. Today, its handsome imperial and early republican 19th-century buildings, many of them covered in *azulejos*, are crumbled and cracked. Others have been pulled down and replaced with ugly concrete warehouses. There are numerous gorgeous baroque churches in a similar state of disrepair, most of them with doors permanently closed. With the exception of the ferry docks, the whole area dangerous and down at heel – especially at night. However, there are plans for restoration. A big hotel group has apparently bought up one of the old colonial mansions and in 2009 musician Carlinhos Brown opened the **Museu du Ritmo** ① *R Torquato Bahia, 84 Edifíc Mercado do Ouro, T071-3353 4333, www.carlinhosbrown.com.br/universo/museu-du-ritmo* and the **International Centre for Black Music** – a complex built around a 1000-sq-concert arena housed in a giant courtyard formed from the walls of a former coloni mansion house which once was home to the gold exchange. The museum has plans f over 100 multi-media installations by 2011, a cinema, art gallery, school and recordi studio on the site. Shows are advertised in the local press and on Carlinhos Brown's website.

There are few sights of interest. Bahia's best souvenir shopping is in the **Mercad Modelo** ① *Praça Visconde Cayru, Cidade Baixa, Wed-Mon 0900-1900, Sun 0900-1300 closed Tue*. This former customs house is thick with stalls selling everything from music instruments to life-size sculptures hacked out of hunks of wood. Look out for the colour handbags, made out of hundreds of can ring-pulls sewn together with fishing twine, a the *orixá* effigies and postcards. There are frequent capoeira shows between 1100 a 1300 on weekdays (you will have to pay to take pictures), occasional live music a numerous cafés and stalls selling Bahian cooking.

Further along the shore to the south is the striking, octaganol church of **Nossa Senho da Conceição da Praia** ① *R Conceição da Praia at Av Contorno*. The church, which dat from 1736, was built in *lioz* marble in Portugal by Manuel Cardoso de Saldan disassembled bit by bit with the stones given numbers, then transported to Salvador a reconstructed. It has an unusual octagonal nave and diagonally set towers, modelled on churches in Portugal such as the Guarda cathedral. Inside it is magnificent, with a stunning ceiling painting of an Italianate panoply of saints gathered around the Madonna in glorious Renaissance perspective – the masterpiece of **José Joaquim da Rocha**.

South of the centre

The modern city, which is dotted with skyscraper apartment blocks, sits to the south of the old centre towards the mouth of the bay. Rua Chile leads to **Praça Castro Alves**, with its monument to the man who started the campaign that finally led to the abolition of slavery in 1888. Two streets lead out of this square: Avenida 7 de Setembro, busy with shops and street vendors selling everything imaginable; and, parallel to it, Rua Carlos Gomes. **Mosteiro São Bento** ① *Av 7 de Setembro, Mon-Fri 0900-1200 and 1300-1600, T071-3322 7749, www.saobento.org, US$3*, another of Bahia's oldest religious buildings, dates from 1582 but was constructed much later. The cool, colonial spaces and cloistered garden are a welcome quiet space within the bustle of the city. The monastery was used as an arsenal by the Dutch during their occupation in 1624 and narrowly avoided going the way of much of colonial Rio and São Paulo in the 20th century – razed to the ground to make way for ugly modern skyscrapers. It houses a religious art museum with some 2000 priceless antiquities.

Just to the south is the **Palacete das Artes and the Museu Rodin** ① *R da Graça 284, Graça, T071-3117 6986, Tue-Sun 1000-1800, free*, a small museum and cultural centre entirely devoted to Rodin sculptures on loan from France until 2012. Some 62 are exhibited, including *The Thinker* and *The Kiss*.

Museu de Arte Sacra da Bahia ① *R do Sodré 276 off R Carlos Gomes, T071-3243 6511, Mon-Fri 1130-1730, US$2*, is in the 17th-century monastery and church of Santa Teresa de Ávila, at the bottom of the steep Ladeira de Santa Tereza. Many of the 400 carvings are from Europe, but there are some beautiful pieces by the artists who worked on the city's finest churches, such as Frei Agostinho de Piedade and José Joaquim da Rocha. Look out for the hauntingly life-like statue of Christ by the latter, carved from a piece of ivory and crucified on a *jacarandá* cross. Among the reliquaries of silver and gold is one made from gilded wood by Aleijadinho (see page 269). The views from the patio, out over the Baía de Todos os Santos, are breathtaking and very little photographed. Opposite is **Impostal** ① *R do Sodré 276, Tue-Fri 0900-1830, Sat and Sun 0900-1800*, a private museum of postcards. Just inland near Campo Belo is the **Dique do Tororo** ① *Av Vasco de Gama*, a lake and leisure area decorated with 3-m-high *orixá* statues by the Bahian sculptor Tatti Moreno. There are large *candomblé* celebrations here at dawn on 2 February before the **Festa da Yemanjá**.

Further south, the **Museu de Arte Moderna and Solar do Unhão** ① *off Av Contorno, T071-3117 6139, Tue-Fri 1300-1900, Sat 1300-2100, free*, is one of the finest modern art museums in northeastern Brazil. The collection includes work by most of Brazil's important artists, including Emiliano di Cavalcanti, the abstract painter Alfredo Volpi, social-expressionist Cândido Portinari and the co-founder of *antropofagismo*, Tarsila do Amaral, alongside pieces by Bahian artists such as Mario Cravo Jr, Carybé and the Franco-Bahian photographer Pierre Verger, and contemporary artists like Jose Bechara, Jon Franco and the photographer Mario Cravo Neto. The gallery is housed in the Solar do Unhão – itself an important historical monument. It sits right on the waterfront and was built in the 17th century initially as a sugar storage way station. It then became a mansion occupied by a series of influential Bahians over the following centuries, all of

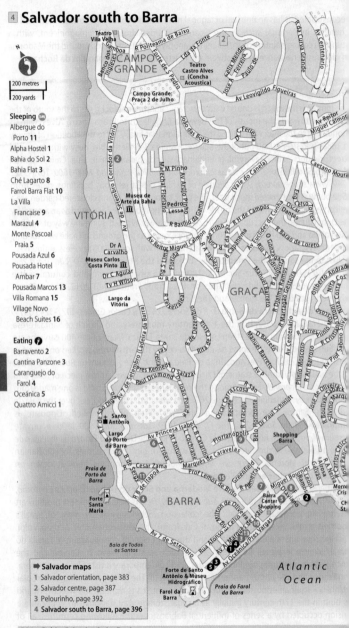

4 Salvador south to Barra

200 metres

200 yards

Sleeping 🛏
Albergue do
  Porto 11
Alpha Hostel 1
Bahia do Sol 2
Bahia Flat 3
Ché Lagarto 8
Farrol Barra Flat 10
La Villa
  Francaise 9
Marazul 4
Monte Pascoal
  Praia 5
Pousada Azul 6
Pousada Hotel
  Ambar 7
Pousada Marcos 13
Villa Romana 15
Village Novo
  Beach Suites 16

Eating 🍴
Barravento 2
Cantina Panzone 3
Caranguejo do
  Farol 4
Oceánica 5
Quattro Amicci 1

Map labels on image:

Teatro Vila Velha
R Politeama de Baixo
R da Curva Grande
Av Centenário
L da da Fonte
Gamboa
Banco dos Ingleses
Forte de Pedra
CAMPO GRANDE
Teatro Castro Alves (Concha Acústica)
Felix Mendes
José A Ferreira
Pátio de
Av Leovigildo Figueiras
Av Reitor Miguel Calmon
Campo Grande; Praça 2 de Julho
João das Botas
D. C Ferreira
Caetano Moura
M Pinho
Av Arujo Pinho
Marechal Floriano
Vale do Canela
Eng Celso Torres
Oscar Dantas
R Celso Torres
Museu de Arte da Bahia
Pedro Lessa
R H de Campos
VITÓRIA
R Basilio da Gama
R da Paz
R Cons Filho
R da Cabamena
Av Euclides da Cunha
R Rio S Pedro
O Gonzaga
R Barão de Loreto
Av Reitor Miguel Calmon
R A Lapassio
Manuel Barreto
Dr A Carvalho
Florida
GRAÇA
Museu Carlos Costa Pinto
Dr C Aguiar
R da Graça
Djalma Ramos
R Martagão Gesteira
Gilberto Andrade
Nila Costa
Tv H Wilson
R Teixeira Leal
R Dezembro
D Barreto
Av Centenário
R Torres
Plínio Moscoso
R Cristóvão
Nila Costa
R Prof Sabino Silva
Largo da Vitória
8 de Dezembro (Ladeira da Barra)
da Costa
Rita
Manuel Barreto
R Art Barroso
Av P
Av 7 de Setembro (Corredor da Vitória)
T P
Pres Kennedy
O Salazar
Raul Drumond
O João Pondé
Oscar Carrascosa
R São
José de Oliveira
R Boulhard
Silvino
Av 7 de Setembro (Ladeira de São Vicente)
Santo Antônio
Largo do Porto da Barra
Av Princesa Isabel
Al Antunes
R Recife
R Araçatu
C B Carain
Florianópolis
Belo Horizonte
Dr Paul Schmidt
Shopping Barra
R A Netto
Alfosa Galvão
Carlos Chico
Praia de Porto da Barra
R B de Itapoã
R César Zama
Marquês de Caravelas
Prof Lemos de Brito
Greenfield
R Palmeira
Miguel Bournier
Leoni Ramos
Morro Cris
Forte Santa Maria
BARRA
Milton de Oliveira
Dr Celso
Av A Marquês de B
Barra Center Shopping
Mariano
Ch St
Baía de Todos os Santos
Av 7 de Setembro
Rua Afonso Celso
Av Oceânica (Pres Vargas)
Atlantic Ocean
Forte de Santo Antônio & Museu Hidrográfico
Farol da Barra
Praia do Farol da Barra

➡ **Salvador maps**
1 Salvador orientation, page 383
2 Salvador centre, page 387
3 Pelourinho, page 392
4 Salvador south to Barra, page 396

whom have left their mark on the building – from little chapels to beautiful painted *azulejos*. The gallery also hosts temporary exhibitions, has an arts cinema (www.saladearte.art.br) and a bar/café with live jazz on Saturdays from 1830. There are many restaurants nearby. The museum is close to a favela and there are occasional muggings particularly after dark; it's best to take a taxi.

Heading towards Porta da Barra, the **Museu de Arte da Bahia** ⓘ *Av 7 de Setembro 2340, Vitória, Tue-Fri 1400-1900, Sat and Sun 1430-1900, US$2*, has interesting paintings by Bahian and Brazilian artists from the 18th to the early 20th century and a collection of 18th- and 19th-century furniture. A kilometre south of here is the **Museu Carlos Costa Pinto** ⓘ *Av 7 de Setembro 2490, Vitória, www.museucostapinto.com.br, Mon and Wed-Fri 1430-1900, Sat and Sun 1500-1800, US$2*, is a modern house with collections of crystal, porcelain, silver and furniture. It ostensibly has the world's only collection of *balangandãs* (slave charms and jewellery). The museum has a pleasant little garden café serving quiches, salads and cakes.

Porto da Barra and the Atlantic beach suburbs

Barra is one of the most popular places to stay in Salvador and the best inner-city beaches are in this area. The strip from Porto da Barra as far as the Cristo at the end of the Farol da Barra beach has some of the city's liveliest cafés, restaurants, bars and clubs. A night out here, in nearby Campo Belo and in the exclusive restaurants and bars of the city's most upmarket venue, **Praça dos Tupinambas**, give an idea of how polarized Salvador society is. The clientele is much more middle class than the Pelourinho; the music, food and conversation are more European and American and, in Brazil's African heart, there's hardly a black face in sight.

There are a few sights of moderate interest around Barra. The **Forte de Santo Antônio** and its famous lighthouse are right at the mouth of the bay where Baía de Todos os Santos and the South Atlantic Ocean meet. On the upper floors, the **Museu Hidrográfico** ⓘ *Tue-Sat 1300-1800, US$2*, has fine views of the coast. A promenade leads away from the fort, along the beach to the **Morro do Cristo** at the eastern end, which is crowned with a statue of Christ, arms outstretched over the bay. The statue is unremarkable in itself, but there are good views from the hill.

Rio Vermelho and the Ocean beaches

From Barra the beach road runs east through the beachfront suburbs of **Ondina** and **Rio Vermelho**. Confusingly, the road is known as both Avenida Oceânica and Avenida Presidente Vargas, and both have different numbering, making finding an address a challenge to say the least. **Rio Vermelho** is the only suburb of interest. It has long been the home of many of Salvador's well-to-do artists and musicians and a centre for candomblé. Unlike the beachfront neighbourhoods around Barra, the clientele is a wealthy mix of middle-class and African-Brazilian. There's a lively market with many little pit-and-sawdust bars, a handful of decent restaurants and small eateries serving some of the city's best *acarajé*. The area is busy at night, especially at weekends, and there are a number of venues playing traditional Bahian music. On 2 February the beach at Rio Vermelho is packed with *candomblé* pilgrims for the **Festa de Yemanjá**. To get here from the city centre, it is a 10-minute taxi ride (US$10-12) or a 20-minute bus journey on the airport–city centre bus. There are some good hotels nearby.

The next beaches along from Rio Vermelho are **Amaralina** and **Pituba**, neither of which are good for swimming but both of which have good surf and small fishing communities. Look out for *Jangadas* – small rafts with sails peculiar to northeast Brazil – in the seashore. Bathing is better at **Jardim de Alah**, **Jaguaripe**, **Piatã** and **Itapoã**, all of which are fairly clean and have fluffy white sand and swaying coconut palms. Any bus from Praça da Sé marked Aeroporto or Itapoã reaches the beaches in about an hour. Near Itapoã is the **Lagoa do Abaeté**, a deep freshwater lake surrounded by brilliant, white sands. This is where local women come to wash their clothes and then lay them out to dry in the sun. The road leading up from the lake offers a panoramic view of the city in the distance with white sands and freshwater less than 1 km from the sea.

Beyond Itapoã are the magnificent ocean beaches of **Stella Maris** and **Flamengo**, both quiet during the week but very busy at the weekends. Beware of strong undercurrents in the sea.

North of the centre: Bonfim, Itapagipe and Ribeira

① Take bus S021-00 marked Ribeira-Pituba from the the parada de onibus (bus stop) on Av da França on the quayside in the Cidade Baixa.

The most famous sight in the northern suburbs is the church of **Nosso Senhor do Bonfim** ① Largo do Bomfim 236, Bonfim, T071-3316 2196, www.senhordobonfim.org.br, museum Tue-Fri 0800-1200 and 1400-1700, free (1745), on the Itapagipe peninsula. It draws extraordinary numbers of supplicants (particularly on Friday and Sunday), making ex-voto offerings to the image of the Crucified Lord set over the high altar. The processions over the water to the church on the third Sunday in January are particularly interesting. The church has some naturalistic interior paintings by Franco Velasco (the modest canvases of the Stations of the Cross) and José Teófilo de Jesus (who painted the ceiling and 34 of the canvases on the church wall). Both almost certainly learnt their technique from the master José Joaquim da Rocha.

The beach south of the church is far too dirty for swimming and is always busy with touts offering fita ribbons. It is the focus for celebrations during the festival of Nosso Senhor dos Navegantes (see page 412). The colonial fort of **Monte Serrat** ① R Santa Rita Durão s/n, T071-3313 7339, Tue-Sun 0900-1700, US$0.50, has unusual round towers. It is one of the best preserved colonial forts in northeast Brazil and was first constructed in 1583 and altered in the 18th and 19th centuries. It sits next to the pretty Portuguese church of **Nossa Senhora do Monte Serrat** on Monte Serrat – a much photographed local beauty spot overlooking the Baía de Todos os Santos and Bonfim beach.

Further north, at Ribeira, is the church of **Nossa Senhora da Penha** (1743), another beautiful colonial building and important syncretistic pilrgrimage site. The beach here has many restaurants, but is polluted.

Ilha de Itaparica and the Baía de Todos os Santos
→ For listings, see pages 402-419. Phone code: 071. Colour map 4, A6.

Salvador sits on a peninsula which forms the northern head of Brazil's largest bay, the Baía de Todos os Santos. The bay is studded with tropical islands, the largest of which, Itaparica, sits immediately opposite Salvador, forming the bay's southern head. Itaparica is the only island close to Salvador with water clean enough for swimming. It is only 29 km long and 12 km wide and can easily be visited on a day trip.

There are two tiny towns on the island and a cluster of hamlets. **Itaparica** is very picturesque and well worth a visit, with a decent beach and many fine residential buildings from the 19th century. The church of **São Lourenço** is one of the oldest in Brazil and a stroll through the old town is delightful. In summer the streets are ablaze with the blossoms of the beautiful flamboyant trees. Itaparica town is connected to the main ferry port at **Bom Despacho** via a coastal road run by small buses and *combi* minivans via the hamlets of **Ponta de Areia** (with good beaches and many *barracas*), **Amoureiras** and **Manguinhos**. Bom Despacho itself is little more than a ferry dock shops and restaurants. Buses to and from Valença arrive and leave from here.

The island's principal town is **Mar Grande**, aka Veracruz. There are many *pousadas* and a cluster of restaurants here, as well as at the beaches of **Mar Grande** and **Penha**, to the south. Beaches get better and more deserted the further south you go. They include the **Barra do Gil** (backed with holiday homes), the **Barra do Pote** (with a white-sand beach and calm waters) and **Tairu** (deserted during the week and with fine, white sand).

Ins and outs The island is connected to the mainland by bridge or boat. The main passenger ferry runs from the São Joaquim terminal in Salvador (see page 383) to **Bom Despacho**, every 45 minutes 0540-2230. A one-way ticket for foot passengers during the week costs US$1, US$1.20 at weekends. A catamaran service for Bom Despacho departs twice daily, US$3. **Mar Grande** can be reached by a small ferry (*lancha*) from the Terminal Marítimo, in front of the Mercado Modelo in Salvador. The ferries leave every 45 minutes and takes 20-40 minutes, US$3 return. There is a bridge on the southwest side of the island. Buses from mainland towns such as Nazaré das Farinhas, Valença and Jaguaribe (a small, picturesque colonial port), arrive at Bom Despacho.

From Bom Despacho there are many buses, *combis* and taxis to all parts of the island. There are no banks on the island. *Combis* and taxis can be rented for trips around the island but be prepared to bargain, US$40-50 for a half-day tour.▸ *See Transport, page 418.*

Bay islands

There are dozens of other islands in the Baía de Todos os Santos. They include the **Ilha do Frades** and the **Ilha do Maré** (with Mata Atlântica forest and tiny fishing villages). These can be visited with organized tours with Ilha Bela or Tatur (see Tour operators, page 416).

Ilha de Itaparica

Nazaré das Farinhas → *Phone code: 075*
Population: 25,000

On the mainland, 60 km inland from Itaparica, Nazaré das Farinhas is reached across a bridge by bus from Bom Despacho. This 18th-century town is celebrated for its market, which specializes in the local ceramic figures, or *caxixis*. There is a large market in Holy Week, particularly on Holy Thursday and Good Friday. From here buses run to southern Bahia. About 12 km from Nazaré (taxi from Salvador US$4.25, bus at 1530) is the village of **Maragojipinha**, which specializes in making the ceramic figures.

Recôncavo Baiano → *For listings, see pages 402-419.*

The area around the bay and immediately south of Salvador is known as the Recôncavo Baiano. This was one of the chief centres of sugar and tobacco cultivation in the 16th century and there is some fine colonial architecture here. Places of interest include the sleepy colonial towns of Cachoeira and São Felix, on the banks of the muddy Rio Paraguaçu, which are famous for their festivals and strong connection to *candomblé*. There are also small fishing villages on the bay that are worth exploring, and dotted throughout the countryside are the decaying ruins of once-productive *engenhos* (sugar refineries), some of which can be visited.

Santo Amaro da Purificação and around → *Colour map 4, A6. Phone code: 075.*

Some 73 km from Salvador, Santo Amaro da Purificação is an old and sadly decaying sugar centre. It is noted for its churches (which are often closed because of robberies), the most famous of which is the **Igreja Matriz Santo Amaro da Purificação** ① *Praça da Purificação, T075-3241 1172, Mon-Fri 0800-1200 and 1400-1700, Sat 0800-1200*, which has a superb painted ceiling by José Joaquim da Rocha. There is also a municipal palace (1769), a fine *praça* and ruined sugar baron mansions including **Araújo Pinto**, the former residence of the Barão de Cotegipe. It is also the birthplace of Caetano Veloso and his sister Maria Bethânia. Other attractions include the splendid beaches of the bay, the falls of Vitória and the grotto of Bom Jesus dos Pobres. There are a number of interesting festivals (see page 414) and craftwork is sold on the town's main bridge. There are no good hotels or restaurants. There are at least 20 buses a day from Salvador to Santo Amaro and onward buses to Cachoeira.

About 3 km beyond Santo Amaro on the BR-420, turn right onto the BA-878 for **Bom Jesus dos Pobres**, a small, traditional fishing village with a 300-year history. There is one good hotel. To get there, take a bus from Salvador's *rodoviária* (four a day, **Camurjipe**, US$3).

Cachoeira and São Felix → *Colour map 4, A6. Phone code: 075.*

Set deep in the heart of some of the oldest farmland in Brazil, **Cachoeira** and its twin town, São Felix, were once thriving river ports that provided a vital supply link with the farming hinterland and Salvador to the east. The region was the centre of the sugar and tobacco booms, which played such an important role in the early wealth of the colony. The majestic *saveiro* (a gaff-rigged boat) traditionally transported this produce down the Rio Paraguaçu to Salvador across the bay. These boats can still occasionally be seen on the river. The town was twice capital of Bahia: once in 1624-1625 during the Dutch invasion and once in 1822-1823 while Salvador was still held by the Portuguese.

With the introduction of roads and the decline of river transport and steam, the town stopped in its tracks in the early 20th century and thus maintains its special charm. As Salvador, *candomblé* plays a very important part in town life (see box, page 389). Easy access by river from Salvador allowed the more traditional *candomblé* temples to move in times of religious repression. Cachoeira was the birthplace of Ana Néri, known as 'Mother of the Brazilians', who organized nursing services during the Paraguayan War (1865-1870).

There are a few interesting sights in Cachoeira. The **Casa da Câmara e Cadeia** ① *Praça de Aclimação, T075-3425 1018, daily 0800-1200 and 1400-1800, US$2* (1698-1712), was, for a brief period when Cachoeira was the state capital in 1822, the seat of the governance of Bahia. Upstairs is the town hall (with stern notices saying no shorts or Havaianas allowed). Downstairs there is a **slavery museum**, housed in the heavy walled dungeon where slaves were imprisoned behind two sets of strong bars. The dungeon has a sad at oppressive atmosphere. The **Museu Regional de Cachoeira** ① *Praça da Aclamação 4, Centro, T075-3425 1123, Mon-Fri 0800-1200 and 1400-1700, Sat 0800-1230, book ahead, US$2*, has a collection of period furniture, sacred images and ecclesiastical items, paintings and documents relating to the history of the town. The dark mark on the walls near the staircase at the entrance show where the river reached during the 1989 flood.

The **Santa Casa de Misericórdia** (1734) was the colonial hospital and has a fine church attached. Other churches include: the 16th-century **Ajuda** chapel (now containing a fine collection of vestments) and the convent of the **Ordem Terceira do Carmo**, whose church has a heavily gilded interior; the **Igreja Matriz** ① *R Ana Nery s/n, Tue-Sat 0900-1200 and 1400-1700, Sun 0900-1200, free*, with 5-m high *azulejos*, and a ceiling painting attributed to José Teolfilo de Jesus (who painted at the Bonfim church in Salvador; and **Nossa Senhora da Conceição do Monte**. All churches are either restored or in the process of restoration.

The **Fundação Hansen Bahia** ① *R 13 de Maio, T075-3425 1453, Tue-Fri 0900-1700, Sat and Sun 0900-1400*, has fine engravings by the German artist **Karl Meinz Hansen**, who was born in Hamburg and lived on the Pelourinho in Salvador during the 1950s. In a series of xylographs he documented the miserable lives of the downtrodden women who prostituted themselves for pennies. The museum itself is the former house of **Ana Néri**, Brazil's Florence Nightingale who nursed the injured during the Paraguayan War.

There is a strong **woodcarving** tradition in Cachoeira and many of its artists can be seen at work in their studios, see page 415.

A 300-m railway bridge built by the British in the 19th century spans the Rio Paraguaçu to **São Felix**, where the **Danneman cigar factory** ① *Av Salvador Pinto 30, 0830-1200 and 1300-1630, T075-3438 3716*, can be visited to see hand-rolling in progress. A trail starting near the **Pousada do Convento** leads to some freshwater bathing pools above Cachoeira. There are beautiful views from above São Félix.

Ins and outs Cachoeira/São Felix are 116 km from Salvador, and 4 km from the BR-420. There are more than 20 daily buses from Salvador to Cachoeira (2½ hours). The quickest way to get back to Salvador is to take a motorbike taxi from Cachoeira to the BR-420 and wait at the bus stop there; buses pass every 15 minutes and are up to an hour quicker because they have fewer stops than buses that leave from Cachoeira's town centre. There is a Bradesco Bank, Praça Dr Aristides Milton 10, with a Visa ATM.

Cachoeira has a **tourist office** ① *R Ana Néri 4, T075-3425 1123*. It is hard to get lost as there are only a handful of streets, all spreading out from the river. The centre of the city and best point for orientation is the Praça da Aclamação and the Igreja da Ordem Terceira do Carmo.

Excursions from Cachoeira

About 6 km from Cachoeira, on the higher ground of the Planalto Baiano, is the small town of **Belém** (the turning is at Km 2.5 on the road to Santo Amaro), which has a healthy climate and is a popular place for summer homes. **Maragojipe**, a tobacco exporting port with a population of 39,000, is 22 km southeast of Cachoeira along a dirt road (BA-123); it can also be reached by boat from Salvador. If you visit, look out for the old houses and the church of São Bartolomeu, with its museum. The main festival is **São Bartolomeu**, in August. Good ceramic craftwork is sold in the town. The tobacco centre of **Cruz das Almas** can also be visited, although transport is poor.

◉ Salvador and the Recôncavo listings

For Sleeping and Eating price codes and other relevant information, see pages 32-37.

● Sleeping

Salvador *p382, maps p383, p387, p392 and p396*

The **Centro Histórico** is the ideal place to stay. The **Pelourinho** is best if you're on a tight budget. **Santo Antônio** has reasonably priced hotels with charm and character. **Barra** also has some reasonable options; especially for apartments with kitchens, and it lies on the seafront. Business visitors will find good services and hotels in **Rio Vermelho**, overlooking the ocean and a 10-min taxi ride from the centre or airport.

Accommodation in the city tends to get very full over Carnaval and New Year, when prices go up. During Carnaval it is a good idea to rent a flat or stay in a shared room in a *pensionato* (private house), as hotels and hostels will be heaving. *Pensionatos* usually charge anything from US$5 to US$35 per person. Be careful with your belongings as not all householders are honest. The tourist office has a list of estate agents for flat rental (eg José Mendez, T071-3237 1394/6) or you can find flats through **Paradise Properties**, www.pp-bahia.com, **Bahia Online**, www.bahia-online.net, or **Bahia Land**, T071-8133 1441, williamwisden@gmail.com. Houses or rooms can be rented from **Pierre Marbacher**, R Carlos Coqueijo 68A, Itapoã, T071-3249 5754 (Caixa Postal 7458, 41600 Salvador), who is Swiss, owns a beach bar at Rua K and speaks English. Prices for the mid- and upper-end hotels are usually considerably cheaper when booked in advance through online travel agencies (OTAs) such as hotels.com and venere.com.

There are various campsites in the area, but be careful of swimming in the sea nearby and be very wary of leaving valuables in the tent. Robbery and assault are frequent.

Camping Clube do Brasil, R Visconde do Rosario 409, Rosario, T071-3242 0482.
Camping de Pituaçu, Av Prof Pinto de Aguiar, Jardim Pituaçu, T071-3231 7143.
Ecológica, R Alameida da Praia, near the lighthouse at Itapoã, T071-3374 3506. Bar, restaurant, hot showers. Highly recommended. To get there, take a bus from Praça da Sé direct to Itapoã, or to Campo Grande or Barra, change there for Itapoã (1 hr), then 30 mins' walk.
Igloo Inn, Terminal Turistico de Buraquinho, Praia Lauro de Freitas, T071-3379 2854.

The Pelourinho

LL Hotel Villa Bahia, Largo do Cruzeiro de São Francisco 16-18, T071-3322 4271, www.hotelvillabahia.com. This boutique hotel, part of the French **Voyeur** group, is housed in a renovated 18th-century town house right next to the the Convento de São Francisco. It has a series of themed rooms, the airiest and brightest of which is the Goa room, with a huge hardwood bed, 2-m-high shuttered windows and polished wood floors. The public areas set the mood with classical music. There's a little mosaic pool out back and a hot tub on the roof.
LL O Convento do Carmo, R do Carmo 1, T071-3327 8400, www.pestana.com. Far and away the best in the city and the best historical hotel in the whole of Brazil, with a range of suites in a beautifully converted baroque convent. Facilities include an excellent restaurant and spa, a small swimming pool and business services.
LL-L Portas Velhas, Largo da Palma 6, Santana, T071-3324 8400, www.casadas portasvelhas.com. A little themed boutique hotel in the square made famous by Jorge Amado's *Dona Flor and Her Two Husbands*. Small but tastefully decorated a/c rooms, 1 larger suite and a good restaurant. The streets running from here to the centre are unsafe at any time of day so take a taxi.

L-AL Casa do Amerlindo, R das Portas do Carmo 6, T071-3266 8550, www.casado amarelindo.com. This refurbished colonial house offers a handful of well-appointed, modern a/c rooms, all with wooden floors and plain white walls decorated with local handicrafts. Those on the coastal side of the hotel have 2-m-tall shutter windows which open onto a sweeping view of the bay. There's an even better view from the rooftop terrace – which serves caipirinhas at sunset – and the hotel is one of the few in the historic centre to have a (tiny) pool and (equally tiny) fitness centre.

AL Studio do Carmo, Ladeira do Carmo 17, T071-3326 2426, www.studiodocarmo.com. This little boutique, which is similar to those further up the hill in Santo Antonio is in a choice location next to the Carmelite churches a stroll from the Largo do Pelourinho. Rooms sit in a converted, tall 18th-century townhouse on the east side of the Largo, so none have bay views – they overlook the street and can be noisy on Tue or weekend nights. But all are large, decked out in wood and white paint and splashed with colour from bed linen and local art. The best are on the top floor and have terraces. Breakfasts are generous spreads of fruit, cakes, cooked meats, cheeses and coffee. The European-Brazilian owners are welcoming and helpful. The hotel also offers a good-value 5-day package in Salvador and Morro de São Paulo. Prices are on the website.

A-B Bahia Café, Praça Da Sé 24, T071-3322 3266, www.bahiacafe.com. This intimate little European-Brazilian boutique hotel is in a great location – 2 mins' walk from the Terreiro de Jesus and the Lacerda Lift. Rooms are rustic chic with chunky beds and brightly coloured counterpanes, but little furniture. Those at the front of the building sit over the street and can be noisy. Breakfasts are ample and there is an internet café serving great coffee on the ground floor.

Hotel Pelourinho, R Alfredo Brito 20, T071-243 2324, www.hotelpelourinho.com. A newly refurbished 1960s hotel with bright red and white-walled a/c en suites. The bathrooms have marble basins and glass shower cubicles and a few offer great views out over the Baía de Todos os Santos.

B-D Hotel Quilombo do Pelô, R Alfredo Brito 13, T071-3322 4371, http://quilombo dopelo.vilabol.uol.com.br. A range of rooms from simple dorms and doubles to the top floor 'Rei Zumbi' suite with its own jacuzzi and views out over the city. All are themed and the restaurant serves Jamaican food.

B-E Albergue das Laranjeiras, R Inácio Acciolli 13, T/F071-3321 1366, www.laranjeirashostel.com.br. A big and brash HI hostel with a range of white-wall and tile-floor dorms and pricey doubles and triples in a colonial building in the heart of the historic centre. The breakfast area doubles up as a café and crêperie. English spoken and a full range of hostel services. The hostel can be noisy but is a good for meeting other travellers.

C-E Albergue do Pelô, R Ribeiro dos Santos 5, T071-3242 8061, www.alberguedopelo. com.br. A bright reception area leads to simple but freshly painted and slate-floored dorms for 4-12, with beds at the bottom end of the price range. Dormitory floors are single sex and despite the privileged, central location, the crowd is quieter than most of the larger, party-orientated hostels nearby. Breakfast included.

C-E Hostel Amizade, R Alfredo Brito 28, T071-3322 0335, www.hostelamizade.com. Spartan rooms with wooden beds and little else, too few bathrooms for the guests and public areas in need of maintenance are made up for only by the good-value, friendly and helpful family who have accommodated the hostel in their home.

C-E Hostel Cobreu, Ladeira do Carmo 22, T071-3117 1401, www.hostelcobreu.com. This good-value, US-run hostel is well-located – 2 mins from the Pelourinho, meaning that lively nightlife is literally on the doorstep (the hostel balcony overlooks a popular hangout). Rooms can therefore be very noisy on a Tue or weekend nights. Rooms and dorms are simple but the owners have made some effort to brighten them up with big blocks of colour and attractive stencils, and there are public spaces to lounge in, booking services and free internet and water. Bring your own padlock for the lockers.

C-E Hostel Nega Maluca, R Dos Marchantes 15, Santo Antônio, T071-3242 9249, www.negamaluca.com. This popular party hostel less than 400 m from one of Pelourinho's biggest Tue night shows, has well-maintained but small rooms and dorms with thoughtful extras -- like a personal bed light and mains socket for each berth. The TV common room comes with complimentary hookahs, a cat and a dog and there's a terrace slung with hammocks and free internet and Wi-Fi, a booking service and a more-generous-than-average hostel breakfast.

D-E Albergue São Jorge, R Alfredo de Brito, T071-3266 7092, www.saojorgehostel.com. This is one of the cheapest hostels in Salvador, offering bright but small single-sex dorms, and a few doubles and triples which, unusually for a hostel, work out at only a little more expensive per person. Internet access and Wi-Fi (in the lobby) come free as does breakfast.

Santo Antônio

Santo Antônio is a quiet district just 5 mins' walk northeast of Pelourinho, beginning immediately after the Largo do Carmo. In recent years it has been a popular place for Europeans to open up carefully designed *pousadas* in beautifully restored buildings. A number have magnificent views of the bay. Most are mid-range, but there are a handful of cheaper options too.

LL-AL Villa Santo Antônio, R Direita de Santo Antônio 130, T071-3326 1270, www.hotel-santoantonio.com. Very stylish, bright and comfortable converted colonial townhouse, the best rooms have magnificent views out over the bay from your bed. All the a/c rooms have en suites and little balconies; all are different. Good service and breakfast.

L-A Pousada das Flores, R Direita de Santo Antônio 442, T071-3243 1836,

www.pflores.com.br. A beautiful, tranquil old house decorated in colonial style and owned by a Brazilian/French couple. The *pousada* serves a great breakfast and supports local community projects -- details of which are on the website.

AL-A Pousada do Pilar, R Direita do Santo Antônio 24 , T071-3241 6278, www.pousada dopilar.com. The a/c rooms are large, modern, very well kept and functional and have cable TV. They are decked out in raw wood and light plaster and have verandas with those excellent Baía de Todos os Santos views. Good breakfast, friendly service. Wi-Fi in reception and a pleasant roof terrace bar.

AL-A Pousada Redfish, Ladeira do Boqueirão 1, T071-3243 8473, www.hotel redfish.com. This English-owned stylish, lime-green boutique has plain, large rooms, some with terraces and open-air showers.

A-B Pousada Villa Carmo, R do Carmo 58, T/F071-3241 3924, www.pousadavillacarmo. com.br. The simple but elegant a/c and fan-cooled rooms in this *pousadas* come with beautiful bay views. Look at several as some are a little cramped. The Italian-Brazilian owners include breakfast and afternoon tea in the price and can organize trips in Salvador and massages.

AL-C Pousada do Boqueirão, R Direita do Santo Antônio 48, T071-3241 2262, www.pousadaboqueirao.com.br. The most stylish of all the *pousadas* in Salvador. Lovingly renovated by the Italian interior designer owner and her brother -- a former merchant seaman. There are a variety of themed rooms; the best at the top of the building, with wonderful views out over the Baía de Todos os Santos. Service and breakfast are excellent. Several languages spoken.

South of the centre: Campo Grande and Vitória

Campo Grande/Vitória make-up a quiet, upmarket residential area, between Barra and the city centre. Whilst few tourists stay here, it's a convenient area for many of the museums and the Mosteiro São Bento and is well connected to the airport, Pelourinho and Barra via bus (see Transport, page 416).

A-B Bahia do Sol, Av 7 de Setembro 2009, T071-3338 8800, www.bahiadosol.com.br. Comfortable and safe family-run hotel in a 1970s tower. Good breakfast and restaurant, bureau de change, but no pool. Rooms have a/c, fridges, safes and en suites. The best are on the upper floors and have recently been refurbished. Ask to see at least a couple.

Porto da Barra and the Atlantic beach suburbs

Barra is the most popular tourist neighbourhood close to the the historic centre and, whilst the sea is none too clean Barra, has has plenty of restaurants, beach bars and nightlife.

A Bahia Flat, Av Oceânica 235, T071-3339 4140, www.bahiaflat.com.br. A range of flats. The best are tastefully decorated and newly refurbished with Miró prints on the walls, patent leather sofas, glass coffee tables, large fridges, sound system and expansive mirror-fronted wardrobes. The best have sea views. The hotel has a pool and sauna and internet.

A Marazul, Av 7 de Setembro 3937, T071-3264 8200, www.marazulhotel.com.br. Blocky 1970s tower in a great location on the seafront with standard 3-star rooms filled with anonymous catalogue furniture. The best rooms are at the top of the building and have magnificent views, but decor is tired and service slow. The restaurant has a pool, gym, conference facilities and business services.

A Monte Pascoal Praia, Av Oceânica 176, Farol beach, T071-2103 4000, www.monte pascoal.com.br. A recently renovated 1970s hotel with simple rooms in tile and white paint, the best of which have views out over the bay. Fittings and decor are a little old-fashioned: counterpanes come in garish colours, walls are a little thin and fittings are old fashioned but rooms are spacious and bright. Facilities include (expensive) Wi-Fi and

internet, a pool, sauna, gym, restaurant and decent service.

B Farol Barra Flat, Av Oceanica 409, T071-3339 0000, www.farolbarraflat.com.br. Over 100 simple yet well-kept apartments with kitchenettes; all with microwaves, TVs and the best with sweeping ocean views. The best are the VIP suites – more spacious and on the top floors.

B Pousada Azul, R Doutor Praguer Fróes 102, T071-3011 9798, www.pousadaazul.com.br. A quiet, brilliant blue *pousada* in a semi-residential street. A handful of spartan a/c rooms decorated in white with splashes of colour from modern art, linen and curtains and wooden floors. All are furnished with solid hardwood beds and commodes. The hotel has free Wi-Fi and offers a generous breakfast.

B Village Novo Beach suites, Av 7 de Setembro 3659, T071-3267 4362, www.villagenovo.com. A 125-year-old converted townhouse with a range of tastefully decorated mock-boutique hotel rooms with terraces, a large roof patio and a pleasant little café restaurant. Look at several – some are far better than others. Many of those with a beach view are obscured by trees. The hotel has an internet café in the basement.

B-C Villa Romana, R Lemos Brito 14, T071-3264 6522, www.villaromana.com.br. Simple a/c rooms with wooden floors, desks, wardrobes and en suites and formal public areas decked out with mock 18th-century furnishings. There is a small patio with a pool behind the main building.

C Pousada Hotel Âmbar, R Afonso Celso 485, T071-3264 6956, www.ambarpousada. com.br. A French-owned *pousada* with very simple, small fan-cooled rooms gathered around a colourful little courtyard. Internet and decent breakfast. The hotel has weekly live music shows, staff are helpful and courteous and the management practices ecotourism: contributing to the *criança familia* social project, recycling waste and conserving water.

D-E Albergue do Porto, R Barão de Sergy 197, T071-3264 6600, www.alberguedoporto. com.br. This HI hostel in a turn-of-the-20th-century house is spacious, high ceilinged fan-cooled and a/c rooms with wooden floors (some with en suites and baths), a comfortable communal area and good breakfasts. Staff speak English and other facilities include, kitchen, laundry, safe, TV lounge, games room and internet. Very popular.

D-E Alpha Hostel, R Eduardo Diniz Gonçalves 128, T071-3237 6282; www.alpha hostel.com. The Salvador branch of this popular Rio hostel is tucked away on a small street a block from the beach and close to bus routes on Av 7 de Setembro. Staff are friendly and courteous and there are airy public areas draped with hammocks. Rooms and dorms are bright and colourful, but are fan-cooled only and can be stuffy – especially in the hotter months. Be wary along the backstreets in the area late at night.

D-E Hostel Che Lagarto Barra, Av Oceânica 84B; T071-3235 2404, www.chelagarto.com. The Salvador branch of a busy South American party hostel chain sits in a big house less than 50 m from the beach and ideally positioned for the carnival parade. Dorms and doubles are spacious and bright, but they can be very noisy.

D-E La Villa Francaise, R Recife 222, Jardim Brasil, T071-3245 6008. This little guesthouse 500 m from the beach behind the Shopping Barra is bright, colourful and well-run and attracts a quieter crowd than many of Barra's brasher establishments. A/c rooms are well-tended, spruce and clean and painted in bright lilacs, lemon yellows and eggshell blues. The helpful and knowledgeable French-Brazilian owners offer a sumptuous breakfast of pastries, fruit and cakes.

D-F Pousada Marcos, Av Oceânica 281, T071-3264 5117, www.pousadamarcos.com.br. A very simple hostel-style guesthouse in a good location near the lighthouse. Always busy.

Rio Vermelho

LL Pestana Bahia, R Fonte de Boi 216, T071-3453 8000, www.pestanahotels.com.br. Newly revamped tower with wonderful views out over the ocean but no access to the beach. Pool, gym, restaurant, sauna and very good business facilities. Online discounts available. With restaurant and bar.

LL Zank, Av Almirante Barroso 161, Rio Vermelho, T071-3083 4000, www.zankhotel. com.br. This discreetly designed, expensive boutique hotel sits in a converted belle époque house 5 mins' cab ride from Rio Vermelho's bars and restaurants. Rooms are decorated in strong monotone blocks – with warm woods offset by cream and white walls. The stylish open plan bathrooms are glass-fronted are separated from the rest of the room by a curtain – meaning that whilst they look superb they offer little toilet privacy. Some rooms (notably No 10) have ocean views.

A-B Catharina Paraguaçu, R João Gomes 128, Rio Vermelho, T071-3334 0089, www.hotelcatharinaparaguacu.com.br. Small colonial-style hotel with attractive courtyards and a range of decent rooms, some of which are distinctly better than others – look carefully and, if booking online, avoid the rooms close to the street. Very good service. Recommended.

B-C Ibis, R Fonte do Boi 215, T071-3330 8300, www.accorhotels.com.br. A vast, anonymous blocky hotel in this budget business chain, with functional rooms some of which have seaviews from the upper floors and all of which have Wi-Fi access.

Ilha de Itaparica *p398, map p399*

B-C Galeria Hotel, Praia do Sol, Barra Grande, T071-3636 8441, www.galeria-hotel.com. German/Brazilian-owned *pousada* with simple tile-floored a/c en suites around a large pool and a good restaurant.

B-C Pousada Arco Iris, Estrada da Gamboa 102, Mar Grande beach, T071-3633 1130, www.parcoiris.na-web.net. Magnificent though dishevelled 19th-century building romantically set in a garden of mango trees. Decent restaurant with slow service, a pool and unkempt but shady camping facilities available in the owners' adjacent property.

C Pousada Canto do Mar, Av Beira Mar s/n, Praia de Aratuba, T071-3638 2244, www.pousadaumcantodomar.com.br. Brightly coloured, simple *cabañas* set in a pretty garden overlooking what is a lively beach in summer and a quiet beach the rest of the year. Friendly staff, decent breakfast.

C-D Jardim Tropical, Estrada da Rodagem, Ponta de Areia, T071-3631 1409, www.jardim-tropical.com. This *pousada* has a series of mock-colonial cabins – which range from simple rooms with nothing but a bed to larger apartments with terracotta-tiled roofs – set in a palm-shaded garden whose lawn is dotted with beach chairs and colourful hammocks. Children are welcome and stay for free under 5 years old. The hotel offers complimentary free transfer to Ponta de Areia beach and Itaparica town.

Cachoeira *p400*

C Pousada do Convento de Cachoeira, R Praça da Aclamação s/n, T075-3425 1716, www.pousadadoconvento.com.br. Newly refurbished rooms in an historic building in the centre of the town. The best are on the upper floor overlooking a grassy courtyard and have high wooden ceilings and chunky, handsome furniture. Those on the ground floor are simpler in whitewash and tile and some are only fan-cooled.

D-E Pousada d'Ajuda, R Largo d'Ajuda s/n, T075-3425 5278. Spacious and clean doubles with little corners cordoned off for showers (ask to see a few rooms, some have saggy mattresses) and dorms for up to 4. Right next to the Igreja da Boa Morte.

D-E Pousada La Barca, R Inocência Boaventura 37, 200 m downstream of the Praça Aclamação, T075-3425 1070, www.labarca.zip.net. Little rooms in a bright orange annexe and public areas decorated with the paintings by the artist-owner Cristina. No a/c.

Eating

Salvador *p382, maps p383, p387, p392 and p396*

The Pelourinho and Santo Antônio

¶¶¶ Maria Mata Mouro, R da Ordem Terceira 8, T071-3321 3929. International menu, excellent service, relaxing atmosphere in a quiet corner in the bustling Pelourinho.

¶¶¶ O Nilo, R das Laranjeiras 44, T071-9159 0937. Superior Lebanese food in an intimate little restaurant decorated with black and white prints. Great tagines and a vegetarian degustation menu.

¶¶¶ Sorriso de Dadá, R Frei Vicente 5, T071-3321 9642, www.dada.com.br. Bahia's most famous chef has cooked for, amongst others, Jorge Amado, Gilberto Gil and Hillary Clinton. Her *moqueca de camarão* and her *vatapas* are signature dishes. But all has sadly fallen somewhat from grace and the food is now very patchy. Lets hope she wakes up from resting on her laurels.

¶¶¶ Uauá, R Gregorio de Matos, 36, T071-3321 3089. Elegant, colonial restaurant and bar serving northeastern cooking and seafood, including some Bahian specialities. The restaurant's name means 'firefly' in Tupi.

¶¶¶-¶¶ Al Carmo, R do Carmo 66, Santo Antônio, T071-3242 0283. A favourite spot to watch the sun sink over the Baía de Todos os Santos, caipirinha or chilled wine in hand. The Italian food is rather stodgy and heavy with cheese. Opt for a starter only. The music (usually a guitarist and singer) has an optional cover charge.

¶¶¶-¶¶ Axego, R João de Deus 1, T071-3242 7481. An established restaurant celebrated for its seafood. The *moquecas* are perhaps the best in the Centro Histórico and there is excellent *feijoada* on Sun lunchtime. Meals are served in a pleasant upstairs dining room. In a great location less than a 1-min walk from the Terreiro de Jesus.

¶¶¶-¶¶ Encontro dos Artistas, R das Laranjeiras 15, T071-3321 1721. Excellent seafood and *moquecas* served in a little streetside restaurant decorated with a mock-Da Vinci *Last Supper*, set in Salvador.

¶¶¶-¶¶ Jardim das Delícias, R João de Deus, 12, T071-3321 1449. An award-winning, elegant restaurant and antiques shop set in a pretty tropical garden serving Bahian and international food accompanied by live classical or acoustic music. Very good value for its quality.

¶¶ Quilombo do Pelô, R Alfredo Brito 13, T071-3322 4371. Daily 1100-2400. Rustic Jamaican restaurant, good food with relaxed, if erratic service. One of the few places offering vegetarian options.

¶¶ Senac, Praça José Alencar 13-15, Largo do Pelourinho, T071-3324 4557. A catering school with 2 restaurants. Upstairs is typical Bahian cooking; downstairs is per kilo and open only for lunch; both are a/c. Dishes are better upstairs but there is plenty of choice in the buffet and options for vegetarians.

¶¶-¶ Pomerô, R Alfredo Brito 33, T071-3321 5556, www.pomero.com.br. Closed Mon. Good value, simple and barely garnished grilled meats, fish steaks, bar snacks and lightly spiced *moquecas* in a popular restaurant housed in a colonial house.

¶ Bahiacafe, Praça da Sé, 20, T071-3322 1266. Smart, Belgian-run internet café with good coffee, a European-style breakfast menu and decent snacks.

¶ Coffee Shop, Praça da Sé 5, T071-3322 7817. Cuban-style café serving sandwiches. Excellent coffee and tea served in china cups. Doubles as cigar shop.

¶ Gramado, Praça da Sé 16, T071-3322 1727. Lunch only. The best of the few per kilo restaurants in the area. Scrupulously clean and with a reasonable choice.

Porto da Barra and Atlantic beach suburbs

There are many a/c restaurants from cheap to medium-priced in **Shopping Barra** and the **Barra Center Shopping**.

¶¶¶¶ Amado, Av Lafayete Coutinho 660, Comércio, T071-3322 3520, www.amado bahia.com.br. The best of Salvador's top-end

restaurants on the Baía de Todos os Santos waterfront. The space is beautiful, set on a deck overlooking the lapping aquamarine of the Baía de Todos os Santos. But the real winner here is the food from Edinho Engel, who had an award-winning restaurant in São Paulo. The emphasis on seafood with dishes such as squid stuffed with crab and garlic in provencale sauce with a white carrot mousseline. The haute cuisine *moquecas* are excellent.

¶¶¶ Barravento, Av Oceanica 814, T071-3247 2577. Very popular beach bar restaurant and hang-out with a marquee roof. Decent cocktails, *chope* and a menu of seafood, *moquecas* and steaks.

¶¶¶ SoHo, Av Contorno 1010, Bahia Marina, Salvador, T071-3322 4554. The restaurant's long bar is where Salvador's 'A-list' drink their caipirinhas. Great sushi and sashimi combinations from Paulistano chef Marcio Fushimi are served in the chic glass-walled dining room and at the open-air veranda tables overlooking the ocean. Come for a late dinner 2130-2200, dress smart casual.

¶¶¶ Trapiche Adelaide, Praça Tupinmbas 2, Av Contorno, T071-3326 2211, www.trapiche adelaide.com.br. Salvador's most self-consciously chic restaurant in a mood-lit glass-walled rectangle built out over the water and with stunning views of the bay. The seafood is excellent but people really come here to be seen in the cavernous modernist open-air dining room or the neighbouring cosy-chic **Bar da Ponta**. Dress well and take a taxi to get here.

¶¶ Cantina Panzone, Av Oceánica 114, T071-3264 3644. Reasonable wood-fired pizza and pasta and a lively crowd in high season.

¶¶ Oceánica, Presidente Vargas 1, T071-3264 3561. A long-established popular Bahian seafood restaurant. Open until late, especially on weekends.

¶¶ Quatro Amicci, R Dom Marcos Teixeira 35. Excellent wood-fired oven pizzas served in a bright modern space in a converted 19th-century house. Lively weekend crowd.

¶ Caranguejo do Farol, Av Oceánica 235, T071-3264 7061. A buzzing bar and seafood

Bahian cuisine

Bahian cooking is spiced and peppery. The main dish is *moqueca* – seafood cooked in a sauce made from coconut milk, tomatoes, red and green peppers, fresh coriander and *dendê* (palm oil). It is traditionally cooked in a wok-like earthenware dish and served piping hot at the table. *Moqueca* is often accompanied by *farofa* (manioc flour) and a hot pepper sauce which you add at your discretion – it's very mild by British or Asian standards. The *dendê* is somewhat heavy and those with delicate stomachs are advised to try the *ensopado*, a sauce with the same ingredients as the *moqueca*, but without the palm oil.

Nearly every street corner has a *Bahiana* selling a wide variety of local snacks, the most famous of which is the *acarajé*, a kidney bean dumpling fried in palm oil, which has its origins in West Africa. To this the *Bahiana* adds *vatapá*, a dried shrimp and coconut milk paté (also delicious on its own), *pimenta* (hot sauce) and fresh salad. For those who prefer not to eat the palm oil, the *abará* is a good substitute. *Abará* is steamed and wrapped in banana leaves.

Bahians usually eat *acarajé* or *abará* with a chilled beer on the way home from work or the beach at sunset. Another popular dish with African origins is *xin-xin de galinha*, chicken on the bone cooked in *dendê*, with dried shrimp, garlic and squash.

Recommended *Bahianas* are: **Chica**, at Ondina beach (in the street behind the Bahia Praia Hotel); **Dinha**, in Rio Vermelho (serves *acarajé* until midnight, extremely popular); **Regina** at Largo da Santana (very lively in the late afternoon); and **Cira** in Largo da Mariquita. Seek local advice on which are the most hygienic stalls to eat from.

restaurant serving great Bahian food in *refeição* portions large enough for 2. Cheap bottled beer. Strong caipirinhas.

Rio Vermelho

Casa da Dinha, R João Gomes 25, just west of the **Catharina Paraguaçu Hotel** and a few yards from the Largo de Santana, T071-3333 0525. One of the best mid-range Bahian restaurants in the city with a varied menu peppered with Bahian specialities, steaks, fish and standard international options like pasta.

Ilha de Itaparica *p398, map p399*

There are many Bahianas selling *acarajé* in the late afternoon and early evening, in the main *praça* and by the pier at Mar Grande.
Philippe's Bar and Restaurant, Largo de São Bento, Mar Grande. The best restaurant on the island with delicious fish dishes cooked by the French owner.
Volta ao Mundo, Largo de São Bento 165, Mar Grande, T071-3633 1031. A good-value buffet restaurant with a fixed price, all-you-can-eat lunchtime menu.

Cachoeira *p400*

Café com Arte Sebo Ana Néri, R 13 de Maio 16, T061-9161 1581. *Petiscos*, good coffee, beer and art from a mixture of local and international artists. Lovely space in a colonial house and a friendly eastern European and fully Bahian owner.
Casa Comercial NS Rosário o Recanto do Misticismo, Praça da Aclamação s/n. Nowhere could be more 'Cachoeira' than this pizza café and restaurant with 2 *candomblé*-inspired shrines – one to the 5 African nations and one to the 5 elements. As well as pizza, there's great *carne do sol* and fried chicken with chips, rice and beans and occasional live music.
Pouso da Palavra, Praça da Aclamação s/n Arty little café opposite the Casa da Camara museum. Great cappuccinos in a cosy period house, owned by poet Damário Da Cruz. Local artists' work decorate the walls and

the café sells some great CDs, souvenirs and beautiful mandala candle shades by Graca Mascarehenses.

◐ Bars, clubs and live music

Salvador *p382, maps p383, p387, p392 and p396*

Centro Histórico

Nightlife is concentrated on and around the **Pelourinho** and the **Terreiro de Jesus**, where there is always a free live street band on Tue and at weekends. The Pelourinho area is also a good place to browse the bars, but be wary after 2300. There are many bars on the **Largo de Quincas Berro d'Água**, and along R Alfredo do Brito. R João de Deus and its environs are dotted with simple pavement bars with plastic tables.

The most famous music from Salvador is the *batucada* of drum orchestras like **Olodum** and **Ilê Aiyê**, whose impressive sound can be heard frequently around the Pelourinho (Olodum played on Paul Simon's *Rhythm of the Saints* album). Both groups have their own venues and play in the individual parades or *blocos* at Carnaval. See box, page 412, for times and venues of the *bloco* rehearsals.

Bar do Reggae and Praça do Reggae, Ladeiro do Pelourinho, by the Nossa Senhora dos Rosarios dos Pretos church. Live reggae bands every Tue and more frequently closer to Carnaval. Be wary of pick-pockets.

Cantina da Lua, Praça Quinze de Novembro 2, Terreiro De Jesus, T071-3322 4041. Open daily. Popular spot on the square with outdoor seating, but gets crowded and the food isn't great.

Casa do Ilê Aiyê, R das Laranjeiras 16, T071-3321 4193, www.ileaiye.org.br. Ilê Aiyê's headquarters and shop, where you can find information about their shows and Carnaval events.

Casa do Olodum, R Gregório de Matos 22, T071-3321 5010, www2.uol.com.br/olodum. Olodum's headquarters where they perform live every Tue and Sun at 1900 to packed crowds.

O Cravinho, Praça 15 de Novembro 3, T071-3322 6759. Dark little bar with occasional live music. Always busy. Greasy bar food is served at tree-trunk tables, usually accompanied by plentiful *cachaça*, which is made here and stored in barrels behind the bar. Be careful in this area after 2300.

Porto da Barra and Atlantic beach suburbs

Barra nightlife is concentrated around the **Farol da Barra** (lighthouse) and **R Marquês de Leão**, which is busy with pavement bars. Like the Pelourinho the whole area is good for a browse, but be wary of pickpockets.

Concha Acústica, Teatro Castro Alves, Praça 2 de Julho, Campo Grande, T071-3339 8000, www.tca.ba.gov.br. The city's premier small concert venue with quality national and international acts such as Tom Zé and Naná Vasconcelos.

Fashion Club, Av Octávio Mangabeira 2471, Jd dos Namorados, T071-3346 0012. Not very fashionable at all – despite the name – but busy (especially on Thu) with a predominantly 20-something crowd.

Habeas Copos, R Marquês de Leão 172. A popular and traditional street-side bar – something of a Salvador institution.

Korunn, R Ceará 1240, Pituba, T071-3248 4208. Lively dance club with a bohemian crowd. Very popular Thu-Sat.

Lotus, Av Almirante Marques de Leão, T071-3264 6787. Salvador's branch of the famous New York and São Paulo club. A little frayed on the inside and populated with a fashionable upper-middle class crowd dancing to old-hat European and US club sounds.

Rio Vermelho and the north

The district of **Rio Vermelho** was once the bohemian section of town and it still has

Bahia's musicians recommend

Mariene de Castro is one of Brazil's most exciting new samba acts. Her debut CD *Abre Caminho* won several of Brazil's top music awards in 2007. She told *Footprint* where to go out in Salvador: "The best and most exciting music in Bahia has its roots firmly in the samba tradition. Some of the best artists are members of the Santo de Casa cultural movement who play in the Praça Pedro Arcanjo near the Pelourinho and the Espaço Cultural Barroquinha, Praça da Barroquinha, (1 km south of the Pelourinho), T061-3334 7350."

Carlinhos Brown is one of Brazil's greatest percussionists and the founder of the Timbalada drum troupe. He is one of the icons of Bahian music and a star of Carnaval. We asked him where to go to hear live music in Salvador: "At our community centre here in Candeal you can hear my band Timbalada as well as great new acts like Candombless and Beat Gabot and in the new African music centre." To get there, take a taxi to Candeal for 1800 on a Sunday and ask for 'A Casa de Carlinhos Brown'.

good live music and exciting bar nightlife. There are a number of lively bars around the **Largo de Santana**, a block west of Hotel Catharina Paraguaçu.

Café Calypso, Trav Prudente Moraes 59, T071-3334 6446. Live Brazilian rock music on Tue and Fri.

Casa da Mãe R Guedes Cabral 81, T071-3334 3041 or T071-9601 6616 (mob). Live *samba de roda* several times a week and roots Bahian music. Ring ahead for schedule.

Havana Music Bar, R Cardeal da Silva 117, T071-3237 5107. Live bands (mostly rock) Wed-Sat. Best after 2230.

Pimentinha, Boca do Rio. One of the few clubs to be lively on a Mon.

Rock In Rio Café, Aeroclube Plaza Show, Boca do Rio, T071-3461 0300. Dance club with a young crowd and an emphasis on rock and MPB. Busiest at the weekends.

Teatro Sesi Rio Vermelho, R Borges dos Reis 9, T071-3334 0668. One of the best venues in the city for contemporary Bahian bands.

Cachoeira *p400*
Casa do Licor, R 13 Maio 25. Interesting bohemian bar with a range of bizarre drinks. Try the banana-flavoured spirit. Live music at the weeeknd.

⊙ Entertainment

Salvador *p382, maps p383, p387, p392 and p396*

The **Fundação Cultural do Estado da Bahia** edits *Bahia Cultural*, a monthly brochure listing the main cultural events for the month. These can be found in most hotels and **Bahiatursa** information centres. Local newspapers *A Tarde* and *Correio da Bahia* have good listing for cultural events in the city.

Cinema
The impressive Casa do Comércio building near Iguatemi houses the **Teatro do SESC** which has a mixed programme of theatre, cinema and music Wed-Sun.

The main shopping malls at Barra and Iguatemi, and **Cineart** in Politeama (Centro), show mainstream Hollywood and international films, almost invariably dubbed (*dublado*). Only a few showings have subtitles (*legendas*).

Theatre and classical music
Associação Cultural Brasil Estados Unidos (**ACBEU**), Corredor de Vitória. US cultural shows and cinema.

Teatro Gregorio de Matos, Praça Castro Alves, T071-3322 2646. Programmes dedicated to showcasing new productions and writers.

Carnaval in Bahia

Carnival in Bahia is the largest in the world and encourages active participation. It is said that there are 1.5 million people dancing on the streets at any one time.

The **pre-carnival festive season** begins with São Nicodemo de Cachimbo (penultimate Sunday of November), followed by Santa Bárbara (4 December), then the Festa da Conceição da Praia, centred on the church of that name (open 0700-1130) at the base of the Lacerda lift. The last night is 8 December (not for those who don't like crowds!). The Festa da Boa Viagem takes place in the last week of December, in the lower city; the beach will be packed all night on 31 December. The new year kicks off on 1 January with a beautiful boat procession of Nosso Senhor dos Navegantes from Conceição da Praia to the church of Boa Viagem, on the beach of that name in the lower city. The leading boat, which carries the image of Christ and the archbishop, was built in 1892. You can follow in a sailing boat for about US$1; go early (0900) to the dock by the Mercado Modelo. A later festival is São Lázaro on the last Sunday in January.

Carnaval itself officially starts on Thursday night at 2000 when the keys of the city are given to the Carnaval King 'Rei Momo'. The unofficial opening though is on Wednesday with the Lavagem do Porto da Barra, when throngs of people dance on the beach. Later on in the evening is the Baile dos Atrizes,

starting at around 2300 and going on until dawn, very bohemian, good fun. Check with **Bahiatursa** for details on venue and time (also see under Rio for Carnaval dates).

There are two distinct musical formats. The **afro blocos** are large drum-based troupes (some with up to 200 drummers) who play on the streets, accompanied by singers atop mobile sound trucks. The first of these groups was the Filhos de Gandhy (founded in 1949), whose participation is one of the highlights of Carnaval. Their 6000 members dance through the streets on the Sunday and Tuesday of Carnaval dressed in their traditional costumes, a river of white and blue in an ocean of multi-coloured carnival revellers. The best known of the recent *afro blocos* are Ilê Aiye, Olodum, Muzenza and Malê Debalê. They all operate throughout the year in cultural, social and political areas. Not all of them are receptive to foreigners among their numbers for Carnaval. The basis of the rhythm is the enormous *surdo* (deaf) drum with its *bumbum bumbum bum* anchorbeat, while the smaller *repique*, played with light twigs, provides a crack-like overlay. Ilê Aiye take to the streets around 2100 on Saturday night and their departure from their headquarters at Ladeira do Curuzu in the Liberdade district is not to be missed. The best way to get there is to take a taxi to Curuzu via Largo do Tanque, thereby avoiding traffic jams. The ride is a little longer but much quicker.

Teatro Vila Velha, Passeio Publico, T071-3336 1384. Márcio Meirelles, the theatre's director, works extensively with **Grupo Teatro Olodum**; although performed in Portuguese, productions here are very visual and well worth investigating.
Teatro XVIII, R Frei Vicente, T071-3332 0018. Experimental theatre in Portuguese.

Theatro Castro Alves, Largo 2 de Julho, Campo Grande, T071-3339 8000. The city's most distinguished performance space and the home of the Bahian Symphony Orchestra and the Castro Alves Ballet Company. The theatre also hosts occasional performances by more cerebral MPB artists and contemporary performers like Hermeto Pascoal or Egberto Gismonti.

A good landmark is the Paes Mendonça supermarket on the corner of the street, from where the *bloco* leaves. From there it's a short walk to the departure point.

The enormous **trios eléctricos**, 12-m sound trucks with powerful sound systems that defy most decibel counters, are the second format. These trucks, each with its town band of up to 10 musicians, play songs influenced by the *afro blocos* and move at a snail's pace through the streets, drawing huge crowds. Each *afro bloco* and *bloco de trio* has its own costume and its own security personnel, who cordon off the area around the sound truck. The *bloco* members can thus dance in comfort and safety.

The traditional Carnaval route is from Campo Grande (by the Tropical Hotel da Bahia) to Praça Castro Alves near the old town. The *blocos* go along Avenida 7 de Setembro and return to Campo Grande via the parallel Rua Carlos Gomes. Many of the *trios* no longer go through the Praça Castro Alves, once the epicentre of Carnaval. The best night at Praça Castro Alves is Tuesday (the last night of Carnaval), when the famous '*Encontro dos Trios*' (Meeting of the Trios) takes place. *Trios* jostle for position in the square and play in rotation until the dawn on Ash Wednesday. It is not uncommon for major stars from the Bahian (and Brazilian) music world to make surprise appearances.

There are grandstand seats at Campo Grande throughout the event. Day tickets for these are available the week leading up to Carnaval. Check with Bahiatursa for information on where the tickets are sold. Tickets are US$10 (or up to US$30 on the black market on the day). The *blocos* are judged as they pass the grandstand and are at their most frenetic at this point. There is little or no shade from the sun so bring a hat and lots of water. Best days are Sunday to Tuesday. For those wishing to go it alone, just find a friendly *barraca* in the shade and watch the *blocos* go by. Avoid the Largo da Piedade and Relógio de São Pedro on Avenida 7 de Setembro: the street narrows here, creating human traffic jams.

The other major centre for Carnaval is Barra to Ondina. The **blocos alternativos** ply this route. These are nearly always *trios eléctricos*, connected with the more traditional *blocos* who have expanded to this now very popular district. Not to be missed here is Timbalada, the drumming group formed by the internationally renowned percussionist Carlinhos Brown.

Ticket prices range from US$180 to US$450. The quality of the *bloco* often depends on the act that plays on the *trio*. For more information see the official Carnaval site, www.carnaval. salvador.ba.gov.br.

Festivals and events

alvador *p382, maps p383, p387, 392 and p396*

Jan Epiphany. Public holiday with many ee concerts and events. Beautiful masses many of the historic churches.
n Festa do Nosso Senhor do Bonfim. eld on the 2nd Sun after Epiphany.

On the preceding Thu there is a colourful parade at the church with many penitents and a ceremonial washing of the church itself. Great for photographs.
Feb Carnaval, see box, above.
2 Feb Pescadores do Rio Vermelho. Boat processions with gifts for Yemanjá, Goddess of the Sea, accompanied by African Brazilian music.

Why I love carnival in Bahia

"I love that Carnival in Salvador is so huge (some 3 million people) and so diverse. We have the popular fun of *axé* music, samba and other styles, alongside Brazil's African heritage, with the *afoxés* – some of which were founded in the first half of the 20th century – and the Afro blocos.

Don't miss the parade by our oldest Afro bloco, Ilê Aiyê (35 years old), which mixes this heritage with exuberant joy and religious reverence."
Tiganá Santana (www.tigana.com.br, www.myspace.com/avozdetigana), a composer and singer from Salvador.

Mar/Apr Holy Week. The week before Easter sees many colourful processions around the old churches in the upper city.

Santo Amaro da Purificação *p400*
24 Jan-2 Feb Festival of Santo Amaro.
2 Feb Nossa Senhora da Purificação.
13 May Bembé do Mercado.

Cachoeira *p400*
24 Jun São João, 'Carnival of the Interior'. Celebrations include dangerous games with fireworks, well attended by tourists.
Mid-Aug Nossa Sehora da Boa Morte.
4 Dec A famous *candomblé* ceremony at the Fonte de Santa Bárbara.

O Shopping

Salvador *p382, maps p383, p387, p392 and p396*
Arts, crafts and cigars
Artesanato Santa Bárbara, R Alfredo Brito 7, Pelourinho, T071-3321 2685. Excellent handmade lace.
Atelier Totonho and Raimundo, Ladeira do Carmo, Pelourinho. 2 adjacent galleries run by a co-operative of some 28 naïve art artists, including Totonho, Calixto, Raimundo Santos and Jô. Good prices.
FIEB-SESI, Av Tiradentes 299, Bonfim; Av Borges dos Reis 9, Rio Vermelho; and Av 7 de Setembro 261, Mercês. Some of the best artisan products in the city ranging from textiles and ceramics to musical instruments.

Goya Lopes. R Gregorio de Mattos, Pelourinho, T071-3321 9428, www.goyalopes.com.br. African Brazilian designer clothing on Goya's Didara label, which features very simple, rustic cotton clothing and beach shawls stamped with intricate motifs in very bright colours from Afro-Brazilian cultural life.
Instituto Mauá, R Gregorio de Matos 27, Pelourinho. Tue-Sat 0900-1800, Sun 1000-1600. Good-quality items, better value and quality than the Mercado Modelo.
Loja de Artesanato do SESC, Largo Pelourinho, T071-3321 5502. Mon-Fri 0900-1800 (closed for lunch), Sat 0900-1300.
Oficina de Investigação Musical, Alfredo Brito 24, Pelourinho, T071-3322 2386. Mon-Fri 0800-1200 and 1300-1600. Handmade traditional percussion instruments (and percussion lessons for US$15 per hr).
Rosa do Prado, R Inacio Aciolly 5, Pelourinho Cigar shop packed with every kind of Brazilian *charuto* imaginable.

Bookshops
Graúna, Av 7 de Setembro 1448, and R Barão de Itapoã 175, Porto da Barra. English titles.
Livraria Brandão, R Ruy Barbosa 4, Centre, T071-3243 5383. Second-hand English, French, Spanish and German books.

Jewellery
Casa Moreira, Ladeira da Praça, just south of Praça da Sé. Exquisite jewellery and antiques. Most are expensive, but there are some affordable charms.

Scala, Praça da Sé, T/F071-3321 8891. Handmade jewellery using locally mined gems (eg aquamarine, amethyst and emerald), workshop at back.

Markets

Feira de Artesanato, Santa Maria Fort, Wed 1700-2100. Arts and crafts in the fort at the far end of Porto da Barra beach.
Feira de São Joaquim, 5 km from Mercado Modelo along the seafront, daily 0800-1900, Sun 0800-1200. The largest and least touristy market in the city selling mainly foodstuffs and a few artisan products. Very smelly.
Mercado Modelo, Praça Cairu, Cidade Baixa, Sat 0800-1900, Sun 0800-1200. Live music and dancing, especially Sat. Expect to be asked for money if you take photos. Many tourist items such as woodcarvings, silver-plated fruit, leather goods, local musical instruments. Lace items for sale are often not handmade (despite labels), are heavily marked up, and are much better bought at their place of origin (eg Ilha de Maré, Pontal da Barra and Marechal Deodoro).

Music and carnival souvenirs

Boutique Olodum, Praça José Alencar, Pelourinho. Olodum CDs, music, T-shirts and musical instruments.
Cana Brava records, R João de Deus 22, T071-3321 0536, www.bahia-online.net. Great little CD shop with a friendly and knowledgeable American owner. Stocks a whole range of classy Brazilian artists, less internationally famous names and back catalogue artists.
Ê Aiyê, R das Laranjeiras 16, T071-3321 193, www.ileaiye.org.br. Bags, clothes, books, music and other such items from this famous Carnaval drum orchestra and *bloco*.

Shopping centres

These are the most comfortable places to shop in Salvador – havens of a/c cool in the heat of the Bahian summer offering a chance to rest over an ice-cold beer, a lunch and to shop for essentials like

Havaianas, bikinis, CDs and beach wraps along with comestibles like batteries, supermarket food and suntan cream.
Shopping Barra, Av Centenário 2992, Chame-Chame, Barra, T071-2108 8288, www.shoppingbarra.com, is the largest shopping mall in easy access of the tourist centres. **Shopping Iguatemi**, Av Tancredo Neves 148, Caminho das Árvores, T071-2126 1111, www.iguatemisalvador.com.br, sits next to the *rodoviária* and has broad spread of mid- to upmarket shops, a large a/c food court and cinemas on the top floor.

Cachoeira *p400*
Woodcarving studios

Worth stopping by to look or to buy are: **Davi Gonçalves**, JJ Seabra 68, Centro T075-3425 2686; **Doidão**, R Ana Nery 42, T075-3425 2764; **Fory**, R Treze de Maio 31, Centro, T075-3425 1142; and **Louco Filho**, R Treze de Maio 18, Centro, T075-3425 4310.

▲ Activities and tours

Salvador *p382, maps p383, p387, p392 and p396*
Capoeira

Associação de Capoeira Mestre Bimba, R das Laranjeiras 1, Pelourinho, T071-3322 0639, www.capoeiramestrebimba.com.br. This school is the inheritor of the teaching of Mestre Bimba, who was the first master to define a system for teaching capoeira regional. There are both male and female teachers.
Escola de Capoeira Angola Irmãos Gêmeos, R Gregório de Mattos 9, Pelourinho, T071-3321 0396, 9963 3562, http://ecaig.blogspot.com (also on Facebook). A school founded by Mestre Curió, who learnt with another legendary capoeirista, Mestre Pastinha. Classes are broad and are good for women, kids and older people. In Curió's absence classes are conducted by the mestre's pupil, Mestra Jararaca (the first woman to earn the Mestra tiltle in Capoeira Angola).

Forte de Santo Antônio Alem do Carmo, T071-3117 1488, www.fortesantantonio. blogspot.com, has a number of schools teaching capoeira – usually in the evenings. They include **Pele da Bahia**, T071-3387 6485, www.mestrepeledabahia.blogspot.com and **Mestre Boca Rica**, T071-3401 3019).

Grupo Cultural de Capoeira Angola Moçambique, R Gregório de Mattos 38, Pelourinho, T071-8113 7455. Offer tuition in Capoeira Angola. Teaching is very flexible, with options for either day classes or full terms and it also offers berimbau and percussion lessons. Famous teachers include Mestres Boca Rica and Neco – alumni of Canjiquinha and Waldemar – 2 of the most celebrated teachers of the 20th century.

Football

Otávio Mangabeira Stadium, Trav Joaquim Maurício, Nazaré, T/F071-3242 3322. 90,000-seat stadium which is home to the **Esporte Clube Bahia** and **Vitória** football clubs. 10 mins away from the Pelourinho, and the Barroquinha terminal.

Tour operators

Bus tours are available from several companies, including: **Alameda Turismo**, T071-3248 2977, US$15 per person; **Itaparica Turismo**, T071-3248 3433; **LR Turismo**, T071-3264 0999, which also offers boat trips; and **Tours Bahia**, T071-3322 3676.

Cultour, R João Gomes, 88 Sala 8 Sobrado da Praça, Rio Vermelho, T071-3335 1062, www.cultour.it. Offer some of the best cultural tours in the city. Less 'touristy' than operators in the Pelourinho area.

Ilha Bela, Av da França, T071-3326 7158, www.ilhabelatm.com.br. Tours around the Baía de Todos os Santos and transfers to Morro de São Paulo.

Tatur Turismo, Av Tancredo Neves 274, Centro Empresarial Iguatemi, Salas 222-224, T071-3114 7900, www.tatur.com.br. Excellent private tours of the city and the state as well as general travel agency services including flight booking and accommodation. Can organize entire packages prior to arrival for the whole of Brazil. Good English, reliable. Owned by Conor O'Sullivan from Cork.

Ilha de Itaparica *p398, map p399*
Tour operators
Small boats for trips around the bay can be hired privately at the small port by the Mercado Modelo in Salvador. A pleasant trip out to the mouth of the bay should take 1½ hrs as you sail along the bottom of the cliff. When arranging to hire any boat check that the boat is licensed by the port authority (Capitânia dos Portos) and that there are lifejackets on board.

Companhia de Navegação Bahiana, T071-3321 7100. Sails 5 times a week to Maragojipe on the Rio Paraguaçu to the west (see page 401). The trip across the bay and up the valley of the river takes 3 hrs. There are some very beautiful views along the way with 2 stops. A good trip would be to continue to Cachoeira by bus from Maragojipe and return to Salvador the following day. Departures from Salvador from the Terminal Turístico in front of the Mercado Modelo, Mon-Thu 1430 (1530 in summer). Fri departure is at 1130. Departures from Maragojipe Mon-Thu 0500 and Fri 0830, US$4.50.

Steve Lafferty, R do Sodré 45, apt 301, T071-3241 0994. A US yachtsman, highly recommended for enjoyable sailing trips around Salvador, for up to 4 people.

Recôncavo Baiano *p400*
Guides Claudio, T075-3982 6080, a local tour guide, doesn't speak much English, but is friendly and knowledgeable.

⊖ Transport

Salvador *p382, maps p383, p387, p392 and p396*
Air
To get to the airport: a/c *combis* leave from Praça da Sé bus stop via the coast road and Barra 0630-2100, US$4, 1-1½ hrs (1 hr from

Barra). Ordinary buses 'Aeroporto' from the same stop cost US$1.50. A taxi to the airport costs around US$30 or US$35-40 after 2200 and on weekends and public holidays. Travel agencies and some hotels can also organize transfers.

There are domestic flights to all of Brazil's major cities, some with connections through **Recife**, **Belo Horizonte** or **São Paulo**; the best prices are usually to **Rio de Janeiro** and **São Paulo**. There are international flights to **Madrid** (3 times weekly with **Air Europa**), **Frankfurt** (once weekly with **Condor**), **Lisbon** (daily with TAP), **Milan** (once weekly with **Air Italy**) and weekly flights to **Miami** in the USA with **American Airlines**.

Airlines flying from Salvador include: **Abaete**, www.abaete.com.br; **Addey**, www.addey.com.br; **Aero Star**, www.aero star.com.br; **Avianca**, www.avianca.com.br; **Azul**, http://viajemais.voeazul.com.br; **Gol**, www.voegol.com.br; **Passaredo**, www.voe passaredo.com.br; **TAM**, www.tam.com.br; and **Webjet**, www.web jet.com.br. International flights are with: **Air Europa**, www.aireuropa.com; **Condor**, www10.condor.com; and TAP, www.flytap.com.

Bus

Local US$1.50, a/c *executivos* US$2, or US$3 depending on the route. On buses and at the ticket sellers' booths, watch your change and beware pickpockets (one scam used by thieves is to descend from bus while you are climbing aboard). Buses marked 'Barra' and 'Campo Grande-Praça da Sé' run between the Praça da Sé in the **Centro Histórico and Barra**. There are a number of lines including M024-00 and M024-01 (both via R Carlos Gomes, Av 7 de Setembro and Praça 2 Julho Campo Grande). To get between the airport and **Centro Histórico**, **Barra** and the beaches, catch the S002-00 'Aeroporto-Praça da Sé' bus, which leaves from the Praça da Se, passing **Av 7 de Setembro** (Centre), Av 7 de Setembro and Av Oceânica in Barra, Av Oceânica in Ondina, R Paciencia, R João

Gomes and R Osvaldo Cruz in Rio Vermelho, continuing on through **Amaralina**, **Pituba** and **Itapoã**, before turning in to the airport (1st bus 0500, last bus 2210). The 1002-00 'Aeroporto-Campo Grande' bus follows a similar route beginning at Av 7 de Setembro in the centre (1st bus 0545, last bus 2300). The most comfortable and quickest of these buses are the a/c *frescão*. For the **ocean beaches**, take buses S011-00, S011-01 and S011-02 marked 'Praça da Sé-Flamengo'. These run to **Flamengo beach** (30 km from the city), following the coastal route, passing through Campo Grande and Barra and all the best beaches (including Stella Maris and Itapoã), and leaving from Praça da Sé, US$3.50; sit on the right-hand side for the best views (1st 0600, last 1930). For **Bonfim** and **Ribeira**, take one of the following: Bus S021-00 marked 'Ribeira-Pituba' calls at Ribeira, R Imperatriz, next to the Igreja do Bonfim, Av da Franca 200 m north of the Mercado Modelo, Av Juracy Magalhaes Jr in Rio Vermelho and Pituba beach; 'Bus S027-00' marked Ribeira Campo Grande calls at Ribeira, the Ladeira do Bonfim near the church, R Itapicuru at R Jacuipe in Mont Serrat, Av da Franca 200 m north of the Mercado Modelo, R Carlos Gomes and the Av 7 Setembro in the centre and in Campo Grande (near the Mosteiro São Bento) and Av Setembro in Barra; Bus 0219-00 runs between Ribeira and the *rodoviária*, leaving from R Travas Fora in Bonfim. For more details on buses in Salvador visit www.transalvador. salvador.ba.gov.br/transporte.

Long distance To get to the *rodoviária* take bus RI or RII, 'Centro-Rodoviária- Circular' (US$1), from the lower city at the foot of the Lacerda Lift; the journey can take up to 1 hr especially at peak periods. On weekdays, a quicker executive bus (US$2) runs from Praça da Sé or Praça da Inglaterra (by McDonalds), Comércio, to **Iguatemi Shopping Centre** from where there is a walkway to the *rodoviária* (take care in the dark). Alternatively take a from the centre, US$15.

There are frequent services to the majority of destinations; a large panel in the main hall of the bus terminal lists destinations and the relevant ticket office. For bus information contact the *rodoviária*, Av Antônio Carlos Magalhães 4362, T071-3460 8300, daily 0600- 2200, and see www.itapemerim.com.br, www.aguiabranca.com.br, www.real expresso.com.br and www.gontijo.com.br.

To **Aracaju**, 3 daily (1st 0630, last 2200, 4½ hrs, US$29, leito US$35 with Bomfim). To **Belém**, US$55 *comercial* with Itapemirim. To **Ilhéus**, 8 daily, 7 hrs, US$36, *executivo* US$46, *leito* US$80 with Bomfim. To **Maceio**, 4 daily, 1st at 0630, last 2200, 4½ hrs, US$42, *leito* US$67 with Bomfim. To **Porto Seguro**, 1 daily at 2000, 10 hrs, US$77 with Aguia Branca. To **Recife**, US$90, 13 hrs, 1 daily and 1 *leito*, with Itapemerim, T071-3358 0037. To **Rio de Janeiro**, leaves at 0700 Mon-Sat, 26 hrs, US$125,*leito* US$145, with Itapemirim and Aguia Branca, good stops, clean toilets, recommended. To **São Paulo**, 30 hrs, US$120, US$155, with São Geraldo (Mon, Wed and Fri at 0830 and 1930, Sun, Mon and Sat at 2000), daily *leito* at 2200. To **Fortaleza**, 20 hrs, US$105 at 0900 with Itapemerim. To **Lençóis** at 2200, 6-8 hrs, US$30 with Real Expresso, via **Feira de Santana**, T071-3358 1591. To **Belo Horizonte**, Gontijo, T071-3358 7448, at 1700, US$120. There are also bus services to **Brasília** along the fully paved BR-242, via Barreiras, 3 daily, 23 hrs; **Palmas**, **Natal**, **João Pessoa**, **Penedo** (via **Maceio**), **Vitória** and **Teresina**. For the shortest route to **Valença**, take the ferry from São Joaquim to Bom Despacho on Itaparica island, from where it is 130 km to Valença via Nazaré das Farinhas (see page 399).

Car hire
There are various car hire booths in the airport: Hertz, www.hertz.com.br, Interlocadora, www.interlocadora.com.br, and Localiza, www.localiza.com.

Taxi
Meters start at US$1.50 and then US$0.70 per 100 m. They charge US$25 per hr within city limits, and 'agreed' rates outside. Taxi Barra-Centro, US$10 daytime; US$12 at night. Watch the meter; the night-time charge should be 30% higher than daytime charges. Teletaxi (24-hr service), T071-3321 9988.

Ferry and boat
See also Ins and outs, page 383, and Ilha de Itaparica, page 398. Boats and catamarans to **Ilha de Itaparica**, other islands in the Baía de Todos os Santos and to **Morro de São Paulo** leave from one of 2 ferry docks in Salvador's Cidade Baixa. From the main ferry dock, **Marítimo de São Joaquim**, Av Oscar Pontes 1051, T071-3254 1020, www.twbmar.com.br, there are 10 car ferries per day to **Itaparica** as well as catamarans to **Morro de São Paulo** (2 hrs). From Salvador's other boat terminal, the **Terminal Marítimo de Mercado Modelo** (or Terminal Marítimo Turistico), ferries and catamarans run to the **Baía de Todos os Santos**, including **Itaparica** around every 30 mins. Catamarans also run to **Morro de São Paulo**, 5 a day. See www.morrodesaopaulo.com.br for the latest ferry timetable.

Ilha de Itaparica *p398, map p399*
Ferry
There are regular ferry services to **Salvador**. The main passenger ferry leaves from Bom Despacho and runs to the **Marítimo de São Joaquim** ferry dock. The 1st ferry to Salvador is at 0515 and the last one at 2300, running at intervals of 45 mins, During the summer months the ferries are much more frequent. (Buses for Calçada, Ribeira stop across the road from the ferry terminal; the 'Sabino Silva– Ribeira' bus passes in front of the Shopping Barra). Enquiries at the Companhia de Navegação Bahiana (CNB), T071-3321 7100, open 0800-1700. A one-way ticket for foot passengers Mon-Fri is US$1, Sat-Sun US$1.20. There is also a catamaran service

which departs from Bom Despacho twice daily, US$3.

From Mar Grande a smaller ferry (*lancha*) runs to the **Terminal Marítimo**, in front of the Mercado Modelo in **Salvador**. The ferries leave every 45 mins and the crossing takes 50 mins, US$3 return.

Recôncavo Baiano *p400*
Bus To **Salvador** (Camurjipe) every hr from 0530. To **Feira Santana**, 2 hrs, US$3.

Directory

Salvador *p382, maps p383, p387, p392 and p396*
Banks Selected branches of major banks have ATMs (which accept Visa and Cirrus cards) and exchange facilities. All shopping centres, the bus station and the airport have branches of **Bradesco**, and there is a branch at R Chile 23, T071-3321 3154. Changing money at banks (open 1000-1600) can be bureaucratic and time-consuming. **Citibank**, R Miguel Calmon 555, Comércio, centre, changes TCs. Branch at R Almte Marquês de Leão 71, Barra, has an ATM. **Banco do Brasil**, Av Estados Unidos 561, Comércio, in the shopping centre opposite the *rodoviária* (also *câmbio* here), very high commission on TCs, at the airport on the 1st floor (Mon-Fri 0830-1530, 1600-2100 and Sat, Sun and holidays 0900-1600); branches in Barra, Miguel Bournier 4, in Shopping Barra and in Ondina. **Cultural centres** Associação Cultural Brasil-Estados Unidos, Av 7 de Setembro 1883, has a library and reading room with recent US magazines, open to all, free use of internet for 30 mins. **Cultura Inglesa**, R Plínio Moscoso 357, Jardim Pipema. German Goethe Institut, Av 7 de Setembro 1809, also with a library and reading room. **Embassies and consulates** France, R Francisco Gonçalves 1, sala 805, Comércio, T071-3241 0168 (Mon, Wed, Thu 1430-1700). Germany, R Lucaia 281, 2nd floor, Rio Vermelho, T071-3334 7106

(Mon-Fri 0900-1200). Holland, Av Santa Luzia, 1136 Edif, Porto Empresarial Sala 302, T071-3341 0410 (Mon-Fri 0800-1200). Italy, Av 7 de Setembro 1238, Centro, T071-3329 5338 (Mon, Wed, Fri 1500-1800). Portugal, Largo Carmo, 4, Sto Antonio, T071-3241 1633. Spain, R Mcal Floriano 21, Canela, T071-3336 1937 (Mon-Fri 0900-1400). Switzerland, Av Tancredo Neves 3343, 5th floor, sala 506b, T071-3341 5827. UK, Av Estados Unidos 4, 18B, Comércio, T071-3243 7399 (Mon-Thu, 0900-1100, 1400-1600, Fri 0900-1100). USA, R Pernambuco, 51 Pituba, T071-3345 1545 (Mon-Fri), 0900-1130, 1430-1630.
Immigration Polícia Federal, Av O Pontes 339, Aterro de Água de Meninos, Lower City, T071-3319 6082. Open 1000-1600. For extensions of entry permits show an outward ticket or sufficient funds for your stay, visa extension US$15. **Internet** There are numerous internet cafés throughout the touristy parts of the city. **Language courses** Casa do Brasil, R Milton de Oliveira 231, Barra, T071-3264 5866, www.casadobrazil.com.br. Portuguese for foreigners. Diálogo, R Dr João Pondé 240, Barra, T071-3264 0007, www.dialogo-brazilstudy.com, with optional dance, *capoeira* and cooking classes and accommodation arranged with host families. Superlearning Idiomas, Av 7 de Setembro 3402, Ladeira da Barra, T071-3337 2824, www.allways.com.br/spl. **Laundry** Kit Lavaderia, Av Amaralina 829, Amaralina. Laundromat, R Oswaldo Cruz, Rio Vermelho. Lav e Lev, Av Manoel Dantas da Silva 2364, loja 7. Unilave, Av Magalhães Neto 18, Pituba. **Medical services** Clinic, Barão de Loreto 21, Graça. Delegação Federal de Saúde, R Padre Feijó, Canela. Free yellow fever vaccinations.

Cachoeira *p400*
Banks Bradesco, in the main square, ATM accepts Visa credit but not debit cards, Mon-Fri 0830-1700. **Post office** In the main square, Mon-Fri 0900-1700.

The Cocoa and Dendê Coast

South of Salvador and the Reconcavo, Bahia descends in a series of glorious beaches, offshore islands and jungly peninsulas, many of them fringed with coral and mangrove or backed by endless kilometres of coconut palms. Sluggish tropical rivers undulate their way across lowland Bahia from the Chapada Diamantina ('diamond mountains') of the interior and interrupt the coastline, while potholed roads connect crumbling colonial towns like Ilhéus and Olivença, which grew fat on the cocoa and dendê oil trade but have since been slowly withering under the tropical sun.

The glorious coast is within easy reach of Salvador and every year an increasing number of tourists are discovering its forgotten fishing villages. The surf mecca of Itacaré is gradually turning chic. The expat community of Morro de São Paulo, on the island of Tinharé, is finding its beach haven is getting crowded; the nightlife here is notoriously lively. Those seeking seclusion should head for the Peninsula de Maraú, a little further south, or to the little-explored wild beaches beyond Una. ►► *For listings, see pages 426-433.*

Valença → *For listings, see pages 426-433. Colour map 4, A5. Phone code: 075.*

Although Valença has a few colonial buildings and two moderately interesting churches, it is essentially an ugly town. The best reason to come here is to take a boat to/from Tinharé, taking an hour or two perhaps to stroll around the dirty market and visit the church of **Nossa Senhora do Amparo**, from where there are good views out over the town, the estuary and the surrounding mangroves. Valença is in the middle of an area that produces black pepper, cloves and *piaçava* (used in making brushes and mats) but it markets itself as the prawn capital of Brazil, and smells the part. Other industries include the building and maintenance of *saveiros* (fishing boats).

Ins and outs
Long-distance buses arrive at the new **rodoviária** ① *Av Maçônica, T075-3741 1280*, while the old rodoviária is for local buses. There are frequent buses between Valença and Salvador. The fastest go via the island of Itaparica (two to three hours including the ferry). Avoid touts at the *rodoviária*; it's better to visit the friendly **tourist office** ① *at the port T075-3641 3311, http://valenca.ba.gov.br*, which has maps and transport information. Boats arrive from Tinharé hourly.

Tinharé and Morro de São Paulo → *For listings, see pages 426-433. Colour map 4, A5. Phone code: 075.*

Depending on whom you ask, Tinharé is either a single large island separated from the mainland by the estuary of the Rio Una and mangrove swamps, or a mini archipelago divided by estuaries, mangroves and an impossibly turquoise sea. Either way it's stunning: a semi-wild of bird-filled *Mata Atlântica* forest fringed with swaying coconut palms and white-sand beaches that until recently were known only to fishermen and a few intrepid Brazilian beach travellers. Before the 1990s the main town here, **Morro de São Paulo**, on the northern tip of the island, was one of the world's great secret tropical island getaways, together with Ko Phi Phi in Thailand and Zanzibar. Now it is rapidly going the same way as these two former Shangri-Las. It began with the Italians who built a string of small-scale but largely tasteful resorts. By the turn of the millennium, Spanish developers with gold Rolexes and nowhere left to turn into concrete on their own crowded coast, were rubbing their hands in glee. Fishermen's houses and environmental concerns are easily bulldozed out of the way by the power of the euro. Indeed many of the original fishermen who lived on the gorgeous beaches that line Tinharé have already been relocated to ugly makeshift villages in the interior. Every beach for 20 km south of town is now backed by hotels and Morro has become a veritable tourist hotspot.

Morro Town itself is dominated by a lighthouse and the ruins of an early 17th-century colonial fort, built as a defence against European raiders. However, this did not stop the Dutch and French using the waters around the island as hiding places for attacks on the Portuguese and even establishing bases here for brief periods of time.

Morro de São Paulo

Morro sits right at the northern tip of Tinharé. Boats from Salvador arrive at a jetty and travellers enter the town through the stone arch that once marked the gateway to the fortress. The battlements are now largely in ruin, perched on top of the craggy hill in front of a series of little streets that branch off a small colonial *praça*. The main thoroughfare runs south to the town's beaches. Another path runs north to the lighthouse and a ruined lookout post complete with cannon (dolphins can be seen in August) and inland to the village of **Gamboa**. From Gamboa it's possible to visit the **Fonte de Ceu** waterfall; make sure you check the tide times, or ask around for a guide. It's possible to take a boat from Gamboa back to Morro (US$10-15).

Morro has five beaches; are all idyllic but are quieter the further from town you go. There is swimming in the sea or in the saltwater coral pools that appear at low tide. The beaches are named prosaically: **Primeira** (first), **Segunda** (second), **Terceira** (third), **Quarta** (fourth) and **Quinta** (fifth). There are boardwalks and a heavy build-up of shacks, beach bars, restaurants and hotels all the way to Terceira. Primeira is barely a beach at all and has the bulk of the hotels. Segunda is a party beach and is very popular with 20-somethings. Quinta is the furthest from town and is the quietest with little noise but the gentle lap of the sea. Before deciding to walk all the way to Quinta (1½ to two hours) check the tide times as the beach gets cut off at high tide. On 7 September there is a big festival at Morro with live music on the beach.

Ins and outs

Getting there There are direct 20-minute flights from Salvador's airport to the third beach at Morro de São Paulo with **Addey Taxi Aereo** ① *T075-3652 1242, www.addey.com.br*, and **Aerostar Taxi Aereo** ① *T075-3652 1312*. Both fly three times daily and cost around US$90 return. Catamarans run from both of Salvador's ferry terminals (see page 383), taking around two hours US$27. Times vary according to the weather but there are usually several a day 0800-1400; check with the tourist office or **Catamarã Gamboa do Morro** ① *T075-9975 6395*. Part of the trip is on the open sea, which can be rough. There are also numerous water taxis. Modified fishing and speed boats also run from Salvador via Valença (which is connected to southern Bahia) and Itaparica. The website www.morrodesaopaulo.còm.br is a useful website with the latest boat times and general information in English, Spanish and Italian. There is a port tax of US$4 payable at the *prefeitura* on arrival to Morro and US$0.80 on leaving the island. It is resented by many. ►► *See Transport, page 432.*

Getting around Morro is tiny and the first four beaches are easily negotiable on foot. A walk from town to Quarta Praia takes around 40 minutes. Until 2008 all roads were sand or dirt tracks but there is now a partially paved section between the town and the beaches, and this is plied by regular VW buses, motorbikes and beach buggies. These leave from the **Receptivo**, a little café that marks the beginning of the road just behind the second and third beaches; it's not hard to find but if in doubt ask for '*Receptivo*' or '*a estrada*'. There are daily transfers to Boipeba by Toyota at 0930, bookable through hotels or the myriad agencies on the island.

Boat trips around Tinharé island can be organized through hotels or agencies in the village; a full day costs US$20-30. Most of these go in a clockwise direction around Tinharé, visiting Boipeba and the villages to the south (including Moreré), the offshore reef pools for snorkelling, followed by the tiny colonial town of Cairu on the mainland and the shores of the Mangrove-line Rio Cairu, before returning.

Best time to visit Morro is expensive between December and March and gets very crowded during public holidays and prices can more than double. Beware of drug dealers and robbery at the busiest times.

Tourist Information There is a tourist booth, **Centro de Informações ao Turista (CIT)** ⓘ *Praça Aureliano Lima s/n, T075-3652 1083, www.morrosp.com.br*. However, the website www.morrodesaopaulo.com.br is more useful and provides lists of agencies, hotels and other information in several languages.

Ilha de Boipeba → *For listings, see pages 426-433. Colour map 4, A5.*

Ilha de Boipeba, a few hours south of Morro, is a similar but far quieter island and with less infrastructure. Accommodation is grouped in three places: the little town on the banks of the Rio do Inferno where the ferry arrives; the adjacent beach, **Boca da Barra**, which is more idyllic; and the fishing village of **Moreré**, a 30-minute boat ride to the south (only possible at high tide). With just a few simple restaurants and a football field on the beach overlooking a beautiful turquoise bay, life here is tranquil even by Bahian standards. Expect to pay at least US$30 for a boat to Moreré. Walking along the beaches will take about two hours. Have your camera at the ready, bring sunscreen and go at low tide as there is a river to ford.

Ins and outs Boat trips leave daily from Morro de São Paulo at 0900; book through a travel agent or your hotel. The return journey costs around US$30, and you have to pay this even if you are intending to stay on the island. Tractors and 4WDs leave from Morro's second beach every morning at around 0800 (one hour, US$15), and return at midday; contact **Zé Balacha**, T075-9148 0343, or ask at your hotel.

South to Itacaré → *For listings, see pages 426-433. Colour map 4, A5.*

Ituberá and Camamu → *Phone code: 073.*

These two towns, which have yet to be overrun by seasonal visitors, are the first stop south on the bus route from Valença. Neither have good beaches but both have access to decent ones by boat. **Ituberá** is a tiny town sitting on a deep inlet; the most beautiful beach in the area, **Barra do Carvalho**, is two hours away by boat. Some 30 km further south, **Camamu** is tucked away in a maze of mangroves. It is the jumping-off point for the peninsula of Maraú; the next stretch of the Bahian coast in line for beach resort development. The town has a handful of pretty colonial buildings, including the 17th century church of **Nossa Senhora da Assunção**.

Itacaré beaches north to south

Do Pontal Immediately across the Rio de Contas from town and reached by passenger ferry. Long, deserted and stretching all the way to Barra Grande some 40 km away – if you're prepared to swim across rivers and camp out.

Coroinha At the harbour, urban and none too clean but with pretty views of the town and the 18th-century church of São Miguel, especially at sunset.

Da Concha Urban and with the bulk of the *pousadas*.

Do Resende A little bay with powdery white sand, swaying coconut palms and a handful of *pousadas*. 10 minutes' walk from Da Concha.

Tiririca The best surf beach in Itacaré, *pousadas* with a beatnik surfer crowd. 10 minutes' walk from Resende.

Do Costa A little bay with strong waves and reasonable surf. 10 minutes' walk from Tiririca.

Do Ribeira The end of the road from town. Very pretty with calm water and rainforest rising at each end. Beach *barracas* sell fish and snacks and there's a little stream for kids. 10 minutes' walk from Do Costa.

Prainha More private and accessible by trail from Ribeira. Good surf. In a protected area (US$1.50 entry fee). 20-30 minutes' walk from Do Ribeira.

Barra Grande and the Peninsula de Maraú → *Phone code: 073.*

This long thin peninsula stretches north from the town of **Maraú**, near Itacaré, towards the southern extremity of the island of Tinharé and is fringed with beautiful beaches along its entire length both on the ocean side and along the beautiful Baía de Camamu. The bay is lined with thick mangrove at its far southern end and sealed at **Tremembé**, with a plunging waterfall that cascades directly into the sea. The main centre of population is the little fishing village of **Barra Grande** at the tip of the peninsula, fronted by a glorious beach and yachts bobbing at the end of a pier. The sandy streets are lined with a handful of *pousadas* and shaded by *casuaring* and palms. Few non-Brazilian tourists make it here.

Ins and outs The peninsula is 200 km south of Salvador, 150 km north of Ilhéus. There is a small airport at Barra Grande, served by scheduled air taxis from Morro de São Paulo and Salvador. Boats run from Camamu to Barra Grande several times a day between October and March and once a day in the morning all year round (boats: one hour, US$3; *lancha*: 40 minutes, US$15). It's also possible to reach the peninsula by road from Itacaré.

Access is difficult to many of the Maraú beaches if you don't have a car (and only possible with a 4WD in wet weather), but some can be reached on foot or by taxi/*combi* from Barra Grande. Tractors run from the village to the more remote beaches further south. There are excellent two- to five-day tours with **Orbitá** (see page 432), leaving from Ilhéus or Itacaré. There are plenty of *pousadas* in Barra (see Sleeping, page 428); the website www.barragrande.net has lots of useful information.

Itacaré → *Phone code: 073.*

Itacaré is a pretty little surfer town at the far end of the Peninsula de Maraú surrounded by glorious forest-fringed beaches. Paulistanos decided it was cool at the turn of the millennium and a handful of beaches are now backed by some of Bahia's most exclusive (and increasingly oversized) resorts, such as **Txai**. Those close to the town itself are more hippy, with an informal surfer-dude feel and a mix of cheaper restaurants and places to stay and more fashionable spots for those swooping in for the evening. Much of the old town remains a simple fishing village whose houses in thick *gouache* shades huddle together under a golden sun around a broad harbour on the banks of the Rio de Contas.

Ins and outs The *rodoviária* is a few minutes walk from town. There are at least four buses a day from Ilhéus (one hour). Porters are on hand with barrows to help with luggage. For information contact the **Secretaria de Turismo de Itacaré** ① *T073-3251 2134, www.itacare.com.br*. *Pousadas* are concentrated on and around **Praia da Concha**, the first beach south of the town centre and the river. More deserted beaches lie along dirt roads to the south and north. To explore the area to the full you will need a car. If you speak some Portuguese, its worth taking the time to find your way to one of the smaller places. Itacaré is very busy with Brazilian tourists in high season but receives relatively few international visitors.

Ilhéus and around → *For listings, see pages 426-433. Colour map 4, A5. Phone code: 073. Population: 242,500.*

Everyone is happy to point out that Ilhéus is the birthplace of Jorge Amado (1912) and the setting of one of his most famous novels, *Gabriela, Cravo e Canela* (Gabriela, Clove and Cinnamon, 1958). Amado also chronicled life on the region's cocoa plantations in two novels, *Cacau* (1933), and the much better-known *Terras do Sem Fim* (The Violent Lands, 1942). A later novel, *São Jorge dos Ilhéus* (1944), continues the story.

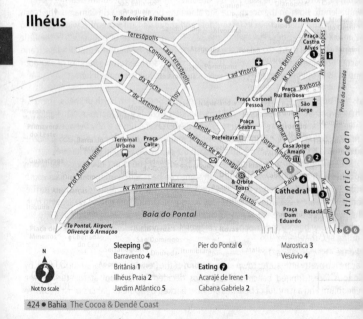

Ilhéus

To Rodoviária & Itabuna
To ④ & Malhado

Teresópolis
Conquista
Lad Teresópolis
da Rocha
F. Eloy
7 de Setembro

Lad Vitória
Berto Berito
M. Vitória
Av Soares Lopes

Praça Castro Alves ①

Praça Barbosa
Praça Rui Barbosa
Praça Coronel Pessoa
Tiradentes
Dantas
Praça Seabra
São Jorge

Dende
Marques de Paranaguá
Prefeitura

Terminal Urbana
Praça Cairu
Jorge Amado
Casa Jorge Amado ② ②

Prof Amélia Nunes
Av Almirante Linhares
& Orbita Tours
Pedro II Sta
Paiva
Cathedral ③

Baía do Pontal
E Bastos
Praça Dom Eduardo
Bataclã

To Pontal, Airport, Olivença & Armação
To ⑤ ⑥

Praia da Avenida
Atlantic Ocean

N
Not to scale

Sleeping 🛏
Barravento 4
Britânia 1
Ilhéus Praia 2
Jardim Atlântico 5
Pier do Pontal 6

Eating 🍴
Acarajé de Irene 1
Cabana Gabriela 2

Marostica 3
Vesúvio 4

Ilhéus's history stretches back to the earliest days of Portuguese colonization, when it was one of the captaincies created by King João III in 1534. Today the port serves a district that produces 65% of all Brazilian cocoa. Shipping lines call regularly. There are good views of the city from the **Convento de Nossa Senhora da Piedade**. Most tourists stay a day or so before heading north towards Itacaré or south towards Porto Seguro.

The town has a number of sights. The church of **São Jorge** ⓘ *Praça Rui Barbosa* (1556), is the city's oldest and has a small museum. The cathedral of **São Sebastião** ⓘ *Praça Dom Eduardo*, is a huge, early 20th-century building. In Alto da Vitória is the 17th-century **Nossa Senhora da Vitória**, built to celebrate a victory over the Dutch. The house where Jorge Amado grew up and wrote his first novel is now a small **museum** ⓘ *R Jorge Amado 21, 0900-1600, US$1*. Immortalized by Amado in *Gabriela, Cravo e Canela*, the **Bataclã** ⓘ *Av 2 de Julho 75, T073-3634 7835*, was once a famous bordello and poker palace. It was used by the region's powerful cacão *coroneis* and linked to other parts of the town by a series of secret tunnels, through which (presumably) the macho men would flee in fear of their wives.

Ins and outs The **airport** ⓘ *3 km from the centre, in Pontal on the south bank of the river, is linked to Ilhéus by bridge; taxi into town US$4*, receives flights from Salvador, Belo Horizonte, São Paulo, Brasília, Curitiba, Porto Seguro and Rio de Janeiro. The **rodoviária** ⓘ *R Itabuna, 4 km from the centre*, has regular bus connections with Salvador. However, the Itabuna–Olivença bus runs through the centre of Ilhéus. The **tourist office** ⓘ *on the beach opposite Praça Castro Alves*, is a few minutes' walk from the cathedral. Staff are friendly and can provide maps (US$2, recommended).

Around Ilhéus

The city beach itself is polluted but the beaches around the town are splendid and increasingly deserted the further you go. North of Ilhéus, two good beaches are **Marciano**, with reefs offshore and good surfing, and **Barra**, 1 km further north at the mouth of the Rio Almada. South of the river, the beaches at **Pontal** can be reached by Barreira' bus; alight just after the **Hotel Jardim Atlântico**. Between Ilhéus and **Olivença** are a number of fine beaches, including **Cururupe**, **Batuba** and **Cai n'Água** (in Olivença itself), both popular surf spots. The **Balneário de Tororomba** ⓘ *on the Rio Batuba, 19 km from Ilhéus, bus from São Jorge, Canavieiras or Olivença*, has ferruginous mineral baths.

From Ilhéus, buses run every 30 minutes to **Itabuna** (32 km), the trading centre of the rich cocoa zone; there are also many lumber mills. **Ceplac installations** ⓘ *Km 8, on the Itabuna– Ilhéus road, T073-214 3000, Mon-Fri 0830-1230*, demonstrates the processing of cocoa. Tours of cocoa plantations can be arranged through the **Ilhéus Praia** hotel (see Sleeping, page 430).

Also at Km 8, the Projeto Mico-Leão Baiano at the **Reserva Biológica de Una** ⓘ *www.ecoparque.org.br, book through Orbitá, see page 432*, was founded to protect the golden-faced tamarin. This is the wettest part of Bahia, most notably in October. Jeeps leave from the *rodoviária*. The reserve lies along a dirt road and most easily reached on a tour or by public jeep which leave when full from the *rodoviária*.

Beyond Ilhéus, the paved coastal road continues south through **Olivença** and **Una**, ending at **Canavieiras**, a picturesque town which benefited from the cocoa boom. It has several fine beaches worth exploring. A rough road continues from there to Porto Seguro.

For Sleeping and Eating price codes and other relevant information, see pages 32-37.

◉ Sleeping

Valença *p420*

A Portal Rio Una, R Maestro Barrinha, T/F075-3741 5050, www.portalhoteis.tur.br. Resort hotel by the riverside. Facilities include a pool, tennis courts and organized activities.
B Do Porto, Av Maçônica 50, T075-3741 3066. Clean, helpful, safe, good breakfast and a reasonable restaurant.
B Guabim, Praça da Independência, T075-3741 3408. Modest but well looked after with singles, doubles and triples.
D Valença, R Dr H Guedes Melo 15, T075-3741 1807. Simple hotel with plain but well-kept rooms and a good breakfast. Recommended.

Tinharé and Morro de São Paulo *p420*

In **Morro de São Paulo**, there are many cheap *pousadas* and rooms to rent near the Fonte Grande (fountain), but this part of town does not get a breeze at night.

There are 4 beaches next to Morro town, which are quieter the further from town you go. The 1st and 2nd beaches are designated party areas, with throbbing bars and shacks selling food and drinks well into the night. There are only *pousadas* and a few restaurants on the final 2 beaches. To reach the beaches turn right at the end of the main street; there is only one trail out of town. You'll have to walk as there are no cars on the island; porters can be hired to transport your luggage to the hotel in a wheelbarrow.
LL-A Hotel Vila dos Orixás, Praia do Encanto, T075-3652 2055, www.hotelvilados orixas.com. A Spanish-run *pousada* on one of Morros loneliest beaches with a series of spacious chalets set in a coconut garden, next to a pool and overlooking the beach. Very peaceful and romantic but a 30-min car ride from town. The hotel runs regular shuttles.

LL-A Pousada da Torre, 2nd beach, T075-3652 1038, www.pousadadatorre.com.br. A very tasteful little boutique hotel on the beach front which looks particularly enticing at night when both the building and the turquoise pool are mood lit under the palms. The plushest rooms are on the upper floor, are decked out in jaqueira wood and raw stone and have balconies with sea views behind big French windows. Rooms in the back annexe are a good deal cheaper, plainer but are large with king-sized beds and rich wood walls.
L-A Pousada Catavento, 4th beach, T/F075-3652 1052, www.cataventopraiahotel.com.br. One of the most luxurious and secluded of the hotels on the island, with well-appointed mock-colonial rooms arranged around a beautiful sculpted swimming pool, a decent restaurant and good service.
A Pousada Vistabella, 1st beach, T075-3652 1001, www.vistabelapousada.com. Good rooms, all with fans and hammocks. Rooms at the front have lovely views and are cooler. The owner Petruska is very welcoming. Recommended.
A-C Agua Viva, 3rd beach, T075-3652 1217, www.pousadaaguavivamorro.com.br. The best rooms in this simple *pousada* are at the front and have little balconies overlooking the beach. They have a/c, fridges and TVs, polished concrete floors and are decorated with art painted by the Morro owners.
A-C Fazenda Vila Guaiamú, 3rd beach, T075-3652 1035, www.vilaguaiamu.com.br. 7 tastefully decorated chalets of various sizes and styles set in their own tropical gardens and visited by marmosets, tanagers and rare cotingas. The hotel has a spa service with wonderful massage. The Italian photographe owner runs an ecotourism project protecting a rare species of crab, which live in the river that runs through the *fazenda*. Guided rainforest walks available. Excellent food. The best option for nature lovers.
B Farol das Estrelas, Terceira Praia, T075-8836 7088, www.faroldasestrelas.com. This squat, mock-colonial building huddled

in a busy terrace of *pousadas* and restaurants has modest a/c rooms, some of which have balconies overlooking the beach and all of which are painted in soft, warm colours and decorated with local paintings. Staff are helpful and speak English, French and Italian. A great breakfast.

B Pousada Colibri, R do Porto de Cima s/n, Centro, near the fountain. In Morro de São Paulo. One of the few that stays cool in this part of town. 6 apartments with pleasant sea views. The owner, speaks English and German.

B Pousada Farol do Morro, 1st beach, T075-3652 1036, www.faroldomorro.com.br. Little huts running up a steep slope. All are a little small but have a sea view and are reached by a private funicular railway. The pool sits perched on the edge of the hill. Brazilian-owned.

B-D Coqueiro Do Caitá, Terceira Praia, T075-3652 1194, www.coqueirodocaita.com. This little 2-storey hotel sits at the end of a leafy alleyway behind the beach and has a series of a/c rooms with little more than a bed and a fan, suites with a jacuzzi and a small swimming pool.

C Pousada Ilha da Saudade, 1st beach, T075-3652 1015, www.ilhadasaudade.com.br. Elegant hillside *pousada* with a beautiful pool with view, a small gym and deluxe suites with jacuzzis. Restaurant, bar and good breakfast.

C-D Hostel Morro de São Paulo, R Fonte Grande at the end of Beco dos Pássaros, T075- 3652 1521, www.hosteldomorro.com.br. This bright HI hostel with terraces slung with hammocks offers small dorms and doubles which are more expensive than those in nearby guesthouses), a tiny pool and a booking service for tours around Morro.

C-D Pousada Grauça, 3rd beach, T075-3652 1099, www.pousadagrauca.com.br. Simple but well-kept a/c and fan-cooled rooms with en suites in concrete *cabañas* away from the beach. Formerly called the 'Gradhia'. Recommended.

C-D Pousada Ilha do Sol, 1st beach, T075-3871 1295, www.pousadailhadosol.com. A big, blocky hotel with modest but well-kept rooms on long balcony corridors. The best have sea views. Generous breakfast.

C-D Tia Lila, 3rd beach, T075-3652 1532, www.pousadatialila.com.br. Very simple a/c rooms with television. Attentive, friendly service. Check a few rooms as some beds are spongy. Very good restaurant with delicious *moqueca de camarão*. Local-owned.

D PousadaTimbalada, Segunda Praia, T075-3652 1366, www.pousadatimbalada.com.br. A simple but welcoming guesthouse tucked away down an alley near party central on the 2nd beach. Small, brightly painted boxy rooms with hammock terraces and barely space for a backpack, and attractive raw stone and terracotta paint public areas.

Ilha de Boipeba *p422*

Accommodation is split between the little town where the riverboat ferry arrives, the adjacent beach, **Boca da Barra**, which is more idyllic, and the fishing village of **Moreré**, 30-mins' boat ride to the south (high tide only).

A Pousada Tassimirim, Tassimirim Beach (a 20 to 30-min walk south of town), T075-3653 6030, www.ilhaboipeba.org.br/en/tassimirim.html. A coconut grove off the beach shades terracotta-roofed bungalows, an al fresco bar, restaurant and pool and a garden visited by dozens of hummingbirds. The price includes breakfast and dinner. Secluded and very tranquil.

A-B Vila Sereia, Boca da Barra beach, T075- 3635 6045, www.ilhaboipeba.org.br/ vilasereia.html. Elegantly simple wooden chalets overlooking the beach. Breakfast on your own private veranda. Very romantic.

A-C Santa Clara, Boca da Barra beach, T075-3653 6085, www.santaclaraboipeba.com. Californian-owned *pousada* with the island's best restaurant and large, tastefully decorated duplex *cabañas*. Very good-value room for 4 (**D** per person). Superlative therapeutic massages available.

B-D Horizonte Azul, Boca da Barra beach, T075-3653 6080, www.pousadahorizonte azul.com. Pretty little *pousada* next door to Santa Clara, with a range of chalets from very comfortable to fairly simple. The hillside garden is visited by hundreds of rare birds from the nearby Atlantic coast rainforest. Very friendly owners who speak English and French. Lunch available.

D-E Geographic Hostel, Praça Santo Antônio 12, T075-3653 6104. This turquoise blue concrete family bungalow, set in gardens in Boipeba village has been converted into a small hostel with boxy dorms and doubles, a large sitting area and a terrace. There is Wi-Fi in public areas.

D-E Sete, Praça Santo Antônio, Boipeba village, T075-3653 6135. This family-run 3-room *pousada* in the village is one of the cheapest options in Boipeba and offers small but very well-maintained a/c rooms with tiled floors and whitewashed walls decorated with floral prints. The restaurant offers ultra-fresh seafood, including hearty *moquecas*.

Ituberá and Camamu *p422*

C Rio Acaraí, Praça Dr Francisco Xavier, T073-3255 2315, www.hotelrioacarai.com.br. Ugly modern *pousada* with a pool and restaurant.

D Tropical, Av Hildebrando Araújo Góes 270, Ituberá, T073-3256 2233. Standard, simple, small town *pousada* with a/c rooms, a restaurant, bar and pool.

E Green House, next to the *rodoviária*, T073-255 2178. Very basic and friendly with breakfast and a simple restaurant.

Barra Grande and the Peninsula de Maraú *p423*

LL Kiaroa, Praia Taipus de Fora, T073-3258 6213, www.kiaroa.com.br. The best of the peninsula's resorts, on a glorious beach, with a range of well-appointed rooms and an excellent restaurant, pampering and various organized activities.

L-AL Lagoa do Cassange, Praia do Cassange (Caixa Postal 23), Camamu, T073-3255 2348, www.maris.com.br. Cabins in a lawned garden between a wild stretch of beach and a lake populated with dozens of water bird species. A/c rooms have coffee-coloured walls, raw dark wood and wicker furniture. Bright raw cotton bedspreads, scatter cushions and rugs add splashes of colour. All have small verandas hung with hammocks.

The hotel practises sustainable tourism – supporting local communities and undertaking some recycling.

AL-A Taipú de Fora, Praia Taipus de Fora, T073-3258 6278, www.taipudefora.com.br. Small upscale mini-resort with a good range of activities including diving and kayaking. The beach is glorious, little-known but one of Bahia's very best, and buried here in text so that only discerning readers will discover it!

C El Capitan, Av Vasco Neto s/n, T073-3258 6078, www.elcapitan.com.br. Cabins in a garden decorated with rusting anchors and nautical bric-a-brac. All are basic in tile and concrete, have terracotta-tile roofs and hammock-slung terraces gathered around a pool a block from the beach at the mainland end of the town, 200 m from the pier.

C-D Eco Village Picaranga, Rio Picaranga, Peninsula de Maraú, T073-9973 9692, www.piracanga.com. A holistic beachside retreat on the south of the peninsula 6 km north of Itacaré, offering treatments, workshops, courses, excursions and alternative weddings. Profits are shared with the local community. Accommodation is in comfortable thatched-roof chalets and bungalows and there is a large maloca-like community space for meditation and movement, a sauna and a wholefood restaurant.

D Meu Sossego, R Dr Chiquinho 17, Barra town, T073-3258 6012, www.meusossego. com. 19 plain a/c rooms with fridges a stroll from the beach.

D Porto da Barra, R Beira Mar, T073-3258 6349, www.pousadaportodabarra.com. Family-run *pousada* right on the beach with simple concrete and tile a/c rooms in long annexes. The best are on the upper floor. Decent breakfast. Friendly owner.

Itacaré *p423*

The area is becoming very popular and prices are going up all the time. Book well ahead in high season.

LL Txai Resort, Praia de Itacarezinho, T073-2627 6363, www.txai.com.br. The most comfortable hotel around Itacaré, set on a deserted beach with very spacious and tastefully appointed bungalows overlooking a long, deep-blue pool shaded by its own stand of palms. Excellent spa and a full range of activities including diving and horse riding.

AL-A Art Jungle, T073-9996 2167, www.art jungle.org. A modern sculpture garden with 6 treehouses in the middle of the forest. All have views out to the sea and to the Rio de Contas. A favourite with celebrities such as Sean Penn, Jade Jagger and Gisele Bündchen.

AL-A Sage Point, Praia de Tiririca, T073-3251 2030, www.pousadasagepoint.com.br. Ocean-front *pousada* with smart wooden chalets in a tropical garden overlooking the sea, each with their own hammock-strewn terraces. Some are a little small but all have wonderful views. The Cuban owner, Ana, speaks English and can organize trips to nearby beaches.

AL-A Vila de Ecoporan, T073-3251 2470, www.villaecoporan.com.br. Brightly coloured spacious chalets gathered around a charming little pool in a hammock-filled garden. Between the town and Praia da Concha. Good Bahian restaurant.

AL-A Villa Bella, Praia da Concha, T073-3251 2985; www.pousadavillabella.com.br. A modern beach hotel with well-appointed rooms set in duplex garden cabins, decked out with wood-panel floors and sitting over a generous pool in a large lawned garden.

AL-A Vira Canoa, Praia da Concha, T073-3251 2525, www.viracanoa.com.br. Maroon bungalows overlooking a lush pool in a pretty garden. Each is decorated with arts and crafts and is filled with heavy wood furniture, plasma-screen TVs and iPod docking stations. The restaurant has good seafood and massages are available.

B-C Maria Farinha, T073-3251 3515, www.mariafarinhapousada.com.br. Simple family-run *pousada* in a concrete annexe overlooking a little pool. Pleasant *maloca*-shaped communal breakfast area, quiet and good for families. Disabled access.

B-C Nainas, Praia da Concha, T073-3251 2983, www.nainas.com.br. Rooms in these colourful cabins and annexes are simple but

comfortable – with little decks, splashes of colour from bedspreads and art and craft decor. They are set in a lush garden close to the beach.

B-C Pousada da Lua, Praia da Concha, T073-3251 2209, http://pousadadalua.com. A handful of terracotta-tile roofed chalets, some of which are large enough for 4 people set in a forest filled with marmosets and parakeets. Great breakfast.

B-C Sítio Ilha Verde, R Ataide Seubal 234, T073- 3251 2056, www.ilhaverde.com.br. These bungalows sitting in a verdant, flower-filled garden are painted in warm tones and are stylishly decorated with local arts and crafts. The largest have space for an entire family.

C-D Estrela, R Pedro Longo 34, Centro, T073-3251 2006, www.pousadaestrela.com.br. A range of well-maintained, pretty duplex chalets and bungalows with rustic wooden fittings and pastel colours on the walls. The *pousada* serves an excellent home-made breakfast with a huge choice. Staff are friendly and services include free Wi-Fi.

D-E Pedra Bonita, R Lodonio Almeida 120, T073-3251 3037, www.itacarehostel.com.br. Pleasant little HI hostel with small doubles and dorms (**E** per person) in an annexe, a small pool, internet and TV area. Friendly staff.

D-E Albergue o Pharol, Praça Santos Dummont 7, Itacaré, T073- 3251 2527, www.albergueopharol.com.br. A pleasant, well-kept hostel 10 mins' walk from the bus stop for Ilhéus in the centre of town and offering simple dorms, triples and doubles and public areas with heavy wooden furniture and lacy hammocks.

Camping

Tropical Camping, R Pedro Longo 187, T073-3251 3531. A small palm-shaded campsite in the centre of Itacaré town.

Ilhéus and around *p424, map p424*
There are plenty of cheap hotels in Ilhéus near the municipal *rodoviária* in centre; not all are desirable (check for hot-pillow establishments that rent rooms by the hour).

LL Fazenda da Lagoa, Rodovia BA-001, Una, T073-3236 6046, www.fazendadalagoa.com. br. Carioca Lia Siqueira and Mucki Skowronski's super-chic beach bungalows offer privacy and intimate designer luxury that lures celebrities. However, the real star here is the wilderness landscape: the vast, empty beach and pounding ocean; the adjacent rainforest and mangrove wetlands; and the beautiful river and lake. This area, as well as the nearby primate sanctuary at Una (see page 425) offers some of the best wildlife and birdwatching in coastal Brazil. Unfortunately the owners have little knowledge of natural history, so nature-lovers are advised to organize their own guides (with prior notice) through **Orbitá** in Ilhéus (see page 432).

A Hotel Barravento, on Malhado beach, R Nossa Senhora das Graças 276, Ilhéus, T/F073-3634 3223, www.barravento.com.br. The smartest hotel in the city. Ask for the penthouse (there is usually no extra charge), which includes breakfast and a fridge.

A Jardim Atlântico, Rodovia Ilheus-Olivenca Km 2, Jardim Atlântico, Ilhéus, T073-3632 4711, www.hoteljardimatlantico.com.br. One of Bahia's few luxurious beach hotels that not only welcomes children but provides kids' clubs, activities and a little water park. There are tennis courts, sauna, gym and activities for the adults. Rooms have their own little garden and hammock terraces and, thankfully, as the restaurant is a long way away, food is decent.

B-C Ilhéus Praia, Praça Dom Eduardo, on the beach, Ilhéus, T073-2101 2533, www.ilheus praia.com.br. A concrete block on the beach offering a/c tile floor rooms with low beds and sea views. Pool, helpful staff.

B-C Pier do Pontal, Av Lomanto Jr, Pontal 3.5 km, T073-3632 4000, www.pierdopontal. com.br. A small-scale beach hotel 20 mins' drive from town with a cluster of rooms in a 3-storey building overlooking a pool. Modern, decent service and a good option if you need to be in the city and have a car (or take a taxi).

C-D Britânia, R Jorge Amado s/n, Ilhéus, T073-3634 1722, www.brasilhotels.com.br/ britania_por.htm. The best value in the town

centre with large rooms in an early 20th-century wooden hotel just west of the cathedral square. Safe area with lots of restaurants.

🍴 Eating

Tinharé and Morro de São Paulo *p420*
There are plenty of restaurants in Morro de São Paulo town and on the 2nd and 3rd beaches. Most of them are okay though somewhat overpriced. For cheap eats stay in a *pousada* that includes breakfast, stock up at the supermarket and buy seafood snacks at the *barracas* on the 2nd beach.

🍴 Tia Dadai, Praça Aureliano Oliveira Lima, T075-3652 1621. Very tasty *casquinha de siri* (baked crab in its shell), and *filé de badejo a Portuguesa* (fillet of bream in tomato and onion sauce). In a great space on the main *praça*. Lively in the evening.

🍴 Tinharé, down a little set off steps off R Caminha de Praia, The food here bursts with flavour, especially the delicious *peixe escabeche* (fresh fish cooked in coconut milk and served in a sizzling cast-iron pot). The portions are so generous they serve for 2 or even 3.

🍴-🍴 Sabor da Terra, R Caminho da Praia, T075-3652 1156. A very popular lunchtime per kilo and à la carte evening restaurant serving great *moquecas* and sea food.

🍴 Pulcinella, 2nd beach. A tiny beach *barraca* run by Luciana from Valença, who serves great *beiju de tapioca*, juices, coffee and snacks, and is eternally cheerful.

Ilha de Boipeba *p422*
Boipeba has cheap eats in the town and surprisingly good food at the **Pousada Santa Clara** and the rustic restaurants in Moreré.

🍴 Santa Clara (see page 427), Boipeba. San Francisco panache in rustic but elegantly decorated tropical surrounds. Come for dinner. Highly recommended.

🍴 Mar e Coco, Moreré, T075-3653 6013. Very fresh seafood in idyllic surroundings, shaded by coconuts and next to a gently lapping bath-warm sea.

Itacaré *p423*

There are plenty of restaurants in Itacaré, most of them on **R Lodônio Almeida**. Menus here are increasingly chic and often include a respectable wine list.

††† Casa Sapucaia, R Lodônio Almeida, T073-3251 3091. Sophisticated Bahian food with an international twist from 2 ex-round-the-world sailors. Try the delicious king prawn caramelized with ginger.

††† Dedo de Moça, R Plinio Soares 26 (next to the São Miguel church), T073-3251 3391. One of Bahia's best restaurants. The chef was trained by Vagner Aguiar, who worked at São Paulo's award-winning **Laurent** restaurant, and her menu of dishes that combine Brazilian ingredients with French and Oriental techniques has been expanded by local chef Carol. Offerings include ultra-fresh fish encrusted with Brazilian nuts. Good cocktails at the little garden bar and a romantic atmosphere.

†† O Casarão Amarelo, Praia da Coroinha, T073-9996 0599. Swiss-owned restaurant in one of the most beautiful colonial buildings in the town. International menu which is good in parts. The fish is always a reliable choice.

† Beco das Flores, R Lodônio Almeida 134, T073-3251 3121. The busiest restaurant in Itacaré, serving good wood-fired pizzas in tastefully decorated surroundings to a well-dressed post-beach crowd.

† La In, R Lodônio Almeida 116, Centro, T073-3251 3054. Great little Bahian and seafood restaurant decorated with colourful art painted by the owner, Marcio, and serving very good value lunches and dinners. Be sure to try the house speciality: fish in prawn sauce baked in a banana leaf.

† O Restaurante, R Pedro Longo 150, T073-3251 2012. One of the few restaurants with a *prato feito*, alongside a mixed seafood menu.

Ilhéus and around *p424, map p424*

Specialities include the local drink, *coquinho*, a coconut filled with *cachaça*, which is only for the strongest heads. There are cheap eats from the various seafood stalls on the *praça* and near the cathedral.

††† Vesúvio, Praça Dom Eduardo, T073-3634 4724. Next to the cathedral, made famous by Amado's novel, now Swiss-owned. Very good but pricey.

†† Marostica, Av 2 de Julho 966, T073-3634 5691. Superior pizzas and pastas, the best in town and very popular on weekend evenings.

† Acarajé de Irene, Praça Castro Alves. Great traditional *acarajé* and other Bahian snacks. Long a local favourite; people come from all over the city just to eat here.

† Cabana Gabriela, R Rui Penalva 109, T073-3632 1836. Good *moquecas* and seafood dishes. Well known to locals as a great place for Bahian food.

Bars and clubs

Tinharé and Morro de São Paulo *p420*

There is always plenty going on in Morro. The liveliest bars are on the 2nd beach where you'll also find the throbbing **Pulsa** nightclub. These tend to get going after 2300 when the restaurants in town empty.

Ilha de Boipeba *p422*

Nightlife on Boipeba is limited to star-gazing or having a beer in town.

Itacaré *p423*

The liveliest bars of the moment are **Toca do Calango**, **Praça dos Cachorros** and **Mar e Mel** on the Praia das Conchas. The **Casarão Amarelo** restaurant becomes a dance club after 2300 on weekends. There is frequent extemporaneous *forró* and other live music all over the city and most restaurants and bars have some kind of music Oct-Apr.

Festivals and events

Ilhéus and around *p424, map p424*
17-20 Jan Festa de São Sebastião.
Feb Shrove Tue, Carnaval.
23 Apr Festa de São Jorge.

28 Jun Foundation day.
Oct Festa do Cacau.

▲ Activities and tours

Tinharé and Morro de São Paulo p420
Tour operators
There are numerous little agencies offering boat, beach and snorkelling tours around Morro and it's an idea to shop around for the best price. They include **Zulu**, T075-3652 1599, zuluturismo@ hotmail.com, www.morrodesaopaulo.com.br/b_zulu.html.

Peninsula de Maraú p427
Maris, T073-3255 2348, www.maris.com.br. Boat trips around the Baía de Camamu (including to the Tremembé falls and to the surrounding islands), trekking along the beaches (including a wonderful 2-day walk between the Praia do Pontal and the Rio Piracanga) and trips to small, traditional fishing villages such as the boat-building community of Cajaíba.

Ilhéus and around p424, map p424
Tour operators
Orbitá, R Marquês de Paranaguá 270, T073-3634 7700, www.orbitaexpedicoes.com.br. Organizes adventure trips, visits to Maraú and general tours. The guides are excellent and knowledgeable. The company also operates out of both Itacaré and Una on a pre-arranged pick-up scheme. Transfers can be arranged to **Fazenda da Lagoa** and throughout Bahia as far as the Chapada Diamantina.

⊙ Transport

Valença p420
Bus Long-distance buses run from the new *rodoviária* on Av Maçônica. Many buses a day to **Salvador**, 5 hrs, US$6, several companies, including **Aguia Branca** T075-3450 4400. **São Jorge** to **Itabuna**, 5 hrs, US$5, very slow. For

the shortest route to **Salvador**, take a bus via Nazaré das Farinhas to Bom Despacho (130 km), and take a ferry from there to the São Joaquim ferry terminal. To **Bom Despacho** on Itaparica, **Camarujipe** and **Águia Branca** companies, 16 a day, 1 hr 45 mins, US$3.60.

Ferry There are boats to **Gamboa** (1½ hrs) and **Morro de São Paulo** (1½ hrs) from the main bridge in Valença, 5 times a day (signalled by a loud whistle). The fare is US$2.50. The *lancha rápida* takes 25 mins and costs US$8. Only Salvador–Valença buses leaving 0530-1100 connect with ferries. If not stopping in Valença, get out of the bus by the main bridge in town, don't wait until you get to the *rodoviária*, which is a long way from the ferry. Private boat hire can be arranged if you miss the ferry schedule. A responsible local boatman is **Jario**, T075-3741 1681; he can be contacted to meet travellers arriving at the *rodoviária* for transfer to Morro. He also offers excursions to other islands, especially Boipeba. There is a regular boat from Valença to **Boipeba** on weekdays 1000-1230 depending on tide, return 1500-1700, 3-4 hrs.

Tinharé and Morro de São Paulo p420
Details on current flights and ferry times to Morro de São Paulo can be found on www.morrodesaopaulobrasil.com.br.
Air There are several daily direct flights from the 3rd beach at Morro de São Paulo to **Salvador**. These cost US$120-130 one way. Times vary seasonally and from year to year but are usually as follows: Salvador–Morro (0830, 1230, 1500, 1530), Morro–Salvador (0915, 1315, 1600, 1615). For further details ask your hotel to contact **Addey** T071-3377 1393, www.addey.com.br, **Aerostar**, T071-3377 4406, www.aerostar.com.br, or drop into the airport office next to the landing strip on Morro.
Ferry Several companies run catamarans from Morro de São Paulo to the Terminal Marítimo in front of the Mercado Modelo

in **Salvador** (1½-2 hrs). Times vary according to the season and weather but there are usually several a day 0800-1400; check with the tourist office or Catamarã Gamboa do Morro, T071-9975 6395. There are also water taxis.

Boats from Morro de São Paulo and Gamboa run to the main bridge in **Valença** (1½ hrs) 5 times a day, US$2.50 (see under Valença, above). There is also a *lancha rápida* which takes 25 mins and costs US$8. Private boat hire can also be arranged, contact Mario, T075-3741 1681 or book through your *pousada*.

Ilha de Boipeba *p422*
Boat Day-trips to the island run from Morro de São Paulo (see page 421). There is regular boat from Boipeba to **Valença** on weekdays 1500-1700, 3-4 hrs. Overnight excursions to the village are possible. Contact Zé Balacha, T075-9148 0343, or book through your *pousada* in Morro or Boipeba.

Barra Grande and the Peninsula de Maraú *p423*
Air There are scheduled air taxis from the airport at Barra Grande to **Morro de São Paulo** and **Salvador**.

Boat Boats run from Barra Grande to **Camamu** several times a day Oct-Mar and once daily year round (boats: 1 hr, US$3; *lancha*: 20 mins, US$15).

Itacaré *p423*
Bus Frequent buses to **Ilhéus** (the nearest town with an airport), 45 mins, US$7 along the newly paved road. To **Salvador**, change at Ubaitaba (3 hrs, US$3), Ubaitaba–Salvador, 6 hrs, US$12, several daily.

Ilhéus and around *p424, map p424*
Air A taxi from town to the airport costs US$8. There are flights to **Salvador**, **Belo Horizonte**, **São Paulo**, **Brasília**, **Curitiba**, **Porto Seguro** and **Rio de Janeiro** with GOL,

www.voegol.com.br, **TAM**, www.tam.com.br, and **Webjet**, www.webjet.com.br. Services are often cut back in low season.

Bus and boat Most long-distance buses leave from the *rodoviária*, 4 km from town. However, the **Itabuna–Olivença** bus goes through the centre of Ilhéus. Several buses run daily to **Salvador**, 7 hrs, US$30 (*leito* US$45, **Expresso São Jorge**), the 0620 bus goes via **Itaparica**, leaving passengers at Bom Despacho ferry station on the island (from where it is a 50-min ferry to **Salvador**). To **Itacaré**, 45 mins-1 hr, US$8. To **Eunápolis**, 4 hrs, US$25, this bus also leaves from the central bus terminal. Local buses leave from Praça Cairu.

Taxi Insist that taxi drivers have meters and price charts.

Directory

Valença *p420*
Banks There is a Bradesco and Banco do Brasil in town, which have ATMs and *câmbios*.

Tinharé and Morro de São Paulo *p420*
Banks There are no banks on the island, but there are Bradesco and Banco do Brasil ATMs in the town and cash dollars can be exchanged in *casas de câmbio* in the village.
Internet There is access in the town in several cafés.

Itacaré *p423*
Banks and internet Theres a Bradesco ATM in the Praça do Forum and a branch of Banco do Brasil at R 31 Março, T073-3251 2212, with a Visa ATM. The town has the usual plethora of internet cafés.

Ilhéus and around *p424, map p424*
Banks Bradesco, R Marquês de Paranaguá 8, T073-3234 5233 will change money and have Visa ATMs.

The Discovery and Whale Coast

The beaches of the far south of Bahia are among the finest in Brazil – long strands of fine white sand washed by bath-warm sea, or pounded by bottle-green surf and backed by swaying rows of coconut palms. Some are remote and completely deserted, others are watched over by busy resorts and party towns like Porto Seguro and Arraial d'Ajuda, or forgotten little villages like Caraíva, Corumbau and Curumuxatiba with only a handful of simple pousadas. Pretty Trancoso is perhaps the chicest beach destination north of Punta del Este in Uruguay, with a ream of gorgeous beach boutiques of the kind that grace the pages of Departures magazine or Taschen coffee-table books. Offshore, in the far south, are the Abrolhos: an archipelago of rocky coral islands fringed with reef. The islands form part of one of Brazil's most carefully protected marine reserves and are one of the best places in South America for seeing humpback whales. Back on the mainland, Bahia's far south is dotted with indigenous Pataxó villages and has extensive areas of Mata Atlântica rainforest. This area, around the pyramidal mountain at Monte Paschoal, is under threat from eucalyptus plantations used to produce toilet paper.

The Discovery Coast takes its name from the first landing by the Portuguese. In AD 1500, Pedro Álvares Cabral became the first European to see Brazil, sighting land at Monte Pascoal south of Porto Seguro. The sea here was too open to offer a safe harbour, so Cabral sailed his fleet north, entering the mouth of the Rio Burnahém to find the harbour he later called 'Porto Seguro' (safe port).

▶▶ *For listings, see pages 443-452.*

Porto Seguro → *For listings, see pages 443-452. Colour map 4, B5. Phone code: 073. Population: 96,000*

Modern Porto Seguro is rapidly developing into southern Bahia's largest and most cosmopolitan coastal city, with residents from all over the world. Located on the Rio Buranhém, which separates the city from Arraial across the water, the attractive dockland area retains a handful of pretty colonial houses.

On the hill above is the higgledy-piggledy **Centro Histórico**, a peaceful place spread out on a grassy slope, with lovely gardens and panoramic views. Brazil began here – on the far side of the grassy square is a block of Cantabrian marble engraved with the Cross Of The Order Of Christ and marking the spot where the conquistador Gonçalo Coelho formally took the Discovery Coast (and by extension the country) from the Tupiniquim people in 1503. Brazil's oldest church sits behind: the **Nossa Senhora da Misericórdia** ① *Praça Pero de Campos Tourinho, T073-3288 5182, Sat-Wed 0930-1330 and 1430-1700, free*, a squat, functional little building in paintbox blue, built in 1526, with heavy fortified walls and a little scrolled Rococo pediment added like a cake decoration. Nearby, and sitting in the ruins of a monastery ransacked by the ancestors of the modern Pataxó, is the Jesuit church of **São Benedito** ① *R Dr Antônio Ricaldi s/n*, built in 1549 with even more heavily fortified walls and the church of **Nossa Senhora da Pena** ① *Praça Pero de Campos Tourinho s/n, T073-3288 6363, daily 0900-1200 and 1400-1700, free*, dating from 1708, but built over another fortified 16th-century structure. Inside is what is said to be the oldest statue in Brazil – an undistinguished effigy of St Francis of Assisi. Next door is the sacred art museum and former jail – the handsome 18th-century **Casa de Câmara e Cadê** ① *Praça Pero de Campos Tourinho s/n, T073-3288 5182, daily 0900-1700, free.*

Ins and outs

Getting there **Aeroporto de Porto Seguro** ⓘ *Estrada do Aeroporto s/n, 2 km north of town, T073-3288 1880*, has connections with Rio de Janeiro, São Paulo, Belo Horizonte, Ilhéus, Salvador, Porto Alegre, Brasília, Curitiba and Vitória. There are banks and a car rental booth in the terminal. A taxi to the centre costs US$8. The **rodoviária** ⓘ *2 km west of the centre, on the road to Eunápolis*, receives direct buses from Ilhéus, Salvador, São Paulo and Rio de Janeiro (direct bus at 1600). Other buses go via via Eunápolis, which has connections with Porto Seguro every 30 minutes (US$5, one hour). The *rodoviária* has cafés and snack bars. Taxis charge US$6 to the town or ferry (negotiate at quiet times). ▶▶ *See Transport, page 450.*

Getting around Buses run throughout the city from the waterfront to the to the old *rodoviária* near the port every 30 minutes, US$0.50. Regular buses run along the seafront from Praça dos Pataxós to the northern beaches, or take a bus to Porto Belo or Santa Cruz Cabrália from the port. For beaches south of the Rio Buranhém, see Arraial d'Ajuda (below) and points further south.

Tourist Information The tourist office, **Secretária de Turismo de Porto Seguro** ⓘ *R Pero Vaz de Caminha 475, Centro, T073-3288 3708, www.portosegurotur.com.br*, has information on tours. Alternatively, contact **Portomondo**, www.portomondo.com. ▶▶ *See Arraial de Ajuda Activities and tours, page 450.*

North of Porto Seguro → *For listings, see pages 443-452.*

Heading north of town, on the BR-367 to Santa Cruz Cabrália (known as Avenida Beira Mar), is Bahia's second most popular tourist area, with a series of hotels and beaches. The best beaches are **Itacimirim**, **Curuípe**, **Mundaí** and **Taperapuã**, which have some lively *barracas*. The biggest (and busiest) are **Barra Point**, **Toá Toa**, **Axé Moi**, **Vira Sol** and **Barramares**. The latter are mainly Brazilian package-tour destinations and offer jet-ski hire and other watersports facilities.

Porto Seguro

CIDADE HISTÓRICA

Farol
NS da Pena
NS da Misericórdia
Gonçalo Coelho Monument
Praça Pero Campos Tourinho
NS do Rosário
Av Beira Mar BR 367
Praia do Cruzeiro
To 🏨 & Santa Cruz de Cabrália
To Airport
Av dos Navegantes
Av 22 de Abril
R 15 de Novembro
R Mal Deodoro da Fonseca
R Cova da Moça
R da Faca
R do Cajueiro
R do Golfo
Banco do Brasil
R Pero Vaz de Caminha
R Antônio Osório
R Batista
Praça Imalá
NS do Brasil
Praça Visconde de Porte Seguro
R Getúlio Vargas
Bradesco
R 2 de Julho
R PA
R São Pedro
Cabral
Praça Chateaubriand
Rio Buranhém
Praça da Bandeira
Praça dos Pataxós

N

00 metres
00 yards

Sleeping
Albergue Porto Seguro 7
Camping Mundaí Praia 9
Estalagem Porto Seguro 1
Navegantes 2
Pousada Casa Azul 3
Pousada dos Raizes 6
Solar da Praça 4
Solar do Imperador 10
Tabapiri Country 8
Vela Branca 5
Xurupita La Torre 11

Eating
Da Japonêsa 2
Portinha 3
Sambuca 1

A few kilometres before Cabrália, a tourist village, **Coroa Vermelha**, has sprouted at the site of Cabral's first landfall and a cross marks the spot where the first Mass was celebrated. It has a rather uncoordinated array of beach bars, hotels, rental houses and souvenir shops selling indigenous Pataxó items. Buses from Porto Seguro take about 20 minutes.

Santa Cruz Cabrália → *Phone code: 073. Colour map 4, B5.*

About 10 minutes north of Coroa Vermelha (25 km north of Porto Seguro), Santa Cruz Cabrália is a delightful small town at the mouth of the Rio João de Tiba. It has a lovely beach, river port, and a 450-year-old church with a fine view. It is believed to be the site of the first landing in Brazil by the Portuguese explorer Pedro Álvares Cabral in 1500. A good trip from here is to **Coroa Alta**, a reef 50 minutes away by boat. It passes along the tranquil river to the reef with crystal waters and good snorkelling. There is a daily departure at 1000. A recommended boatman is Zezé (T/F073-3282 1152), who can usually be found on the square by the river's edge; he is helpful and knowledgeable. The trip costs around US$25 without lunch.

A 15-minute river crossing by ferry to a new road on the opposite bank gives easy access to the deserted beaches of **Santo André** and **Santo Antônio**. As yet, few tourists make it to here, but the new road is certain to change this. Hourly buses run between Santa Cruz and Porto Seguro (23 km).

Estação Veracel Veracruz

ⓘ *Rodovia BR-367 Km 37; T073-3166 1535, T073-8802 0161, www.veracel.com.br/veracruz, pre-booking necessary for visits Tue and Thu 0830-1630 and Sat 0830-1130.*

This 6000-ha private reserve half way between Santa Cruz Cabrália and Porto Seguro is one of the best locations in southern Bahia for wildlife- and birdwatching. There are some 307 species of birds (with 21 threatened or endangered species and 32 endemics) and 40 mammals (including tapir, jaguar, thin-spined arboreal porcupine, brown howler monkey, Geoffroy's marmoset, crested capuchin and coastal black-handed titi monkey). There are scores of reptiles and amphibians and bird-watching is excellent, with rare species such as the red-billed curassow and banded and white-winged cotingas. This is one of the few locations outside the

Around Porto Seguro

▲ To Itabuna & Salvador

Guaiú
Santo Antônio
Santo André
Santa Cruz Cabrália
Eunápolis   Estação Veracel Veracruz   Ponta do Mutá
                 Coroa Vermelha   Recife de Fora
BR 367   Taperapuã
            Jaqueira Pataxó   Mundaí
Rio Buranhém   Porto Seguro   Curuípe
Parque Nacional ♦ Arraial da Ajuda   Araçaipe
do Pau-Brasil   Mucugê
Itabela   Parracho
                    Rio da Barra   Pitinga
Rio dos Frades   Lagoa Azul
                                              Taípé
            Monte Pascoal Trancoso   Nativos
                                              Coqueiros
                                              Itapororoca
                           Espelho
            Caraíva
        Parque Nacional
        de Monte Pascoal
                           Corumbau
Itamaraju   ● Barra do Caí
BR 101
Curumuxatiba

Praia das Ostras

Prado   Atlantic
                           Ocean
Guaratiba

Rio Itanhém Alcobaça   Abrolhos Islands
                           (70km from Caravelas)
                                    N

                           Barra de
                           Caravelas
Caravelas   20 km
                           20 miles

To Teixeira de Freitas, Linhares & Vitória

To Teixeira de Freitas

To Reserva Nacional Marinho dos Abrolhos

The Pataxó

"This is our land. You have to respect the land you are walking on because it is ours. When you arrived here this land was already ours. And what did you do to us? You stopped our progress with riot squads, gunfire and tear gas. With our blood we commemorate once more the Discovery of Brazil". (Pataxó indigenous leader during the response to the celebration of Brazil's discovery in 2000.)

The Pataxó are descendants of the Gê speaking warrior tribes who lived in the mountains along the Bahian coast, and who inflicted the heaviest defeats on the Bahian Portuguese in the first years of the colony. Since contact was made the tribe have suffered greatly. The greatest destruction was in 1951 when one of the most important villages was, ostensibly, caught in a gun battle between bandits and police. Hundreds of Pataxó, including women and children, were murdered. The Pataxó had long been campaigning to have their tribal lands in the Monte Pascoal national park returned to them. The battle was part of a concerted and ongoing effort to rid the Pataxó of their ancestral lands. In 1961 the federal government converted 22,500 ha of land traditionally occupied by the Pataxó into the Monte Pascoal National Park. The Pataxó were violently evicted. Much of their territory was later ceded to big landowners for farming cacau and planting eucalyptus. On 19 August 1999, numerous indigenous Pataxó people set up camp at the national park, declaring that 'Monte Pascoal belongs to the Patoxó' and demanding the transformation of 'what the authorities call Monte Pascoal National Park into an indigenous park, the land of the Pataxó, to preserve it and to rehabilitate it'. Another Pataxó group, the Pataxó

Hã-Hã-Hãe were treated equally badly. By the 1970s they had been shunted around from one piece of land to another as successive farmers and land speculators moved into the area, eventually settling on the São Lucas ranch where they were denied proper access to drinking water and consistently persecuted. Whilst prospects remain bleak for the Pataxó they continue to fight to preserve their cultural identity. In the new millennium, two remarkable Pataxó sisters began a cultural renovation project in their village of Jaqueira. They re-introduced the Pataxó language, traditional agricultural methods and implemented an ecotourism project to provide income for the community. Young Pataxó people have found new pride in their culture rather than leaving the community. And the tribe are utilizing the tools of the outside world to strengthen their voice. They were instrumental in a change in the Brazilian law in 2008 which declared that "the study of the history and culture of African-Brazilian and Indigenous Brazilian culture ... would be mandatory". The journalist Aricema Pataxó of the University of Bahia publishes a blog on the Pataxó (http://aricemaindiosdabahia. blogspot.com). A visit to Jaqueira is one of the highlights of a journey through southern Bahia (see page 438). And meanwhile the Pataxó continue to lobby for the right to live on their ancestral lands. The World Rainforest Movement have details on their latest effort (www.wrm.org.uy) and provide international support for their campaign. For further information see http://pib.socioambiental.org/ en/povo/pataxo-ha-ha-hae, http://www.indiosonline.org.br/novo.

Amazon where Harpy eagles are known to nest. Specialist birding tours are available with Ciro Albano (see page 450).

Jaqueira Pataxó village

Some 8 km north of Porto Seguro, the beautiful and inspiring *Pataxó* indigenous reserve of Jaqueira is well worth a visit. Its traditional houses lie in the heart of a stand of native-owned rainforest. All the food is either grown or hunted using traditional techniques. And a small craft shop selling beautiful ceramics, sacred incense and art provides extra revenue. The project was conceived by two impressive *Pataxó* sisters who despaired at the loss of *Pataxó* culture in the villages of southern Bahia. Their eco-tourism and cultural recuperation model has completely rejuvenated *Pataxó* culture. Young people are speaking their own language again and rediscovering their identity. It is possible to visit or even stay in the village. Trips can be organized with **Portomondo**, www.portomondo.com, who work closely with the *Pataxó*. For further information visit www.rabarsa.com/pataxo.

South of Porto Seguro → *For listings, see pages 443-452. Colour map 4, B5.*

Arraial da Ajuda → *Phone code: 073.*

A five-minute float across the Rio Buranhém from the docks at Porto Seguro brings you to Arraial da Ajuda, a pretty little colonial village turned beach-party town and a more popular base for travellers than Porto. Arraial is an ideal place to get stuck, with a string of gorgeous beaches that begin at the mouth of the river at **Araçaipe** and continue south indefinitely. The little hotels behind the sand are on a far smaller scale than Porto's package-tourist towers and cater to shallow as well as deep pockets. The town itself has a string of pleasant little bars and restaurants; all of which are easily manageable on foot. Arraial is also one of the best places in Brazil to learn capoeira. At Brazilian holiday times (especially New Year and Carnaval) it is very crowded, almost to bursting point

The town centre is clustered around the pretty 16th-century church of **Nossa Senhora da Ajuda** (1549), which sits high on a cliff, affording great views of the palm-covered coast. The principal streets extend off the square in front of the church. The largest, which is lined with shops, bars, restaurants and *pousadas*, is called Broadway. There's a party here or on one of the beaches almost every night in high season.

Arraial's beaches are splendid: some pounded by surf, others are little bays gently lapped by an Atlantic tamed by offshore reef. Most have *barracas* selling good simple seafood and chilled drinks, and playing music. From north to south they are as follows. **Araçaipe** is popular with families and day-visitors from Porto, and has several pretty beach hotels and *pousadas*. **D'Ajuda** is in front of the town and has a small protected area **Mucugê** just to the south of town, has good surf, plenty of beach *barracas* for forró and lambada parties in the summer. To reach these, take Rua da Praia out of town. South beyond Mucugê is **Parracho**, which is popular for windsurfing and kayaking (rental available); followed by **Pitinga**, with strong waves breaking on the offshore reef creating some decent surf. The penultimate beach is **Lagoa Azul**, backed by cliffs, with gorgeous sand and strong surf. Few make it to the beach farthest south, **Taipé**, an hour's walk from Arraial. It is backed by sandstone cliffs and has glassy water and a handful of *barracas*. At low tide it is possible to walk to from Taipé to Trancoso (see below) along the beach via the village of **Rio da Barra**; allow two hours. A dirt road behind the beach follows the same route and is plied by taxis and cars; it is easy to hitch a lift.

Ins and outs Ferries from Porto Seguro run across the Rio Buranhém to the south bank, every 30 minutes day and night (three minutes, US$0.60 for foot passengers, US$5 for cars). From there, it is a further 5 km to Arraial da Ajuda town centre (US$1 by bus, *combis* charge US$1.50 per person, taxis US$5), although the first *pousadas* are literally on the Arraial river bank. It is not necessary to return to Porto Seguro to venture into the rest of Bahia. Arraial is connected by bus to Eunápolis and Caraíva, and Trancoso to the south. Various agencies in town offer transfers by buggy or Land Rover to Corumbau and beyond all the way to Abrolhos. **Portomondo** (see Activities and tours, page 450) is by far the best and most reliable.

Trancoso → *Colour map 4, B5. Phone code: 073.*

In the last five years this once-sleepy little village, 15 km south of Arraial, has become Bahia's chicest beach destination, beloved of the Brazilian and international jet-set for its combination of low-key atmosphere and high-fashion labels. The coolest São Paulo names fill the tiny shopping centre and the town and beaches are dotted with smart designer boutiques and haute-rural restaurants offering the best food outside Rio de Janeiro and São

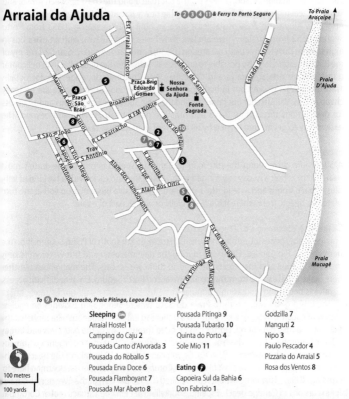

Arraial da Ajuda

To ② ③ ④ ❶ & Ferry to Porto Seguro
To Praia Araçaipe

Est Arraial Trancoso
R do Campo
Manoel A dos Santos
Praça São Brás
Broadway
Praça Brig Eduardo Gomes
Nossa Senhora da Ajuda
Ladeira de Santa
Fonte Sagrada
Beco do Jeque
Estrada do Arraial
Praia D'Ajuda
R FM Nobre
R CA Parracho
R São João
Trav S Antônio
R Vista Alegre
R Capoeira
R Iequitiha
R do Ipê
Alam dos Flamboyant
Alam dos Oitis
Est do Mucugê
Est Alto do Mucugê
Est da Pitinga
Praia Mucugê

To ⑨, Praia Parracho, Praia Pitinga, Lagoa Azul & Taipé

N
100 metres
100 yards

Sleeping
Arraial Hostel 1
Camping do Caju 2
Pousada Canto d'Alvorada 3
Pousada do Roballo 5
Pousada Erva Doce 6
Pousada Flamboyant 7
Pousada Mar Aberto 8

Pousada Pitinga 9
Pousada Tubarão 10
Quinta do Porto 4
Sole Mio 11

Eating
Capoeira Sul da Bahia 6
Don Fabrízio 1

Godzilla 7
Manguti 2
Nipo 3
Paulo Pescador 4
Pizzaria do Arraial 5
Rosa dos Ventos 8

Paulo. Celebrities come here to be recognized only by those they wish to be recognized by, especially the Mario Testino set. Despite its status, Trancoso remains a simple little town at heart, and herein lies its charm. It is glossy but intimate, with life focusing on the **Quadrado**, a long grassy square where locals play football in the evening. The square is crowned with the little whitewashed 17th-century church of **São João Batista**, and lined with colourful little *casas*, each housing a bikini boutique, crafts shop, fashionable restaurant, bar or guesthouse. The houses are particularly enchanting at night, when they contrast with the dark indigo canvas of the rainforest, under a dome of stars.

Below the Quadrado are a stretch of beaches extending away to the north and south. The most famous and the closest to town are **Praia do Trancoso** and **Praia dos Nativos**, both washed by gentle waves, with coral far off shore and a cluster of chic-shack *barracas* that host parties for the designer-label brigade during the summer months. **Coqueiros** across the little river to the north is quieter, with one simple restaurant and a view. To the south beyond Trancoso beach are **Rio Verde**, with a little river, and beyond it **Itapororoca** a deserted beach with just a few very expensive houses and good clear-water snorkelling.

Ins and outs In high season, *combis* ply the dirt road along the coast between Arraial and Trancoso, leaving when full. Buses run along the newly paved road between Porto Seguro, Arraial de Ajuda and Trancoso at least once an hour in high season (US$3 from Porto Seguro, US$2 from Arraial). There are two daily buses from Caraíva; with an extra bus in high season. Taxis from Arraial cost around US$30; from Porto airport US$40-50. Like any of the Bahian resorts, It is also possible to organize air taxis from Rio or São Paulo or helicopter transfers from Arraial, Caraíva and Corumbau. See **Portomondo**, page 450, for details. Trancoso can be packed out in high season. Be sure to book ahead. There are no really cheap rooms. Various tour operators around the main square sell *combi*, bus and air tickets for destinations throughout Bahia and organize day trips to Espelho and beyond. The easiest way to get around town is by bike, on foot or motorbike taxi.

Espelho

A 50-minute drive along the dirt road to Caraíva, Espelho is one of the state's most beautiful beaches: a glassy bay fringed with white sand and rocks with a handful of very plush beach hotels and a delightful restaurant. The Caraíva bus will drop you at the turn off to the beach, from where it is a 5-km walk; or visit as part of a tour.

Caraíva → *Colour map 4, B5. Phone code: 073.*

This incredibly peaceful, atmospheric fishing town, 65 km south of Porto Seguro, is on the banks of the Rio Caraíva. Electricity (during the daytime only) and hot water were only installed in 2008 and the streets are sand so there are no cars. The marvellous beaches here make a real escape from Trancoso, Arraial and Porto Seguro. Despite difficult access Caraíva is becoming increasingly popular.

There is a good walk north to **Praia do Satu** (where Señor Satu provides an endless supply of coconut milk), or 6 km south to a rather sad Pataxó indigenous village; watch the tides as you may get cut off. Horses can be hired through any of the *pousadas* and buggy rides to Corumbau (from where buses connect to Cumuruxatiba) can be organized from the town square with the Pataxó (US$40). Or you can walk the 12 km along the beach to the river that separates Caraíva's last beach with Corumbau village; there is a boatman here for crossings (US$2, 10 minutes). Boats can be hired (US$50 per day) at the river port in Caraíva for excursions to Caruípe beach, Espelho, snorkelling at Pedra de Tatuaçu reef or Corumbau (take your own mask and fins), or for trips up the beautiful river Rio Caraíva which gets into wild, pristine rainforest some 10 km inland. **Prainha** river beach, about 30 minutes away, and mangrove swamps can also be visited by canoe or launch.

Ins and outs Caraíva is connected to Trancoso by two daily (three in high season), along a very poor dirt road. The journey involves a river crossing and can take as long as three hours in the wet season (April to June). If arriving by bus from the south, change buses in Itabela (departs at 1500), or take a taxi; about 50 km. The high season is December to February and July. There are plenty of cheap *pousadas* and restaurants along the rustic sandy streets. Most bars have live *forró* in the summer. Flip-flops are best for walking along the sand streets, and take a torch as it is very dark at night.

Parque Nacional de Monte Pascoal
① *16 km north of Itamaraju, Caixa Postal 076, CEP 45830-000, Itamaraju, T073-3281 2419.*
The national park was set up in 1961 to preserve the flora, fauna and birdlife of the coast where Europeans first landed in Brazil. There is a bus from Itamaraju at 0600 (Monday to Friday); taxis run from Itamaraju cost around US$50 for the round trip including waiting time. Or the park can be visited with a tour group such as **Portomondo**, see page 450.

Corumbau
This tiny fishing village sits on a little promontory of land that sticks out into the deep blue of the Bahian Atlantic. It's a one-beach buggy town, with a tiny church and a handful of very cheap *pousadas* and restaurants; but it is fringed with beaches every bit as gorgeous as any of those around Caraíva or Trancoso. There is great snorkelling from the beach to the south of town. Foreigners are few and far between, except for a handful who come to stay at the exclusive and beautifully designed resorts to the south of the town.

Ins and outs Corumbau is not easy to reach. The best way is to organize a transfer with an agency like **Portomondo** (see page 450). However, it is possible to get here by catching the bus to Caraíva and then either sharing a buggy ride from the main square (US$40) or walking the 12 km to the river and catching the ferry boat (see above). There is one daily bus from Itamaraju.

Cumuruxatiba → *Colour map 4, B5. Phone code: 073.*
The road from Itamaraju leads to Cumuruxatiba (www.cumuru.com.br), which is also connected to Corumbau (and across the river to Caraíva) via a dirt road. In low season, Cumuruxatiba is a sleepy local beach resort; in high season it is a lively, young party town, popular with families and 20-something groups from the south of Brazil. There are plenty of little *pousadas* and restaurants. As yet the region is unspoilt and there are some almost completely deserted beaches both to the north and south, great for hours of wandering.

Ins and outs Cumuruxatiba is 29 km south of Corumbau and 21 km north of Prado and is served by daily buses from both, with more frequent services in high season. Buses from Salvador, Porto Seguro and elsewhere in the state run via Itamaraju, 60 km inland on the BR-101, from where there is a daily bus to Cumuruxatiba.

Prado → *Colour map 4, B5. Phone code: 073.*
Prado is a scruffy town sandwiched between a long sand spit and the sluggish Rio Jucuruçú, lined with mangroves. There are two species of mangrove: stately, tall red

mangroves near the sea, and white mangroves in the fresher water. The river and trees are a haven for birdlife with at least three kingfisher species, ospreys and numerous herons and waders. There are southern otters and, further upstream, spectacled caiman. The beaches around town, especially near the **Barra do Prado** about 3 km downstream, are some of the best in southern Bahia: vast, lonely stretches of powder-soft sand that disappear into the distant horizon. It is possible to walk to the beaches from the town centre (about 45 minutes), or boats run from the quay. Bring plenty of sun shade, water and snacks, as there are no facilities except in the highest season.

Ins and outs Prado is well connected to the rest of Bahia, with direct buses to Caravelas (for Abrolhos), numerous daily connections to Itamaraju (for the rest of the state) and three daily buses to Cumuruxatiba. Day-trips to the beaches cost around US$40 for a boat.

Caravelas → *Colour map 4, B5. Phone code: 073.*
Continuing south, Caravelas is a charming little town on the banks of the Caravelas estuary, surrounded by mangroves. There are eight fine white-sand beaches nearby. The town is well known for its Catholic festivals, which attract thousands of pilgrims. Caravelas was a major trading port in the 17th and 18th centuries and the town's name was taken from the Portuguese sailing boats whose technology opened up the world to Lisbon. It is now slowly developing as a resort for Brazilian tourism. The best beaches are about 10 km away at the fishing village of **Barra de Caravelas** (hourly buses). There is a helpful tourist information, **Ibama Centro de Visitantes** ① *Barão do Rio Branco 281.*

Ins and outs Caravelas is 36 km south of Prado on the BA-001, on the banks of the Rio Caravelas and is served by frequent buses from Eunápolis and Itamaraju from where there are connections to the rest of the state. There are two weekly buses from Porto Seguro and daily connections to Prado to the north. The town is the departure point for the Abrolhos islands.

Parque Nacional Marinho dos Abrolhos
Abrolhos is an abbreviation of *Abre os olhos*, 'Open your eyes', from Amérigo Vespucci's exclamation when he first sighted the reef in 1503. Established in 1983, the park consists of five small islands: **Redonda**, **Siriba**, **Guarita**, **Sueste** and **Santa Bárbara**, which are volcanic in origin. There are also abundant coral reefs and good diving. Darwin visited the archipelago in 1830 and Jacques Cousteau studied the marine environment here.

The archipelago national park protects the most extensive coral reefs in the south Atlantic with four times as many endemic species than the reefs and atolls in the Caribbean. There are numerous endemic species, including giant brain corals, crustaceans and molluscs, as well as marine turtles and mammals threatened by extinction and huge colonies of nesting seabirds. In addition, the seas around the islands are one of the most important south Atlantic nurseries for humpback whales – which can always be seen in season.

In 2002, the Abrolhos region was declared an area of Extreme Biological Importance by the Brazilian Ministry of Environment, based on the Brazilian commitment to the international Convention on Biodiversity. For more information see **Conservation International**, www.conservation.org. The archipelago is administered by **Ibama** and a navy detachment mans a lighthouse on Santa Bárbara, which is the only island that may be visited. Visitors are not allowed to spend the night on the islands, but may stay overnight on schooners.

Capoeira

Capoeira is the most visually spectacular and gymnastic of all martial arts and the only one to have originated in the Americas. Salvador is the capoeira centre of Brazil and seeing a fight between good Bahian capoeristas is an unforgettable experience. Fighters spin around each other in mock combat, never touching but performing a series of lunges, kicks and punches with dizzying speed and precision. Some wear razor blades on their feet. A ring or *roda* of other capoeiristas watches, clapping, singing and beating time on a *berimbau* and hand-held drum. Every now and then they exchange places with the fighters in the centre of the ring.

Although many claim that capoeira derives from an Angolan foot-fighting ritual, this is incorrect. Capoeira originated in Brazil and there is strong evidence to suggest that it was invented by indigenous Brazilians. Padre José de Anchieta a 16th-century ethnologist makes an aside in his 1595 book *The Tupi Guarani Language* that the 'Indians amuse themselves by playing capoeira' and other Portuguese explorers like Martim de Souza recall the same.

The word capoeira itself comes from Tupi-Guarani and means 'cleared forest' and the postures, including many of the kicks, spins and the crouching position taken by those in the circle are all Brazilian-Indian. It was in indigenous capoeiras that the fight was passed on to African plantation slaves who modified them, added African chants and rhythms and the *berimbau*; an instrument probably brought to Brazil from West Africa. The art was used as a weapon against the soldiers of the enslaved African king Zumbi who established the Americas' only free slave state just north of Bahia in the 1700s.

Ins and outs The Parque Nacional Marinho dos Abrolhos is 70 km east of Caravelas. The journey to the islands takes three to four hours depending on the sea conditions. Between July and early December, humpback whale sightings are almost guaranteed. Boats leave at 0700 from the Marina Porto Abrolhos some 5 km north of Caravelas town centre (around US$50 depending on numbers) and they return at dusk. It is possible to dive or snorkel at Abrolhos. If you are coming from Porto Seguro everything including transfers and accommodation in Caravelas can be arranged by **Portomondo**, T073-3575 3686, www.portomondo.com. In Caravelas, book with **Abrolhos Turismo**, or **Catamarã Veleiro Sanuk**, see page 450, through any of the hotels listed above; or directly at the Marina Porto Abrolhos. For further information see www.ilhasdeabrolhos.com.br.

◉ The Discovery and Whale Coast listings

For Sleeping and Eating price codes and other relevant information, see pages 32-37.

◓ Sleeping

Porto Seguro *p434, map p435*
Prices rise steeply Dec-Feb and Jul. Off-season rates can drop by 50%, negotiate the rate for stays of more than 3 nights. Room capacity is greater than that of Salvador. Outside Dec-Feb, rooms with bath and hot water can be rented for about US$150 per month.

There are no hotels of character on the beach; all are huge, brash affairs that look like they belong in 1970s Benidorm. The best beach boutiques are in Trancoso or Arraial. But Porto is better value than either if you opt to stay in town.

L Xurupita, Rua B 25, Taperapuã, T073- 2105 9500, www.xurupita.com. This is one of the few Porto Seguro resort hotels which doesn't feel like a brash 1970s throwback. Annexes of plain, rooms given splashes of colour from big floral murals and furnished with dull catalogue furniture sit on a shady lawn surrounded by lush Atlantic coastal rainforest. Some have views out over the coast (which is just over 1 km away). The hotel run transfers to the beach and into town and have a pool, restaurant and a sports centre with gym coaching, squash and tennis.

L La Torre, Av Beira Mar 9999, Praia do Mutá, T073-2105 1700, www.resortlatorre.com. One of the best big beach resorts in Porto, close to the barraca action on the thronging Praia Mutá. Rooms range from spacious family suites with sea views to boxier options for two, there's restaurant low-lit for courting couples in the evening and a big, sculpted pool. Cheapest rates are through the internet and are all-inclusive with meals, drinks (only Brazilian alcoholic drinks are provided) and sport activities. The hotel provides entertainment for adults and children – from light tree-top and zip line adventures and organized play times to ultralight scenic flights and scuba diving, has a sauna, gym, tennis courts and volleyball, together with regular free transfer to their own barraca at the beach and to the airport.

B Estalagem Porto Seguro, R Mcal Deodoro 66, T073-3288 2095, www.hotelestalagem.com.br. Terraced rooms in a deep blue colonial house in the town centre. Great atmosphere and a stroll from nearby restaurants. The hotel help with tours and transfers.

B Solar do Imperador, Estr do Aeroporto, T073-3288 8450, www.solardoimperador.com.br. Well-appointed, spacious and modern a/c rooms with en suites and balconies in a medium-sized resort hotel on the road to the airport. Large pool and wonderful views from the upper deck in the public area.

B-C Vela Branca, R Dr Antonio Ricaldi, Cidade Alta, T073-3288 2318, www.vela branca.com.br. This enormous family resort with 3 pool, 4 tennis courts, restaurants, bars and anonymous package hotel rooms caters to groups from Brazil and Europe – many of whom choose never to leave the hotel except on a tour bus. It is an intimate as a shopping mall but offers cheap rates when booked through online and it's a great option for children – the hotel offers kids clubs and a kid's pool and has plenty of play areas – including a football pitch, and a volleyball court on the beach.

C Solar da Praça, R Assis Chateaubriand 75, Passarela do Álcool, Centro, T073-3288 2585, www.pousadasolardapraca.com. Pretty little renovated colonial townhouse with a range of basic but well-kept rooms dominated by a bed. Some with a/c and en suites in an adjacent annexe. Opt for those on the upper floors as they are less musty. The staff can organize excursions.

C-D Hotel Navegantes, Av 22 de Abril 212, T073-3288 2390, www.portonet.com.br/navegantes. Simple, plain white wall and tile floor a/c rooms, with en suites and TVs, crowding over a little pool and concrete deck in the centre of town.

C-D Pousada dos Raizes, Praça dos Pataxós 196, T/F073-3288 4717, pousadaraizes@hotmail.com.br. Well-kept unpretentious city hotel with helpful staff. Cheaper without breakfast. Recommended.

C-F Albergue Porto Seguro, R Cova da Moça 720, T073-3288 1742, www.porto segurohostel.com.br. HI hostel. Cheaper prices per person in dorms. Smart little hostel in the centre, with internet, excursions and discount rates at their sister beach hostel on Praia Taberapuan north of town.

Camping

Camping Mundaí Praia, 5 km north of the town centre, T073-3679 2287, www.campingmundai.com.br. Great-value beachside camping sites with power, restaurant/snack bars. There are plans to construct chalets; phone ahead to check.

Santa Cruz Cabrália *p436*

L Toca do Marlin, Estr BA-001, Km 40.5, Santo André, T073-3671 5041, www.tocado marlin.com.br. One of the most luxurious beach resorts in South America, with spacious a/c *cabañas* next to a ranch overlooking a quiet, beautiful beach some 50 km north of Porto Seguro. Excellent food and excursions.

A-B Baía Cabrália, R Sidrack de Carvalho 141, centro, T/F073-3282 8000, www.baiacabralia. com.br. Medium-size family resort with a large pool, sauna and gym.

B-C Victor Hugo, Villa de Santo André, Km 3, Santa Cruz Cabrália, T073-3671 4064, www.pousadavictorhugo.com.br. Smart, tastefully decorated little *pousada* right on the beach on the edge of an environmentally protected area. Rooms are plain in whitewash and thick oil paint colours, with heavy wooden furniture, lacey bedspreads and dark wood floors and they sit under the palms in a small garden. Stays here are wonderfully tranquil.

C-D Pousada do Mineiro, T073-3282 1042. A/c rooms around a pool and with a sauna, friendly staff and a *churrascaria* barbecue. Recommended.

Arraial da Ajuda *p438, map p439*
At busy times such as New Year's Eve and Carnaval, don't expect to find anything under US$15 per person in a shared room, with a minimum stay of 5-7 days.

A Pousada Pitinga, Praia Pitinga, T073-3575 067, www.pousadapitinga.com.br. Wooden chalets in a coconut-filled rainforest garden on hill overlooking the sea. Tranquil atmosphere, great food and a pool. A member of the Roteiros de Charme group, see page 34.

A-C Pousada Canto d'Alvorada, on the road to the Arraial d'Ajuda ferry, T073-3575 1218, www.cantodalvorada.com.br. Cheaper out of season. Pretty, Swiss-run *pousada* facing the beach on the edge of town with 21 cabins, a restaurant, pool, sauna and laundry facilities.

B-C Privillage Praia, Estrada da Pitinga 300, Praia de Pitinga, T073-3575 1646, www.privillage.com.br. This tranquil *pousada* is in secluded forest overlooking an almost

deserted beach 10 mins from Arraial d'Ajuda town. Rooms are less beautiful than the setting – set in concrete chalets and with raw brick walls, tiled floors and heavy wicker furniture. All have international TV and comfortable king-sized beds and a number have ocean views. The *pousada* has a good restaurant and a pool whose waters appear to merge with the sea.

A-C Quinta do Porto, Ponta do Apaga Fogo 1, T073-3575 1022, www.quintadoporto.com.br. Rooms in long corridors above a smart pool set in tropical gardens right on the river opposite Porto Seguro. Convenient for both Arraial and Porto towns (*combis* from Porto every 10 mins, ferries from Porto every 15 mins), and with an excellent travel agencies for onward excursions. The beach is 10-15 mins' walk.

C Pousada do Roballo, Estr do Mucugê, T073-3575 1053, www.pousadadoroballo. com.br. Welcoming *pousada* with a set of small rooms, each with a tiny hammock-hung veranda. Set in pleasant garden surroundings and with a pool.

C Pousada Erva Doce, Estr do Mucugê 200, T073-3575 1113, www.ervadoce.com.br. Well-appointed chalets and a decent restaurant, set in a lawned garden and with a pool.

C Pousada Mar Aberto, Estr do Mucugê 554, T/F073-3575 1153, Pretty little *pousada* with brick chalets set on the crest of a hill and set in lush gardens close to Mucugê beach and the centre. With a pool. At the lower end of the price category.

C Sole Mio, T073-3575 1115, just off the beach road leading from the ferry to Arraial. French owners, English spoken, laid-back with 4 chalets and an excellent pizzeria.

D Pousada do Mel, Praça São Bras. Simple but clean and with a good breakfast. Recommended.

D Pousada Flamboyant, Estr do Mucugê, T089-3875 1025. Rooms arranged around a little courtyard. Good breakfast and a pool.

E-F Arraial Hostel, R do Campo 94, T073-3575 1192/1998, www.arraialdajudahostel. com.br. Price per person. Smart well equipped modern backpacker hostel with IYHA discount in a large and colourful little house on the edge of town. Good facilities include a pool, bar, internet and book exchange.

Camping

Camping do Caju, T073-3575 2257, www.campingdocaju.com.br. Campsites and simple thatched roof chalets in a pretty garden surrounded by forest, just off the Estrada da Balsa (ferry road) – 2 km from the centre of Arraial and 5 km from the Porto-Arraial ferry point. To get there take R Portugal from the beach where there are signposts for the campsite.

Trancoso *p439*

LL Villas de Trancoso, Estr Arraial D'Ajuda, T073-3668 1151, www.villasdetrancoso.com. A series of luxurious cabins gathered on a lawn next to a pool and a relaxed bar and rustic wood-weight gym area on the adjacent beach. The duplex suite is perhaps the most luxurious in the town. American-run and owned and with a Californian feel. Can be hot as there isn't much shade.

L Etnia, R Principal, T073-3668 1137, www.etniabrasil.com.br. This captivating eco-chic *pousada* is a stroll from the Quadrado is a glossy magazine favourite, with a series of elegant and individually style bungalows gathered around a lush designer pool and set in a tropical forest garden filled with brilliantly coloured birds and butterflies. Run with *gaúcho* and Italian style, panache and efficiency.

L Pousada Estrela d'Água, Estrada Arraial D'Ajuda, Praia dos Nativos, T073-3668 1030, www.estreladagua.com.br. An infinity pool with waters melding into the turquoise sea leads to a light-flooded living area and a garden with luxurious faux-fishermen's cottages decorated with minimalist, clean whites and deep blues. There is free Wi-Fi throughout and the hotel follows the PNUMA UN programme for nature, installing solar power, recycling and engaging in some small welfare programmes. The bar is a favourite sunset cocktail spot and is open to non-residents who arrive from the beach.

L-AL Mata N'ativa Pousada, Estr Velha do Arraial s/n (next to the river on the way to the beach), T073-3668 1830, www.matanativa pousada.com.br. The best in town for nature lovers and those seeking a quiet, relaxed retreat. A series of elegant and romantic cabins are set in a lovingly maintained orchid and heliconia garden with a pool by the riverside, which is a good few degrees cooler than anywhere else in Trancoso in the heat of the day. Nothing is too much trouble for the warm-hearted owners Daniel and Daniela. Both are knowledgeable about flora and fauna in the Mata Atlântica rainforest and can organize wildlife or birdwatching excursions. Good English, Spanish and Italian. Great breakfast.

A Capim Santo, to the left of the main square, T073-3668 1122, www.capim santo.com.br. Friendly, beautifully designed little *pousada* right on the edge of Quadrado and with a series of well-appointed rustic chic rooms and cabins. The restaurant is one of the best and most romantic in town. Superb breakfasts and dinners.

B Pousada Calypso, Parque Municipal, T073-3668 1113, www.pousadacalypso.com.br. Comfortable, spacious rooms, jacuzzis, a library and sitting area and helpful staff who speak German and English. Just off the Quadrado.

C Pousada Quarto Crescente, R Principal, T073-3668 1014, www.quartocrescente.net. About 500 m inland, away from main square, on the main road to the beach. With cooking facilities, laundry and helpful owners who speak English, German, Dutch and Spanish. Map, bus times and directions on the website.

C Pousada Som do Mar, Beco da Praia dos Nativos, Praia dos Nativos, T073- 3668 1812, www.pousadasomdomar.com.br. Simple little mock-colonial cubes with terraces hung with hammocks overlooking a tiny pool 5 mins' walk from the Nativos beach. Internet and Wi-Fi.

D-E Café Esmeralda, T073-3668 1527, www.trancosonatural.com. Tiny white-washed rooms in rather airless fan-cooled, tile-roofed bungalows right on the Quadrado The *pousada* restaurant serves good breakfa (extra) and some of the cheapest lunches in Trancoso, and is one of the few establishments to be locally owned.

Caraíva p440

AL-A Vila do Mar, R 12 de Outubro s/n, T073-3668 5111, www.pousadaviladomar. com.br. The plushest hotel in town, with spacious, stylish airy, wooden *cabañas* overlooking the beach set on a lawn around an adult and children's pool.

C Pousada Flor do Mar, R 12 de Outubro s/n, Caraiva, on the beach, T073-9985 1608, www.caraiva.tur.br/flordomar. Charming beachfront *pousada* with airy rooms with a view – the best right at the beachfront.

C Pousada San Antônio, Praia de Caraíva, T073-9962 2123, www.pousadasanantonio. com.br. Very simple but colourful fan-cooled rooms right on the beach and breezy public areas decorated with marine bric-a-brac and furnished with wicker chairs and hammocks.

C Pousada Terra, Praia de Caraíva, T073-9985 4417, www.terracaraiva.com.br. Simple cabins on the edge of the town and on the outskirts of the Monte Pascoal forest.

C-D Pousada da Praia, Praia de Caraíva; T073-9985 4249; www.pousadapraiacaraiva. com.br. Very simple little boxes with no more than a bed, a table, chair and wardrobe. Public areas are furnished more comfortably, with an outdoor deck area hung with hammocks and dotted with wicker sofas.

Camping

Camping Caraíva Praia de Caraíva, Praia de Caraiva, T073-2231 4892, 9993 9087, www.campingcaraiva.com.br. Basic but shady plots by the riverside with a communal cooking area and showers, and a selection of simple shacks with hard beds (**D-E**).

Corumbau p441

L Fazenda São Francisco, T011-3078 4411, www.corumbau.com.br. Spacious, well-appointed hard wood and cream cabins gathered around a pool in a palm-shaded garden 5 mins' walk from the beach.

LL Vila Naia, T011-3061 1872, www.vila naia.com.br. Tastefully appointed, luxurious bungalows set in a little garden back from the beach. Very popular with fashionable Paulistanos. Intimate and romantic but not of the same standard as Tauana.

AL Pousada Corumbau, T073-3573 1190, www.corumbau.tur.br. It's difficult to miss this big red 2-storey house in tiny Corumbau. There are a range of rooms – from simple concrete huts (with space for up to 4 at a push), to big tiled rooms in the main building. All are homey but decorated in brash colours with little of the sense of style evident at the other Corumbau *pousadas* only a little above this price range. The latter all have verandas with sea views, satellite TV and the *pousada* has a simple restaurant.

A Jocotoka Village, T073-3288 2291, www.jocotoka.com.br. Brilliantly coloured, higgledy-piggledy, thatched-roof chalets grouped on a shady lawn between the beach and patchy *restinga* forest. The interiors come in lurid oranges, brilliant blues and more sombre creams and are spacious and breezy. All have shaded terraces. The *pousada* has a large pool and a bar and offers a range of light adventure activities, including whale watching, snorkelling and kayking. Children under 5 and pets are not permitted. Breakfast and dinner are included, making stays here good value.

D-F Vila Pousada & Camping Segovia, Corumbau s/n, T073-9986 2305, www.corumbaunet.com.br. There are only 5 small, fan-cooled and barely furnished chalets in this little family-run guesthouse close to the beach. They include breakfast and there are plots for camping out back.

Cumuruxatiba p441

B-C Vereda Tropical, Av Beira Mar s/n, T073-3573 1070, www.pousadavereda tropical.com.br. A series of terracotta-roofed apartments in a little garden right in front of the beach. The lime green rooms have tiled floors, pretty palm-frond lamps and a small veranda with wooden chairs. Rooms have queen-sized beds, mosquito nets and a/c. Book ahead for chalets close to the sea.

C Pousada Axé, Av Beira Mar 1030, T073-3573 1030, www.pousadaaxe.com.br. 20 beachside chalets gathered around a pool. Generous breakfast and friendly service.

C-D Pousada Urupê, Estrada rural s/n, Cumuruxatiba, T073-3573 1444, www.nossa casa.net/urupe. Plain white-wall and tile rooms with bathrooms in a mock colonial building next to the Rio do Peixe Pequeno at the Corumbau end of town.

E Aleksandro, Av 13 Maio s/n, T073-3573 1050, www.pradobahiabrasil.com.br/pousadascumu ru.html. A very simple space a block from the beach with fan-cooled rooms in a wind next to a garden. Cool even in the heat of the day.

Prado p441

A-B La Isla Resort, Prado, T073-3021 1111, www.ilhadaalegria.com.br. A large family-orientated resort on an island 10 mins' downstream from Prado town centre, and reached via the river docks. Functional, plain rooms are in a series of annexes gathered around an artificial lake and there is a big pool and water park area (with slides) for children. Excursions include trips on the river and to local beaches and tours to the Abrolhos islands.

C Casa de Maria, R Seis, Novo Prado, Prado, T073-3298 1425, www.casademaria.com.br. Annexes of rooms in a 2-storey building built around a pool near the beach. Abrolhos excursions organized. Claims to serve the best breakfast in southern Bahia.

C Novo Prado, Praia Novo Prado, Prado, T073-3298 1455, www.novoprado.com.br. Pleasant beachside *pousada* near the town centre, with colourful rooms, airy public areas, a little library, sauna and pool and a range of a/c and fan-cooled rooms.

C-D Abaetê, R IV, lote 35, Novo Prado, T073-3298 1611, www.portonet.com.br/ abaete. Modest tiled, a/c en suites dominated by a double bed and with a little fridge and

a/c. All overlook a concrete deck and pool and the hotel is a block from the town beach at the north end of the city. There are many other options nearby, including the slightly cheaper **D Vivenda da Praia**, next door.

Caravelas p442

B Marina Porto Abrolhos, R da Baleia, 5 km outside of town, T073-3674 1060, www.marina portoabrolhos.com.br. One of the most comfortable hotels in the region, with a range of individual and family suites housed in faux-Polynesian chalets and gathered in a palm-tree garden around a large pool. Activities include trips to the Abrolhos.

C Pousada Liberdade, Av Ministro Adalicio Nogueira 1551, Caravelas, T073-3297 2076, www.pousadaliberdade.com.br. Spacious but simple chalets in a large, lawned garden area next to a lake and just outside the town centre. Excursion organized to the Abrolhos islands.

C-D Pousada dos Navegantes, R das Palmeiras 45, Centre, T073-3297 1830, www.pousadanavegantes.com.br. Simple *pousada* with a pool near the beach organizing tours to the Abrolohos, dive excursions and dive certification. Friendly and helpful.

⊘ Eating

Porto Seguro *p434, map p435*

¶¶ Sambuca, Praça Pataxós 216, T073-3288 2366. Right next to the ferry port to Arraial. Varied à la carte menu and decent wood-oven cooked pizzas.

¶¶-¶ Portinha, R Saldanha Marinho 33, T073-3288 2743. The most popular buffet in Porto with a huge choice of hot and cold dishes and juices for lunch and dinner and great deserts. A very popular meeting point, always busy and buzzing with people.

¶ Da Japonêsa, Praça Pataxós 38. Open 0800-2300. Excellent value with a varied Brazilian and Japanese menu. Recommended

Arraial da Ajuda *p438, map p439*

Food in Arraial is pricey and restaurants tend to look better than the dishes they serve. There are numerous *barracas* selling simple seafood, juices and beer on Mucugê beach, as well as the popular **Barraca de Pitinga** and **Barraca do Genésio** on Pitinga beach.

♦♦♦ Don Fabrizio, Estrada do Mucugê 402, T073-3575 1123. The best Italian in town, in an upmarket open air-restaurant with live music and reasonable wine.

♦♦♦ Manguti, Estrada do Mucugê, T073-3575 2270, www.manguti.com.br. Reputedly the best in town, though the food looks like mutton dressed as lamb. Meat, pasta, fish served as comfort food alongside other Brazilian dishes. Very popular and informal.

♦♦♦ Rosa dos Ventos, Alameda dos Flamboyants 24, T073-3575 1271. This romantic little spot decorated with arts and crafts by local artists cooks fresh food pulled from their own organic garden and the Atlantic. The menu is quite varied, with dishes like fish slow-roasted in banana leaf, braised lamb and crawfish lobster (which should be ordered 24 hrs in advance).

♦♦ Godzilla, Estrada do Mucugê 200, T073-3575 3302. East Asian and Japanese fusion cooking from a vivacious and enthusiastic Japanese expat, Fumiaka Yamada.

♦♦ Pizzaria do Arraial, Praça São Bras 28. Basic pizzeria and and popular pay-by-weight restaurant.

♦ Paulo Pescador, R São Bras 116, T073-3575 1242, www.paulopescador.com.br. One of the best options for lunch – with 6 different *pratos feitos* (set meals) to choose from and good fresh seafood. English spoken, good service. *Bobó de camarão* highly recommended. Very popular, there are often queues for tables.

Trancoso *p439*

Food in Trancoso is expensive. Those on a tight budget should shop at the supermarket between the main square and the new part of town. There are many fish restaurants in the *barracas* on the beach. Elba Ramalho, when in town, gigs at her restaurant, **Para Raio**.

♦♦♦ Cacau, Quadrado 96, T073-3668 1296. The restaurant of choice for those who want to eat Bahian in Trancoso. The menu is strong on flavour and spices which includes starters like mini *acarajé* balls with *vatapá* or *caruru* and mains like *camarão nativo* (local prawns), served twitchingly fresh.

♦♦♦ Capim Santo, R de Beco 55, Quadrado, T073-3668 4112, www.capimsanto.com.br. Paulistana ex-pat Sandra Marques' cooking is quintessentially Trancoso. Seafood dishes with a Bahian twist like prawn in manioc flour balls or tuna carpaccio are served under the stars by candlelight in a little tropical garden just off the Quadrado. Be sure to begin the evening with a *caipisake com abacaxi e gengibre* (sake with crushed ice, fresh crushed pineapple and root ginger).

♦♦♦ Japaiano, Quadrado 1, in the **Hotel da Praça**. A Brazilian-Asian fusion menu created by Rio's hot young kitchen maverick Felipe Bronze who learnt his trade at **Le Bernardin** and **Nobu** in New York and his name at **Zuka** and **Z Contemporâneo** in Rio. Dishes include *moqueca de camarões e lulas com curry verde tailandês* (prawn and squid *moqueca* with a green Thai curry sauce).

♦♦♦ Maritaca, Quadrado, T073-3668 1258. A Marrakech theme may seem odd in hippy-chic Trancoso. But the sumptuous back deck at this new restaurant – with its open sky and beautiful drop-off view out to the sea – attracts a faithful cocktail crowd. The Italian food is adequate but lacks sparkle; slow service.

♦♦ Barraca Do Andrea, Coqueiros beach. The most fashionable place to sip and sun. Run by a Sardinian who serves great Italian wood-fired pizza, super-fresh ceviche and a gamut of fruity caipirinhas and tropical juices.

♦ Dona Maria. This joyful old lady and her 9-year-old grandson sell delicious home-baked bread, tiny prawn, chicken *empadas* (meat pies) and steaming hot treacle-sweet black coffee to fishermen (or visiting surfers) who rise with the sun. You can find them before 0900 on a tiny little tile stall on the Quadrado in front of the Ainarí boutique.

Portinha, Quadrado. Good-value pay-by-weight options and a wealth of juices.

🎵 Bars and clubs

Arraial da Ajuda *p438, map p439*
Porto Seguro does not have much in the way of nightlife; most visitors stay in Arraial across the water. In Arraial, the *lambada* is danced at the **Jatobar** bar (in summer), by the church on the main square (opens 2300, *pensão* at the back is cheap, clean and friendly). **Limelight** has raves all year round. Many top Brazilian bands play at the beach clubs at **Praia do Parracho** in summer, entry is about US$20. Entry to other beach parties is about US$10.

⛰️ Activities and tours

Estação Veracel Veracruz *p436*
Ciro Albano, www.nebrazilbirding.com. The best birding guide for the northeast of Brazil offering tips to birding and wildlife sites, including Estação Veracruz, Canudos and the Chapada Diamantina.

Arraial da Ajuda *p438, map p439*
Portomondo, Ponta do Apaga Fogo 1, Marina Quinta do Porto Hotel, T073-3575 3686, www.portomondo.com. The best operator in southern Bahia with tours from around Trancoso, Caraíva and Corumbau to Monte Pascoal and Abrolhos. Excellent diving and ecotourism itineraries and car or helicopter transfers to hotels in Trancoso and further south.

Trancoso *p439*
Joácio, T073-3668 1270, or ask at **Bouganvillea** restaurant on the main square. Good day trips to Espelho Beach, Caraíva and other beaches and forested areas in the area. Expect to pay US$10-15 per person depending on group size and distance.

Parque Nacional Marinho dos Abrolhos *p442*
See also Ins and outs, page 443. All-inclusive trips from Porto Seguro can be arranged with **Portomondo** (see above). From Caravelas, book with **Abrolhos Turismo**, Praça Dr Emílio Imbassay 8, T073-3297 1149, www.abrolhosturismo.com.br or **Catamarã Veleiro Sanuk**, T073-3297 1344, www.catamarasanuk.cjb.net.

⊖ Transport

Porto Seguro *p434, map p435*
Air Taxi to airport (T073-3288 1880), US$15. Flights to **Belo Horizonte**, **Rio de Janeiro**, **Salvador**, **São Paulo** and **Ilhéus** in high season with **GOL**, www.voegol.com.br, **Tam**, www.tam.com.br, and **Webjet**, www.webjet.com.br.

Boat Boats cross the river to **Arraial da Ajuda** on the south bank, 5 mins, US$1 for foot passengers, US$5 for cars, every 15-30 mins day and night.

Bus At Brazilian holiday times, all transport should be booked well in advance. **Expresso Brasileiro** buses run from Praça dos Pataxós along the BR-367 stopping at the beaches north of town. Buses for **Caraíva** go via Eunápolis and Itabela (leaving Eunápolis at 1330, 2 hrs), or from Arraial D'Ajuda, via Trancoso daily at 0700 and 1600, extra bus at 1100 in high season (**Viação Águia Azul**, T073-3875 1170). To **Eunápolis**, 1 hr, US$5, very frequent. To **Curumuxatiba**, **Prado** and destinations further south, take a bus to Eunápolis, Texeira de Freitas or Itamaraju and an onward bus from there. For **Caraíva** bus leaves at 0700, 1330 (high season) and 1500 (via Trancoso). To **Trancoso**, 2 daily buses, but easier to take the ferry to Arraial and catch one of the more frequent buses or *combis* from there. Other services via Eunápolis (those going north avoid Salvador) or Itabuna (5 hrs, US$25).

To **Rio de Janiero**, daily, direct, 1745, US$80, *leito* US$70 (São Geraldo), 18 hrs (very cold a/c, take warm clothes); or take the 1800 to Ilhéus and change at Eunápolis. To **Belo Horizonte**, daily, direct, US$80 (São Geraldo). To **São Paulo** direct, 1045, 25 hrs, not advisable, very slow; much better to go to Rio then take the Rio–São Paulo express. To **Salvador** (Águia Branca), daily, 12 hrs, US$80. To **Vitória**, daily, 11 hrs, US$60. To **Ilhéus**, daily 0730, 4½ hrs, US$45.

Car hire Several companies at the airport, including **Localiza**, T073-3288 1488 (and R Cova da Moça 620, T073-3288 1488) and **Nacional**, T073-3288 4291.

Cycle hire Oficina de Bicicleta, Av Getúlio Vargas e R São Pedro, US$15 for 24 hrs; also at Praça de Bandeira and at 2 de Julho 242.

Arraial da Ajuda *p438, map p439*
Ferry Take a bus or *combi* to Rio Buranhém, from where boats cross the river to **Porto Seguro**, on the north bank, 5 mins, US$1 for foot passengers, US$5 for cars, every 15-30 mins day and night.

Trancoso *p439*
Bus Buses run regularly on the newly paved road between **Porto Seguro**, **Arraial d'Ajuda** and **Trancoso**, at least every hr from Arraial in high season. To Porto Seguro US$4, to Ajuda US$2.40. Arriving from the south, change buses at Eunápolis from where the newly paved Linha Verde road runs to Trancoso. Buses for **Caraíva** leave twice daily at 0800 and 1700, with an extra bus at 1200 in high season.

Caraíva *p440*
Access roads are poor and almost impossible after heavy rain. **Aguia Azul** buses run to **Porto Seguro** twice daily (3 times in high season), along a very poor dirt road involving river crossing. If heading south, take a bus to **Itabela** or **Eunápolis** (0600, 3 hrs).

Parque Nacional de Monte Pascoal *p441*
To **Caraíva** there is a river crossing by boats which are always on hand. There is 1 bus a day Mon-Fri to **Itamaraju**, 16 km to the south.

Corumbau *p441*
Beach buggy taxis take you to the river crossing (US$40) to **Caraiva**, or it's about a 10-km walk. The punt ferry across the river costs around US$10. Buses run to **Itmaraju** and beyond to **Curumuxatiba**.

Cumuruxatiba *p441*
There are 3 daily buses to **Prado** and **Itamaraju** and a bus every other day direct to **Porto Seguro**. 1 bus a day to **Corumbau** via Itamaraju.

Prado *p441*
Frequent buses to **Itamaraju**, 3 daily to **Curumuxatiba** and **Caravleas** (via Alcobaça).

Caravelas *p442*
Air There are flights to **Belo Horizonte**, **São Paulo** and **Salvador**. Another option is to fly via **Porto Seguro**.

Bus Caravelas is well connected, with buses to **Texeira de Freitas** (4 a day), **Salvador**, **Nanuque**, **Itamaraju** and **Prado**.

❶ Directory

Porto Seguro *p434, map p435*
Banks Agência do Descobrimento, Av Getúlio Vargas, also arranges flight tickets and house rental. Banco do Brasil, Av Beira Mar, 1000-1500, changes TCs and US$ cash, also Visa ATMs. Also at airport. Bradesco, Av Getulio Vargas, Visa ATMs. Deltur, in the new shopping centre, near Banco do Brasil. **Internet** Dotted throughout town. **Laundry** New Porto, Shopping Av, daily 0900-2230, priced per item. **Post office** In the mini-shopping centre on the corner of R das Jandaias and Av dos Navegantes. **Telephone** Shopping Av, daily 0700-2300,

corner of Av dos Navegantes and Av Beira Mar, also at Praça dos Pataxós, beside ferry terminal. Daily 0700-2200, cheap rates after 2000, receives and holds faxes, F073-3288 3915.

Arraial da Ajuda *p438, map p439*
Banks There is a Banco do Brasil with a *câmbio* and ATM, and Bradesco and HSBC ATMs in the small shopping centre on Estrada do Mucugê. Several bars on Broadway change US$ cash, but rates are poor. **Internet** Dotted throughout town. **Post office** Praça São Bras. **Telephone** Telemar on the main square. Daily 0800-2200, number for receiving faxes is F073-875 1309, US$1.

Trancoso *p439*
Banks Banco do Brasil ATM which only sometimes works with international Visa cards. Best to bring cash from Arraial. Most places accept TCs. **Internet** Several on the main square.

Prado *p441*
Banks There is a Bradesco with ATM in the town centre.

Caravelas *p442*
Banks The Banco do Brasil, Praça Dr Imbassahi, does not change money but has an ATM. There is also a Bradesco.

Linha Verde and the northern coast

Heading north from Salvador airport, the BA-099 coast road, or Estrada de Coco (Coconut Highway), passes many coconut plantations and 50 km of beautiful beaches. From south to north the best known are Ipitanga (famous for its reefs), Buraquinho, Jauá, Arembepe, Guarajuba, Itacimirim, Castelo Garcia D'Ávila (where there is a 16th-century fort) and Forte. North of the smart mini-resort town of Praia do Forte, the road is called the 'Linha Verde' (Green Line), which runs for 142 km to the Sergipe state border. The road is more scenic than the BR-101, especially near Conde. There are very few hotels or pousadas in the more remote villages. Among the most picturesque are Subaúma and Baixio; the latter, where the Rio Inhambupe meets the sea, is very beautiful. Buses serve most of these destinations. ▸▸ *For listings, see pages 454-456.*

Arembepe → *Colour map 4, A6. Phone code: 071.*
Some 45 km north of Salvador, this former fishing village is now a quiet resort. There is a hippy palm-hut community, which has been here since the 1970s, 30 minutes' walk along the beach, behind the sand dunes, with a café, arts and crafts shops and swimming. The best beaches are 2 km north of town. A music festival is held on the following Carnaval celebrations and there is a **Tamar** turtle centre.

Praia do Forte → *Colour map 4, A6. Phone code: 071.*
Some 80 km north of Salvador, is this pleasant mini resort town much beloved of wealthy people from Salvador. Praia may no longer be a fishing village but it still feels low key. Aside from the town's main street, Alameda do Sol, most of the streets are sand. Much of the area around the town is protected, with turtle-nesting beaches, remnant coastal *restinga* forest, and a small area of marshland, which is home to a large number of birds, caymans and other animals. Birdwatching trips on the Pantanal wetlands, which is home to many species of wading birds, spectacled caiman and capybara, are rewarding and can be organized through the town's large-scale 'eco' resort.

The **Projeto Tamar** ① *Caixa Postal 2219, Rio Vermelho, Salvador, Bahia, T071-3876 1045, www.tamar.org.br*, is a national project that studies and preserves the sea turtles that lay their eggs in the area. Praia do Forte is the headquarters of the **national turtle preservation programme** and is funded by the Worldwide Fund for Nature. There is a visitor centre at the project (US$1.50 for turtle sanctuary). The coast here is ideal for windsurfing and sailing, owing to constant fresh Atlantic breezes.

Praia do Forte takes its name from the castle built by a Portuguese settler, Garcia D'Avila, in 1556, to warn the city to the south of enemy invasion. He was given a huge area of land, from Praia do Forte to Maranhão, on which he made the first farm in Brazil. He brought the first herd of cattle to the country, cleared the virgin Atlantic forest and brought the first coconut and mango trees to Brazil.

Imbassaí → *Colour map 4, A6. Phone code: 071.*

About 14 km from Praia do Forte is the simple village of Imbassaí, named after the adjacent river that winds along the coast next to the sea forming a pretty sand spit and offering both salt and fresh water swimming. When the Portuguese arrived there was a substantial Tupinambá village here, which was destroyed under Me de Sa, becoming a fishing village and then, in the late 20th century, a weekend retreat for Soterpoletanos (people from Salvador). Their holiday homes cluster along the river banks and along **Praia de Santo Antônio**, beach, 4 km from the town. Imbassaí remains far quieter, however, than its neighbour **Porto Sauípe**, 22 km to the north. The fishing village charm here has been drowned out by purpose-built hotels and condominiums on the **Costa do Sauipe**, beach. Resorts here come with corporate-designed village colour and names like 'Breezes'. They are meant to appeal to the international tourism market, but are expensive and look old-fashioned. As they sit on one of the rockiest, roughest stretches of beach in northern Bahia, it's hard to fathom why anyone would choose to stay here rather than on one of Bahia's other beaches.

Conde and Sítio do Conde → *Colour map 2, C5. Phone code: 075.*

These twin towns 185 km north of Salvador are sufficiently far from the state capital to have been spared the ravages of condominium and resort development. Conde lies away from the coast and preserves a small colonial centre with a 17th-century church. Sítio do Conde is 6 km from the town, on the coast. It has a string of small *pousadas* and beach homes but, unlike the larger resort towns to the south, it remains a fishing village at heart. The beach is thin and rocky but south and north of the town the sands get increasingly broad, white and deserted. South, they stretch through **Corre Nu** and **Jacaré** to **Barra do tariri**, 16 km south, which has good swimming and fine sunsets. **Siribinha**, 13 km north of Sítio do Conde, is long, broad and deserted but for a tiny fishing hamlet.

Mangue Seco → *Colour map 2, C5. Phone code: 075.*

The last stop on the Linha Verde is Mangue Seco. The town was immortalized in Jorge Amado's book *Tieta*. A steep hill rises behind the village to white-sand dunes that offer superb views of the coast. The encroaching dunes have caused the mangrove to dry up.

The peninsula is connected to Pontal in the state of Sergipe by boat or canoe on the Rio Real 10-minute crossing). Buses run between Pontal and Estancia twice a day. The ferry across the river usually leaves before 1000 in the morning. A private launch will cost US$10, but it is usually possible to find someone to share the ride and cost.

⊚ Linha Verde and the northern coast listings

For Sleeping and Eating price codes and other relevant information, see pages 32-37.

⊜ Sleeping

Arembepe *p452*
B-C Arembepe Refúgio Ecológico, Estr Aldeia Hippie, T071-3624 1031, www.hostel bahia.com. A handful of very simple but well-appointed a/c concrete chalets gathered around a pool and overlooking the beach in a protected area next to the **Tamar** turtle project. Very peaceful.
C-D Cores do Mar, R das Flores s/n, T071-3624 1155, www.pousadacoresdomar.com. br. This unprepossessing concrete cube in the middle of town offers well-kept, modern a/c rooms with little more than a bed sitting on floor tiles and a tiny attached shower room.
C-D Gipsy, R Eduardo Pinto, Km 3, T071-3624 3266, www.gipsy.com.br. A good-value, 40-room hotel with a/c rooms and a pool.

Praia do Forte *p452*
The town's main street had its name changed from Alameda do Sol to **Av ACM**. This street doesn't have numbers marked, so you just have to walk along to find your hotel. Prices rise steeply in the summer season. It may be difficult to find very cheap places to stay.
LL-AL Praia do Forte Eco-Resort, Av do Farol, T071-3676 4000, www.praiadoforte ecoresort.com.br. A large-scale family resort set in tropical gardens on the beach and with programmes to visit the nearby protected areas. Room are spacious, well appointed and comfortable. Service, which includes a Thalasso spa and entertainment, is excellent. Beautiful pool.
L-AL Aloha Brasil Pousada, R da Aurora, T071-3676 0279, www.pousadaalohabrasil. com.br. Relaxing tropical garden and pool. Rooms are not big but are charming with king-sized beds and verandas.
L-AL Porto Zarpa Hotel, R da Aurora, T071-3676 1414, www.portozarpa.com.br.

Large 2-storey building surrounded by garden, close to the beach, cable TV, parking, pool, good for families.
AL-A Sobrado da Vila, Av ACM, T/F071-3676 1088, www.sobradoda vila.com.br. The best in the village itself with a range of individually decorated rooms with balconies and a good-value restaurant, convenient for the town.
A Ogum Marinho, Av ACM, T071-3676 1165, www.ogummarinho.com.br. A/c, cheaper with fan, nice little courtyard garden, good restaurant and service. It has an art gallery with work by Brazilian artists.
A-B Pousada Casa de Praia, Praça dos Artistas 08-09, T071-3676 1362, www.casa depraia.tur.br. Good value and location, rooms with and without a/c, popular.
B-C Pousada João Sol, R da Corvina, T071-3676 1054, www.pousadajoaosol.com.br. 6 well-appointed and newly refurbished chalets. The owner speaks English, Spanish and German. Great breakfast.
C Pousada Tatuapara, Praça dos Artistas 1, T071-3676 1466, www.tatuapara.com.br. Spacious and well-maintained, fan, fridge. Good breakfast. Recently refurbished. Pool.
D Pousada Tia Helena, just east of Praça dos Artistas, at Alameda das Estrelas, T071-3676 1198, T071-9901 2894 (mob), www.tiahelenapraiadoforte.com.br. Helena, the motherly proprietor provides an enormous breakfast, simple rooms. Recently refurbished reductions for 3-day stays.
E Albergue da Juventude, Praia do Forte, R da Aurora 3, T071-3676 1094, www.albergue.com.br. Price per person. Smart youth hostel with decent shared rooms and rooms with en suites (**B-C**), a large breakfast, fan, kitchen and shop, cheaper for HI members.

Imbassaí *p453*
B Pousada Caminho do Mar, T/F071-3832 2499. Bungalows with a/c, restaurant, German-run.

B Pousada Imbassaí, T/F071-3876 1313. A/c chalets and apartments.
C Pousada Lagoa da Pedra, T071-3248 5914, www.lagoadapedra.com.br. Chalets set in large grounds, some English spoken, friendly.
D Pousada Anzol de Ouro, T071-3322 4422, www.anzoldeouro.com.br. Modest fan-cooled chalets around a simple pool.

Sítio do Conde p453
A Hotel Praia do Conde, T075-3429 1129 (in Salvador T071-3449 1129, www.hotelpraiadoconde.com.br. Smart a/c chalets with en suites around a pool.
C Pousada Oasis, T075-3449 1105, www.portaldoconde.com. Very simple, plain accommodation either fan-cooled or a/c rooms. With breakfast.

Mangue Seco p453
There are plenty of small cheap places along the seafront from the jetty, none with addresses or phone numbers (the village is tiny). There are simple restaurants around the main square next to the church. The beach has a handful of *barracas* serving cheap fish.
B-C Fantasias do Agreste, T075-3445 9011, www.pousadafantasiasdoagreste.com. Bright rooms with terraces overlooking a pool, decked out in tiled floors, whitewash and blocks of primary colour and furnished with wicker beds and light wood wardrobes.
B-C Village Mangue Seco, T075-3224 2965, www.villagemangueseco.com.br. Mock-adobe concrete chalets (some a/c, some fan-cooled), sitting around a pool in a large palm-shaded lawn dotted with tropical flowers.

Eating

Arembepe p452
Mar Aberto, Largo de São Francisco 43, T071-824 1257. Good seafood with a French twist.

Praia do Forte p452
Bar Do Souza, Av do Sol, on the right as you enter the village. Best seafood in town, open daily, live music at weekends. Recommended.
O Europeu, Av ACM, T071-3676 0232. Anglo-Brazilian owned, with the most adventurous menu in town with well-prepared homely dishes. The owners, William and Vera, are very friendly and knowledgeable about the area. Recommended.
Restaurante Casa da Nati, Av ACM, T071-3676 1239. Per kilo and Bahian food from a Praia do Forte native.
Restaurante Point do Ivan, Av ACM, T071-9997 1711. Bahian food, good *moqueca*, *bobo de camarco* and cheap *prato feito*.
Café Tango, Av ACM, T071-3676 1637. Pleasant open-air tea and coffee bar with great pastries and cakes.

Shopping

Praia do Forte p452
Galeria de Arte Claudia Ferraris, Alameda das Estrelas, T071-9125 1191 or T071-9165 8325, www.claudiaferraris.com. Incredible European-born artist who paints small capoeira pictures that beautifully capture the movement and colour of the martial art dance.
Joia Rara, Av ACM, T071-3676 1503. Tailor-made jewellery using Brazilian precious stones set in white gold, gold or silver. The client chooses the stone which is then polished. These include Bahian emeralds, aquamarines, tourmalines and amethysts, The shop doubles up as the artists studio. Authentic and good value.
Nativa, Av ACM, T071-3676 0437. Artisan clothing from Brazils northeast region. Beautiful hand work embroidered shirts, skirts, and bags. Quite chic and unusual.

▲ Activities and tours

Praia do Forte p452
Tour operators
Praia do Forte is ideal for windsurfing and sailing owing to constant fresh Atlantic breezes. **Odara Turismo**, in the EcoResort Hotel, T071-3676 1080. Imaginative tours to surrounding areas and outlying villages and beaches using 4WD vehicles. They are very friendly and informative. Recommended. The owners, Norbert and Papy, speak English and German.

⊖ Transport

Arembepe and Imbassaí p452 and p453
Bus To the Terminal Francês in **Salvador**, every 2 hrs, 1 hr, US$7, to Arembepe, last bus at 1800. Buses also run to **Itapoã**. Hourly Linha Verde buses run from Salvador's *rodoviária* along the BA-099 and will drop visitors at the crossroads for Imbassaí or **Sauípe**.

Praia do Forte p452
Bus It is easy to flag down buses from the crossroads on the main highway out of town. To get there take a *combi* (every 15 mins, US$1) from town. Taxis are a rip-off. To **Salvador** buses run 5 times daily, 1 hr, US$5 (Santa Maria/Catuense). To **Estancia** in Sergipe, 4-5 daily, US$5.

Conde and Sítio do Conde p453
Hourly Linha Verde buses run from Salvador's *rodoviária* along the BA-099 and will drop visitors at the crossroads for **Conde**. There are 9 buses daily from Salvador to Conde. 2 buses a day run north from Conde and Sítio do Conde to **Siribinha**. 3 buses a day run south from Sítio do Conde to **Barra do Itariri**.

Mangue Seco p453
Any **Aracaju**-bound bus will drop visitors at the town of **Estancia** – just across the border from Bahia in Sergipe state, from where there are 2 southbound buses a day to **Pontal** (a port comprising little more than a jetty, sitting opposite Mangue Seco) and more frequent Toyotas (leaving when full) from in front of the Estancia hospital. Infrequent slow boats cross the river from Pontal to **Mangue Seco** – usually 2-3 times daily. A private launch will cost US$10-15, but there are invariably other people willing to share the boat – and it is just a matter of waiting a while for them to turn up.

Chapada Diamantina and the sertão

The beautiful Chapada Diamantina national park comprises a series of escarpments covered in cerrado, caatinga and moist tropical forest, dripping with waterfalls and studded with caves. It is one of the highlights of inland Bahia. Although little of the forest is original, there is still plenty of wildlife including jaguar and maned wolf, and the area is good for birdwatching. Various trails cut through the park offering walks from a few hours to a few days, and many leave from the little colonial mining town of Lençóis, the ideal base for visiting the region.

The road from Salvador to Lençóis and the chapada passes through Feira de Santana, famous for its Micareta, an extremely popular out-of-season carnival. The harsh beauty of the sertão and its hospitable people are the reward for those wanting to get off the beaten track. The region has been scarred by droughts and a violent history of bandits, rebellions and religious leaders. Euclides da Cunha and Canudos are good places to start exploring this history. The Raso da Catarina, once a hiding place for Lampião, and the impressive Paulo Afonso waterfalls, can both be visited from the town of Paulo Afonso located on the banks of the São Francisco. This important river runs through the sertão, linking agricultural settlements such as Juazeiro, Ibotirama and Bom Jesus da Lapa and has its headwaters in northern Minas Gerais. ▸▸ *For listings, see pages 462-464.*

Lençóis and around → *For listings, see pages 462-464. Colour map 4, A5. Phone code: 075.*
Population: 9000.

Lençóis is the best place from which to explore the *chapada*. It's a pretty little colonial
village set on the banks of the fast-flowing Rio Lençóis, in the middle of the park. Many of
the sights can be visited on foot from town. Lençóis was established as a mining town in
1844 and takes its name from the tents assembled by the prospectors who first arrived
here (*lençóis* means 'white sheets' in Portuguese) set on the brown and green of the
hillside. While there are still some *garimpeiros* (gold and diamond prospectors) left,
tourism is now the main economic mainstay. Rather than precious metals, visitors are
attracted by the cool climate, the relaxed atmosphere and the wonderful trekking in the
Diamantina hills. The streets of Lençóis are lined with rustic houses, many of which are
now *pousadas*, restaurants or shops selling quirky handicrafts and semi-precious stones.

Ins and outs The **airport** ⓘ *20 km from town, Km 209, BR-242, T075-3625 8100*, has weekly
flights (on Saturdays) with **TRIP** (www.voetrip.com.br) to and from São Paulo via Salvador.
There are direct buses from Salvador and other cities in Bahia via Feira de Santana. Buses
from Recife and the northeast come via Seabra, west of Lençóis. There is a tourist office,
Sectur, inside the market next to the river.

Lençóis

Sleeping 🛏
Camping &
 Pousada Lumiar **1**
Canto das Aguas **2**
Casa da Geleia **3**
Casa de Hélia **4**
Estalagem de Alcino **5**
Lençóis **6**
Pousada dos Duendes **7**
Pousada Vila Serrano **8**
Pousada Violeiro **9**

Eating 🍴
Artistas da Massa **1**
Cozinha Aberta **2**
Gaya **3**
Neco's **4**

Bars & clubs 🍸
Fazedinha e Tal **5**

Excursions from Lençóis

On walking trips from Lençóis it is possible to visit the *serrano* (in the hills above town), which has wonderful natural pools in the river bed, which give a great spring-water massage when you sit under them; or the **Salão de Areia**, where the coloured sands for the bottle paintings come from. **Ribeirão do Meio** is a 45-minute walk from town; here locals slide down a long natural water chute into a big pool (it is best to watch someone else first and take something to slide in). Also near Lençóis are two very pretty waterfalls: the **Cachoeira da Primavera**; and the **Cachoeira Sossego**, a calendar photo cascade plunging into a deep blue pool.

Other towns in the chapada

There is simple accommodation and a handful of tour operators in **Palmeiras**, some 55 km west of Lençóis. The town makes a far quieter alternative base for exploring the *chapada*. **Combis** run sporadically between Palmeiras and Lençóis. **Mucugê** town in the far south, 134 km from Lençóis is sleepier still, and has a fascinating whitewash cemetery filled with elaborate mausoleums and set against the dark granite of the hillside. There are bus connections with Lençóis and Feira de Santana. The adjacent **Parque Municipal de Mucugê** was set-up to protect the *sempre viva* or *chuveirinho* plant – a beautiful globe of white flowers whose popularity with flower arrangers in Brazil almost led to their extinction in the late 20th century. **Igatu** has a population of approximately 350 people, some of them live in the largely abandoned stone houses built into or around Cyclopean boulders that dot the landscape. Wandering around the village and the ruins is a haunting experience. There are two *pousadas* in the village.

Feira de Santana → *Colour map 2, C4. Phone code: 075. Population: 450,500.*

Located 112 km northwest of Salvador, Feira de Santana is the centre of a great cattle breeding and trading area. Its Monday market, known as **Feira do Couro** (leather fair), is said to be the largest in Brazil and attracts great crowds to its colourful display of local products. The **artesanato market** in the centre, however, has a bigger selection. The *rodoviária* has an interesting wall of painted tiles (made by **Udo-Ceramista**, whose workshop is in Brotas, Avenida Dom João VI 411, Salvador). The **Micareta**, held in late April, is the biggest out-of-season carnival in Bahia and attracts many popular *axé* music groups from Salvador. Buses run to Salvador every 20 minutes, 1½ hours and there are connections to other towns throughout the state.

Parque Nacional da Chapada Diamantina

The Chapada Diamantina national park was founded in 1985 and comprises 1500 sq km of escarpment broken by extensive tracts of *caatinga* scrub forest, *cerrado*, patches of moist Atlantic coast forest and pântano (wetlands with permanent plant growth). The diversity of ecosystems have an associated diversity of flora and fauna. There is very little primary forest left, but the area is nonetheless home to rare large mammals such as maned wolf, jaguar and ocelot and birds endemic to all of the ecosystems. Spectaculars include the king vulture, crowned eagle, red-legged seriema and blue-winged macaw. There are birding guides available in Lençóis (see page 463).

Ins and outs

The **park headquarters** ① *R Barão do Rio Branco 25, T075-3332 2420*, is at Palmeiras 50 km from Lençóis. However, Lençóis is a much more practical source of information and the numerous agencies make it easy to find out what's what. See also www.infochapada.com.

Roy Funch, an American who used to manage the park and who now offers guided walks (see page 464), has written an excellent book on the *chapada*: *A Visitor's Guide to the Chapada Diamantina Mountains* (Collection Apoio 45), in English and Portuguese. The book includes history and geology of the region, an itinerary of all the principal sights, with instructions on how to reach them, and a thorough, though not comprehensive checklist of birds and mammals. It is widely available in Lençóis.

Chapada Diamantina

Background

The *chapada* forms part of the Brazilian shield, one of the oldest geological formations on earth, dating from the when the world was only one land mass. It extends north into the Serra da Capivara and Jalapão, and south into the Serra do Espinhaço and Serra da Canastra in Minas and the mountains of Mato Grosso and northern Bolivia.

Cave paintings and petroglyphs suggest that people have been living in and around the *chapada* for millennia. However, there were no permanent settlers in the hills in recorded history until the arrival of Portuguese prospectors in the 1700s, who discovered gold and diamonds in the extreme south of the *chapada* near Livramento de Nossa Senhora and in the north near Jacobina. The Portuguese kept the findings secret for fear of driving down world gem prices, and ceding the *chapada* to other European powers, notably the Dutch and Spanish, who were invading and occupying Brazilian territory repeatedly during this period.

The *chapada* didn't open up fully to mining until 1844, when Mucugê, Rio de Contas and subsequently Lençóis were founded and settled by miners from neighbouring Minas Gerais and western Bahia, followed by Portuguese noblemen from the Bahian coast. The latter evolved into *coroneis*: robber barons who set-up ruthless local fiefdoms run by gun-toting *jangada* henchmen. The most famous was

Horácio de Mattos, a prototype for many modern-day rural Brazilian politicians. De Mattos sucked all the money out of the *chapada* with his personal campaigns. He carried out famous vendettas against two other *coroneis*, Manuel Fabrício de Oliveira and Militão Rodrigues Coelho, to establish patriarchal dominance, overthrew the state government, routed the federal army and chased the infamous communist Prestes column all the way across Brazil and into Bolivia. He was in the back in Salvador in 1930.

Visiting the park

The *chapada* is cut by dirt roads, trails and rivers, which lead to waterfalls, viewpoints on table-top mountains, caves and natural swimming holes. There are many different hikes, and many of the routes have been used for centuries by the local farmers and miners, but finding your own way is difficult and it is best to visit on a guided trip.

There are more than 24 tour operators in Lençóis and organizing a trip to even the most distant sights is straightforward. Most tours tend to be car-based and rather sedentary as these are more profitable. But there are plenty of great hikes and sights around Lençóis, so consider all the options before signing up. Brazilian tourists are often more interested in chatting loudly among themselves than in hearing the quiet music of nature, so it can be difficult to see wildlife. ➤➤ *See Activities and tours, page 463.*

The most impressive sights in the *chapada* are included in the standard packages. Most have an entrance fee. These include: the extensive **Gruta do Lapa Doce** (US$5) and **Pratinha** caves (US$5); the latter of which are cut through by glassy blue water. The table-top mountains at the **Morro de Pai Inácio**, US$2, 30 km from Lençóis, offer the best view of the *chapada*, especially at sunset. The 384 m high **Cachoeira da Fumaça** (Smoke or Glass Waterfall) is the second highest in Brazil and lies deeper within the park 2½ hours hike from the village of **Capão**. The view is astonishing; the updraft of the air currents often makes the water flow back up creating the 'smoke' effect. The **Rio Marimbus** flows through and area of semi-swamp reminiscent of the Pantanal and very rich in birdlife whilst the **Rio Mucugezinho** plunges over the blood-red **Cachoeira do Diabo** in an extensive area of *cerrado* just below the craggy **Roncador** ('snorer') waterfall.

Hiking in the chapada

It is essential to use a guide for treks as it is easy to get lost. Trail-walking in the park can involve clambering over rocks and stepping stones so bring strong shoes. A reasonable level of physical fitness is advisable. There are a lot of mosquitos in campsites so carry repellent. For overnight trips it is highly advisable to bring a fleece and sleeping bag as nights in the 'winter' months can be cold. Sometimes, guides can arrange these. A tent is useful but optional; although many camps are beside reasonably hospitable caves. Torches (flashlights) and a water bottle are essentials.

The **Morro do Pai Inacio to Capão** trail is a 25-km day-hike that leads from the summit of the Pai Inácio escarpment around other table-top mountains, passing through *cerrado* *caatinga* and arable areas to the Capão valley. Another day hike is from **Lençóis to Capão** along a series of rivers (great for swimming) and around the base of the mountains, with a car ride back at the end of the walk.

The **Cachoeira da Fumaça** trail leaves direct from Lençóis and takes two to three days to reach the base of the falls, from where there is a steep hike to the top. If you only have one day, it's possible to drive the 70 km to the **Vale do Capão** and hike the steep 6-km trail to the top of the falls. Both trails are very popular in high season.

Introduction

Brazil is one of the world's great musical countries, and your travels here will be accompanied by a rich and varied soundtrack. Brazilians dance to, or play, a bewildering array of musical styles, which are unique to their country – from the lilting flow of bossa nova, to the funk of samba, or the up-close and intimate *forró* jigs of the northeastern desert. There's always a live band on somewhere, any night of the week, no matter how small the town, and it seems that everyone plays something, whether it's a guitar, a bow and arrow-shaped twanging *berimbau*, a drum or a mandolin. And they generally play it with the dexterity they play football.

Brazilian music has very little in common with that of the rest of Latin America. No one has heard of the Buena Vista Social Club or Shakira, and the locals dance neither tango nor salsa. Music here comes from a more diverse set of roots than the rest of the continent: from half a dozen West African nations; from the wistful melancholy of Portuguese folk, whose mood is altogether different from that of Spain; from the calls and trance choruses of the forest *indígenas*; and from Galician Celtic dances and German campfire songs. Brazilians add to this an unfailing musical curiosity, which scours the world for new sounds and which crosses generations and transcends trends. In Brazil, people love music for its own sake not because it's in vogue. Music you might say, is always in fashion here, but fashion is never in music.

Previous page: Seu Jorge, international film actor, style icon and the foremost samba funk singer in Brazil. **Above**: Nelson da Rabeca (see page 488) in his living room in Marechal Deodoro, Alagoas.

Above: Rio's Clube dos Democráticos is one of the best places in Brazil for live big band or gafieira samba.

Rio: samba and the boys from Ipanema

If you've heard one Brazilian tune it's likely to be either the joyful, summery chorus of *Mas que Nada* or a lift-music version of *The Girl from Ipanema*. Both songs come from Rio de Janeiro and from a time before men had walked on the moon. *Mas que Nada* is a **samba** – the country's most ubiquitous and enduring music style, and the sound of Rio carnival. Samba was born in the poor, black district of Gamboa in the early 20th century (see page 90) and it comes in many forms, from the big drum troupes whose chorus of *tambores* and giant *surdo* bass drums can fill a stadium, to quieter, acoustic sung samba. But it is invariably best heard live, and preferably in Rio de Janeiro itself (see pages 126-130 for a list of venues). Despite its age, samba lives on and remains very popular with young Brazilians, particularly as **samba soul** and **samba funk** (also known as Rio samba, whose most famous exponent is **Seu Jorge**) and in its close-danced beach-and-barbecue form, **pagode**. Both samba and pagode are also dance styles, characterized by fast feet and leg movements with stiff upper body and hips. They are incredibly tricky to master. For the first half of its life, samba was working class, poor and black. But in the 1950s its rhythms were adopted by a group of young, nerdy, white middle-class boys from Ipanema and Copacabana. Musicians like the conservatory-trained **Antônio Carlos (Tom) Jobim**, the poet and diplomat **Vinícius de Moraes**, and Bahian émigré **João Gilberto** began to play a kind of samba on the acoustic guitar or piano, which they accompanied with witty lyrics and more complex chord progressions drawn from French impressionist composers and a jazzier Brazilian musical style called **choro** (which is still popular today). Few of these new samba singers could

Above: Bossa nova has lived on abroad far more than it has in Brazil. Rio session musicians *Os Ipanemas* are one of the most popular acts in Europe. **Opposite page**: Locals gather to dance samba on weekend nights at the Rio Scenarium club in Lapa, Rio de Janeiro.

sing and their breathy, almost spoken vocal style became a trademark of the their sound, which was christened the new wave or **bossa nova**.

Bossa nova became internationally famous when its soft sound was adopted by a series of US 'cool jazz' musicians in the 1960s. The foremost of these was the saxophonist **Stan Getz** who in 1964 released one of the best-selling jazz albums of all time, *Getz/Gilberto*, with João Gilberto. It included a single version of Tom Jobim and Vinícius de Moraes' *The Girl from Ipanema* (with English lyrics vastly inferior to Vinícius'). This rocketed into the billboard chart and João's wife, **Astrud Gilberto**, who sang the song, was propelled to stardom. Her success defined and continues to define the Brazilian vocal style in the minds of foreigners: light, happy and invariably female. It also stimulated an exodus of musicians from Brazil, which included a Carioca session pianist called **Sergio Mendes**.

He repeated Astrud's success with a popular samba song by Carioca singer Jorge Ben – *Mas Que Nada*. Bossa largely died in Brazil in the 1970s, and it can be hard to hear it beyond the tourist bars, but it lived on in the USA as jazz-bossa and hotel lobby music, and was resurrected in Europe in the new millennium with Bebel Gilberto's club chill-out room re-recordings of her father João's music. Her sound is slowly beginning to filter back to Brazil's club and cocktail bar scene today.

Essential CDs
Choro: anything by Pixinguinha
Samba: Bezerra da Silva, *O Partido Alto da Samba*
Bossa nova: Elis Regina and Tom Jobim, *Elis e Tom*
Rio funk: Seu Jorge, *America Brasil*
Rio soul: Tim Maia, *O Melhor de Tim Maia*
Pagode: Zeca Pagodinho, *Ao Vivo MTV*

Brazil's other great musical capital city is Salvador. From the late 1960s to the 1980s, this most African of Brazilian cities produced some of Brazil's most creative and exciting musicians. Choro, samba and bossa nova were all acoustically driven. When the Beatles and Hendrix rose to global stardom in the 1960s and even Dylan picked up an electric guitar, there was something of a revolution in Brazil. Conservatives wanted to keep the country's music 'authentic' and unpolluted by foreign influences. Liberals, spearheaded by a group of avant garde musicians from Bahia led by **Tom Zé**, **Gilberto Gil** and **Caetano Veloso**, and a São Paulo trio called **Os Mutantes**, embraced electric instruments and psychotropic drugs and took Brazilian music in a new electric direction. This was christened **tropicália** after a fusion

ALEX ROBINSON

Naná Vasconcelos from Recife (see page 500) has consistently been voted the best percussionist in the world by *Down Beat* magazine. He opens the Recife/Olinda Carnaval.

Essential CDs
Tropicália: various artists, *Tropicália Panis e Circenses*; Caetano Veloso, *Bicho*; Gilberto Gil, *Parabolicamará*; Tom Zé, *Fabrication Defect*
Blocos afros: Olodum, *20 Anos*; Carlinhos Brown, *Alfagamabetizado*
Samba de roda: Mariene de Castro, *Abre Caminho* (see page 425)

of the words tropical and psychedelia. The seeds of *tropicália* blew from Bahia over the whole of Brazil to produce myriad musical fruits, fusions of rock, soul, funk and Brazilian rhythms. Collectively these came to be known as **MPB**, or Música Popular Brasileira.

Acoustic music lived on in Bahia after *tropicália*. The late 1970s saw the emergence of a string of heavily percussive bands focused around drum troupes and called **blocos afros**. These were cultural organizations associated with Salvador carnival and rooted in the ritual music of the African Brazilian spirit religion of *candomblé*, traditional **Samba de Roda** (sung in a ring of people and accompanied only by percussion), and the martial art dance of **capoeira**. Bands like **Olodum**, **Ilê Aiyê** and Carlinhos Brown's **Timbalada** (see page 425) promoted African-Brazilian issues and solidarity through their music. Seeing them up close in the streets of Salvador, with dozens of drummers playing together in perfect syncopated unison, is an incredibly powerful experience. But even the drums of the *blocos afros* are being drowned out by Bahia's most popular music, **axé**, which sounds a little like salsa sexed-up, fused with rock and roll and overdosing on speed. It's energetic but shallow, with slushy lyrics and little sophistication. It's also relentlessly commercial and it's sweeping through the carnivals and clubs of the northeast leaving musical variety and the more traditional musical styles in its wake. Salvador is sadly not at its best musical moment as this book goes to press (see box, page 406). For a list of what to hear where, see pages 423-425.

The rhythms of the African-indigenous Brazilian martial art dance of capoeira have strongly influenced Brazilian music in general, especially in Bahia.

Recife and São Luís: back to Africa and into the mangroove

Salvador's crown as the musical capital of the northeast has, at least for now, passed to São Luís, the new centre of African-Brazilian music, and Recife, where the spirit of *tropicália* lives on as *mangue beat*. On a Saturday night in the colonial centre of São Luís, large groups gather in impromptu bands to play the local equivalent of samba, **cacuriá**. Women dance and swirl in flowing dresses, and everyone is sucked into the throng. The city is at its liveliest

> **Essential CDs**
> **Cacuriá**: Dona Teté, *O Divino Cacuriá de Dona Teté*
> **Brazilian reggae**: Tribo de Jah, *Essencial*
> **Mangue beat**: Nação Zumbi, *Afrociberdelia*; Mundo Livre S/A, *Samba Esquema Noise*
> **Siba**: *Fuloresta de Samba*

during the **Bumba-Meu-Boi** festivals, which have their own costumed dances (see pages 18 and 607) and it preserves a strong connection with the Caribbean through **reggae**, which is played in many of the small bars in the city centre.

Recife in Pernambuco state is more avant garde and intellectual. At weekends, the smoky bars of the old city centre vibrate to the guitars, drums, desert fiddles and electrified accordions of experimental bands and singers, whose sound is a fusion of the **maracatu** rhythms of African Pernambuco, with folk sounds from the arid backlands and international rock influences from bands like Nick Cave and the Bad Seeds, and British Sea Power (see page 499). There's a great diversity of sound, but the scene as a whole emerged as **mangue beat** in the 1990s. This was a deliberate attempt to re-discover Pernambuco's African and poor rural majority and re-articulate their heritage in a modern context. It was led by the charismatic singer **Chico Science** and his band **Nação Zumbi** (see page 684), **Fred Zeroquatro**, lead singer of **Mundo Livre S/A** (see page 515), and rootsier **Mestre Ambrósio**. Chico died in a car crash in 1997 but Mundo Livre and Mestre Ambrósio's lead singer, **Siba**, can be heard at carnival time. Their legacy and spirit lives on.

ALEX ROBINSON

ALEX ROBINSON

ALEX ROBINSON

Opposite page: Fred Zeroquatro of Mundo Livre S/A from Recife – one of the founders of the *mangue beat* movement. **Top**: An *aparelhagem* techno-brega club night in Belém.
Middle: Banda Glória playing at the Aldeia Turiassu in São Paulo.
Bottom: Moreno Veloso, Domenico Lancelotti and Alexandre Kassin of Mais 2 – one of the freshest new bands from Rio.

Northeast and the backland barn dance jig

Above: *Forró* is danced at the Festas Juninhas celebrations in Campina Grande, Paraíba.
Opposite page: MPB singer Maria Rita, the new face of intelligent Brazilian pop.

Essential CDs
Forró: Sivuca, *Cabelo do Milho*; Mel com Terra, *Forró Mel com Terra*; Elba Ramalho, *Flor de Paraíba* ; Dorivã, *Taquarulua*

The rest of northeastern Brazil is dominated by **forró**, a kind of punchy jig originally driven by triangle, accordion and a deep bass drum, but now usually played by a full band. Popular wisdom says that the name derives from a Brazilianized pronunciation of 'for all' and comes from the 'for all' dances held for railway workers by their British bosses in the early 20th century. In reality, the dance is probably far older, dating from the 19th century. At this time, dance hall floors in the *sertão* were made of baked mud and, in order for them not to get dusty, people would drag their feet as they danced. The name probably comes from an abbreviation of *forrobodó* meaning 'dragged feet'. *Forró* is party music, and the biggest parties of all are the **Festas Juninhas** (see pages 18 and 535) in the *sertão* backlands in Caruaru, Pernambuco and Paraíba in June, when hundreds of thousands gather to dance at breakneck speed, yet so close that they are literally entwined. You can do the same at any time of year, though, in the beach bars in Maceió, Fortaleza and half a dozen other little resorts. But get a Brazilian to show you the dance steps first or you'll feel like a rugby player dancing ballet.

Brazilian pop: rodeo crooning and spangly skirts

As in any country, the music visitors are most frequently exposed to is chart pop, and in Brazil it's no better than anywhere else. And no worse. But unlike almost everywhere else, it is home grown. Brazilian pop loosely falls into two styles: up tempo *axé* carnival music and its variants; and a kind of romantic crooning, *sertanejo*. The former originates largely from Bahia and Para and is generally sung by scantily clad, supremely energetic, muscular divas like Ivete Sangalo or Joelma from Banda Calypso. They front a band of precisely choreographed session musicians and even more scantily clad dancers. Lyrics are crass and cheesy, and the music as basic as the Spice Girls. But the shows are supremely professional and they attract crowds of hundreds of thousands, as does *sertanejo*. But here the singers are male duos with mullet haircuts, usually dressed in checked shirts and stetsons, who sing desperately cheesy romantic power ballads about 'grande amor'. Videos are often intercut with shots of prize bulls and rodeos.

The Amazon: surf guitar and carimbó rock

There's only one place in the Amazon for music – Belém. The city pounds to the springy West-Africa-meets-the-Caribbean rhythm of **carimbó** and strums to the psychedelic sixties Dick Dale surf twang of **guitarrada**. A night out on the town is unforgettable and quite unlike anywhere else in the world. At the weekend *aparelaghem* parties, DJs housed in giant space-pod sets as large as a truck and covered in shimmering flashing lights, play pounding techno-*guitarrada* or techno-*brega* to warehouse-sized crowds of revellers. Psychedelic *carimbó*-reggae bands

made up of 20 year olds and fronted by 70-year-old rockers in dark glasses and satin suits, play in sweaty clubs on the riverside, sharing a stage with surf guitar bands or red hot power metal samba bands fronted by a wispy woman with dreadlocks and tattoos. There's nowhere else like it anywhere, even in Brazil. Come here for the Círio festival if you can and dive in.

Essential CDs

Carimbó: Curimbó de Bolso, *Cantação Amazónida*
Techno-guitarrada: Pio Lobato, *Technoguitarrada*
Guitarrada: Guitarradas do Pará
Amazon metal: Madam Sataan, *Madam Sataan*
Carimbó psychedelia: Coletivo Radio Cipo, *Formigando na Calcada do Brasil*
Surf pyschedelic pop: La Pupuña, *The Shark Side of the Moon*

Top: Mestre Laurentino of Coletivo Rádio Cipó, the self-proclaimed oldest rocker in the world.
Above: Coletivo Rádio Cipó, one of many bands making Belém one of Brazil's most exciting musical cities.

xii

Minas Gerais: Milton Nascimento and metal from the mines

The state of Minas is Brazil's lyrical, reflective heart. Many of the country's finest poets and writers grew up in its pretty villages of whitewashed sugar-cube houses and colonial bell towers set in rolling hills. Many associate the Minas sound with Milton Nascimento and his band, the **Clube da Esquina**. Clube da Esquina formed as a loose association of like-minded musicians in 1970s Belo Horizonte, and together they forged a new Brazilian musical style whose influence has spread far beyond their country. Herbie Hancock, Wayne Shorter and Stevie Wonder are admirers of Milton Nascimento and the great French modern jazz and classical composer, Lionel Belmondo, has called him as important a composer as Ravel. Unlike much Brazilian music, the Clube da Esquina sound is textural and melodic rather than rhythmic and dancy, owing more to folk and church music than samba and bossa nova. Soaring, melancholy vocal lines interplay with sweeping, rich harmonies, the chants of Africa and indigenous Brazil, and catholic choral lines, children's voices, gentle acoustic guitar, mandolin, the orchestra, a distant organ or drum, a ringing bell tower ... all rising and falling with the dynamic breadth of a Villa-Lobos or Vaughan Williams tone poem. Above this rich, pastoral landscape of sound, Milton's voice soars in golden baritone or searing falsetto telling hundreds of stories of Minas Gerais, of Brazil itself, of its marginalized and

Milton Nascimento, one of the towering greats of international music (see page 264).

> **Essential CDs**
> **Clube da Esquina**: Milton Nascimento, *Clube da Esquina*; *Clube da Esquina II*
> **Modern Minas**: Erika Machado, *No Cimento*; Uakti and Philip Glass, *Aguas da Amazonia*

innocent, its slaves, serfs and *indigenas*, woven together with deeply personal impressions and reflections from Milton's own life. Although his legacy lives on in a hundred singer-songwriters who play in the bars and theatres of Belo Horizonte, Minas continues to produce some of Brazil's most individual voices: the all-instrumental band **Uakti** who build their own unique percussion instruments and play a kind of mesmerizing minimalist trance on them, collaborating with composers like Philip Glass; **Érika Machado** (see page 260) who sings beautifully crafted, catchy pop with quirky, witty lyrics; **Proa**, a kind of new-wave indie electronica; and Brazil's most commercially successful band, **Sepultura**, who play some of the world's most driving, exciting virtuoso death metal.

Street musicians gather for an impromptu jam in Vila Madalena, one of São Paulo's many musical neighbourhoods.

São Paulo: the avant garde

Everything from the Brazilian musical continent comes together in São Paulo. It is Brazil's nexus, its default capital where the talent gravitates in search of money. On any night anywhere you can hear a bizarre *carimbó*-metal act from Belém, Recife *mangue beat*, an off-the-wall Mineiro songwriter, cowboy ballads from Goiás or some old-school samba. Yet the city has its own sound too, a kind of avant garde art rock samba formulated by one of Brazil's great unsung musical geniuses, **Itamar Assumpção**. Itamar was the Zappa of Brazil, a supremely odd, witty, individual musical and lyrical voice who gathered a group of immensely talented musicians around him in the 1980s and performed strings of famously bizarre, theatrical shows. His work inspired numerous other mavericks such as baroque music-hall samba rockers, **Karnak**, and the electronica pioneer, **Max de Castro** (see page 215). Together their sound became known as **vanguarda**. São Paulo has also produced many of Brazil's internationally famous DJs, notably **Patife** and **Marky**, both of whom had a predilection for drum 'n' bass.

> **Essential CDs**
> **Avant garde**: Itamar Assumpção, *Preto Bras*; Karnak, *Karnak*; Max de Castro, *Max de Castro*
> **Club**: DJ Patife, *Cool Steps*

Brazilian instruments glossary

Atabaque: the Brazilian equivalent of the conga drum
Bandolim: Brazilian pear-shaped mandolin
Tambor: a tight-skinned samba drum
Repinique: a tight-skinned samba drum
Surdo: a deep, booming samba drum
Reco reco: a friction percussion instrument that looks like a cheese grater
Cavaquinho: a four-stringed miniature Portuguese guitar
Caxixi: a little basket full of pebbles or beads used in capoeira and general percussion
Cuica: a friction drum whose call sounds like a crying monkey
Xequere: a gourd or wooden shell enclosed in a basket of beads, used in samba and *maracatu*
Tamborim: a small hand-held drum
Pandeiro: a small-hand held drum with bells on the edge (tambourine in English)
Zabumba: a deep sonorous drum used in *forró*
Violão: a guitar
Timbal: a clear high-tone drum used in Bahian music and most famously by Carlinhos Brown
Rocar : a series of little plate bells in a metal frame
Berimbau: a bow-shaped twanging percussion instrument used in capoeira
Gongue: a metal bell used in *maracatu*

bove: Berimbaus, Xequeres, Timbales and other assorted percussion instruments for sale in the treets of Salvador. **Next page**: Carioca MPB singer Marisa Monte playing live at the Barbican in London.

A trail runs from **Igatu to Andaraí**, leaving from the central square of the former town past the cemetery and following the Xique-Xique river. The walk takes four hours and offers wonderful views of the mountain landscape. There are plenty of river bank stops for a cooling swim. There are longer treks too.

The **Vale do Paty** hike is a four- to six-day walk running through the heart of the Serra along a valley surrounded by imposing *meseta* table-top mountains. There are many good stopping places with viewpoints, caves, swimming holes and waterfalls. The route usually departs from Capão in the north or from the village of Guiné just west of Andaraí town.

For a full cross-section of the park, hike the 112-km **Travessia Diamantina**, which runs from the Vale do Capão in the north right across the park via the Vale do Paty, to the Cachoeira do Buracão in the far south. Accommodation is in tents and rustic *pousadas* and there are side-trips off to the Cachoeira da Fumaça (near Capão), Igatu, Poço Encatado, and the Marimbus pantanal area and Roncador falls. Establish which of the sights you would like to visit with the tour company before setting off.

The sertão → *For listings, see pages 462-464. Colour map 2, C4.*

Most of Bahia is arid: a rock and scrub semi-desert covered in leafless *caatinga* forest, cut by the blue vein of the majestic Rio São Francisco and dotted with little settlements where local people scratch a meagre living from the sun-baked earth. This is the *sertão* – a backland that has produced some of Brazil's most enduring mythical figures. **Antônio Conselheiro**, a purple-robed desert prophet whose rag-tag band of marauders and bandits converted to Christianity in the late 19th-century and built Canudos, crushed two armies and almost broke the Brazilian state. **Lampião** – the *sertão*'s brutal Robin Hood – who pillaged the rich *coroneis*, distributed wealth and brutal justice to the desert villages in the early 20th century and died in a gun battle in a town famous for its troubadours and poets. Their legacy, the iron hand of *coroneis* who impose rough justice to this day and countless forgotten, timeless festivals and rites still characterize the dust and dirt towns of this vast interior. Tourists are seldom seen and are always a curiosity.

Euclides da Cunha and Monte Santo → *Phone code: 075.*

North of Feira da Santana, at Km 225 on the BR-116 road to Fortaleza, **Euclides da Cunha**, is a good base for exploring the Canudos area with a couple of standard hotels. The bus station is on the BR-116, T075-3271 1365.

About 38 km west is the famous hill shrine of **Monte Santo** in the *sertão*, reached by 3.5 km of steps cut into the rocks of the **Serra do Picaraça**. It's a 45-minute walk each way, so set out early. This is the scene of pilgrimages and great religious devotion during Holy Week. The shrine was built by an Italian who had a vision of the cross on the mountain in 1765. One block north of the bottom of the stairs is the **Museu do Sertão**, with pictures from the 1897 Canudos rebellion.

Canudos → *Phone code: 075.*

Canudos itself is 100 km away. Religious rebels, led by Antônio Conselheiro, defeated three expeditions sent against them in 1897 before being overwhelmed. The Rio Vaza Barris, which runs through Canudos, has been dammed, and the town has been moved to **Nova Canudos** by the dam. Part of the old town is still located 10 km west in the **Parque Estadual de Canudos**, created in 1997.

The 1500-ha **Estação Biológica de Canudos** lies a few kilometres from the state park. It was founded in 1989 by the Fundação Biodiversitas (www.biodiversitas.org.br) to protect the only remaining nesting sites of the critically endangered giant blue Lear's macaw. Fewer than 100 birds nest here, on a large sun-baked clay cliff within the reserve. The park and reserve can only be visited with a hire car, or a taxi from Canudos town. The Estação Biológica de Canudos can also be visited on a birding tour with guides such as Ciro Albano (see page 464). There are direct buses to Canudos from Salvador. For tourist information see www.canudosnet.com.br.

◉ Chapada Diamantina and the sertão listings

For Sleeping and Eating price codes and other relevant information, see pages 32-37.

◉ Sleeping

Lençóis *p457, map p457*

L Canto das Águas, Av Senhor dos Passos, T/F075-3334 1154, www.lencois.com.br. Medium-size riverside hotel with modest a/c or fan-cooled rooms, a pool and efficient service. The best rooms are in the new wing; others can be musty.

AL Hotel de Lençóis, R Altinha Alves 747, T075-3334 1102, www.hoteldelencois.com.br. Plain, dark wood and white-tiled rooms with terracotta roofs set in a handsome colonial house in a grassy garden on the edge of the park. Good breakfast, pool and a restaurant.

A Pousada Vila Serrano, R Alto do Bonfim 8, 3334 1486, www.vilaserrano.com.br. Warm and welcoming mock-colonial *pousada* overlooking a patio and little garden 5 mins from town. Excellent service, breakfast, trips organized. Very friendly and knowledgeable.

C-D Estalagem de Alcino, R Gen Viveiros de Morais 139, T075-3334 1171, www.alcino estalagem.com. An enchanting and beautifully restored period house with a range of rooms furnished with 19th-century antiques. Most have shared bathrooms. The superb breakfast is served in the little garden with hummingbirds, near the owner's pottery workshop. Great library and book exchange.

D Casa da Geleia, R Gen Viveiros 187, T075-3334 1151. A handful of smart chalets set in a huge garden at the entrance to the town. English spoken, good breakfast, including

sumptuous jams and honeys made or collected by the owner. Zé Carlos is a keen birdwatcher and an authority on the region.

D Casa de Hélia, R da Muritiba, T075-3334 1143, www.casadehelia.com.br. Attractive and welcoming little guesthouse. English spoken. Good facilities, legendary breakfast.

D Pousada dos Duendes, R do Pires, T/F075-3334 1229, www.pousadadosduendes.com. Run by English Olivia Taylor and often crowded with backpackers. Rooms are basic with shared showers, modest breakfast and dinner (with veggie options). Their tour agency, H2O Expeditions, arranges tours and treks from 1 to 11 days. Check with other agencies in town before committing.

D Pousada Violeiro, R Prof Assis 70, T075-3334 1259, www.pousadavioleiro.com.br. Very simple rooms with room for up to 4 (**E**) just behind the bus stop near the river. Quiet and conservative.

D-E HI Lençóis, R Boa Vista 121, T075-3334 1497, www.hostelchapada.com.br. A large, friendly and well-run hostel with an adventure sports agency in one of the town's grand old colonial houses. The building has been completely restored and has singles, en suite doubles and single-sex 4- to 6-bed dorms; shared kitchen and a large, airy garden with hammocks and littered with outdoor chairs.

Camping

Camping and Pousada Lumiar, near the Rosário church in the town centre, T075-3334 1241. A large grassy area for pitching tents and a series of very simple rooms (**D**) tents and bungalows (**C**). Popular restaurant. Friendly.

Feira de Santana *p458*

There are several cheap hotels in Praça da Matriz and near the *rodoviária* (fairly central). **A Feira Palace**, Av Maria Quitéria 1572, T075-3221 5011, www.feirapalacehotel.com.br. Blocky 1970s hotel in need of renovation, but the best in town; with a restaurant and pool. **B-C Acalanto**, R Torres 77, T075-3625 3612, www.hotelacalanto.com.br. Modern, standard, small-town hotel with around 50 modest rooms with en suites. **D Paládio**, Av Getúlio Vargas 294, T075-3623 8899. Far less grand than its name but well kept.

Euclides da Cunha and Monte Santo *p461*

B Do Conselheiro, Av Mcal Juarez Tavora 187, Euclides, T075-3275 1814. Standard town hotel with breakfast in the price. **C Grapiuna**, Praça Monsenhor Berenguer 401, Euclides, T075-3275 1157. Basic rooms with a/c and cheaper options without bath. Recommended.

Canudos *p461*

E Brasil, Nova Canudos. Very simple rooms with en suites and fans. Cheaper without breakfast.

🍽 Eating

Lençóis *p457, map p457*
¶¶¶ **Cozinha Aberta**, Rui Barbosa 42, T075-3334 1309, www.cozinhaaberta.com.br. The best in town with organic and slow food from Paulistana chef Deborah Doitschinoff. Just east of the main *praça*. ¶¶ **Artistas da Massa**, R Miguel Calmon. Italian dishes, mainly pasta and pizza. ¶¶ **Neco's**, Praça Maestro Clarindo Pachêco 15, T075-3334 1179. Set meal of local dishes of the kind once eaten by the *garimpeiro* miners, such as saffron-stewed mutton accompanied by prickly pear cactus, crisp, tart *batata da serra* and fried green banana.

¶ **Gaya**, Praça Horácio Matos s/n, T075-3334 1167. Organic and wholefood with large salads generous juices and sandwiches. The owners organize trips into the *chapada*.

🍸 Bars and clubs

Lençóis *p457, map p457*
Clube Sete, R das Pedras. Little dance club open Fri and Sat nights.
Doce Barbaros, R das Pedras, 21. Lively little bar almost any night of the week.
Fazendinha e Tal, R das Pedras 125. Very popular bar with rustic *garimpeiro* decoration serving hundreds of different *cachacas*.

🛍 Shopping

Lençóis *p457, map p457*
There is a little market in the main square selling arts and crafts.
Instrumentos, R das Pedras 78, T075-3334 1334. Unusual faux-Brazilian and African musical instruments by quirky ex-pat Argentinian Jorge Fernando.
Zambumbeira, R das Pedras at Tamandare, T075-3334 1207. Beautiful ceramics by reknowned artisans like Zé Caboclo, jewellery, walking sticks and arty bric-a-brac.

🥾 Activities and tours

Lençóis *p457, map p457*
Guides
Guides offer their services at most *pousadas* (about US$20-30 per trip); most of them are very young. The following are recommended:
Chapada Adventure, Av 7 de Setembro 7, T075-3334 2037, www.chapadaadventure.com.br. A small operator offering good value car-based tours and light hiking throughout the *chapada*.
Edmilson (known as Mil), R Domingos B Souza 70, T075-3334 1319. Knows the region extremely well, knowledgeable and reliable.

For a da Trilha, R das Pedras 202, www.for
adatrilha.com.br. Longer hikes and light
adventures, from canyoning to rapelling.
Gaya, Praça Horácio Matos s/n, T075-3334
1167, T075-9992 2820 (mob), rafa.gaya@
yahoo.com.br, see Eating, page 463. Rafa
organizes budget backpacker trips in and
around the *chapada* in an old Toyota
Bandeirante. Tours cost around US$200
for 300-km round trips for up to 10 people,
and include unusual locations such as the
Cachoeira do Mosquito. Book ahead if possible.
Luiz Krug, contact via Vila Serrano, T075-3334
1102. An independent, English-speaking guide
specializing in geology and caving.
Roy Funch, T/F075-3334 1305, www.fcd.org.
br. The ex-director of the Chapada Diamantina
National Park is an excellent guide and has
written a visitors' guide to the park in English.
It is recommended as the best for information
on history, geography and trails of the
chapada. Highly recommended. He can be
booked through www.elabrasil.com.
Trajano, contact via Vila Serrano or Casa da
Hélia, T075-3334 1143. Speaks English and
Hebrew and is a good-humoured guide for treks
to the bottom of the Cachoeira da Fumaça.
Venturas e Aventuras, Praça Horácio
de Matos 20, T075-3334 1304. Excellent
trekking expeditions, up to 6 days.
Zé Carlos, T075-3334 1151, contact through
Casa da Geleia or Vila Serrano. The best
guide for birdwatching.

Canudos *p461*
Birdwatching
Ciro Albano, www.nebrazilbirding.com.
The best birding guide for the northeast
of Brazil offering tips to birding and wildlife
sites, including Estação Veracruz, Canudos
and the Chapada Diamantina.

Body and soul
The *chapada* is a centre for alternative
treatments. All the practitioners listed
come highly recommended.

Anita Marti, T075-9989 8328. Healing
and therapeutic massage and treatments.
Dieter Herzberg, T075-9984 2720,
dieterherzberg@yahoo.com.br. All manner
of therapeutic and healing massage.
Jaques Gagnon, T075-3334 1281,
www.janeladaalma.com. Neuro-structural
therapy and healing massage.

⊖ Transport

Lençóis *p457, map p457*
Air Airport, Km 209, BR-242, 20 km from town
T075-3625 8100. Weekly flights from São Paulo
and Salvador with TRIP (www.voetrip.com.br).

Bus Real Expresso to **Salvador** 3 a day,
US$24, *comercial* via **Feira de Santana**.
Book in advance, especially at weekends and
holidays. For the rest of Bahia state change at
Feira de Santana; it is not necessary to go via
Salvador. Buses also to **Recife**, **Ibotirama**,
Barreiras or **Palmas** (for Jalapão), **Chapada
dos Veadeiros** and **Brasília**, 16 hrs, US$60 (all
with transfer in Seabra, several buses daily).

Canudos *p461*
At least 4 buses daily leave Salvador's
rodoviária for the city of Euclides da Cunha.
From here there are regular connections
to Canudos. Taxis in Canudos town can be
hired for a full day for around US$40.

❶ Directory

Lençóis *p457, map p457*
Banks and post office There is a
Bradesco with an ATM, and a post office
(Mon-Fri 0900-1700) on the main square.

Feira de Santana *p458*
Banks Banco 24 Horas, Av Senhor dos
Passos 1332. **Banco do Brasil**, Av Getúlio
Vargas 897. There is also a **Bradesco** in town.

Contents

Footprint features

Recife & the northeast coast

At a glance

Getting around Mostly by bus. Car hire recommended for the coast but not for the interior as roads can be poor.

Time required 2 days for Recife and Olinda, 3-5 days for the coast, 2-3 days for Fernando de Noronha.

Weather Hot and wet summers (Mar-Jul), hot and drier winters (Sep-Feb).

When not to go Apr and May are wet. Jun and Jul are wetter but are the best months for festivals.

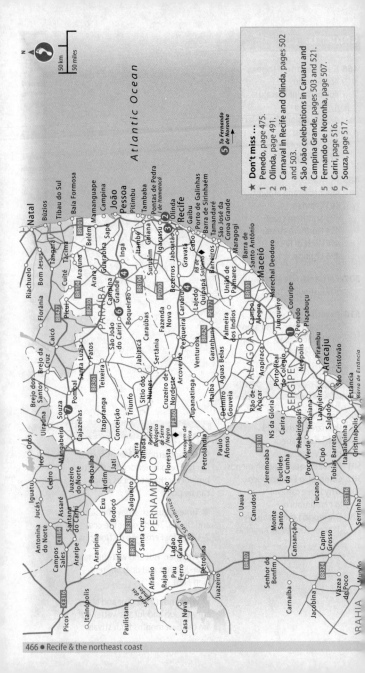

★ Don't miss ...
1 Penedo, page 475.
2 Olinda, page 491.
3 Carnaval in Recife and Olinda, pages 502 and 503.
4 São João celebrations in Caruaru and Campina Grande, pages 503 and 521.
5 Fernando de Noronha, page 507.
6 Cariri, page 516.
7 Souza, page 517.

To Fernando de Noronha

Atlantic Ocean

50 km
50 miles

N

The four states that comprise this region – Sergipe, Alagoas, Pernambuco and Paraíba – are often overlooked by visitors. Most travellers whizz through, perhaps stopping for a beach break at Porto de Galinhas or Fernando de Noronha, and a few days in colourful, colonial Olinda. But those who spend time in the region, exploring its buildings, sampling the music and arts scene in Recife or getting lost in the crowds at the great festivals in the *sertão* find it one of the most interesting, diverse and least spoilt parts of Brazil.

In the first centuries of its colonial history, the region grew rich through sugar and became the commercial and intellectual centre of Brazil. Pernambuco, in particular, retains many magnificent buildings from that period, while the convents in Olinda and Igarassu are fine examples of Iberian baroque. In the late 19th century, the sugar boom subsided and poverty began to spread across the state. Yet the proud intellectual tradition continued, with notables such as Marechal Deodoro, the founder of the Brazilian republic, Gilberto Freyre, who helped forge Brazil's identity and Francisco Brennand, the surreal artist, all from the area.

The region has never been more culturally exciting than today. In the 1990s Recife saw the explosion of an artistic movement called *mangue beat*, which sought to fuse the rich heritage of Pernambuco folk art and music with social activism and post-modernism. The resulting cultural fluorescence has helped to make Pernambuco Brazil's most vibrant cultural state. Artists have ateliers on every other corner in Olinda, while numerous festivals showcase the country's most innovative film-making and resurrect popular culture. Carnaval in Recife or Olinda is considered by many to be the best and most traditional in the country.

Sergipe and Alagoas

Few tourists stop off in these two tiny states between Bahia and Pernambuco, but herein lies their charm. Both have fine beaches, easily accessible from the state capitals: Aracaju and Maceió. And both have a series of very pretty Portuguese towns where visitors are still a novelty. The most impressive are Penedo (on the banks of Brazil's 'other' great river, the São Francisco, which forms the border between the two states), Marechal Deodoro (the birthplace of the founder of the Brazilian Republic) and the Portuguese capital of Sergipe, São Cristóvão (which is Brazil's fourth oldest town and its newest World Heritage Site). Of the capitals, Maceió is by far the more salubrious, with some excellent beaches and lively nightlife. ▶▶ *For listings, see pages 477-483.*

Aracaju → *For listings, see pages 477-483. Colour map 2, C5. Phone code: 079. Population: 462,600.*

Founded in 1855, this state capital stands on the south bank of the Rio Sergipe, about 10 km from its mouth and 327 km north of Salvador. The river itself is pleasant enough and lined with handsome buildings, but the city centre is tawdry and unpleasant, especially at night, and there is very little to see. Most visitors stay at **Praia Atalaia** (see below), a 10-minute taxi (US$15) or 20-minute bus ride south of town.

Overlooked by most international visitors, Aracaju has a lively off-season carnival immediately prior to the one in Salvador, with the same music and floats. The commercial area is on Rua Itabaianinha and Rua João Pessoa, leading up to Rua Divina Pastora and Praça General Valadão.

Ins and outs

Getting there **Santa Maria airport** ① *12 km from the centre, Av Senador Júlio César Leite, Atalaia, T079-3243 1388,* receives flights from Maceió, Rio de Janeiro, São Paulo, Recife, Salvador, and other towns. Interstate buses arrive at the **rodoviária** ① *4 km west of the centre,* which is linked to the local bus system from the adjacent terminal (buy a ticket before going on to the platform). Bus 004 'T Rod/L Batista' goes to the centre, US$0.50. Buses from Laranjeiras and São Cristóvão (45 minutes) arrive at the **old bus station** at Praça João XXIII. Look for routes written on the side of buses and at bus stations in town. ▶▶ *See Transport, page 482.*

Tourist information The principal tourist office, **Bureau de Informações Turísticas de Sergipe** ① *Centro de Turismo, Praça Olímpio Campos s/n, Centro T079-3179 1947, daily 0800- 2000,* has town maps and staff speak some English. **Emsetur** ① *Trav Baltazar Goís 86, Edif Estado de Sergipe, 11th-13th floors, T079-3179 7553, www.emsetur.se.gov.br, Mon-Fri 0700-1300,* also has information. There is a tourist booth on the seafront on **Praia Atalaia** ① *Arcos da Orla de Atalaia 243, between R Maynard and Rotary, daily 1000-2100, www.visitearacaju.com.br,* but staff do not speak English and information is limited. There are other branches at the airport (0600-2400) and the *rodoviária* (0800-2230).

Private tour operators offer trips around the city, including rafting on the Rio São Francisco and the river delta. The best is **Brisamar Tur** ① *on the beach, Av Rotary s/n, Hotel Beira Mar, Praia de Atalaia, T079-3223 1781, www.brisamartur.com.br,* English spoken.

Aracaju beaches

Praia Atalaia is the nearest beach to Aracju and a much better place to stay. Although it can't compete with Bahia or Alagoas, there is a long beach of fine white sand, lined with *forró* clubs, restaurants and bars. The beach is lively with families and smooching couples who wander along the esplanade at sunset and the entire area feels as safe and old fashioned as a British Butlins seaside resort. There's even an artificial lake in a tiny theme park where you can hire pedal boats.

Continuing south along the Rodovia Presidente José Sarney, is a long stretch of sand between the mouths of the Rio Sergipe and Rio Vaza Barris; the further you go from the Sergipe, the clearer the water. One of the best beaches is the 30-km-long **Nova Atalaia**, on Ilha de Santa Luzia across the river. It is is easily reached by ferry from the **Terminal Hidroviária** ① *Av Rio Branco, near Praça General Valadão*. Boats cross the river to **Barra dos Coqueiros** every 15 minutes (US$1). Services are more frequent at weekends, when it is very lively with with fishing and pleasure craft.

Excursions from Aracaju

By far the most interesting excursion is to the canyons and beaches of the **Rio São Francisco**. The blue waters course their way through the hills of Minas Gerais and the desert backlands of Bahia before cutting through a series of dramatic gorges near the **Xingó** dam, and subsequently through fields of windswept dunes before washing out into the deep green Atlantic in northern Sergipe. **Brisamar Tur** (see above) runs day-trips down the river stopping at deserted beaches along the way; US$30-50 per person, depending on numbers.

About 23 km northwest from Aracaju is **Laranjeiras**, a tiny and sleepy colonial town with a ruined church on a hill. It is reached by taking the São Pedro bus from the old *rodoviária* in the centre of Aracaju (45 minutes). The town was originally founded in 1605 and has several churches dating back to the imperial period, when it was an important producer of sugar. The 19th-century **Capela de Sant'Aninha** has a wooden altar inlaid with gold.

South of Aracaju → *For listings, see pages 477-483. Colour map 2, C5.*

São Cristóvão

The old Sergipe capital lies 17 km southwest of Aracaju on the road to Salvador, sitting pretty on a little hill and on the shores of a briny lake. Founded by Cristóvão de Barros in 1590, it is Brazil's fourth oldest town, and one of many pretty, crumbling towns that dot this part of the country. The colonial centre focuses on Praça São Francisco, which was inscribed on the World Heritage List in August 2010. It is surrounded on all sides by unspoilt Portuguese buildings. The **Igreja e Convento de São Francisco** ① *Praça São Francisco, Tue-Fri 0900-1700, Sat and Sun 1300-1700, US$2*, has a beautiful, simple, baroque façade with a scrolled pediment, and an interior covered with lavish paintings. It also houses a sacred art museum, the **Museu de Arte Sacra e Histórico de Sergipe**, which has more than 500 priceless 18th- and 19th-century ecclesiastical objects. Other buildings on the square include the **Museu de Sergipe** (same opening hours), in the stately former **Palácio do Governo**, and the churches of **Misericórdia** (1627) and the **Orfanato Imaculada Conceição** (1646, permission to visit required from the sisters).

The streets surrounding Praça São Francisco are equally unspoilt, with whitewashed mansions, townhouses and churches offset by the oil-paint yellows and blues, green slat-shutters and woodwork. As tourirsts are few and far between, São Cristóvão is far

Palmares and Zumbi

From the first days of slavery in Brazil, *fujões* (runaways) would disappear into the interior and set up villages or *mocambos*. Between the 1630s and the end of 17th century these *mocambos* prospered (especially during times of crisis such as the Dutch invasion in 1630) and together formed *quilombos*, free territories which accepted not only runaway slaves but freed ones and whites who had fallen out with the re-established Portuguese colony. The most famous of these *quilombos*, established in what is now the state of Alagoas, was called Palmares after the large number of palm trees in the area. It consisted of 30,000 people living in several *mocambos* in an area of 17,000 square miles (44,000 sq km). According to reports from Bartholomeus Lintz, the leader of a Dutch expedition in 1640, the largest settlement in Palmares had 220 buildings, a church, four smithies and a meeting house.

The political and social structures were very similar to those found in West Africa, and although Catholicism was practised, so was polyandry, mainly due to the lack of women in the republic. The leader of Palmares was Ganga-Zumba who was revered like a king, but it appears he was killed by his followers in 1680 after making some concessions to the Portuguese two years earlier. He was succeeded by the republic's brave military commander, Zumbi, who is said to have been an African king.

The existence of Palmares was a constant thorn in the side of Portuguese domination of Brazil and dozens of attempts were made to destroy it. However, Zumbi managed to defend the republic until it was finally smashed in 1695 by the Portuguese with *bandeirante* help. Zumbi was killed and his decapitated head was put on display in Recife to discourage other potential runaways and prove that he was not immortal as his followers believed. He is still remembered every year on 20 November, Brazil's Black Consciousness Day. He has also become a popular icon at Carnaval time. There are still small *quilombo* communities throughout Brazil.

The site of the Palmares Republic is situated on the Serra da Barriga, close to modern União do Palmares in Alagoas state, reached by driving north out of Maceió on the BR-101, turning left after Messias and driving for 40 km along a paved road.

more tranquil than the colonial cities of Minas or Bahia. There are other squares in town. The Praça Senhor dos Passos is lined by more Portuguese buildings and churches, including **Igreja Senhor dos Passos** and **Terceira Ordem do Carmo** (both built 1739), while on the Praça Getúlio Vargas (formerly Praça Matriz) is the 17th-century **Igreja Matriz Nossa Senhora da Vitória** ① *all are open Tue-Fri 0900-1700, Sat and Sun 1500-1700*. Also worth seeing is the old **Assembléia Legislativa** ① *R Coronel Erundino Prado*. The town is lively only during both the Sergipe pre-Carnaval celebrations, Carnaval itself and Easter, when the streets are strewn with mosaics created with hundreds of thousands of flower petals.

Ins and outs São Cristóvão lies 23 km south of Aracaju. Several buses an hour run between Aracaju's *rodoviária* and São Cristóvão (30 minutes, US$2). Agencies in Atalaia organize excursions to São Cristóvão.

Estância → *Phone code: 079. Population: 57,000.*

Estância is 247 km north of Salvador, on the BR-101, almost midway between the Sergipe-Bahia border and Aracaju. It is one of the oldest towns in Brazil. Its colonial buildings are decorated with Portuguese tiles (none are open to the public). The town's heyday was at the turn of the 20th century and it was one of the earliest places in Brazil to get electricity and a telephone system. Estância is also called 'Cidade Jardim' because of its parks. The month-long festival of **São João** in June is a major event.

Maceió → *For listings, see pages 477-483. Colour map 2, C6. Phone code: 082. Population: 780,000.*

The capital of Alagoas is one of coastal Brazil's most attractive and safest cities, with a string of beautiful white-sand beaches, a pretty little colonial centre and a low-key feel. There are a handful of low-key beach resorts a short bus ride away; the best is at **Praia do Frances**, near the old Portuguese capital of Marechal Deodoro. The city has a lively street carnival and traditional **Festas Juninas**.

Ins and outs

Getting there Flights arrive at **Zumbi dos Palmares airport** ① *Rodovia BR-104, Km 91, T082-3214 4000, 25 km from the city centre and beaches*, from Aracaju, Brasília, Rio de Janeiro, Florianópolis, Salvador, São Paulo, Recife, Belo Horizonte and Porto Alegre. A bus runs from the airport to most popular city beach, Ponta Verde/Pajuçara, every 30 minutes 0630-2100 (allow 45 minutes); look for name of the beach on the front of the bus. Taxis charge a flat rate of around US$23. Interstate buses arrive at the **rodoviária** ① *5 km from the centre*, situated on a hill, with good views. Luggage store is available. Take bus Nos 711 or 715 to Ponta Verde/Pajuçara or buses marked 'Ouro Preto p/centro'; these run every few minutes. A taxi from the bus station to Pajuçara costs around US$15. ▸▸ *See Transport, page 482.*

Getting around and orientation Ponta Verde, Pajuçara and adjacent Praia de Jaticúa are easy to walk around as is the commercial centre. You will need to take public transport between them. Local buses connect Ponta Verde and Pajuçara with the tiny historic city centre every few minutes, leaving from the the the beachside road Avenida Robert Kennedy/Alvaro Otacilio and stopping at various points including the cathedral. Bus stops are little blue elongated concrete stands. *Combis* for the nearby beaches like Praia do Frances and Marechal Deodoro leave from in front of the Hospital Santa Casa.

Tourist information **Semptur** ① *Av da Paz 1422, Centro, T082-3336 4409, www.maceio turismo.com.br*, offers information on the city and environs, including maps. The state tourism authority **Setur** ① *R Boa Vista 453, Centro, T082-3315 5700, www.turismo.al.gov.br*, also has branches at the airport and *rodoviária*. The website has a comprehensive list of public services, hotels, restaurants, bars and other contacts. Far more convenient is the **tourist information post** on Pajuçara beach, next to the Sete Coqueiros artisan centre. For very entertaining city tours or trips to Marechal Deodoro, Praia do Francês and beyond contact **Del** (see Activities and tours, page 481), who speaks several languages including English.

Maceió beaches

The sea in Maceió is an impossibly brilliant shade of misty greens and blues and it washes onto some of the finest white-sand beaches in urban Brazil. **Trapiche**, **Sobral** and

Avenida, immediately in front of the city, look appetizing and are pounded by an impressive surf but they are far too filthy for anything but brown trout. The best beaches for bathing (and the best places to stay in Maceió) are **Pajuçara**, **Ponta Verde** and **Jatiúca**, becoming increasingly plush the further they are from the centre.

Pajuçara has the bulk of the budget accommodation and a nightly crafts market. At weekends there are wandering musicians and entertainers here, and patrols by the cavalry on magnificent *Manga Larga Marchador* horses. Periodically, especially on *candomblé* anniversaries, there are rituals to the *orixá* of the sea, *Yemanjá*. There is a natural swimming pool 2 km off the beach, **Piscina Natural de Pajuçara**, and low tide leaves lots of natural pools to explore in the exposed reef. Check the tides; there is no point going at high tide. *Jangadas* (simple platforms with sails) cost US$10 per person per day (or about US$40 to have a *jangada* to yourself). On Sunday or local holidays in the high season it is overcrowded. At weekends lots of *jangadas* anchor at the reef, selling food and drink.

The next beach is **Ponta Verde**, which is quieter and forms the cape separating Pajuçara from the best of the urban beaches, **Jatiúca**. The better hotels are here and the beach is

Maceió

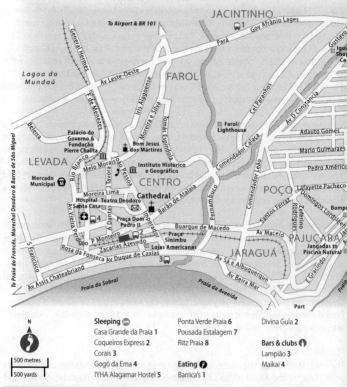

Sleeping [bed]	Ponta Verde Praia 6	Divina Gula 2
Casa Grande da Praia 1	Pousada Estalagem 7	
Coqueiros Express 2	Ritz Praia 8	**Bars & clubs** [music]
Corais 3		Lampião 3
Gogó da Ema 4	**Eating** [fork/knife]	Maikai 4
IYHA Alagamar Hostel 5	Barrica's 1	

fronted by a pretty esplanade, lined with cafés and smart restaurants. It is tastefully lit at night. The principal restaurant area in Maceió lies just inland of northern Jatiúca.

After Jatiúca the beaches are: **Cruz das Almas**, **Jacarecica** (9 km from the centre), **Guaxuma** (12 km), **Garça Torta** (14 km), **Riacho Doce** (16 km), **Pratagi** (17 km) and **Ipioca** (23 km). Cruz das Almas and Jacarecica have good surf. Bathing is best three days before and after a full or new moon because tides are higher and the water is more spectacular.

Sights

The centre of Maceió can easily be wandered around in less than an hour. It is pretty, with a handful of handsome Portuguese buildings and some half-decent art deco. On Praça dos Martírios (Floriano Peixoto is the **Palácio do Governo**, which also houses the **Fundação Pierre Chalita** (Alagoan painting and religious art) and the church of **Bom Jesus dos Mártires** (built 1870 and covered in handsome *azulejo* tiles). These are two of the oldest buildings in the city and well worth visiting. The **cathedral**, Nossa Senhora dos Prazeres (1840) is on Praça Dom Pedro II. The **Instituto Histórico e Geográfico** ⓘ *R João Pessoa 382, T082-3223 7797*, has a small but good collection of indigenous and Afro- Brazilian artefacts.

Lagoa do Mundaú, a lagoon, whose entrance is 2 km south at **Pontal da Barra**, limits the city to the south and west. Excellent shrimp and fish are sold at its small restaurants and handicraft stalls and it's a pleasant place for a drink at sundown. Boats make excursions in the lagoon's channels (T082-3231 7334).

Buses 🚌
Rodoviária 1
To Marechal Deodoro
& Praia do Francês 2
To Riacho Doce 3
To Praia Francês 4

Excursions from Maceió
→ *For listings, see pages 477-483.*

Marechal Deodoro and around
The former capital of Alagoas is 22 km south of Maceió across the impressive brackish lakes that give the state its name, and just behind one of the best resort beaches in the northeast, **Praia do Francês**. The town is well worth a visit, not only for its delightful crumbling buildings and expansive lake, but because of it has a wonderful, laid-back feel and is unspoilt by tourism. It's built on a hill, overlooking **Lake Manguaba**. Boat trips can be organized through tour guides such as **Del** (see Activities and tours, page 481).

The town is named after Marechal Deodoro da Fonseca, the charismatic general who founded the Brazilian republic

Nelson da Rabeca

There are more orchestras in Marechal than in any town of this size in Brazil and the town has produced some famous musicians. They include **Nelson da Rabeca**, whose smiling statue stands at the gateway to the town. In the 1960s, Nelson was an illiterate 54-year-old sugar-cane cutter who had barely left Alagoas. When television first came to the town locals would congregate in a local bar to watch TV programmes. Nelson would join them, and became especially fond of the regular music shows. On one show Nelson saw an orchestra perform for the first time. He became fascinated with an instrument which was entirely new to him – the violin. Knowing he'd never be able to afford to buy one he determined to make one of his own, heading into the forest and cutting a sapling. He carved the instrument from the raw wood, together with a bow, which he fitted with horsehair. It was a failure. So he built another, and then another, until he had a working fiddle, or *rabeca*, as they are called in Portuguese. Nelson spent all his spare hours learning to play his *rabeca*, and as he progressed he began to perform locally with his wife. Nelson's story and reputation spread during the 1970s and 1980s, and today he is one of the most famous folk violinists in Brazil. His hand-crafted *rabecas* are owned and played by the finest musicians in South America, including fellow Alagoan, Hermeto Pascoal. It's possible to visit Nelson's home and see his workshop as part of a guided tour, see page 481.

after the deposition of Emperor Dom Pedro II. The modest townhouse where he grew up is now the **Museu Marechal Deodoro** ① *R Marechal Deodoro, daily 0800-1700, free*. It offers an interesting insight into the simplicity of life in Brazil at the end of the 19th century, even for those in the upper middle classes. Marechal Deodoro's large family lived in a few simple rooms; it is easy to imagine them dining together by oil lamp around the plain hard-wood table, watched over by the family patriarch. Typical northeastern *macramé* lace can be bought outside the museum in the adjacent houses.

The town is very pleasant to wander around, which takes all of 20 minutes. The cobbled streets are lined with attractive colonial houses, some of which have been converted into modest restaurants and *pousadas*. These lead to a series of squares watched over by impressive if decrepit Portuguese churches. Some are almost beyond repair, but the most impressive, the **Igreja Matriz de Nossa Senhora da Conceição** built in 1783 has undergone full restoration, returning to its full baroque glory in late 2008. Be sure to take a peek inside. The 17th-century **Convento de São Francisco** on Praça João XXIII, has another fine baroque church, **Santa Maria Magdalena**, with a superb wooden altarpiece tha t has been badly damaged by termites. You can climb the church tower for views of the town. Adjoining it is the **Museu de Arte Sacra** ① *Mon-Fri, 0900-1300, US$0.50, guided tours available, payment at your discretion*.

It is easy to visit Marechal on a day trip from Maceió and still have time left over to enjoy the sun and surf on **Praia do Francês**. It is one of the state's most beautiful beaches, pounded by glass-green surf at one end, protected by a fringing reef at the other and shaded by towering coconut palms along its entire length. There are plenty of *barracas*, restaurants and bars selling drinks and seafood.

There are more beaches beyond Francês, including **Barra de São Miguel**, entirely protected by the reef. It gets crowded at weekends. Several good, cheap *barracas* serve food and drink and there are some decent places to stay. Carnaval is very lively here.

Ins and outs

Minivans run to Marechal Deodoro and Praia do Francês from in front of Hospital Santa Casa next to the Texaco station on Avenida Rio Branco in the city centre. They run 0430-2200 and leave when full (every 20 minutes or so) in high season and at weekends. The journey takes 20 minutes and costs around US$1. Taxis cost around US$30. Tour operators in Maceió offer day trips and can organize air-conditioned private transport (see page 481).

Praia do Francês and Marechal Deodoro have accommodation. For more information see www.praiadofrances.net and www.turismo.al.gov.br.

Penedo → *For listings, see pages 477-483. Colour map 2, C5. Phone code: 082. Population: 57,000.*

A more interesting crossing into Alagoas than the usual arrival, along the coast from north or south, can be made by frequent ferry crossings from **Neópolis** in Sergipe, to Penedo some 35 km from the mouth of the Rio São Francisco.

Penedo is a delight – a kind of forgotten Ouro Preto sweltering in the tropical heat on the banks of the sluggish Rio São Francisco, just across the water from Sergipe. Its colonial streets clamber up a series of hills from the banks of the river and are lined with wonderful old buildings. There's a stunning baroque church at every other turn, and barely a tourist in sight. The town was founded in 1565; it was overthrown by the Dutch (who built a fort here) in 1637, and then re-taken by the Portuguese shortly after. It developed as a trading port in the 17th and 18th centuries and grew rich from the gold and diamonds transported down the Rio São Francisco from the interior of Bahia and Minas. Very few of the long two-masted sailing vessels that used to cruise on the river can be seen now, although there are plenty of smaller craft. Boats travel down the river to a series of beautiful white-sand beaches in both Sergipe and Alagoas; these include **Arambipe** and **Peba**. The latter (in Alagoas) is also reachable by road. Either side of the river mouth are turtle nesting grounds, which are protected.

Ins and outs

The *rodoviária* is on the river front on Avenida Beira Rio, near the service station. There is one daily bus from Salvador (via Aracaju). Four buses a day run from Maceió, as well as *combis* 0500-1620. ▸▸ *See Transport, page 482.*

The very friendly and helpful **tourist office** ⓘ *T082-3551 3907, Praça Barão de Penedo 2, www.penedo.al.gov.br, Mon-Fri 0730-1330*, has useful maps of the city marked with all the principal sights, hotels and restaurants and can organize guided tours of the baroque buildings, sometimes in English.

Sights

The most impressive building in the city is the church of **Nossa Senhora da Corrente** ⓘ *Praça 12 de Abril s/n, Centro, Tue-Sun 0800-1700* (1784), named 'Our Lady of the Current' presumably in homage to the river, which ran swiftly and powerfully past the town until the construction of the Rio São Francisco dam in the late 20th century. It is one of the finest pieces of Portuguese baroque in northeastern Brazil, built on an intimate scale such as those in Ouro Preto, rather than being grand like the churches of

Olinda or Salvador. The simple façade hides a rich interior covered in gold leaf and centred on a splendid painted and gilt altarpiece replete with blue and rose marble. The nave is lined with masterful *azulejo* panels, and paintings by the Pernambucan Portuguese artist Libório Lázaro Lial, who was also responsible for much of the ecclesiastical decoration in the city. According to legend, fugitive slaves were hidden inside the church by a trap door behind one of the side altars.

On Praça Barão de Penedo is the neoclassical **Igreja Matriz** (closed to visitors) and the 18th-century **Casa da Aposentadoria** (1782). East and a little below this square is the Praça Rui Barbosa, where you'll find the **Convento de São Francisco** (1783) and the church of **Nossa Senhora dos Anjos** ① *Praça Rui Barbosa s/n, Centro, Tue-Fri 0800-1100 and 1400-1700, Sat and Sun 0800-1100*, whose façade is topped with typically Portuguese-baroque filigree flourishes. As you enter the church, the altar on the right depicts God's eyes on the world, surrounded by the three races (indigenous, black and white). The church a fine trompe l'oeil ceiling (1784), also by Libório Lázaro Lial, which recalls Mestre Atahyde's ceiling in the Igreja São Francisco de Assis in Ouro Preto (see page 262). The convent is still in use.

The church of **Rosário dos Pretos** ① *Praça Marechal Deodoro*, (1775-1816), is open to visitors, as isis **São Gonçalo Garcia** ① *Av Floriano Peixoto, Mon-Fri 0800-1200, 1400-1700*, (1758-1770). The latter has a particularly fine baroque interior. Lively markets are held outside on weekdays. A wander around them feels like a trip back in time to an older Alagoas. Fishermen sell estuary bream straight out of the wheelbarrow, hacked up bits of cow hang unrefrigerated from meat-hooks in the heat next to stalls offering everything from baskets of home-made soap to pocket calculators. Vast sacks of grain, rice, flour and beans sit next to little hand-drawn carts in front of algae-covered walls of 400-year-old buildings and above the flurry and fluster megaphones blare out special offers and political slogans, broken by the occasional peel of a baroque church bell.

On the same street is the pink **Teatro 7 de Setembro** ① *Av Floriano Peixoto 81, Mon-Fri 0800-1200, 1400-1730, Sat morning only*, with a lovely little conch-shaped auditorium dating from 1884. There are river views from the **Rocheira** just behind **Pousada Estylos**. Before the construction of the São Francisco dam, the river used to wash against the stones immediately below the parapet; you can still see the tide mark, some 4 m higher than it is today.

There are two museums. The most interesting is the **Paço Imperial** ① *Praça 12 de Abril 9, Centro, T082-3551 2498, Tue-Sat 1100-1700, Sun 0800-1200*. Emperor Dom Pedro II stayed in this handsome mansion in 1859 and the building has been trading on the glory ever since. It now preserves a wonderful ceiling painting by Francisco Lopes Ruis, as well as furniture and artefacts that once belonged to the Portuguese high society families and church art. There are great views over the river from the second floor. The **Casa de Penedo** ① *R João Pessoa 126, signs point the way up the hill from Floriano Peixoto, T082-551 2516, Tue-Sun 0800-1200 and 1400-1800*, displays photographs and books on, or by, local figures.

North of Maceió → *For listings, see pages 477-483.*

There are many interesting stopping points along the coast between Maceió and Recife. At **Paripueira**, a 40-minute bus ride from the *rodoviária* in Maceió, the beach is busy only during high season; low tide leaves lots of natural swimming pools.

Barra de Santo Antônio → *Colour map 2, C6.*

Some 45 km north of Maceió is this busy fishing village, with a palm-fringed beach on a narrow peninsula, a canoe ride away. The beaches nearby are beautiful: to the south, near the village of Santa Luzia, are **Tabuba** and **Sonho Verde**. To the north is **Carro Quebrado**, from where you can take a beach buggy to **Pedra do Cebola**, or further to **Praia do Morro**, just before the mouth of the Rio Camaragibe.

Maragogi → *Colour map 2, C6.*

Unlike many of the resorts just to the north (such as Porto de Galinhas), this little beach town has preserved its local character. Outside the high season, when the Maragogi gets crowded, life goes on pretty much as it has done before tourists began to arrive in the 1980s. And yet the beach is glorious: a seemingly infinite stretch of broad, fine sand washed by a turquoise sea. Some 6 km offshore, a fringing reef reveals a series of deep swimming pools at low tide. The current is rich with sergeant majors and wrasse and with the occasional visiting turtle. Trips out there are easy to organize (expect to pay around US$10).

Ins and outs From Maceió there are two buses a day and frequent *combis* and shared taxis to Maragogi. *Combis* leave from the Maxi service station (Maxi *posto*) at Cruz de Almas on the BR-101 highway in Maraju on the northern outskirts of Maceió city (taxi from the *rodoviária* US$5). There are also two buses daily from Recife; or take a bus to São José da Coroa Grande, and take a *combi* from there.

Beyond Maragogi, a coastal road, unpaved in parts, runs to the Pernambuco border and **São José da Coroa Grande**. The main highway, BR-101, heads inland from Maceió before crossing the state border to Palmares.

⊙ Sergipe and Alagoas listings

For Sleeping and Eating price codes and other relevant information, see pages 32-37.

◉ Sleeping

Aracaju *p468*

The city centre is unpleasant and seedy at night and pretty much all the hotels are scruffy and home to more than just humans. Staying here is not recommended. The beach is only 10-20 mins away.
D Amado, R Laranjeiras 532, T079-3211 9937, www.infonet.com.br/hotelamado. The best of a poor selection, with a range of a/c and fan-cooled rooms, a decent breakfast and laundry facilities. Look at several rooms before deciding.
D Brasília, R Laranjeiras 580, T079-3214 2964. It's hard to believe that these corridors of gloomy and often windowless rooms with

damp, old air offer the second best sleeping option in the city centre … but they do.

Aracaju beaches *p469*

Hotels are invariably blocky affairs but there are plenty of them, along the main thoroughfare, Av Santos Dumont, next to the beach.
L-A Celi Praia, Av Oceânica 500, T079-2107 8000, www.celihotel.com.br. This big beige block looks like a set of offices – which is appropriate as it caters principally to business clientele. Rooms are plain but large, modern and comfortable. All have balconies, internet and there is a gym, 24-hr business centre, pool, sauna and one of the best restaurants on the beach. Good online rates.
B San Manuel, R Niceu Dantas 75, Atalaia, T079-3218 5203, www.sanmanuelpraia hotel.com.br. Pleasant, modern, well-appointed rooms decorated in tile and

cream walls with Wi-Fi, international TV and business facilities (including conference rooms). The best views have sea views and terraces.

C-D Oceânica, Av Santos Dumont 413, Atalaia, T079-3243 5950, www.pousadaoceanica-se.com.br. A lemon yellow block facing the beach with scrupulously clean simple rooms tiled, painted light blue and furnished with little wooden tables and commodes.

D Relicário, Av Santos Dumont 622, Atalaia, T079-3243 1584. A mock-Chinese hotel with simple plain a/c and fan-cooled rooms right next to one of the main beach nightlife areas.

Excursions from Aracaju *p469*
D-E Pousada Vale dos Outeiros, Av José do Prado Franco 124, Laranjeiras, T079-3281 1027. A handful of a/c and fan-cooled rooms and a restaurant. Look at several – the best are on the upper floors and have views.

São Cristóvão *p469*
There are no hotels, but families rent out rooms near the *rodoviária* at the bottom of the hill.

Estância *p471*
There are a number of cheap, very simple hotels around the Praça Barão do Rio Branco. **C-D Jardim**, R Joaquim Calazans 202, Estância, T079-3522 1656, www.hoteljardim-se.com.br. A modern home in a what looks like a converted town house. A range of tile and whitewash a/c rooms and a a huge buffet breakfast.

D Turismo Estanciano, Praça Barão do Rio Branco 176, T079-3522 1404, www.hotel estanciano.com. Very simple en suites with little more than a bed, fridge and a table.

Maceió *p471, map p472*
There are many hotels on **Pajuçara** mostly along Av Dr Antônio Gouveia and R Jangadeiros Alagoanos but many of the cheapest are not to be trusted with your belongings. The best rooms are on the beaches **Ponta Verde** and **Jatiúca**. It can

be hard to find a room during the Dec-Mar holiday season, when prices go up.

L Ponta Verde Praia, Av Álvaro Otacílio 2933, Ponta Verde, T082-2121 0040, www.hotel pontaverde.com.br. The best option on the beach in an enviable location with easy walking access to the *forró* clubs and restaurants to the north and Praia Pajuçara to the west. The range of a/c rooms are all well-appointed and comfortable and with international TV and Wi-Fi. The best on the upper floors have wonderful sweeping views out over the sea. Generous buffet breakfast.

B Pousada Estalagem, R Engenheiro Demócrito Sarmento Barroca 70, T082-3327 6088, www.pousadaestalagem.com.br. Flats with little cookers in a quiet back street above a photo shop. Some have space for up to 6 in one room, making this in the **D** category for groups.

B Ritz Praia, R Eng Mário de Gusmão 1300 Laranjeiras, Ponta Verde, T082-2121 4600, www.ritzpraia.com.br. This is a hotel of 2 halves. The refurbished rooms on the upper 4 floors are bright and airy and have views. Those yet to be refurbished are rather gloomy but well-maintained have frowsty en suites with marble fittings. The hotel is only a block from the beach and there is a sun deck on the top floor with a pool the size of a small car.

B-C Coqueiros Express, R Desportista Humberto Guimarães 830, Ponta Verde, T082-4009 4700, www.coqueirosexpress.com.br. The best rooms in this spruce, well-run hotel are on the upper floors and have partial sea views. All are well appointed (refurbished in 2006) and decorated in tile and light green and hanging with faux-modernist minimalist *jangada* prints. There's a garden-pond sized pool next to reception and breakfast is hearty.

D Casa Grande da Praia, R Jangadeiros Alagoanas 1528, Pajuçara, T082-3231 3332, www.hotelcasagrandedapraia.com.br Check the rooms here as some have spongy beds and are rather musty. The best by far are on the upper floor annexe overlooking a small garden. Staff are friendly and offer a decent service which includes a good breakfast. Very close to the beach.

D Gogó da Ema, R Laranjeiras 97, T082-3327 0329, www.hotelgogodaema.com.br. Very simple tile and lime green rooms dominated by large double beds with decent mattresses. En suites come with little marble sinks. The hotel lies in a quiet back street a hop from the sand and offers a generous breakfast.

D-E Corais, R Desportista Humberto Guimarães 80, Pajuçara, T082-3231 9096. Very basic, musty rooms in corridors around a little garden courtyard. All are frayed, fan-cooled and en suites. Perfect if you plan to spend as little time as possible asleep and as much time as possible on the beach, which is only a few hundred metres away.

D-E HI Alagamar Hostel, R Pref Abdon Arroxelas 327, T082-3231 2246, www.maceio praiaalbergue.com. It can be hard to get a room here; you'll need to book 2 months in advance in high season and about a week in advance in low season. In either case the hostel requires a 50% upfront deposit into their bank account – a bureaucratic ritual in Brazil. The rooms have all been given a much-needed fresh lick of paint, but look at a few before committing – those on the lower floors are musty and all can be uncomfortably hot at night. Dorms are single-sex.

Marechal Deodoro and around *p473*

A Village Barra Hotel, R Sen Arnon de Mello, Barra de São Miguel, T082-3272 1000, www.villagebarrahotel.com.br. A modern, 4-storey, concrete hotel with rooms over-looking a large pool and sundeck, and the beach at Barra de São Miguel. There's a restaurant and staff can organize excursions to Marechal Deodoro and other locations. The hotel lies 10 km south of Praia do Francês and 16 km from Marechal Deodoro (buses from Praia do Francês and Maceió).

B Pousada Bougainville e Restaurant Chez Patrick, R Sargaço 3, T082-3260 1251, www.praiadofrances.com. A pretty little *pousada* near the beach with a/c, rooms with TVs, a pool, seafood and a good French and seafood restaurant cooking.

C Pousada da Barra, Av Oceanica 249, Praia Sta Irene, Barra de São Miguel, T022-2771 3109, www.pousadadabarra-rj.com.br. Good.

C Pousada Le Soleil, R Carapeba 11, Praia do Francês, T082-3260 1240, www.pousadalesoleil.kit.net. An anonymous concrete block of a hotel with balconies close to the beach. Decent breakfast. Wi-fi.

C-D Capitães de Areia, R Vermelha 13, Praia do Francês, 100 m from the beach, T082-3260 1477, www.capitaesdeareia.com.br. A terracotta-coloured block with terraces of rooms near the beach, a pool and a restaurant. Good low season discounts.

Penedo *p475*

C São Francisco, Av Floriano Peixoto, T082-3551 2273, www.hotelsaofrancisco.tur.br. A big, ugly 1970s block with boxy little balconied rooms all with a/c, TV and fridge. Showing its age far more than the colonial hotels.

C-D Pousada Colonial, Praça 12 de Abril 21, 5 mins' walk from the bus station, T082-3551 2355. A converted colonial building with creaky wooden floors and huge rooms – the best with views out over the river. All are fan-cooled but for the suites. Friendly, efficient reception staff.

D-E Pousada Estylos I, Praça Jácome Calheiros 79, T082-3551 2465; with another branch, **Pousada Estylos II** at R Damaso do Monte 86, T082-3551 2429. A modest modern hotel near the river with a range of a/c and fan-cooled rooms. Open sporadically, but always in high season.

D-F Imperial, Praça Coronel Peixoto 43, T082-3551 4749. Simple a/c and fan-cooled rooms with a bath, fan and hot water. The best are on the upper floors and have river views. **F** for single rooms and doubles with shared bathrooms.

Barra de Santo Antônio *p477*

This is a tiny place with no visible addresses. Locals will point you to *pousadas* but it is a struggle to get lost.

D São Geraldo. Very simple but very clean, and with a restaurant.

D-E Pousada Buongiorno, T082-2121 7577
(Maceió). 6 modest rooms in a farmhouse,
bathrooms but no electricity, many fruit trees.

Maragogi *p477*

C Jangadeiros, Beira Mar s/n, T082-3296
2167, www.pousadadosjangadeiros.com.br.
Plain but modern tile-floor and whitewash
rooms in a concrete hotel a block from the
beach 5 mins north of the town centre.
A little pool and good breakfast. Friendly staff.
C-D Agua de Fuego, Rodovia AL 101 Norte,
T082-3296 1326, www.aguadefuego.com.
The best small hotel in Maragogi with a range
of spacious tile floor rooms right overlooking
the beach. Friendly Argentinian owner, great
breakfast and a pool. In a quiet area 15 mins'
walk south of town along the beach.
D-E O Tempo e o Vento, Trav Lourenco
Wanderley 22, T082-3296 1720. Tiny little
rooms right near the beach. The best are
closest to the seafront. Those overlooking
the town *praça* can be noisy. **F** for single.

🍴 Eating

Aracaju *p468*

🍴🍴 **Cantina d'Italia**, Av Santos Dumont s/n,
T079-3243 3184. The chicest option on the
beachfront serving pizza and pasta to the
city's middle classes. The best tables are
on the upper deck.
🍴-🍴 **O Dragão**, Av Santos Dumont, Atalaia,
T079-3243 0664. Japanese and Chinese food,
including a bottomless sushi and sashimi
buffet. Served in a large mock-oriental
pavilion right on the beach next to the lake.
🍴 **Cariri**, Av Santos Dumont 243, T079-3243
1379, www.cariri-se.com.br. Northeastern
cooking including *frango caipira* (chicken
cooked in a tomato and onion sauce) and
carne do sol (beef jerky). Live *forró* music
Tue-Sat. One of several similar lively
clubs on this part of the beach.

São Cristóvão *p469*

🍴 **Senzala do Preto Velho**, R Messias Prado
84. Recommended northeastern specialities.

Maceió *p471, map p472*

The best restaurants, bars and clubs are on
and around R Engenheiro Paulo B Nogueira
on **Jatiúca** beach. There are many other
bars and restaurants in **Pajuçara** and along
Av Antônio Gouveia.
  For 5 km from the beginning of Pajuçara,
through Ponta Verde and Jatiuca in the
north, the beaches are lined with *barracas*
(thatched bars) with music, snacks and
meals until 2400 (later at weekends).
Vendors on the beach sell beer and
food during the day; clean and safe.
  There are many other bars and *barracas* at
Ponto da Barra, on the lagoon side of the city
and a string of cheap but high-quality stalls
next to the **Lampião club** in Jatiúca in front
of the **Maceió Atlantic** suites hotel. Local
specialities include oysters, *pitu*, a crayfish
(now scarce), and *sururu*, a type of cockle.
The local ice cream, 'Shups', is recommended.
🍴🍴🍴 **Divina Gula**, R Engenheiro Paulo B
Nogueira 85, T082-3235 1016, www.divina
gula.com.br. Closed Mon. The best restaurant
in the city, with a lively atmosphere and busy
crowd. The large menu includes many overly-
cheesed Italian options, pizzas, seafood and
northeastern meat dishes. Portions are large
enough for 2.
🍴🍴-🍴 **Barrica's**, Av Álvaro Calheiros 354, Ponta
Verde, www.barricaspizzaria.com.br. One of
the liveliest of the waterfront bars in Maceió
with live music every night, a buzzing crowd
and a range of dishes from pasta to grilled
or fried meat or fish, the inevitable pizzas
and a handful of veggie options.

🍸 Bars and clubs

Maceió *p471, map p472*

The bars here are relaxed and varied and
there are nightclubs to suit most tastes.

Lampião, Praia de Jatiúca s/n, diagonally opposite the Maceió Atlantic suites hotel. A very lively beachside *forró* bar with live bands every night playing live music to an eager crowd. The house band dress up as Lampião himself – in straw hats and with yokely shirts and leather jerkins and they are fronted by a bottle-blonde in a sparkly cap who has everyone up and dancing. Packed on Fri and Sat. Food available.
Maikai, R Engenheiro Paulo B Nogueira quadra 14, T082-3305 4400, www.maikai maceio.com.br. Restaurant and adjacent club with space for thousands and a range of northeastern acts, playing music from *forró* to *axé*. Currently the busiest and most popular club in town.

✪ Entertainment

Maceió *p471, map p472*
Cinema Arte 1 and 2, Pajuçara and Iguatemi shopping centres. Cinema São Luiz, R do Comércio, in the centre. All show foreign films dubbed except the cinema in Shopping Farol.

✪ Festivals and events

Aracaju *p468*
1 Jan Bom de Jesus dos Navegantes, procession on the river.
1st weekend in Jan Santos Reis (Three Kings/Wise Men).
Feb/Mar Pre-carnival Carnaval.
Jun Festas Juninas.
8 Dec Both Catholic (Nossa Senhora da Conceição) and *umbanda* (*Iemanjá*) festivals.

Excursions from Aracaju *p469*
Jan The main festival in Laranjeiras is São Benedito in the 1st week of the month.

São Cristóvão *p469*
Mar Senhor dos Passos, held 15 days after Carnaval.

8 Sep Nossa Senhora de Vitória, the patron saint's day.
Oct/Nov Festival de Arte (moveable).

Estância *p471*
Jun The month-long festival of São João is a major event.

Maceió *p471, map p472*
27 Aug Nossa Senhora dos Prazeres.
16 Sep Freedom of Alagoas.
8 Dec Nossa Senhora da Conceição.
15 Dec Maceiofest, a great street party with *trios elêctricos*.
24 Dec Christmas Eve.
31 Dec New Year's Eve, half-day.

○ Shopping

Aracaju *p468*
The *artesanato* is interesting, with pottery figures and lace a speciality. A fair is held in Praça Tobias Barreto every Sun afternoon. The municipal market is a block north of the *hidroviária* (ferry terminal).

Penedo *p475*
There is a daily market on the streets off Av Floriano Peixoto, with good hammocks. Ceramics are on sale outside Bompreço supermarket, on Av Duque de Caxias.

▲ Activities and tours

Maceió *p471, map p472*
José dos Santos Filho (Del), T082-3241-4966, Mb082-8859 3407, jalbino.filho@ hotmail.com. Bespoke tourist guide offering trips along the coast and in the city – including visits to Nelson da Rabeca's house in Marechal Deodoro. Very friendly, knowledgeable and with a comfortable a/c car and reasonable command of English.

⊖ Transport

Aracaju *p468*

Air The airport is 12 km from the centre. Flights to **Brasília**, **Maceió**, **Rio de Janeiro**, **Salvador**, **São Paulo** and **Recife**, with Avianca, www.Avianca.com.br, Azul, www.voeazul.com.br, GOL, www.voegol.com.br and TAM, www.tam.com.br.

Bus Buses run from the old bus station at Praça João XXIII to **Laranjeiras** and **São Cristóvão** (45 mins, US$3).

Long-distance buses run from the *rodoviária*, 4 km from the centre. Buses to the *rodoviária* run from Praça João XXIII, the terminal near the *hidroviária* and from Capela at the top of Praça Olímpio Campos. To **Salvador**, 6-7 hrs, at least 11 a day with Bonfim, US$25, executive service at 1245, US$35 (1 hr quicker). To **Maceió**, US$25 with Bonfim. To **Recife** at 2330, US$35, 10 hrs. To **Rio**, US$20, 30 hrs. To **São Paulo**, US$120, 35 hrs **Belo Horizonte** US$85, 20 hrs, **Foz de Iguaçu**, US$200, 22 hrs. To **Estância**, US$5, 1½ hrs. To **Penedo**, 3 hrs, US$7, 2 a day.

São Cristóvão *p469*

Bus São Pedro buses run to the old *rodoviária* in the centre of **Aracaju** (45 mins, US$1.25).

Estância *p471*

Bus Many buses stop at the *rodoviária*, on the main road. To **Salvador** 4 hrs, US$12-14.

Maceió *p471, map p472*

Air Buses marked 'aeorporto' run to the airport from Ponta Verde/Pajuçara, every 30 mins 0630-2100; allow 45 mins. Taxis charge a flat rate of around US$23. There are flights to **Aracaju**, **Brasília**, **Florianópolis**, **Rio de Janeiro**, **Salvador**, **São Paulo**, **Recife**, **Belo Horizonte** and **Porto Alegre** with Azul, www.voeazul.com.br, GOL, www.voegol.com.br, TAM, www.tam.com.br, and Webjet Linhas Aéreas, www.webjet.com.br.

Bus Taxis from town go to all the northern beaches (for example 30 mins to Riacho Doce), but buses run as far as Ipioca. The Jangadeiras bus marked 'Jacarecica-Center, via Praias' runs past all the beaches as far as **Jacarecica**. From there you can change to 'Riacho Doce-Trapiche', 'Ipioca' or 'Mirante' buses for **Riacho Doce** and **Ipioca**. These last 3 can also be caught in the centre on the seafront avenue below the Praça Sinimbu (US$1 to Riacho Doce). To return take any of these options, or take a bus marked 'Shopping Center' and change there for 'Jardim Vaticana' bus, which goes through Pajuçara. *Combis* to **Marechal Deodoro**, **Praia do Francês** and **Barra de São Miguel** leave from opposite the Hospital Santa Casa in front of the Texaco service station. *Combi* US$2 to Marechal Deodoro, 30 mins, calling at Praia do Francês in each direction. Last bus back from Praia do Francês to Maceió at 1800.

Long distance The 'Ponte Verde/Jacintinho' bus runs via Pajuçara from the centre to the *rodoviária*, also take 'Circular' bus (25 mins Pajuçara to *rodoviária*). Bus to **Recife**, 10 a day, 3½ hrs express (more scenic coastal route, 5 hrs), US$15. To **Aracaju**, US$18, 5 hrs (potholed road). To **Salvador**, 10 hrs, 4 a day, US$50 (*rápido* costs more). To **Penedo**, 4 buses a day and *combis* from outside the *rodoviária*.

Car hire Localiza, and others in the airport and through hotels.

Penedo *p475*

Bus Daily bus to **Salvador** via **Aracaju**, 6 hrs, at 0600, US$25, book in advance. Also a bus direct to Aracaju, 3 hrs, US$7. Buses south are more frequent from **Neópolis**, 6 a day 0630-1800, change here for **Aracaju**, 2 hrs, US$7. To **Maceió**, 115 km, 4 buses a day in either direction, US$12, 3-4 hrs and *combis*.

Ferry Frequent launches for foot passengers and bicycles across the river to **Neópolis**, 10 mins, US$0.50, for connections by bus to **Aracaju**. The dock in Penedo is on Av Duque de Caxias, below Bompreço. The ferry makes 3 stops in Neópolis, the 2nd is closest to the *rodoviária* (which is near the **Clube Vila Nova**, opposite the Texaco station). There is also a car ferry (every 30 mins, US$3, take care when driving on and off).

ⓘ Directory

Aracaju *p468*
Banks Visa ATMs at shopping centres, Banco do Brasil, Praça Gen Valadão and Bradesco in the city centre. MasterCard ATMs at Banco 24 hrs, Av Francisco Porto and Av Geraldo Sobral, in the city centre close to the Shell gas station.

Maceió *p471, map p472*
Banks Open 1000-1500. Good rates at Banespa. Plenty of branches of Bradesco for ATMs. Cash against MasterCard at Banorte, R de Comércio, 306, Centro.
Internet There are myriad internet cafés

throughout the city. **Laundry** Lave-Sim, R Jangadas Alagoanas 962, Pajuçara. Washouse, R Jangadas Alagoanas 698, Pajuçara. **Medical services** Unimed, Av Antonio Brandao 395, Farol, T082-221 1177, used to be São Sebastião hospital. **Pediatria 24 horas**, R Durval Guimaraes 519, Ponta Verde, T082-3231 7742/7702. **Dentist:** Pronto Socorro Odontologico de Maceio, Av Pio XV11, Jatiuca, T082-3325 7534. **Post office** R João Pessoa 57, Centro, 0700-2200.

Penedo *p475*
Banks Bradesco, on Av Duque de Caxias, opposite Bompreço supermarket, with Visa ATM. Open 0830-1300. **Restaurant e Bar Lulu**, Praça 12 de Abril, will change cash if conditions suit the owner, fair rates.
Post office Av Floriano Peixoto, opposite Hotel Imperial. **Telephone** On Barão de Penedo.

Maragogi *p477*
Banks Bradesco in the town centre.

Pernambuco

Once the main producer of the world's sugar, today the state of Pernambuco offers a variety of attractions from beaches to traditional culture, colonial cities and museums. Recife, the state capital, is the main industrial and commercial centre with a very lively cultural scene and extensive urban beaches, while Olinda offers colonial elegance and a number of magnificent churches. Towns such as Caruarú and Nova Jerusalém, in the sertão, host very lively festivals and have some of the country's strongest artisan traditions working with clay, straw and leather handicrafts.

Pernambuco is saturated with music. In the 1970s, musician Naná Vasconcelos took the traditional beats of forró, ciranda and maracatú to New York, Miles Davis and beyond. In the 1980s and 1990s the mangue beat movement fused them with rock, electronica and trance. Many of Brazil's most famous contemporary avant-garde musicians are from Pernambuco, and Recife is considered Brazil's musical capital. Carnaval in the city of Recife and nearby Olinda is one of the best in the country. Nana Vasconcelos opens the festival leading a drum orchestra that dwarfs those in Bahia, and the maracatu prepares the way for three days of African-Brazilian cultural processions and relentless partying. ▶▶ *For listings, see pages 496-506.*

Recife and around → For listings, see pages 496-506. Colour map 2, B6. Phone code: 081.
Population: 1.2 million.

Recife is one of the most attractive large cities in Brazil. From afar it looks as blighted by skyscrapers as Rio de Janiero or Belo Horizonte, but in the shadows are many fine colonial buildings from the sugar boom, watching over little shady squares or sitting on the edge of the filigree of canals and waterways that divide up the city. The colonial heart is **Recife Antigo**. This was a no-go area like Rio's Lapa until 15 years ago, but it's now the centre of the city's booming music and alternative culture scene. To the south of the centre are a string of urban beach suburbs – **Pina**, **Boa Viagem** and **Piedade** – which, although frequented by bull sharks, are among the cleanest urban beaches in the country (outside the busy weekends when locals leave rubbish on the sand). The city prides itself on good food and unique fashion and has many fine restaurants and boutiques. Although they retain separate names, Recife and Olinda have long ceased to be two cities. Olinda is now Recife's colonial suburb.

Ins and outs

Getting there International and domestic flights arrive at **Gilberto Freyre airport** ① *Guararapes, 12 km from the city centre, near the hotel district of Boa Viagem.* The airport is modern and spacious, with a tourist office, banks, shops, post office and car rental and tour agencies. Airport taxis cost US$5 to the seafront; bus No 52 runs to the centre, US$0.40.

Long-distance buses arrive at the **Terminal Integrado dos Passageiros (TIP)** ① *12 km outside the city near the Oficina Brenn and cultural museum at São Lourenço da Mata, T081-3452 1999,* pronounced 'chippy'. To get to the centre from the *rodoviária*, take the metrô to Central station, 30 minutes. If going to Boa Viagem, get off the metrô at Central station (Joanna Bezerra station is unsafe) and take a bus or taxi (US$8) from there. ►► *See Transport, page 505.*

Getting around **City buses** cost US$0.90-1.50; they are clearly marked and run frequently until about 2230. Many central bus stops have boards showing routes. On buses, especially at night, look out for landmarks as street names are hard to see. Commuter services, known as the **metrô** but not underground, leave from the Central station; they have been extended to serve the *rodoviária* (frequent trains, 0500-2300, US$0.40 single). Integrated bus-metrô routes and tickets (US$1) are explained in a leaflet issued by **CBTU Metrorec**, T081-3251 5256. Trolleybuses run in the city centre. Taxis are plentiful; fares double on Sunday, after 2100 and during holidays.

Orientation The city centre consists of three sections sitting on islands formed by the rivers Capibaribe, Beberibe and Pina: **Recife Antigo**, **Santo Antônio** and **São José**. The inner city neighbourhoods of **Boa Vista** and **Santo Amaro** lie immediately behind to the east. The centre is always very busy by day; the crowds and narrow streets, especially in the Santo Antônio district, can make it a confusing city to walk around. But this adds to its charm. This is one of the few cities in Brazil where it is possible to get lost and chance upon a shady little square or imposing colonial church or mansion. Recife has the main dock area with the commercial buildings associated with it. South of the centre is the residential and beach district of **Boa Viagem**, reached by bridge across the Bacia do Pina. **Olinda**, the old capital, is only 7 km to the north (see page 491). Although the streets are generally too full to present danger it is wise to be vigilant where the streets are quiet. Always take a taxi after dark if you are walking alone or in a pair.

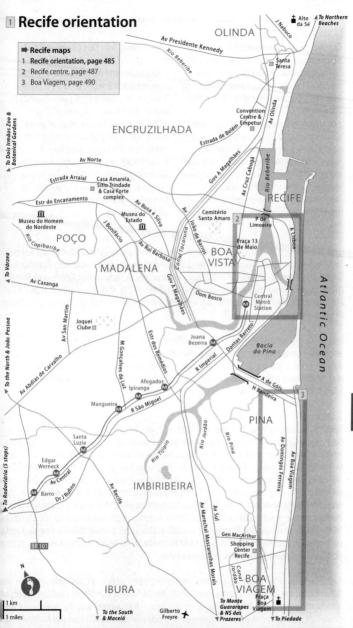

1 Recife orientation

➡ **Recife maps**
1 Recife orientation, page 485
2 Recife centre, page 487
3 Boa Viagem, page 490

To Dois Irmãos Zoo & Botanical Gardens

OLINDA

Av Presidente Kennedy

Alto da Sé

To Northern Beaches

J Nabuco

Rio Beberibe

Santa Teresa

Convention Centre & Empetur

Av Olinda

ENCRUZILHADA

Estrada de Belém

Av Norte

Gov A Magalhães

Av Cruz Cabugá

Rio Beberibe

RECIFE

Estrada Arraial

Casa Amarela, Sítio Trindade & Casa Forte complex

Estr do Encanamento

Av Rosa e Silva

Museu do Estado

Cemitério Santo Amaro

P de Limoeiro

Museu do Homem do Nordeste

J Bonifácio

Av João de Barros

2

A Lisboa

POÇO

Praça 13 de Maio

Rio Capibaribe

Av Rui Barbosa

BOA VISTA

To Várzea

MADALENA

Canal Tacaruna

Gov A Magalhães

Av Caxanga

Dom Bosco

Central Metrô Station

Av San Martim

Joquei Clube

Estr dos Remédios

M Gonçalves da Luz

Joana Bezerra

Dantas Barreto

Bacia do Pina

To the North & João Pessoa

Av Abdias de Carvalho

R Imperial

A de Góis

Afogados Ipiranga

H Bandeira

3

Mangueira

R São Miguel

Rio Tijipió

PINA

Av Domingos Ferreira

Santa Luzia

Rio Pina

Av Boa Viagem

Edgar Werneck

Rio Jordão

Atlantic Ocean

Av Central

To Rodoviária (5 stops)

Barro

Dr J Rufino

IMBIRIBEIRA

Av Recife

Av Sul

Av Marechal Mascarenhas Morais

BR 101

Gen MacArthur

Shopping Center Recife

Canal Jordão

N

BOA VIAGEM

1 km

1 miles

IBURA

Gilberto Freyre

To Monte Guararapes & NS das Prazeres

Praça Boa Viagem

To the South & Maceió

To Piedade

Naná Vasconcelos

Brazilian music without Recife's master percussionist Naná Vasconcelos would be like jazz without Charles Mingus. Bossa nova had been introduced into the USA by Stan Getz. But it was Naná and Paranense Airto Moreira who placed Brazilian percussion in the upper echelons of the serious jazz world. Naná was introduced to the US jazz scene by Miles Davis who went to one of the percussionist's concerts in the 1970s. And during a 25-year sojourn in New York he added his trademark *berimbau* and percussion to scores of records by artists like the CODONA trio (which he led with Don Cherry and Colin Walcott), Jan Garbarek, Pat Metheny, Gato Barbieri and numerous others. His most remarkable work, though, is purely Brazilian. Together with Egberto Gismonti and on albums like *Dança das Cabecas* (ECM), he created a new musical genre which fused jazz, classical and Brazilian styles. And his *Fragmentos* (Nucleo Contemporaneo/Tzadik) and *Storytelling* (EMI) albums are complex, mesmerizing tapestries of percussion and vocals that beautifully evoke Brazilian landscapes and local people.

Tourist information The main office for the Pernambuco tourist board, **Setur** ① *Centro de Convenções, Complexo Rodoviário de Salgadinho, Av Professor Andrade Bezerra s/n, Salgadinho, Olinda, T081-3182 8300, www.setur.pe.gov.br*, is between Recife and Olinda. There are other branches in Boa Viagem (T081-3463 3621), and at the airport (T081-3224 2361, open 24 hours); they cannot book hotels, but the helpful staff speak English and can offer leaflets and decent maps.

Safety Opportunistic theft is unfortunately common in the streets of Recife and Olinda (especially on the streets up to Alto da Sé). Keep a good hold on bags and cameras, and do not wear a watch. Prostitution is reportedly common in Boa Viagem, so choose nightclubs with care. Should you have any trouble contact the **tourist police** ① *T081-3326 9603/ T081-3464 4088*.

Sights

Recife's architecture is far less celebrated than its pretty neighbour, the former Portuguese capital of Olinda, but it retains some very attractive buildings. Rua da Aurora, which watches over the Capibaribe river, is lined with stately palladian and neoclassical buildings. The islands to the south, over the filigree of bridges, are dotted with imposing churches and surprisingly lavish civic structures, especially around the Praça da República. The city began with the Dutch at the twin forts – the **Forte do Brum** on the island of **Recife Antigo** (Old Recife) which faces the open ocean, and the **Forte das Cinco Pontas** on the neighbouring island of Santo Antonio. Both were built by the Dutch in 1630, seven years before Maurice of Nassau sacked and burned Olinda. The two forts controlled access to the Dutch port of **Mauritsstadt**, as Recife was first known, at the northern and southern entrances respectively.

Recife Antigo This 2-km-long island, facing the open ocean on one side and the Rio Beberibe on the other, lays at the heart of old Recife. Until the 1990s its cobbled streets of handsome colonial buildings were a no-go area – frequented only by drug users and prostitutes. However, the area has been almost completely rehabilitated and Recife Antigo

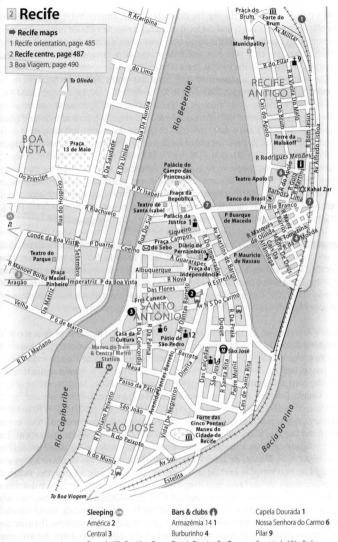

2 Recife

➡ Recife maps
1 Recife orientation, page 485
2 **Recife centre, page 487**
3 Boa Viagem, page 490

Labels on map:

Praça do Brum
Forte do Brum
Av Militar
New Municipality
R do Pilar
RECIFE ANTIGO
R B Vieira do Melo
Cais do Apolo
R Da Bom
R Bom Jesus
Torre da Malakoff
R Alfredo Lisboa
R Rodrigues Mendes
Teatro Apolo
Barbosa Lima
Kahal Zur
Banco do Brasil
Av Rio Branco
R Marques de Olinda
R Bra
R do Moeda
R Tomazina
Mde R
Cais de Santa Deus
P Buarque de Macedo
P Mauricio de Nassau
R Araripina
do Lima
Rio Beberibe
Do Príncipe
BOA VISTA
Praça 13 de Maio
R Da Saudade
Rua Da União
Rua Do Hospício
Palácio do Campo das Princessas
Praça da República
Teatro de Santa Isabel
Palácio da Justiça
R Riachuelo
R Da Aurora
P Pr Isabel
Siqueiro
Conde da Boa Vista
P Duarte
Rua Do Sul
7 de Setembro
Praça Campos
do Sebo
Diário de Pernambuco
A Guararapes
Praça da Independência
Teatro do Parque
R Manoel Borba
Praça Maciel Pinheiro
Imperatriz
R Matriz
P da Boa Vista
Albuquerque
R Nova
R Estreitos
Aragão
Velha
Das Flores
Frei Caneca
SANTO ANTÔNIO
Av N S Do Carmo
Av Dantas Barreto
Duque
Av Martins de Barros
R Coelho
P 6 de Março
R Dr J Mariano
Casa da Cultura
R Da Concordia
R Da Palma
Pátio de São Pedro
Barreto
Direita
Duque
São José
Das Calcadas
R Santa Rita
Cais de Santa Rita
Padre Muniz
São Luiz
Museu do Trem & Central Metró Station
Mauá
Passo da Pátria
São João
Avenida Dantas Barreto
Vidal De Negreiros
SÃO JOSÉ
R Floriano Peixoto
R do Peixoto
R do Muniz
Forte das Cinco Pontas/ Museu do Cidade de Recife
Av Sul
Estelita
Rio Capibaribe
Bacia do Pina
To Olinda
To Boa Viagem

Sleeping
América **2**
Central **3**
Pousada Villa Boa Vista **5**

Eating
Gelattos **2**
Leite **3**

Bars & clubs
Armazémia 14 **1**
Burburinho **4**
Depois Dancing Bar **5**
Estacío Pirata **6**
Marco Zero **7**

Churches
Basílica de Nossa Senhora de Penha **14**

Capela Dourada **1**
Nossa Senhora do Carmo **6**
Pilar **9**
Concatedral São Pedro dos Clérigos **12**

Buses
To Itamaracá & Igarassu **1**
To Porto da Galinhas **2**
To Boa Viagem **3**

N
200 metres
200 yards

is now the spiritual heart of the city. The **Marco Zero** point, sitting in the Praça Rio Branco is the official centre of the city and the locus of activity for Recife's vibrant carnival. The best Pernambucan bands play on the stage here until dawn during carnival week and the streets nearby are busy with bars and little makeshift restaurants most evenings and especially at weekends. The liveliest street is Rua da Moeda.

The well-preserved whitewashed and terracotta-roofed **Forte do Brum** ① *Praça Comunidade Luso Brasileira s/n, T081-3224 8492, Tue-Fri 0900-1600, Sat and Sun 1300-1700, US$1* (1629), is now an army museum, with huge Dutch and Portuguese canons on its bulwarks, exhibition rooms with photographs and memorabilia from Brazil's Second Word War campaign in Italy and a dusty collection of colonial documents, including some early Dutch maps of Brazil. At the other end of Recife Antigo is the **Kahal Zur Israel Synagogue** ① *R do Bom Jesus 197, T081-3224 2128, Tue-Fri 1000-1200 and 1400-1700, US$2*, an exact replica of the first synagogue to be built in the Americas – in 1637. Under the Dutch, the 'New Christians' (Jews and Muslims forced to convert under the Inquisition), were given freedom to worship. After the city was re-conquered by the Portuguese the synagogue was destroyed and the Jews either fled or were expelled. Many went north to the Dutch colony of Suriname, which retains a large Jewish population to this day.

There are two other sights worth seeing in passing. One of the city's first churches, the elegant, sky-blue **Igreja de Nossa Senhora do Pilar** ① *R de São Jorge s/n*, dating from 1680 is undergoing extensive refurbishment after being badly looted and lying decrepit for decades. The intention is to return the crumbling church to its former glory, complete with its magnificent ceiling paintings. The **Torre** ① *Praça do Arsenal da Marinha, T082-3424 8704, Tue-Sun 1500-2000, free*, is a 19th-century mock-Mudejar tower with a small observatory on its upper floor. It's worth visiting if only for the sweeping view out over the city.

Santo Antônio and São José The bulk of Recife's historical monuments lie in the twin neighbourhoods of Santo Antônio and São José on the island immediately to the south of Recife Antigo (and linked to that neighbourhood by the Buarque de Macedo and Mauricio de Nassau bridges). These neighbourhoods are interesting just to wander around (during the day only) and are replete with magnificent baroque churches. Most impressive of all is the **Capela Dourada da Ordem Terceira do São Francisco** ① *R do Imperador, Santo Antônio, T081-3224 0530, Mon-Fri and Sun 0800-1100 and 1400-1700* (1695-1710 and 19th century), in the church of Santo Antônio of the Convento do São Francisco. This is one of the finest baroque buildings in northeast Brazil and is another national monument. The lavish façade conceals a gorgeous gilt-painted interior with ceiling panels by Recife's Mestre Athayde, **Manuel de Jesus Pinto**. It is his finest work. Pinto was born a slave and bought his freedom after working on a series of Recife's magnificent churches, including the Concatedral de São Pedro dos Clérigos (see below). The chapel was designed and paid for in 1695 by a wealthy Franciscan lay brotherhood, the Ordem Terceira de São Francisco de Assis. The church sits immediately south of the **Praça da República**, one of the city's stateliest civic squares, graced by a fountain, shaded by palms and overlooked by a number of handsome sugar-boom buildings. These include the **Palácio do Campo das Princesas** ① *Praça da República s/n, Mon-Fri 0900-1700, free*, a neoclassical pile with a handsome interior garden by Roberto Burle Marx, which was formerly the Governor's Palace; the pink **Teatro de Santa Isabel** ① *Praça da República s/n, T081-3355 3323, www.teatrosanta isabel.com.br, guided visits Sun 1400 and 1700 in English, and almost nightly performances*, which has a lavish auditorium; and the imposing mock-French **Palácio da Justiça**, topped with a French Renaissance cupola.

Colonial Recife's other great church is the **Concatedral de São Pedro dos Clérigos** ⓘ *Pátio de São Pedro, R Barão da Vitória at Av Dantas Barreto, T081-3224 2954, Mon-Fri 0800-1200 and 1400-1600*, which overlooks one of the city's best-preserved colonial squares, is only a little less impressive. It's a towering baroque building with a beautiful painted and carved octagonal interior with a trompe l'oeuil ceiling (also by Manuel de Jesus Pinto (see Capela Dourada, above). The area has been renovated and is filled with little shops, restaurants and bars. There are sporadic music and poetry shows in the evenings from Wednesday to Sunday. Also worth visiting is the 18th-century **Basílica e Convento de Nossa Senhora do Carmo** ⓘ *Av Dantas Barreto, Santo Antônio, T081-3224 3341, Mon-Fri 0800-1200 and 1400-1900, Sat 0700-1200, Sun 0700-1000*, named after the city's patron saint, which has a magnificent painted ceiling and high altar. One of the best places in northeast Brazil to buy arts and crafts lies a stroll to the south, next to the Ponte 6 de Março. The **Casa da Cultura** ⓘ *R Floriano Peixoto s/n, Santo Antônio, T081-3224 0557, www.casadaculturape.com.br, Mon-Fri 0900-1900, Sat 0900-1800, Sun 0900-1400*, is a gallery of hundreds of shops and stalls selling clay figurines, leatherwork, lace and ceramics from all over Pernambuco, including the famous arts and crafts town of Caruaru. The building is the former state penitentiary. Immediately west of the Casa da Cultura is Recife's other Dutch fort, the **Forte das Cinco Pontas**. This is now home to the **Museu da Cidade do Recife** ⓘ *Mon-Fri 0900-1800, Sat and Sun 1300-1700, US$1 donation*, which shows a cartographic history of the settlement of Recife.

The **Basílica de Nossa Senhora de Penha** ⓘ *Praça Dom Vital, São José, T081- 3424 8500, Tue-Thu 0800-1200 and 1500-1700, Fri 0600-1800, Sat 1500-1700, Sun 0700-0900*, is an Italianate church a few streets north of the fort, which holds a traditional 'blessing of São Felix' on Fridays, attended by hundreds of sick Pernambucans in search of miracles.

Suburban Recife

The **Oficina Brennand** ⓘ *Propriedade Santos Cosme e Damião s/n, Várzea, T081-3271 2466, www.brennand.com.br, Mon-Fri 0800-1700, US$3*, is a Dali-esque fantasy garden and museum preserving hundreds of monumental ceramic sculptures by Latin America's most celebrated ceramic artist, Francisco Brennand. Enormous snake penises in hob-nailed boots are set in verdant lawns; surrealist egret heads look out over a Burle Marx garden from 10-m-high tiled walls; haunting chess-piece figures in top hats gaze at tinkling fountains. The museum has a very good air-conditioned restaurant and gift shop. There is no public transport here so take a taxi from Recife (around US$15 including waiting time; alternatively take a local bus to the *rodoviária* or to Varzea suburb and do a round trip from there, US$10).

The Brennands are one of the wealthiest old-money families in Brazil and Ricardo Brennand – as if not to be outdone by his cousin – has his own museum 10 minutes' taxi ride away. The **Instituto Ricardo Brennand** ⓘ *Alameda Antônio Brennand, Várzea, T081-2121 0352, www.institutoricardo brennand.org.br, Tue-Sun 1300-1700 (last entry 1630), US$3*, is a priceless collection of European and Brazilian art (including the largest conglomeration of Dutch-Brazilian landscapes in the world), books, manuscripts and medieval weapons housed in a fake Norman castle with its own moat and giant swimming pool.

3 Boa Viagem

To & Recife Centre

Boa Viagem detail

Atlantic Ocean

➡ **Recife maps**
1 Recife orientation, page 485
2 Recife centre, page 487
3 Boa Viagem, page 490

200 metres
200 yards

Sleeping
Aconchego **1**
Coqueiral **2**
Piratas da Praia **4**
Pousada da Julieta **5**
Pousada da Praia **5**
Recife Monte **7**

Eating
Chica Pitanga **2**
Churrascaria Porção **3**
É Gastronomia **4**
Ilha da Kosta **5**
La Capannina **6**
La Maison **7**
Parraxaxa **8**
Peng **9**
Tempero Verde **12**

Boa Viagem → *See map page 490.*

Recife's beach neighbourhood, and the site of most of the hotels, lies around 6 km south of town in the neighbourhood of Boa Viagem. The 8-km promenade lined with high-rise buildings commands a striking view of the Atlantic, but the beach is backed by a busy road, is crowded at weekends (when it is strewn with rubbish), and is plagued by bull sharks who lost their mangrove homes to the south after a spate of ill-considered coastal development. You can go fishing on *jangadas* at Boa Viagem at low tide. The main *praça* has a good market at weekends.

Ins and outs To get there from the centre, take any bus marked 'Boa Viagem'; from Nossa Senhora do Carmo, take buses marked 'Piedade', 'Candeias' or 'Aeroporto', which run along Avenida Domingos Ferreira, two blocks parallel to the beach, all the way to Praça Boa Viagem (at Avenida Boa Viagem 500). To get to the centre, take the bus marked 'CDU' or 'Setubal' from Avenida Domingos Ferreira. The PE-15 Boa Viagem to Olinda bus runs along the Avenida Boa Viagem and stops at the Praça Boa Viagem. It is fast and frequent.

Olinda → *For listings, see pages 496-506. Colour map 2, B6. Phone code: 081. Population: 350,000.*

About 7 km north of Recife is the old capital, a UNESCO World Heritage Site, founded in 1537. The compact network of cobbled streets is steeped in history and very inviting for a wander. Olinda is a charming spot to spend a few relaxing days, and a much more appealing base than Recife. A programme of restoration, partly financed by the Dutch government, was initiated in order to comply with the recently conferred title of 'national monument', but much is still in desperate need of repair.

Ins and outs

Getting there and around From Recife, take any bus marked 'Rio Doce', No 981, which has a circular route around the city and beaches; or No 33 from Avenida Nossa Senhora do Carmo, US$1.30; or 'Jardim Atlântico' from the central post office at Siqueira Campos (US$1.30, 30 minutes). From the airport, take the 'Aeroporto' bus to Avenida Domingos Ferreira in Boa Viagem and change to one of the buses mentioned above. From the Recife *rodoviária*, take the metrô to Central station (Joana Bezerra is unsafe) and then change. In all cases, alight in Olinda at Praça do Carmo. The PE-15 Boa Viagem bus runs between Olinda and Boa Viagem every 10-20 minutes (US$1.30, 20 minutes). Taxi drivers between Olinda and Recife often try to put their meters on rate 2 (only meant for Sundays, holidays and after 2100), but should change it to rate 1 when queried. A taxi from Boa Viagem should cost around US$14, US$20 at night. From Olinda to the centre of Recife, take a bus marked 'Piedade/Rio Doce' or 'Barra de Jangada/Casa Caiada'.

Tourist information The **Secretaria de Turismo** ① *Praça do Carmo, T081-3429 9279, daily 0900-2100*, provides a complete list of all historic sites and a useful map, *Sítio Histórico*. Guides with identification cards wait in Praça do Carmo. They are former street children and half the fee for a full tour of the city (about US$12) goes to a home for street children. If you take a guide you will be safe from mugging, which does unfortunately occur.

Sights

Whilst Olinda city boasts an ornate church on almost every corner, there are two which rank among the finest in South America – the Igreja e Convento Franciscano de Nossa

Senhora das Neves (Brazil's first Franciscan convent) and the Basilica e Mosteiro de São Bento. The **Igreja e Convento Franciscano de Nossa Senhora das Neves** ① *Ladeira de São Francisco 280, T081-3429 0517, Mon-Fri 0700-1200 and 1400-1700, US$2, children free, mass Tue at 1900, Sat at 1700 and Sun at 0800,* (1585), is one of the oldest religious complexes in South America. It has a modest, weather-beaten exterior, but an interior that preserves one of the country's most splendid displays of woodcarving, ecclesiastical paintings and gilded stucco. The Franciscans began work on the buildings, which comprise the convent, the church of Nossa Senhora das Neves and the chapels of São Roque and St Anne, in 1585. Even if you are in a rush, be sure to visit the cloisters, the main church and the São Roque chapel, which is covered with beautiful Portuguese *azulejo* tiles.

The **Basilica e Mosteiro de São Bento** ① *R São Bento, T081-3429 3288, Mon-Fri 0830-1130, 1430-1700, Mass Sat 0630 and 1800; Sun 1000, with Gregorian chant; monastery closed except with written permission, free,* is another very early Brazilian church, founded

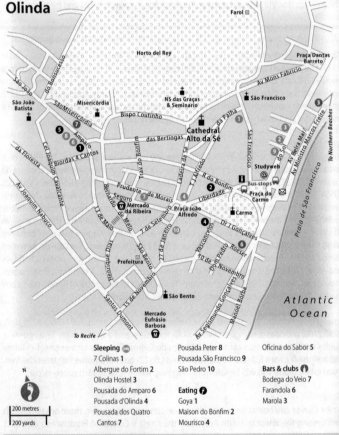

Olinda

Sleeping
7 Colinas 1
Albergue do Fortim 2
Olinda Hostel 3
Pousada do Amparo 6
Pousada d'Olinda 4
Pousada dos Quatro
Cantos 7

Pousada Peter 8
Pousada São Francisco 9
São Pedro 10

Eating
Goya 1
Maison do Bonfim 2
Mourisco 4

Oficina do Sabor 5

Bars & clubs
Bodega do Veio 7
Farandola 6
Marola 3

in 1582 by Benedictine monks, burnt by the Dutch in 1631 and restored in 1761. It is the site of Brazil's first law school and was the first place in Brazil to abolish slavery. The vast, cavernous nave is fronted by a towering tropical cedar altarpiece covered in gilt. It is one of the finest pieces of baroque carving in the Americas and was on loan to the Guggenheim museum in New York for much of the first decade of the new millennium. There are fine carvings and paintings throughout the chapels.

It's worth making the short, but very steep, climb up the **Alto da Sé** to the plain and simple **Igreja da Sé** ⓘ *Mon-Fri 0800-1200, 1400-1700* (1537), for the much- photographed views out over Olinda, the palm tree-fringed beaches and the distant skyscrapers of Recife. The chuch was the first to be built in Olinda and has been the city's cathedral since 1677. In the late afternoon and especially at weekends, there are often *repentista* street troubadours playing in the little cathedral square and women selling *tapioca* snacks. The **Igreja da Misericórdia** ⓘ *R Bispo Coutinho, daily 1145-1230, 1800-1830* (1540), a short stroll downhill from the cathedral, has some beautiful *azulejo* tiling and gold work but seemingly random opening hours. The **Igreja do Carmo** (1581), on a small hill overlooking Praça do Carmo, is similarly impressive, but has been closed for years despite assurances that it would be refurbished. Olinda has many handsome civic buildings too, including streets of 17th-century houses with latticed balconies, heavy doors and brightly painted stucco walls. Some, like the mansion housing the **Mourisco** restaurant (Praça João Alfredo 7), are in the Portuguese Manueline style, their façades replete with Moorish architectural motifs.

There's a thriving arts and crafts community in Olinda and this is a good place to stock up on regional souvenirs. Look out for terracotta figurines and woodcarvings. The figurines are often by named artisans (look for their autograph imprinted in the clay on the base) and are becoming collectors' items. You'll find shops selling arts and crafts near the cathedral and in the handicraft shops at the **Mercado da Ribeira** ⓘ *R Bernardo Vieira de Melo*, and the **Mercado Eufrásio Barbosa** ⓘ *Av Segismundo Gonçalves at Santos Dumont, Varadouro*. Every Friday at 2200 there are serenades in Olinda, with a troupe of musicians leaving the Praça João Alfredo (aka Praça da Abolição) and walking throughout the old centre.

The beaches close to Olinda are polluted, but those further north, beyond Casa Caiada, at **Janga**, and **Pau Amarelo**, are beautiful, palm-fringed and usually deserted (although the latter can be dirty at low tide). There are many simple cafés where you can eat *sururu* (clam stew in coconut sauce), *agulha frita* (fried needle-fish), *miúdo de galinha* (chicken giblets in gravy), *casquinha de caranguejo* (seasoned crabmeat) and *farinha de dendê* (served in crab shells). Visit the Dutch fort on Pau Amarelo beach where there is a small craft fair on Saturday nights. To get to the beaches, take either a 'Janga' or 'Pau Amarela' bus; to return to Recife, take a bus marked 'Varodouro'.

Southern coast → *For listings, see pages 496-506.*

Gaibú and around

Heading south from Recife are some of the best beaches in the state. The first stop is the beautiful and quiet beach at **Gaibú**, 30 km south, where there are *pousadas* and cheap restaurants. The scenic **Cabo de Santo Agostinho**, with a ruined fort, is 5 km to the east. About 1 km on foot from Gaibú is the beautiful **Praia Calhetas**. The beach at **Itapuama** is even emptier. Buses to Gaibú and the beaches run frequently from **Cabo**, Pernambuco's main industrial city, which has a few interesting churches and forts and a **Museu da**

Abolição, which has dusty displays about the history and abolition of the slave trade. To get to Cabo take a bus signed 'Centro do Cabo' from the airport in Recife.

Nearby, **Suape** has many 17th-century buildings, while the **Reserva Biológica de Saltinho**, www.museudouna.com.br/saltinho.htm, preserves some of the last vestiges of Atlantic forest in the northeast.

Porto de Galinhas → *Phone code: 081.*

Some 60 km south of Recife, Porto de Galinhas – whose name means 'port of chickens' because slaves were smuggled here in chicken crates – was one of the first of a string of low-key beach resorts discovered in the 1990s. Back then it was little more than a beach and two sandy streets; the myth of its tranquil charm endures – but it is only a myth. Today Porto de Galinhas is well on its way to becoming a full-scale resort comparable those near Porto Seguro in Bahia. The sandy streets are asphalted and lined with shops and restaurants, while the beaches are backed with *pousadas* and resort hotels for several kilometres north and south. There is a reef close to the shore, so swimming is only possible at high tide.

Buses and minivans run from Avenida Dantas Barreto and Rua do Peixoto in Recife, at least hourly. Taxis cost around US$50. The **Centro de Informacões Turisticas** ① *R da Esperança s/n, T081-3552 1728, www.bureaudeinformacoes.tur.br*, has maps, information on transport, hotels and tour operators and a few English-speaking staff.

South of Porto de Galinhas

Some 80 km south of Recife are the beaches of **Barra do Sirinhaém**, with some tourist development and three hotels, including **Dos Cataventos** (D). Fishermen make trips to offshore islands (good views). Beyond these are the little towns of **Tamandare** and **São José da Coroa Grande**, which are quieter than Porto de Galinhas, and have a few simple places to stay.

Northern coast → *For listings, see pages 496-506.*

Igarassu → *Colour map 2, B6. Phone code: 081. Population: 77,500.*

Some 39 km north of Recife on the road to João Pessoa, Igarassu has the first church built in Brazil, **SS Cosme e Damião** (1535) and the convent of **Santo Antônio**, a beautiful baroque building with some very fine gilt work and *azulejos*.

Itamaracá → *Phone code: 081. Population: 14,000.*

North of Igarassu the road passes through coconut plantations to **Itapissuma**, where there is a bridge to **Itamaracá** island. According to the locals, this is where Adam and Eve spent their holidays (so does everyone else on Sunday now). It has the old Dutch **Forte Orange**, built in 1631; an interesting penal settlement with gift shops, built round the 1747 sugar estate buildings of Engenho São João, which still have much of the old machinery, charming villages and colonial churches, as well as some fine, wide beaches At one of them, **Praia do Forte Orange**, the **Instituto Chico Mendes de Conservação da Biodiversidade (ICMBio)** has a centre for the study and preservation of manatees, **Centro Nacional de Conservação e Manejo de Sirênios** or **Peixe-boi** ① *Tue-Sun 1000-1600*.

There are pleasant trips by *jangada* from Praia do Forte Orange to **Ilha Coroa do Avião** a recently formed sandy island, which has rustic beach bars and a research station for the development of wildlife and migratory birds. The beaches of **Sossego** and **Enseada** also have some bars but are quiet and relatively undiscovered. The crossing is 3 km north of Itamaracá town; recommended for sun worshippers.

Further north again, two hours from Recife by bus, is **Pontas de Pedra**, an old fishing village with a nice beach, lots of bars and opportunities for fishing and diving.

At the Pernambuco–Paraíba border, a 27-km dirt road goes to the fishing village of **Pitimbu**, with *jangadas*, surf fishing, lobster fishing and lobster-pot making. There are no tourist facilities but camping is possible and food is available from **Bar do Jangadeiro**. To get here, take a bus from Goiana, US$1.

West of Recife → *For listings, see pages 496-506.*

Bezerros → *Colour map 2, B6. Phone code: 081. Population: 52,000.*

The town of Bezerros, 15 km west of Recife on the BR-232, is set next to the Rio Ipojuca. It has some old houses, fine *praças* and churches. Some, like the **Igreja de Nossa Senhora dos Homens Pretos**, **São José** and the **Capela de Nossa Senhora**, date from the 19th century. The former railway station has been converted into the **Estação da Cultura**, with shows and other cultural performances. The best known artist and poet is José Borges (born 1935), whose work has been exhibited internationally. The city's main attraction is handicrafts, which are found in the district of **Encruzilhada de São João**. Most typical are the Papangu masks, made of painted papier mâché, and used at Carnaval as interior decoration. Wooden toys are also popular, as well as items made from leather and clay. About 10 km from the centre of Bezerros, near the village of Serra Negra, a small eco-tourism park, **Serra Negra ecological tourism trail**, has been set up. Trails lead to caves and springs; the flora is typical of the *agreste*.

Carnaval here is famed throughout Brazil and is known as **Folia do Papangu**, see Festivals, page 503. For tourist information contact the **Departamento de Turismo** ① *Praça Duque de Caxias 88, Centro, T081-3328 1286.* The artisans association, **Associação dos Artesãos de Bezerros**, is at the same address.

Caruaru → *Colour map 2, B6. Phone code: 081. Population: 254,000. Altitude: 554 m.*

Situated 134 km west of Recife, this small town in the *sertão* is famous for its huge **Festas Juninas**, held throughout June (see Festivals and events, page 503), and its little clay figures (*figurinhas* or *bonecas de barro*) originated by Mestre Vitalino (1909-1963), and very typical of northeast Brazil. Most of the potters live at **Alto da Moura**, 6 km away, where you can visit the **Casa Museu Mestre Vitalino** ① *buses from Caruaru, a bumpy 30-min ride, US$0.50*, once owned by Vitalino and containing personal objects and photographs, but no examples of his work. UNESCO has recognized the area as the largest centre of figurative art in the Americas. It is also possible to buy the arts and crafts in Caruaru itself. The town hosts a number of markets, which were originally devoted to foodstuffs but which now also sell arts and crafts. The most famous is the **Feira da Sulanca**, held in the city centre on Tuesdays, with some 10,000 stalls and 40,000 visitors.

ns and outs The *rodoviária* is 4 km west of town; buses from Recife stop in the town centre. Alight here and look for the **Livraria Estudantil**, on the corner of Vigário Freire and Rua Anna de Albuquerque Galvão; this is a useful landmark. Follow Galvão down hill from the bookshop, turn right on Rua 15 de Novembro to the first junction, 13 de Maio; turn left, and finally cross the river to the Feira do Artesanato (arts and crafts market).

During the **Festas Juninas**, there is a tourist train, **Train do Forró**, from Recife, which is a very spirited affair with bars, and bands playing in the carriages. See www.tremdo forro.com.br and www.caruaru.pe.gov.br for information.

Fazenda Nova and Nova Jerusalém

During Easter Week each year, various agencies run package tours to the little country town of Fazenda Nova, 23 km from Caruaru. Just outside the town is Nova Jerusalém. Every day from the day before Palm Sunday up to Easter Saturday, an annual Passion play is enacted here, on an open-air site about one third the size of the historic quarter of Jerusalem. Nine stages are used to depict scenes from the Passion of Christ, which is presented using 50 actors and 500 extras to re-enact the story with the audience following in their footsteps. *TV Globo* stars often play the starring roles and the sound and lighting effects are state of the art. Performances begin at 1800 and last for about three hours.

There is little accommodation in Nova Jerusalém/Fazenda Nova and it is usually full during the Passion. **Empetur** in Recife/Olinda has details of agencies that offer trips. During the Easter period there are direct bus services from Recife (and from Caruaru at other times).

◉ Pernambuco listings

For Sleeping and Eating price codes and other relevant information, see pages 32-37.

● Sleeping

Recife *p484, maps p485 and p487*
For the city centre, the best pace to stay is **Boa Vista**. Be careful walking back to hotels after dark. During **Carnaval** and for longer stays, individuals rent private rooms and houses in Recife and Olinda; listings can be found in the classified ads of *Diário de Pernambuco*. This accommodation is generally cheaper, safer and quieter than hotels.
A Pousada Villa Boa Vista, R Miguel Couto 81, Boa Vista, T081-3223 0666, www.pousada villaboavista.com.br. The only modern hotel in town, with plain, comfortable a/c rooms (all en suites have modern bathrooms and powerful showers), around a courtyard. Quiet, safe and a 5-min taxi ride from the centre.
D América, Praça Maciel Pinheiro 48, Boa Vista, T081-3423 2707, www.hotelamerica recife.com.br. Frayed, very simple rooms with low, foamy beds, lino floors and tiny en suites. The best rooms are on the upper floors with views out over the city.
D Central, Av Manoel Borba 209, Boa Vista, T081-3222 2353. A splendid 1920s building

with its original French open lifts and plain, but freshly painted rooms with parquet flooring and flat-pack furniture. The bathrooms have enormous iron tubs (without plugs). The upper floors have wonderful views of the city.

Boa Viagem *p491, map p490*
Boa Viagem is the main tourist district and although it has plenty of hotels it is a long way from the centre of Recife. The beach is notorious for shark attacks. The main beachfront road is **Av Boa Viagem**; hotels here are mostly tower blocks and tend to be more expensive.
B Aconchego, Félix de Brito 382, T081-3464 2960, www.hotelaconchego.com.br. Motel-style rooms around a pleasant pool area, a/c, sitting room. English-speaking owner, will collect you from the airport.
B Recife Monte, on the corner of R Petrolina and R dos Navegantes 363, T081-2121 0909, www.recifemontehotel.com.br. A big tower with 150 rooms and a string of smarter duplex suites watching over a gloomy atrium with a small shaded pool, Rooms are good value for the category and the crowd are predominantly business travellers.

C Coqueiral, R Petrolina, 43, T081-3326
5881, www.hotelcoqueiral.com.br. Dutch-
owned (English and French spoken). Small,
homely rooms with a/c and a pretty breakfast
room. Recommended.

C-D Pousada da Praia, Alcides Carneiro Leal
56, T081-3326 7085, www.hpraia.com. This
ungainly blue block 50 m from the beach has
very simple tiled rooms – some pocket-sized
and with little more than a spongey bed,
others larger suites with space for up to 6. All
are a/c and come with a TV, safe and Wi-Fi and
there is a rooftop breakfast and lounge area.

D Pousada da Julieta, R Prof José Brandao
135, T081-3326 7860, hjulieta@elogica.com.br.
Friendly and clean. One block from beach,
very good value. Recommended.

E Piratas da Praia, Av Conselheiro Aguiar
2034, 3rd floor, T081-3326 1281, www.piratas
dapraia.com. This popular hostel sits close to
bakeries, *botecos* and a number of bars and
a block back from the beach. Fan-cooled rooms
and dorms are colourful but a little pokey,
but pleasant public areas include a living area
with rather uncomfortable plastic seats and
a well-appointed kitchen. Staff speak some
English can organize trips and give local
travel advice, and there is free Wi-Fi.

Olinda p491, map p492

Travellers generally tend to use Olinda as a
base rather than Recife as it is safer, prettier
and its sights, restaurants and bars are
concentrated in a relatively small area.
Transport to Recife is straightforward (see
page 506). Prices at least triple during Carnaval
when 5-night packages are sold. Rooms at
regular prices can often be found in Boa
Viagem during this time. In the historic
centre, accommodation is mostly in converted
mansions, which are full of character. If you
can afford it, staying in one of these *pousadas* is
the ideal way to absorb Olinda's colonial
charm. All *pousadas*, and most of the cheaper
hotels outside the old city, have a pool.

AL 7 Colinas, Ladeira de Sao Francisco 307,
T/F081-3439 7766, www.hotel7colinas.
com.br. Spacious, new hotel with all mod

cons, set in private, gated gardens and
with a large swimming pool.

AL Pousada do Amparo, R do Amparo 199,
T081-3439 1749, www.pousadadoamparo.
com.br. Olinda's best hotel is a gorgeous,
18th-century house, full of antiques and
atmosphere in the Roteiros do Charme
group (see page 34). Rooms have 4-poster
beds and each is decorated differently. The
public areas include a spacious foyer with a
high ceiling decorated with art, a pool and
sauna area surrounded by a little flower-
filled garden and an excellent, delightfully
romantic restaurant.

B-C Pousada dos Quatro Cantos,
R Prudente de Morais 441, T081-3429 0220,
www.pousada4 cantos.com.br. A large
converted townhouse with a little walled
garden and terraces. The maze of bright
rooms and suites are decorated with
Pernambuco arts and crafts and furnished
mostly with antiques. Warm, welcoming
and full of character.

C Pousada São Francisco, R do Sol 127,
T081-3429 2109, www.pousadasao
francisco.com.br. Well-kept and airy a/c
rooms with little terraces, slate floors and
pokey bathrooms housed in a modern
2-storey hotel overlooking a pool and bar
area and set in pleasant gardens, which
are visited by hummingbirds in the early
morning. The hotel has a small restaurant
and parking. Outside the historic centre
but within walking distance.

C-D Pousada Peter, R do Amparo 215, T081-
3439 2171, www.pousadapeter.com.br.
The rather pokey white-tiled a/c rooms in
this converted town house contrast with
the spacious lobby lounge decorated with
Pernambuco crafts and colourful artwork.
Breakfast is served on the terrace overlooking
distant Recife and the modest pool.

C-E Olinda Hostel, R do Sol 233, T081-
3429 1592, www.alberguedeolinda.com.br.
HI youth hostel with fan-cooled 8-bed dorms
with shared en suites, and doubles. The
hostel has a tropical garden, TV room, and a
shady area with hammocks next to a pool.

C-E Pousada d'Olinda, P João Alfredo 178, T/F081-3494 2559, www.pousadadolinda. com.br. Basic but well-kept dorms and doubles around a pool, garden and communal breakfast area and lunchtime restaurant. Discount of 10% for owners of **Footprint** guides. English, French, German Arabic and Spanish spoken.

D São Pedro, R 27 Janeiro 95, T081-3439 9546, www.pousadapedro.com. Quiet little *pousada* with a walled garden, a small pool shaded by frangipani and bamboo. Has a delightful breakfast area and lobby decorated with art and antiques. The rustic rooms are tiny but tastefully decorated and all a/c. The best are on the upper floor.

D-E Pousada do Fortim, R do Sol 151, T081-3439 7124, www.pousadadofortim.com.br. Very simple but clean boxy rooms with a/c at the cheapest rates in Olinda. Some are big enough for 4. Breakfast is US$2 extra.

Camping

Olinda Camping, R Bom Sucesso 262, Amparo, T081-3429 1365. US$5 per person, space for 30 tents, 5 trailers, small huts for rent, quiet, well-shaded, town buses pass outside. Recommended.

Gaibu *p493*

L-E Casa dos Golfinhos, Gaibu beach, T081-8861 4707, www.gaibu-bedandbreakfast.com. Bed and breakfast accommodation close to the beach, under German management.

Porto de Galinhas *p494*

There are plenty of cheap *pousadas* and hotels in town along **R da Esperança** and its continuation **R Manoel Uchôa**; also along **R Beijapurá**, which runs off R da Esperança.

L Village Porto de Galinhas, T081-3552 2945, www.villageportodegalinhas.com.br. All-inclusive family beach resort right on the ocean and with a large pool, restaurant, a/c rooms. Some 7 km from town.

C-E HI Pousada A Casa Branca, Praça 18, T081-3552 1808, www.pousadaacasabranca. com.br. Very clean, well-kept, newly opened

hostel with some a/c rooms and several dorms. To get there take the right turn (away from the sea) off R Beijupira opposite R Carauna and walk inland for 400 m. The *pousada* is in a little square 150 m before the Estrada Maracaipe.

C-E La Vila delle Rose, R Manoel Uchôa 11, T081-3552 1489, www.laviladellerose.com.br. Simple, bright and well-kept doubles and shared rooms in a large house very close to the beach. Good breakfast and friendly service. All en suites.

Igarassu *p494*

Camping

Engenho Monjope, 5 km before Igarassu coming from Recife, T081-3543 0528, US$5. A Camping Clube do Brasil site on an old sugar estate, now a historical monument (bus US$1, alight at the 'Camping' sign and walk 5-10 mins).

Itamaracá *p494*

B Casa da Praia, Av da Forte Orange, T081-3544 1255. With pool, minibar, breakfast and optional dinner.

C Pousada Itamaracá, R Fernando Lopes 205/210, T081-3544 1152, www.pousada deitamaraca.com.br. Away from the beach, but has a pool.

Caruaru *p495*

A large number of cheap *hospedarias* can be found around the central square, Praça Getúlio Vargas.

A Grande Hotel São Vicente de Paulo, Av Ric Branco 365, T081-3721 5011, www.grandehotel caruaru.com.br. A good, centrally located hotel with a/c, laundry, garage, bar, restaurant, pool, TV. It also houses the local cinema.

C Centenário, 7 de Setembro 84, T081-3722 4011. Also has more expensive suites and a pool. The breakfast is good. As the hotel is in the town centre it can be noisy, but otherwise recommended.

C Central, R Vigario Freire 71, T081-3721 5880. Suites or rooms, all with a/c, TV, good breakfast, in the centre. Recommended.

🍴 Eating

Recife *p484, maps p485 and p487*
The best Recife restaurants are in Boa Viagem (see below) and adjacent Pina. Be careful of eating the local crabs, known as *guaiamum*; they live in the mangrove swamps which take the drainage from Recife's *mocambos* (shanty towns).

There are many cheap *lanchonetes* catering to office workers, they tend to close in evening.

ʔʔʔ Leite, Praça Joaquim Nabuco 147/53 near the Casa de Cultura, Santo Antônio. This formal Portuguese-Brazilian fusion restaurant, with black-tie waiters and a live pianist, is one of the oldest in the country and has been serving Portuguese standards like bacalhau (smoked salted cod) for 120 years. More modern options on the 50+ dish menu include king prawns fried in garlic butter and served with cream cheese sauce and Brazil nut rice. It is frequently voted the best in the city.

ʔ Gelattos, Av Dantas Barreto, 230. Great juices (*sucos*) – try the delicious *guarana do amazonas* with nuts. Snacks include, hamburgers and sandwiches.

Boa Viagem *p491, map p490*
Restaurants on the main beach road of Av Boa Viagem are pricier than in the centre. Venture a block or 2 inland for cheaper deals. There are many a/c cheapies in the Shopping Center Recife, T081-3464 6000. Many of the better restaurants are closed on Mon.

ʔʔʔ Churrascaria Porção, R Ernesto de Paula Santos 1368, T081-3465 3999, www.porcao. com.br. This widespread upmarket Brazilian *churrascaria* chain is good for meat- and salad-eaters alike – with a huge salad and pasta bar as well as the usual waiters whisking sizzling spit roast cuts of meat from the kitchen.

ʔʔʔ É Gastronomia, R do Atlantico 147, Pina, T081-3225 9323, www.egastronomia.com.br. Warm reds, mirrors, low light, candles on the table and chill out music make this recent opening feel like a lounge room in a swish

London club. Chef Douglas Van Der Ley serves classic French dishes with a Brazilian twist, with plates like fillet steak with foie gras, accompanied with sweet potato puree and cheese tartlet. The dessert menu changes daily.

ʔʔʔ La Maison, Av Boa Viagem, 618, T081-3325 1158. This fondue restaurant in a low-lit basement has an illicit dive bar feel and cheesy 1970s decor, but its good fun, attracts a lively crowd and has stodgy desserts like peach melba on the menu.

ʔʔ Chica Pitanga, R Petrolina, 19, T081-3465 2224. Upmarket, excellent food by weight. Be prepared to queue. Recommended.

ʔʔ Ilha da Kosta, R Pe Bernardino Pessoa 50, T081-3466 2222, www.ilhadakosta.com.br. One of half a dozen good-value restaurants serving everything from steaks and Bahian stews to sushi and roast chicken. These sit alongside a variety of *petisco* snacks. Open from 1100 until the last client leaves.

ʔʔ La Capannina, Av Cons Aguiar 538, T081-3465 9420. Italian pizzas, salad, pasta and sweet and savoury crêpes. Recommended.

ʔʔ Parraxaxa, R Baltazar Pereira, 32, T081- 3463 7874, www.parraxaxa.com.br. Rustic-style, award-winning buffet of north-eastern cuisine, with tapioca breakfasts and a generous spread of dishes at lunch and dinner time. The dining room is decorated with effigies of the *sertão* bandit Lampião and his consort Maria Bonita.

ʔ Peng, Av Eng Domingos Ferreira, 2886, T081-3326 9149. Self-service, some Chinese dishes. Bargain, rather than gourmet food.

ʔ Tempero Verde, R SH, Cardim, opposite Chica Pitanga. Where the locals go for a bargain meal of beans, meat and salad, US1.50. Simple, self-service, street tables.

ʔ TioDadá, R Baltazar Pereira, 100. Loud, TV screens, good-value portions of beef.

Olinda *p491, map p492*
Try *tapioca*, a local dish made of manioc with coconut or cheese. The traditional Olinda drinks, *pau do índio* (with 32 herbs) and *retetel* are manufactured on R do Amparo.

There are a number of *lanchonetes* and fast-food options along the seafront, including **Mama Luise** and **Gibi**, Av Min Marcos Freire, and **Leque Moleque**, Av Sigismundo Gonçalves 537.

Goya, R do Amparo 157, T081-3439 4875. Regional food, particularly seafood, beautifully presented.

Oficina do Sabor, R do Amparo 355, T081-3429 3331. Chef Cesar Santos runs the kitchen at what is probably the city's best restaurant, serving traditional Lusitanian dishes like Portuguese *bacalhau* (salted codfish) and surubim catfish in passionfruit soubise with sautéed sweet potato and rice. Tables sit in a colourful dining room and on an al fresco terrace with sea views. There are plenty of vegetarian options.

Maison do Bonfim, R do Bonfim 115, T081-3429 1674. English-trained chef Jeff Colas serves a choice of European dishes like mini vol-au-vent de Roquefort and *carpaccio com rúcula e tomate seco e mostarda francesa* (carpaccio with rocket and sun-dried tomato with French mustard) in this attractive Portuguese town house on the most elegant colonial street in the city. The wine list is one of the best in Olinda, with a choice of Argentine and Chilean reds.

Samburá, Av Min Marcos Freire 1551. With terrace, try *caldeirada* and *pitu* (crayfish), also lobster in coconut sauce or daily fish dishes, very good.

Grande Pequim, Av Min Marcos Freire 1463, Bairro Novo. Good Chinese food.

Mourisco, Praça João Alfredo. Excellent, good-value food by weight in lovely, part-covered garden. Delicious deserts. A real find. Warmly recommended.

Caruaru *p495*

Alto da Moura is a real tourist spot and gets very busy.

Catracho's, close to São Sebastião hospital. Has a Caribbean feel and the Honduran owner mixes great cocktails.

Costela do Baiano, close to Igreja do Rosário. Very good value northeastern cooking with good seafood.

A Massa, R Vidal de Negreiros. The best of a number of cheap lunch restaurants in the centre near Banco do Brasil. With respectable pizzas and pasta.

⊕ Bars and clubs

Recife *p484, maps p485 and p487*

Recife and Olinda are reknowned for their lively nightlife. There is frequent live music – both in public spaces and in Recife and Olinda's numerous theatres. The website http://bacarau.com.br has details of what's on where.

Recife Antigo is the best place in the city for weekend nightlife. Many exciting bands post mangue beat fusion bands and DJs play in the bars and clubs around **R Tomazino** (R do Burburinho); and there is always a lively crowd. The area is not safe to walk to so take a taxi. The best listings site is www.reciferock.com.br and has information on live post-mangue beat music.

Armazém 14, Av Alfredo Lisboa s/n, Cais do Porto, Recife Antigo. One of the top live music venues for the alternative scene. Big names like Mundo Livre and Mombojo play here.

Boratcho, Galeria Joana Darc, Pina, T081-3327 1168. Tex Mex restaurant and live music venue for alternative *mangue beat* bands. Alternative and gay crowd.

Burburinho, R Tomazina 106, T081-3224 5854. The best of the live music spots in Recife Antigo. Grungy, arty crowd and a range of sounds from psychedelic *forró* funk to *frevo* rock and all things mixed. Other bars lie near by – start here and wander.

Fred Zeroquatro recommends

Mundo Livre S/A, www.mundolivresa.com, are one of the most exciting Recife bands. Together with **Chico Science** they invented *mangue beat* in the 1990s. Their iconic lead singer, Fred Zeroquatro gave us his tips for what to do when in Recife and Olinda.

→ All the great alternative Recife bands play at carnival usually at the *Marco Zero* event. Contacting Marco Zero productions (T081-3222 2720) for information. And be sure not to miss carnaval's *A Noite dos Tambores Silenciosos* (the night of the silent drums), in the Pátio do Terço (held by the church of Nossa Senhora do Terço next to Rua Direita). It's one of the best percussion events in the northeast; very African and with a strong sacred and ritualistic feel.

→ For roots and alternative Pernambuco music head for the **Casa da Rabeca** (Rua Curupira 125, Cidade Tabajara, Olinda; bus from PE-15 bus terminal). This little showhouse was founded by Mestre Salustiano, who sadly died in 2008, and showcases traditional and emerging artists. Come after 2100 on a weekend night.

→ Every Tuesday and Saturday there are *Terça Negra* and *Sabado Mangue* shows. These are free concerts given by the best new musicians at the **Pátio de São Pedro** (in front of São Pedro church, Recife Antigo).

Central, R Mamede Simões 144, Boa Vista, T081-3222 7622, www.centralrecife.com.br. The drinking hole of choice for the city's musical and artistic middle-class community. Decent bar food, lunches and breakfast.
Depois Dancing Bar, Av Rio Branco 66, T081-3424 7451. Well-established alternative dance club with live bands.
Estação Pirata, R do Apolo, Recife Antigo. Good live bands – look out for Eddie and Tine who play here.

Olinda *p491, map p492*

Beginning at dusk, but best after 2100, the **Alto da Sé** becomes the scene of a small street fair, with arts, crafts, makeshift bars, barbecue stands, and impromptu traditional music. Every Fri night band musicians walk the streets serenading passers-by. Each Sun from 1 Jan to Carnaval there is a mini carnival in the streets of the city, with live music and dancing.
Bodega do Veio, R do Amparo 212, T081-3429 0185. An Olinda institution with live music Thu-Sun. Sat nights are hosted by a famous local fiddle player, Mestre Saluciano, and his band, who play traditional *pe na serra forró*. Great *petiscos* (especially the *prato frio*) and caipirinhas.

Cantinho da Sé, Ladeira da Sé 305, T081-3439 8815. Lively, good view of Recife, food served.
Farandola, R Dom Pedro Roeser, 190, tucked away behind Igreja do Carmo church. Mellow bar with festival theme and big top-style roof. Live music nightly, plans for a circus next door. Drinks are cheap; try *bate bate de maracuja* (smooth blend of *cachaça*, passionfruit juice and honey) or *raspa raspa* fruit syrup. Warmly recommended.
Marola, Tr Av Dantas Barreto 66, T081-3429 2499. Funky wooden *barraca* on rocky shore-line specializing in seafood. Great *caiprifrutas* (frozen fruit drink with vodka). Can get crowded. Recommended.
Pernambucanamente, Av Min Marcos Freire 734, Bairro Novo, T081-3429 1977. Live, local music every night.

Itamaracá *p494*

Bar da Lia, R do Jaguaribe, close to the Forte Orange, weekends feature *cirandas* danced at the bar, led by the well-known singer, Dona Lia, and her band. Also serves food. In high season only – from Sep to after carnival.

Carnaval in Pernambuco

The most traditional and least touristy big carnival in Brazil takes place in Recife, its twin city Olinda, and the little towns nearby. Whilst there are few international tourists, Brazilian visitor numbers are as high as those in Bahia. The music is the most exciting in Brazil, and it is Pernambuco's own. Whilst Salvador pounds to *afoxé* and *axé*, and Rio to samba, Recife and Olinda reverberate to pounding *maracatú*, up-tempo, brassy *frevo* and alternative raucous *mangue beat*. The dancing is some of the best and most acrobatic in the country, with *frevo* dancers leaping, falling into the splits, twirling and throwing tiny, sparkly miniature umbrellas.

Pernambuco carnival is held in the street – unlike Rio and like Salvador. The difference is that, whilst you have to pay in Salvadoro, in Pernambuco, the celebrations here are almost all free. The crowds are big but only oppressive at the opening parade. Recife's carnival takes place in the old city centre, which is dotted with gorgeous Portuguese baroque churches and crumbling mansions, while sitting on two islands between the Beberibe and Capibare and the Atlantic. On the Friday, in the streets around the **Pátio de São Pedro** (Marco Zero) in Recife Antigo, there are big, spectacular *maracatú* parades with troupes of up to 100 drummers and blocos dressed in colourful costumes and swirling white dresses. This square forms the focus of Recife carnival for the following week, with a big sound stage hosting wonderful live acts. Carnival officially opens with the huge **Galo da Madrugada** (Cock of the Dawn parade), which is said by locals to be the largest street gathering in the world. Despite its name the parade usually begins at around 1000 on Carnival Saturday. Floats with many of the most famous stars – such as **Lenine**, **Alceu Valença** and **Eddie** – pass through the teeming crowds under a baking tropical sun. Try and get a place in one of the shaded bandstands at the side of the street as the heat can be oppressive. These can be booked up to a fortnight in advance at the central post office on Avenida Guararapes in Recife. Carnival shows continue until dawn on stages dotted around old Recife for the next five nights. In neighbouring Olinda the party is on the steep cobbled streets, between pretty 18th-century houses and opulent churches and overlooking the shimmering Atlantic. Troupes of *frevo* dancers wander through the throng playing and dancing with effortless gymnastic dexterity.

There are parties in other areas throughout both cities. These include the parade of the **Virgens do Bairro Novo** (Bairro Novo Virgins) in Olinda, led by outrageously camp drag queens, and the **Noite dos Tambores Silenciosos** (the Night of the Silent Drums), held in a pretty colonial church square in one of the poorest inner-city neighbourhoods. It's one of the most spectacular percussion events in Latin America, with a strongly African, sacred, ritualistic feel.

The most spectacular of the Carnival celebrations near Recife are held at **Nazaré da Mata**, where there are traditional parades and music.

⊛ Festivals and events

Recife *p484, maps p485 and p487*
For **Carnaval**, see box, above.
1 Jan Universal Brotherhood.

12-15 Mar Parades to mark the city's foundation.
Mid-Apr Pro-Rock Festival, a week-long celebration of rock, hip-hop and *mangue beat* SP at Centro de Convenções, Complexo de

Why I love carnival in Pernambuco

"Brazil's best carnival takes place in Pernambuco – with over 15 days of partying freely in the streets – with no charge for anything (unlike in Salvador or Rio) and with the full integration of rich and poor in the frenzy of joyful celebration. The state was colonized by the Portuguese. But the Dutch, French, English, Arabs, Jews and Africans – together with scores of indigenous nations – were all here. And this mix of nations has produced a unique carnival brew whose other ingredients include the *frevo* dancing of Recife and Olinda, the *maracatu* beats of the Pernambuco rainforests, the *caboclinho* rhythms of the tropical coast and the raw fusion of *mangue beat*.

Aquiles Lopes is the former chief of Empetur in Pernambuco (www.empetur.com.br).

Salgadinho and other venues. Check *Diário de Pernambuco* or *Jornal de Comércio* for details.
Jun Festas Juninas, see box, page 520.
11-16 Jul Nossa Senhora do Carmo, patron saint of the city.
Aug Mes do Folclore.
1-8 Dec Festival of Lemanjá, with typical foods and drinks, celebrations and offerings to the goddess.
8 Dec Nossa Senhora da Conceição.

Olinda *p491, map p492*
Feb Carnaval. Thousands of people dance through the narrow streets of the old city to the sound of the *frevo*, the brash energetic music that normally accompanies a lively dance performed with umbrellas. The local people decorate them with streamers and straw dolls, and form themselves into costumed groups (*blocos*), which you can join as they pass (take only essentials). Among the best-known *blocos*, which carry life-size dolls, are O homem da meianoite (Midnight Man), A Corda (a pun on 'the rope' and 'acorda' – wake up!), which parades in the early hours, **Pitombeira** and **Elefantes**. Olinda's carnival continues on Ash Wed, but is much more low-key, *a quarta-feira do batata* (Potato Wednesday), named after a waiter who claimed his right to celebrate Carnaval after being on duty during the official celebrations). The streets are very crowded with people dancing and drinking non-stop.

The local cocktail, *capeta* (guaraná powder, sweet skimmed milk and vodka) is designed to keep you going.
12-15 Mar Foundation Day, 3 days of music and dancing, night-time only.

Bezerros *p495*
Feb Carnaval celebrations are famous throughout Brazil and known as **Folia do Papangu**. Papangu characters wear masks that resemble a cross between a bear and a devil and are covered from head to foot in a costume like a bear skin (or an all-covering white tunic).
Jun São João.

Caruaru *p495*
Mar/Apr Semana Santa, Holy Week, with lots of folklore and handicraft events.
18-22 May The city anniversary.
13 Jun Santo Antônio.
24 Jun São João, a particularly huge *forró* festival, part of Caruaru's **Festas Juninas**. The whole town lights up with dancing, traditional foods, parties like the **Sapadrilha**, when the women dress as men, and the **Gaydrilha**, where the men dress as women, and there is even a *Trem do Forró*, which runs from Recife to Caruaru, rocking the whole way to the rhythms.
Sep Micaru, a street carnival. Also in Sep is **Vaquejada**, a Brazilian cross between rodeo and bullfighting; biggest in the northeast.

O Shopping

Recife *p484, maps p485 and p487*
Markets
The permanent craft market is in the **Casa da Cultura**; prices for ceramic figurines are lower than Caruaru.
Cais de Alfândega, Recife Barrio. With local artisans work, 1st weekend of the month.
Domingo na Rua, Sun market in Recife Barrio, stalls of local *artesanato* and performances.
Hippy fair, Praça Boa Viagem, seafront. Sat-Sun only. Life-sized wooden statues of saints.
Mercado São José (1875), for local products and handicrafts.
Sítio Trindade, Casa Amarela. Sat craft fair during the feast days of 12-29 Jun, fireworks, music, dancing, local food. On 23 Apr, here and in the Pátio de São Pedro, one can see the *xangô* dance. Herbal remedies, barks and spices at Afogados market.

Shopping malls
Shopping Center Recife, between Boa Viagem and the airport, www.shopping-recife.com.br. One of the largest in the country, with clothes, CDs, bookshops and lots more.
Shopping Tacaruna, Santo Amaro. Buses to/from Olinda pass.

Bezerros *p495*
The city's main attraction is handicrafts, which are found in the district of **Encruzilhada de São João**; items in leather, clay, wood, papier mâché and much more.

Caruaru *p495*
Caruaru is most famous for its markets which, combined, are responsible for about 70% of the city's income. The **Feira da Sulanca** is basically a clothes market supplied mostly by local manufacture, but also on sale are jewellery, souvenirs, food, flowers and anything else that can go for a good price. The most important day is Mon. There is also the **Feira Livre** or **do Troca-Troca** (free, or barter market). On the same site, Parque 18 de Maio, is the **Feira do Artesanato**,

leather goods, ceramics, hammocks and basketware, all the popular crafts of the region; it is tourist orientated but it is on a grand scale and is open daily 0800-1800.

▲ Activities and tours

Recife *p484, maps p485 and p487*
Diving
Offshore are some 20 wrecks, including the remains of Portuguese galleons; the fauna is very rich.
Mergulhe Coma, T081-3552 2355, T081-9102 6809 (mob), atlanticdivingasr@hotmail.com. English-speaking instructors for PADI courses.
Seagate, T081-3426 1657, www.seagaterecife.com.br. Daily departures and night dives.

Football
Recife's 3 clubs are Sport, Santa Cruz and Náutico. **Sport** play at Ilha do Retiro, T081-3227 1213, take Torrões bus from the central post office on Av Guararapes. **Santa Cruz** play at Arruda, T081-3441 6811, take Casa Amarela bus from the central post office. **Náutico** play at Aflitos, T081-3423 8900, take Água Fria or Aflitos bus. Local derbies are sometimes full beyond safe capacities. Avoid *arquibancada* tickets for Santa Cruz-Sport games. For games at Arruda, dress down.

Tour operators
Jacaré e Cobra de Água Eco-Group, T081-3447 3452, T081-3968 7360 (mob), www.truenet.com.br. Regular excursions in Pernambuco.
Souto Costa Viagens e Turismo Ltda, R Felix de Brito Melo 666, T081-3465 5000, and Aeroporto de Guararapes (American Express representative).
Student Travel Bureau (**STB**), R Padre Bernardino Pessoa 266, T081-3465 4522, stbmaster@stb.com.br. ISIC accepted, discounts on international flights but not domestic Brazilian flights.

Trilhas, T081-3222 6864, recommended for ecologically oriented excursions.

Olinda *p491, map p492*
Tour operators
Viagens Sob O Sol, Prudente de Moraes 424, T/F081-429 3303, T081-971 8102 (mob). English spoken, transport, car hire.
Victor Turismo, Av Santos Domont 20, loja 06, T081-3494 1467. Day and night trips to Recife.
Victor Turismo, **Felitur**, R Getulio Vargas 1411, Bairro Novo, T/F081-439 1477.

Porto de Galinhas *p494*
Diving
AICA Diving, Nossa Senhora do Ó, T/F081-552 1290 or T081-968 4876 (mob), run by Mida and Miguel. For diving and canoeing trips, as well as excursions to Santo Aleixo island.
Porto Point Diving, Praça Principal de Porto de Galinhas, T081-552 1111. Diving and canoeing trips, as well as excursions to Santo Aleixo island.

☉ Transport

Recife *p484, maps p485 and p487*
Air
Bus No 52 runs to the airport, US$1.40, from the city and Bus 033 runs between the airport and Boa Viagem. International flights to **Lisbon** and **Milan**. Domestic flights to **Brasília**, **Campina Grande**, **Fernando de Noronha**, **Fortaleza**, **João Pessoa**, **Juazeiro do Norte**, **Maceió**, **Natal**, **Paulo Afonso**, **Petrolina**, **Rio de Janeiro**, **Salvador** and **São Paulo**.

Airline offices Avianca, www.Avianca.com.br. Azul, airport, www.voeazul.com.br. Gol, T081-3464 4793, www.voegol.com.br and the airport. TAM, T081-342 5011, at airport, T081-3462 4466. TAP/Air Portugal, Av Conselheiro de Aguiar 1472, Boa Viagem T081-3465 8800, at airport T081-3341 0654. TRIP, T081-3464 4610 (for flights to Noronha) www.voetrip.com.br and the airport.

Bus
To get to the *rodoviária*, take the metrô from the central railway station, entrance through Museu do Trem, opposite the Casa da Cultura, 2 lines leave the city, take train marked 'Rodoviária', 30 mins. From Boa Viagem a taxi all the way costs US$20, or go to central metrô station and change there. Bus from the centre (1 hr) or from Boa Viagem. Bus tickets are sold at Cais de Santa Rita (opposite EMTU).

Bus PE-15 runs between Av Segismundo Gonçalves in Olinda and Av Dom Ferreira in Boa Viagem every 15-20 mins.

Buses to the nearby destinations of **Igarassu** (every 15 mins) and **Itamaracá** (every 30 mins) leave from Av Martins de Barros, in front of Grande Hotel. To **Olinda** take any bus marked 'Rio Doce', No 981, which has a circular route around the city and beaches, or No 33 from Av Nossa Senhora do Carmo, US$1, or 'Jardim Atlântico' from the central post office at Siqueira Campos.

To **Cabo** (every 20 mins) and beaches south of Recife from Cais de Santa Rita. To **Salvador**, daily 1930, 12 hrs, US$18-25, 4 a day (all at night) (1 *leito*, 70). To **Fortaleza**, 12 hrs, US$20 *convencional*, US$30 *executivo*. To **Natal**, 4 hrs, US$9. To **Rio**, daily 2100, 44 hrs, US$58-65. To **São Paulo**, daily 1630, 50 hrs, US$60-70. To **Santos**, daily 1430, 52 hrs, US$60. To **Foz do Iguaçu**, Fri and Sun 1030, 55 hrs, US$90. To **Curitiba**, Fri and Sun, 52 hrs, US$76. To **Brasília**, daily 2130, 39 hrs, US$49-60. To **Belo Horizonte**, daily 2115, 34 hrs, US$41. To **São Luís**, 28 hrs, Progresso at 1430 and 1945, US$75. To **Belém**, 34 hrs (Boa Esperança bus recommended). To **João Pessoa**, every 30 mins, US$2.50. To **Caruaru**, every hr, 3 hrs, US$3. To **Maceió**, US$9, 3½ hrs (express), 6 hrs (slow), either by the main road or by the coast road daily via 'Litoral'.

Car hire

Budget, T081-3341 2505. 24 hrs, just outside Guararapes airport. Hertz, T081-462 3552. Localiza, Av Visconde de Jequitinhonha 1145, T081-3341 0287, and at Guararapes airport, T081-3341 2082, freephone, T0800-992000.

Olinda *p491, map p492*

Bus To Recife, the No 981 bus has a circular route around the city and beaches. The No 33 runs to Av Nossa Senhora do Carmo, US$1. Or take the metrô from Praça do Carmo to Central station.

Taxi To Boa Viagem US$8, US$12 at night. Make sure the meter is set to rate 1, except on Sun, holidays or after 2100, when rate 2 applies.

Igarassu *p494*

Bus Buses run to Cais de Santa Rita, Recife, 45 mins, US$1.

Itamaracá *p494*

Bus Buses run to Recife (Av Martins de Barros opposite the Grande Hotel), US$1.10, very crowded) and Igarassu.

Caruaru *p495*

Bus Buses from the centre, at the same place the Recife buses stop, to *rodoviária*, US$0.40. Many buses run to TIP in Recife, 2 hrs express, US$3. Bus to Maceió, 0700, 5 hrs, US$9. Bus to Fazenda Nova 1030, 1 hr, US$2, returns to Caruaru 1330.

① Directory

Recife *p484, maps p485 and p487*

Banks Open 1000-1600, hours for exchange vary between 1000 and 1400, sometimes later. Banco do Brasil, R Barão da Souza Leão 440, Boa Viagem; Av Dantas Barreto, 541, Santo Antonio, exchange and credit/debit cards, TCs. Bradesco, Av Cons Aguiar 3236, Boa Viagem, T081-3465 3033; Av Conde de Boa Vista, Boa Vista; R da Concordia 148, Santo Antônio, 24-hr VISA ATMs, but no exchange. Citibank, Av Marquês de Olinda 126, T081-3216 1144, takes MasterCard. Av Cons Aguiar, 2024, ATM. Lloyds Bank, R AL Monte 96/1002. MasterCard, Av Conselheiro Aguiar 3924, Boa Viagem, cash against card. There are money changers at Anacor, Shopping Center Recife, loja 52, also at Shopping Tacaruna, loja 173. Monaco, Praça Joaquim Nabuco, *câmbio*, TCs and cash, all major currencies, no commission but poor rates. Norte Cambio Turismo, Av Boa Viagem 5000, also at Shopping Guararapes, Av Barreto de Menezes. Cultural centres British Council, Av Domingos Ferreira 4150, Boa Viagem, T081- 3465 7744, www.britcoun. org/br. 0800-1500, reading room with current British newspapers, very helpful. Alliance Française, R Amaro Bezerra 466, Derby, T081-3222 0918. Embassies and consulates Denmark, Av Marques de Olinda 85, Edif Alberto Fonseca 2nd floor, T081-3224 0311 (0800-1200, 1400-1800). France, Av Conselheiro Aguiar 2333, 6th floor, T081-3465 3290. Germany, Av Dantas Barreto 191, Edif Santo Antônio, 4th floor, T081-3425 3288. Japan, R Pe Carapuceiro, 733, 14th floor, T081-3327 7264. Netherlands, Av Conselheiro Aguiar 1313/3, Boa Viagem, T081-3326 8096. Spain, R Sirinhaem, 105, 2nd floor, T081-3465 0607. Switzerland, Av Conselheiro Aguiar 4880, loja 32, Boa Viagem, T081-3326 3144. UK, Av Eng Domingos Ferreira 4150, Boa Viagem, T081-3465 7744 (0800-1130). USA, R Gonçalves Maia 163, Boa Vista, T081-3421 2441. Medical services Dengue fever has been resurgent in Recife. Previous sufferers should have good insurance as a 2nd infection can lead to the haemorrhagic form, requiring hospitalization. Hospital Santa Joana, R Joaquim Nabuco 200, Graças, T081-3421 3666. Unicordis, Av Conselheiro Aguiar 1980, Boa Viagem, T081-3326 5237 and Av Conselheiro Rosa de Silva 258, Aflitos, T081-3421 1000, equipped for cardiac emergencies.

Fernando de Noronha

This small volcanic island rising from the deep, on the eastern edge of the mid-Atlantic ridge 350 km off the coast, is the St Barts of Brazil and one of the world's great romantic destinations. It is blessed with exceptional natural beauty; rugged like the west of Ireland, covered in maquis like Corsica and fringed by some of the cleanest and most beautiful beaches in the Atlantic. Many of the beaches are exposed to the full force of the ocean and pummelled by a powerful bottle-green surf that has earned the island the nickname 'the Hawaii of the Atlantic'. Surf championships are held on Cacimba do Padre beach. However, there are numerous coves where the sea is kinder and the broad beaches are dotted with deep clear-water rock pools busy with juvenile reef fish. The water changes through shades of aquamarine to deep indigo and is as limpid as any on earth. Diving here rivals Mexico's Cozumel and the Turks and Caicos.

Despite the fact that two-thirds of the island is settled, it is an important nesting ground for turtles and marine birds: both the island itself and the seas around it are a marine park, protected by Instituto Chico Mendes de Conservação da Biodiversidade (ICMBio). All that is needed to make it a sanctuary of international standing is to remove the non-native feral monitor lizards (brought here in the 20th century to kill rats), the goats and the abundant cats and dogs. Tourism, however, is controlled and only limited numbers can visit the island at any time. Book well in advance.

▶▶ *For listings, see pages 509-510.*

Ins and outs

Getting there and around Flights to the island from Recife and Natal are run by **TRIP**, www.voetrip.com.br. **CVC**, www.cruisevacationcenter.com, operates a small cruise liner, which sails from Recife to Noronha and then back to Recife via Fortaleza and Natal. Buggy hire, motorbike hire and jeep tours are available in town.

Best time to visit The rains are April to July. The vegetation turns brown in the dry season (August to March), but the sun shines all year round. Noronha is one hour later than Brazilian Standard Time. There are far fewer mosquitos here than on the coast but bring repellent.

Tourist information **Instituto Chico Mendes de Conservação da Biodiversidade (ICMBio)** has imposed rigorous rules to prevent damage to the nature reserve and everything, from development to cultivation of food crops to fishing, is strictly administered. Many locals are now dependent on tourism and most food is brought from the mainland. Entry to the island is limited and there is a tax of US$30 per day for the first week of your stay. In the second week the tax increases each day. Take sufficient reais as it's difficult to change money. For information see www.fernandodenoronha.com.br.

Sights

The island was discovered in 1503 by Amerigo Vespucci and was for a time a pirate lair. In 1738 the Portuguese built a charming little baroque church, **Nossa Senhora dos Remedios**, some attractive administrative buildings and a fort, **O Forte dos Remédios**, which was used as a prison for political dissidents by the military dictatorship in the late 20th century. The most famous was the communist leader Luis Carlos Prestes, who led the famous long march, the Prestes Column, in 1925-1927. Many people were tortured and murdered here. The islands were occupied by the USA during the Second World War and used as a naval base. US guns sit outside the *prefeitura* in the centre of the main town, **Vila dos Remédios**, which overlooks the coast on the eastern shore.

Some of the best beaches lie immediately south of the town, clustered around an imposing granite pinnacle, the **Morro do Pico**. The most beautiful are **Conceição**, **Boldró**, **Americano**, **Baía do Sancho**, **Cacimba do Padre** and the turquoise cove at **Baía dos Porcos**, which sits on the edge of the beginning of the marine park. Beyond is the **Baía dos Golfinhos**, with a lookout point for watching the spinner dolphins in the bay. On the south, or windward side, there are fewer beaches, higher cliffs and the whole coastline and offshore islands are part of the marine park. As with dive sites, **Instituto Chico Mendes de Conservação da Biodiversidade (ICMBio)** restricts bathing in low-tide pools and other sensitive areas to protect the environment.

There are good possibilities for hiking, horse riding and mountain biking. A guide will take you to the marine park and to beaches such as **Atalaia**, which has the best snorkelling.

Wildlife and conservation

The island is a UNESCO World Heritage Site. It may look like an ecological paradise but it has been the victim of much degradation. Almost all of the native vegetation was chopped down in the 19th century, when the island was used as a prison, to prevent prisoners from hiding or making rafts. A giant native rodent, recorded by Amerigo Vespucci was wiped out and linseed, feral cats, dogs, goats, rats, mice, tegu (*teju* in Portuguese) lizards and cavies were introduced in the 16th century. These continue to damage bird and turtle nesting sites and native vegetation. Nonetheless, the island remains an important sanctuary for sea-bird species. Ruddy turnstone, black and brown noddy, sooty tern, fairy tern, masked booby, brown booby and white-tailed tropicbird all nest here. Some endemic bird species

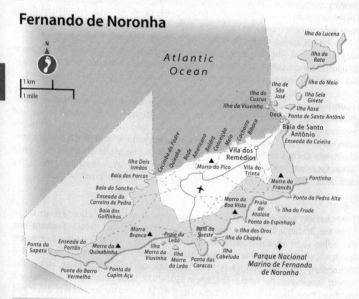

Fernando de Noronha

still survive: the Noronha vireo (*Vireo gracilirostris*); a tyrant flycatcher, the Noronha elaenia or cucuruta (*Elaenia spectabilis reidleyana*); and the Noronha eared dove or arribaçã (*Zenaida auriculata noronha*). There is an endemic lizard (*Mabuya maculate*) and at least 5% of the fish species are unique to the archipelago. The most spectacular animals are the nesting hawksbill and green turtles, and the spinner dolphins. Good terrestrial wildlife guides are non-existent on Noronha and even **Instituto Chico Mendes de Conservação da Biodiversidade (ICMBio)** spell the species names incorrectly on their information sheets. There are a number of reasonable dive shops; though biological knowledge is minimal.

⊙ Fernando de Noronha listings

For Sleeping and Eating price codes and other relevant information, see pages 32-37.

● Sleeping

Fernando de Noronha *p507, map p508*
Some of the most luxurious hotels on the island are built on illegally occupied land and are not listed here.
L Zé Maria, R Nice Cordeirol, Floresta Velha, T081-3619 1258, www.pousadazemaria. com.br. Spacious bungalows with cream tile floors, hardwood ceilings and generous beds. Verandas and hammocks have views out to the Morro do Pico. The highlight is the delicious, but small deep-blue half-moon pool.
L-AL Solar dos Ventos, T081-3619 1347, www.pousadasolardosventos.com.br. With a spectacular bay view, well-appointed wood, brick and tile bungalows and friendly owners.
AL Pousada do Vale, T081-3619 1293, www.pousadadovale.com. Friendly, well-run *pousada* with comfortable en suite rooms decorated with mosaics. The best are the duplex wooden bungalows. 300 m from Vila dos Remedios town centre.
A-B Pousada dos Corais, Conj Residencial Floresta Nova, T081-3619 1147, www.pousada corais.com.br. 8 simple a/c rooms, small pool.

● Eating

Fernando de Noronha *p507, map p508*
† **Ecologiku's**, Estr Velha do Sueste, T081-3619 1807. Bahian cooking served in an open-sided, mood-lit restaurant with a little garden.

† **Açai e Raizes**, BR-363, Floresta Velha. Roadside sandwich bar with snacks, puddings and delicious cream of Cupuaçu and Açai.
† **Cia da Lua**, Bosque dos Flamboyantes. Coffee, snacks, internet, car and buggy rental.
† **Jacaré**, Praça Presidente Eurico Dutra. The best-value on the island, with seafood buffet.

⊙ Bars and clubs

Fernando de Noronha *p507, map p508*
Vila dos Remédios town, which is the size of a postage stamp, has several bars with lively weekend *forró* from 2200 on weekends, and a bar with live reggae nightly in high season.

▲ Activities and tours

Fernando de Noronha *p507, map p508*
Tour and dive operators
It is possible to see hatching turtles in season. For details, contact **Fundação Pró-Tamar**, Caixa Postal 50, CEP 53990-000, Fernando de Noronha, T081-3619 1269.
Atlantis Divers, T081-3619 1371, www.atlantis divers.com.br. **Águas Claras** and **Noronha Divers** all offer the same dive locations around Noronha and the offshore islands, as well as dive 'baptism' for complete beginners. Diving costs US$50-75 for 2 tanks and is by far the best in Brazil aside from Atol das Rocas, 2 days off Bahia.
Barco Naonda, Vila do Porto, T081-3619 1307, www.barconaonda.com.br. One of many companies offering boat trips around the

island. The best leave at lunchtime, catching the late afternoon light on their return.
Locadora Ilha do Sol, T081-3619 1132, www.pousadadovale.com. Offers buggy rental and guided tours of the island.

⊖ Transport

Fernando de Noronha *p507, map p508*
Air Daily flights to **Recife** with TRIP (1 hr 20 mins, US$400 return). To **Natal** with TRIP (1 hr, US$300 return).

Paraíba

Travellers used to bypass Paraíba, but they are beginning to discover that there are many reasons to stop. The beaches are some of Brazil's best and least spoilt. Some of the most important archaeological sites in the Americas are tucked away in the haunting, rugged landscapes of its interior and the state capital, João Pessoa, is an attractive colonial city with a lively nightlife. Each year in June, Campina Grande, on the edge of the sertão, hosts one of the country's biggest festivals, the Festa do São João, with live music and up to a million people dancing forró into the small hours.

The dense tropical forest that once covered the entire coastal strip now only survives in patches, one of which is within the city of João Pessoa; forming one of the largest areas of wilderness within any city in the world. The seaboard is marked for much of its length by offshore reefs. Inland from the coastal plain the Zona da Mata is an abrupt line of hills and plateaux, a transitional region between the humid coast and the much drier interior. Most people live in this zone, especially in and around the state capital and a couple of other industrial centres. ▸▸ *For listings, see pages 517-522.*

João Pessoa and around → *For listings, see pages 517-522. Colour map 2, B6. Phone code: 083. Population: 598,000.*

João Pessoa is the state capital yet retains a small town atmosphere. It has some attractive colonial architecture and is set on the Rio Paraíba amid tropical forest. The atmosphere is restful and laid-back, yet there are plenty of bars and restaurants along the beachfront, particularly popular at weekends. The main beach, **Tambaú**, is pleasant but rather built up.

Ins and outs

Getting there and around It is a two-hour bus ride through sugar plantations on a good road from Recife (126 km) to João Pessoa. **Presidente Castro Pinto airport** ① *11 km south of the centre, T083-3232 1200*, receives flights from São Paulo, Brasília, Recife and Rio de Janeiro. A taxi from the airport to centre costs US$15, to Tambaú US$20. Alternatively, the airlines **GOL** flies from São Paulo or Rio to Recife, then provides free bus transport to João Pessoa. The **rodoviária** ① *R Francisco Londres, Varadouro, 10 mins west of the centre, T083-3221 9611*, has a luggage store and helpful **PBTUR**, www.pbtur.pb.gov.br, information booth. A taxi to the centre costs US$3.50, to Tambaú US$9. All city buses stop at the *rodoviária* and most go via the Lagoa (Parque Solon de Lucena). From the centre take No 510 for Tambaú, No 507 for Cabo Branco. The **ferroviária** ① *Av Sanhauá, Varadouro, T083-3221 4257*, has train connections to Bayeux and Santa Rita in the west and Cabedelo to the north.

Tourist information PBTUR ① *Centro Turístico Almte Tamandaré 100, Tambaú, T083-3214 8279 or T0800-3281 9229, 0800-1900*, and others at the *rodoviária*, and airport, provide useful information, pamphlets and maps. Some staff speak good English, and some French.

Background

The Portuguese did not gain a foothold on this part of the coast until the end of the 16th century. Their fort became the city of Filipéia, which grew to become the third largest in Brazil. This was later re-named Parahyba and then João Pessoa, in honour of the once state governor who refused to form alliances with other powerful politicians during the 1930s run for the vice-presidency. This led to his assassination, an event that swept his running mate, the fascist, Getúlio Vargas to power. Pessoa's '*nego*' ('I refuse') is written on the state's flag.

Sights

The well-preserved Centro Histórico has several churches and monasteries that are worth seeing. The **Centro Cultural São Francisco** ① *Praça São Francisco 221*, one of the most important baroque structures in Brazil, includes the beautiful 16th-century church of São Francisco and the Convento de Santo Antônio, which houses the **Museu Sacro e de Arte Popular** ① *T083-3218 4505, Tue-Sun 0900-1200 and 1400-1700, U$2*, with a magnificent collection of colonial artefacts. This is the best point to see the sunset over the forest.

Other tourist points include the **Casa da Pólvora**, an old gunpowder store which has become the city museum, and **Museu Fotográfico Walfredo Rodríguez** ① *Ladeira de São Francisco, Mon-Fri 0800-1200 and 1330-1700*. The **Teatro Santa Rosa** ① *Praça Pedro Américo, Varadouro, T083-3218 4382, Mon-Fri 0800-1200 and 1330-1800*, was built in 1886 with a wooden ceiling and walls. The **Espaço Cultural José Lins de Rego** ① *R Abdias*

1 Joâo Pessoa orientation

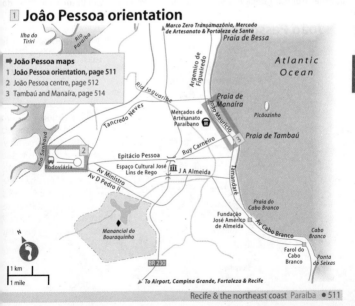

➡ Joâo Pessoa maps
1 Joâo Pessoa orientation, page 511
2 Joâo Pessoa centre, page 512
3 Tambaú and Manaíra, page 514

Gomes de Almeida 800, Tambauzinho, T083-3211 6222, a cultural centre named after the novelist (see Literature, page 786), includes an art gallery, history and science museums, several theatres, cinema and a planetarium. The **Fundação José Américo de Almeida** ⓘ *Av Cabo Branco 3336, Cabo Branco*, should be visited by those interested in modern literature and politics; it is in the former house of the novelist and sociologist.

João Pessoa prides itself in being a green city and is called 'Cidade Verde'. Its parks include the 17-ha **Parque Arruda Câmara**, also known as Bica, located north of the centre in the neighbourhood of Roger; it has walking trails, an 18th-century fountain, an aviary and a small zoo. **Parque Solon de Lucena** or **Lagoa** is a lake surrounded by impressive palms in the centre of town, the city's main avenues and bus lines go around it. **Mata** or **Manancial do Bouraquinho** is a 471-ha nature reserve of native *Mata Atlântica*, one of the largest urban forest reserves in Brazil. It is located south of the centre and administered by **Instituto Chico Mendes de Conservação da Biodiversidade (ICMBio)** ⓘ *T083-3244 2725*, which organizes guided walks; access is otherwise restricted.

Urban beaches

João Pessoa's urban beachfront stretches for some 30 km from Ponta do Seixas (south) to Cabedelo (north); the ocean is turquoise green and there is a backdrop of lush coastal vegetation. By the more populated urban areas the water is polluted, but away from town the beaches are reasonably clean; some spots are calm and suitable for swimming while others are best for surfing. The beach of **Tambaú** lies right in the centre of this 30-km strip and is, for all intents and purposes, the centre of the João Pessoa. It has many hotels, restaurants, the state tourism centre and clean sand. It is about 7 km from the old colonial city centre along Avenida Presidente Epitáceo Pessoa. The pier by **Hotel Tambaú** affords pleasant views (bus No 510 'Tambaú' from outside the *rodoviária* or the city centre, alight at **Hotel Tropical Tambaú**). South of Tambaú are **Praia de Cabo Branco** and **Praia do**

2 João Pessoa centre

➡ **João Pessoa maps**
1 João Pessoa orientation, page 511
2 João Pessoa centre, page 512
3 Tambaú and Manaíra, page 514

Sleeping ⬛
Guarany 2

JR 3

N
Not to scale

Seixas and, to the north, are the beaches of **Manaíra**, **Bessa**, **Intermares**, **Poço** and **Camboinha**, before reaching the port of Cabedelo (see below).

Excursions from João Pessoa

About 14 km south of the centre, down the coast, is the **Cabo Branco** lighthouse at the little forested cape of **Ponta do Seixas**, the **cape of the rising sun**, the most easterly point of continental Brazil and South America (34° 46' 36" W), and thus the first place in the Americas where the sun rises. There is a panoramic view from the clifftop and the beautiful beach below, **Praia Ponta do Seixas,** and coming here to watch sunrise is one of João Pessoa's most traditional romantic experiences. This beach and adjacent, more urbanized, **Praia do Cabo Branco** to the north and **Praia do Penha** to the south are much better for swimming than Tambaú. Penha has a 19th-century church where devotees petition the saints for succour, leaving notes all over the building and crawling up the steps to the nave in obeisance. Take bus No 507 'Cabo Branco' from outside the *rodoviária* to the end of the line and hike up to the lighthouse from there. Or at low tide you can walk from Tambaú to Ponta do Seixas in about two hours.

The port of **Cabedelo**, on a peninsula between the Rio Paraíba and the Atlantic Ocean, is 18 km north by road or rail. Here, Km 0 marks the beginning of the **Transamazônica highway**. At the tip of the peninsula are the impressive but run-down walls of the 17th-century fortress of **Santa Catarina**, in the middle of the commercial port. The **Mercado de Artesanato** is at Praça Getúlio Vergas in the centre.

The estuary of the Rio Paraíba has several islands; there is a regular boat service between Cabedelo and the fishing villages of **Costinha** and **Forte Velho** on the north bank; Costinha had a whaling station until the early 1980s.

The beaches between João Pessoa and Cabedelo have many bars and restaurants and are very popular with the locals on summer weekends (**Bar do Sumé**, Rua Beira Mar 171, Praia Ponta do Mato, Cabedelo, has good fish and seafood). Take a bus marked Cabedelo-Poço for the beach as most Cabedelo buses go inland along the Transamazônica. A taxi from Tambaú to Cabedelo costs US$24.

At Km 3 of the Transamazônica, about 12 km from João Pessoa, is the access to **Jacaré**, a pleasant beach on the Rio Paraíba (take the 'Cabedelo' bus and walk 1.5 km or take the train and walk 1 km, taxi from Tambaú US$10). There are several bars along the riverfront where people congregate to watch the lovely sunset to the sounds of Ravel's *Bolero*. Here you can hire a boat along the river to visit the mangroves or ride in an ultralight aircraft. ▶ *See Activities and tours, page 521.*

From Tambaú tour boats leave for **Picãozinho**, a group of coral reefs about 700 m from the coast which at low tide turn into pools of crystalline water, suitable for snorkelling (US$20 per person). Further north, boats leave from Praia de Camboinha to **Areia Vermelha**, a large sandbank surrounded by corals. This becomes exposed at low tide, around the full and new moon, and is a popular bathing spot (US$20 per person tour, US$5 per person transport in a *jangada*). Floating bars are set up at both locations, travel agencies arrange trips.

Paraíba coast → *For listings, see pages 517-522.*

The Paraíba coastline has 117 km of beautiful beaches and coves, surrounded by cliffs and coconut groves. These are among the least developed of the northeast.

3 Tambaú & Manaíra

João Pessoa maps
1 João Pessoa orientation, page 511
2 João Pessoa centre, page 512
3 Tambaú and Manaíra, page 514

Sleeping	Eating
Caiçara 2	Adega do Alfredo 1
Littoral 1	Cheiro Verde 4
Pousada Mar Azul 10	Gulliver 2
Royal Praia 5	Mangaí 3
Solar Filipéia 9	
Tambiá Praia 7	**Bars & clubs**
Tropical Tambaú 3	Fashion Club 5
Victory Business Flat 6	Incognito 6
Villa Mare Apt Hotel 8	Mr Caipira 8
Xênius 4	Zodiaco 7

Tambaba → *Colour map 2, B6.*

The best-known beach of the state is Tambaba, the only official nudist beach of the northeast and one of only two in Brazil. It is located 49 km south of João Pessoa in a lovely setting: the green ocean, warm water, natural pools for swimming formed by the rocks, cliffs up to 20 m high full of caves, palms and lush vegetation. Two coves make up this famous beach: in the first bathing-suits are optional, while the second one is only for nudists. Strict rules of conduct are enforced, unaccompanied men are not allowed in this area and any inappropriate behaviour is reason enough to be asked to leave. The only infrastructure is one bar, where meals are available.

Access is from **Jacumã**, via the BR-101, 20 km south from João Pessoa to where the PB-018 goes 3 km east to Conde and continues 11 km to the beach of Jacumã; from here a dirt road goes 12 km south to Tambaba. Buses run hourly to Jacumã from the João Pessoa *rodoviária*. In summer, dune buggies can be hired at Jacumã to go to Tambaba. Buggy from João Pessoa to Tambaba US$25 per person return (leaves 0930, returns 1730). A day-trip by taxi costs US$95.

Between Jacumã and Tambaba are several good beaches such as **Tabatinga**, which has many summer homes built on the cliffs, and **Coqueirinho**, which is surrounded by pleasant vegetation, and is good for bathing, surfing and exploring caves. There are plenty of cheap and mid-range *pousadas* at both and a very good seafood restaurant at Coqueirinho, **Canyon de Coqueirinho**, on the beach. Near the border with Pernambuco is the 10-km long beach of **Pitimbu**.

Campina and around

The best beaches of northern Paraíba are in the vicinity of the fishing village of **Campina**; although there is little infrastructure in this area, the shore is worth a visit. Access is via a turnoff to the east at Km 73.5 of the BR-101, 42 km north of João Pessoa. It is 28 km along a dirt road (PB-025) to Praia Campina, with a wide beach of fine sand, palms and hills in the background. Nearly 3 km south is **Praia do Oiteiro**, in which the white sand stands out in contrast with the multicoloured cliffs and calm blue ocean. About 2 km north of Campina is **Barra do Mamanguape**, where Instituto Chico Mendes de Conservação da Biodiversidade (ICMBio) runs a preservation centre for marine manatee.

Some 85 km from João Pessoa is **Baia da Traição**, a fishing village and access point for a number of beaches. Its name means 'Bay of Betrayal' and refers to the massacre of 500 residents of a sugar plantation in the 16th century. There is a reserve near town where wood and string crafts are made by the local indigenous people; an annual festival, **Festa do Toré**, takes place on 19 April. Fisherman offer boat tours to the area's less accessible beaches (US$15 per person). **Barra de Camaratuba**, 17 km north of Baia da Traição, is a popular surfing beach.

The sertão → *For listings, see pages 517-522.*

The semi-arid region of thorn and bush that makes up the hinterland of the northeast is known as the *sertão*. The Transamazônica runs right through the heart of the region, due west of João Pessoa as the BR-230, and along the axis of the state of Paraíba.

Campina Grande → *Colour map 2, B6. Phone code: 083. Population: 340,500.*

Set in the Serra da Borborema, 551 m above sea level and 130 km west of João Pessoa, the second city in Paraíba has a very pleasant climate. Known as the '*porta do sertão*' (door of the sertão), it is an important centre for light industry and an outlet for goods from most of northeast Brazil. In the 1920s it was one of the most important cotton producing areas in the world; a decline in this industry brought a decrease in prosperity in the 1940s and 1950s and the diversification of industry to areas such as sisal and leather. The city's two universities have been instrumental in technological development and reactivation of the local economy and today Campina Grande has the honour of making every single pair of Brazil's famous fashion flip-flops, Havaianas, which are sold all over the world.

Ins and outs The **João Suassuna airport** ① *7 km south of centre on the road to Caruaru, T083-3331 1149*, receives daily flights from Recife. A taxi from the airport to the centre costs US$15. A city bus runs to Praça Clementino Procópio, behind Cine Capitólio. The **rodoviária** ① *Av Argemiro de Figueiredo, T083-3321 5780*, is a 20-minute bus ride from the centre. Tourist information is available from **PBTUR** ① *T156*, or **DEMTUR** ① *T083-3341 3993*.

Sights Avenida Floriano Peixoto is the main street running east–west through the entire city, with Praça da Bandeira at its centre. The **Museu Histórico de Campina Grande** ① *Av Floriano Peixoto 825, Centro, T083-3310 6182, Tue-Sat 0800-1200, 1300-1700*, is the city museum housed in a 19th-century building, with a very well-displayed photo and artefact collection reflecting the cycles of prosperity and poverty in the region. The **Museu da História e Tecnologia do Algodão** ① *R Benjamin Constant s/n, Estação Ferroviária, T083-3341 1039, Tue-Sat 0800-1200 and 1300-1700, free*, has machines and related equipment used in the cotton industry in the 16th and 17th centuries. The **Museu Regional de São João** ① *Largo da Estação Velha, Centro, T083-3341 2000, daily 0800-1300*, houses an interesting collection of objects and photographs pertaining to the June celebrations.

The **Teatro Municipal Severino Cabral** ⓘ *Av Floriano Peixoto*, is a modern theatre where there are regular performances. The main parks in town are: the **Parque do Açude Novo** (Evaldo Cruz), a green area with playgrounds, fountains and restaurants; the nearby **Parque do Povo** with its *forródromo* where the main festivities of the city take place; and the **Açude Velho**, a park around a dam south of the centre. The **Mercado Central**, where a large roof has been built over several blocks of old buildings, has regional crafts and produce, is worth a visit.

Excursions from Campina Grande

About 10 km north from Campina Grande is **Lagoa Seca**, where figures in wood and sacking are made, and there is a **Museu do Índio**.

Some 35 km east of Campina Grande, off the road to João Pessoa, is **Ingá**, site of the **Pedra de Itacoatiara** archaeological centre, where inscriptions dated as 10,000 years old were found on a boulder 25 m long and 3 m high. A small museum at the site contains fossils of a giant sloth and a Tyrannosaurus rex. During the June festivities there is a train service to Itacoatiara.

The **Boqueirão** dam on the Rio Paraíba, 70 km southeast of town, is where locals flock on holidays for watersports; there is a hotel-*fazenda* (T081-3391 1233).

Cariri

The *sertão* proper begins near São João do Cariri an hour or so from Campina Grande. This is an area of fascinating rock formations, with giant weather-worn boulders sitting on top of gently curved expanses of rock that look out over a plain of low bushes and stunted trees. Although the vegetation is quite different to the landscape itself; the arid conditions and the size of the trees recalls the Australian outback (the rocks themselves have been compared to the Devil's Marbles). The most spectacular of all the formations sit in the private grounds of **Fazenda Pai Mateus** (see Sleeping, page 519). Like various other sites in Paraíba and Rio Grande do Norte, boulders here are covered in important pre-Columbian rock art, some of which has been controversially dated as pre-Clovis (making it older than the accepted datings for the first waves of American population coming from over the Bering Strait). A famous local holy man lived inside one of the giant hollowed-out stones and the views from his former home at sunset are particularly spellbinding. The *fazenda* itself is a very pleasant place to stay and there is rich, though depleted wildlife in the area and good birdwatching. Tours can be organized with **Cariri Ecotours** (see Essentials, page 53), who provide fascinating information about the archaeological sites but have little knowledge of the fauna in the region. The *fazenda*'s guides are informative about life in the *sertão* and the use of medicinal plants, but again as ever in Brazil, knowledge of birds and animals is poor.

North of Cariri, 46 km from Campina Grande, is **Areial**, the main town of the Brejo Paraibano, a scenic region of green hills and valleys, with a pleasant climate, where colonial sugar *fazendas* have been transformed into hotels.

Patos → *Colour map 2, B5. Population: 84,500.*

West of Campina Grande the landscape turns to vast, flat expanses, flanked by rolling hills and interesting rock formations; very scenic when green, but a sad sight during the prolonged *sertão* droughts. Situated 174 km from Campina Grande is Patos, the centre of a cattle-ranching and cotton-growing area. It's also an access point for the **Serra do Teixeira**, 28 km away, which includes **Pico do Jabre**, the highest point in the state, at 1130 m above sea level. There are various hotels and restaurants in Patos.

Souza → *Colour map 2, B5. Phone code: 081. Population: 59,000.*

About 130 km northwest of Patos, the pleasant *sertão* town of Souza, has high temperatures year-round and is gaining fame for the nearby dinosaur tracks and prehistoric rock carvings. The *rodoviária* is 1 km from the centre, there are no city buses, walk (hot), take a moto-taxi (US$1) or a taxi (US$5). The **Igreja do Rosário** at the Praça Matriz has paintings dating to the Dutch occupation of the area. It currently functions as a school. About 3 km from the centre, atop a hill, is a **statue of Frei Damião**, an important religious leader of the northeast who died in 1997. Frei Damião was an Italian friar who came to Brazil in the 1930s and stayed to become an inspiration for the faith of its most recent generation of dispossessed. He is seen as belonging to the same tradition as O Conselheiro and Padre Cícero.

Fossilized dinosaur prints of up to 90 different species, which inhabited the area between 110 and 80 million years ago, are found in a number of sites in the Souza region. These were extensively studied by the Italian palaeontologist Giussepe Leonardi in the 1970s and 1980s. The **Vale dos Dinossauros**, on the sedimentary river bed of the Rio do Peixe, is one of the closest sites to Souza; it has some impressive Iguanodontus prints. Access is 4 km from town along the road north to Uiraúna; the best time to visit is the dry season, July to October. The area has no infrastructure and is best visited with a guide. Try to contact Robson Marques of the **Movisaurio Association** ① *R João Rocha 7, Souza, PB 58800-610, T083-3522 1065*, who is very knowledgeable; otherwise contact the Prefeitura Municipal. Tours can be organized through **Cariri Ecotours** in Natal (see Essentials, page 53), these can be combined with visits to Cariri.

⊚ Paraíba listings

For Sleeping and Eating price codes and other relevant information, see pages 32-37.

⊜ Sleeping

João Pessoa *p510, maps p511 and p512*
The town's main attractions are its beaches, where most tourists stay. Hotels in the centre are poorer and tend to cater for business clients. The centre is very quiet after dark and it is difficult to find a restaurant. Cheaper hotels can be found near the *rodoviária*; look carefully as some are sleazy. The most convenient beach and the focus of nightlife and restaurants is **Tambaú**. There are good restaurants and a few hotels in **Manaíra**, north of Tambaú. There are also a few in the southern beach suburb of **Cabo Branco**, but this is quieter and has fewer eating options.
B-C Hotel JR, R João Ramalho de Andrade, T083-2106 8700, www.hoteljr.com.br. 1990s business hotel with basic facilities

and a restaurant. The largest and most comfortable in the centre.
C-D Guarany, R Almeida Barreto 181 and 13 de Maio, T/F083-2106 8787, www.hotel guarani.com.br. Cheaper in low season, or without a/c and TV. A pleasant, safe, extremely good-value establishment with a self-service restaurant.
D Ouro Preto, R Idaleto 162, T083-3222 7074, Varadouro near *rodoviária*. Very simple rooms with baths and a fan.

Urban beaches *p512, map p514*
Accommodation can also be found in the outer beaches such as **Camboinha** and Seixas, and in **Cabedelo**.
AL Best Western Caiçara, Av Olinda 235, T/F083-3247 2040, www.hotcaicarara.com.br. A slick, business-orientated red and white apartment block with business facilities, a pleasant restaurant and a rooftop pool with a view.

AL Littoral, Av Cabo Branco 2172, T083-2106 1100, www.hotellittoral.com.br. An unprepossessing block in a great seafront location. With a pleasant swimming pool set in leafy gardens and modern, simply appointed rooms with small balconies. There are often discounts for online advanced bookings.

AL Tropical Tambaú, Av Alm Tamandaré 229, T083-2107 1900, www.tropicalhotel.com.br. An enormous round building on the seafront which looks like a rocket-launching station and has comfortable motel-style rooms around its perimeter. Good service. Recommended.

AL Xênius, Av Cabo Branco 1262, T083-3015 3519, www.xeniushotel.com.br. Popular standard 4-star hotel with a pool, good restaurant. Well-kept but standard a/c rooms, low-season reductions.

A-B Nobile Inn Royal Praia, Coração de Jesus, T083-2106 3000, www.royalhotel.com.br. Comfortable a/c rooms with fridges, pool.

A-B Victory Business Flat, Av Tamandaré 310, T083-3041 3011, www.victoryflat.com.br. Furnished apartments with a pool and sauna. Cheaper in low season.

B Pouso das Águas, Av Cabo Branco 2348, Cabo Branco, T083-3226 5103. A homely atmosphere with landscaped areas and a pool.

B Tambía Praia, R Carlos Alverga 36, T083-3247 4101, www.tambiahotel.hpg.com.br. Centrally located and 1 block from the beach. Intimate, with balconies and sea view. Recommended.

B Villa Mare Apartment Hotel, Av Négo 707, T083-3226 2142. Comfortable apartments for 2 or 3 people with full amenities per night or from US$400-500 per month. Helpful staff. Recommended.

C-D Solar Filipéia, Av Incognito Coração de Jesus 153, T083-3219 3744, www.solarfilipeia.com.br. A recently opened, smart hotel with large, bright rooms with bathrooms in tile and black marble and excellent service. Good value.

E Pousada Mar Azul, Av João Maurício 315, T083-3226 2660. Very clean large rooms, the best are on the upper level, on the oceanfront road. Some have a/c and private bath, others have fans. Well kept, safe and a real bargain.

E-F Hostel Manaíra, R Major Ciraulo 380, Manaíra, T083-3247 1962, www.manaira hostel.br2.net. Friendly new hostel close to the beach, with a pool, internet, barbecue, cable TV and breakfast. A real bargain.

Camping

Camping Clube do Brasil, Praia de Seixas, 13 km from the centre, T083-3247 2181.

Tambaba *p514*

B Chalé Suiço, R Chalé Suiço 120, Tabatinga, T083-3981 2046. Small, shared bath, restaurant, upstairs rooms have ocean-view balconies.

B Pousada Corais de Carapibus, Av Beira Mar, Carapebus, T083-3290 1179, www.coraisdecarapibus.com.br. A few kilometres south of Jacumã. With bath, pool, restaurant and a nice breeze since it is located on a cliff across from the ocean.

C Jacuma's Lodge, PB008, T083-3290 1977, www.jacuma.tur.br. Very simple tiled a/c rooms decorated with lacey rugs, curtains and counterpanes sitting in a small hotel right on the beach. There's a pleasant shady pool area with tables, sun loungers and a paddling pool for children.

Campina Grande *p515*

Many hotels around Praça da Bandeira.

AL-A Garden, R Engenheiro José Bezerra 400, Mirante Km 5, T083-3310 4000, www.gardenhotelcampina.com. The vast hotel complex is Campina Grande's best hotel, sitting on a hill 5 km (3 miles) from the centre, with views out over the city. There are 5 swimming pools, a well-equipped gym, squash courts and aerobics classes. Rooms are vast and spartan, with verandas and all come with broadband internet.

B Mahatma Gandhi, Floriano Peixoto 338, T/F083-3321 5275. With bath, a/c, fridge.

B Souto Maior, Floriano Peixoto 289, T083-3321 8043. Rooms include bath a/c and fridge.

B-C Village, R Octacílio Nepomuceno 1285, Catole, Rodoviária Nova 4km, T083-3310 8000, www.hoteisvillage.com.br. This large business hotel is in a good location near the shopping centre mall and is equipped with tennis courts swimming pools, hot tubs and a spa.

C Regente, Barão do Abiaí 80, T083-3321 3843. With bath, a/c or fan, fridge.

C-D Pérola, Floriano Peixoto 258, T083-3341 5319. With bath and a/c, cheaper with fan, parking and a very good breakfast.

D Avenida, Floriano Peixoto 378, T083-3341 1249. With fan, good value, cheaper with shared bath.

D Verona, 13 de Maio 232, T083-3341 1926. With bath, fan, good value, friendly service.

D-E Eliu's, Maciel Pinheiro 31B, 1st floor, T083-3321 4115. Clean, friendly, a/c and bath (cheaper with fan/without bath), good value.

E Aurora, 7 de Setembro 120, T083-3321 4874. Shared bath, very basic and run down.

Cariri *p516*

A visit to **Fazenda Pai Mateus**, www.pai mateus.com.br, can be organized through Cariri Ecotours, see Essentials, page 53.

B Gadelha Palace, Trav Luciana Rocha 2, Cariri, T081-3521 1416. With bath, a/c, fridge, pool and restaurant.

C Dormitório Sertanejo I, R Col Zé Vicente, Cariri. Rooms nice and clean with bath and fan. No breakfast, but good value. Recommended.

E Dormitório Aguiar, R João Gualberto, Cariri. Very basic.

🍴 Eating

João Pessoa *p510, maps p511 and p512*
There are few eating options in the city centre. Locals eat at the stalls in **Parque Solon de Lucena** next to the lake, where there are a couple of simple restaurants.

Urban beaches *p512, map p514*
Every evening on the beachfront, stalls sell all kinds of snacks and barbecued meats. At **Cabo Branco** there are many straw huts on the beach serving cheap eats and seafood.

♦♦♦ **Adega do Alfredo**, Coração de Jesus. Very popular traditional Portuguese restaurant in the heart of the club and bar area.

♦♦♦ **Gulliver**, Av Olinda 590, Tambaú. Trendy French/Brazilian restaurant frequented by João Pessoa's middle classes.

♦♦ **Cheiro Verde**, R Carlos Alverga 43. Self-service, well established, regional food.

♦♦ **Mangaí**, Av General Édson Ramalho 696, Manaíra, T083-3226 1615. This is one of the best restaurants in the northeast to sample the region's cooking. There are almost 100 different hot dishes to chose from, sitting in copper tureens over a traditional wood-fired stove some 20 m long. The open-sided dining area is very welcoming and spacious. Very good Italian too with a charming atmosphere.

♦♦ **Sapore d'Italia**, Av Cabo Branco 1584, Standard Italian fare including pizza.

Campina Grande *p515*
Rua 13 de Maio by Rui Barbosa in the centre has several good restaurants. There are many bars near **Parque do Povo**, busy at weekends.

♦♦ **A Cabana do Possidônio**, 13 de Maio 207 T083-3341 3384. A varied menu of regional and international dishes.

♦♦ **La Nostra Casa**, R 13 de Maio 175, T083-3322 5196. Modest but friendly pasta and pizza restaurant.

♦ **Carne & Massa**, R 13 de Maio 214, T083-3322 8677. Regional cooking including *carne de sol*, pasta and a range of desserts.

♦ **La Suissa**, Dep João Tavares 663. Good savoury and sweet snacks.

♦ **Lanchonette Casa das Frutas**, Marquês de Herval 54. Good-value meals, fruit juices and snacks.

♦ **Manoel da Carne de Sol**, Félix de Araújo 263. T083-3321 2877. One of the city's best-value regional restaurants including an excellent *carne de sol* lunch with runner beans, *farofa* manioc flour and vegetables.

The world's greatest barn dance – the Festas Juninas

Carnaval is essentially an urban, black Brazilian celebration. The Festas Juninas, which take place throughout Brazil during June, are a rural celebration. While carnival pounds to samba, the Juninhas pulsate to the triangle and accordion of *forró*. Rather than wearing feathers and sequins, Juninas revellers dress up as *caipiras* (yokels) in tartan shirts and reed hats; and they eat *canjica* (maize porridge) and drink *quentão* (a Brazilian version of mulled wine). And they do it in enormous numbers. During the most important weekend of the festivals – the eve of St John's Day on 23 June – over one million mock-*caipiras* descend on the little backland towns of Campina Grande in Paraíba and Caruaru in Pernambuco. Both towns are entirely taken over by *forró* bands, cowboys, stalls selling *doce de leite* and other country produce, and the percussion of fireworks and bangers. Foreign visitors are still a rare curiosity.

† **Vila Antiga**, R 13 de Maio 164, T083-3341 4718. A popular pay by weight restaurant with a broad range of regional dishes, pastas, salads and desserts.

Souza *p517*
Several restaurants are on R Col Zé Vicente.
† **Diagonal**, Getúlio Vargas 2. Ordinary but reasonable pizzeria.

🎵 Bars and clubs

João Pessoa *p510, maps p511, p512 and p514*
There are many open bars on and across from the beach in Tambaú and Cabo Branco; the area known as **Feirinha de Tambaú**, on Av Tamandaré by the Tambaú Hotel and nearby streets, sees much movement even on weekend nights, with R Coração do Jesus being the epicentre. There are numerous little bars and *forró* places here and this is the place for a night-time browse. Other beachfront neighbourhoods also have popular bars.
Fashion Club, Mega Shopping, Manaíra. The most popular nightclub in the city, with a 20-something crowd and mostly techno and MPB. Large beachfront *baracca* restaurant with live music at weekends.

Incognito, R Coração do Jesus. A very popular and lively bar and dance club. There are many others here including KS.
Mr Caipira, Av João Maurício 1533, Manaíra, T083-246 7597. Live acoustic music, Brazilian barbecued food, *feijoada* and a smart 30-something crowd. On the seafront road.
Zodiaco, Incognito Coração do Jesus 144. One of several nightclubs in the area attracting a lively young crowd especially at the weekends.

🎊 Festivals and events

João Pessoa *p510, maps p511, p512 and p514*
Feb Pre-carnival celebrations in João Pessoa are renowned: the *bloco* **Acorde Miramar** opens the celebrations the Tue before Carnaval. On Wed, known as **Quarta Feira de Fogo**, thousands join the **Muriçocas de Miramar**, forming a *bloco* second only to Recife's **Galo da Madrugada** with as many as 300,000 people taking part.
5 Aug The street celebrations for the patroness of the city, **Nossa Senhora das Neves**, last for 10 days to the rhythm of *frevo*.

Campina Grande *p515*

Apr **Micarande**, the out-of-season Salvador-style carnival.

Jun-Jul Campina Grande boasts the largest São João celebrations in Brazil; from the beginning of Jun into the 1st week of Jul the city attracts many visitors; there are bonfires and *quadrilhas* (square dance groups) in every neighbourhood; *forró* and invited artists at the Parque do Povo; *quentão*, *pomonha* and *canjica* are consumed everywhere.

Aug The annual **Congresso de Violeiros**, which gathers singers and guitarists from all across the northeast.

O Shopping

João Pessoa *p510, maps p511, p512 and p514*

Cheaper arts and crafts can be bought at **Mercado de Artesanato**, Centro de Turismo, Almte Tamandaré 100, Tambaú, daily 0800-1800; **Mercados de Artesanato Paraibano**, Av Rui Carneiro, Tambaú, daily 0900-1700; **Bosque dos Sonhos**, by the Cabo Branco lighthouse. Weekends only. **Terra do Sol**, R Coração do Jesus 145, T083-3226 1940, www.terradosol.art.br. The best place to buy regional crafts, including lace, embroidery and ceramics. Very elegant, high-quality bedspreads, bath robes, hammocks and tablecloths made from natural cotton. Also sells work by Paraíba artists and artisans.

▲ Activities and tours

João Pessoa *p510, maps p511, p512 and p514*

Cliotur, Av Alm Tamandaré 310, Sala 2, T083-3247 4460. Trips to the *sertão*. Also offers light adventure activities.

Roger Turismo, Av Tamandaré 229, T083-3247 1856. Half-day city tours (US$6), day trips to Tambaba (US$8) and Recife/Oldina (US$12). A large agency with some English-speaking guides and a range of other tours.

Excursions from João Pessoa *p513*

Flaviano Gouveia, Jacaré, T083-3982 1604. Ultralight aircraft rides, US$19 for 8-min ride or US$115 for 1 hr.

Sea Tech, PO Box 42, João Pessoa, 56001-970, T083-3245 1476. Run by Brian Ingram, originally from England. Boatyard and frequent port of call for international yachtspeople plying the Brazilian coast.

⊖ Transport

João Pessoa *p510, maps p511, p512 and p514*

Air A taxi to the airport costs US$8 from the centre or US$12 from Tambaú. Flights to **São Paulo**, **Brasília**, **Recife** and **Rio de Janeiro**. Gol flies to **São Paulo** or **Rio** from Recife, and provides free bus transport from João Pessoa.

Airline offices Avianca, www.Avianca.com.br. GOL, www.voegol.com.br, and at the airport. TAM, T083-3247 2400, Av Senador Rui Carneiro 512, T083-3247 2400.

Bus From the *rodoviária* or Lagoa (Parque Solon de Lucena), take bus No 510 for **Tambaú**, No 507 for **Cabo Branco**.

Buses to **Recife** with Boa Vista or Bonfim, every 30 mins, US$2.50, 2 hrs. To **Natal** with Nordeste, every 2 hrs, US$8 *convencional*, US$7.50 *executivo*, 3 hrs. To **Fortaleza** with Nordeste, 2 daily, 10 hrs, US$18. To **Campina Grande** with Real, every 30 mins, US$4, 2 hrs. To **Juazeiro do Norte** with Transparaíba, 2 daily, US$14, 10 hrs. To **Salvador** with Progresso, 4 weekly, US$30, 14 hrs. To **Brasília** via Campina Grande, with Planalto, 2 weekly, US$57, 48 hrs. To **Rio de Janeiro** with São Geraldo, daily, US$67 *convencional*, US$80 *executivo*, 42 hrs. To **São Paulo** with Itapemirim, daily, US$73 *convencional*, US$76 *executivo*, 47 hrs. To **Belém** with Guanabara, daily, US$46, 36 hrs.

Car hire Avis, Av Nossa Senhora dos Navegantes, 402, T083-3247 3050. Localiza, Av Epitácio Pessoa 4910, T083-3247 4030, and at the airport, T0800-992000. **Tempo**, Almte Tamandaré 100, at the Centro de Turismo, T083-3247 0002.

Train Regional services west to **Bayeux** and **Santa Rita**, and **Cabedelo** in the north.

Tambaba *p514*
Bus From Tambaba a dirt road leads 12 km north to the beach of **Jacumã**, from where the PB-018 goes 11 km west to **Conde** and continues 3 km to the BR-101, which runs 20 km north to **João Pessoa**. There are hourly buses from Jacumã to **João Pessoa** 0530-1900.

Campina Grande *p515*
Air Daily flights to **Recife** with Nordeste. Taxi to airport US$7. City bus Distrito Industrial from Praça Clementino Procópio, behind Cine Capitólio.

Bus To **João Pessoa**, with Real, every 30 mins, US$3, 2 hrs. To **Souza** with Transparaíba, 6 daily, US$7, 6 hrs. To **Juazeiro do Norte** with Transparaíba, 2 daily, US$10, 9 hrs. To **Natal** with Nordeste, 0800 daily, US$6, 18 hrs. To **Rio** with Itapemirim, 1600 daily, US$65, 42 hrs. To **Brasília** with Planalto, 2 weekly, US$55, 46 hrs.

Car hire On R Tavares Cavalcante are **Intermezzo**, No 27, T083-321 4790; **Kelly's**, No 301, T/F083-3322 4539. Also **Localiza**, R Dr Severino Cruz 625, T083-3341 4034, and at the airport, T083-3331 4594.

Souza *p517*
Bus To **Campina Grande** with Transparaíba, 6 daily, US$7, 6 hrs. To **João Pessoa** with Transparaíba, 6 daily, US$10, 8 hrs. To **Juazeiro do Norte** with Transparaíba or Boa Esperança,

4 daily, US$4, 3½ hrs. To **Mossoró**, RN, with **Jardinense**, 4 daily, US$6, 4½ hrs.

❻ Directory

João Pessoa *p510, maps p511, p512 and p514*
Banks Banco 24 horas, Av Almirante Tamandaré 100, Tambaú, ATM for Cirrus, Visa and MasterCard. Banco do Brasil, Praça 1817, 3rd floor, Centro, Isidro Gomes 14, Tambaú, behind Centro de Turismo. HSBC, R Peregrino de Carvalho, 162, Centre, ATM for cirrus and visa. Mondeo Tour, Av Négo 46, Tambaú, T083-3226 3100. 0900- 1730, cash and Tcs. PB Câmbio Turismo, Visconde de Pelotas 54C, Centro, Mon-Fri 1030-1630, cash and TCs. **Internet** Cyberpointy Café, Av Almirante Tamandaré, 100, in Centro Turístico Tambaú, daily 0800-2100, US1.60 per hr. **Post office** Main office is at Praça Pedro Américo, Varadouro; central office is at Parque Solon de Lucena 375; also by the beach at Av Rui Carneiro, behind the Centro de Turismo. **Telephone** Calling stations at: Visconde de Pelotas and Miguel Couto, Centro; Centro de Turismo, Tambaú; Av Epitácio Pessoa 1487, Bairro dos Estados; *rodoviária* and airport.

Campina Grande *p515*
Banks Banco do Brasil, 7 de Setembro 52, cash and TCs at poor rates. Mondeo Tour, R Índios Cariris 308, cash at good rates and TCs, Mon-Fri 1000-1600. **Post office** R Marquês do Herval, Praça da Bandeira. **Telephone** Floriano Peixoto 410 by Praça da Bandeira in the industrial district and at the *rodoviária*.

Contents

Footprint features

Fortaleza & the far northeast

At a glance

○ **Getting around** Bus and internal flights. Car hire is not recommended as roads can be poor and badly signposted, especially in the interior.

◎ **Time required** 1 day for Fortaleza; 2-3 days for São Luís and Alcântara; 2-3 days for the Lençóis Maranhenses; 10 days for the whole region.

☼ **Weather** Hot and wet Jan-Jun, hot and dry Jul-Dec.

✕ **When not to go** Mar and Apr have the most rain and least sunshine.

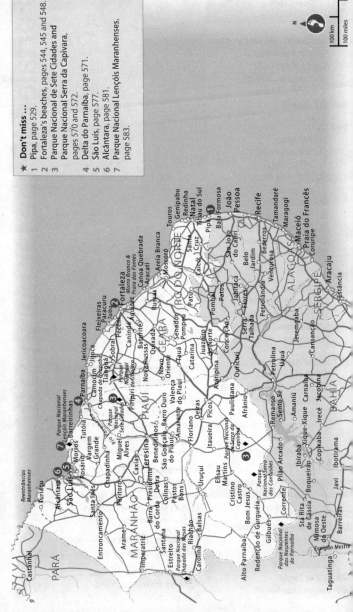

★ Don't miss ...

1 Pipa, page 529.
2 Fortaleza's beaches, pages 544, 545 and 548.
3 Parque Nacional de Sete Cidades and Parque Nacional Serra da Capivara, pages 570 and 572.
4 Delta do Parnaíba, page 571.
5 São Luís, page 577.
6 Alcântara, page 581.
7 Parque Nacional Lençóis Maranhenses, page 583.

Bahia may have the prettiest stretches of coastline in Brazil but the northeast has some of the most dramatic. In Rio Grande do Norte, broken, striated cliffs and imposing dunes tower above the wild and deserted beaches of Natal, Genipabu, Pipa and Areia Branca. In neighbouring Ceará the coast becomes touristy again, especially around the state capital, Fortaleza, a sunny, planned city whose charm is somewhat sullied by a plethora of cheap package tours. Just to the north is the Western hemisphere's kitesurfing capital, Cumbuco, where the only Brazilians you'll see are working in the hotels and restaurants.

Beyond the state border at Jericoacoara, the cliffs and dunes give way to the wilderness of the Delta do Parnaíba, the largest delta in the Western hemisphere. The wetlands of the Rio Parnaíba spread like an outstretched palm to divide the land into myriad islands and a maze of narrow channels, which hide some of Brazil's least visited and least spoilt beaches. Most visitors head for Maranhão state and the coastal desert of the Lençóis Maranhenses: a huge sea of coastal dunes, pocked with freshwater lakes and fringed by deserted beaches and forgotten wind-blown fishing villages. Further north, and almost inaccessible, the swamps and inlets of the Reentrâncias Maranhenses preserve the largest bank of coral in Atlantic South America, the Parque Estadual Marinho do Parcel Manoel Luís, which is just beginning to open up to diving.

Maranhão's capital, São Luís, is famous for its Bumba-Meu-Boi festival in June and its historic centre, whose colonial buildings are covered in blue and white Portuguese *azulejos* and filled with decaying baroque churches. The city is one of two World Heritage Sites in the region, the other being the Parque Nacional da Serra da Capivara, whose bizarre honeycomb domes tower over canyons covered in what may be the oldest rock painting in the Americas.

Rio Grande do Norte

This state is famous for its beaches and dunes, especially around Natal. The coastline begins to change here, becoming gradually drier and less green, as it shifts from running north–south to east–west. The vast sugar cane plantations and few remaining stands of Mata Atlântica (coastal forest) are replaced by the dry caatinga vegetation and caju orchards. The people are known as 'Potiguares', after an indigenous tribe that once resided in the state.» *For listings, see pages 532-539.*

Natal and around → *For listings, see pages 532-539. Colour map 2, B6. Phone code: 084. Population: 713,000.*

The state capital, located on a peninsula between the Rio Potengi and the Atlantic Ocean, is pleasant enough but has few sights of interest. Most visitors head for the beaches to the north and south. During the Second World War, the city was, somewhat bizarrely, the second largest US base outside the United States and housed 8000 American pilots.

Ins and outs

Getting there Flights arrive at **Augusto Severo International Airport** ① *Parnamirim, 18 km south of centre, 10 km from Ponta Negra, T084-3644 1070*, from Belém, Brasília, Fernando de Noronha, Fortaleza, Recife, Rio de Janeiro, Salvador and São Paulo. A taxi to the centre costs US$25; US$20 to Ponta Negra. Buses run every 30 minutes to the old *rodoviária* near the centre, US$1 from where there are connections to Ponta Negra on route 54 or 56 amongst others, or take the 'Aeroporto' bus to the city centre and then bus Nos 54 or 46 south to Ponta Negra.

Interstate buses arrive at the new **Rodoviária Cidade do Sol** ① *Av Capitão Mor Gouveia 1237, Cidade da Esperança, 6 km southwest of the centre, T084-3205 4377*. A taxi to Ponta Negra costs around US$18; to the Via Costeira around US$25. Alternatively, take bus No 66 to Ponta Negra. This passes close to the hotel strip whilst not taking Avenida Erivan Franca (the street that runs along the seafront). For Praia do Meio beach and the Via Costeira take bus No 40 and alight at Praia do Meio for an easy walk to any of the hotels on that beach or Praia dos Artistas. Or take any of the Via Costeira buses.

Buses from the south pass Ponta Negra first, where you can ask to alight. The city buses 'Cidade de Esperança Avenida 9', 'Areia Preta via Petrópolis' or 'Via Tirol' run from the new *rodoviária* to the centre. It is also possible to travel between Natal and Fortaleza by beach buggy: an exciting trip but not a very environmentally responsible one as buggies have seriously eroded the coast. » *See Transport, page 538.*

Getting around Unlike most Brazilian buses, in Natal you get on the bus at the front and get off at the back. The **Old Rodoviária** ① *Av Junqueira Aires, by Praça Augusto Severo, Ribeira*, is a central point where many bus lines converge. Buses to some of the nearby beaches also leave from here. Taxis are expensive compared to other cities (eg four times the price of Recife); typical 10-minute journey costs US$15. Buses are the best option. Route 54 and 46 connect Ponta Negra with the city, the former via Via Costeira and the old *rodoviária*.

Tourist information The state tourist office, **SETUR** ① *Centro de Turismo R Aderbal d Figueiredo 980, Petrópolis, T084-3211 5013 www.setur.rn.gov.brwww.rosaleao.com.br clientes/setur*, covers the whole of Rio Grande do Norte state, although their informatio

Natal

Natal orientation

Sleeping
Bruma 4
Casa Grande 1
Imirá Plaza 2
Maine 3
Porto Mirim 5

Eating
A Macrobiótica 1
Raro Sabor 2

N
Not to scale

and English is very limited, and the office is not conveniently located. However, there are **tourist information booths** at the airport, the bus station, on Avenida Presidente Café Filho on Praia das Artistas beach and Erivan Franca on Ponta Negra, all open daily 0800-2100. See www.natal trip.com, www.natal.com.br and www.rn. gov.br for more information.

Sights

No-one comes to Natal for sightseeing, but the city is not without culture. The oldest part is the **Ribeira** along the riverfront, where a programme of renovation has been started. This can be seen on Rua Chile and in public buildings restored in vivid art deco fashion, such as the **Teatro Alberto Maranhão** ① *Praça Agusto Severo, T/F084-3222 9935*, built 1898-1904, and the **Prefeitura** ① *R Quintino Bocaiuva, Cidade Alta*. The **Cidade Alta**, or Centro, is the main commercial centre and Avenida Rio Branco its principal artery. The main square is made up by the adjoining *praças*, **João Maria, André de Albuquerque, João Tibúrcio** and **7 de Setembro**. At Praça André de Albuquerque is the old **cathedral** (inaugurated 1599, restored 1996). The modern cathedral is on Avenida Deodoro. The church of **Santo Antônio** ① *R Santo Antônio 683, Cidade Alta, Tue-Fri 0800-1700, Sat 0800-1400*, dates from 1766, and has a fine, carved wooden altar and a sacred art museum.

The **Museu Câmara Cascudo** ① *Av Hermes de Fonseca 1440, Tirol, T084-3212 2795, www.mcc.ufrn.br, Tue-Fri 0800-1130, 1400-1730, Sat, Sun 1300-1700, US$2.50*, has exhibits on *umbanda* rituals, archaeological digs, the sugar, leather and petroleum industries; there is also a dead whale.

The 16th-century **Forte dos Reis Magos** ① *T084-3202 9006, daily 0800-1630, US$1.50*, is at Praia do Forte, the tip of Natal's peninsula. Between the fort and the city is a military installation. Walk along the beach to the fort for good views (or go on a tour, or by taxi).

At Mãe Luiza is a **lighthouse** with beautiful views of Natal and surrounding beaches (take a city bus marked 'Mãe Luiza' and get the key from the house next door).

South to Ponta Negra

The urban beaches of **Praia do Meio**, **Praia dos Artistas** and **Praia de Areia Preta** have recently been cleaned up. The first two are sheltered by reefs and good for windsurfing. The beachside promenade, **Via Costeira**, runs south beneath the towering sand dunes of **Parque das Dunas** (access restricted to protect the dunes), joining the city to the neighbourhood of Ponta Negra. A cycle path parallels this road and provides great views of the coastline.

The vibrant and pretty **Ponta Negra**, 12 km south of the centre (20 minutes by bus), is justifiably the most popular beach and has many hotels. The northern end is good for surfing, while the southern end is calmer and suitable for swimming. **Morro do Careca**, a 120-m-high sand dune, surrounded by vegetation, sits at its far end. It is crowded on weekends and holidays. The poorly lit northern reaches can be unsafe after dark.

Excursions from Natal

The beautiful beaches around Natal – some of which are developed, others are deserted and accessible only by trails – are good all year round for day trips or longer stays. Those north of the city are known as the **Litoral Norte**, where there are extensive cashew plantations; those to the south form the **Litoral Sul**. The areas closest to the city are built-up and get busy during the summer holidays (December to Carnaval), when dune-buggy traffic can become excessive.

Popular tours from Natal include boat trips on the **Rio Potengi**, along the nearby beaches of the Litoral Sul, and to **Barra do Cunhaú**, 86 km south of Natal. The latter goes through mangroves and visits an island and a salt mine, **Passeio Ecológico Cunhaú** ① *T084-9934 0017, www.barradocunhau.com.br*. Other popular pastimes include buggy tours, marlin fishing (11 km from shore, said by some to be the best in Brazil) and microlight flights over the Rio Potengi and sand dunes north of Natal.» *See Activities and tours, page 537.*

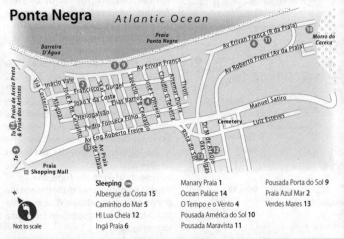

Ponta Negra

Atlantic Ocean

Praia Ponta Negra
Morro do Careca
Barreira D'Água
Av Erivan França (R da Praia)
Av Roberto Freire (Av da Praia)
To Praia de Areia Preta & Praia dos Artistas
Via Costeira
Inácio Vale
Alagoas
José R de Carvalho
Francisco Gurgel
João V da Costa
Heliogalvão
Pedro Fonseca Filho
Av Eng Roberto Freire
Lisádio José
Elias Barros
Cláudio G Teixeira
José T Oliveira
Atemar Dutra
Tivoli
B Cearalho
Av Erivan França
Dr M de Araújo
Rota do Sol
das Algas
Av Praia de Tibaú
Manuel Satiro
Cemetery
Luiz Esteves
Praia
Shopping Mall
Not to scale

Sleeping
Albergue da Costa 15
Caminho do Mar 5
HI Lua Cheia 12
Ingá Praia 6
Manary Praia 1
Ocean Paláce 14
O Tempo e o Vento 4
Pousada América do Sol 10
Pousada Maravista 11
Pousada Porta do Sol 9
Praia Azul Mar 2
Verdes Mares 13

The **Centro de Lançamento da Barreira do Inferno** ① *11 km south of Natal on the road to Pirangi, T084-3216 1400, www.clbi.cta.br, visits by appointment on Wed from 1400,* is the launching centre for Brazil's space programme.

Southern coast → *For listings, see pages 532-539.*

South of Natal, the Rota do Sol/Litoral Sul (RN-063) follows the coastline for some 55 km and provides access to beaches south of Ponta Negra. From here the coast becomes more remote and long curves of white sand backed by multicoloured sandstone cliffs and sweeping dunes, fragments of Atlantic forest alive with rare birds, black tea lagoons and bays filled with dolphins, make this one of the most popular stretches in the northeast. Thankfully development is small scale and it still feels relaxed (outside high season). Several species of turtles, including giant leatherbacks, still nest here, although numbers are declining as the popularity of beach buggy tourism grows. The best place to stay along this stretch of coast is **Pipa**, a lively little town with good *pousadas* and restaurants.

Ins and outs

Buses run along Litoral Sul from both Natal's bus stations, every 30 minutes in summer, stopping at **Pirangi** (US$4, one hour), and **Tabatinga** (US$5, 1¼ hours); there are six daily buses to **Tibau** and **Pipa** (two to three hours).

From João Pessoa in Paraíba you will have to change at Goaianinha on the main road to Natal. This route is also run by *combis*, which leave when full up and cost about 20% more than the buses. *Combis* connect Pipa and Tibau until around 2300.

Rota do Sol

Praia do Cotovelo, 21 km from Natal, offers a view of the Barreira do Inferno rocket-launching centre to the north. At its southern end it has some cliffs and coconut palms where camping is possible.

Pirangi do Norte, 25 km from Natal (30 minutes by bus) has calm waters and is popular for watersports and offshore bathing (500 m out) when natural pools form between the reefs. Nearby is the world's largest *cajueiro* (cashew tree); branches springing from a single trunk cover 7300 sq m. The snack bar by the tree has schedules of buses back to Natal. Lacemakers offer bargains for clothing and tableware. Pirangi has a lively **Carnaval**.

Búzios, 35 km from Natal, has a pleasant setting with vegetation-covered dunes and coconut palms. The water is mostly calm and clear, making it good for bathing.

Barra de Tabatinga, 45 km from Natal, is surrounded by cliffs used for parasailing. Waves are strong here, making it a popular surfing beach. A new 'shark park' complete with resident biologist is its latest attraction.

Camurupim and **Barreta**, 46 km and 55 km from Natal respectively, have reefs near the shore, where bathing pools form at low tide; this area has many restaurants specializing in shrimp. Beyond Barreta is the long, pristine beach of **Malenbar** or **Guaraíra**, accessible on foot or on a 10-minute boat ride across the Rio Tibau. Buggy tours from Natal cost US$100.

Tibau do Sul and Pipa → *Colour map 2, B6. Population 6124.*

The little fishing town of **Tibau do Sul** has cobbled streets and sits high on a cliff between surf beaches and the manatee-filled Lago de Guaraíra. Boat trips can be arranged from here to the *lago* or to see dolphins in the calm waters offshore. Although most tourists head straight for Pipa, which is more developed, the beach *barracas* in Tibau are lively at

Lampião – Brazil's bloodthirsty Robin Hood

Cangaceiros: were they subversives, common criminals or heroes? The debate rages on about the armed band led by Virgulino Ferreira da Silva, better known as Lampião. He is regarded by some as a Robin Hood of the northeast, stealing from the *coroneis* (wealthy landowners) and urban gentry, to give to the ubiquitous poor of the *sertão*. Others look on Lampião and his followers as nothing more than common criminals; looting, raping and killing as they terrorized towns in the northeast during the 1920s and 1930s. This was the *Cangaço*, the reign of banditry, which inspired so much fear and fascination throughout Brazil and attracted worldwide attention.

The controversial religious leaders of the *sertão* were also involved. Lampião claimed the spiritual protection of Padre Cícero, and the legacy of the Cangaço retains an unusual religious dimension. For example, the tomb of Jararaca (one of Lampião's lieutenants who was captured during the band's unsuccessful 1927 siege of Mossoró and supposedly buried alive), is attributed miraculous powers and has become a site of pilgrimage. Yet Jararaca is reputed to have been a ruthless killer.

Several early cinematographers from the US, Germany and France tried to film Lampião and his band, but only Lebanese-born Benjamin Abrahão was sufficiently taken into his confidence to do so. Abrahão spent almost seven months recording the day-to-day life of the *cangaceiros*. His footage was considered so subversive that he was subsequently murdered under mysterious circumstances and his film confiscated by the government of Getúlio Vargas. It languished in an official vault for 20 years, much of it destroyed by time and the elements.

Today the Sociedade Brasileira de Estudos do Cangaço is one of the organizations which collects data, anecdotes and artefacts from this important episode in the region's and the nation's history. It also carries on the unresolved debate as to whether the *cangaceiros* were really heroes or villains.

---

night with *forró* and MPB. Natal's finest restaurants are also here (see Eating, page 535 and there are a handful of decent *pousadas* in town.

From Tibau, a series of white-sand crescents, separated by rocky headlands and backed by high cliffs crowned with coconut groves and remnant coastal forest, stretche south to **Pipa**. This is one of Natal's most enchanting little tourist towns, whose mix o local fishermen and settlers from all over Brazil has formed an eclectic alternative community. There are excellent *pousadas* and restaurants in all price ranges and the nightlife is animated. The town is becoming increasingly popular and the number o people can feel overwhelming during Carnaval and New Year.

The town beach is somewhat developed, but there are plenty of others nearby. **Praia dos Golfinhos** to the south and **Madeiro** beyond it have only a few hotels and **Praia de Amor** to the north is surrounded by cliffs and has reasonable surf. Access to the shore i down the steps built by the few clifftop hotels or by walking along the beach from Pipa a low tide. There are tours to see dolphins from US$10 per person and also around th mangrove-lined **Lagoa Guaraíra** at Tibau, particularly beautiful at sunset.

Just north of town, on a 70-m-high dune, is the **Santuário Ecológico de Pipa** ① *T084 3211 6070, www.pipa.com.br/santuarioecologico, 0800-1600, US$3*, a 60-ha park create in 1986 to conserve the *Mata Atlântica* forest. There are several trails and lookouts ove the cliffs, which afford an excellent view of the ocean and dolphins. Although large animals like cats and howler monkeys are long gone, this is one of the few areas in the state where important indicator bird species, such as guans, can be found.

Genipabu and the northern coast → *For listings, see pages 532-539.*

The coast north of Natal is known for its many impressive, light-coloured sand dunes, some reaching a staggering 50 m in height. **Genipabu**, a weekend resort for the Natal middle classes, is the most famous of these and is only a very short bus ride from the city. The country beyond the resort is well off the tourist trail, with vast long beaches backed by multicoloured cliffs, dunes and salt lakes. It is dramatic terrain, so much so that it has been used as the backdrop to numerous biblical films. Three crosses stand over the cliffs at **Areia Branca**, left there by one of the most recent productions, *Maria, A Mãe do Filho de Deus*. The best way to experience the majesty of the coastal landscape is to walk and listen to the wind on the sand. Buggy tourism has led to the degradation of many of the northeast's dunes. Fixed dunes are protected and should not be disturbed, but shifting dunes can be visited by buggy, camel or horse. Ask locally for advice.

Ins and outs
Areia Branca and the other small towns along the northern coast are reachable from Mossoró, the second largest town in the state but with little in the way of tourist attractions. Galinhos, in the far north, sits on a long broad sandspit and is connected to the mainland by ferry from the little village of Guamaré. From here, there are buses to both Mossoró and Natal via the small town of Jandaíra.

Redinha → *Colour map 2, B6.*
A 25-minute ferry crossing on the Rio Potengi or a 16-km drive from Natal up the Rota do Sol/Litoral Norte, takes you to Redinha, an urban beach with ocean and river bathing and buggies for hire. The local delicacy is fried fish with tapioca, served at the market. About 5 km north of Redinha, on a point, is **Santa Rita**. From its high dunes there is a great view of the surrounding coastline.

Genipabu and around
The best-known beach in the state, Genipabu, is 30 km north of Natal. Its major attractions are some very scenic dunes and the **Lagoa de Genipabu**, a lake surrounded by cashew trees where tables are set up on a shoal in the water and drinks are served. There are also many bars and restaurants on the seashore. Buggy rental and microlight flights can be arranged. → *See Activities and tours, page 538.*

North of Genipabu, across the Rio Ceará Mirim, are several beaches with coconut groves and dunes, lined with fishing villages and summer homes of people from Natal; access is via the town of Extremoz. One of these beaches, **Pitangui**, 35 km from Natal, is 6 km long and has a crystalline lake where colourful schools of fish can be seen. **Jacumã**, 49 km from Natal, has a small waterfall and the inland Lagoa de Jacumã, a lake surrounded by dunes where sand-skiing is popular.

Muriú, 44 km from Natal, is known for its lovely green ocean where numerous small boats and *jangadas* anchor; the beach has attractive palms (buggy tour from Natal, including shifting dunes US$100). About 5 km to the north is **Prainha** or **Coqueiro**, a beautiful cove with many coconut palms and strong waves.

Lovely beaches continue along the state's coastline; as you get further away from Natal the beaches are more distant from the main highways and access is more difficult. Around 83 km north of Natal, in the centre of a region known for its coconuts and lobsters, is the ugly resort town of **Touros**. From here the coastline veers east–west.

Far north → Phone code: 084.

As the coast turns to the west, the terrain becomes more dramatic and bleak. Sheltered coves are replaced by vast beaches stretching in seemingly interminable broad curves. Behind them are pink, brown and red cliffs, or large expanses of dunes. Highlights are the sleepy little village of **Galinhos**, with its sand streets and beautiful, gentle beach washed by a calm sea, and the **Costa Branca** near the little fishing towns of **Areia Branca**, **Ponta do Mel** and **Rosadao**, where huge pink and white dunes converge behind magnificent long beaches.

◉ Rio Grande do Norte listings

For Sleeping and Eating price codes and other relevant information, see pages 32-37.

◉ Sleeping

Natal and around *p526, map p527*
Economical hotels are easier to find in Natal than at the outlying beaches or Ponta Negra, but very few people stay here and what they save by doing so is often spent on public transport to and from the beaches.

The distinction between **Praia do Meio** and **Praia dos Artistas** is often blurred. Most hotels are on the beachfront **Av Pres Café Filho**, the numbering of which is illogical.

The **Via Costeira** is a strip of enormous, upmarket beachfront hotels, which are very isolated, with no restaurants or shops within easy walking distance.
L Maine, Av Salgado Filho 1741, Lagoa Nova, T084-4005 5774, www.hotelmaine.com.br. A business-orientated 4-star in a concrete tower in Natal town, with reasonable service and a restaurant.
AL-A Imirá Plaza, Via Costeira 4077, Praia Barreira d'Agua, T084-3211 4104, www.imiraplaza.com.br. A vast, sprawling package resort on the beach and with a pool and tennis court. Popular with families. Cheaper in low season.
AL-C Porto Mirim, Av Café Filho 682, Praia dos Artistas, T084-3220 1600,

www.portomirim.com.br. A smart, modern seafront hotel with spacious public areas but small tiled rooms and little rooftop pool and deck with nice views. Cheaper off season.
A-B Bruma, Av Pres Café Filho 1176, T/F084-3202 4303, www.hotelbruma.com.br. A small, family-run beachfront hotel with 25 balconied rooms around a little pool. Popular with Brazilian families.

Ponta Negra *p528, map p528*
Ponta Negra is the ideal place to stay, with its attractive beach and concentration of restaurants. The most popular hotels are those right on the beach, on **Av Erivan França** facing the sea, and on **R Francisco Gurgel** behind that street. The latter is quieter.
LL Ocean Paláce, Km 11, near Ponta Negra, T084-3220 4144, www.oceanpalace.com.br. A 5-star with large, comfortable suites, smaller, pokier family rooms and a string of bungalows in a regimented line near the beach. Public areas include a lovely ocean-front pool and terrace. Relaxed and friendly.
LL-L Manary Praia, R Francisco Gurgel 9067, T/F084-3204 2900, www.manary.com.br. The best and most tranquil hotel facing the beach and the only one with a trace of style. The rooms, which are decorated in hardwood and pastel colours, have ample bathrooms and secluded private terraces. Good food. A Roteiros de Charme hotel, see page 34.

AL Praia Azul Mar, R Franscisco Gurgel 92, T084-4005 3555, www.praia-azul.com. Pleasant and well-run package holiday hotel, with a/c rooms and a pool overlooking the beach.

A-B Hotel e Pousada O Tempo e o Vento, R Elias Barros 66, T/F084-3219 2526, www.otempoeovento.com.br. Small terracotta and whitewash hotel a block back from the beach with a range of a/c rooms gathered around a pool. The *luxo* rooms are by far the best, others have a fan and there are low season discounts.

B Caminho do Mar, R Dr Ernani Hugo Gomes 365, T084-3219 3761. Simple plain rooms and breakfast, a short walk from the beach.

B Ingá Praia, Av Erivan França 17, T084-3219 3436, www.ingapraiahotel.com.br. A pink cube on the beach with comfortable well-kept rooms and a rooftop terrace. Wi-Fi in all rooms.

C Pousada América do Sol, R Erivan França 35, T084-3219 2245, www.pousada americadosol.com.br. Very simple a/c rooms with pokey bathrooms and TVs. Good breakfast in a terrace overlooking the beach and substantial off-season reductions.

C Pousada Porta do Sol, R Erivan França 9057, T084-3236 2555, www.pousadaporta dosol.com.br. Basic rooms with TV, fridge, fan and an excellent breakfast, pool, beachfront, good value.

D Pousada Maravista, R da Praia 223, T084-3236 4677, http://maravistabrasil.com. Plain and simple but with a good breakfast, English spoken, TV, fridge.

D-F Albergue da Costa, Av Praia de Ponta Negra 8932, T084-3219 0095, www.albergue dacosta.com.br. A simple hostel in a great location, with public areas strewn with hammocks and with rather scruffy little rooms and dorms. The low prices are per person.

D-F HI Lua Cheia, R Dr Manoel Augusto Bezerra de Araújo 500, T084-3236 3696, www.luacheia.com.br. One of the best youth hostels in Brazil; in a 'castle' with a 'medieval' **Taverna Pub** in the basement. The price includes breakfast.

D-F Verdes Mares, R das Algas 2166, Conj Algamar, T084-3236 2872, www.hostel verdesmares.com.br. HI youth hostel, price per person, includes breakfast, discount in low season.

Rota do Sol *p529*

B-C Varandas de Búzios, Av Beira Mar s/n, Búzios, T084-3239 2121, www.rcentrium.com/cl/varandasbuzios. Regimented rows of cabins and a large central restaurant and public area with a pool right on the beach. Reasonable restaurant.

C Pousada Esquina do Sol, Av Deputado Márcio Marinho 2210, Pirangi do Norte, T084-3238 2078, www.esquinadosol.com.br. Small hotel a stroll form the beach with a range of fan-cooled and a/c rooms and kitchenettes in a low-rise concrete block with verandas. Small pool and generous breakfast.

Tibau do Sul and Pipa *p529*

In Pipa more than 30 *pousadas* and many private homes offer accommodation.

LL-A Sombra e Água Fresca, Praia do Amor, T084-3246 2144, www.sombraeagua fresca.com.br. Cheaper in low season. Tastefully decorated but small chalet rooms and vast luxury suites with separate sitting and dining areas. All with magnificent views.

LL-A Toca da Coruja, Praia da Pipa, T084-3246 2226, www.tocadacoruja.com.br. One of the best small luxury hotels in northeastern Brazil, with a range of chalets set in forested gardens and decorated with northeast Brazilian antiques and art. Beautiful pool and an excellent restaurant. A member of the **Roteiros de Charme** group, see page 34.

L Ponta do Madeiro, R da Praia, Estr para Pipa Km 3, T/F084-3246 4220, www.pontado madeiro.com.br. Very comfortable spacious a/c chalets, beautiful pool with bar and spectacular views over the Praia do Madeiro. Excellent service and a good restaurant. Highly recommended.

L Village Natureza, Canto do Madeiro, Pipa, T/F084-3246 4200, www.villagenatureza. com.br. Beautifully appointed a/c chalets nestled in tropical wooded gardens overlooking the sea and Madeiro beach. Gorgeous circular pool, pleasant grounds, lovely views and a long series of steep steps leading to the beach.

AL-A Marinas Tibau Sul, Tibau do Sul, T/F084-3246 4111, www.hotelmarinas. com.br. Cabins for 4, pool, restaurant, watersports, horse riding and a boat dock.

A-B Mirante de Pipa, R do Mirante 1, Praia da Pipa, T084-3246 2055, www.mirante depipa.com.br. A/c and fan-cooled chalets with a veranda set in a forested garden. Wonderful views.

C-D A Conchego, R do Ceu s/n, Praia da Pipa, T084-3246 2439, www.pousada-aconchego. com. Family-run *pousada* with simple chalets with red-tiled roofs and terraces, in a garden filled with cashew and palm trees. Tranquil and central. Good breakfast.

D Pousada da Pipa, Praia da Pipa, T084-3246 2271, www.pipa.com.br/pousada dapipa.com. Small rooms decorated with a personal touch. The best are upstairs and have a large shared terrace with glazed terracotta tiles, sitting areas and hammocks. Large breakfast.

D Vera-My house, Praia da Pipa, T084-3246 2295, www.praiadapipa.com/veramyhouse. Good value, friendly and well maintained though simple rooms with bath, **E-F** per person in dormitory, use of kitchen, no breakfast. Recommended.

Camping

Eco-Camping da Pipa, Av Baía dos Golfinhos 10a, Praia da Pipa, T084-3222 0432/9413 5337, www.ecopipa.com. Great full-powered campsite with cooking facilities, showers and cabins (**D**) for those who don't want to use a tent. Right near Golfinhos beach.

Genipabu and the northern coast p531
A Genipabu, Estr de Genipabu s/n, 2 km from beach, T084-3225 2063, www.genipabu.com. br/portugues. A very relaxing spa hotel on a hillside outside of town with wonderful views out over the beaches and sea. Smart and very

well-kept a/c rooms with en suites. Treatments include Ayurvedic massage, reiki, yoga, body wraps and facials, see www.spanaturalis. com.br. Attractive pool and a sauna. Sister hotel on the beach, **Peixe Galo**, www.pousadapeixegalo.com.br.

B do Gostoso, Praia Ponta de Santo Cristo, 27 km west of town, T084-3263 4087, www.pousadadogostoso.com.br. Rustic chalets on a lonely stretch of beach and in the style of *sertão* houses. Simple restaurant.

B Pousada Villa do Sol, Enseada do Genipabu, Km 4, T084-3225 2132, www.villa dosol.com.br. 20 attractive a/c chalets, the best of which are the 5 newest, with views over the river. Small pool and restaurant with good service.

C Soleil, Av Beira Mar 91, Res Tabu, T084-3225 2064, www.pousadadosoleil.com.br. 10 simple rooms in a brightly painted *pousada* right on the beach. Facilities include a pool, a BBQ and internet.

Far north p532
There are plenty of *pousadas* in **Tibau** and many restaurants and bars along the beach. Although there are some *pousadas* in **Areia Branca**, it isn't a good base for the beaches. **Ponta do Mel**, which is flanked by 2 magnificent beaches, is better and has a couple of very basic *pousadas* in the town.

Galinhos town is very sleepy and *pousadas* often close up for a few days whilst their owners go away. There are at least 7 in town so it is always possible to find a room, either on the ocean or the coastal side.

A Pousada Costa Branca, Ponta do Mel, Costa Branca, T084-3332 7062, www.costa branca.com.br. The best hotel between Genipabu and Ceará with a range of cabins on a bluff with magnificent views over an endless stretch of beach. Organized tours to the dunes to the south, which are among the most spectacular in the state. Good restaurant, service and pool, and Lord Byron tribute bar with live music.

B-C Chalé Oásis Galinhos, R Beira Rio s/n, Galinhos, T084-3552 0024, www.oasis

galinhos.com. The best option in Galinhos, with 6 brightly painted a/c wooden chalets with palm-thatch roofs. All are individually decorated in lush pinks or cool blues, and come with wicker furnishings and arty bric-a-brac. Public areas are splashed with tropical colours and include a TV room lounge with comfy armchairs and a pool and sundeck overlooking the beach. The *pousada* organizes trips around Galinhos.

D Panorama, Tibau, T084-3236 2208. Very basic rooms with a bath and more expensive options with fans.

D Pousada e Restaurante Brasil Aventura, Galinhos, T084-3552 0085. One of several very simple beachfront *pousadas* with a fish restaurant. Plain but well kept and popular with backpackers.

🍴 Eating

Natal and south to Ponta Negra
p526, map p527

Prawns feature heavily on menus as Natal is the largest exporter of prawns in Brazil. Check out the beach *barracas* for snacks and fast food.

♥♥♥ Chaplin, Av Pres Café Filho 27, Praia dos Artistas. Traditional seafood restaurant with sea views. Part of a leisure complex with a bar, English pub and a nightclub.

♥♥♥ Doux France, R Otávio Lamartine, Petrópolis. Authentic French cuisine, outdoor seating.

♥♥♥ Estação Trem de Minas, Av Pres Café Filho 197, Praia dos Artistas, T084-3202 2099. Charming rustic style, distinctly upmarket. 40 brands of *cachaça*, live music nightly, terrace and cocktails. Self-service lunch and dinner.

♥♥♥ Raro Sabor, R Seridó 722, Petrópolis, T084-3202 1857. Exclusive bistro with Russian caviar on the menu.

♥♥ A Macrobiótica, Princesa Isabel 524, Centro. Vegetarian restaurant and shop. Lunch only.

♥♥ Bob's, Av Sen Salgado Filho. Daily 1000-2200. Hamburger chain.

♥♥ Camarões Express, Av Sen Salgado Filho, Centro. Open for lunch only at weekends. Express prawns in 15 styles.

♥♥ Carne de Sol Benigna Lira, R Dr José Augusto Bezerra de Medeiros 09, Praia do Meio. Traditional setting, regional cuisine.

♥♥ Fiorentina, Augusto Bezerra de Medeiros 529, delivery T084-3202 0020. An Italian pizzeria with a huge range of seafood, try the lobster with spaghetti. Friendly service.

♥♥ Peixada da Comadre, R Dr José Augusto Bezerra de Medeiros 4, Praia dos Artistas. Lively seafood restaurant with popular prawn dishes.

♥♥ Saint Antoine, R Santo Antônio 651, Cidade Alta, Centro. Mediocre self-service pay by weight establishment.

♥-♥ Farol Bar, Av Sílvio Pedrosa 105 (at the end of Via Costeira on Praia Areia Preta). Famous dried meat dishes -- a local speciality.

Ponta Negra *p528, map p528*

♥♥♥ Manary, Manary Praia Hotel, R Francisco Gurgel (see page 532). The best seafood in the city in a poolside restaurant overlooking Ponta Negra beach.

♥♥♥ Roschti, Av Erivan França, T084-3219 4406. International cuisine in a relaxed beachfront bistro and more formal upstairs dining room.

♥♥♥ Sobre Ondas, Av Erivan França 14, T084-3219 4222. Average seafood and international dishes in an intimate beach-front setting with an underwater theme.

♥♥ Atlântico, Av Erivan França 27, T084-3219 2762. Relaxed, warm service, semi open air, beachfront. Portuguese-owned, Italian and Portugese dishes, fish and *carne do sol*. Recommended.

♥♥ Barraca do Caranguejo, Av Erivan França 1180, T084-3219 5069. Eight prawn dishes for US$8 and live music nightly from 2100.

♥♥ Camarões, Av Eng Roberto Freire 2610. Also at Natal shopping centre. Touristy, but very good seafood.

♥♥ Cipó Brasil, Av Erivan 3, T0800-3284051. Funky little Playa del Carmen-style bar with a jungle theme, 4 levels, sand floors, lantern-lit, very atmospheric. Average food (pizzas, crêpes), good cocktails, live music from 2100.

†† Ponta Negra Grill, Av Erivan 20, T084-3219 3714. A large, popular restaurant with live music and several terraces overlooking the beach. Steaks, seafood and cocktails.

† Ponta Negra Mall. Stalls sell sandwiches and snacks.

Tibau do Sul and Pipa *p529*

There are many restaurants and bars along Pipa's main street, Av Baía dos Golfinhos.

††† Al Buchetto, Av Baía dos Golfinhos 837, Pipa, T084-3246 2318. Decent, Italian-made pasta and a lively atmosphere.

††† Camamo Beijupirá, Tibau do Sul, T084-3246 4195. One of the best restaurants in Brazil with an eclectic mix of fusion dishes like prawns and slices of leek in a spicy cashew sauce with raisins and ginger, served with fervent enthusiasm by owner Tadeu Lubambo. Excellent wine list.

††† Toca da Coruja, Praia da Pipa (see page 533). Superlative and beautifully presented regional food in a tropical garden setting. Intimate and romantic. Highly recommended.

††† Vivendo, Av Baía dos Golfinhos, Pipa. One of the town's best seafood restaurants and a good place to watch the passers-by.

† Casa de Taipe and Shirley-My House, Av Baía dos Golfinhos 1126 and 1213, Praia da Pipa. Very cheap but decent self-service restaurants, the latter owned by the sister of Vera of **Vera-My House** (see page 534).

† São Sebastião, R do Ceu, Pipa. Vegetarian and wholefood. Good value. Good juices.

† Sopa de Patrick/Chez Lisa, Av Baía dos Golfinhos s/n, Praia da Pipa. Generous portions of various delicious soups, in a little shack beyond the main square.

† Tatoo Batata, R do Ceu, Pipa, T084-9419 7181. Enormous baked potatoes with fillings like cheese and sweet corn. Salads and juices too. Friendly owner. Next to **A Conchego** *pousada* (see Sleeping).

◐ Bars and clubs

Natal and around *p526, map p527*

Dance is an important pastime in Natal. In an area in the centre known as **Ribeira**, there are a few popular bars/nightclubs in restored historic buildings in R Chile.

Amiça, Av Engenheiro Roberto Freire s/n. New club with techno and house, popular with locals and tourists.

Blackout B52, R Chile 25, T084-3221 1282. Lively venue with a 1940s theme. The best night is 'Black Monday'. There is live rock, blues and MPB on other nights. The crowd is 20s and early 30s.

Budda Pub, Av Engenheiro Roberto Freire (an annexe of the Tiberius). A little bar with good bar food and a laid-back atmosphere.

Centro de Turismo (see Shopping, below) has *Forró com Turista*, a chance for visitors to learn this fun dance, Thu at 2200. There are many other enjoyable venues where visitors are encouraged to join in.

Chaplin, Av Presidente Café Filho 27, Praia dos Artistas, T084-3202 1188. Different zones with everything from MPB and *forró* to techno and progressive house.

Novakapital, Av Presidente Café Filho 872, Praia dos Artistas, T084-3202 7111. With *forró*, live music, especially rock and foam parties, US$4, from 2400.

Ponta Negra *p528, map p528*

Although there is a handful of respectable clubs, Ponta Negra beach is now somewhat seedy. The municipal authorities are coming down very hard on the sex industry and its clients, and are installing video cameras all along the beach. Alto Ponta Negra is very lively and has live music and a range of bars and clubs open until dawn.

Baraonda, Av Erivan França 44, T084-9481 3748. Live music nightly except Tue, including *forró* and MPB from 2300 until late.

Taverna Pub, R Dr Manoel, Araújo 500, Alta Ponta Negra, T084-3236 3696. Medieval-style pub in youth hostel basement. Eclectic (rock,

Brazilian pop, jazz, etc) live music Tue-Sun from 2200, best night Wed. Recommended.

In front of the Taverna is a cluster of small venues including **Tapiocaria Salsa Bar** and the **Calderão da Bruxa**.

Tibau do Sul and around *p529*

Tibau do Sul has various beach *barracas*. There is always something going on in Pipa, whatever the night and whatever the month.
Aruman, Av Baía dos Golfinhos, Pipa. Good cocktails and a trendy crowd.
Blue Bar, Av Baía dos Golfinhos, Pipa. Live *pagodé* and samba on Wed.
Calangos, Baía dos Golfinhos s/n (at the southern end of Pipa). A club with famous DJs like Patife. Techno and MPB Thu-Sun.
Carvalho do Fogo, Tibau do Sul. *Forró* until dawn every Wed.
Reggae Bar, just off Av Baía dos Golfinhos, Pipa centre. Live reggae bands, usually on Tue.

⊛ Festivals and events

Natal and around *p526, map p527*
Jan Festa de Nossa Senhora dos Navegantes, when numerous vessels go to sea from Praia da Redinha, north of town.
Mid-Oct Country show, Festa do Boi (bus marked Parnamirim to the exhibition centre), gives a good insight into rural life.
Mid-Dec Carnaval, the Salvador-style out-of-season carnival, a lively 4-day music festival with dancing in the streets.

◎ Shopping

Natal and around *p526, map p527*
Centro de Turismo, R Aderbal de Figueiredo, 980, off R Gen Cordeiro, Petrópolis, T084-3212 2267. Sun-Wed 0900-1900, Thu 2200. A converted prison with a wide variety of handicraft and antiques shops, art gallery and tourist information booth. Good view of the Rio Potengi and the sea.

Centro Municipal de Artesanato, Av Pres Café Filho, Praia dos Artistas. Daily 1000-2200. Sand-in-bottle pictures are very common in Natal and there are plenty here alongside other touristy items.
Natal Shopping, Av Senador Salgado Filho, 2234, between Via Costeira and Ponta Negra. Large mall with restaurants, cinemas and 140 shops. Free shuttle service to major hotels.

Tibau do Sul and around *p529*
Pipa is a good place for raw cotton and costume jewellery made from tropical seeds.
The Bookshop (next to the **Reggae Bar**, see Bars and clubs, above). Run by the wonderfully knowledgeable and eccentric Cyntia, who rents out books of all genres from Oscar Wilde to Dostoyevsky.

▲ Activities and tours

Natal and around *p526, map p527*
Boat trips
Boat trips on the Rio Potengi and along the nearby beaches of the Litoral Sul. A 2-hr tour includes hotel pickup, a snack, and allows time for a swim, US$25 per person. Boat trips to Barra do Cunhaú, 86 km south of Natal, go through mangroves, visit an island and a salt mine (Passeio Ecológico Cunhaú).

Buggy tours
Buggy tours are by far the most popular, US$40-90 and can be organized through the hotels. Be sure to check that only shifting dunes are visited. Fixed dunes are protected by Brazilian environmental law. It is possible to hire a buggy, or take a tour, all the way to Fortaleza (US$800 for 4 people) with companies like **Buggy e Compania**, www.buggyecia.com.br. Avoid the huge operators like **Brésil-Aventure** who journey in huge convoys. **Cariri Ecotours**, below, can recommend environmentally sensitive operators.

Dromedary rides

Cleide Gomes and Philippe Landry of
Dromedunas, www.dromedunas.com.br,
offer dromedary rides on the dunes above
Genipabu. Walks last around 30 mins and
they make a far more peaceful alternative to
buzzing dune buggies. You'll find them on
Genipabu beach from 0900 every day.

Ecotourism

Cariri Ecotours, R Francisco Gurgel 9067,
Ponta Negra, T/F084-9928 0198, www.cariri
ecotours.com.br. Excellent tours to some of
the most interesting sights in the northeastern interior, such as Souza, Cariri and the
Serra da Capivara. Short on information about
local fauna but good on history and geology.

Tibau do Sul and Pipa *p529*
Buggy tours to Barra de Cunhaú US$50,
from Pipa to Natal US$115.

Genipabu *p531*
Associação dos Bugueiros, T084-3225 2077.
US$25 for dune buggy tour. Microlight flights
are also available.

⊕ Transport

Natal and around *p526, map p527*
Air Buses to the airport run every 30 mins
from the old *rodoviária* and are marked
'Aeroporto'. A taxi to the airport costs
US$25; US$20 from Ponta Negra. There
are flights to **Brasília**, **Fortaleza**, **Recife**,
Rio de Janeiro, **Salvador**, **São Paulo**; **Belo
Horizonte**, **Goiânia**, **São Luís**, **Fernando de
Noronha**, **Vitória**, **Porto Alegre**. There are
international flights to **Lisbon** with TAP.

   Airline offices GOL, www.voe
gol.com.br, at airport. Oceanair,
www.Avianca.com.br. TAM, Av Campos
Sales 500, Tirol, T084-3201 2020, at airport,
T084-3643 1624, freephone T0800-123100,
www.tam.com.br. TAP, www.flytap.com,
has connections with Portugal. TRIP,

T084-3234 1717, freephone T0800-2747,
www.voetrip.com.br. Varig, R Mossoro 598,
Centro, T084-3201 9339, at airport, T084-
3743 1100, freephone T0800-997000, www.
varig.com.br. **Webjet**, www.webjet.com.br.

Bus
Local Regional tickets are sold on street
level of the new *rodoviária* in Cidade da
Esperança; interstate tickets are available
on the 2nd floor. A taxi to the bus station
costs around US$25 from town, or US$18
from Ponta Negra, or there are regular local
buses (see Ins and outs, page 526).

   From the old *rodoviária* Viação Campos
runs to **Pirangi**, US$0.60, 5 times a day
0630-1815, 3 on Sun 0730, 0930, 1645.
In summer, buses run from both *rodoviárias*,
every 30 mins to **Pirangi**, US$2, 1 hr;
to **Tabatinga** US$3, 1¼ hrs.

   Long-distance From the new
rodoviária, there are 6 buses a day to **Tibau
do Sul**, US$5, 2 hrs, starting at 0600, and
going on from Tibau to **Pipa**, US$7, 15 mins
more.To **Recife** with Napoles, 5 daily, US$15
convencional, US$12 *executivo*, 4 hrs. With
Nordeste to **Mossoró**, US$10 *convencional*,
US$15 *executivo*, 4 hrs. To **Aracati**, US$14,
5½ hrs. To **Fortaleza**, US$15 *convencional*,
US$210 *executivo*, US$35 *leito*, 8 hrs. To **João
Pessoa**, every 2 hrs, US$4 *convencional*,
US$8 *executivo*, 3 hrs. With São Geraldo to
Maceió, buses both direct and via Recife,
US$21 *convencional*, US$30 *executivo*, 10 hrs.
To **Salvador**, US$50 *executivo*, 20 hrs.
To **Rio de Janeiro**, US$90. To **São Paulo**,
US$90 *convencional*, US$100*executivo*,
46-49 hrs. With Boa Esperança to **Teresina**,
US$40 *convencional*, US$45 *executivo*,
17-20 hrs. To **Belém**, US$70, 32 hrs.

Car hire Car hire offices can be found at the
airport and through mid- to top-range hotels.
Avis, at airport, www.avis.com. Hertz, airport,
www.hertz.com. Localiza, Av Nascimento de
Castro 1792, www.localiza.com.

Tibau do Sul and Pipa *p529*
Bicycle hire From **Blue Planet**, Pipa.
US$5 for a half day, US$10 full day.

Buggy It is possible to travel all the way
to **Fortaleza** by buggy with **Top Buggy**,
www.topbuggy.com.br, via the stunning
Rio Grande do Norte dunes and beaches.

Bus *Combis* connect Pipa and Tibau until
around 2300. 6 buses a day to **Natal**'s new
rodoviária, US$5, 2 hrs, from Pipa via Tibau
do Sul, leaving Pipa 0500-1600. Minivans
also do this run and are easiest to catch
from the beach.
   Buses to **Paraíba** pass through Goianinha
on the interstate road. Frequent *combis* connect
Goianinha with Pipa (30 mins, US$1.50).

Taxi Carlos, T084-9977 0006, after-hours
taxi, speaks basic English.

Redinha *p531*
Bus Regular bus service from the old
rodoviária to **Genipabu**.

Ferry There is a frequent ferry service
to Cais Tavares de Lira, **Ribeira**, weekdays
0530-1900, weekend and holidays 0800-
1830, US$1 per person, US$5 for car.

---

❶ Directory

Natal and around
p526, map p527
Banks There are **Bradesco** and **HSBC** banks
for international ATMs at the *rodoviária*,
airport and throughout the city: **Banco
24 horas**, Natal Shopping, Cirrus, Visa,
MasterCard and Plus. Also, Av Rio Branco 510,
Cidade Alta, US$ cash and TCs at poor rates,
cash advances against Visa, Mon-Fri
1000-1600. **Banespa**, Av Rio Branco 704,
Cidade Alta, US$ cash and TCs at **dolar
turismo** rate, Mon-Fri 1000-1430. **Sunset
Câmbio**, Av Hermes da Fonseca 628, Tirol,
T084-3212 2552, cash and TCs, 0900-1700.
Dunas Câmbio, Av Roberto Freire 1776,
Loja B-11, Capim Macio (east of Parque
das Dunas), T084-3219 3840, cash and TCs,
0900-1700. **Embassies and consulates**
Germany, R Gov Sílvio Pedrosa 308, Areia
Preta, T084-3222 3596. **Italy**, R Auta de Souza
275, Centro, T084-3222 6674. **Spain**,
R Amintas Barros 4200, Lagoa Nova,
T084-206 5610. **Internet** Internet cafés
on Ponta Negra and around the main beach
areas. **Post office** R Princesa Isabel 711,
Centro; Av Rio Branco 538, Centro; Av
Engenheiro Hildegrando de Góis 22, Ribeira.
Poste restante is in Ribeira, near the old
rodoviária, at Av Rio Branco and Av General
Gustavo Cordeiro de Farias, hard to find.
Police Tourist police (Delegacia do Turista):
T084-3236 3288, 24 hrs. **Telephone**
R Princesa Isabel 687 and R João Pessoa,
Centro, also a the *rodoviária*.

Ponta Negra *p528, map p528*
Banks Banco do Brasil, Seafront ATM for
Cirrus, Visa, MasterCard and Plus. **Embassies
and consulates** Canada, Av Roberto
Freire 2951, bloco 01, loja 09-CCAB Sul,
T084-3219 2197. **Internet** Sobre Ondas
(also bar and restaurant, see Eating),
0900-2400, 10 centavos 1 min. **Post
office** Av Praia de Ponta Negra 8920.
Telephone Av Roberto Freire 3100,
Shopping Cidade Jardim, Av Roberto Freire.

Ceará

Ceará calls itself the 'Terra da Luz' (Land of Light) and much of its 573-km coastline and bone-dry interior is baked under permanent sunshine. It could just as well be called the land of wind: kitesurfers and windsurfers are quickly discovering that there is nowhere better in the world for their sports. Locations such as Cumbuco and Jericoacoara are blown by strong winds almost 365 days a year, and the Atlantic Ocean offers varied conditions from glassy flat through to rolling surf. Ceará boasts some beautiful beaches, too – though poor when compared to the rest of Brazil perhaps – with long, broad stretches of sand backed by ochre cliffs or towering dunes. Sadly they are increasingly populated by expat and profiteering foreigners. Many of the little fishing villages that lay undiscovered for decades are losing their character to ugly condos and concrete hotels. In places like Canoa Quebrada, Jericoacoara and Cumbuco, other European languages are spoken as much as Portuguese. Even the state capital Fortaleza has been affected. Plane-loads of foreign tourists have turned its once-lively nightlife increasingly tawdry; and while the state authorities are cracking down hard on the exploitation locals in the main tourist towns are often cynical about foreigners.
▶▶ For listings, see pages 555-567.

Fortaleza → *For listings, see pages 555-567. Colour map 2, A5. Phone code: 085. Population: 2.1 million.*

Brazil's fifth largest city is a stretch of concrete towers along a series of white-sand beaches behind a gloriously misty green and blue Atlantic dotted with rusting wrecks. The water temperature is permanently in the high 20s and there's a constant sea breeze. The sea is surprisingly clean, even in Iracema near the centre, but the best beaches for swimming are further east and west.

Fortaleza has a long history and a number if sights of historic interest. However, most tourists are drawn here by the city's reputation for lively nightlife. The sound of *forró* still reverberates in the streets behind Iracema beach, but nowadays it's hard to find anywhere that isn't overrun with groups of single foreign men and professional local women. Many locals are angry about their city's poor reputation and are wary of tourists. There are signs that this is changing, however – police and local hotel owners have been making concerted efforts to discourage the growth of this kind of tourism and are coming down increasingly hard on any locals and foreigners involved.

Ins and outs

Getting there International and domestic flights arrive at **Aeroporto Pinto Martins** ① *Praça Eduardo Gomes, 6 km south of the centre, T085-3392 1200.* There are connections with São Luís and Belém, as well as the Guianas, various destinations in Portugal and Italy. The airport has a 24-hour tourist office, T085-3477 1667, car hire, a food hall, internet facilities, bookstore, **Banco do Brasil** for exchange and **Bradesco** and **HSBC** for international ATMs. Bus No 404 runs from the airport to Praça José de Alencar in the centre, US$1.50. **Expresso Guanabara** minibuses run to the *rodoviária* and Beira Mar (US$2). Bus No 066 runs from Papicu to Parangaba; bus No 027 runs from Papicu to Siqueira. Taxis to the centre, Avenida Beira Mar or Praia do Futuro charge a fixed fee of US$25, or US$30 at night (30 minutes, allowing for traffic).

Interstate buses arrive at the **Rodoviária São Tomé** ① *Av Borges de Melo 1630, Fátima, 6 km south of the centre, T085-3256 2100.* Information is available from *Disque Turismo* booth, open 0600-1800, which also has lockers for storing luggage.

Opposite the *rodoviária* is **Hotel Amuarama**, which has a bar and restaurant; there's also a *lanchonete*. Many city buses run to the centre (US$1) including No 78, which goes to Iracema via the Centro Dragão do Mar. If in doubt, the tourist information booth will point you in the right direction. A taxi to Praia de Iracema, or Avenida Abolição costs around US$15. Minivans to Jericoacoara leave from in front of the Hotel **Casa Blanca** (see Sleeping, page 556). ▸▸ *See Transport, page 564.*

Getting around The city is spread out, with its main attractions in the centre and along the seashore; transport from one to the other can take a long time. The city bus system is efficient if a little rough; buses and vans cost US$1 per journey. The cheapest way to orientate yourself within the city is to take the 'Circular 1' (anti-clockwise) or 'Circular 2' (clockwise) buses which pass Avenida Beira Mar, the Aldeota district, the university (UFC) and cathedral via Meireles, Iracema, Centro Dragão do Mar and the Centre, US$1.50. Alternatively, take the new *Top Bus* run by **Expresso Guanabara** ① *T0800-991992, US$2.50*, an air-conditioned minibus starting at Avenida Abolição.

When driving outside the city, have a good map and be prepared to ask directions frequently as road signs are non-existent or are placed after junctions.

Tourist information The main office of the state tourism agency, **Setur** ① *Secretária do Turismo do Estado do Ceará, Av General Afonso Albuquerque Lima, Fortaleza T085-3101 4688, www.setur.ce.gov.br*, has maps and brochures and can help with hotels and tours. There are also information booths at the airport and *rodoviária*, and at the Farol de Mucuripe (old lighthouse), open 0700-1730. The **Posta Telefônica Beira Mar** ① *Av Beira Mar, almost opposite Praiano Palace Hotel*, provides information, sells *combi* tickets to Jericoacoara, and has postcards, clothes and magazines. If you have problems, contact the **tourist police** ① *R Silva Paulet 505, Aldeota, T085-3433 8171.*

Safety The city is generally safe for visitors. However, tourists should avoid the following areas: Serviluz favela between the old lighthouse (Avenida Vicente de Castro), Mucuripe and Praia do Futuro; the favela behind the railway station; the Passeio Público at night; and Avenida Abolição at its eastern (Nossa Senhora da Saúde church) and western ends.

Sights

Walking through the centre of Fortaleza, it is hard to ignore the city's history, which dates back to the 17th century. Pedestrian walkways radiate from the **Praça do Ferreira**, the heart of the commercial centre, and the whole area is dotted with shady green squares. The **Fortaleza Nossa Senhora da Assumpção** ① *Av Alberto Nepomuceno, T085-3255 1600, telephone in advance for permission to visit, daily 0800-1100, 1400-1700,* originally built in 1649 by the Dutch, gave the city its name. Near the fort, on Rua Dr João Moreira, is the 19th-century **Praça Passeio Público** (or Praça dos Mártires), a park with old trees and statues of Greek deities. West of here a neoclassical former prison (1866) houses a fine tourist centre, the **Centro de Turismo do Estado (Emcetur)** ① *Av Senador Pompeu 350, near the waterfront, T0800-991516, closed Sun*, with museums, theatre and craft shops. It houses the renovated **Museu de Arte e Cultura Populares** and the **Museu de Minerais** ① *T085-3212 3566*. Further west along Rua Dr João Moreira, at **Praça Castro Carreira** (commonly known as Praça da Estação), is the nicely refurbished train station, **Estação João Felipe** (1880), which runs commuter services.

The **Teatro José de Alencar** ⓘ *Praça José de Alencar, T085-3229 1989, Mon-Fri 0800-1700, hourly tours, some English-speaking guides, US$1, Wed free*, was inaugurated in 1910 and is worth a visit. It is a magnificent iron structure imported from Scotland and decorated in neoclassical and art nouveau styles. It also houses a library and art gallery. The **Praça dos Leões** or Praça General Tibúrcio has bronze lions imported from France. Around it stand the 18th-century **Palácio da Luz** ⓘ *T085-3231 5699*, former seat of the state government, and the **Igreja Nossa Senhora do Rosário**, built by slaves in the 18th century. Also here is the former provincial legislature, dating from 1871, which houses the **Museu do Ceará** ⓘ *R São Paulo, next to Praça dos Leões, T085-3251 1502, Tue-Fri 0830-1730, Sat 0830-1400, US$0.80*. The museum has displays on history and anthropology. To get there, take bus marked 'Dom Luís'.

The new **cathedral** ⓘ *Praça da Sé*, completed in 1978, in Gothic style but constructed out of concrete with beautiful stained-glass windows, stands beside the new semi-circular **Mercado Central**.

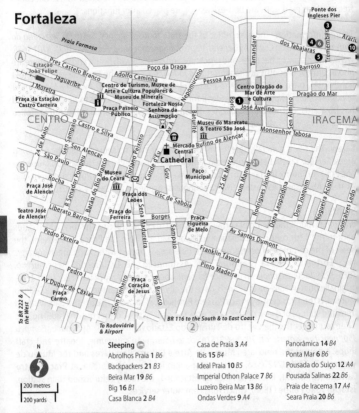

Fortaleza

	Sleeping 🛏	Casa de Praia **3** *A4*	Panorâmica **14** *B4*
	Abrolhos Praia **1** *B6*	Ibis **15** *B4*	Ponta Mar **6** *B6*
	Backpackers **21** *B3*	Ideal Praia **10** *B5*	Pousada do Suiço **12** *A4*
	Beira Mar **19** *B6*	Imperial Othon Palace **7** *B6*	Pousada Salinas **22** *B6*
	Big **16** *B1*	Luzeiro Beira Mar **13** *B6*	Praia de Iracema **17** *A4*
	Casa Blanca **2** *B4*	Ondas Verdes **9** *A4*	Seara Praia **20** *B6*

There are several worthwhile museums to visit in and around Fortaleza. The **Museu do Maracatu** ⓘ *Rufino de Alencar 231*, at Teatro São José, has costumes of this ritual dance of African origin. The new and exciting **Centro Dragão do Mar de Arte e Cultura** ⓘ *R Dragão do Mar 81, Praia de Iracema, T085-3488 8600, www.dragaodomar.org.br, Tue-Thu 1000- 1730, Fri-Sun 1400-2130, US$0.75 for entry to each museum/gallery, free on Sun*, hosts concerts, dance performances and exhibitions of art and photography. It has various entrances, from Rua Almirante Barroso, Rua Boris, and from the junction of Monsenhor Tabosa, Dom Manuel and Castelo Branco. The latter leads directly to three museums: on street level, the **Memorial da Cultura Cearense**, with changing exhibitions; on the next floor down is an art and cultural exhibition; in the basement is an excellent audio-visual museum of **El Vaqueiro**. Also at street level is the **Livraria Livro Técnico**. There is a **planetarium** with a whispering gallery underneath. The centre also houses the **Museu de Arte Contemporânea do Ceará**. This area is very lively at night.

Some 15 km south of the centre, the **Museu Artur Ramos** ⓘ *in the Casa de José de Alencar, Av Perimetral, Messejana, T085-3229 1898, Mon 1400-1730, Tue-Sun 0800-1200,*

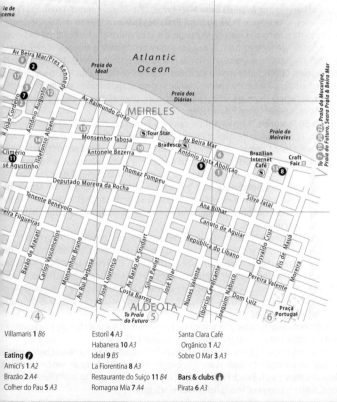

Villamaris **1** *B6*	Estoril **4** *A3*	Santa Clara Café
	Habanera **10** *A3*	Orgânico **1** *A2*
Eating 🍴	Ideal **9** *B5*	Sobre O Mar **3** *A3*
Amici's **1** *A2*	La Fiorentina **8** *A3*	
Brazão **2** *A4*	Restaurante do Suíço **11** *B4*	**Bars & clubs** 🍸
Colher do Pau **5** *A3*	Romagna Mia **7** *A4*	Pirata **6** *A3*

1400-1700, displays artefacts of African and indigenous origin collected by the anthropologist Artur Ramos, as well as documents from the writer José de Alencar.

Beaches

The urban beaches between Barra do Ceará (west) and Ponta do Mucuripe (east) are polluted and not suitable for swimming. Minibus day tours for other beaches, from US$6, and transfers to Jericoacoara, US$15, leave from along the seafront. The agency **CPVTUR** ⓘ *Av Monsenhor Tabosa 1001, T085-3219 2511*, also runs trips.

Heading east from the centre, **Praia de Iracema** is one of the older beach suburbs, with some original early 20th-century houses. It is not much of a sunbathing beach as it has little shade or facilities and swimming is unsafe, but at night it is very lively. Of its many bars and restaurants, the **Estoril**, housed in one of the earliest buildings, has become a landmark. The Ponte Metálica or **Ponte dos Ingleses**, nearby, was built by the British Civil engineering firm, Norton Griffiths and Company, in 1921 as a commercial jetty for the port, but was never completed due to lack of funds, and re-opened as a promenade pier in imitation of English seaside piers. It was and is now a very popular spot for watching the sunset and the occasional pod of visiting dolphins.

East of Iracema, the **Avenida Beira Mar** (Avenida Presidente Kennedy) connects **Praia do Meireles** (divided into **Praia do Ideal**, **Praia dos Diários** and Praia do Meireles itself) with Volta da Jurema and Praia do Mucuripe; it is lined with high-rise buildings and most luxury hotels are located here. A *calçado* (walkway), following the palm-lined shore, becomes a night-time playground as locals promenade on foot, roller skates, skateboards and bicycles. Children ride mini-motorbikes, scooters or the 'happiness' train with its Disney characters. Take in the spectacle while sipping an *agua de coco* or *caiprinha* on the beachfront, where there are volleyball courts, bars, open-air shows and a **crafts fair** in front of the Imperial Othon Palace Hotel.

Praia do Mucuripe, 5 km east of the centre, is Fortaleza's main fishing centre, where *jangadas* (traditional rafts with triangular sails) bring in the catch; there are many restaurants serving *peixada* and other fish specialities. The symbol of this beach is the statue of Iracema, the main character of the romance by José de Alencar (see Background, page 782). From the monument there is a good view of Mucuripe's port and bay. At Mucuripe Point is a **lighthouse** built by slaves in 1846, which houses the **Museu de Fortaleza** (now sadly run down and not a safe area, according to the tourist office). There is a lookout at the new lighthouse, good for viewing the *jangadas*, which return in the late afternoon, and the sunset.

Praia do Futuro, 8 km southeast of the centre, is the most popular bathing beach. It is 8 km long with strong waves, sand dunes and freshwater showers, but no natural shade. Vendors in straw shacks serve local dishes such as crab. On Thursday nights it becomes the centre for the city's nightlife, with people enjoying live music and *forró*. The south end of the beach is known as **Caça e Pesca**; water here is polluted because of the outflow of the Rio Cocó. Praia do Futuro has few hotels or buildings because the salt-spray corrosion is among the strongest in the world.

At **Praia de Sabiaguaba**, 20 km southeast of the centre, is a small fishing village known for its seafood; the area has mangroves and is good for fishing.

Some 29 km southeast of the centre is **Praia Porto das Dunas**, a pleasant beach that is popular for watersports, such as surfing. Buggies and microlight tours can be arranged. The main attraction is **Beach Park** ⓘ *US$20*, the largest water park in South America, with pools, water toboggans, sports fields and restaurants.

The coast east of Fortaleza → For listings, see pages 555-567.

The most prominent feature of the eastern coast is the impressive coloured sand cliffs. There are also freshwater springs near the shore, along with palm groves and mangroves. Lobster fishing is one of the main activities. It is possible to hike along much of the eastern coast: from Prainha to Águas Belas takes seven hours (bring plenty of water and sun protection). Where there are rivers to cross, there is usually a boatmen. Fishing villages have accommodation or hammock space.

Aquiraz and around → *Colour map 2, A5. Phone code: 085. Population: 61,000.*
Some 31 km east of Fortaleza, Aquiraz was the original capital of Ceará. It retains several colonial buildings and has a religious art museum. It is also the access point for a number of beaches.

Six kilometres east of Aquiraz, **Prainha** is a fishing village and weekend resort with a 10-km beach and dunes. The beach is clean and largely empty and the waves are good for surfing. You can see *jangadas* coming in daily in the late afternoon. The village is known for its lacework; the women using the *bilro* and *labirinto* techniques at the **Centro de Rendeiras**. In some of the small restaurants it is possible to see displays of the *carimbó*, one of the north Brazilian dances. Just south of Prainha is **Praia do Presídio**, with gentle surf, dunes, palms and *cajueiros* (cashew trees).

About 18 km southeast of Aquiraz is **Praia Iguape**, another fishing village known for its lacework. The beach is a large, elbow-shaped sandbank, very scenic especially at Ponta do Iguape. Nearby are high sand dunes where sand-skiing is popular. There is a lookout at Morro do Enxerga Tudo; one-hour *jangada* trips cost US$8.50. Lacework is sold at the **Centro de Rendeiras**. Locals are descendants of Dutch, Portuguese and indigenous peoples; some traditions such as the *coco-de-praia* folk dance are still practised. Some 3 km south of Iguape is **Praia Barro Preto**, a wide tranquil beach, with dunes, palms and lagoons.

Ins and outs There are regular buses to the beaches and to the city of Aquiraz from the *rodoviária* in Fortaleza. For further information on the area, including accommodation and restaurants, visit www.aquiraz.ce.gov.br.

Cascavel → *Phone code: 085.*
Cascavel, 62 km southeast of Fortaleza, has a Saturday crafts fair by the market. It is the access point for the beaches of Caponga and Águas Belas, where traditional fishing villages coexist with fancy weekend homes and hotels. **Caponga**, 15 km northeast of Cascavel, has a wide, 2-km-long beach lined with palms. *Jangadas* set sail in the early morning; arrangements can be made to accompany fishermen on overnight trips, a 90-minute ride costs US$14 for up to five people. There is a fish market and crafts sales (ceramics, embroidery and lacework) on the beach. A 30-minute walk south along the white-sand beach leads to **Águas Belas**, at the mouth of the Rio Mal Cozinhado, offering a combination of fresh and saltwater bathing (access also by road, 15 km from Cascavel, 4 km from Caponga). The scenery here, and 5 km further east at Barra Nova, changes with the tide. A walk north along the beach for 6 km takes you to the undeveloped **Praia do Batoque**, which is surrounded by cliffs and dunes.

Morro Branco and Praia das Fontes → *Phone code: 085.*
Beberibe, 78 km from Fortaleza, is the access point for Morro Branco and Praia das Fontes, some of the better-known beaches of the east coast.

About 4 km from Beberibe, **Morro Branco** has a spectacular beach, coloured craggy cliffs and beautiful views. *Jangadas* leave the beach at 0500, returning at 1400-1500. Lobster is the main catch in this area. The coloured sands of the dunes are bottled into beautiful designs and sold along with other crafts such as lacework, embroidery and straw goods. *Jangadas* may be hired for sailing (one hour for up to six people US$30). Beach buggies cost US$100 for a full day; taxis are also available for hire. The beach is lined with summer homes and can get very crowded during peak season.

South of Morro Branco and 6 km from Beberibe is **Praia das Fontes**, which also has coloured cliffs with freshwater springs. There is a fishing village and, at the south end, a lagoon. Near the shore is a cave, known as **Mãe de Água**, visible at low tide. Buggies and microlights can be hired on the beach. A luxury resort complex has been built here, making the area expensive.

South of Praia das Fontes are several less developed beaches including **Praia Uruaú** or **Marambaia**, about 6 km from Praia das Fontes along the beach or 21 km by road from Beberibe, via Sucatinga on a sand road. The beach is at the base of coloured dunes; there is a fishing village with some accommodation. Just inland is **Lagoa do Uruaú**, the largest in the state and a popular place for watersports. A buggy from Morro Branco costs US$45 for four people.

About 50 km southeast of Beberibe is **Fortim**. From here, boats run to **Pontal de Maceió**, a reddish sand point at the mouth of the Rio Jaguaribe, from where there is a good view of the eastern coast. In the winter the river is high and there is fishing for shrimp; in the summer it dries up, forming islands and freshwater beaches. There's a fishing village about 1 km from the ocean with bars, restaurants and small *pousadas*.

Prainha do Canto Verde → *Phone code: 085.*

Some 120 km east of Fortaleza, in the district of Beberibe, is Prainha do Canto Verde, a small fishing village on a vast beach, which has an award-winning community tourism project. There are guesthouses or houses for rent (see Sleeping, page 557), restaurants (good food at **Sol e Mar**) and a handicraft cooperative. Each November there is a **Regata Ecológica**, with *jangadas* from up and down the coast competing. *Jangada* and catamaran cruises are offered, as well as fishing and a number of walking trails. This simple place, where people make their living through artesanal fishing, without the use of big boats or industrial techniques. The village has built up its tourism infrastructure without any help from outside investors, and has been fighting the foreign speculators since 1979. The people are friendly and visitors are welcome to learn about the traditional way of life, although knowledge of Portuguese is essential.

Ins and outs   To get to Prainha do Canto Verde, take a São Benedito bus to Aracati or Canoa Quebrada, buy a ticket to Quatro Bocas and ask to be let off at Lagoa da Poeira, two hours from Fortaleza. If you haven't booked a transfer in advance, Márcio at the **Pantanal** restaurant at the bus stop may be able to take you, US$2.75. The website www.fortal net.com.br/~fishnet, is a good source of information.

Aracati → *Phone code: 088. Population: 62,000.*

Situated on the shores of the Rio Jaguaribe, Aracati is the access point to the Ceará's most southeasterly beaches. The city is best known for its **Carnaval** (the liveliest in the state) and for its colonial architecture, including several 18th-century churches and mansions with Portuguese tile façades. There is a **religious art museum** (closed lunchtime and

Sunday afternoon), a Saturday morning crafts fair on Avenida Coronel Alexandrino, and a number of simple *pousadas* (**B-E**) on the same street.

Canoa Quebrada → *Colour map 2, A5. Phone code: 088.*

Canoa Quebrada stands on a sand dune 10 km from Aracati backed by crumbling, multi-coloured sandstone cliffs. It remained an isolated fishing village until 1982, when a road was built. It is now a very popular resort, with many package hotels, busy bars and restaurants. But the village is almost entirely devoid of its once legendary laid-back, weed smoking hippy beach feel. The nightlife is good in season (especially over Christmas, New Year and Carnaval, when it can be very difficult to find a room). Canoa is famous for its *labirinto* lacework, coloured sand sculpture and beaches. Sand skiing is popular on the dunes and there is good windsurfing and kitesurfing on the Jaguaribe estuary, just outside town, with plenty of options for lessons and equipment rental (see page 564).

Local fishermen have their homes in **Esteves**, a separate village also on top of the cliff; they still live off the sea and rides on *jangadas*, buggy tours and light adventure on zip lines and sandboards can easily be organized in town or on the beach.

Ins and outs Canoa is served by at least four daily buses from Fortaleza; *expresso* or *leito* are fastest. Very frequent *combi* vans connect to Arati from where there are connections into Rio Grande do Norte. Note that the nearest place to change money or find an international ATM is in Aracati. To avoid biting insects and *bicho do pé* (burrowing fleas that frequent dirty beaches), it is best to wear shoes or sandals. For more information, including extensive accommodation listings, visit www.portalcanoaquebrada.com.br.

South of Canoa Quebrada

Heading south from Canoa Quebrada, **Porto Canoa** is a resort town that opened in 1996, fashioned after the Greek islands. It includes beach homes and apartments, shopping areas, restaurants and hotels, and there are facilities for watersports, horse riding, microlight flights, buggy and *jangada* outings.

South of here, **Majorlândia** is a very pleasant village with multi-coloured sand dunes, used in bottle pictures and cord crafts, and a wide beach with strong waves that are good for surfing. The arrival of the fishing fleet in the evening is an important daily event; lobster is the main catch. It is a popular weekend destination with beach homes for rent and plenty of *pousadas*. Unlike many beach locations in Ceará, the area is predominantly Brazilian. **Carnaval** here is quite lively, but you will have no trouble finding a room outside the peak season. The town is easy to find your way around.

About 5 km south along the beach from Majorlândia is the village of **Quixaba**, on a beach surrounded by coloured cliffs, with reefs offshore and good fishing. At low tide you can reach the popular destination of **Lagoa do Mato**, some 4 km south. The *lagoa* can also be reached by buggy from Canoa Quebrada beach (US$30 for four people). There's a hotel, restaurant and pristine beach surrounded by dunes, cliffs and palms.

Ponta Grossa → *Phone code: 088.*

Ponta Grossa, 30 km southeast of Aracati near Icapuí, is the last municipality before Rio Grande do Norte (access from Mossoró) and is reached via a sand road just before Redonda. It's a very pretty place, nestled at the foot of the cliffs, with a beautiful beach.

Ponta Grossa has its own tourism development initiative. The fishing community has many members of Dutch origin, following a shipwreck in the 19th century, and many people have fair hair. It is also one of the few places where *peixe boi marinho* (manatees) can be spotted. There's a good lookout from the cliffs (four-hour buggy ride, US$75 for four).

Beach trips go from Canoa Quebrada (see above) to Ponta Grossa for lunch, but it is possible to stay here (it helps if you can speak Portuguese). A number of cabins are being built and there are several restaurants/bars. The tourism coordinator is Eliabe, T088-3432 5001/9964 5846. For information on community tourism and the preservation of traditional ways of life in Ceará, contact **Instituto Terramar** ① *R Pinho Pessoa 86, Joaquim Távora, Fortaleza, T085-3226 4154/8804 0999*, ask for Esther Neuhaus, *www.terramar.org.br*.

To the south are the beaches of **Redonda**, another very pretty place, and **Barreiras**, which is good for surfing and has a handful of hotels.

The coast west of Fortaleza → *For listings, see pages 555-567.*

The coast northwest of Fortaleza has many wide beaches backed by fixed or shifting dunes, and surrounded by swathes of coconut groves. The main roads are some distance from the shore, making access to the beaches more difficult than on the eastern coast. This means the fishing villages have retained a more traditional lifestyle and a responsible attitude towards travel is especially important.

Praia Barra do Ceará
This long beach lies 8 km northwest of the centre of Fortaleza, where the Rio Ceará flows into the sea (take a 'Grande Circular 1' bus). Here are the ruins of the 1603 **Forte de Nossa Senhora dos Prazeres**, the first Portuguese settlement in the area, partially covered by dunes, from which you can watch the beautiful sunsets. The palm-fringed beaches west of the Rio Ceará are cleaner but have strong waves. An iron bridge has been built across this river, making the area more accessible and open to development, as at **Praia de Icaraí**, 22 km to the northwest, and **Tabuba**, 5 km further north.

Cumbuco → *Colour map 2, A5.*
Cumbuco is a long, white-sand beach backed by foreign-owned hotels and condominiums, a few palms and a handful of little beach shacks; and has a problem with rubbish. The beach itself is nothing special, unless you're a kitesurfer in which case you'll be amazed. There is no better place in Brazil and perhaps the world to learn how to kitesurf; ideal conditions can be guaranteed almost every day of the year. Sadly, as Cumbuco is largely European-owned and locals can no longer afford to buy property here, the town has entirely lost its Brazilian personality. Portuguese is rarely heard and the only locals that remain work in the hotels or restaurants. As well as kitesurfing and windsurfing, there are buggies, horse riding and *jangadas*, as well as dunes (known locally as *skibunda*), which you can slide down into the freshwater **Lagoa de Parnamirim**. A buggy tour costs around US$15 per person.

Cumbuco is served by regular buses from Fortaleza. Allow one to two hours for the journey. For more information visit www.kite-surf-brazil.com.

Pecém and Taíba → *Phone code: 085. Population: 5500 (Pecém).*
Some 58 km northwest of Fortaleza, **Pecém** is a village set in a cove with a wide beach, dunes and inland lagoons. There is strong surf and surfing and fishing championships are held here. From Pecém it is 19 km by road to **Taíba**, a 14-km-long beach with a long palm-covered point extending into the sea. Nearby is **Siupé**, a village that maintains colonial characteristics, where embroidered hammocks, a trademark of Ceará, are made.

Pecém and Taíba are serviced by regular buses from Fortaleza; both have a few simple *pousadas*. The town's central telephone exchange can be reached on T085-344 1064 and T085-3340 1328; any three-digit numbers listed are extensions on these central lines.

Paracuru and Lagoinha → *Phone code: 085. Population: 28,000 (Paracuru).*

Some 106 km northwest of Fortaleza, **Paracuru** is a fishing port which hosts the most important **Carnaval** on the northwest coast, including street dancing and parades, decorated boats, sports championships and a beauty contest. It has some lovely deserted white-sand beaches with good bathing and surfing, and the people are very friendly. There are several *pousadas* in the centre. Restaurant **Ronco do Mar** has good fish dishes. **Boca do Poço** bar has *forró* at weekends. Buses from Fortaleza run at least every hour during the day to the central *rodoviária*, US$5.

West of Paracuru and 12 km from the town of Paraipaba is **Lagoinha**, a very scenic beach with hills, dunes and palms by the shore. There's a fishing village on one of the hills and nearby are some small but pleasant waterfalls. About 3 km west of town is **Lagoa da Barra**, a lake surrounded by dunes. Local legend says that one of the hills, Morro do Cascudo, has hidden treasure left by French pirates. There are six daily buses from Fortaleza to Paracuru and frequent transfers from there to Lagoinha (**Brasileiro**, three hours, US$6); there are plenty of cheap seafood restaurants and *pousadas*.

Fleixeiras and around → *Colour map 2, A4. Phone code: 085.*

Further northwest, some 135 km from Fortaleza, is **Trairi**, access point to a series of beaches that have kept their natural beauty and, until the mid-1990s, were untouched by tourism. North of Trairi, 15 km by road, is **Fleixeiras**, where pools that are good for snorkelling form near the beach at low tide. There are three daily buses from Fortaleza to Fleixeiras (US$7, information T085-3272 4128).

About 5 km west is **Imboaca**, a scenic beach with interesting rock formations and shifting dunes. Further west, at the mouth of the Rio Mundaú, is **Mundaú**, another beautiful area, with a beach, palms, dunes and an old working lighthouse. Take a raft across to the spit and walk for hours on deserted sands, see wind-eroded dunes or take a boat from the quay up the river to see the mangroves. Access roads from Imboaca and Cana to the south are often impassable because of shifting dunes; at low tide it is possible to reach it along the beach from Fleixeiras. There is a fishing village near the beach with some *pousadas* and restaurants.

Jericoacoara → *For listings, see pages 555-567. Colour map 2, A4. Phone code: 088.*

Jericoacoara is another of the northeast's paradise beaches that is getting spoilt. Up until the 1980s it was a magical place: a collection of little fishermen's shacks lost under towering dunes and surrounded by wonderful long, sweeping beaches. São Paulo middle-class hippies used to live here for months, surfing, dancing *forró* and smoking copious amounts of weed. Slowly Jeri began to grow. Then buggies began to race up and down the dunes – including the most delicate, those with fixed vegetation – and local villages started to become tourist attractions. In the 1980s, the Italians discovered Jeri and building began, much of it with braggadocio and little or no environmental considerations; buggies whizzed up and down from dawn to dusk like a plague of motorized flies. Today, few properties or tourism businesses are locally owned and the fishermen and their families are being sidelined and priced out of town.

Environmental concerns in Jericoacoara

Jericoacoara is ostensibly part of an environmental protection area that includes a large coconut grove, lakes, dunes, mangroves and hills covered in *caatinga* vegetation. Degradation, over-building and the marginalization of the local community led Jericoacoarans to write a letter to the World Bank at the turn of the millennium, expressing their concerns about the exploitation of the area and corruption within the federal environmental body, Ibama. The issues persist and there is a growing rubbish problem, but Jeri's beautiful landscape has not been destroyed beyond recuperation. Whether it remains beautiful and wild depends largely on visitors' spending choices. Here are some tips – gleaned from talking to local people.

→ Avoid staying in large hotels, especially the European-run hotels on the beach. One of the largest has cut down protected mangroves to build its facilities.

→ Avoid buying property in Jeri or anywhere along the Ceará coastline. This increases property prices and forces locals off their own land.

→ Where possible we have tried to recommend local, or at least Brazilian businesses or hotels in Jeri. Choosing them will ensure that local families have enough income to continue living in their home town.

→ Buggy tourism has disturbed the dunes and their flora and fauna and has been responsible for a proliferation of plastic litter and cans. Choose to walk on the dunes instead and if you decide to take a buggy tour choose a local small operator and take responsibility for the disposal of your rubbish.

→ Make an effort to speak Portuguese. Generally only non-local Brazilians will speak English. By insisting on speaking English you help create tourist demand that most local fishermen cannot fulfil.

That said, Jeri remains beautiful and it has a long way to go before it becomes as spoilt as Morro de São Paulo, Canoa Quebrada or Cumbuco. If careful choices are made by tourists (such as supporting local businesses, trying to speak Portuguese, participating in Brazilian culture and avoiding buggy tours and large European-run beachfront resorts), it could turn itself into an inspiring sustainable, small-scale resort (see box, above). The nearby beaches offer superb conditions for kitesurfing and windsurfing – both practices that do little to damage the environment – and there is excellent walking and cycling along the long flat beaches to beauty spots like the crumbling chocolate-coloured rock arch at **Pedra Furada**. Sandboarding is popular and watching the sunset from the top of the large dune just west of town, followed by a display of *capoeira* on the beach, is a tradition among visitors.

Ins and outs

There are two direct buses a day from Fortaleza to Jijoca from where *jardineiras* (Toyota pickups) do the 45-minute transfer to Jeri. Be sure to take a *VIP* or *executivo* as the journey takes five to six hours (seven to eight hours on other buses). It is far more comfortable to take an air-conditioned mini-van; these can be organized through *pousadas* in Jeri. Hotels and tour operators run two- to three-day tours from from Fortaleza. If not on a tour, 'guides' will besiege new arrivals in Jijoca with offers of buggies, or guiding cars through the tracks and dunes to Jeri for US$8. If you don't want to do this, ask if a pickup is going or contact **Francisco Nascimento** ⓘ *O Chicão, at Posta do Dê, or T088-3669 1356*, who charges US$5 per person for the 22-km journey (30 minutes). There are connections with the rest of the state through Sobral. Arrivals from Maranhão and Piauí come via Parnaíba (see page 571) and Camocim. There are no banks in town; most *pousadas* and restaurants accept Visa but it is wise to bring plenty of cash in reais. ➤ *See Transport, page 566.*

Around Jericoacoara

Going west along the beach takes you through a succession of sand dunes and coconut groves; the views are beautiful. After 2 km is the beach of **Mangue Seco**, and 2 km beyond this is an arm of the ocean that separates it from **Guriú** (across the bridge), where there is a village on top of a fixed dune. There is good birdwatching here and if you wish to stay hammock space can be found. The village musician sings his own songs in the bar. It's a four-hour walk from Jericoacoara, or take a boat across the bay.

The best surfing, kitesurfing and windsurfing is 10 minutes from town on the pebbly **Praia de Malhada**, reachable either by walking east along the beach or by cutting through town. Top-quality equipment can be rented in Jeri. A 3- to 4-km walk to the east takes you to the **Pedra Furada**, a stone arch sculpted by the sea, one of the landmarks of Jeri, only accessible at low tide (check the tide tables at the **Casa do Turismo**). Swimming is dangerous here as waves and currents are strong. In the same direction but just inland is **Serrote**, a large hill with a lighthouse on top; it is well worth walking up for the magnificent views.

The best kitesurfing and windsurfing beaches are beyond Jeri, some 15 km east of town (43 km by road via Jijoca and Caiçara), at **Praia do Preá** and **Praia de Guriú**. Both beaches are reachable on day tours for around US$50 if you have your own kitesurf. Tours including equipment (US$60) can be arranged in Jeri through www.kiteclubprea.com. There is accommodation on both beaches. At low tide on Preá, you can visit the **Pedra da Seréia**, a rock pocked with natural swimming pools.

Some of the best scenery in the area is around **Nova Tatajuba**, about 35 km west of Jerí. One Toyota a day passes through the town on the way to the ferry point at Camocim and almost all buggy tours visit. There are simple *pousadas* and restaurants and the village is far smaller and less touristy than Jeri. ➤ *See Sleeping, page 558.*

Some 10 km beyond Praia do Preá (62 km by road) is the beach of **Barrinha**, with access to the picturesque **Lagoa Azul**. From here it's 10 km inland through the dunes (20 km along the road) to **Lagoa Paraíso** or **Jijoca**, a turquoise, freshwater lake, great for bathing (buggy US$10 per person).

Cruz

Some 40 km east of Jijoca is Cruz, an obligatory stop if travelling by bus from Sobral to Jericoacoara. It is a small pleasant town, surrounded by a *carnauba* palm forest (used in making brooms). At the south end is a large wooden cross dating from 1825, nearby is a statue to São Francisco. There is a lively market on Sunday when, at dawn, *pau d'arara* trucks, mule carts and bicycles converge on the town. There are two very basic hotels.

Western Ceará → *For listings, see pages 555-567.*

Sobral → *Colour map 2, A4. Phone code: 088. Population: 145,000.*

Sobral, 238 km west of Fortaleza (four hours by bus, US$5), is the principal town in western Ceará and the access point to beaches in the west of the state. The city has a handful of well-preserved colonial buildings including the **Catedral da Sé**, **Teatro São**

João and a mansion on the Praça da Sé. There is a **Museu Diocesano** ① *Praça São João*, a Cristo Redentor statue and a monument to the 1919 solar eclipse. Near town is the **Parque Ecológico Lagoa da Fazenda**.

Chapada de Ibiapaba

Brazil's smallest national park lies in the heart of the Chapada de Ibiapaba mountains in the far northwest of the state. The Chapada is an area of tablelands, caves, rock formations, rivers and waterfalls, most of which is unprotected. There are many small towns and places to visit: **Tianguá** is surrounded by waterfalls; 3 km to the north is Cachoeira de São Gonçalo, a good place for bathing; 5 km from town are natural pools at the meeting place of seven waterfalls; and about 16 km from town, on the edge of the BR-222, is Cana Verde, a 30-m-high waterfall surrounded by monoliths and thick vegetation.

Some 30 km north of Tianguá is **Viçosa do Ceará**, a pretty colonial town also within the *chapada*, known for its ceramics, hang-gliding, food and drink. Climb to the Igreja de Nossa Senhora das Vitórias, a stone church on top of the 820-m-high **Morro do Céu** (reachable by walking up 360 steps), for a good view of the town, the surrounding highlands and the *sertão* beyond. Near the town are interesting rock formations, such as the 100-m-wide **Pedra de Itagurussu** with a natural spring. There is good walking in the area. Basic walking maps are available at the **Secretaria de Turismo**, near the old theatre to the right of the *praça* on which the church stands. Ask about visiting the community that makes sun-baked earthenware pots. There are five buses a day from Fortalezavobral.

Parque Nacional Ubajara → *Colour map 2, A4.*

Some 18 km south of Tianguá, at an altitude of 840 m, is the town of **Ubajara**, with an interesting Sunday morning market selling produce of the *sertão*. Some 3 km from the town is the **Parque Nacional Ubajara**, with 563 ha of native highland and *caatinga* brush. It is the smallest of Brazil's national parks and its main attraction is the **Ubajara cave** on the side of an escarpment. Fifteen chambers extending for a total of 1120 m have been mapped, of which 360 m are open to visitors. Access is along a 6-km footpath and steps (two to three hours, take water) or by a **cable car** ① *T088-3634 1219, 0900-1430, last up at 1500, US$1.50*, which descends the cliff to the cave entrance. Lighting has been installed in nine caverns of the complex. The cave is completely dry and home to 14 types of bat. Several rock formations look like animals, including a horse's head, caiman and a snake; a fact which guides spend much of the tour explaining. In 1979 a speleological expedition found a giant skull in one of the caves, belonging to what was later identified as a previously unknown species of bear related to the Andean spectacled bear, and suggesting that the Serra was far colder 10,000 years ago than it is today.

Ins and outs A guide from the **Instituto Chico Mendes de Conservação da Biodiversidade (ICMBio)** leads visitors through the cave. At the park entrance is an **ICMBio office** ① *5 km from the caves, T085-3634 1388, www.icmbio.gov.br*, and a bar by the entrance serving juices, snacks and drinks. In the park there is a new easy walkway through the woods with stunning views at the end. Start either to the left of the park entrance or opposite the snack bar near the cable-car platform. There is a good 8-km trail to the park from Araticum (7 km by bus from Ubajara). This route is used by locals and passes through *caatinga* forest. There are six buses daily from Fortaleza to Ubajara town. From Jericoacoara it is necessary to change buses in Sobral (which is itself reachable from Jijoca). For more information, including accommodation, see http://portalubajara.com.br and www.ubajara.ce.gov.br.

South from Ubajara

The Chapada de Ibiapaba continues south from Ubajara for some 70 km. Other towns in the highlands are: **Ibiapina**, with the nearby Cachoeira da Ladeira, reached by a steep trail, a good place for bathing; **São Benedito**, known for its straw and ceramic crafts and a working *engenho* sugar mill; and **Carnaubal**, with waterfalls and a bathing resort.

Ipu, 80 km south of Ubajara, is a town at the foot of the Serra de Ibiapaba, on the edge of the *sertão*. It's an interesting transition as you descend from the green serra, with its sugar cane, tall *babaçu* palms and cattle, down the escarpment to the *sertão*. Ipu's main claim to fame is the **Bica do Ipu**, a 180-m waterfall plunging off the sheer edge of the *serra* into a pool; it is said to be the site of the legendary love affair between *Iracema*, a local indigenous Brazilian woman, and the founder of Fortaleza. You can cool off under the falls and there are basic facilities and a few places to stay around town.

If driving, you can cross the *sertão* on good roads via **Varjota** on the large lake of the **Açude de Araras** (33 km), **Santa Quitéria** (a further 41 km) to **Canindé** (111 km on the CE-257).

Monsenhor Tabosa, in the centre of the state, has the highest peak in Ceará, the Pico da Serra Branca, which rises to 1156m, and which is the source of two of the states principal rivers, the Acaraú and the Quixeramobim. The area around the mountain, in the **Serra das Matas**, has been made into an environmental protection area, with *caatinga* and patches of *Mata Atlântica*. There is good day hiking in the hills – none is available through organized tours so you'll have to take a taxi or local bus from Monsenhor Tabosa (ask in the *pousadas*). This remote town is very friendly, with a a handful of very simple hotels (see Sleeping, page 559). It can get very wet in the rainy season (around March). The easiest way to get there is by car or **Horizonte** bus on the CE032 from Canindé, but there are roads from Nova Russas, south of Ipu, and the BR-020 from Boa Viagem (which is very rough).

Continuing south, the greenery of the Chapada de Ibiapaba eventually gives way to the dry **Sertão dos Inhamuns**. One of the main towns in this area is **Crateús**, about 210 km south of Sobral, a remote settlement with rich folkloric traditions seen during the festivals of **Mergulho Folclórico** in August, and the **Festival de Repentistas**, in September. Nearby are archaeological sites with rock inscriptions. There is a regular bus service on the paved road to Fortaleza (347 km). The bus service from Crateús runs along the very bad road to Teresina, every other day.

South of Fortaleza → *For listings, see pages 555-567.*

The Maciço de Baturité mountains → *Colour map 2, A5. Phone code: 085. Population: 32,000. Altitude: 171 m.*

The town of **Baturité**, the largest in the area, is surrounded by the hills and waterfalls of the **Maciço de Baturité**, an irregular massif with beautiful scenery, many waterfalls and good **birdwatching** (which can be organized through the excellent Ciro Albano, see page 564). Baturité is more in the foothills than in the *serra* proper. It has some colonial buildings and a historical museum and is home to the **Pingo de Ouro** distillery, which can be visited. There are several hotels and restaurants, or you can also stay in the **Jesuit seminary** ⓘ *T085-3347 0362 in advance*, where a few monks still work in the local community and tend the cloister garden (**E** per person, full board US$11.10 per day including morning and afternoon coffee with local fruits, ask for 'Jesuitas' if taking a taxi, or walk up). The *rodoviária* is beyond town on the way out to Guaramiranga.

Some 16 km northwest of Baturité, is **Guaramiranga**, the centre of a fruit and flower growing area. At 365 m above sea level, it is reached by a very twisty road through lush vegetation and fruit trees full of birds. There are several *pousadas* along the way. The town is packed with visitors at weekends; if you want to stay overnight you must book in advance. During **Carnaval** (February) there is a **Festival de Jazz and Blues**. To ensure a bed during this time you must book in November. The town also holds a **Festival Nordestino de Teatro** in September in the **Teatro Municipal Rachel de Queiroz**. This is in the centre of town and around it are a number of restaurants including **Café com Flores**, **Taberna Portuguesa**, **O Alemão**, **Confrari** (for pasta and fondue). For information contact secultguaramiranga@hotmail.com.

About 7 km further north is **Pacoti**, with large botanical gardens (*horto forestal*). There are trails for viewing the highland flora, and several waterfalls that are good for a dip. On the main road to Pacoti, turn left at Forquilha to climb **Pico Alto** (1115 m above sea level), previously thought to be the highest peak in Ceará, which offers special views and sunsets. You can go up by car, or if you leave early in the morning you may be able to catch a lift with the school bus.

Juazeiro do Norte → *For listings, see pages 555-567. Colour map 2, B4. Phone code: 088.* *Population: 200,000.*

The south of the state is known as the **Cariri region**, the name of an indigenous group that lived in the interior and resisted Portuguese colonization for a long time. The main centre in this area is Juazeiro do Norte, the second largest city in Ceará. Along with its two satellites, **Crato** and **Barbalha**, 10 km to the west and south respectively, they form an oasis of green in the dry *sertão*.

Juazeiro was home to one of Brazil's most venerated Catholic figures: the miracle-working priest, Padre Cícero Romão Batista, a controversial and very popular figure who championed the rights of Ceara's poor from the 1870s to the 1930s. Even before his death, Padre Cícero had become a legend after a consecrated communion wafer he passed to a woman at Mass reportedly bled in her mouth, and Juazeiro do Norte an important pilgrimage site, drawing the faithful from throughout the northeast and, increasingly, from the whole nation. Today it is the most important pilgrimage centre of the region and visiting during a pilgrimage is an incredible experience. The town is dominated by the imposing Italianate **Sanctuário do Sagrado Coração de Jesus** basilica and a huge sombre **statue of Padre Cicero**, gazing at a distant horizon from the top of the **Colina do Horto** hill, 8 km from the town centre. To get there, either take the pilgrim trail up the hill (one hour, start early because of the heat) or take the **Horto** city bus to the summit. There are also two museums devoted to the priest. The **Memorial Padre Cicero** ① *R São José 242, T088-3512 2240, Mon-Sat 0800-1100 and 1300-1600, Sun 0900-1100 and 1400-1700, free*, is based in the house where he lived and preserves some of his personal belongings and myriad messages from pilgrims including lottery tickets and football coupons that provided winnings after Cicero answered pilgrims prayers. There are even more covering the walls of the **Museu Vivo do Padre Cicero** ① *Colina do Horto, daily 0800-1200 and 1400-1700, free*, together with numerous effigies and devotional books. The priest is buried in the simple church of **chapel of Nossa Senhora do Perpétuo Socorro** ① *Praça do Cinqüentenário, daily 0800-1800, free*, which is completely packed with pilgrims during religious celebrations. Also worth seeing is the **church of Nossa Senhora das Dores** with the adjacent pilgrimage grounds, roughly fashioned after St Peter's Square in Rome.

The town receives six main annual pilgrimages (see Festivals and events, page 563) but visitors arrive all year round and religious tourism is the principal source of income

Another cultural manifestation seen throughout the Cariri region is the *bandas cabaçais ou de pífaros*, musical groups that participate in all celebrations. As well as playing instruments, they dance, imitating animals, and perform games or fights.

Ins and outs

Cariri airport ① *Av Virgílio Távora 4000, T088-3572 0700*, is 6 km from the city and receives flights from Brasília, Fortaleza, Recife, Rio de Janeiro and São Paulo (Guarulhos). A taxi to the centre costs US$5.75 (motorcycle taxi US$3); a taxi to the bus station costs US$8.40. The **rodoviária** ① *Av Delmiro Gouveia s/n, T088-3571 2309*, is on the road to Crato. A taxi to the centre costs US$3 (motorcycle taxi US$0.60). ⯈ *See Transport, page 567.*

ⓔ Ceará listings

For Sleeping and Eating price codes and other relevant information, see pages 32-37.

ⓔ Sleeping

Fortaleza *p540, map p542*
Almost all hotels offer reduced prices in the low season. There are many *pousadas* in the Iracema/Meireles area, but they change frequently. Most hotels in Fortaleza have a strict policy of not accepting overnight visitors except with prior reservations.
C Caxambu, Gen Bezerril 22, opposite the cathedral, T085-3231 0339, caxambu@accvia.com.br. Discounts in low season. Rooms have a/c, TV and fridge. Room service available, breakfast included. Probably best bet in centre, good value.
D-E Backpackers, R Dom Manuel 89, T085-3091 8997, www.backpacksersce.com.br. Central, basic, shared bathrooms, no breakfast, linen, toilet paper or towels but free Wi-Fi, a helpful owner and a lively mixed foreign and Brazilian crowd. 10-min walk from the beach.
E Big, Gen Sampaio 485, Praça da Estação, Centro, T085-3212 2066. All rooms have fan, old lino and clean sheets. Cheaper without TV, even cheaper without bath, simple breakfast, OK, but caution needed at night as it's right in thick of the central scrum.

Beaches

LL-L Beira Mar, Av Beira Mar 3130, T085-4009 2000, Meireles, www.hotelbeiramar.com.br. Newly reformed beachfront hotel with some seafront rooms, others have a side view. Comfortable and safe, with a pool, 24-hr business centre with internet and parking. Good value, especially in low season.
LL-L Imperial Othon Palace, Av Beira Mar 2500, Meireles, T085-3466 5500, www.othon.com.br. Large hotel on the beachfront with all the usual facilities, business and tourists catered for, pool, sauna, massage (recommended *feijoada* on Sat).
LL-L Luzeiro Beira Mar, Av Beira Mar 2600, Meireles, T085-4006 8585, www.hotel luzeiros.com.br. A tall tower built at the turn of the millennium and with functional, business-like rooms with perfunctory design touches, a large pool, sauna and Wi-Fi in public areas and rooms.
LL-L Seara Praia, Av Beira Mar 3080, Meireles, T085-4011 2200, www.hotelseara.com.br. 30% cheaper in low season, smart, comfortable luxury hotel with pool, gym, cyber café, French cuisine.
L Ponta Mar, Av Beira Mar 2200, Meireles, T085-4006 2200, www.ponta mar.com.br. Aimed more at the business market, but still a good and similar facilities.
A Ibis, Atualpa Barbosa de Lima 660, Iracema, T085-3052 2450, www.ibishotel.com. In anonymous **Accor** boardroom-designed style, with functional furniture, modest workstations and Wi-Fi at a price, together with a small pool. Breakfast is extra and discount rates are available online, pushing the hotel into the **B** and very occasionally the **C** price range.

A-B Casa Blanca, R Joaquim Alves 194, T085-3219 0909, www.casablancahoteis.com.br. The best rooms on the upper floors of this tall tower have wonderful sweeping ocean views. All are a/c, well-appointed (if anonymous) and have international TV. Breakfasts are a feast and there's a tiny rooftop pool, a little gym and massage service. Minivans leave from in front of the hotel to Jericoacoara; if waiting for a minivan, an a/c room costs US$50 for 4 hrs.

B Abrolhos Praia, Av Abolição 2030, 1 block from the beach, Meireles, T/F085-3248 1217, www.abrolhospraiahotel.com.br. Pleasant, TV, fridge, hot shower, a/c, rooms look a bit sparse but no different from others in this category, soft beds, discount in low season, internet.

B Praia de Iracema, Raimundo Girão 430, Iracema, T085-3219 2299, www.hotelpraia deiracema.com. 20% discount in low season, a/c, TV, fridge, safe in room, coffee shop, pool, brightly coloured bedcovers, on corner so traffic outside, but OK for value and comfort.

B Villamaris, Av Abolição 2026, Meireles, T085-3248 0112, www.hotelvillamaris.com.br. **C** Plain, simple a/c rooms with cream painted, crinkle concrete walls a tiny work table and international TV. Good location.

B Casa de Praia, R Joaquim Alves 169, T085-3219 1022, www.hotelcasadepraia.com.br. Well-kept, modest a/c rooms in warm colours and with international TV, Wi-Fi. The best are above the 4th floor and have partial ocean views. There's a little rooftop pool. Minivans leave from in front of the hotel of Jeri.

B-C Ideal Praia, R Antonele Bezerra 281, T085-3248 7504, www.hotelideal.com.br. A mock-colonial hotel in a quiet little back street offering 2 kinds of rooms. Those on the ground floor are decorated with mock-marble tiles and have little windows. Those on the upper floors have ocean views and little terraces. All are well kept, homey and have international TV and a/c. There's a mouse-size pool on the roof.

B-D Pousada do Suíço, R Antônio Augusto 141, Iracema, T085-3219 3873, www.pension-vom-schweizer.com. A justifiably popular, well-kept and well-run budget hotel in an excellent location near the beach. It is quiet, discreet and on one of the less noisy streets. There are a variety of rooms, some more spacious than others, a number with kitchens, and all a/c and with a TV and fridge. The Swiss owner runs a decent restaurant a few blocks away and can organize tours and give travel advice. Be sure to reserve mid-Oct-Feb.

C Pousada Salinas, Av Zezé Diogo 3300, Praia do Futuro, T085-3234 3626, www.pousadasalinas.com.br. **D** in low season, popular, a/c, TV, fridge, parking, just across from sea, some English spoken.

C-D Ondas Verdes, Av Beira Mar 934, Iracema, T085-3219 0871, www.centernet. psi.br/hotelondasverdes. Scruffy hotel beloved of backpackers even though there are better options nearby. Rooms are musty; be sure to look at several.

C-D Panorâmica, R Idelfonso Albano 464, T085-3219 8347, www.portalde hospedagem.com.br. Very simple peach and grey tile boxes. The best by far are on the upper floors, have partial ocean views and little terraces. In a quiet location.

Camping

Fortaleza Camping Club (do Professor), R Vereador Pedro Paulo Moreira 505, Águas Frias, T085-3273 2544. Around 10 km east of the airport. Lots of shade, US$7 per person.

Pousada dos Pinheiros, R Paulo Mendes 333, Praia do Futuro, T085-3234 5590, marcosacleite@ig.com.br. On the beach.

Aquiraz and around *p545*

In Águas Belas, there are simpler rooms available in private houses.

B Kalamari, Av Beira Mar, Porto das Dunas beach, T085-3361 7500, www.kalamari.com.br. Small beach hotel with balconied rooms overlooking a smart pool. Equidistant between Fortaleza and Aquiraz. Tours organized.

B Pousada Villa Francesa, Av Beira Mar, Prainha, 1.5 km from the beach, T085-3361 5007, www.villafrancesa.com. Tiny 8 room, French-run beach hotel that opened in 2005.

Rooms are gathered around a smart pool and the hotel offers tours and internet.

B-C Pousada Mama Rosália Via Local 19, Porto das Dunas beach T085-3361 7491, www.pousadamamarosalia.com.br. Family-run beach hotel with simple tile-floor and whitewash rooms with en suites, a restaurant and a pool.

Morro Branco and Praia das Fontes *p545*

L Praia das Fontes, Av A Teixeira 1, Praia das Fontes, T085-3338 1179, www.oasisatlantico.com. Luxurious resort, watersports, horse hire, tennis courts and a simple spa. Recommended.

B Das Falésias, Av Assis Moreira 314, Praia das Fontes, T085-3327 3052, www.hotel falesias.com.br. Pleasant German-owned cliff-side *pousada* with a pool and tidy rooms.

B Recanto Praiano, Morro Branco, T085-3338 7229, www.recantopraianopousada.com.br. Peaceful little *pousada* with a good breakfast. Recommended.

C Pousada Sereia, on the beach, Morro Branco, T085-3330 1144. Lovely simple *pousada* with an excellent breakfast and friendly staff. Highly recommended.

D Rosalias, Morro Branco, T085-3330 1131. Very simple and somewhat run down but only 50 m from the bus stop, and with a shared kitchen.

Prainha do Canto Verde *p546*

There are also houses for rent (eg **Casa Cangulo** or **Vila Marésia**). Note that prices rise by 30% for the regatta and over Christmas and Semana Santa.

E Dona Mirtes. Price includes breakfast, will negotiate other meals.

Canoa Quebrada *p547*

Villagers will let you sling your hammock or will put you up cheaply. **Verónica** is recommended, European books exchanged. **Sr Miguel** rents good clean houses for US$10 a day.

AL Tranqüilândia, R Camino do Mar, T088-3421 7012, www.tranquilandia.it.

A range of thatched roofed, a/c chalets around a smart pool in a lawned tropical garden. Decent restaurant. Italian-owned and with facilities for kitesurfers.

B Pousada Latitude, R Dragão do Mar (Broadway), T088-3241 7041, www.pousada latitude.com.br. Large a/c 2-storey bungalows in a large complex off the main street. Not intimate but with decent service.

B-C Pousada Lua Estrela, R Nascer do Sol 106, T088-3421 7040, www.portalcanoaquebrada. com.br. A smart hostel/*pousada* with with fan-cooled rooms with great sea views, fridges and hot showers and a/c rooms without views in the garden. 20 m off R Dragão do Mar.

C Pousada Alternativa, R Francisco Caraço, T088-3421 7278, www.pousada-alternativa. com.br. Rooms with or without bath. Centrally located and recommended.

C Pousada Oásis do Rei, R Nascer do Sol 112, T088-3421 7081, www.pousadaoasisdorei. com.br. Simple rooms around a pool in a little garden, with polished concrete or tiled floors; some with sea views and some with bed space for 3 or 4.

C Pousada Via Láctea, just off R Dragão do Mar (Broadway), www.pousadavialactea.com. This chunky brick building may not be beautiful, but the views are and the beach is only some 50 m away. English spoken and tours organized. Highly recommended.

C-E Pousada Azul, R Dragão do Mar (Broadway) s/n, T088-9932 9568 (mob), www.portalcanoaquebrada.com.br/. Very simple, small concrete and blue tile a/c or fan-cooled boxes, a sunny upper deck, miniature pool and warm service from the owner Saméa.

E-F Albergue Ibiza, R Dragão do Mar (Broadway) s/n, T088-8804 7603 (mob), www.portalcanoaquebrada.com.br/canoa_ quebrada_albergue_ibiza.htm. Tiny, boxy but astonishingly cheap and fairly spruce doubles and dorms 200 m from the beach.

Paracuru and Lagoinha *p549*

There are a number of cheaper hotels on both beaches; it's worth shopping around.

C Dunas, Paracuru, T085-3344 1965, http://hoteldunas.com.br. Family-orientated hotel with a small water park next door and range of very simple rooms gathered around a pool.

C-D Mar e Vista, Av Francisco Azevedo 170, Lagoinha, T085-3363 5038, www.pousada-maravista.com. The are great views from this clifftop hotel more than make up for the very simple rooms; ask for one at the front with a shared terrace and hammock area.

Jericoacoara *p549*

There are crowds at weekends mid-Dec to mid-Feb, in Jul and during Brazilian holidays. Many places full in low season too. For New Year's Eve, 4- to 5-day packages are available. Prices rise by as much as 40% in peak season (New Year and Carnaval).

L Vila Kalango, R do Instituto Chico Mendes de Conservação da Biodiversidade (ICMBio) s/n, T088-3669 2289, www.vilakalango.com.br. The smartest option in town with well-appointed rooms in stilt house cabins in a tree-filled garden just set-back from the beach. Lovely pool and bar area, a decent restaurant and excellent facilities for kitesurfers and windsurfers. There's a sister hotel, Rancho do Peixe, on Praia da Preá. Shuttle buses to/from Fortaleza.

A-B Espaço Nova Era, R do Forró s/n, T088-3669 2056, www.novaerapousada.com.br. A mock-Mediterranean lobby house leads to a set of circular a/c or fan-cooled cabins in terracotta brick and polished concrete. These sit in an Italianate garden shaded by trees and coloured with tropical flowers. Room for 5 in the larger cabins making this an economical option. Italian-owned.

B Barão, R do Forró 433, T088-3669 2136 www.recantodobarao.com. Duplex rooms in 2 corridors strung with hammocks. All overlook the corridors and *pousada* gardens and the brightest and best-kept rooms are on the upper floors. The *pousada* has a small pool and attractive sitting areas furnished with sun beds. There is a popular *churrascaria* next door. São Paulo owned.

C Papagaio, Trav do Forró s/n, T088-3669 2142, pousadapapagaio@hotmail.com, Attractive, stone-floored a/c rooms with pretty pebble-dash bathrooms and hammock-strung verandas overlooking a courtyard garden shaded by prickly pears and with a tiny pool. Brazilian owned.

C Pousada Tirol, R São Francisco 202, T088-3669 2006, www.jericoacoarahostel.com.br HI-affiliated hostel with dorms (**E** per person) with hot water showers and scrupulously cleaned doubles (**C-D** in low season) with barely room for a double and a single bed. Very friendly and popular with party-loving travellers. Very busy cybercafé, US$3 per hr; 10 mins free use for all guests.

C Pousada Zé Patinha, R São Francisco s/n, T088-3669 2081, www.sandjeri.com.br, Simple, a/c or fan-cooled tiled rooms and plain white rooms in 2 parallel corridors. No outside windows, just overlooking the corridor. Cool in the heat of the day, quiet, with decent mattresses and locally owned.

D Pousada Zé Bento, R São Francisco s/n, T088-3669 2006, Small, tiled rooms with white walls and little en suites off a small, palm shaded and sandy garden annex. Friendly, tours organized, locally owned.

Around Jericoacoara *p551*

D Rancho do Peixe, Praia do Preá, T088-9966 2111, www.ranchodopeixe.com.br. Chic bungalows set right on the beach next to a long pool. All have hammock verandas and are fan-cooled. Special rates and excellent facilities for kitesurfers and windsurfers.

Tatajuba

There are a handful of very simple *pousadas* in this village between Camocim and Jericoacoara. These include:

E Pousada Brisa do Mar, T088-9961 5439 with spartan and very basic rooms some with en suites. There are plenty of simple seafood restaurants in town, the most famous of which is the **Barraca de Dona Delmira**.

Cruz p551

F Hospedaria, R 6 de Abril 314. Very basic, simple little *pousada* with tiny rooms.
F Hotel Magalhães, R Teixeira Pinto 390. Very basic, shared bath, friendly, meals available.

Western Ceará p551

D Pousada Doce Lar, R Felipe Sampaio 181, Centro, Itapajé, T085-3346 1432. Clean and comfortable; ask for a room with a mountain view. No restaurant on site but some close by.

Sobral p551

A Beira Rio, R Conselheiro Rodrigues 400 across from the *rodoviária*, T088-3613 1040. A/c (cheaper with fan), fridge.
A Visconde, Av Lúcia Saboia 473, 10 mins from the *rodoviária*, T088-3611 4222. Friendly, a/c (cheaper with fan), good breakfast.
B Cisne, Trav do Xerez 215, T/F088-3611 0171. A/c, cheaper with fan, friendly.
B Vitória, Praça Gen Tibúrcio 120, T088-3613 1566. Bath, a/c (cheaper with fan), some rooms without bath (**C**), restaurant.
D Francinet's, R Col Joaquim Ribeiro 294. With fan, bath (cheaper with shared bath).

Chapada de Ibiapaba p552

A Serra Grande, about 2 km from town, BR-222, Km 311, T088-3671 1818. All the usual amenities, good.
C Complexo de Lazer Rio's, Viçosa do Ceará, Km 4.5 on the road from Tianguá, T088-3632 1510/1099. Swiss-style chalets, water park, good local food in the restaurant.

Parque Nacional Ubajara p552

B-D Pousada Sítio do Alemão, Estrada do Teleférico, near the park, 2 km from town, T/F088-9961 4645, www.sitio-do-alemao. 20fr.com. Take Estrada do Teleférico 2 km from town, after the **Pousada da Neblina** turn right, signposted, 1 km to Sítio Santana/Klein (Caixa Postal 33, Ubajara, CEP 62350-000, T088-9961 4645). Herbert Kelin's 5-chalet *pousada* sits in an old coffee and banana plantation surrounded by beautiful cloud-forest, and with sweeping views over the

serra and plains. The chalets vary in size. The largest has 2 bedrooms and the smallest and cheapest, shared bathrooms. A generous breakfast is included in the price and **Casa das Delícias** in Ubajara will send lasagne for other meals (the restaurant is owned by Mrs Klein). The *pousada* will pick-up from the *rodoviária* in Ubajara town, given notice. Excursions organized and bicycle hire.
C Pousada Gruta da Ubajara, T088-3634 1375, portalubajara.com.br/pousadagruta. htm. Sits just 50 m from the entrance to the park, and has a dozen lemon and orange concrete chalets, some with room for 4 people, and a restaurant serving spit-roast meat, stewed chicken and the owner's potent, home-made *cachaça*.
C-D Paraíso, in the centre, Ubajara, T085-3634 1913. The best of a poor lot in Ubajara town, with plain, but bright rooms decked out in granite and whitewash, the best of which have small terraces. Rooms at the back are quietest.

Camping

Sítio do Bosco, 8 km from Tianguá on the BR 222 towards Teresina, T088-9413 0269, www.sitiobosco.com.br. With shady sites, great views over the hills, a cave on site, spring-water swimming pool, restaurant and organized hang-gliding and excursions.

South from Ubajara p553

C-D Pousada de Inhuçu, R Gonçalo de Freitas 454, São Benedito, T088-3626 3232, www.clubepousada.com.br, in Inhuçu village, 7 km from São Benedito and 30 km from Ubajara NP. A welcoming, small, country hotel with 16 modest, white-wall and raw wood fan-cooled rooms all of which have hammock terraces, some of which are large enough for families (children under 5 stay free). The hotel has a sauna, swimming pool and can organize trips to nearby waterfalls and Ubajara NP.
C-D Queda d'Agua, R Cel Félix 897, Ipu, T088-3683 1885, www.pousadaquedadagua. com.br. An excellent-value, family-run town

hotel with corridors of plain but well-kept rooms, all with a shared terrace, a/c and bathrooms. Friendly owners offer a large breakfast and can give advice on excursions in the serra, which is almost on the doorstep. A map on the website gives full details of how to reach the *pousada*.

Monsenhor Tabosa

The town is tiny. There are 3 basic *pousadas*: **dos Viajantes**, **São Sebastião** and **Pousada Gaia**, just behind the cemetery on the road out to Santa Quitéria (T088-3696 1904); ask for Márcia or Honório Júnior. Honório will draw rough walking maps in the Serra and, if asked, can arrange for the *forró* band to play.

The Maciço de Baturité Mountains *p553*
B Senac Hotel Escola de Guaramiranga, Guaramiranga, T/F088-3321 1106, www.ce. senac.br. A large concrete complex with a big swimming pool and a pleasant wooded setting, some 500 m outside town up a road from the main street (past Parque das Trilhas). Rooms are all a/c suites, with fridge and hot water and the hotel has a reasonable restaurant. The grounds have forest walks, orchards and an old convent. As the hotel doubles as a tourism school and hosts lots of events it's an idea to enquire ahead.
B-C Hofbräuhaus, Estrada de Aratuba, Chapada de Lameirão, Mulungu, T085-3221 6170, www.hofbrauhaus-brasil.com. Run by Wolfgang Helmut Rühle, who has restaurants in Guaramiranga (O Alemão), Pacoti and Fortaleza; he speaks German, English and Portuguese. Rooms are homely and each one is designed in a different style (Spanish, Arabic, Japanese, etc). All are very clean and smart. Rooms with veranda cost a little more. Prices are cheaper Mon-Thu (a bargain). The restaurant is German and Cearense. All vegetables and herbs (for all the restaurants) are grown on the property; it, also has a snail farm for the house speciality. Lots of flowers and grapes, far-reaching views over the *sertão*, mini-disco, small business centre, completely safe. Exceptional.

B-C Remanso Hotel da Serra, 5 km north of Guaramiranga, T088-3231 7088, www.remansohoteldeserra.com.br. A big mountain resort, with serroed ranks of chalets lined up on the shore of a small artificial lake. The complex is set in pretty remnant cloudforest and trails lead directly from the grounds into the woods. There are swimming pools for both adults and children, 2 restaurants and a playground. Excursions are available through reception. Avoid weekend stays which can be noisy. Rooms cheapest on triple or quadruple share. Breakfast not included in the price.
B-D Parque das Cachoeiras, Estrada CE 356, Km 7 between Baturité and Guaramiranga, T085-8886 5575/3302 1416, www.hotelparque dascachoeiras.com.br. One of the newest openings in the Maciço de Baturité, with very simple, rooms (with no more than a bed and a wardrobe) in a beautiful setting in cloudforest and next to a rushing mountain stream. The owners organize trail walks and excursions into the park and to the Jesuit seminary (which is in walking distance of the hotel).

Juazeiro do Norte *p554*
Expect prices to be higher during pilgrimages. There are many basic hotels and *hospedarias* for pilgrims on R São José and around Nossa Senhora das Dores basilica.
AL Verde Vales Lazer, Av Plácido Alderado Castelo s.n, Lagoa Seca, 3 km from town on the road to Barbalha, T/F088-3566 2544, www.hotel verdesvales.com.br. A resort housed in a large modern mansion house next to a water park on the edge of the city. The 97 rooms are in the annexe – spread along long corridors. All are modern, spruce and orientated to both families and business travellers. Facilties include a games room, pool, internet access, tennis courts, sauna and restaurant.
B-C Panorama, Santo Agostinho 58, T088-3566 3150, www.panoramhotel.com.br. An 8-storey tower conveniently located in the centre of the city with great views from the upper floors. Rooms are simple but fairly well-appointed and with decent beds. The best

are the 5 suites. There's a tiny, unappealing pool, restaurant and internet access.

C-D Plaza, Padre Cícero 148, T088-3511 0493. With bath, a/c, cheaper with fan and cheaper still with shared bath.

D Hotel Aristocrata, R São Francisco 402, T088-3511 1889. A very simple family-run 2-star option in the city centre, with a/c rooms, the cheapest without fridges and a small restaurant.

D San Felipe, Av Dr Floro Bartolomeu 285, T088-3511 7904, www.sanfelipehotel.com.br. A range of plain but recently refurbished a/c rooms in a little concrete block in the town centre. Those on the upper floors have with a good view of Padre Cícero's statue.

🍴 Eating

Fortaleza *p540, map p542*
Iracema and Dragão do Mar
2 good areas for restaurants, with plenty of variety. There are many eateries of various styles at the junction of **Tabajaras** and **Tremembés**, mostly smart.

♥♥ Amici's, R Dragão do Mar 80. Pasta, pizza and lively atmosphere in music-filled street, evenings only. Some say it's the best at the cultural centre.

♥♥ Colher do Pau, R Tabajaras 412, Iracema. Daily from 1830. *Sertaneja* food, seafood, indoor and outdoor seating, live music. Recommended.

♥♥ Estoril, R dos Tabajaras 397, Iracema. Varied food in this landmark restaurant, which is also a catering school.

♥♥ Romagna Mia, R Joaquim Alves 160. Very good fresh seafood, pasta and genuine thin crust Italian pizza made by an Italian ex-pat resident of at least 20 years and served in a little garden shaded by vines tiled with mock-Copacabana dragon's tooth paving.

♥♥ Sobre O Mar, R dos Tremembés 2, T085-3219 6999, www.sobreomardiracema.com.br. The perfect vantage point for watching the sky fade from deep red through to lilac over the pier and the green sea at the end of the

day. Sit with an icy batida in hand (the *vodka com abacaxi* is excellent) or a petit gateau with chocolate sauce under your spoon. But eat your main course elsewhere.

♥ Brazão, R João Cordeiro corner of Av R Girão, Iracema. The only place open 24 hrs, but the food is not that special.

♥ Habanera, R Tabajaras at Ararius, T088-3219 2259. Cuban cigars, great coffee and pastries or, as they are known in Portuguese, *salgados*. Try the *empadas*.

♥ Santa Clara Café Orgânico, R Dragão do Mar 81, at end of red girder walkway (or upstairs depending which way you go), www.santaclara.com.br. Café, delicious organic coffees, juices, cold drinks, plus sandwiches and desserts.

Beaches

Several good fish restaurants at **Praia de Mucuripe**, where the boats come ashore 1300-1500. R J Ibiapina, at the Mucuripe end of Meireles, 1 block behind the beach, has pizzerias, fast food restaurants and sushi bars.

♥♥♥-♥♥ La Fiorentina, Osvaldo Cruz 8, corner of Av Beira Mar, Meireles. Some seafood expensive, but there's also fish, meats and pasta. Unpretentious, attentive waiters, good food, frequented by tourists and locals alike.

♥♥♥-♥ Ideal, Av Abolição e José Vilar, Meireles. Open 0530-2030. Bakery serving lunches, small supermarket and deli, good, handy.

Cumbuco *p548*
Accommodation can be organized through **Hi Life** (see Activities and tours, page 564).

Jericoacoara *p549*
There are several restaurants serving vegetarian and fish dishes.

♥♥ Bistrogonoff, Beco do Guaxelo 60, T088-3669 2220. Fish and meat combinations, stroganoffs and a healthy selection of pastas. Convivial atmosphere, very popular in the evenings. Owners from São Paulo.

♥♥ Na Casa Dela, R Principal, T088-3669 2024. Northeastern Brazilian and Bahian cooking from owners from São Paulo and Rio Grande do Norte, including delicious sun-dried meat with onions, manioc flour, rice and pureed squash. The dining is intimate with tables mood-lit and sitting in the sand under their own private *palapa*. Waitresses are dressed in colourful regional dresses.

Ⅲ Sky, R Principal on the beach. A popular sunset bar and evening chill-out space with tables under the stars, mood-music and decent though somewhat over-priced cocktail standards.

Ⅰ Do Sapão, R São Francisco s/n, T088-9905 8010. Good-value *prato feito*, set meals including a delicious vegetarian pizzas and pastas. Live music. Named in homage to the giant toads that appear everywhere in Jeri after dark.

Ⅰ Kaze Sushi, R Principal. Decent, fresh sushi and sashimi, miso soups and fruit juices.

Ⅰ Restaurante do Suiço, R Antônio Augusto and José Agustinho, Iracema, T085-3219 3873. Expats and locals flock to this lively little restaurant, a few blocks inland from Iracema beach, to eat the superior wood-fired pizzas, fondues and rosti, and sip caipirainha cocktails and cheap, very cold beer. There's table football and live music some evenings.

🌙 Bars and clubs

Fortaleza p540, map p542
Fortaleza is renowned for its nightlife and prides itself on having the liveliest Mon night in the country. Some of the best areas for entertainment, with many bars and restaurants are: **Av Beira Mar**, **Praia de Iracema**, the hill above **Praia de Mucuripe** and **Av Dom Luís**. *Forró* is the most popular dance and there is a tradition to visit certain establishments on specific nights. The most popular entertainment areas are the large **Dragão do Mar** complex and the bars just east of the Ponte dos Ingleses and around O Pirata.
Mon *Forró* is danced at the **Pirata Bar**, Iracema, US$15, open-air theme bar, from 2300, and other establishments along R dos Tabajaras and its surroundings.

Tue Live golden oldies at **Boate Oásis**, Av Santos Dumont 6061, Aldeota.
Wed Regional music and samba-reggae at **Clube do Vaqueiro**, city bypass, Km 14, by BR-116 south and E-020, at 2230.
Thu Live music, shows at Pirata and in the adjacent bars.
Fri Singers and bands play regional music at **Parque do Vaqueiro**, BR-020, Km 10, past city bypass.
Sat *Forró* at **Parque Valeu Boi**, R Trezópolis, Cajueiro Torto, **Forró Três Amores**, Estrado Tapuio, Eusébio and **Cantinho do Céu**, CE-04, Km 8.
Sun *Forró* and *música sertaneja* at **Cajueiro Drinks**, BR-116, Km 20, Eusébio.

The streets around Centro Cultural Dragão do Mar on R Dragão do Mar are lively every night of the week. Brightly painted, historic buildings house restaurants, where musicians play to customers and the pavements are dotted with cocktail carts.
Caros Amigos, R Dragão do Mar 22. Live music at 2030: Tue, Brazilian instrumental; Wed, jazz; Thu, samba; Sun, Beatles covers, US$1 (also shows music on the big screen).
Restaurant e Crêperie Café Crème, R Dragão do Mar 92. Live music on Tue.

Jericoacoara p549
There are frequent parties to which visitors are welcome. About once a week in high season there is a folk dance show that includes *capoeira*. There is nightly *forró* in high season at the **Casa do Forró**, R do Forró, a couple of blocks inland from the beach (low season on Wed and Sat only); starts about 2200. This is the centre of Jeri nightlife, aside from the bars near or along the beach like the European-orientated **Planeta Jeri** on R Principal.

🎭 Entertainment

Fortaleza p540, map p542
Cinema For information about cinema programming, T139.

Theatre In the centre are **Teatro José de Alencar**, Praça José de Alencar (see page 542), and **Teatro São José**, R Rufino de Alencar 363, T085-3231 5447, both with shows all year.

⊛ Festivals and events

Fortaleza p540, map p542
6 Jan Epiphany.
Feb Ash Wed.
19 Mar São José.
Jul Last Sun in Jul is the **Regata Dragão do Mar**, Praia de Mucuripe, with traditional *jangada* (raft) races. During the last week of Jul, the out-of-season Salvador-style carnival, **Fortal**, takes place along Av Almte Barroso, Av Raimundo Giro and Av Beira Mar. In Caucaia, 12 km to the southeast, a **vaquejada**, traditional rodeo and country fair, takes place during the last weekend of Jul.
15 Aug, the local *umbanda terreiros* (churches) celebrate the **Festival of Iemanjá** on Praia do Futuro, taking over the entire beach from noon till dusk, when offerings are cast into the surf. Well worth attending (members of the public may '*pegar um passo*' – enter into an inspired religious trance – at the hands of a *pai-de-santo*). Beware of pickpockets and purse-snatchers.
Mid-Oct **Ceará Music**, a 4-day festival of Brazilian music, rock and pop, is held in Marina Park.

Canoa Quebrada p547
Jul In the second half of the month is the **Canoarte** festival, which includes a *jangada* regatta and music festival.

Juazeiro do Norte p554
6 Jan Reis Magos (Epiphany).
2 Feb Candeias (Candelmas), Nossa Senhora da Luz.
24 Mar **Padre Cícero's birth** and one of the biggest pilgrimages and celebrations of the year.

20 Jul **Padre Cícero's death**. With up to 300,000 pilgrims from all over the northeast.
10-15 Sep Nossa Senhora das Dores, the city's patron saint.
1-2 Nov **Finados**, the city receives 600,000 visitors for the All Saints' Day pilgrimages.

⊙ Shopping

Fortaleza p540, map p542
Bookshops
Livraria Livro Técnico, see Dragão do Mar, page 543. Several branches including on Dom Luís, Praça Ferreira, **Shopping Norte** and at UFC university.
Livraria Nobel bookstore and coffee shop in **Del Paseo** shopping centre in Aldeota.
Siciliano, bookstore and coffee shop in new part of **Iguatemi** shopping mall, with just a bookstore in the old part.

Handicrafts
Fortaleza has an excellent selection of locally manufactured textiles, which are among the cheapest in Brazil, and a wide selection of regional handicrafts. The local craft specialities are lace and embroidered textile goods; hammocks (US$15-100); fine alto-relievo woodcarvings of northeast scenes; basket ware; leatherwork; and clay figures (*bonecas de barro*). Bargaining is okay at the **Mercado Central**, Av Alberto Nepomuceno (closed Sun), and the **Emcetur Centro de Turismo** in the old prison. Crafts also available in shops near the market, while shops on R Dr João Moreira 400 block sell clothes. Every night (1800-2300) there are stalls along the beach at Praia Meireles. Crafts also available in the commercial area along Av Monsenhor Tabosa.

Shopping centres
The biggest is **Iguatemi**, south of Meireles on way to Centro de Convenções; it also has modern cinemas. Others are **Aldeota** and **Del Paseo** in Aldeota, near Praça Portugal.

▲ Activities and tours

Fortaleza p540, map p542
Kitesurfing, windsurfing and surfing
Ceará is one of the best palces in the world
for kitesurfing and windsurfing. The major
centres are Cumbuco and Jericoacoara.
The sport is also popular in Canoa Quebrada.
Rental equipment can be found at all 3 (see
the relevant section, below). In Fortaleza,
equipment for kitesurfing and windsurfing
can be rented at some of the popular
beaches, such as Porto das Dunas. Surfing
is popular on a number of Ceará beaches.
Bio Board, Av Beira Mar 914, T085-3242 1642,
www.bioboard.com.br. A windsurfing and kitesurfing school. Looks after equipment for you.
Hi Life, Av Beira Mar 2120, Praia dos Diários,
T085-9982 5449, www.kite-surf-brazil.com.
The best kitesurf school in the area (see
Cumbuco, below, for further details).

Tour operators
Many operators offer city and beach tours.
Others offer adventure trips further afield,
most common being off-road trips along
the beaches from Natal in the east to the
Lençois Maranhenses in the west.
Ceará Saveiro, Av Beira Mar 4293, T085-3263
1085. *Saveiro* and yacht trips, daily 1000-1200
and 1600-1800 from Praia de Mucuripe.
Dunnas Expedições, R Silva Paulet 1100,
Aldeota, T085-3264 2514, www.dunnas.com.br.
Off-road tours with a fleet of white Land Rovers.
Experienced, environmentally and culturally
aware, very helpful and professional staff.
Martur, Av Beira Mar 4260, T085-3263 1203.
Sailing trips, from Mucuripe, same schedule
as Ceará Saveiro.
Sunny Tour, Av Prof A Nunes Freire 4097,
Dionísio Torres, T085-3258 2337, also has
a stand on Av Beira Mar near the craft fair.
Beach tours and trips to Jericoacoara.

Canoa Quebrada p547
Kite Flat Water, R Dragão do Mar, T085-9604
4953, www.brasilkiteflatwater.com. Kite-surfing
rental and excursions at Canoa Quebrada.

Cumbuco p548
Hi Life, Av Dos Coqueiros s/n, Cumbuco,
Caucaia, T085-3318 7195, www.kite-surf-
brazil.com. One of the leading kitesurf schools
in Ceará. Can arrange full tours from Europe
and organize hotels in Cumbuco and transfers.

Jericoacoara p549
Buggy tours cost US$44.45 for a buggy to all
the sites; contact the Associação de Bugueiros
(ABJ), R Principal, *barraca* near Instituto Chico
Mendes de Conservação da Biodiversidade
(ICMBio). If seeking a *bugueiro* who speaks
English, Spanish, Italian and French, ask for
Alvaro, the school teacher, who is Uruguayan.
Vila Kalango and **Peixe Galo**, are orientated
to kitesurfers and organize some of the
best kitesurf excursions in Jeri.
Clube dos Ventos, R das Dunas, T088-621
0211, www.clubventos.com. Windsurfing
and kitesurfing at Preá and Lagoa Jijoca.
Equipment hire, courses and transfers.

Parque Nacional Ubajara p552
Birdwatching
Ciro Albano Birding Brazil, T085-9955 5162,
www.nebrazilbirding.com. The best and most
experienced birdwatching guide in the northeast of Brazil, offering bespoke and scheduled
trips to the Maciço de Baturité and other
locations in Ceará, as well as further afield in
Bahia, Alagoas, Pernambuco, Sergipe and Minas.
Speaks English and will pick-up from airports
in Fortaleza or Salvador and organize transport
and accommodation in an all-in package.

Hang-gliding
Sítio do Bosco, T088-9413 0269, www.sitio
bosco.com.br. Hang-gliding from the Serra
de Ibiapaba near Ubajara.

⊖ Transport

Fortaleza p540, map p542
Air
To get to the airport, bus No 404 runs from
Praça José de Alencar in the centre, US$1.50.

Expresso Guanabara minibuses run from the *rodoviária* and Beira Mar (US$2). Taxis to the centre cost US$25, US$30 at night (30 mins, allowing for traffic). There are regular international flights to **Portugal** (Lisbon), **Italy** (Milan, Rome and Verona) and the **Guianas** via Belém.

Airline contacts Air Italy, www.airitaly. it. GOL, Av Santos Dumont 2727, Aldeota, T085-3266 8000, freephone T0800-997000, www.voegol.com.br. **Avianca**, www.Avianca. com.br. TAF, www.voetaf.com.br. TAM, www.tam.com.br. TAP Air Portugal, www.fly tap.com. Webjet, www.webjet.com.br, Azul, www.voeazul.com.br.

Bus

Local Many city buses run to the *rodoviária* (US$1.50), including 'Aguanambi' 1 or 2 which go from Av Gen Sampaio, 'Barra de Fátima-Rodoviária' from Praça Coração de Jesus, 'Circular' for Av Beira Mar and the beaches, and 'Siqueira Mucuripe' from Av Abolição. A taxi from Praia de Iracema or Av Abolição costs about US$15.

For the eastern beaches near Fortaleza (**Prainha**, **Iguape**, **Barro Preto**, **Batoque**) and towns such as **Aquiraz**, **Eusêbio** or **Pacajus**, you must take São Benedito buses, T085-3272 2544, from the *rodoviária*. To **Beberibe**, 10 a day US$8. To **Cascavel** US$1.10. To **Morro Branco** at 0745, 1000, 1515, 1750, US$2.25. To **Canoa Quebrada** at 0830, 1100, 1340, 1540 (plus 1730 on Sun) US$4.25. To **Aracati** at 0630, 0830, 1100, 1340, 1540, 1900 last back at 1800, US$4.90. There are regular buses to the western beaches near Fortaleza, including **Cumbuco**, from the *rodoviária*.

Long-distance Redenção buses from Fortaleza to **Jericoacoara** from the *rodoviária* 0900, 1700 and the Av Beira Mar at the Posta Telefônica opposite **Praiano Palace Hotel** 30 mins later. The day bus goes via **Jijoca** and the night bus via **Preá**. The journey takes 6 hrs and costs US$25 one way. Always check times of the Redençao buses from Fortaleza as they change with the season. The night

bus requires an overnight stop in Preá; make your own way to Jeri next day. A *jardineira* (open-sided 4WD truck) meets the Redenção bus from Fortaleza at Jijoca (included in the Redenção price). Several a/c *combis* a day leave from outside the Casa Blanca hotel for to **Jeri** via **Jijoca** (US$50, 4 hrs).

Nordeste to **Mossoró**, 10 a day, US$30; to **Natal**, 8 daily, US$25 *semi-leito*, US$40 *executivo*, US$50 *leito*, 7½ hrs; to **João Pessoa**, 2 daily, US$40 *semi-leito*, US$45 *leito*, 10 hrs. Boa Esperança stops at Fortaleza on its **Belém–Natal** route. Itapemirim to **Salvador**, US$85, 1900, 23 hrs. Guanabara to **Recife**, 5 daily, US$45 *executivo*, US$60 *leito*, 12 hrs, book early for weekend travel; to **Teresina**, several daily, US$40, *leito* US$50, 10 hrs; to **Parnaíba** US$40; to **Belém**, 2 daily, US$65 *executivo*, 23 hrs; to **São Luís**, 3 daily, US$65, 18 hrs; **Sobral** US$10; **Ubajara** 0800, 1800, return 0800, 1600, 6 hrs, US$12; to **Piripiri** for **Parque Nacional de Sete Cidades**, US$30, 9 hrs, a good stop en route to Belém. Ipu Brasília to **Sobral**, US$14, and to **Camocim**, 1120, 1530; to **Majorlândia**, US$7, **Campina Grande**, US$40, 13 hrs; to **Juazeiro do Norte**, Rio Grande/Rápido Juazeiro, 5 a day from 1230-2145, 8-9 hrs, US$50, *leito* US$90. Redenção to **Quixadá**, many daily, US$7; to **Redentora**, 0600,1200 via Baturité. Redenção to **Almofala** 0700, 1730, US$10; to **Cruz** 0900, 1030, 1630, 1830, US$10. Redenção from *rodoviária* to **Gijoca**, US$12, 1030, 1830 and **Jeri**, 0900, 1830, US$10. Tickets are also sold at the **Posta Telefônica** Beira Mar, on Beira Mar almost opposite **Praiano Palace**.

Bus companies Açailândia, T085-3256 8525; Boa Esperança, T085-3256 5006; Eucatur/União Cascavel, T085-3256 4889, run Pantanal–Palmas, Gontijo–São Paulo, São Gonçalo–Belo Horizonte; Guanabara, T085-3256 0214; Nordeste, T085-3256 2342; Rio Grande/ Rápido Juazeiro, T085-3254 3600; Transbrasiliana, T085-3256 1306.

Car hire

Many car hire places on Av Monsenhor Tabosa: **Amazônia**, No 1055, T085-3219 0800; Reta, No 1171, T085-3219 5555; **Shop**,

No 1181, T085-3219 7788, and many more at the junction with Ildefonso Albano. Brasil Rent a Car, Av Abolição 2300, T085-3242 0868, www.brasillocadora.com.br. Localiza, Av Abolição 2236, T0800-992020. There are also many buggy rental shops.

The coast east of Fortaleza p545
Bus Daily bus service to Fortaleza *rodoviária* to **Prainha**, 11 daily, US$3; to **Iguape**, hourly 0600-1900, US$3. To **Caponga**: direct bus from Fortaleza *rodoviária* (4 a day, US$3) or take a bus from Fortaleza to **Cascavel** (80 mins) then a bus from Cascavel (20 mins); bus information in Caponga T088-3334 1485. For bus information in Fortaleza, São Benedito, T088-3272 2544, at *rodoviária*: to **Beberibe**, 10 a day, US$4; to **Cascavel**, US$3; to **Morro Branco**, 0745, 1000, 1515, 1750, US$4; to **Canoa Quebrada**, 0830, 1100, 1340, 1540 (plus 1730 Sun), US$7; to **Aracati**, more than 10 per day first at 0500, last at 1900, last back at 1800, US$7; onward connections from Arati to **Natal** (at least 10 per day), **Recife** (2 per day), **Salvador** (1 per day). **Natal– Aracati** bus via **Mossoró**, 6 hrs, US$7.50; from Mossoró (90 km) US$2.50, 2 hrs; **Fortaleza– Aracati** (142 km), besides São Benedito, Guanabara or Nordeste many daily, US$7, 2 hrs; Aracati to **Canoa Quebrada** from Gen Pompeu e João Paulo, US$3; taxi US$15.

Pecém and Taíba p548
Bus There are 11 daily buses to **Fortaleza** and 4 daily buses to **Siupé**.

Paracuru and Lagoinha p549
Bus There are 8 daily buses to **Fortaleza** *rodoviária*, US$3 to **Paracuru**. For information contact T085-272 4483 (in Fortaleza).

Jericoacoara p549
Bus Redenção buses to **Fortaleza**, twice daily at 1400 (via **Preá**) and 2230 (via **Jijoca**). The journey takes 6 hrs and costs US$15 one way. Always check times of the Redenção buses as they change with the season. A *jardineira* (4WD truck) meets the bus and transfers to **Jijoca**

(included in the price). *Combis* also run to **Fortaleza** via Jijoca, US$50, 4 hrs.

If heading to **Belém** (US$28.25, 20 hrs) or other points north and west, take the *jardineira* to **Jijoca**, from where buses run to **Cruz**. In Cruz, you can change for **Sobral**; there is only one bus a day Cruz–Sobral, US$7.25, 3-4 hrs, but Redenção runs from Cruz to **Fortaleza** several times daily, US$6.40.

To get to **Parnaíba**, take a Toyota to **Camocim** (US$10) from leaving at around 0900; book through your hotel or ask around for buggy or *jardineira* (US$25 per person).

Motorcycle If on a motorcycle, it is not possible to ride from Jericoacoara to **Jijoca** (unless you have an excellent scrambler). Safe parking for bikes in Jijoca is not a problem.

Cruz p551
Bus The bus to **Jijoca** goes through town at about 1400, US$4 or US$7 to **Jericoacoara**, wait for the bus by 1330. To **Jijoca** daily at about 1400, US$1.25; the bus meets *jardineira* for Jericoacoara (US$2.20). Alternatively, take an *horário* pick-up from Cruz to **Jijoca**.

Parque Nacional de Ubajara p552
Bus 6 daily to and from **Fortaleza** to Ubajara town, US$20. From **Jericoacoara** take a combi to Jijoca and then to Sobral from where there are buses to both Ubajara and Tinguá. 2 buses daily to and from **Teresinha** (onward to São Luis and Belém), 3 to and from **Parnaíba** and buses every hr from Tinguá to Ubajara. 5 buses a day between Sobral (with connections to Jijoca (for Jericoacoara) and Fortaleza) and Viçosa do Ceará (6 hrs, US$21).

The Maciço de Baturité Mountains p553
Bus From **Baturité**, there are 4 Redentora buses a day to **Fortaleza** *rodoviária*, 3 hrs. To **Guaramiranga** Mon-Fri 0830, daily 1030, 1700, also to **Aratuba**. Pinheiro, T085-3256 3729, also runs to **Guaramiranga** and **Aratuba**.

Juazeiro do Norte p554

Air A taxi to the airport from the centre costs US$5.75; US$2 by motorcycle taxi. There are flights to **Brasília**, **Fortaleza**, **Recife**, **Rio de Janeiro** and **São Paulo** (Guarulhos), with Gol, www.voegoel.com.br and Oceanair, www.oceanair.com.br.

Bus To **Fortaleza** with Rio Negro, 2 daily, US$17 *convencional*, US$35 *executivo*, 8 hrs. To **Picos** with Boa Esperança, 2 daily, US$5.75, 5 hrs. To **Teresina** with Boa Esperança, Progresso or Aparecida, 3 daily, US$16, 11 hrs. To **São Luís** with Progresso, US$20, 16 hrs. To **Belém** with Boa Esperança, 1 daily (often full), US$70, 25 hrs. To **Campina Grande** with Transparaiba, 2 daily, US$25, 9 hrs. To **João Pessoa** with Braga, 1 daily, US$50, 10 hrs. To **Recife** with Braga, 1 daily, US$35, 11 hrs. To **Salvador** with Itapermirim, 2 weekly, US$17.50, 14 hrs. To **São Paulo** with Itapemirim, 1 daily, US$90, 40 hrs.

Car hire IBM, Santo Agostinho 58, T088-3511 0542. Localiza, at the airport and at Av Padre Cícero Km 3, No 3375, T088-3571 2668. Unidas, Av Padre Cícero, Km 2 on road to Crato, T088-3571 1226.

❶ Directory

Fortaleza p540, map p542

Banks Bradesco, Av Pontes Vieira 357, and Av Santos Dumont 2110, for international ATM. Banco do Brasil, R Barão do Rio Branco 1500, also on Av Abolição (high commission on TCs). Banco Mercantil do Brasil, R Mayor Facundo 484, Centro, Praça do Ferreira, cash against MasterCard. Exchange at Tropical Viagens, R Barão do Rio Branco 1233, T085-3221 3344, English spoken. Libratur, Av Abolição 2194, T085-3248 3355, Mon-Fri 0900-1800, Sat 0800-1200 Recommended. More *câmbios* on Av Mons Tabosa: eg TourStar, No 1587, Sdoc, No 1073, T085-3219 7993. **Embassies and consulates** France, R Bóris 90, Centro, T085-3254 2822. Germany, R Dr Lourenço

2244, Meireles, T085-3246 2833, gja435@sec.secrel.com.br. Italy, R E 80, Parque Wáshington Soares, T085-3273 2606. Netherlands, Av Pe Antônio Tomás 386, T085-3461 2331. UK, c/o Grupo Edson Queiroz, Praça da Imprensa s/n, Aldeota, T085-3466 8888. US, Nogueira Acioli 891, Centro, T085-3252 1539. **Internet** Many internet cafés around the city. Beira Mar Internet Café, Av Beira Mar 2120A, Meireles, US$2.60 per hr also international phones. Cyber Net, Av Beira Mar 3120 in small mall, smart, US$2.20 per hr. Internet Express, R Barão de Aracati opposite Colonial Praia, opens 0800. **Laundry** Laundromat, Av Abolição 3038, Meireles. **Medical services** Instituto Dr José Frota (IJF), R Barão do Rio Branco 1866, T085-3255 5000, recommended public hospital. **Post office** Main branch at R Senador Alencar 38, Centro; Av Monsenhor Tabosa 1109 and 1581, Iracema; at train station; opposite the *rodoviária*. Parcels must be taken to Receita Federal office at Barão de Aracati 909, Aldeota (take 'Dom Luís' bus). **Telephone** International calls from Emcetur hut on Iracema beach and from Telemar offices: R Floriano Peixoto 99, corner of R João Moreira, Centro; also at *rodoviária* and airport.

Coast east of Fortaleza p545

Banks Canoa Quebrada has a Banco do Brasil ATM but these do not usually accept international cards. Aracati has money changers, banks and international ATMs.

Jericoacoara p549

Internet There are plenty of internet cafés in town but no banks.

Juazeiro do Norte p554

Banks Banco do Brasil, R São Francisco, near Praça Pradre Cícero, poor rates, Mon-Fri 1100-1600, Bradesco, R Conceição 503, Centro T088-3512 2830 and at R Sta Luzia 321, T088-3512 2966. No *câmbios* in town. **Post office** R Conceição 354 and at *rodoviária*. **Telephone** R São Pedro 204, half a block from Praça Padre Cícero and at *rodoviária*.

Piauí

But for a sliver of coast Piauí is dry sertão, pocked with jagged hills cut by canyons and dotted with weather-worn ancient mounds of rock. Few tourists stop here, but those that do seldom regret it. Torrid Teresina is a friendly and well-planned capital where foreigners are a curiosity, Parnaíba is a pretty colonial river port, and the dry interior is broken by a number of stunning and intriguing state and national parks. These include the enigmatic Serra da Capivara, Sete Cidades and the almost inaccessible Serra dos Confusões, beehive mounds sticking up out of the desert whose canyon walls are daubed with some of the oldest rock art in the Americas. And while Piauí's coast is tiny it includes the magnificent Delta do Parnaíba: one of the largest river deltas in the world, replete with mangrove swamps and tiny islands fringed with golden beaches and home to traditional communities who seldom see tourists. After neighbouring Maranhão, Piauí is the poorest state in Brazil. Its population is about 2.7 million, but many leave to seek work elsewhere. The economy is almost completely dependent upon agriculture and livestock, both of which in turn depend on how much rain, if any, falls.» For listings, see pages 574-577.

Background

The state's long, thin, wineskin shape derives from its history and the course of the Parnaíba river, which winds 1480 km through the arid *sertão* to the Piauí coast. Piauí is the only state to have been founded from the interior rather than as a coastal port. It was initially explored from the Bahia and Pernambuco through the sertão by 18th-century ranchers looking for fresh pasture land. Long forgotten colonial towns such as Oerias date from this period. Other towns sprung up along the Parnaíba river, like Floriano, Amarante and, in 1852, Teresina. The latter remains the only northeastern capital to lie inland. The river's delta eventually became the coastal frontier of the state.

Until the early 19th century Piauí was under the control of neighbouring Maranhão. At Independence, there was bitter, bloodthirsty fighting between supporters of the Portuguese colony and the Brazilians who sought their freedom. And well into the 20th century Piauí maintained a strong tradition of Portuguese-inspired *Coronelismo*, see box, page 530, whose vestiges persist to this day.

Teresina → *For listings, see pages 574-577. Colour map 2, A3. Phone code: 086. Population: 716,000.*

Piauí's capital is a pleasant friendly city with abundant woodland, some attractive colonial buildings and the usual gamut of Brazilian concrete apartment blocks. It lies about 350 km from the coast, at the confluence of the Rio Poti and the Rio Parnaíba. It is flat with a grid of streets, some of which are lined with handsome terracotta roofed 19th-century buildings. There are more than 30 urban parks. The city was founded in the 18th century as the Vila do Poti and was renamed in honour of the empress of Brazil and wife of Dom Pedro II, Teresa Cristina, who had supported the idea of moving the capital from Oreias. Teresina has a lively cultural scene and a famously vibrant nightlife. The city itself is reputed to be the hottest after Cuiabá, with temperatures up to 42°C and an annual mean of around 30°C.

Ins and outs

The **Senador Petrônio Portela airport** ① *5 km from the centre, Av Centenário s/n, T086-3133 6270*, receives flights from Fortaleza, Brasília, Rio de Janeiro, São Paulo, Goiâna and

São Luís. Outside the airport, buses run straight into town and to the *rodoviária*. The **rodoviária** is 4 km the centre. There are buses running into the town every few minutes. There are direct bus connections with Fortaleza (a scenic nine-hour journey), Belém, Recife and São Luís. ▸▸ *See Transport, page 576.*

For tourist information, there are several offices of **Piemtur** ⓘ *R Álvaro Mendes 2003, Caixa Postal 36; R Magalhães Filho, next to 55 N; and R Acre, Convention Centre, T086-3221 7100.* There are also kiosks at the *rodoviária* and the airport. The **Sindicato dos Guiás de Turismo de Piauí (Singtur)** ⓘ *R Paissandu 1276, T086-3221 2175,* has information booths at the Centro de Artesanato, Praça Dom Pedro II (helpful, friendly), the Encontro das Águas, Poty Velho and on the shores of the Rio Poty. Another office is **Ana Turismo** ⓘ *R Álvaro Mendes 1961, Centro, T/F086-3221 2272. The website www.teresina.pi.gov.br is* also a useful source of information.

Sights
Praça Pedro II lies at the heart of the city and is the hub of Teresina life. There are many bars and restaurants in the surrounding streets, where diners are frequently serenaded by *violeiros* (Brazil's equivalent of *mariachis*). Many *violeiros* also congregate at the **Casa do Cantador** ⓘ *R Lucia 1419, Vermelha, T086-3211 6833, 1400-2000, Wed is the best night,* a little *boteco* outside the city centre surrounded by mangroves. There is live poetry, a gallery of art and shows at the **Oficina da Palavra** ⓘ *R Benjamin Constant 1400, Centro, T086-3223 4441, www.oficinadapalavra-pi.com.br, Mon-Fri 0800-1200 and 1400-2000, Sat and Sun 0800-1200.* The centre has some attractive buildings including the **Teatro 4 Setembro** and the old art deco cinema, the **Rex**. There's a decent crafts market at the **Central do Artensato**, which is well-known for its opals, carved wood and hammocks. The **Museu do Piauí** ⓘ *Praça Marechal Deodoro s/n, Tue-Fri 0730-1730, Sat and Sun 0800-1200, US$1.50,* is in a mansion house dating from 1859 and has been completely refurbished. It preserves a collection of sacred art by local artists from the 19th century, as well as impressive woodcarvings by Mestre Dezinho Nonato de Oliveira and an extensive collection of frowsty fossils. The **Palácio de Karnak** ⓘ *just west of Praça Frei Serafim,*

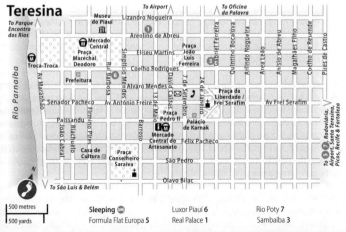

Teresina

500 metres
500 yards

Sleeping 😴
Formula Flat Europa **5**

Luxor Piauí **6**
Real Palace **1**

Rio Poty **7**
Sambaíba **3**

T086-3221 9820, Mon-Sat 0800-1800 (visits to the inside of the palace by appointment only), is a grand neoclassical edifice set in pretty gardens landscaped by Roberto Burle Marx, and has been the governor's palace since 1926. Inside is a collection of period furniture and artefacts and a rare set of lithographs of the Middle East in 1839 by the Scottish artist David Roberts, famous for his depictions of unexcavated temples throughout the Middle East and most notably in Egypt. The **Casa da Cultura** ① *R Rui Barbosa 348, Centro, T086-3215 7849, Mon-Fri 0800-1900, Sat 0900-1300, Sun 1300-1600*, is devoted to the history of the city and to the lives of famous ex-residents such as the journalist Carlos Castelo Branco and the photographer Jose de Medeiros. The reception desk has a programme of cultural events taking place in Teresina.

Every morning along the picturesque river, with washing laid out to dry on its banks, is the *troca-troca* (market), where people buy, sell and swap. Most of the year the rivers are low, leaving sandbanks known as *coroas* (crowns). The confluence of the two rivers is at the **Parque Encontro dos Rios** ① *Av Boa Esperança s/n, Poti Velho, T086-3217 5020, daily 0800-1800*, where there is a statue of the Cabeça de Cuia river demon, Crispim. Canoes are available for hire on the river.

Around Teresina → *For listings, see pages 574-577.*

Parque Nacional de Sete Cidades → *Colour map 2, A3.*

Some 190 km northeast of Teresina, this interesting 6221 ha park has strange eroded rock formations which, from the ground, look like a medley of weird monuments. They are grouped into *cidades* (cities), each of which holds a different view. The best is from Segunda Cidade, especially in the late afternoon when the golden light brings out the panoply of colours on the rocks and casts haunting shadows. Inscriptions on some of the rocks have never been deciphered and are thought to be from between 5000 and 10,000 years old. One theory suggests links with the Phoenicians, and the Argentine Professor Jacques de Mahieu considers them to be Nordic runes left by the Vikings.

With 22 springs, the park is an oasis in the dry surroundings and forms a transition zone between *caatinga* vegetation and *cerrado*. There is abundant wildlife including white-tailed deer, paca, various armadillos, tamandua anteaters and well over 100 bird species, some of them rare *sertão* endemics. Large iguanas descend from the trees in the afternoon.

The park spans 12 km and can be walked across in a long day, beginning at the Portaria Sul (south gate) and finishing at the Portaria Norte (north gate). Trails are well signposted, but beware of rattlesnakes when hiking.

Ins and outs The park is 26 km northeast of the little town of Piripiri on the BR-343. There are buses to Piripiri from Parnaíba and Teresina as well as Fortaleza, Ubajara and São Luís (though these buses have many stops). From Piripiri there is an **Instituto Chico Mendes de Conservação da Biodiversidade (ICMBio)** bus direct to the park at 0700 daily, from by the Telemar office in front of the Praça da Bandeira (it is ostensibly for employees, but usually possible to hitch a ride). The bus passes in front of the **Hotel Fazenda Sete Cidades** at 0800, reaching the park 10 minutes later; it returns at 1630. *Moto-táxis* in Piripiri charge (US$10) to the park, or a standard taxi costs US$20.

If coming from Parnaíba, Barreirinhas (in the Lençóis Maranhenses) or Jericoacoara, agencies such as **Eco Dunas**, offer trips often as part of an interstate transfer. ▸▸ *See Activities and tours, page 591.*

The park is open daily 0800-1700. There is accommodation in Piripiri and right next to the park. Information and maps are available from **Instituto Chico Mendes de Conservação da Biodiversidade (ICMBio)** ① *Av Homero Castelo Branco 2240, Teresina, T086-3343 1342, www.icmbio.com.br*. Another useful website is www2.uol.com.br/mochilabrasil/setecidades.shtml.

Parnaíba and around → *For listings, see pages 574-577. Colour map 2, A3. Phone code: 086. Population: 133,000.*

Parnaíba makes a good break in the journey north or south. It's a relaxed, friendly place, with a pretty colonial centre overlooking the Parnaíba river. If crossing the delta, buy all provisions here. There are beaches at **Luís Correia**, 14 km from Parnaíba, with radioactive sands. About 18 km from Parnaíba is **Pedra do Sal**, with dark blue lagoons and palm trees. At **Lagoa do Portinho**, 12 km from Parnaíba, there are bungalows, a bar, restaurant and canoes for hire; it is possible to camp. **Praia do Coqueiro** is a small fishing village with natural pools formed at low tide. Seafood is good at **Alô Brasil** and **Bar da Cota**.

Ins and outs The **rodoviária** ① *5 km south of centre on BR-343, T086-3323 7300*, has bus connections with São Luís, Tutóia (for the Lençóis Maranhenses), Piripiri (for Parque Nacional da Sete Cidades) and Camocim (for Jericoacoara). Buses marked Praça João Luíz run to the centre; taxi US$6. About 14 km from the town centre, on the Parnaíba river, is the Porto dos Tatus, where boats leave for the delta. ⏵ *See Transport, page 576.*

For tourist information contact **Piemtur** ① *R Dr Oscar Clark 575, T086-3321 1532*; there is another branch at **Porto da Barca**, a pleasant shopping and entertainment complex in the colonial centre, with several good restaurants and an open-air bar on the riverside.

Delta do Parnaíba
The Delta do Parnaíba, which separates Piauí from Tutóia (see page 584) and the spectacular Lençóis Maranhenses (see page 583) in neighbouring Maranhão, is one of the largest river deltas in the world. It's a watery labyrinth of mangroves, broad rivers and narrow creeks, with unspoilt tropical islands fringed by gorgeous deserted beaches. The interiors of these islands are home to largely unstudied wildlife, including many rare birds, and traditional Caiçara fishing communities, who seldom see tourists. Renting hammock space with them is straightforward and simple makeshift *pousada* accommodation can be arranged. Many people in this region live as they have done for generations, in adobe houses, on a diet of fresh fish cooked in baked-earth ovens. Illiteracy is the norm. There is no mains electricity and the nearest shopping is at Parnaíba or Tutóia.

Ins and outs Crossing the delta is no longer possible by public ferry, but it's possible to charter a launch (up to 12 people, US$175) in Tutóia or at Porto dos Tatus (also called Porto da Barca), 10 km north of Parnaíba. Recommended boatmen include **Capitão Báu** ① *T086-3323 0145, T086-8831 9581 (mob)*. Alternatively, take a boat from Parnaíba to the crab-fishing village of Morro do Meio on Ilha das Canarias (Monday at high tide, usually in the small hours). It is sometimes possible to hitch a lift from Ilha das Canarias to Tutóia with a crab fisherman. It's more interesting and better value to cross the delta rather than returning to the same place, but allow plenty of time. ⏵ *See Transport, page 576.*

Tours can be arranged from Parnaíba for US$30-50 per person (minimum four people) with **Delta do Rio Parnaíba** ① *Porto das Barcas 13, Parnaíba, Parnaíba, T086-3321 1969*, *www.deltadorioparnaiba.com.br*. The company also offers excursions to other locations in Piauí and Maranhão states. The Delta do Parnaiba can be visited as part of a tour between Jericoacoara and the Lençóis Maranhenses, with EcoDunas (see page 591). Day trips also run from Porto dos Tatus, either on a huge boat full of noisy people or a smaller launch. The former include food and drink and cost around US$15 per person. The latter are by charter only (US$250-300 for up to six).

Ilha do Caju → *Population: 70. www.ilhadocaju.com.br.*
① *Trips are arranged through Pousada Ecológica Ilha do Caju, see Sleeping, page 575.*
This beautiful island, named after the extensive stands of cashew tree that fringe its shores, has an astonishing variety of terrain, with lakes, forest, marshes and an expanse of white dunes to the northwest. It has remained virtually unchanged for four centuries, thanks in part to the conservation efforts of the Englishman James Frederick Clark, who stumbled here in 1847. The whole island is environmentally protected and no chemical pesticides are used.

Much of the water, including the sea, is *salobre* (a mixture of fresh and salt). Swimming from the vast, shimmering beach through the currents of alternating sea and river water is a recommended experience. There are lakes on the island, caused by flooding, in which trees that have been killed by the brine content stand bleached and knotted – an unnerving image of lifelessness surrounded by vigorous vegetation. Walking through the forest surrounding the lake is magical: nesting herons, ospreys and kingfishers take off in clouds of flashing green; tiny, long-legged jacanas and gallinules hop from leaf to leaf on the water lilies; and myriad butterflies hover around your head.

Southern Piauí → *For listings, see pages 574-577.*

Oeiras
The old capital of Piauí, 320 km from Teresina, is a pretty colonial treasure almost completely unknown to most Brazilians – let alone international tourists. The state government is restoring some of the colonial buildings, such as the bishop's palace and the church of Nossa Senhora da Vitória. There are some impressive celebrations during holy week, including a huge fireworks display and costumed parade on Maundy Thursday, serenaded by local mandolin players.

Parque Nacional Serra da Capivara → *Colour map 2, B3.*
① *35 km from São Raimundo Nonato. The agency Trilhas da Capivara, T089-3582 1294, trilhascapivara@uol.com.br, runs excursions from US$40. For the most up-to-date information on transport and logistics, contact Fundham, below.*
About 500 km south of Teresina is this 130,000-ha park, on the UNESCO World Heritage List. Some 30,000 prehistoric rock paintings on limestone have been found, dating from between 6000 and 12,000 years ago. The paintings are of daily life, festivities and celebrations, as well as hunting and sex scenes. Excavations by Brazilian and French archaeologists have uncovered fossilized remains of extinct animals such as the sabre-toothed tiger, giant sloths larger than elephants and armadillos the size of a car.

Nearly 400 archaeological sites have been identified in the park since research began in 1970. About 22 of them have been set up to receive tourists. Roads and all-weather paths allow visitors to view the sites with ease. Specially trained guides are available. The area is good for hiking in the *caatinga*, with its canyons and mesas. It is also possible to see much of the *caatinga* wildlife, in particular the birds.

Much investment has gone into the park, not just for visitors' facilities, but also to educate the local population about protecting the paintings and to establish a bee-keeping project to provide income in times of drought.

São Raimundo Nonato

São Raimundo Nonato is best known as the administration centre and access point for the Parque Nacional Serra Da Capivara. The **Fundação Museu do Homem Americano (Fundham)** ① *Centro Cultural Sérgio Motta, Bairro Campestre, T089-3582 1612, www.fumdham.org.br*, has a fascinating collection of artefacts found in the *serra*. These are well displayed, though the information in English is poor. In September, the city hosts the **Festival Internacional Serra da Capivara** with music, theatre and parades.

There are bus connections with Teresina (a bumpy 540-km journey) and Petrolina in Pernambuco (300 km away).

Parque Nacional Serra dos Confusões

The largest and most remote national park in northeastern Brazil covers over 5000 sq km of rugged weather-beaten sandstone escarpments and towering crags surrounded by *cerrado* and *caatinga* forests. Like the Serra da Capivara to the north, its canyons and caves are covered in rock art. The park is replete with rare and endangered wildlife – particularly birds. Species include puma, jaguar, pampas deer, red-handed howler monkey yellow-legged tinamou and black-fronted piping-guan.

The park is 640 km south of Teresina. There is currently no administration or infrastructure. Although it is not officially open to tourism, visits are possible. Guides can be organized in the nearby *sertão* town of Caracol.

Parque Nacional das Nascentes do Parnaíba and hyacinth site

This huge 733,162-ha park in the far south of Piauí, straddling the border with Tocantins, Maranhão and Bahia, preserves pristine areas of *cerrado* and *caatinga* forest. Ochre table-top mountains covered in waterfalls form part of the ancient rocks of the Brazilian shield. The wildlife is exuberant, including more than 60 mammal species and 211 birds – many of them endemic or endangered.

In the far southwest of the park, 20 km from **São Gonçalo do Piauí**, is the best place in the world for seeing the very rare **hyacinth macaw**. The hyacinth site is on private land in a region of *cerrado* with red sandstone cliffs where the macaws nest. An illegal bird trade used to flourish in the area, but local people now guard the site, which is supported by the **Kaytee Avian Foundation** and others. Many other *cerrado* birds may be seen, together with black-and-gold howlers and, less commonly, maned wolves and giant anteaters.

Accommodation is in very simple huts with mosquito nets, sand floors and shared bathrooms. Meals are served at the site. Access is via the airport at **Barreiras** (see page 548) in western Bahia, 340 km south, and a five- to six-hour drive. Currently tours are only possible through **Focus Tours**, www.focustours.com.

For Sleeping and Eating price codes and other relevant information, see pages 32-37.

● Sleeping

Teresina *p568, map p569*

There are many cheap places on R São Pedro and R Alvaro Mendes. The cleanest and best is **Glória**, No 823, blocks 800 and 900. There are other cheap hotels and *dormitórios* around Praça Saraiva.

AL-A Rio Poty, Av Mcal Castelo Branco 555, Ilhota, T086-4009 4009, www.riopoty.com. 5 stars. One of the better options in town with rooms in a large concrete Benidorm-style block overlooking a big swimming pool.

B Real Palace, R Areolino de Abreu 1217, T086-2107 2700, www.realpalacehotel.com.br. Business orientated hotel with a range of old-fashioned rooms and suites and a small business centre.

B-C Luxor Piauí, Praça Mal Deodoro 310, Centro, T086-3221 3306, www.luxor.com.br. Business hotel with small, simply appointed rooms with a bed, desk and armchair squeezed in. The hotel has a business centre with broadband and a small pool.

B-C Sambaíba, R Gabriel Ferreira 230-N, T086-3222 3460. A functional 2-star with very simple a/c rooms.

C Formula Flat Europa, R José Olímpio de Melo 3330, Ilhotas, T086-3223 7100, www.formulaflateuropa.com.br. Bright, modern and well-appointed flats with microwaves, kitchenettes and living areas. Space for up to 3 people making this an **E-F** option per person.

D Santa Teresinha, Av Getúlio Vargas 2885, opposite the *rodoviária*, T086-3211 0919. With a/c or fan, clean, friendly.

Parque Nacional de Sete Cidades *p570*
Piripiri, 26 km from the park, is a cheap place to break the Belém–Fortaleza journey. As well as those listed, there are other options near bus offices and behind the church.

C-D Fazenda Sete Cidades, 8 km from the park entrance, T086-3276 2222. A converted farmhouse with large though simple fan-cooled and a/c rooms, horse riding, river water swimming pools and a play area for kids.

C-D Parque Hotel Sete Cidades, Km 63 on BR-222, 6 km from the park entrance, T086-9424 0024, www.hotelsetecidades.com.br. Tile-floor chalets with private bath and room for 3-4 (in double beds). Natural river-water swimming pool, good restaurant and bicycle or horse transport; also has a free pickup to the park (and a most unpleasant zoo). At the bottom end of this price range.

D-E Hotel Rodoviário I and **Hotel Rodoviário II**, in front of the terminal *rodoviária* Luiz Menezes, Piripiri, Av Estado Pernambuco 779, T086-3276 2838. Pink concrete blocks hiding a series of very simple fan-cooled or a/c rooms with shared baths or en suites. Convenient for transit passengers.

E Hotel California, R Dr Antenor de Araujo Freitas 546, Piripiri, T086-3276 1645. There's plenty of room in the Hotel California, with 32 rooms all with a/c and en suites. 24-hr reception so you can check out any time you want. Convenient for the 0700 bus to the park from nearby Praça da Bandeira.

E Instituto Chico Mendes de ICMBio (Ibama) hostel, in the park, T086-3343 1342. Price per person. Rooms with bath, pleasant, good restaurant, natural pool nearby, camping. Recommended. Not open all year round, so book ahead or check with **Instituto Chico Mendes de Conservação da Biodiversidade (ICMBio)**, www.ICMBio.com.br, in Teresina.

Parnaíba and around *p571*
AL-A Pousada dos Ventos, Av São Sebastião 2586, Universidade, T086-3322 2555, www.pousadadosventos.com.br. The best business hotel in town, a 10-min taxi ride from the centre, with spacious, simple rooms and an attractive breakfast area next to the pool.

C Pousada Chalé Suiço, Av Padre R J Vieira 448, Fátima, T086-3321 3026, www.chale suico.com.br. Cheaper without a/c or breakfast, bar, laundry, pool, tours arranged, windsurfing, sandboarding, buggies and bikes.

D-E Igaraçu, R Almirante Gervasio Sampaio 390, T086-3322 3342. Right next to **Bradesco** bank, 5 mins walk from the centre. Very plain rooms, some with no windows, and with only a chair and table for furniture gathered around a scruffy courtyard. The best are the a/c doubles with bunks (these have firmer mattresses).

D-E Residencial, R Almirante Gervásio Sampaio 375, T086-3322 2931, www.residencialpousada.com.br. Very plain, simple doubles, dorms and plusher en suites with cold water showers gathered around a plant-filled courtyard. There are many other basic hotels nearby in the centre.

Delta do Parnaíba *p571*

F Ilha das Canarias, Morro do Meio Caiçara Comunidade. Bring a hammock and ask at the **Raimundo Aires** restaurant (US$15 per person per night) great fish in the restaurant and idyllic beaches nearby. Very simple, no showers – just the river.

Ilha do Caju *p572*

A Pousada Ecológica Ilha do Caju, contact: Av Presidente Vargas 235, Centro, Parnaíba, T086-3321 1179, www.ilhadocaju.com.br. Comfortable rustic cabins, each has its own hammock outside, but inside there is a huge bed, handmade by the same craftsmen who made much of the *pousada*'s highly individual furniture. The owner, Ingrid, and senior staff speak English and are helpful and welcoming. Children must be aged 14 or over. The *pousada* will organize all transfers.

Oeiras *p572*

D-E Pousada do Cônego, Praça das Vitórias 18, Centro, T089-3462 1219. Very simple hotel housed in a large and somewhat decrepit town house and a small pizza restaurant with tables on the sunny veranda under the shade of tropical trees.

Parque Nacional Serra da Capivara *p572*
D Serra da Capivara, Estrada PI-140 exit for Teresina, Km 2, T089-3582 1389. Intimate country hotel near the park, with a pool and 18 a/c cabins and a restaurant.

São Raimundo Nonato *p573*

D Pousada Lelinha, R Dr Barroso 249, Aldeia, T089-3582 2993, www.lelinhapousada. com.br. One of the better options in the town with large, airy rooms the biggest of which have room for up to 5. Breakfasts are generous and the staff can give advice on visiting the *serra*.

D Pousada Zabelê, Praça Major Toinho 280, Centro, T089-3582 2726. Simple standard town hotel with a range of fan-cooled and a/c rooms. Helpful staff.

🍴 Eating

Teresina *p568, map p569*
There are many places for all budgets around Praça Dom Pedro II.
🍴🍴🍴 **Camarão do Elias**, Av Pedro Almeida 457, T086-3232 5025. Best restaurant in the city, with fish and prawn dishes. Try the fish of the day in caper and lemon sauce.
🍴🍴 **Pesqueirinho**, R Domingos Jorge Velho 6889, Poty Velho district, T086-3225 2268. Excellent fish restaurant on the riverbank.
🍴 **Sabores Rotisserie**, R Simplício Mendes 78, Centro. Per kilo food, good quality and variety.

🎉 Festivals and events

Teresina *p568, map p569*
Feb/Mar Teresina is proud of its **Carnaval**, which is then followed by **Micarina**, a local carnival in Mar.
Jul/Aug There is much music and dancing at the **Bumba-Meu-Boi**, which takes place in Teresina on a smaller scale to São Luís **Festidanças**, and a convention of itinerant guitarists.

Oeiras *p572*

Feb/Mar Procissão do Fogaréu aka O Procissão de Bom Jesus dos Passos on Maundy Thursday. Also Easter parades.

O Shopping

Teresina *p568, map p569*
Crafts Teresina is an excellent and cheap place to buy *artesanato*, for which Piauí is renowned throughout Brazil. Panels of carved and painted hardwood, either representing stylized country scenes or images of religious significance, are a good buy, as are clay or wooden models of traditional rural characters. Many of these eccentric figures come from the region's rich fund of myths and legends. Hammocks, straw and basket ware are also made here, as well as leather and clothes.

Parnaíba and around *p571*
Crafts Artesanato de Parnaíba, R Dom Pedro II 1140, and **Cooperativa Artesanal Mista de Parnaíba**, R Alcenor Candeira, both sell local handicrafts.

▲ Activities and tours

Parque Nacional de Sete Cidades *p570*
Tours can be arranged with **Eco Dunas** (see page 591) and **Delta do Parnaíba** (see page 571) as well as most agencies in Jericoacoara (see page 564).

Parque Nacional Serra da Capivara *p572*
Trips can be organized via **Trilhas da Capivara**, T089-3582 1294, and **Cariri Ecotours** (see page 538) in Natal. See **Fundham**, www.fundham.org.br, for information.

O Transport

Teresina *p568, map p569*
Air Flights to **Fortaleza**, **Brasília**, **Rio de Janeiro**, **São Paulo**, **Goiânia** and **São Luís**.

Bus The bus journey to **Fortaleza** is scenic and takes 9 hrs (US$13.50). There are direct buses to **Belém** (13 hrs, US$23.40), **Recife** (16 hrs, US$27) and **São Luís** (7 hrs, US$12).

Parnaíba and around *p571*
Bus If travelling west up the coast from Parnaíba, there are 3 buses a day to **Tutóia** (2½ hrs, US$8) with **Nazaré** at 0700, 1200 and 1400. From Tutóia, Toyotas leave when full from the dock area for **Paulinho Neves** (1 hr, US$6), further Toyotas leave from here to **Barreirinhas** (2 hrs, US$10) near the **Parque Nacional Lençóis Maranhenses**.

It's also possible to take a bus inland to **São Luís** (4-6 hrs, US$12, US$48 – a very bad road, better to go via Tutóia) and from there to **Barreirinhas** (Cisne Branco, 3-3½ hrs on a new road, US$20, 4 per day). See São Luís transport, page 591.

If travelling east down the coast to **Jericoacoara** take a bus to **Camocim** (2 daily with **Guanabara**, 1½-2 hrs, US$12). To avoid getting stuck in Camocim, take the early bus at around 0700. This connects with the 1100 Toyota to **Jericoacoara** (2 hrs, US$10) via the ferry (US$1 per foot passenger) across the river separating Piauí and Ceará, and the village of Tatajuba.

Parnaíba is also connected to **Fortaleza** (10 hrs, US$50) and **Teresina** (6 hrs, US$50). Buses for the **Porto da Barca** (Tatuís) leave from the *rodoviária* every hour and take 10 mins. Taxis cost around US$10.

Delta do Parnaíba *p571*
Boat Boats can be chartered from **Tutóia** (connected to Barreirinhas and Caburé in the Lençóis Marnahenses, via Paulino Neves, and direct to São Luís) or at **Porto dos Tatus** (also called Porto da Barca), 10 km north of Parnaíba. A boat for 12 people costs for around US$175 with **Capitão Báu**, T086-3323 0145, T086-8831 9581 (mob) or contact **Clipe Turismo**, www.clipecoturismo.com.br.

Oerias p572

Bus The *rodoviária* is on Av Transamazônica s/n, T089-3462 2006. Buses to **Teresina** (310 km), **São Raimundo Nonato** (280 km) and connections to **Tocantins**.

Parque Nacional Serra da Capivara p572

Bus The *rodoviária* is at R Cândido Ferraz, T089-3582 1266. There are buses to **Teresina** (530 km) and connections to **Pernambuco**.

🌐 Directory

Teresina p568, map p569

Banks Banks with ATMs include: Banco do Brasil and Bradesco, R Alvaro Mendes 991, Centro, T086-3221 5050 and in the airport. Itaú, in same avenue at P Center Shopping.

Parnaíba and around p571

Banks There is a Bradesco and an HSBC in the town centre for international ATMs and numerous branches around town including: Banco do Brasil, Praça da Graça 340, and Bradesco, Av Pres Getúlio Vargas 403, T086-3321 3032. **Medical services** Pró- Médica, Av Pres Vargas 799, T086-322 3645, 24-hr emergency ward. **Post office** Praça da Graça. **Telephone** Av Pres Getúlio Vargas 390.

Maranhão

Although far less visited than neighbouring Ceará, Maranhão is one of Brazil's most fascinating states with spectacular natural sights and a rich traditional culture with a strong African heritage. The capital, São Luís, was founded by the French but built by the Portuguese, whose azulejos and ornate baroque flourishes grace the elegant buildings of its colonial centre. Every Friday and Saturday night its little praças erupt to the riotous rhythms of cacuria, and in June the city becomes the backdrop for one of the most colourful spectacles in the northeast: the Bumba-Meu-Boi pageant.

The city is enclosed on both sides by natural beauty. To the southeast are the Lençóis Maranhenses, a 155,000-ha coastal desert of vast shifting dunes and isolated communities, cut by broad rivers and in the rainy season (between June and September), pocked with lakes, whose clear reflective waters are a vivid sky blue against brilliant white sand. To the northwest are the little- explored deltas of the Reentrâncias Maranhenses, which preserve the largest concentration of mangrove forest in Brazil, and which are fringed by the south Atlantic's longest coral reef.

Inland, Maranhão is remote and desperately poor but filled with fascinating forgotten villages and wilderness areas such as the Chapada das Mesas in Carolina: a forest-shrouded escarpment dripping with waterfalls that forms the transition zone between the hot, dry northeast and the wet and warm Amazon. ▶▶ *For listings, see pages 587-592.*

São Luís → *For listings, see pages 587-592. Colour map 2, A2. Phone code: 098. Population: 870,000.*

The capital and port of Maranhão state, founded in 1612 by the French and named after St Louis of France, stands upon São Luís island between the bays of São Marcos and São José. It's a beautiful city that rivals Recife and Salvador for colonial charm, and following extensive refurbishment it is in better condition than both. Like both cities, São Luís was a slaving port, initially for indigenous Amazonians who were brought in here in huge numbers to grow sugar cane, and subsequently for Africans. São Luís retains an African identity almost as strong as Salvador and Recife. The city is as Amazonian as it is northeastern and is subject to heavy tropical rains. However, a large proportion of the surrounding deep forest has been cut down to be replaced by *babaçu* palms, the nuts and oils of which are the state's most important products.

Ins and outs

Getting there **Marechal Cunha Machado airport** ① *13 km from centre, Av Santos Dumont, T098-3217 6100*, receives flights from most Brazilian capitals via Fortaleza or Belém, as well as direct flights from Parnaíba and Teresina and international flights from the Guianas and Portugal. **Gol** and **Tam** have offices in the terminal, there is car rental, a tourist office (daily 0800-2200), cyber-café, a **Banco do Brasil** and an office for the Lençóis Maranhenses tour company **Eco Dunas**. *Colectivo* mini-vans run from outside the terminal to Praça Deodoro in the city centre (every 40 minutes until 2200, US$1, one hour). A taxi to the centre costs US$20 but it is cheaper to call a radio taxi, T098-3232 3232, US$12.

From the **rodoviária** ① *12 km from the centre on the airport road*, the bus marked 'Rodoviária via Alemanha' runs to Praça João Lisboa in the centre (US$1).

Ferries cross the bay from Alcântara to the São Luís docks, **Terminal Hidroviário** ① *Rampa Campos Mello, Cais da Praia Grande, US$4 foot passenger, US$25 car*, usually in the afternoon. To check ferry times call T098-3222 8431.▶▶ *See Transport, page 591.*

Tourist information **Central de Servicos Turísticos** ① *Praça Benedito Leite, T098-3212 6211, www.turismo.ma.gov.br*, and **São Luís Turismo** ① *www.saoluisturismo.com.br*, have useful websites. Also see http://saoluis-ma.com.br. Look out for Corbis photographer Barnabás Bosshart's masterfully photographed map-guides to São Luís and Alcântara.

Sights

The old part of the city, on very hilly ground with many steep streets, has been beautifully restored and is replete with colonial art nouveau and art deco buildings. The damp climate encouraged the use of ceramic *azulejo* tiles for exterior walls. *Azulejos* are a common sight in Portugal but their civic use is relatively rare in Brazil; São Luís displays a greater quantity and variety than anywhere else in the country. Most of the tiles are Portuguese (particularly from Porto), with a handful of print designs from Holland and France.

A good place to start a tour of the centre is **Avenida Dom Pedro II**. This was the heart of the original Tupinambá island village of Upaon Açu. When the French arrived in 1612, captained by Daniel de la Touche, they planted a huge wooden cross in the ground and, with a solemn Mass, decreed the land for France. La Touche renamed the village after Louis XIII, the emperor of France, and declared it the capital of the new land of 'France Equinoxiale' (Equinoctial France). There is a bust of La Touche in the 17th-century **Palácio de la Ravardière** ① *Av Dom Pedro II s/n, T089-3212-0800, Mon-Fri 0800-1800*.

Part of the original wall of the French fort still remains in the bulwarks of the **Palácio dos Leões** ① *Av Dom Pedro II, T089-3214 8638, Mon, Wed and Fri 1500-1800, US$3*, which was extensively embellished by the Portuguese after they re-conquered the city in 1615. When Maranhão became part of the newly independent Brazil in the 19th century, the palace was taken over by the governor. The rooms are furnished with period antiques from Portugal, France and the UK, with a series of paintings by artists including Vitor Meirelles, who was responsible for Imperial Brazil's most famous painting: *A Batalha de Guararapes*. The building is replete with stunning tropcial dark *jacarandá* wood and light *cerejeira* polished floors; visitors are required to use carpet slippers. There are marvellous views from the terrace.

Together with neighbouring Belém, Portuguese São Luís was the centre of a voracious slave trade. *Banderiante* expeditions roamed far into the interior capturing

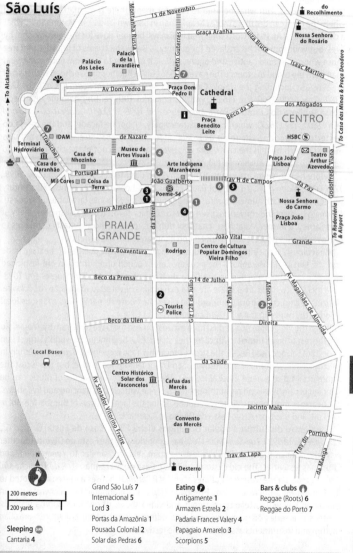

São Luís

Sleeping 🛏
Cantaria 4

Grand São Luís 7
Internacional 5
Lord 3
Portas da Amazônia 1
Pousada Colonial 2
Solar das Pedras 6

Eating 🍴
Antigamente 1
Armazen Estrela 2
Padaria Frances Valery 4
Papagaio Amarelo 3
Scorpions 5

Bars & clubs 🍸
Reggae (Roots) 6
Reggae do Porto 7

indigenous men, murdering their wives and children and bringing the prisoners to Maranhão to work on the cane fields. Entire Amazon civilizations, including the *Omagua*, were wiped-out this way. The Jesuits were appalled by the cruelty and their most famous politician-priest, Antônio Vieira (see box, page 266), came to São Luís as a missionary to protest against the slave trade in 1653: "At what a different price the devil buys souls today compared with what he used to offer for them! There is no market in the world where the devil can get them more cheaply than in our own land … In Maranhão … what a cheap market! An Indian for a soul! That Indian will be your slave for the few days that he lives; but your soul will be enslaved for eternity… Break the chains of injustice and free those whom you hold captive and oppressed! … It is better to live from your own sweat than from the blood of others". The naves of São Luís's churches once echoed with his hell fire sermons, including the simple **Catedral da Sé** ① *Praça Dom Pedro II, s/n, T089-3222 7380, daily 0800-1900, free* (1629), with its beautiful 19th-century baroque altarpiece, **Nossa Senhora do Carmo** ① *Praça João Lisboa 350, T098-3222 6104, daily 0700-1115 and 1430-1800, free* (1627), which has an extraordinary, elaborate façade, and the **Igreja do Desterro** ① *Largo do Desterro s/n, daily 0800-1130 and 1500-1830, free*, which was perhaps the first church built in the city. Vieira was eventually driven out of the city and went to Pará where he met with similar failure.

Before he left, Vieira inaugurated the **Convento das Mercês** ① *R da Palma 506, T098-3211 0062, Mon-Fri 0800-1800, Sat 0800-1400*, which houses copies of his 17th-century sermons, along with numerous rare Portuguese and French books (available on request). The main body of the convent is given over to exhibits devoted to Brazilian presidency of Jose Sarney, a former Maranhão senator of dubious repute, whose dynasty continues to rule over Brazil's poorest state with an iron hand, and reap the benefits.

Miraculously some indigenous groups managed to avoid the ravages of the slave trade and still survive in Maranhão. Their cultures are touched upon, from an old-fashioned anthropological perspective, in the **Casa de Nhozinho** ① *R dos Portugueses s/n, T098-3218 9951, 0900-1900, free*. There are also exhibitions devoted to Maranhão *caboclo* life. Nhozinho, who came from Curupuru and gives the house its name, was a famous local wooden toy maker in the mid-20th century.

When the *indigenous people* died from exhaustion and the slave trade ran dry, Maranhão and the rest of Brazil turned to Africa for their slaves, thus beginning the world's largest skin trade. Like Salvador and Recife, the strong African heritage is celebrated most powerfully in the city's exuberant music and festivals. São Luís is famous for reggae, but this is just the commercial tip of a huge musical iceberg. The exuberance and variety of music can be sampled on any weekend night throughout the year with *cacuriá* dancing and live shows, but becomes most obvious in May and June during the local festivals of **Bumba-Me-Boi** in São Luís, and the syncretistic **Festo do Divino** in Alcântara.

The **Centro de Cultura Popular Domingos Vieira Filho (Casa da Festa)** ① *R do Giz 225, T098-3218 9924, Tue-Sun 0900-1900*, has exhibitions on the **Festa do Divino**, together with the African-Brazilian *Tambor-de-Mina* spirit religion (similar to *candomblé*), and Christmas festivities. The old customs building, **Casa do Maranhão** ① *R do Trapiche s/n, Praia Grande, on the waterfront at the far end of R Portugal*, houses a museum devoted to the **Bumba-Meu-Boi** festival (see box, page 590) and Maranhão music. Downstairs is an exhibition hall with artefacts, costumes and video shows of previous Bumba festivals. Upstairs is a series of rooms devoted to a different Bumba-Meu-Boi African-Brazilian rhythm and instruments associated with the festival.

The centre of the African slave trade in the city was the **Cafua das Mercês** ① *R Jacinto Maia 54, Praia Grande, Mon-Fri 0900-1800*. It is now a museum of African-Brazilian culture with an extensive collection of musical and religious instruments, clothing and cultural artefacts. The **Casa das Minas** ① *R do Sol 302, T098-3221 4537, Tue-Sun 0900-1800*, is one of the oldest sacred spaces in Brazil for African-Brazilian religions and is an important centre of black culture in São Luís.

There are numerous other buildings of interest. Although the prettiest and liveliest colonial streets are **Rua Portugal** and **Rua do Giz** (28 de Julho), it is Caixa Econômica Federal in the 19th-century **Edifício São Luís** ① *R da Nazare at R do Egíto*, that preserves what is probably the largest *azulejo*-fronted building in the Americas. It now houses a bank. The **Teatro Arthur de Azevedo** ① *R do Sol 180, T089-3232 0299, daily 1500-2000 or when there are shows*, is a very handsome 19th-century theatre restored to its original spendour in the 1990s. Some of the city's best performances are held here. The **Centro Histórico Solar dos Vasconcelos** ① *R da Estrela 462, Praia Grande, T098-3231 9075, Mon-Fri 0800-1900, Sat and Sun 0900-1900, free*, is a fine colonial town house devoted to the history of the city with many interesting paintings, photographs and exhibits. The first floor of the **Museu de Artes Visuais** ① *R Portugal 293, Praia Grande, T098-3231 6766, Tue-Fri 0900-1900, Sat and Sun 0900-1800*, has a collection of some of the city's most precious and intricate European *azulejos*, mostly from Portugal but with some pieces from England, Holland and Belgium. Upstairs is a collection of important Brazilian art including pieces by Tarsila do Amaral, Cícero Dias and Alfredo Volpi.

Excursions from São Luís

Calhau is a huge beach, 10 km away. **Ponta D'Areia** is nearer to São Luís but more crowded. **Raposa**, a fishing village built on stilts, is a good place to buy handicrafts; there are a few places to stay on Avenida Principal. To get there, take a bus from the Mercado Central in São Luís (one hour with **Viação Santa Maria**, every 30 minutes). Another fishing village, **São José de Ribamar**, has a church dedicated to the patron saint and is a centre for *romeiros* in September. Many bars on the seafront serve local specialities such as fried stonefish. It is a 30-minute bus ride with **Maranhense** from the market in São Luís.

Alcântara → *Colour map 2, A2. Phone code: 098. Population: 22,000.*

The former state capital, Alcântara, is on the muddy mainland bay of São Marcos, 22 km by boat from São Luís across the turbid Rio Bacanga. It's a sleepy, but beautifully preserved colonial town with one of the largest and least modified groups of 17th- and 18th-century colonial buildings in Brazil, whose terracotta roofs and brightly painted façades sit under a baking sun. The town is another of Maranhão's World Heritage sites. During the sugar boom, Alcântara was the preferred retreat of Portuguese plantation owners. The crop was initially harvested by enslaved Indians captured from the Amazon. Most were wiped out by cruelty and disease in the 17th century, and it is the descendants of the African slaves brought in to replace their numbers who give contemporary Alcântara its distinctive Afro-Brazilian culture and cuisine. The town is reknowned for its *cacuriá* dancing (from which lambada is derived), its spicy food and the practice of the *candomblé* spirit religion.

The town clusters around a pretty grassy square called the **Praça da Matriz**, which retains a pillory at its centre. Some 50 of the city's few hundred houses, civic buildings and churches are protected by the federal heritage bureau, IPHAN, and many have been restored. The **Museu Histórico** ① *Praça da Matriz, s/n, daily 0900-1400*, houses some fine *azulejos* and colonial miscellanea, including a bed which was built especially for a scheduled, but cancelled, visit by the Emperor Dom Pedro. It has never been slept in. Another small museum, the **Casa Histórica** ① *Praça da Matriz, Mon-Fri 1000-1600*, has some 18th-century English furniture and porcelain imported by the Alcântara aristocracy. There is a ruined fort on the southern edges of town and a number of crumbling churches and mansions, These include the 17th-century. **Igreja de Nossa Senhora do Carmo** ① *Praça da Matriz, Mon-Fri 0800-1300, 1400-1800, Sat-Sun 0900-1400, free*, with a finely carved rococo interior, the ruined **Matriz de São Matias** (1648), and colonial mansions, such as the **Casa** and **Segunda Casa do Imperador**. These sit alongside numerous old plantation aristocracy mansions with blue, Portuguese-tile façades.

Canoe trips go to **Ilha do Livramento**, where there are good beaches and walks around the coast. It can be muddy after rain, and watch out for mosquitoes after dark. A rocket-launching site has been built nearby.

Ins and outs Launches run to Alcântara from the **Terminal Hidroviário** ① *Rampa Campos Mello, Cais da Praia Grande, São Luís*, at around 0700 and 0930 (US\$20), returning to São Luís at about 1630, depending on the tide. The journey takes about an hour. The sea can be very rough between September and December. Catamaran tours can be booked through in São Luís. ▸▸ *See Activities and tours, page 591.*

Alcântara

To Fonte de Miritituia (500m)

Nova

Ruins

Ruins

Ruins

de Pindaré

da Viola

de Baixo

Direita

Sol

Imperatriz

da Baronesa

Nossa Senhora do Rosario dos Pretos

To 2

To 1 & Praia da Baronesa

Contorno

Ticket Office

Ladeira do Jacare

Inacio Raposo

Fonte das Pedras

das Mercés

Barão de Grajau das Flores

Grande

Casa do Imperador

Praça da Matriz

Colonial Mansion House

Nossa Senhora do Desterro

Lighthouse

Matriz de São Matias (Ruined)

Pelourinho

Forte de São Sebastião (Ruined)

Baía de São Marcos

To Ilha do Livramento

N

200 metres
200 yards

Sleeping ⬭
Pousada Bela Vista **2**
Pousada da Josefa **4**
Pousada dos Guarás **1**

Sítio Tijupá **3**

Eating 🍴
Bar do Lobato **1**

Parque Nacional Lençóis Maranhenses → For listings, see pages 587-592.

Colour map 2, A3. Phone code: 098. www.parquelencois.com.br.

Northeastern Brazil's windswept coast is broken by extensive dunes all the way from Natal to the Amazon. In eastern Maranhão they become so vast that they form a coastal desert stretching for some 140 km between Tutóia on the Delta do Parnaíba and Primeira Cruz, east of São Luís. The Parque Nacional Lençóis Maranhenses, which encloses only a part of the *lençóis*, covers an area of 1550 sq km. The sand extends up to 50 km inland and is advancing by as much as 200 m a year. Dumped by the sea and blown by the wind, it forms ridges 50 m high in long flowing patterns that change constantly. From the air the undulating, talcum powder-white dunes look like giant wrinkled bed sheets ('lençóis' in Portugese). Between December and June the dunes are pocked with freshwater lakes that shine a brilliant blue under the tropical sky and provide a startling contrast with the brilliant white sand.

The coast of the Lençóis Maranhenses provides a refuge for severely endangered species including manatee. Leatherback and green turtles come here to lay their eggs in late summer; while in the forests and scrubland around the Rio Preguiças there are resident puma, jaguar and spectacled caiman. The Lençóis are home to numerous rare species of fish including the South American lungfish, which cocoon themselves in moist mud under the seasonally flooded lake beds in the dry, and shoals of huge game fish like *camurupim* (tarpon) live in the estuaries and rivers. The dunes are a breeding ground for migratory birds such as the lesser yellowlegs, which come all the way from the Arctic to feed here. Recent studies have shown the sparse vegetation to include grasses that are unknown elsewhere.

Excavations begun in 1995 on the supposed site of a Jesuit settlement which, according to local rumour, was buried intact by a sandstorm.

The *lençóis* are not difficult to visit. Travellers who have a few days to spare are rewarded by an amazing panorama of dunes reaching from horizon to horizon, deserted beaches washed by a powerful surf, boat rides on the aptly named **Rio Preguiça** (Lazy River), and tiny, quiet towns and hamlets where strangers are still a relative novelty.

Visiting the park

The *lençóis* are divided into two areas. To the west of Rio Preguiça is the park proper and the **Grandes Lençóis**, which stretch between Ponta Verde in the far west and the town of **Barreirinhas** on the banks of the Preguiça. Barreirinhas is the tourist capital for the region and has plenty of

Barreirinhas

To Parque Nacional
Lençóis Maranhenses

Siqueira Campos
Antonio Dias
Rodoviária
Inacio Neves
Monsenhor Gentil
Coronel Godinho
Major Gaio
Conrado Ataíde
Eco Dunas
Inacio Lins

Av Brasília
Preguiças
Av Beira Rio
Joaquim Spiro de Carvalho

Toyotas for
Paulino Neves
& Tutóia

To Vassouras,
Mandacaru
Atins & Caburé

Dunes

31 de Março

N

200 metres
200 yards

Sleeping 🛌
Belo Horizonte 4
Buriti 1

Pousada Igarapé 2
Tia Cota 3

Eating 🍴
Barlavento Carlão 1
Bona Mesa Pizzaría 3
Maré Mansa Mineiro 4
Paladar 5

pousadas and restaurants and tour operators, such as **Eco Dunas**, offering trips into the park. From here it is easy to arrange tours and transfers along the Rio Preguiça both up and downstream and onwards through the Delta do Parnaíba to Jericoacoara.

The dunes east of the Rio Preguiça form the **Pequenos Lençóis**, which extend to **Tutóia**. These are easier to travel through than the Grandes Lençóis but less easy to visit on an organized tour. **Paulino Neves**, a town rather than a hamlet on the Rio Cangata, is just south of a series of large dunes at the eastern end of the *lençóis*.

There are several small, friendly settlements in the Pequenos Lençóis. Most lie on the Rio Preguiça. The two-shack town of **Vassouras** is literally at the feet of the *lençóis*; its make-shift huts are watched over by a spectacular, looming dune whose crest affords wonderful views. Further downstream at **Mandacaru** there is a lighthouse with great views out over the coast and some craft shops selling Buriti palm-weave work and carvings. **Atins** and **Caburé** are miniature beach resorts sandwiched between a rough and windy Atlantic and the lazy blue waters of the Preguiça. Both are surrounded by a bleak sea of sand.

You can walk into parts of the Grandes Lençóis from Atins and into the Pequenos Lençóis from Caburé (see below). Many of the overland tours from Jericoacoara finish in Caburé. Be careful of broken glass – especially in Caburé where rubbish is buried rather than collected.

Ins and outs

There are four buses a day to Barreirinhas from São Luís (four hours, US$7) and numerous transit combis and Toyotas bookable through São Luís hotels. There is Toyota transport east between Barreirinhas and Paulino Neves and further connections from here to the scruffy port town of Tutóia and the Delta do Parnaíba, or onward buses to Parnaíba town for the rest of Piauí and Jericoacoara and Fortaleza in Ceará. Many of the towns along the route have a bad wind-blown rubbish problem and their streets are littered with billowing plastic bags and the corpses of discarded bottles.

Traversing the Pequenos Lençóis

It is possible to walk or cycle along the coast in front of the Pequenos Lençóis between **Caburé** and **Tutóia** in either direction; allow about three days. Camping is permitted, but you must take all supplies with you including water, since some dune lakes are salty. The

Barreirinhas to Jericoacoara

Drastic plastic

There are few places on the planet where the ravages of plastic waste are more apparent than in the windswept far northeast of Brazil. It is everywhere: snagged and billowing in trees on the edges of the Lençóis Maranhenses, floating like jellyfish in the wild waters of the Delta do Parnaíba, piled up as drift on the beaches of Ceará and strewn along roadside verges between towns and cities throughout the region. The UN Environment Programme estimates that there are now 46,000 pieces of plastic litter floating in every square mile of ocean on earth.

In 1993 the Brazilian Newton Diniz invented a type of plastic that bio-degrades in 18-48 months and invested money in a biodegradable plastics factory. His company, Polibag, www.polibag.com.br, now provides the whole of the city of Porto Seguro, including all the supermarkets and hotels, with biodegradable plastic as well as myriad clients in the USA, Europe and Japan. This is despite forceful resistance from the petro-chemical industry who set up an NGO campaigning against Polibag's work.

area is very remote and you may not see another person for the duration of the walk. Because of the hot and sandy conditions, this is a punitive trek, only for the very hardy. Do not try the treacherous hike inland across the dunes or a hike into the Grandes Lençóis without a guide. The dunes are disorientating and there have been a number of cases of hikers becoming lost and dying of heat exposure or starvation.

Northern Maranhão and the Reentrâncias Maranhenses → For listings, see pages 587-592.

Northern Maranhão is separated from neighbouring Para by the Reentrâncias Maranhenses, the wildest, most remote and least visited stretch of coast in Brazil's northeast. It is made up of deep inlets thick with mangroves and brackish swamps, jewel-like forested islands and vast dunes of shifting sand. The *reentrâncias* are home to a scattered handful of fishing communities and millions of rare and endangered endemic and migratory waterbirds, making them one of the world's most important wetland areas, protected by **Ramsar**, www.ramsar.org (see also www.wetlands.org). This is pioneer territory for tourists of any kind, including birders.

Offshore, in the **Parcel Manoel Luís State Marine Park**, are the most extensive reef systems in South America dotted with the broken remains of some 200 ships, from Portuguese Caravels to modern tankers and with very rich marine life, with many endemics and abundant potato cod and large sharks. Visibility is around 35 m, with an average depth of 30 m and water temperature a balmy 32°C. The reef is

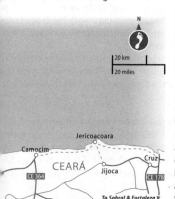

almost completely unexplored by divers as it is almost 70 km offshore and some 200 km from São Luís. There are few operators and tides and currents are very strong.

Ins and outs

The *reentrâncias* span the coast between Alcântara and Carutapera on the Para border. Access is difficult as there are few roads, little infrastructure and scant accommodation. The main centre for the little tourism that exists are the coastal fishing villages of **Apicum- Açu** and **Cururupu**, both connected by daily, bumpy bus to Alcântara. Only part of the road is paved to the former and access is tough in the wet and there a very simple *pousadas* in both villages.

Boats leave Apicum-Açu for the **Ilha dos Lençóis**, a small fishing community lost in time, huge dunes and mangroves near Parcel Manoel Luís State Marine Park. At present diving in that park can be organized (with plenty of notice) only through larger dive shops in São Paulo.

Southern Maranhão → *For listings, see pages 587-592.*

Carolina → *Phone code: 099. Population: 23,000.*

Carolina is a pretty colonial town of whitewashed houses and terracotta roofs on the banks of the Tocantins river. The climate is hot and damp, the sunsets over the river spectacular and the town is set in the midst of the **Parque Nacional Chapada das Mesas**, a vast area of some 160 000 ha of waterfalls and escarpments covered in a mix of *cerrado* and tropical forest and replete with wildlife.

The **Cachoeira da Pedra Caída**, on the Rio Farinha just off the BR-010, 35 km outside town is one of the northeast's most beautiful: a three-tiered waterfall that plunges into a rocky gorge. The **Cachoeiras do Itapecuru** off the BR-230, 33 km from Carolina are two conjoined falls that fall into a huge swimming hole surrounded by pretty white-sand beaches. The Rio Farinha, a tributary of the Tocantins, has a further series of spectacular falls including the **Cachoeira São Romão** a thundering curtain of water more than 100 m and Farinha itself which falls into wide, deep and clear plunge pool. You'll need a guide with a 4WD to visit them. But come soon as they are threatened by a hydroelectric project.

The **Cachoeira da Prata** 40 km from town, are next to the **Morro das Figuras**, which is covered with rock inscriptions thought to have been carved by the ancestors of the Tup people. Access is by unsealed road from the BR-230, requiring a 4WD. The Chapada das Mesas has a series of other table top mountains, including the **Morro do Portal**, which affords wonderful views and is easy to reach from Carolina.

Between June and August the Tocantins river is low and lined with beaches, the best o which are on the opposite side of the river in the little town of **Filadélfia**, in Tocantins. The city's goes out at night on the **Ilha dos Botes**, a river island 5 km from town filled with simple bars and restaurants.

Ins and outs Carolina lies 221 km south of Imperatriz on a road which joins the BR-010 There are frequent buses. The **rodoviária** ① *T099-3531 2076*, is in the centre. A ferry connects the town with Filadelfia in Tocantins on the opposite bank of the rive (10 minutes). For information contact **Secretaria de Turismo** ① *R Duque de Caxias 522 T098- 3731 1613, Mon-Fri 0800-1300*. Guides and transport cost US$20-30 per half day and can be organized through *pousadas*.

Maranão listings

For Sleeping and Eating price codes and other relevant information, see pages 32-37.

Sleeping

São Luís *p577, map p579*

Although many Brazilians opt to stay on the beach the sand is not as clean as it is in Piauí and Ceará, while the city centre is charming and full of life. Cheap hotels can be found in R das Palmas, very central, and R Formosa.

AL Pestana São Luís, Av Avicência, Praia do Calhau, T098-2106 0505, www.pestanasao luis.com.br A fully renovated resort hotel housed in a former 1970s grand hotel. This is much the best option for families or business. Rooms are well appointed with work stations and good desks, there's a full business centre and the various leisure options include a large pool, games area and tennis courts.

A Grand São Luís Hotel, Praça Dom Pedro II 299, T098-2109 3500, www.atlantica hotels.com.br. A newly refurbished 1960s grand dame with plain rooms, the best of which have sea views. Business facilities, pool and gym.

B Portas da Amazônia, R do Giz 129, T098-222 9937, www.portasdaamazonia.com.br. Tastefully converted wood-floor rooms in a colonial building in the heart of the centre. Smart and well run. Internet.

B-C Pousada Colonial, R Afonso Pena 112, T098-3232 2834, www.clickcolonial.com.br. Clean, well-kept rooms set in a beautiful restored, tiled house, a/c, comfortable, quiet.

C-D Lord, R de Nazaré 258, facing Praça Benedito Leite, T/F098-3221 4655. The carpets and scruffy walls in the lobby and on the stairs don't look as if they've been changed since the hotel opened in the 1970s, but the long, plain red rooms are spacious and clean, and they offer views out over the colonial centre from tiny terraces. Noisy a/c, cheapest with shared bathroom. Check for spongy mattresses.

C Hotel Cantaria, R da Estrela 115, T098-221 3390. Spartan but bright single, double,

a/c or fan-cooled triple rooms with good views out over R da Estrela.

D-E Internacional, R da Estrela 175, T098-3231 5154. Very scruffy, tiny fan-cooled boxes with button-sized windows in a dilapidated house reached by rickety stairs. Bizarrely very popular with backpackers but definitely only for the desperate. Other options nearby.

D-E Solar das Pedras, R da Palma 127, T098-3232 6694, www.ajsolardaspedras.com.br. This HI-affiliated hostel is by far the best backpacker option in town, well-run, with tidy 4- to 6-person dorms (**E** pp) and doubles, internet, lockers and a little garden.

Excursions from São Luís *p581*

In Raposa there are hotels on Av Principal.
C Hotel Sol e Mar, Av Gonçalves Dias 320, São José de Ribamar. With a restaurant.

Alcântara *p581, map p582*

B Pousada dos Guarás, Praia da Baronesa, T098-3337 1339. A beach front *pousada* with a series of bungalows with en suites, a good restaurant, canoe hire and advice on excursions around the town.

D Pousada Bela Vista, Vila Jerico s/n, Cema, T098-3337 1569, danniloalcantara@ ig.com.br. Cabins and pretty suites with great views out over the bay and a restaurant with delicious Maranhense food.

D-E Sítio Tijupá, R de Baixo s/n at the Post Office, T098-3337 1291. Tiny simple *pousada* with 4 small but well-kept, fan-cooled rooms.

E Pousada da Josefa, R Direita, T098-3337 1109. A friendly, family-run restaurant and *pousada* right in the centre with a range of very simple, plain rooms. Look at several.

Parque Nacional Lençóis Maranhenses *p583, map p583*
Barreirinhas

Most hotels can organize tours. Bring a hammock for flexibility; in the smaller hamlets it is always possible to rent space in a beach bar or restaurant for a few dollars.

A Buriti, R Inácio Lins s/n, T098-3349 1800, www.pousadadoburiti.com.br. Corridors of large, plain rooms with concrete terraces near a pool and breakfast area. Simple but the best in the centre of town.

C Belo Horizonte, R Joaquim Soeiro de Carvalho 245, T098-3499 0054, www.bh mirante.com.br. Well-kept tiled and white-washed rooms near the central square. The quietest are at the front. Good service from the welcoming owner, Albino and a pleasant rooftop breakfast area. Sister *pousada* in Caburé.

C-D Pousada Igarapé, R Coronel Godinho 320, T098-9111 0461. Small, boxy fan-cooled or a/c doubles set in corridors opposite the Assembleia de Deus church, which has noisy hellfire sermons at weekends.

D Tia Cota, R Coronel Godinho 204, T098-3349 1237. Simple fan or a/c whitewashed rooms, with decent beds and mattresses, ranging from phone box-sized with shared baths to more spacious en suite doubles.

Caburé, Vassouras, Mandacaru and Atins

It is possible to rent hammock space in the restaurant shacks in Vassouras or Mandacaru for around US$20 per day with food included.

C-D Rancho Pousada, R Principal, Praia do Atins, Atins, T098-9616 9646, www.rancho pousada.com. Comfortable, though simple beach chalets cooled by the constant sea breeze. The best are close to the waterfront. The *pousada* has a simple restaurant and a pool. There are a couple of other, simpler options in the village.

D-E Pousada do Paulo (aka Pousada Lençóis de Areia), Praia do Caburé, T098-9143 4668. Rooms for up to 4. Well- kept. The owner was the first to settle here and named the town after a local bird. Best food in the village. Watch out for glass on the vast, sweeping Atlantic beach. There are other options in town and rooms are always available outside peak season.

Paulino Neves and Tutóia

Tutóia is an ugly, scruffy town surrounded by wastelands of billowing plastic bage. It's a good idea to try and arrive early and leave quickly.

C Tutóia Palace Hotel, Av Paulino Neves 1100, Tutóia, T098-3479 1247, Lençóis de Areia. Crumbling mock colonial hotel in garish pink with 12 fading rooms, 5 of which have a/c and none of which are palatial.

D-E Oasis dos Lençóis, Av Rio Novo, Centro, Paulino Neves T098-9966 1351. A very friendly river bank *pousada* run by Dona Mazé and her family. Public areas are decorated with old photos of the Lençóis, the breakfasts generous, but the fan-cooled rooms are very simple and in need of refurbishment.

E-F Tremembés, Praça Tremembés, Tutóia, T098-3479 1354. Very, very simple, with fan-cooled plain boxes and shared bathrooms. Look at several.

Reentrâncias Maranhenses *p585*
Cururupu

D-E Hotel Kelma, R Cesario Coimbra, Centro, T098-3391 1252. 20 very simple rooms with shared baths and fans.

D-E Hotel Natalia, Av Liberalino Miranda 53, Jacaré, T098-3391 2359. A friendly family-run guesthouse with 8 plain little rooms with shared bathrooms and a large breakfast,

Carolina *p586*

There are a handful of very simple *pousadas* near the bus station.

B-C Chalés da Pedra Caída, Praça do Estudante 460, T099-3531 2318. Chalets with fan, restaurant, natural pool and 3 neighbouring waterfalls.

C-D Pousada do Lajes, Estr por Riachão (BR-230), Km 2, T099-3531 2452, www.pousadadolajes.com.br. Chalets with a/c gathered around a little pool outside town with a restaurant and a small play area for kids

🍴 Eating

São Luís p577, map p579

Bases provide simple home cooking, although most are found away from the centre and beaches. Typical dishes are *arroz de cuxá* and *torta de camarão* and desserts or liqueurs made from local fruits. Try the local soft drink *Jesús* or *Jenève*. **R da Estrela** has many eating places with outdoor terraces. **R dos Afogados** has good places for lunch. There is further choice in the **São Francisco** district, just across bridge. The centre is very lively on Fri and Sat but on Sun most people go to **Praia Calhau**.

¶¶¶-¶¶ Antigamente, R da Estrela 210. Portuguese and Brazilian standards, decent fish and pizza in this restaurant decorated with local art, colourful bottles and bric-a-brac. Lively on weekends and Mon-Fri after 0800.

¶¶¶-¶¶ Armazen Estrela, R da Estrela 401, T098- 3254 1274. A fine dining restaurant upstairs, offering French-Brazilian dishes like partridge in *cajá* sauce and standards like steak diane. Downstairs there's a great little *botequin* in a long, stone-walled cool room with Romanesque brick arches, offering good *petisco* snacks and live music on weekends.

¶¶¶-¶¶ Papagaio Amarelo, R da Estrela 210. Varied menu with excellent fish and regional standards and tables that spill out into the plaza. Both this restaurant and neighbouring **Antigamente** are the liveliest spots in this busy streets and have good live music at weekends.

¶ Padaria Frances Valery, R do Giz (28 de Julho) 164. Delicious cakes, eclairs, quiches, tropical fruit juices and coffee, friendly.

¶ Scorpions, R da Palma 83. Great value per kilo with a good choice of stews, salads and *pratos feitos*. Near the HI.

Alcântara p581, map p582

¶ Bar do Lobato, Praça da Matriz. Pleasant with good simple food, fried shrimps highly recommended.

Parque Nacional Lençóis Maranhenses p583, map p583
Barreirinhas

¶¶-¶ Barlavento Carlão, Av Beira Rio s/n, T098- 3349 0627. Fillet of fish in Passion fruit sauce, açai pulp with guarana and various simple meat and poultry dishes and fresh juices.

¶ Bona Mesa Pizzaria, R Inacio Lins s/n. Wide choice of pizzas cooked in a traditional wood-fired oven and delicious *doce de buriti* dessert.

¶ Maré Mansa Mineiro, Rio Preguicas at Joaquim Diniz. A floating restaurant, bar and dance club with live reggae every Wed and Sat. Very busy after 2300 with a crowd ranging from 18 years old to 80.

¶ Paladar, Coronel Godinho 176. Very cheap but hearty *prato feitos* with meat, chicken or fish options, rice, beans, vegetables and salad.

🍷 Bars and clubs

São Luís p577, map p579
There is *cacuriá* dancing, drum parades and buzzing nightlife every Fri and Sat along the north end of **R do Giz** and along **R João Gualberto**.

Antigamente, Praia Grande. Live music Thu-Sat.

Reggae Bar do Porto, R do Portugal 49, T098-3232 1115. One of the best reggae bars in the city with a broad range of live acts and DJs and a vibrant crowd at weekends.

Reggae (Roots) Bar, R da Palma 86, T098-3221 7580. Live reggae and Maranhão roots music most nights. Especially lively at weekends.

🎭 Entertainment

São Luís p577, map p579
Cinema Colossal, Av Mcal Castelo Branco 92, São Francisco. Passeio, R Oswaldo Cruz 806.
Theatre Teatro Artur de Azevedo, see page 581. Teatro Viriato Correa, Av Getúlio Vargas, Monte Castelo, T098-3218 9019.

Bumba-Meu-Boi

Throughout the month of June the streets of São Luís are alive to the sound of *tambores* and dancers recreating the legend of Catirina, Pai Francisco and his master's bull. Although this mixture of African, indigenous and Portuguese traditions exists throughout the north, it is in Maranhão that it is most developed, with around 100 groups in São Luís alone. Here there are various styles called *sotaques*, which have different costumes, dances, instruments and *toadas*. These are Boi de Matraca da Ilha and Boi de Pindaré, both accompanied by small percussion instruments called *matracas*, Boi de Zabumba marked by the use of a type of drum, and Boi de Orquestra accompanied by string and wind instruments. Although there are presentations throughout June the highlights are the 24th (São João) and the 29th (São Pedro) with the closing ceremony lasting throughout the 30th (São Marçal), particularly in the bairro João Paulo. The shows take place in an *arraial*, which are found all over the city, with the ones at Projeto Reviver and Ceprama being more geared towards tourists (however be aware that a livelier more authentic atmosphere is to be found elsewhere in other *bairros*, such as Madre Deus). The Centro de Cultura Popular Domingos Vieira Filho at Rua do Giz 221, Praia Grande is the place to learn more about these variations as well as many other local festivals and traditions such as Tambor de Crioula or Cacuriá, both sensual dances derived from Africa. A good location to see these dances and capoeira practised is Labouarte, Rua Jansen Muller, Centro (Cacuriá de Dona Tetê is particularly recommended, with participation encouraged).

⊛ Festivals and events

São Luís *p577, map p579*
24 Jun Bumba-Meu-Boi, see box, above. For several days before the festival, street bands parade, particularly in front of São João and São Benedito churches. There are dances somewhere in the city almost every night in Jun and a whole string of smaller Boi-related festivals and very lively *cacuriá* and reggae at weekends all year round, especially on R Giz.
Aug São Benedito, at the Rosário church.
Oct Festival with dancing, at **Vila Palmeira** suburb (take bus of same name).

Alcântara *p581, map p582*
Jun Festa do Divino, at Pentecost (Whitsun). On 29 Jun is **São Pedro** saint day.
Aug São Benedito.

○ Shopping

São Luís *p577, map p579*
Arts and crafts
IDAM, Coisa da Terra and Mil Cores Rua Portugal, on R Portugal sell wicker and weave work, pottery and figurines from Maranhão. **Arte Indígena Maranhense**, R do Giz at João Gualberto, T098-3221 2940. Sells Maranhão art made by indigenous peoples.

Music and books
Poeme-Sé, R João Gualberto 52, Praia Grande, T098-3232 4968. Cosy little bookshop and cybercafé with a selection of Maranhão music. **Rodrigo CDs Maranhenses**, R João Vital s/n between Estrela and Giz, T098-3232 4799, sells a huge selection of Maranhão and north-eastern roots, traditional and contemporary music. This is one of the best music shops in northeastern Brazil.

Parque Nacional Lençóis
Maranhenses *p583, map p583*
Barreirinhas
There is an arts and crafts market next to the river selling *buriti* palm waevework bags, mats and homeware. Light and excellent value.

⛰ Activities and tours

São Luís *p577, map p579*
Eco Dunas, with an office in São Luís airport T098-3349 0545, also at R Inácio Lins 164, Barreirinhas, T011-4654 1200, www.eco dunas.tur.br. The best option for tours of Lençóis Maranhenses, the delta and tours all the way from São Luís to Jericoacoara or vice versa. Excellent guides, infrastructure and organization. English spoken and flights organized. Can arrange wonderful scenic flights over the Lençóis with pilot Amirton for around US$100. The company also run 1-day tours around São Luís, trips to the Parque Nacional das Sete Cidades and visits to Alcântara.
Francinaldo dos Santos, T098-8839 0578, fran-live@hotmail.com. Freelance guide in Barreirinhas. Good for groups only. Excellent rates and adventure trips. A local who grew up in the area. Portuguese only.
Phylipi, T098-8118 1710, phylipi@hotmail. com. Very good guide for São Luís and Alcântara. Fluent English and French. US$25 for a 2- to 3-hr city centre tour. Around US$80

per day for groups of up to 10. Trips run to the Lençóis Maranhenses; also offers transfers to the Delta do Parnaíba and Jericoacoara.

Reentrâncias Maranhenses *p585*
For those interested in diving in the Parcel Manoel Luís State Marine Park contact **SCAFO**, Universitário SENAC, Av Eng Eusébio Stevaux 823, Santo Amaro, São Paulo, T011-5682 7766, www.scafo.com.br. Can organize dive operators and boats in São Luís. Give plenty of notice.

🚌 Transport

São Luís *p577, map p579*
Air Minivans run to the airport from Praça Deodoro in the centre, every 40 mins until 2200, US$1, 1 hr. As well as local flights, there are connections through **Belém**, **Teresina** or **Fortaleza** to the rest of Brazil and international flights to the **Guianas** and **Portugal**.
  Airline offices GOL, www.voegol. com.br and TAM, www.tam.com.br have offices at the airport. Other airlines include: Litoranea, www.voelitoranea.com.br; Oceanair, www.oceanair.com.br; TAF, www.voetaf.com.br; and TAP Air Portugal, www.flytap.com.

Boat Boats to **Alcântara** leave from the Terminal Hidroviario da Praia Grande Rampa Campos Melo s/n, Cais da Praia Grande, São Luís, T098-3232 0692. There are departures

in the morning usually at 0700 and 0930 but times vary according to the tide. The trip takes 1 hr, US$4.

Bus To **Fortaleza**, US$270, 4 a day, 18 hrs. To **Belém**, 13 hrs, US$30, **Transbrasiliana** at 1900 and 2000 (no *leito*). Also to **Recife**, US$50, 25 hrs, all other major cities and local towns. To **Barreirinhas**, 3 hrs on a newly paved road US$10. More comfortable on a private bus, US$30 – organize through **Eco Dunas** (see page 591) or your hotel.

Alcântara *p581, map p582*
Boat Boats from Alcântara to **São Luís** leave daily at 0830 and 1600.

Parque Nacional Lençóis Maranhenses *p583, map p583*
Hotels in São Luís can book minivan trips for the same price as the bus. See Ins and outs page 584. A regular boat service plies the river between **Barreirinhas** and **Caburé** and/or **Atins** stopping at **Vassouras** and **Mandaracu** on the way. Boats leave daily at 1000-1100 from the end of the **Orla** next to the town dune (US$4, 3-4 hrs to Caburé or Atins; both 4 hrs, US$10); the boat returns with the tide. Speedboats can be organized at Barreirinhas through **Eco Dunas** (see page 591), and it is possible to reach both **Paulino Neves** or even **Tutóia** by boat.

Marcelo T098-3349 1964, organizes freelance boat trips for a good price to anywhere in the region. **Mão**, T098-9608 0624, has 4WD transfers to Tutóia from Barreirinhas via the other towns and villages.

ⓘ Directory

São Luís *p577, map p579*
Banks There are branches of all the major Brazilian banks. **Bradesco** Av Magalhães Almeida 300, T098-3212 2359 and at the airport. **Banco do Brasil**, Praça Deodoro, for TCs and Visa ATMs and at the airport HSBC, off Praça João Lisboa, accepts MasterCard/Cirrus/ Maestro at ATMs. Agetur, R do Sol 33A. **Embassies and consulates** France, R Santo Antônio 259, T098-3231 4459. Germany, Praça Gonçalves Dias 301, T098-3232 7766. Italy, R do Genipapeiro, Jardim São Francisco, T098-3227 0270. Spain, Praça Duque de Caxias 3, João Paulo, T098-3223 2846. USA, Av Daniel de La Touche, Jardim Buriti, T098-3248 1769. **Internet** Plenty of internet cafés in the centre of town. HCG, R Paparaúbas 11, São Francisco. **Language courses** Senhora Amin Castro, T098-3227 1527, for Portuguese lessons. Recommended. **Laundry** Nova China, R da Paz 518. **Libraries** Arquivo Público, R de Nazaré 218, rare documents on local history. **Medical services** Clínica São Marcelo, R do Passeio 546, English-speaking doctor. Hospital Monte Sinai, R Rio Branco 156, T098-3232 3260, 24 hrs. **Post office** Praça João Lisboa 292. **Telephone** Embratel, Av Dom Pedro II 190.

Alcântara *p581, map p582*
Banks There are no longer any **Bradesco** banks in Alcântara – bring cash from São Luís. Banco do Estado do Maranhão, R Grande 76, changes US$ and TCs. **Post office** R Direita off Praça da Matriz. **Telephone** Telemar, R Grande, 0700-2200.

Carolina *p586*
Banks Banco do Brasil, A Mascarenhas 159. **Medical services** FNS, R Benedito Leite 57, T098-3731 1271. **Telephone** Av E Barros, 0730-2230.

Contents

Border crossings

The Amazon

At a glance

Getting around Internal flights and boats; some buses, but very few passable roads.

Time required 3 days for Manaus or Belém. 2-3 days for Cristalino Jungle Lodge or Mamirauá. 10 days to travel between Manaus and Belém. 2-4 weeks to get off the beaten track.

Weather Hot and wet year round. Belém wettest Dec-Apr, Manaus Mar-May; Sep-Nov is the wettest in the southern Amazon.

When not to go Good to visit year round but least comfortable in the wetter months.

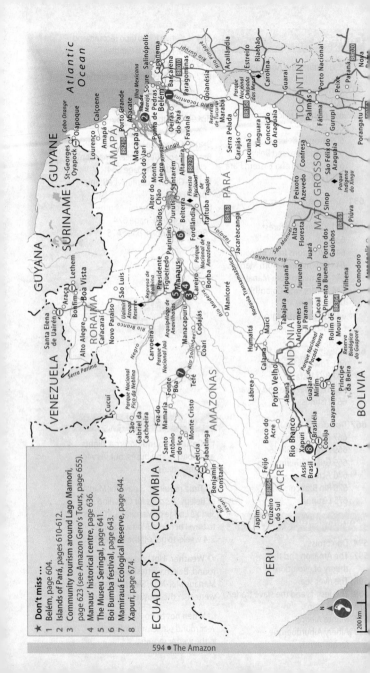

Don't miss ...

★ Belém, page 604.

1 Islands of Pará, pages 610-612.

2 Community tourism around Lago Mamori, page 623 (see Amazon Gero's Tours, page 655).

3 Manaus' historical centre, page 636.

4 The Museu Seringal, page 641.

5 Boi Bumba festival, page 643.

6 Mamirauá Ecological Reserve, page 644.

7 Xapuri, page 674.

The Amazon is far more than a river. It is a continent of forests, savannahs and mountains, coursed by myriad veins of flowing water, pocked with lakes, overflowing with flooded forests and home to several million people. The wildlife is spectacular but the forests are dense and animals are far easier to spot in the Pantanal or cerrado. What is magical about the Amazon are its vast landscapes – its oceanic rivers, shimmering skies and labyrinthine backwaters – and the unique human drama which is played out here day after day.

The Amazon offers great diveristy. In the north, along the border with Venezuela and Colombia, are the forests and savannahs of the Guiana Shield where vegetation grows like a giant filigree over white sand and recycles 99.9% of its water and nutrients. West of here, the magnificent Rio Negro, black as coffee and fringed with pearly beaches, gushes past giant boulders the size of mountains before winding through the world's largest river archipelago, the Anavilhanas, and spreading out over several kilometres as it reaches the teeming port of Manaus.

In the east, the Amazon is joined by a series of rivers which are in their own right some of the largest in the world: the glassy blue Tapajos, the inky Xingu and, just as the river reaches its mouth, the Tocantins. Here the Amazon divides around an island the size of Denmark, the Ilha de Marajó, before spilling into the Atlantic, turning it fresh 100 miles offshore. Two cities lie on its banks: sleepy Macapá, with road connections to the Guianas; and bustling Belém, a historic colonial city with some of the best nightlife and cuisine in Brazil.

In the far west, the forests are gentler, more fertile and filled with life. Deforestation has been minimal and many tribal people remain uncontacted. The floating Uakari lodge is one of the Amazon's best.

In the southern Amazon state of Rondônia, the trees are broken by giant soya fields and cattle pasture, which cut into the green with geometric order. The state of Acre is far wilder and offers the chance to stay in indigenous villages or explore the forests around Xapuri – protected thanks to the world's first eco-martyr, Chico Mendes.

Visiting the Amazon → *See also page 802.*

The Amazon belongs to six Brazilian states: **Amapá** and **Pará** in the northwest, **Amazonas** in the east, **Roraima** in the north on the borders of the Guianas and Venezuela, and **Rondônia** and **Acre** in the southwest on the borders of Bolivia and Peru. Further areas extend into northern **Mato Grosso** and **Tocantins**, whose Amazon territories and sights are dealt with in the Pantanal and the Brasília, Goiás and Tocantins chapters, respectively.

Contrary to many people's expectations, the Amazon is not the best place in Brazil for seeing wildlife. Forest provides excellent cover and most animals live in the canopy. Even in the small rainforest lodges on the tiniest, remotest tributaries, animals are hard to spot. Whilst there are locations within the Amazon that specialize in wildlife (notably Mamirauá, see page 644, and Cristalino Jungle Lodge, see page 755), far more can be seen in the Pantanal. Visitors using any operator listed in the text can, however, expect to see caiman, several species of monkey and at least one species of river dolphin. They will also see many birds, especially on dawn or dusk trips on the smaller rivers.

The Amazon is, though, far more than a wild safari park. It is the last great preserve of tropical wilderness on Earth. There are few places in the world where the power of living nature can be felt more potently or where a way of life in tune with that power survives more successfully. Come here for the landscapes, for vast skies and interminable views, for rivers that feel like a sea and the hypnotic, trance-like music of the rainforest – sung by a chorus of millions.

Ins and outs

Getting there

There are a number of entrance points to the Amazon: **Manaus**, a city of 1.5 million people in the middle of the Amazon Basin, is the best place to organize safari cruises and lodges. It also offers the best access (by boat or air) to smaller towns further into the forest, such as Tefé. This is where one of the two best Amazon rainforest lodges lies: **Mamirauá Ecological Reserve**, see page 644 (the other being **Cristalino Jungle Lodge** in Mato Grosso – see page 755). Manaus is also the point of departure for a string of jungle lodges within a few hours of the capital – the best of which offer fascinating glimpses of both the forest and a timeless way of life – through some of the best community tourism projects in Brazil. It is also the jumping off point for the waterfalls of **Presidente Figueiredo** (see page 642), and the **Boi Bumba** festival in Parintins (see page 643).

Belém, at the mouth of the Amazon, began as a colonial slaving port and grew into a city with one of the best alternative cultural scenes in the north of Brazil. There are no forest lodges near Belém but it is possible to visit the rainforest on a cruise, with a small operator, or whilst staying on one of the river islands, such as **Marajó**. It is also possible to visit the forest from **Santarém**, a small city at the meeting of the Tapajós river and the Amazon.

Acre, in the south, is rapidly emerging as an alternative entrance point. The state lies right on the border with Peru and is served by regular flights and buses from Cuzco. **Xapuri**, which was the home of the first eco-martyr Chico Mendes (see box, page 672) is now the entrance point to the **Reserva Extrativista Chico Mendes** – a sustainable reserve where it is possible to see rubber tappers at work, and where there is abundant wildlife. Tour operator **Maanaim Amazônia**, see page 677, runs tours throughout Acre, including to indigenous villages far off the beaten track.

The Amazon and the theory of evolution

While the Spanish and Portuguese came to the Amazon to plunder, pillage and enslave, the Europeans who followed them in the 18th and 19th centuries were more interested in beetles and botany than gold. Among the first was the Frenchman Charles Marie de la Condamine, who came to the Andes in the mid-1700s to ascertain whether the earth was a perfect sphere. He narrowly escaped being stoned by a superstitious mob in Cuenca, Ecuador, and fled to Cayenne. In doing so he was obliged to cross the Amazon, producing the first accurate map of the basin along the way and bringing rubber back to Europe. De la Condamine inspired other Enlightenment scientists to follow him. The greatest was Alexander von Humboldt, today known for the Humboldt Current (which he did not discover) and the Humboldt River (which he never saw), but who, in his time, was considered the pre-eminent scientist in Europe. During his stay on the upper Rio Negro, this great German collected some 12,000 specimens and survived shocks by electric eels, *curaré* poison and bathing with piranhas. He captured and dissected a 7-m caiman and established the region as the best in the world for the study of natural sciences. The English followed him: Henry Bates, Richard Spruce and, in 1848, Alfred Russel Wallace, who wrote: "I'd be an Indian here, and live content, to fish and hunt, and paddle my canoe, and see my children grow, like wild young fawns, In health of body and peace of mind, rich without wealth, and happy without gold! "

The seemingly infinite variety of plants and animals in the Amazon caused Wallace to reflect on how all this variety had come about: "so alike in design yet so changeable in detail? "Places not more than fifty or a hundred miles apart have species of insects and birds at the one which are not found at the other. There must be some boundary which determines the range of each species, some external peculiarity to mark the line which each one does not pass."

Charles Darwin had the same thought two years earlier after his return from Brazil and while reading an essay by Thomas Malthus on population. In his essay the economist argued that the realization of a happy society will always be hindered by its tendencies to expand more quickly than its means of subsistence. If this is true of animals, thought Darwin, then they must compete to survive and Nature must act as a selective force, killing off the weak, and species must evolve each from another through this process. Darwin was terrified by the implications of his thought and did not commit it to paper for six years, then sealing it and handing it to his wife with instructions to publish it after his death.

Alfred Russel Wallace was younger and less timid. While in a high fever on a field trip in Indonesia he was pondering over the thoughts that had haunted him since his days on the Amazon, and he too recalled the same essays by Malthus. The same thought which had struck Darwin, flashed into his own mind: "I saw at once that the ever-present variability of all living things would furnish the material from which, by the mere weeding out of those less adapted to the actual conditions, the fittest alone would survive the race." Wallace wrote to Darwin who was, at that time, the most famous natural scientist in Britain, explaining his theory and asking for his advice. Darwin's hand was forced and, after papers written by both scientists were presented at the Linnean Society on the same day, the theory of evolution was born.

The river sea

Many people imagine the Amazon as a single river but, in reality, it is a huge network of rivers extending into nine countries. Before the Andes were formed, some 15 million years ago, the Amazon flowed west into the Pacific. However, as the crash of continental plates pushed up the mountains, the river was cut off from its ocean and became a vast inland sea, hemmed in by the Guiana Shield to the east. Over millions of years this sea eroded the ancient conglomerate shield, until it eventually burst through into the Atlantic. It left behind a vast filigree of veins that today make up the Amazon river system, populated by prehistoric, air-breathing fish like the pirarucu, and unique freshwater species such as the Amazon stingrays (Potamatrygonidae), whose closest relatives still live in the Pacific.

International flights into the Amazon Flights from the USA or Europe tend to come via Fortaleza, Rio de Janeiro, São Paulo or Salvador, with airlines such as **TAP**, www.flytap.com. The region also has the following direct international connections:

To **Manaus** from Miami with **TAM**, www.tam.com.br; from Panama (with connections onward to cities in Central America and the USA) with **Copa**, www.copaair.com; from Atlanta with **Delta**, www.delta.com.

To **Belém** from Haiti and Martinique via Cayenne (Guyane) with **Air Caribes**, www.aircaraibes.com, with connections from Paris; from Georgetown (Guyana) and Paramaribo (Suriname) with **META**, www.voemeta.com; from Paramaribo with **Surinan**.

To **Boa Vista** in Roraima from Georgetown and Paramaribo with **META**.

To **Rio Branco** in Acre from Lima and Cuzco with **Star Peru**, www.starperu.com.

To **Cruzeiro do Sul** in Acre from Pucallpa in Peru with **Star Peru**, www.starperu.com.

Destinations in Colombia can be reached through **Leticia**, which is conjoined with Tabatinga on the far western Amazonian border.

International borders The Brazilian Amazon has a number of borders permitting overland or river crossings.

Venezuela can be reached from Boa Vista (Roraima) via Santa Elena, from where there are buses to Caracas; or with far more difficulty from São Gabriel da Cachoeira (Amazonas) via Cucuí (Amazonas) and San Carlos de Río Negro in Venezuela for Puerto Ayacucho, which also has buses to Caracas and the rest of the country. See page 664.

Peru can be reached easily from Rio Branco in Acre with daily buses to Puerto Maldonado (via Assis Brasil and Iñapari in Peru), for onward land connections to Cusco. There are also numerous *combis* running between Assis Brasil and Iñapari. Peru can also be reached from Tabatinga or Benjamin Constant (Amazonas), from where there are boats running to Iquitos in Peru and onward boats to Pucallpa or flights to Lima. See page 645.

Bolivia is reached from Guajará-Mirim (Rondônia), from where launches cross the river to Guayará Merin in Bolivia for buses to Rurrenabaque and La Paz. There are also connections from Rio Branco in Acre, via the border town of Brasiléia to Cobija in Peru, from where there are flights to La Paz and buses in the dry season. See pages 674 and 675.

Colombia is easily reached from Tabatinga (Amazonas) which is twinned and contiguous with the Colombian city of Leticia, from where there are flights to Bogotá. See page 645.

Guyane (French Guiana) can be reached from Macapá (Amapá) by bus to Oiapoque, from where there are onward *combis* to St Georges Oyapock (Guyane), onward to Cayenne and all the way through Suriname to Guyana. See page 604.

Guyana is easily reached by bus from Boa Vista via Bonfim (Roraima) to Lethem (Guyana), from where there are buses to Georgetown. See page 664.

Getting around

By road Aside from routes to Belém from the Atlantic Coast and from Tocantins, bus routes are limited to the following: **Amazonas/Roraima:** Manaus–Boa Vista (via Presidente Figuieredo), paved. **Roraima:** Boa Vista–Venezuela, paved. Boa Vista–Guyana, paved. **Amazonas:** São Gabriel da Cachoeira–Cucuí, paved and dirt. **Amapá:** Macapá–Oiapoque (from where there is boat and road access to French Guiana), dirt. **Pará:** Santarém–Cuiabá (in the Pantanal) is being improved and buses now run intermittently along the route through Pará into Mato Grosso with changes at Itauba for Alta Floresta and the Rio Cristalino; enquire at the *rodoviária* in Cuiabá or Santarém for the latest details. **Amazonas/Rondônia:** Humaitá–Porto Velho. **Rondônia/Acre:** Porto Velho–Rio Branco with onward buses to Cruzeiro do Sul and to Peru and Bolivia via Assis Brasil and Brasiléia. There are services to Guajará-Mirim along a small branch road, paved and dirt. **Rondônia/Mato Grosso:** Porto Velho–Cuiabá and onwards to the rest of Brazil, paved. There are dirt roads Manaus–Porto Velho, and Santarém–Porto Velho. These were overgrown and impassable when this book went to press, but there are plans to re-pave the road between Manaus and Porto Velho for the 2014 World Cup.

By plane Flight networks within the Amazon are extensive. **Trip**, www.voetrip.com.br, have the largest Amazonian network, which includes Manaus–São Gabriel da Cachoeira via Barcelos, and Manaus– Tabatinga via Tefé. **Trip** also connect Manaus with Brasília, Cuiabá and Campo Grande and Alta Floresta with Brasília and the rest of Brazil. **META**, www.voemeta.com, flies Belém–Boa Vista and Belém–Santarém. **Sete**, www.voesete. com.br, flies Belém to Brasília with stops in the Xingu in Mato Gross, and to a number of smaller towns. **TAM**, www.tam.com.br, links Alta Floresta, Altamira, Santarém and all the Amazon state capitals with the rest of Brazil. **GOL**, www.voegol.com.br, connects all of the Amazonian state capitals with the rest of Brazil. **Avianca**, www.avianca.com.br, links Porto Velho with São Paulo, Rio and other major cities in Brazil.

Flight schedules are constantly changing and routes frequently close and re-open. Check the airline websites for the latest details and for prices.

By boat River boats are the buses of the Amazon and serve an extensive network, connecting both major and minor settlements. You won't see a great deal from the deck, especially if travelling downstream, as the boats stay in the middle of the river to catch the current. Going upstream, you will see an endless line of trees broken by the occasional village. However, the atmosphere on board is lively. Food is served, usually consisting of meat, beans and rice (which is brown as it is cooked in river water) and there is often a bar serving drinks and snacks. The size and quality of the boats varies greatly. The best boats ply the busiest routes: Manaus–Santarém–Belém and Manaus–Tabatinga. Overcrowding can be a problem.

The cheapest way to travel is **hammock class**, out in the open on the deck. Be sure to take water, a cable and padlock for your bags, a jumper (nights on the water can be cool) a good book and, most importantly, a *rede* (hammock) with two pieces of rope (each about 1 m long) to string it up across the beams. The boats that travel on the Amazon itself are largely mosquito free – except when they moor; it's a good idea to bring a *mosquiteiro para rede* (mosquito net) for your hammock. Hammocks and nets can be bought easily in any of the larger Amazon towns, usually in the downtown area near the river. Arrive early to get a good spot. Some boats also have air-conditioned berths and **cabins** and, for a higher price, **suites** with attached bathroom.

Many boats ply the following routes: Manaus–Belém via Parintins, Óbidos and Santarém (four days); Manaus–São Gabriel da Cachoeira via Barcelos and Santa Isabel (six days); Manaus–Porto Velho via Manicoré and Humaitá (four days); Manaus–Tefé (36 hours); Manaus–Parintins (20 hours); Manaus–Tabatinga (six days); Belém–Santarém (two to three days); Belém–Macapá (36 hours); Macapá–Manaus (seven to 10 days).
▶▶ *See Transport, page 656.*

Banks, mobile phones and internet

There are plenty of ATM facilities in all the Amazon's main towns (the state capitals, Santarém, Cruzeiro do Sul, Marabá, Parintins and São Gabriel da Cachoeira), where there is an **HSBC, Bradesco** or **Banco 24 horas**. Small amounts of US dollars cash can usually be exchanged away from banks at a poor rate, but are not accepted as local currency. The rate of exchange for traveller's cheques is appalling. There is mobile coverage in all the large cities and even in many remote outposts. There are numerous internet cafés and LAN houses in all the major cities.

Health

There is a danger of **malaria** in Amazônia, especially on the brown-water rivers. Mosquito larvae do not breed well in the black-water rivers as they are too acidic. Mosquito nets are not required when in motion as boats travel away from the banks and are too fast for mosquitos to settle. However, nets and repellent can be useful for night stops. Wear long, loose trousers (tight ones are easy to bite through) and a baggy shirt at night and put repellent around shirt collars, cuffs and the tops of socks.

A **yellow fever** inoculation is strongly advised. It is compulsory to have a certificate when crossing borders and those without one will have to get inoculated and wait 10 days before travelling. Other common infections in the Amazon are **dengue**, which is widespread in the Amazon – as it is throughout South America – **cutaneous larva migrans** (a spot that appears to move), which is easily treated with **Thiabendazole**, and **tropical ulcers**, caught by scratching mosquito bites, which then get dirty and become infected. ▶▶ *See Health, page 44.*

Amazon food

The Amazon has a distinctive range of dishes that make use of the thousands of fruits and vegetables and the abundant fish of the area. Regional food here vies with Bahia as the best in Brazil – especially in Belém, Manaus and Rio Branco. Must-tries include *tacacá*, a soup made with jambo leaves, which numbs the tongue and stimulates energy. The best fish are *pacu* and *tambaqui*, both types of vegetarian piranha (the carnivorous ones can be eaten too). *Jaraqui* is very common in Amazonas – often in a delicious broth. *Pirarucu*, one of the world's largest freshwater fish, is delicious; however, due to overfishing it is in danger of becoming extinct and should only be eaten when sustainably sourced from locations such as Mamirauá. Specialities of Pará state include duck, often served as *pato no tucupi*, in a yellow soup made from the sieved off cassava (manioc) juice and served with *jambo*. *Maniçoba* is made with the poisonous leaves of the *cassava* (bitter manioc), simmered for eight days to get rid of the cyanide. It is jet black but deliciously tangy. *Caldeirada* is a fish and vegetable soup, served with *pirão* (manioc puree), and is a speciality of Amazonas. There is also an enormous variety of tropical and jungle fruits, many unique to the region. Try them fresh, or in ice creams or juices. The best include *tapereba*, *cupuaçu*, *cajú* (the fruit of the cashew nut), *cacau* (the fruit of the cocoa bean) and *camu camu*, which has the highest vitamin C content of any fruit in the world. Avoid food from street vendors, except those selling *tacacá* at the Boi bumba or from **Gisela** in the Praça São Sebastião in Manaus who has been selling delicious *tacacá* for decades, from 1600-2200.

Amapá and Pará

Sometimes called Brazilian Guyana, the isolated border state of Amapá was once exploited for its natural resources and suffered from heavy deforestation. However, efforts are now being made towards sustainable development. Located near the French territory of Guyane, with its cheap air links to Paris, it is another good port of entry into northern Brazil. Tourist infrastructure outside the provincial riverside capital of Macapá is negligible. The state is a quarter of the size of France and has a population of just under half a million.

Pará is just across the river from Amapá – a distance that would span Switzerland. In the 1990s, the state capital, Belém, was dangerous and down at heel, but extensive refurbishment in the last decade has transformed it into an attractive colonial city. The state itself is barely aware of the existence of tourists. Although there are many beautiful natural sights, such as the vast river island of Marajó in the Amazon delta and the Amazônia National Park on the River Tapajós, infrastructure is poor, with no jungle lodges at all in the extensive rainforests. While areas north of the Amazon have been afforded at least nominal protection since 2006, in the south of the state rapid deforestation is making space for vast soya plantations.

Santarém, a quiet little town at the junction of the Tapajós and Amazon rivers, is the world's largest soya-export port. Thankfully ecotourism is gradually catching on here: a few tour companies offer trips to the river beaches at Alter do Chao and the failed rubber plantation towns of Belterra and Fordlândia – set up by Henry Ford in the early 20th century. Monte Alegre, whose caves have revealed evidence of a significant pre-Columbian Amazon culture, are a day's boat ride away upstream. Travel in Pará takes time (as it does anywhere in the Amazon) and the more isolated parts of the state are often linked only by boat and air. Even when there are roads, rain and forest encroachment makes even asphalted areas impassable. ▸▸ *For listings, see pages 617-630.*

Macapá → For listings, see pages 617-630. Colour map 1, A5. Phone code: 096. Population: 284,000.

The capital of Amapá is a pleasant city on the banks of the northern channel of the Amazon delta. It has an impressive fortress as well as a monument to the equator, which divides the city. There is a museum detailing the research being carried out in the rainforest and at nearby Curiaú, a village originally formed by escaped slaves.

The town was founded around the first Forte de São José do Macapá, built in 1688. In 1751 more settlers from the Azores arrived to defend the region from Dutch, English and French invasions and the *aldea* became a *vila* in 1758. Many slaves were later brought from Africa for the construction of the fort.

Ins and outs

Getting there The **airport** ⓘ *R Hildemar Maia, 3 km from the centre, T096-3223 4087,* receives flights from Belém, Brasília, Foz do Iguaçu, Rio de Janeiro, São Paulo, São Luís, Fortaleza, Marabá and Cayenne (Guyane). Taxis to the centre cost around US$7.

Buses arrive at the new **rodoviária** ⓘ *on the BR-156, 3 km north of Macapá.* Buses from Oiapoque pass through the city centre after a long and uncomfortable journey over mainly unsurfaced roads. This journey can take even longer during the rainy season (January to May). Boats from Belém and Santarém arrive at nearby Porto Santana, which is linked to Macapá by bus or taxi. ▸ *See Transport, page 626.*

Getting around There is an air-taxi service to some towns, however, most are linked by the trucks, buses and community minibuses, which leave from the new *rodoviária.* Buses to other parts of the city leave from a bus station near the fort. The centre and the waterfront are easily explored on foot.

Tourist information **SETUR** ⓘ *Av Binga Uchôa 29, T096-3212 5335, www.setur.ap.gov.br, Mon-Fri 1000-1800,* also has a branch at the airport. For information on national parks, contact **Instituto Chico Mendes de Conservação da Biodiversidade (ICMBio)** ⓘ *www.icmbio.gov.br.* The website www.macapaturismo.com.br is also useful.

Macapá

Sleeping		Eating
Atalanta 1	Ceta Ecotel 8	Pousada Ekinox 2	Cantinho Baiano 2
	Frota Palace 3	Santo Antônio 7	Chalé 1
	Gloria 4	Vista Amazônica 10	Divina Arte 5
	Holliday 9		Divina Gula 6
	Macapá 5	Eating	Flora 7
	Mercúrio 6	Bom Paladar Kilo's 3	Sarney 8

Sights

Each brick of the **Fortaleza de São José do Macapá**, built between 1764 and 1782, was brought from Portugal as ballast. Fifty iron cannon still remain and there is a museum. The *fortaleza* is used for concerts, exhibitions and colourful festivities on the anniversary of the city's founding on 4 February. **São José cathedral**, inaugurated by the Jesuits in 1761, is the city's oldest landmark. The **Centro de Cultura Negra** ① *R General Rondon*, has a museum and holds frequent events. The **Museu do Desenvolvimento Sustentável** ① *Av Feliciano Coelho 1509, Tue-Fri 0830-1200, 1500-1800, Mon and Sat 1500-1800*, exhibits research on sustainable development and traditional community life in Amazônia. The museum shop sells arts and crafts.

The riverfront has been landscaped with trees, lawns and paths and is a very pleasant place for an evening stroll. The **Complexo Beira Rio** has food and drink kiosks and a lively atmosphere. The recently rebuilt *trapiche* (pier) is a lovely spot for savouring the cool of the evening breeze, or watching the sun rise over the Amazon.

There is a monument to the equator, **Marco Zero** (take Fazendinha bus from Avenida Mendonça Furtado). The equator also divides the enormous football stadium nearby, aptly named O Zerão. The Sambódromo stadium is located nearby. South of here are the **botanical gardens** ① *Rodovia Juscelino Kubitschek, Km 12, Tue-Sun 0900-1700*.

Excursions from Macapá

Some 16 km from the centre, **Fazendinha** is a popular local beach, which is very busy on Sunday and has many seafood restaurants. **Curiaú**, 8 km from Macapá, is inhabited by the descendants of African slaves, who have maintained many of the customs of their ancestors. They are analogous to the Bush Negroes of Suriname, making the village the only one of its kind in Brazil. It is popular at weekends for dancing and swimming. The surrounding area is an environmental reserve with many water buffalo.

North of Macapá → *For listings, see pages 617-630.*

North of Macapá the road divides at **Porto Grande**, and a branch heads northwest to **Serra do Navio** where manganese extraction has now ended (**Hotel Serra do Navio** and several bars and restaurants). The BR-156 continues north, passing the turnings for two jungle hotels. The paved road goes as far as **Ferreira Gomes** on the shores of the Rio Araguari. Further on is **Amapá**, formerly the territorial capital and location of a Second World War American airbase. There are a few hotels. Beyond Amapá is **Calçoene**, with a government- owned hotel that serves expensive food in an adjoining canteen; very cheap sleeping space is also advertised in a café on the Oiapoque road. North of Calçoene a road branches west to **Lourenço**, whose goldfields still produce even after decades of prospecting. The main road continues north across the Rio Caciporé and on to the border with French Guyane at **Oiapoque**, on the river of the same name.

Oiapoque → *Colour map 1, A5. Population: 13,000.*

This is a ramshackle little gold-mining town with dirt streets lined with little guesthouses, spit-and-sawdust bars and shops buying the precious metal by the gram. It lies 90 km inland from **Cabo Orange**, Brazil's northernmost point on the Atlantic Coast and the site of one of its wildest and remotest national parks. Access to the park is very difficult although guides can sometimes be arranged through the boatmen on the river docks in Oiapoque.

Border essentials: Brazil–Guyane

Oiapoque (Brazil)–St-Georges Oyapock (Guyane)

From Macapá, only the first section of the road north to the Guyane border (BR-156) is paved. It is precarious in places but open year-round with buses and pickups operating even in the wet season. Take food and water for the journey as services are scarce. Petrol and diesel are available along the road, but drivers should take extra fuel at Macapá. There are at least two buses a day to from Macapá to Oiapoque. From Oiapoque there are frequent launches to Guyane across the river (US$5, 10 minutes). A bridge is being built and should be complete in 2011. *Combis* to Cayenne leave from St-Georges Oyapock before lunch so be ready by 1000.

Oiapoque town has its share of contraband, illegal migration and drug trafficking and can be a little rough; visitors should be cautious, especially late at night. With the building of the road between St-Georges Oyapock and Cayenne, the town has become a popular spot for French Guianan weekenders, most of them single men and in search of more than a drink. The **Cachoeira Grande Roche** rapids can be visited, upstream along the Oiapoque river, where it is possible to swim, US$30 by motor boat. The **Associação dos Povos Indigenous Brazilians de Oiapoque**, in front of the Banco do Brasil, provides information about the indigenous peoples that live in the area, and the indigenous Uaçá reserve.

The road construction has led to significant environmental damage with much deforestation along the Brazilian side of the road in Amapá, and Brazilian *garimpeiros* and hunters illegally flooding into Guyane have been causing havoc in pristine forests.

Belém → *For listings, see pages 617-630. Colour map 1, A6. Phone code: 091. Population: 1.3 million.*

Belém do Pará is the great port of the eastern Amazon. The city received an extensive facelift in the new millennium and is now a very pleasant capital with much of cultural interest – with streets of freshly painted, impressive 19th-century buildings from the rubber boom era and one of Latin America's liveliest contemporary music scenes. The reforms included opening up the waterfront and converting the derelict docks into a breezy promenade, which leads to one of Brazil's more colourful markets – Ver o Peso. Belém is a good base for boat trips along the river – either as cruises or public transport to Santarém, Manaus and beyond. An archipelago of beautiful, unspoilt tropical river islands lies a short boat trip offshore. The largest, Marajó, is as big as Denmark. With mean temperatures of 26°C, Belém is hot, but frequent showers and a prevailing breeze freshen the streets. The city has its fair share of crime and is prone to gang violence. Take sensible precautions, especially at night.

Ins and outs

Getting there Val-de-Cans international airport ① *Av Júlio César s/n, 12 km from the city, T091-3210 6000*, receives flights from the, Caribbean, the Guianas and the major Brazilian capitals. The airport bus 'Perpétuo Socorro-Telégrafo' or 'Icoaraci' runs every 15 minutes to the Prefeitura on Praça Felipe Patroni (US$1.50, allow 40 minutes). A taxi from the airport into town costs US$18. Ordinary taxis are cheaper than co-operatives, buy ticket in advance in departures side of airport. There are ATMs in the terminal, tourist information, cafés and car rental.

There are road connections from São Luís and the northeastern coast as well as a three-day bus link from São Paulo via Brasília. Interstate buses arrive at the **rodoviária** ① *end of Av Gov José Malcher, 3 km from the centre*. There are showers (US$0.10), a good snack bar, and agencies with information and tickets for riverboats. Buses to the centre cost US$0.50; taxis charge US$5-7. At the *rodoviária* you are given a ticket with the taxi's number on it; threaten to go to the authorities if the driver tries to overcharge.

Boats arrive at the port from Macapá, Manaus and Santarém as well as other parts of the Amazon region and delta. ›› *See Transport, page 627.*

Getting around The city centre is easily explored on foot. City buses and taxis run to all the sites of interest and to transport hubs away from the centre.

Tourist information Paratur ① *Praça Waldemar Henrique, Reduto, on the waterfront, T091-3224 9493, www.paraturismo.pa.gov.br*, has information on the state and city. Some staff speak English and can book hotels and tours to Marajó island. For information on national parks contact the **Instituto Chico Mendes de Conservação da Biodiversidade (ICMBio)** ① *www.icmbio.gov.br.* The website www.belemonline.com.br is also useful.

1 Belém orientation

➡ **Belém maps**
1 Belém orientation, page 605
2 Belém centre, page 606

Background

Established in 1616 because of its strategic position, Belém soon became the centre for slaving expeditions into the Amazon Basin. The Portuguese of Pará, together with those of Maranhão, treated the indigenous Brazilians abominably. Their isolation from the longer-established colonies allowed both places to become relatively lawless. In 1655, the Jesuits, under Antônio Vieira, attempted to lessen the abuses, while enticing the indigenous Brazilians to descend to the *aldeias* around Belém. This unfortunately led to further misery when smallpox spread from the south, striking the Pará *aldeias* in the 1660s.

2 Belém

➡ **Belém maps**
1 Belém orientation, page 605
2 Belém centre, page 606

200 metres
200 yards

Sleeping 🛏
Grão Pará **1**
Itaoca Belém **2**
Le Massilia & Restaurant **3**

Machado's Plaza **8**
Novo Avenida **4**
Regente **6**
Unidos **10**

Eating 🍴
Açaí (Hilton Hotel) **6**
Boteco das Onze **4**
Cantina Italiana **1**
Churrascaria Rodeio **8**

Churrascaria Tucuruvi **9**
Doces Bárbaros **2**
Govinda **10**
Lá em Casa **5**
Mãe Natureza **11**
Manjar das Garças **7**
Portinha **12**
Sabor Paraense **3**

Bars & clubs 🍸
A Pororó **13**
Bar do Gilson **16**
Café Com Arte **15**
Carrousel **14**
Mormoço **17**
São Mateus **18**

Soon after Brazil's Independence, the Revolta da Cabanagem, a rebellion by the poor blacks, indigenous Brazilians and mixed-race *cabanos*, was led against the Portuguese-born class that dominated the economy. The movement came to an end in 1840 when the *cabanos* finally surrendered, but the worst years of violence were 1835-1836. Some estimates say 30,000 were killed. The state's strategic location once again became important during the Second World War, when Belém was used as an airbase by the Americans to hunt German submarines in the Atlantic.

Sights

Belém used to be called the 'city of mango trees' and there are still many such trees remaining. There are some fine squares and restored historic buildings set along broad avenues. The largest square is the **Praça da República**, where there are free afternoon concerts; the main business and shopping area is along the wide Avenida Presidente Vargas, leading to the river, and the narrow streets which parallel it.

The recently restored neoclassical **Teatro da Paz** ① *R da Paz, T091-4009 8750, www.theatrodapaz.com.br, Mon-Fri 0900-1700, Sat 0900-1200, tours US$3*, (1878), is one of the largest theatres in Brazil and its handsome ballrooms, polished floors, extensive murals and paintings and overall opulence are every bit as impressive as those of the theatre's more famous counterpart in Manaus. It was inspired by the Scala in Milan and is stuffed with imported materials from Europe – an iron frame built in England, Italian marble, French bronzes and a Portuguese mosaic stone floor. The auditorium once featured a magnificent ceiling painting by Domenico de Angelis (see page 608 and 609) who also worked in the Teatro Amazonas in Manaus, which crumbled and fell to the floor only decades after it was painted. The theatre stages performances by national and international stars, and offers free concerts and shows.

West of here, at the **Estação das Docas**, the abandoned warehouses and quays of the port have been restored into a waterfront complex with an air-conditioned interior with a gallery of cafés, restaurants and boutiques. It's a great place to come in the late afternoon when the sun is golden over the Baía do Guajará and locals promenade along the cobbles under the towering 19th-century cranes. There are three converted warehouses in the Estação das Docas – each a 'boulevard'. The Boulevard das Artes contains the **Cervejaria Amazon** (brewery), with good beer and simple meals, an archaeological museum and arts and crafts shops. The Boulevard de Gastronomia has smart restaurants and the five-star **Cairu** ice cream parlour (try *açaí* or the *pavê de capuaçu*). In the Boulevard das Feiras there are trade fairs. Live music is transported between the boulevards on a moving stage. There are also ATMs and an internet café within the complex.

Heading south, the 17th-century **Mercês church** (1640) is the oldest in Belém. It forms part of an architectural group known as the Mercedário, the rest of which was heavily damaged by fire in 1978 and has now been restored.

Near the church, the Belém market, known as **Ver-o-Peso** ① *Blvd Castilhos França 27, T091-3212 0549*, was the Portuguese Posto Fiscal, where goods were weighed to gauge taxes due, hence the name: 'see the weight'. Inside are a flurry of stalls selling all manner of items – herbal remedies, Brazil nuts, açaí, bead jewellery, African-Brazilian religious charms, incense and, in the main gallery, scores of tiled slabs covered with bizarre river fish – from piraiba as big as a man to foot-long armour-plated cat fish. You can see them being unloaded at around 0530, together with hundreds of baskets of açaí. A colourful, if dirty, dock for fishing boats lies immediately upriver from the market and whole area swarms with people, including armed thieves and pickpockets.

The Jesuits and the slave trade

Cristobal de Acuna, a Jesuit who visited the Amazon in the 1620s, describes an incredible density of villages along the lower Amazon. He writes of the happy and abundant life of the Omagua people, the largest of the tribal nations, who lived in large towns with handsome houses, fired pottery as fine as any in Europe, baked bread, wove cotton and farmed turtles. Within 100 years of his visit they and all the slaves of the lower Amazon nations were killed and their cultures and achievements lost for ever.

The were lost to 'Red Gold', the little-known Amazon slave trade. The indigenous people were rounded up in droves and brought to São Luís and Belém to farm the burgeoning sugar plantations where they were forced to live in appalling conditions and work until they died. Only the Jesuits sought to abate this human traffic. They had long defended the Guaraní in southern Brazil by persuading them to move into settlements organized along European lines, which were known as reductions or *aldeias*. They were determined to do the same in the Amazon. Their leader, Antônio Viera, berated the people of São Luís and Belém with hellfire sermons: "What is a human soul worth to Satan?" he asked; "There is no market on earth where the devil can get them more cheaply than right here in our own land ... What a cheap market! An Indian for a soul! Christians, nobles," he begged "break the chains of injustice and free those whom you hold captive and oppressed!"

Viera was successful... for a while. The captives would be sent to Jesuit reductions from where they would be on loan to plantation owners for six months each year. The locals were certainly treated with less cruelty by the Jesuits. However, the Order were, in effect, equally responsible for the loss of indigenous life and culture. The reductions were breeding grounds for European disease and the native people were forced to completely abandon their religious and social practices. And when the Order was forced to leave Iberian America after a campaign against them by Portugal's Marquis de Pombal, the indigenous people who had been under their charge were enslaved and treated with renewed viciousness.

A typical Jesuit reduction was rectangular and built around a large *praça de armas*. To the rear of the plaza stood the church. On one side of the church was the cemetery and on the other the claustro, where the Jesuits themselves lived and studied. Near this were the workshops in which the works of art were produced. Behind the church were the gardens. Around the other sides of the plaza were the houses in which the Indians lived. The streets between the buildings were at right angles to each other and the settlement could easily be expanded along this plan. Chapels were built on the sides of the plaza. Other buildings included the *cabildo* (the municipal building of the indigenous people), the *cotiguazu* (a house for widows), a prison, a hospital and an inn for visitors.

Around Praça Dom Pedro II is a cluster of interesting buildings. The **Palácio Lauro Sodré** and **Museu do Estado do Pará** ① *Praça Dom Pedro II, T091-3225 3853, Mon-Fri 0900-1800, Sat 1000-1800*, is a gracious 18th-century Italianate building. It contains Brazil's largest framed painting, *The Conquest of Amazônia*, by Domenico de Angelis. The building was the work of the Italian architect Antônio Landi, who also designed the cathedral, and was the administrative seat of the colonial government. During the rubber boom many new decorative features were added. Also on Praça Dom Pedro II is the **Palácio Antônio Lemos,** which houses the **Museu de Arte de Belém** as well as the **Prefeitura** ① *Tue-Fri 0900-1200, 1400-1800, Sat and Sun 0900-1300*. It was originally built as the Palácio Municipal between 1868 and 1883, and is a fine example of the Imperial neoclassical style. In the downstairs rooms there are old views of Belém; upstairs, the historic rooms, beautifully renovated, contain furniture and paintings, which are all well explained.

The **cathedral** ① *Praça Frei Caetano Brandão, Mon 1500-1800, Tue-Fri 0800-1100, 1530-1800* (1748), is also neoclassical, and contains a series of brilliantly coloured paintings by the Italian artist Domenico de Angelis – famous for his work on the Teatro Amazonas in Manaus, but whose first visit to the Amazon was to Belem in 1884 at the invitation of the bishop to paint this cathedral and the Teatro da Paz. Directly opposite is the restored 18th-century **Santo Alexandre church** ① *Praça Frei Caetano Brandão s/n, Mon 1500-1800, Tue-Fri 0800-1100, 1530-1800*, with a fabulous rococo pediment and fine woodcarving. This was once the Jesuit headquarters in Belém – where Father Antonio Vieira (see box, page 266) would have preached his hellfire sermons denouncing the indigenous slave trade; inciting the wrath of the locals, Pombal and eventually contributing to the disestablishment of the order.

Also in the old town is the **Forte do Castelo** ① *Praça Frei Caetano Brandão 117, T091-3223 0041, daily 0800-2300*, which was rebuilt in 1878. The fort overlooks the confluence of the Rio Guamá and the Baía do Guajará and was where the Portuguese first set up their defences. There is a good restaurant, the **Boteco Onze**, where you can watch the sunset (entry US\$1, drinks and *salgadinhos* served on the ramparts from 1800). At the square on the waterfront below the fort, the açaí berries are landed nightly at 2300, after being picked in the jungle. Açaí berries, ground up with sugar and mixed with manioc, are a staple food in the region.

East of the centre, the **Basílica de Nossa Senhora de Nazaré** ① *Praça Justo Chermont, Av Magalhães Barata, Mon-Sat 0500-1130, 1400-2000, Sun 0545-1130, 1430-2000*, was built in 1909 from rubber wealth. It is romanesque in style and has beautiful marble and stained-glass windows. The *basílica* feels very tranquil and sacred, especially when empty. A museum here showcases one of the largest and most colourful festivals in the north of Brazil, the **Círio de Nazaré** (see page 625). The Nossa Senhora de Nazaré sits illuminated in a shrine in the sacristy.

The botanic gardens, **Bosque Rodrigues Alves** ① *Av Almirante Barroso 2305, T091-3226 2308, Tue-Sun 0800-1700*, is a 16-ha public garden (really a preserved area of original flora), with a small animal collection. To get there, take the yellow bus marked 'Souza' or 'Cidade Nova' (any number), 30 minutes from Ver-o-Peso market, or from the cathedral. The **Museu Emílio Goeldi** ① *Av Magalhães Barata 376, Tue-Thu 0900-1200, 1400-1700, Fri 0900-1200, Sat and Sun 0900-1700, US\$1*, takes up an entire city block and consists of the museum proper (with a fine collection of indigenous Marajó pottery and an excellent exhibition of Mebengokre tribal lifestyle), a rather sad zoo and botanical exhibits including Victoria Régia lilies. Buses run from the cathedral.

The **Murucutu** ruins, an old Jesuit foundation, are reached by the Ceará bus from Praça da República; entry is via an unmarked door on the right of the Ceará bus station.

Around Belém → *For listings, see pages 617-630.*

A *foca* (passenger ferry) to the small town of **Barcarena** ① *daily departures from Ver-o-Peso, but best Tue-Fri, US\$1*, makes an interesting half-day trip. A return trip on the ferry from Ver-o-Peso to Icaoraci provides a good view of the river. Several restaurants here serve excellent seafood; you can eat shrimp and drink coconut water and appreciate the breeze coming off the river. **Icoaraci** is 20 km east of the city and is well known as a centre of ceramic production. The pottery is in Marajóara and Tapajonica style. Artisans are friendly and helpful, will accept commissions and send purchases overseas. A bus from Avenida Presidente Vargas in Belém runs to Icoaraci.

The nearest beach to Belém is at **Outeiro** (35 km), on an island near Icoaraci. It takes about an hour by bus and ferry (the bus may be caught near the **Maloca**, an indigenous-style hut near the docks that serves as a nightclub). A bus from Icoaraci to Outeiro takes 30 minutes.

Salinópolis → *Colour map 1, A6. Population: 33,500.*
Some 223 km from Belém, at the extreme eastern end of the Amazon delta, this seaside resort has many small places where you can eat and drink at night by the waterfront. There is a fine sandy beach nearby (buses and cars drive onto the beach), but the water is murky. It is a peaceful place mid-week but very busy at weekends and in high season and is at its peak during the holiday month of July.

Atalaia, an island opposite Salinópolis, is pleasant and can be reached by taxi (US$6) or by boat. Salinópolis is four hours from Belém by bus on a good road, US$6.

The little riverside village of **Tomé-Açu**, south of Belém on the Rio Acará-Mirim, affords a view of life on a smaller river than the Amazon. Three buses a day run from Belém, US$8. The **Hotel Las Vegas** has a friendly owner, Fernando. The boat back to Belém on Sunday leaves at 1100, arriving 1800, US$5.

Islands around Belém

The mouth of the Amazon, formed by the confluence of that river in the north and the Tocantins in front of Belém, is dotted with myriad islands and mangrove lined backwaters. There are 27 islands around Belém; the largest of which, **Marajó** (see below), is as big as Switzerland. Many of the islands can be visited on a day trip from the capital, others are a longer haul. Most are lined with long beaches of fine sand broken by strands of clay and dark stones heavy with iron ores. The water that washes them looks as expansive as an ocean, stretching to a vast horizon, but even out in what is geographically the Atlantic, it is fresh water and brown.

Ilha do Cotijuba, www.cotijuba.com, and the more built-up **Ilha do Mosqueiro**, www.mosqueiro.com.br, are reachable from Belém in a couple of hours. Both have a number of *pousadas* and small restaurants, stretches of forest and, on Cotijuba, gorgeous beaches. The islands get very crowded at Christmas and during Carnaval. The **Ilha da Mexiana** in the Marajó archipelago is more remote and less visited.

Ins and outs Boats run to **Cotijuba** from the docks in Belém (especially at the weekends), however, the quickest way to reach all the islands is from the port in **Icoaraci**, 20 km north of Belém (30 minutes bus ride from the *rodoviária* or from near the Ver-o-Peso market; taxi US$25). There are at least four boats a day from here to Cotijuba; the first at 0900. Others only leave when full. The fastest take 20 minutes, the slowest one hour.

Mosqueiro is connected to the mainland by road. At least four buses a day leave from the *rodoviária* taking around 90 minutes to get to the main towns (Praia do Paraíso, Carandaduba and Vila Mosqueiro). There are no banks on any of these islands, so bring cash from Belém.

Ilha de Maiandeua and Vila do Algodoal

This sandy estuarine island with long sweeping beaches is more commonly known by the name of its principal town, Vila do Algodoal – a small-scale traveller resort very popular with French backpackers. The island is a semi-protected area at the junction of the sea, the Amazon and the Rio Maracanã. It is very tranquil and has sand dunes, small lakes and a number of isolated beaches lapped by an Atlantic heavy with the silt of the Amazon. The main town is tiny with a cluster of sandy streets lined with little houses, many of them *pousadas*, and fronted by a muddy beach, the Praia Caixa d'Agua. Donkey carts connect it with the island's other beaches, which include (running north and clockwise from Algodoal town), **Farol** (separated from Algodoal by a fast-flowing estuary and with flat tidal sands), and its continuation, the 14-km-long **Princesa** (with dunes, the best swimming and many of the cheap beach *pousadas*), **Fortalezinha** (some 20 km from Algodoal, with grey sands and weak waves, also reached across an estuarine inlet, but with with dangerously strong currents – cross on a ferry only), **Mococa** (around 23 km from Algodoal and with sharp stones and a small fishing community) and, on the other side of the bay from Algodoal town (reachable by boat – 30 minutes), **Marudá** (muddy and with a small town) and to its north **Crispim** (which has beach bars, dunes, and good windsurfing and which is very popular with Paraenses at weekends). All accommodation is low-key and simple. Be wary of stingrays on the beaches – especially in muddier areas – and of strong rip tides, sharks and strong waves on the beaches beyond Mococa – notably Enseada do Costeiro.

Ins and outs Buses run from Belém to Marudá town (2-3 hours, US$7, from Belém *rodoviária* from where you catch a ferry (30 minutes, US$3, around five ferries a day, last at 1700). There are onward bus connections from Marudá to Salinópolis and from there south to Maranhão. It is easy to find a room on arrival, except during weekends and holidays. There are no banks or ATMs in Algodoal. For more information see www.algodoal.com.br.

Ilha de Marajó → *Colour map 1, A5.*

The largest island near Belém is also the largest riverine island in the world (although some claim that as it abuts the Atlantic the title belongs to Bananal, see page 710). Like the rest of the Amazon, Marajó is partly flooded in the rainy season between January and June. The island is home to feral water buffalo, which can be seen in large numbers; they are said to have swum ashore after a shipwreck. Many are now farmed and Marajó is famous throughout Brazil for its *mozarela* cheese. The island's police force use the buffalo instead of horses to get around the beaches. The island is also home to numerous bird species, including thousands of roseate spoonbills, and black caiman, river turtles and other wildlife. There is good **birdwatching** on the fazendas – especially on **Fazenda Bom Jesus**, 5 km from Soure. This *fazenda*, owned by local matriarch Eva Abufaiad, has a delightful colonial chapel on more than 6000 ha of land, and has rehabilitated much of its land for wildlife – a visit here is a real delight. Visits are easily organized through the Casarão da Amazônia (see page 619).

Marajo was was the site of the pre-Columbian **Marajóaras** civilization, celebrated for its ceramics, beautiful replicas of which can be bought from artisans in Soure. It is also a centre for candomble. Many of the communities here are descended from Africans who escaped slavery in Belém and fled to the forest to found their own villages or *quilombos*. A number of beaches around Soure are sacred candomble sites. The *quilombolas* did not remain altogether free of slavery, however. As Marajo was settled ranchers laid claim to the land, and much of the territory around Soure and Salvaterra which was originally community land is now privately owned. According to the news agency Brasil de Fato (www.brasildefato.com.br), many of the *quilombolas* are employed, and a system of semi-debt peonage – where their wages are offset against the cost of their rent and accommodation – is organized in such a way that they can never earn enough to pay off their employers. In 2007 the Ministry of Work and Employment freed a number of people from such slavery on the fazenda Santa Maria. Other *fazendas* – including Bom Jesus – stand accused of having their farm hands impede access to roads, including the PA-154 state road linking the *quilombo* community of Caju-Una with Soure.

The capital of Marajó is **Soure** (with a handful of restaurants, arts and crafts shops and one of the best *pousadas* on the island), with the other principal town being **Salvaterra** (fine beaches and more choice of accommodation); both are on the eastern side of the island, which has the only readily accessible shore. There are many fine beaches around both towns: **Araruna** (2 km from Soure; take supplies and supplement with coconuts and crabs), from where it's a beautiful walk along the shore to **Praia do Pesqueiro** a magnificent beach 13 km from Soure; (bus from Praça da Matriz at 1030, returns 1600, or on horseback from the Casarão da Amazônia, food available at maloca); and **Caju-Una** and **Céu** 15 km and 17 km from Soure. These are equally magnificent beaches – 400-m broad stretches washed by a limpid fresh-water sea. Both are almost completely deserted, and at the far end Céu extends north into a seemingly interminable expanse of beach and virgin rainforest which stretches over 100 km north to the gentle mangrove-lined cape where Marajo eventually meets the open (but still sweet ocean).

Praia de Joanes between the point of arrival on Marajó (Porto de Camará) is another popular place to stay. It has a laid-back feel, some impressive Jesuit ruins and cliffs overlooking the beach. In the far south of the Marajó archipelago are the little towns of **Ponta de Pedras**, which has a few colonial buildings and a fine beach, and **Breves** in the midst of towering rainforest, which runs northwest to unexplored areas inhabited only by indigenous people.

Fishing boats make the eight-hour trip to **Cachoeira do Arari** (one hotel, **D**), where there is a fascinating **Marajó museum**. A 10-hour boat trip from Ponta de Pedras goes to the **Arari Lake** where there are two villages: **Jenipapo** and **Santa Cruz**. The latter is less primitive and less interesting; a hammock and a mosquito net are essential.

Ins and outs A ferry from **Belém** sails twice daily (once daily at weekends), from the Armazem 10 dock in town (US$5). Boats also run from **Porto de Icoaraci**, 20 km north of Belém (30 minutes bus ride from the *rodoviária* or from near the Ver-o-Peso market; taxi US$25). Boats take three hours for the 30 km crossing to the island's main arrival point, **Porto de Camará** (20 km south of Salvaterra). From here, small craft await to transfer passengers to Salvaterra village (US$12, 30 minutes), Soure (US$14, 40 minutes, including a ferry crossing) or Praia de Joanes (US$4, 15 minutes). Each is clearly marked with the destination. There is also a taxi-plane service direct to Soure from Belém. The capital has a **Banco do Brasil** ATM, but this is unreliable. Changing money is only possible at very poor rates. There is internet in both Soure and Salvaterra. Take plenty of insect repellent. Bicycles and horses can be rented in both Slavaterra and Soure for around US$1/US$10 per hour respectively, to explore beaches and the interior of the island.

Santarém → *Colour map 1, B4. Phone code: 093. Population: 262,500.*

The third largest city on the Brazilian Amazon is small enough to walk around in a morning. It was founded in 1661 as the Jesuit mission of Tapajós; the name was changed to Santarém in 1758. There was once a fort here, and attractive colonial squares overlooking the waterfront still remain. Standing at the confluence of the Rio Tapajós with the Amazon, on the southern bank, Santarém is halfway (three days by boat) between Belém and Manaus. Most visitors breeze in and out of town on a stopover.

In front of the market square, the yellow Amazon water swirls alongside the green blue Tapajós river at the **meeting of the waters**, which is nearly as impressive as that of the Negro and Solimões near Manaus (see page 641). A small **Museu dos Tapajós** ① *Centro Cultural João Fora, on the waterfront, downriver from where the boats dock*, has a collection of ancient Tapajós ceramics, as well as various 19th-century artefacts. The unloading of the fish catch between 0500 and 0700 on the waterfront is interesting.

There are good beaches nearby on the Rio Tapajós. Prainha, a small beach, is between town and the port, by a park with many mango trees (Floresta–Prainha bus from centre). On the outskirts of town is Maracanã, with sandy bays (when the Tapajós is low) and some trees for shade (Maracanã bus from the centre, 20 minutes). Santarém has been at the centre of rapid deforestation in the last decade – fuelled by soya (see box, page 614).

Santarém

N

Not to scale

Sleeping		Eating
Brasil 1	Mirante 4	Mascote 2
Brasil Grande 2	New City 5	Mascotinho 3
Grão Rios 6	Santarém Palace 7	Piracaia 4
Horizonte 3		Sabor Caseiro 5

Blood crop

Ten years ago Santarém was surrounded by trees. Since then, the ranchers have arrived and the trees are disappearing, just as they are further south in Mato Grosso and the Goiás *cerrado* forests, in order to make way for lucrative soya plantations. In 2003 the huge multinational company Cargill built a soya grain terminal in Santarém so that the crop could be transferred to ocean going vessels in the north of the country and not the south. The decision had a far reaching impact. The road cutting up to Santarém from the centre west was renovated and agriculture began to expand into the Amazon. With such an easy means of export on the city's doorstep, developers moved in to Santarém itself, claiming they would bring food and jobs to the poor. The area occupied by farms around the city rose rapidly to over 750 sq km and was planted on land that had been cleared from secondary forest, as well as some 10% on newly felled rainforest Indigenous *caboclo* communities who had made their homes on the land coveted by the farmers were displaced. The ranchers came armed with a ream of false title deeds – just as they did with the *caiçairas* on the Costa Verde (see page 161). Some *caboclos* sold up. Others were forced off through threats of violence. A few stubbornly stayed. They were intimidated, then beaten. Some were killed. Very few found work on the plantations where the machinery is high tech and the manpower required minimal. And the soya plantations continued to expand. In 2006 Brazil became the world's biggest soya exporter. After a long Greenpeace campaign, in June 2008 the Brazilian environmental minister Carlos Minc called for a deal to curb appropriation of land for soya farms. But Brazil has a powerful elite and a long history of lip service. The country's current strict environmental legislation is rarely enforced. So for now the vegetarian option is as complicit in death and deforestation as hardwood tables or beef.

Ins and outs **Aeroporto Maestro Wilson Fonseca** ① *15 km from town, Praça Eduardo Gomes, s/n, T093-3523 4328*, receives flights from Fortaleza, Belém, Salvador, Brasília, Manaus and other towns in the Amazon. From the **rodoviária** ① *outskirts of town, T093-3522 3392*, buses run to the waterfront near the market, US$1. Boats from Belém and Manaus dock at the **Cais do Porto**, 1 km west of town (take 'Floresta-Prainha', 'Circular' or 'Circular Externo' bus; taxi US$7); boats from other destinations, including Macapá, dock by the waterfront near the centre of town. The tourist office, **Comtur** ① *R Floriano Peixoto 777, T/F093-3523 2434, Mon-Fri 1000-1700*, has good information available in English. Also see www.paraturismo. pa.gov.br. ►► *See Transport, page 628.*

Alter do Chão → *Colour map 1, B4.*
Alter do Chão (http://alterdochao.tur.br) is a friendly village sitting next to a brilliant white spit of talcum-powder fine sand (known cheesily as Love Island to locals) which juts into the deep blue Rio Tapajós 34 km west of Santarém. It is a very popular beach destination and has a proliferation of restaurants and *pousadas*. There is kayaking and light ecotours on Lago Verde, a lake lined with white-sand beaches in the dry season next to Alter do Chão village. Increasing numbers of tour operators offer trips into the forest from Alter do Chão rather than Santarem. Every second week of September, and Alter do Chao celebrates one of Para's biggest festivals, the **Festa do Çairé**, which sees

big-costumed processions in the sandy streets and a pageant depicting the seduction of a river dolphin by a beautiful *cabocla* (river peasant) girl.

Floresta Nacional do Tapajós → *Colour map 1, B4.*
ⓘ *Information from Paratur in Belém, www.paraturismo.pa.gov.br.*

This 545,000-ha reserve on the eastern banks of blue Tapajós river, some 120 km south of Santarém, is home to 26 riverine communities who eke a living from harvesting Brazil nuts, rubber and from fishing. The protected area forms part of a larger reserve spanning both banks of the river. On the less accessible west shore is the 648,000-ha **Reserva Extrativista Tapajós Arapiuns**, created to allow local people to extract rubber and nuts, hunt on a small scale to reduce environmental impact on the forest. Both areas are open to tourism and agencies in Santarém offer trips which include Amazon homestays with riverine communities. The forests themselves are not as wild as those in similar reserves in Acre (see page 670) but the area is stunningly beautiful, with white-sand beaches, pink river dolphins and the forest itself with its many towering Kapok and Brazil nut trees.
» *Trips can be organized with tour operators in Santarém, see page 626.*

Belterra and Fordlândia → *Colour map 1, B4. Phone code 093.*
Fordlândia, 300 km south of Santarém, was Henry Ford's first rubber plantation. He founded it in 1926 in an attempt to provide a cheaper source of rubber for his Ford Motor Company than the British and Dutch controlled plantations in Malaya. There is **Hotel Zebu**, in old Vila Americana (turn right from the dock, then left up the hill), one restaurant, two bars and three shops on the town square. There is a little pebble beach north of town.

Around Santarém

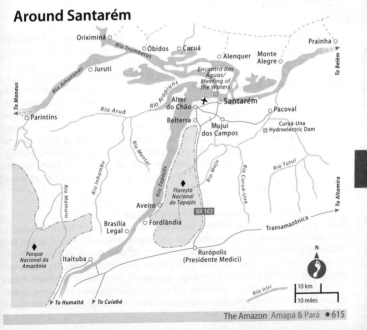

Closer to Santarém, 37 km south on a dirt road, is **Belterra**, where Henry Ford established his second rubber plantation. In the highlands overlooking the Rio Tapajós. It is nearer to the town than his first project, which was turned into a research station. At Belterra, Ford built a well laid-out town, where the houses resemble the cottages of Michigan summer resorts, many with white paint and green trim. The town centre has a large central plaza that includes a bandstand, the church of Santo Antônio (circa 1951), a Baptist church and a large educational and sports complex. A major hospital, which at one time was staffed by physicians from North America, is now closed.

Ford's project, the first modern attempt to invest in the Amazon, was unsuccessful. It was difficult to grow the rubber tree in plantation conditions, where it was unprotected from the heavy rains and harsh sun, and indigenous parasites were attracted by the concentrations of trees. Boats could only come this far upriver in the rainy season and there was a series of disputes between the American bosses and the local employees. Ford sold up in 1945 and the rubber plantation is now deserted.

Alenquer

This tiny town on the opposite bank of the Amazon river to Santarém sits in pretty forest dotted with waterfalls, clear-water streams and strangely eroded tower-like rock formations, the most impressive of which is the Cidade dos Deuses (City of the Gods), some 40 km from town. The easiest way to visit the attractions is either on an organized tour from Santarém or through a *pousada* in Alenquer itself. There are daily boats to Alenquer from the docks in Santarém (speed boats take two to three hours, US$15) or slow boats (US$5, six hours). Boats to and from Belém stop at Alenquer. For more information see www.alenquerpara.com.br.

Monte Alegre

There's not much to this small village, which may have changed ideas about the history of Brazil, and perhaps the Americas (see box, page 617) – just a collection of low, scruffy buildings gathered around a street on a shallow hill rising from the vast swampy expanses of the Amazon river. Outside the town, in the municipality of Campina, is the **Parque Estadual de Monte Alegre** (Monte Alegre State Park) – 5800 ha of lowland forest broken by sedimentary escarpment. This was where Anna Roosevelt made her excavations in the 1990s and is an extraordinary place. The cliffs, crags and caves in the escarpment are covered with hundreds of blood-red paintings. Some show strange figures with pyramidical bodies and bulbous heads surrounded by halos, others symmetrical checker board designs, dancing figures and vibrant hand patterns. Visiting the state park is difficult. Trips can be organized through *pousadas* in town, or with advance notice through Gil Serique (see page 626) in Santarém. For more information see www.montealegre.rec.br.

Óbidos → *Colour map 1, A4. Phone code: 093. Population: 46,500.*

Óbidos is the last major town between Santarém and the border with Amazonas state. It is located at the narrowest and deepest point on the river where, millions of years ago, the Amazon (which at that stage was a giant lake in the middle of Brazil) squeezed through the gap in the Guyana and Brazilian highlands to meet the Atlantic. The town was strategically important in the Portuguese expansion of the Amazon. The **Forte Pauxi** (Praça Coracy Nunes, 1697) is a reminder of this fact. Today, Óbidos is a picturesque and clean city with many beautiful tiled buildings and some pleasant parks. Worth seeing are

Monte Alegre

Monte Alegre is the site of archaeological discoveries that have threatened to radically alter current views of the spread of civilization in South America. In the 1990s, Dr Anna C Roosevelt, of the Field Museum of Natural History, Chicago, found pottery fragments in a cave which, according to radiocarbon dating, appear to be from 7000-8000 BC. This pre-dates by some 3000 years what was thought to be the earliest ceramic ware in South America (from Colombia and Ecuador). Subsequent artefacts discovered here, however, have radiocarbon dates of 15,000 BC, which calls for a significant rethink of the original idea that people moved from the Andes into the Amazon Basin. These finds suggest that the story of the people of the Americas is more diverse than hitherto understood. The cave that Dr Roosevelt excavated is called Caverna da Pedra Pintada. Also in the area are pictographs, with designs of human and animal figures and geometric shapes. Trips can be arranged; many thanks to Philip W Hummer, who sent us a description of a tour led by Dr Anna Roosevelt.

the **Prefeitura Municipal** ⓘ *T093-3547 1194*, the *cuartel* and the **Museu Integrado de Óbidos** ⓘ *R Justo Chermont 607, Mon-Fri 0700-1100 and 1330-1730*. There is also a **Museu Contextual**, which consists of a system of plaques with detailed explanations of historic buildings throughout town. Boating and fishing trips can be arranged and there is a popular beach at **Igarapé de Curuçambá** (with bus connections).

Ins and outs The small airport has flights to Manaus, Santarém and Parintins. Óbidos is five hours upriver from Santarém by boat (110 km). A poor road runs east to Alenquer, Monte Alegre and Prainha and west to Oriximiná, impassable in the wet season.

⊚ Amapá and Pará listings

For Sleeping and Eating price codes and other relevant information, see pages 32-37.

⊜ Sleeping

Macapá *p601, map p602*

AL Ceta Ecotel, R do Matodouro 640, Fazendinha, T096-3227 3396, www.ecotel.com.br. A rainforest-themed hotel with sloths and monkeys in the trees and a series of trails. All the furniture is made on site. 20 mins from the town by taxi.

AL-A Atalanta, Av Coracy Nunes 1148, T096-3223 1612, www.atalantahotel.com.br. By far the best hotel in town with a rooftop pool and comfortable modern a/c rooms with bathrooms. Includes a generous breakfast. 10 mins' walk from the river.

A Macapá, Av Francisco Azarias Neto 17, on the waterfront, T096-3217 1350, www.macapahotel.com.br. The city's grandest hotel, overlooking the river, with a pool, tennis courts and children's play area. Rooms are past their best. Popular with families from Guyane.

A-B Pousada Ekinox, R Jovino Dinoá 1693, T096-3223 0086, www.ekinox.com.br. One of the best in town, with chalets set in a little tropical garden and with a library. Helpful, French-speaking staff and a good restaurant.

B Frota Palace, R Tiradentes 1104, T096-2101 3999, www.hotelfrota.com.br. Plain, faded rooms with en suites. Airport pickup service for US$7.

C Gloria, Leopoldo Machado 2085, T096-3222 0984. A clean, well-kept, simple hotel with a/c rooms all with en suite, TV and hot water. Breakfast included in the price.

D Mercúrio, R Cândido Mendes 1300, 2nd floor, T096-3224 2766. Very basic, but close to Praça São José (where the bus from Porto Santana stops).

D-E Holliday, Av Henrique Gallúcio 1623, T096-3223 3122. Very simple, though recently repainted, little boxy a/c rooms 20 mins' walk from the river. Breakfast included.

D-E Vista Amazônica, Av Beira Rio 1298 (about 1.5 km beyond the Cantino Baiano restaurant away from town), T096-3222 6851. A simple *pousada* and restaurant sitting right opposite the Amazon, with simple but well-maintained tiled rooms with en suites.

E-F Santo Antônio, Av Coriolano Jucá 485, T096-3222 0226. Very simple and slightly musty downstairs rooms and brighter a/c rooms upstairs.

Oiapoque *p603*

There are plenty of cheap hotels in Oiapoque, but they are not well maintained. The noisiest and least reputable are closest to the river; the best a few blocks behind.

Belém *p604, maps p605 and p606*

A series of new openings and renovations has seen Belém's hotels improve greatly, although they are still not up to much. All are fully booked during **Círio** (see Festivals, page 624). There are many cheap hotels close to the waterfront (none too safe) and several others near the *rodoviária* (generally OK).

A Itaoca Belém, Av Pres Vargas 132, T091-4009 2400, www.hotelitaoca.com.br. Well-kept, bright, no-nonsense a/c rooms with writing desks and en suites. The best are on the upper floors away from the street noise, and with river views. Decent breakfast.

A Machado's Plaza, R Henrique Gurjão 200, T091-4008 9800, www.machadosplaza hotel.com.br. Bright, brand-new boutique hotel with smart and tastefully decorated a/c rooms, a small business centre, plunge pool and a pleasant a/c breakfast area. Good value.

A Regente, Av Gov José Malcher 485, T091-3181 5000, www.hregente.com.br. Small, newly refurbished a/c rooms decorated in cream and white tile and with standard 3-star fittings, above a noisy street. Popular with US tour groups.

B Le Massilia, R Henrique Gurjão 236, T091-3224 2834, www.massilia.com.br. An intimate, French-owned boutique hotel with chic little duplexes and more ordinary doubles. Excellent French restaurant and a tasty French breakfast.

C-D Grão Pará, Av Pres Vargas 718, T091-3321 2121, www.hotelgraopara.com.br. Well-kept, new a/c rooms with contemporary fittings and smart en suites in black marble, and a boiler for hot water. The best have superb river views. Excellent breakfast. Great value.

D Novo Avenida, Av Pres Vargas 404, T091-3223 8893, www.hotelnovoavenida.com.br. Slightly frayed but spruce en suite rooms. Decent breakfast. Groups can sleep in large rooms for **E-F** per person. Good value.

D Unidos, Ó de Almeida 545, T091-3224 0660. Simple but spruce, spacious a/c rooms with cable TV and clean en suites. There are other cheap hotels a few doors away if this one is full.

D-E Amazônia Hostel, Av Governador Jose Malcher 592, T091-4141 8833, www.amazoniahostel.com.br. It's necessary to make a reservation at this popular hostel. Rooms are a cut above the other very cheap hotels dotted around the decrepit and dank Trav Frutuoso Guimarães and they are situated in a brightly painted rubber boom mansion in a salubrious part of town. Dorms and doubles are very simple; there's no a/c so they can be hot when the windows are closed, and popular with mosquitoes when they aren't. Staff are helpful and some speak English, there's a book exchange, kitchen and breakfast.

Salinópolis *p610*

A Atalaia, Ilha Atalaia, 15 km from Salinópolis, T/F091-3464 1122. A simple

pousada in a pleasant setting. Reserve in advance for the weekend, take a taxi.
A Joana d'Arc, Av João Pessoa 555, T/F091-3823 1422. Modest but well looked after and with a generous breakfast.
A Solar, Av Beira Mar, T091-3823 1823. The best in town with smart en suite rooms and a good restaurant.
B Diolindina, Av Pres Médici 424, Capanema, T091-821 1667. Small clean a/c rooms with fridge and bath. The price includes breakfast and safe parking. Recommended. There are good restaurants and a supermarket opposite.

Islands around Belém *p610*
Cotijuba
C-D Pousada Farol, T091-3259 7144, T091-9943 0237 (mob). Chalets and rooms in annexes set in a little garden right in front of the beach. Good rates during the week. Friendly owners. On the opposite side of the island from the port.

Mosqueiro
There are plenty of opportunities for camping on Mosqueiro and a wealth of *pousadas* in all price brackets.
B Farol, Praia Farol, Olha do Mosqueiro, T091-3771 1219. With 1920s architecture but in good repair, small restaurant, rooms face the beach, good views.
B-C Porto Arthur, Av Beira Mar, Praia do Porto Arthur, T091-8145 1438, bookable through www.paratur.com.br. Concrete chalets with verandas, and plain though clean a/c rooms with fridges. These sit over a pool and patio less than 2 mins' walk from the beach. The hotel has a BBQ restaurant, a sauna and paddling pool for kids.

Ilha de Maiandeua and Vila do Algodoal *p611*
B-C Jardim do Éden, http://onlinehotel.com.br/para/ilha-do-algodoal/jardim-do-eden-pousada/index.htm. A series of bizarre neo-Gothic brick *cabañas* with kitchenettes overlooking the beach on Praia do Farol. Well kept and well run and with more

personality than most on the island. Tours available and camping in the grounds (on the beach). Discounts available online.
B-C Pousada Bela-Mar, Av Beira Mar, Vila do Algodoal beach, T091-3854 1128, belamarhotel.blogspot.com. A very simple beachside hotel with tiny rooms, set in a garden. Close to the boat jetty.
B-C Pousada Chalés do Atlântico, Vila do Algodoal, T091-3854 1114, www.algodoal.com.br. Recently renovated. 11 simple little *cabañas* with mosquito screening, en suites and cold showers.

Ilha de Marajó *p611*
Marajó gets very busy in the Jul holiday season – be sure to reserve ahead at this time.
AL-A Fazenda Araruna, 14 Rua, Trav 18, outside Soure, T091-3741 1474. A pretty bungalow set on a vast buffalo farm owned by the charming Dona Amélia Barbosa. Offer horse riding, boat and kayak trips and buffalo rides on the beach. Rooms are rustic but comfortable and the price includes an evening meal.
AL-D Casarão da Amazonia, 4 Rua 646, Soure, T091-3741 2222, www.amazzonia.info. The only grand rubber boom mansion in Soure was a ruin until Italian Giancarlo lovingly restored it into this fabulous sky-blue belle époque boutique hotel in the new millennium. The building sits in its own tropical garden next to a pool and restaurant (serving crispy Neapolitan pizzas). Rooms are comfortable, well-appointed and cool and Giancarlo offers wonderful horseback and boat tours around Marajo. Come for several days.
A Pousada dos Guarãs, Av Beira Mar, Salvaterra, T/F091-3765 1133, www.pousadadosguaras.com.br. Well-equipped little resort hotel on the beach with an extensive tour programme.
B-C Canto do Frances, 6 Rua, Trav 8, Soure, T091-3741 1298, www.ocantodofrances.blogspot.com. This French/Brazilian-owned *pousada* 20 mins' walk from the centre offers well-kept, whitewash and wooden-walled

rooms in a pretty bungalow sitting in a garden filled with flowers and fruit trees. Breakfast is generous and the owners organize horse riding, canoe and bike trips around Soure. Book ahead to be met at the ferry port.
C Paracuary, Rio Paracuary, Soure, T091-3225 5915, www.paracauary.com.br. A/c rooms with en suites in mock colonial chalets around a pool 3 km from Soure and on the banks of the Rio Paracuary.
C Ventania, Praia de Joanes, T091-3646 2067, www.pousadaventania.com. Pretty little cliff-top *pousada* in a lawned garden a stroll from the beach. Each apartment has room for 2 couples **D**. Bike rental, French, Dutch, English and Spanish spoken.
D-E Araruna, Rua 7, Trav 14, Soure. Very simple fan-cooled rooms some of which are decidedly musty (look at a few), but this is the best cheapie in town.

Santarém p613, map p613
All hotels, except **Amazon Park**, are in the compact grid of streets in the heart of the city near the waterfront.
A Amazon Park, Av Mendonça Furtado 4120, T091-3523 2800, amazon@stm.interconect.com.br. Large 1970s hotel, 4 km from the centre, with a swimming pool and friendly, competent staff.
C Brasil Grande Hotel, Trav 15 de Agosto 213, T091-522 5660. Family-run. Restaurant.
C New City, Trav Francisco Corrêa 200, T091-523 3149. Standard town hotel with plain a/c rooms and an airport pickup service. River trips can be organized from here.
C-D Santarém Palace, Rui Barbosa 726, T091- 3523 2820. A 1980s hotel with 44 comfortable but simple a/c rooms with TV and fridge.
D Brasil, Trav dos Mártires 30, T091-3523 5177. Pleasant, family-run, with fan-cooled rooms with shared bathrooms, breakfast and a small restaurant.

D Mirante, Trav Francisco Correa 115, T091-3523 3054, freephone T0800-707 3054, www.mirantehotel.com. One of the new and cleaner cheapies. A/c rooms with fridges, TVs, and some with a balcony and individual safes. Internet facilities available. Recommended.
D-F Horizonte, Trav Senador Lemos, 737, T091-3522 5437, horizontehotel@bol.com.br. Plain, simple, well-kept rooms with a/c or fan.
E Grão Rios, in a little alley off Av Tapajós between Trav dos Mártires and 15 de Agosto. Well-kept a/c rooms, some with a river view.

Alter do Chão p614
B Belas Praias Pousada, R da Praia s/n at the *praça*, T093-3527 1365. Belaspraias@gmail.com. Located on the river front of the beaches, and offering the best rooms – a/c and well appointed with river views.
B-C Agualinda Hotel, R Dr Macedo Costa s/n, T093-3527 1314. A comfortable, clean modern hotel with friendly staff who can help organize forest and river tours.
D-E Albergue Pousada da Floresta, T093-3527 1172, www.alberguedafloresta.com. A simple backpacker hostel with basic cabanas and a very cheap open-space for slinging hammocks. Facilities include tour organizing, canoe and bike rental, kitchen and in a great location next to the forest just south of the village. Prices include breakfast. Ask for Angelo.

Belterra p615
E Hotel Seringueira. 8 simple fan-cooled rooms and a pleasant restaurant.

Óbidos p616
C Braz Bello, R Corrêia Pinto, on top of the hill. Clean rooms with shared bathrooms. Optional full board.
C-D Pousada Brasil, R Corrêia Pinto. Basic with fan-cooled rooms with en suites or shared bathrooms.

🍴 Eating

Macapá p601, map p602

The waterfront *praça* has many open-air restaurants and bars, concentrated at the *trapiche* (pier). These are lively after 1800, especially at weekends.

🍴🍴🍴 Chalé, Av Pres Vargas 499, T096-3222 1970. The best restaurant in the city with good fish, Brazilian dishes and a pleasant atmosphere.

🍴🍴 Cantinho Baiano, Av Beira-Rio 1, T096-3223 4153. Overlooking the river 10 mins' walk south of the fort and with some of the best river fish in town. There are many other restaurants along this stretch about 1.5 km beyond the Cantinho Baiano.

🍴🍴 Flora, Rodovia Salvador de Diniz 1370-A, Km 15, T096-3283 2858. A lively little restaurant on the riverside next to a little marina 15 km from the fort (travelling away from town). Good fish and local dishes; try the fish infused with energetic Amazon fruits.

🍴 Bom Paladar Kilo's, Av Pres Vargas 456, T096-223 0555. Pay-by-weight buffet with excellent ice cream made from local fruits; make sure you try the *cupuaçu*.

🍴 Divina Arte, Av Pres Vargas 969, T096-3222 1877. A decent lunchtime menu restaurant and per kilo buffet. Plenty of choice.

🍴 Divina Gula, Av Pres Vargas 993, T096-3083 2091. Pleasant little café serving coffee, cakes and snacks.

🍴 Sarney, R Gal Rondon 1501. Simple but very cheap and filling per kilo restaurant. Good value. Lunchtime only.

Oiapoque p603

Gourmets will find themselves in a desert but there are many cheap places serving fish, beans and rice, and several spit-and-sawdust bars in the blocks around the river.

Belém p604, maps p605 and p606

All the major hotels have upmarket restaurants. There are numerous outdoor snack bars serving far cheaper meals. Good snack bars serving *vatapá* (Bahian dish) and

tapioca rolls are concentrated on **Assis de Vasconcelos** on the eastern side of the Praça da República. There are many decent a/c restaurant, bar and café options in the smart and newly renovated **Estação das Docas** on the riverfront where the boats dock.

🍴🍴🍴 Açaí, Hilton Hotel, Av Pres Vargas 882, T091-3242 6500. Come for lunch or dinner daily, or Sun brunch. Regional dishes such as roasted duck with *tucupi* sauce and jambo leaves.

🍴🍴🍴 Boteco das Onze, Praça FC Brandão s/n, T091-3224 8599. Just about the best regional cooking in Belém with live music every night and a view out over the river. Packed at weekends. Try the *filetena brasa* or the excellent *tambaqui*.

🍴🍴🍴 Churrascaria Rodeio, Rodovia Augusto Montenegro, Km 4, T091-3248 2004. A choice of 20 cuts of meat and 30 buffet dishes for a set price. Well worth the short taxi ride to eat all you can.

🍴🍴🍴 Churrascaria Tucuruvi, Trav Benjamin Constant 1843, Nazaré, T091-3235 0341. Enormous slabs of pork, beef, lamb and a range of sausages; all in vast portions and served with salads and accompaniments.

🍴🍴 Cantina Italiana, Trav Benjamin Constant 1401, T091-225 2033. Excellent Italian, with hotel delivery.

🍴🍴 Lá em Casa, Estação das Docas. Very good local cooking, especially the buffet and the à la carte *menu paraense*. Try the excellent *tacacá no tucupi* (an acrid soup with prawns cooked with jambo leaves that make the mouth go numb).

🍴🍴 Le Massilia, see Sleeping. French-owned and run with dishes including frogs' legs, *sole meunière* and *magret de canard*. Excellent cocktails.

🍴🍴 Manjar das Garças, Praça Carniero da Rocha s/n, Arsenal da Marinha, Mangal das Garças, T091-3242 1056. Huge lunch and evening buffet. The restaurant sits next to the river in a small park filled with scarlet ibis on the edge of town. Taxis US$5. Well worth it for an all you can eat meal at weekends.

Ħ Sabor Paraense, R Sen Manoel Barata 897, T091-3241 4391. A variety of fish and meat dishes such as crab in coconut milk served in a bright, light dining room.

Ħ-Ħ Mãe Natureza, R Manoel Barata 889, T091-3212 8032. Lunch only. Vegetarian and wholefood dishes in a bright clean dining room.

Ħ Doces Bárbaros, R Benjamin Constant 1658, T091-3224 0576. Lunch only. Cakes, snacks, sandwiches and decent coffee in a/c surrounds.

Ħ Govinda, R Ó de Almeida 198. Lunch only. Basic but tasty vegetarian food.

Ħ Portinha, R Dr Malcher 434, T091-3223 0922. Thu-Sun evenings only. Wonderful pastries, *takaka*, *cames* and juices.

Salinópolis *p610*

Ħ Bife de Ouro, Av Dr Miguel Santa Brígida, opposite petrol station. Simple, but excellent for fish and shrimp. Always busy at lunchtime.

Ħ Gringo Louco, 15 km (take taxi or hitch), at Cuiarana beach (follow signs). The US owner serves good, unusual dishes, and some 'wild' drinks known as 'bombs'. Popular.

Islands around Belém *p610*

Ħ Hotel Ilha Bela, Av 16 de Novembro 409, Mosqueiro. No evening meals. Recommended for fish.

Ħ Marésia, Praia Chapeu Virado, Mosqueiro. Highly recommended.

Ħ Sorveteria Delícia, Av 16 de Novembro, Mosqueiro. Serves good local fruit ice creams and the owner buys dollars.

Ilha de Marajó *p611*

There are a number of cheap places to eat in Soure but few restaurants of any distinction.

Ħ Canecão, Praça da Matriz, Soure. Sandwiches and standard beans, rice and cheap meals. Recommended.

Santarém *p613, map p613*

As with other small towns in the interior of Brazil, most restaurants in Santarém serve basic café-style food, lunch (consisting

of rice, beans, chips and a choice of beef, chicken or fish) and juices. The best choice is to be found along the waterfront in the centre.

Ħ Mascote, Praça do Pescador 10, T091-3523 2844. Open 1000-2330. Fish-orientated restaurant with a bar and ice cream parlour. Avoid *piraracu*.

Ħ Mascotinho, Praça Manoel de Jesus Moraes, on the riverfront. Bar and pizzeria attracting a lively crowd at sunset. Great river view.

Ħ Santo Antônio, Av Tapajós 2061, T091-3523 2356. Barbecued meat and fish.

Ħ Piracaia, R Floriano Peixoto 557, Centro, T091-3522 2881. The best value quality per kilo restaurant in town with a great choice of meat, fish and a few veggie options. General Brazilian cuisine.

Ħ Sabor Caseiro, R Floriano Peixoto 521, Centro, T091-3522 5111. Northern cooking with Takaka soups, river fish and prawn dishes alongside the usual chicken/meat and rice, beans and chips.

Alter do Chão *p614*

Ħ Lago Verde, Praça 7 de Setembro. Good fresh fish, try *calderada de tucunaré*.

Óbidos *p616*

There are plenty of cheap fish restaurants near the waterfront and in the upper town.

♪ Bars and clubs

Macapá *p601, map p602*

The food and drink kiosks in **Complexo Beira Rio** have live music most evenings. **ETNA** is the current dance club of choice, vibrating to the frenetic local rhythm *brega*, which sounds like *forró* on speed.

Belém *p604, maps p605 and p606*

Belém has some of the best and most distinctive live music and nightlife in northern Brazil. It's well worth heading out on the town at weekends.

Albery Albuquerque recommends

There is no one quite like Albery Albuquerque, www.myspace.com/alberyalbuquerque. He makes music from the rainforest by spending months recording birds and wild animals in the heart of the Amazon and precisely reproducing their calls with keyboard, voice and stringed instruments within his complex instrumental music. Here are his recommendations for what to do in Belém.

→ Take a taxi to Ver-o-Rio (Pedro Alvares Cabras near to Moinho Santa Rosa) for sunset. The views out over the river and the colours in the sky are magical.
→ If you have only a little time in Belém be sure to visit Cotijuba island for a taste of the forest and a sense of the size and magnificence of Amazonian nature.

A Pororó, Av Senador Lemos 3316, Sacramenta, T091-3233 7631. Bands like Calypso made their names in these vast, steaming warehouse clubs. Every Fri and Sat they are packed to the girders with scantily-clad blue-collar locals dancing wildly to techno *brega* acts – usually comprising a platinum blonde with a tiny skirt and Amazonian thighs backed by a band and a troupe of male dancers. A few hours here may be as cheesy as it comes but they are immense fun and barely known even to Brazilian tourists.

Baía Cool Jazz Club, Av Almirante Tamandaré 1, between R do Arsenal and R de Breves, T091-3289 6632. The jazz café of Belém, with national and international acts and local bands of all kinds – from rock, carimbó-fusion, reggae and jazz. Shows are followed by DJs who play underground sounds in the dark cellar bar.

Bar do Gilson, Trav Padre Eutíquio 3172, T091-3272 1306. A covered courtyard space decorated with arty black and white photography and with live Rio de Janeiro *samba* and *choro* on weekends. The bar owner, Gilson often plays mandolin in the band.

Boteco das Onze, Praça Frei Caetano Brandão s/n, Complexo Feliz Lusitânia, T091-3224 8599. This restored colonial fort and mansion is a favourite haunt for Belém's 20- and 30-something upper-middle classes who gather to sip cold draught beer on the veranda or dance inside to live Belém MPB.

Wonderful views out over the river and decent food.

Café Com Arte, Av Rui Barbosa 1436 (between Braz de Aguiar and Nazaré), Nazaré, T091-3224 8630. A brightly painted colonial house turned bar and club and with 3 floors devoted to live Belém rock, MPB fusion and DJs – some of whom play avante garde techno *brega*. Attracts an alternative studenty crowd and is especially busy on Fri. At its best after 2300.

Carrousel, Av Almirante Barroso at Antônio Baena. Up-tempo techno-*brega* with twanging guitars, played by DJs on a sound stage that looks like the flight control gallery for a 1970s starship. The club is invariably jam-packed with revellers and the atmosphere and spectacle have to be experience to be believed. Every Fri.

Ibiza, R Jerônimo Pimentel 201, between Av Visconde de Souza Franco and Av Almirante Wandenkolk, Umarizal; T091-3222 0562, www.ibizabelem.com.br. Lively club-bar with live rock, funk and MPB and DJs. Very popular but far from cutting edge.

Mormaço, Passagem Carneiro da Rocha s/n, next to Mangal das Garças, T091-3223 9892, www.mormaco.net. A warehouse-sized building on the waterfront which showcases some of the best live bands in Belém at weekends, playing local rhythms like *carimbó* and Brazilianized reggae and rock.

São Mateus, Trav Padre Eutíquio 606, next to the Praça da Bandeira, Campina, T091-

Coletivo Radio Cipo recommend

Coletivo Radio Cipo, www.myspace.com/coletivoradiocipo, play a vibrant mix of reggae, *carimbó*, roots and rock. They are one of the most exciting bands on the vibrant Belém music scene and often play life in the city. Their singer Carlinhos recommends the following: 'For me the **Bar do Gilson** (see page 623) is a great spot to listen to music, eat and chat. In the 1970s when a group of friends who loved *chorinho* and other such music found there was nowhere to play it in Belém they began to gather here. Some great names have played at the venue over the years, when they pass through Belém, such as Paulino da Viola, Beth Carvalho, Cristina Buarque and Sivuca, together with musicians from Japan, Cuba and other countries. It's a great place and there's always a good show.'

3252 5338. Another of Belém's pretty colonial houses turned street bar. Live bands of every kind; including new acts and space for some 300 people sipping ice-cold beer, caipirinhas and munching *comidinha* bar snacks.

down is respectable and there are plenty of multiplexes in the city's shopping malls.

Theatre Margarida Schiwwazappa, Av Gentil Bittencourt 650, T091-3222 2923.

● Entertainment

Macapá *p601, map p602*
Art galleries Cândido Portinari, corner of R Cândido Mendes and Av Raimundo Álvares da Costa. Exhibitions of local art.

Cinemas In Macapá Shopping, R Leopoldo Machado 2334.

Theatre Teatro das Bacabeiras, R Cândido Mendes. Concerts, poetry and plays.

Belém *p604, maps p605 and p606*
Art galleries Debret, R Arcipreste Manoel Theodoro 630, Batista Campos, T091-222 4046. Contemporary painting and sculpture, also has library specializing in art and philosophy.
Casa das 11 Janelas (1768), Praça Frei Caetano Brandão, T091-3219 1105. Cultural performances and art exhibitions, panoramic view.

Cinema Olímpia, Av Pres Vargas 918, T091-3223 1882. The 1st cinema in Belém, opened over 80 years ago, but now shows films for lonely men. But **Nazaré** a few doors

● Festivals and events

Macapá *p601, map p602*
Apr/May Marabaixo is the traditional music and dance festival held for 40 days after Easter.
Jun The Sambódromo has parades of Escolas de Samba at **Carnaval** and Quadrilhas during São João.
14 Aug Festa de São Joaquim held in Curiaú.

Belém *p604, maps p605 and p606*
Apr Maundy Thu, half-day; Good Fri, all shops closed, all churches open and there are processions.
9 Jun Corpus Christi.
15 Aug Accession of Pará to Independent Brazil.
7 Sep Independence Day, commemorated on the day with a military parade, and with a student parade on the preceding Sun.
Sep Festa do Çairé, Santarém and Alter do Chão. Parades in the streets in Alter do Chão with 2 teams competing to out-dance and out-costume each other – the Boto Cor do Rosa (pink river dolphin) and the Boto Tucuxi (gray river dolphin) teams.

The Festival of Candles

Our Lady of Nazareth has been celebrated with syncretistic festivals in Spain and Portugal since an image of the Virgin arrived in the monastery of Caulina in Spain in AD 361. It lay buried for many years under Saint Bartholomew's peak in Caulina, in protection against the Muslim invaders, but was recovered and taken to Portugal in 1119 where the effigy was said to have been the source of countless miracles.

The effigy in the Basílica de Nossa Senhora de Nazaré church was discovered by Plácido José de Souza, a caboclo, in 1700, buried in mud on an igarapé near Belém. De Souza built a chapel for the image, and over the following century the statue became associated with miracles in Pará; so much so that it began to be carried around the streets in veneration every October. In 1793, the Vatican authorized the first official processions in Belém, in celebration of Our Lady of Nazareth. Today the effigy forms the focus of the largest festival in this part of northern Brazil, the Círio de Nazaré.

On the second Sunday in October, a procession carries a copy of the Virgin's image from the Basílica to the cathedral, in a procession which attracts up to a million visitors. On the Monday, two weeks later, the image is returned to its usual resting place. Alongside the Sunday procession there's a lively festival known as the **Carnabelém**, which attracts many major Brazilian artists and musicians; carnival performers attend, along with an increasing contingent of international artists. There is a Círio museum in the crypt of the Basílica, enter at the right side of the church; free entry. For dates check with Paratur (see page 605).

---

30 Oct Círio. The festival of candles, based on the legend of Nossa Senhora de Nazaré whose image was found on the site of her Basílica around 1700. On the 2nd Sun in Oct a procession carries the Virgin's image from the Basílica to the cathedral; it is returned 2 weeks later. The festival attracts many artists and musicians and has become a massive national celebration with carnival performers and rock groups. Highly recommended. See www.ciriodenazare.com.br
2 Nov All Souls' Day.
8 Dec Immaculate Conception.
24 Dec Christmas Eve, half-day.

Santarém *p613, map p613*
22 Jun Foundation of the city.
29 Jun São Pedro, with processions of boats on the river and Boi-Bumba dance dramas.
8 Dec Nossa Senhora da Conceição, the city's patron saint.

Alter do Chão *p614*
2nd week in Sep Festa do Çairé, religious processions and folkloric events. Recommended.

O Shopping

Macapá *p601, map p602*
Macapá and Porto Santana were declared a customs-free zone in 1992. There are now many cheap imported goods available from shops in the centre. In the handicraft complex **Casa do Artesão**, Av Azárias Neto, Mon-Sat 0800-1900, craftsmen produce their wares on site. A feature is pottery decorated with local manganese ore, also woodcarvings and leatherwork.

Belém *p604, maps p605 and p606*
There is an arts and crafts market in the **Praça da República** every weekend selling attractive seed and bead jewellery, wicker,

hammocks and raw cotton weave work, toys and other knick-knacks. Belém is a good place to buy hammocks: look in the street parallel to the river, 1 block inland from **Ver-o-Peso**. There is a bookshop with English titles in the arcade on **Av Pres Vargas**.

Complexo São Brás, Praça Lauro Sodré. Has a handicraft market and folkloric shows in a building dating from 1911.

Ná Figueredo, Av Gentil Binttencourt 449, Nazaré and Estação das Docas, T091-3224 8948, www.nafigueredo.com.br. One of the best music shops in the north of Brazil selling a wealth of local sounds from the very best bands and unusual music from throughout Brazil. Funky T-shirts and casualwear.

Parfumaria Orion, Trav Frutuoso Guimarães 268. Has a wide variety of perfumes and essences from Amazonian plants, much cheaper than tourist shops.

Shopping Iguatemi, Trav Padre Eutique 1078. Belém's shopping mall.

Ilha de Marajó *p611*

Carlos Amaral, 3 Rua, Trav 20. Beautiful Marajo ceramics, made using the same techniques and materials as the Marajoara use themselves. Pieces include large pots and lovely jewellery – with pendants, bracelets and necklaces.

Santarém *p612, map p613*

Muiraquitã, R Lameira Bittencourt 131. Good for ceramics, woodcarvings and baskets.

▲ Activities and tours

Macapá *p601, map p602*
Tour operators

Amapá Turismo, Hotel Macapá, T096-3223 2667. **Fénix**, R Cândido Mendes 374, T/F096-3223 8200, and R Jovino Dinoá 1489, T096-3223 5353.

Belém *p604, maps p605 and p606*
Tour operators

Amazon Star, R Henrique Gurjão 236, T091-3241 8624, T091-3982 7911 (mob), www.amazonstar.com.br. Offers 3-hr city tours and river tours. The company also books airline tickets and hotel on Marajó.

Santarém *p613, map p613*
Tour operators

Amazon Tours, Trav Turiano Meira 1084, T091-3522 1928, T091-3975 1981 (mob), www.amazonriver.com. Owner Steve Alexander is very friendly and helpful and has lots of tips on what to do, he also organizes excursions for groups to Bosque Santa Lúcia with ecological trails. Recommended.

Gil Serique, 80 R Adriano Pimentel, T093-9973 8951, www.gilserique.com. Enthusiastic, larger-than-life, English-speaking tour guide who visits the creeks, flooded forest, primary forests and savannahs around Santarém, including the Tapajos National Park and Maica wetlands. Good on conservation.

Milly Turismo, R Siqueira Campos 277-A, Centro, T091-3523 5938. millyturismo@ bol.com.br. Flights, bus tickets tours and very efficient friendly service.

Santarém Tur, R Adriano Pimental 44, T091- 3522 4847, www.santaremtur.com.br. Branch in **Amazon Park Hotel** (see Sleeping). Friendly, helpful foreign-owned company offering individual and group tours (US$50 per person per day for a group of 5), to Tapajós National Forest, Maiça Lake and Fordlândia. Recommended.

⊖ Transport

Macapá *p601, map p602*
Air Taxis to the airport cost around US$7. There are flights **Belém**, **Brasília**, **Foz do Iguaçu**, **Rio de Janeiro**, **São Paulo**, **São Luís**, **Fortaleza**, **Marabá** and **Cayenne** (Guyane), amongst others.

   Airline offices Gol, www.voegol. com.br. META, airport, T0300-789 5503, www.voemeta.com. **Puma**, T096-3039 3939, www.pumaair.com.br. **TAM**, airport, T096-4002 5700, www.tam.com.br. **Varig**, R Cândido Mendes 1039, T096-3223 4612, www.varig.com.br.

Boat Boats leave from Porto Santana, which is linked to Macapá by bus or taxi. To **Belém**, *Atlântica*, fast catamaran 8 hrs, 3 times a week, US$30, reservations at **Martinica**, Jovino Dinoá 2010, T096-2235 777. Slower but slightly cheaper boats are *Bom Jesus*, *Comandante Solon*, *São Francisco de Paulo*, *Silja e Souza* of **Souzamar**, Cláudio Lúcio Monteiro 1375, Porto Santana, T096-3281 1946, car ferry with **Silnave**, T096-3223 4011. Purchase tickets from offices 2 days in advance (**Agencia Sonave**, R São José 2145, T096-3223 9090, sells tickets for all boats). Also smaller boats to **Breves** as well as a regular direct service to **Santarém**).

Bus **Estrela de Ouro**, office on the main square in front of the cathedral, leaves daily at 2000; and **Cattani**, office on Nunes between São José and Cándido Mendes, leaves daily at 0630 to **Amapá** (US$20), **Calçoene** (US$25, 7 hrs) and **Oiapoque** (12 hrs in the dry season with several rest stops, 14-24 hrs in rainy season, US$35). The Oiapoque bus does not go into Amapá or Calçoene and it is therefore inconvenient to break the trip at these places.

Pickup trucks run daily to various locations throughout Amapá: crowded on narrow benches in the back, or pay more to ride in the cab. Despite posted schedules, they leave when full. To **Oiapoque** at 0800, 10-12 hrs, US$35 cab, US$15 in back, to **Lourenço** at 0900.

Car hire **Localiza**, R Independência 30, T096-3223 2799, and airport T096-3224 2336. **Sila Rent a Car**, Av Procópio Rola 1346, T096-3224 1443.

Train Limited services between **Porto Santana** and **Serra do Navio**.

Oiapoque *p603*
Air Flights to **Macapá** 3 times a week.

Boat Frequent launches across the river to **Guyane** (US$5, 10 mins). Occasional cargo vessels to **Belém** or **Macapá** (Porto Santana).

Bus **Estrela de Ouro** leaves for **Macapá** from the waterfront, twice daily at 1000 and after lunch, 10-12 hrs (dry season), 14-24 hrs (wet season), US$35, also **Cattani**. Pickup trucks depart from the same area when full, US$35 in cab, US$15 in the back. *Combis* to **Cayenne** leave from St-Georges Oyapock in the morning.

Belém *p604, maps p605 and p606*
Air To get to the airport, take bus 'Perpétuo Socorro-Telégrafo' or 'Icaraci', every 15 mins, from the prefeitura, Praça Felipe Patroni (US$1.50, 40 mins). A taxi to the airport costs US$15. There are flights to most state capitals and many others. Internationally, there are flights to **Cayenne** (Guyane), **Fort-de-France** (Martinique), **Port au Prince** (Haiti), **Paramaribo** (Surinam) and **Miami** (USA).

Airlines Air Caribe, www.caribbean-airlines.com; GOL, www.voegol.com.br; META, www.voemeta.come; SETE, www.voe sete.com.br; TAM, www.tam.com.br. TOTAL, www.total.com.br.

Boat Boats leave from the Companhia das Docas at the Armazém 10 dock in town to Porto de Camará near Salvaterra on **Ilha de Marajó**, Mon-Sat 0630 and 1430, Sun 1000. Boats to Marajó also run from the port at Icoaraci (20 km north of Belém, 30 mins by bus from the *rodoviária* or from the Ver o Peso market, taxi US$25), Mon-Fri 0630, 0730, Sat 1600, 1700, Sun 1600, 1700 and 1800.

There are river services to **Santarém**, **Manaus** (see Routes in Amazônia, page 656) and intermediate ports. The larger ships berth at Portobrás/Docas do Pará (the main commercial port), either at Armazém (warehouse) No 3 at the foot of Av Pres Vargas, or at Armazém No 10, a few blocks further north (entrance on Av Marechal Hermes, corner of Av Visconde de Souza Franco). The guards will sometimes ask to see your ticket before letting you into the port area, but tell them you are going to speak with a ship's captain. Ignore the touts who approach you. Smaller vessels (sometimes cheaper, usually not as clean, comfortable or safe) sail from small docks along the Estrada Nova (not a safe part of town). Take a Cremação bus from Ver-o-Peso.

There is a daily service to **Macapá** (Porto Santana) with *Silja e Souza* of **Souzamar**, Trav Dom Romualdo Seixas, corner of R Jerônimo Pimentel, T091-222 0719, and Comandante Solon of **Sanave** (Serviço Amapaense de Navegação, Av Castilho Franca 234, opposite Ver-o-Peso, T091-3222 7810). To **Breves**, ENAL, T091-3224 5210. There are 2 desks selling tickets for private boats in the *rodoviária*; some hotels (eg **Fortaleza**) recommend agents for tickets. Purchase tickets from offices 2 days in advance. Smaller boats to Macapá also sail from Estrada Nova.

Bus To get to the *rodoviária* take **Aeroclube**, Cidade Novo, No 20 bus, or **Arsenal** or **Canudos** bus, US$0.50, or taxi, US$5 (day), US$7 (night).

Regular bus services to all major cities: Transbrasiliana go direct to **Marabá**, US$20 (16 hrs). To **Santarém**, via Marabá once a week (US$45, more expensive than by boat and can take longer, goes only in dry season). To **São Luís**, 2 a day, US$20, 13 hrs, interesting journey through marshlands. To **Fortaleza**, US$35-40 (24 hrs), several companies. To **Salvador**, US$50.

Car hire Avis, R Antônio Barreto 1653, T091-3230 2000, www.avis.com, also at airport, T0800- 558 066. Localiza, Av Pedro Álvares Cabral 200, T091-3212 2700, www.localiza.com.br, and at airport, T091-3257 1541.

Ilha do Marajó *p611*
Air
There is a taxi-plane service between Soure **Belém**. There are regular flights at weekends and its is worth ringing ahead to see if there is any space on a plane.

Airline offices Aeroval Táxi Aéreo, Av Senador Lemos (Aeroclube do Pará), T091-3233 3528; **Táxi Aéreo Soure**, Av Senador Lemos, Pass São Luiz s/n (Aeroclube do Pará), T091-3233 4986; **Táxi Aéreo Cândido**, Av Senador Lemos, Pass São Luiz s/n (Aeroclube do Pará), T091-9608 9019.

Boat
Boats run from Porto de Camará near Salvaterra to **Porto de Icoaraci** (Mon-Fri 1600 and 1700, Sat 1600 and 1700, Sun 1600, 1700 and 1800). Henvil sell tickets through their booth at the *rodoviária* (T091-3246 7472). Boats also run from Camará do Porto to the Armazém 10 dock in **Belém**, Mon-Sat 0630, 1500, Sun 1500 (3 hrs, US$5). Timetables regularly change so check beforehand.

Boat companies Arapari Navegação, R Siqueira Mendes 120, Cidade Velha, Belém, T091-3242 1870 and Companhia Docas do Pará, portão 15, T091-3242 1570. Henvil Navegação, Av Bernardo Sayão 4440, Praça Princesa Isabel, Jurunas, Belém, T091-3249 3400/3246 7472 and Porto de Icoaraci, R Siqueira Mendes s/n.

Santarém *p613, map p613*
Air
The bus to the airport from the centre leaves from Rui Barbosa every 80 mins, 0550-1910; taxis US$8. The hotels **Amazon Park, New City** and **Rio Dourado** have free buses for guests; you may be able to take these. There are flights to **Belém, Fortaleza, Manaus, Recife, Salvador, São Luís; Altamira, Itaituba, Monte Dourado, Oriximiná, Manaus; Araguaína, Belo Horizonte, Brasília, Carajás, Parintins, Trombetas, Tucuruí, Uberaba** and **Uberlândia**.

Airline offices GOL, www.voegol.com.br, META, R Siqueira Campos 162,

T091-3522 6222, www.voemeta.com.br.
Penta, Trav 15 de Novembro 183, T091-3523 2532. **TRIP**, www.voetrip.com.br.
TAM, www.tam.com.br.

Bus

To get to the *rodoviária* take the 'Rodagem' bus from the waterfront near the market, US$0.50. To **Itaituba**, US$11, 11 hrs, 2 a day. To **Marabá** on the Rio Tocantins (via **Rurópolis** US$7.50, 6 hrs, and **Altamira** US$23, 28 hrs), 36 hrs (can be up to 6 days), US$41, with **Transbrasiliana**. Also to **Imperatriz**, via Marabá; office on Av Getúlio Vargas and at the *rodoviária*. Enquire at the *rodoviária* for other destinations. Beware of vehicles that offer a lift, which frequently turn out to be taxis. Road travel during the rainy season is always difficult, often impossible.

Buses to **Belterra** leave from Trav Silvino Pinto between Rui Barbosa and São Sebastião, Mon-Sat 1000 and 1230, US$4, about 2 hrs. There is a 1-hr time difference between Santarém and Belterra, so if you take the 1230 bus you'll miss the 1530 return.

Boats

There are local services to **Óbidos** (US$10, 4 hrs), **Oriximiná** (US$12.50), **Alenquer**, and **Monte Alegre** (US$10, 5-8 hrs). Boats for **Belém** and **Manaus** leave from the Cais do Porto, 1 km west of town (take 'Floresta-Prainha', 'Circular' or 'Circular Externo' bus; taxi US$4); boats for other destinations, including **Macapá**, leave from the waterfront near the centre of town. For further information on services to Manaus, Belém, Macapá, Itaituba and intermediate ports, see Routes in Amazônia for details, page 656.

Alter do Chão *p614*

Bus Tickets and information from the bus company kiosk opposite **Pousada Tupaiulândia**. Buses to **Santarém** leave from the bus stop on Av São Sebastião, in front of Colégio Santa Clara, US$1, about 1 hr.

Belterra and Fordlândia *p615*

Bus Bus from Belterra to **Santarém** to Belterra Mon-Sat 1300 and 1530, US$4, about 2 hrs. There is a 1-hr time difference between Santarém and Belterra.

Boat Boats that run **Santarém–Itaituba** stop at Fordlândia if you ask (leave Santarém 1800, arrive 0500-0600, US$12 for 1st-class hammock space); ask the captain to stop for you on return journey, about 2300. The alternative is to take a tour with a Santarém travel agent.

❶ Directory

Macapá *p601, map p602*

Banks Banco do Brasil, R Independência 250, and **Bradesco**, R Cândido Mendes 1316, have Plus ATMs for VISA withdrawals. For *câmbios* (cash only), **Casa Francesa**, R Independência 232. **Monopólio**, Av Isaac Alcoubre 80. Both US$ and euros can be exchanged here. Best to buy euros in Belém if heading for Guyane as *câmbios* in Macapá are reluctant to sell them and they are more expensive and hard to obtain at the border.
Embassies and consulates France, at Pousada Ekinox (see Sleeping, page 617). Visas are not issued for non-Brazilians.
Internet @llnet in Macapá Shopping and numerous others. **Medical services** Hospital Geral, Av FAB, T096-3212 6127. Hospital São Camila & São Luiz, R Marcelo Candia 742, T096-3223 1514. **Post office** Av Corialano Jucá. **Telephone** R São José 2050, open 0730-2200.

Oiapoque *p603*

Banks It is possible to exchange US$ and reais to euros, but dollar rates are low and TCs are not accepted anywhere. Banco do Brasil, Av Barão do Rio Branco, 1000-1500, reais to euros and Visa facilities. Visa users can also withdraw reais at **Bradesco**, exchanging these to euros. Gold merchants, such as **Casa Francesa** on the riverfront and a *câmbio* in the market, will sell reais for US$ or euros. Rates are even worse in St Georges. Best to buy euros in Belém, or abroad. **Immigration** Polícia Federal for Brazilian exit stamp is on the road to Calçoene, about 500 m from the river. **Post office** Av Barão do Rio Branco, open 0900-1200, 1400-1700.

Belém *p604, maps p605 and p606*
Banks Banks open 0900-1630, but foreign exchange only until 1300. Banco do Brasil, Av Pres Vargas, near Hotel Itaoca, good rates, ATMs; Bradesco throughout the city for ATMs. HSBC, Av Pres Vargas near Praça da República has MasterCard Cirrus and Amex ATMs. **Embassies and consulates** Suriname, R Gaspar Viana 488, T091-3212 7144. For visas allow 4 days. Colombia, Av Almirante Barroso, 71, apt 601, bloco B, Ed. Narciso Braga, T091-3246 5662. Venezuela, R Presidente Pernambuco 270, T091-3222 6396, convenbelem@canal13.com.br. Allow at least 1 day for visas. UK, Av Governador José Malcher, 815 – SL 410, T091-3222 0762; USA, www.embaixada.americana.org.br. **Internet** Throughout the city including: Amazon, 2nd floor of Estação das Docas; Convert, Shopping Iguatemi, 3rd floor, US$1.40 per hr; InterBelém, Av Jose Malcher 189, US$1 per hr, helpful South African owner, English spoken. **Language schools** Unipop, Av Sen Lemos 557, T091-3224 9074, Portuguese course for foreigners. **Laundry** Lav e Lev, R Dr Moraes 576. Lavanderia Paraense, Trav Dom Pedro 1104, T091-3222 0057, dry and steam cleaning. **Libraries** UFPA, Av Augusto Correa 1, T091-3211 1140, university library with many titles on Amazônia. **Medical services** A yellow fever certificate of

inoculation is mandatory (see Health, page 44) It is best to get one at home (always have your certificate handy). Medications for malaria prophylaxis are not sold in Belém pharmacies. You can theoretically get them through the public health service, but this is hopelessly complicated. Such drugs are sometimes available at pharmacies in smaller centres, eg Santarém and Macapá. Bring an adequate supply from home. Clínica de Medicina Preventativa, Av Bras de Aguiar 410 (T091-3222 1434), will give injections, English spoken, open 0730-1200, 1430-1900 (Sat 0800-1100). Hospital da Ordem Terceira, Trav Frei Gil de Vila Nova 59, T091-3212 2777, doctors speak some English, free consultation. Surgery Mon 1300-1900, Tue-Thu 0700-1100, 24 hrs for emergencies. The British consul has a list of English-speaking doctors. **Police** For reporting crimes, R Santo Antônio and Trav Frei Gil de Vila Nova. **Post office** Av Pres Vargas 498. Also handles telegrams and fax. **Telephone** Telemar, Av Pres Vargas.

Santarém *p613, map p613*
Banks There are Bradescos in town with Visa ATMs. **Internet** Amazon's Star Cyber, Av Tapajos, 418 em frente a Orla, T093-3522 3648. Fast connection. English speaking. Tips and information available. Global Cyber, R Siqueira Campos 175 B, Centro. Hip grunge/graffiti decor, fast connection, good a/c, drinks, friendly staff. **Laundry** Storil, Trav Turiano Meira 167, 1st floor. **Post office** Praça da Bandeira 81. **Medical services** Hospital São Raimundo Nonato, Av Mendonça Furtado 1993, T091-3523 1176. **Telephone** Posto Trin, R Siqueira Campos 511. Mon-Sat 0700-1900, Sun 0700-2100.

Amazonas and the Amazon River

Amazonas is the largest state in Brazil (1.6 million sq km), bigger than any country in South America except Argentina, but with a population of just 2.8 million. Half of the inhabitants live in the capital, Manaus, with the rest spread out in remote communities often linked only by air and river.

The scenery in Amazonas is magnificent. Nothing can prepare you for the vast skies, the pure air, the endless shades of green, and rivers that stretch to the horizon. Nowhere does the Amazon feel more like the inland sea it once was than here. Rivers merge in vast swirls of myriad shades, from the translucent black of strong iced tea to café-au-lait brown, through vast forest-fringed lakes covered with giant water lilies or through eerie strands of flooded igapó or varzea forest. And in the rivers' depths swim 4-m-long horny-tongued fish, bull sharks, dolphins, stingrays and catfish big enough to swallow a man whole.

Amazonas state preserves Brazil's most extensive and unspoilt areas of lowland tropical forest, and the tourist industry here is developing fast. Most tours and trips to jungle lodges begin in Manaus, a sprawling rubber-boom town with good national and international connections. Beyond Manaus are the giant boulder mountains of the upper Rio Negro, which rise to Brazil's highest peak, the flooded wilds of Mamirauá Ecological Reserve near Tefé, and the Javari near Tabatinga, which are among the best places in the Amazon for spotting wildlife.

But the vast forests of Amazonas are not uninhabited. Civilizations have been living here from anywhere between 11,000 and 5000 BC and these people and their caboclo descendants maintain a rich cultural life. Although indigenous villages are very difficult to visit, their heritage can be experienced at the festivals in São Gabriel and the Boi Bumba in Parintins. The latter is the largest and most spectacular in the country after Carnaval and takes place on an island in the middle of the Amazon river at the end of June. ‣‣ *For listings, see pages 647-660.*

Visiting the forest

What to visit
The scenery is at its best on the **Rio Negro**, especially around the **Anavilhanas** archipelago, and further upstream where the mountains of the Guiana Shield punctuate the forest like giant worn crocodile teeth. However, the Rio Negro is an acidic, black-water river and consequently has a lower level of biodiversity than the more PH-neutral brown-water rivers like the Solimões (Amazon). So if you are intent on seeing wildlife, you will see far more in the regions south of Manaus, on the smaller river tributaries, creeks (*igarapés*) and flooded forest areas (*varzea* and *igapós*), especially those that are farthest from people. The **Lago Mamori**, **Lago Piranha** and the **Rio Urubu** are popular destinations for operators in Manaus. These are semi-protected areas which mix wild forests, rivers, creeks, igapo lakes and riverine communities living within nature at minimum impact. Only the farther reaches of either have prolific wildlife, but all offer a taste of the forest, and there are fascinating community tourism projects at Mamori (see **Amazon Gero Tours**, page 655). The best area for wildlife and genuine, accessible wilderness is the **Mamirauá Ecological Reserve** near Tefé, 30-40 minutes by plane from Manaus or 11-12 hours by fast boat. Some of the lodges very close to Manaus have their own reserves, which have been populated with rescued primates and birds. The best of these is **Amazon Ecopark** (see page 650). There are other jungle lodges in Acre and Mato Grosso that are good for wildlife.

When to visit

There is no best time to visit the forest; it depends what you want to see. The Amazon around Manaus is far more than a big river; think of it rather as an inland sea. Water is everywhere, especially during the **wet season**, which lasts from November to May. During the floods, the water rises by 5-10 m and the forests around the main rivers form areas known as *varzea* (on brown-water rivers) and *igapós* (on black-water rivers). Trees are submerged almost to their canopies and it is possible to canoe between their trunks in search of wildlife. In the morning you can often hear the booming call of huge black caiman and the snort of dolphins. And as the boats pass through the trees, startled hatchet fish jump into the bows. It is possible to canoe for tens of kilometres away from the main river flow, as *varzea* and *igapós* often connect one river to another, often via oxbow lakes covered in giant lilies. The lakes are formed when a meandering river changes course and leaves part of its previous flow cut off from the stream. In the **dry season** the rivers retreat into their main flow, exposing broad mudflats (on the brown-water rivers) or long beaches of fine white sand. Caiman and giant river turtles can often be seen basking on these in the evening sun, and wildlife spotting is generally a little easier at this time of year. Trees in the Amazon bear fruit at different times throughout the year; whenever a particular tree is in fruit it attracts large parrots, macaws and primates.

Choosing a tour or lodge

Once you have decided on when and where to go, the next decision is to choose a lodge or an operator. Those used to the quality of wildlife information supplied by rainforest tour operators in Costa Rica, Peru, Ecuador or Bolivia will be disappointed by the lack of professional wildlife knowledge and ecotourism services offered by many of the operators in Manaus. If you are interested first and foremost in wildlife and want accurate information, be sure to request a specialist wildlife guide (see page 654) and question your tour company carefully to test their knowledge. A good way of doing this is to ask whether they can supply a species list for the area around their lodge or for the forests they visit during their tours. Few can. Serious wildlife enthusiasts and birders looking to visit the Brazilian Amazon should think about heading for **Mamirauá Ecological Reserve** near Tefé (see page 644) or **Cristalino Jungle Lodge** (see page 755) in Mato Grosso.

That said, the better Manaus tours offer a fascinating glimpse of the forest and filigree of rivers, and insights into river people's lives. And they are far cheaper than either Mamirauá or Cristalino. **Standard tours** involve a walk through the forest looking at plants and their usage, caiman spotting at night (many guides drag caiman out of the water, which has negative long-term effects and should be discouraged), piranha fishing and boat trips through the *igapós* (flooded forests) or the *igarapés* (creeks). They may also visit a *caboclo* (river village) or one of the newly established indigenous villages around the city. Other trips involve light adventure such as rainforest survival, which involves learning how to find water and food in the forest, and how to make a shelter and string up a hammock for a secure night's sleep.

Trips vary in length. A half-day or a day trip will usually involve a visit to the 'meeting of the waters' and the Lago de Janauri nature reserve, where you are likely to see plenty of birds, some primates and river dolphins. The reserve was set up to receive large numbers of tourists so there are captive parrots on display and numerous tourist shops. Yet ecologists agree that the reserve helps relieve pressure on other parts of the river. Boats for day trippers leave the harbour in Manaus constantly throughout the day, but are best booked at one of the larger operators. Those with more time can take the longer cruises with a company like **Amazon Clipper** (see page 655) or stay in one of the rainforest lodges. To see virgin rainforest, a five-day trip by boat is needed.

Prices vary but usually include lodging, guide, transport, meals (but not drinks) and activities. The recommended companies charge around US$110-125 per person for a day trip, or US$300-350 for three days.

Beware of the touts

There are many hustlers at the airport in Manaus and on the street (particularly around the hotels and bars on Joaquim Nabuco and Miranda Leão), and even at hotel receptions. It is not wise to go on a tour with the first friendly face you meet. All go-betweens earn a commission so recommendations cannot be taken at face value and employing a freelance guide not attached to a company is potentially dangerous as they may not be qualified; check out their credentials. Tourist offices are not allowed by law to recommend guides, but can provide you with a list of legally registered companies. Unfortunately, disreputable companies are rarely dealt with in any satisfactory manner, and most continue to operate. Book direct with the company itself and ask for a detailed, written contract if you have any doubts. Above all avoid the cheapest tours. They are almost invariably the worst. Choosing a once in the lifetime tour on the basis of price alone is as clever as using plastic bags instead of shoes because they're cheaper.

What to take

Leave luggage with your tour operator or hotel in Manaus and only take what is necessary for your trip. Long-sleeved shirts and long trousers made of modern wicking fabrics, walking boots, insect repellent and a hammock and/or mosquito net, if not provided by the local operator, are advisable for treks in the jungle, where insects can be voracious. A hat offers protection from the sun on boat trips. Powerful binoculars are essential for spotting wildlife (at least 7x magnification is recommended, with the ability to focus at between 2.5 m and infinity). Buying bottled water at the local villages is a sure way to help the local economy, but it can be expensive in the lodges and it produces a great deal of waste plastic that is usually just chucked into the river directly or indirectly. Bring iodine, purification tablets or a modern water filter like PUR Scout or Aquapure (best with iodine for Amazon river water).

Ecotourism best practice in Manaus→ See page 649 for a list of recommended lodges.

Most of the lodges around Manaus do not adhere to proper ecotourism practices; this guide lists the exceptions. Good practice includes integration and employment for the local community, education support, recycling and proper rubbish disposal, and trained guides with good wildlife lodges. Ecotourism in Brazil is often a badge for adventure tourism in a natural setting and few operators conform to the best practices of the **International Ecotourism Society**, www.ecotourism.org. In Manaus, a relatively small number of communities have benefited from a boom which has seen the total number of beds rise from just six in 1979 to more than 1000 today. Only 27% of labour derives from local communities and very few of the lodges are locally owned. We would love to receive feedback about lodges and operators you feel are (or aren't) making a difference.

Manaus, the state capital, sits at 32 m above sea level some 1600 km from the Atlantic. The city sprawls over a series of eroded and gently sloping hills divided by numerous creeks, and stands at the junction of the liquorice-black Rio Negro and the toffee-coloured Solimões, whose waters flow side by side in two distinct streams within the same river. The city is the commercial hub for a vast area including parts of Peru, Bolivia and Colombia, and ocean-going container vessels often dock here.

New-found wealth has turned Manaus from tawdry to tourist-friendly in the last 10 years and the city will be one of the host cities for the 2014 World Cup. The **Centro Histórico** (old rubber boom city centre), which huddles around the green and gold mock-Byzantine dome of the **Teatro Amazonas** opera house, has been tastefully refurbished and now forms an elegant pedestrian area with cafés, galleries, shops and musuems. The area is a pleasant place to stroll around and sip a cool juice or a strong coffee, and many of the best hotels and guesthouses are found here. There are plenty of restaurants, bars and clubs, which support a lively, colourful nightlife.

Despite the city's size, the forest is ever present on the horizon and always feels just a short boat trip away. Beaches fringe its western extremities at Ponta Negra, whose sands are backed by towering blocks of flats, making it feel like a kind of Amazonian Ipanema.

There are plenty of sights near Manaus. The most vaunted are generally the least interesting. However, the **Anavilhanas** – the largest river archipelago in the world, comprising a beautiful labyrinth of forested islands, some fringed with white-sand beaches lapped by the jet-black waters of the Rio Negro – should not be missed. Try to be there for sunset when thousands of swifts descend to roost and the light is a deep, rich gold.

Manaus is also the main departure point for rainforest tours. There are many lodges around the city, from 20 minutes to four hours away. And although animals here are not as easy to see as in Tefé or on the **Rio Cristalino**, the scenery is breathtaking.

Ins and outs

Air The modern **Eduardo Gomes airport** ① *10 km north of the city centre, T092-3652 1120*, receives flights from all of Brazil's principal cities and there are international connections with Ecuador, Bolivia, Panama and the USA. Airport buses run to the Praça da Matriz restaurant (aka Marques da Santa Cruz), next to the cathedral in the centre of town (every 30 minutes 0500-2300, US$1.50). A taxi to the centre costs around US$29 on the meter. Taxi drivers often tell arrivals that no bus to town is available – be warned.

Road The only usable road runs north to Boa Vista, Guyana and Venezuela (although there are plans afoot to pave the road to Porto Velho for 2014). Visitors almost invariably arrive by plane or boat. The only long-distance buses arriving in Manaus **rodoviária** ① *5 km out of town at the intersection of Av Constantino Nery and R Recife*, are from Boa Vista, Presidente Figueiredo and Itacoatiara. To get to the centre, take a bus marked Praça Matriz or Cidade Nova, US$1.50, taxi US$20.

River Boats run to Santarém, Belém, Parintins, Porto Velho, Tefé, Tabatinga (for Colombia and Peru), São Gabriel da Cachoeira, and intermediate ports. Boat passengers arrive at the newly renovated **floating docks** ① *in the centre, a couple of blocks south of Praça da Matriz*, with direct access to the main artery of Avenida Eduardo Ribeiro, and 10 minutes' walk from the opera house and main hotel area. The docks is open to the public 24 hours a day. Bookings can be made up to two weeks in advance at the ticket sales area by the port's pedestrian entrance, bear left on entry and walk past the cafés. The names and itineraries of departing vessels are displayed here.

Boats for **São Gabriel da Cachoeira**, **Novo Airão**, and **Caracaraí** go from São Raimundo, upriver from the main port. Take bus No 101 'São Raimundo', No 112 'Santo Antônio' or No 110, 40 minutes; there are two docking areas separated by a hill, the São Raimundo *balsa*, where the ferry to Novo Airão, on the Rio Negro, leaves every afternoon (US$10); and the Porto Beira Mar de São Raimundo, where the São Gabriel da Cachoeira boats dock (most departures are on Friday).

Manaus

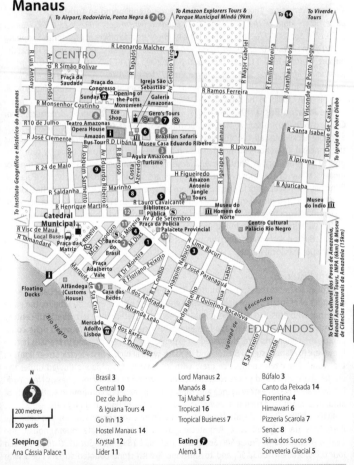

N
200 metres
200 yards

Sleeping
Ana Cássia Palace 1

Brasil 3
Central 10
Dez de Julho
 & Iguana Tours 4
Go Inn 13
Hostel Manaus 14
Krystal 12
Lider 11

Lord Manaus 2
Manaós 8
Taj Mahal 5
Tropical 16
Tropical Business 7

Eating
Alemã 1

Búfalo 3
Canto da Peixada 14
Fiorentina 4
Himawari 6
Pizzeria Scarola 7
Senac 8
Skina dos Sucos 9
Sorveteria Glacial 5

Many boat captains will allow you to sleep on the hammock deck of the boat for a day before departure or after arrival. Be careful of people who wander around boats after they've arrived at a port; they are almost certainly looking for something to steal. Agencies in town can book boat tickets for a small surcharge. ⟫ *See Transport, page 656.*

Getting around The Centro Histórico and dock areas are easily explored on foot. All city bus routes start on Marquês de Santa Cruz next to the Praça da Matriz and almost all then pass along the Avenida Getúlio Vargas (two blocks east of the Opera House). Taxis can be found near the opera house, at the *rodoviária*, airport and in Ponta Negra. Many of the upmarket hotels are in Ponta Negra, which is 13 km from the city centre and can feel somewhat isolated.

Tourist information There are several **Centros de Atendimento ao Turista (CAT)** ① *main office: 50 m south of the opera house, Av Eduardo Ribeiro 666, T092-3622 0767, Mon-Fri 0800-1700, Sat 0800-1200*, throughout the city. There are also offices in **Amazonas Shopping** ① *Av Djalma Batist 482, Chapada, T096-3236 5154, Mon-Sat 0900-2200, Sun 1500-2100*; at the **airport** ① *T096-3652 1120 or T0800-280 8820, daily 0700-2300*; at the **port** ① *regional terminal, R Marquês de Santa Cruz, armazém 07, Mon-Fri 0800-1700*, and ① *international terminal, R Marquês de Santa Cruz, armazém 10*, which opens only when cruise liners dock. There is a **CAT** trailer in the **rodoviária** ① *R Recife s/n, Flores, Mon-Sat 0800-1200*.

The **Amazon Bus** ① *T092-2324 5071, www.tucunareturismo.com.br, departures from CAT next to Teatro Amazonas, Mon-Sat 0900 and 1430, US$35, US$17 for children under 12*, is a double decker bus (air-conditioned ground floor and open-top upper deck), which visits the principal attractions in the Manaus on a three-hour, principally drive-by tour with guided commentary in Portuguese. It doesn't represent very good value for time or money. Many of the more interesting sights are not included (notably the Palacete Principal, the floating docks and INPA), there are some bizarre inclusions (like the football stadium, the Olympic village and the Federal University) and there's only one proper stop – at Ponta Negra beach (where the bus breaks for snacks and a breath of warm air).

The website for tourism in the Amazon, www.amazonastur.am.gov.br, has extensive information on accommodation throughout the state in Portuguese and English. *A Crítica* newspaper lists local events.

Centro histórico

The colonial streets that spread out from Teatro Amazonas and Praça São Sebastião are a reminder of Manaus's brief dalliance with wealth and luxury. Eduardo Ribeiro, the state governor who presided over these golden years, was determined to make 19th-century Manaus the envy of the world: a fine European city in which the nouveau riche could parade their linen and lace. He spared no expense. Trams were running in Manaus before they were in Manchester or Boston and its roads were lit by the first electric street lights in the world. The city's confidence grew with its majesty. Champagne flowed under the crystal chandeliers and prices rose to four times those of contemporaneous New York. Extravagance begot extravagance and rubber barons eager to compete in statements of affluent vulgarity fed their horses vintage wine or bought lions as guard cats.

In the 1890s, Ribeiro decided to put the icing on his cake, commissioning the Gabinete Português de Engenharia e Arquitetura to build an Italianate opera house, the **Teatro Amazonas** ① *Praça São Sebastião, T096-622 1880, Mon-Sat 0900-1600, 20-min tour US$6, students US$2.50*, and to surround it with stone-cobbled streets lined with elegant houses, plazas, and gardens replete with ornate fountains and gilded cherubs. Masks adorning the theatre walls were made in homage to great European artists, including Shakespeare, Mozart, Verdi and Molière and the driveway was paved in rubber to prevent the sound of carriage wheels spoiling performances. For the lavish interior, Ribeiro turned to the Roman painter **Domenico de Angelis** (who had painted the Opera House in Belém in 1883) and **Giovanni Capranesi** (an Italian colleague who had worked with Angelis on the Igreja de São Sebastião near the Teatro). Their grandiose decorations are magnificent both in their pomp and their execution. They include a series of trompe l'oeuil ceilings – showing the legs of the Eiffel Tower from beneath (in the auditorium) and the muse of the arts ascending to heaven surrounded by putti in the Salão Nobre reception room. Ribeiro also commissioned a Brazilian artist to paint a stage curtain depicting *Iara*, the spirit of the river Amazon at the centre of the meeting of the waters, and a series of scenes of idealized indigenous Brazilian life based on Paulistano Carlos Gomes' opera, *O Guarany*, in the ballrooms. The steel for the building was moulded in Glasgow, the mirrors made in Venice and priceless porcelains from France, China and Japan were purchased to grace mantelpieces, stairwells and alcoves. After the theatre doors were opened in 1896, Caruso sang here and Pavlova danced.

But for all its beauty and expense the theatre was used for little more than a decade. In the early 20th century the rubber economy collapsed. Seeds smuggled by Englishman Henry Wickham, to the Imperial Gardens at Kew and thence to Malaysia, were producing a higher yield. The wild-rubber economy dwindled and the doors to the opera house closed. Over the decades, the French tiles on the dome began to crack, the Italian marble darkened and the fine French furniture and English china slowly began to decay. What you see today is the product of careful restoration, which has returned the *Teatro* to its original glory. There are regular performances, which sell out very quickly, and an arts festival every April.

The Teatro Amazonas sits at the head of a handsome square, the **Praça São Sebastião**, paved with black and white dragon's tooth stones and surrounded by attractive, freshly painted late 19th- and early 20th-century houses. Many are little cafés, galleries or souvenir shops and the area is a safe and pleasant place to while away an hour or two. There are often free concerts on weekend evenings. In the middle of the square is another grand rubber boom construction, the bronze monument to the **Opening of the Ports**. It depicts *Iara* (see Teatro Amazonas, above), embraced by Mercury – representing commerce and standing over five ships, representing the continents of Europe, Africa, America, Oceania and Antarctica. In front of the monument is the modest **Igreja de São Sebastião** ⓘ *R 10 de Julho 567, T092-3232 4572*, whose interior is filled with more brilliantly coloured romantic paintings by Domenico de Angelis, Giancarlo Capranesi (who painted in the Teatro Amazonas and in Belém) and canvases by Bellerini and Francisco Campanella, both also Italian.

Eduardo Ribeiro's house sits on the southwestern edge of the *praça*, opening in late 2010 as a museum, the **Museu Casa de Eduardo Ribeiro** ⓘ *R José Clemente s/n, Centro, Mon-Fri 0900-1700, Sun 1600-2100, free guided tours (in Portuguese)*. The house is a tall town mansion built in a typically late-Victorian, eclectic style – with a neoclassical façade topped with balcony finished with a Baroque flourish. The two floors of the three-storey interior are devoted to Ribeiro. They are sober when you consider his excesses, bringing together items known to have belonged to the ex-state governor along with photographs, letters and memorabilia, and furniture and decorations from the rubber boom period.

On the waterfront

The city's other sights are huddled around the waterfront. The **Mercado Adolfo Lisboa** ① *R dos Barés 46*, was built in 1882 as a miniature copy of the now-demolished Parisian Les Halles. The wrought ironwork, which forms much of the structure, was imported from Europe and is said to have been designed by Eiffel. It was closed for refurbishment in early 2011.

The remarkable harbour installations, completed in 1902, were designed and built by a Scottish engineer to cope with the Rio Negro's annual rise and fall of up to 14 m. The large **floating dock** is connected to street level by a 150-m-long floating ramp, at the end of which, on the harbour wall, can be seen the high-water mark for each year since it was built. The highest so far recorded was in 2009. When the river is high, the roadway floats on a series of large iron tanks measuring 2.5 m in diameter. The large beige **Alfândega** (**Customs House**) ① *R Marquês de Santa Cruz, Mon-Fri 0800-1300*, stands at the entrance to the city when arriving by boat. Said to be have been modelled on the one in Delhi, it was entirely prefabricated in England, and the tower once acted as a lighthouse.

Dominating the streets between the opera house and the waterfront; and right next to the local bus station, is the **Catedral Municipal**, on Praça Osvaldo Cruz, built in simple Jesuit style and very plain inside and out. Originally constructed in 1695 in wood and straw, it was burnt down in 1850. Nearby is the main shopping and business area, the tree-lined **Avenida Eduardo Ribeiro**, crossed by Avenida 7 de Setembro and bordered by ficus trees.

Some 200 m east of the cathedral is the **Biblioteca Pública** (**Public Library**) ① *R Barroso 57, T096-3234 0588, Mon-Fri 0730-1730*, inaugurated in 1871, is part of the city's architectural heritage. Featuring an ornate European cast-iron staircase, it is well stocked with 19th-century newspapers, rare books and old photographs, and is worth a visit. Nearby, on the leafy, fountain-filled Praça Heliodoro Balbi (aka Praça da Policia) is a new museum complex, the **Palacete Provincial** ① *Praça Heliodoro Balbi s/n, Centro, T092-3635 5832, Tue-Fri 0900-1700, Sat 1000-1900, Sun 1600-2100, free* . The Palacete is a stately late-19th-century civic palace which was once the police headquarters. It is now home to six small museums: the Museu de Numismática (with a collection on Brazilian and international coins and notes), the Museu Tiradentes (profiling the history of the Amazon police and assorted Brazilian military campaigns), the Museu da Imagem e do Som (with free internet, cinema showings and a DVD library), the Museu de Arqueologia (preserving a handful of Amazon relics), a restoration atelier and the Pinacoteca do Estado – one of the best art galleries in northern Brazil, with work by important painters such as Oscar Ramos, Moacir Andrade and Roberto Burle Marx. The Palacete is a very pleasant place to while away a few hours and has decent air-conditioned café serving tasty coffee, cakes and savouries.

Other museums and cultural centres

The **Museu do Homem do Norte** ① *Av 7 de Setembro 1385, near Av Joaquim Nabuco, T096-3232 5373, Mon-Thu 0900-1200, 1300-1700, Fri 1300-1700, US$1*, is an interesting review of the way of life of the Amazonian population, or 'men of the north', although it has deteriorated in recent years and is now gathering dust. Social, cultural and economic aspects are displayed with photographs, models and other exhibits.

The **Palácio Rio Negro** ① *Av 7 de Setembro 1546, T096-3232 4450, Mon-Fri 0900-1400, free*, was the residence of a German rubber merchant until 1917 whereupon it became the state government palace. It underwent a major refurbishment in 2010 and now has an assortment of rooms presenting potted hagiographies of Amazonas state governors, exhibition spaces and a little café.

The **Museu do Índio** ⓘ *R Duque de Caxias 296, near Av 7 Setembro, T096-234 1422, Tue-Fri 0930-1730, Sat, Sun and holidays 1300-1700, US$1.70, free on Sun*, is managed by the Salesian missionaries who have been responsible for the ravaging of much of the indigenous culture of the upper Rio Negro. It is rather run down and betrays a Victorian view of indigenous culture. The displays are dusty and poorly displayed, but there are plenty of artefacts, including handicrafts, ceramics, clothing, utensils and ritual objects from the various indigenous tribes of the upper Rio Negro. There is also a small craft shop.

West of the centre

The **Instituto Geográfico e Histórico do Amazonas** ⓘ *R Frei José dos Inocentes 132, Manaus, T092-3622 1260, Mon-Fri 0900-1200 and 1300-1600, US$1.50*, is located in the oldest part of Manaus – a cluster of streets of tiny cottages dotted with grand, rubber boom buildings. It houses a museum and library of over 10,000 books, which thoroughly document Amazonian life through the ages.

The **Zoo** ⓘ *Estrada Ponta Negra 750, T096-625 2044, Tue-Sun 0900-1630, US$3, free on Sun, take bus No 120 from R Tamandaré by the cathedral, US$0.70, every 30 mins, get off 400 m past the 1st infantry barracks*, a big white building, is run by **CIGS**, the Brazilian Army Unit specializing in jungle survival. It has recently been expanded and improved. About 300 Amazonian animals are kept in the gardens, including anacondas in a huge pit.

Further afield

The **Bosque da Ciência INPA** are maintained by the **Instituto Nacional de Pesquisas da Amazônia (INPA)** ⓘ *R Otavio Cabral, Petropolis, T092-3643 3293, US$3, Tue-Fri 0900-1130, 1400-1630, Sat and Sun 0900-1630, take bus No 519 from the Praça da Matriz*, which conducts research into all aspects of the Amazon. There is a small park that is good for a taste of rainforest flora and fauna before you head out to the forest. The animals here are kept in less distressing conditions than in the city zoo. Paca (*Agouti paca*), agouti (*Myoprocta exilis*), squirrel monkeys (*Saimiri scicureus*) and tamarins (*Saguinus sp*) roam free, and among the other animals on display are Amazonian manatee (*Trichechus inunguis*) and giant otter (*Pternura brasiliensis*). A small museum within the park has displays on indigenous peoples use of the forest, medicinal plants and bottles of pickled poisonous snakes. INPA also manages what is probably the largest urban rainforest reserve in the world, on the northeastern edge of Manaus. Pedro Fernandes Neto (T092-9090 9983, pedroffneto@hotmail.com), takes guided tours and other adventure tourism activities in and around the city. This is far more interesting than the Jardim Botânico Chico Mendes – which isn't really worth visiting.

The **Centro Cultural dos Povos da Amazônia** ⓘ *Praça Francisco Pereira da Silva s/n, Bola da Suframa, Centro, T092-2125 5300, www.ccpa.am.gov.br*, is a large cultural complex devoted to the indigenous peoples of the Amazon. Outside the building there are Desano and a Yanomami *maloca* (traditional buildings), and the large, modern and well-curated museum in the main building preserves many artefacts, including splendid headdresses, ritual clothing and weapons. Explanatory displays are in Portuguese and passable English. It's a far better museum than the old-fashioned Museu do Indio. There are also play areas for the kids, a library and internet.

There is a curious little church, **Igreja do Pobre Diabo**, at the corner of Avenida Borba and Avenida Ipixuna, in the suburb of Cachoeirinha. It is only 4 m wide by 5 m long, and was built by a local trader, the 'poor devil' of the name. To get there, take the 'Circular 7 de Setembro Cachoeirinha' bus from the cathedral to Hospital Militar.

The **Museu de Ciências Naturais da Amazônia (Natural Science Museum)** ① *Av Cosme Ferreira, Cachoeira Grande suburb, 15 km from centre, T092-3644 2799, Mon-Sat 0900-1200 and 1400-1700, US$6, best to combine with a visit to INPA, and take a taxi from there (see above)*, is one of the city's little-known treasures. The remote museum is run by Japanese, with characteristic efficiency, and the exhibits are beautifully displayed and clearly labelled in Japanese, Portuguese and English. The main building houses hundreds of preserved Amazon insects and butterflies, together with stuffed specimens of a selection of the river's bizarre fish. You can also see live versions, including the endangered pirarucu (*Arapaima gigas*), which can grow up to 3.5 m, and a primitive osteoglottid fish that breathes air.

Beaches

Manaus has two sandy beaches on the outskirts of the city. The **Praia da Ponta Negra**, which lies upstream of the city's pollution, is the most popular and the most heavily developed. It is backed by high-rise flats and lined with open-air restaurants, bars and areas for beach volleyball and football. Nightlife here is lively, especially at weekends.

Around Manaus

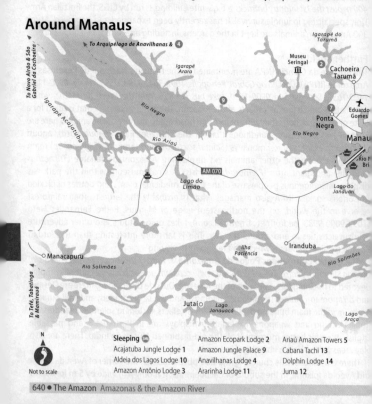

Sleeping
Acajatuba Jungle Lodge 1
Aldeia dos Lagos Lodge 10
Amazon Antônio Lodge 3

Amazon Ecopark Lodge 2
Amazon Jungle Palace 9
Anavilhanas Lodge 4
Ararinha Lodge 11

Ariaú Amazon Towers 5
Cabana Tachi 13
Dolphin Lodge 14
Juma 12

However, on most nights at least one of the bars (such as **O Laranjinha**, see page 652) will have Boi Bumba dance shows. Many of the better hotels, including the **Tropical**, are situated here. To get here take any bus marked 'Ponta Negra' (eg No 120) from the local bus station next to the cathedral. The beach can also be reached on the Tropical's shuttle bus (see Sleeping, page 647). Boats also leave from here for other beaches on the Rio Negro.

The meeting of the waters

About 15 km from Manaus is the confluence of the coffee-coloured **Rio Solimões** (Amazon) and the black-tea coloured **Rio Negro**, which is itself some 8 km wide. The two rivers run side by side for about 6 km without their waters mingling. This phenomenon is caused by differences in the temperature, density and velocity of the two rivers. Tourist agencies run boat trips to this spot (US$60-160). The simplest route is to take a taxi, or bus No 713 'Vila Buriti', to the Porto de CEASA dock, and take the car ferry across to Careiro. Ferries leave all the time when full and there are many other smaller boats too. The last departure from CEASA is at 1800 and the last return to CEASA from Careiro is 2000. Motor boats for the meeting of the water charge US$15 per person or US$80 per boat (up to five people). Boats also leave from the hotel **Tropical** (US$90 per boat, up to five people). You should see dolphins, especially in the early morning. Alternatively, hire a motorized canoe from near the market in the city centre (about US$30; per person or US$180 per boat for up to eight people). Allow three to four hours to experience the meeting properly. A 2-km walk along the Porto Velho road from the CEASA ferry terminal leads to some ponds, some way from the road, in which huge Victoria Regia water lilies can be seen from April to September.

To Boa Vista & Presidente Figueiredo

To Silves, Itacoatiara

To Parintins

Rio Puraquequara

Rio Amazonas

Ceasa Ferry Dock
Encontro das Águas
Meeting of the Waters

Ilha do Careiro

Lago do Rei

Ilha Xiborema

Careiro

Rio Mamori

Rio Amazonas

Lago Comprido

BR 319

Pousada dos Guanavenas 8
Tiwa Amazone Resort 6
Tropical 7

Tropical Business 7
Zequinha Lodge 15

Excursions from Manaus

Museu Seringal

① *Igarapé São João, 15 km north of Manaus up the Rio Negro, Tue-Sun 0800-1600, T092-3234 8755, US$3 and US$15 round trip on a private launch from the Hotel Tropical.* This museum sitting at the end of a pretty *igarapé* (creek) off the Rio Negro is a full-scale reproduction of an early 20th-century rubber-tapping mansion house, with serf quarters, a factory and a shop complete with authentic products. It was built as a film set for the 2002 Portuguese feature film, *A Selva*. A guided tour – especially from one of the former rubber tappers brings home the full horror of the system of debt peonage that enslaved Brazilians up until the 1970s. The museum can be visited with **Amazon Flower** or **Amazon Gero Tours**.

Arquipélago de Anavilhanas

This filigree of more than 350 brilliant-green islands in the jet-black Rio Negro – some fringed with white-sand beaches, others anchored only by their roots – is one of the area's must-see sights. The scene is particularly beautiful at the end of the day when the sky looks vast and warm and the light on the trunks of the partially submerged trees is a thick orange-yellow. Birds fly into the Anavilhanas to roost and millions of bats leave for their night hunt. The air is silent but for bird calls, the lapping of the river and the bluster of river dolphins surfacing for air. The islands are 80 km upstream of Manaus. Several companies arrange visits to the archipelago (US$195-285, per person, one day – it takes four hours to reach the islands), as can most of the Rio Negro lodges. Rio Negro safari cruises almost all visit the Anavilhanas.

It is possible to see botos (pink river dolphins) being fed, and even to swim with them at the **Boto Cor-de-Rosa restaurant** in the Anavilhanas village of Novo Airão. Visits should be booked through a Manaus tour operator in as small a group as possible.

Presidente Figueiredo

There are hundreds of waterfalls dotted through the forest and scrubby savannah that surrounds the sleepy town of Presidente Figueiredo, 117 km north of Manaus on the shores of the vast artificial lake Balbina, formed by the ill-fated Figueiredo dam. It's possible to visit three or four on a day trip from Manaus. With an overnight stay it's also possible to see the beautiful and (in Brazil) very rare Guianan Cock of the Rock (Rupicola rupicola). This is one of South America's most spectacular sights. Males are pigeon-sized, and brilliant tangerine, with an exuberant, almost iridescent half-moon crest which completely obscures the beak, an orange-tipped black tail and silky-orange filaments which stick out at bizarre angles around the wings and tail. Females are a dull brown with a yellow-tipped black bill. Up to 40 males at a time perform elaborate courtship dances for the females in forest clearings called *leks*, twisting and trilling and displaying their extraordinary crests until a female settles behind her chosen mate and pecks him on the rump. Cock of the rocks can only be seen on an organized tour (see page 654).

Figueiredo has so many waterfalls and caves, it's hard to know where to begin. The most spectacular are arguably the following: The **Cachoeira Gruta da Judeia**, which plummets off the lip of a gargantuan cave in the heart of the forest; the **Cachoeira Arco Iris** and **Cachoeira Iracema** both of which are a series of stepped falls plunging through rocky gorges and over huge boulders; and the **Cachoeira Pedra Furada**, which rushes through a series of holes in an enormous rock. There are light adventure activities too. Ask for Johnny (bookable through **Pedro Neto** – see Guides, page 656) who organizes abseiling, canyoning and whitewater rafting around Figueiredo.

Presidente Figueiredo town – often called **Balbina** – is an uninteresting place, built in the 1970s as a settlers' camp for construction workers on the dam. Its grid of streets lead to a long beach which gets packed with visitors from Manaus at weekends and a small centre for rehabilitiating distressed Amazonian manatees (intermittently open).

Ins and outs Presidente Figueiredo's attractions are spread out over a large area, and whilst even the remotest falls are no more than two hours walk off a road, driving distances are relatively large and there is no public transport. The only practical way to visit

Festa do Boi Bumba

The Boi Bumba festival in Parintins is a competition between two rival groups, similar to the samba schools in Rio, called Caprichoso (whose colour is blue) and Garantido (red). The two teams present a pageant, which originates from Braga in Portugal, but has been heavily syncretized with indigenous and Afro-Brazilian themes. It was brought to Parintins in the early 20th century by settlers from São Luís in Maranhão. The pageant tells the story of Pai Francisco and his wife Mãe Catirina who steal the prize bull from the landowner that they work for, and kill it. The landowner discovers this and threatens to kill them if they fail to resurrect his bull by midnight. The couple employ the talents of a shaman, a priest and an African *pai santo*, and these characters invoke the female spirit of rainforest fertility, the Cunhã-poranga, played by a beautiful young dancer. The story is told to the backdrop of vast four-storey floats with moving parts and troupes of hundreds of dancers. It is performed in the purpose-built *bumbódromo* stadium which holds almost 40,000 spectators. Previews of the festival in miniature are held in the **Hotel Tropical** in Manaus throughout the year and there are always Boi Bumba dancers on weekend evenings in the Ponta Negra bars in Manaus.

Figueiredo is with a hire car from Manaus, or on an organized tour. Operators and guides in Manaus organize open or multi-day visits. If you are passing through on the way to or from Boa Vista, excursions can be organized through the **Pousada das Pedras** or the **Pousada Wal** in Balbina. There are at least six buses a day to Balbina from the Manaus *rodoviária*. Boa Vista buses will stop at Balbina on request.

Downstream from Manaus → *For listings, see pages 647-660.*

Parintins → *Colour map 1, B4. Phone code: 092. Population: 90,000.*

Parintins is situated between Manaus and Santarém, just before the Amazonas-Pará border, on the Ilha Tupinambana. In the dry season, boat trips run to the river beaches and to nearby lakes. In colonial times, this was the resting point of a group of coastal indigenous Brazilians who made an astonishing trek through thousands of miles of dense forest to escape the ravages of the Portuguese slave trade. However, they didn't evade it for long. Within a generation they had been found by slavers from Belém who took all the women and children and murdered all the men. Ironically the island is now the site of one of the country's most important and spectacular festivals, Boi Bumba, which celebrates the triumph of the indigenous and *caboclo* poor over a *coronel* (tyrannical landowner).

The **Festa do Boi Bumba** (see box, above) is the most vibrant in Brazil after Carnaval and draws tens of thousands of visitors to Parintins on the last three days of June each year. But since the town has only two small hotels, finding a room can be a challenge. Everyone sleeps in hammocks on the boats that bring them to the festival from Manaus and Santarém (a large vessel will charge about US$130 per person, including breakfast, for the duration).

Ins and outs The **airport** ⓘ *Estrada Odovaldo Novo s/n, Parintins, T092-3533 2700*, receives flights from Manaus, Óbidos and Santarém and others. Boats stop here on the Belém–Manaus route. there are also sailings from Óbidos and Santarém. ↠ *See Transport, page 656.*

Upstream from Manaus → *For listings, see pages 647-660.*

Tefé and the Mamirauá Ecological Reserve → *Colour map 1, B2. Phone code: 097.*
Population: 65,000.

Tefé is a scruffy town roughly halfway between Manaus and the Colombian border. The local airport authorities confiscated all of the city's rubbish lorries in a dispute over the municipal dump, and now it is piled up willy-nilly. But few come here for the town itself, for this is the access point to one of the world's most important primate and waterfowl reserves, the **Mamirauá Ecological Reserve** ① *T097-3343 4160, www.mamiraua.org.br and www.uakarilodge.com.br*. This is a **Ramsar**, www.ramsar.org, site set up with British support to protect huge areas of terra firme, gallery, *varzea* and *igapó* forest at the confluence of the Solimões and Japurá rivers, and to manage them sustainably with the local riverine people. There are abundant birds including numerous rare trogons, cotingas, currasows, hoatzin, harpy eagle and five species of macaw. There are black caiman (one of which lives under the floating lodge), both species of Amazon dolphin, and numerous rare primates – the most spectacular of which are the endemic black-headed squirrel monkey and the endangered white uakari, known locally as the 'macaco Ingles' because of its red complexion and its genitalia. A visit is unforgettable.

The reserve has a small floating lodge, the **Pousada Uacari** (see Sleeping, page 651) on the Mamirauá river and visitors stay here in simple but elegant wooden rooms. Trips include walks in terra firme forest, boat and canoe trips to *igarpe* creeks, *varzea* and *igapó* forest and the vast Mamirauá lake. Visits must be booked in advance.

Ins and outs Tefé is connected to Manaus by air daily on **Trip** (www.voetrip.com.br), with onward flights to Tabatinga. There are regular slow boats (at least one a day) from Manaus or from Tabatinga and fast speed boats from Manaus (see page 656). The town is small enough to negotiate on foot.

Border with Colombia and Peru

Benjamin Constant → *Colour map 1, B1. Phone code: 097. Population: 23,000.*
This tiny town, with a big sawmill and a series of little tiled houses set in bougainvillea gardens, sits on the frontier with Peru, just opposite Leticia in Colombia. There is an interesting **Ticuna indigenous cultural centre and museum** ① *Av Castelo Branco 396, T096-415 5624*, with artefacts, information panels and a gift shop. The music is haunting but sadly not for sale. Ticuna people run the museum.

Ins and outs There are boat services from Manaus (seven days or more), to Manaus (four days or more) and from Iquitos in Peru. There are no facilities in Benjamin Constant, but it is possible to buy supplies for boat journeys. Benjamin Constant is two hours from Tabatinga and Leticia (ferry/*recreio* US$2; 25 minutes by speedboat, US$4 per person, cheaper if more passengers). ▶▶ *For boats to/from Manaus, see Routes in Amazônia, page 656.*

Tabatinga → *Colour map 1, B1. Phone code: 097. Population: 38,000.*
Tabatinga is theoretically 4 km from Leticia (in Colombia) but, in reality, it is the scruffy half of the same town: a long street buzzing with mopeds, a port and some untidy houses in between. There is an important Ticuna centre here, and the town is the headquarters of one of the country's most important indigenous NGOs, **FIUPAM**, fiupam@yahoo.com.br.

Border essentials: Brazil–Colombia–Peru

It is advisable to check requirements and procedures before arriving at this multiple border. No foreign boats are allowed to dock at the Brazilian, Colombian and Peruvian ports, so travellers should enquire carefully about embarkation/disembarkation points and where to go through immigration formalities. If waiting for transport, the best place for accommodation, exchange and other facilities is Leticia in Colombia.

Brazilian immigration Entry and exit stamps are given at the **Polícia Federal**, 2 km from the Tabatinga docks (Monday to Friday 0800-1200, 1400-1800); through the docks to the end of the road, turn right at this T-junction for one block to a white building opposite Café dos Navegantes; also at the airport (Wednesday and Saturday only). Proof of sufficient funds (US$500) or an onward ticket may be asked for. One week's transit in Tabatinga is permitted. In this area, carry your passport at all times. The **Colombian consulate** (0800-1400) is near the border on the road from Tabatinga to Leticia, opposite Restaurant El Canto de las Peixadas. Tourist cards are issued on presentation of two passport photos. **Note** If coming from Peru, you must have a Peruvian exit stamp and a yellow fever certificate.

Colombian immigration Exit stamps to leave Colombia by air or overland are given by **DAS**, Calle 9, No 8-32, Leticia, no more than one day before you leave. If flying into Leticia prior to leaving for Brazil or Peru, get an exit stamp while at the airport. Check both offices for entry stamps before flying into Colombia. To enter Colombia you must have a tourist card to obtain an entry stamp, even if you are passing through Leticia en route between Brazil and Peru (the Colombian consul in Manaus may tell you otherwise; try to get a tourist card elsewhere). The Colombian consulate in Tabatinga (see above) issues tourist cards; 24-hour transit stamps can be obtained from DAS. If visiting Leticia without intending to go anywhere else in Colombia, you may be allowed to enter without immigration or customs formalities (but traveller's cheques cannot be changed without an entry stamp). The **Brazilian consulate** in Leticia is at Calle 11, No 10-70 (Monday to Friday 1000-1600); onward ticket and two black-and-white photos needed for visa (photographer nearby); allow 36 hours. The **Peruvian consulate** is at Cra 11, No 6-80 (0830-1430); no entry or exit permits are given here.

Peruvian immigration Peruvian entry/exit formalities take place at Santa Rosa; reais and dollars can be exchanged here. Every boat leaving and entering Peru stops here. Entry formalities into Brazil takes place at Tabatinga; for Colombia, In Leticia. There is an immigration office in Iquitos (Mcal Cáceres 18th block), where procedures for leaving can be checked. Also in Iquitos are the **Brazilian consulate** (Calle Sargento Lores 363, T005194-232081), and **Colombian consulate** (Calle Putumayo 247).

However, there is little of interest for tourists, who are better off staying in Leticia. Flights arrive in Leticia (see below) from where a minibus to Tabatinga costs US$1.

The port area in Tabatinga is called Marco and the port captain is very helpful and speaks good English. There are regular boats from Manaus and from Benjamin Constant, across the water, and from Iquitos in Peru. A mosquito net for a hammock is essential if sailing upstream from Tabatinga, much less so downstream. A good hammock will cost US$15 in Tabatinga (try **Esplanada Teocides**).

Ins and outs Travel between Tabatinga and Leticia (Colombia) is very informal. Taxis between the towns charge US$5 (more if you want to stop at immigration offices or change money), or US$0.80 in a *colectivo* (more after 1800). Beware of taxi drivers who want to rush you expensively over the border before it 'closes'. It is not advisable to walk the muddy path between Tabatinga and Leticia as robberies occur here. Boats from Manaus normally start from Tabatinga and spend a day or two here before returning; you can stay on board. ➤➤ *For boats to/from Manaus, see Routes in Amazônia, page 656.*

Leticia (Colombia) → *Colour map 1, B1. International phone code +57. Phone code: 9859.*

This riverside city is clean and modern, though run down, and is rapidly merging into one town with neighbouring Marco in Brazil. Leticia is a good place to buy indigenous products typical of the Amazon, and tourist services are better than in Tabatinga or Benjamin Constant. The best time to visit the area is in July or August, the early months of the dry season. At weekends, accommodation may be difficult to find.

The **museum** ① *Cra 11 y Calle 9*, set up by **Banco de la República**, covers local ethnography and archaeology and is set in a beautiful building with a library and a terrace overlooking the Amazon. There is a small **Amazonian zoo** ① *US$1*, and botanical garden on the road to the airport, within walking distance of town (20 minutes).

Ins and outs The **airport** ① *1.5 km from town*, receives flights from Manaus (three times a week with **Rico**) via Tefé. It is a small terminal with few facilities. A taxi to the centre costs US$1.60. There is a **tourist office** ① *C 10, No 9-86, Ministerio del Medio Ambiente, Cra 11, No 12-05*, for general information on national parks.

Up the Rio Negro

It is possible to get a public passenger boat from São Raimundo port on the outskirts of Manaus up the Rio Negro (see Routes in Amazônia, page 656). There are hardly any villages of more than a few houses, but these places are important in terms of communications and food resources. It is vital to be self-sufficient in terms of food and cash and to be able to speak Portuguese or have a Brazilian guide. **Nova Airão**, on the west bank of the Negro, next to the southern extremity of the Anavilhanas islands, is a three-hour bus trip across the newly opened Rio Negro road bridge. It has a large boat-building centre at the south end, and a fish and vegetable market at the north end. Ice and bread can also be purchased here. It has a telephone, from which international calls can usually be made. There is road access and a bus service from Manaus.

North of Nova Airão and 220 km from Manaus on the Rio Negro, is the UNESCO World Heritage-listed **Parque Nacional Jaú**. This is Brazil's largest national park and, at 2,272,000 ha, is the largest protected area of tropical forest in the world. It encompasses the entire Jáu river basin, from its headwaters to its source. The only way to get here is with a tour; there is no transport or facilities (guides or tour operators charge US200-230 per person per day for a minimum of four people). Permits are necessary. Guides and operators can organize these or you can contact the **Instituto Chico Mendes de Conservação da Biodiversidade (ICMBio)** ① *www.icmbio.gov.br*. Like most Brazilian parks, Jaú is a paper park – meaning that whilst it is delineated on the map it is not policed or practically protected. However, it is, in the main, pristine wilderness. The park is little visited and little studied but, according to ICMBio, so far they have recorded 400 species of vascular plants, a number of which are endemic; 263 species of fish (almost half as many as the entire continent of Europe); and all the large terrestrial Amazonian mammals.

Moura is about five days upstream from Manaus. It has basic medical facilities and the military base has an airstrip (only usable September to December) and tele-communications. About a day further upstream is **Carvoeira**, almost opposite the mouth of the Rio Branco. There is a vibrant festival in the first week of August. A couple of days beyond is **Barcelos**, with a daily air service, except Sundays, the centre for bass fishing on the Amazon. There are a couple of places to stay here.

São Gabriel da Cachoeira and on towards Venezuela → *Colour map 1, A2.*

A great distance further upstream is São Gabriel da Cachoeira, some 900 km and 10 days from Manaus by boat. The city is tiny and sits under a hulking boulder mountain in front of a series of dramatic rapids. There are fine white-sand beaches on the Negro during the dry season. São Gabriel is near the **Pico da Neblina National Park**, named after the highest mountain in Brazil (3014 m). The park can be visited with **Roraima Adventures** (from Boa Vista, see page 665).

Ins and outs There are flights four times a week with **Trip**, www.airtrip.com.br. You can continue from São Gabriel to Venezuela or to Colombia; be sure to get an exit stamp for Brazil here and an entry stamp for Colombia. Visas for Venezuela must be obtained in Manaus. There is a Colombian consulate in São Gabriel near the **FOIRN** indigenous headquarters. In São Gabriel there are two banks but no exchange facilities and the **Vaupes** hotel (**E**). Cargo boats go to **Cucuí** at the border between Brazil, Colombia and Venezuela. There is also a twice-weekly bus, US$5 (one hotel, ask for Elias, no restaurants). From Cucuí there are daily boats to Guadalupe (Colombia) and infrequent boats to Santa Lucía (Venezuela).

◉ Amazonas and the Amazon River listings

For Sleeping and Eating price codes and other relevant information, see pages 32-37.

● Sleeping

Manaus *p634, map p635*
Whilst there are a number of hostels and cheap guesthouses, Manaus lacks hotels of quality in the Centro Histórico. The best establishments are in Ponta Negra or close to the airport; both very inconvenient for seeing almost all that is interesting in the city. The best area to stay in the city centre is around the **Teatro Amazonas**, where the Italianate colonial houses and cobbled squares have been newly refurbished.

Although the area around Av Joaquim Nabuco and R dos Andradas has lots of cheap hotels, this is a low-key red-light district which is very sketchy at night, as is the Zona Franca – around the docks. Things are expected to change in the years approaching the World Cup.
L Tropical, Av Coronel Teixeira 1320, Ponta Negra, T092-3659 5000, www.tropical hotel.com.br. A lavish though increasingly frayed 5-star hotel 20 km outside the city in a semi-forested parkland setting next to the river. The hotel has a private beach, tennis court and a large pool with wave machine. There are several restaurants including a decent *churrascaria*. The river dock is a

departure point for many river cruises. To get here take a Ponta Negra bus from the Praça da Matriz, US$1.50, then walk or take a taxi. A taxi to the centre costs around US$30. Service can be slow. The hotel tour agency organizes excursions.

L Tropical Business, Av Coronel Teixeira 1320, Ponta Negra, T092-2123 3000, www.tropicalhotel.com.br. The business companion to the **Tropical**, just a few doors away, is far better, cleaner and more contemporary. Rooms and suites are modern and well appointed, housed in a large tower block with great views out over the river from the upper floors. The hotel has the best business facilities in the city and has a lovely infinity pool set in gardens overlooking the beach. Like the other hotels in Ponta Negra, it's a long way from the centre.

AL Taj Mahal Hotel, Av Getúlio Vargas 741, Centre, T092-3627 3737. A large, business hotel in a superb location overlooking the Opera House in the city centre. Facilities include a revolving rooftop restaurant and a spa. The hotel could be one of the city's best but it's looking very, very tired nowadays, and the staff seem equally so. Rooms and public areas are in sore need of refurbishment, but this is one of the very few hotels in the centre it's possible to reserve through email.

A Ana Cássia Palace, R dos Andradas 14, Centre, T092-3303 3637, www.anacassia. com.br. Faded, poorly renovated, unsecure, but bright and spacious rooms, some with great views of the port. The hotel has a rooftop restaurant and breakfast area and a pool.

A Lord Manaus, R Marcílio Dias 217, T092-3622 2844, www.lordmanaus.com.br. Pleasant, spacious lobby and standard a/c rooms with writing desks and beds, all of which are in some need of refurbishment. Conveniently located for boats and shops, in the heart of the Zona Franca but it is not safe to walk around this area at night.

A Manaós, Av Eduardo Ribeiro 881, T092-3633 5744, www.hotelmanaos.com.br. Recently renovated and right next to the Teatro Amazonas. Spruce a/c rooms with marble floors and smart bathrooms. Decent breakfast.

A-B Go Inn, R Monsenhor Coutinho 560, Centro Histórico, T092-3306 2600, www.atlanticahotels.com.br. This 2010 opening is one of the very few decent, modern a/c accommodation options in the city centre – with undistinguished but no-nonsense corporate-designed rooms with tiny work desks, queen-sized beds and wall-mounted TVs. Facilities include a café, disabled rooms, gym and paid Wi-Fi in all rooms.

B-C Central, R Dr Moreira 202, T092-3622 2609, www.hotelcentralmanaus.com.br. A business hotel tucked away behind the Palacete Provincial, with a range of rooms, many very scruffy although some well kept; look at a few. Excellent large breakfast.

B-C Krystal, R Barroso 54, T092-3233 7535, www.krystalhotel.com.br. A range of small, boxy a/c rooms in soft colours, with polished tile floors, TVs a fridge and wardrobe and little else.

B-C Lider, Av 7 de Setembro 827, T092-3621 9700, www.liderhotelmanaus.com.br. Small modern a/c rooms with marble floors, little breakfast tables and en suite bathrooms. The best are at the front of the hotel on the upper floors. Very well kept.

C-D Brasil, Av Getúlio Vargas 657, T092-2101 5000, hotel-brasil@internext.com.br. Faded cavernous a/c rooms decorated with tacky art and with tiny en suite bathrooms and even tinier balconies. Small pool.

D Dez de Julho, R 10 de Julho 679, T092-3232 6280, www.hoteldezdejulho.com. One of the better cheap option, with clean though simple rooms (some with a/c and hot water). One of the best tour operators (**Amazon Gero**) in the lobby and efficient, English-speaking staff. In a great location next to Praça São Sebastião.

E Hostel Manaus, R Lauro Cavalcante 231, Centro, T092-3233 4545, www.hostelmanaus. com. **F** for HI members. HI hostel in one of the city's original houses. Good-value dorms and private rooms. Quiet and reasonably central with views of the city from the rooftop patio. Australian-run. Great place to join a jungle tour – with a good tour operator in the lobby. Not to be confused with a non-HI hostel in the city using a similar name.

Lodges accessible from Manaus

When reserved in advance, either direct or through an operator (see page 654), lodges will organize all transfers from either a Manaus hotel or in many cases the airport.
LL-L Amazon Jungle Palace, office at R Emilio Moreira 470, Manaus, T092-3212 5600, www.amazonjunglepalace.com.br. A floating lodge with very comfortable a/c 4-star rooms and a pool, on a black-water tributary of the Rio Negro some 5 km from the Anavilhanas. Excellent guides and service but, as ever with lodges close to Manaus, somewhat depleted forest.
L Acajatuba Jungle Lodge, Lago Acajatuba, 4 hrs up the Rio Negro from Manaus. Office at Av 7 de Setembro 1899, Manaus, T092-3234 3199, www.acajatuba.com.br. This Rio Negro lodge sits in a beautiful location on the edge of Acajatuba lake – a large igarapé visited by boto dolphins, at the far southern end of the Anavilhanas islands. 40 apartments, a bar and a restaurant. Accommodation is in simple, round, thatched roof bungalows with mosquito screens (but no nets – bring your own). The lodge does not conform to best ecotourism practice – guides handle wild animals.

L Anavilhanas Lodge, Edifício Manaus Shopping Centre, Av Eduardo Ribeiro 520, sala 304, T092-3622 8996, www.anavilhanas lodge.com. This is the nearest jungle lodges get to boutique. Minimalist rooms with high thread count cotton on the beds, low-lighting, flatscreen TVs and tasteful rustic chic hangings and decor sit in thatch-roofed cabins whose front walls are entirely glass-fronted – giving spectacular views out over the Rio Negro and the adjacent Anavilhanas archipelago. There's a lodge bar serving *cupuaçu* caipirinhas, amongst other drinks, and a range of comfortable lounging areas. But bring a mosquito net. The large menu of activities includes the standard piranha fishing, community visits, hikes and dolphin spotting alongside more meditative kayaking and sunset tours of the Anavilahnas.
L Ariaú Amazon Towers, 60 km and 2 hrs by boat from Manaus, on the Rio Ariaú, 2 km from Archipélago de Anavilhanas; office at R Leonardo Malcher 699, Manaus, T092-2121 5000, www.ariautowers.com.br. With 271 rooms in complex of towers connected by walkways, a pool, meditation centre, large restaurant and gift shop, this is a jungle hotel more than a jungle lodge. If you are after intimacy with the forest you won't find it here. But the hotel is a good option for older people or those with small children. The guided tours are generally well run, although specialist wildlife guides are not available and tame wildlife hangs around the lodge.

L Pousada dos Guanavenas, Ilha de Silves, 300 km from Manaus on the road to Itacoatiara, then by boat along the Rio Urubu. T092-3656 1500, www.guanavenas.com. A large lodge in cleared grounds overlooking the black-water Lago Canacari, some 4-5 hrs from Manaus. The hotel has a pool, excellent restaurant and very comfortable a/c rooms with hot water. The hotel's tours run like clockwork – sometimes too much so.

L-AL Amazon Ecopark Lodge, Igarapé do Tarumã, 20 km from Manaus, 15 mins by boat, T092-2547 7742 or T092-9146 0594 www.amazonecopark.com.br. The best lodge within an hour of Manaus, in a private forest that would otherwise have been deforested. The lodge makes a real effort at conservation and good practice. The apartment cabins are very comfortable (hot showers) and set in the forest. The lodge has a lovely white-sand beach and is close to the **Amazon Monkey Jungle**, an ecological park where primate species (including white uakari) are treated and rehabilitated in natural surroundings. The **Living Rainforest Foundation**, which administers the ecopark, also offers educational jungle trips and overnight camps (bring your own food), entrance US$20.

A Ararinha Lodge, Paraná do Araçá, exclusively through **Amazon Gero Tours**, www.amazongerotours.com. One of the more comfortable lodges in the Mamori area. This lodge sits on a riverbank overlooking the Paraná do Araça – a little visited and unspoilt river running off the Lago do Mamori lake regions. Accommodation is in smart wooden chalets housing suites of individual rooms which come complete with double or single beds with mosquito nets. The area is one of the best for wildlife in the Mamori region.

A Dolphin Lodge, Paraná do Mamori, T092-3877 9247, through **Maia Expeditions**, www.maiaexpeditions.com. A small lodge with simple wooden cabins perched on a grassy bluff overlooking the Parana do Mamori river (off Lago Mamori). The lodge runs tours and has kayaks for guests to use.

A Juma, Lago da Juma, T092-3232 2707, www.jumalodge.com. A newly refurbished lodge in a beautiful location on the outer reaches of Lago Mamori at Juma. Accommodation is in comfortable wooden and palm-thatch huts on stilts right on the riverbank. The owners have a burgeoning interest in birdwatching and proper wildlife tours.

A Tiwa Amazone Resort, Lago Salvador, 10 mins across the Rio Negro from Ponta Negra, T092-3088 4676, T092-9995 7892, www.tiwaamazone.com. A medium-sized resort lodge with very comfortable spacious cabanas with en suites and a/c, built out over a small caiman-filled lake. The resort itself has a large pool and bar. Too close to Manaus for much wildlife, but an option as an alternative city hotel, especially for a business trip. Good tours.

A-B Amazon Antônio Lodge, through Antonio Jungle Tours, www.antonio-jungletours.com. A thatched roof wooden lodge with plain, fan-cooled wooden rooms and an observation tower. Set in a beautiful location overlooking a broad curve in the river Urubu some 200 km from Manaus.

A-B Aldeia dos Lagos Lodge, near Silves, run by the **Silves Project**, T092-3248 9988, through **Viverde** tours (see page 655), www.aldeiadoslagos.com. A community-based eco-project run in conjunction with an NGO. Accommodation is in a simple floating lodge set in a system of lakes near the tiny town of Silves and with high environmental diversity. Good for birds and caiman. Profits are fed back into local communities.

C Cabana Tachi, through Amazon Jungle Tours, T092-9627 4151, www.amazon jungletours.com. A simple, rustic community-owned lodge run in ecotourism partnership with **Amazon Gero Tours** in a pioneering project which sees money and resources returning to the community. In one of the most pristine stretches of forest in the region. Good for wildlife.

C Zequinha, through Amazon Gero Tours, www.amazongerotours.com. Very simple wooden fan-cooled rooms and 1 a/c suite in a round maloca building 100 m from a bluff overlooking the Lago Mamori.

Presidente Figueiredo p642

B-C Pousada das Pedras, Av Acariquara 2, Presidente Figueiredo, T092-3324 1296, www.pousadadaspedras.am.com.br. Simple tiled rooms in a tropical garden, a generous breakfast of fruit, rolls, juices and coffee and tours organized to waterfalls and caves by the enthusiastic owner.

B-C Pousada do Wal, BR-174, T092-3324 1267, www.pousadadawal.com.br. A pretty little *pousada* with terracotta-tile and whitewashed bungalows set in a little garden pation off a quiet Balbina street. Rooms are very simple with TVs, fridges, simple wooden furnishings and a bed, and public areas are strung with hammocks. The hotel can help organize excursions.

Tefé p644

L Pousada Uacari, T097-3343 4672 or T097- 3343 4160, www.uakarilodge.com.br. Together with **Cristalino Jungle Lodge** (see page 755), this is the best lodge for wildlife, guiding and ecotouristic practice in the Brazilian Amazon. The lodge is in a magical location in the Mamirauá reserve, floating on a river, with 10 suites of 25 sq m each linked by floating bridges. Tours are excellent. Look out for the friendly black caiman which lives in the water under the restaurant. The lodge and the trips in the reserve can be booked in Manaus through **Iguana Tours**, at either their shop or their office in Manaus airport. Book well in advance.

D Anilce, Praça Santa Teresa 294. Clean, a/c, very helpful. Don't leave valuables in your room.

E Hotel Panorama, R Floriano Peixoto 90. Recommended, with a good restaurant.

Benjamin Constant p644

There are a number of very cheap and very simple *pousadas* in town.

B Benjamin Constant, R Getúlio Vargas 36, beside the ferry, T092-3415 5638; postal address Apdo Aéreo 219, Leticia, Colombia. All rooms have a/c, some with hot water and TV. Good restaurant, arranges tours.

Tabatinga p644

C Pousada do Sol, General Sampaio, T092-3412 3355. Simple rooms but in a hotel with a sauna and a pool. Friendly owners.

D-E Travellers Jungle Home, R Marechal Rondon 86. A little hostel and tour operator with Brazilian/French owners and a pet snake.

Leticia (Colombia) p646

The international phone code for Colombia is +57. The code for Leticia is 9819.

AL Anaconda, Cra 11 No 7-34, T9819-27119. The plushest in town with large a/c rooms, hot water, a restaurant, good terrace and swimming pool.

B Colonial, Cra 10 No 7-08, T9819-27164. A/c or fans, swimming pool, cafeteria, noisy.

C-D Residencias Fernando, Cra 9, No 8-80, T9819-27362. Simple but well appointed and clean. Recommended.

D Residencias La Manigua, C 8 No 9-22, T9819-27121. Friendly staff and modest but well-maintained rooms.

D Residencias Marina, Cra 9 No 9-29, T9819-26014. Standard cheap hotel rooms, TV, some with a/c, cold water, good breakfast and meals at attached restaurant.

E Residencia Internacional, Av Internacional, between the centre and the Brazilian border. Basic rooms with attached bathrooms and fans. Hard beds.

F Residencias Colombia, C 10 at C 8. Very basic rooms with a shared bathroom. Good value.

🍴 Eating

Manaus p634, map p635

Many restaurants close Sun night and Mon. The best are a 10-15-min taxi ride from the Centro Histórico.

¶¶¶ Banzeiro, R Libertador 102, Adrianópolis, T092-9204 7056, www.restaurante banzeiro.com.br. Chef Ivar Schaedler cooks gourmet workings of traditional Amazonian and Brazilian dishes, served in a pretty dining room. 10-min taxi ride from the Centro Histórico. Plates include *pato no tucupi* (see page 600), *moqueca do banzeiro* (made with Pirarucu) and *caldeirinha de tucanaré* (peacock bass fish broth). Delicious drinks include *batidas de cacau* (made with the chocolate bean fruit) and *caipiroska amazonica* (made with *cupuacu*).

¶¶¶ Village, R Mario Ypiranga Monteiro 948, Adrianópolis, T092-3234 3296, www.village restaurante.com.br. The favourite dining room of Manaus' burgeoning wealthy elite is a contemporary space flooded with warm natural light through big glass windows or low-lit for intimate after-dark dining. The best options from the big menu are the river fish and regional dishes.

¶¶¶-¶¶ Himawari, R 10 de Julho 618, opposite Teatro Amazonas, T092-3233 2208. A conveniently located a/c Japanese restaurant serving reasonable sushi, sashimi, steamed pastries and salads by Teruko Sakai who was born and spent his early years in Nagasaki. Attentive service, good sake and open Sun night when many restaurants close.

¶¶ Búfalo, Av Joaquim Nabuco 628, T092-3633 3733, www.churrascariabufalo.com.br. The best *churrascaria* in Manaus, with a US$12 all-you-can-eat Brazilian BBQ and a vast choice of meat. Come with an empty stomach.

¶¶ Canto da Peixada, R Emílio Moreira 1677 (Praça 14 de Janeiro), T092-3234 3021. One of the longest-established *peixadas* (simple fresh fish restaurants) in Manaus. Unpretentious, always vibrant and with excellent Amazon fishes from Jaraqui to Tambaqui. A short taxi ride from the centre.

¶¶ Fiorentina, R José Paranaguá 44, Praça da Polícia, T092-3232 1295. Fan-cooled traditional Italian with cheesy vegetarian dishes and even cheesier piped music.

Great *feijoada* on Sat, half-price on Sun. Dishes are served with mugs of wine.

¶¶ Pizzeria Scarola, R 10 de Julho 739, corner with Av Getúlio Vargas, T092-3232 6503. Standard menu and pizza delivery, popular.

¶ Alemã, R José Paranaguá, Praça da Polícia. Food by weight with great pastries, hamburgers, juices, sandwiches.

¶ Senac, R Saldanha Marinho 644, T092-3633 2277. Lunch only. Cookery school with a self-service restaurant. Highly recommended.

¶ Skina dos Sucos, Eduardo Ribeiro and 24 de Maio. A large choice of Amazonian fruit juices and bar snacks.

¶ Sorveteria Glacial, Av Getúlio Vargas 161, and other locations. Recommended for unusual ice creams such as *açai* and *cupuaçu*.

Tefé *p644*
¶¶-¶ Au Bec d'Or by the port. With simple but very tasty French cuisine using Amazon ingredients.

Leticia (Colombia) *p646*
There are plenty of lunchtime *almuerzo* restaurants serving cheap dishes of the day in the centre of town. Fried banana and meat, fish and fruit is sold at the market near the harbour and there are many cheap café/bars overlooking the market on the river bank. Take your own drinking water or beer.
¶ Sancho Panza, Cra 10 No 8-72. Good-value meat dishes, big portions, Brazilian beer.

⊙ Bars and clubs

Manaus *p634, map p635*
Manaus has lively nightlife with something going on every night. O Laranjinha in Ponta Negra is popular any week night and has a live Boi Bumba dance show on Wed.

The scene is constantly changing and clubs and bars are often in different neighbourhoods far from the centre. The most economical way of of exploring Manaus's nightlife is with a guide.

DJ (Djalma) Oliveira, T092-9112 3942/ 9185 4303, djalmatour@hotmail.com (or book through **Amazon Gero Tours**), will take visitors out to sample Manaus' club life. He is cheaper than a taxi and speaks a little English.

Entertainment

Manaus *p634, map p635*
Cinema
In R 10 de Julho and 8 screens at the **Manaus Plaza Shopping**, Av Djama Batista 2100, www.manausplazashopping.com (3 km from the centre), has the cities best multiplexes. Films are usually dubbed into Portuguese.

Performing arts
For **Teatro Amazonas** and **Centro Cultural Palácio Rio Negro**, see pages 636 and 638. In Praça da Saudade, R Ramos Ferreira, there is sometimes a Sun **funfair** from 1700; try prawns and *calaloo* dipped in *tacaca* sauce. **Teatro da Instalação**, R Frei José dos Inocentes 445, T/F092-3234 4096. Performance space in restored historic buildings with free music and dance (everything from ballet to jazz), May-Dec Mon-Fri at 1800. Charge for performances at weekends. Recommended.

Festivals and events

Manaus *p634, map p635*
6 Jan Epiphany.
Feb Carnaval in Manaus has spectacular parades in a *sambódromo* modelled on Rio's, but with 3 times the capacity. Tourists may purchase grandstand seats, but admission at ground level is free (don't take valuables). Carnaval lasts for 5 days, culminating in the parade of the samba schools.
3rd week in Apr A Semana do Indio (Indigenous Brazilian week), a festival celebrating all aspects of indigenous life. Tribal people arrive in Manaus, there are small festivals and events (contact the tourist

office for details, see page 636) and indigenous handicrafts are on sale throughout the city.
Jun Festival do Amazonas, a celebration of all the cultural aspects of Amazonas life, indigenous, Portuguese and from the northeast, especially dancing. Also in Jun is the **Festival Marquesiano**, with typical dances from those regions of the world which have sent immigrants to Amazonas, performed by the students of the Colégio Marquês de Santa Cruz.
29 Jun São Pedro, boat processions on the Rio Negro.
Sep Festival de Verão do Parque Dez, 2nd fortnight, festival with music, fashion shows, beauty contests and local foods at the Centro Social Urbano do Parque Dez. In the last week of Sep is the **Festival da Bondade**, with stalls from neighbouring states and countries offering food, handicrafts, music and dancing at SESI, Estr do Aleixo, Km 5.
Oct Festival Universitário de Música (FUM), the most traditional festival of music in Amazonas, organized by the university students, on the university campus.
8 Dec Processão de Nossa Senhora da Conceição, from the Igreja Matriz through the city centre and returning to Igreja Matriz for a solemn Mass.

Parintins *p643*
Jun Festa do Boi Bumba. Huge 3-day festival attracting 40,000 people (see box, page 643).
24 Dec-6 Jan Parintins' other main festival is the **Pastorinhas**.

São Gabriel da Cachoeira *p647*
Sep Festribal is a very lively indigenous festival in the city. Reachable through **Amazon Gero Tours**.

Shopping

Manaus *p634, map p635*
All shops close at 1400 on Sat and all day Sun. Since Manaus is a free port, the whole

area a few blocks off the riverfront is full of electronics shops. This area, known as the **Zona Franca**, is the commercial centre, where the shops, banks and hotels are concentrated.

Markets and souvenirs

To buy a hammock head to the **Casa das Redes** and other shops on R dos Andradas. There are now many handicrafts shops in the area around the theatre. The souvenir shop at the INPA (see page 639) has some interesting Amazonian products on sale. The markets near the docks are best in the early morning. There is a very good Sun market in the **Praça do Congresso**, Av E Ribeiro. **Ponta Negra** beach boasts a small 'hippy' market, very lively at weekends. There is a good supermarket at the corner of Av Joaquim Nabuco and R Sete de Setembro.
Central de Artesanato Branco e Silva, R Recife 1999, T092-3642 5458. A gallery of arts and crafts shops and artist's studios selling everything from indigenous art to wooden carvings by renowned Manaus sculptor Joe Alcantara.
Ecoshop, Largo de São Sebastião, T092-3234 8870 and Amazonas Shopping, T092-3642 2026 www.ecoshop.com.br. Indigenous arts and crafts from all over the Amazon, including Yanomami and Tikuna baskets, Wai Wai necklaces and Baniwa palm work.
Galeria Amazonica, R Costa Azevedo 272, Largo do Teatro, T092-3233 4521, www.galeriamazonica.org.br. A large, modern space filled with Waimiri Atroari indigenous arts and crafts, from weapons, basketware, jewellery and clothing. One of the best places for buying indigenous art in Brazil.

▲ Activities and tours

Manaus *p634, map p635*
Swimming
Swimming is possible at **Ponta Negra** beach, 13 km from the centre (Soltur bus, US$0.70), although the beach virtually disappears beneath the water Apr-Aug.

There is good swimming at waterfalls on the Rio Tarumã, where lunch is available, shade, crowded at weekends. Take the Tarumã bus from R Tamandaré or R Frei J dos Inocentes, 30 mins, US$0.70 (very few on weekdays), getting off at the police checkpoint on the road to Itacoatiara. There is also superb swimming in the natural pools and under falls of clear water in the little streams which rush through the woods, but take locals' advice on swimming in the river; electric eels and various other kinds of unpleasant fish, apart from the notorious piranhas, abound, and industrial pollution of the river is growing.

Every Sun, boats depart from the port in front of the market for beaches along **Rio Negro**, US$2, leaving when full and returning at the end of the day. This is a real locals' day out, with loud music and foodstalls on the sand.

Amazon tours

Águia Amazomas Turismo, R 24 de Maio 440 CA-H sala 1, Vila Baipendi, T092-3231 1449, www.aguiaamazonas.com.br. Bespoke trips, lodge stays and cruises conducted by Samuel Basilio – an experienced guide from the upper Rio Negro specializing in long expeditions (who has worked on many BBC documentaries as a location finder), and his brother-in-law Antonio João da Silva. When booked ahead, agencies listed here will meet visitors at the airport, book Manaus hotels and organize all transfers.
Amazon Antonio Jungle Tours, c/o Hostel Manaus, R Lauro Cavalcante 231, T092-3234 1294 and T092-9961 8314, www.antonio-jungletours.com. Jungle stays on the Rio Urubu, a blackwater river 200 km northeast of Manaus and some of the best-value packages for backpackers and a reliable, well-run service with local, English-speaking guides.
Amazon Explorers, Av Djalma Batista 2100, T092-2133 4777, www.amazonexplorers.com.br. Day tours including the 'meeting of the waters', Lago do Janauari, rubber collecting and lunch a number of lodges

(all listed on the website) and booking and transfers for Mamirauá and the Boi Bumba and Parintins. From around US$150 per person per day.

Amazon Gero Tours, R 10 de Julho 695, T092-3232 4755 or T092-9983 6273, www.amazongerotours.com. Excellent tours to a series of lodges around Lago Mamori, transfers to São Gabriel for the festivals, day trips to Presidente Figueiredo and around the city of Manaus (including 'meeting of the waters'), and bookings made for lodges everywhere. Gero, the owner, is very friendly and dedicated and one of the few operators in Manaus genuinely to contribute shares of his profits to the local riverine communities. They also run a lodge at Ararinha lake.
Iguana Tour, R 10 de Julho 679 (hotel 10 de Julho), T092-3663 6507, www.amazon brasil.com.br. Offers an extensive range of trips of various lengths. Good facilities

including riverboat, Juma lodge and campsite in the forest.
Manati Amazonia, Av Getúlio Vargas 334, sala 6 at Huascar Figueiredo, T092-3234 2534, www.manatiamazonia.com. A Franco-Brazilian company offering excursions to the Anavilhanas, riverboat cruises and tours in the forests around Mamori with accommodation at **Juma** lodge.
Viverde, R das Guariúbas 47, Parque Acariquar, T092-3248 9988, www.viverde. com.br. A family-run agency acting as a broker for a broad range of Amazon cruises and lodges (including the beautiful **Aldeia dos Lagos** lodge in Silves) and running their own city tours and local excursions.

Amazon cruises
Amazon Clipper, T092-3656 1246, www.amazonclipper.com.br. The leading small boat cruise operator. Excellent trips

along the Rio Negro with knowledgeable wildlife guides, including wildlife cruises, sports fishing and bespoke tours. Accommodation is in comfortable cabins, the best of which are private, with en suites and work desks. Set departure dates are listed on the company website. From US$180 per person per day.

Iberostar Grand Amazon, www.iberostar.com.br/amazon/. This leviathan cruises the Amazon (Solimões) river from Manaus on 3 or 4 night trips. With a pool, dance hall, piped music, vast sundeck and space for 200+ people this is hardly an intimate rainforest experience. Each day is peppered with 3 or 4 optional forest and creek excursions on smaller launches. These are often fairly crowded. Those who are environmentally concerned might like to enquire about waste management and the treatment of cruise ship's sewage before booking a trip.

Mamori Community Houseboat tours, through Geraldo Mesquita, T092-3232 4755, geroexpeditions@hotmail.com. River tours on traditional wooden Amazon river boats – some of which are over 40 years old – with sleeping in cabins or hammocks on board and the option of nights camping in the rainforest or spent in traditional riverine communities. Proceeds from the trips revert to the local people. Great value and fascinating.

Guides

Guides sometimes work individually as well as for tour agencies, and the best ones will normally be booked up in advance. Some will only accompany longer expeditions and often subcontract shorter trips. The easiest way to find a guide, however, is through an agency. Advance notice and a minimum of 3 people for all trips is required by the following guides, who are among the best in the city. All can organize bespoke trips (given notice) and can reserve hotels and jungle lodges.

Cristina de Assis, T092-9114 2556, amazonflower@bol.com.br. Cultural city tours telling the story of the city and the rubber boom with visits to the historic buildings and the Museu Seringal. Also trips to the Rio Negro to swim with pink dolphins (these need to be organized at least a week in advance), to the waterfalls at Presidente Figueiredo, the Boi Bumba party in Parintins and the forest. Cristina speaks excellent English and has worked with the Waimiri-Artroari indigenous people.

Matthias Raymond, T092-8115 5716, raymathias@hotmail.com. A Waipixana indigenous guide offering trips to further reaches of the forest including the Pico da Neblina (book in advance). Many languages.

Pedro Neto, T092-8831 1011, pedroffneto@hotmail.com. An adventure tour specialist offering light adventure trips to the large INPA rainforest reserve, the forest around Manaus and the waterfalls at Presidente Figueiredo – where there is trail-walking, abseiling and birdwatching for spectaculars such as The Guianan Cock of the Rock. Light-hearted but erudite and resolutely great company.

Leticia (Colombia) *p646*

Amazon Jungle Trips, Av Internacional, 6-25, T9819-27377. Lodge-based tours offering a variety of adventure options.

Anaconda Tours, Hotel Anaconda, T9819-27119. Tours to Amacayacu, Isla de los Micos and Sacambu Lodge.

Elvis Cuevas, Av Internacional, 6-06, T0819- 27780. An independent guide offering trips to Amacayacu and indigenous communities nearby.

⊖ Transport

Routes in Amazônia

Belém–Manaus Via **Breves**, **Almeirim**, **Prainha**, **Monte Alegre**, **Curua-Uná**, **Santarém**, **Alenquer**, **Óbidos**, **Juruti** and **Parintins** on the lower Amazon. 5 days upriver, 4 days downriver, including an 18-hr stop in Santarém, suite US$350 upriver,

US$250 down, double berth US$180 upriver, US$150 down, hammock space US$75 upriver, US$65 down. Vehicles: small car US$250, *combi* US$320 usually including driver, other passengers extra, 4WD US$450 with 2 passengers, motorcycle US$80. *Nélio Correa* is best on this route. *Defard Vieira*, very good and clean, US$75. *São Francisco* is largest, new and modern, but toilets smelly. *Cisne Branco* of similar quality. *Cidade de Bairreirinha* is the newest on the route, a/c berths. *Lider II* has good food and pleasant atmosphere. *Santarém* is clean, well organized and recommended. *João Pessoa Lopes* is also recommended. The Belém–Manaus route is very busy. Try to get a cabin if you can.

Belém–Santarém Same intermediate stops as above. 2½ days upriver, 1½ days downriver, suite US$150, berth US$135, hammock US$45 upriver, US$38 down. All vessels sailing Belém–Manaus will call at Santarém.

Belém–Macapá (Porto Santana) Non-stop, 8 hrs on fast catamaran, **Atlântica**, US$30, 3 days a week, or 24 hrs on large ships, double berth US$110, hammock space US$30 per person, meals not included but can be purchased onboard (expensive), vehicle US$90, driver not included. *Silja e Souza* (Wed) is best. *Comandante Solon* (Sat) is state run, slightly cheaper, crowded and not as nice. Same voyage via Breves, 36-48 hrs on smaller riverboats, hammock space US$25 per person including meals. *ENAL* (Sat); *Macamazônia* (every day except Thu), slower and more basic; *Bartolomeu I* of Enavi, food and sanitary conditions OK, 30 hrs; *Rodrigues Alves* has been recommended. *Golfinho do Mar* is said to be the fastest.

Macapá (Porto Santana)–Santarém Via **Vida Nova**, **Boca do Jari**, **Almeirim**, **Prainha**, and **Monte Alegre** on the lower Amazon (does not call at Belém). 2 days upriver, 1½ days downriver,

berth US$130, hammock US$40. Boats include *Viageiro V* (nice) and *São Francisco de Paula*.

Santarém–Itaituba Along the Rio Tapajós, 24 hrs (bus service on this route is making the river trip less common).

Manaus-Parintins-Santarém Same intermediate stops as above. 2 days upriver, 1½ days downriver, fares berth US$85, hammock US$30. All vessels sailing Belém–Manaus will call in Santarém and there are others operating only the Santarém–Manaus route, including: *Cidade de Terezinha III* and *IV*, good. *Miranda Dias*, family-run and friendly. Speedboats (*lanchas*) are sometimes available on this route, 16 hrs sitting, no hammock space, US$35. **Ajato** fast boats run Manaus–Parintins (*Pérola*, Thu-Fri, 7 hrs, US$90, **Princesa Lana**, Wed, 6 hrs, US$90).

Manaus–Porto Velho Via **Borba**, **Manicoré** and **Humaitá** on the Rio Madeira. 4 days upriver, 3½ days downriver (up to 7 days when the river is low), double berth US$280, hammock space US$85 per person.

Manaus–Tefé Via **Codajás** and **Coari**, 24-36 hrs, double berth US$70, 1st-class hammock space US$20 per person. *Capitão Nunes* is good. *Jean Filho* also okay. Note that it is difficult to continue west from Tefé to Tabatinga without first returning to Manaus. **Ajato** fast boats run Manaus–Tefé (*A Jato 2001*, Wed and Sat, 7 hrs, US$85.

Manaus–Tabatinga Via **Fonte Boa**, **Foz do Mamaria**, **Tonantins**, **Santo Antônio do Iça**, **Amataura**, **Monte Cristo**, **São Paulo de Olivença** and **Benjamin Constant** along the Rio Solimões. Up to 8 days upriver (depending on cargo), 3 days downriver, double berth US$280, hammock space US$65 per person (can be cheaper downriver). When going from Peru into Brazil, there is a thorough police check some 5 hrs into Brazil.

Voyagers, *Voyagers II* and *III* recommended; *Almirante Monteiro*, *Avelino Leal* and *Capitão Nunes VIII* all acceptable; *Dom Manoel*, cheaper, acceptable but overcrowded. Ajato fast boats run Manaus–Tabatinga (A Jato 2000, Tue, 30 hrs, US$150).

Manaus–São Gabriel da Cachoeira
Via **Novo Airão**, **Moura**, **Carvoeiro**, **Barcelos** and **Santa Isabel do Rio Negro** along the Rio Negro. Berth US$180, hammock US$60, most locals prefer to travel by road. Boats on this route: *Almirante Martins I* and *II*, *Capricho de Deus*, *Manoel Rodrigues*, *Tanaka Netto* departing from São Raimundo dock, north of main port.

Manaus *p634, map p635*
Air
Taxi fare to airport US$17.50, fixed rate, or take bus marked 'Aeroporto Internacional' from Marquês de Santa Cruz at Praça Adalberto Vale, near the cathedral, US$1, or from Ed Garagem on Av Getúlio Vargas every 30 mins. No buses 2200-0700. It is sometimes possible to use the more regular, faster service run by the **Hotel Tropical**; many tour agencies offer free transfers without obligation. Check all connections on arrival. Allow plenty of time at Manaus airport, formalities are very slow especially if you have purchased duty-free goods.

Many flights depart in the middle of the night and while there are many snack bars there is nowhere to rest. Local flights leave from Terminal 2. Check in advance which terminal you leave from.

There are international flights to **Panama City**, **Miami** and **Atlanta**. For the **Guianas**, a connection must be made in Boa Vista. Domestic flights to **Belém**, **Boa Vista**, **Brasília**, **Cruzeiro do Sul**, **Macapá**, **Parantins**, **Porto Velho**, **Rio Branco**, **Rio de Janeiro**, **Santarém**, **São Paulo**, **Tabatinga**, **Tefé** and **Trombetas**.

Make reservations as early as possible; flights get booked up quickly.

Boat
See Manaus, Ins and outs, page 634, and Routes in Amazônia, above.

Bus
To get to the *rodoviária* take a local bus from the centre, US$0.70, marked 'Aeroporto Internacional' or 'Cidade Nova' (or taxi, US$5). There are many daily services to **Boa Vista** on Eucatur; the best are at night leaving at 2030 and 2100 (10 hrs, US$28). Most go via **Presidente Figueiredo** (3 hrs, US$10). There are also 8 daily buses to **Itacoatiara** (4 hrs, US$15).

Other towns in the state are best visited by air or boat, especially during the Nov to May wet season when road travel is next to impossible.

Car
The road north from Manaus to **Boa Vista** (770 km) is described on page 661. The Catire Highway (BR-319), from Manaus to **Porto Velho** (868 km), has been officially closed since 1990 but is ostensibly set to re-open by 2014. Several bridges are out and there is no repair in sight. The alternative for drivers is to ship a car down river on a barge, others have to travel by boat (see above). To **Itacoatiara**, 285 km east on the Amazon; now paved route AM-010, 266 km, through Rio Preto da Eva.

There are car hire agencies in the airport, including major international companies such as **Localiza** and **Hertz**.

Parintins *p643*
Air A taxi or motortaxi to the airport costs US$5. Flights to **Manaus** (1¼ hrs), **Belém**, **Santarém** (1 hr 20 mins) with Trip, www.voe trip.com.br and TRIP, www.trip.com.br.

Boat Boats call on the Belém–Manaus route: 60 hrs to **Belém** (depending on boat and if going up or down river), 10-26 passengers. There are irregular sailings to **Óbidos** (ask at the port), 12-15 hrs. A boat to **Santarém** takes 20 hrs.

Tefé p644
Air The airport has a connection to **Manaus** with Trip, 3 times a week.

Boat If travelling on to **Tabatinga**, note that Manaus–Tabatinga boats do not usually stop at Tefé. You must hire a canoe to take you out to the main channel and try to flag down the approaching ship.

Benjamin Constant p644
Boat Boats to **Iquitos** leave from a mudbank called **Islandia**, on the Peruvian side of a narrow creek, a few metres from Benjamin Constant. The journey takes a minimum of 2 days upstream, 8-36 hrs downstream, depending on the speed of the boat. On ordinary boats, fares range from US$30-40 per person, depending on standard of accommodation, food extra. Speedboats charge US$75 per person, three a week are run by **Amazon Tours and Cruises**. All boats call at Santa Rosa (2-3 days upstream to Iquitos were immigration formalities are carried out).

Tabatinga p644
Air The airport has a connection to **Manaus** with Trip, 3 times a week.

Boat Amazon Tours and Cruises operates a luxury service between **Iquitos** and Tabatinga leaving Sun, returning from Tabatinga on Wed, US$695 per person in the Río Amazonas. Also *Arca* US$495 per person, return journey Wed-Sat.

Leticia (Colombia) p646
Air Expect to be searched before leaving Leticia airport, and on arrival in Bogotá from Leticia. Trip fly to **Manaus** (sporadically via **Tefé**). There are onward flights from Leticia to **Bogota**. For the border crossing, see box, page 645.

ℹ Directory

Manaus p634, map p635
Banks Banco do Brasil, Guia Moreira, and airport changes US$ cash, 8% commission, both with ATMs for Visa, Cirrus, MasterCard and Plus. Most offices shut at 1500; foreign exchange operations 0900-1200 only, or even as early as 1100. **Bradesco**, Av 7 de Setembro 895/293, for Visa ATM. **Credicard**, Av Getúlio Vargas 222 for Diner's cash advances. Cash at main hotels; **Câmbio Cortez**, 7 de Setembro 1199, converts TCs into US$ cash, good rates, no commission. **HSBC**, R Dr Moreira 226, ATM for Visa, Cirrus, MasterCard and Plus. Do not change money on the streets. **Embassies and consulates** Most open in the morning only. **Bolivia**, Av Efigênio Sales 2226, Qd B No 20, T092-3236 9988. **Colombia**, R 24 de Maio 220, Rio Negro Centre, T092-3234 6777, check whether a Colombian tourist card can be obtained at the border. **France**, Av Joaquim Nabuco 1846, T092-3234 2947. **Germany**, R 24 Maio 220, Rio Negro Centre, sala 812, T092-3234 9045, 1000-1200. **Italy**, R Belo Horizonte 240, Adrianópolis, T092-3611 4877. **Japan**, R Fortaleza 460, T092-3232 2000. **Netherlands**, R Miranda Leão 41, T092-3622 1366. **Peru**, R A, casa 1, Conj Aristocrático, Chapada, T092-3236 3012. **Portugal**, R Terezina 193, T092-3234 5777. **Spain**, Al Cosme Ferreira 1225, Aleixo, T092-3644 3800. **UK**, R Paraquê 240, T092-3237 7869. **USA**, R Recife 1010, Adrianópolis, T092-3633 4907, will supply letters of introduction for US citizens. **Venezuela**, R Ferreira Pena 179, T092-3233 6004 (0800-1200), everyone entering Venezuela overland needs a visa. The requirements are 1 passport photo, an onward ticket and the fee, usually US$30 (check in advance for changes to these regulations – it is reported that a yellow fever certificate is not needed). Takes 24 hrs. **Immigration** To extend or replace a Brazilian visa, take bus from Praça Adalberto Vale to Kissia Dom Pedro for Polícia Federal

post; people in shorts not admitted.
Internet Many around the Teatro, including
Loginet, R 10 de Julho 625. **Amazon Cyber
Cafe**, Av Getúlio Vargas, 626, corner with R 10
de Julho, US$1.50 per hr. **Discover Internet**,
R Marcílio Dias 304, next to Praça da Polícia,
cabins in back of shop with internet phones
and scanners, US$1.50 per hr. Free internet
access is available from all public libraries
in city, eg **Biblioteca Arthur Reis**, Av 7 de
Setembro 444, open 0800-1200 and 1400-
1700, with virtual Amazon library and English
books. **Laundry** Lavanderia Amazonas,
Costa Azevedo 63, near Teatro Amazonas,
US$0.40 per item, closed Sat afternoon and
Sun. **Lavanderia Central**, R Quintino Bocaiúva
602. **Lavalux**, R Mundurucus 77, fast service
washes. **Lavlev**, Av Sen A Maia 1108. One
of few self-service laundries is opposite
the cemetery, open Sun, a taxi ride away.
Medical services Clínica Sao Lucas,
R Alexandre Amorin 470, T092-3622 3678,
reasonably priced, some English spoken,
good service, take a taxi. **Hospital Tropical**,
Av Pedro Teixeira (D Pedro I) 25, T092-3656
1441. Centre for tropical medicine, not for
general complaints, treatment free, some
doctors speak a little English. Take bus Nos
201 or 214 from Av 7 de Setembro in the
city centre. **Pronto Soccoro 28 de Agosto**,
R Recife, free for emergencies. **Post office**

Main office including poste restante on Mcal
Deodoro. On the 1st floor is the philatelic
counter where stamps are sold, avoiding the
long queues downstairs. Staff don't speak
English but are used to dealing with tourists.
For airfreight and shipping, **Alfândega**,
Av Marquês Santa Cruz (corner of Marechal
Deodoro), sala 106. For airfreight and sea
mail, **Correio Internacional**, R Monsenhor
Coutinho and Av Eduardo Ribeiro (bring
your own packaging). **UPS**, T092-3232 9849
(Custódio). **Telephone** International calls
can be made from call boxes with a phone
card. Also at **Telemar**, Av Getúlio Vargas 950.

Tabatinga *p644*
Banks There is a Banco do Brasil, Av
da Amizade, which changes TCs at a poor
rate and has a Visa ATM. It is easier to
get Peruvian money for reais in Leticia.
Internet Infocenter, Av Amizade 1581.

Leticia (Colombia) *p646*
Banks Banco de Bogotá, will cash Tcs,
has ATM on Cirrus network, good rates for
Brazilian reais. **Banco Ganadero**, Cra 11, has
a Visa ATM. There are street money changers,
plenty of *câmbios*, and banks for exchange.
Shop around. **Post office** Avianca office,
Cra 11 No 7-58. **Telephone** Cra 11/C 9,
near Parque Santander.

Roraima

This extreme northern state is one of the country's newest and is only just beginning to exploit its strategic position on the border with Gran Sabana in Venezuela and the stunning Parakaima mountains in Guyana. The state capital is Boa Vista, a safe, tidy modern city with a very lively out-of-season carnival. Beyond the city, the rainforest gives way to extensive grasslands overlooked by precipitous table-top mountains. The most famous of these is Conan Doyle's lost world, Roraima, which can be visited from Boa Vista. Others, such as Tepequen and those on the upper Rio Branco, are more remote and less visited, their wildernesses replete with wildlife. Guyana and Venezuela are a couple of hours from Boa Vista and all visa formalities can be sorted out in that city. Contrary to popular belief, crossing into both countries is easy and painless and there are excellent onward transport services to Caracas or Georgetown. ▶▶ *For listings, see pages 665-666.*

Background

Roraima covers an area nearly twice the size of England but supports a population of just 325,000. Land grants in the 1970s to encourage agricultural development resulted in a rapid increase in population (from only 25,000 in 1960). Then, in the late 1980s a gold rush in the northwest of Roraima drew prospectors from all over the country. The mining took place on the indigenous Yanomami reserve, devastating their traditional way of life. Further tragedy came in January 1998 when forest fires spread across the state, causing massive destruction. The forest cover gives way to grasslands in the northeast and there is a pronounced dry season. The *várzea* (flood plain) along the main rivers irrigates the southeast of the state. Cattle ranching is important as is rice cultivation on the flood plain of the Rio Branco. Other crops are maize, beans, manioc and banana. Some mining continues but at a reduced level.

Towards Boa Vista

The road that connects Manaus and Boa Vista (a ferry crosses the Rio Branco at Caracaraí) is fully paved and regularly maintained. There are service stations with toilets and camping sites every 150-180 km; all petrol is low octane. At Km 117 is **Presidente Figueiredo**, with many waterfalls and a famous cave with bats. There are also shops and a restaurant. About 100 km further on is a service station at the entrance to the **Uaimiri Atroari Indian Reserve**, which straddles the road for about 120 km. Private cars and trucks are not allowed to enter the reserve between sunset and sunrise, but buses are exempt from this regulation. Nobody is allowed to stop within the reserve at any time. At the northern entrance to the reserve there are toilets and a place to hang your hammock (usually crowded with truckers overnight). At Km 327 is the village of **Vila Colina** where **Restaurante Paulista** is clean with good food, and you can use the shower and hang your hammock. At Km 359 there is a monument to mark the **equator**. At Km 434 is the clean and pleasant **Restaurant Goaio**. Just south of Km 500 is **Bar Restaurante D'Jonas**, a good place to eat; you can also camp or sling a hammock. Beyond here, large tracts of forest have been destroyed for settlement, but already many homes have been abandoned.

The capital of the extreme northern state of Roraima, 759 km north of Manaus, is a very pleasant, clean, laid-back little town on the Rio Branco. Tourism is beginning here and there are a number of interesting new destinations offering a chance to explore far wilder country than that around Manaus, with correspondingly richer wildlife. The landscape is more diverse, too, with tropical forest, savannah and highlands dotted with waterfalls. However, the area immediately around the city has been heavily deforested.

Boa Vista lies within easy access of both Venezuela and Guyana and crossing the border to either is straightforward. When the river is low, it is possible to swim in the Rio Branco, 15 minutes by bus from the town centre (too polluted in Boa Vista). As a result of heavy international pressure, the Brazilian government expelled some 40,000 gold prospectors from the Yanomami Reserve in the west of the state in the early 1990s. The economic consequences were very severe for Boa Vista, which went from boom to bust. An increase in cattle ranching in the area has not taken up the slack.

Ins and outs

The **airport** ① *4 km from the centre*, receives national and international flights. There are no exchange or left luggage facilities. A taxi to the centre costs US$20; to the *rodoviária*, US$10. There is a bus to the centre, US$1, or a 45-minute walk.

The **rodoviária** ① *Av das Guianas, 3 km out of town at the end of Av Ville Roy, T095-3224 0606*, receives several daily buses from Manaus, Bonfim (from the Guyanese border) and Santa Elena in Venezuela. A taxi to the centre costs US$5, or the 10-minute bus ride costs US$0.45. The local bus terminal is on Avenida Amazonas, by Rua Cecília Brasil, near the central *praça*.

The city has a modern, functional plan, which often means long, hot treks from one place to another. The rather ineffectual state tourism office **Detur** ① *R Coronel Pinto 267, Centro, Boa Vista, T095-2121 2525, www.turismo.rr.gov.br*, also has booths at the *rodoviária*, T095-3623 1238, and the airport. ►► *See Transport, page 666.*

To Venezuela and Guyana
→ *For listings, see pages 665-666.*

Boa Vista has road connections with the Venezuelan frontier at **Santa Elena de Uairén**, 237 km away. The road is paved, but the only petrol available is 110 km

Boa Vista

To Airport

L Tiradentes

Av Major Williams

Av Ene Garcez
R Pedro Rodrigues
Gal Ene Garcez
Gal Penha Brasil
Prof A Bitencourt
Brig Eduardo Gomes

Homem de Melo

Buses to
Rodoviária
& Airport

Roraima
Adventures

Venezuelan
Consulate

Av Glaycon
de Paiva

Banco
do Brasil

Palácio do
Governo

R Alfredo Cruz

Coronel Pinto

Cathedral

Praça do
Centro
Cívico

Ceará

Av Ville Roy

Aguía
Tours

Jaime Brasil

RNS da Consolação

R Benjamin Constant

Cecília Brasil

Ataíde Teive

Bradesco

Amazonas

R Floriano Peixoto

Av Getúlio Vargas

Auriacha

Sebastião Diniz

Orla Taumanan
Toca Boat

Bento Brasil

Amatari

Rio Branco

N

500 metres
500 yards

Sleeping 🛏
Aipana Plaza 1
Barrudada Palace 5

Euzébio's 2
Ideal 4
Uiramutam Palace 3

Eating 🍴
Churrascaria La Carreta 4
1000 Sabores 1
Frangão 2
Peixada Tropical 3

south of Santa Elena. Boa Vista is also linked to Bonfim for the Guyanese border at **Lethem**. Both roads are open all year.

Santa Elena de Uairén (Venezuela) → *International phone code +58.*

Santa Elena de Uairén is the gateway to the Venezuelan Highlands for those entering the country from Brazil. It is a pleasant frontier town, 10-12 hours by bus from Ciudad Bolívar, which is nine hours from Caracas. The road is paved all the way and there are also flights. The landscape is beautiful, an ancient land of flat-topped mountains and waterfalls. The road skirts the **Parque Nacional Canaima**, which boasts the highest waterfall in the world, the **Angel Falls** (Salto Angel). Not far north of Santa Elena is the route to Mount Roraima.

Santa Elena has plenty of hotels and places to eat, as well as money-changing facilities, a phone office with international connections, and tour companies for trips into the Gran Sabana – as the region is known.

Ins and outs The **rodoviária** ⓘ *C Mcal Sucre*, receives arrivals from Ciudad Bolívar (Venezuela) several times daily; the journey takes 10-12 hours and buses are run by a number of companies. There are plenty of accommodation options in Santa Elena de Uairén, but just one basic hotel on the Brazilian side of the border. ▶ *See Transport, page 666.*

Lethem (Guyana)

A small but scattered town on the Brazilian border (see below), this is the service centre for the Rupununi and for trade with Brazil. There are many small stores, a small hospital (T772 2006), a police station (T772 2011) and government offices. A big event at Easter is the rodeo, visited by cowboys from all over the Rupununi. Prices are about twice as high as in Georgetown. About 2.5 km south of town at St Ignatius there is a Jesuit mission

Around Boa Vista

Border essentials: Brazil–Venezuela–Guyana

Pacaraima (Brazil)–Santa Elena de Uairén (Venezuela)

Searches are thorough and frequent at this border crossing. Officials may give only two months' stay and car drivers may be asked to purchase an unnecessary permit; ask to see the legal documentation. Everyone who crosses the border must have a 30-day tourist card or a visa for Venezuela and a yellow fever vaccination certificate (this is also a requirement when coming from Venezuela into Brazil). Citizens of the EU, Mercosur, North America (with the exception of Mexico), Japan, Malaysia, Taiwan, South Africa, Australia and New Zealand do not require visas. Citizens of Israel require a visa. The current procedure is to take a filled-out visa form, onward ticket, passport photo and deposit slip from the Banco do Brasil (US$30) to the **Venezuelan consulate** in Boa Vista; be prepared to wait an hour. Visas will take longer (up to 24 hours). It may be possible to get an entry card at the border; check requirements in advance. There is also a Venezuelan consulate in Manaus which issues one-year, multiple-entry visas (see page 659). The **Brazilian consulate** in Uairén is near the bus terminal, opposite the Corpoven petrol station (open 0800-1200, 1400-1800). Buses leave Boa Vista *rodoviária* at 0730, 1000 and 1400 for Santa Elena de Uirén, stopping at all checkpoints, US$15, 3½ to six hours; take water for the journey.

Bonfim (Brazil)–Lethem (Guyana)

The main border crossing between Brazil and Guyana is from Bonfim, 125 km (all paved) northeast of Boa Vista, to Lethem. The towns are separated by the Rio Tacutu, which is crossed by small boats for foot passengers (five minutes, US$3). Vehicles cross by ferry on demand, US$7, or drive across in the dry season. The river crossing is 2.5 km from Bonfim, about 1.5 km north of Lethem. A bridge is under construction. It is essential to have a yellow fever vaccination both to leave Brazil and to enter Guyana. Citizens of the following countries do not need a visa to enter Guyana (they get a tourist stamp at the border): EU countries (except Bulgaria, Czech Republic, Hungary, the Baltic states, Malta, Cyprus, Poland, Romania, Slovakia and Slovenia), USA, Canada, Australia and New Zealand, Japan, the DPRK and the Republic of Korea. Citizens of all other countries must apply for a visa beforehand. The Guyanese consulate in Boa Vista is closed as of January 2011 (though it may re-open – see www.guyana.org/govt for the latest). Consular services in Brazil are available through the Guyanese embassy in Brasília or the consulate in Rio de Janeiro (both listed on the site). The bus passes through **Brazilian immigration** where you receive your exit stamp before crossing the river. On the other side, there are taxis to take you to **Guyanese immigration** office (US$5). You are given a visa for the exact amount of time you stipulate. The border is open 24 hours but officials tend to leave immigration after 1800.

dating from 1911. In the nearby mountains there is good birdwatching and there are waterfalls to visit.

There is another border crossing at **Laramonta** from where it is a hard but rewarding walk to the Guyanese town of Orinduik.

⊕ Roraima listings

For Sleeping and Eating price codes and other relevant information, see pages 32-37.

⊜ Sleeping

Boa Vista *p662, map p662*
B Aipana Plaza, Joaquim Nabuco 53, Praça do Centro Cívico, T095-3224 4800, www.aipanaplaza.com.br. The best in town with plain rooms decorated in cream and dark tiles, and photos of Roraima. Hot water, a/c, marble bathrooms and cable TV. Attractive pool area with a shady little bar.
B Uiramutam Palace, Av Capt Ene Garcez 427, T095-3624 4700, www.uiramutam. com.br. A business hotel with modest a/c rooms with writing desk and armchair, cable TV and large bathrooms. Decent pool.
C Barrudada Palace Hotel, R Araújo Filho 228, T095-2121 1700, www.hotelbarrudada. tur.br. Simple a/c rooms in a modern tower block with a pool and restaurant, very close to the centre. Rooms on the upper floors have views of the river. Breakfast and lunch included.
D Euzébio's, R Cecília Brasil 1107, T095-2121 0300, www.hoteleuzebios.com.br. Spruce, modest rooms with a/c and en suites with cold showers. The best are airy and on the upper floors. Pleasant pool and a laundry service.
F Hotel Ideal, R Araújo Filho 533, T095-3224 6342. Very simple but well-kept rooms with en suites. Some have a/c. Friendly staff and generous breakfast. Convenient for the centre.

Camping
Rio Cauamé, 3 km north of town. Pleasant unofficial site with small bar and clean river.

⊕ Eating

Boa Vista *p662, map p662*
Most restaurants close at night, except for pizzerias. There are a number of restaurants

serving snacks and juices on the riverside along R Floriano Peixoto and several open-air restaurants and cafés on the **Orla Taumanan**, a complex of little bars and eating places overlooking the river. Nightlife and bars are concentrated here; it is quiet during the week but livelier at weekends. There are many little juice stands around **Praça do Centro Cívico**.
♨ Churrascaria La Carreta, R Pedro Rodrigues 185, 500 m from **Euzébio's**, T095-3224 0165. With a good-value US$5 buffet,with plenty of choice and a vibrant, friendly atmosphere. Recommended.
♨ Euzébio's (see Sleeping). Decent fish, *feijoada* and meat dishes. Generous breakfast.
♨ Peixada Tropical, R Pedro Rodrigues at Ajuricaba 1525, T095-3224 6040. River fish dishes in a variety of styles from Bahian sauces to *milanesa* accompanied by beans, rice and salads.
♦ 1000 Sabores, R Araújo Filho at Benjamin Constant. Opens early and closes late. Pizzas, snacks and juices.
♦ Frangão, R Homem de Melo at Cecília Brasil 965, T095 3224 8240. Chicken and river fish with salads, rice, beans.

⊕ Bars and clubs

Boa Vista *p662, map p662*
R Floriano Peixoto is lively after dark at weekends when there is live music in and around the Orla Taumanan.

▲ Activities and tours

Boa Vista *p662, map p662*
Aguia Tours, R Benjamin Constant 1683, T095-3624 1516. Can book buses and flights and the owner speaks some English.
Roraima Adventures, R Coronel Pinto 86, sala 106, T095-3624 9611, T095-3623 6972, www.roraima-brasil.com.br. Interesting trips to little-known and little-visited parts of

Roraima state, including the spectacular Tepequen and Serra Grande mountains and the Rio Uraricoera, which is replete with wildlife. Also regular expeditions to the Pico da Neblina and Mount Roraima itself. Groups get the best prices, which are competitive with those in Manaus. Helpful with visas for Venezuela, reliable and professional.

⊖ Transport

Boa Vista p662, map p662
Air
A taxi to the airport costs US$20. Flights and buses and flights can be booked through **Aguia Tours** or **Roraima Adventures** (see Activities and tours, above).

The airport has flights to the **Guianas**, **Belém**, **Brasília**, **Macapá**, **Manaus**, **Santarém** and **São Paulo**. Confirm flights before reaching Boa Vista as they are often fully booked. Air taxis can be booked with **Rondônia**, Praça Santos Dumond, T095-3224 5068.

Airline offices GOL, www.voe gol.com.br. META, Praça Santos Dumont 100, T095-3224 7677, www.voe meta.com.br. TAM, www.tam.com.br.

Bus
Note that it is difficult to get a taxi or bus to the *rodoviária* in time for early morning departures; as it's a 25-min walk, book a taxi the previous evening. To **Manaus**, with Eucatur, US$35, 10-12 hrs, 4 daily each way, can be crowded, advisable to book at least a few hours in advance. To **Caracaraí** US$12, 3 hrs. **Amatur** to **Bonfim**, daily 0730, 1430, 1700, 2 hrs, US$7.

Car hire
Localiza, Av Benjamin Constant 291E, T/F095-3224 5222. **Yes**, Av Maj Williams 538, T/F095-3224 3723.

Taxis
For radio taxis contact **Tupã**, R Monte Castelo 318, T095-3224 9150.

Border with Venezuela p662
Bus Buses from Santa Elena to **Boa Vista** leave at 0830, 1200, 1500 and 1600, stopping at all checkpoints, US$15, 3½-6 hrs, take water. It is possible to share a taxi.

Border with Guyana p662
Bus Bonfim–Boa Vista at least 3 a day, US$7. Weekly jeep **Laramonta–Boa Vista** US$30.

Boat To cross the river, take a canoe, US$0.25. No boats at night.

⊖ Directory

Boa Vista p662, map p662
Banks US$ and Guyanese notes can be changed in Boa Vista. TCs and cash in **Banco do Brasil**, Av Galycon de Paiva 56, 1000-1300 (minimum US$200), will not change *bolívares*. There is no official exchange agency and the local rates for bolivares are low. **Bradesco**, Jaime Brasil e Getúlio Vargas, Visa ATM. Best rate for dollars, **Casa Pedro José**, R Araújo Filho 287, T095-3224 4277, also changes TCs and bolivares. **Embassies and consulates** Venezuela, Av Benjamin Constant 968, T095-3623 9285, open mornings only. Visas available. Laid-back service. Allow 24-48 hrs. Guyana, there is currently no consular service for Guyana in Roraima, this may change – see www.guyana. org/govt for the latest information. **Medical services** Geral, Av Brig Eduardo Gomes, T095-3623 2068. Free yellow fever inoculations at a clinic near the hospital.

Rondônia and Acre

The state of Rondônia is largely populated by migrants from other parts of Brazil. Foreigners are welcomed without question or curiosity and there is no regional accent. A local academic described the state as 'a land where nobody has a name and everyone can have a dream'. Most visitors tend to arrive via the BR-364 from Cuiabá or the Rio Madeira from Manaus.

The intriguing state of Acre, rich in natural beauty, history and the seringueiro culture, was very much off the beaten track until 2010, when regular bus services and flights connected the state, and its capital city Rio Branco, with Cusco in Peru. Acre is now a viable entry or exit point for Brazil and the state is beginning to develop its considerable potential for adventure, with some of the best indigenous and ecotourism projects in the Amazon region, many of them in very remote country.
▸▸ *For listings, see pages 675-678.*

Porto Velho → *For listings, see pages 675-678. Colour map 1, B2. Phone code: 069. Population: 330,000.*

Porto Velho stands on a high bluff overlooking a curve of the Rio Madeira, one of the Amazon's main tributaries. The city has seen the rubber, gold and timber booms come and go. Service and IT industries are now the major employers. The city is a large sprawl of streets, laid out in blocks stretching 8 km into the interior. The lack of town planning means that many of the best shops, hotels and banks are now a fair distance from the old centre near the river. The city is increasingly prosperous as the result of government money flooding in to fund huge twin hydroelectric dam projects on the Rio Madeira, a few kilometres upstream of the city centre. This is one of the largest civil engineering projects in the world. And whilst the scheme may be of dubious environmental pedigree, it is renovating a once tawdry Porto Velho. Some 80% of the city's sewage will be treated by 2011 making Porto Velho one of the first Brazilian cities not to pump most of its raw discharge into a river or the sea. Buildings in the centre are being renovated and by 2012

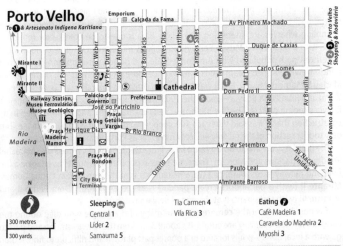

Porto Velho

Sleeping
Central **1**
Líder **2**
Samauma **5**
Tia Carmen **4**
Vila Rica **3**

Eating
Café Madeira **1**
Caravela do Madeira **2**
Myoshi **3**

the city will be graced with a very attractive waterfront promenade. That said, there is little in Porto Velho for tourists and very little organized tourism in the Rondônia Amazon, and the only real reason to come here is en route to or from Bolivia or Acre.

Ins and outs

Getting there Porto Velho is well connected, with flights on **Gol**, **Avianca**, **TAM** and **TRIP** to destinations including Cuiabá, Campo Grande, Rio Branco, Manaus, Brasília, São Paulo, Belém and Fortaleza. These arrive at the **Aeroporto Gov Jorge Teixeira De Oliveira** ① *8 km west of town, T069-3225 1755*. A taxi to downtown costs US$25 and 'aeroporto' buses run every 40 minutes 0700-1900 between the aiport and Rua Carlos Gomes in the city centre. There is a CAT (Centro ao Atendimento Turistico) at the airport – with no English and a few pamphlets. Interstate buses from Rio Branco and Cuiabá arrive at the **rodoviária** ① *east of the centre, Jorge Teixeira, between Carlos Gomes and Dom Pedro II*. There are buses to downtown. ›› *See Transport, page 678.*

Getting around Urban bus services are good. Consider hiring a car if you're going to stay for some time, as the city is very spread out. Be patient as even local residents get confused with directions. Taxis in town are cheap and plentiful. Find your favourite driver and stick with him; all have mobile phones and work with partners to give prompt 24-hour service.

Tourist office CMTUR ① *R Jose do Patrocinio 852, Centro, T069-3901 3186, www.portovelho. ro.gov.br*, is helpful, though staff speak little to no English. The office publishes a glossy pamphlet and is enthusiastic about improvements being made to the city. They can also recommend sports fishing operators and a handful of destinations to visit around the city.

Sights

At the top of the hill on Praça João Nicoletti is the **cathedral**, built in 1930, with beautiful stained-glass windows. The **prefeitura** (town hall) is across the street. The principal commercial street is Avenida 7 de Setembro, which runs from the railway station to the upper level of the city, near the *rodoviária*. The centre is hot and noisy, but not without its charm, and the port and old railway installations with their steam locomotives and crumbling wharves are interesting. The whole area is due to be completely rebuilt in 2012, with a refurbished **Museu Ferroviário** (railway museum – currently closed) and a waterfront park populated with Amazon wildlife and dotted with Amazon-lily-covered ponds. Newly polished steam trains will run once more on a short stretch of the old Rio **Madeira-Mamoré** railway. Brazil was required to construct this railway – between Porto Velho and Riberalt in Bolivia – under the 1903 Treaty of Petrópolis, in part exchange for Bolivia's ceding of Acre. The line barely reached Guajará-Mirim, and so many died in its construction that it was said that each 100 sleepers were paid for with a human life. The new tourist section of the railway will only run as far as Porto Velho's suburbs.

The neoclassical **Palácio do Governo** faces Praça Getúlio Vargas, while Praça Marechal Rondon is spacious and modern. There are several popular viewpoints overlooking the river and railway yards. **Mirante I** (with restaurant) is at the end of Rua Carlos Gomes; **Mirante II** (with a bar and ice cream parlour) is at the end of Rua Dom Pedro II and **Mirante III** (with restaurant) is at the end of Benjamin Constant.

It is possible to visit the **cemetery**, where many of the people who died during the construction of the railway are buried. It's about 3 km from the railway station and best to go with a local guide, as it is located in a poorer part of town and difficult to find. It is an eerie place, with many of the tombstones overgrown, some of which have been tampered with by practitioners of *macumba*, and there are rumoured to be ghosts.

Parque Nacional Municipal de Porto Velho ① *Av Rio Madeira s/n, 10 km, T069-221 2769, Thu-Sun, volunteer guides*, is a small zoo with 12 km of marked trails.

Excursions from Porto Velho

The **Banho do Souza** is a bar, restaurant and swimming area, 36 km out of town on the BR-364. A coolbox of beers and soft drinks is left by your table and you pay for what you've drunk at the end of the afternoon, swimming is free.

Along the BR-364 → *For listings, see pages 675-678.*

The **Marechal Rondon Highway**, BR-364, runs 1550 km from Porto Velho to Cuiabá in Mato Grosso. The paving of this road has led to the development of farms and towns. Cattle ranches can be seen all along the road, with the lowest population density in the south between Pimenta Bueno and Vilhena.

Pousada Ecológica Rancho Grande ① *contact Caixa Postal 361, Ariquemes, Rondônia 78914, T/F069-3532 2300, www.ranchogrande.com.br*, is a working *fazenda* about 250 km south of Porto Velho. It contains millions of rare butterflies, about 450 bird species and numerous mammals, all of which can be seen on the 20 km of trails. Owner, Harald Schmitz, speaks English, German and Spanish. Highly recommended, especially for butterfly lovers. Reservations and tours can be arranged through the fazenda's website.

Parque Nacional dos Pacaás Novos protects some 765,800 ha of *cerrado*, rainforest and tropical savannah and lies west of the BR-364. The fauna includes all the spectacular mammals such as jaguar, brocket deer, puma, tapir, peccary and maned wolf. The average annual temperature is 23°C, but this can fall as low as 5°C when the cold front known as the *friagem* blows up from the south pole. Information is available from **Instituto Chico Mendes de Conservação da Biodiversidade (ICMBio)** ① *www.icmbio. gov.br*. There is another large reserve, the **Jaru Biological Reserve** in the east of the state. No tour operators visit either to date.

On the Rio Guaporé, the **Guaporé Biological Reserve** ① *Av Limoeira, CEP 78971, Guaporé, T069-3651 2239*, contains the Forte Príncipe da Beira. The fort was constructed in 1777 to defend the border with Bolivia and is currently being restored. It can be reached from Costa Marques (20 km by road), which is some 345 km by unpaved road west of Rolim de Moura. This unplanned town, 40 km west of Pimenta Bueno, relies on agriculture, livestock and a small furniture industry. There are a few basic hotels and guesthouses, which are easy to find and do not require reservations.

Guajará-Mirim → *For listings, see pages 675-678. Colour map 1, C2. Phone code: 069. Population: 39,000.*

From Porto Velho, the paved BR-364 continues 220 km southwest to **Abunã** (with a few cheap hotels), where the BR-425 branches south to Guajará-Mirim. About 9 km east of Abunã is a ferry crossing over the Rio Madeira, where it receives the waters of the Rio Abunã. The BR-425 is a fair road, partly paved, which uses the former rail bridges. It is sometimes closed from March to May. Across the Mamoré from Guajará-Mirim is the Bolivian town of **Guayaramerín**, which is connected by road to Riberalta, from where there are air services to other Bolivian cities.

Guajará-Mirim is a charming town. The **Museu Municipal** ① *T069-3541 3362, 0500-1200, 1400-1800*, at the old Guajará-Mirim railway station beside the ferry landing, is interesting, diverse, and recommended. An ancient stern wheeler plies the Guaporé. Return trips of 1250 km, taking 26 days, can be made from Guajará-Mirim to Vila Bela in Mato Grosso; the fare includes food.

Ins and outs There are seven buses daily between Porto Velho and Gujará-Mirim, taking three to five hours and one to Rio Branco (10 hours). Speedboats cross the river for Bolivia at least every 30 minutes (when full). There are plenty of money changers on both sides of the river. **Brazilian immigration** is at the Polícia Federal, Avenida Presidente Dutra, 70 Cristo Rei, T069- 3541 2437, 0830-1200 and 1400-1800.

Guayaramerín (Bolivia) → *International phone code +591.*

The Bolivian town of Guayaramerín is a cheerful, prosperous little place, on the bank of the Río Mamoré. It has an important **Zona Libre**. There are flights to Trinidad, La Paz, Cobija, Cochabamba and Santa Cruz, as well as buses to La Paz, Santa Cruz, Trinidad, Cobija and other destinations, but the roads are in poor shape and appalling in the wet season. Boats run upriver to Trinidad. **Bolivian immigration** is at Avenida Costañera at Calle Mariscal Santa Cruz, T(+591) 855 4413, Monday-Friday 0800-1200 and 1400-1800, Saturday 0830-1200.

Acre

In the mid-19th century, what is now Acre was disputed land between Brazil and Bolivia. The Treaty of Ayacucho, 1866, gave the territory to Bolivia. However, the onset of the rubber boom in the 1880s upset this arrangement because many of the landowners who were exporting rubber from Acre and down the Rio Madeira were Brazilian. They resented the fact that the Bolivian government had nominal control, exacting duties, but had signed economic rights over to North American interests. Many *Nordestinos* also migrated to this western frontier at the time in search of fortune. In 1899 the Brazilians rebelled. Four years later the Bolivian government yielded the territory to Brazil under the Treaty of Petrópolis and the American company received US$2 million compensation. In 1913, Rio Branco became capital of the new Território Federal do Acre, which attained statehood in 1962.

Acre has a population of only 500,000 but, as its land is much more productive than that of Rondônia. In the 1990s there was a flood of migration from Acre's landless south into the its neighbouring state, and conditions have yet to be improved. Acre is slightly drier than Rondônia, with 1.5-2 m of rain a year.

Rio Branco → *For listings, see pages 675-678. Colour map 1, B2. Phone code: 068. Population: 253,000.*

Remote Rio Branco, 4287 km from Rio, is one of Brazil's surprises. Rather than being the scruffy frontier of most Brazilians' popular imagination, it's one of the country's neatest, safest (and smallest) state capitals, with manicured public spaces, orderly cycleways and a lively waterfront promenade, the Mercado Velho, which buzzes with bar life in the evenings and at weekends. The city is a pleasant place to stopover en route to the attractions further east – the great forests of Acre and beyond to the Andes, Bolivia and Peru.

The Rio Acre divides Rio Branco into two districts – **Primeiro** (west bank) and **Segundo** (east bank), on either side of the river, linked by two bridges. The central Primeiro district contains most of the sights including the shady main square, **Praça Plácido de Castro**.

This is lined with modest buildings of state, including the handsome, neoclassical **Palácio Rio Branco** ① *Av Getúlio Vargas s/n, T068-3223 9240, Wed-Fri 0800-1800, Sat-Sun 1600-2100, free*, looking like a mini-White House and housing a museum devoted to the story of Acre. Nearby, along Avenida Brasil, is the **Nossa Senhora de Nazaré** ① *Av Brasil s/n, T068-3224 1932, Mon-Fri 0800-1800, Sat 0700-1230, Sun 0600-0900 and 1600-2000, www.diocesriobranco.com.br, free*, which is worth a quick visit to see the huge psychedelic murals and stained-glass windows showing the stations of the cross. A large park, the **Parque da Maternidade**, runs through the entire city centre in the *Primeiro* for 6 km, with cycle paths, shady areas and hundreds of hummingbirds flitting through the trees. There are plenty of cafés for a juice or snack and a museum, the **Casa Povos da Floresta** ① *Parque da Maternidade s/n, T068-3224 5667, Wed-Fri 0800-1800, Sat-Sun 1600-2100, free*, devoted to Acre's indigenous peoples and *caboclos*. A small arts and crafts centre nearby, the **Casa de Artesão** ① *Parque da Maternidade s/n, T068-3223 0010, Mon-Sat 0900-2000, free*, sells work by a cooperative of craftsmen from all over Acre.

The city's prettiest streets line the riverbank around the **Mercado Velho** (Rio Acre at Avenida Epaminondas). The latter building was built in the 1920s and was recently refurbished. The streets overflow with cafés, bars and craft shops and it is always busy with people drinking and chatting al fresco in the evenings.

Acre's oldest street, **Rua Eduardo Assmar**, lies on the other side of the river in *Segundo*. It is lined with tiny art deco shops dating from the 1920s. Look out for the old cinema, the **Cine Teatro Recreio**, which must have been one the remotest picture house in the world when it was constructed during the rubber boom.

Sleeping 🛏
Afa Hotel & Restaurant 1
Imperador Galvez 3
Irmãos Inácio Palace 2
Loureiro 4
Ouro Verde 5
Papãi 6
Terra Verde 7

Eating 🍴
Elcio 1
Mata Nativa 2

Chico Mendes – eco-martyr

The most famous *seringueiro* (rubber tapper) was Francisco (Chico) Alves Mendes, born in 1944. Chico's father had come to Acre from northeast Brazil as a *soldado da borracha*, engaged in providing rubber for the Allies during the Second World War. Chico learnt the trade of his father, became a leader of the Xapuri Rural Workers' Union and was a founder member of the CNS. He was instrumental in setting up a number of extractive reserves, parcels of land preserved for sustainable exploitation by those that lived there. He was shot dead on 22 December 1988 by cattle ranchers, to whose land-grabbing Mendes was in open opposition. He was by no means the only *seringueiro* who had been killed in such circumstances (he was the 90th rubber tapper to be killed in 1988 alone), but his murder was the culmination of a decade of *fazendeiro-seringueiro* confrontation. Over 4000 people attended his funeral; the world's media latched onto the story and Chico Mendes became the first globally-recognized eco-martyr. He was honoured by the United Nations for his efforts to stop the destruction of the rainforest. The universal outcry at his assassination led to the arrest, trial and imprisonment of his killers, members of the family of Darly Alves da Silva; a rare event in the history of Amazon land disputes. His death inspired changes in government policy on environmental protection, greater involvement of rubber tappers and other forest workers in local organizations, and the development of extractive reserves, first promoted in 1985 as protected areas for the *seringueiros*. Father Andre Ficarelli, assistant to the Bishop of Acre, said that Mendes' murder was like "the lancing of a tumour, exposing all the corruption and problems which the government [chose] to ignore". To others it was an opportunity to portray the whole affair in Hollywood-style melodrama; there was fierce competition for the film rights to Mendes' life story.

But Chico has left a lasting legacy. The forests he fought to preserve remain protected as the **Reserva Extrativista Chico Mendes**. It is possible to visit, staying in comfortable lodge accommodation and seeing both the rubber tappers – who continue their way of life – and abundant wildlife. **Chico Mendes'** house in Xapuri has been preserved as a museum (see page 674).

There are a few other sights. The **Museu da Borracha** ⓘ *Av Ceará 1144, T068-3223 1202, Tue-Fri 0800-1800, Sat-Sun 1600-2100, free*, which tells the story of the Acre rubber trade and the guerrilla war against Bolivia by the Cearenses who came here from Fortaleza – 6500 km away. The **Parque Chico Mendes** ⓘ *Rodovia AC-40, km 07, Vila Acre, T068-3221 1933, Wed-Sun 0700-1700, free*, preserves tropical forests, which are cut with trails and rich with birdlife, a replica of a rubber-tapper settlement, a zoo and a memorial to Chico Mendes who died in nearby Xapuri (see page 674). The **Horto Forestal**, in Vila Ivonete (Primeiro), 3 km north of the centre, is popular with joggers and has native Amazonian trees, a small lake, walking paths and picnic areas (take a city bus to 'Conjunto Procon' or 'Vila Ivonete'). The Brazilian spiritual movement of **Santo Daime**, devoted to taking Ayahuasca (daime) in group sessions, was founded in Rio Branco by Sebastião Mota de Melo, and has numerous churches and facilities in Rio Branco, including the Céu do Mapiá (www.ceudomapia.org), on the outskirts of the city.

Ins and outs The airport on the AC-40, Km 1.2, in the Distrito Segundo, T068-3224 6833, receives flights from several Brazilian cities. A taxi from the airport to the centre costs a flat rate of US$20, or take a bus marked 'Custódio Freire' or 'Terminal Urbano', US$0.90. Buses arrive at the **rodoviária** ① *Av Uirapuru, Cidade Nova, Segundo distrito, T069-3224 1182*. To get to the centre, take a city bus marked 'Norte–Sul'. For tourist information, contact the **Secretaria de Indústria e Comércio** ① *Av Getúlio Vargas 659, Centro*, or the **Departamento de Turismo** ① *BR-364, Km 5, Distrito Industrial, T068-3224 3997*.

The **Aeroporto Internacional de Rio Branco-Plácido de Castro** ① *Estrada BR- 364 km 18, Sena Madureira, T068-3211 1003*, is just under 10 km from the city centre. Taxis cost US$15, or take any bus marked 'Custódio Freire' (US$1) to the urban bus terminal in the city centre. Buses also run from here to the *rodoviária*, 5 km from the city centre at Avenida Uirapuru, Cidade Nova, Distrito Segundo, T068-3224 6984. The **Secretária de Turismo (SETUL)** ① *at the Estádio (football stadium), Av Chico Mendes, T068-3201 3024, Mon-Fri 1000-1800, Sat 1200-1700, www.ac.gov.br*. There is a **CAT office** ① *Praça Povos da Floresta (Praça Eurico Dutra), T068-3901 3029, Mon-Sat 0900-1800*.

Excursions from Rio Branco

About 8 km southeast of town, upriver on the Rio Acre, is **Lago do Amapá**, a U-shaped lake good for boating and water sports; access is by river or by land via route AC-40. About 2 km beyond along the AC-40 is **Praia do Amapá**, a bathing beach on the Rio Acre; an annual arts festival is held here in September. Excursions can be made to **rubber plantations** and rubber extraction areas in native forest (*seringais nativos*).

Some 13 km from Rio Branco is **Colônia Cinco Mill** (access along AC-10), a religious centre of the followers of the Santo Daime doctrine. Its members, many originally from outside Acre and Brazil, live a communal life, working in agriculture and producing crafts made of latex. The religion centres around the use of *ayahuasca*, a hallucinogenic potion. Visitors are usually welcome, but enquire beforehand.

Cruzeiro do Sul and around → *Colour map 1, B1. Population: 65,000.*

From Rio Branco, the BR-364 continues west to Cruzeiro do Sul, Japim and the Peruvian frontier, running through cleared ground around the capital but quickly entering towering forest, which continues to the snaking rivers and jagged mountains of the **Serra do Divisor** in Acre and Brazil's far western frontier. This is pioneer country for tourism, wild in the main and with large numbers of indigenous Brazilians, especially in the forests of the **Vale do Juruá**. One of the best tour operators in the Amazon, **Maanaim Amazônia** (see page 677) run visits here several times a year.

Cruzeiro do Sul itself feels about as isolated as a medium-sized town can feel. Amazonas state, whose border is just north of town, stretches in unbroken trees for more than 1000 km before reaching the tiny outpost of Benjamin Constant; itself unreachable by road; and it's a similar story to the south and the west. Cruzeiro is a sleepy place. Cheap excursions can be made on the river, for example to the village of **Rodrigues Alves**, two to three hours' return by boat or 15 km by road. In the jungle it's possible to see rubber tapping and the collecting of latex in *borrachas*. It's difficult to change money in Cruzeiro do Sul.

Ins and outs The BR-364 is unpaved and a single bus a day makes the 672-km journey between Rio Branco taking anything from 14 to 20 hours, depending on conditions. There are daily flights. The road is frequently impassable and open, on average, around 20 days a year. Flights connect the town with Rio Branco (**Gol & Trip**) and Pucallpa in Peru. In the wet

Guajará-Mirim (Brazil)–Guayaramerín (Bolivia)

Immigration Brazilian exit/entry stamps can be obtained from the Polícia Federal, Avenida Pres Dutra 70, corner of Avenida Quintino Bocaiúva, T069-3541 4021.

Transport Speedboats take five minutes to cross the Rio Mamoré (border), US$2.65, and run all day. There is also a 20-minute ferry crossing for vehicles, T069-3541 3811, Monday to Saturday 0800-1200, Monday to Friday 1400-1600.

season there are sporadic boats to Manaus (seven to 10 days). There are a few basic, boxy hotels in town (near the cathedral and facing the river), many offer fullboard. West of Cruzeiro do Sul the Amazonian forests stretch to one of the world's remotest and largest national parks, the 843,000-ha **Parque Nacional da Serra do Divisor**. It is made up of a series of ancient, craggy table-top mountains dripping with waterfalls which mark a transition between the Amazon lowlands and the foothills of the Andes. The park has been little studied, but according to the Instituto Chico Mendes de Conservação da Biodiversidade it has one of the highest levels of biodiversity in the Brazilian Amazon. Visits can be made with **Maanaim** (see page 677).

Xapuri

Chico Mendes' home town is little more than a few houses and shops straddling the BR-317, which runs from Rio Branco to Assis Brasil and Brasiléia on the borders of Peru and Bolivia. But it's well worth stopping for a day or two. Chico's house is one of two buildings preserved as a small cultural centre and museum, the **Fundação Chico Mendes** ① *T068-3542 2651, Mon-Sat 0900-1700, US$3*. The main building showcases memorabilia associated with the environmentalist, including prizes and awards given by international and Brazilian bodies, photographs and letters. His very simple wooden house is preserved as it was when Chico was shot by cattle ranchers Darly Alves da Silva and Darcy Alves Ferreira when he left his back door to go for a pee in his outhouse. There are still blood stains on the door frame. Xapuri has very basic lodging and two restaurants and a huge condom factory – with prophylactics made from rubber harvested in the surrounding forests.

Chico Mendes' rubber-tappers community near Xapuri is still extant, as is the forest he sought to protect – preserved as the **Reserva Extrativista Chico Mendes**. Jaguar, harpy eagle and tapir are still abundant, as are towering Brazil nut and kapok trees. As well as a functioning rubber tapping community, Xapuri is now an ecotourism venture. Chico Mendes' cousin works as a guide. A one- or two-night stay here is a magical experience and well worth undertaking. Book through **Maanaim**, see page 677.

Brasiléia, Assis Brasil and onwards to Bolivia and Peru

The BR-317 is paved all the way to the borders at **Brasiléia**, opposite the Bolivian town of Cobija, and **Assis Brasil**, where the Peruvian, Bolivian and Brazilian frontiers meet and there is an easy crossing to the Peruvian town of **Iñapari**. There is little reason to stop in either town. Brasiléia is a provincial town of a handful of streets. The Bolivian town of **Cobija** is busier as it's a duty-free port – and a good place to pick up electronics bargains. Unless you want to fly, onward transport into Bolivia is poor – the town is roughly 500 km northwest of La Paz and the road is impassable much of the year. Assis is smaller still, and

Border essentials: Brazil–Bolivia

Brasiléia (Brazil)–Cobija (Bolivia)

There are two official crossings between Cobija and Brasiléia: one is by ferry to Cobija's boat wharf, just off Calle Bolívar, at the west end of town. The other is via the international bridge, east of the ferry. The former is often quicker, and certainly cheaper (US$1.35), as taxis are expensive (US$12). All visitors must carry a yellow fever certificate. The *polícia federal* in Brasiléia gives entry/exit stamps. For more details see page 55.

as the bus passes straight through, whisking visitors through emigration and immigration, there is even less of a reason to stop. Neither town has a bank with an ATM (though there are abundant moneychangers and, in Brasiléia, a Banco do Brasil which will change dollars or TCs with a commission heavy enough to make you whince). Both towns have café-restaurants, pharmacies and taxi stands.

⊚ Rondônia and Acre listings

For Sleeping and Eating price codes and other relevant information, see pages 32-37.

⊜ Sleeping

Porto Velho *p667, map p667*
AL Vila Rica, Av Carlos Gomes 1616, T/F069-3224 3433, www.hotelvilarica.com.br. Tower block hotel with a restaurant, pool and sauna.
B Central, R Tenreiro Aranha 2472, T069-2181 2500, www.enter-net.com.br/hcentral. A big, functional, red and white concrete block with friendly staff and plain but well-kept modern a/c rooms with TVs, work desks and fridges and views on the upper floors. Good breakfast, a laundry service and Wi-Fi for free in all rooms and public areas. 2 mins' walk from the a/c shops, restaurants and cinemas of the new Porto Shopping mall.
C Líder, R Carlos Gomes 3189 immediately behind the *rodoviária* to the northeast, T069-3225 2727. Boxy but bright rooms which, despite needing a fresh lick of paint, are clean. All come with en suites with solar-heated hot water and breakfast is included.
C Por do Sol, R Carlos Gomes 3168 immediately behind the *rodoviária* to the northeast, T069-3222 9161, hotelpordosol

@yahoo.com.br. A corridor of peach and brown tile a/c rooms, the best of which have large windows and are in the middle of the corridor. Some have space for 3 people, making this **E** per person. Free Wi-Fi, breakfast included.
C Samauma, R Dom Pedro II 1038, T069-3224 5300, hotelsamauma@hotmail.com. Much the best mid-range option in the city centre with brick annexes of cosy, comfortable rooms all with a/c, international TV and en suites gathered around a popular restaurant. Free Wi-Fi in all areas, breakfast and friendly, welcoming staff.
C-D Tía Carmen, Av Campos Sales 2995, T069- 3221 7910. Very friendly and with simple well-kept rooms. The snack bar in front of the hotel serves good cakes. Refurbished in 2009 and with fre Wi-Fi in all rooms.

Guajará-Mirim *p669*
AL-A Pakaas Palafitas Lodge, Km 18, Estrada do Palheta, T/F069-3541 3058, www.pakaas. com.br. 20 mins by taxi from town centre (US$15). 28 smart bungalows in a beautiful natural setting out of town. The hotel is set in forest cut by walking trails and offers canoeing on the river, and has an attractive pool.

C Jamaica, Av Leopoldo de Matos 755, T/F069-3541 3721. Simple but the best hotel in town. Rooms have a/c and fridges. Parking.
C Lima Palace, Av 15 de Novembro 1613, T069-3541 3421. Similar to the *Jamaica* but with scruffier rooms.
D Chile, Av Q Bocaiúva. Basic but well run. Includes breakfast, good value but pretty run down.
D Mamoré, R Mascarenhas de Moraes 1105, T069-3541 3753. Clean, friendly and popular with backpackers.

Rio Branco *p670, map p671*
There are few economical hotels in the centre, but a reasonable selection by the *rodoviária*.
AL-A Imperador Galvez, R Santa Inés 401, T068-3223 7027, www.hotelimperador. com.br. 2 annexes of comfortable, quite modern rooms with international flatscreen TV and free Wi-Fi gathered around a large pool. Breakfasts are enough to last all the way through until the evening.
AL-A Terra Verde, R Marechal Deodoro 221, T068-3213 6000, www.terraverdehotel. com.br. One of the best in the city – with well-appointed a/c rooms and more luxurious Terra Verde suites which come with 2 flatscreens and separate living and sleeping areas. A pool, breakfast and free Wi-Fi throughout.
A Irmãos Inacio Palace, R Rui Barbosa 450-69, T068-3214 7100, www.irmaospinheiro.com.br. The bright, spacious rooms in this hotel were refurbished in early 2010, receiving fresh light peach decor, bathrooms with granite basins and new tiles and functional work desks. The hotel has a pool, free Wi-Fi, serves a generous breakfast and has some English-speaking staff. There's a *churrascaria* restaurant next door.
A Loureiro, R Marechal Deodoro 304, T068-3224 3110. A/c rooms in this freshly refurbished, blocky hotel are scrupulously clean and come with faux-parquet floors, tiled bathrooms and flatscreen TVs. The building is close to the river with many shops and restaurants a stroll away.

B-C Afa, R Franco Ribeiro 108, T068-3224 1396. Simple whitewash and wall tile rooms, which, whilst clean, quiet and well-kept, have small windows. Breakfast is generous and there is a very good per kilo lunch restaurant downstairs. Triples are **D** per person.
C Papai, R Floriano Peixoto 849, T068-3223 6868. This centrally located hotel has simple but garish pink and lime green a/c rooms the best of which are on the upper floors – those in the basement can be musty. Free Wi-Fi.
D Ouro Verde, R Uirapuru 326, next to *rodoviária*, T068-3223 2378. This no-frills option has rooms only a little larger than the twin or double beds they contain. But they are clean and set on a long sunny terrace and have plenty of natural light, and each comes with an en suite. Triples work out at **F** per person. With breakfast.

🍴 Eating

Porto Velho *p667, map p667*
🍴 **Caravela do Madeira**, R José Camacho 104, Agricolândia, T069-3221 6641. Closed Mon. The best formal restaurant in Porto Velho, in a long wooden dining room perched over the Madeira river. The menu is strong on river fish (the tambaqui is excellent) and the restaurant is one of the few in the city to have a wine list.
🍴 **Myoshi**, Av Amazonas 1280, Bairro NS das Graças, T069-3224 4600, www.myoshi.com.br. This large open-plan dining room serves the best Japanese food in the city with an evening sushi and sashimi buffet. Brazilian fusion options include salmon and cream cheese, sushi tucumã – made with an Amazon river fish – and a desert banana and chocolate sushi. It's a 15-min cab ride from the centre. Also delivers.
🍴-🍴 **Emporium**, Av Presidente Dutra 3366, T069-3221 2665. A very popular restaurant-bar serving hearty portions of river fish, steaks and a wide choice of very cold beer, caipirinhas and juices. The street behind Emporium is known as the Calçada da Fama

and is replete with bars and restaurants. It's very busy at weekends.

Ψ Café Madeira, Majo Amarantes at Carlos Gomes on the riverfront, T069-3229 1193. The tables perched on a little promontory overlooking the Madeira are a favourite spot for an ice sunset *chopp* draught beer and a *petisco* bar snack. Main courses include steak, river fish and chicken fillets with rice and Brazilian rose coco beans.

Rio Branco *p670, map p671*

There are boats on the river serving cheap but good food. The local specialities are *tacacá*: a soup served piping hot in a gourd, made from *goma* (manioc starch), cooked *jambu* leaves which numb the mouth and tongue, shrimp, spices and hot pepper sauce and a delicious Amazonian take on moqueca, rendered tangy and seet with rainforest herbs and spices.

ΨΨ-Ψ Mata Nativa, Estrada Via Verde Km 2 1971, Rio Branco, T069-3221 3004. Regional food served in an open-sided maloca set in a garden on the road to Sena Madureira some 6 km from the centre. Plates are big enough for 4 people and include *moqueca de tambaqui* (Bahian spicy coconut soup with tambaqui fish) and *galinha caipira* (herb-coated chicken served with *pirão* manioc gruel and *vatapa* prawn paste). Very popular on weekends.

Ψ Afa, R Franco Ribeiro 108, T069-3224 1396, www.afabistro.com.br. The best and best-value per kilo restaurant in the city, with a wide choice of dishes from tambaqui fish stew, lentils, spit-roast beef, decent.

Ψ Elcio, Av Ceará 2513. Superb fish *moquecas* as good as anythign you'll find in Espírito Santo or Bahia in a rich coconut sauce flavoured with an Amazon leaf, *xicoria* and fresh coriander and accompanied with rice, *pirão*, *farofa* and delicious chilli and *tucupi* sauce. Serves 2-3 people.

O Shopping

Porto Velho *p667, map p667*
Artesanato Indigena Karitiana, R Rui Barbosa 1407 between Jose Camacho and Calama), T069-3229 7591. Daily 0800-1200 and 1400-1700. A Karitiana-run cooperative shop selling indigenous art including beads, earrings and necklaces, ritual items and weapons.
Porto Velho shopping, 2.5 km east of the *rodoviária*, www.pvshopping.com.br. With many a/c boutiques, travel agencies and restaurants in the food emporium and a 6-screen multiplex cinema with films in English.

Markets

There is a clean fruit and veg market at the corner of R Henrique Dias and Av Farquhar and a dry goods market 3 blocks to the south, near the port. On Sun there's a general market off Av Rogério Weber near port, excellent bargains but no souvenirs. Watch out for pickpockets.

▲ Activities and tours

Guajará-Mirim *p669*
Alfatur, Av 15 de Novembro 106, T/F069-3541 2853. Tour operator.

Rio Branco *p670, map p671*
Maanaim Amazônia, R Colombia 39, Bairro Bosque, T068-3223 3232, www.maanaim-amazonia.com. One of the best tour operators in the Brazilian Amazon, with a fascinating range of trips, including expeditons to the remote Serra do Divisor National Park, visits to Ashaninka, Yawanawa and other indigenous communities, and stays in the Serengal Cachoeira Chico Mendes rainforest reserve in Xapuri (see page 674).

⊖ Transport

Porto Velho *p667, map p667*
Air
To get to the airport take bus 'Aeroporto' (last one between 2400 and 0100). Flights to **Brasília**, **Manaus** and **Rio Branco** and other destinations – see Ins and outs, page 668.

Boat
See Routes in Amazônia, page 656. There is a regular passenger service from the port – **Porto Cai N'Água** (which means 'fall in the water') up the Madeira to Manaus. For the best price buy directly on the boat, avoid touts on the shore. The Rio Madeira is fairly narrow, so the banks can be seen and there are several 'meetings of waters'.

Bus
Many restaurants and snack bars in the *rodoviária*, 24-hr ATM. Any **Esperança da Communidade** or **Presidente Roosevelt** local bus runs the 1.5 km from the cathedral in the city centre to the *rodoviária*. There are buses to **Campo Grande** (27 hrs, US$155), 2 daily 1st at 0600; **Cuiabá** (24 hrs, US$75), 6 daily; **Guajará-Mirim** (5-6 hrs, US$22) 6 daily from 0630, fastest at midday; **Rio Branco** (8 hrs, US$32), 5 daily; **São Paulo** (40 hrs, US$185), 1 daily at 1000.

Guajará-Mirim *p669*
Bus To **Porto Velho**, 5½ hrs or more depending on season, 8 a day with **Viação Rondônia**, US$18. A taxi to the Porto Velho *rodoviária* costs US$25 per person for 4-5 people, 3 hrs, and leaves when full.

Rio Branco *p670, map p671*
Air For transport to and from the airport see Ins and outs, page 673. There are flights to **Porto Velho**, **Manaus**, **Brasília**, **São Paulo**, **Cuiabá** and **Campo Grande** and to **Cruzeiro do Sul**.

Bus To **Porto Velho**, Viação Rondônia, 5 daily, 8-10 hrs, US$50. To **Guajará-Mirim**,

daily with **Rondônia** at 1130 and 2200, 8 hrs, US$50; or take **Inácio's Tur** shopping trip, 3 per week.

Car hire Car rentals with nationwide agencies are more expensive in Acre than other states. **Locabem**, Rodovia AC-40, Km 0, 2nd district, T069-3223 3000. **Localiza**, R Rio Grande do Sul 310, T069-3224 7746, airport T069-3224 8478. **Unidas**, T069-3224 5044.

⊕ Directory

Porto Velho *p667, map p667*
Banks Open until 1400 only. There are numerous **Bradesco** and **HSBC** banks with ATMs in town, including in the airport and at Bradesco, Av 7 de Setembro 711, Centro and HSBC, Av Campos Sales, 2645, Centro. **Laundry** Lavanderia Marmoré, Pinheiro Machado 1455B. **Medical services** Hospital Central, R Júlio de Castilho 149, T/F069-3224 4389, 24-hr emergencies. Dentist at Carlos Gomes 2577; 24-hr clinic opposite. **Post office** Av Pres Dutra 2701, corner of Av 7 de Setembro. **Telephone** Av Pres Dutra 3023 and Dom Pedro II, daily 0600-2300.

Guajará-Mirim *p669*
Banks Banco do Brasil, foreign exchange in the morning only. Loja Nogueira, Av Pres Dutra, corner Leopoldo de Matos, cash only. There is no market in Brazil for bolivianos. **Embassies and consulates** Bolivia, Av C Marquês 495, T069-3541 2862, visas are given here. **Medical services** Regional, Av Mcal Deodoro, T069-3541 2651. **Post office** Av Pres Dutra. **Telephone** Av B Ménzies 751.

Rio Branco *p670, map p671*
Banks There are plenty in town and at the airport, including Bradesco, Praça Eurico Dutra 65, T068-3223 2016. **Medical services** Santa Casa hospital, R Alvorada 178, T068-224 6297. **Post office** On the corner of R Epaminondas Jácome and Av Getúlio Vargas.

Contents

Brasília, Goiás & Tocantins

At a glance

◒ **Getting around** Internal flights and buses. Car hire is a possibility when using one location as a base but is not good over the whole region, which is vast.

◉ **Time required** 1 day for Brasília; 7 days for Brasília and Goiás; 5-7 days for Jalapão.

☽ **Weather** Varies across the region. The north of Tocantins is similar to the northern Amazon – hot and wet Dec-Apr. Brasília and Goiás are hot and dry Apr-Sep and warm and wet Oct-Mar.

✖ **When not to go** Brasília, Goiás and southern Tocantins in Dec and Jan.

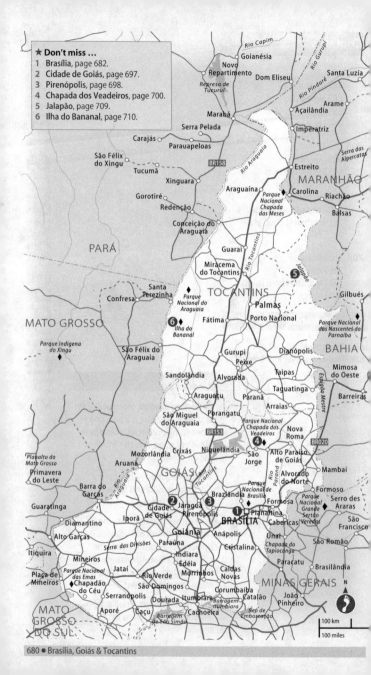

★ **Don't miss ...**
1 Brasília, page 682.
2 Cidade de Goiás, page 697.
3 Pirenópolis, page 698.
4 Chapada dos Veadeiros, page 700.
5 Jalapão, page 709.
6 Ilha do Bananal, page 710.

The country's capital, Brasília, is the symbol of the nation's commitment to its empty centre. Although not generally viewed as a tourist attraction, it is interesting as a city of pure invention similar to Australia's Canberra or Washington in the United States. Its central position makes it a natural crossroads for visiting the north and interior of Brazil and, when passing through, it is well worth undertaking a city tour to view its innovative modern design.

Like Brasília, Goiás is rarely on the itinerary for first-time visitors to Brazil. But those who know the country well often consider it their favourite state. There is so much of interest here: colonial cities as beautiful as any in Minas and far less visited; colourful and bizarre festivals; national parks as wild as the Pantanal; and trekking, wildlife- and birdwatching that is second only to the Pantanal and the Amazon. Its people are among the country's most welcoming. They are quietly spoken, poetic and obsessed with dreadful *sertanejo* music, which laments lost love through videos of girls in little shorts intercut with prize bulls. The state is easily visited from Brasília or on the way to or from the Pantanal and the coast.

Further north is the state of Tocantins, dominated by vast rivers, *cerrado* forests and, increasingly, soya plantations. The deserts of Jalapão lie here: landscapes that at first sight seem a strange fusion of North Africa and outback Australia but which, unlike both, are broken by myriad lakes and waterfalls. Further to the west on the frontier of Mato Grosso is the Bananal – one of the biggest river islands in the world and home to large groups of indigenous Brazilians.

Brasília

→ *Colour map 4, A2. Phone code: 061. Population: 2.1 million.*
This planned and impersonal capital city, sitting like a monument to the space age in a vast plain surrounded by ever-expanding favelas and chaos, may seem very un-Brazilian to those who are new to the country. This is, after all, a nation famous for its laissez-faire attitude. But it also has 'Order and Progress' written proudly on its flag, in homage to the ideas of Comte. And the grandiose schemes of many of its 20th-century leaders have long been influenced by a desire to propel the country into a Positivist vision of the future. Brazil's capital was intended by its conceivers, Lúcio Costa and Oscar Niemeyer, and then president Juscelino Kubitschek, as a statement of that future in concrete; an attempt perhaps to make real the cliché repeated by every other Brazilian leader that this is 'the country of the future'. Although many of the remarkable buildings, such as the the dome and saucer of the Congresso Nacional, would in themselves make a trip here worthwhile, Brasília is every bit as Brazilian as Rio Carnaval and Pelé and a visit here is a must for those interested in the psychology of the country. ▸▸ *For listings, see pages 690-695.*

Ins and outs

Getting there

Air Flights arrive at the **international airport** ① *12 km south of the centre, T061-3364 9000, www.infraero.com.br.* Tourist information is available from **Setur** ① *T061-3214 2742, www.setur.df.gov.br, daily 0730-2230.* **Infraero** ① *2nd floor, open 24 hrs,* has information on airport buses. A taxi to the centre costs around US$25, meter rate two is used. Alternatively, take bus No 102 or 118 (US$1.50, 30 minutes) from outside the terminal building to the municipal bus station at the western end of the Eixo Monumental. There are left-luggage facilities at the airport (locker tokens US$1.50), banks, car rental agencies, a post office and various restaurants and shops.

Bus and train Interstate buses arrive at the combined bus and train station, the **rodoferroviária** ① *west of town, T061-3363 2281; information from Setur daily 0800-2000.* From here bus No 131, US$1.50, runs to the **municipal bus station** ① *T061-3327 4631, www.guiadebrasilia.com.br/cidade/turistas/rodoferroviaria.htm,* in the city centre. Both bus stations have large luggage lockers. The *rodoviária* has a post office, telephone facilities and showers (US$1.50). A taxi to the northern hotel zone (Setor Hoteleiro Norte) costs US$18.

Getting around

Inner-city Brasília's main transport hub is the municipal bus station, at the western end of the Eixo Monumental and Avenida W3, which is connected by regular services to both the aiport and *rodoviaria* (see above for details). A good and cheap way of seeing Brasília is by taking bus rides from here around the city: the destinations are clearly marked: the circular bus routes 106, 108 and 131 go around the city's perimeter. If you go around the lake by bus, you must change at the Paranoá Dam; to or from Paranoá Norte take bus 101, 'Rodoviária'; and to and from Sul, take bus 100, bypassing the airport. If staying in a hotel outside the centre, it's worth contacting them in advance to ask how to get there. A new urban railway, the metrô, runs to the southwest suburbs but is very limited. Brasília is not pedestrian friendly. Despite the fact that most Brazilians cannot afford to buy a car, there are no pavements in the city. Be careful after dark. ▸▸ *See Transport, page 694.*

City tours **Brasília City Tour** ① *T061-9298 9416, www.brasiliacitytour.com.br, US$15, children 6-12 US$7, children under 6 free.* Open-topped double decker buses leave from the Brasília shopping centre and Torre de TV (TV Tower) at the eastern end of the Eixo Monumental. They call at some 20 of the key city sights, including the Palácio do Itamaraty, Palácio da Justiça, Catedral and Congreso Nacional at the following times: Monday 1030, 1400, 1600 and 1900 (from Brasília Shopping), Tuesday-Wednesday 1030, 1400, 1600 and 1900 (from Brasília Shopping and the Torre de TV), Thu-Sun 1030, 1200, 1330, 1500, 1630 and 1900 (from Brasília Shopping and the Torre de TV). Private companes like **BSB** ① *SCLN 310 Bloco D Loja 71, T061-3340 0067, www.bsbtour.tur.br*, offer a range of half- and full-day tours of the city in air-conditioned cars, for roughly twice the price (and therefore cheaper when divided between several people). English-speaking guides are available (at extra cost) on request.

Orientation

A competition for the best general plan was won by Professor Lúcio Costa, who laid out the city in the shape of a bent bow and arrow. The design has also been described as intending to appear as a bird or aeroplane in flight, interpretations Costa was quick to reject in his lifetime. The official name for central Brasília is the **Plano Piloto**.

The **Eixo Monumental** divides the city into **Asa Norte** and **Asa Sul** (north and south wings) and the **Eixo Rodoviário** divides it east and west. Buildings are numbered according to their relation to them. For example, 116 Sul and 116 Norte are at the extreme opposite ends of the city. The 100s and 300s lie west of the Eixo and the 200s and 400s to the east; *quadras* 302, 102, 202 and 402 are nearest the centre, and 316, 116, 216 and 416 mark the end of the Plano Piloto. Residential areas are made up of large six-storey apartment blocks called 'Super- Quadras'. Each Super-Quadra houses 3000 people and has a primary school and playgroup. Each group of four Super-Quadras should have a library, police station, club, supermarket and secondary school. All *quadras* are separated by feeder roads, along which are the local shops. There are also a number of schools, parks and cinemas in the spaces between the *quadras* (especially in Asa Sul), though not as systematically as was originally envisaged. On the outer side of the 300s and extending the length of the city is **Avenida W3**, and on the outer side of the 400s is **Avenida L2**, both of these being similarly divided into north and south according to the part of the city they are in.

Asa Norte is growing very fast, with standards of architecture and urbanization that promise to make it more attractive than Asa Sul in the near future. The main shopping areas, which have more cinemas, restaurants and other facilities, are situated on either side of the municipal bus station (*rodoviária*). There are now several parks and green areas. The private residential areas are west of the Super-Quadras, and on the other side of the lake.

At right angles to these residential areas is the 'arrow', the 8-km-long, 250-m wide **Eixo Monumental**. The **Eixo Rodoviário** (the main north–south road), in which fast-moving traffic is segregated, follows the curve of the bow, the radial road is along the line of the arrow; intersections are avoided by means of underpasses and cloverleaves. Motor and pedestrian traffic is segregated in the residential areas.

Best time to visit

The climate is mild and the humidity refreshingly low, but overpowering in the dry season (May to mid-October). The noonday sun beats hard, but summer (October to April) brings heavy rains and the air is usually cool by night. It's best to visit in the dry season when the stark modernist buildings stand out against the deep blue sky.

Tourist information

The tourist office, **Setur** ① *Centro de Convenções (convention centre), 3rd floor, T061-3214 2767, 0800-1200 and 1300-1800*, has helpful English-speaking staff, and can provide a good map of Brasília. There are branches at the *rodoferroviária* and at the airport (see above), which have more limited information but will book hotels and provide city maps. **Embratur** ① *Setor Comercial Norte, quadra 2, bloco G, T061-224 9100, www.braziltour.com*, also has a branch at the airport. The **tourist office** in the centre of Praça dos Tres Poderes has a colourful map and lots of information. The staff are friendly and have interesting information about Brasília and other places in Goiás, but only Portuguese is spoken. Other useful information is available from www.infobrasilia.com.br, www.dicasde brasilia.com.br, www.guiade brasilia.com.br and www.aboutbrasilia.com.

Maps Maps of Brasília showing individual streets are almost impossible to find. But city maps with each *quadra* marked are available from larger newsagents and at the airport. Slightly less detailed maps are available from **Setur**.

① Brasília: Plano Piloto

Sleeping 🛏	Eating 🍴		La Chaumière **4**
Albergue Brasília **1**	Alice **1**		Le Français **5**
Royal Tulip Alvorada **2**	Aquavit **2**		Oca da Tribo **6**
	Kosui **3**		O Convento **7**

Sights

Brasília was a project powered by the indefatigable will of one man. Plans to build a new capital in the centre of the country had been drawn up as early as 1822. But it took Juscelino Kubitschek, Brazil's self-proclaimed great modernizer, whose famous election winning catchphrase was "50 years in five", to realize the dream. His capital was rushed through from start to finish within one term of presidential office. The blueprint was cleared by Congress in 1956. Work began the following year and by the time Eisenhower laid the cornerstone of the US embassy in February 1960, accompanied by a great media fanfare, the new capital was largely complete.

Most of the interesting sights are concentrated on or around the **Eixo Monumental**, an inner-city highway forming the 'arrow' of Brasília's bow. They can be visited by car, taxi or tour over the course of a morning. The **television tower** ① *Mon 1400-2000, Tue-Sun 0800-2000, closed Mon morning*, between the Setor Hoteleiro Norte and the Setor Hoteleiro Sul is a good place to begin a tour and to orientate oneself. It offers excellent panoramic views from the observation platform 75 m up, as do many of the tall hotels nearby.

➡ **Brasília maps**
1 Brasília: Plano Piloto, page 684
2 Brasília hotel zone, page 688

go Do
ranoá

Estr Hotéis de Turismo

Palácio da
Alvorada

Palácio
do Jabaru

cio do
nalto

Panteão
Tancredo
Neves

Avenida das Nações

N I Leste

Sces Trecho 3

Sces Trecho 2

Estrada Parque Dom Bosco

To ① ② ③

atu Anu 8
orcão 9
attoria da Rosa 10
niversal Diner 11

Vercelli 12
Zuu aZdZ 13

Praça dos Três Poderes and around

The most important buildings are clustered together at the western end of the Eixo Monumental around the Praça dos Três Poderes; named after the three powers of the federal state that flank it. To the north is the seat of presidential power, the **Palácio do Planalto** ① *Praça dos Três Poderes, 30-min tours available on Sun 0930-1330*. A wall of glass between twin white concrete platforms, it is reached by a long low ramp flanked by guards in red and white uniforms. Opposite, the **Supremo Tribunal Federal** is smaller and more perfectly formed, with Niemeyer's trademark fluted columns hiding patrolling secret service guards in sharp suits. The famous modernist statue of blind justice sitting in front of the building is by the Mineiro sculptor Alfredo Ceschiatti. To the west, the seat of the Senate and Congress, **Congresso Nacional** ① *Praça dos Três Poderes, Mon-Fri 0930-1200, 1430-1630, take your passport, free guided tour in English 1400-1600*, is the most famous and stately group of buildings in Brasília – a tour de force of simple lines and curves. The concave and convex domes of the Chamber of Deputies and the Senate are juxtaposed and balanced by the twin towers of the executive: a geometric tension and harmony in which Niemeyer intended to

Oscar Niemeyer and Brasília

Oscar Niemeyer Soares Filho (born 1907 in Rio de Janeiro) was educated at the Escola Nacional de Belas Artes and in 1936 joined the group of architects charged with developing Le Corbusier's project for the Ministry of Education and Health building in Rio de Janeiro. His first international project was the Brazilian pavilion at the New York International Fair in 1939 in partnership with Lúcio Costa. In the 1940s he was one of the main designers of Pampulha and in 1947 he worked on the United Nations headquarters in New York. This was the period in which he affirmed his style, integrating architecture with painting and sculpture. He transformed utilitarian constructions with the lightness of his designs, his freedom of invention and the use of complex, curved surfaces. Throughout the 1950s he was commissioned to design a wide variety of national and international projects, but it was the years 1956-1959 that stamped his signature on the architectural world. This was when he worked on Brasília, specifically the Palácio da Alvorada, the ministries, the Praça dos Três Poderes, the cathedral, university and, in 1967, the Palácio dos Arcos e da Justiça. After Brasília Niemeyer continued to work at home and abroad; among his more famous later projects were the Sambódromo in Rio (1984) and the Memorial da América Latina in São Paulo (1989). The Royal Institute of British Architects awarded him the prestigious Royal Gold Medal for Architecture in 1998.

Many of Brazil's most famous architects, sculptors and designers were involved in Brasília. The city was built during Juscelino Kubitschek's term as president (1955-1960) and was unparalleled in scale and architectural importance in Latin America at that time. A description of the city, and its effect on the economy at the time of its construction are dealt with elsewhere in the book. Niemeyer was appointed chief architecture and technical adviser to Novacap, the government authority which oversaw the new capital. But while it is common knowledge who the famous names were, it is also worth noting that 30,000 workers were involved in bringing the plan to reality. Most of them came from the northeast. The city has been honoured not just for its architecture, but also for being the first purpose-built capital of the 20th century. In 1987 it was named a Unesco World Cultural Heritage Site, the first contemporary city to gain such protection from the United Nations.

Niemeyer himself has said "The modern city lacks harmony and a sense of occasion. Brasília will never lack these". And it is true that the principal buildings, and the overall plan itself, are strikingly powerful. The whole enterprise is deeply rooted in the 20th century, not just in its design, but also in the idea that it is a city you jet into and out of. If you arrive by road (which most people do not), the experience is even more fantastic. After hours and hours in the bus, travelling across the unpopulated central plateau, you come to this collection of remarkable buildings and sculptures in the middle of nowhere. The vastness of the landscape demands a grand city and yet, for all its harmony, it is almost as if not even Brasília can compete with the sky and the horizon.

Niemeyer is still working in his late 90s. In 2002, a museum designed by the architect himself opened in Curitiba. It is spectacular, sitting like a giant black eye on a pedestal in one of the city's parks, fully living up to Niemeyer's proclamation that 'the most important element in any work of art is to surprise, to startle'. His mostly recently opened grand buildings are the Biblioteca Nacional and the dome-shaped and Oca-like Museum of Brasília, which opened in the capital in 2006.

symbolize that of government. These monumental buildings are offset beautifully by the vast expanse of the square, the artificial ponds and the lawns.

There are a handful of other interesting buildings in the plaza: the **Espaço Lucio Costa** ⓘ *Tue-Sun 0900-1800, free*, with a scale model of the city; a monument to Juscelino Kubitschek; the **Panteão da Liberdade e Democracia** built in homage to Democracy and Liberty; and Bruno Giorgio's **Candangos** – twin bronze figures sculpted in homage to the Candango workers who built the city from nothing in the middle of what was a vast plain, and who received the satellite favelas that ring the city as their reward.

Beyond the *praça* to the east and on the shores of Lago Paranoá is the **Palácio Alvorada**, residence of the president and not open to the public.

Less than a kilometre west of the *praça* are two further Niemeyer buildings of note. The **Palácio de Itamarati** is one of the finest pieces of modernist architecture in Brazil; its elegant columns rising from a lily pond, which acts like a huge mirror for the entire building. Inside there is a series of rooms each decorated with fine sculpture and paintings including Pedro Américo's *O Grito de Ipiranga*, showing the moment when Dom Pedro shouted his declaration of Brazilian Independence, and Jean-Baptiste Debret's painting of the emperor's subsequent coronation. There are also works by Brazilian modernists Alfredo Volpi, Candido Portinari and Pedro Correia de Araújo. The building is named after the Rio de Janeiro palace of Francisco José da Rocha Leão, a wealthy industrialist who became the Conde de Itamaraty. This building served as the first ministry of the exterior in the early republican era. Opposite Itamarati is the **Palácio da Justiça** ⓘ *Mon-Fri 0900-1200, 1500-1700*, its walls broken by a series of broad fountains that climb up the façade of the building and drop water into the pond that sits at the building's feet.

West along the Eixo Monumental

The Eixo stretches for some 8 km west of Praça dos Três Poderes eventually reaching the *rodoferroviária*. Almost all of the city's other important monuments lie on either side of the road. We follow them here from east to west.

The government ministry buildings line the Eixo east of the *praça* like dominos, or a series of commissars standing to attention. Eventually they reach Niemeyer's striking **Catedral Metropolitana Nossa Senhora Aparecida** ⓘ *Esplanada dos Ministérios, Eixo Monumental, T061-3224 4073, 0800-1930*; a crown of thorns in concrete and glass sitting in a toroidal lake and watched over by Alfredo Ceschiatti's four evangelists, standing sentinel-like in concrete. The entrance to the cathedral is via a subterranean tunnel, emerging from relative darkness into an arena bright with stained glass and light marble.

Next to the cathedral are two of the most recently built Niemeyer buildings, which opened to the public in 2008: the **Museu Nacional de Brasília** ⓘ *Eixo Monumental s/n, Mon 0800-1700, Tue-Fri 0800-1800, Sat 0800-1700, free*, a striking dome-shaped building, which currently only shows temporary exhibitions, and which has an entrance halfway up its side reached by a snaking ramp; and the cuboid **Biblioteca Nacional** next door ⓘ *Eixo Monumental s/n, Mon 0800-1700, Tue-Fri 0800-1800, Sat 0800-1700, free, free internet on ground floor (bring ID)*. Less than 1 km west, a few blocks south, is the **Santuário Dom Bosco** ⓘ *Av W3 Sul, quadra 702, T061-3223 6542, 0800-1800*, a modernist cube with tall Gothic arches filled with stained glass, which shades from light blue to indigo as it ascends. It is particularly beautiful in the late afternoon when shafts of light penetrate the building. The church is named after the 19th-century saint and founder of the Salesian order, who proclaimed that a new civilization would arise in the third millennium between the 15th and 16th parallels and on the edge of an artificial lake. The trunk of the enormous cross hanging over the altar was carved from a single piece of tropical cedar.

Beyond the TV tower, which lies at the intersection of the Eixo and the hotel zones, are two other interesting groups of buildings. A monument to the man whose ego and ambition created the city, the **Memorial Juscelino Kubitschek (JK)** ① *Tue-Sun 0900-1800, US$1.50, toilets and café*, has the former president standing high above a marble plinth waving towards the Praça dos Três Poderes. His tomb lies beneath the marble together with a collection of memorabilia. In front of the memorial is the **Memorial dos Povos Indígenas** ① *Tue-Sun 0900-1800, US$3*; a round concrete building shaped like a *Bororo* communal house or *maloca* and reached by a tongue-like ramp. Inside is a small but fascinating collection of indigenous art and cultural artefacts. On the other side of the Memorial JK, east of Praça do Cruzeiro, is the city's second Niemeyer cathedral, the **Catedral Militar de Nossa Senhora da Paz** ① *Tue-Sun 0900-1800*. This is a brilliant white wedge of concrete cut with jagged windows, whose design echoes Notre Dame du Haut, designed by Niemeyer's mentor, Le Corbusier. The church marks the entrance to the **Quartel General do Exército**; an enormous and imposing complex of military buildings centred on an elliptical auditorium made of a single wave of concrete and added to Brasília during the military dictatorship, as if to compensate for the lack of army presence on the Praça dos Três Poderes. All are by Niemeyer. There is a small **military museum** ① *Tue-Sun 0900-1800*, on the site. Die-hard Niemeyer fans should also visit the city's first church – which was in a sense a precursor to the design and partnerships that created the city; the **Igrejinha Nossa Senhora de Fatima** ① *SGAS 906 Bl. D lote 10, ASA SUL, T061-3443 2869*, was inaugurated in 1958 as a petition to Our Lady to cure the President and First Lady's sick daughter. It was designed by Niemeyer and is covered in tiles by *Athos Bulcão* – whose work adorns many of Brasília's buildings. The flags and angels inside are the work of Alfredo Volpi one of post-War Brazil's leading modernist artists.

The **Templo da Boa Vontade** ① *Setor Garagem Sul 915, lotes 75/76, T061-3245 1070, www.tbv.com.br, open 24 hrs*, is a seven-faced pyramid dedicated to all philosophies and religions topped by one of the world's largest rock crystals. To get there, take bus No 151 from outside the Centro do Convenções or on Eixo Sul to Centro Médico.

Brasília hotel zone

Brasília maps
1 Brasília: Plano Piloto, page 684
2 Brasília hotel zone, page 688

N

400 metres
400 yards

Sleeping	Kubitschek
Alvorada 1	Plaza 7
Aristus 2	Nacional 4
Bittar Inn 6	
Casablanca 3	
El Pilar 5	

The **Panteão Tancredo Neves** is a 'temple of freedom and democracy', built 1985-1986 by Niemeyer. It includes an impressive homage to Tiradentes (see box, page 266).

The **Monumental Parade Stand** has unique and mysterious acoustics (the complex is north of the Eixo Monumental, between the 'Memorial JK' and the *rodoferroviária*). There are remarkable stained-glass panels, each representing a state of the Federation, on the ground floor of the Caixa Econômica Federal.

Around Brasília

About 15 km along the Belo Horizonte road is the small wooden house, designed by Niemeyer, erected in only 10 days and known as **O Catetinho**. President Kubitschek stayed here in the late 1950s during his visits to the city when it was under construction; it is open to visitors and houses memorabilia and some of JK's furniture and personal items.

Some 40 km northeast of the Plano Piloto via Saída Norte is **Planaltina**, originally a settlement on the colonial pack route from the mines of Goiás and Cuiabá to the coast. The old part still contains many colonial buildings. There are two good *churrascarias* on the main street and it is a good place for a rural Sunday lunch. About 5 km outside Planaltina is the **Pedra Fundamental**, the foundation stone laid by President Epitácio Pessoa in 1922 to mark the site that was originally chosen for the new capital.

Also outside Planaltina, at Km 30 on the BR-020, lies **Águas Emendadas**. From the same point spring two streams that flow in opposite directions to form part of the two great river systems: the Amazon and the Plate. Permission from the biological institute in Brasília is required to visit. At Km 70 is the town of **Formosa**. Some 20 km north of the town is the **Itiquira waterfall** (158 m high). From the top are spectacular views and the pools at the bottom offer good bathing, but it gets crowded at weekends. There are four smaller falls in the area and camping is possible. To get there from the centre of Formosa, follow the signs or ask. The only bus from Formosa to Itiquira leaves at 0730 and returns at 1700.

Parque Nacional de Brasília → *Colour map 3, A6.*

ⓘ *10 km northwest of the rodoferroviária, around 15 mins by car. Contact Instituto Chico Mendes de Conservação da Biodiversidade (ICMBio), Via L Quatro Norte, www.ibama.gov.br, or at the park's office, Via Epia SMU, T061-3233 3251.*

This park was founded in 1961 to preserve a remnant of the original *cerrado* flora and fauna that Brasília replaced. The park covers some 28,000 ha, but only a small portion is open to the public without a permit. There is a swimming pool fed by clear river water, a snack bar and a series of trails through gallery forest, which is popular with joggers in the early morning and at weekends. The rest of the park is rolling grassland, gallery forest and *cerrado* vegetation. There are large mammals include tapir, maned wolf and pampas deer; birdwatching is good, especially for Brasília tapaculo, horned sungem, yellow-faced parrot and nighthawk.

⊛ Brasília listings

For Sleeping and Eating price codes and other relevant information, see pages 32-37.

⊜ Sleeping

Brasília *p682, maps p684 and p688*
The best area to base yourself is in the northern hotel zone, which has lots of shops and restaurants nearby. Prices usually include breakfast. Weekend discounts of 30% are often available if you ask. The best area for cheap accommodation is around W3 703 and 704 in the Asa Sul where many residential houses have been turned into hostels. The quietest areas are northwest of the main Av W3 Sul. Beware of bus station touts. The tourist office has a list of *pensões*.

Southern hotel zone
L Nacional, quadra 1, bloco A, T061-3321 7575, www.hotelnacional.com.br. This huge old-fashioned city landmark was *the* place to stay in the 1970s and 1980s. Now rooms look rather old-fashioned, but on the upper floors they offer sweeping views. Several restaurants.
A Alvorada, quadra 4, bloco A, T061-2195 1122, www.alvoradahotel.com.br. Another relic with simple, well-kept small rooms and good views from the roof terrace. Avoid the noisy streetside rooms on the lower floors.

Northern hotel zone
LL-L Kubitschek Plaza, quadra 2, bloco E, T061-3319 3543, www.plazabrasilia.com.br. Popular business hotel with modern rooms and excellent facilities. Broadband access in each room, pool, sauna and gym. The **Manhattan Plaza**, next door is similar and also run by the **Plaza** group (same website).
AL-A Aristus, quadra 2, bloco O, T061-3328 8675, www.aristushotel.com.br. Newly painted and delightfully dated 1970s block with simple a/c rooms and breakfast. Free Wi-Fi.
A Casablanca, quadra 3, bloco A, T061-3328 8586, www.casablancabrasilia.com.br.

A mock-Niemeyer block complete with modernist Gothic arches echoing the Palácio do Itamarati. Rooms are newly refurbished 1970s shells with fitted desks in light wood and smart marble bathrooms behind glass petitions. The best rooms are on the quieter north side. Free Wi-Fi.
B El Pilar, quadra 3, bloco F, T061-3328 5915, www.elpilar.com.br. Plain, well-kept fan-cooled and a/c rooms with tiled floors and en suites. Avoid those below street level as they collect car fumes.
C Bittar Inn, quadra 2, bloco N, T/F061-3328 7150, www.hoteisbittar.com.br. Simple rooms with a fan but good value for the area.

Other areas
LL-L Royal Tulip Alvorada, SHTN, Trecho 1, Conjunto 1B, Bloco C 70800 200, T061-3424 7000, www.royaltulipbrasiliaalvorada.com. This huge, brilliant red, horseshoe-shaped hotel designed by Unique Hotel (see page 205) architect Ruy Ohtake has a variety of luxurious suites and simpler doubles, catering mostly to visiting businessmen and politicians. Facilities include several swimming pools, tennis courts, spa, gym and sauna. The most interesting accommodation is in the upper-floor suites, which were refurbished recently with Niemeyer sketches, new carpets and fresh bedding. The restaurants are adequate but pricey, so eat elsewhere.
C-E Albergue Brasília, Setor Recreativo Parque Norte, quadra 2, T061-3343 0531, www.brasiliahostel.com.br (take bus 143 from the municipal bus station). A large HI hostel in a bright concrete building in a semi-rural area on the outskirts of the city. Modern, sparse but well-appointed a/c and fan-cooled doubles with en suites and dorms sit along corridors that are flooded with plenty of natural light. Staff are helpful and speak some English. Breakfast included.

🍴 Eating

Brasília *p682, maps p684 and p688*
The Southern Hotel Sector has more restaurants than the north. At weekends, few restaurants in central Brasília are open. There is plenty of choice in all price brackets in the **Pier 21** entertainment mall on the lakeshore. Other cheaper options are along R 405/406.

Snack bars serving *prato feito* or *comercial* (cheap set meals) can be found all over the city, especially on **Av W3** and in the **Setor Comercial Sul**. Other good bets are the **Conjunto Nacional** and the **Conjunto Venâncio**, 2 shopping/office complexes on either side of the municipal *rodoviária*. Tropical fruit flavour ice cream can be found in various parlours, eg **Av W3 Norte 302**. Freshly made fruit juices are available in all bars.

Asa Sul

There are good mid-range options on and around Av Anhaguera between Tocantins and Goiás; but by far the best choice is on and around **Praça Tamandaré** and **Av República Líbano**. For cheap bars/restaurants, try around Praça Tamandaré and on R 68 in the centre. There are many cheap places on **Av W3 Sul**, eg at **Blocos 502 and 506**.

Kosui, SCES, Trecho 4, lote 1B, Academia de Tênis, T061-3316 6900. The best of the city's Japanese food, from Tokyo-born chef Ryozo Koniya. Great Japanese banquet.

La Chaumière, Av W3 Sul, quadra 408, bloco A, loja 13, T061-3244 3875, lunch only on Sun. The city's favourite French cuisine in classical surroundings.

Le Français, Av W3 Sul, quadra 404, bloco B, loja 27, T061-3225 4583. French food served in bistro atmosphere, classic and modern dishes, 40-bottle wine list.

O Convento, SHIS, QI 9, conjunto 9, casa 4, T061-3248 1211, www.oconvento.com.br. The best for regional and Brazilian cuisine in a mock-farmhouse dining room decorated with antiques and arts and crafts.

Piantella, SCLS 202, bloco A, loja 34, T061-3224 9408, www.piantella.com.br. A favourite

of senior politicians for decades and is a good place to watch power lunches in action. The vast menu combines *feijoada*, Italian food, steaks and seafood. The wine list is excellent.

Porção, Sector de Clubes Sul, Trecho 2, cj 35, rest 3, T061-3223 2002, www.porcao.com.br. Upmarket chain restaurant specializing in *churrasco*, piano bar, large veranda.

O Espanhol, Av W3 Sul, quadra 404, bloco C, loja 07, T061-3224 2002. Open daily. Host to the city's annual Spanish festival and serving respectable seafood.

Oca da Tribo, SCES Trecho 2, opposite Agepol, T061-3226 9880, www.ocadatribo.com.br. A wholefood restaurant in a mock-indigenous communal house decorated with artefacts from the Xingu. Plenty of vegetarian options and others by Dutch Cordon Bleu chef Gabriel Fleijsman and a good lunch buffet.

Vercelli, SCLS 410, bloco D, loja 34, T061-3443 0100, www.vercelli.com.br. Lunch only. Pizzas, pastas and lots more on a huge menu.

Naturama, SCLS 102, bloco B, loja 9, T061-3225 5125. Vegetarian and wholefood dishes. Lunchtime only.

Asa Norte

All of the large hotels in this area have upmarket restaurants.

Trattoria da Rosario, SHIS QI 17, bloco H, Loja 215, Lago Sul, Fashion Park, T061-3248 1672. Closed Mon, lunch only on Sun. Northern Italian food from chef Rosario Tessier. Excellent Uruguayan lamb.

Universal Diner, SCLS 210, bloco B, loja 30, T061-3443 2089, www.universaldiner.com.br. Lunch only on Sun. One of the city's best contemporary restaurants with strong Asian influences from New York-trained chef Mara Alcamim who also runs Zuu aZdZ.

Zuu aZdZ, 210 Sul, Bloco C, Loja 38, T061-3244 1039, www.zuuazdz.com.br. Mara Alcamim's chic, glass-sided restaurant is always busy. Beautifully presented dishes from the menu of Brazilian-Asian molecular gastronomy. There are lots of meat and chicken options, and daring side dishes like chantilly cream infused with hot wasabi.

Boa Saúde, Av W3 Norte, quadra 702, edif Brasília Rádio Center. Sun-Fri 0800-2000. Respectable vegetarian with a range of salads, quiches and pies.

Bom Demais, Av W3 Norte, quadra 706. Comfortable, serving fish, beef and rice, live music at weekends (cover charge US$0.50).

Conjunto Nacional, SDN, Cj A. Enormous mall and food court with 50 restaurants.

Beyond the central areas

Alice, SHIS QI 17 Comércio Local, Lago Sul, T061-3248 7743, www.restaurantealice. com.br. This homely restaurant offers French home cooking in a faux-Provencale dining room in Brasília's plushest neighbourhood, Lago Sul, around 8 km from the city centre. It has been voted the best restaurant in Brasília by *Veja* magazine innumerable times. Excellent wine list.

Aquavit, Mansões do Lago Norte, ML 12, conjunto 01, casa 05, T061-3369 2301, www.restauranteaquavit.com. Opened in 2005 just a few doors from Patu Anu and run by Danish architect-turned-chef Simon Lau Cederholm. The location is stunning – the dining room is a glass-walled and floored rectangle suspended over a tropical garden and with the same marvellous views as Pat Anu. The dinner to get is the Babette's Feast Banquet – an ingredient-by-ingredient reproduction of the meal in Gabriel Axel's Academy Award-winning film, from (sustainably sourced) turtle soup to roast quail.

Patu Anu, Brasília's best restaurant is tucked away in the forest and offers sweeping views of the city. The kitchen is run by Argentine star chef, Lucas Fernandes Arteaga, who learnt his tricks at the Michelin 3-star **Martín Berasategui** in San Sebastian. His Franco-Latin American *degustation*-only menu includes dishes like grilled caiman with *pupunha* berry and coconut, and duck in tucupi sauce with crispy *farofa* (manioc flour) and *mandioquinha* (a Brazilian root vegetable like a large salsify).

Bars and clubs

Brasília *p682, maps p684 and p688*
Arena Café, CA 7, bloco F1, loja 33, T061-3468 1141, www.cafearena.hpg.com.br. Popular gay bar with DJs from Thu to Sat.
Bar Brasília, SHC/S CR, quadra 506, bloco A, loja 15, parte A, T061-3443 4323. Little *boteco* with 1950s decor, draught beer and wooden tables. Lively after 1900, especially on Fri.
Bier Fass, SHIS, quadra 5, bloco E, loja 52/53, T061-3248 1519, www.bierfass.com.br. Cavernous bar/restaurant with live music Tue-Sun and 20/30s crowd. Happy hour from 1800.
Café Cancún, Shopping Liberty Mall, SCN, Quadra 3, bloco D, loja 52, T061-3327 1566, www.cafecancun.com.br. Tacky Mexican restaurant by day, 20-something beautiful people club after dark.
Clube de Choro, SDC, quadra 3, bloco G, T061-3327 0494, www.clubedechoro.com.br. (Wed-Sat). One of the best clubs in the country devoted to the music that gave rise to samba. Top names from the city and all over Brazil. Great atmosphere. Tickets sold 9 days in advance.
Frei Caneca, Brasília Shopping, SCN, quadra 5, bloco A, lojas 82s/94s, T061-3327 0202. Similar to *Café Cancún*. Dreadful 'flashback' night on Thu. Most interesting at weekends.
Gates Pub, Av W3 Sul 403, T061-3225 4576, www.gatespub.com.br. Great for *forró* dancing and live music with a young middle-class crowd.
UK Brasil Pub, SCLS 411, bloco B, loja 28, T061-3346 5214. Some of the best live bands in the city play here to a crowd of all ages. Guinness, sandwiches.

Entertainment

Brasília *p682, maps p684 and p688*
Entertainment listings are available in 2 daily papers, *Jornal de Brasília* and

Correio Brasiliense. Any student card (provided it has a photograph) will get you a 50% discount at the cinema/theatre/concert hall. Ask for *'uma meia'* at the box office.

Cinema

There are 15 cinemas in the Plano Piloto. For programme details call T139. Tickets are half price on Wed.
Pier 21, SCCS, Trecho 2, Cj 32/33. An enormous complex with 13 cinema screens, nightclubs, restaurants, video bars and children's theme park.

Live music

Concerts are given at the **Escola Parque**, quadras 507-508 Sul; the **Ginásio Presidente Médici**, Eixo Monumental, near TV tower; the **Escola de Música**, Av L2 Sul, quadra 602; and the outdoor **Concha Acústica**, at the edge of the lake in the northern hotel zone.

Other

Planetarium, Setor de Divulgação Cultural, T061-325 6245, next to the TV tower. Re-opened in early 2008.

Theatre

Teatro Nacional, Setor Cultural Norte, Via N 2, next to the bus station, T061-3325 6109, foyer open 0900-2000, box office opens at 1400. There are 3 auditoria: the **Sala Villa-Lobos** (1300 seats), the **Sala Martins Pena** (450), and the **Sala Padre José Maurício** (120).
   The Federal District authorities have 2 theatres, the **Galpão** and **Galpãozinho**, between Quadra 308 Sul and Av W3 Sul.

⊛ Festivals and events

Brasília *p682, maps p684 and p688*
Feb Ash Wednesday.
Apr Maundy Thursday (half-day).
8 Dec Immaculate Conception.
24 Dec Christmas Eve.

○ Shopping

Brasília *p682, maps p684 and p688*
Books
Good selection of English books at **Livraria Sodiler** in Conjunto Nacional and at the airport.

Handicrafts

For handicrafts from all the Brazilian states try **Galeria dos Estados** (which runs underneath the *eixo* from Setor Comercial Sul to Setor Bancário Sul, 10 mins' walk from the municipal *rodoviária*, south along Eixo Rodoviário Sul). For Amerindian handicrafts, **Artíndia** SRTVS, quadra 702, also in the *rodoviária* and at the airport. There is a **feira hippy** at the base of the TV tower at weekends and holidays selling leather goods, woodcarvings, jewellery and bronzes.

Jewellery

H Stern, branches in the **Nacional** and Carlton hotels and at the **Conjunto Nacional** and **Parkshopping**. Fine jewellery.

Shopping centres

The best shopping centres are **Shopping Brasília** below the southern hotel zone and **Patio Brasília** below the northern hotel zone. Both have a wide range of boutiques and fast food restaurants. Others include the vast **Conjunto Nacional** on the north side of the *rodoviária*; the **Conjunto Venâncio** on the south side; the **Centro Venâncio 2000** at the beginning of Av W3 Sul; the **Centro Venâncio 3000** in the Setor Comercial Norte; **Park-shopping** and the **Carrefour** hypermarket just off the exit to Guará, 12 km from the centre.

▲ Activities and tours

Brasília *p682, maps p684 and p688*
Tour operators
Many tour operators have their offices in the shopping arcade of the **Hotel Nacional**. 3- to 4-hr city tours with English commentary can be booked on arrival at the airport –

a convenient way of getting to your hotel if you have heavy baggage.

However, we have received criticism that some tours are too short or that the guides speak poor English. For night-time tours, the floodlighting is inadequate on many buildings. **3 Turismo**, SCLS 402, bloco A, lojas 27/33, Asa Sul, T061-225 2686, www.burititurismo.com.br. Tours around the city and Goiás and American Express representative.

Presmic Turismo, SHS Q 1, bloco A, loja, 35, T061-3233 0115, www.presmic.com.br. Full-day, half-day and night-time city tours (at 0845, 1400 and 1930 respectively).

⊖ Transport

Brasília *p682, maps p684 and p688*
Air
To get the airport take bus Nos 102 from the municipal bus station, 30 mins US\$1.50. Brasília airport has connections with most major cities in Brazil and a number of international destinations. **TAP**, www.flytap.com, has flights to **Lisbon**.

Airline offices BRA, SHS quadra 1, bloco A, loja 71/72, in front of Hotel Nacional, and in Shopping Flamingo and Shopping Sia, T061-2105 0909, www.voebra.com.br. GOL, airport, T061-3364 9370, premium rate number, T0300-789 2121, www.voegol.com.br. Oceanair, T0300-789 8160, www.oceanair.com.br. Passaredo, www.voepassaredo.com.br. Sete, www.voesete.com.br. TAM/Brasil Central, SHN Hotel Nacional, Gallery Store, 36/37, T061-3325 1300; airport, T061-3365 1000, www.tam.com.br. TOTAL, www.total.com.br. Webjet, www.webjet.com.br.

Bus
Local bus No 131 goes from the municipal bus station at the junction of the Eixo monumental and Av W3, to the *rodoferroviária*. All major destinations served. Bus tickets for major companies are sold in a subsidiary office in Taguatinga, Centro Oeste, C8, lotes 1 and 2, loja 1; and at the city *rodoviária*.

To **Rio**, 17 hrs, 6 *comuns* daily (US\$60) and 3 *leitos* (about US\$100). To **São Paulo**, 16 hrs, 7 *comuns* (about US\$60) and 2 *leitos* (about US\$90) daily (**Rápido Federal** recommended). To **Goiânia**, numerous daily. Change in Goiânia for **Cidade de Goiás**. To **Pirenópolis**, 2 daily; the quickest in the morning. To **Palmas**, 2 daily, best in the afternoon; via **Alto Paraíso** in the Chapada dos Veadeiros. To **Belo Horizonte**, 12 hrs, 9 *comuns* (US\$60) and 2 *leitos* (US\$90) daily. To **Belém**, 36 hrs, 4 daily (US\$85, **Trans Brasília**, T061-3233 7589), buses are poorly maintained, but no alternative. To **Recife**, 40 hrs (US\$100). To **Salvador**, 24 hrs, 3 daily (US\$100). To **Campo Grande**, **São Luís**, 15 hrs, 1915, US\$120, or **Viação Motta** via São Paulo 0930, 1930, or 1820 direct. To **Corumbá**, US\$90. To **Cuiabá**, 17½ hrs (US\$80) daily at 1200 with São Luís. **Mato Grosso**, generally Goiânia seems to be the better place for Mato Grosso destinations. **Barra do Garças**, 0830 and 2000, takes 9 hrs with **Araguarina**, T061-3233 7598, US\$60 return.

Car hire
All large companies are represented at the airport. **Avis**, T/F061-3365 2780. **Interlocadora**, T061-3365 2511 and **Localiza**, Setor Locadoras, T0800-992000. **Unidas**, T061-3365 1412.

⊕ Directory

Brasília *p682, maps p684 and p688*
Banks Foreign currency can be exchanged at branches of **Banco Regional de Brasília** and **Banco do Brasil**, Setor Bancário Sul, latter also at airport, US\$20 commission for TCs. **American Express**, Buriti Turismo, CLS 402 bloco A, lojas 27/33, T061-3225 2686. **Diners Club**, Av W3 Norte 502. **MasterCard**, for cash against a card, SCRN 502, bloco B, lojas 30 e 31, Asa Norte. Good exchange rates at **Hotel Nacional** and from hotels with 'exchange-turismo' sign. **HSBC**, SCRS 502, bloco A, lojas 7/12, ATM. **Cultural centres** Aliança

Francesca, Sul Entrequadra 707-907, bloco A, T061-3242 7500. **American Library**, Casa Thomas Jefferson, Av W4 Sul, quadra 706, T061-3243 6588. **British Council**, Setor C Sul, quadra 01, bloco H, 8th floor, Morro Vermelho building, T061-3323 6080. **Cultura Inglesa**, SEPS 709/908 Conj B, T061-3243 3065. Instituto Cultural Goethe, Edif Dom Bosco, Setor Garagem Sul 902, lote 73, bloco C, T061-3224 6773. Mon-Fri, 0800-1200, also Mon, Wed, Thu 1600-2000. **Embassies and consulates** Australia, Caixa Postal 11-1256, SHIS QI-09, Conj 16, Casa 1, T061-3248 5569. Austria, SES, Av das Nações 40, T061-3243 3111. Canada, SES, Av das Nações 16, T061-3321 2171. Denmark, Av das Nações 26, T061-34438 188 (0900-1200, 1400-1700). Germany, SES, Av das Nações 25, T061-3443 7330. Guyana, SDS, Edif Venâncio III, 4th floor, sala 410/404, T061-3224 9229. Netherlands, SES, Av das Nações 5, T061-

3321 4769. **South Africa**, SES, Av das Nações, lote 06, T061-3312 9503. **Sweden**, Av das Nações 29, Caixa Postal 07-0419, T061-3243 1444. **Switzerland**, SES, Av das Nações 41, T061-3443 5500. **UK**, SES, quadra 801, Conjunto K, or Av das Nações, Caixa Postal 070586, T061-3225 2710. **USA**, SES, Av das Nações 3, T061-3321 7272. **Venezuela**, SES, Av das Nações 13, T061-223 9325. **Internet** Café.Com.Tato, CLS 505, bloco C, loja 17, Asa Sul, open daily. Liverpool Coffee Shop, CLS 108, R da Igreijinha. **Laundry** Lavanderia Laundromat, CLN 104, bloco C, loja 106, Asa Norte. Self-service. **Post office** Poste restante, Central Correio, 70001; SBN-Cj 03, BL-A, Edif Sede da ECT, the central office is in the Setor Hoteleiro Sul, between hotels Nacional and St Paul. Also at Ed Brasília Rádio, Av 3 Norte.

Goiás

With an area of 364,714 sq km and some 4 million inhabitants, Goiás is one of Brazil's most rapidly developing frontier agricultural areas. The land is used for producing coffee, soya and rice, most of Brazil's tin and tungsten, and for raising beef on some of the country's largest cattle ranches. ▶▶ *For listings, see pages 701-707.*

Goiânia → *For listings, see pages 701-707. Colour map 3, B5. Phone code: 062. Population: 1.1 million.*

Just off the BR-060, 209 km southwest of Brasília, is the second of Brazil's planned state capitals, after Belo Horizonte. Goiânia was founded in 1933 and replaced Goiás Velho as capital four years later. The city is famous for its street cafés and is a good place to stop between Brasília and the rest of the interior. Tourism is not as developed here as in other parts of the country, but the city is pleasant and there are some interesting sights within easy reach. Goiânia is spacious with more parks and gardens than any other of Brazil's large cities and many are filled with interesting forest and *cerrado* plants, as well as marmosets and remarkably large numbers of birds.

Ins and outs
Getting there Santa Genoveva airport ① *R Capitão Frazão s/n, T062-3265 1500, 8 km from the centre off R 57,* receives flights from several of Brazil's main cities. There are several car hire firms at the airport. A taxi to the centre costs US$10. Buses arrive at the **rodoviária** ① *R 44, No 399 in the Norte Ferroviário sector, T062-3224 8466.* Buses to the centre 'Rodoviária-Centro' (No 404) and 'Vila União-Centro' (No 163) leave from the stop on the city side of the terminal, US$1.50; No 163 goes on to the Praça Tamandaré.

Tourist information **AGETUR** ⓘ *R 30 at R 4, Centro de Convenções, 2ª Andar, T062-3201 8122, www.goiasbrasil.com.br.* Useful websites include www.goias.gov.br.

Sights

The centre of the city is **Praça Cívica**, with well-lit main avenues radiating out in all directions. On the *praça* stand the government palace, the main post office and the **Museu Zoroastro Artiaga** ⓘ *Praça Cívica 13, T062-3201 4676.* The museum has a small but interesting collection of historical objects, fossils and religious items as well as cases

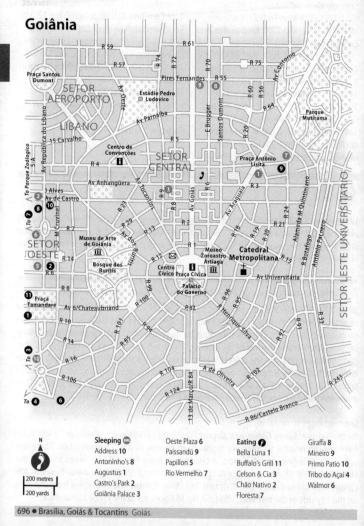

Goiânia

Sleeping 🛏		Eating 🍴	
Address **10**	Oeste Plaza **6**	Bella Luna **1**	Giraffa **8**
Antoninho's **8**	Paissandú **9**	Buffalo's Grill **11**	Mineiro **9**
Augustus **1**	Papillon **5**	Celson & Cia **3**	Primo Patio **10**
Castro's Park **2**	Rio Vermelho **7**	Chão Nativo **2**	Tribo do Açai **4**
Goiânia Palace **3**		Floresta **7**	Walmor **6**

depicting indigenous and early settler life in Goiás. The museum was twice the size before it was cherry-picked by local politicians for their private collections.

From the *praça*, Avenida Araguaia runs northeast to the shady **Parque Mutirama**, with recreational facilities and a **planetarium** ① *Sun 1530 and 1630*.

More tranquil is the **Bosque dos Buritis** ① *1 km west of Praça Cívica along R 10*, which has shaded walks in *buriti*-filled tropical gardens and a turtle-filled pond. In the gardens of the Bosque dos Buritis is the **Museu de Arte de Goiânia** ① *R 1 605, T062-524 1190, Mon-Fri 0800-1700, Sat 0800-1300, free*, which showcases the work of a number of local artists including Siron Franco, who is nationally renowned. The **Parque Zoológico** ① *Av Anhangüera, Tue-Sun 0700-1800*, 1 km west of the **Castro's Park** hotel is set in large gardens and is a good place to while away an afternoon.

A kilometre east of Praça Cívica, the **Museu Antropológico do UFG** ① *Praça Universitária, Mon-Fri 0900-1700*, houses wide-ranging ethnographic displays on the indigenous peoples of the Centre West.

The **Casa do Índio** ① *Av Jamel Cecílio 2000, Pedro Iudovico*, is a centre for indigenous arts and craft production and an important meeting place for indigenous peoples such as the Xavantes. The shop there sells a variety of handicrafts.

The **Memorial do Cerrado Museum** ① *Av Bela Vista, Km 2, Jd Olímpico, T062- 562 4141, Mon-Sat 0800-2200, Sun 0800-1800, US$2*, just outside the city towards Cidade de Goiás, provides an interesting introduction to *cerrado* life, with reconstructions of indigenous villages, *quilombos* and colonial streets as well as planted *cerrado* vegetation.

Cidade de Goiás (Goiás Velho) → *For listings, see pages 701-707. Colour map 3, A5.*
Phone code: 062. Population: 30,000.

This delightful town, nestled in the midst of *cerrado*-covered ridges, is one of central Brazil's hidden beauties. Cobbled streets lined with colourful yellow and blue Portuguese buildings gather around a little river watched over by a collection of elegantly simple baroque churches. Horses and old VWs clatter along the heavy stone flags and the local residents go about their day-to-day business as they always have done, treating visitors like guests or curiosities rather than tourists.

The town was founded in 1727 as Vila Boa and, like its Minas counterparts, became rich on gold, before becoming the capital of Goiás state, which it remained until just before the Second World War. But while towns like Ouro Preto and Tiradentes lavished their churches in gilt, Goiás chose modesty, erecting simple façades whose more classical lines stand strong against the intense blue of the sky. Interiors, too, were plain with simple panelling that beautifully offset both the richly painted wooden ceilings and the virtuoso sculpture of the *Goiás Aleijadinho* by Veiga Valle.

Ins and outs
Cidade de Goiás is well connected by bus with Goiânia, 130 km away, but there are few services from anywhere else. The **rodoviária** ① *Av Dario da Paiva, Bairro João Francisco*, is 2 km out of town. All buses also stop at the *rodoviária velha* (old bus station) next to the Mercado Municipal, 500 m west of the central Praça do Coreto. The **tourist office** ① *Praça da Bandeira, T062-3371 1996, daily 0900-1700*, is housed in the Quartel do Vinte, a former barracks where many of the German soldiers who fought in the Paraguayan war were housed. The Museu Casa de Cora Coralina is a better source of information.

Sights

The most interesting streets in the colonial part of town spread out from the two principal *praças*: **Praça Brasil Caiado** and immediately below it towards the river **Praça do Coreto**. The former is dominated by the Chafariz de Cauda, a lavish baroque fountain, which once supplied all the town's water. The best of the churches and museums are in the small cobbled town centre that radiates out from the two central plazas and spreads a little way along the riverbank. It is easily navigable on foot. The oldest church, **São Francisco de Paula** ① *Praça Zacheu Alves de Castro*, built in 1763, sits on a platform overlooking the market and the Rio Vermelho. It has a beautiful 19th-century painted ceiling by André Antônio da Conceição, depicting the life of St Francis de Paula. **Nossa Senhora da Abadia** ① *R Abadia s/n*, has a similarly understated but impressive painted ceiling, while the other 18th-century churches like **Nossa Senhora do Carmo** ① *R do Carmo*, on the riverside, and **Santa Bárbara** ① *R Passo da Pátria*, are almost Protestant in their simplicity. The latter sits on a hill a kilometre or so east of the town from where there are wonderful sunset views.

Cidade de Goiás has some interesting museums. The **Museu das Bandeiras** ① *Praça Brasil Caiado/Largo do Chafariz, T062-3371 1087, Tue-Fri 0900-1700, Sat 1200-1700, Sun 0900-1300, US$1*, was once the centre of local government. The museum tells the story of the Goiás Bandeira exhibitions, which sit over a small but forbidding dungeon. The former governor's palace, the **Palácio Conde dos Arcos** ① *Praça do Coreto, T062-3371 1200, Tue-Sat 0800-1700, Sun 0900-1300, US$1*, sits in the square below Praça Brasil Caiado and was the governor's palace before the state capital moved to Goiânia. It has a display of 19th-century furniture, portraits of all the governors, and a pretty little walled garden. Across the way the **Museu de Artes Sacras** ① *Praça do Coreto, T062-3371 1207, Tue-Sat 0800-1700, Sun 0900-1300, US$1*, houses some clunky 18th-century church silverware and a series of painted wooden statues by one of Brazil's most important religious sculptors, José Joaquim da Veiga Valle. Veiga Valle was entirely self taught and had little knowledge or access to the Latin American baroque style that he was later seen to represent. Look out for the double 'V' signatures in the patterns of the fingers and the uncannily realistic stained-glass eyes.

From Praça do Coreto, a stroll downhill and across the river, will bring you to the **Museu Casa de Cora Coralina** ① *R do Candido 20, T062-3371 1990, Tue-Sun 0900-1700, US$1*, the former home of Goiás's most respected writer, with a collection of her belongings and a beautifully kept riverside garden at the back. Staff here are extremely helpful and knowledgeable about the city, though they speak no English. The 18th-century **Mercado Municipal**, next to the old *rodoviária*, is a wonderful spot for a snack and photography. All manner of interesting characters gather here and the small stall shops sell everything from shanks of beef to Catholic kitsch. **Espaço Cultural Goiandira do Couto** ① *R Joaquim Bonifacio 19, T062-3371 1303, Tue-Sun 0900-1700, US$1*, has chocolate box-style paintings of the city made entirely from different coloured sands from the surrounding *serra*. The artist, now in her 90s, has exhibited all over the world.

Pirenópolis → *For listings, see pages 701-707. Colour map 3, A/B5. Phone code: 062.*
Population: 23,000. Altitude: 770 m.

This lovely colonial silver mining town, 165 km due west of Brasília, sits in the midst of rugged hills dripping with waterfalls and covered in rapidly disappearing but still pristine *cerrado*. Like Cidade de Goiás it was founded by *bandeirantes* in search of gold and then by small-scale cattle ranchers. Its centre remains well preserved and only a little less pretty than Cidade de Goiás, leading it to be declared a National Heritage Site in 1989. Pirenópolis's proximity to Brasília has made it a favourite weekend playground for the capital's middle classes who congregate in the lively restaurants and bars, which line the northern end of Rua do Rosario. But the town's home-grown culture still thrives; one of Central Brazil's most unusual and vibrant festival takes place here every May/June (see Festivals and events, page 706) and on weekends the Praça Central fills to the brim with *peões* in stetsons and spurs blasting out *sertanejo* music from their souped-up cars. Pirenópolis is a great place to pass a few days or even weeks. The surrounding countryside offers good walking and light adventure activities and there are plenty of tour operators, though as elsewhere in Brazil, little English is spoken.

Ins and outs

The bus station is in the centre of town. Pirenópolis is served by two buses a day from Brasília. Tourist information is available at the **Centro de Atendimento ao Turista** ① *R do Bonfim, Centro Histórico, T062-3331 2729*, but they don't speak much English.

Sights

The **Igreja Matriz Nossa Senhora do Rosário** has undergone restoration after being gutted by a fire in 2002. It is the oldest church in the state, dating from 1728, and before the fire had one of the most magnificent painted interiors in Goiás; sadly unrestored. **Nosso Senhor do Bonfim** (1750-1754), which houses an impressive life-size crucifix from Bahia, was transported here on the backs of 260 slaves. The more subtly beautiful image of Our Lady is Portuguese. The church of **Nossa Senhora do Carmo** ① *daily 1300-1700*, serves as a museum of religious art. Another, the **Museu Família Pompeu** ① *R Nova 33, Tue-Fri 1300-1700, Sat 1300-1500, Sun 0900-1200*, displays regional historical items and documents. The tiny, privately owned **Museu das Cavalhadas** ① *R Direita 37, Fri and Sat 0800-1700, US$1*, has a collection of masks, photographs and costumes from the Festa do Divino. **Fazenda Babilônia** ① *25 km southwest, no public transport, Sat and Sun 0800-1700, US$2*, is a fine example of an 18th-century sugar *fazenda*. It's now a small museum with the original mill and a lovely little chapel.

Around Pirenópolis

The *cerrado* and hills around the town have so far managed to resist the onslaught of soya and there are still opportunities to get out into the midst of some genuine wild country. There are plenty of walks and adventure activities on offer, birdwatching is good and there is a reasonably healthy population of maned wolf and various South American cats, including jaguar. The landscape is rugged, with many waterfalls and canyons. Guides are essential as many of the attractions are well off the beaten track.

Santuário de Vida Silvestre Vagafogo ① *T062-3335 8490, www.vagafogo.com.br, visits through Padilha or Savannah Tur (see Activities and tours, page 706)*, is the labour of love of Evandro Engel Ayer, who bought an area of the *cerrado* intending to start a farm. After falling in love with the plants and animals living here he instead decided to create a wildlife reserve. There is good birdwatching, with various rare species, a species list and a library. Mammals seen here include ocelot, brown capuchin and a rare subspecies of tufted-eared marmoset. Evandro is helpful and knowledgeable, speaks good English and serves one of the best lunches in Goiás.

The **Mosteiro Buddhisto** ① *information through Padilha, see Activities and tours, page 706*, is a simple Zen monastery near a series of beautiful waterfalls in the heart of pristine *cerrado* forest. Day visits can be arranged that involve light walks or longer term retreats. This is particularly magical at sunset.

Chapada dos Veadeiros → *For listings, see pages 701-707. Colour map 3, A6.*

ⓘ *Entry only with a guide. The park is reached by paved state highway BR-118. Tours can be arranged from Alto Paraíso de Goiás or São Jorge, see below.*

These table-top mountains, drained by countless fast-flowing rivers that rush through deep gorges and plummet over spectacular waterfalls, are less famous than Diamantina or Guimarães, but are less spoilt and more subtly beautiful. The national park, which protects only a fraction of their area, is almost twice the size of Diamantina and eight times the size of Guimarães. And unlike both those areas, its forests have never been felled. It was designated as a UNESCO World Heritage Site in 2001. At present trips within the park itself are limited to day visits only; but there are plans to change this. Walks of up to nine days can be easily organized at a good price within the wilderness areas in the park's environs, together with a range of adventure activities from canyoning to rappelling. There is plenty of accommodation in Alto Paraíso and São Jorge and transport to and from Brasília is straightforward.

Like most of wild Goiás, the Chapada is covered in *cerrado* forest – a habitat of such floral diversity that it has recently been declared a biological hot-spot by **Conservation International**. Rare mammals including jaguar, maned wolf, puma, tapir, ocelot and giant anteater are abundant and, although no one has yet compiled a serious bird list, spectaculars and rarities include red-shouldered macaw, coal-crested finch, helmeted manakin and various key indicator species like rusty-margined guan and bare-face currasow; king vultures are abundant.

There are numerous waterfalls and beauty spots both within and outside the park. The **Cânions do Rio Preto** are steep gorges cut from the ancient sandstone of the Brazilian shield by the Rio Preto. They terminate in the park's most spectacular waterfalls, the **Saltos do Rio Preto**, which fall in two strands into a deep pool surrounded by pristine cerrado. The two-tier **Cachoeira Almeçegas** drop over 80 m into deep plunge pools which are good for swimming. Access is along a tortuous trail. The Rio Raizama plunges over the **Salto do Rio Raizama** after cutting through a narrow canyon lined by bromeliads and mosses. It is possible to clamber upriver over giant boulders. The **Cachoeira Morada do Sol** is a smaller waterfall, dropping just 5 m into a series of shallow pools surrounded by pretty forest. The **Macaco and Macaquinho** falls sit in large private reserve run by a local character intent on preserving his land from the onset of soya. They are popular with abseiling groups. There are many trails from the falls into the surrounding cerrado woodland. The **Vale da Lua** is a popular beauty spot outside the park. It is a shallow canyon whose rocks have been sculpted into organic shapes by the rushing São Miguel river. The late-afternoon light here is particularly beautiful.

Alto Paraíso and São Jorge → *Colour map 3, A6.*

The ramshackle town of **Alto Paraíso de Goiás** is filled with crystal shops and has become famous over the years as a centre for alternative therapies. Judging only by appearance many of these seem superficial. But there are some serious practitioners here doing excellent work, and at a fraction of the price of those in other parts of the world. The town is connected to Brasília and the rest of Goiás state by the paved state highway BR-118. There are bus connections to Brasília and to Palmas in Tocantins. Alto

Paraíso is the best point to stock up on provisions before a trek in the Chapada dos Veadeiros and has the best of the tour operators and hotels. Access to the eastern attractions like the Vale de Lua are only really possible from Alto Paraíso. There is a small **tourist booth** on the main street (no English).

The tiny village of **São Jorge** is 40 km from Alto Paraíso on a partly paved road. With its three dirt streets, it is smaller and prettier than Alto Paraíso but has fewer restaurants and tour services. Several buses run daily between Alto Paraíso and São Jorge. The town lies only 1 km from the park entrance itself but the guides are less professional.

Southwest Goiás state → *For listings, see pages 701-707.*

Serranópolis → *Colour map 3, B4.*

This little town is close to some remnant *cerrado* forest that clings to a series of small table-top mountains in the flat sea of soya, which is gradually taking over Goiás. Important cave paintings have been found here; these are now carefully protected and can be reached via a series of well-maintained trails. There are a few simple hotels in town and two excellent forest *pousadas*, which are carefully designed, wonderfully peaceful and great for birdwatching or just relaxing.

Parque Nacional das Emas → *Colour map 3, B4.*

This 133,000-ha park, protecting low *campo sujo cerrado* forests, black water rivers and savannah is Goiás's third UNESCO World Heritage Site – the others being Chapada dos Veadeiros and Cidade de Goiás. The park protects large populations of maned wolf, puma and jaguar as well as many rare *cerrado* bird species. These include red-shouldered and blue-winged macaw, greater rhea, bare-face currasow and diverse tyrant flycatchers and woodpeckers, as well as several species of macaw. It is a favourite destination for wildlife documentary film crews.

Ins and outs The most convenient base for visiting the park is **Chapadão do Céu**, www.chapadaodoceu.go.gov.br, about 30 minutes to the east. This newly created soya town has some decent hotels and tour operators to take visitors to the park. Four-day, three-night visits to the park can be arranged through agencies and tour operators such as **Padilha** in Pirenópolis, www.padilhaecoturismo.pirenopolis.tur.br or Savannah Tur (see page 706), the **Pantanal Bird Club** in Cuiabá (see page 758), or **Focus Tours** (see page 52).

◉ Goiás listings

For Sleeping and Eating price codes and other relevant information, see pages 32-37.

◒ Sleeping

Goiânia *p695, map p696*
The best hotels are 1 km from the centre in the Setor Oeste with restaurants and bars. Hotels in the centre are frayed 1970s blocks.
L Castro's Park, Av República do Líbano 1520, Setor Oeste, T062-3212 4428,

www.castrospark.com.br. A 5-star hotel in a tower a few blocks from the centre, with gym and swimming pool.
L-A Address Hotel, Av República do Líbano, 2526, Setor Oeste T062-3257 1000, www.addresshotel.com.br. The best hotel in the city with good promotional rates. Modern suites with comfortable beds; the best with separate living areas and good views. Excellent business facilities. Plenty of restaurants and bars nearby.

AL-A Papillon, Av República do Líbano 1824, T062-3219 1500, www.papillonhotel.com.br. A tower in the new centre with modern tiled rooms and suites, a pool, gym, sauna, business facilities and 24-hr room service. Very popular, book ahead.

B Oeste Plaza, R 2 No 389 Setor Oeste, T062-3224 5012, www.oesteplaza.com.br. Well-maintained modern tower with small a/c rooms with tiled floors and en suites. Those on the higher floors have good views. Small pool and gym.

C Augustus, Praça Antônio Lisita 702, T062-3224 1022, www.augustushotel.com.br. Blocky B-grade 1970s business hotel with rather gloomy apartment rooms, a pool, sauna and gym. Conveniently located for the centre. Official rates are higher but not adhered to.

D Rio Vermelho, R 4 No 26, T062-3213 2555, www.hotelriovermelho.com.br. Simple hotel in a quiet street with lots of cheap restaurants. The cheapest rooms are fan cooled. With breakfast. Close to the centre.

D-F Goiânia Palace, Av Anhangüera 5195, T062-3224 4874, goiâniapalace@terra.com.br. Art-deco building with a range of rooms from simple fan-cooled doubles to suites. Good breakfast. Friendly and well located.

F Antoninho's, R 68 No 41, T062-3223 1815. Very basic but clean and well looked after. Only a few rooms have windows. Friendly, safe and with good breakfasts.

F Paissandú, Av Goiás 1290 at R 55, T062-3224 4925. Very simple fan-cooled or a/c rooms 8 blocks north of the centre. Breakfast.

Camping

Itanhangá municipal site, Av Princesa Carolina, Km 13, T062-292 1145. Attractive wooded location, reasonable facilities..

Cidade de Goiás *p697*

AL Fazenda Manduzanzan, on the road to Cachoeira das Andorinhas, 8 km, T062-9982 3373, www.manduzanzan.com.br. 10 apartments in the *cerrado* near the region's prettiest waterfalls. Sauna, horse riding, spring- water swimming pools. Lunch included in the price.

AL-B Vila Boa, Av Dr Deusdete Ferreira de Moura, 1 km southeast on the Morro do Chapéu do Padre, T062-3371 1000. The best option, but out of town and inconvenient for the centre. Pool, bar, restaurant and good views. The best rooms are the 4 suites.

B Casa da Ponte, R Moretti Foggia s/n, T062-3371 4467. An art deco building next to the bridge across the Rio Vermelho with small well-maintained a/c rooms with en suites and parquet flooring. The best overlook the river.

C-D Pousada do Ipê, R Cel Guedes de Amorim 22, T062-3371 2065. Cloisters of rooms gathered around a courtyard dominated by a huge mango tree. The annexe has a swimming pool and bar area. Breakfast is included.

C-D Pousada do Vovô Jura, R Sta Barbara 38, T062-3371 1746. A colonial house set in a little garden with views out over the river and *serra*.

D-E Pousada do Sol, R Americano do Brasil, T062-3371 1717. Well-maintained, plain, fan-cooled rooms with lino or wood floors.

E Pousada do Sonho, R 15 Novembro 22, T062-3372 1224. A simple, well-kept residential house with plain rooms with shared bathrooms. Good breakfast.

E Pousada Reis, R 15 Novembro 41, T062-3371 1565. A simple cheapie next to the *Sonho* offering similar rooms to **Pousada do Sonho** but shoddier service.

Camping

Attractive, well-run **Cachoeira Grande** campground, 7 km along the BR-070 to Jussara (near the tiny airport), with bathing place and snack bar. More basic site (**Chafariz da Carioca**) in town by the river.

Pirenópolis *p698*

There are plenty of rooms in town, but they fill up during Festa do Divino so book ahead or visit from Brasília (about a 90-min drive).

A Casa Grande, R Aurora 41, T062-3331 1758, www.casagrandepousada.com.br. A big old house near the centre decorated with colonial furniture and with chalet rooms in a small garden visited by many birds.

A O Casarão, R Direita 79, T062-3331 2662, www.ocasarao.pirenopolis.tur.br. A colonial home decorated with period furniture, there's a little pool set in heliconia-filled gardens. Rooms have 4-poster beds and mosquito nets.

B-C Do Arvoredo, R Direita s/n, T062-3331 3479, www.arvoredo.tur.br. Peaceful little *pousada* set in a little wood. Clean, modest fan-cooled rooms are set around a small pool and there are good rates on weekdays.

C Pouso do Sô Vigario, R Nova 25, T062-3331 1206, www.pousadaspirenopolis.com.br. Small rooms but pleasant public spaces with objets d'art and posters from European painting exhibitions. Good location. Decent breakfast in a little garden next to the pool.

E Rex, Praça da Matriz 15, T062-3331 1121. 5 rooms, all with fridge and TV, around a courtyard. Good breakfast and location.

Camping

Camping Roots, R dos Pireneus 96, T062-3331 2105, camproots@yahoo.com. Sites with electricity, hot showers and English-speaking staff. 10-min walk from the centre.

Alto Paraíso and São Jorge *p700*

Prices in São Jorge often go up at weekends.

AL Casa das Flores, T061-9976 0603, São Jorge, www.pousadacasadasflores.com.br. Elegant little *pousada* with tasteful rooms (lit only by candlelight), sauna, pool and great breakfast in the decent attached restaurant. The best in town, but overpriced.

A-B Camelot, on the main road just north of Alto Paraíso, T061-3446 1581, www.pousada camelot.com.br. Delightfully kitsch mock-Arthurian castle with proper hot showers and comfortable a/c rooms with satellite TV.

A-B Portal da Chapada, 9 km along the road from Alto Paraíso to São Jorge, T061-3446 1820, www.portaldachapada.com.br. The best choice for birdwatchers, with comfortable a/c wooden cabins in the midst of the *cerrado*.

B Casa Rosa, R Gumersindo 233, Alto Paraíso, T061-3446 1319, www.pousadacasarosa. com.br. The best in town with a range of

well-kept a/c rooms, the best are in chalets near the pool. Also known as 'As Cerejeiras'.

B Trilha Violeta, São Jorge, T061-3455 1088, www.trilhavioleta.com.br. Fan-cooled violet rooms with private bathrooms around a bougainvillea-filled garden. Reasonable restaurant. Friendly.

B-C Aquas de Março, São Jorge, T061-3347 2082, www.chapadadosveadeiros.com.br. Simple duplex rooms decorated with paintings by local artist, Moacir. Pleasant garden, saunas, *oforo* baths and decent breakfast.

D-E Pousada do Sol, R Gumersindo 2911, Alto Paraíso, T061-446 1201. Small and simple, with a range of rooms, the best with balconies and fridges.

E Casa Grande, São Jorge, T061-9623 5515, www.pousadacasagrande.com.br. Simple but well-kept rooms and a good breakfast.

Camping

Tattoo, at the top of São Jorge, tattoo@travessia.tur.br. Powered sites from only US$3. Decent wood-fired pizzas and a small bar. English spoken. Very friendly and helpful.

Serranópolis *p701*

A-B Aldeia Ecológica Guardiões do Cerrado, about 15 km south of Serranópolis at Km 70 off the BR-184, take a taxi from the town (about US$20). A magical forest *pousada* with a ring of beautifully appointed chalets all decorated individually, many with Xavantes indigenous art and tasteful photographs. Great food and walks and much wildlife. Currasows and maned wolf visit the camp for breakfast each morning.

A-B Araras, T064-3668 1054, www.pousada dasararas.com. Tasteful little chalets in an armadillo-filled garden next to a clear-water river with a natural swimming area. Trails lead to the various archaeological sites.

Parque Nacional das Emas *p701*

A Fazenda Santa Amélia, Estrada Serranópolis, Chapadão do Céu, T064-3634 1380. A working *fazenda* with a range of wildlife tours in the property's remnant *cerrado* forest (none in Emas except with special arrangement). Comfortable chalets, a pool and full board in the price.

D Paraná, Av Indiaiá, Chapadão do Céu, T064-3634 1227. Simple, clean and well run with fan-cooled rooms.

E Rafael, Av Indiaiá, Chapadão do Céu, T064-3634 1247. Very simple and clean with fan-cooled rooms and shared bathrooms.

⦿ Eating

Goiânia *p695, map p696*
Goiânian cooking is like that of Minas – lots of meat with huge portions of vegetable dishes and, of course, beans and rice. Local specialities include *arroz com piqui*, rice with a cruel *cerrado* fruit, a practical joke of evolution whose outer flesh is soft and sweet but if bitten leaves the mouth full of sharp spines that have to be surgically removed. Beware!

The city has a good range of restaurants and bars, especially around **Praça Tamandaré** and **Av República Líbano** in the Setor Oeste where there are options in all price brackets.

Pamonharías (street stands) sell *pamonha* snacks, tasty pastries made with green corn, sweet, savoury, or *picante* (spicy); all are served hot and have cheese in the middle, some include sausage.

⫟⫟⫟ Bella Luna, R 10 704, Praça Tamandaré, T062-3214 3562. Some of the best Italian food in Goiânia, including excellent pizza, pasta and northern Italian seafood dishes.

⫟⫟⫟ Celson & Cia, R 15 539 at C 22, T062-3215 3043, www.celsonecia.com.br. Very popular meat restaurant with a good cold buffet. Evenings only except at weekends.

⫟⫟⫟ Chão Nativo, Av República Líbano 1809 (opposite hotel **Papillon**), T062-3223 5396. The city's most famous Goiânian restaurant also serving local and Mineira food. Lively after 2000 and lunchtime on weekends.

⫟⫟ Tribo do Açai, R 36 590, T062-3281 6971. Buzzing little fruit juice bar with excellent buffet salads and health food. Just round the corner from **Shopping Bougainville**.

⫟⫟⫟ Walmor, R 3 1062 at R 25-B, T062-3215 5555, www.churrascariadowalmor.com.br. Large portions of excellent steaks served in an attractive open-air dining area.

⫟⫟-⫟ Floresta, R 2 at R 9, T062-3224 9560. Lively corner bar with grilled steaks, standard rice and beans dishes, and snacks. Open until late. Good draft lager.

⫟ Buffalo's Grill, Praça Tamandaré, T062-3215 3935. Pizzas, grilled meat and chicken, sandwiches and crêpes. Open 24 hrs.

⫟ Giraffa, Av República Líbano 1592, T062-3225 1969. Fast food joint with some sumptuous set plates including steak/chicken with rice, beans and chips.

⫟ Mineiro, R 4 53 (opposite **Rio Vermelho**, see Sleeping), T062-3224 9113. Cheap, good per kilo buffet with lots of choice and some veggie options. One of several on this block.

⫟ Primo Patio, Av República Líbano (opposite Castro's Plaza), T062-3213 3366, Pizza, pasta and grilled steak and chicken (with the inevitable rice, beans and chips).

Cidade de Goiás *p697*
For the best very cheap options head for the **Mercado Municipal** between the São Francisco church and the river.

⫟⫟ Dali, R 13 de Maio 26, T062-3372 1640. Riverside restaurant with a little patio offering a wide range of international and local dishes.

⫟⫟ Flor do Ipê, Praça da Boa Vista 32, at the end of the road leading from the centre across the bridge, T062-3372 1133. The best in town for Goiânian food, with an enormous variety on offer, a lovely garden setting with views of the river and *serra*. Highly recommended.

⫟ Degus't Fun Pizzeria, R Quinta Bocaiuva, next to Praça do Coreto, T062-3371 2800. Pizza, casseroles, soups and very friendly service from a mother-and-daughter team.

Pirenópolis *p698*
There are plenty of options along **R do Rosário**, serving a surprising range of international food including some vegetarian and Asian options. Many have live music at night (and an undisclosed cover charge – be sure to ask).

There are cheaper options near the Igreja Bonfim in the upper part of town.

¶¶ **Caffe Tarsia**, R do Rosário 34, T062-3331 1274, www.caffetarsia.com.br. Much the best in town with a menu of Mediterranean dishes, Goiás food and steaks. Live music and weekends. Good caipirinhas.

¶¶ **Chiquinha**, R do Rosário 19, T062-3331 3052. Local cuisine with an emphasis on meat.

¶¶ **Emporio do Cerrado**, R do Rosário 21, T062-3331 3874. Great Goiás food like Pequi risotto with chicken in orange sauce served in a dining room decorated with black and white photos. Live music at weekends.

¶ **Alma Vegetariana**, R dos Pireneus at Praça do Correto, T062-3331 2938. Vegetarian pies, pastas, sandwiches and good juices.

¶ **O Cafeteria**, R do Rosário 38, T062-9972 7953. Light food and about the cheapest option in town.

Alto Paraíso p700

The best of the restaurants are in Alto Paraíso. São Jorge has a few basic options.

¶¶-¶ **Oca Lila**, Av João Bernades Rabelo 449, T061-3446 1773. Decent pizza and sandwiches, live music at the weekend, good atmosphere and a decent veggie buffet at lunch.

¶ **Jatô**, R Coleto Paulino 522, T061-3446 1339. Open Thu-Sun. Self-service; veggie options.

¶ **Pizza 2000**, Av Ari Valadão 659, T061-3446 1814. The centre of the town's early evening social life. Respectable pizzas.

🍸 Bars and clubs

Goiânia p695, map p696

Goiânia is surprisingly lively, with some of the best nightlife in central Brazil. This is especially true during the various festivals and Carnaval. There is an active gay scene and plenty of choices of clubs and bars. Most locals tend to drink in the restaurants (many of which double up as bars) before heading to a club at around 2300.

Café Cancún, Shopping Flamboyant and Av Jamel Cecilio 3, T062-3546 2035, www.cafe cancun.com.br. With a lively forró night on Wed and a mix of club music on others.

It's, Av 136, 960, Edifício Executive Tower, Térreo, Setor Marista, T062-3241 8477, www.its.art.br. The city's current favourite with a range of different music on different nights – from techno and hip hop to MPB.

Pulse, R9 1087, T062-215 6133, www.pulse.com.br. Crowded little club with a small sound system and rather tired decoration. Sweaty and packed on Sat.

Pirenópolis p698

Bars along **R do Rosário** cater for those from Brasília and the children of the hippies who migrated here in the 1970s. Locals hang out near the **Igreja Bonfim** where there are 2 spit-and-sawdust bars and booming car stereos.

🎉 Festivals and events

Cidade de Goiás p697

Feb Carnaval is joyous and still little known to outsiders. There are plans to make it into a traditional 19th-century masked parade with formal balls.

Apr The streets of Cidade de Goiás blaze with torches during the solemn Fogaréu processions of Holy Week, when hooded figures re-enact Christ's descent from the cross and burial.

Apr-May Festa Divino Espírito Santo processions, serenades and the formal distribution of food to the poor.

May Encontro Afro Brasileiro, a celebration of black Brazilian culture with live music, Afro-Brazilian food. Attended by people come from all over Brazil.

Jun International Film Festival, live music by acts like Gilberto Gil and Titãs and films from almost 100 different countries and especially from Latin America.

24-26 Jul Birthday of the City, the city becomes once more the capital of the state and there are processions in homage to the patron saint, Santa Ana, and various shows.

Pirenópolis p698

May/Jun Festa do Divino Espírito Santo, held 45 days after Easter (Pentecost), is one of Brazil's most famous and extraordinary folkloric/religious celebrations. It lasts 3 days, with medieval costumes, tournaments, dances and mock battles between Moors and Christians, a tradition held annually since 1819. The city throbs with life over this period and there are numerous and frequent extemporaneous *forró* and *sertanejo* parties.

O Shopping

Goiânia p695, map p696

Ceramic, sisal and wooden handicrafts from **Centro Estadual do Artesanato**, Praça do Trabalhador (0800-1800); **Sun handicrafts markets** at the Praça Cívica (morning) and Praça do Sol (afternoon). The latter starts after 1530, until 2100, known as the **Honey Fair** as all types of honey are sold; also good for a Sun snack, with many sweets and tarts sold along the street. See also **Casa do Indio**, page 697.

Cidade de Goiás p697

Frutos da Terra, R Dom Cândido Penso 30, next to Cora Coralina Museum. Wide range of items from bags and belts to leather sandals and ceramics. Most is made in the town.

Pirenópolis p698

There are many jewellery and arts and crafts shops in the streets in the historic centre.

▲▲ Activities and tours

Goiânia p695, map p696

Visitors are welcome to the sporting facilities throughout Goiânia. For sunbathing, swimming and waterskiing try the **Jaó Club**, T062-261 2122, on a reservoir near the city.
Turisplan Turismo, R 8 Q 7, 388 lt 50 s 1 – Setor Central, T062-3224 7076. Tours to Paraúna and the mining villages. Also sells bus tickets.

Cidade de Goiás p697

Massage and treatments

Cleonice Albino, T062-3372 1119/062-9902 7344. Very good-value Ayurvedic massage and colour therapy. Either at the therapist's clinic, or can come to your hotel.

Wildlife and adventure tours

Frans and Susana Leeuweenberg, contact through **Serra Dourada**, below. A husband-and-wife team of biologists who have been working hard to protect the *cerrado* for many years. English, French and Dutch spoken.
Serra Dourada Aventura, T062-3371 4277/T062-9238 5195, www.vilaboadegoias.com.br. Hikes in the surrounding forest and within the state park, visits to waterfalls, kayaking and canyoning and longer distance trips to the Rio Araguaia. Very good value.

Pirenópolis p698

Padilha, T062-3331 2998, www.padilhaecoturismo.pirenopolis.tur.br. Walks, adventure activities and visits to the Vagafogo private reserve and the Mosteiro Buddhisto and trips further afield to destinations such as Emás and the Rio Araguaia. Good value, well organized and excellent English spoken. Can organize transfers from Brasília to Pirenópolis, hotel booking and trekking, rafting and sightseeing around Pirenópolis.
Savannah Tur, R Pirineus 100, T062-3331 1267, www.savannah.tur.br. Trekks in the hills around Pirenópolis and visits to the numerous waterfalls that dot the hills, whitewater rafting, rappelling and visits to the Santuário de Vida Silvestre Vagafogo.

Chapada dos Veadeiros p700

Alpatour, R dos Nascentes, T062-3446 1820, www.altoparaiso.com. Van-based tours to the principal sights. Suitable for all ages.
Alternativas, T062-3446 1000, www.alternativas.tur.br. Very well-organized tours, walks and adventure trips including canyoning, rapelling and abseiling, throughout the region. Enthusiastic guides, some of whom

speak English and the only tour operator in the region owned and run by locals. **Ecorotas**, T062-3446 1820, www.altoparaiso. com.br. Light adventure trips and visits to the major sights.

Travessia, T062-3446 1595, www.travessia. tur.br. Treks from a few days to over a week with rappelling and canyoning from one of the most respected instructors, Ion David.

Alto Paraíso and São Jorge *p700*
Massage and treatments
Atash, R do Segredo 37, Alto Paraíso, T061-3446 1028. Ayurvedic and classical Thai massage and breathing meditation from a long-experienced practitioner.
Sílvia Luz, R 12 Dezembro 217, Alto Paraíso, T061-3446 1585, T061-9956 9685, silviapraxis @hotmail.com. One of Brazil's best Ayurvedic and Reiki practitioners. Also works with Tuiná and Shiatsu. Highly recommended.

Parque Nacional das Emas *p701*
Tours are available through **Padilha** (see above), www.padilhaecoturismo.pirenopolis. tur.br. Alternatively, contact the tourist office in the **Prefeitura Municipal**, Chapadão do Céu, www.chapada odoceu.go.gov.br, for a list of authorized operators. Interest is growing but visits to Emas are still in the early stages.

⊖ Transport

Goiânia *p695, map p696*
Air Flights to **Brasília**, **Palmas**, **Rio de Janeiro**, **São Paulo**, **Belo Horizonte** (Pampulha), **Cuiabá**, **Ribeirão Preto**, **Rio de Janeiro** (Santos Dumont), **São José do Rio Preto**, **São Paulo** (Guarulhos), **Uberlândia**, **Campo Grande** and **São Félix do Araguaia**.
   Airline offices GOL, www.voegol.com.br, and TAM, www.tam.com.br, have offices at the airport.

Bus To **Brasília**, 207 km, at least 15 departures a day, 2½ hrs, US$5, and **São Paulo**, 900 km via Barretos, US$25, 14½ hrs,

leito services at night. To **Goiás Velho**, 136 km, hourly from 0500, 2½ hrs, US$5. **Pirenópolis**, 0700 and 1700, 2 hrs, US$5. **Campo Grande**, 935 km, 4 services daily, 18 hrs, US$30. To **Cuiabá** (Mato Grosso), 916 km on BR-158/070 via Barra do Garças, or 928 km on BR-060/364 via Jataí (both routes paved, most buses use the latter route), 4 buses a day, US$25, 15-16 hrs, continuing to Porto Velho (**Rondônia**) and Rio Branco (**Acre**), a very trying journey.

Car hire Millenium, T062-9612 7842 (24 hrs); **Siga**, T062-207 8388.

Cidade de Goiás *p697*
Bus Hourly bus services to **Goiânia** (2½ hrs) 0530-2000, change here for other places.

Pirenópolis *p698*
Bus 2 buses a day to **Brasília** (2½-4 hrs).

Chapada dos Veadeiros *p700*
Bus Brasília–Alto Paraíso–São Jorge leaves at 1100 (3-4 hrs), returning 0900. There is a night bus **Palmas–Brasília**, arriving from Brasília 2200.

Parque Nacional das Emas *p701*
Bus One daily bus from **Serranópolis** to Chapadão do Céu, leaving at 0800. To get to Chapadão do Céu from Campo Grande, go via Costa Rica or Chapada do Sul.

⊙ Directory

Goiânia *p695, map p696*
Banks There are several branches of Bradesco, HSBC and Banco do Brasil. In the centre and along Av Rep Líbano. Travel agents will exchange cash, poor rates for TCs. **Immigration** Immigration office, R 235, Setor Universitário. **Internet** There are numerous internet cafés throughout the city.

Parque Nacional das Emas *p701*
Banks There is a Banco do Brasil with a Visa ATM in Chapadão do Céu.

Tocantins

Tocantins is not on the tourist track but it offers some of the most exciting opportunities for adventure tourism in Brazil's interior. Jalapão – an enormous wilderness of cerrado forest, table-top mountains, dune deserts, waterfalls and whitewater rivers – lies on the borders of Tocantins and Piauí. It is as spectacularly beautiful as the Chapada dos Veadeiros or the Chapada Diamantina but far less visited. The world's largest river island, Ilha do Bananal, lies at the southern end of the state. Its northern extremes are almost as rich in wildlife as the Pantanal and the interior of the island is home to numerous indigenous groups (who cannot be visited without authorization from FUNAI). The serra around the planned modern capital, Palmas, is covered with rainforest dotted with beautiful waterfalls. The northwestern corner of the state sees the end of the cerrado and the beginnings of the Amazon rainforest. ▶▶ For listings, see pages 710-711.

Palmas → *For listings, see pages 710-711. Colour map 1, B5. Phone code: 063. Population: 130,000.*

Palmas, the newest capital city in the country's newest state (Tocantins was carved out of Goiás in the late 1980s), sits on the banks of the flooded Tocantins river at the foot of low forested mountains. It is a city built for mathematicians and cars, with an arcane street numbering system and wide, long avenues broken by roundabouts. Rather fascistic monuments to the autocrat who founded the state (and whose family still largely run Tocantins like a private fiefdom) can be seen around town, especially on Praça dos Girassóis in the centre. Palmas is an essential jumping-off point for trips to Bananal and Jalapão and there are many waterfalls and forest trails in the surrounding hills.

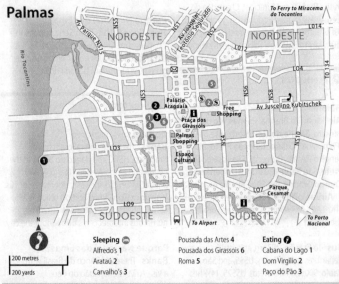

Palmas

Sleeping 🛏
Alfredo's 1
Arataú 2
Carvalho's 3
Pousada das Artes 4
Pousada dos Girassois 6
Roma 5

Eating 🍴
Cabana do Lago 1
Dom Virgílio 2
Paço do Pão 3

Ins and outs

Palmas airport ⓘ *20 km from town, Av NS 5, T063-3321 61237*, receives flights from Brasília, São Paulo and Belém. A taxi into town costs around US$20 and there is an irregular shuttle bus. The **rodoviária** ⓘ *ACSUSO 40, T061-3216 1603*, is 10 km from the centre; city buses are plentiful and cheap. The city is divided into four sectors: **Noroeste (NO)**, **Nordeste (NE)**, **Sudoeste (SO)** and **Sudeste (SE)**. Like Brasília, the different blocks are named by use and location. Some address abbreviations are **Área Central (AC)**, **Área de Comércio** and **Serviço Urbano (ACSU)** and **Área Administrativa (AA)**. For tourist information contact SETUR ⓘ *Praça dos Girassóis, T061-3218 2015*, on the *praça*.

Sights

It is worth spending a few hours wandering across the central **Praça dos Girassóis**, an enormous grassy square dotted with monuments and imposing public buildings. The most impressive is the **Palácio Araguaia**, a massive government palace topped with a golden globe that looks like it has been dragged here from North Korea. It is surrounded by other monuments; most whiff of totalitarianism. The state's founding *caboclo* pioneers hold their arms up in adulation as if they had discovered the promised land. Carlos Prestes – the communist leader who was, bizarrely, much admired by the fascist governor and state founder, José Wilson Siqueira Campos – stands with his troops around a tattered flag. And Siqueira Campos is everywhere, immortalized by himself out of love for the people of Tocantins, on plaques and public buildings. There's a forgotten Niemeyer building too: a long low rectangle next to the Prestes sculpture, also built in homage to the leader.

Excursions from Palmas → *For listings, see pages 710-711.*

There are numerous waterfalls in the nearby **Serra do Lajeado**, most of them reached via light trails through primary rainforest rich with birdlife. These include the **Cachoeira de Taquaruçu** near the town of the same name, **Macaco** and **Brejo do Chiqueiro**. The first trail to the falls is at Km 18 on the Estrada do Rio Negro. At Km 36 there are trails along the river to the **Brejo da Lagoa** waterfall and eventually to the 60-m-high **Cachoeira do Roncador**. Most of the falls have deep pools good for swimming. About 8 km away at Canelas is the **Praia da Graciosa**, a beach on the River Tocantins, with floating bars, sports courts, shows, and a campsite. It is particularly busy at weekends.

Jalapão → *Colour map 1, B5. Phone code 062.*

Jalapão is one of the highlights of a visit to the Brazilian interior: table-top mountains tower over seemingly endless plains covered in *caatinga* and *cerrado* forest, fast-flowing black-water rivers lead to plunging waterfalls, sweeping sand dunes, bubbling clear-water springs and sleepy *caboclo* villages. The air so clear you can see for over 100 km and, other than the Serra dos Confusões in Piauí, there is probably nowhere in Brazil where *sertão* and *cerrado* is more pristine. It is still possible to see the world's rarest large parrot, Spix's macaw, in the stands of *buriti* palms and one of the world's rarest water birds, the Brazilian merganser duck, on the smaller rivers. There's plenty of other wildlife too, best seen at dawn and in silence (avoid trips with Brazilian groups if possible). Maned wolf, giant anteater and white-tailed deer are numerous and there is a healthy population of all the larger cat species.

Jalapão is a six-hour drive from Palmas on the border of Tocantins, Piauí, Maranhão and Bahia. At present only **Korubo Expeditions** offers trips here, staying at their very comfortable safari camp next to one of the larger rivers (see page 711 for details). It's possible to visit on a self-drive trip, though only with a 4WD; prepare as if for the Australian outback, with plenty of spare fuel, two ropes and at least 20 litres of water. There is simple accommodation in the scattered small towns.

Ilha do Bananal → *Colour map 1, B5. Phone code 062.*

ⓘ *Permission to visit the park should be obtained in advance from Instituto Chico Mendes de Conservação da Biodiversidade (ICMBio), R 219, No 95, Setor Universitário, 74605-800, Goiânia. Access is through the small but pleasant town of Santa Teresinha. It is far easier, however to visit on an organized trip with Bananal is the world's largest river island and is located on the northeastern border of Mato Grosso. The island is formed by a division in the south of the Rio Araguaia and is approximately 320 km long. The entire island was originally a national park (called Parque Nacional Araguaia), which was then cut in half and later further reduced to its current size of 562,312 ha. But there are still plenty of wild areas that are rich in fauna, several permanent lakes, marshland areas and seasonally flooded habitats similar to those in the Pantanal. The vegetation is a transition zone between the* cerrado *(woody savannah),* varzea, igapó, *Amazon* terra firme *forest and gallery forest.*

The fauna is also transitional. More than 300 bird species are found here, including the hoatzin, hyacinth macaw, harpy eagle and black-fronted piping guan. The giant anteater, maned wolf, bush dog, giant otter, jaguar, puma, marsh deer, pampas deer, Brazilian tapir, yellow anaconda and South American river turtle can also be spotted. The island is flooded most of the year, with the prime visiting time being the dry season from June to early October, when the beaches are exposed.

◉ Tocantins listings

For Sleeping and Eating price codes and other relevant information, see pages 32-37.

● Sleeping

Palmas *p708, map p708*
AL Pousada das Artes, 103 Sul, Av, LO1 78, T063-3219 1500, www.arteshotel.com.br. Very comfortable, well-kept a/c rooms with marble and mosaic bathrooms, restaurant, sauna and swimming pool. Only the master suite has external windows.
A Hotel Arataú, Av JK 104 Norte 123, T063-3215 5323, hotelaratau@bol.com.br. Spacious tiled rooms; the best are on the upper floors.
A Pousada dos Girassois, Av NS 1, 103 Sul, conj 03, lote 44, T063-3219 4500, www.pousadadosgirassois.com.br. Over-looking the main grassy square. Rooms are small and modern with a/c and cable TV but tiny windows. Very good restaurant. The departure point for **Korubo's** Jalapão tours.

B Hotel Roma, Av LO2-104 Norte, lote 23, T063-3215 3033, www.hotelroma-to.com.br. Pleasant, intimate hotel with bright, airy tiled rooms in terracotta and cream. Internet access.
C Carvalho's, Av 103 Sul, SOO1, lote 11, T063-3215 5758. Modest, well-kept a/c en suites some with no external windows.
D-E Alfredo's, Av JK, 103 Sul, Quadra 101, lotes 23/24, T063-3215 3036. Simple fan-cooled and a/c rooms gathered around a garden courtyard visited by hummingbirds. Trips to the Ilha do Bananal and Jalapão. Cheapest with 4 or more people.

Ilha do Bananal *p710*
A Bananal, Praça Tarcila Braga 106, CEP 78395 (Mato Grosso). Full board. There is only room for 10 people so reserve well ahead.

There is some simple accommodation for scientists at the park, which can sometimes be reserved at the address above or from the national parks department in Brasília. Bring your own food and bedding. The severely underpaid but dedicated staff appreciate any extra food or financial help, although it will not be solicited. A boat to the park can be arranged at **Hotel Bananal**, above.

⊘ Eating

Palmas p708, map p708
₩ **Cabana do Lago**, Praia da Graciosa, T063-3215 6055. Local fish grills and sauce dishes like *tucunaré* (peacock bass) and Goiás meat dishes like *carne do sol* beef and guinea fowl in coconut milk. Overlooking the river.
₩ **Dom Virgilio**, Av JK 103, Norte 159, T063-3212 1400. Great buffet lunch with generous salads and pizzas in the evening.
₩ **Paço do Pão**, Av JK 154, 103 Sul, T063-3215 5665. Very good, large wood-fired pizzas.

⊙ Shopping

Palmas p708, map p708
Na Natureza, Av JK 103 Sul, Conj 01, lote 150, Sala 04, T063-3215 2391. Beautiful baskets and earrings in Capim Dourado, indigenous ceramics and bead necklaces and bracelets made with Amazonian and *cerrado* seeds.
Palm Blue Shopping, ACSUSO 10, Conj 2.

▲ Activities and tours

Palmas p708, map p708
Also see *pousada* **Carvalho's**, Sleeping, above.
Korubo Expeditions, São Paulo, T011-3667 5053, www.korubo.com.br. Excellent but expensive tours to Jalapão. Guides are very good (specialist wildlife guides should be booked in advance) and accommodation is in very comfortable African-style safari tents with beds. Activities included in the price are whitewater rafting, treks, 4WD tours, wildlife spotting and visits to typical Jalapão villages. Avoid going with a large group of Brazilians as noise means wildlife spotting is difficult.

Ilha do Bananal p710
Bananal can be visited from São Félix do Araguaia (with permission from Funai in the town) by crossing the river to the Carajá village of Santa Isabela de Morra and asking to see the chief, who can tell you the history of the tribe. The island can be crossed from São Félix to São Miguel de Araguaia by taking an 8-hr trip. From São Miguel, a 5-hr bus trip brings you to Porangatu (**D Hotel Mauriti**, restaurant) on the Belém–Brasília highway.

⊖ Transport

Palmas p708, map p708
Air Daily flights to **Brasília**, **São Paulo**, **Curitiba Florianópolis** and **Goiânia** with GOL, and **TAM**. Offices at the airport.

Boat The port is 9 km from the city. Ferries to **Miracema do Tocantins** and **Paraíso do Tocantins**.

Bus Buses to Brasília often run via the Chapada dos Veadeiros. To **Brasília** (12 hrs), **Belém** (10 hrs), **Goiânia** (14 hrs), **Salvador** (20 hrs), **São Luís** (14 hrs), **Teresina** (12 hrs).

Car hire Hertz, Av Nossa Senhora, T063-3978 1900, and Localiza, ACSO 11-CL02, lote 41, T063-3216 1104, and at the airport.

Taxi Rádio Táxi Palmas, T063-3213 2001.

⊙ Directory

Palmas p708, map p708
Medical services Hospital Regional and Proctology, Praça ARSE, quadra 51, Setor Serrano, T063-3214 1424. **Post office** Av Joaquim Teotônio Segurado.

Contents

Footprint features

Border crossings

At a glance

⊖ **Getting around** Plane, bus, jeep,
boat and horseback.

◎ **Time required** 3-4 days for
one of the cities and a *fazenda* or
Pantanal tour. 1-2 days for Bonito.

☼ **Weather** Hot and wet Oct-Feb,
hot and drier Mar-Apr, dry May-Sep.

✗ **When not to go** Dec-Feb is very
wet, the Pantanal is flooded and
there are many mosquitos.

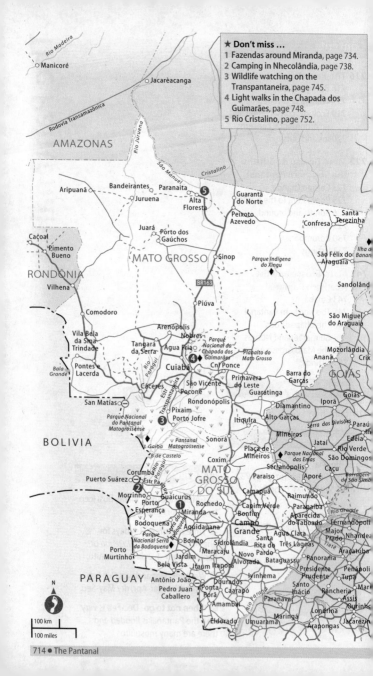

★ **Don't miss ...**
1 Fazendas around Miranda, page 734.
2 Camping in Nhecolândia, page 738.
3 Wildlife watching on the Transpantaneira, page 745.
4 Light walks in the Chapada dos Guimarães, page 748.
5 Rio Cristalino, page 752.

The Pantanal, which is an enormous seasonally flooded wetland on the borders of Brazil, Paraguay and Bolivia, is the best place in the Americas for spotting wild animals, and one of the best places in the world to see birds. Capybara, anaconda, peccary, giant otter, metre-long macaws and ocelots are common sights and it is even possible to see that most elusive of South American mammals, the jaguar. At the end of the dry season, between June and August, the number of water birds, raptors and parrots has to be seen to be believed. Visiting the wetlands is easy with a large choice of camping tours from Campo Grande, Cuiabá, Corumbá or Miranda; or there's the more comfortable option of staying at one of the *fazenda* ranch houses that are increasingly opening their doors to tourists. Families with children will enjoy the little resort town of Bonito, which is famous for its clear-water rivers and caves, and makes a good base for visiting the Pantanal.

The Pantanal lies within two Brazilian states: Mato Grosso do Sul and Mato Grosso. Until the second half of the 20th century these were little-explored wildernesses of table-top mountains, *cerrado*, savannah and dense rainforest. The famous British explorer, Colonel Percy Fawcett, was lost, and perhaps murdered, in the forests of the Xingu, and Theodore Roosevelt contracted a fatal disease on an expedition here in previously uncharted territory. These days, even the Pantanal is grazed by cattle, and the great Amazonian forests of northern Mato Grosso state are steadily giving way to soya beans, planted for the vegetarians of the USA and Europe and the kitchens of China. However, substantial pockets of forest still remain for now, particularly around the Rio Cristalino near the town of Alta Floresta, where one of the best jungle lodges in the Americas can be found.

The Pantanal

The Pantanal UNESCO Biosphere Reserve is the world's largest freshwater wetland and one of the best places on earth for seeing wildlife, particularly birds. Within Brazil it comprises a plain of around 21,000 sq km but the Pantanal extends beyond Brazil into Bolivia, Paraguay and Argentina to form an area totalling 100,000 sq km. The plain slopes 1 cm in every kilometre north to south and west to east to the basin of the Rio Paraguai and is rimmed by low mountains. From these, 175 rivers flow into the Pantanal and after the heavy summer rains they burst their banks, as does the Paraguai itself, to create vast shallow lakes broken by patches of high ground and stands of cerrado forest. Plankton then swarm in the water to form a biological soup that contains as many as 500 million micro algae per litre. Millions of amphibians and fish spawn or migrate to consume them. And these in turn are preyed upon by waterbirds and reptiles. Herbivorous mammals graze on the stands of water hyacinth, sedge and savannah grass and at the top of the food chain lie South America's great predators – the jaguar, ocelot, maned wolf and yellow anaconda. In June, at the end of the wet season, when the sheets of water have reduced, wildlife concentrates around the small lakes or canals and then there is nowhere else on earth that you will see such vast quantities of birds or such enormous numbers of crocodilians. Only the plains of Africa can compete for mammals and your chances of seeing a jaguar or one of Brazil's seven other species of wild cat are greater here than anywhere on the continent.

Background

To the indigenous groups who arrived in the area tens of thousands of years before the Europeans, the Pantanal was a sea, which they called 'Xaraes'. Myths about this sea quickly reached the ears of the Spanish and Portuguese *conquistadores*, who set out to explore it. As if to presage the future, the first to arrive, in 1543, was a Spaniard called Cabeza de Vaca (Cow Head) who complained about the swarms of mosquitoes and vampire bats and promptly turned westward into the Paraguayan *chaco*. The fate of the Pantanal and its myriad indigenous residents was left to the ruthless Portuguese and their *bandeirantes*. Apart from a few skirmishes they left the Pantanal alone for 200 years, but then gold was discovered glittering in a stream they called the River of Stars (or 'Cuiabá' by the local people). A settlement was established and soon the Portuguese were scouring the area for native slave labour for their mines. The *indígenas* were understandably aggrieved by this and two of the fiercest tribes, the Guaicurú and the Paiaguá, combined forces to attack the Portuguese. Their tactics were highly effective: they worked in small guerrilla bands, laying ambushes when the Europeans least expected it. The Guaicurú were horsemen, charging into battle naked but for jaguar skins, clubs, lances and machetes; crouched low on their stolen Andalusian horses, or riding on the horse's sides rather than their backs and thus invisible to the Portuguese. They used no saddles or stirrups and had just two chords for reins. The Paiaguá attacked by water and were excellent swimmers, advancing in their canoes and then leaping into the water and using the sides of the boats as shields. They would then suddenly right their boats and fire several volleys of arrows during the time it took the *bandeirantes* to fire one. They soon defeated the Europeans, regaining control of the Pantanal for almost 100 years. The Portuguese were furious and accused the Guaicurú in particular of dishonourable tactics. "They fight only to win," the Portuguese claimed, "attacking only when the enemy seemed weaker". The Guaicurú responded by exposing the hypocrisy of the Portuguese:

"Since the Portuguese and Spaniards claim to go to heaven when they die, they do well to die quickly. But, since they also claim that the Guiacurú go to hell after death, in that case the Guiacurú want to die as late as possible." (John Hemming, *Red Gold*). But through subterfuge the pact was broken and in 1734 the Portuguese regained control by means of a devastating ambush that decimated the Paiaguá. The tribes then retreated into the depths of the Pantanal where their numbers slowly diminished as a result of punitive *bandeirantes* expeditions, inter-tribal conflict and European diseases.

Today Pantaneiros boast of their proud traditions, which are barely three generations old. Nearly 25 million of their cattle roam the Pantanal and the true indigenous Pantaneiros have largely disappeared. Of the 25,000 Guiacurú present in 1500, some 200 survive in their Kadiweu and Mbayá subgroups. The Paiaguá have been reduced to a sad remnant living on an island reservation near Asunción in Paraguay. Other tribes, such as the Parecis, who were enslaved in the mines, fared even worse and, of the great indigenous groups of the Pantanal, only the Bororo, who allied with the Portuguese, retain any significant numbers. Even their traditions have been greatly damaged by the aggressive missionary tactics of the Salesians in the 20th century.

Wildlife and vegetation

Wildlife → *See Ecology, conservation and environmental issues, page 719.*

Mammals Outside Africa there is nowhere better for seeing wild mammals than the Pantanal, especially between July and late September. During this time, there are groups of **capybara** – the world's largest rodent – at just about every turn. Critically endangered **marsh deer** (who have webbed feet to help them run through the swamp), or their more timid cousins, the **red brocket**, and the **pampas deer** wander in every other stretch of savannah alongside **giant anteaters**. Few visitors leave without having seen both species of peccary (which resemble pigs but are in a different family) – the solitary **collared peccary** and the herd-living **white-lipped peccary**, **giant otters** and at least one species of cat. Lucky visitors may even see a jaguar or **tapir**. There are at least 102 mammal species here and, although most of them are bats (including vampires), the list includes eight of South America's 10 wild cats, four dog species and numerous primates ranging from the tiny palm-sized **pygmy marmoset** to South America's second largest primate, the **red howler monkey**.

The cats are usually top of everyone's 'most wanted' list. The largest is the **jaguar** (most easily seen here at **Fazenda San Francisco** in the south, or at **Porto Jofre** on the Transpantaneira), followed by the more elusive **puma**, which has the widest distribution of any feline in the world. Even more common is the retriever-sized **ocelot** and the tawny or black **jaguarundi**, which is about twice the size of a domestic cat, though more slender. The most elusive creature is the **pampas cat**, which has a fawn body and striped legs, but scientists are yet to agree on its species. The other cats are all spotted and are, in size order, the **margay**, **geoffroy's cat** (the most hunted in the Americas) and, the most beautiful of all, the **oncilla** or tiger cat.

Other carnivores include **crab-eating foxes**, **coatis** and **racoons** (who often hang around the *fazendas* at night), the **maned wolf**, **short-eared dog**, and **bush dog** (Cachorro Vinagre, found in the drier semi-deciduous forests). Monkeys are not as varied here as they are in the Amazon, but visitors will hear or see **red howler monkey** or **black howler monkey**, the smaller **brown capuchin**, and possibly the **pygmy marmoset** or the **silvery marmoset**. Other species present include various **titi monkeys** and **night**

monkeys, which are most easily seen around **Fazenda Bela Vista** on the Estrada Parque in the south. Woolly monkeys can be found in the dry forests.

Reptiles After birds, the easiest animals to see in the Pantanal are caimans, of which the dominant species is the **jacaré caiman**, a smaller sub-species of the spectacled caiman found in the Amazon. Jacaré caimans reach a maximum length of about 1.5 m. **Yellow anaconda**, the world's heaviest snake, are abundant but difficult to see; your best chance is on the Estrada Parque in the south, which they frequently cross during the day. Other snakes, the majority of which are not venomous, are also abundant but hard to spot. The venomous species, which include pit vipers, such as the **fer de lance** or jararaca, are nocturnal.

Birds There are more than 700 resident and migratory bird species in the Pantanal. Birding on the Transpantaneira road in the north or at one of the *fazendas* in the south can yield as many as 100 species a day. From late June to early October the vast numbers of birds have to be seen to be believed. Try to visit as many habitat types as possible and, as well as trail-walking, jeep rides and horseback excursions, be sure to include river trips in your itinerary. Night safaris will maximize sightings of more unusual **heron**, such as the boat-billed, agami and zigzag, and the numerous nightjars and potoos. Specialities in the Pantanal include the metre-long **hyacinth macaw** (the world's largest parrot), the **golden-collared macaw**, **blue-fronted parrot**, **blue-crowned nanday**, **blaze-winged and green-cheeked parakeets**, the giant flightless **rhea**, chestnut-bellied and spix's **guan**, **crowned eagle**, **bare faced currasow** and **helmeted manakin**. Remember to bring good binoculars and a field guide. A book such as Nigel Wheatley's *Where to watch birds in South America* can give far greater detail than this book has space for, though it is now very out of date.
➤ *For recommended birding guides, see Books, page 807.*

Forest types and what lives where

Although the Pantanal is often described as an ecosystem in its own right, it is actually made up of many habitats, which have their own, often distinct, biological communities. The Pantanal is of recent geological origin and has very few endemic plant species. Botanically it is a mosaic: a mixture of elements from the Amazon region including *varzea* and gallery forests and tropical savannah, the *cerrado* of central Brazil and the dry *chaco* region of Paraguay.

Pantanal cerrado forest The *cerrado* is found both in the upland areas, which are not prone to flooding, and in some areas that may be inundated for a short period. It is dominated by the *cerrado* **pequi tree** (*Caryocar brasiliense*) whose fruits have a famous spiny interior, the beautiful flowering legume **Sucupira** (*Bowdichia virgiloides*) and the **sandpaper tree** (*Curatella americana*). But the most conspicuous trees in the *cerrado* are **trumpet trees** (various *ipê*); these are characterized by their brilliant colours (indigo in *Tabebuia impetignosa* and yellow in *Tabebuia aurea*) and no leaves in the dry season. Sometimes these trees stand as the dominant species in vast areas of semi-agrarian parkland. Within the dry *cerrado* are numerous stands of **bocaiúva palm** (*Acrocomia aculeate*) characterized by its very spiny trunk and leaves. Its fruit is an important food source for macaws and larger parrots. In the wetter *cerrado* are numerous islands of dense savannah forest or *cerradão*, often thick with **acuri palm** (*Attalea phalerata*), whose woody fruit is the principal food for the hyacinth macaw and, when fallen, for peccaries (*javali* in Portuguese) and agouti (rabbit-sized, tailless rodents; *cutia* in Portuguese). *Cerrado* habitats are also important refuges for the larger sheltering mammals, such as jaguar and tapir, who will flee into the densest wet *cerrado* to escape predators.

Semi-deciduous tropical forest This taller, denser forest occurs on higher ground such as the Serra do Bodoquena south of Miranda, and comprises a mix of species from the Paraguayan *chaco* and the Amazon. For instance **jutaí** (*Hymenaea courbaril*), from which the sacred copal resin is extracted, comes from the Amazon; while the **monkey-ear plant** (*Enterolobium contortisquam*), recognized by its curved seed pods, is a common *chaco* species. More primate species can be found here than elsewhere in the Pantanal, along with smaller toucans, such as the **chestnut eared aracari**, and rare mammals like bush dog and **tayra** (*Iara*).

Swamp and seasonally flooded land This varies greatly, from Amazonian habitats characterized by riverine forests such as *varzea* (seasonally flooded riverbank forest) to seasonally flooded grassland and palm savannah dominated by **carunda palm** trees. Alongside these are permanently marshy areas and open lakes and oxbows thick with floating plants. This diversity of habitats means a great diversity of species and nowhere is better than these areas for seeing large concentrations of birds and mammals. *Varzea*, which is best seen by canoe or paddle boat, is good for mammals such as tapir and giant otter, and for riverine birds like the **southern screamer** (*tachã*), the five species of Brazilian **kingfisher** (*Martim pescador*), **black-collared hawks** (*Gaviao belo*) and the myriad species of heron and stork, including the giant 1.2-m-tall **jabiru** (*tuiuiu*). Apart from *varzea*, much swampland is dominated by the papyrus-like sedge (*Cyperus giganteus*) or reed mace (*Typha dominguensis*) or by floating plants like **water hyacinth** (*Eichhornia crassipes*), which caiman and capybara use as cover.

Xeric vegetation This permanently dry scrub forest found in elevated areas is dominated by *chaco* species such as various types of **cacti** (such as *Cereus peruvianus* and *Opuntia stenartha*) together with the swollen-trunked, baobab-like pot-bellied **chorisia** (*Bombacaceae*). Many distinct species occur here, including one of the world's rarest cats, the pampas cat, and rare birds, such as **black-legged seriemas** and *chaco* **earthcreepers**.

Ecology, conservation and environmental concerns

Only one area of the Pantanal is officially a national park, the 135,000-ha **Parque Nacional do Pantanal Matogrossense** in the municipality of Poconé, only accessible by air or river. You can obtain permission to visit from **Ibama** ① *R Rubens de Mendonça, Cuiabá, T065-3644 1511/1581*. **Hunting is strictly forbidden** throughout the Pantanal and is punishable by four years' imprisonment. However, most *fazendeiros* regularly shoot and kill jaguar, many locals still offer their services as jaguar hunters and some landowners even allow illegal private hunts.

   Fishing is allowed with a licence, US$40, according to strict quotas. It is not permitted in the spawning season or *piracema* (1 October to 1 February in Mato Grosso do Sul; 1 November to 1 March in Mato Grosso). There are also restrictions on the size of fish that may be caught, but poaching is rife and there are plans to halt all fishing for four years due to severe stock depletion. Application forms are available through travel agents with advanced notice. Catch and release is the only kind of fishing allowed on rivers Abobral, Negro, Perdido and Vermelho. Like other wilderness areas, the Pantanal faces significant threats to its integrity. Agrochemicals and *garimpo* mercury, washed down from the neighbouring *planalto*, are a hazard to wildlife.

The **International Union for the Conservation of Nature** (IUCN), www.iucn.org, is concerned at the amount of poaching, particularly of *jacaré* skins, birds and capybara. The forestry police have built control points on all major access roads to the Pantanal. Biologists interested in research projects should contact the **Coordenador de Estudos do Pantanal** ① *Departamento de Biologia, Universidade Federal do Mato Grosso do Sul, Campo Grande, T067-3787 3311 ext 2113*, or the **IUCN** about their **Fazenda Rio Negro programme** ① *T067-3326 0002, www.fazendarionegro.com.br*, or **Projeto Gadonça** ① *Fazenda San Francisco, www.fazendasanfrancisco.tur.br*. See also **Fazenda San Francisco**, page 735.

There have been serious concerns about the **Jaguar Research Center**, on the Transpantaneira, who stands accused, by the Ministério Público de Mato Grosso, of feeding wild jaguar in order to lure them to the camera, building on national park land and of attempted animal trafficking. We do not recommend this operator in this guide nor any who guarantee a jaguar sighting.

Visitors can make an important contribution to protecting the Pantanal by acting responsibly and choosing guides accordingly. Take your rubbish away with you, don't fish out of season, don't let guides kill or disturb fauna, don't buy products made from endangered species, don't buy live birds or monkeys, and report any violation to the authorities. The practice of catching caiman, even though they are then released, is traumatic for the animals and has potentially disruptive long-term effects.

Ins and outs

Getting there and around

The Pantanal can be reached from both Mato Grosso and Mato Grosso do Sul states. In Mato Grosso access is from the capital city, Cuiabá, which has an airport. In Mato Grosso do Sul, access is from the state capital, Campo Grande, or from Corumbá on the border with Bolivia (both cities have airports); or from the little cattle ranching town of Miranda (connected to the rest of Brazil by bus and train), which lies between them.

There are three ways to visit the Pantanal. The cheapest (and most popular with backpackers) is to take an **organized tour**. These involve camping, perhaps with a night in a *fazenda* (ranch house), and a range of activities, including hiking, canoeing and wildlife and birdwatching. Guides tend to emphasize light adventure and have reasonable general knowledge of the Pantanal but poor knowledge of specific plants or animals.

Another option is to organize a tour through a **fazenda**. Although some are very modest, *fazendas* are generally comfortable with air-conditioned rooms and good home cooking. Many (if requested in advance) can organize decent wildlife guides who know English and scientific names for birds and animals. *Fazendas* can also be booked through tour operators, such as **Brazil Nature Tours** in Campo Grande (see page 738), **Aguas do Pantanal Turismo** in Miranda (see page 739) or **Pantanal Nature Tours** in Cuiabá (see page 758).

It is also possible to visit the Pantanal on a **self-drive tour**, by hiring a 4WD in Cuiabá or Campo Grande. Those considering this option should speak good Portuguese and stick to the two principal dirt roads that enter the Pantanal: the Transpantaneira in Mato Grosso and the Estrada Parque in Mato Grosso do Sul.

For further information on the Pantanal, consult www.braziltour.com, www.brazil tourism.org, www.turismo.ms.gov.br and www.sedtur.mt.gov.br.

Visiting the Southern Pantanal → *For details see Mato Grosso do Sul, page 722.*

Access to the southern Pantanal is from Campo Grande (see page 723), Miranda (see page 729) and Corumbá (see page 730), all in Mato Grosso do Sul.

Campo Grande offers most of the tours, both upmarket (through agencies such as **Saab**) and the myriad budget operators like **Ecological Expeditions**, whose touts are ready and waiting for buses arriving from destinations in eastern Brazil like Foz do Iguaçu.

Corumbá, near the Bolivian border, was once the capital of backpacker tourism in the Pantanal but, although many of the budget operators maintain offices here and cheap tours can be readily organized, the town is now used more as a departure point for boat trips. ▶▶ *See page 739.*

Miranda lies half way between Campo Grande and Corumbá at the turn off to Bonito. It is still a Pantanal ranching town free of touts, and the best of the *fazendas* (ranch house safari hotels) are situated close by. There are two excellent operators and the town is friendly and relaxed. Although there are excellent *fazendas* off the Estrada Parque road, there are also an increasing number opening up to tourism around Miranda. These include the stylish, upmarket **Refúgio Ecológico Caiman**, the closest thing central Brazil has to a Mexican hacienda (and similarly beloved of the chic) and **Fazenda San Francisco**, which is probably the best spot in the entire Pantanal for big cats, especially ocelot, which you can almost be guaranteed to see. ▶▶ *See Sleeping, pages 734 and 735.*

Many of the tours and some of the *fazendas* lie off a dirt road running off the BR-262 Campo Grande to Corumbá highway. This road, which is known as the **Estrada Parque**, begins halfway between Miranda and Corumbá at a turn-off called Buraco da Piranha (the Piranha hole), heads north into the Pantanal and then, after 51 km, turns west to Corumbá at a point called the Curva do Leque. This is the overland access point to **Nhecolândia** – a region particularly rich in wildlife. Four-wheel drives run by the tour operators or the *fazendeiros* wait at the Buraco da Piranha to meet tour buses arriving from Campo Grande. They then take visitors either to *fazendas* or to campsites in Nhecolândia. *Fazendas* in this area include **Fazenda Rio Negro**, a project run in conjunction with Conservation International and now closed to tourism, **Fazenda Barra Mansa, Fazenda Barranco Alto** and **Fazenda Santa Sophia, Fazenda Bela Vista**, which has a wealth of primates; and **Fazenda Rio Vermelho**, which is famous for sightings of the larger carnivores. ▶▶ *See Sleeping, page 735 and 736.*

Visiting the Northern Pantanal → *For details see Mato Grosso, page 722.*

There are two main access points to the northern Pantanal: the **Transpantaneira road** (see page 745), which cuts through the wetland and is lined with *fazendas*; and the town of **Barão de Melgaço** (see page 746), which is surrounded by large lakes and rivers and is not as good for wildlife. Both are reached from Cuiabá in Mato Grosso.

The Transpantaneira was built in 1976 and was originally planned to connect Cuiabá with Corumbá, but it currently goes only as far as the border at Porto Jofre on the Rio Cuiabá. Work has been suspended indefinitely – ostensibly because of the division of the two Mato Grosso states – and is a superb spot for wildlife watching. Hundreds of thousands of birds congregate here, particularly between June and September, to wade through the shallow wetlands to either side of the road. And at any time of year there seems to be a raptor on every other fence post. Mammals and reptiles can often be spotted crossing the road or even sitting on it, particularly at dawn and dusk. Most of the northern Pantanal's tourist-orientated *fazendas* are here. The road is unpaved, potholed and punctuated by numerous rickety wooden bridges and, although it can be driven in a standard hire car, progress is slow. It is probably better to see the Transpantaneira as part of a tour as most of the guides have access to the *fazendas* along the way. If you choose to go alone, be sure to book in advance; private individuals who turn up unannounced may or may not be welcome at some *fazendas*.

The easiest access is in the dry season (July to September). In the wet, especially January and February, there is no guarantee that you will get all the way to Porto Jofre. Bring plenty of water and some extra fuel as petrol stations often run out. If you choose not to take a tour or hire a car you can hitch a ride along the Transpantaneira from Poconé. Do not travel alone and be prepared for a bumpy ride in the back of a truck. There are several excellent companies based in Cuiabá who offer trips along the Transpantaneira to Porto Jofre, often combining them with visits to the Chapada dos Guimarães (see page 746), Nobres or the Mato Grosso Amazon. They include **Pantanal Nature** and the **Pantanal Bird Club**. ▸ *For further information, see Sleeping, page 753, Activities and tours, page 757, and Transport, page 759.*

When to go

The Pantanal is worth visiting at any time of year. However, the dry season from June to October is the ideal time to see wildlife as animals and birds congregate at the few remaining areas of water. This is also the breeding season, when birds form vast nesting areas, with thousands crowding the trees, creating an almost deafening cacophony of sounds. The white-sand river beaches are exposed, *jacarés* bask in the sun, and capybara frolic in the grass. It is during these months you are most likely to see jaguars, however, July sees lots of Brazilian visitors and the increased activity decreases the chances of sightings. From the end of November to the end of March (wettest in February), most of the area, which is crossed by many rivers, is subject to flooding. At this time mosquitoes abound and cattle crowd onto the few islands remaining above water. In the southern part of the Pantanal, many wild animals leave the area, but in the northern Pantanal, which is slightly higher, the animals remain.

Mato Grosso do Sul and the Southern Pantanal

Mato Grosso do Sul is dominated by the Pantanal wetlands in the north and by the low Serra da Bodoquena mountains in the south, which surround the family-orientated ecotourism town of Bonito. The mountains are honeycombed by caves and cut by numerous glassy clear streams. There are only a few towns of any size and the state is a centre of soya plantations and cattle ranching. Many of the designated backpacker tours of the Pantanal leave from the state capital, Campo Grande, which is a prosperous, modern city with lively nightlife. However, they take half a day to reach the Pantanal itself, which begins in earnest east of Campo Grande, near the cattle-ranching town of Miranda. Many of the best fazenda ranch houses are in the area surrounding Miranda, as well as a handful of small, upmarket tour operators. The town also has one of the Pantanal's liveliest festivals, O Festa do Homen Pantaneiro, in November. Corumbá, on the banks of the Rio Paraguai, is another popular departure point for the Pantanal, and lies close to the Estrada Parque dirt road (which runs through the wetlands) and to Nhecolândia, a wilderness area visited by most of the Campo Grande backpacker tours. ▸ For listings, see pages 733-742.

Campo Grande → *For listings, see pages 733-742. Colour map 3, C3. Phone code: 067. Population: 665,000.*

A major gateway to the Pantanal, Campo Grande is a pleasant, modern city on a grid system, with wide avenues. It was founded in 1899 and became the state capital in 1979. Because of the *terra roxa* (red earth), it is known as the 'Cidade Morena'.

In the centre is a shady park, the **Praça República**, commonly called the Praça do Rádio after the Rádio Clube on one of its corners. Three blocks west is **Praça Ari Coelho**. Linking the two squares, and running east–west through the city, is the broad Avenida Afonso Pena; much of its central reservation is planted with yellow *ypé* trees. In spring, their blossom covers the avenue, and much of the city besides. The avenue's eastern reaches

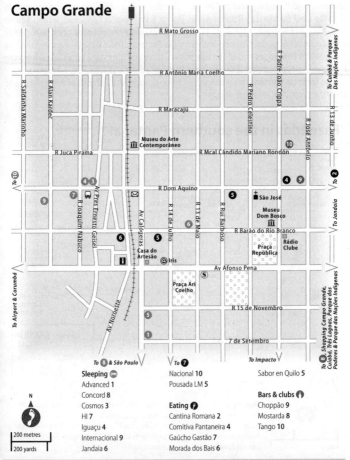

Campo Grande

Sleeping 🛏
Advanced **1**
Concord **8**
Cosmos **3**
HI **7**
Iguaçu **4**
Internacional **9**
Jandaia **6**
Nacional **10**
Pousada LM **5**

Eating 🍴
Cantina Romana **2**
Comitiva Pantaneira **4**
Gaúcho Gastão **7**
Morada dos Bais **6**
Sabor en Quilo **5**

Bars & clubs 🍸
Choppão **9**
Mostarda **8**
Tango **10**

are the centre of a burgeoning restaurant and nightlife scene. City tours are on offer everywhere but they are generally expensive and there are few obvious sights.

Ins and outs

Getting there The **airport** ⓘ *Av Duque de Caxias, 7 km, T067-3368 6000*, receives flights from Cuiabá, Londrina, São Paulo and Santa Cruz (Bolivia). A bus leaves every 10 minutes from outside the airport terminal for the city centre and bus station. A taxi costs US$6 (10 minutes). It is safe to spend the night at the airport if you arrive late. Banco do Brasil at the airport exchanges dollars; the Bradesco just outside has a Visa ATM. The airport also has a tourist information booth (little English, many pamphlets), a post office, car rental and airline offices.

Campo Grande is well connected by bus to cities in the southern Pantanal and onwards to Bolivia and Paraguay, and to São Paulo, Cuiabá and Brasília/Goiânia. The **rodoviária** ⓘ *in the block bounded by R Barão do Rio Branco, R Vasconcelos Fernandes, R Dom Aquino and R Joaquim Nabuco, T067-3383 1678*, has shops, *lanchonetes* and a cinema, together with a number of budget tour operators for the Pantanal. Town buses leave from the Rua Vasconcelos Fernandes end of the bus station; state and interstate buses leave from the Rua Joaquim Nabuco end. A taxi to Praça República costs US$4, or it's a 1-km walk.

The **Trem do Pantanal** train connects Campo Grande with Miranda at weekends – see Miranda, page 729, for more details.

Fazendas in the southern Pantanal

Sleeping
Cacimba de Pedra **4**
Fazenda 23 de Março **1**
Fazenda Baia Grande **2**
Fazenda Barra Mansa **3**

Fazenda Barranco Alto **9**
Fazenda Campo Lourdes **5**
Fazenda Meia Lua **7**
Fazenda San Francisco **6**
Fazenda Santa Ines **11**

Fazenda Santa Sophia **13**
Fazenda Xaraés **12**
Pousada Rio Vermelho **10**
Refúgio Ecológico Caiman **8**

The BR-262 is paved most of the way from Campo Grande to Corumbá and the Bolivian border; a rail service along this route is due to recommence in early 2009 and is likely to be expensive. It is best to make this journey during the day to take advantage of the marvellous scenery. ▸▸ *See Transport, page 740.*

Tourist information There are **Centro de Atendimento ao Turista** ⓘ *www.prefeiturade campogrande.com.br, Mon-Fri 0900-1800*, tourist booths throughout the city: at the airport, T067-3363 3116; in the rodoviária, T067-3382 2350; and in the Mercado Municipal, T067-3314 9949.

Sights
Just north of the Praça República, is the **Museu Dom Bosco** ⓘ *Av Alfonso Pena, Parque Naçoes Indígenas, T067-3312 6491, www.museu.ucdb.br, usually Tue-Sat 0800-1800, Sun 0800-1200 and 1400-1700, US$1.50, but with a temporary restriction on visits in early 2009, contact Professor Dirceu or Señor Juliano on T067-3326 9788,* which contains relics of the tribes who suffered at the hands of aggressive Salesian missionaries in the early and mid-20th century. The largest collections are from the Tukano and Bororo people from the upper Rio Negro and Mato Grosso respectively, both of whose cultures the Salesians were responsible for almost completely wiping out. Traditional practices such as sleeping in *malocas* or wearing indigenous clothing were banned, and the *indígenas* were indoctrinated in rigorous, literalistic pre-Vatican II Catholicism. These exhibits sit alongside a rather depressing display of stuffed endangered species (mostly from the Pantanal), as well as peculiarities such as a two-headed calf, and seashells from around the world.

Next to the railway line, the **Museu do Arte Contemporâneo** ⓘ *Marechal Rondón and Av Calógeras, Mon-Fri 1300-1800, free,* displays modern art from the region.

The **Parque dos Poderes**, a long way from the centre, covers several hectares. As well as the Palácio do Governo and state secretariats, there is a small zoo for rehabilitating animals from the Pantanal. Contact the **Centro de Reabilitação de Animais Silvestres (CRAS)** ⓘ *T067-3326 1370,* to arrange a visit. There are many lovely trees in the park, along with cycling and jogging tracks. Plenty of capybara live in the lakes.

Coxim → *Phone code: 067. Population: 28,500.*
Coxim, 242 km north of Campo Grande on the BR-163 and halfway between Campo Grande and Rondonópolis, also provides access to the Pantanal. It sits in a green bowl, on the shores of the Rio Taquari. The area has great potential for tourism, with waterfalls nearby at Palmeiras, and the Pantanal in close proximity. But as yet there are no official tours other than a few small charter boat operators at the town port. There are a few hotels including some cheap options around the bus station.

Ponta Porã to the border → *For listings, see pages 733-742. Colour map 3, C2.*
Phone code: 067. Population: 54,000.

Right on the border, Ponta Porã is separated from the town of **Pedro Juan Caballero** in Paraguay by only a broad avenue. With paved streets, good public transport and smart shops, Ponta Porã is decidedly more prosperous than its neighbour, although Brazilian visitors flock across the border to play the casino and buy cheaper foreign goods. An animal show is held each October at the **Parque das Exposições**, by the *rodoviária*.

Border essentials: Brazil–Paraguay

Ponta Porã (Brazil)–Pedro Juan Caballero (Paraguay)

Immigration There are no border posts between the two towns and people pass freely for local visits. For entry/exit visas, go to the **Brazilian Federal Police office**, Rua Marechal Floriano 1483 (second floor of the white engineering supply company building), T067-3431 1428, Monday to Friday 0730-1130, 1400-1700. The two nations' consulates face each other on Rua Internacional (border street), a block west of Ponta Porã's local bus terminal; some nationalities require a visa from the **Paraguayan consul**, Rua Internacional, next to Hotel Internacional, Monday to Friday 0800-1200. Check requirements carefully, and ensure your documents are in order; without the proper stamps you will inevitably be sent back somewhere later on in your travels. Taking a taxi between offices can speed things up if pressed for time; drivers know about border crossing requirements, US$7.

Transport From the border, there are frequent buses (around six hours) to Asunción, and flights there from Pedro Juan Caballero. A road also runs to Concepción on the Rio Paraguai, where boat connections can be made.

The town can be reached by bus or plane from Campo Grande. The *rodoviária* is 3 km out on the Dourados road, from where the 'São Domingos' bus runs to the centre, taxi US$3.

Bonito and around → *For listings, see pages 733-742. Colour map 3, C2. See also map, page 727. Phone code: 067. Population: 17,000.*

The designated tourist town of Bonito lies just south of the Pantanal in the **Serra da Bodoquena** hills. It is surrounded by beautiful *cerrado* forest cut by clear-water rivers rich with fish and dotted with plunging waterfalls and deep caves. The town was 'discovered' by *Globo* television in the 1980s and has since grown to become Brazil's foremost ecotourism destination. There are plenty of opportunities for gentle adventure activities such as caving, rafting and snorkelling, all with proper safety measures and great even for very small children. Those looking to see animals and contemplate nature should opt for the forest walks of the Sucuri river. Despite the heavy influx of visitors, plenty of wildlife appear on and around the trails when it is quiet. **Paca** and **agouti** (large, tailless foraging rodents), **brown capuchin** monkeys and **toco toucans** are abundant, as are endangered species like the tiny and aggressive **bush dog** and cats such as **ocelot** and **jaguarundi**. **Bare-faced currasows** (magnificent turkey-sized forest floor birds) can often be seen strutting around the pathways. Rarely seen small toucans such as the **chestnut-eared aracari** are relatively easy to spot here, flitting in and out of the trees.

For all its attractiveness, many of Bonito's prices are becoming almost offensively steep and many of the attractions would simply not be worth the entry ticket at half the price.

Ins and outs

Getting there and around The *rodoviária* is on the edge of town. Several buses daily run to/from Campo Grande (five hours), Miranda (two to three hours) and Corumbá (five hours). Bonito town is a grid layout based around one principal street, Rua Coronel Pilad

Bonito

Sleeping 🛏
Albergue do Bonito **3**
Canaã **2**
Pira Miuna **6**
Pousada Muito Bonito **1**
Pousada Olho d'Água **4**
São Jorge Hostel **5**
Tapera **7**

Eating 🍴
Cantinho do Peixe **3**
Da Vovó **2**
Mercado da Praça **5**
Santa Esmeralda **1**
Tapera **4**

Bars & clubs 🍸
Bollicho **7**
O Taboa **8**

Rebuá, which extends for about 2 km. The town is easily negotiated on foot. ▸▸ *See Transport, page 740.*

Tourist information The tourist office: **Conselho Municipal de Turismo (COMTUR)** ① *Rodovia Bonio, Guia Lopes da Laguna km1, T067-3255 2160, www.bonito-ms.com.br,* has limited information and staff do not speak English. The private website www.portalbonito.com.br is a more useful source of information. Prices in Bonito have risen sharply over the years, making the area prohibitively expensive for those on a budget. Local attractions can only be visited with prior booking through one of the town's numerous travel agents. With the exception of specialist activities like cave diving, all agents offer exactly the same products at exactly the same price, but only a few offer transport. Taxis to the sights are exorbitantly expensive; an alternative would be to hire a car. ▸▸ *See Activities and tours, page 739, and Car hire, page 740.*

Best time to visit The number of visitors to Bonito is limited so pre-booking is essential during December and January, Carnaval, Easter and July; prices during these times are also very high. The wet season is in January and February; December to February are the hottest months; July and August coolest.

Sights

There are scores of different sights in Bonito and those sketched out below are a mere representative selection. The website www.bonito-ms.com.br has a full list, with pictures and links to each individual attraction's website.

Gruta Lagoa Azul ① *Rodovia para Tres Moros 22 km, daily 0700-1700, US$20,* is a cave with a lake 50 m long and 110 m wide, 75 m below ground level. The water's temperature is 20°C, and it is a jewel-like blue, as light from the opening is refracted through limestone and magnesium.

Prehistoric animal bones have been found in the lake. The light is at its best in January and February, from 0700 to 0900, but is fine at other times. A 25-ha park surrounds the cave. The cave is filled with stalactites and stalagmites. It is reached via a very steep 294-step staircase which can be slippery in the rain and is completely unilluminated.

Nossa Senhora Aparecida cave has superb stalactites and stalagmites and can be visited, although there is no tourism infrastructure.

On the banks of the Rio Formoso, the **Balneário Municipal** ① *7 km on road to Jardim, US$4*, has changing rooms, toilets, camping, swimming in clear water and plenty of colourful fish to see. Strenuous efforts are made to keep the water and shore clean. The **Horminio waterfalls** ① *US$1*, consist of eight falls, which are suitable for swimming. There's a bar and camping is possible. **Rafting** is also a popular activity. The 2½-hour trip combines floating peacefully downriver, swimming and shooting down the four waterfalls.

The **Aquário Natural** ① *Estrada para Jardim 8 km and then 5.5 km of dirt road, daily 0900-1800, US$70 including lunch*, is a 600-m-long clear-water river lagoon filled with dourado and other fish and is formed by one of the springs of the Rio Formoso. This is the most child-friendly snorkelling in Bonito – easy and with almost no current.

It is possible to snorkel further along the **Rio Formoso** ① *Estrada para Ilha do Padre 12 km, daily 0800-1700, US$28*, or float on rubber dinghies over gentle rapids.

One of the better value, and more peaceful tours involves birding and swimming or snorkelling in crystal-clear water from the springs of the **Rio Sucuri** ① *Rodovia Bonito, Fazenda São Geraldo, Km 18, T067-3255 1030, daily 0900-1800, US$75 with lunch*, to its meeting with the Formoso, followed by horse riding or trail walking. Other tours include **Rio da Prata** (US$40), a beautiful spring with underground snorkelling for 2 km. There are also plenty of chances for walking along ecological trails, horse riding and fishing trips. The **fishing** season is from 1 March to 31 October. In late October and early November is the *piracema* (fish run). The fish return to the spawning grounds and hundreds can be seen jumping the falls.

Abismo Anhumas ① *Fazenda Anhumas, Estrada para Campo dos Indios s/n, T067-3225 3313, US$210 (for abseiling and snorkelling) or US$310 (for rapelling and scuba diving)*, is another of Bonito's spectacular caves, filled with a glassy pool. The ticket gives visitors an abseil (of just a few metres) into the cave, followed by three to four hours snorkelling or scuba diving.

Bonito Aventura ① *Estrada para Jardim 8 km, daily 0900-1800, US$28, including lunch*. This little reserve comprises a stand of pretty cerrado forest with many rodents like paca and agouti as well as capuchin monkeys and toco toucans in the trees. Trails cut through it to a clear-water river filled with fish.

Jardim

Jardim, reached by paved road (60 km from Bonito) could be an alternative base to Bonito for trips on clear-water rivers and visits to caves. There is far less infrastructure and consequently far fewer tourists and cheaper accommodation, restaurant and taxi prices. The town itself has a wide, tree-lined main street, a handful of hotels and basic café- restaurants. The official town website, www.jardim.ms.gov.br, has information and photos of what to see and do. The *rodoviária* has regular bus connections with Campo Grande and other towns (see Transport, page 740). From Bonito a road leads to **Porto Murtinho**, where a boat crosses to Isla Margarita in Paraguay (entry stamp available on the island).

Miranda → *For listings, see pages 733-742. Colour map 3, B2. Population: 23,000.*

This little farming town built around a now disused mill and a railway station lies some 200 km west of Campo Grande at the turn-off to Bonito. It has long been overlooked as a gateway to the Pantanal and Bonito, but is actually far closer to both than either Corumbá or Campo Grande. Many of the best of the southern Pantanal *fazendas* are found here: **San Francisco** has an impressive big cat project and almost guaranteed ocelot or jaguar sightings, while **Refúgio Ecológico Caiman** would sit comfortably within the pages of *Condé Nast Traveller*. Miranda is also a real town, preoccupied more with its own local economy and culture than with tourism. It lies in the heart of indigenous Terena land and the communities have a large **cultural and arts centre** ⓘ *at the entrance to town, Mon-Fri 0700-2200, Sat and Sun 0800-2200, free*, with panels on Terena history and arts and crafts for sale. Every October Miranda throws the spectacular **Festa do Homem Pantaneiro**: four days of rodeos, lassoing and general revelry that combine well with the water festival in Corumbá. For dates ask tour operators (see page 739). The crystal-clear river Salobrinho just outside town has great birdlife and a community of giant otters. There is a wonderful British girder bridge just west of town given as a gift to Brazil by King George V.

Ins and outs The Campo Grande–Corumbá road crosses the Rio Miranda bridge (two service stations before it), then continues paved all the way to cross the Rio Paraguai.

Miranda

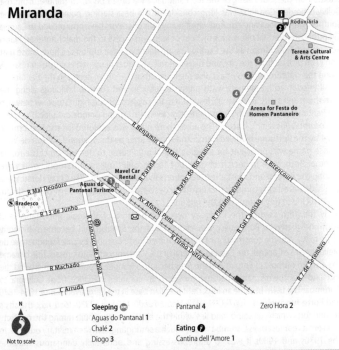

N
Not to scale

Sleeping 🛏
Aguas do Pantanal 1
Chalé 2
Diogo 3

Pantanal 4

Eating 🍴
Cantina dell'Amore 1

Zero Hora 2

Miranda is served by numerous daily buses from Corumbá, Campo Grande and Bonito. There is a tourist booth just outside the *rodoviária*, opposite the **Zero Hora** bakery and supermarket. Rail services to Corumbá, onwards to Bolivia and eventually to Campo Grande are due to recommence in 2009. There is no tourist office but Aguas do Pantanal can provide information in English, see also www.mirandaemfoco.com. The town is tiny and can be walked from end to end in less than 10 minutes.

Trem do Pantanal

① *Estação Ferroviaria s/n, T067-3384 6755, Sat-Sun 1 departure, US$20 or US$400 for a private cabin for up to 8 people, bookable only through tour operators like SAAB tourism or Brazil Nature Tours, see page 738 .*

Miranda is the terminus for the Trem do Pantanal. This is a tourist-designated diesel train which takes 11 hours to make the 220-km trip across the southwestern Pantanal from Campo Grande. The journey includes a two-hour stop for lunch in the tiny town of Aquidauana and breaks at stations to buy indigenous arts and crafts. There's little wildlife to see along the way– the occasional rhea strinding across the pasture, distant lakes filled with birds – but the journey is more comfortable and leisurely than on the bus.

Corumbá → *For listings, see pages 733-742. Colour map 3, B1. Phone code: 067. Population: 95,000.*

Situated on the south bank of the Rio Paraguai, by a broad bend, 15 minutes from the Bolivian border, Corumbá was long considered the best starting point for visiting the southern part of the Pantanal. And whilst many tour operators have now moved to Campo Grande, Corumbá still offers trips by boat or jeep and access to the major hotel and farm accommodation. Almost all the Campo Grande agencies have sub-offices here, those that don't can pick up from the city, and there are still a number of upmarket cruise companies along the waterfront. Corumbá is also the most attractive urban centre in the Pantanal – small enough to be intimate, with pretty Republican and colonial buildings along the waterfront and a very lively annual festival. It makes a pleasant one-night stopover between the Pantanal and Bolivia and is far more attractive than Campo Grande or Cuiabá.

Corumbá has a long history. The area where it lies was explored for the first time in 1524 by the Portuguese Aleixo Garcia and shortly after by the Spaniard Cabeza de Vaca whose name was prescient for a region that would come to depend on cattle for its income. Both were in search of gold but found only Guiacurú warriors, who were among the fiercest and most effective fighters in Brazil, and who, like Crazy Horse, were finally defeated only through trickery. Their descendants are the modern-day Kadiweu, who still life in tiny numbers in the region.

By the 18th century the Paraguay river had become of strategic importance and skirmishes between Portuguese *bandeirantes* and the Spanish had become sufficiently tense to warrant the construction of the now ruined Forte Coimbra by Luiz Albuquerque de Mello Pereira e Cáceres, the Capitão-General of the Captaincy of Mato Grosso. This became the eastern outpost of Empire and the river became a frontier. A port grew up around the fort and the town's name became corrupted in common parlance from Coímbra to Corumbá. The town became an important Brazilian base in the Parguayan war of 1864-1870 and **Forte Junqueira** ① *T067-3231 5828, Mon-Fri 0800-1100 and 1330-1630, R$2*, the city's second fort (which still stands and lies within the city limits), was built during the conflict.

From its earliest days Corumbá was as much a smuggling town as a military outpost. In the 1970s and 1980s it was so unprepossessing and potentially dangerous that the railway that ferried passengers in and out of Bolivia was popularly known as the Death Train. Whilst there is still illicit trade in Corumbá, Mato Grosso do Sul's prosperity has seen the town become more salubrious. The colonial buildings are freshly painted and there are even a smattering of smart restaurants. It is a pleasant town to spend a day or so; especially during the annual Festa de Nossa Senhora de Candelária when the streets are filled with processions and as much water is thrown about as in the Thai Songkran.

There are beautiful views from the quays out over the Paraguay river, especially at sunset, and some remnant colonial architecture. The compact streets include the spacious **Praça da Independência** and **Avenida General Rondon** (between Frei Mariano and 7 de Septembro), which has a palm-lined promenade that comes to life in the evenings. There is also hiking in the rugged Serra do Urucum hills to the south, where the world's greatest reserve of manganese is now being worked.

Corumbá

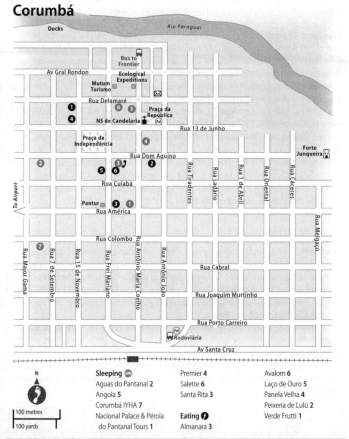

Sleeping	Premier **4**	Avalom **6**
Aguas do Pantanal **2**	Salette **6**	Laço de Ouro **5**
Angola **5**	Santa Rita **3**	Panela Velha **4**
Corumbá IYHA **7**		Peixeria de Lulú **2**
Nacional Palace & Pérola	**Eating**	Verde Frutti **1**
do Pantanal Tours **1**	Almanara **3**	

Border essentials: Brazil–Bolivia

Corumbá (Brazil)–Puerto Suárez (Bolivia)

You will need to present a yellow fever vaccination certificate to enter Bolivia. If you arrive in Brazil without a yellow fever vaccination certificate, you may have to go to Rua 7 de Setembro, Corumbá, for an inoculation. There are money changers only at the border and in Quijarro (Bolivia).

Immigration Formalities are constantly changing, so check procedures in advance at the tourist office or *policía federal*. At present passports are stamped at the *rodoviária* Monday to Friday 0800-1130 and 1330-1700, and at the **Brazilian Polícia Federal** (Praça da República 37, Corumbá) at weekends 0800-1130 and 1330-1700. The visa must be obtained on the day of departure. If exiting Brazil in order to get a new visa, remember that exit and entry must not be on the same day.

Transport Leaving Brazil, take Canarinho city bus marked 'Fronteira' from the port end of Rua Antônio Maria Coelho to the Bolivian border (15 minutes, US$0.35), walk over the bridge to Bolivian immigration (blue building), then take a *colectivo* to Quijarro or Puerto Suárez. Taxis to the border cost US$6-8.

When entering Brazil from Quijarro, take a taxi or walk to the Bolivian border to go through formalities. Just past the bridge, on a small side street to the right, is the bus stop for Corumbá. Take a bus marked 'Fronteira' or 'Tamengo' to Praça da República (US$0.80, every 45 minutes 0630-1915); don't believe taxi drivers who say there is no bus. Taxi to the centre US$6. Brazilian immigration formalities are carried out at the *policía federal*.

Into Bolivia Over the border from Corumbá are Arroyo Concepción, Puerto Quijarro and Puerto Suárez. From Puerto Quijarro a 650-km railway runs to Santa Cruz de la Sierra. There is a road of sorts. A better road route is from Cáceres to San Matías, then to San Ignacio (see page 747). There are internal flights from Puerto Suárez.

Ins and outs

The **airport** ① *4 km west of town*, receives flights from Campo Grande, Cuiabá, Londrina and São Paulo (via Campo Grande). There is no public transport from the airport to town; you have to take a taxi (US$6). The **rodoviária** ① *R Porto Carreiro at the south end of R Tiradentes*, is next to the railway station. A city bus to Praça da República costs US$0.80. Taxis are extortionate, but moto-taxis charge only US$0.65. Corumbá is well connected by bus to Campo Grande and Bolivia.

The municipal tourist office, **Sematur** ① *R América 969, T067-231 7336*, provides general information and city maps. The combination of economic hard times and drug running make the city unsafe late at night.

There is a lively festival every October. Corumbá is hot (particularly between September and January), with 70% humidity; June and July are cooler. Mosquitoes can be a real problem from December to February.

For Sleeping and Eating price codes and other relevant information, see pages 32-37.

⊜ Sleeping

Campo Grande *p723, map p723*
The better hotels lie near the city centre. There are lots of cheaper hotels in the streets around the *rodoviária* so it is easy to leave bags in the *guarda volumes* and shop around. This area is not safe at night.
L Jandaia, R Barão do Rio Branco 1271, T067-3316 7700, www.jandaia.com.br. The city's best hotel, aimed at a business market. Modern well-appointed rooms (with Wi-Fi) in a tower. The best are above the 10th floor. Pool, gym and some English spoken.
A-B Advanced, Av Calógeras 1909, T067-3321 5000, www.hoteladvanced.com.br. Clean, spacious, spartan rooms with en suites and boiler-heated showers, in a 1980s block with a very small pool. Cheaper with fan.
A-B Internacional, R Alan Kardec 223, T067-3384 4677, www.hotelinternacional.com.br. Small but comfortable rooms with a/c or fans and flatpack furniture, or newly renovated suites with smart bathrooms in slate and tile and cable TV. Pool and restaurant. Quiet street near the *rodoviária*.
C Concord, Av Calógeras 1624, T067-3384 3081, www.hotelconcord.com.br. A standard town hotel with a small pool and renovated a/c rooms with modern fittings.
D-E Iguaçu, R Dom Aquino 761, T067-3322 4621, www.hoteliguacu.com.br. Very popular well-kept hotel next to the *rodoviária* with smart, simple a/c rooms with cable TV. Good breakfast.
D-E Nacional, R Dom Aquino 610, T067-3383 2461, hotelnacional@ig.com.br. Quiet, well-kept hotel with simple rooms with fans and proper mattresses. Some en suites. TV room and internet. Better value than the nearby HI.
E HI, R Joaquim Nabuco 185, opposite *rodoviária*, T067-3042 0508, www.hostel

campogrande.com. Simple, musty little rooms with saggy foam mattress beds and frayed en suites. Laundry, kitchen, internet, reception open 24 hrs. **Ecological Expeditions** (see Activities and tours, page 738) offers Pantanal trips from their office next door.
E-F Cosmos, R Dom Aquino 771, near the *rodoviária*, T067-3384 4270. Very simple but bright and well-kept 1980s rooms with decent mattresses and en suites.
E-F Pousada LM, R 15 de Novembro 201, by Praça Ari Coelho, T067-3321 5207, www.lmhotel.com.br. Tiny, basic en suites set around a courtyard, all with TV and fridge, some with terraces. Cheaper with fan.

Ponta Porã *p725*
Brazilian hotels include breakfast in tariff; Paraguayan ones do not.
A-B Barcelona, R Guia Lopes 45, T067-3437 2500. Simple but well kept, with a/c or fan-cooled rooms. Bar and sauna.
C Alvorada, Av Brasil 2977, T067-3431 5866. With a good café, close to post office, good value but often full.
C-D Internacional, R Internacional 1267, T067-3431 1243. Cheaper without a/c. Hot water, good breakfast. Recommended.
E Dos Viajantes, R Albino Torraca 591, T067-3421 8817, across park opposite the railway station. Very basic and only for those on the tightest budget.

Bonito *p726, map p727*
AL Pira Miuna, R Luís da Costa Leite 1792, T067-3255 1058, www.piramiunahotel. com.br. Huge, ugly brick building with the most comfortable a/c rooms in the centre and a large pool area with jacuzzis and a bar.
AL Pousada Olho d'Água, Rod Três Morros, Km 1, T067-3255 1430, www.pousadaolho dagua.com.br. Comfortable accommodation in fan-cooled cabins set in an orchard next to a small lake. Horse riding, bike rental, solar-powered hot water and great food from the vegetable garden. Recommended.

A Tapera, Estrada Ilha do Padre, Km 10, on the hill above the Shell station on the road to Jardim, T/F067-3255 1700, www.tapera hotel.com.br. Peaceful location with fine views and cool breezes. Very comfortable, but own transport an advantage.

C Canaã, R Col Pilad Rebuá 1376, T067-3255 1255, www.hotelcanaabonitoms.com.br. A scruffy lobby leads to gloomy though reasonably well-maintained 1980s motel-style rooms with a/c and en suites. Also has a tour agency.

C-E Albergue do Bonito, R Lúcio Borralho 716, Vila Donária, T/F067-3255 1462, www.aj bonito.com.br. IYHA youth hostel. A well-run hostel with a travel agency, pool, kitchen and laundry facilities. English spoken, very friendly. Price per person for dorms.

D Pousada Muito Bonito, R Col Pilad Rebuá 1448, T/F067-3255 1645, www.muito bonito.com.br. Price per person in en suites or dorm-style rooms with bunk beds, all with a nice shared patio. Clean, excellent and with helpful owners and a tour operator (Mario Doblack at the tour office speaks English, French and Spanish). The price includes breakfast.

Camping

Camping Rio Formoso, Rodovia Bonito/ Guia Lopes da Laguna Km 06, T067-9284 5994, www.campingrioformoso.com.br. With space for 60 tents.

Miranda *p729, map p729*

A-D Aguas do Pantanal, Av Afonso Pena 367, T067-242 1242, www.aguasdopantanal. com.br. Much the best in town with a good range of very comfortable a/c rooms and cheaper backpacker accommodation, an attractive pool surrounded by tropical flowers and a very helpful travel agency (see page 739). They usually have a rep waiting at the *rodoviária*.

C Hotel Chalé, Av Barão do Rio Branco 685, T067-242 1216, hotelchale@star5.com.br. Plain a/c motel-like rooms with tiled floors and en suites, and a pool.

C Pantanal Hotel, Av Barão do Rio Branco 609, T067-3242 1068. Standard town hotel with pool and well-maintained a/c rooms with en suite, set along a gloomy corridor.

D-E Diogo, Av Barão do Rio Branco s/n, T067-242 1468. Very simple but well-kept doubles, triples and quadruples, some with a/c.

Fazendas around Miranda

Prices below include accommodation, all food and at least 2 guided trips per day. Standard packages include jeep trips, trail walks, horse riding, boat trips (where the *fazenda* has a river) and night safaris. They do not always include transfer from Miranda or the Buraco da Onca and this should be checked when booking. Unless otherwise indicated the standard of wildlife guiding will be poor, with common familial or generic names known only for animals and little awareness of species diversity or numbers. Keen birdwatchers should request a specialist birding guide through their tour operator or *fazenda*. Also take a good pair of binoculars and some field guides (see Books, page 809). The following *fazendas* can be booked through **Brazil Nature Tours** in Campo Grande, page 739, or **Aguas do Pantanal Turismo** in Miranda, page 739. Tours are the same price even if you are on your own, but there are almost always other guests.

LL Refúgio Ecológico Caiman, 36 km from Miranda, T011-3706 1800, www.caiman.com.br. The most comfortable, stylish accommodation in the Pantanal in a hotel reminiscent of a Mexican hacienda. Tours and guiding are excellent. Part of the **Roteiros de Charme** group (see page 34).

AL Cacimba de Pedra, Estr Agachi, T067-9982 4655, www.cacimbadepedra.com.br. A Jacaré caiman farm and *pousada* in beautiful dry deciduous forest cut by trails and dotted with lakes. A/c rooms are simple but spruce and sit in front of an inviting pool. The forest is abundant with wildlife. There is a hyacinth macaw nest on the farm and tapir sightings are common.

AL Fazenda Campo Lourdes, T067-3026 5786, www.campolourdes.com.br. One of the most remote *fazendas* in the heart of wild country. Rustic but comfortable accommodation.

AL Fazenda San Francisco, turn off BR-262 30 km west of Miranda, T067-3242 3333, www.fazendasanfrancisco.tur.br. One of the best places in the Pantanal to see wild cats, which are preserved through Roberto Coelho's imaginative **Gadonça** project, www.procarnivoros.org.br, a pioneering initiative that encourages the preservation of natural big cat prey to reduce losses from jaguar kills on cattle. The scheme has been a great success. Birding is also excellent. Accommodation is simple but very well kept in rustic a/c cabins around a pool in a garden filled with rheas. There are plans to build chic new cabins. Food and guides are excellent. Birdwatchers should request Alyson (see Activities and tours, page 738) at least a week in advance.

AL Fazenda Santa Ines, Estr La Lima, Km 19, www.fazendasantaines.com.br. A very comfortable family-orientated *fazenda* overlooking an artificial lake. Tours are aimed firmly at the Campo Grande weekend market and although there is little wildlife here, food is excellent and there is a range of light adventure activities for kids.

AL-A Fazenda Baia Grande, Estr La Lima, Km 19, T067-3382 4223, www.fazendabaia grande.com.br. Very comfortable a/c rooms set around a pool in a bougainvillea and *ipê*-filled garden. The *fazenda* is surrounded by savannah and stands of *cerrado* broken by large lakes. The owner, Alex, is very friendly, eager to please and enthusiastic.

A Fazenda 23 de Março, T067-3321 4737, www.fazenda23demarco.com.br. Simple rustic *fazenda* with only 4 rooms near Miranda in Aquidauna. There are programmes orientated to budget travellers, and **Centrapan**, a centre for the preservation of Pantanal culture, where visitors can learn to lasso, ride a bronco and turn their hand to other Pantanal cowboy activities.

Fazendas on the Estrada Parque

The Estrada Parque is a dirt road that cuts through the Pantanal near Miranda – running in a right angle through the wetlands and eventually arriving in Corumbá town. See map page 724.

LL-L Fazenda Xaraés, www.xaraes.com.br. One of the most luxurious *fazendas*, with a pool, tennis court, sauna, airstrip and modest but well-appointed a/c rooms in cream and terracotta. The immediate environs have been extensively cleared, but there are some wild areas of savannah and *cerrado* nearby and there are giant otters in the neighbouring Rio Abodrai.

L-AL Fazenda Barra Mansa, www.hotel barramansa.com.br. One of the better lodges in the region in a wild area right on the banks of the Rio Negro and between 2 large tracts of wetland. Like all the Rio Negro *fazendas* it is famous for its jaguars. Specialist guiding is available on request; be sure to stipulate this in advance. The farm also offers sport fishing, horse riding and canoe trips on the river. Accommodation for up to 16 is in rustic a/c rooms with hammocks. There is a small library of field guides at the *fazenda*.

L-AL Fazenda Barranco Alto, Caixa postal 109, Aquidauana, Mato Grosso do Sul, T067-3241 4047, www.fazendabarrancoalto. com.br. A beautiful, remote large ranch on the banks of the Rio Negro and owned and run by and agronomist and his biologist wife. Along with the neighbouring **Fazenda Rio Negro**, it is one of the oldest *fazendas* in the Pantanal with farm buildings dating from the first half of the 20th century. The surrounding area has stands of *cerrado* set in seasonally flooded savannah cut by the river. Guiding is good but stipulate your interest in wildlife in advance, especially if you are a birder.

L-AL Fazenda Santa Sophia, T067-9648 9352, www.fazendasantasophia.com.br. A beautiful old wood and plaster *fazenda* on the Rio Negro near Barranco Alto. There are no specialist nature guides (organize your own) but the scenery is wonderful and rich in wildlife and the accommodation simple but comfortable. All excursions are on horseback.

AL Fazenda Rio Vermelho, T067-3382 2046, A rustic *fazenda* in a wild area on the banks of a river famous for its population of jaguars. Simple but well-kept a/c rooms, with fridge. Organize your trip well in advance as the *fazenda* lies a long way off the Parque Estrada road.

Corumbá *p730, map p731*

There are hostels around the bus station, however this is a 10-min walk from the centre of town where most of the hotels, restaurants and tour agencies are found.

A-B Aguas do Pantanal Palace hotel, R Dom Aquino Corrêa 1457, T067-3234 8800, www.aguasdopantanalhotel.com.br. The smartest in town together with the **Nacional Palace**, with a/c rooms in a 1980s tower, a pool and sauna.

A-B Nacional Palace, R América 936, T067-3234 6000, www.hnacional.com.br. Smart, modern a/c rooms, a decent pool and parking.

C-D Angola, R Antônio Maria Coelho 124, T067-3231 7727. Huge, scruffy a/c and fan-cooled rooms with en suites. Internet access. Safe as it lies in front of the *polícia federal*.

C-E Salette, R Delamaré 893, T067-3231 6246. Cheap and cheerful with a range of rooms, the cheapest with fans and shared bathrooms. Recommended.

D Premier, R Antônio Maria Coelho 389, T067-3231 4937. Basic *pousada* with small a/c rooms without windows. Prices negotiable.

D Santa Rita, R Dom Aquino 860, T067-3231 5453. Modern, well-kept hotel with a/c rooms, all with TVs and en suites.

D-E HI Corumbá, R Colombo 1419, T067-3231 1005, www.corumbahostel.com.br. A newly opened, well-equipped modern hostel with helpful staff and a pool. A/c or fan-cooled rooms and dorms.

🍴 Eating

Campo Grande *p723, map p723*

Local specialities include *caldo de piranha* (soup), *chipa* (Paraguayan cheese bread, sold on the streets, delicious when hot) and the local liqueur, *pequi com caju*, which contains *cachaça* (sugar-cane rum). There are many cheap restaurants around the *rodoviária* and many others in the **Shopping Campo Grande** mall.

†††† Comitiva Pantaneira, R Dom Aquino 2221, T067-3383 8799. Hearty, tasty and very meaty regional dishes served by waiters in cowboy gear or as a buffet. Lunchtime only.

††† Gaúcho Gastão, R 14 de Julho 775, T067-3384 4326. The best *churrascaria* in town, famous for its beef. Comfortable. Lunch only.

†† Cantina Romana, R da Paz, 237, T067-3324 9777. Established for more than 20 years, Italian dishes, salads and a lunchtime buffet, good atmosphere.

††-† Sabor en Quilo, R Barão do Rio Branco 1118 and R Dom Aquino 1786, T067-3383 3911. Lunchtime only. Self-service per kilo restaurants with plenty of choice including sushi on Sat.

† Morada dos Bais, Av Noroeste, 5140, corner with Afonso Pena, behind tourist office. Brazilian and Italian dishes, snacks and coffee served in a pretty courtyard, Lunchtime only.

Bonito *p726, map p727*

†††-†† Santa Esmeralda, R Col Pilad Rebuá 1831. Respectable Italian food in one of the few a/c dining rooms.

†† Cantinho do Peixe, R 31 de Março 1918, T067-3255 3381. À la carte Pantanal fish dishes including good *pintado na telha* (grilled surubim).

†† Tapera, R Col Pilad Rebuá 480, T067-3255 1110. Good, home-grown vegetables, breakfast, lunch, pizzas, meat and fish dishes, opens 1900 for the evening meal.

¶ **Da Vovó**, R Sen F Muller 570, T067-3255 2723. A great per kilo restaurant serving Minas and local food all cooked in a traditional wood-burning aga. Plenty of veg and salads.

¶ **Mercado da Praça**, R 15 Novembro 376, T067-3255 2317. The cheapest in town. A snack bar housed in the local supermarket, offering sandwiches and juices 0600-2400.

Miranda *p729, map p729*

¶¶ **Cantina Dell'Amore**, Av Barão do Rio Branco 515, T067-3242 2826. The best in town with fish, pasta and *jacaré* steak.

¶ **Zero Hora**, Av Barão do Rio Branco at the *rodoviária*, T067-3242 1330. 24-hr snack bar, provision shop and, at the back, there's an average but good-value per kilo restaurant, with its own private waterfall.

Corumbá *p730, map p731*

Local specialities include *peixadas corum-baenses*, a variety of fish dishes prepared with the catch of the day; as well as ice cream, liquor and sweets made of *bocaiúva*, a small yellow palm fruit, in season Sep-Feb. There is a range of decent restaurants in R Frei Mariano including a number of *churrascarias* and pasta restaurants. You'll find plenty of good simple fish restaurant bars on the waterfront.

¶¶¶-¶¶ **Avalom**, R Frei Mariano 499, T067-3231 4430. Chic little restaurant bar with streetside tables and decent pasta, pizza and fish. Buzzing with a young middle-class crowd, especially after 2100 on Fri.

¶¶ **Almanara**, R América 961. Arabic and Turkish food from felafel to *baba ganoush*.

¶¶ **Laço de Ouro**, R Frei Mariano 556, T067-3231 7371. Very popular fish restaurant with a lively atmosphere and tables spilling out onto the street. Similar crowd to **Avalom**.

¶¶-¶ **Peixeria de Lulú**, R Dom Aquino 700, T067-3232 2142. A local institution that has been selling good river fish for many years.

¶ **Panela Velha**, R 15 de Novembro 156, T067-3232 5650. Popular lunchtime

restaurant with a decent, cheap all-you-can-eat buffet.

¶ **Verde Frutti**, R Delamaré 1164, T067-3231 3032. A snack bar with a wide variety of juices and great, ice-cold *acai na tigela*.

◑ Bars and clubs

Campo Grande *p723, map p723*

The best of the chic bars are on **R Afonso Pena**, beyond the monument, and along the streets to the north of Afonso Pena.

Choppão, R Dom Aquino 2331, T067-3383 9471. Lively open-sided bar with live music from Thu to Sat.

Morada dos Bais, see Eating, above. Restaurant and *choperia*, live music in the courtyard, daily from 2030, free.

Mostarda, Av Afonso Pena 3952, T067-3026 8469. Popular 20- and 30-something bar which is always lively after 2200 and hosts live music at weekends.

Clubs

There are a number of clubs open Thu-Sat, including **Tango**, R Cândido Mariano 2181, www.tangobar.com.br, and for something a little more alternative try **Bazar** or **Garagem**, R Doutor Temístocles 94.

Bonito *p726, map p727*

Bollicho Bar, R Col Pilad Rebuá 1996, T067-3255 3299. Always thronging with young people any night of the week and serving hot chocolate, caipirinhas, snacks and *chopp* to the sound of live music at weekends.

O Taboa, R Col Pilad Rebuá 1837, T067-3255 1862. The liveliest in town with occasional bands and good caipirinhas and *chopp*.

✺ Festivals and events

Miranda *p729, map p729*

Mid-Oct/early Nov Festa do Homem Pantaneiro, rodeos, lasso competitions,

live *sertanejo* bands, barn dances and
4 days of cowboy revelry. Can be combined
with Corumbá's water festival. For dates
contact **Aguas do Pantanal Turismo** in
Miranda (see page 739).

Corumbá *p730, map p731*
2 Feb Festa de Nossa Senhora da
Candelária, Corumbá's patron saint,
all offices and shops are closed.
24 Jun Festa do Arraial do Banho de São
João, fireworks, parades, traditional food,
processions and the main event – the
bathing of the image of the saint in
the Rio Paraguai.
21 Sep Corumbá's anniversary, includes
a Pantanal fishing festival held on the eve.
Mid-Oct Festival Pantanal das Águas, with
street parades featuring giant puppets, street
dancing and occasional water fights.

O Shopping

Campo Grande *p723, map p723*
Local native crafts, including ceramics,
tapestry and jewellery, are of good quality.
A local speciality is *os bugres da conceição*
(squat wooden statues covered in moulded
wax). Very good selections are found at **Casa
do Artesão**, Av Calógeras 2050, on the corner
with Av Afonso Pena. Mon-Fri 0800-2000,
Sat 0800-1200. Also try: **Barroarte**, Av Afonso
Pena 4329, and **Arte do Pantanal**, Av Afonso
Pena 1743. There is a market (*Feira Livre*) on
Wed and Sat. **Shopping Campo Grande**,
Av Afonso Pena 4909, www.shoppingcampo
grande.com.br, is the largest shopping
mall in town, on its eastern edge.

Corumbá *p730, map p731*
Shops tend to open early and close by 1700.
Casa do Artesão, R Dom Aquino 405, in a
converted prison. Mon-Fri 0800-1200,
1400-1800, Sat 0800-1200, good selection
of handicrafts and a small bookshop.
CorumbArte, Av Gen Rondon 1011. Good
silk-screen T-shirts with Pantanal motifs.

Frutal, R 13 de Junho 538. Open 0800-
2000. Supermarket.
Livraria Corumbaense, R Delamaré 1080.
Useful for state maps.
Ohara, Dom Aquino 621, corner Antônio
João. Supermarket.

▲ Activities and tours

Wildlife guides for the Pantanal
See also tour operators and guides for the
northern Pantanal, page 757.
Alyson is a Londrina-based birding guide
who works with **Neblina Forest Tours**
(www.neblinaforest.com); available
through **Fazenda San Francisco**.
Juan Mazar Barnett, T+54 (0)11-4312
6345, www.seriemanaturetours.com.
Very experienced Buenos Aires-based
birding guide and editor of *Cotinga*
magazine. Expert on *chaco* and Pantanal
birds. Book well ahead; expensive.

Campo Grande *p723, map p723*
City Tour, T067-3321 0800, or through the
Campo Grande Pantanal visitor centre and
most larger hotels. Half-day tours of the city's
sights including the Museu Dom Bosco and
the Parque das Nações Indígenas.

Tours to the southern Pantanal
Brazil Nature Tours, R Guia Lopes 150,
1st floor, T067-3042 4659, www.brazil
naturetours.com. Booking agents for
nature-based tours throughout Brazil,
flights, buses and the *fazendas* of the
Pantanal, north and south.
Ecological Expeditions, R Joaquim Nabuco
185, T067-3321 0505, www.ecological
expeditions.com.br; with another office in
Corumbá, see below. Attached to the youth
hostel at the bus station. Offers budget
camping trips and lodge-based trips in
Nhecolândia (sleeping bag needed)
for 3, 4 or 5 days ending in Corumbá.
The 1st day, which involves travel to
the Buraco da Piranha, is free.

Impacto, R 7 de Setembro 1090, T067-3325 1333, www.impactotour.com.br. Very helpful Pantanal and Bonito tour operator established over 10 years. Prices vary according to standard of accommodation; a wide range is offered. 2-day packages for 2 people US$190-600. Transfers and insurance included. English spoken.

Bonito and around *p726, map p727*
There is very little to choose between agencies in Bonito. English speakers are hard to come by. We list only those who also offer transport or a specialist service such as cave diving.
Impacto, R Col Pilad Rebuá 1515, T067-3255 1414. English-speaking staff. Can be pre-booked through their efficient head office in Campo Grande or through **Aguas do Pantanal Turismo** in Miranda (see below).
City Tour, R Col Pilad Rebuá 1515, T067-3255 1414. English-speaking staff. Can be pre-booked through their efficient head office in Campo Grande or through **Aguas do Pantanal Turismo** in Miranda (see below).
Ygarapé, R Col Pilad Rebuá 1956, T067-3255 1733, www.ygarape.com.br. English spoken. PDSE accredited cave diving.

Miranda *p729, map p729*
Tours to the southern Pantanal
Both of the operators below can organize accommodation during the **Festa do Homem Pantaneiro** (see Festivals and events, above).
Aguas do Pantanal Turismo, Aguas do Pantanal hotel, Av Afonso Pena 367, T067-3242 1242, www.aguasdopantanal.com.br. Very well-organized tours to the *fazendas* around Miranda, to those on the Estrada Parque, and to the sights around Bonito. Also offers exclusive 1- or 2-day trips on the Rio Salobrinha to the Sanctuario Baía Negra. This is a little-visited clear water river that's great for snorkelling and teeming with life – particularly birds. Expect to see 4 species of kingfisher, screamers, bare-faced currasow and cocoi, boat-billed heron and numerous

other varieties, storks and ibises. Bring insect repellent. Can also organize scenic flights.
Explore Pantanal, R Dr Alexandre 305, Miranda, T067-3242 4310, T067-9638 3520, www.explore pantanal.com. Run by a Kadiweu indigenous guide and his Swiss partner, with many years of experience. Very good English, German, French, Spanish and Italian and decent Hebrew. Great for small groups who want to get off the beaten track. A range of excursions, including fascinating stays with indigenous people in the Pantanal. Trips to Bonito (including pre-arranged transport), camping tours and day tours. Prices are competitive with budget operators in Campo Grande and Corumbá. For best rates book ahead.

Corumbá *p730, map p731*
Tours to the southern Pantanal
Ecological Expeditions, R Antônio Maria Coelho 78. Main office in Campo Grande.
Mutum Turismo, R Frei Mariano 17, T067-3231 1818, www.mutumturismo.com.br. Cruises and upmarket tours (mostly aimed at the Brazilian market) and help with airline, train and bus reservations.
Pantur, R América 969, T067-3231.2000, www.pantur.com.br. Packages to Bonito and the *fazendas* on the Estrada Parque, including some of the less visited, such as the luxurious **Xaraes**. Flights and bus tickets can be booked here too. Confusing website; click on the flags for tour details.
Saab Eco Adventure, T067-9283 1785, http://saabtourecoadventure.blogspot.com. Excellent, comfortable, light adventure tours of the Pantanal and stays at their own designated *fazenda* the **Pousada Mangabal**.

Pantanal fishing and river cruises
Pérola do Pantanal, Nacional Palace (see Sleeping), T067-3231 1470, www.peroladopantanal.com.br. Fishing and 'eco' tours on their large river boat, *Kalypso*, with options of added jeep trips on the Estrada Parque.

⊖ Transport

Campo Grande *p723, map p723*
Air The airport is 7 km from the city centre; to get there take city bus No 158, which stops outside the airport; taxi US$6.

As ever, the cheapest flights are available on line. Agencies in the city (many offices in front of the *rodoviária*) will book online and charge to credit cards. Campo Grande has flights to **Brasília, Cuiabá, Manaus, Porto Alegre, Santa Cruz** (Bolivia), **São Paulo, Porto Velho, Corumbá, Goiânia, Londrina, Belo Horizonte, Campinas, Corumbá, Cuiabá, Curitiba, Salvador** and many others.

Airlines include: **Avianca,** www.Avianca. com.br; **Azul,** www.voeazul.com.br; **GOL,** www.voe gol.com.br; **TAM,** www.tam. com.br; **TRIP,** www.voetrip. com.br.

Bus Town buses leave from the R Vasconcelos Fernandes end of the *rodoviária*, while state and interstate buses leave from the R Joaquim Nabuco end.

To **São Paulo,** US$80, 14 hrs, 9 buses daily, 1st at 0800, last at 2400, 3 *leito* buses US$105. To **Cuiabá,** US$45, 10 hrs, 12 buses daily, *leito* at 2100 and 2200, US$55. To **Brasília,** US$80, 23 hrs at 1000 and 2000. To **Goiânia,** with São Luís at 1100, 2000, 15 hrs on 1900 service, US$65, others 24 hrs, but only US$5 cheaper. **Rio de Janeiro,** US$80, 21 hrs, 4 buses daily, *leito* at 1540, US$100. To **Belo Horizonte,** 22 hrs, US$80. To **Corumbá,** with Andorinha, 8 daily from 0600, 6 hrs, US$35. Campo Grande–Corumbá buses connect with those from Rio and São Paulo, similarly those from Corumbá through to Rio and São Paulo. To **Ponta Porã,** 5 hrs, 9 buses daily, US$15. To **(Queiroz),** US$14. Beyond Dourados is **Mundo Novo,** from where buses go to **Ponta Porã** (0530) and to **Porto Frajelli** (very frequent). From Mundo Novo, ferries for cars and passengers go to **Guaíra** for US$3. Twice daily direct service to **Foz do Iguaçu** (17 hrs) with Integração, 1600,

US$45; same company goes to **Cascavel,** US$40. To **Pedro Juan Caballero** (Paraguay), del Amambay company, 0600, US$21. Amambay goes every Sun morning to **Asunción** (Paraguay).

Car hire Hertz, Av Afonso Pena 2620 and airport, T067-3383 5331. Locagrande, Av Afonso Pena 466, T067-3721 3282. Localiza, Av Afonso Pena 318, T067-3382 8786, and at the airport, along with various others T0800- 992000. Unidas, Av Afonso Pena 829, T067-3384 5626, at airport, T067-3363 2145.

Ponta Porã *p725*
Bus To **Campo Grande,** 9 a day 0100-2130, 4 hrs, US$15.

Bonito *p726, map p727*
Bus To **Campo Grande,** 0530, US$15, 5½-6 hrs. Buses use the MS-345, with a stop at Autoposto Santa Cruz, Km 60 (all types of fuel, food and drinks available). Several daily buses to **Miranda.** Some buses to Corumbá and Campo Grande buses call in here; check at the *rodoviária*. There is a bus that runs Corumbá– Miranda–Bonito–Jardim–Ponta Porã, Mon-Sat, leaves either end at 0600, arriving Bonito at 1230 for **Ponta Porã** or 1300 for **Miranda;** for **Campo Grande** it's also possible to change in Jardim (1400 for 1700 bus) or Miranda, which have better connections. The fare to **Corumbá** is US$15. There are also connections on the 1230 route to **Bela Vista** at 2000 or **Asunción** (Paraguay) and **Col Oviedo** (Paraguay). Ticket office opens at 1200.

Car hire Unidas, R das Flores s/n, T067-255 1066. Yes Rent a Car, R Senador Filinto Muller 656, T067-255 1702.

Jardim *p728*
Bus To **Campo Grande,** 0530, 1200, 1600 and 2 at night, US$25, 5 hrs. To **Bonito** (US$6.50), **Miranda** and **Corumbá** at 1130. To **Dourados,** 0600. To **Bela Vista**

(Paraguayan border) 0200, 1030, 1500, 1930.
To **Porto Murtinho**, 0010 and 1530 (bus
from Bonito connects). To **Ponta Porã**,
0600, 1500; Sun only at 1400 to **São Paulo**.

Miranda *p729, map p729*
Bus To **Campo Grande**, 12 a day (2- 3 hrs),
US$15. To **Corumbá**; 10 daily (3-4 hrs), US$15.
To **Bonito**, 1 daily (2-3 hrs), US$9 at 1630.

Car hire Mavel, Av Afonso Pena 31,
T067-3242 1734 or through **Aguas do
Pantanal** hotel. Also bookable through
Explore Pantanal (with a surcharge).

Corumbá *p730, map p731*
Air The airport is 3 km from the city centre;
taxi US$6 or there is an infrequent bus.
Flights to **Brasília** and **Campo Grande**
with **Tam**, www.tam.com.br, and **Trip**,
www.voetrip.com.br.

Boat The *Acurí*, a luxury vessel, sails
between Corumbá and **Cáceres** once a week,
US$600 including return by air. For further
details, see Cáceres transport, page 760.

Bus **Andorinha** services to all points east.
To **Campo Grande**, 7 hrs, US$25, 13 buses
daily 0630-2400, interesting journey ('an
excursion in itself'); take an early bus for a
chance of seeing wildlife, connections from
Campo Grande to all parts of Brazil. To **São
Paulo** direct, 22 hrs, US$90, 1100 and 1500,
confirm bus times in advance as these
change (T067-3231 2033). To **Rio de Janeiro**
direct, 30 hrs, US$105, daily 1100. **Cruzeiro
do Sul** operates the route south to the
Paraguayan border. To **Ponta Porã**,
12 hrs, US$40, Bonito (6 hrs, US$20) and
Jardim (9 hrs, US$25). At least 4 daily to
Miranda. Mon-Sat at 0600; ticket office
open 0500-0600 only, at other times
call T067-3231 2383.

Car hire Localiza, airport and R Cabral
2064, T067-231 6000. **Unidas**, R Frei
Mariano 633, T/F067-231 3124.

❻ Directory

Campo Grande *p723, map p723*
Banks Banco do Brasil, 13 de Maio and
Av Afonso Pena, open 1100-1600, charges
commission US$10 for cash, US$20 for TCs,
regardless of amount exchanged. Visa ATMs
at **Bradesco**, 13 de Maio and Av Afonso Pena;
at **HSBC**, R 13 de Maio 2837; and at **Banco
24 horas**, R Maracaju, on corner with 13 de
Junho. Also at R Dom Aquino and Joaquim
Nabuco. **Overcash Câmbio**, R Rui Barbosa
2750, Mon-Fri 1000-1600. **Embassies and
consulates** Bolivia, R João Pedro de Souza
798, T067-382 2190. Paraguay, R 26 Agosto
384, T067-324 4934. **Internet** Cyber Café
Iris, Av Afonso Pena 1975, and **Cyber Café**,
R Alan Kardec 374, T067-3384 5963 near
the Hotel Turis. Also in the IYHA. **Medical
services** Yellow and dengue fevers are
both present in Mato Grosso do Sul; the
former only in very remote areas. There is a
clinic at the railway station, but it's not very
hygienic, best to get your immunizations at
home. **Post office** On corner of R Dom
Aquino and Av Calógeras 2309, and Barão
do Rio Branco on corner of Ernesto Geisel,
both locations offer fax service, US$2.10 per
page within Brazil. **Telephone** Telems,
R 13 de Maio and R 15 de Novembro,
daily 0600-2200.

Ponta Porã *p725*
Banks Banco do Brasil changes TCs.
Many in the centre of town (but on Sun
change money in hotels). **Bradesco**
has a Visa ATM.

Bonito *p726, map p727*
Banks The town has a Bradesco bank for
Visa ATM on Av Coronel Pilão Rebuá, 535.
Banco do Brasil, R Luís da Costa Leite 2279
for Visa. Some hoteliers and taxi drivers may
change money. **Post office** R Col Pilad
Rebuá. **Telephone** Santana do Paraíso.

Jardim *p728*
Banks Elia, a taxi driver, will change money; ask around.

Miranda *p729, map p729*
Banks The town has both a **Bradesco** and a Banco do Brasil. **Internet** Star Informatica, R Francisco Rebúa 149, T067-3242 2100.

Corumbá *p730, map p731*
Banks Banco do Brasil, R 13 de Junho 914, ATM. HSBC, R Delamaré 1068, ATM. HSBC, R Delamaré 1068, ATM. **Câmbio Mattos**, R 15 de Novembro 140, Mon-Fri 0800-1700, good rates for US$ cash, US$5 commission on TCs. **Câmbio Rau**, R 15 de Novembro 212, Mon-

Fri 0800-1700, Sat 0900-1200, cash only, good rates. **Embassies and consulates** Bolivia, R Antônio Maria Coelho 881, T067-231 5605, Mon-Fri 0700-1100, 1500-1730. A fee is charged to citizens of those countries that require a visa. A yellow fever vaccination certificate is also required. **Internet** Pantanalnet, R América 430, US$2.50 per hr. **Laundry** Apae, R 13 de Junho 1377, same day service. **Post office** Main office at R Delamaré 708, fax service. Branch at R 15 de Novembro 229. **Telephone** R Dom Aquino 951, near Praça da Independência, daily 0700-2200. To phone Quijarro/Puerto Suárez, Bolivia, costs slightly more than a local call; dial 214 + the Bolivian number.

Mato Grosso and the Northern Pantanal

Mato Grosso, immediately to the north of Mato Grosso do Sul, shares the Pantanal with that state and has equally well-developed tourism facilities. Although there are just as many opportunities for seeing wildlife, trips to the Pantanal near the state capital, Cuiabá, tend to be more upmarket than those leaving from Corumbá in Mato Grosso do Sul. The state also has abundant though rapidly depleting areas of Amazon forest; Alta Floresta, in the north, has an excellent birdwatching and wildlife lodge and one of the Amazon's most comfortable lodges, the Jardim da Amazônia, lies in the middle of vast fields of soya to Alta Floresta's southwest. The much-vaunted Chapada dos Guimarães hills, near Cuiabá, afford good light walking and birdwatching, although the natural landscape has been greatly damaged by farming and development. ▸▸ *For listings, see pages 753-760.*

Background

The area that is now Mato Grosso and Mato Grosso do Sul was first demarcated as Spanish territory, but it was the Portuguese Aleixo Garcia who was the first to explore it in 1525. Jesuits and then *bandeirantes* entered the Mato Grosso for their different ends during the 17th and early 18th centuries, and, when gold was discovered near Cuiabá, a new influx of explorers began. Mato Grosso became a captaincy in 1748 and the borders between Portuguese and Spanish territories were decided in the following years. Throughout the 19th century, after the decline in gold extraction, the province's economy stagnated and its population dwindled. This trend was reversed when the rubber boom brought immigrants in the early 20th century to the north of the region. Getúlio Vargas's 'March to the West' in the 1940s brought added development, accompanied first by the splitting off of Rondônia and by the formation of Mato Grosso do Sul in 1977.

Cuiabá → *For listings, see pages 753-760. Colour map 3, A2. Phone code: 065. Population: 470,000.*

An important starting point for trips into the Pantanal, Cuiabá, a state capital, is an ordered and increasingly wealthy city; rich on soya from the vast plantations to the north. There are few sights of more than a passing interest, but the city has a number of leafy *praças* leading it to be called the 'Cidade Verde' (green city) by Matogrossenses. Cuiabá is in reality two twinned cities – separated by the sluggish Rio Cuiabá, an upper tributary of the Rio Paraguai – **Cuiabá** on the east bank of the river, and **Várzea Grande** on the west. They vie with Teresina in Piauí and Corumbá in Matto Grosso do Sul as the hottest cities in Brazil, with temperatures pushing up to the high 40s in the Antipodean summer months. The coolest months are June, July and August in the dry season.

Ins and outs

Getting there Flights arrive at **Marechal Rondon airport** ① *Av João Ponce de Arruda, s/n, Várzea Grande, T065-3614 2500, 10 km from the centre*, from Alta Floresta, Brasília, Campo Grande, São Paulo, Rio and Salvador, amongst others. There are ATMs outside the airport, as well as a post office, car hire booths and **Sedtur** office. To get to the centre, take any white **Tuiuiú** bus (the name will be written on the side), from in front of the airport to Avenida Tenente Coronel Duarte. Taxis cost US$20. Interstate buses arrive at the **rodoviária** ① *north of the centre at R Jules Rimet, Bairro Alvorada*. Town buses stop at the entrance of the *rodoviária*. ▸▸ *See Transport, page 759.*

Getting around Many bus routes have stops in the vicinity of Praça Ipiranga. Bus Nos 501 or 505 ('Universidade') to the university museums and zoo (ask for 'Teatro') leave from Avenida Tenente Coronel Duarte by Praça Bispo Dom José, a triangular park just east of Praça Ipiranga.

Tourist information **Sedtur** ① *R Marechal Rondon, Jardim Aeroporto, Várzea Grande and with a smaller office at R Ricardo Franca at Voluntarios da Patria, T065-3613 9300, Mon-Fri 0900-1800, www.sedtur.mt.gov.br*, provides maps and general information on hotels and car hire and has a website in English. Staff are friendly and speak English and Spanish. They are very helpful in settling disputes with local tour companies.

Sights

The most pleasant public space in Cuiabá is the lush **Praça da República** which is surrounded by a cluster of imposing buildings and dotted with sculptures and shady trees. Other pedestrian shopping streets and further squares lead off the *praça*. The

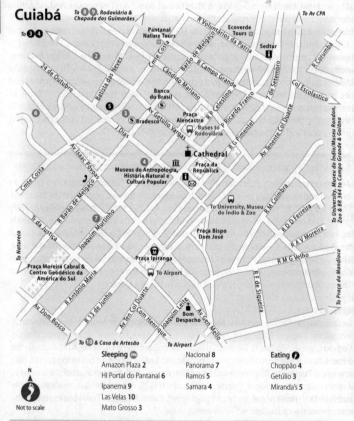

Cuiabá

Sleeping 🛏
Amazon Plaza 2
HI Portal do Pantanal 6
Ipanema 9
Las Velas 10
Mato Grosso 3

Nacional 8
Panorama 7
Ramos 5
Samara 4

Eating 🍴
Choppão 4
Getúlio 3
Miranda's 5

Not to scale

brutalist façade of the **cathedral**, flanked by two functionalist clock towers, dominates the square. Until the late 1960s a beautiful 18th-century baroque church stood here but this was demolished to make way for the current building in a sweep of modernization that saw almost all the city's colonial charm destroyed.

On **Praça Ipiranga**, at the junction of avenidas Isaac Póvoas and Tenente Coronel Duarte, a few blocks southwest of the central squares, there are market stalls and an iron bandstand from Huddersfield in the UK, or Hamburg in Germany, depending on which story you believe. There is live acoustic music on Thursday and Friday on the **Praça da Mandioca**, a small square just east of the centre.

On a hill beyond the square is the extraordinary church of **Bom Despacho**, built in the style of Notre Dame. It is best viewed from afar as it is sadly run down and not open to visitors. In front of the Assembléia Legislativa on Praça Moreira Cabral, is a point marking the **Geodesic Centre of South America** (see also under Chapada dos Guimarães, below).

The rather dusty **Museus de Antropologia, História Natural e Cultura Popular** ① *Fundação Cultural de Mato Grosso, Praça da República 151, Mon-Fri 0800-1730, US$0.50*, are worth a look. There are interesting historical photos, a contemporary art gallery, indigenous weapons, archaeological finds and pottery. The section of stuffed wildlife from the Pantanal is disturbingly compelling.

At the entrance to the Universidade de Mato Grosso by the swimming pool, 10 minutes by bus from the centre, is the small **Museu do Índio/Museu Rondon** ① *T065-3615 8489, www.ufmt.br/ichs/museu_rondon/museu_rondon.html, Tue-Sun 0800-1100, 1330-1700, US$1*, with artefacts from tribes mostly from the state of Mato Grosso. Particularly beautiful are the **Bororo** and **Rikbaktsa** headdresses made from macaw and currasow feathers, and the **Kadiwéu** pottery (from Mato Grosso do Sul). Continuing along the road through the campus, signed on the left before a right turn in the road, is the **Zoológico** ① *Tue-Sun 0800-1100, 1330-1700, free*. The jacaré, capybara, tortoise and tapir pen can be seen at any time, but are best in the early morning or late afternoon. It also has coatis, otters, rhea, various monkeys and peccaries and a few, birds.

The **Águas Quentes** hot springs are 86 km away (9 km south of the BR-163, 77 km east of Cuiabá) and can be visited as a day trip

---

The Northern Pantanal → For listings, see pages 753-760. Colour map 3, A1 and A2.

The Mato Grosso Pantanal is well-developed for tourism only along the Transpantaneira dirt road, which is superb for seeing wildlife – especially jaguars. Other areas around Barão do Melgaço and the colonial river port of Cáceres are pioneer country where you will probably not encounter another tourist.

The Transpantaneira

The main access point to the northern Pantanal is the **Transpantaneira dirt road**, which runs south from the main Cuiabá to Cáceres, beginning in earnest at the scruffy town of Poconé. The Transpantaneira cuts through the heart of the Pantanal wetland and is one of the best places for seeing wildlife in the Americas. Capybara, jaguarondi, oncilla, pacas and agoutis are common sights on the road itself, and the wetland areas immediately to either side – which begin as ditches and stretch into wilderness – are filled with hundreds of thousands of egrets, ibises, herons and metre-tall jabiru storks. Caiman bask on the banks of the ditches and ponds and anaconda snake their way through the water hyacinth and reeds. The road is lined with a string of *fazendas* (see page 753), of various levels of comfort, which are used by tour operators from Cuiabá as bases for deeper ventures into the wetlands.

The few towns that lie along the Transpantaneira are most interesting when seen from a wing mirror, but they do sell petrol. **Poconé** is an unprepossessing dusty little place, founded in 1781 and known as the 'Cidade Rosa' (pink city) by over-romantic locals. Until 1995 there was much *garimpo* (illicit gold mining) activity north of town and many slag heaps can be seen from the road. There are numerous cheap hotels in town but there is no real advantage in staying here. From Poconé it is 63 km (two to three hours) south to the one-horse town of **Pixaim**, where there is a petrol station, a few cafés and little else, and then a further two to three hours to **Porto Jofre**, at the end of the road and on the banks of the **Rio Piquiri**. The town is one of the best locations in the Americas for seeing jaguar and has a few hotels and restaurants. For information on visiting the Transpantaneira see Pantanal ins and outs page 720.

Barão de Melgaço and around → *Colour map 3, A2.*

Barão de Melgaço, 130 km from Cuiabá on the banks of the Rio Cuiabá, is far less visited than the Transpantaneira – you'll see far fewer tourists here, and far fewer animals. The town sits on the edge of extensive areas of lakeland and seasonally flooded *cerrado*, and is reachable by two roads. The shorter, via Santo Antônio do Leverger, is unpaved from Santo Antônio to Barão (closed in the wet season). The route via São Vicente is longer but more extensively paved. The best way to see the Pantanal from here is by boat down the

Around Cuiabá

Sleeping
Araras Lodge 1
Fazenda Piuval 2
Pousada Rio Clarinho 3
Pousada Rio Claro 4
Pouso Alegre 5

Border essentials: Brazil–Bolivia

Cáceres (Brazil)–San Matías (Bolivia)

An unpaved road runs from Cáceres to the Bolivian border at San Matías. Exit and entry formalities are carried out at **Brazilian immigration**, Rua Col Farías, Cáceres, closed Sunday. When closed, go to the **Polícia Federal**, Avenida Rubens de Medarca 909. **Bolivian immigration** in San Matías is open 1000-1200, 1500-1700. If crossing from Bolivia into Brazil, there are three luggage checks for drugs before the border.

San Matías is a busy little town with hotels, restaurants and a bank. The next major town in Bolivia is San Ignacio de Velasco, which is on the road route to Santa Cruz de la Sierra. Buses run from San Matías to San Ignacio and San Ignacio to Santa Cruz; there are also flights. See Transport, page 755.

Rio Cuiabá. Near the town, the riverbanks are lined with farms and small residences but become increasingly forested with lovely combinations of flowering trees (best seen September to October); and the environs become increasingly wild and filled with birds, rodents and reptiles. After a while, a small river to the left leads to the **Chacororé** and **Sia Mariana lakes**, which join up via an artificial canal. The canal has resulted in the larger of the two lakes draining into the smaller one, and it has begun to dry out. Boats can continue beyond the lakes to the **Rio Mutum** but a guide is essential because there are many dead ends. The area is rich in birdlife and the waterscapes are beautiful.

Boat hire costs up to US$85 for a full day and is available from restaurants along the waterfront – ask at the **Restaurant Peixe Vivo**, or enquire with travel agencies in Cuiabá, who can organize a bespoke trip. The best time for a boat trip is sunset, when birds gather in huge numbers. Bring a powerful torch to do some caiman spotting for the return trip in the dark.

Cáceres → *For listings, see pages 753-760. Colour map 3, A1. Phone code: 065. Population: 86,000.*
Cáceres is a hot, steamy but hospitable provincial town on the far western edge of the Pantanal, sitting between the stunning **Serra da Mangabeira** mountains (15 km to the east), and the broad Rio Paraguai. The city is 200 km west of Cuiabá. It has little tourist infrastructure for Pantanal visits, but makes a possible pit stop on the long road between Cuiabá and Rondonia. It's a pleasant place, with a lovely waterfront and a number of well-preserved 19th-century buildings painted in pastel colours. It's easy to organize a short boat trip on the river. Until 1960, Cáceres used to have regular boat traffic downstream to the Rio de Plata. Occasional boats still run down river as far as Corumbá, and though there is no reliable service, if you're prepared to wait around for a few days you could probably hitch a ride. Travel in a pair or group if possible as the river route is a back door to Bolivia for cocaine traffickers.

The **Museu de Cáceres** ⓘ *R Antônio Maria by Praça Major João Carlos*, is a small local history museum. Exhibits include indigenous funerary urns. The main square, **Praça Barão de Rio Branco**, has one of the original border markers from the Treaty of Tordesillas, which divided South America between Spain and Portugal. The *praça* is pleasant and shady during the day and, in the evenings between November and March, the trees are packed with thousands of chirping swallows (*andorinhas*); beware of droppings. The square is full of bars, restaurants and ice-cream parlours and comes to life at night. Vitória Regia lilies can be seen north of town, just across the bridge over the Rio Paraguai along the BR-174 and there are archaeological sites on the river's edge north of the city.

The Pantanal is wild near Cáceres, and was the site of a horrific jaguar attack in 2008 when a large female cat killed and partially ate a hunter. Excursions are difficult to organize, however, there is excellent wildlife and birdwatching in the Serra da Mangabeira – a steep, jagged range covered in forest and traversed by the BR-070 federal highway running from Cuiabá to Porto Velho.

Ins and outs The **rodoviária** ① *Terminal da Japonesa, T065-3224 1261*, has bus connections with Cuiabá and Porto Velho. It is also possible to arrive on the *Acuri*, a luxury boat that travels between Corumbá and Cuiabá. At the waterfront you can hire a boat for a day trip, US$5 per person per hour, minimum three people; on holidays and some weekends there are organized day trips on the river. ▶▶ *See Transport, page 760.*

The Chapada dos Guimarães and Nobres → *For listings, see pages 753-760.*
Colour map 3, A2. Phone code: 065. Population: 13,500. www.chapadadosguimaraes.com.br.

Although consumed by agriculture and blighted by ill-considered careless tourism development, the craggy, cave-pocked escarpments of the Chapada dos Guimarães constitute one of the oldest plateaux on earth and one of the most scenic areas in Mato Grosso. They are very easy to visit in a day trip from Cuiabá. They begin to rise from the hot plains around Cuiabá some 50 km from the city, forming a series of vertiginous stone walls washed by waterfalls and cut by canyons. A dramatic, winding road, the MT-020, ascends through one to an area of open savannah standing at around 700 m, broken by patches of *cerrado* forest and extensive areas of farmland, dotted with curiously eroded rocks, perforated by dripping caves and grottoes, and leading to whole series of viewpoints out over the dusty Mato Grosso plains. There is one small settlement, the tranquil and semi-colonial village of **Chapada dos Guimarães**, where life focuses on a single *praça* and people snooze through the week until the crowds rush in from Cuiabá on Fridays and Saturdays.

The Chapada is said to be the geodesic heart of the South American continent and, about 8 km east of Chapada dos Guimarães town, at the **Mirante do Ponto Geodésico**, there is a monument officially marking this. It overlooks a great canyon with views of the surrounding plains, the Pantanal and Cuiabá's skyline on the horizon.

As the geodesic centre, the highlands are rich with **New Age folklore**. Crystals tinkle in the shops in Chapada dos Guimarães village, and peyote people in tie-dye clothing gather in cafés to murmur about apocalypse and a new human evolution, over hot chocolate and soggy cake. The Chapada's rocks are said to have peculiar energizing properties; a fact more solidly grounded in truth than you may suspect – a local magnetic force that reduces the speed of cars has been documented here by the police.

The Chapada is pocked with caves. These include the **Caverna Arroe-jari** ① *43 km of Chapada dos Guimarães village, daily 0900-1800, US$5, allow 3-4 hrs for the walk to and from the cave*, whose name means the 'home of souls' in a local Brazilian language. It's a haunting place – an 800-m-long cavern coursed by a little mountain stream running into a deep aqua blue lake, set in boulder-strewn grassland. It's best visited early in the day during the week, to ensure the fewest numbers of visitors possible, and to soak up the atmosphere. The walk to the cave cuts through waterfall-filled rainforest before emerging in open cerrado. Birdlife is rich.

The Chapada is a popular destination for birders, who often combine it with the Pantanal and Alta Floresta to up their species count. **Birdwatching** here is fruitful, in open country and with grassland and *cerrado* species not found in Alta Floresta and the Pantanal. Guides listed under the northern Pantanal (see page 758) can organize one- or two-day trips here and many are even based in the little town of Chapada dos Guimarães. Mammals, such as puma, jaguarundi, giant river otter and black-tailed marmoset can also be seen with time and patience.

Chapada dos Guimarães village
The colourful village of Chapada dos Guimarães, 68 km northeast of Cuiabá, is the most convenient and comfortable base for excursions. It's a pretty little place, with a series of simple, brightly painted buildings clustered around a small *praça* graced with the oldest church in the Mato Grosso, **Nossa Senhora de Santana**, dating from 1779 and with a simple whitewashed façade. It is open intermittently. Just outside the town, there's a big **piscina publica** ⓘ *R Dr Pem Gomes*, a spring-water fed, public swimming pool.

Ins and outs Frequent, regular buses run between Cuiabá and Chapada dos Guimarães town (about 1½ hours). The *chapada* can be visited in a long day trip either by self-drive (although access is via rough dirt roads that may deteriorate in the rainy season), bus or most easily through agencies such as **Pantanal Nature** or **Natureco** (see page 757-758). The **tourist office** ⓘ *R Quinco Caldas 100, 4 blocks from the praça*, near the entrance to the town, provides a useful map of the region and can help organize tours. The **Festival de Inverno** is held in the last week of July; during this time, and around **Carnaval**, the town is very busy and accommodation is scarce and expensive.

Parque Nacional da Chapada dos Guimarães
This begins just west of Chapada dos Guimarães town, near where the Salgadeira tourist centre offers bathing, camping and an unsightly restaurant right beneath the **Salgadeira waterfall**. The beautiful 85-m **Véu da Noiva waterfall** (Bridal Veil), 12 km from the town, near Buriti (well signposted; take a bus to Cuiabá and ask to be dropped you off), is less blighted and can be reached by either a short route or a longer one through forest. Other sights include: the **Mutuca** beauty spot, named after a vicious horsefly that preys on tourists there; the viewpoints over the breathtaking 80-m-deep **Portão do Inferno gorge** off the MT-020 road; and the **Cachoeirinha falls**, where there is another small, inappropriately situated restaurant.

About 60 km from town are the archaeological sites at **Pingador** and **Bom Jardim**, which include caverns with petroglyphs dating back some 4000 years.

Nobres and Bom Jardim
Some 100 km north of the Chapada is the little town of **Nobres**, which, like Bonito in Mato Grosso do Sul (see page 726), is surrounded by clear water rivers full of dourado fish and many beautiful caves. Unlike Bonito, there are few tourists and, whilst over-priced, the attractions are a good deal cheaper and far less spoilt. Nobres is the name for the area, but the main village, with a couple of small *pousadas* and a single restaurant, is called **Bom Jardim**. The town sits 2 km from the **Lago das Araras** ⓘ *Bom Jardim, US$5*, a shallow lake surrounded by stands of buriti palm where hundreds of blue and yellow macaws roost overnight. Come at dawn for a wonderfully raucous dawn chorus. The restaurant **Estivado** ⓘ *Rodovia MT-241, Km 66, 500 m northeast of Bom Jardim on the ponte Rio*

Estivado, US$4 for swimming (bring your own snorkel), US$7 for lunch, offers a taste of what Nobres has to offer. It sits over the slow-flow of the Rio Esitvado, which forms a wide pool next to the restaurant and is filled with fish.

Nobres' other attractions dot the countryside around Bom Jardim, and as in Bonito they are on private ranch land. There is good snorkelling at the **Reino Encantado** ① *18 km from Bom Jardim at Alto Bela Vista, T065-9237 4471, US$50 for full day use including lunch, guide and equipment, US40 per night for a double room in the adjacent pousada;* the **Recanto Ecológico Lagoa Azul** ① *14 km from Bom Jardim at Alto Bela Vista, US$25 for entry, guide and equipment, US$8 extra for lunch;* and at the **Rio Triste** ① *18 km from Bom Jardim village, US$30 for a 2-hr float with guide and equipment rental.* The former two are half-kilometre floats down the Rio Salobra, which is filled with piraputanga (*Brycon microlepis*), piova (*Schizodon Borelli*) and piauçu (*Leporinus macrocephalus*) fish. The Rio Triste is filled with these species as well as fierce, salmon-like dourado (*Salminus maxillosus*) and spectacular mottled fresh-water stingrays, which should be treated with caution as they will inflict a painful wound if stepped on or handled. The most spectacular cave is the **Gruta do Lagoa Azul**, which was closed as this book went to press, and is set open according to the whims of **Ibama**, Brazil's environmental protection agency.

Ins and outs Bom Jardim town is served by a single daily bus from Cuiabá. However, there are at least four buses daily from Cuiabá (as well as services from Sinop and Alta Floresta) to Nobres town, from where there are regular connections to Bom Jardim. Taxis can be booked through the Pousada Bom Jardim to take visitors to the various attractions – there is no public transport. This can prove expensive (up to US$45 for a round trip to any single attraction, with waiting time), and the most practical way of visiting Nobres is with a tour agency in Cuiabá, such as **Pantanal Nature** or **Trip Nobres** (see page 759). The former can include the trip in conjunction with the Chapada dos Guimarães or Jardim da Amazônia and is better for wildlife.

The Mato Grosso Amazon → *For listings, see pages 753-760.*

Northern Mato Grosso is an enormous sea of soya which has washed much of the Amazon rainforest out of northern Mato Grosso under waves of agricultural expansion powered by the policies of the world's largest soya farmer, Mato Grosso's governor Blairo Maggi, who is number 62 on the Forbes power list. On ascending to the governership of Mato Grosso, Maggi talked of tripling the area of soya planted in the Amazon. In an interview conducted with Larry Rohter of the *New York Times*, Maggi defended his destruction of the forest stating: "To me, a 40% increase in deforestation doesn't mean anything at all, and I don't feel the slightest guilt over what we are doing here. We're talking about an area larger than Europe that has barely been touched, so there is nothing at all to get worried about." He has been strongly supported by Lula, who declared in the same year that 'The Amazon is not untouchable', and is an ally of Lula's expansionist successor, Dilma Roussef. In 2003, Maggi's first year as governor, loggers cleared 4560 sq miles of Mato Grosso forest, an area twice the size of Delaware. The forests disappeared and Maggi profited: the André Maggi Group produces 5% of Brazil's soybeans and, with annual sales reaching US$2 billion in 2008, is the world's largest soy producer. Maggi received the Golden Chainsaw Award from Greenpeace international in 2005. Since exposure in the world's press, he has since attempted to re-invent himself as a champion of the environment, buying heavily into the carbon credit market. But the damage is largely done, and only islands of forest remain in northern Mato Grosso. Thankfully some are large.

The Xingu
The largest section of Mato Grosso forest by far is the indigenous reserves of the Xingu, which stretch into neighbouring Pará. These are home to dozens of tribal Brazilians, including the powerful Kayapó, and are protected under federal law since the indigenous cause was championed by the indefatigable Villas Boas brothers in the mid-20th century. The reserves are under threat from the Belo Monte dam – the third largest hydroelectric project in the world, which will alter the course of the Xingu river and prevent the migration of fish upriver, flood some 500 sq km of land and force some 40,000 indigenous and Caoboclo people to re-locate or become dependent on government handouts for food.

São Félix do Araguaia → *Colour map 1, C5. Population: 14,500.*
This town is the main population centre in the Mato Grosso Xingu region. It has a high population of indigenous Carajás, whose handicrafts can be found between the pizzeria and **Mini Hotel** on Avenida Araguaia. There is some infrastructure for fishing. Indigenous *fazenda* owners may invite you as their guest. If you accept, remember to take a gift: pencils, radio batteries, a few sacks of beans or rice, or a live cockerel will be much appreciated. Many river trips are available for fishing or wildlife spotting.
➤➤ *See Activities and tours, page 759.*

Ins and outs Access to São Félix and Santa Teresinha is by bus from Cuiabá. The *rodoviária* is 3 km from the centre and waterfront, taxi US$15.

Jardim da Amazônia
Arriving at this private reserve by car is an incredible experience. The road from Cuíabá takes some five hours to drive, and is lined by soya, stretching to the horizon in every direction across the ceaseless plains. Thunderstorms flicker on the horizon and every hour or so you pass through a new agricultural town full of Stetsons and pick-ups. The turn-off to **Jardim da Amazônia** ① *300 km north of Cuiabá on the Rodovia MT-10, Km 88, São José do Rio Claro, Mato Grosso, T066-3386 1221, www.jdamazonia.com.br, book through Pantanal Nature to ensure you have a wildlife guide as they are not available at the reserve,* main road cuts immediately into thick forest. The horizon disappears and all is exuberant and full of life. Birds flit, paca and agouti run across the dirt road and, after a mile, forest clears to reveal a beautiful house, set in tropical gardens and sitting on a lake at the bend of a healthy Amazon river. Behind are a cluster of little boutiquey cabins. While it is entirely an island of forest (with no ecological corridors connecting it to the rest of the Amazon) the Jardim da Amazônia reserve is sufficiently large to maintain healthy populations of large neotropical mammals. There are jaguar and puma here, anaconda and giant otter. Capybara graze on the garden lawns at twilight and a tapir comes to steal cashew fruits from trees near the rooms in the dead of night. The reserve is also one of the few places in the Amazon to which you can safely bring children. It offers a range of activities, including canoeing on the river, rainforest walks and wildlife watching.

Cristalino Rainforest Reserve → *Phone code: 065. Colour map 1, B4. Population: 71,500.*
The road that runs due north from Cuiabá to Santarém (1777 km) is passable in all weather conditions as far as **Sinop**, and has recently been asphalted as far as **Santarém**.

This will enable soya from Mato Grosso to be shipped via the Amazon to the Atlantic, out of a vast plant owned by **Cargill** but currently closed thanks to lobbying from Greenpeace Brazil. The areas around the road are among the principal victims of active deforestation, with land being cleared for cattle and soya farms. Soya is spreading beyond Mato Grosso into southern Pará.

There are, however, still extensive tracts of forest intact, especially near the **Rio Cristalino**, which is home to one of the Amazon's most spectacular rainforest reserves, the **Cristalino Rainforest Reserve** ⓘ *Alta Floresta, T066-3512 7100, www.cristalino lodge.com.br*. This is the best location in the Brazilian Amazon for wildlife enthusiasts, with superb guided visits to pristine rainforest, comfortable accommodation and wildlife-watching facilities as good as the best of Costa Rica or Ecuador. Cristalino is a private reserve the size of Manhattan. It is contiguous with the 184,940-ha **Cristalino State Park**, which is itself connected to other protected Amazon areas, forming an important large conservation corridor in the Southern Amazon. **Ecotourism** at Cristalino is a model of best practice and is streets ahead of anywhere else in Brazil. The management fulfill all four of the key conservational tourism criteria: conserving natural resources and biodiversity, conducting environmental education activities with the local community (leading to employment), practising responsible ecotourism (with recycling, water treatment, small group sizes and excellent guiding) and funding a research foundation.

Wildlife is abundant. Cristalino has so far recorded **600 bird species**, with new ones added almost monthly. This amounts to half of the avifauna in the Amazon and a third of all species found in Brazil. All the spectacular large mammals are found here alongside very rare or endemic species such as **bush dogs**, **red-nosed bearded saki monkey** and the recently-discovered **white-whiskered spider monkey**. And whilst wildlife is difficult to see (as it is anywhere in the Amazon), the reserve offers some of the best facilities for seeing wildlife in the Americas – on trail walks, boat trips on the river or from the lodge's enormous **birdiwatching tower**, which offers viewing in and above the forest canopy. There is also a hide next to a **clay lick** for seeing tapir, peccary and big cats, and harpy eagles nest in the grounds of the reserve's twin hotel, the **Floresta Amazônica** in Alta Floresta town. Scopes, binoculars and tape recorders are available and there is an excellent small library of field guides. The reserve also offers **adventure activities** including kayaking, rappelling and camping in the forest; sleeping in hammocks slung between the trees.

Ins and outs Cristalino is reachable from Alta Floresta town, which is connected to Cuiabá by regular buses and flights. The airport, **Aeroporto Deputado Benedito Santiago** ⓘ *4 km from the city centre, Av Ariosto da Rivas s/n, T066-3521 2159*, has connections with both Cuiabá and Brasília with two of Brazil's larger airlines. There are also daily overnight buses from Cuiabá, 12 hours. The town was built in the late 1970s and laid out on a grid pattern. Finding your way around in straightforward. Cristalino Reserve representatives will meet you at the airport or bus station and transfer you to their hotels in the reserve by 4WD. Packages including transfers are available through the reserve's website.

For Sleeping and Eating price codes and other relevant information, see pages 32-37.

Sleeping

Cuiabá *p743, map p744*

L Amazon Plaza, Av Getúlio Vargas 600, T065-2121 2000, www.hotelamazon.com.br. By far the best in the centre with very smart modern rooms in a tower with good views. The chairs and decking in the relaxing, shady pool area are painted with pictures of Amazon wildlife. Excellent service. Broadband internet in all rooms.

A Las Velas, Av Filinto Müller 62, Várzea Grande, T065-3682 3840, resvelas@terra. com.br. Less than 100 m from the airport. Clean, spacious a/c rooms (the executive ones are best and only a little more expensive) with newly renovated bathrooms, cable TV and boiler-heated showers. Free airport transfer for luggage.

B Nacional, Av Jules Rimet 22, T065-3621 3277. Opposite the front of the bus station and convenient for those who are just passing through. Plain a/c rooms with newly renovated en suites.

B-C Mato Grosso, R Comandante Costa 643, T065-3614 7777, www.hotelmt.com.br. The best-value mid-range option in the centre with newly renovated a/c or fan-cooled rooms with tiled floors and chintzy beds, the brightest of which are on the 2nd floor or above.

B-C Panorama, Praça Moreira Cabral 286, T065-3322 0072. A frayed 1980s tower with very simple, plain a/c or fan-cooled rooms with en suites; some have good views.

C HI Portal do Pantanal, Av Isaac Póvoas 655, T/F065-3624 8999, www.portaldopantanal. com.br. Large, bare dorms (segregated by sex) and doubles, a TV lounge area and a small kitchen. Price per person, breakfast included, internet access (US$2.50 per hr), laundry, kitchen.

C Ipanema, Av Jules Rimet 12, T065-3621 3069. Opposite the front of the bus station. Very well-kept a/c or fan-cooled rooms, some with armchairs, cable TVs and smart en suites. Internet access and a huge lobby TV for films or football. Many other options between here and the **Nacional**.

C Samara, R Joaquim Murtinho 270, T065-3322 6001. Very simple, scruffy rooms with en suite cold showers. No breakfast. Only come here if the other options are full.

C-D Hotel Ramos, R Campo Grande 487, T065-3624 7472, www.hotelramos.com.br. The best-value economy option with an array of well-kept, frayed but clean rooms, some with huge brown-tile bathrooms with tubs and showers, others with simple shower cubicles. These are set in a converted townhouse on a quiet, leafy back street close to the centre. Facilities include excellent tour agency, **Pantnanal Nature**, laundry service (with self-service machines), free Wi-Fi and airport/bus station pickup (with 12 hrs' notice). As with hostels, the lower price band for this hotel is per person.

The Northern Pantanal *p745*
Fazendas on the Transpantaneira

All prices here include tours around the *fazenda's* grounds with a guide – either on foot and or horseback or in a jeep, and full board.

See also page 734. Distances are given in kilometres from Poconé town. For tour operators, see Activities and tours, page 757.

L Araras Lodge, Km 32, T065-3682 2800, www.araraslodge.com.br. Book direct or through **Pantanal Nature** or any of the other opertors in Cuiabá as part of a tour. One of the most comfortable places to stay, with 14 a/c rooms. Excellent tours and food, home-made *cachaça*, a pool and a walkway over a private patch of wetland filled with capybara and caiman. Very popular with small tour groups from Europe. Book ahead.

L Fazenda Piuval, Km 10, T065-3345 1338, www.pousadapiuval.com.br. The 1st *fazenda* on the Transpantaneira and one of the most touristy, with scores of day visitors at weekends. Rustic farmhouse accommodation, a pool, excellent horseback and walking trails as well as boat trips on the vast lake, but whilst the *fazenda* is great for kids it's not a good choice for those looking to spot wildlife and really get into the sticks.

L Pousada Rio Clarinho, Km 42, book through **Pantanal Nature** (see page 748). Charming option on the Rio Clarinho. What it lacks in infrastructure, it makes up for in wildlife. The river has rare waterbirds such as agami heron and nesting hyacinth macaw, as well as river and giant otters and, occasionally, tapir. The boatman, Wander, has very sharp eyes – be sure to ask for him – and there is a 20-m birding tower in the grounds. Not to be confused with the nearby Pousada Rio Claro (see below).

L Pousada Rio Claro, Km 42, www.pousada rioclaro.com.br, book through **Eco do Pantanal** or **Natureco**. Comfortable *fazenda* with a pool and simple a/c rooms on the banks of the Rio Claro, which has a resident colony of giant otters. The *pousada* is most popular with Brazilian families and is very child-friendly; however, few Brazilians who visit here are as interested as in foreigners in seeing wildlife, or in the silent contemplation of pristine nature.

L Pouso Alegre, Km 36, T065-3626 1545, www.pousalegre.com.br. Rustic *pousada* with simple a/c or fan-cooled accommodation on one of the Pantanal's largest *fazendas*. It's overflowing with wildlife and particularly good for birds (especially on the morning horseback trail). Many new species have been catalogued here. The remote oxbow lake is particularly good for waterbirds (including agami and zigzag herons). The lodge is used by a number of birding tour operators. Proper birding guides can be provided with advance notice. Best at weekends when the very knowledgeable owner Luís Vicente is there.

AL-B Caranda Fundo, Km 43, book through Pantanal Nature (see page 748). One of the best options for budget travellers. Visitors sleep in hammocks in a large room (bring a hammock mosquito net). Tours include horseback rides, treks and night safaris. Hyacinth macaws nest on the *fazenda* and there are many mammals, including abundant howler monkeys, peccaries and huge herds of capybara.

Barão de Melgaço *p746*

There is a handful of cheaper options near the waterfront.

L do Mutum Pantanal Ecolodge, T065-3052 7022, www.pousadamutum.com.br, reservations through Pantanal Nature, or through other agencies in Cuiabá. One of the region's most comfortable lodges, with rooms housed in mock-colonial round houses or whitewash and tile-roofed cabins and set in a broad shady lawn around a lovely pool. The *pousada* organizes excursions on horseback around the surrounding Pantanal, or by jeep and by boat on the adjacent river.

C Pousada Baguari, R Rui Barbosa 719, Goiabeiras, Barão de Melgaço, T065-3322 3585. Rooms with a/c, restaurant, boat trips and excursions.

Cáceres *p747*

A Caiçaras, R dos Operários 745 corner R Gen Osório, T065-3223 2234. Modern town hotel with a/c rooms and cheaper options without a fridge.

B Riviera Pantanal, R Gen Osório 540, T065-3223 1177, rivierapantanalhotel@ hotmail.com. Simple town hotel with a/c rooms, a pool and a restaurant.

B-D Rio, Praça Major João Carlos 61, T065-3223 3387. A range of rooms, the cheapest have shared bathrooms and no a/c.

C-D Charm, Col José Dulce 405, T/F065-3223 4949. A/c and fan-cooled rooms, with or without a shared bath.

D-E União, R 7 de Setembro 340. Fan-cooled rooms, cheaper with shared bath, basic but good value.

The Chapada dos Guimarães *p748*
See www.chapadadosguimaraes.tur.br
for further details.

L Pousada Penhasco, 2.5 km on Av
Penhasco, Bom Clima, T065-3301 1555,
www.penhasco.com.br. A medium-sized
resort complex perched on the edge of
the escarpment (for wonderful views),
with modern chalets and bungalows,
heated indoor and an outdoor pools
(with waterslides), tennis courts and
organized activities. A long way from
quiet and intimate, but good for kids.
AL Solar do Inglês, R Cipriano Curvo 142,
Centro, T065-3301 1389, www.solardo
ingles.com.br. In an old converted house
near the town centre with 7 cosy rooms with
dark wood floors, faux antiques and oriental
rugs, each with private bathroom, TV and
frigobar. Garden, swimming pool and sauna.
Breakfast and afternoon tea included.
B Turismo, R Fernando Corrêa 1065, a
block from the *rodoviária*, T065-3301 1176,
www.hotelturismo.com.br. A/c rooms with
a fridge, cheaper with fan, restaurant,
breakfast and lunch excellent, very popular,
German-run. Ralf Goebel, the owner, is
very helpful in arranging excursions.
B-D Rio's Hotel, R Tiradentes 333, T065-
3301 1126, www.chapadadosguimaraes.
com.br/pousadarios. Simple a/c doubles,
triples and quadruples with a fridge, cheaper
with fan, cheaper with shared bath and a
good breakfast. Price in lower category is
per person in a quadruple.
C Pousada Bom Jardim, Praça Bispo Dom
Wunibaldo 461, T065-3301 2668. A bright,
sunny reception in a colonial building on
the main square leads to a corridor of
either simple fan-cooled rooms or more
comfortable a/c rooms painted light orange,
and with wicker and wood furnishings, local
art on the walls and private bathrooms.
C-D São José, R Vereador José de Souza 50,
T065-3301 1574, www.pousadasaojose.tur.br.
This bright yellow cottage with a terracotta
tiled roof just off the southeastern corner of
the main square, and near the church, has an

annexe of very plain fan-cooled or a/c singles,
doubles with little more than a wardrobe
and a bed (and a TV and fridge with a/c),
and windows overlooking a small yard.
The cheapest have shared bathrooms.

Camping
Oasis, 1 block from the main *praça*, T065-
3301 2444, www.campingoasis.com.br.
In an excellent central location in the large
lawned garden dotted with fruit trees and
sitting behind a townhouse. Facilities include
separate bathrooms for men and women,
cooking facilities and a car park.

Nobres *p749*
C-D Pousada Bom Jardim and Bom Garden,
Vila Bom Jardim, T065-3102 2018,
www.pousadabomjardim.com. 2 hotels
joined as 1 – Bom Garden – out the back
has modern, well-kept a/c rooms with en
suites and TVs, Bom Jardim is simpler, with
less-well-appointed, older and smaller rooms.
The restaurant has a central restaurant and can
organize tours (though no English is spoken).

São Félix do Araguaia *p751*
C Xavante, Av Severiano Neves 391, T062-
3522 1305. A/c, frigobar, excellent breakfast,
delicious *cajá* juice, the owners are very
hospitable. Recommended.
E Pizzeria Cantinho da Peixada,
Av Araguaia, next to the Texaco station,
overlooking the river, T062-3522 1320. Rooms
to let by the owner of the restaurant, better
than hotels. He also arranges fishing trips.

Cristalino Rainforest Reserve *p751*
L Cristalino Jungle Lodge, reservations
Av Perimetral Oeste 2001, Alta Floresta, T065-
3512 7100, www.cristalinolodge.com.br.
A beautifully situated and well-run lodge
on the Cristalino river in a private reserve
the size of Manhattan island. This reserve is
contiguous with the 185,000-ha Cristalino
State Park (which is linked to other protected
areas to form a huge conservation corridor in
the Southern Amazon). Trips from the lodge

include canoeing and snorkelling in clear-water rivers, as well as the usual caiman spotting and piranha fishing as well as more adventurous options such as rapelling and canyoning. But the emphasis is on wildlife, with more than 600 species of birds (half of the avifauna in the Amazon and a third of all species found in Brazil) and unique mammals such as the newly discovered white-whiskered spider monkey as well as very rare species like jaguar, puma, tapir, bush dog and giant otter. Facilities are the best in the Amazon – with a library of wildlife books, scopes and binoculars, canoes and launches, a 50-m canopy lookout tower and superb guiding. The lodge supports the local community, practices recycling and water treatment and funds a scientific research programme.

B Floresta Amazônica, Av Perimetral Oeste 2001, Alta Floresta, T065-3521 3601. In the park with lovely views, pool, sports, all facilities.

C Pirâmide Palace, Av do Aeroporto 445, Alta Floresta, T065-3521 2400. A/c rooms with fridges, restaurant.

D Grande Hotel Coroados, R F1 No118, Alta Floresta, T065-3521 3022. Not very well kept but has a/c, pool and bar.

🍴 Eating

Cuiabá *p743, map p744*
Many of the restaurants in the centre are only open weekdays for lunch. On **Av CPA** there are many good restaurants and small snack bars. **R Jules Rimet**, across from the *rodoviária*, has several cheap restaurants and *lanchonetes*.
♥♥♥ Getúlio, Av Getúlio Vargas 1147, at São Sebastião, T065-3264 9992. An a/c haven to escape from the heat. Black-tie waiters, excellent food with meat specialities and pizza, and a good buffet lunch on Sun. Live music upstairs on Fri and Sat from significant Brazilian acts.

♥♥♥-♥♥ Choppão, Praça 8 de Abril, T065-3623 9101. Established 30 years ago, this local institution is buzzing at any time of day or night. Huge portions of delicious food or *chopp*. The house speciality chicken soup promises to give diners drinking strength in the early hours and is a meal in itself. Warmly recommended.
♥♥ Panela de Barro, R Cmte Costa 543. Self-service, a/c lunchtime restaurant with a choice of tasty regional dishes.
♥♥-♥ Miranda's, R Cmte Costa 716. Decent self-service per kg lunchtime restaurant with good value specials.

Cáceres *p747*.
♥♥ Corimbá, R 15 de Novembro s/n, on the riverfront. Fish and general Brazilian food.
♥ Gulla's, R Col José Dulce 250. Per kg buffet, good quality and variety. Recommended.
♥ Panela de Barro, R Frei Ambrósio 34, near the *rodoviária*. Brazilian *comida caseira* (home cooking) with the usual range of meat dishes with squash, rice, black beans and salads.

Chapada dos Guimarães *p748*
Pequi is a regional palm fruit with a deadly spiky interior used to season many foods; *arroz com pequi* is a popular local rice and chicken dish.
♥♥ Fellipe 1, R Cipriano Curvo 596, T065-3301 1793. One of the few per kilo restaurants in the village, on the southwestern corner of the square next to the church serving mostly meaty options, beans, rice, unseasoned salads and sticky puddings. In the evenings, the menu becomes à la carte.
♥♥ Nivios, Praça Dom Wunibaldo 631. A popular spit for meat and regional food.

Nobres *p749*
♥ WF, T065-3102 2020. Lunch every day and dinner with reservation only from Senhora Fatima who serves a hearty meal of meat/chicken/fish with beans, rice, salad and condiments, washed down with fresh tropical fruit juice.

São Félix do Araguaia *p751*
🍴 **Pizzeria Cantinho da Peixada**,
Av Araguaia, next to the Texaco station,
overlooking the river. As well as serving
pizza, the owner, Klaus, also rents rooms.

🎶 Bars and clubs

Cuiabá *p743, map p744*
Cuiabá is quite lively at night, bars with
live music and dance on Av CPA.
Café Cancun, R Candido Mariano at São
Sebastião. One of a chain of popular Brazilian
club-bars attracting a mid-20s to 40s crowd.
Choppão, see Eating, above.
Tucano, Av CPA. Daily 1800-2300. Restaurant-
bar specializing in pizza, with beautiful view.

🎭 Entertainment

Cáceres *p747*
Traditional folkloric dance groups: **Chalana**,
T065-3223 3317, and **Tradição**, T065-223
4505, perform shows at different locations.

🎉 Festivals and events

Cáceres *p747*
Mid-Mar Piranha Festival.
Mid-Sep International Fishing Festival.
There's also an annual cattle fair.

🛍 Shopping

Cuiabá *p743, map p744*
Local handicrafts in wood, straw, netting,
leather, skins, Pequi liquor, crystallized caju
fruit, compressed guaraná fruit and
indigenous crafts are on sale at the airport,
rodoviária, craft shops in the centre and at
the daily market in the Praça da República,
interesting. There's a picturesque fish and
vegetable market at the riverside.

Casa de Artesão, Praça do Expedicionário
315, T065-3321 0603. All types of local
crafts in a restored building.

The Chapada dos Guimarães *p748*
Ispiaaió, R Cipriano Curvo, Praça Dom
Wunibaldo, T065-9214 8420. Regional arts
and crafts, including mobiles (of the hanging
from the ceiling variety), wall hangings,
lacework and clothing.

⛰ Activities and tours

Cuiabá *p743, map p744*
Travel agencies in Cuiabá also offer
trips to the *chapada*.

Tours to the northern Pantanal
You should expect to pay US$70-100 per
person per day for tours in the Pantanal.
Budget trips are marginally more expensive
(around US$10-15 per day more) than those
in the southern Pantanal, but accommodation
in the *fazendas* is more comfortable. For longer
tours or special programmes, book in advance
and be very wary of cut-price cowboy
operators, some of whom hang around in
the airport alongside those we list below.
Ecoverde Tours, R Pedro Celestino 391,
Centro, T065-9638 1614 or 3624 1386,
www.ecoverdetours.com.br. No-frills, but
well-run backpacker tours of the Pantanal
with Joel Souza, who has many years guiding
experience, knows his birds and beasts and
speaks good English. Ask if he is available
as other guides are not always of the same
standard. The best option in Cuiabá for a
budget trip to the Pantanal.
Natureco, R Benedito Leite 570, Cuiabá,
T065-3321 1001, www.natureco.com.br.
A range of *fazenda*-based Pantanal tours,
trips to the Xingu, Cáceres, Alta Floresta and
Barão de Melgaco. Specialist wildlife guides
available with advance notice. Some English
spoken. Professional and well run.

Pantanal Nature Tours, R Campo Grande 487, Centro, T065-3322 0203, T065-9955 2632 (mob), www.pantanalnature.com.br. Great trips to the northern Pantanal – both to the *fazendas* along the Transpantaneira and to Porto Jofre, from where the company runs the best jaguar safari in the Pantanal, and to Nobres, the Chapada dos Guimarães and Pousada Jardim da Amazônia. Guiding is excellent (bilingual) and service professional.

Pantanal wildlife and birding guides

All guides work freelance; companies employ extra guides for trips when busy. Most guides wait at the airport for incoming flights; compare prices and services in town if you don't want to commit yourself. The tourist office recommends guides, however, their advice is not always impartial. Those recommended below can be booked with advance notice through **Eco do Pantanal** or **Natureco**.

Ailton Lara, T065-3322 0203, ailton@pantanal nature.com.br. Excellent and good-value birding trips to the Chapada, the Pantanal and other destinations around Mato Grosso.

Boute Expeditions, R Getúlio Vargas 64, Várzea Grande, near airport, T065-3686 2231, www.boute-expeditions.com. Paulo Boute is one of the most experienced birding guides in the Pantanal; works from home and speaks good English and French. His standard tours operate in Mato Grosso (including the Amazon

and the Chapada alongside the Pantanal). He also runs tours to the Atlantic coastal forests and other bespoke destinations on request.

Fabricio Dorileo, fabriciodorileo18@ yahoo.com.br or through Eduardo Falcão – rejaguar@bol.com.br. Excellent birding guide with good equipment, good English and many years' experience in the Pantanal and Chapada dos Guimarães. Trained in the USA. Book him through the Cuiabá operators.

Giuliano Bernardon, T065-8115 6189, T065-9982 1294, giubernardon@gmail.com. Young birding guide and photographer with a good depth of knowledge and experience in the Chapada, Pantanal, Mato Grosso, Amazon and Atlantic coastal forest.

Pantanal Bird Club, T065-3624 1930, www.pantanalbirdclub.org. Recommended for even the most exacting clients, PBC are the most illustrious birders in Brazil with many years of experience. Braulio Carlos, the owner, has worked with Robert Ridgely and Guy Tudor and his chief guide, Juan Mazar Barnett, is one of the editors of *Cotinga* magazine. Tours throughout the area and to various parts of Brazil.

The Chapada dos Guimarães *p748*

Chapada Pantanal, Av Fernando Correa da Costa 1022, T065-3301 2757. Tours to all the principal sights in the Chapada and trips further afield to Nobres.

Nobres p749

The Cuiabá agencies listed under the Pantanal, and **Chapada Pantanal Tours** in Chaoda dos Guimarães village visit Nobres. **Pantanal Nature** (see above). Trips to all the attractions in Nobres. These can be combined with the Chapada dos Guimarães and Jardim da Amazonia. Excellent for wildlife.
Trip Nobres, T065-3023 6080, www.tripnobres.com. Boisterous light adventure activities in and around Nobres, including abseiling, rafting, snorkelling and diving. The owner is one of the few PADI-accredited dive instructors in the area.

São Félix do Araguaia p751
Boat trips

Icuryala, Goiânia, T062-223 9518. Excellent food and service, US$100 per day, independent visitors welcome. Recommended.
Juracy Lopes, contact through Hotel Xavante (see Sleeping, page 755). A very experienced guide with many friends, including the chief and council in Santa Isabela. Trips to the village or to see wildlife cost US$15 for 2; longer trips can be made to the meeting of the waters with the Rio das Mortes, or for a night in the jungle sleeping in hammocks.

⊖ Transport

Cuiabá p743, map p744

Air Marechal Rondon international airport is 10 km from the city; taxi US$18, or take the white Tuiuiú bus from Av Tenente Coronel Duarte in the city centre, US$1.50, or the terminal. There are also aeroporto buses from the *rodoviária*. Flights can be booked in the airline offices at the airport or through Pantanal Nature, or other tour operators in town, which also handle bus tickets. Cuibá has connections with **Alta Floresta**, **Belo Horizonte**, **Brasília**, **Campo Grande**, **Curitiba**, **Foz de Iguaçu**, **Goiânia**, **Manaus**, **Salvador**, **Santarem**, **Porto Alegre**, **Porto Velho**, **Salvador**, **São Paulo**, **Rio de Janeiro** and onward connections, with **Asta**,

www.voeasta.com.br, **Avianca**, www.Avianca. com.br, **Azul**, www.voeazul.com.br, **GOL**, www.voegol.com.br, **Pantanal**, www.voe pantanal.com.br, **Passaredo**, www.voe passaredo.com.br, **TAM**, www.tam.com.br and **TRIP**, www.voetrip.com.br.

Bus Bus No 202 runs to the *rodoviária* from R Joaquim Murtinho by the cathedral, 20 mins. A taxi costs US$10 to the centre. There is a Bradesco ATM, cafés and restaurants in the *rodoviária*.

Buses to **Alta Floresta**, 3 daily, 12 hrs, US$85; **Brasília**, 2 daily morning and evening, 18 hrs, US$90; **Campo Grande**, 12 hrs, 12 daily, US$55-65; **Foz de Iguaçu**, 2, both in the small hours, 23 hrs, US$100-115; **Goiânia**, 5 daily, 15 hrs, US$75; **Palmas**, 1 daily, 25 hrs, US$110 (via Goiânia); **Porto Velho**, 3 daily, US$75, 23 hrs; **Rio**, 36 hrs, US$150; **Salvador**, on Mon, Wed and Fri, 48 hrs, US$150; **Santarem**, 1 daily, 48 hrs, US$140; **Rio Branco**, 1 daily, 37 hrs, US$100 (or change in Porto Velho); **São Paulo**, 2 daily US$85-95, 24 hrs.

Car hire **Atlântida**, Av Isaac Póvoas, T065-3623 0700. **Localiza**, Av Dom Bosco 965, T065-3624 7979, and at airport, T065-3682 7900. **Unidas**, airport, T065-3682 4062. **Vitória**, R Comandante Costa 1350, T065-3322 7122.

The Transpantaneira p745
Bus From Poconé to **Cuiabá**, US$10 with TUT, T065-3322 4985, 6 a day 0600-1900.

Car Poconé has a 24-hr petrol station with all types of fuel, but closed on Sun.

Border with Bolivia p747
Bus From Cáceres to **San Matías**, US$20 with **Transical-Velásquez**, Mon-Sat at 0630 and 1500, Sun 1500 only (return at same times). Trans Bolivia to **San Matías**, Sun, Mon, Fri at 1500, Tue, Wed, Thu and Sat at 0700. For details of crossing the border, see box, page 747.

Cáceres p747

Bus Colibrí/União Cascavel buses
to **Cuiabá**, US$15, many daily 0630-2400
from the *rodoviária* (book in advance, very
crowded), 3½ hrs. To **Porto Velho**, US$50.

Boat Intermittent sailings to Corumbá –
ask at the docks when you arrive.

Car hire Localiza, R Padre Cassimiro 630,
T065-3223 1330, and at airport. **Locavel**,
Av São Luís 300, T065-3223 1212.

The Chapada dos Guimarães p748

Bus 7 departures daily to **Cuiabá** (Rubi,
0700-1900, last return 1800), 1½ hrs, US$5.

Nobres p749

See Ins and outs, page 750.

São Félix do Araguaia p751

Bus To **Barra do Garças** at 0500, arrive
2300; or 1730, arrive 1100 next day. Also
to **Tucumã**, 6-8 hrs, and to **São José do
Xingu**, 10 hrs. No buses to Marabá.

Jardim da Amazônia p751

With tour opertors from Cuiabá only –
or self drive. Pantanal Nature, page 758,
are the best option.

Cristalino Rainforest Reserve p751
Alta Floresta

Air Cristalino Jungle Lodge offers a free
pick-up and drop-off for guests. There's little
reason to come if you're not going to the
lodge. There are flights to **Brasília**, **Cuiabá**,
Curitiba, **Porto Alegre**, **Campinas**,
Cascaval, **Ji-Paraná**, **Londrina**, **Maringá**,
Rondonópolis, **Sinop** and **Vilhena**,
with **Avianca**, www.Avianca.com.br,
or **Trip**, www.voetrip.com.br.

Bus To **Cuiabá** daily, several (12 hrs, US$35).
The *leito* night bus is the best option.

ⓘ Directory

Cuiabá p743, map p744

Banks Banco do Brasil, Av Getúlio Vargas
and R Barão de Melgaço, commission US$10
for cash, US$20 per transaction for TCs (there
are several branches of **Bradesco**, R Barão
Melgaco 3435, for ATMs.

Cáceres p747

Banks Banco do Brasil, R Col Jose Dulcé
234. HSBC, R Col Jose Dulcé 145. **Casa de
Câmbio Mattos**, Comte Bauduino 180,
next to main *praça*, changes cash and
TCs at good rates.

The Chapada dos Guimarães p748

Banks Bradesco R Fernando Correia 868
With an ATM. **Post office** R Fernando
Corrêa 848.

Contents

Footprint features

History

Indigenous peoples

Origins

The Clovis people Until the 1980s, scientists thought they understood how people had arrived in the Americas – over a land bridge from Russia. It was an opinion which had changed little since 1949 when Willard Libby and his associates invented radio carbon dating. It seemed that none of the archaeological sites found in the Americas contained artefacts that dated earlier than 11,200 years Before the Present (BP) and archaeologists were of the opinion that these were left behind by Siberian nomads who came to be known as the Clovis people (after the distinctively bi-facially worked flint spear and arrow heads first found near Clovis, New Mexico). Archaeological remains showed that the Clovis People were hunter-gatherers who followed the migrations of herds of giant woolly elephants (mammoths and mastodons), horses and camels over North America from the Yukon to Panama. The Clovis gradually settled and spread to the Pacific coast and north to the Arctic, becoming the ancestors of the native North Americans and the Inuit of the Arctic. They also came to be considered the donor culture for South America.

The Clovis model tied in nicely with evidence from other sciences. Geologists had long known that Northern Canada was covered in a great ice sheet from 100,000 years BP that began to melt back in about 13,000 BP, exposing a land bridge at the Bering Straits between the Asian and American continents, and the model became widely accepted until the early 1980s, when it was subtly modified: anthropological, genetic and linguistic analyses suggested that the Beringia migration had occurred in three stages. The first wave of Siberian migrants, who crossed in about 11,200 BP, entering the Yukon and migrating south through the great plains, east of the Rockies, became the Clovis. The second and third waves crossed many thousands of years later, the first group migrating southwest of the Rockies and settling on the North American Pacific coast – ancestors of the Pacific Coast native Americans, and the second populating the Arctic; making the Inuit the most recently arrived native Americans.

Controversy from Serra da Capivara and the Amazon In the 1980s, Brazilian archaeologists working in Brazil's northeast and the Amazon began to question the accepted Clovis model. Brazilians had long had their doubts about Clovis. **Walter Neves** at the University of São Paulo noted that native Americans are too great physiologically diverse to be descended only from the one group of migrants whose ancestors established the Clovis culture. Paulista archaeologist **Nième Guidón** found human remains at Pedra Furada in the **Serra da Capivara**, suggesting human presence from some 47,000 years BP – long before Clovis. Guidón's claims sparked hot debate among other experts, many of whom argued that what she described as ash from fireplaces was in fact the remains of naturally caused forest fires. This claim has led to some accusations of racism by Brazilians, who argue that if Guidón were American she would have been taken more seriously. This appears not to be the case, for similar controversy was sparked by the findings of a scion of one of the most famous American families, **Anna Roosevelt**. In 1992, a Brazilian team led by Roosevelt, unearthed evidence for a sedentary Amazon civilization, based in caves at **Monte Alegre**, near Santarém. These 'Pedra Pintada' people had been living off the rainforest as long as 11,000 years ago, making them roughly contemporary to, or only a little later than, the North

American Clovis. But the Pedra Pintada were very different to Clovis; even at this early stage, they lived more like the indigenous Brazilians who met the first *conquistadores*; foraging in the forest, making use of a wide variety of plants and animals, manufacturing rock tools and crafting their own, triangular, and distinctly un-Clovis spear points. They were also artists: the Pedra Pintada caves are called so because of their painted walls. Fastidious carbon-dating has shown that they were the first artists in the western hemisphere. In 1997, the year Roosevelt's results were published, discoveries at Monte Verde, a peat bog in southern Chile, presented further problems for the Clovis model. Chunks of mastodon meat, fossilized footprints, charcoal and bits of llama bone found at Monte Verde dated to 12,500 BP; 1300 years before the Clovis were meant to have arrived in the New World. 1999 findings at 30 sites near Las Vegas in Ecuador and Quebrada Jaguay in Peru were equally surprising. It seems that these coastal communities, far from being oafish Flintstones, were trading with Central America, cultivating gourds, squash and maize, and offshore fishing.

First American shamanism Guidon and Roosevelt's research, together with that being undertaken by ethno-biologists such as **Wade Davis**, anthropologists such as **Gerardo Reichel-Dolmatoff** and Mesoamerica archaeologists and epigraphers such as **Linda Schele**, began to change radically once widely accepted ideas about pre-Columbian Americans. Gone is a notion based on an analysis of their technology and concluding that they were prehistoric, primitive peoples, instead is an analysis based on their rich societal structure, speculative philosophy and the mythology which sustained it. We now see the first Americans as a divergent range of peoples who arrived in the Americas at varying times and probably from various locations. Between them they shared a common philosophical world map that was radically different from our own Greco-Roman idea and which was rooted in **shamanism**. In philosophical terms, shamanism assumes that being is as vital a component of reality as energy and matter; and like those two it is shared. In other words the basic stuff of the Universe is threefold – matter (energy), space and time (position) and the perception of those two (being), on which they both depend for their existence. The essence of being can be directly apprehended behind the mind by seers or shaman (Portuguese *pajé*). In most first American societies it was shaman – together with powerful civic leaders (Portuguese *cacique*) – who guided tribal societies; be they Mayan or Ticuna.

Lifestyle of the first Brazilians Little is known about how these people lived in Brazil, largely because of the colonial ideas that were handed down to Western archaeologists by the Spanish and Portuguese, who burned and plundered many of the artefacts and books of the first Americans. The Amazonian peoples were decimated by the Portuguese slave trade long before their knowledge could be shared; and as most of their treasures were made from perishable materials like feather, bark and reed, the products of their labour and their knowledge rotted into the forest floor. Some ceramics remain, as well as a few other more resilient items. The pottery produced by the early peoples was of a high standard. Early ceramics have been found on **Marajó island** at the mouth of the Amazon. The **Annatuba** culture lived here in small villages by the river. Most of their ceramics found are round bowls and jars, including huge funeral urns, which have been dated with increasing antiquity; the earliest from around 980 BC. Textile production was done mainly with hand-twisted fibres, using both cotton and bast. Objects found in Rio Grande do Sul, dating from AD 550 or earlier, included twined bags, nets and ropes. Most of the textiles found throughout Brazil were simple everyday items, such as hammocks and straps, with little decoration. Despite this, what we know is scant and trivial. The earliest people lived mainly on the flood plains of the great rivers and caught fish and manatee using spears thrown from the shore, or from dugout canoes. Besides fishing, these people also cultivated manioc and other plants found on the forest floor. They kept turtles in corrals at the river's edge, for eating and also for making tools and other artefacts from their shells.

Their nomadic lifestyle was carefully planned, and they followed planting and harvesting seasons in accordance with the periodic rising and falling river levels. At first, as hunters and gatherers, they built simple, temporary houses out of tree trunks and palm leaves, and slept in hammocks made from plant fibres. Where clothing was used it was simple; a large, ankle-length tunic called a *kushma* was the main garment worn. Although this may sound impractical wear for people living in a warm, humid climate, the *kushma* provided much-needed protection against biting insects. Compensating for their plain clothing, the people painted their bodies and wore colourful jewellery, such as feather head-dresses; the designs for which were often rich and elaborate and drawn from an extensive mythology. Little has remained of the perishable adornments, but cylindrical and flat ceramic stamps have been found throughout Amazônia, which may have been used to apply ink designs onto the face and other parts of the body, still common today among Brazilian ethnic groups.

The migration to the coast

Around 7000-4000 BC a climatic change increased the temperature throughout the south of Brazil, drawing people down from the inland *planalto* region to the coasts, and leading to an upsurge in population here. These coastal inhabitants lived on shellfish collected from the water's edge, as evidenced by *sambaquis* (huge shell mounds), discovered on the coast. In rare cases they also fed on whales that had probably been beached, but they did not go far out to sea to fish. Some of the *sambaquis* found measure up to 25 m high; many of them also served as dwellings, with floors and fireplaces, and as burial sites, with graves often underneath the houses. The dead were buried with personal adornments and some domestic artefacts.

The Marajó Kingdoms of the Amazon

By about 100-200 BC, people throughout Brazil were settled in structured, fixed communities by the coasts and rivers, living increasingly by farming instead of nomadic hunting and gathering. The subsequent population growth spread communities further along river courses and into seasonally flooded savannah lands.

Until Anna Roosevelt's research it had been thought that unlike the great empires of the Andes, the lowland peoples did not form political groupings much larger than a few villages. However it is now suggested that much of Brazil was settled by chiefdoms, some of which were substantial and the seat of sophisticated civilizations. The most notable of these was probably **Marajó** which Roosevelt has called 'one of the outstanding indigenous achievements of the New World.' The Marajó people occupied thousands of square kilometres in the lower portion of the Amazon Basin in a civilization which perhaps numbered around 100,000 people and which endured for some 1000 years. They had an advanced tropical rainforest agriculture in which fruit-bearing and utilitarian trees were planted within the forest (as opposed to in cleared areas); in much the same way as the Lacandon Maya today. The Marajó people were either influential on Brazilian indigenous people as a whole or they were part of a widespread practice, for by about 2000 BC peoples throughout the lower Amazon were planting at least 138 species of crop plant; including manioc which remains a staple in Brazilian diet to this day.

Tribal nations

The most widespread linguistic grouping in Brazil at the time of the European conquest was the Tupi-Guaraní. These people originated from the Atlantic coast around AD 500-700. By the 1500s the Tupi-Guaraní, who often moved from place to place could be found from north of the Amazon south to Rio de la Plata, and west into Paraguay and Bolivia; they were probably the first Americans the Portuguese encountered

One of the biggest groups of Tupi-speaking people were the **Tupinambá**. They lived on the coast, from the mouth of the Amazon south to São Paulo state, cultivating crops, such as manioc, sweet potato, cotton, gourds and tobacco. They lived in villages of four to eight large, rectangular, thatched houses, each containing up to 30 families and usually built on an elevation to catch the breeze. They moved to new sites every five years or so.

The Tupinambá were cannibals. This was a highly ritualized military practice, carried out on prisoners of war. The victims were kept as slaves, often for long periods, being well fed and looked after; in some cases even marrying the owner's daughter or sister, who had their children. But all such slaves were eventually eaten, after an elaborate ceremony with much singing and dancing. An appointed executioner would kill them with a club and they were then cooked and different parts of the body divided up among various participants in the ritual. There have been many theories as to why people practised cannibalism; since they tended to eat victims of war it was thought that it gave them power over the spirits of their dead enemies. It is most commonly argued that human flesh supplemented the diet for large populations who had scarce resources. But this was not the case for the Tupinambá, who had ample food supplies. When the Tupinambá themselves were asked why they ate human meat they simply said they liked the taste of it.

European colonization

Arrival of the Portuguese

Pedro Álvares Cabral is believed to be the first Portuguese explorer to land on the Brazilian coast, having been blown off his course to India and making landfall on 22 April 1500. He claimed the territory for Portugal as a result of agreements with Spain under the papal bull of 1493 and the Treaty of Tordesillas (1494), but it was some years before the Portuguese realized that this was not just another island as the Spanish had found in the Caribbean – and that they had stumbled across a huge new continent. Further expeditions were sent out in 1501 and 1503-1504 and a few trading stations were set up to export the only commodity they felt was of commercial interest: a species of dyewood known as 'pau do brasil'. Little attention was paid to the new colony, as the Portuguese concentrated on the more lucrative trade with Africa, India and the Far East. Some settlers, often banished criminals as well as merchants, gained acceptance with the local indigenous tribes and intermarried, fathering the first hybrid cultural Brazilians.

Colonization

The coastal trading stations at Salvador da Bahia, Pernambuco, São Vicente and Cabo Frio soon attracted the attention of French and British traders, who seized Portuguese ships and started to trade directly with the indigenous tribes. The French even proclaimed the right to trade in any part of Brazil not occupied by the Portuguese. This forced the Portuguese Crown to set up a colony and in 1530, Martim Afonso de Sousa was sent out with about 400 men. Faced with the impossibly huge task of colonizing the Brazilian coastline, the Crown turned to private enterprise to stake its claim. In 1534 the coast was divided into 15 donatories – given by the Portuguese crown to an individual captain to develop on behalf of Portugal. Although successful settlements were established in Pernambuco in the north and São Vicente in the south, the problems faced in most captaincies – indigenous resistance, lack of capital and the difficulty of attracting settlers – led to the reassertion of Crown control in 1549. The indigenous Brazilians had been happy to barter brazil wood with the Portuguese and had helped in the logging and transporting of timber, but the introduction of sugar plantations was a different matter and the hunter-gatherers had no experience of such exhausting work. When they refused to co-operate in this profitable enterprise, the Portuguese took them as slaves on a massive scale, which destroyed the good relations previously enjoyed and led to attacks on Portuguese settlements.

The First Brazilian capital and the Jesuits

Fighting broke out throughout the donatory colonies – especially in the largest sugar-growing area in Bahia. Plantations and mills were ransacked and the Portuguese murdered and ritually eaten. The Portuguese responded with increased violence – sending an old soldier to establish a capital in Brazil from which order would be imposed with an iron fist. **Tomé de Sousa** and a fleet of ships left Lisbon in 1549. The new colonists were made up principally of 'New Christians' (Jews and Arabs forced to convert to Christianity under the threat of the Inquisition), soldiers and priests, including a group of firebrand Jesuits led by the charismatic Manoel de Nobrega. The King gave de Sousa clear instructions – to convert the locals to Christianity, to begin more plantations and to punish any indigenous people who resisted, 'destroying their villages and settlements, and killing and enslaving whatever part of them you consider sufficient to act as a punishment and an example.' The new capital of Portuguese Imperial Brazil was built on a bluff above a huge sheltered bay that formed a natural harbour, and which the governor cleared of its three Tupinambá villages before beginning construction. It was named São Salvador da Bahia de Todos os Santos (the city of the Holy Saviour of All Saints Bay) – now known as Salvador. As a result of disagreements with the first Bishop of Brazil, Fernandes Sardanha, the Jesuits moved in 1554 from Bahia to the captaincy of São Vicente, where they set up a mission at Piratininga, which later became the city of **São Paulo**, then going on to found missions throughout Brazil. Their opposition to the indigenous slave trade led to increasing conflict with the colonists and eventually to their expulsion from the Americas in the 18th century. Troubles with the indigenous Brazilians did not end with de Sousa or his successor, and in 1557 a new and even tougher governor was appointed, **Mem de Sá** – with a mission to quell the unruly indigenous people and prevent the fledgling colony falling into rival European hands.

French and Dutch incursions

As Brazil became wealthier on pau brasil wood and sugar from the plantations in Pernambuco and Bahia, the Portuguese had increasing difficulties in consolidating their hold on Brazil in the face of growing interest from France and Holland. French Calvinists found a colony on an island in Guanabara Bay, which they christened **France Antarctique**. Mem de Sá ousted them after a series of bloody battles which led to the formal founding of a Portuguese colony in the bay, **São Sebastião de Rio de Janeiro**, in 1567. Mem de Sa crushed the indigenous Brazilians in Bahia in a ruthless scorched earth policy which devastated their morale and their numbers. The threats from Europe arose again the following century. **São Luís** was occupied by the French in 1612-1615, but it was the **Dutch** who posed the greatest threat on both sides of the Atlantic. They seized Pernambuco in

1630, Portuguese Angola in 1641 and dominated the Atlantic trading routes until the Portuguese managed to regain Angola in 1648-1649 and Pernambuco in 1654.

Sugar and slaves

Throughout the colonial period Brazil produced raw materials for Portugal. The colonial economy experienced a succession of booms and recessions, the first of these was based on sugar, as during the 17th century the northeastern provinces of Pernambuco, Bahia and Paraíba were the world's main producers of sugar. As European settlement had led to the death of much of the native population (over a third of the indigenous Brazilians in coastal areas died in epidemics in 1562-1563 alone) and slavery was unsuccessful, the Portuguese began what was to become the biggest **Atlantic slave trade** of all – transporting almost 40% of all the the Africans who were brought to the Americas to meet the demand for labour on the sugar plantations (*engenhos*). "The most solid properties in Brazil are slaves", wrote the Governor in 1729, "for there are lands enough, but only he who has slaves can be master of them." As many as 10 million African slaves may have survived the dreadful conditions of the Atlantic crossing before the trade was abolished in 1854 and slavery was abolished in Brazil in 1888.

The gold rush

As the sugar industry declined in the late-17th century in the face of competition from British, French and Dutch Caribbean colonies, **gold** was discovered inland in 1695 in Ouro Preto in Minas Gerais, and then in Mato Grosso and other areas. Despite the lack of communications, prospectors rushed in from all over Europe. Shortly afterwards, diamonds were found in the Serra do Frio. The economy was largely driven by gold until the 1760s and a revival of world demand for sugar in the second half of the 18th century. Thereafter, there was diversification into other crops such as cocoa, rice, cotton and coffee, all of which were produced for export by large numbers of slaves.

The gold rush shifted the power centre of Brazil from the northeast to the centre, in recognition of which new captaincies were created in Minas Gerais in 1720, Goiás in 1744 and Mato Grosso in 1748, and the capital was moved from Salvador to Rio de Janeiro in 1763. Legacies of the period can be seen today in the colonial towns of Mariana, Congonhas, São João del Rei, Diamantina and, above all, in the exceptionally beautiful city of Ouro Preto, a national monument full of glorious buildings, paintings and sculpture.

Marquês de Pombal

The decline of gold in the mid-18th century made economic reform necessary and the Marquês de Pombal was the minister responsible for a new programme for Portugal and her empire. Imbalances had arisen particularly in trade with Britain. Portugal imported manufactured goods and wheat but her exports of oil and wine left her in deficit, which for a while was covered by Brazilian gold. Pombal was a despotic ruler from 1750 to 1777, modernizing and reforming society, education, politics and the economy. In order to revive Portugal he concentrated on expanding the economy of Brazil, increasing and diversifying exports to cover the deficit with Britain. Cocoa, cotton and rice were introduced by the new monopoly company of **Grão Pará e Maranhão** in the north and a similar company for Paraíba and Pernambuco revitalized the sugar industry in the northeast. The monopoly companies led to high prices and were not entirely successful so were closed in 1778-1779, but the effects of Pombal's reforms were felt in the latter part of the 18th century and Portugal's trade with Britain turned into a surplus. From 1776 when the American colonies revolted, Britain was constantly at war and Portugal was able to supply rising British demand.

Rebellion

Pombal's influence on society enabled the Portuguese Empire to last much longer than the Spanish Empire. He deliberately offered posts in the militia and the bureaucracy to Brazilians and was careful not to alienate the Brazilian elites. White Brazilians were on the same standing as the Portuguese and identified strongly with the mother country. Although rebellion was rare, it still occurred, influenced partly by the turmoil that was going on in Europe with the French Revolution. In 1788-1789 a famous plot was uncovered in Minas Gerais called the **Inconfidência Mineira** (see box, page 266), which aimed to establish an independent republic in protest at the decline of the gold industry and high taxes. The rebels, who included many people from the upper echelons of society, were punished and the most prominent leader, **Tiradentes** (the tooth-puller), was hanged. Other plots were discovered in Rio de Janeiro in 1794, Pernambuco in 1801 and Bahia in 1807, but they were all repressed.

The Brazilian empire

At the beginning of the 19th century, Napoleon Bonaparte caused a major upheaval in the monarchies of Europe. His expansion into the Iberian peninsula caused panic in both Spain and Portugal. In August 1807 he demanded that Portugal close its ports to British ships but the British sent a fleet to Lisbon and threatened to attack Brazil if that happened. In November of the same year the French invaded and occupied Portugal. The Prince Regent decided to evacuate the court to Brazil and under British escort sailed to Rio de Janeiro, which became the **capital of the empire** in 1808. The court stayed there even after 1815 when Napoleon was defeated and Portugal was ruled by the regency council, but King João VI was forced to return to Portugal in 1820 after a series of liberal revolts in the mother country, leaving his son Dom Pedro as prince regent in Brazil.

Independence from Portugal

Dom Pedro oversaw a growing rift between Portugal and Brazil as the liberals in Lisbon tried to return Brazil to its former colonial status, cancelling political equality and the freedom of trade granted when the King left Portugal in the hands of the French. In October 1821 the government in Lisbon recalled the prince regent but Brazilians urged him not to go. Encouraged by his chief minister, **José Bonifácio de Andrada e Silva**, a conservative monarchist, Dom Pedro announced on 9 January 1822 that he would stay in Brazil, thereby asserting his autonomy. After another attempt to recall the prince regent, **Dom Pedro** made the final break with Portugal, proclaiming Brazil's independence on 7 September 1822. He was crowned emperor and Brazil became a constitutional monarchy in its own right. There was resistance in the north and northeast, particularly from the militia, but by 1824 violence had subsided. In 1825, under pressure from Britain, Portugal recognized the independent state of Brazil.

The first years of independence were unsettled, partly because of the emperor's perceived favouritism for the Portuguese faction at court and lack of attendance to the needs of the local oligarchy. De Andrada e Silva resigned as opposition grew. In 1823 Dom Pedro dissolved the constituent assembly amidst fears that he had absolutist designs. However, he set up a royal commission to draft a new constitution which lasted from 1824

Estimated slavery statistics

Country	Voyages	Slaves transported
Denmark	250	50,000
British North America and USA	1500	300,000
Holland	2000	500,000
France (including French Caribbean)	4200	1,250,000
Spain (including Cuba)	4000	1,600,000
Britain	12,000	2,600,000
Portugal (including Brazil)	30,000	4,650,000

Cited from *The Slave Trade Hugh Thomas Phoenix Press*

until the fall of the monarchy in 1889. This gave the emperor the right to appoint and dismiss cabinet ministers, veto legislation and dissolve parliament and call for elections. The parliamentary government consisted of two houses, a senate appointed by the monarch and a legislature indirectly elected by a limited male suffrage. A council of state advised the monarch and ensured the separation of the executive, the legislature and the judiciary. Catholicism remained the official religion and the monarchy was supported by the church.

Abdication
Dom Pedro still failed to gain the trust of all his people. A **republican rebellion** broke out in Pernambuco in 1824, where the elite were suffering from the declining sugar industry, and there was further resentment from all the planter oligarchy as a result of the **Anglo-Brazilian Treaty of 1826**. This treaty granted British recognition of the independent Brazil in return for certain trading privileges, but, almost more importantly, stipulated that the Atlantic slave trade should come to an end in three years. There was also a territorial dispute in 1825 with the Argentine provinces over the left bank of the Río de la Plata, called the *Banda Oriental*, which flared up into war and was only settled in 1828 with the creation of Uruguay as a buffer state. The mistrust between the Portuguese and the Brazilians became even more pronounced. Portuguese merchants were blamed for the rising cost of living and in 1831 rioting broke out in Rio de Janeiro. Dom Pedro shuffled and reshuffled his cabinet to appease different factions but nothing worked and on 7 April he abdicated in favour of his five-year-old son, **Dom Pedro II**, choosing to leave Brazil a week later on a British warship.

Regency and rebellion
During the 10 years of the young prince's boyhood, there were many separatist movements and uprisings by the oppressed lower classes. In 1832-1835 there was the War of the Cabanos, in Pernambuco, a guerrilla war against the slave-owning plantocracy of the northeast; in 1835 the **Revolta da Cabanagem** (Cabanagem rebellion) of free indigenous tribes and *mestizos* took place in Pará after a white secessionist revolt and sporadic fighting continued until 1840 (see page 607); in 1837-1838 in Bahia there was a **federalist rebellion**; in 1835 Rio Grande do Sul proclaimed itself a republic, remaining independent for nearly 10 years, with the movement spreading into Santa Catarina, which also declared itself a republic. By 1840 there was a general consensus that although he had not come of age, it

was imperative that the 14 year old, Pedro, should **ascend to the throne**. He was duly crowned. Administration of the country was centralized again, the powers of provincial assemblies were curtailed, a national police force set up and the council of state restored.

The second empire
It took a couple of years for the balance of power to be worked out between the conservative elites of Rio de Janeiro and the liberal elites of São Paulo and Minas Gerais, but once the interests of different groups had been catered for, the constitutional monarchy worked smoothly for 20 years. **Coffee** was now the major crop in São Paulo and Minas Gerais and it was important that the wealthy oligarchy who produced it shared in the power structure of the nation in order to prevent secessionist movements.

Abolition of slavery
Despite the Anglo-Brazilian Treaty of 1826, the slave trade continued until the British Royal Navy put pressure on Brazilian ships carrying slaves in 1850 and the trade was halted soon afterwards. As slaves in Brazil did not reproduce at a natural rate because of the appalling conditions in which they lived and worked, it was clear that an alternative source of labour would eventually have to be found. Anti-slavery movements gathered strength and in 1871 the first steps towards abolition were taken. A new law gave freedom to all children born to slaves from that date and compensation was offered to masters who freed their slaves. During the 1870s large numbers of European immigrants, mostly from Italy and Portugal, came to work on the coffee plantations, and as technology and transport improved, so the benefits of slavery declined. During the 1880s the abolition movement became unstoppable and, after attempts to introduce compensation for slave owners failed, a **law abolishing slavery** was finally passed on 13 May 1888. Some plantation owners went bankrupt, but the large majority survived by paying immigrant workers and newly freed slaves a pittance. Those freed slaves who left the plantations to find employment in the cities were equally exploited and lived in poverty.

Proclamation of the Republic

The first Republic: 1889-1930
The monarchy did not long survive the end of slavery. The São Paulo coffee producers resented abolition and resented their under-representation in the structures of power nationwide, while being called upon to provide the lion's share of the treasury's revenues. The republican movement started in the early 1870s in cities all over Brazil, but grew strongest in São Paulo. It gradually attracted the support of the military, who also felt under-represented in government, and on 15 November 1889 a **bloodless military coup d'état** deposed the monarchy and instituted a federal system. The constitution of the new republic established 20 states with wide powers of self-government, a directly elected president of a national government with a senate and a chamber of deputies. Suffrage was introduced for literate adult males (about 3% of the population) and the church and state were separated. Although the birth of the republic was bloodless, there were pockets of resistance in rural areas such as the northeast, where the sugar estates were in recession. In the 1890s **Antônio Conselheiro** led tens of thousands of followers against the secular republic at Canudos, nearly all of whom were eventually killed by government troops. In 1911 there was another rebellion in the southern states of Paraná

and Santa Catarina, led by a Catholic visionary in defence of the monarchy. The **Contestado** movement lasted until 1915, when it too was destroyed by the military.

Brazilian politics were now dominated by an alliance known as **café com leite** (coffee with milk), of the coffee growers of São Paulo and the cattle ranchers of Minas Gerais, occasionally challenged by Rio Grande do Sul, with periodic involvement of the military. The first two presidents of the republic were military: **Marshal Deodoro da Fonseca** (1889-1891) and **Marshal Floriano Peixoto** (1891-1894). In some ways the military took the place of the Crown in mediating between the states' oligarchies, but its interventions were always unconstitutional and therefore gave rise to political instability. By the 1920s tensions between São Paulo and Minas Gerais had come out into the open with the cattle ranchers resenting the way in which the coffee growers used their position to keep the price of coffee artificially high at a time when there was an oversupply. Other social groups also became restive and unsuccessful coup attempts were launched by junior army officers in 1922, 1924 and 1926.

The end of the First World War saw the rise of the USA as an industrial power and the decline of Britain's traditional supremacy in trade with Latin America. Although Brazil was still exporting its raw materials to Europe at ever lower prices, it now imported its manufactured goods from the USA, leading to difficulties with finance and fluctuating exchange rates. Brazil's terms of trade had therefore deteriorated and the profitability of its export-led economy was declining before the crash of Wall Street in 1929. The cost of stockpiling excess coffee had led to a rise in debt and by 1930 the government was spending a third of its budget on debt servicing. The growth of nationalism was a key feature of this period as well as the emergence of new political factions and parties such as fascists and communists.

Vargas and the Estado Nôvo: 1930-1945

The Wall Street crash led to a sudden decline in demand for coffee and the São Paulo elite saw its hegemony wiped out. The elections of 1930 saw another win for the São Paulo candidate, but the results were disputed by a coalition of opposition forces. After several months of tension and violence, the army intervened, deposed the outgoing president and installed the alternative candidate of Rio Grande do Sul, **Getúlio Vargas**, a wealthy rancher, as provisional president. Vargas in fact held office until 1954, with only one break in 1945-1950. His main aim, when he took office, was to redress the balance of power away from São Paulo and in favour of his own state. However, the effects of his reforms were more far-reaching. He governed by decree, replacing all state governors with 'interventors' who reduced the state militias, and reorganized the system of patronage within the states in favour of his own. São Paulo naturally resisted and there was a rebellion in 1932, but it was soon put down by federal troops, effectively wiping out the threat to Vargas' authority. In 1934 a constituent assembly drew up a new constitution that reduced the power of the states and gave more power to the president. The assembly then elected Vargas as president for a four-year term.

With the decline of traditional oligarchic blocs came the rise of political parties. The first to fill the vacuum were the fascists and the communists, who frequently took to street violence against each other. The fascists, called Integralists, were founded by Plínio Salgado in 1932. The **Aliança Libertadora Nacional (ALN)**, a popular front including socialists and radical liberals, was founded by the Brazilian Communist Party in 1935. The ALN attempted to gain power by infiltrating the junior ranks of the army and encouraging rebellions, but Vargas clamped down on the movement, imprisoning its leaders. The fascists aimed to take power in 1938, the year elections were due, at which Vargas was not eligible to stand. However, in October 1937, Vargas declared a state of siege against an alleged communist plot and suspended the constitution which had prevented him being re-elected. Instead, he proclaimed a new constitution and a new state, Estado Nôvo. The fascists tried to oust him but failed, leaving Vargas with no effective opposition whatsoever.

The Estado Nôvo was also a response to an economic crisis, brought on by a fall in coffee prices, rising imports, a resulting deficit in the balance of payments, a high level of debt and soaring inflation. Vargas assumed dictatorial powers to deal with the economic crisis, censoring the press, banning political parties, emasculating trade unions and allowing the police unfettered powers. There followed a transition from export-led growth to import substitution and industrialization with heavy state intervention. Agricultural resources were channelled into industry and the government became involved in mining, oil, steel, electricity, chemicals, motor vehicles and light aircraft. The military were allowed free rein to develop their own armaments industry. As war approached in Europe, Vargas hedged his bets with both Nazi Germany and the USA, to see who would provide the greatest assistance for Brazil's industrialization. It turned out to be the USA, and in return for allowing US military bases to be built in northern Brazil he secured loans, technical assistance and other investments for a massive steel mill at Volta Redonda and infrastructure projects. Brazil did not declare war on Germany until 1944, but it was the only Latin American country to send troops to join the allies, with a force of 25,000 men going to Italy.

The elections of 1943 had been postponed during the War, but Vargas scheduled a vote for December 1945 in an attempt to dispel his fascist image. He allowed the formation of political parties, which included two formed by himself: the Social Democratic Party (PSD), supported by industrialists and large farmers, and a Labour Party (PTB), supported by pro-Vargas trade unions. There was also the National Democratic Union (UDN), opposed to Vargas, and the newly legalized Communist Party. However, there were growing fears that Vargas would not relinquish power, and when he appointed his brother as chief of police in Rio de Janeiro, the military intervened. Faced with the prospect of being deposed, Vargas chose to resign in October 1945, allowing the **elections** to take place as planned in the December. They were won by the PSD, led by General Eurico Dutra, a former supporter of the Estado Nôvo, who had encouraged Vargas to resign.

The second Republic: 1946-1964

Yet another constitution was drafted by a constituent assembly in 1946, this one based on the liberal principles of the 1891 constitution but including the labour code and the social legislation of the *Estado Nôvo*. Industrialization through state planning was retained, the foreign-owned railways were nationalized, hydroelectric power was developed, but deflation was necessary to bring down spiralling prices. The Communist Party was banned again in 1947. Meanwhile Vargas was elected Senator for Rio Grande do Sul, his home state, and kept active in politics, eventually being **elected as candidate** for the PSD and PTB alliance in the 1950 presidential elections. Although it was his third presidency, it was only his first by direct elections.

The third Vargas presidency was beset by the problems of fulfilling populist election promises while grappling with debt and inflation. Rapid industrialization required levels of investment which could only be raised abroad, but the nationalists were opposed to foreign investment. He failed to reconcile the demands of the USA and the nationalists, particularly with regards to oil and energy, and he failed to control inflation and stabilize the economy. There were rumours of corruption, and after the president's bodyguard was implicated in a plot to kill a journalist, which went wrong and another man was shot, the army issued him with another ultimatum to resign or be ousted. Instead, on 24 August 1954, **Vargas shot himself**, leaving a suicide note denouncing traitors at home and capitalists abroad.

The next president was Juscelino Kubitschek, who took office in January 1956 with the aim of achieving economic growth at any cost, regardless of inflation and debt. He is best known for building the new capital of Brazil, **Brasília**, nearly 1000 km northwest of Rio de Janeiro in the state of Goiás. This massive modernist project served in the short term to expand the debt and in 1961, the next president, Jânio Quadros, inherited huge economic problems which brought his government down after only seven months and Congress unexpectedly accepted his resignation. Power passed to his vice-president, João Goulart, a populist and former labour minister under Vargas, who was mistrusted by the armed forces and the right wing. His powers were curtailed with the appointment of a prime minister and cabinet who would be jointly answerable to Congress. The 1960s were a turbulent time in Brazil as elsewhere, with the universities a hotbed of revolutionary socialism after the Cuban Revolution, Trotskyist and Communist agitators encouraging land occupations, strikes in industry and a move to secure trade union rights for the armed forces. A nationalist Congress passed legislation cutting foreign companies' annual profit remittances to 10% of profits, which sparked a massive outflow in foreign capital and a halving of US aid. Goulart was forced to print money to keep the economy going, which naturally put further pressure on an already soaring inflation rate. When Goulart clashed with Congress over approval of an economic adjustment programme and tried to strengthen his position by appealing for popular support outside Congress, he alarmed the middle classes, who unexpectedly supported a **military coup** in March 1964. Goulart took refuge in Uruguay.

Military rule: 1964-1985

The 1964 coup was a turning point in Brazilian political history. This time the armed forces did not return to barracks as they had before. Opposition leaders were arrested, the press censored, labour unions purged of anyone seen as left wing, and the secret police were given wide powers. The political parties were outlawed and replaced by two officially approved parties: the government Aliança Renovadora Nacional (ARENA) and the opposition Movimento Democrático Brasileiro (MDB). Congress, consisting only of members of these two parties, approved a succession of military presidents nominated by the armed forces. A new constitution, introduced in 1967, gave the president broad powers over the states and over Congress. The worst period of repression occurred between 1968 and 1973 with a wave of urban guerrilla warfare. Around this time, the military government's economic adjustment programme paid dividends and the economy began to grow, making life easier for the middle classes and reducing any potential support for **guerrilla groups**. In 1968-1974 the economy grew at over 10% a year, which became known as the Brazilian 'economic miracle'. This spectacular growth, achieved because of the authoritarian nature of the regime, masked a widening gulf between the rich and poor, with the blacks and mulattos, always at the bottom in Brazilian society, suffering the most. Edwin Williamson (*The Penguin History of Latin America*) quotes statistics showing that in 1960 the richest 10% of the population received 40% of the national income; by 1980 they received 51%, while the poorest 50% received only 13%. In the shanty towns, or favelas, which had mushroomed around all the large cities, but especially São Paulo, disease, malnutrition and high mortality rates were prevalent and their citizens battled constantly in appalling housing lacking sewerage, running water and electricity.

By 1973 some military officers and their civilian advisors had become alarmed at the rising level of opposition. Arguing that repression alone would merely lead to further opposition and even to attempted revolution, they pressed for 'decompression': policies to relax the repression while remaining in power. The attempt to carry out this policy by legalizing political parties, permitting freer trade unions and strikes and reducing censorship, gave greater space for the opposition to demand an end to military rule. Attempts to introduce elections to Congress which were less controlled faced the same obstacle: they tended to result in victories for candidates who favoured civilian rule.

One of the main reasons for the military deciding to return to their barracks was the dire state of the economy. The armed forces had taken over in 1964 when the economy had hit rock bottom, their authoritarian regime had allowed rapid expansion and change which brought about the **'economic miracle'**, yet by 1980 the economy had gone full circle. Inflation was running at 100% a year and was set to go through the roof, foreign debt was the highest in Latin America, estimated at over US$87 billion, and unemployment was soaring. When international interest rates rose sharply in 1982, Brazil was no longer able to service its debt and it suspended interest payments. Unwilling to go through another round of authoritarianism and repression, the military decided to let the civilians have a go. Elections in 1982 produced a majority for the pro-government Social Democratic Party (PDS) in the electoral college which was to elect the next president, but splits in the PDS led to the election in January 1985 of the opposition candidate (see under São João del Rei, page 273).

The return to democracy

Corruption and impeachment

In 1985 **Tancredo Neves** was elected as the first civilian president for 21 years. Before he could take office he fell ill and died. His vice-president José Sarney became president at a time of economic crisis, with inflation at 300%. Sarney introduced the Cruzado Plan in 1986, freezing prices and wages, but inflation exploded when the freeze was lifted.

A new constitution brought direct presidential elections in November 1989. After two rounds of voting **Fernando Collor de Melo**, of the small Partido da Reconstrução Nacional, won 53% of the vote to narrowly defeat his left-wing rival, Luís Inácio da Silva (popularly known as Lula). Collor launched controversial economic reforms, including opening the economy to imports, privatization and a freeze on savings and bank accounts. The policies failed and by 1991 inflation reached 1500% and foreign debt payments were suspended.

Just over half way through his term, Collor was suspended from office after Congress voted overwhelmingly to impeach him for corruption. He avoided this by resigning on 29 December 1992. Vice-president Itamar Franco took over, but had scant success in tackling poverty and inflation until the introduction of an anti-inflation package that introduced the *real* as the new currency.

The plano real

The architect of the *real* plan was finance minister **Fernando Henrique Cardoso**. Three decades earlier he had been a high-profile leftist and opponent of military rule, forced into exile after the 1964 military coup. The success of the *real* plan led to his election as president in October 1994. After trailing Lula of the Workers Party (PT), Cardoso gained such popularity that he won the election in the first round of voting. However, his alliance of the Brazilian Social Democrat Party (PSDB), the Liberal Front (PFL) and the Labour Party (PTB) failed to gain a majority in either house of Congress. This severely hampered plans to reform the tax and social security systems and the civil service. The government was also criticized for its slowness in addressing social problems. Such problems ranged from the need for land reform and violence associated with landlessness, to the slave-like working conditions in agricultural areas and the human rights of the indigenous Brazilians and of street children in large cities.

Towards the end of 1997 the financial crisis in Asia sapped investor confidence throughout the world, and threatened Brazil's currency and economic stability. The failure to cut public spending had swollen the budget deficit and the *real* was exposed to speculation. Cardoso was obliged to take actions to prevent an upsurge in inflation and devaluation of the currency, but at the cost of slowing down economic growth. Crisis was avoided and inflation remained in single figures, in contrast to the hyperinflation of earlier periods.

The government still faced the serious social imbalances that it had failed to redress. However, Cardoso managed to beat Lula again in October 1998 without the need for a second poll. In doing so he became the first Brazilian president to be elected for a second term.

Cardoso's second term

Cardoso and his PSDB party emerged victorious from the 1998 elections with 99 Deputies, but they needed allies both in the 513-seat Chamber of Deputies and in the Senate. Political opponents had also won many powerful state governorships. The PSDB's relations with its major ally, the PFL, came under increasing strain. Unlike the PSDB, the PFL was a conservative group dominated by old-style politicians, typified by its leader, the Bahian coronel **Antônio Carlos Magalhães**, who increasingly controlled Congress. There were rumours of corruption in Cardoso's government, with not even the president himself above implication. Another financial crisis threatened, which was averted by an IMF loan of US$18 billion at the end of 1998, but the delayed social security reforms had still not been passed. Finally when ex-president Itamar Franco, governor of Minas Gerais, refused to pay his state's debts to the Federal Government in January 1999, foreign investors lost confidence. The pressures on the *real* became too great and the central bank had to let it float freely against the dollar. It lost 50% of its value in the process. Two more stable years followed, but with its economic credibility eroded and shifting alliances in Congress the Cardoso government made little progress with its policies.

The 2002 elections

As in the USA, Brazilian presidents cannot run for a third term. Four front-runners emerged in the 2002 elections. Taking an early commanding lead in the opinion polls was **Luiz Inácio Lula da Silva**, best known as Lula, who was making his fourth bid for the presidency. With a refurbished image, a new suit, moderated policies and a millionaire running mate, the veteran firebrand, gained support from all classes.

Against a backdrop of global crises, the *real* again lost some 50% of its value in less than a year. Foreign investors were concerned about repeated budget deficits, and the prospect that a more left-wing government might default on debts. In August 2002, the IMF again came to the rescue, this time with a record US$30-billion loan, subject to tough conditions. On 27 October 2002 Lula won a convincing victory against government-backed José Serra. The new president – once shoe-shine boy, ex-leader of the Metal Workers' Union and head of the Workers' Party – set out to lead the first left-wing government in Brazil for 40 years.

For foreigners, what was perhaps most remarkable about Lula's first term of office was how little changed. Whilst Chávez in Venezuela and Ivo Morales in Bolivia forged policies allying their countries with Cuba and Cuban ideology, which included preaching a gospel of hatred and mistrust against the United States, Lula forged a middle way. In one of the first meetings with George Bush, the new president made it clear that Brazil was open for business and that he expected the USA to be open to Brazilian exports, particularly agricultural products that had long been denied access to US markets. Lula also wanted to acknowledge Brazil as a regional power. Nor did Brazil plummet into economic crisis as was predicted by the likes of George Soros. Its economy continued to grow steadily, albeit at a slower rate than its counterparts in Asia. And publicly Lula distanced himself from firebrand left-wing Latin Americans like Chávez; preferring to foster closer trade relations with China and India. Lula also attempted to introduce reforms that ran against the grain of Brazilian society and political practice, by filtering money from the elite and the public service establishment to the less privileged. Brazil's public services are among the most cumbersome, financially draining, bureaucratic and corrupt in the world. And none are more so than the pension system. Many public sector professionals collect several pensions and many retire on pensions higher than their final salary. In contrast state pensions to the private sector average US$120 per month. In 2002 the state pension ran a deficit worth 4.3% of GDP or US$18 billion. One of Lula's early achievements was to get the Senate to pass a bill on pensions reform, capping public pensions at US$750 per month (still two times higher than the average middle-class salary), raising the retirement age and introducing new pension taxes. This resulted in strikes by half of the country's federal workers and the blocking of the bill by judges; a process which can take years to unravel in Brazil's equally bureaucratic courts.

Lula returns to power and the 2010 elections

In mid-2004 Lula published an impressive proposed bill on Agrarian Reform which promised far more than any Brazilian government ever has: 400,000 families are to be settled via expropriation, 200,000 to be settled on land purchased by a Credito Fundiário small loans bank, designed to sell to small farmers at subsidized interest rates. He also launched a *Fome Zero*, or 'no hunger' programme, designed to give all poor Brazilians enough to eat.

But the second half of Lula's first term saw his good intentions frustrated by a combination of incompetence and corruption. Municipal governments, principally individual mayors, tried to control the disbursement of funds both for the Credito Fundiário and the Fome Zero programme; raking off public money has long been a way of life in Brazil. As so often in Brazil's history, money dedicated for the poor was ending up in private bank accounts. And in 2005 a corruption scandal called the **Mensalão** rocked Lula's federal government. Public funds had been used to bribe smaller parties to vote for Lula's government in the two federal chambers. Lula's deputy resigned, together with several senior PT members. Lula denied involvement but was severely compromised and was branded either oblivious and therefore incompetent or corrupt himself. A savage press campaign against him boded ill for the federal elections of 2006. But Lula won again; buoyed by popular support from the poor urban majority. In November 2010, **Dilma Rousseff**, Lula's preferred successor and former chief of staff,was elected Brazil's first ever woman president, promising to "overn for all Brazilians" and eradicate poverty. Shortly after rising to power another huge oil field was discovered off the coast of Rio de Janeiro, further consolidating the country's wealth. Rousseff is the daughter of a Bulgarian immigrant and his school teacher wife who became a leftist guerila and was tortured by the secret police during the dictatorship. She is expected to continue Lula's economic legacy and to make inroads, physically and economically, into the Amazon; whilst Brazil's impoverished are set to benefit under her leadership, the environment is expected to suffer.

Culture

People

Indigenous peoples

There were probably between three and five million indigenous people in Brazil when the Portuguese arrived. Today there are between 200,000 and 300,000. The effects of European colonization were devastating – whole tribes were wiped out under the Portuguese Amazon slave trade and others set to fight against each other for Portuguese advantage. Present-day tribal groups number about 220; each has a unique dialect, but most languages belong to four main linguistic families, Tupi-Guarani, Gê, Carib and Arawak. A few tribes remain uncontacted, others are exclusively nomadic, others are semi-nomadic hunter-gatherers and farmers, while some are settled groups in close contact with non-indigenous society. There is no agreement on precisely how many tribes are extant, but the Centro Ecumênico da Documentação e Informação (CEDI) of São Paulo said that of the 200 or so groups it documented, 40% have populations of less than 200 people and 77% have populations of less than 1000. Hemming underlines this depressing statistic when he reports that tribes contacted in recent decades have, as have others in previous centuries, suffered catastrophic reductions in numbers as soon as they encounter diseases which are common to non-indigenous people, but to which their bodies have no immunity.

Most of Brazil's indigenous people live in the Amazon region; they are affected by deforestation, encroachment from colonizers, small- and large-scale mining, and the construction of hydroelectric dams. Besides the Yanomami, other groups include the Xavante, Ticuna, Tukano, Kreen-Akrore, Kaiapó, Bororo and Arara. The struggle of groups such as the Yanomami to have their land demarcated in order to secure title is well-documented. The goal of the Statute of the Indian (Law 6.001/73), for demarcation of all indigenous land by 1978, is largely unmet. It was feared that a new law introduced in January 1996 would slow the process even more. However all is not bleak. The populations of many indigenous groups have grown over the last decade and a number have their land rights, which have been protected under Brazilian Law, by Fernando Henrique Cardoso and by Lula (although the latter is alleged to have reneged on a promise to enshrine an important area territory in Roraima into law at the 11th hour in exchange for support by powerful members of the state elite). On occasion indigenous land rights are enforced. A flight out over the Xingu in northern Mato Grosso shows this starkly, with the indigenous territory as a huge green island in a sea of soya and cattle plantations. Funai, the National Foundation for the Support of the Indian, a part of the Interior Ministry, is charged with representing the indigenous interests, but lacks resources and support. There is no nationwide, representative body for indigenous people, although the Amazon indigenous lobbying group, COIAB, is increasingly powerful and Manoel Moura's FIUPAM (fiupam@yahoo.com.br) is growing daily.

Mestiços

At first the Portuguese colony grew slowly. From 1580 to 1640 the population was only about 50,000 apart from the million or so indigenous Brazilians. In 1700 there were some 750,000

Indigenous people of Brazil

As a percentage of population Brazil has few indigenous people. But total numbers are large, with estimates varying between 450,000 and almost a million; in some 227 tribal nations. These are scattered throughout the country from the far south to the Amazon; with the greatest numbers in that region. In addition some 30% of Brazilians are part indigenous, many being *caboclo* (a word in the interior or north and northeast) or *caiçara* (used on the south and southeast coast) peoples leading traditional semi-indigenous largely self-sufficient lives. There are also traditional communities founded by African fugitives from slavery – or *quilombos*. It is possible to visit all of these communities. This should always be organized beforehand. Visitors who arrive unannounced will not be welcome and in some areas may be putting themselves at considerable risk. Details of how to visit are given in the relevant section of the text.

non-indigenous people in Brazil. Early in the 19th century Humboldt computed there were about 920,000 whites, 1.96 million Africans, and 1.12 million indigenous Brazilians and people of mixed Portuguese and indigenous origin (*mestiços*): after three centuries of occupation a total of only four million, and over twice as many Africans as there were whites.

The arid wastes of the *sertão* remain largely uncultivated. Its inhabitants are *mestiço*; most live off a primitive but effective method of cultivation known as 'slash and burn'. This involves cutting down and burning the brushwood for a small patch of ground, which is cultivated for a few years and then allowed to grow back.

Afro-Brazilians

Racism is culturally rife in Brazil and often openly expressed in all-white company. Though there is no legal discrimination against black people, the economic and educational disparity – by default rather than intent of the Government – is such that successful Afro-Brazilians are active almost exclusively in the worlds of sport, entertainment and the arts.

Brazilian culture, however would be nothing without its African influences. Those interested in the development of Afro-Brazilian music, dance, religion, arts and cuisine will find the cities of Rio de Janeiro, Bahia and São Luís, which retain the greatest African influences, particularly fascinating. Black Pride movements are particularly strong in Bahia.

After the rigours of transatlantic shipment in tiny rat-infested spaces, the Africans suffered further trauma on arrival at the Brazilian ports. They were often sold in groups that were segregated to avoid slaves from the same family or speaking the same language being together. By breaking all cultural and sentimental ties, the Portuguese hoped to eradicate ethnic pride and rebellions on the estates. As a result African spiritual cults became mixed and syncretistic even before they mixed with Portuguese Catholicism and indigenous spirituality. In what is now modern day Nigeria, for instance, there were different groups of people, each with its own divinity or *orixá* (pronounced 'orisha'). These *orixás* were normally the spirit of a distinguished ancestor or a legendary hero and were worshipped only in a particular region. As the slaves went to Brazilian estates in groups made up of people from different African regions, they soon started to worship all the *orixás*, instead of just one. As a result uniquely Afro-Brazilian religions were born out of the template of African spirituality, notably *candomblé*, *umbanda*, and *macumba*, which are devoted to integration with the natural world and archetypal energies through the intervention of spirits, or **Orixas**.

Europeans

Modern immigration did not begin effectively until after 1850. Of the 4.6 million immigrants from Europe between 1884 and 1954, 32% were Italians, 30% Portuguese, 14% Spanish, 4% German, and the rest of various nationalities. Since 1954 immigrants have averaged 50,000 a year. Most of the German immigrants settled in Santa Catarina, Rio Grande do Sul, and Paraná. The Germans (and the Italians, Poles and other Slavs who followed them) did not, in the main, go as wage earners on the big estates, but as cultivators of their own small farms. Here there is a settled agricultural population cultivating the soil intensively.

Asians

There are some two million Japanese-descended Brazilians; they grow a fifth of the coffee, 30% of the cotton, all the tea, and are very active in market gardening. Today the whites and near-whites make up about 53% of the population, people of mixed race about 34%, and Afro Brazilians 11%; the rest are either indigenous or Asian. There are large regional variations in the distribution of the races: the whites predominate greatly in the south, which received the largest flood of European immigrants.

Arts and crafts

Woodcarving

Woodworking has two principal origins, the African and the Jesuit. In northeastern Brazil, many woodcarving and sculpting techniques are inherited from the African slaves who were brought across the Atlantic to work the sugar plantations. One of the most prominent examples is the *carranca*, the grotesque figurehead that was placed on a boat's prow to ward off evil spirits. *Carrancas* are an adaptation of the African mask-making tradition and other carved and sculpted masks can be found in the northeast. The Jesuits passed on skills in the carving and painting of religious figures in wood. Originally they encouraged their indigenous converts in the techniques, but today others practice the art. Woodcarving is widespread in Pernambuco and Bahia in the northeast. In Rio de Janeiro many contemporary artists work in wood and Embu, near São Paulo, is a centre for wooden sculptures and furniture making.

Ceramics

In northeastern Brazil, religious figures are also made in clay, for instance the unglazed, life-sized saints made from red clay in Tracunhaém, near Recife. Another centre for similar work is Goiana, also in Pernambuco. A third place from which the ceramics are even more famous is Alto da Moura, near Caruaru (Pernambuco – see page 495). Here, Mestre Vitalino began modelling scraps of clay into little figures depicting everyday life (work, festivals, dancing, political events). He died in 1963, but the tradition that he started has continued and is known throughout Brazil.

The pots that are made in the Amazon region come in various styles, some of them quite strange. Bahian and other northeastern pottery shows African influence.

Textiles, clothing and leather

Ceará, in the north, is famous for its lace-making, and beautiful pieces are sold all over Brazil. In other parts of the north, hammocks and other woven items are found. The hammock is, of course, an essential household item and you may well need to buy one if you are travelling up the Amazon on a boat. Other utilitarian articles which have become craft items are the rugs and capes made in the highlands further south, such as Minas Gerais, to keep out the night-time cold.

In the northeast, traditional costumes have their roots in the rituals of the African religions that came to Brazil with the slave trade. In southern areas where European immigration was heaviest, many traditional costumes can be seen, usually at the festivals and dances that have survived. Another type of clothing from the south is that associated with the *gaúchos*, the Brazilian cowboys of Rio Grande do Sul. As well as the clothes, which normally use hide in their manufacture, you may also buy saddlery, stirrups, silverware and the gourds used for drinking *maté*.

Leatherwork is not confined to the south, but can be found in any region where cattle are raised.

Musical instruments

The most popular instruments that tourists like to buy are those connected with African music, especially the hand and friction drums like the *zabumba*, cuica and *reco reco*, shakers and the *berimbau* (the one-stringed bow that is twanged in accompaniment to capoeira). Here again, the best place to look is in the northeast where the African heritage is strongest. You can also purchase guitars and other stringed instruments. For a glossary of musical instruments, see Music and dance colour section (page xv) in the centre of the book.

Basketware

In Amazônia, a huge variety of raw materials are available for making baskets, nets, hammocks, slings for carrying babies, masks and body adornments. In the northeast, too, baskets come in all shapes and sizes, especially in Bahia, Pernambuco and Paraíba. Another northeastern craft, which does not fit into the above categories, is pictures made in bottles with coloured sands (Lençóis, Bahia, and Natal, Rio Grande do Norte, are good places to buy them). In Minas Gerais, two very common things to see and buy are soapstone carvings (for instance birds and animals) and the cooking pots used in *mineira* kitchens.

Gemstones

Even before the discover of rich mineral deposits in the interior of the country, legends told of mountains full of precious stones. Prospectors looked for diamonds and emeralds as well as gold and silver to make them wealthy. The existence of gems was known about almost from the earliest days of the Portuguese colony, from the reports given to the new arrivals by the indigenous Brazilians and from scattered discoveries of different stones. But there was nothing to bring riches on the scale of the silver and gold found in the Spanish colonies. Gold was found in Minas Gerais in the 17th century and diamonds in 1725 at Diamantina (Minas Gerais) and thus Brazil's mineral wealth began to appreciate. The search for new deposits has never flagged.

Commercially mined stones include: **diamonds**, found in Minas Gerais, Roraima, Bahia, Tocantins, Mato Grosso and Mato Grosso do Sul. Brazil was the world's largest producer of diamonds until South Africa entered the market in the 19th century. **Emeralds**, not discovered in Brazil until 1963 (many green beryls had been mined before then, but were known not to be true emeralds), are now mined in Bahia, Minas Gerais and Goiás. **Aquamarine** is a clear blue beryl from Rio Grande do Norte, Paraíba, Bahia, Minas Gerais and Espírito Santo. **Ruby** and **sapphire** are two shades of the same mineral, corundum, the former rich red, the latter a deep blue. Rubies are found in Santa Catarina, sapphires in Minas Gerais. The two most valued forms of **topaz** found are the rare Imperial Topaz from

Ouro Preto (Minas Gerais), which comes in a range of colours from honey-coloured through shades of red to pink, and Blue Topaz from Minas Gerais and Rondônia.

Tourmalines are also found and come from Minas Gerais, Ceará and Goiás; they have the widest range of colours of any gemstone, from colourless (white) to red, yellow, greens, blues, lilac and black. They even come in bi- and tri-coloured varieties. **Opals**, unique for their rainbow flecks, are mined in Piauí and Rio Grande do Sul. **Amethyst**, a quartz which ranges in colour from pale lilac to deep purple, is mined in Tocantins, Pará, Bahia, Mato Grosso do Sul and Rio Grande do Sul. From the last three states, plus Minas Gerais, comes **citrine**, another quartz which is predominantly yellow. Less well-known, but equally beautiful are **kunzite**, a rare pinkish-violet stone, and **chrysoberyl**, both found in Minas Gerais. Chrysoberyl is found in a variety of forms, a golden-yellow-brown, 'cat's eye' chrysoberyl, which has an luminous thread running through it, and the very rare **alexandrite**, which changes colour according to the light. Its most spectacular form changes from green in daylight to red in artificial light.

Festivals

Brazilians love a party and the mixing of different ethnic groups has resulted in some particularly colourful and varied celebrations. The difficulties of daily life are often relieved by the fantasy and release of Carnaval as well as the many other popular festivals held throughout the year. Wherever you go you will find street vendors selling ice-cold beer and the smell of *churrasco* coming from improvised barbecues accompanied by loud vibrant music and dancing in the streets. ▸▸ *For festival dates, see Essentials page 39, and relevant chapters throughout the book.*

Carnaval

Almost all Brazilian towns have some form of Carnaval festivities. Although the most famous is Rio de Janeiro, there are equally spectacular and different traditions in Bahia and Pernambuco, as well as a number of other good locations for those who wish only to party. The colonial mining towns of Diamantina and Ouro Preto in the interior of Minas Gerais are good locations to spend Carnaval in atmospheric surroundings. Florianópolis and Laguna on the coast of Santa Catarina have less traditional but still very popular and lively carnivals.

Out of season carnivals

Street carnivals with *trios eléctricos* in the style of Bahia are held throughout Brazil at various times of the year. Some of the most popular are **Micareta** in Feira de Santana (April), **Fortal** in Fortaleza (July) and **Carnatal** in Natal (December). Although by no means traditional they are nonetheless exuberant and enjoyable.

Other popular festivities

There are several other festivals which are almost as important to Brazilians as Carnaval. **Reveillon** (New Year's Eve) is a significant event and is generally celebrated on beaches. This can be either a hedonistic party as at Copacabana and Arraial D'Ajuda with the revellers dressed in white for luck, or as a respectful *candomblé* ceremony in which flowers are launched into the sea at midnight as an offering to Yemanjá.

The **Festas Juninas** (São João) are extremely popular especially in the northeast and are held around 24 June (St John's day). Fires are built and *forró* is the music of choice with the festivities lasting for over a week at times. Fireworks and the co-ordinated dancing of groups called *quadrilhas* are also part of the celebrations.

50 of the best Brazilian musicians
→ *See Music and dance in the centre of the b*

1 **Albery Albuquerque**, www.myspace.com/alberyalbuquerque. Jungle jazz with real forest animals.

2 **Acid-X**, www.acidx.com.br. Carioca Acid Jazz. *Na Estrada* is a classic.

3 **Adriana Calcanhotto**, www.adriana calcanhotto.com. Smoochy, clever, smooth.

4 **Afro Reggae**, www.myspace.com/afroreggae. *Capa de Revista* is the real sound of the favela funk outrage.

5 **Airto Moreira**, www.airto.com. Along with Naná Vasconcelos, perhaps the world's greatest ever percussionist. *Identity* is the album.

6 **Ana Cascardo**, www.anacascardo.com.br. Classic contemporary MPB à la Milton Nascimento.

7 **Andreia Dias**, www.andreiadias.com.br. Sultry, smoky and the modern São Paulo sound; her first CD *Vol 1* is sumptuous.

8 **Antônio Carlos Jobim**, one of the inventors of bossa nova and great innovators of Brazilian music. *Garota da Ipanema* is the most famous, but *Matita Pere* is also recommended.

9 **Arkestra One**, www.cosmicsounds-london.com. Nina Miranda of *Smoke City's* greatest Brasil-trip hop moment.

10 **Axial**, www.axialvirtual.com. Wonderful percussion, seductive singing. *Papaloko* is gorgeous.

11 **Baden Powell**, not the scout master but Brazil's greatest ever samba guitarist.

12 **Banda Black Rio**, www.banda blackrio.com. Rio funk soul maestros, go for *Gafieira Universal*.

13 **Bezerra da Silva**, the father of political samba and an all round joyfully cynical genius.

14 **Cabruera**, www.myspace.com/cabrueramusic. Mangue beat samba rock from Paraíba.

15 **Caetano Veloso**, www.caetano veloso.com.br. Brazil's Bowie and the co-founder of *tropicália*.

16 **Carlinhos Brown**, www.carlinhos brown.com.br. Salvador's great musical iconoclast and a thorn in the side of the white elite. Is there anything funkier than *Pandeiro-Deiro*? See box, page 411.

17 **Cassia Eller**, if Kurt Cobain had been a lesbian from Brasília he'd have sounded like this. She even did a version of *Smells like Teen Spirit*.

18 **CéU**, www.myspace.com/ceuambulante, Where samba, *electronica* and intelligence meet. *Vagarosa* is as sumptuous as melted chocolate.

19 **Chico Science**, this genius invented mangue beat, died young, and went to rock Olympus. *Macô* is a track that should be listened to loud and in an altered state.

20 **Clara Moreno**, www.myspace.com/claramoreno. *Forget Tanto Tempo Electromblé* is what Brazilian *electronica* should always sound like.

21 **Clepsidra**, www.myspace.com/clepsidrarelogiodeagua. Clever art electronica-samba-bossa nova-indie rock-jazz fusion from Belém. With violins.

22 **Coletivo Radio Cipo**, www.my space.com/coletivoradiocipo. See our opener and download *Cowboy Sem Lei*.

23 **Curimbó de Bolso**, it's hard to find but *Cantação Amazônica* is a sonic sliver of pure trance-inducing tropical jungle joy. Get it from Ná Figueredo in Belém.

24 **DJ Dolores**, www.myspace.com/djdoloresaparelhagem. Where mangue beat goes club.

25 **DJ Patife**, www.djpatife.com.br. The father of Brazilian drum 'n bass with DJ Marky, djmarky.uol.com.br.

26 **Djavan**, www.djavan.com.br. Brazil's Stevie Wonder. We like *Bicho Solto O XIII*.

27 **Dori Caymmi**, www.doricaymmi.com. Carefully crafted, beautiful jazz-tinged music from Bahia. We love his fusion work with Larry Coryell and Billy Cobham on *Live from Bahia*.

28 Dorival Caymmi, Brazil mourned when he died in 2008. The father of Bahian music.

29 Ed Motta, one of the most important musicians in Rio soul and jazz. *Aystelum* is a classic.

30 Elis Regina, to many she's Brazil's greatest ever singer. *Elis e Tom* is a landmark album.

31 Érika Machado, www.erika machado.com.br. Quirky Mineira.

32 Hermeto Pascoal, www.hermeto pascoal.com.br. If Stockhausen were genetically fused with Mingus and raised in Alagoas perhaps he'd play something like this extraordinary *Música Universal*.

33 Gilberto Gil, www.gilbertogil.com.br. Funky, smart ex-minister of culture and co-founder of *tropicália*. His albums are patchy. Cherry pick.

34 Itamar Assumpção. Difficult, odd, witty, intensely rewarding and impossible to play. Try *Navalha Na Liga*.

35 João Bosco, www.joaobosco.com.br. The pinnacle of erudite sung samba. *Casa de Marimbundo* is like a bolt of pure rhythmic energy.

36 Jorge Ben, www.jorgeben.com.br. One of Rio's great funkster tunesmiths – including *Mas que Nada*.

37 Karnak, www.andreabujamra.com. São Paulo art rock samba.

38 Madame Sataan, www.myspace.com/madamesaatan, Superb power metal from the Amazon. Singer Sammliz sings like Elis Regina and is as beautiful as bossa.

39 Marcel D2, www.marcelod2.com.br. Irresistibly funky samba-rap. Try *Loadeando*.

40 Mariene de Castro, www.mariene decastro.com.br. Great modern Bahian samba. See box, page 411.

41 Marlui Miranda, her *Tudos os Sons* brought the music of the indigenous Amazonians to the world. A masterpiece.

42 Max de Castro. Vanguard experimentalism from São Paulo. *Silêncio No Brooklyn* twists and turns with endless inventiveness. Wonderful.

43 Milton Nascimento. *Clube da Esquina* is simply one of the greatest records of all time.

44 Naná Vasconcelos, www.nana vasconcelos.com.br. Vies with Airto for the title of world's greatest ever percussionist. Endlessly inventive. *Fragmentos* is the album. Or *Storytelling*. See box, page 486.

45 Orchestra Imperial, www.myspace. com/orquestraimperial. Joyful, masterful, delicious tongue-in-cheek big band samba from master producer Kassin and his pals.

46 Rappin Hood, www.trama.uol.com.br/ rappinhood. Infectious samba funk rapper whose *Sou Negao* (with Possumente Zulu) bursts with danceability.

47 Relogios de Frederico, www.relogiosdefrederico.mus.br. Inventive funk rockers from Porto Alegre.

48 Seu Jorge, www.seujorge.com. The current Brazilian ambassador to the musical world plays Jorge Ben samba funk with a political theme, We love all of *America Brasil*, especially *Mina do Condomínio*.

49 Zeca Baleiro, www2.uol.com.br /zecabaleiro. *Meu Tribo Sou Eu* should be a national anthem for the post-racial world. He also wrote a very funny song about Stephen Fry.

50 Zé Ramalho, www.zeramalho. com.br. A kind of desert troubadour whose gravel voiced post-psychedelia would be great in David Lynch film. His most famous track is called *Brave New Cow* and is a work of genius.

Brasil Musica e Artes, www.bmabrazil.band camp.com, is a non-profit organization which promotes Brazilian music.

In the north, the African and indigenous cultures have mixed to form the Boi-Bumba tradition. In Amazonas, the **Festa do Boi** has become more commercialized but is still very impressive and popular. In Maranhão, where it is known as **Bumba-Meu-Boi**, the festivities are more traditional but equally as popular.

There are many Catholic saints' days that are sometimes celebrated in conjunction with African deities (especially in Bahia). Every town has a patron saint and his or her day will be an excuse for civic festivities, in addition to those of the foundation day of the town.

Immigrants from Europe to the south of Brazil and elsewhere have brought festivals from their own cultures such as the **Oktoberfest** held in Blumenau, believed to be second only to Munich.

Literature

The colonial period

Some of the major differences between Brazil and Spanish America spring from the history of colonization in the two areas. There were no great empires with large cities like those of the Incas or the Aztecs, and Portuguese exploitation concentrated first on extractive, then on cultivated export products (brazil-wood, then sugar). Although cities like Recife, Bahia and Rio de Janeiro did finally develop, there was, incredible as it may seem, no printing press in Brazil until the flight of the Regent, King João VI to Rio in 1808. This is not to say that there was no colonial literature, though scholars can still quarrel about how 'Brazilian' it was. When the Portuguese set foot in Brazil in 1500, the letter sent back to King Manuel by Pero Vaz de Caminha, already wondering at the tropical magnificence of the country and the nakedness of the inhabitants, set themes that would recur in many later works. The first plays to be put on in Brazil were religious dramas, staged in three languages – Portuguese, Spanish, and Tupi – by the Jesuit **José de Anchieta** (1543-1597). The most notable 17th-century poet is **Gregório de Matos** (1636- 1696), famous for his sharp satires on the corrupt life of the city of Salvador, and its tempting black and mulatta women. In the late 18th century, a group of poets from the gold-mining area of Minas, foremost among them **Tomás Antônio Gonzaga** (1744- 1810), were at the centre of the early, abortive move for independence, the *Inconfidência* (1789; see page 266). Although best known as a lyric poet, Gonzaga has been proved to be the author of the anonymous satirical poem *Cartas chilenas*, which gives a vivid portrait of colonial society.

The 19th century

It is helpful to understand Brazilian literature, even long after political independence, as a gradual and, to some extent, contradictory process of emancipation from foreign models. Every European literary movement – Romanticism, Realism, Symbolism, etc – had its Brazilian followers, but in each there was an attempt to adjust the model to local reality. A good example is the first of these, Indianism, which flourished in the mid-19th century, and produced two central figures: the poet **Antônio Gonçalves Dias** (1823-1864), himself partly of indigenous descent, and the novelist **José de Alencar** (1829-1877). It is a form of Romanticism, idealizing the noble savage, and with plots adapted from Walter Scott, and it happily ignored what was happening to real indigenous tribes at the time. However, it does express national aspirations and feelings, if in nothing else, in the nostalgia for a kind of tropical Eden expressed in perhaps the most famous Brazilian poem, Gonçalves Dias *Canção do exílio*: "My land has palm-trees/ where the sabiá sings. /The birds that sing here/ don't sing like those back home." Alencar's novels, not all of them about Indians, are a systematic attempt to portray Brazil in its various settings, including the city. *O guarani* (1857), turned into a famous opera by Carlos Gomes, and *Iracema* (1865), are his most popular. The latter is perhaps the most complete mythical version of the Portuguese conquest, allegorized as a love affair between a native woman and an early colonist, Martim Soares. Iracema, "the virgin with the honeyed lips" dies in childbirth at the end, but the future lies with their mixed-blood son, Moacir.

After his death, Alencar was succeeded as the chief figure in Brazilian letters by **Joaquim Maria Machado de Assis** (1839-1908). Perhaps Brazil's best writer, and certainly the greatest to appear in Latin America until well into the 20th century, he had to fight against formidable obstacles: he was of relatively poor origins, was mulatto, he had a stammer and, in later life, was subject to epileptic fits. He wrote nine novels and more than 200 short stories as well as poetry and journalism. He ended his life as an establishment figure and founder of the Brazilian Academy of Letters. But his novels, especially those written after 1880, when he published *Memórias póstumas de Brás Cubas*, and the best of his stories are surprisingly subversive, covert attacks on slavery and on male power, for instance. He avoided detection by not using his own voice, hiding behind quirky, digressive narrators who are not always trustworthy. All the novels and most of the stories are set in Rio, which he hardly left, and give a remarkably varied account of the city and its different social levels. His most famous novel, *Dom Casmurro* (1900) is one of the best-disguised cases of an unreliable narrator in the history of the novel, and still arouses critical polemics.

Machado's atmosphere is predominantly that of the empire, which fell in 1889, a year after the abolition of slavery. In the Republic, a younger generation, more overtly rebellious in their aims, and affected by new scientific ideas from Europe, came to the fore. If Machado is the most famous Brazilian author, perhaps *Os sertões*, by **Euclides da Cunha** (1866-1909) is the most famous book. It is an account of the Canudos campaign in the interior of the state of Bahia in 1896-1897. The campaign was a horrific failure, victory being won only at a huge cost in casualties, and Euclides da Cunha, sent to cover it as a journalist, turned this failure into an indictment of a social system, which excluded huge groups of people. Written in a dramatic, somewhat self-indulgent style, with extensive use of scientific words, it has been excellently translated as *Rebellion in the Backlands*.

The other important prose writer of this period, the novelist **Afonso Lima Barreto** (1881-1922), was mulatto like Machado, but there resemblances end. Much more openly rebellious and less of a conscious artist than Machado, his novels, the most notable of which is *Triste fim de Policarpo Quaresma*, are overt attacks on intellectual mediocrity, and the corruption and despotism into which the Republic soon fell. A passing mention ought to be made, too, of one of the 'unclassifiable' books in which Brazilian literature abounds: **Helena Morley**'s *Minha vida de menina* (translated by Elizabeth Bishop as *The Diary of Helena Morley*), and only published in 1942. It is the precocious, funny, and remarkably perceptive teenager's diary, written in Diamantina, Minas Gerais, at the end of the 19th century.

The 20th century

In general, the poetry of the turn of the century was imitative and stuffy. Renewal did not come until the early 1920s, when a group of intellectuals from São Paulo, led by the unrelated **Mário de Andrade** (1893-1945) and **Oswald de Andrade** (1890-1954) began the movement known as modernism. This is conveniently supposed to have begun in 1922, the centenary of political independence, with a Week of Modern Art in São Paulo; in fact it began earlier, and took until the mid-1920s to spread to the provinces. In great part, modernism's ideology was nationalist, and though the word spanned the political spectrum, at its best it simply meant the discovery of a real Brazil behind stereotypes. Mário travelled throughout the country, attempting to understand its variety, which he embodied in his major prose-work, the comic 'rhapsody' *Macunaíma* (1928), which in its plot and language attempts to construct a unity out of a complex racial and regional mix. Also in 1928, Oswald launched the 'anthropophagist', or cannibalist programme, which proclaimed that Brazilian writers should imitate their native predecessors, and fully digest European culture: a new kind of Indianism, perhaps.

The most enduring artistic works to have emerged from modernism, however, are poetic – two of Brazil's major modern poets, **Manuel Bandeira** (1886-1968) and **Carlos Drummond de Andrade** (1902-1987) were early enthusiasts of modernism, and corresponded at length with Mário. Bandeira, the older man, made a slow transition to the new, freer style; his poems, often short and based on everyday events or images, nevertheless have a power and rhythmic accuracy that are deceptively simple. Drummond's poetry is more self-conscious, and went through a complex intellectual development, including a period of political enthusiasm during the Second World War, followed by disillusionment with the beginning of the Cold War. His themes, including some remarkable love-poetry addressed by a 50-year-old to a younger woman, and a lifelong attachment to Itabira, the small town in Minas Gerais where he was born, are very varied. Readers without Portuguese can best approach Drummond, widely regarded as Brazil's greatest poet, through an excellent anthology, *Traveling in the Family*.

The 1930s were a crucial decade. With increasing political mobilization, the growth of cities, and of an aspiring middle class, literature began to look to a wider audience; however, at first, it still reflected the dominance of rural life. The realism of this period, which often had a strong regionalist bias, had its raison d'être in a society still divided by huge social and/or geographical differences, and indeed played its part in diminishing those differences. Many of the first group came from the economically and socially backward northeast. **José Lins do Rego** (1901-1957) is perhaps the most characteristic figure. He was highly influenced by the ideas of **Gilberto Freyre** (1900-1987), whose *Casa grande e sensually* (*The Masters and the Slaves*), published in 1933, was one of the most important and readable of Brazilian books. It is a study of the slave-based, sugar- plantation society, and one of the first works to appreciate the contribution made by Blacks to Brazil's culture. It remains, however, very paternalist, and Lins do Rego's fiction, beginning with the semi-autobiographical *Menino de engenho*, reflects that, commenting on the poverty and filth of the (ex-)slave-quarters as if they were totally natural. His 'sugar-cane cycle' sold in large editions, in part because of its unaffected, simple style.

A greater novelist belonging to the same group is **Graciliano Ramos** (1892-1953). His fiction is much more aggressive, and in later life he became a communist. His masterpiece, turned into an excellent film in the 1960s, is *Vedas secas*, which returns to the impoverished interior of *Os sertões*, but concentrates on an illiterate cowhand and his family, forced from place to place by drought and social injustice; it is a courageous attempt to enter the mental world of such people. *Memórias do cárcere*, published after Ramos's death, is his unflinching account of his imprisonment for a year during the Vargas regime.

The essential novelist to read for anyone visiting the south of Brazil is **Érico Veríssimo** (1905-1975), especially his epic trilogy collectively entitled *O tempo e o vento* (*O continente* [1949], *O retrato* [1951], and *O arquipélago* [1961]) spread over two centuries of the turbulent history of Rio Grande do Sul.

Gradually, in the 1940s and 1950s, a subtler and more adventurous fiction began to be published alongside the regionalist realism that was the major heritage of the 1930s. Three writers stand out: João Guimarães Rosa, Clarice Lispector and João Cabral de Melo Neto. **João Guimarães Rosa** (1908-1967) published his major novel, *Grande sertão: veredas* in 1956. Almost Joycean in its aspirations and linguistic innovations, it is a kind of mixture of a cowboy story and a modern version of Faustian pact with the devil. For those without stamina (and excellent Portuguese), the translation (*The Devil to Pay in the Backlands*) is unfortunately not an adequate alternative. Rosa is best approached through his stories, those of Sagarana (particularly *A hora e vez de Augusto Matraga*) being perhaps the best.

The stories and novels of **Clarice Lispector** (1920-1977) now have a considerable audience outside Brazil, as well as a huge one inside it. Her stories, especially those of *Laços de família* (1960), are in general set in middle-class Rio, and usually have women as their central characters. The turbulence, family hatreds, and near-madness hidden beneath routine lives are conveyed in unforgettable ways, with a language and symbolism that is poetic and adventurous without being exactly difficult (she said she fought with the Portuguese language daily). Some of her novels have over-ambitious metaphysical superstructures, and may not be to some readers' tastes – *A paixão segundo G H*, for instance, concerns a housewife's confrontation with a dead cockroach in her maid's room, and her final decision to eat it, seen as a kind of "communion". When at her best, in some of her journalism, in her late, deliberately semi-pornographic stories, and above all in the posthumous novel, *A hora da estrela*, which approaches the poor in an utterly unsentimental way, Lispector can stimulate and move like no one else.

The greatest poet of this generation is **João Cabral de Melo Neto** (1920-1999), whose best poetry concerns his home state, Pernambuco. The drought-ridden interior, the lush but oppressive landscape of the sugar-plantations, and the city slums are all present in the verse-play *Morte e vida severina* (1956), and his tight, sparse poetry often returns to the same places, or analogous ones in the several countries (most importantly, in Spain) in which he has resided as a diplomat.

The 1964 military coup, and the increasing use of torture and censorship in the late 1960s and early 1970s, had profound effects on literature, especially as they were accompanied by vast economic changes (industrialization, a building boom, huge internal migration, the opening up of the Amazon). At first, censorship was haphazard, and the 1960s liberation movements had their – increasingly desperate – Brazilian equivalents. Protest theatre had a brief boom, with *Arena conta Zumbi*, about a 17th-century rebel slave leader, produced by **Augusto Boal** (born 1931), being one of the most important. The best fictional account of those years can be found in two novels by **Antônio Callado** (born 1917), *Quarup* (1967), set in the northeast and centred on a left-wing priest, and *Bar Don Juan* (1971), whose focus is on the contradictions of a group of middle-class guerrillas; and in **Ivan Ângelo**'s *A festa* (1976), set in Belo Horizonte, a funny and hard-hitting account of a varied set of people, which chronicles the impact of the 'sex and drugs' revolution alongside its political concerns. A remarkable documentary account of the period is ex- guerrilla (subsequently leader of the Green Party) **Fernando Gabeira**'s *O que é isso companheiro?* (1982), which chronicles his involvement in the kidnapping of the American ambassador in 1969. Poetry at this time went through a crisis of self-confidence, and it was widely thought that it had emigrated into the (marvellous) lyrics of such popular composers as **Chico Buarque de Holanda** and **Caetano Veloso**, who were also the foremost standard-bearers of political protest in the 1970s.

It is impossible in the space available to give more than a few suggestions of some of the best work published in recent decades, concentrating on books which have been translated. A brilliant satirical novel by **Paulo Emílio Salles Gomes** (1916-1977) about the

São Paulo upper middle class is *Três mulheres e três Pppês* (1977); **Darcy Ribeiro** (born 1922), an anthropologist and politician, took time off to write *Maíra* (1978), an updating of Indianism, but with real indigenous Brazilians and a threatened Amazon environment; **Rubem Fonseca** (born 1925), whose story *Feliz ano novo* (1973) created a scandal because of its brutal treatment of class differences, has dedicated himself to the writing of hard-nosed thrillers like *A grande arte* (1983); **Caio Fernando Abreu** (1948-96) is a short-story writer of considerable talent, dealing with the alienated urban young in such books as *Morangos mofados* and *Os dragões não conhecem o paraíso*; finally, **Milton Hatoum**'s *Relato de um certo oriente* (1989) is a vivid novel set in Manaus, amongst the Lebanese immigrant community. He followed it with the highly acclaimed *The Brothers*. Patricia Melo has devoted her writing to exploring social problems in her native Rio. Several of her books have been filmed; most notably *O Matador* (*O Homen do Ano* or *Man of the Year*), the story of a man who accidentally becomes a ruthless hired gun. The country's leading literary export is without a doubt the popular mystical novelist, Paulo Coelho, most famous for his whimsical novel, *The Alchemist*.

Recommended reading

Essays and books that can be wholeheartedly recommended for those who want more information are: Ray Keenoy, David Treece and Paul Hyland, *The Babel Guide to the Fiction of Portugal, Brazil and Africa in English Translation* (London: Boulevard Books, 1995). Irwin Stern (ed) *Dictionary of Brazilian Literature* (New York: Greenwood Press, 1988). Mike González and David Treece, *The Gathering of Voices* (Verso, 1992) (on 20th-century poetry). Elizabeth Bishop and Emanuel Brasil (eds) *An Anthology of Twentieth-Century Brazilian Poetry* (Wesleyan University Press, 1972); John Gledson, *Brazilian Fiction: Machado de Assis to the Present*, in John King (ed), *Modern Latin American Fiction: A Survey* (Faber, 1987). Many of the essays in Roberto Schwarz, *Misplaced Ideas: Essays on Brazilian Culture* (Verso, 1992), especially those on *Machado de Assis*, and *Culture and Politics in Brazil, 1964-1969* are very stimulating. »» See also Books, page 807.

Fine art and sculpture

The colonial era: 16th and 17th centuries

No visitor to Brazil should miss visiting a colonial church. During the colonial period in Brazil the Church dominated artistic patronage, with the religious orders vying with each other to produce ever more lavish interiors. In the 17th century the Benedictines included several notable sculptors among their ranks. Much of the magnificent gilded interior of the monastery of São Bento in Rio de Janeiro is by **Frei Domingos da Conceição** (circa 1643-1718), who worked there during the 1660s. His *Crucifixion* of 1688 in the monastery of São Bento in Olinda sets up a deliberately shocking contrast between the sinuous elegance of Christ's body and the terrible lacerations of his flesh. **Frei Agostinho de Piedade** (died 1661) of the Benedictine community in Salvador produced some old-fashioned terracotta reliquary busts during the 1630s and 1640s (Museu de Arte Sacra, Salvador) but the powerful *Penitent Peter* in Salvador's Nossa Senhora do Monte (circa 1636), also attributed to him, prefigures the emotional intensity of subsequent generations.

A distinctive feature of colonial interiors is the incorporation of decorative scenes in blue and white painted tiles, *azulejos*, around the walls. These were imported from Portugal from the earlier 17th century onwards, with subject matter as often secular as religious. Good examples include the Franciscan foundations in Olinda, Salvador and

Recife, and the church of Nossa Senhora da Glória in Rio de Janeiro, which has hunting scenes in the sacristy, Old Testament figures in the choir, and in the nave, astonishingly, scenes of pastoral love loosely based on the *Song of Songs*.

The 18th century

Although 17th-century church decoration is often lavish there is little warning of the extraordinary theatricality which characterizes the work of the 18th century. Behind their sober façades churches open out like theatres, with the equivalent of balconies and boxes for the privileged, and a stage for the high altar with a proscenium arch and wings of carved and gilded wood. Cherubs whisper to each other or gesticulate from their perches amongst the architectural scrolls; angels, older and more decorous, recline along a cornice or flutter in two dimensions across an illusionist ceiling. The object of devotion is usually placed high above the altar on a tiered dais, surrounded by a Bernini-esque sunburst of gilded rays. A skilled exponent of this type of design was the Portuguese-born sculptor **Francisco Xavier de Brito** (died 1751), as in Nossa Senhora do Pilar, Ouro Preto and São Francisco de Penitência, Rio.

Xavier de Brito was largely responsible for bringing the Baroque style to Brazil and this style reaches its most ornate and theatrical in the work of Xavier de Brito's pupil, **Aleijadinho**, the 'Little Cripple' (1738-1814) a mulatto artist who worked in the province of Minas Gerais. As by far the most famous artist in the colonial period in the whole of Latin America it is perhaps not surprising to find his name attached to an impossible number of projects, but a consideration even of the securely documented reveals a man of extraordinary passion and energy who worked as a painter, architect and, above all, sculptor. The church at Congonhas do Campo offers the most dramatic example of Aleijadinho's art. Pilgrims paying homage to the miracle-working Bom Jesus do Matozinhos approach the church along a penitential road winding up the hill between six small chapels, each housing scenes from Christ's Passion represented by life-size expressive statues of polychrome wood. The final ascent is up an imposing double staircase under the stony gaze of 12 judgmental prophets who variously lament, threaten or cajole, addressing the heavens, the distant horizon, each other, or the faithful on the stone steps below them. In a building beside the church a fascinating display of drawings and photographs of the many accidents and emergencies from which the Good Jesus has saved people, testifies to the continuing popularity of this shrine.

The paint equivalent to Aleijadinho's sculptures can be found in the work of his contemporary, **Manuel da Costa Ataíde** (1762-1830) from Mariana, whose vividly colourful narrative scenes decorate numerous churches in Minas Gerais. Ataíde's rococo settings are populated with solidly-built saints and angels whose rolling eyes and exaggerated gestures give them an earthy vigour sometimes at odds with the spirituality of the subject matter, as in the illusionist ceiling of São Francisco de Assis, Ouro Preto, a church whose design is traditionally attributed to Aleijadinho. Both Aleijadinho and Athayde were probably friends of the insurrectionist Tiradentes and criticisms of the Portuguese and the appalling treatment of non-European Brazilians is implicit in their work (for more details see box, page 262).

In Bahia, **José Joaquim da Rocha** (1737-1807), see pages 390 and 391, was one of the most successful artists of his day and his slightly Italianate ceiling paintings survive in many churches in Salvador. The best sculptor of the late colonial period in Bahia was **Manuel Inácio da Costa** (1763-1857) whose figures, often dramatically gaunt with protruding veins and large eyes, are reminiscent of Aleijadinho's work (see, for example, his *Christ at the Column* in the Museu de Arte Sacra in Salvador). It is in Rio that sculpture first begins to sober up again, as for example in the work of the sculptor Valentim de Fonseca e Silva, known as **Mestre Valentim** (circa 1750-1813), which can be seen in several churches including São Francisco de Paula and Nossa Senhora da Glória. Valentim also designed the first public gardens in Rio: the *Passeio Público* was inaugurated in 1783 and included walks, seats decorated with *azulejos* and pavilions. A unique series of six painted views of Rio and Guanabara Bay by **Leandro Joaquim** (1738-1798), originally made for one of the pavilions, are now in the Museu Histórico Nacional in Rio.

French influence in Imperial Brazil

After the transfer of the Imperial court to Rio in 1808, João VI made a determined effort to renovate Brazilian culture, and in 1816 the French Artistic Mission – a boatload of painters, sculptors, architects, musicians and craftsmen – arrived from France to found what was to become the Imperial Academy. Two artists were particularly influential: **Nicolas-Antoine Taunay** (1755-1830) and **Jean-Baptiste Debret** (1768-1848). Taunay's luminous landscapes of the area around Rio and Debret's lively street scenes helped to open up new areas of secular Brazilian subject matter, and inspired artists throughout the 19th century. The Academy provided scholarships to send promising young artists to Paris, so reinforcing the French influence, and there are echoes of Delacroix in the work of **Vítor Meireles** (1832-1903) as for example, in his *Battle of the Guararapes* of 1879 in the Museu Nacional de Belas Artes, Rio, and of Ingres in *La Carioca* (1882) of **Pedro Américo** (1843-1905) in the same museum. The influence of Courbet can be seen in the so-called belle époque of the first republican years (1889-1922), in particular in the work of Meireles' pupil, **José Ferraz de Almeida Júnior** (1850-1899).

The 20th century, towards a Brazilian vision

Brazil moved from this essentially academic tradition straight into the radicalism of the early 20th century, and movements such as Cubism, Futurism, Fauvism and Constructivism were quickly translated into distinctively Brazilian idioms. **Lasar Segall** (1891-1957), **Anita Malfatti** (1896-1964) and the sculptor **Vitor Brecheret** (1894-1955) were pioneers of modernism, working in relative isolation before the 1922 Semana da Arte Moderna (Modern Art Week) in São Paulo drew together a group of artists and intellectuals whose influence on Brazilian culture can still be felt today. They sought to challenge established bourgeois attitudes, to shake off the traditional cultural subservience to Europe, and to draw attention to the cultural diversity and social inequality of contemporary Brazil. **Emilio di Cavalcanti** (1897-1976) mocked the artificiality of white middle-class socialites and championed Blac Brazilian beauty (examples in the Museu de Arte Contemporânea, São Paulo). **Tarsila do Amaral** (1886-1973) borrowed her loud colours from popular art while her imagery includes ironic reworkings of European myths about the savage cannibalistic indigenous Brazilians supposed to inhabit the Brazilian jungle. **Cândido Portinari** (1903-1962) used murals to expose the exploitation and injustice suffered by workers and peasants, while **Osvaldo Goeldi** (1895-1961) explored similar themes in his powerful wood engravings. Portinari, in an interesting revival of the colonial use of *azulejos*, created murals in blue and white painted tiles for modern architecture such as the MES building by Costa and Niemeyer of Rio, begun in 1937, and Niemeyer's church of São Francisco in Pampulha, Belo Horizonte (1943).

The economic strength of the middle years of the century encouraged state patronage of the arts. President Getúlio Vargas recognized that art and architecture could be used to present an image of Brazil as a modern industrialized nation, with Brasília being the culmination of this vision. Museums of Modern Art were founded in São Paulo and Rio, and in 1951 São Paulo hosted its first **Bienal Internacional**, which attracted abstract artists from Europe and the US and confirmed Abstraction – symbol of progress and technological modernization – as the dominant mode in Brazil during the 1950s. Rivalry between the artistic communities of Rio and São Paulo helped to produce some outstanding avant-garde art. In the 1950s **Waldemar Cordeiro** (1925-1973), leader of the São Paulo Grupo Ruptura, painted what at first sight appear to be rather simple geometric patterns in bright, contrasting colours, but on closer attention the flat surface seems to break up, suggesting recession, space and restless movement, in some ways prefiguring the British Op Art movement of the 1960s. The Neo-Concrete group of artists of Rio argued for the integration of art into daily life, and experimented with art that made sensory and emotional demands on the 'spectator' whose participation leads in turn to creation. During the early 1960s, **Lygia Clark** (1920-1988) made *bichos* (*animals*) out of hinged pieces of metal which, as the name implies, are like creatures with a life of their own: they can be rearranged indefinitely but because of their complexity it is impossible to predetermine what shape will result from moving a particular section. Nowadays, unfortunately, they are displayed in museums where touching is not encouraged (as in the Pinacoteca do Estado, São Paulo). **Hélio Oiticica** (1937-1980) took the idea further, working with people (poor and often black) from the samba schools in the Rio favela to create artistic 'happenings' involving dance, music and flamboyant costumes called *parangolés* (capes). The notion that a key function of art should be to shock the bourgeoisie was first voiced in the 1922 Week of Modern Art. Oiticica often succeeded, and he and other artists of the 1960s also realized another of the aims of the first modernists: to create Brazilian modern art that was not the poor relation of developments in Europe or the US. A museum of his work is now open in Rio. Other important figures of this generation include the neo-concretist painter **Ivan Serpa** (1923-1973), **Sérgio Camargo** (1930-1990), who produced textured rhythmic constructions of white on white but because they are made with off-cuts of wood they suggest the tensions between form and material, geometry and nature; and **Amílcar de Castro** (born 1920) whose deceptively simple sculptures are often cut from one large panel of cast iron.

The military coup of 1964 marked the beginning of a period of political repression and of renewed artistic energy, with figurative tendencies re-emerging. In 1970 **Antônio Enrique Amaral** (born 1935) took as his theme the banana, so often used in dismissive references to Latin America, and in an extended series of paintings monumentalized it into an extraordinary symbol of power and productivity. In an ironic neo-colonial altarpiece (circa 1966) installed in the Museu de Arte de São Paulo, **Nelson Leirner** (born 1932) makes the object of devotion the neon-lit head of pop star Robert Carlos. Conceptual art offers different ways of confronting the dominant ideology. Both **Cildo Meireles** (born 1948) and **Jac Lierner** (born 1961) have used, misused or forged banknotes, for example, and both they and **Waltercio Caldas** (born 1946) and **Tunga** (born 1952) have created installations which draw attention, directly and indirectly to environmental issues. The painter **Siron Franco** (born 1947) also often addresses the issue of the destruction of the Amazon rainforest, but his disturbing surreal images explore many other areas – industrial pollution, sexual fantasy, political corruption, national identity – making him one of the most exciting artists in Brazil today.

Architecture

Brazilian colonial style: houses and civic buildings
The earliest Portuguese colonizers to arrive in Brazil in the 16th century faced many problems in building their houses, forts, churches and other necessary structures. First of all there was a lack of building materials, such as bricks, roof tiles and mortar. Second, there were few trained craftsmen, such as carpenters and bricklayers, in the colony. They therefore had to improvise by developing unusual building techniques and trying different materials. In the hinterland, in places like São Paulo, Goiás and Minas Gerais the majority of the houses were built with *taipa de pilão*. This technique consisted of using a wooden form to build thick walls. These forms were filled with a mixture of clay, vegetable fibres, horsehair, ox blood and dung. This paste was then compacted with a pestle and allowed to dry for two to three days before the next layer was added. The roof tiles were often moulded on a female slave's thigh and dried in the sun.

It is quite easy to identify a house in Brazilian colonial style. Their shapes, colours and building techniques remained virtually unchanged for almost three centuries. Firstly, they always had large, visible roofs, made with red clay tiles, finishing in eaves extending beyond the walls. All the buildings were painted in a white wash, with bright colours used only on window and door frames. These were made of wood and had, mostly, elegant arches at the top. In the 19th century, sash windows with squared 10 sq cm pieces of glass were added in many houses, as can be seen in cities like Paraty, Ouro Preto and Salvador.

Urban colonial houses had doors and windows opening directly onto the street. Courtyards were never placed in front of the house, but internally, forming airy patios which protected the privacy of the family. The furniture was extremely simple and rough. Often, the only pieces of furniture in a bedroom would be the bed itself and a leather box to store clothes and personal belongings. In the colonial period, the highest status symbol was to live in a *sobrado* (a house with more than one floor, usually two). The ground floor was normally a commercial business and above it the residence of the owner's family.

Churches, convents and religious buildings: the baroque in Brazil
Houses, public buildings and other colonial civic edifices were generally unelaborate. All the refinement, style and sophistication in art, architecture and decoration was lavished on churches, convents and monasteries. The great religious orders, such as the Jesuits, Franciscans, Carmelites and Benedictines brought to Brazil the latest artistic trends from Europe, mainly the Baroque and Rococo.

Two separate strands in Brazilian religious architecture evolved. In the most important cities, close to the seaboard and more influenced by European culture, the churches and convents were built according to designs brought from Portugal, Italy and Spain. Some were merely copies of Jesuit or Benedictine temples in Europe. Examples of this can be found in Salvador (the main cathedral, the São Francisco church), Rio de Janeiro (the Mosteiro de São Bento, the Convento de Santo Antônio) and Olinda (church and convent of Nossa Senhora das Neves).

Brazilian baroque
At the end of the 17th century gold was found in the region of Minas Gerais. One of the first administrative acts of the Portuguese crown in response to this discovery was to banish the traditional European orders from the mining region. The royal administration wanted to control the mining itself, taxation and traffic in gold and, as the friars were regarded as

among the most shameless of smugglers of the metal, the orders in this instance were denied the support they were given elsewhere in the Portuguese colonies. Therefore the majority of the churches in cities like Ouro Preto, Mariana, Congonhas and Sabará were built by local associations, the so-called 'third orders'. These lay orders had the gold and the will to build magnificent temples but, although they wanted their projects to be as European as possible, the original designs were hard to obtain in such out-of-the-way places. So the local artists had to find their own way. Inspired by descriptions and second-hand information, they created their own interpretation of the Baroque, thoroughly infused with regional influences and culture. This is the reason why the 'Barroco Mineiro' is so original.

Curved churches and the decline of the Gold Era

At the beginning of the 18th century, when gold was easily found in Minas Gerais, the main attraction was the inside of the church; richly and heavily decorated in carved wood and gold. Many of the churches built in this period will be a total surprise for the visitor. Their façades and exteriors are so simple and yet the naves and altars are so highly and artistically decorated. As the mines started to decline, the outside of the buildings became more sophisticated, with curves, round towers and sinuous walls, such as the churches of São Francisco de Assis and Rosário, in Ouro Preto. As the gold for covering walls ran out, it was replaced by paintings and murals.

The 19th century and the neoclassic style

The beginning of 19th century brought a major change in the history of Brazilian architecture. When Napoleon invaded Portugal in 1808, the Portuguese royal family and some 15,000 nobles and wealthy families fled to Rio de Janeiro, bringing with them their own view of what was sophisticated in the arts. In 1816 the king, Dom João VI, invited a group of French artists (The French Artistic Mission) to Brazil to introduce the most recent European trends in painting, sculpture, decoration and architecture. This was the beginning of the neoclassic style in Brazil. An Imperial Academy of Fine Arts was created and all the new government buildings were built in neoclassic style. The great name of this period was the French architect Grandjean de Montigny, who planned and built many houses and public buildings throughout the city of Rio de Janeiro.

The rich and famous also wanted their houses in this newly fashionable style, which revolutionized the Brazilian way of building. The large roofs were now hidden by a small wall, the plat band. Windows and doors acquired round arches and walls were painted in ochres and light tones of pink. Public buildings and churches started to look like ancient Greek temples, with triangular pediments and columns. This new style was not best suited to Brazil's climate. The earlier, large colonial roofs were much more efficient in dealing with heavy tropical rains and, in consequence, the neoclassic style never became popular in the countryside.

Even when the coffee planters, in the second half of 19th century, started to become extremely rich and fond of imported fashions, they would build their urban mansions in the neoclassic style, but still keep their farm houses with large roofs, sometimes adding small neoclassic details in windows, doors and internal decoration. Good examples of this 19th-century rural architecture can be found very close to Rio de Janeiro, in cities like Vassouras, Valença, Barra do Piraí and Bananal, where some of the old farm houses are open to visitors.

There are many examples of urban neoclassic building in Rio de Janeiro, such as the Museu Nacional, the Santa Casa da Misericórdia, the Casa de Rui Barbosa and the Instituto

Benjamin Constant. Also very close to Rio, in Petrópolis, the Museu Imperial (formerly the emperor's summer palace) is also a perfect example of the style. This neoclassic style remained popular in Brazil until the end of the 19th century, being also the 'official' style of the first and the second Brazilian empires.

The early 20th century and the eclectic style

After the republic, in 1889, the neoclassic style lost favour since it had been serving the king and the emperors for such a long time. A new style, or better, a new harmony of different styles started to gain popularity, also under the influence of Paris and the belle époque. There were elements of neoclassic architecture, but also an excess of decoration and adornment on the façades. A broad 'boulevard' was constructed in Rio de Janeiro in 1906, the Avenida Central (today Avenida Rio Branco), with the idea of creating a 'Paris in the Tropics'. There are many examples of buildings in the eclectic style on this avenue: the Biblioteca Nacional, the Teatro Municipal (opera house) and the Museu Nacional de Belas Artes, all of them built within the first decade of 20th century. Also in Manaus, during the rubber boom, many buildings adopted this style, such as the Teatro Amazonas (opera house). During the first two decades of this century, the eclectic style remained very popular.

The 'Modern Art Week' of 1922 and national pride

In 1922 a group of artists, painters, poets and architects organized in São Paulo 'A Semana da Arte Moderna' or the Modern Art Week, during which they exhibited their distaste at the influence of foreign standards in Brazilian art. They considered their role to be a quest for a genuine Brazilian form of expression. This resulted in the rejection of all imported standards and, as far as architecture was concerned, two main currents emerged: neocolonial and modernism.

The Neocolonial

The first movement sought its true Brazilian style in the past, in the colonial period. Architects like Lúcio Costa, studied the techniques, materials and designs of the 16th, 17th and 18th centuries, soon producing houses with a colonial look, but also combining elements which were only previously found in baroque churches. These included pediments and decorated door frames. The style was called neocolonial and remained popular until the 1940s, especially in Rio de Janeiro and São Paulo.

In search of greater authenticity, architects employed original materials brought from demolished old houses. A good example of this can be found in Rio de Janeiro, in the Largo do Boticário (very close to the train station for Corcovado, in Cosme Velho), a small square surrounded by neocolonial houses painted in fancy, bright colours.

Modernism

The other current generated by the Semana da Arte Moderna looked to the future for its inspiration for Brazilian-ness. Architects such as Oscar Niemeyer, Lúcio Costa, Affonso Eduardo Reidy, the landscape designer Roberto Burle Marx and many others started to design functional and spacious buildings, with large open areas and *pilotis* (pillars carrying a building, leaving the ground floor open). The use of concrete and glass was intense and the masterpiece of the Brazilian architectural modernism is Brasília, the capital, planned from scratch in the 1950 by Lúcio Costa and Oscar Niemeyer.

Many examples of modernist building can be found all over Brazil: in Brasília, the cathedral, the National Congress, the Palácio do Planalto (the presidential palace), in fact the whole city, with its broad freeways and spacious urban blocks, called *quadras*; in Belo Horizonte, the church of São Francisco de Assis, in Pampulha; in São Paulo, the MASP (Museum of Art of São Paulo), the Memorial da América Latina, and many commercial buildings along the Avenida Paulista; in Rio de Janeiro, the Ministério da Educação e Saúde, the Museu de Arte Moderna, the Catedral Metropolitana, the Petrobrás building (Brazilian State Petrol Company), the BNDES building (National Bank of Social and Economic Development), all in the central area of the city.

Brazilian contemporary architecture

The most recent trend is the postmodern. Many business centres, shopping malls and residential buildings are being designed in a style which uses coloured mirror glass, granite and stylized structures reminiscent of classical temples.

Brazilian architects are also famous worldwide for their techniques in designing houses for construction on steeply-inclined hills. In Rio de Janeiro, if you are driving along the coastal road in the neighbourhoods of Barra and São Conrado you can see many of these astonishing projects, which are homes of the very wealthy.

Religion

Amazon Spirituality – rainforest shamanism

The spirituality of the Amazon peoples, like that of their cousins throughout the Americas, is based firmly in shamanism; a religion that underlies all our belief systems, and is found all over the world. Like Inca or Maya shamanism, Amazon shamanism finds its roots in Siberia; the homeplace of America's ancestors. In the rainforest, it has long developed into its own, complex, form.

Above all, shamanism is a way of life; a journey of spiritual evolution in which the teacher and guide is the shaman. Although the ultimate goal is spiritual realization, few indigenous Brazilians opt for the long, almost monastic path that takes them there. Shamanism is more often concerned with the correct ordering of day-to-day life and the marking out of ritual and symbolic space. Everything from a hunt to the positioning of a building has to mimic the higher, divine world. For indigenous Brazilians, as for Catholic or Orthodox Christians, symbols are more than mere representations; they are the means by which the material world is tuned to the spiritual. Shamans, who both educate would-be shamans, and oversee all the tribes spiritual activities, are therefore priests and spiritual professors. Some have attained spiritual realization; either through intense deprivation or suffering, or the long process of shamanisitic education, others are merely the holders of tradition that has been passed on to them.

Spiritual realization

For the shaman, spiritual realization involves complete existential awareness of the fundamental absence of dualism. The shamanistic universe comprises two worlds, that co-exist. Most obvious is the visible 'material' world, which is the realm of the senses and is governed by the quest for food. But underlying this is a spiritual 'invisible' world that we share with all objects and beings in the Universe. This is the realm of pure being, archetype and spirit, and is the place in which we apprehend and even meet the cosmic and divine powers. Whilst we tend to regard only the visible as real, Indians traditionally see the opposite as being true: *mári ariri kéro dohpá inyarí* – 'our-existence-dream-like-appears'. All actions in the visible world must therefore be evaluated in terms of the invisible world – for this is ultimately where they derive their form and meaning: what we do belongs to the material world; what we are, belongs to the spiritual.

When a shaman reaches the point of realization, he is like the enlightened of Buddhism or Hinduism: the scales fall from the eyes, the two realms are perceived as one and 'what-he-realizes-himself-to-be' completely informs what he does. As with Zen, such spiritual realization is accomplished through a journey of direct experience, but in shamanism, it is guided by symbol, tradition and Psychotropic pharmacy. The Tucanoan concept of mind-brain relationships are an indication of this. The following is a very crude outline.

Tucanoan Mind-Brain symbolism

The Tucanoan equate the invisible world with the left cerebral hemisphere, and the visible with the right. The left hemisphere, is the hemisphere of the mature, enlightened adult – the 'older brother'. It is the seat of intuition, moral authority, order, all intellectual and spiritual endeavours, music, dreams and abstract thought. Its name – *ëmëkóri mahsá turí* – means 'Sun-people-dimension'; the sun being the manifestation of the power of the creator of the Universe – the 'Sun-Father'. It is also the home of the *gahí turí* – the other dimension/house/world, where we apprehend and interact with the archetypes and forms of the invisible world. And it is the instrument for interpreting the *bogári* – energy fields and 'transmissions' that emanate from the natural world. The right hemisphere is called *mahsá turí*, or 'human dimension'. It is subservient and is associated with the younger brother. Here lies all practical knowledge and skill; tradition; customary rules and rituals; and everything pertaining to the physical.

The fissure between the two hemispheres has a very complex symbolism associated with it. Simply speaking, it can be seen as an anaconda-river, with the dark patterns on the snake-river's back as stepping stones. The shamanic student learns to navigate the river, stepping on the stones to move from immature, materialistic, right-hemisphere orientated life, to enlightened, spiritual, left-hemisphere orientated life. Just in front of the anaconda's head is a rock crystal – symbolizing the seat of cosmic (solar) illumination – like grace in Christianity or Da'at in kabbalism. For the Tucanoan, the rock crystal is a model of the Universe and the holy shape and the hexagon infuses the structures of daily life.

Psychotropic remedies such as Ayahuasca are common vehicles of spiritual intuition, used to shift perception from right to left hemisphere, or from the 'visible' to 'invisible world' orientation. Such remedies collapse the ego; Ayahuasca is said to completely silence the inner voice which most of us use to think, and shift the perception away from the human tendency to regard himself as separate to the rest of world. It has been known to send those who identify themselves with their powers of reason to madness. Shamans use Ayahuasca and other such remedies very carefully, and with Chinese pharmaceutical precision. All tribal members use them at one time or another, to mark key events like puberty, and help the individual perceive the spiritual significance of such events.

The ordering of daily life to the spiritual

Shamans are informed not only by intuition but by age-old tradition. If intuition is shaminic prayer, then tradition is the text of shamanic life. It comes in the form of myriad taboos and rituals passed down through generations, and a giant cosmological map, in which positions and movements are imbued with Biblical significance. This map is comprised of the stars above and the forest around, and their harmonic movements. It is used to plot and interpret everything; from the timing of different harvesting seasons to the construction of buildings.

For the Tucanoan people of the Upper Rio Negro, Orion is the single most important feature on this map. This constellation is a macrocosmic model of the primal or cosmic human being: The Master of Animals. This figure is to the indigenous people, like Adam before the fall might be to a mystical Christian, is the archetypal, cosmic man whose correct relationship with the spiritual world ensures harmony within the Garden of Eden. In his path across the night sky The Master of Animals drags his catch behind him over a forest trail; the Milky Way. He is watched carefully – by following The Master of Animals, divine harmony is brought to bear on Earth: constellations along his path announce different harvesting and hunting seasons.

The six stars within Orion are linked together in a hexagonal pattern. Another hexagon links the stars that surround this constellation. These astronomical hexagons are the macrocosmic representation of rock crystal, which Tucanoans regard as sacred. They serve as the basic architectural models for the construction of the communal longhouse – the *maloca*. Six points of reference mark the positions of the strongest house posts; one at each corner of the hexagon, and correspond to the stars surrounding Orion. Six further posts delimit a central hexagon in the heart of the *maloca*, corresponding to Orion itself. An imaginary line bisects the *maloca* through both hexagons, representing both the Equator and the belt of Orion. The indigenous people perform ritual dances within this inner hexagon, whose movements are also symbolically related to pattern of the constellation of Orion. Two groups of dancers – one male and one female, move back and forth over the imaginary dividing line in triangular formations, tracing the hour-glass shaped outline of Orion. Like a dancing, living Yin and Yang, they represent the relationship between feminine and masculine archetypes: light and darkness, sun and moon, fertility and restraint. And as Orion is the macrocosmic model of Man, the *maloca* represents man within the Universe, and the dances represent the eternal play that occurs within the soul.

Land and environment

Geography

Brazil is the largest country in South America and the fifth largest in the world. It is almost as large as the USA and over covers 4300 km from north to south and the same from east to west, with land borders of 15,700 km and an Atlantic coastline of 7400 km. It borders all the other mainland South American countries except Chile and Ecuador and occupies almost half the total area of the continent. Its population of 162 million is the fifth largest in the world, and over half that of South America.

Geology

Although Brazil is dominated by the vast river basins of the Amazon and the Paraná which account for about three-fifths of the country, not much of it is 'lowlands'. Ancient rock structures, some of the oldest in the world, underlie much of the area creating resistant plateaux and a rounded hilly landscape. These ancient Pre-Cambrian rocks culminate in the Guiana highlands to the north and the crystalline ranges which run close to the coastline all the way from near the Amazon to the Uruguayan frontier.

It is believed that South America and Africa were joined in the geologic past, and there is a tolerable fit between the easterly bulge of Brazil and the Gulf of Guinea. Persuasive evidence has been found of identical ostracod fossils (freshwater fish) in corresponding Cretaceous rocks in both Brazil and Gabon, overlain by salt deposits that could have been the first appearance of the South Atlantic Ocean. This suggests that the split began some 125 million years ago. What is now accepted is that the South American Plate continues to move westwards with the consequent elevation of the Andes on the other side of the continent where it meets the Pacific Plates.

Amazon Basin

The Amazon river is the greatest in the world in area of drainage, about 7,000,000 sq km, and in volume of discharge into the sea averaging 180,000 cu m per second (or 170 billion gallons per hour), 10 times that of the Mississippi, and more than all the rivers of Europe put together. Such is the flow that the salinity of the Atlantic Ocean is affected for 250 km out from the river delta. It is 6400 km long (marginally shorter than the Nile) from its sources in the Andes of Peru, and still has over 3000 km to go through Brazil when it leaves Leticia on the Colombia/Brazil border, yet with only a fall of 80 m to sea level. Unlike most major world rivers, the basin is reduced in width near its mouth, indeed hills come down to the river near Monte Alegre only 200 km from the delta. Some 200 km above this at Óbidos, the river is over 75 m deep, that is the bottom is well below sea level. This reflects the more recent geological history of the basin which until the latter part of the Tertiary Period (say 25 million years ago) was connected to the Pacific and drained through what is now Ecuador. With the uplift of the Andes, this route was closed off, and a huge inland sea was formed, helped by a downward folding of the older rocks (some geologists believe there was also significant rifting of the strata) to create a huge geosyncline. Eventually the water broke through the crystalline rocks to the east and made the new connection to the Atlantic. Deep layers of sediment were laid down and have been added to ever since, with today's heavy tropical rains continuing to erode the surrounding mountains. This gives the largest, more or less, level area in Brazil, but it is so heavily forested and the soils so continually leached by the climate, with vast expanses frequently under floodwaters, that the potential for agriculture is strictly limited.

A characteristic of virtually all the tributaries which join the Amazon from the south is that upstream navigation ends where the rivers tumble off the plateaux of central Brazil creating dramatic waterfalls and in many cases now providing hydroelectric power.

Centre West

South of the Amazon Basin is a large area of undulating highlands, a dry plateau mostly between 200 m and 800 m. These are ancient rocks, back as far as Pre-Cambrian crystallines. They produce poor soils but sufficient to provide the grasslands or cerrado of the Mato Grosso, Goiás, western Paraná and adjacent areas, widely used for ranching, though now increasingly found suitable for soya bean production, one of Brazil's foremost exports.

From Minas Gerais southwards, the rivers drain into the second largest basin of Brazil, the Paraná, which eventually reaches the Atlantic by way of the River Plate of Argentina/Uruguay. This is another large river system, 4000 km long, of which about half is in Brazil. A principal tributary of the Paraná is the Rio Paraguai which, in its early stages, flows into a wide depression now filled with many thousands of metres of sediments and known in Brazil as the Pantanal. Further south, the swamps continue into the Chaco of Paraguay and Argentina. To the east of this, again the rivers fall off the old highland strata to form rapids and waterfalls, the largest of which was the former Sete Quedas Falls (Salto de Guaíra) on the Paraná, sadly drowned by the Itaipu Dam lake in 1982. Nearby however are the Iguaçu Falls, the most impressive of South America, created by very resistant layers of basalt.

The coast and escarpment

Highlands follow the coastline, only a short distance inland, for 3000 km. The ancient crystalline/granite ridges, known as *serras*, stretch from Porto Alegre in the south to near Belém in the north, just short of the Amazon estuary. Long stretches are in the form of a single or stepped escarpment, abrupt in the east and sloping more gently inland to the west. They are not high in South American terms – the highest point, Pico da Bandeira is only 2890 m – but it is no more than 120 km from the ocean near Vitória. The narrowness of the coastal strip has had a profound effect on the history of settlement. Until comparatively recent times, the lack of natural access to the hinterland confined virtually all economic activity to this area, and today most of the major cities of Brazil and 80% of the population are on or near the coast.

Because of varying erosion over many millions of years, there are a number of interesting natural features in these highlands. The many granite 'peaks' in and around Rio de Janeiro are the resistant remnants of very hard rocks providing spectacular viewpoints, Pico da Tijuca (the highest, 1012 m), Corcovado (710 m) and Pão de Açúcar (396 m) the best known. There are others in the neighbouring state of Espírito Santo. Near Curitiba are the eroded sandstones of Vila Velha and the wild scenery through the Serra do Mar towards the coast. In the state of Bahia, there are remarkable caves and waterfalls in the Chapada da Diamantina National Park. In many places, what rivers there are flowing eastwards necessarily have to lose height quickly so that gorges and waterfalls abound. There are also many kilometres of spectacular coastline and fine beaches. South of Porto Alegre, eroded material moved down the coast by the southerly ocean currents added to alluvials brought north from the River Plate by subsidiary currents, have created long sand bars to form several large freshwater lagoons. The longest, Lagoa dos Patos, is over 250 km long.

Rio São Francisco

The escarpment forces most of the rain run-off to flow west into the interior to feed the Amazon and Paraná river systems. However, one major river breaks through the barrier to flow into the Atlantic. The São Francisco rises south of Belo Horizonte – one important tributary starts only 250 km from the sea – but flows, north then east, for 2900 km before it gets there. Almost 500 km of rapids through the escarpment culminate in the 75 m Paulo Afonso falls, before completing the final 240 km to the sea. Where it turns east is one of the driest areas of the country, known as the *sertão*. The river is therefore of great significance particularly as the rains there are so unreliable. Together with the link it provides to so much of the interior and its course wholly within the country (unlike the Amazon and the Paraná), the São Francisco is revered by the Brazilians as the 'river of national unity'. Its value for irrigation, hydroelectric power, fish and navigation above the rapids is inestimable, but because of sand bars at its mouth and close proximity to the fall line, the river has not proved useful for shipping or access generally to the ocean in spite of being the third largest river system on the continent.

Northern highlands

After sinking below the Amazon estuary, the Brazilian highlands reappear to the north and sweep round to the west to form the border with the Guianas and Venezuela. The highest tabular uplands are near where Guyana, Venezuela and Brazil meet at Monte Roraima (2810 m) and further west along the border where a national park has been set up focussed on Pico de Neblina, 3014 m, the highest point in Brazil.

Climate

The climate of Brazil is a function of latitude and altitude. The average annual temperature exceeds 26°C along the northeast coast and in the central Amazon with little variation throughout the year. The highlands are cooler and further south there are seasonal variations: Brazil extends to 34° south, which is equivalent to the latitude of North Carolina. High summer temperatures can occur almost anywhere here, yet frosts are not uncommon in July and August as coffee producers know only too well. Rainfall is more complicated. The northeast trade winds bring moist air to the coast north of the Amazon, where there is heavy precipitation all year round. The same winds push saturated air into the Amazon Basin where rainfall is progressively greater from east to west throughout the year and virtually on a daily basis. The abrupt rise of the Andes beyond the borders of Brazil increases the precipitation and feeds the many tributaries.

During the period December-May, the northeast trade winds move north and Brazil between Belém and Recife receives less rain-bearing winds. From Salvador, the southeast trade winds bring moisture from the South Atlantic and it is the gap between these two systems, known as the 'doldrums', that explains the dry areas of northeast Brazil. On average there is significant rainfall here, but sometimes it fails to arrive causing prolonged periods of drought. Precipitation in the southern states of Brazil is concentrated in the escarpment thus feeding the Paraná system and is well distributed throughout the year.

Although there are occasional storms causing local damage, for example in the favelas (shanty towns) of Rio, Brazil is not subject to hurricanes or indeed to other natural disasters common elsewhere in Latin America such as earthquakes, volcanic eruptions or unexpected widespread and catastrophic floods.

Ecosystems, flora and fauna

The neotropical region is a land of superlatives, it contains the most extensive tropical rainforest in the world, and is drained by the Amazon, which has by far the largest volume of any river system. The fauna and flora are abundant. There are more birds, primates, reptiles, amphibians, freshwater fish and plant species here than in any other region in the world. Ecosystems are to a large extent determined by the influence of the great rivers and mountains: the Amazon river system and the Andes (which, although not part of Brazil, dramatically affect the climate and river drainage) and the far older iron and sandstone hills and depleted soils of the Guiana and Brazilian shields that lie at the heart of the continent in the north along the border with Venezuela and in the heart of Brazil in Goiás, Tocantins and large parts of the Mato Grossos around the world's largest wetland, the Pantanal.

South America's isolation from the rest of the world, until the joining of the continent with North America some four million years ago years ago, has been another crucial contributing factor to its biodiversity. Unique families of birds called the sub-oscine passerines (which are unable to sing in the same way as other songbirds because of a physical peculiarity in their larynx) developed because of this isolation. And prior to the invasion from the north by more aggressive and competitive mammals (like the coatimundi and the puma) South America was home to large numbers of marsupials; a few of which cling on in the numerous opossum families.

Brazil can be divided into biogeographical zones: two huge **river basins** comprising the River Amazon and the River Plate; **mountains**, comprising the Guiana highlands to the north and the Brazilian highlands to the south where the *cerrado* forests lie; and a **coastal strip** of Atlantic rainforest.

Mata Atlântica (Atlantic rainforest)

The Atlantic rainforest used to cover 2,600,000 sq km in a coastal strip 160 km wide and 4200 km long but now covers less than 5% of that. As the forest ranges from sea level to over 2000 m and has been isolated biologically from the Amazon and Andes, it is one of the most biodiverse regions in the world; so much so; that it is one of Conservation International's designated world biodiversity hotspots: see www.biodiversityhotspots.org, for further details. There are 21 different primate species found here (compared to, for example Costa Rica's four). Seventeen of these are endemic to the *Mata Atlântica*, and of these, 13 species including the golden lion tamarin, are endangered. South America's largest primate, the woolly spider monkey, known locally as *muriqui*, was hunted close to extinction by European colonists who first settled along this coastal zone and subsequently by Brazilian peasant farmers. But the monkey still clings on in private reserves like REGUA in Rio de Janeiro state (see page 152) and the Parque Nacional Caparaó in Minas Gerais.

Where it is still extant, the lush **Mata Atlântica** coastal rainforest itself extends to 800 m in elevation and grades into cloud forest between 800 m and 1700 m and, although greatly depleted is still abundant in parts of Bahia, São Paulo, Paraná and Rio de Janeiro. In the cloud forests (which can be seen in Itatiaia), drenching by mist, fog and rain leads to a profusion of plant growth, trees and shrubs that are covered with a great variety of epiphytes, orchids (including the famous Cattleya which comes from Rio state), mosses, lichens and bromeliads. At the highest elevations, the forest gives way to mountain grasslands or *campos de altitude*. In the southern zone of the Atlantic forest, in Rio Grande do Sul and Santa Catarina, there are large stands of *araucária*, a relative of the monkey puzzle tree. The best places to see the *Mata Atlântica* are Itatiaia national park in Rio, the mountains behind Paraty and Ubatuba, and the coastal zone between Cananéia in São Paulo and Paranaguá in Paraná. The forest is immensely rich in bird life, with over 930 bird species, 144 of which are endemic species. The Serra dos Tucanos in Rio is perhaps the best place in Brazil for *Mata Atlântica* birding – with excellent guiding and facilities, followed closely by REGUA (see page 152). Self-guided birding is immensely rewarding – from the hills above Paraty, in the Serra dos Órgãos, in Itatiaia or the forests on the Ilha do Cardoso near Cananéia. The latter island is one of the few places where caiman still bask on coastal beaches. The best places to see the *Mata Atlântica* itself are Itatiaia national park, in Rio, the mountains behind Paraty and Ubatuba and the coastal zone between Cananéia in São Paulo and Paranaguá in Paraná.

Overfishing and mangrove destruction Drift net and long line fishing in the 1960s decimated one of the healthiest populations of fish in the tropical Atlantic and the once abundant dolphin fish and tunny are now rarely seen and small fishing villages cannot survive on their catch. This loss in fish stocks has been exacerbated by the destruction of coastal mangroves throughout Brazil. Mangroves provide a breeding ground for numerous species including many that are commercially important and the shallow lagoons near the swamps are important for one of Brazil's two species of manatees. Now extensive areas of mangroves are limited to the Delta da Parnaíba in Piauí and stretches around Boipeba in Bahia and Cananéia in São Paulo. The once abundant *restinga* that lies behind the mangrove forests has also been greatly depleted. *Restinga* consists of shrub forest, coastal sand dunes, ponds and wetlands; there are remnants in areas like **REGUA** (see page 152) and in the Delta do Parnaíba (see page 571).

Amazon rivers

The Amazon Basin, which is made-up of myriad different rivers; more than four of which are by water volume the largest rivers in the world, contains the greatest area of tropical rainforest in the world, 6,000,000 sq km, 60% of which is located in Brazil. It is home to 20% of the world's plant and bird species; perhaps 10% of mammal species; an inestimable number of insects and perhaps some 2000 species of fish inhabiting the 1000 tributaries of the Amazon. When in flood the great river inundates the forest for a short period in its upper reaches to create a unique habitat called *várzea*; in the lower reaches this flooding may last for four to seven months forming *igapó* swamp forest.

The rivers of the Amazon are either classified as blackwater or whitewater rivers. The former are black-tea coloured due to the brown humic acids derived from the decomposing materials on the forest floor but contain little suspended material. The white waters owe their colour to the suspended soil particles which originate in the run-off from the Andes. Each has its characteristic fish. Within a 30-km radius of Manaus, there are estimated to be over 700 species of fish. Many are biologically curious. The pirarucu or *arapaima,* which can reach over 3 m and weigh in at over 150 kg has a primitive lung that enables it to live in oxygen-depleted water. Its habit of surfacing for air makes it easy prey for fishermen. Despite being served on tables throughout the Amazon it is a threatened species, protected by Ibama; the state environmental body. The piraiba is one of the world's largest catfish; aggressive and big enough to swallow a human. The candiru is one of the world's smaller catfish. It is parasitic, swimming into the gill spaces of other fish and lodging there to gorge blood. It is said to be attracted to urea and to swim up the urethra of swimmers who pee in the water, with unpleasant or even fatal consequences. The various species of piranha, are much maligned. The largest and most fearsome are the red piranhas and the grey piranhas, but although these fish can be dangerous when trapped in small pools in the dry season Amazonians quite happily swim in oxbow lakes filled with the fish in the wet. The pacu is one of the various species of vegetarian piranha, which feeds on fruit falling from trees in the flooded forest. More dangerous than piranhas are electric eels and sting rays; both of which are relatively common; as are bull sharks. An electrical shock of 650 volts has been recorded from a captive electric eel and the German naturalist and explorer Alexander Von Humboldt talked of them being able to knock out a fully grown horse.

Amazon forests

There are various forest types associated with and largely unique to the Amazon rivers. All the Amazonian forests are highly species rich. It has been estimated that 4 sq km of forest can harbour some 1200 vascular plants, 600 species of tree, and 120 woody plants. Gallery forests are those which are found along the banks of rivers; and which are subject to rapid erosion when the river changes course. These forests tend to grow on nutritionally rich soil and are often high in fruiting plants. *Várzea* is a biodiverse seasonally flooded forest found along the banks of the whitewater rivers; it is very nutritionally rich as a consequence of the huge amount of silt and nutrients washed out of the mountains and trapped by the massive buttress-rooted trees. It can be flooded for as much as seven months of the year and is found throughout the Amazon system. One of the most common *várzea* trees, the Pará rubber tree (*Hevea brasiliensis*), is the source of latex. The Brazilian rubber industry foundered in the 19th century when seeds of this tree were smuggled to Asia by the British and grown in vast rubber plantations, which flourished in the absence of Amazonian pest species. Another *varzea* tree is camu-camu, whose juice has by far the highest vitamin C content of any fruit in the world; despite claims made for various Australian berries. *Varzea* forests are good places to spot waterbirds such as the Amazon's many heron, egret, ibis, duck, cormorant and stork species, at least five kingfisher species, numerous raptors like black-collared hawks and endemic birds like hoatzin. These are generally found along waterways where it feeds on leaves and fruit. The newly hatched chicks of this primitive bird have claws at the tip of each wing which enable them to crawl around in the foliage. *Varzea* is frequently visited by parrots and macaws and by primates, who are all after seasonal fruit and nuts.

Igapó forests are seasonally inundated forests found on blackwater rivers. They grow in sandy soil, which lies as beautiful exposed beaches in the dry. The largest areas of *igapó* are found in the Rio Negro system, which joins the Amazon in Manaus. Despite being flooded for up to seven months of the year to a possible depth of 15 m, palms dominate the *igapó*, interspersed with large hardwood trees like kapok. During the wet season, these flooded forests are inhabited by turtles and small fish, and the predators that feed upon them – like giant otters and various species of caiman, which can be heard calling to each other at dawn. Bird and primate life is rich with similar families to *várzea*, though with less diversity as *igapó* has fewer fruiting trees.

Flooded meadows are frequently found in the still-flowing reaches of the *várzea*. These vast carpets of floating waterlilies (including the metre-wide *Vitória regia*), water lettuce and water hyacinth are home to the Amazonian manatee, a large herbivorous aquatic mammal, only a little smaller than the manatee associated with Florida and the Caribbean and the dugong of Australia. It is very difficult to see. Two species of dolphin hunt for fish in the *várzea* and *igapó*, as well as in the larger rivers, using sonar to catch their prey. The Amazonian dolphin, or *boto* is unique to the river system, and is bubble-gum pink. There are also enormous numbers of spectacled caiman that populate the forest and feed on the highly productive fish community. The most common species are the spectacled caiman (with a yellow eyelid) and the far larger black caiman.

Várzea and *Igapó*, together with terra firme forest, are the best places to spot wildlife in the wet. In the dry the best locations are the river corridors. Caiman and turtles are commonly seen basking on the riverbanks, and if you are really lucky you may see a jaguar or ocelot draped over a branch or a tapir, the largest South American mammal, taking a bathe or a drink. Birdlife is only a little less rich in the dry than the wet, with fewer migratory species but greater concentrations of water birds hunting for the dwindling supplies of fish. **Giant otters** are found in *várzea* and *igapó* as well as in oxbow lakes and on smaller Amazonian tributaries. They can grow to up to 2 m in length and are active by day when they hunt for food, often in small groups.

In the terra firme forests, which grow on permanently dry soil, the soaring canopy some 45 m overhead is home to the greatest numbers of animals. It is a habitat thick with strangling vines and numerous epiphytic plant species amongst which troupes of squirrel monkeys, in various species, and **capuchins** forage, alongside **uakari**, **saki** and **titi**

Animal trafficking

The number of animals facing extinction in Brazil has tripled since the early 1990s. In 2009 federal authorities caught one trafficking ring that was responsible for poaching an estimated 500,000 animals from the wild every year.

Poaching of wild animals is big business in Brazil. The Brazilian government estimates that as many as 12 million animals are poached every year. Despite there being posters all over every airport denouncing animal trafficking, between 1998 to 2009 the legislation against trafficking weakened and prosecutions became weak and confused. Large-scale trafficking is undertaken by gangs, yet Brazilian law does not distinguish between large-scale poaching for the trafficking industry and individuals poaching a single animal from the wild as a pet.

monkeys. In the high canopy groups of **spider monkeys** perform their lazy aerial acrobatics, whilst lower down, clinging to epiphyte-clad trunks and branches, groups of tiny **tamarins** and **marmosets** forage for gums, blossom, fruit and the occasional insect prey. Small arboreal cats such as **margay** and large weasels, and racoons like **tayra** and **coatimundi**, prey on them. Families of **howler monkeys** noisily roar out their territorial boundaries at dawn and dusk. Birdlife is very rich, with high numbers of uniquely neotropical species such as turkey-sized **currasows** and **guans**, spectacularly coloured **cotingas**, **trogons** and **motmots**, myriad **tyrant flycatchers** and as many **woodpeckers**, **woodcreepers** and **foliage gleaners**; many associated with particular tree families. Brilliant **tanagers** and **hummingbirds** flit through the canopy flowers and all are watched over by a succession of **raptors**; the largest of which is the elusive metre-tall **harpy eagle**, with ankles as thick as a woman's wrist. These are big and powerful enough to pluck the larger monkeys and the various species of sloth out of the tops of trees. **Antbirds** and **manakins** flutter silently through the forest below; the former in various species each of which follow troupes of specific army ant families through the forest eating the insects they startle as they pass. The best places to see the Amazon wildlife are Cristalino Jungle Lodge (see page 755), Mamirauá Reserve (see page 644), the Anavilhanas Islands (see page 642), preferably on a cruise, and from the best of the jungle lodges around Manaus (see page 649).

The Pantanal

This ecologically diverse zone includes the largest area of wetlands in the world and is the best place in South America for seeing wild animals. Alongside the wetlands are dry savannahs, *cerrado*, chaco scrublands as well as gallery forest. The area is very flat and flooded by the rising rivers leaving isolated islands or cordilheiras between vast lakes or *baías*, which become saline as the waters evaporate. This mixed ecosystem supports a highly diverse fauna characteristic of the constituent habitat types which includes 200 species of mammal. **Capybara** (a large aquatic rodent that looks like a giant guinea pig), **tapir** and South America bush pigs or **peccaries** are common along the waters edge as are the **web-footed marsh deer**. **Jaguar**, the largest cat in the Americas weighing up to 150 kg, and **puma**, which are only a little smaller are more commonly associated with the forest and savannahs and prey on these herbivores and the cattle and feral pigs which graze here. **Giant anteater**, **armadillos** and **rhea** (South American ostrich(are seen in the grassland areas. Spectacular assemblages of **wading birds** such as egrets, jabiru storks, ibises, spoonbills and herons prey on the abundant invertebrate and fish. **Anacondas** and **Pantanal caiman** (a sub-species of spectacled caiman) are still common, although the large black caiman has been hunted out. The best places to see animals in the Pantanal are the Transpantaneira (see page 745) in Mato Grosso and the *fazendas* around Miranda (see page 734).

The cerrado

The *cerrado* is Brazil's outback and makes up most of the interior of the country between the coast and the Amazon Basin, much of Mato Grosso and Mato Grosso do Sul including parts of the Pantanal, almost all of Goiás, Tocantins, Minas Gerais and the far west of the northeastern states are *cerrado*. It is the most extensive woodland-savannah region in South America. Like the Australian outback, the *cerrado* comprises forest, grassland and scrub broken by rivers and underground streams. Also like the outback it grows on ancient, eroded rock and it bursts into bright bloom in the wet. Within the *cerrado*, there is a tapestry of different vegetation types, including tree and scrub savannah, grassland with scattered trees, and occasional patches of a dry, closed canopy forest called the *cerradão*. Gallery forests are found throughout the region, although they are technically not considered part of the typical *cerrado* formations. Unlike the outback the *cerrado* gets plenty of rain (around 1500 m per year), usually between October and April. For the rest of the year the *cerrado* is dry – so much so that many of the plants have adapted to drought conditions – with leathery or waxy leaves and some deciduous tendencies. Much of the vegetation is also adapted to fire. The *cerrado* is Brazil's most critically threatened biome. It is also one of the world's greatest botanical repositories with an estimated 10,000 plant species, of which about 4400 are endemic. Herbaceous species, which include herbs rather than woody plants, are almost entirely endemic. Some of the most remarkable plants in the *cerrado* include the conspicuous *Mauritia flexuosa* palms (known locally as *buritis*) that grow along the swampy headwaters of streams and rivers, and the spectacular *ipê* trumpet flower trees (*tabebuia*), which are leafless when in bloom and have brilliant purple, pink, yellow or white flowers. There are some 600 bird species, nearly 20 of which are endemic and all of Brazil's spectacular mammals can be seen here. The best places to see the *cerrado* are Chapada dos Veadeiros (see page 716), Jalapão (see page 725), the Parque Estadual São Gonçalo do Rio Preto near Diamantina (see page 285), the Serra da Canastra, the Serra do Cipó and Parque Nacional das Emás (see page 717).

The sertão and caatinga

The sertão is a region which lies in the dry hinterlands of northeastern Brazil; ecologically it is made up principally of *caatinga*. This is South America's least scientifically studied biome and is completely unique to Brazil. The *caatinga* is made up of xeric desert-adapted plants – small, thorny deciduous trees, cacti, succulent plants, and fire-adapted grassland savannahs. There are many unique flowering plants that burst into brilliant bloom in the wet. The biome has two seasons: winter (May-November) when it is very hot and dry, and the summer (January-April) when it is very hot and wet. During the dry winter periods trees are bare and their roots begin to protrude through the surface of the stony soil which can reach temperatures of up to 60°C. When the rains begin in January, the bleak, desert-like landscape of the *caatinga* is transformed in an exuberance of green and bright flowers; the rivers start to fill up and birds begin to sing in the trees.

Caatinga makes up some 11% of Brazilian territory, yet only 1% of its habitats are protected – a reflection on the respect given to the sertão by both federal and state governments. And there are no tour operators offering wildlife trips to the region. Animal life in the *caatinga* has been adversely affected by hunting and human occupation. Many species have become extinct locally, while others, such as the **three-banded armadillo**, **collared anteater, jaguar** and **tufted capuchin**, survive in reduced numbers. Bird species include some of the world's rarest parrots – Lear's and Spix's **macaws** live in tiny numbers on the fringes of Jalapão (see page 725) and near the Serra da Capivara (see page 572) and **cactus parakeets, long-billed wrens, scarlet-throated tanagers** and **yellow-faced siskins** occur throughout the biome. Beyond hearsay, little is known about the *caatinga* except that it is critically vulnerable. There are no statistics available for flora or fauna species or numbers. The best places to see *caatinga* are anywhere in the sertão, especially the Serra da Capivara and the remote Serra dos Confusões in southern Piauí.

National parks

On paper Brazil has stringent environmental legislation and a large system of very well-protected national parks. However, hunting is rife as none of the parks have rangers. Until recently, unscrupulous and influential businessmen and politicians logged and abused the parks with impunity; a situation which began to change only with the exposure of a logging scandal involving the state governments and **Ibama** (Instituto Brasileiro do Meio Ambiente e dos Recursos Naturais Renováveis – the Brazilian Institute for the Environment and Renewable Natural Resources) in Brazil's southern Amazon and Central West in the new millennium. This still compares favourably with Britain though where agriculture, logging and road construction is permitted within national parks even when they are world heritage sites. Ibama has in its care 57 national parks (Parques Nacionais, or PARNA). They are by no means the whole picture, though. They form part of a system of protected areas which go under different titles and which have varying degrees of public access. The network comprises, in addition to the national parks: *estações ecológicas* (ecological stations), *reservas biológicas* (biological reserves), *reservas ecológicas* (ecological reserves), *áreas de relevante interesse ecológico* (areas of relevant ecological interest), *reservas particulares do patrimônio nacional* (private national heritage reserves) and *áreas sob proteção especial* (areas of special protection). In all these entities, the exploitation of natural resources is completely forbidden. They are for research, education and recreation only. Three other types of entity are designed to allow the sustainable use of natural resources, while still preserving their biodiversity: *florestas nacionais* (national forests), *áreas de proteção ambiental* (areas of environmental protection) and *reservas extrativas* (extractive reserves, such as the rubber-tapping zones in Acre state). A new initiative is the **Projeto Corredores Ecológicos** (Ecological Corridors Project), which aims to create avenues of forest between isolated protected areas so that fauna may move over a greater area to breed, thus strengthening the stock of endangered animals, which might otherwise suffer the ills of inbreeding. An example of this is a project to link the *Mata Atlântica* of Poço das Antas with other pockets of coastal forest to help the survival of the golden lion tamarin.

Ibama was created in 1989 by uniting four separate bodies: the environmental secretariat (SEMA), the Brazilian Institute of Forest Development (IBDF), and the superintendencies for the development of fishing and rubber (SUDEPE and SUDHEVEA). Brazil has a long history of passing laws to protect natural resources, such as that of 1808 that excluded from international trade the export of *pau-brasil* and other woods. At the same time though, enforcement of such laws has not been easy. Today, the achievement of Ibama's goals is determined by resources, but funds are insufficient to commit either enough money or staff to the job of protecting the areas that have been designated for preservation. Sad though this is, there are still a large number of parks open to visitors that can give a good idea of the variety of Brazil's natural resources and the value that they hold for the country.

This book does not describe all of Brazil's national parks or other conservation entities, but only those which have easy access. Nor does it list all the offices of Ibama or its related departments throughout the country, but those nearest to the parks described are given and it is to these that you should apply to if a permit is needed to visit a specific park.

For more information, contact **Ibama** ① *national headquarters, SAIN, Av L-4, bloco B, Térreo, Edifiço Sede do Ibama, CEP 70 800-200, Brasília DF, T061-3226 8221/9014, www.ibama.gov.br*, or at a local branch listed throughout the text.

Information can also be obtained from the environment ministry, **Ministério do Meio Ambiente (MMA)** ① *Esplanada dos Ministérios, bloco B, 5-9 andar, CEP 70068-900, Brasília DF, www.mma.gov.br*. See also the book *Nacionais Brasil, Guias Philips* (1999), which has a good map, beautiful photographs, sections on history, flora and fauna and tourist services, US$15.

Books

History and anthropology

Hemming, J *Red Gold, Amazon Frontier* and *Die if You Must*, Pan. The little-known history of Brazil's indigenous people is alternately shocking and inspiring. This wonderful, scholarly and beautifully written account is as readable and exciting as Prescott's *Conquest of Peru* and will in time rank alongside it. A must for anyone with an interest in Brazil. **Reichel-Dolmatoff, G** *Rainforest Shamans*, Themis books. The best introduction to the philosophy of an Amazon people available in English.

Literature

Amado, J et al, *Gabriela, Clove and Cinnamon, Dona Flor and her two Husbands* (Avon Books). Very poor translations of these captivating novels, almost all of which are set in Bahia, and which read like a cross between Poldark and Angelique. Romps through 19th- and 20th-century Bahia. Ripping yarns though not literary masterpieces. Over a long

career Amado published many best sellers, most of which are available in English. He is often criticized for producing an overly optimistic, sexily tropical view of the country, and of Bahia, his home state. **Andrade, Mário de** *Macunaíma*. Written in the 1920s, this is a comic statement in picaresque form about Brazilian nationality, by the leader of modernism. **Ângelo, I** *The Celebration* (Avon Books). Much the best novel about the political, social and economic crisis at the end of the 1960s, the worst period of the military regime. **Buarque, C** *Turbulence* and *Budapest* (Bloomsbury). The first is a short, pacey allegory of modern Brazil, the second which has been recently translated, is a labyrinthine Borgesian magic realist novel set in Budapest. It was top of the best sellers list in Brazil for many months – something unusual for literary fiction. Buarque is the son of a distinguished social historian and is most famous as a singer and composer. **da Cunha, E** *Rebellion in the Backlands* (University of Chicago Press). The book that inspired Mario Vargas Llosa and which is the country's most famous piece of sustained journalistic writing.

Freyre, Gilberto *The Masters and the Slaves*, out of print. One of the central figures in the story of Brazil's struggle to define its identity. Controversial and sometimes viewed as implicitly racist, this account traces the psychology of Brazil to its sugar plantation past.

Guimarães Rosa, J *The Jaguar and Other Stories* (Boulevard Books). Decent translations of Brazil's greatest novelist are hard to come by. There are none at all of his masterpiece, *Grande sertão, veredas: As trilhas de amor e guerra de Riobaldo*. Guimarães Rosa is, in a sense, the first great magic realist author, and is by far the most respected author within Brazil. He is credited with having invented a new kind of poetically colloquial literary Portuguese. This draws its inspiration from the mystical and lyrical language of the interior of Brazil, a region which was gradually cut off from the rest of the country. *The Jaguar* is little more than an introduction to his writing.

Hatoum, M *The Brothers*. One of the most interesting of Brazilian contemporary writers who focusses on the experience of being Brazilian-Lebanese in the dangerous world of the early 20th-century Amazon. Wonderfully evocative.

Lins do Rego, J *The Masters and the Slaves* (University of California Press). Highly influenced by Gilberto Freyre, this is an evocative account of childhood on a northeastern sugar plantation.

Lispector, C *Family Ties, The Hour of the Star* and *Soulstorm* (University of Texas Press, Carcanet Press and New Directions). Brazil's other great modernist and the country's most highly revered woman's writer.

Llosa, M V *The War of the End of the World* (Penguin). An enthralling dramatization of the Canudos rebellion. Very hard to put down and beautifully structured.

Machado de Assis, J M *The Posthumous Memoirs of Bras Cubas, Dom Casmurro*

(Oxford University Press) and *Philosopher or Dog,* (Bloomsbury). At last some decent translations of Brazil's most acerbic and witty literary social commentator. With a black mother and white Portuguese-descended father, Machado de Assis was a bridge between the 2 Brazil's: the haves and the have nots.

Morley, H *The Patriot* (London: Rex Collings). The diary of a girl's life in Diamantina, in Minas Gerais. Translated by the great American poet Elizabeth Bishop who lived in Brazil for many years. A delightfully intimate and frank portrait of small-town life.

Ramos, G *São Bernardo* (Peter Owen) *Anguish* (Knopf, 1972) and *Barren Lives* (University of Texas Press, 1965). The greatest of the novelists of the 1930s and 1940s: a harsh realist.

Torres, A *Blues for a Lost Childhood* (Readers International,1989). An idealistic Brazilian journalist leaves his rural town for Rio only to be crushed by the realities of the city. Sobering and not very cheerful reading.

Ubaldo Ribeiro, J *The Lost Manuscript* (Bloomsbury). A panoramic historical novel, originally entitled *Long Live the Brazilian People*.

Poetry

Bandeira, M *This Earth, that Sky: Poems by Manuel Bandeira* (University of California Press). The oldest member of the modernist movement, and one of Brazil's greatest poets, master of the short, intense lyric.

Drummond de Andrade, C *Plantation Boy* (New York: Knopf). Perhaps Brazil's greatest poet, with a varied, lyrical, somewhat downbeat style.

Photography

Andujar, Claudia *A vulnerabilidade do ser* (Cosacnaify). Wonderful evocative and masterful images that capture the poetry of Brazil's landscapes and people; often fused in a double exposure. Her Amazon images are startlingly original.

Bassit, José *Imagens Fiéis*. A moving account of traditional religious life in the backlands of the northeast. Again, masterfully shot.

Salgado, S *Migrations* (Aperture). The most recent volume from the world's most highly respected photojournalist renowned for transcendental images of the world's silent majority and their daily lives. Incredible.

Social comment

Bellos, A *Futebol: The Brazilian Way of Life* (Bloomsbury, 2003). A loving look at the beautiful game, its history, its players, supporters and its legendary feats. Alex Bellos is one of the UK's leading Brazilian experts and was the *Guardian* correspondent based in Rio.

Castro, R *Rio de Janeiro* (Bloomsbury, 2004). An anecdotal history and profile of Rio de Janeiro written by a Carioca.

Fausto, B *A Concise History of Brazil* (Cambridge University Press). Dry as dust but the only readily available, reliable history of the country available in English.

Harvey *Liberators* (Constable and Robinson, 2002). A wonderful romp through the Liberation of South America from Europe with a colourful section on imperial Brazil. How all history should be written.

McGowan, C and **Pessanha, R** *The Brazilian Sound: Samba, Bossa Nova and the Popular Music of Brazil* (Temple University Press, 1998). An encyclopaedic survey of Brazilian popular music with interviews from many of the key players.

Page, J *The Brazilians* (Da Capo Press,1995). One of the few popular books on Brazil which really gets under the country's skin. With excellent chapters on Carnaval, football, Brazilian society and character and plenty of information on Rio.

Travel writing

Davis, W *One River*. A remarkable travel book: Hunter S Thompson meets George Forrest and Levi Strauss in the heart of the Amazon.

Fawcett, P *Exploration Fawcett* (Weidenfeld & Nicholson, 2001). The diaries of the intrepid explorer who disappeared in Mato Grosso in the 1920s and whose descriptions of the table-top mountains there inspired Conan Doyle to write *The Lost World*. Some beautiful writing on the Amazon, Rio de Janeiro and the Andes.

Fleming, P *Brazilian Adventure* (Pimlico, 1998). The sparkling, delightfully humorous account of a 1930s expedition in search of Colonel Percy Fawcett.

Robb, P *A Death in Brazil* (Bloomsbury, 2004). A poetic odyssey through Brazil's history, culture and landscape.

Wildlife field guides

General

Kricher, J *A Neotropical Companion* (Princeton University Press). A very clear, intelligent introduction to the ecosystems, biology and botany of the neotropical region.

Pearson, D and **Beletsky, L** *Brazil – Amazon & Pantanal* (Academic Press). By far the best introductory wildlife and botanical guide.

Birds

de la Peña, M and **Rumboll, M** *Birds of Southern South America and Antarctica* (Harper Collins & Princeton University Press). A slim volume, but with comprehensive information on most of Brazil's non-neotropical species.

Dunning, J *South American Birds: A Photographic Aid to Identification* (Harrowood Books, Pennsylvania, 1987). The best of the current photoguides with more than 2700 species, over 1400 colour photographs.

Hilty, S and **Brown, W** *Birds of Colombia*. The best book for the northern Amazon region.

Ridgely, R and **Tudor, G** *The Birds of South America, Volume 1 & II* (University of Texas Press & Oxford University Press, UK). One of the most important bird books of the century.

Sibley, D and **Alfred, A** *Sibley's Birding basics* (Knopf, 2002). Very useful aid to bird identification giving clues through appearance, behaviour, flight and song. Invaluable for inexperienced bird wathchers.

Sick, H *The Birds of Brazil* (Princeton University Press). Currently the only widely available book covering almost all Brazil's species (there are more species added almost monthly).

Souza, D *All the Birds of Brazil* (Gráfica Santa Helena, 2002). Covering most Brazilian species and include illustrations, albeit rather poor ones. English and Portuguese.

Wheatley, N *Where to Watch Birds in South America* (Princeton University Press). A little out of date but with an interesting list of places and useful bird inventories.

Zimmer, K and **Whittaker, A** *Birds of Brazil* (Princeton University Press). The 1st comprehensive, modern illustrated field guide to the birds of Brazil. Originally due out in 2008. Now delayed until 2010.

Mammals
Eisenberg, J F and **Redford, K** *Mammals of the Neotropics Vol 3: The Central Neotropics – Ecuador, Peru, Bolivia, Brazil*.

Emmons, L H *Neotropical Rainforest Mammals: A Field Guide* (University of Chicago Press). Excellent illustrated field guides which between them cover pretty much everything in tropical Brazil.

Plants
Henderson, A, **Galeano, G** and **Bernal, R** *A Field Guide to the Palms of the Americas* (Princeton University Press). A comprehensive illustrated guide. Well worth having.

Reptiles and amphibians
Bartlett, R D and **Pope Bartlett, P** *Reptiles and Amphibians of the Amazon: An Ecotourist's Guide* (University of Florida Press). With 250 common species.

Footnotes

Contents

Basic Portuguese for travellers

Learning Portuguese is a useful part of the preparation for a trip to Brazil and no volume of dictionaries, phrase books or word lists will provide the same enjoyment as being able to communicate directly with the people of the country you are visiting. It is a good idea to make an effort to grasp the basics before you go. As you travel you will pick up more of the language and the more you know, the more you will benefit from your stay. ▸▸ *See also Language in Essentials, page 45.*

General pronunciation

Within Brazil itself, there are variations in pronunciation, intonation, phraseology and slang. This makes for great richness and for the possibility of great enjoyment in the language. A couple of points which the newcomer to the language will spot immediately are the use of the tilde (~) over 'a' and 'o'. This makes the vowel nasal, as does a word ending in 'm' or 'ns', or a vowel followed by 'm' + consonant, or by 'n' + consonant. Another important point of spelling is that for words ending in 'i' and 'u' the emphasis is on the last syllable, though (unlike Spanish) no accent is used. This is especially relevant in place names like Buriti, Guarapari, Caxambu, Iguaçu. Note also the use of 'ç', which changes the pronunciation of c from hard [k] to soft [s].

Personal pronouns

In conversation, most people refer to 'you' as *você*, although in the south and in Pará *tu* is more common. To be more polite, use *O Senhor/A Senhora*. For 'us', *gente* (people, folks) is very common when it includes you too.

Portuguese words and phrases

Greetings and courtesies

hello	*oi*
good morning	*bom dia*
good afternoon	*boa tarde*
good evening/night	*boa noite*
goodbye	*adeus/tchau*
see you later	*até logo*
please	*por favor/faz favor*
thank you	*obrigado* (if a man is speaking)
	/obrigada (if a woman is speaking)
thank you very much	*muito obrigado/muito obrigada*
how are you?	*como vai você tudo bem?/tudo bom?*
I am fine	*vou bem/tudo bem*
pleased to meet you	*um prazer*
no	*não*
yes	*sim*
excuse me	*com licença*
I don't understand	*não entendo*
please speak slowly	*fale devagar por favor*

what is your name?	*qual é seu nome?*
my name is …	*o meu nome é …*
go away!	*vai embora!*

Basic questions

where is?	*onde está/onde fica?*
why?	*por que?*
how much does it cost?	*quanto custa?*
what for?	*para que?*
how much is it?	*quanto é?*
how do I get to … ?	*para chegar a … ?*
when?	*quando?*
I want to go to …	*quero ir para …*
when does the bus leave?/arrive?	*a que hor sai/chega o ônibus?*
is this the way to the church?	*aquí é o caminho para a igreja?*

Basics

bathroom/toilet	*banheiro*
police (policeman)	*a polícia (o polícia)*
hotel	*o (a pensão, a hospedaria)*
restaurant	*o restaurante (o lanchonete)*
post office	*o correio*
telephone office	*(central) telefônica*
supermarket	*o supermercado*
market	*o mercado*
bank	*o banco*
bureau de change	*a casa de câmbio*
exchange rate	*a taxa de câmbio*
notes/coins	*notas/moedas*
traveller's cheques	*os travelers/os cheques de viagem*
cash	*dinheiro*
breakfast	*o caféde manh*
lunch	*o almoço*
dinner/supper	*o jantar*
Meal	*a refeição*
drink	*a bebida*
mineral water	*a água mineral*
soft fizzy drink	*o refrigerante*
beer	*a cerveja*
without sugar	*sem açúcar*
without meat	*sem carne*

Getting around

on the left/right	*à esquerda/à direita*
straight on	*direto*
to walk	*caminhar*
bus station	*a rodoviária*
bus	*o ônibus*

bus stop	*a parada*
train	*a trem*
airport	*o aeroport*
aeroplane/airplane	*o avião*
flight	*o vôa*
first/second class	*primeira/segunda clase*
train station	*a ferroviária*
combined bus and train station	*a rodoferroviária*
ticket	*o passagem/o bilhete*
ticket office	*a bilheteria*

Accommodation

room	*quarto*
noisy	*barulhento*
single/double room	*(quarto de) solteiro/(quarto para) casal*
room with two beds	*quarto com duas camas*
with private bathroom	*quarto com banheiro*
hot/cold water	*água quente/fria*
to make up/clean	*limpar*
sheet(s)	*o lençol (os lençóis)*
blankets	*as mantas*
pillow	*o travesseiro*
clean/dirty towels	*as toalhas limpas/sujas*
toilet paper	*o papel higiêico*

Health

chemist	*a farmacia*
doctor	*o coutor/a doutora*
(for) pain	*(para) dor*
stomach	*o esômago (a barriga)*
head	*a cabeça*
fever/sweat	*a febre/o suor higiênicas*
diarrhoea	*a diarréia*
blood	*o sangue*
condoms	*as camisinhas/os preservativos*
contraceptive (pill)	*anticonceptional (a pílula)*
period	*a menstruação/a regra*
sanitary towels/tampons	*toalhas absorventes/absorventes internos*
contact lenses	*lentes de contacto*
aspirin	*a aspirina*

Time

at one o'clock (am/pm)	*a uma hota (da manhã/da tarde)*
at half past two/two thirty	*as dois e meia*
at a quarter to three	*quinze para as três*
it's one o'clock	*é uma*
it's seven o'clock	*são sete horas*
it's twenty past six/six twenty	*são seis e vinte*

it's five to nine	*são cinco para as nove*
in ten minutes	*em dez minutos*
five hours	*cinco horas*
does it take long?	*sura muito?*

Days

Monday	*segunda feiro*
Tuesday	*terça feira*
Wednesday	*quarta feira*
Thursday	*quinta feira*
Friday	*sexta feira*
Saturday	*sábado*
Sunday	*domingo*

Months

January	*janeiro*
February	*fevereiro*
March	*março*
April	*abril*
May	*maio*
June	*junho*
July	*julho*
August	*agosto*
September	*setembro*
October	*outubro*
November	*novembro*
December	*dezembro*

Numbers

one	*um/uma*
two	*dois/duas*
three	*três*
four	*quatro*
five	*cinco*
six	*seis* ('*meia*' half, is frequently used for number 6 ie half-dozen)
seven	*sete*
eight	*oito*
nine	nove
ten	*dez*
eleven	*onze*
twelve	*doze*
thirteen	*treze*
fourteen	*catorze*
fifteen	*quinze*
sixteen	*dezesseis*
seventeen	*dezessete*
eighteen	*dezoito*

nineteen	*dezenove*
twenty	*vinte*
twenty-one	*vente e um*
thirty	*trinta*
forty	*cuarenta*
fifty	*cinqüe*
sixty	*sessenta*
seventy	*setenta*
eighty	*oitenta*
ninety	*noventa*
hundred	*cem, cento*
thousand	*mil*

Useful slang

that's great/cool	*que legal*
bloke/guy/geezer	*cara* (literally 'face')
biker slang for bloke/guy	*mano*
cheesy/tacky	*brega*
posh, spoilt girl/boy with rich parents	*patricinha/mauricinho*
in fashion/cool	*descolado*

Glossary

→ See also Music and dance colour section.

azulejo	tile	ferroviária	train station
baía	bay	forró	music and dance style from northeast Brazil
bairro	area or suburb		
bandas	marching bands that compete during Carnaval	frevo	frenetic musical style from Recife
bandeirantes	early Brazilian conquistadors who went on missions to open up the interior	gaúcho	cowboy, especially from Rio Grande do Sul
		garimpeiro	miner or prospector
barraca	beach hut or stall	igreja	church
berimbau	stringed instrument that accompanies capoeira	ilha	island
		jangada	small fishing boats, peculiar to the northeast
biblioteca	library		
bilhete	ticket	jardim	garden
botequim	small bar, open-air	lanchonete	café/deli
caboclo	rural workers of mixed descent	largo	small square
cachaça	cane liquor	leito	executive bus
cachoeira	waterfall	litoral	coast/coastal area
caipirinha	Brazilian cocktail, made from cachaça, lime, sugar and ice	mata	jungle
		mercado	market
câmbio	bureau de change	Mineiro	person from Minas Gerais
candomblé	African-Brazilian religion	mirante	viewpoint
capela	chapel	mosteiro	monastery
capoeira	African-Brazilian martial art	Paulista	person from São Paulo
Carioca	person from Rio de Janeiro	ponte	bridge
carnaval	carnival	praça	square/plaza
cerrado	scubland	praia	beach
cerveja	beer	prancha	surfboard
churrascaria	barbecue restaurant, often all-you-can-eat	prefeitura	town hall
		rio	river
empadas	mini pasties	rodoviária	bus station
estrada	road	rua	street
favela	slum/shanty town	sambaquis	archaeological shell mounds
fazenda	country estate or ranch	sertão	arid interior of the northeast
feijoada	black-bean stew	Sertanejo	person who lives in the sertão
		vaqueiro	cowboy in the north

Acronyms and official names

FUNAI	Fundacao Nacional do Indio (National Foundation for Indigenous People)
IBAMA	Instituto Brasileiro do Meio Ambiente E Dos Recursos Naturais Renováveis (Brazilian Institute of Environment and Renewable Natural Resources)
MPB	Música Popular Brasileira
RAMSAR	Wetlands Convention

Index → Entries in bold refer to maps.

Advertisers' index

Credits

Footprint credits

Project editor: Felicity Laughton
Layout and production: Emma Bryers
Proofreading: Jen Haddington
Maps: Kevin Feeney
Colour section and cover design: Pepi Bluck

Managing Director: Andy Riddle
Commercial Director: Patrick Dawson
Publisher: Alan Murphy
Publishing Managers: Felicity Laughton,
Nicola Gibbs
Digital Editors: Jo Williams, Jen Haddington
Marketing and PR: Liz Harper
Sales: Diane McEntee
Advertising: Renu Sibal
Finance and administration: Elizabeth Taylor

Photography credits

Front cover: Cachoeira, Bahia/Frédéric Soreau/
photolibrary.com
Back cover: Touros beach, Rio Grande do
Norte, Natal/Bertrand Gardel/hemis.fr
Page 1: Adrián Domínguez/age fotostock.com
Pages 2-9 and page 11: Alex Robinson
Pages 10: Bumba-Meu-Boi/Franck Camhi/
Alamy
Page 12: Frédéric Soreau/photolibrary.com

Manufactured in India by Nutech Print Services
Pulp from sustainable forests

Footprint feedback

We try as hard as we can to make each guide as
up to date as possible but things always change.
If you want to let us know about your experiences
then go to **footprinttravelguides.com** and send
in your comments.

Publishing information

Footprint Brazil
7th edition
© Footprint Handbooks Ltd
February 2011

ISBN: 978 1 907263 26 2
CIP DATA: A catalogue record for this book
is available from the British Library

® Footprint Handbooks and the Footprint
mark are a registered trademark of Footprint
Handbooks Ltd

Published by Footprint
6 Riverside Court
Lower Bristol Road
Bath BA2 3DZ, UK
T +44 (0)1225 469141
F +44 (0)1225 469461
footprinttravelguides.com

Distributed in the USA by Globe Pequot Press,
Guilford, Connecticut

Footprint Mini Atlas
Brazil

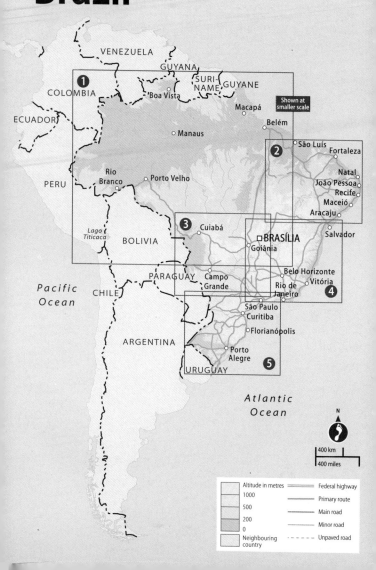

VENEZUELA

GUYANA

SURI-
NAME

GUYANE

COLOMBIA

1

Boa Vista

Macapá

Shown at
smaller scale

ECUADOR

Belém

Manaus

São Luís

2

Fortaleza

PERU

Rio
Branco

Porto Velho

Natal

João Pessoa

Recife

Maceió

Aracaju

*Lago
Titicaca*

BOLIVIA

3

Cuiabá

□BRASÍLIA

Goiânia

Salvador

Pacific
Ocean

PARAGUAY

Campo
Grande

Belo Horizonte

Vitória

4

CHILE

Rio de
Janeiro

São Paulo

Curitiba

Florianópolis

ARGENTINA

5

Porto
Alegre

URUGUAY

*Atlantic
Ocean*

N

400 km

400 miles

Altitude in metres		Federal highway
1000		Primary route
500		Main road
200		Minor road
0		Unpaved road
Neighbouring country		

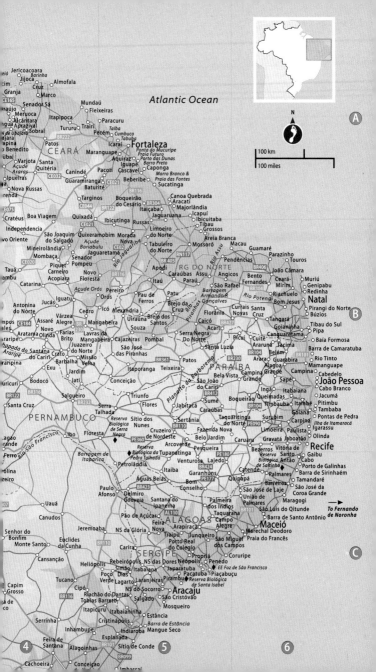

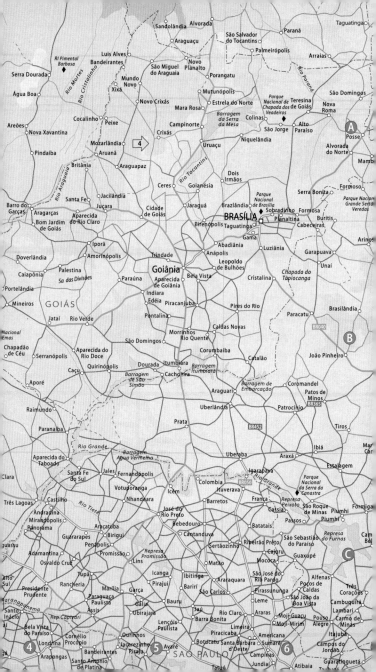

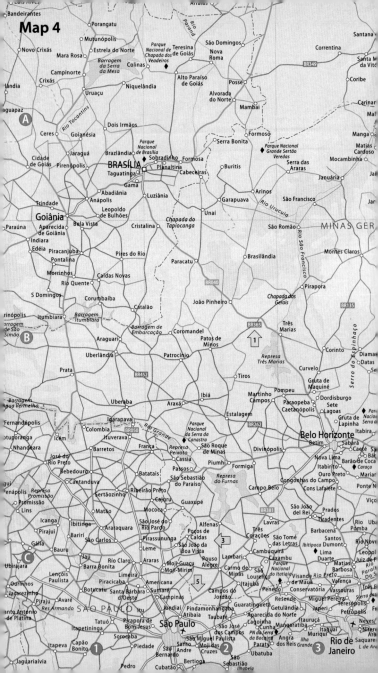

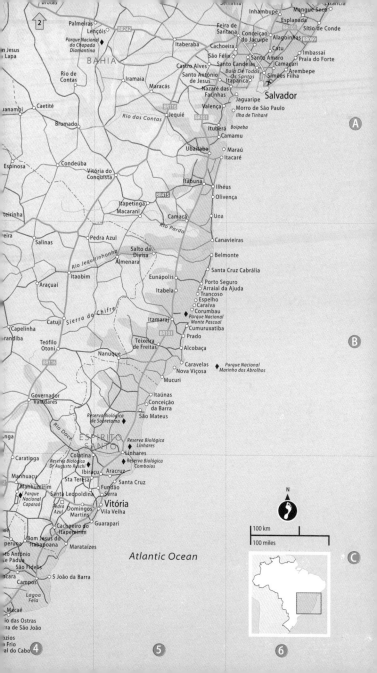

Index

Distance chart

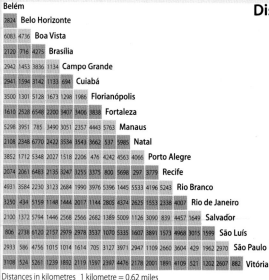

	Belém	Belo Horizonte	Boa Vista	Brasília	Campo Grande	Cuiabá	Florianópolis	Fortaleza	Manaus	Natal	Porto Alegre	Recife	Rio Branco	Rio de Janeiro	Salvador	São Luís	São Paulo
Belo Horizonte	2824																
Boa Vista	6083	4736															
Brasília	2120	716	4275														
Campo Grande	2942	1453	3836	1134													
Cuiabá	2941	1594	3142	1133	694												
Florianópolis	3500	1301	5128	1673	1298	1986											
Fortaleza	1610	2528	6548	2200	3407	3406	3838										
Manaus	5298	3951	785	3490	3051	2357	4443	5763									
Natal	2108	2348	6770	2422	3534	3543	3662	537	5985								
Porto Alegre	3852	1712	5348	2027	1518	2206	476	4242	4563	4066							
Recife	2074	2061	6483	2135	3247	3255	3375	800	5698	297	3779						
Rio Branco	4931	3584	2230	3123	2684	1990	3976	5396	1445	5533	4196	5243					
Rio de Janeiro	3250	434	5159	1148	1444	2017	1144	2805	4374	2625	1553	2338	4007				
Salvador	2100	1372	5794	1446	2568	2566	2682	1389	5009	1126	3090	839	4457	1649			
São Luís	806	2738	6120	2157	2979	2978	3537	1070	5335	1607	3891	1573	4968	3015	1599		
São Paulo	2933	586	4756	1015	1014	1614	705	3127	3971	2947	1109	2660	3604	429	1962	2970	
Vitória	3108	524	5261	1239	1892	2119	1597	2397	4476	2178	2001	1891	4109	521	1202	2607	882

Distances in kilometres   1 kilometre = 0.62 miles

Map symbols

- ▢ Capital city
- ○ Other city, town
- ⟂⟂ International border
- ⟂⟂ Regional border
- ⊖ Customs
- ◯ Contours (approx)
- ▲ Mountain, volcano
- ⟋⟍ Mountain pass
- ⏤⏤ Escarpment
- Glacier
- Salt flat
- Rocks
- Seasonal marshland
- Beach, sandbank
- ⟨⟨⟨ Waterfall
- ⌒ Reef
- ━━ Motorway
- ─── Main road
- ─── Minor road
- ─ ─ ─ Track
- ······ Footpath
- Railway
- ┼▬ Railway with station
- ✈ Airport
- 🚌 Bus station
- Ⓜ Metro station

- ---- Cable car
- ┼┼┼┼ Funicular
- ⛴ Ferry
- ▭▭▭ Pedestrianized street
- Ⅺ Ⅽ Tunnel
- → One way-street
- ▦▦▦ Steps
- ⤫ Bridge
- ▬▬▬ Fortified wall
- Park, garden, stadium
- ● Sleeping
- ❶ Eating
- ❶ Bars & clubs
- ▦ Building
- ▪ Sight
- ✝ Cathedral, church
- 🏯 Chinese temple
- 🕉 Hindu temple
- 🕎 Meru
- 🕌 Mosque
- 🛕 Stupa
- ✡ Synagogue
- 🅘 Tourist office
- 🏛 Museum
- ✉ Post office
- Ⓟ Police

- Ⓢ Bank
- @ Internet
- ♪ Telephone
- 🛒 Market
- ✚ Medical services
- 🅿 Parking
- ⛽ Petrol
- ⛳ Golf
- ∴ Archaeological site
- ♦ National park, wildlife reserve
- ✤ Viewing point
- ▲ Campsite
- 🏠 Refuge, lodge
- 🏰 Castle, fort
- Diving
- 🌴 Deciduous, coniferous, palm trees
- ⌂ Hide
- 🍇 Vineyard, winery
- 🏺 Distillery
- Shipwreck
- ⚔ Historic battlefield
- 1️⃣ Detail map
- 1️⃣ Related map

Alex and Gardênia Robinson

Alex Robinson is a photographer and writer who has been published by *New York Times*, *Sunday Times Travel*, the *Independent*, *Vanity Fair* and *Departures* magazine, amongst others. He was part of a team who won a national magazine award in the USA, an Editora Abril journalism award in Brazil, and was runner-up in the Friends of the Earth International photography competition. Gardênia Robinson is a former investment banker from São Paulo who ran her own NGO in Brazil, working with sustainable tourism in local communities. She has researched and photographed books on the Amazon, Brazil and Mexico. They have been greatly assisted in the new edition of the Brazil book by their seven-year-old son Raphael.

Acknowledgements

Ed Stocker and Clemmy Manzo updated the Paraná and Santa Catarina sections of the Iguaçu and the south chapter. Ed is a freelance current affairs journalist who has written for the *New Statesmen* and *New Internationalist*, and the former deputy editor of *Songlines* magazine. Clemmy is editor of *Time Out Buenos Aires*.

Thanks goes to Alessandra Ribeiro, David at BMA for all the help and pointers on Brazilian music and culture, Carlos Magno, João Vergara, Marcos Sacchi, Jean Barbosa and Marcelo in Belem, Jody Gillett, Scubidu, Andre Dias, Cassio in Acre, Geraldo Mesquita a true local hero, Pedro Neto for great company, a crack and effortless professionalism, Ailton Lara another true professional, Raphael Robinson, SEBRAE in Rio, Milton Nascimento for the interview and candomble tips, Fred 04, Michelle in Pernambuco and her beautiful new baby Liz, Aquiles in Pernambuco, Roberto Constante and Chriz Fuzinatto in Embratur, Carlinhos Brown, Mariene de Castro, Moyses Lopes in Porto Alegre, Ben Box, Felicity Laughton and Alan Murphy at Footprint – for their patience, hard work and faith in the book.